THE
OXFORD COMPANION TO
MEDICINE

THE OXFORD
COMPANION TO
MEDICINE

Edited by
JOHN WALTON
PAUL B. BEESON
RONALD BODLEY SCOTT

Associate Editors and Principal Contributors
S. G. OWEN
PHILIP RHODES

VOLUME II · N–Z

Oxford   New York
OXFORD UNIVERSITY PRESS
1986

Oxford University Press, Walton Street, Oxford OX2 6DP

Oxford New York Toronto
Delhi Bombay Calcutta Madras Karachi
Kuala Lumpur Singapore Hong Kong Tokyo
Nairobi Dar es Salaam Cape Town
Melbourne Auckland

and associated companies in
Beirut Berlin Ibadan Nicosia

Oxford is a trade mark of Oxford University Press

British Library Cataloguing in Publication Data

The Oxford companion to medicine
1. Medicine—Dictionaries
I. Walton, Sir, John, 1922–   II. Beeson, Paul
B.   III. Scott, Sir, Ronald Bodley
IV. Owen, S. G.   V. Rhodes, Philip
610'.3'21   R125

ISBN 0–19–261191–7

Library of Congress Cataloging in Publication Data

Main entry under title:
The Oxford companion to medicine.
1. Medicine—Dictionaries.   2. Medicine—
Biography—Dictionaries.   I. Walton, John Nicholas.
II. Beeson, Paul B. (Paul Bruce), 1908–
III. Scott, Ronald Bodley.   IV. Owen, S. G. (Samuel
Griffith)   V. Rhodes, Philip.
R121.088   1986   610'.3'21   85-29846
ISBN 0–19–261191–7 (set)

Set by Wyvern Typesetting, Bristol
Printed in Great Britain by
Billing & Sons Ltd
Worcester

A NOTE TO THE READER

Entries are listed in a simple letter-by-letter alphabetical order, with spaces, hyphens, and the definite and indefinite articles being ignored. Names beginning with Mc are ordered as if spelt Mac and St as if spelt Saint. In addition, biographies of individuals whose surnames have a prefix (de, van, von, etc.) occur under the capital letter of the main surname. The Companion contains a system of cross-references that is designed to inform the reader of related entries; this should be particularly useful for anyone less familiar with the more specialized medical vocabulary encountered in some of the entries. A cross-reference is shown in three ways: (i) by the use of an asterisk before a word (e.g. *biochemistry), indicating that there is an entry for that word; (ii) by the use of 'See' followed by the entry title in SMALL CAPITALS, indicating that further discussion will be found under that entry; and (iii) by the use of 'See also' followed by the entry title in SMALL CAPITALS, indicating that there is a related entry that might interest the reader. The cross-referencing does not attempt to be comprehensive but aims to guide the reader towards entries that might enhance the understanding of the entry being consulted. Thus the absence of a cross-reference does not necessarily imply that there is no related entry, and the reader may benefit from checking. A cross-reference is given the first time a particular word appears in an entry but not thereafter, regardless of the length of the entry (save in a few exceptional circumstances). In order to save space the titles of various entries have been abbreviated when they appear in cross-references. As a general rule SI units have been used throughout the text, and these units are described in the entry SI UNITS. Occasionally non-SI units have been used where this reflects common medical practice, for example, millimetres of mercury (mmHg) to record blood pressure. Appendix I contains a list of medical qualifications and Appendix II a list of common medical abbreviations. A list of main entries to be found within the Companion appears at the front of Volume I.

N

NAEGELI, OTTO (1871–1938). Swiss haematologist, MD Zurich (1897). Naegeli was appointed professor of medicine and director of the medical clinic in Zurich in 1918. For many years he was the leading European clinical haematologist and his book *Lehrbuch der Blutkrankheiten und Blutdiagnostik* (1931) was the bible of *haematology for many years. He described myelomonocytic *leukaemia and a cell called the micromyeloblast.

NAEVUS. Birthmark; any congenital mark or discoloration on the skin or mucous membrane of the mouth.

NAILS, like hair, are composed of *keratin and their normal growth is sensitive to the general state of *nutrition; transverse furrows often follow acute severe illnesses, after growth is resumed. In iron-deficiency anaemia they become characteristically soft and concave (koilonychia). Nail changes occur in many cutaneous disorders, particularly *psoriasis and fungus infections like *ringworm.

NALIDIXIC ACID is an oral antibacterial drug of value in urinary tract infections. It is effective against some gram-negative bacteria but not against *Pseudomonas* species. Side-effects include gastrointestinal disturbances and allergic reactions.

NARCISSISM, or excessive self-love, is held by some psychoanalysts to be regression to or persistence of a normal early phase of *psychosexual development. In Greek mythology Narcissus was a youth who fell in love with his own image reflected in a fountain and pined away until transformed into the flower of the same name.

NARCOANALYSIS is *psychoanalysis assisted by the administration of a drug (usually a short-acting *barbiturate like thiopentone sodium) which causes mental disinhibition and so facilitates expression of thoughts, ideas, and memories.

NARCOLEPSY. Periodic attacks of an uncontrollable urge to sleep during normal waking hours. Narcolepsy is often associated with *cataplexy. See also SLEEP.

NARCOSIS is a state of stupor or insensibility produced by drugs which depress the central nervous system.

NARCOTIC. Any drug which produces *narcosis.

The term is often used synonymously with 'narcotic analgesic' to mean a drug like *morphine which is used primarily to relieve pain. Since morphine and related compounds are strongly addictive, 'narcotic' is sometimes loosely used for any drug of *addiction.

NASOPHARYNX. That part of the *pharynx which lies above the soft palate and behind the nose.

NATIONAL ACADEMY OF SCIENCES (NAS). A private organization of scientists and engineers dedicated to the advancement of science and its use for the general welfare. The Academy, which has its headquarters in Washington, DC, and which has an official advisory role to the US government on matters concerned with science and technology, was given its charter by Congress in 1863. Membership is conferred on the basis of major contributions to scientific research or development, and is by election only; members at present number about 1250. The NAS carries out its work of bringing together scientists and engineers to exchange information and to further research by means of institutes, boards, committees, subcommittees, panels and *ad hoc* groups. It is organized into scientific sections; these include sections of mathematics, astronomy, physics, engineering, geology, chemistry, botany, geophysics, biochemistry, neurobiology, population biology, evolution, medical genetics, anthropology, psychology, social and political studies, and economic sciences.

The Institute of Medicine was organized under the NAS charter in 1970. It makes studies of public health policy, with special emphasis on the provision of adequate health services for all sectors of society. It has about 300 members.

NATIONAL BLOOD TRANSFUSION SERVICE. In England and Wales, the National Blood Transfusion Service (NBTS) operates in conjunction with the Department of Health and Social Security and 15 regional Blood Transfusion Centres to provide a service for the collection (from voluntary unpaid donors), storage, and distribution of blood and blood products. There is a separate Scottish National Blood Transfusion Service with five regional Blood Transfusion Centres and a Headquarters Laboratory.

NATIONAL BOARD OF HEALTH (USA). See HEALTH, NATIONAL BOARD OF (USA).

NATIONAL FORMULARY, BRITISH. See
PHARMACY AND PHARMACISTS.

NATIONAL FORMULARY (USA). The *United
States Pharmacopoeia* has been published since
1820, and has gone through many new editions. Its
purpose has been to describe drugs regarded as
appropriate and essential by the medical profession. Presently it is revised at five-year intervals,
but supplements are issued when appropriate.

In 1888 the first *National Formulary* of unofficial
preparations was published by the American
Pharmaceutical Association. For some time the
Pharmacopoeia was then looked upon as limited to
the 'best' drugs, whereas the *Formulary* included
some 'second best' agents, approved by some, but
not all of the profession. Gradually a tendency
developed for the *National Formulary* to
emphasize the standards for inactive ingredients
(excipients) used in making drug dosage forms. In
1975 the US Pharmacopoeial Convention, Inc.,
took over the publication of both reference works,
and in 1980 they were published together in a single
volume. This presented standards of strength,
quality, and purity for about 2800 drugs. There is a
Committee on Revision, which distributes proposed revisions for both publications, and invites
comments before issuing supplements or new
editions.

NATIONAL HEALTH INSURANCE ACT 1911.
Lloyd George's famous enactment represented a
landmark in the development of state provision for
health in the UK. Because of fierce opposition
from the medical 'establishment', including the
British Medical Association, the Act did not come
into force on the appointed day (12 July 1912) but
was delayed until the end of 1913. By this time
there were 15 000 000 insured persons, and the
government had recruited 10 000 general practitioners willing to participate in the scheme. Under
the Act, insured workers (wage earners with an
income of less than 160 pounds per annum, excluding civil servants and teachers) but not their
families, were entitled to free advice and treatment
from 'panel doctors' and to sickness benefit paid
through approved societies such as trade unions,
workmen's clubs, etc. Hospital treatment for the
seriously ill or injured was not included. Panel
doctors were paid an annual capitation fee of 7s.
6d. per patient. Another pioneering feature of the
Act was the provision of a subsidy for medical
research of 1d. per patient per annum; from this
modest beginning, the *Medical Research Council
was eventually to emerge.

**NATIONAL HEALTH SERVICE ACTS 1946,
1977.** The National Health Service (NHS), which
came into being in the UK on 5 July 1948, was
established by the National Health Service Act
1946. The latter followed, and was largely based
on, the *Beveridge Report* of 1942 and a subsequent government White Paper of 1944. It became:

the duty of the Minister of Health to promote the
establishment in England and Wales of a comprehensive
health service designed to secure improvement in the
physical and mental health of the people and the prevention, diagnosis and treatment of illness and for that
purpose to provide or secure the effective provision of a
service in accordance with the provisions of the Act.
Services so provided shall be free of charge, except where
any provision of the Act expressly provides for the making
and recovery of charges.

The NHS comprised: central administration;
hospital and specialist services; the health services
of local health authorities; general medical, dental,
and pharmaceutical services; and mental health
services. The administrative bodies for hospitals
were Regional Hospital Boards, with Boards of
Governors and Hospital Management Committees; those for general practice, Executive
Councils; while the Local Health Authorities
administered personal health services.

The 1946 Act, as amended, was superseded by
the National Health Service Act 1977, which consolidated much of the law relating to the NHS in
England and Wales and re-enacted many of the
provisions of the *National Health Service
(Reorganization) Act 1973.

**NATIONAL HEALTH SERVICE (AMEND-
MENT) ACT 1949.** This Act made consequential
amendments to the *National Health Service Act
1946, which after modification by the *National
Health Service (Reorganization) Act 1973, was
superseded by the *National Health Service Act
1977.

**NATIONAL HEALTH SERVICE IN THE UK:
ITS STRUCTURE.** The National Health Service
(NHS) began on 5 July 1948, the appointed day on
which the legislative measures of the first NHS Act
of 1946 (1947 for Scotland) were brought into
effect. The structure of the service established at
that time remained unchanged until the
reorganization of 1974 and its main feature was its
three organizational branches, interdependent but
unrelated below government level. The three branches provided a public health service, hospital and
specialist services, and a framework for general
practice provided by independent contractors.
Certain health functions were retained at national
level, for example the responsibility for the special
hospitals (secure *psychiatric hospitals) which
were administered directly for England and Wales
by the then *Ministry of Health, continuing in 1985
to be the responsibility of the present *Department
of Health and Social Security (DHSS). Such
Ministerial responsibilities were not integral to the
NHS which consisted from its inception, therefore,
of services provided through its own national structure. There was no management link with a
government department through which political
accountability could be related to service activity.

The public health service. The public health
service continued as before 1948 to be a responsi-

bility of local government with only some of the major component tiers of local government in the UK being identified as health authorities. Health functions were fulfilled by these health authorities through a committee system of authority members who had been elected by local government elections. The same authorities had to discharge substantial welfare responsibilities under the National Assistance Act 1948 and many combined health and welfare functions in their committees and in the duties of the officers concerned. The chief officer for health, and frequently therefore also for welfare, was the *Medical Officer of Health whose office involved him personally in certain statutory responsibilities for public health. Invested in the office was a significant level of independence derived from the right and duty of the Medical Officer of Health to report publicly on health matters, continuing the spirit of the historical development of public health and legislation from the previous century.

The public health service provided environmental health services, control measures for infectious diseases, maternity and child welfare services including vaccination and immunization, home nursing, school health services, and some other services concerned with occupational health and employment. The ambulance services (except in Scotland) were also a local authority responsibility. Welfare services included residential care for the elderly and the handicapped, and domiciliary support services for such individuals. At this time services for children were somewhat fragmented locally by responsibilities being shared between local authority health and education committees, sometimes separate welfare committees, and by the Home Office's local responsibilities towards children in such matters as parental rights, fostering and adoption. The Medical Officer of Health, either through the formal nature of his appointment to his own authority or through informal mechanisms of collaboration and persuasion, fulfilled a co-ordinating role over all these local activities which could be broadly defined as being concerned with health and laid the foundations of a comprehensive community health and welfare service. The public health service encompassed the duties and functions of all preventive health measures and the other two branches of the NHS largely ignored this aspect of health care as a result.

Funding for the public health services was partly through local rates and partly from direct government support. There was great variation in the spending pattern on health and welfare from one locality to another and capital assets, many of which were retained by local government when the NHS passed from its sphere of responsibility in 1974, differed in scale and quality.

Hospital and specialist services. The hospital and specialist services, government-funded from general taxation, were administered between 1948 and 1974 through a structured system of boards and committees which relied heavily on the voluntary services of appointed lay members and the participation of health professionals in management. Regions were defined upon the principle that each should have at least one medical school and associated teaching hospital to form a focus for teaching and research and all that was implied in terms of excellence in medicine. Teaching hospitals were managed by boards of governors on which the universities were strongly represented, and it was through these boards that the responsibilities of the NHS to provide hospital facilities for the teaching of medical students was discharged. The London postgraduate teaching hospitals were also each managed by boards of governors and all were largely independent—employing their own senior medical staff and dealing directly with the Ministry of Health in relation to major capital developments and revenue allocations. Chairmen and members of boards and boards of governors were appointed by the Minister. (See also MEDICAL EDUCATION IN THE UK AND EUROPE.)

The Regional Hospital Boards appointed Hospital Management Committees for the non-teaching hospitals in each Region and allocated revenue, developed capital programmes, and employed senior medical staff at Regional level. Regions undertook the responsibilities for postgraduate medical education which flourished during that period, and it was through this activity that the relationship between Regions and universities was maintained.

After some redefinition of 13 Regions in 1959 in order to match the developing Southampton Medical School, a pattern of 14 English Regions was established which continues (with slight variations in 1974) to the present day. Wales functioned as a single Region as did Northern Ireland, and Scotland had the equivalent of four Regions. The division of functions between the English Regions and the Ministry of Health and the Scottish Regions and the Scottish Home and Health Department was somewhat different, management in Scotland being more directly a government responsibility. Within Regions hospitals were grouped under Hospital Management Committees. At first groups were small, and psychiatric and general hospitals tended to be in separate groups. As time went on, and particularly after the *Mental Health Act 1959, there was a good deal of merging into larger and mixed groups under Management Committees with wider responsibilities. There was amending legislation in 1968 which enabled Management Committees to undertake teaching hospital responsibilities as University Hospital Management Committees. The *National Blood Transfusion Service was run by the Regional Hospital Boards in conjunction with the Ministry of Health.

General practitioner services and other independent contractors. The independent contractor services consisted (as now) of general medical and dental practitioners, opticians and pharmacists who offered services for NHS patients through contracts made with Executive Councils. These Councils were established broadly on County, Metropolitan, or County Borough scale and their unpaid 30-strong membership was 15 professional and 15 lay. Lists of patients registered with general medical practitioners were maintained as the basis for payment through capitation fees with very limited extra allowances. The other professions were paid through the Executive Councils on an item of service basis, and the financial commitment to this branch of the NHS was open-ended. The Executive Councils' functions were those of contract administration, acting as paymaster according to nationally negotiated scales, and the handling of complaints. There was no planning, research, or educational function and no management function directly related to the independent contractors. Medical and management information systems were not developed as in the other branches of the NHS. A Medical Practices Committee at national level controlled the distribution of general practitioners by influencing new practices and vacancies in a system of 'closed', 'open', and 'intermediate' practice areas. In 1968 the Ministries of Health and Social Security were merged to form the large Department of Health and Social Security (DHSS). Although the NHS became the responsibility of a Secretary of State, and a similar change occurred in Wales in 1969, the structure of the NHS continued as before. The government changes, however, heralded the reorganization of local government which in turn raised the question of its role in the provision of health services.

Changes in community health services. Local government's role in welfare was redefined in 1968 following the *Seebohm Report* (1968). Local Authority Social Services Departments were to be established and these would absorb welfare and children's services creating new boundaries thereby for activities defined as health. This demarcation in an area crucial for health planning, as a preliminary constraint on all subsequent NHS organization, was of profound significance. It is proving difficult, 15 years later, to find the mechanism to rebuild the health and welfare bridges which were broken down at that time. A strong sense was developing in the NHS of the need to bring primary health care, preventive services, and specialist care together to bear upon the growing needs of the elderly and to develop common aims for health and welfare services. Integrated planning and management was seen as the key to the future, and the division of the NHS into three separate branches was believed to be a major obstacle. Quite apart from the question of local government reorganization, therefore, there was a demand for a management structure which would unify the NHS.

The 1974 reorganization. Six years of intensive consultation and study culminated in the reorganization of 1974. During that time it became

apparent that not only were social services slipping from the sphere of influence of health, but also that the position of the independent contractors was unassailable by those involved in planning and management. After two Green Papers (Ministry of Health, 1968; DHSS, 1970) a consultative document (DHSS, 1971), reports on collaboration with local government (DHSS, 1973, 1974), on medical administration (DHSS, 1972), on DHSS reorganization and a White Paper (DHSS, 1972), the reorganized NHS came into effect on 1 April 1974 (NHS Reorganization Act 1973). New Health Authorities were set up throughout the UK and every post in the NHS carrying any management responsibility was affected. The main aim of integration was achieved only in so far as the remnants of the public health service were incorporated from local government into a new NHS management structure. The structure itself was, however, the aggregate of all the options which the long period of study and consultation had produced.

The arrangement in England was for 14 Regional Health Authorities (RHA), covering geographical areas only slightly changed from the previous Regions, with 90 Area Health Authorities (AHAs) accountable to them and matching County Council and Metropolitan Districts. In London some boards of governors for postgraduate hospitals were preserved, accountable directly to the DHSS. Lines of accountability were a great feature of the 1974 structure. An AHA was accountable as a corporate body to the appropriate RHA, but the chairmen were both accountable to the Secretary of State who appointed them. AHAs whose responsibilities included the supervision of one or more undergraduate teaching hospital were known as AHAs (Teaching) or AHAs(T). Authorities delegated functions to multidisciplinary teams of officers as well as to individual chief officers who formed the teams. Teams managed by consensus and were accountable as a team. Regions had one team, Areas had an Area team, also one or more District teams including a general medical practitioner and a consultant, to cover local services by officer management (i.e. there was no member authority for a District). Teams were not accountable to teams and there was no officer line management between Region and Area nor from Area to District officers. Formal committees (Joint Consultative Committees) were established with the aim of ensuring collaboration with the matching local authorities. Community Health Councils (CHCs) were introduced as independent bodies with the right to be consulted as representing the consumer. Professional advisory committees changed their nature—they had formerly been committees of the Boards and Management Committees but now became committees of the professions themselves with a statutory right to be consulted.

The new management arrangements were detailed by a study group of DHSS and NHS officers, management consultants, and a university research unit whose report was published as the *Grey Book* (DHSS, 1972). This book, which had advisory rather than statutory status, covered objectives, roles, and relationships for Authorities and officers and defined management style and structure. Notwithstanding the scope for variation, the *Grey Book* was closely adhered to in England and its 'red' and 'black' counterparts drawn up for Wales and Northern Ireland respectively were also adopted.

Wales adopted a similar pattern to England and reorganized at the same time, the Welsh Office taking on approximately the same role as the English Regions. Northern Ireland and Scotland reorganized before England with Area tiers (Boards) but no Regional tiers. Common or central services agencies fulfilled some of the functions which in England were undertaken by Regions. Integration of health with personal social services was achieved in Northern Ireland. Arrangements for the independent contractors remained almost untouched in England and Wales by this reorganization. Family Practitioner Committees (FPCs) emerged from the old Executive Councils with similar functions although accountable to AHAs. In Scotland and Northern Ireland former Executive Council functions were taken over by the new Health Boards.

The Regional functions could now be summarized as resource allocation (for Regional purposes and to AHAs including the AHAs(T)), strategic planning, and support for teaching and research. It was intended that all day-to-day management should be undertaken by AHAs who could delegate extensively to officer teams. A feature of the Authorities' business was that it had to be conducted in public and without recourse to committees.

The 1974 reorganization proved almost immediately to be costly and complex. Many of the posts in the new management structure were unfilled for lack of funds. The formal structures involved greatly extended lines of communication, and a network for consultation which slowed decision-making.

The importance of planning care for patient groups at local level and for structures within Districts—sectors and units—began to emerge and a standardized NHS Planning System was developed. A Royal Commission on the NHS, sitting between 1976 and 1979, heard much evidence on the need for simplification and on the apparent failure to have achieved integration. Their report (Royal Commission, 1979) included a recommendation that there should be one organizational tier below Region or Health Department.

By December 1979 the DHSS and Welsh Office had published *Patients First*, a consultative paper on the structure and management of the NHS in England and Wales. DHSS Circular HC(80)8 (1980) launched the further reorganization which was to be effective from 1982.

The 1982 reorganization. The 1982 reorganization was aimed at simplifying the NHS management structure below Regional level and achieving a 10 per cent reduction in management costs in so doing. Very little legislative change was necessary compared with 1974. The 90 English AHAs were abolished and replaced by 192 District Health Authorities (DHAs) directly accountable to the RHAs which were unaffected. Those Districts with continuing responsibility for Teaching Hospitals were recognized for this purpose by their Regional Health Authority but the word 'Teaching' was dropped from their titles. Chairmen of the new Authorities were appointed by the Secretary of State, members by the RHA. Total membership was reduced to a basic 15, but this included nominations from local government authorities in the District and some variations upwards were allowed to take account of the number of local authorities involved. A university-nominated member and not more than three medically qualified members were also included in the total. All members were unpaid in respect of their services but a modest honorarium for chairmen which had been introduced in 1974 was continued.

In Scotland, Wales, and Northern Ireland the 1982 reorganization did not involve the abolition of a management tier but other features of the English reorganization were introduced so that a closely similar pattern of management now exists throughout the UK. The differences are mainly those of terminology, with Northern Ireland continuing its system of combined health and social services. 'Common services agencies' survived in Scotland and Wales for the management of multi-District services which are mostly the responsibility of English Regions. Following several reports on the best means of procurement, a Supply Council (Special Health Authority) was set up for England. Another such Authority was established for NHS training at national level. Ambulances became a District responsibility with some co-ordinating functions at Regional level other than in the Metropolitan situations and in London.

The management pattern for the operational authority (DHA) since 1982 retains most of the features of the 1974 reorganization in a simplified structure. The DHA appoints four officers: medical, nursing, administrative, and finance. These officers are joined by a medical consultant and a general practitioner nominated by their peers, and in teaching Districts by a representative of each medical school concerned. A multidisciplinary team of officers is thus formed which has a collective management responsibility for the District's services. Decisions are taken by consensus and the team as a whole is accountable to the DHA which resolves any failures of the team to form a consensus view. Officers in the team continue to carry individual responsibility for specified professional functions.

A similar team management method is adopted in the English Regions, but the team consists of five officers appointed by the RHA: medical, nursing, administrative, finance, and works (i.e. there are no clinical, non-officer, members of the team). There is no accountability of the District team to the Regional team or of individual officers from one tier to another. The DHA is, however, accountable to the RHA, while the District and Regional chairmen are both accountable to the Secretary of State.

A further feature of the 1982 reorganization was the development of a management structure within Districts, and this has its counterparts throughout the UK. The new structure is made up of Units which may have geographical, functional, or a mixed make-up. A single hospital or a locality with its catchment population, a defined psychiatric service, or a comprehensive maternity service may all be found as examples of this very flexible management Unit. A nursing officer and an administrator are appointed with management responsibilities at Unit level, and a medical representative is nominated by the profession locally to make a medical management input. In many cases these three individuals function collectively as a consensus-forming management team, but this is not a requirement. Officers in such Unit Management Groups are directly accountable to the District officers of the same discipline, except for the medical members who are accountable to their electorate and in England, except in teaching hospitals, are employed by the RHA.

Financing of the NHS. Capital and revenue funding for the NHS is derived from general taxation and allocated by the government departments to the Regional Authorities in England and to the operational authorities elsewhere. Within England it has been long-standing government policy to effect a fair distribution of funds, and particularly to move funds from the relatively richer south to the less well-off Regions in the north. Little progress was made with this redistribution until a methodology was developed by a Resource Allocation Working Party which reported in 1976 (RAWP, 1976). (Similar reports followed for Scotland, Wales, and Northern Ireland.) The report advocated the calculation of revenue targets which are a per caput share for the population served, greatly modified by adjustment of that population by weightings related to the local need for services. Movement gradually towards targets was intended through the allocations made but the usefulness of the method has been somewhat attenuated by the very limited revenue growth available in recent years. A method of distributing capital also advocated by the Working Party never gained acceptance and after six years of use is being reviewed.

Revenue funding is particularly significant in NHS management as it represents the means by which change can be managerially effected. Politicians, members, and the Community Health Councils tend to point to the level of spending as an indicator of the level of service although the relationship is far from direct. Authorities are legally required to keep within their annual cash limits, and the cash-limited allocation is a powerful system of control. The performance of the NHS is almost exemplary in respect of its overall cash limit. The other major force in NHS management is the practical approach voluntarily adopted by health professionals in the face of limited resources for meeting health demands. Advisory committees of health professionals (medical, dental, pharmaceutical, and optical being formally recognized) are established at every level and have the right to be consulted and to offer advice. In changing situations, it is peer group pressures, especially within the medical profession, that can speed or obstruct management decisions to effect changes and influence the way in which financial allocations are used. In recognition of this power the NHS has developed a highly participative management style, involving the professionals and predominantly the doctors at every level of decision-making.

At the time of writing the recommendations in the report of a management enquiry undertaken for the Secretary of State by R. Griffiths and presented in the form of a letter with accompanying notes (November 1983) are being implemented. No further legislation or structural change is involved but radical alterations in the DHSS include the setting up of Supervisory and Management Boards concerned with the NHS. There is great emphasis on personal accountability for a general management function which is being introduced at every level of the NHS through the appointment of regional, district, and unit general managers. It is expected that clinicians will become general managers in some instances and will be able to participate in a revised system of management budgeting. The recently introduced system of management review, from level to level up to the Secretary of State's review of Regions is strongly endorsed. This exercise represents a distinct change in management style for the NHS with less reliance on a multi-disciplinary approach and more adaptation of business methods to the management of health services. Whereas cost control has not caused difficulties hitherto, the current search for cost improvements, value for money, and increased productivity seems likely to place the organization under severe pressure. There is, however, considerable scope for diversity in the way the new measures are introduced and no doubt some developments will emerge as worthwhile. The evaluation of the results of management change remains elusive in terms of health and health services.   E. R. RUE

References

Committee on Local Authority and Allied Personal Social Services (1968). *Seebohm Report.* Cmnd. 3703. London.

Department of Health and Social Security (1970). *The Future Structure of the National Health Service.* London.

Department of Health and Social Security (1971). *The National Health Service Reorganisation; consultative document.* London.

Department of Health and Social Security (1972a). *Report of the Working Party on Medical Administrators.* London.

Department of Health and Social Security (1972b). *National Health Service Reorganisation: consultative document.* London.

Department of Health and Social Security (1972c). *Management Arrangements for the Reorganised National Health Service.* London.

Department of Health and Social Security (1973, 1974). *Reorganisation of the National Health Service and Local Government in England and Wales: a report from the working party on collaboration between the NHS and Local Government on its activities.* (To the end of 1971, 1973; January to July 1973, 1973; July 1973 to April 1974, 1974.)

Department of Health and Social Security (1979). *Patients First. Consultative paper on the structure and management of the National Health Service in England and Wales.* London.

Department of Health and Social Security (1980). *Health Service Development. Structure and management.* DHSS circular HC(80)8. London.

Ministry of Health (1968). *The Administrative Structure of Medical and Related Services in England and Wales.* London.

Resource Allocation Working Party (1976). *Sharing Resources for Health in England. Report of the Resource Allocation Working Party.* London.

Royal Commission on the National Health Service (1979). *Merrison Report.* Cmnd. 7615. London.

Further reading

Chaplin, N. W. (ed.) (1982). *Health Care in the United Kingdom.*

NATIONAL HEALTH SERVICE (REORGANIZATION) ACT 1973. The 1973 Act made some changes in the arrangements provided for the *National Health Service in the *National Health Service Act 1946. Local health authorities were abolished and their responsibilities including public health and all personal health services were transferred to a reorganized health authority system comprising two tiers, namely, Regional Health Authorities (replacing Regional Hospital Boards) and Area Health Authorities (newly created). Executive Councils were replaced by Family Practitioner Committees, and brought under the control of the AHAs. Two other important changes were: the creation of the office of Health Service Commissioner or '*ombudsman'; and the setting up of *Community Health Councils to represent the 'consumer interest'.

NATIONAL HOSPITALS FOR NERVOUS DISEASES, THE, have arisen from the amalgamation of several hospitals. The National Hospital for the Paralysed and Epileptic was founded by Louisa Chandler and her sister in 1860 to care for these patients, who were inadequately treated in the general hospitals of that day. It had eight beds in Queen Square in London. Also there is the Maida Vale Hospital, founded as the London Infirmary for Epilepsy and Paralysis by Dr Julius Althaus in 1866, which was originally in Marylebone, moving to its site in Maida Vale in 1903. These two hospitals were responsible for the founding of neurology and neurosurgery as independent specialties in the UK. In 1948, with the advent of the *National Health Service, they were amalgamated under one Board of Governors, becoming then the National Hospitals for Nervous Diseases. The research and postgraduate medical educational activities were brought together in 1951 under the Institute of Neurology, as part of the British Postgraduate Medical Federation, which is a school of the University of London. Later came the incorporation at Finchley of occupational therapy and physiotherapy facilities (1976). The Audrey Fleming Speech Therapy School in Hampstead and the West End School in Portland Place have combined (1972) and are now the National Hospitals' College of Speech Sciences, the only one of its kind in the UK.

Among the great names in neurology to have worked in these hospitals were John Hughlings *Jackson, David *Ferrier, Henry *Head, Charles Edouard *Brown-Séquard, James Collier, S. A. Kinnier *Wilson, and Gordon *Holmes, while in the early years of neurosurgery Victor *Horsley was pre-eminent.

NATIONAL INSTITUTE FOR MEDICAL RESEARCH. The National Institute for Medical Research (NIMR), Mill Hill, London, is the UK *Medical Research Council's major institute for research in the basic laboratory sciences subserving medicine. The concept of such an institute dates from the beginning of the Council itself, immediately prior to and following the First World War. The first of the Institute's two sites, at Hampstead, was occupied in 1920; in 1949, it moved to larger purpose-built accommodation in Mill Hill, six miles further north of central London.

Many noted biomedical scientists have worked for shorter or longer periods at the NIMR. The first three directors, spanning the period from 1928 to 1971, were in order Sir Henry *Dale, Sir Charles Harington, and Sir Peter Medawar. Among the many topics upon which major research achievements have been either initiated or developed there may be mentioned: the methonium compounds which provided the first effective treatment of *hypertension; the isolation of *ergometrine; many physical methods including *ultramicroscopy and gas *chromatography; *protein synthesis; *vitamin D; virology, particularly with respect to *influenza and transmissible tumours; *immunology; *insulin and *carbohydrate metabolism; sex *hormones and reproductive physiology; environmental physiology; and methods for biological standards and control. (See also RESEARCH INSTITUTES.)

NATIONAL INSTITUTES OF HEALTH (NIH) arose out of a small bacteriological laboratory at the Marine Hospital, Staten Island, New York, established by the US government. It was for research into *cholera and other *infectious diseases. For its first 25 years it is concentrated on these though in 1891 it moved to Washington, DC, as the Hygienic Laboratory. It gradually expanded its interests into *public health under the auspices of the US Public Health Service. In 1930 the name was changed by enactment to National Institute of Health, with the wide remit of 'ascertaining the cause, prevention and cure of disease'. Later the NIH moved to Bethesda, Maryland, where it now employs a staff of about 12 000, some in the Clinical Centre. As funding for research has become increasingly a government concern the administration was handed over to the NIH, which supports research in universities, hospitals, and medical centres of all kinds. The funds used for this purpose now amount to $3150 million annually. With the addition of the National Heart Institute, the National Cancer Institute, and some others the enterprise became the National Institutes of Health. See also RESEARCH INSTITUTES.

NATIONAL INSURANCE ACT 1946. This was one of the enactments which arose out of the *Beveridge Report* and which formed the legislative basis of the British version of the 'welfare state' that has existed since 1948. The Act, which was largely replaced by the National Insurance Act 1965, established an extended system of national insurance providing pecuniary payments by way of unemployment benefit, sickness benefit, maternity benefit, retirement pension, widows' benefit, guardian's allowance, and death grant; it also provided for the making of payments towards the cost of a *national health service. Earlier legislation regarding unemployment insurance, national health insurance, widows', orphans', and old age contributory and non-contributory pensions was repealed by the Act.

NATIONAL INSURANCE (INDUSTRIAL INJURIES) ACTS. These UK Acts, beginning with that of 1946, replaced the Workmen's Compensation Acts 1925–45, repealing most of their provisions, and established a system of compulsory insurance against personal injury caused by accidents arising out of and in the course of an insured person's employment and against prescribed diseases and injuries due to the nature of a person's employment. Compensation was in the form of insurance benefits administered by the state. Compensation in respect of employment prior to the operation of the Act (i.e. to 1946) has been retained under the Industrial Injuries and Diseases (Old Cases) Act 1975. The Acts were in turn superseded by the Social Security Acts of 1975 and 1978.

NATIONAL MEDICAL ASSOCIATIONS. See MEDICAL COLLEGES, ETC. OF THE UK; MEDICAL INSTITUTIONS, ETC, IN THE USA AND CANADA.

NATURAL CHILDBIRTH, also known as the Grantly Dick Read method of childbirth, was first advocated by Read in 1933. The principle is the avoidance of pain and muscular tension by relaxation methods which allow the birth to proceed naturally and render *analgesic drugs unnecessary. Some advocates of natural childbirth feel also that the mother should be allowed to choose her own posture during labour.

NATURAL SELECTION is the process by which life forms best adapted to their environment survive and reproduce in the greatest numbers, propagating their *genetic characteristics. Genetic *mutations producing new characteristics favourable to survival and reproduction are propagated, those unfavourable are not.

Charles *Darwin in 1859 proposed natural selection as the principal mechanism of evolutionary change and hence as the origin of species.

NATURISM is a movement based on the practice of communal nudity in private grounds or on beaches set aside for the purpose.

NATUROPATHY is a system which eschews the use of medicinal drugs and the consumption of other than 'natural' foods.

NAUNYN, BERNHARD (1839–1925). German clinical physician, MD Berlin (1863). Naunyn was professor of clinical medicine in Strasbourg, and also in Dorpat, Berne, and Königsberg. His special interest was in metabolism and diseases of the liver and pancreas, and *diabetes mellitus.

NAUSEA is an unpleasant sensation of being about to vomit, sometimes culminating in the act of vomiting. The original meaning was seasickness.

NAVY, ROYAL: MEDICAL SERVICES

Origins. Prior to the 16th c., sick and wounded seamen were nursed in hospitals on the Channel coast, which were independently endowed, owned by the town or attached to religious houses. With the decline of the monasteries towards the end of the 15th c., independent almshouses were provided by mariners' guilds at Hull, Newcastle, and Bristol. Elsewhere, the sick were quartered in private houses and inns under government contract or were admitted to *St Bartholomew's and *St Thomas's hospitals in London. During the early Tudor period, seamen continued to receive pay while sick and, if discharged, were given travelling expenses and a small terminal grant. Howard, Drake, and Hawkyns, concerned about the plight of seamen after the Armada battle, established the Chatham Chest in 1590 as an independent charity supported by subscriptions of sixpence a month from all seamen; this was the earliest form of health insurance. In 1592, Sir John Hawkyns founded his hospital in Chatham to provide twelve almshouses for pensioners and Elizabeth's Poor Law Act of 1601 included provision for wounded seamen. Fifteenth-century voyages of discovery and Henry VIII's revolutionary innovations in shipbuilding and naval gunnery resulted in ships of greater size, firepower, and seakeeping capability, with augmented crews living in overcrowded conditions and exposed, not only to wounds and burns from missiles, splinters, and gun explosions, but also to devastating epidemics. *Plague and *dysentery were first recorded in 1545 (Oppenheim, 1896). *Scurvy appeared with the long Elizabethan voyages, and *typhus resulted from the activities of the press-gang in time of war. An epidemic of dysentery in 1588 led to the appointment of two physicians and one, Roger Marbeck, subsequently sailed with the fleet to Cadiz.

Henry VIII was first to realize the need for a permanent medical service at sea. Lists of surgeons in his *navy royal* appear throughout his reign, coordinated by the Company of Surgeons. The first evidence of a structured medical service is provided by the Cotton MSS (Galba, BIII, fol. 154, British Library), which lists the pay of the chief surgeon, of eight 'other surgions being most expert', and of more junior surgeons, who served in Howard's fleet against France in 1512 or 1513. Certainly, in 1513, there were 32 naval surgeons serving under four masters and a chief surgeon (Exch. Accts, 56(10), 1513, Public Record Office). Henry's pharmacopoeia of plasters and ointments (Sloane MSS 1047, British Library) appears to have been used by naval surgeons. It marked a break with classical tradition by introducing simple practical remedies.

Evolution and structure. The size and complexity of Henry's navy required an effective administration and Henry created a Navy Board in 1546. Naval surgeons served their apprenticeship with masters of varying calibre, but were examined and appointed by the London Company, on behalf of the Board which granted their warrants, to ships appropriate to their qualifications and experience. A liaison between the Board and Surgeons' Hall was established, in the Elizabethan era, by William Clowes, who acted as *de facto*, if not *de jure*, surgeon-general. He served in the flagship *Ark Royal* against the Spanish Armada in 1588 and, in that year, published the first book on naval surgery. This was based upon 20 years of sea experience, and established the practical and sturdily independent tradition of naval medical writing. Clowes was followed, under the early Stuarts, by John *Woodall, first surgeon-general of the East India Company, whose book, *The Surgeon's Mate* (1617), listed the contents of the surgeon's chest, described the use of his instruments and called for high professional standards, continuing postgraduate education, and a journal of clinical practice. Woodall was probably responsible for ensuring that the 1629 barber-surgeons' charter of Charles I provided for the mandatory

examination of sea surgeons at Surgeons' Hall and for the inspection of their chests and instruments, towards which the cost the surgeon was awarded a 'free gift'. Woodall was succeeded by James Pearse, who became the first official surgeon-general of the Navy in 1670 and followed Knight as surgeon-general of the Forces in 1680 to establish a joint directorate of Army and Navy medical services until William's accession in 1688. From 1703, chests were supplied by the *Society of Apothecaries and Queen Anne's Bounty, which replaced the free gift, was given presumably to meet their increased cost.

The Dutch wars of the 17th c. demonstrated the need for a central medical department to co-ordinate arrangements for the reception, treatment, and disposal of casualties. The first of six wartime Sick and Hurt Boards was established in 1653 and took over surgeons' appointments. Whereas continuity was provided by senior surgeons and, later, the surgeon-general, physicians were often responsible for regional arrangements and medical advice to the Board until, in 1654, Cromwell chose Paul de Laune as first physician of the Fleet. During this period, naval sick quarters were established in home ports and, later, overseas. They were administered by a 'Surgeon and Agent'. Surgeons also held permanent appointments in naval dockyards. The Fifth Board (1702) was given responsibility for prisoners of war and acted with the scrupulous care and impartiality of the *Red Cross today. The Sixth Board (1740) was not dissolved, but continued throughout the wars of the 18th c. In 1796, its prisoner-of-war commitment was transferred to the Transport Board with which the Sick and Hurt Board was itself amalgamated in 1805. The Transport Board with its single remaining medical commissioner was absorbed into the Victualling Board in 1817. Sir William Burnett, an able administrator, became its physician in 1822. When the Admiralty Board was reorganized in 1832, Burnett was made Physician-General of the Navy to head an independent medical department. In 1841 he was styled Inspector General of Hospitals and Fleets, and in 1844 Director-General of the Medical Department of the Navy; this marked belated recognition by the Admiralty of the value of professional men. Surgeons did not achieve commissioned rank and a uniform until 1805, and assistant surgeons had to wait until 1855 for these privileges. Staff Surgeons were introduced in 1855 and Fleet Surgeons—a grade higher—in 1875, in order to prove parity with the Army and reward experience and responsibility. Agitation for better conditions of service continued until the highly professional service of recent years was established. In 1918, surgeons were given the equivalent executive rank that they still hold: surgeons entered as Surgeon Lieutenants; Staff Surgeons became Surgeon Lieutenant Commanders; Fleet Surgeons, Surgeon Commanders; Deputy Inspectors, Surgeon Captains; and Inspectors General, Surgeon Rear-Admirals. The

Medical Director-General has since held the rank of Surgeon Vice-Admiral and is accountable to the Admiralty Board through the Second Sea Lord. Today, approximately 370 medical officers hold commissions of varying length. A large reserve, representing every medical specialty, is used to augment training, research and clinical care at home and overseas and can be readily integrated into emergency surgical teams in support of operations by Royal Marines.

Hospitals. A need for hospitals became evident during the 17th c. when fleets were deployed far afield. The *Goodwill,* a hospital-storeship, supplied a solution in the Mediterranean in 1625 and hospital ships have been employed ever since, enjoying particular success in both World Wars and in the Falklands operation of 1982. The heavy casualties of the three Dutch wars overwhelmed local facilities, and naval hospitals appeared at Rochester in 1666 and Plymouth in 1673. There were probably others and the Commonwealth, in 1642, also requisitioned Henry VII's Savoy Hospital and Ely House in London. The large number of disabled led William III to develop Greenwich Palace as a hospital for naval pensioners in memory of Queen Anne. Under naval executive, rather than medical, administration, standards of hygiene and care rapidly deteriorated, in contrast to its infirmary for those acutely ill, under medical direction, which a Royal Commission in 1860 found efficient and spotlessly clean. The infirmary became the Dreadnought Seamen's Hospital in 1870 and Greenwich Hospital passed to the Royal Naval College in 1873. Haslar Hospital (Fig. 1) at Gosport, with accommodation for 1800 patients, was built between 1746 and 1762 and a new hospital at Plymouth for 950 patients, between 1758 and 1762. They were administered by the senior physician and a council. The Melville Hospital at Chatham (1827–8) was superseded by a new hospital in 1905, while Great Yarmouth Hospital (1809) became the naval asylum in 1863. With the territorial gains of the 18th c., overseas hospitals were established and, by the end of the century, there were naval hospitals at Haslar, Plymouth, Chatham, Yarmouth, Cork, Portland,

Fig. 1. Royal Navy Hospital, Haslar

Deal, in Scotland, Malta, Halifax, Victoria, Jamaica, Bermuda, Cape Town, Trincomalee, and Hong Kong. Today, hospitals remain only at Haslar, Plymouth, and Gibraltar. Executive officers were installed as governors of Haslar and Plymouth in 1794. With a few notable exceptions (Parry at Haslar), they were not a success. They brought discipline and better organization, but also pomposity, interference, and the imposition of unworkable dockyard routines until, in 1870, following a civil commission on naval hospitals which found the medical arrangements admirable, they reverted to medical administration under Inspectors-General.

Nursing. Until the end of the 18th c., nursing on board ships was provided by 'loblolly boys' (loblolly was a kind of porridge);they were seamen or marines of good character. From 1808, a separate sick berth below the forecastle was established. In hospital ships, an all-male sick watch had been the rule since 1703, with women used for domestic duties only, although, assisted by pensioners, some nursed in hospitals . In 1853, sick-berth staff were provided for all sea-going ships and, in 1854, men replaced women in hospital. The Sick Berth Branch, recruited primarily from boys of Greenwich Hospital School, stemmed from the Hoskins Committee of 1883. With a recognized career structure, it was the forerunner of the modern Medical Branch with its medical assistants and technicians.

Elizabeth Alkin devoted all her private resources to the nursing of wounded sailors during the Dutch wars and, during the Crimean war, three naval hospitals operated under a matron and two nursing sisters to achieve an excellent health record. The Hoskins Committee recommended a female nursing service, which was established in 1885 and developed into Queen Alexandra's Royal Naval Nursing Service in 1902, accepting suitably qualified male (naval) nurses in 1982.

Reformers. The evolution of the modern naval medical service has been due entirely to the courageous efforts of scientifically orientated medical officers in the face of Admiralty hostility. In the process, the sailor has been the principal beneficiary, for almost every improvement in his health, diet, and conditions of service has derived directly from individual medical initiative. Clowes, Woodall, Wiseman, Yonge and Moyle made important contributions to surgery during the 17th c. Their emphasis upon professionalism, clinical observation and record-keeping led directly to 18th and 19th c. reforms, spearheaded by James *Lind (Fig. 2) and his disciples, Sir Gilbert *Blane and Thomas Trotter. Lind towers above them all and is specially remembered for the world's first controlled *clinical trial, which he conducted on board HMS *Salisbury* (Fig. 3) in 1747, to prove the power of oranges and lemons to cure scurvy in matched scorbutic cases on a scorbutic diet. His *Treatise of the Scurvy* (1753) described the pathological

Fig. 2. Dr James Lind, after a portrait painted upon Lind's retirement from the Royal Naval Hospital, Haslar, in 1783

features, scurvy's association with other nutritional disorders, and the adverse influence of environmental and psychological stress; it included a masterly review of the world literature. His *Health of Seamen* (1757) provided the basis of modern sanitary science and his *Hot Climates* (1768), the first authoritative handbook on tropical medicine. At Haslar, Lind lowered the rate of hospital infection, introduced high-energy/*protein diets with vitamin-rich foods of high fibre content and demonstrated an enlightened administration. He showed the feasibility of distilling sea water, was first to demonstrate the clinical signs and correct treatment of *hypothermia, and described modern methods of *resuscitation. Although they were ignored by the Admiralty until Blane became a commissioner of the Sick and Hurt Board in 1795, the introduction of Lind's measures

Fig. 3 HMS *Salisbury*, from a painting by Leonard Pearce

contributed as significantly to the defeat of Napoleon as their adoption by Captain Cook led to the success of his three great voyages of discovery between 1768 and 1779. Scurvy and typhus were eliminated from the fleet and the incidence of *malaria and of *yellow fever was markedly reduced. Blane (1815) claimed that the number of sick fell by 75 per cent between 1806 and 1811. His pursuit of medical audit was taken up by statisticians such as Robertson and Bryson, and the *Health of the Navy Statistical Reports* from 1830 reflected this favourable trend.

Postgraduate education. Lind wrote his first paper for the Association of Surgeons of the Royal Navy, an intellectually active group founded in 1746 to advance knowledge of the sea diseases which had caused devastating mortality during Anson's circumnavigation (1740–4). This group had rooms in Covent Garden and William *Hunter as lecturer, and followed the tradition established during the Dutch wars, of surgeons holding shipboard clinical meetings after each engagement. Cockburn attempted to put such informal gatherings on an official basis by using hospital ships for postgraduate teaching; this was one of a number of reforms that he proposed in 1702, which were rejected by the Admiralty. Meetings continued in ports and, in 1732, John Atkins propounded a scheme for a postgraduate medical centre in Portsmouth Naval Academy. No more was heard about the Association after 1762, but the gold medal it awarded for the best case presentation was endowed by Sir Gilbert Blane and is still given for outstanding work. The *Journal of the Royal Naval Medical Service* is the Association's natural successor. Trotter, in 1797, recognizing the teaching potential of Haslar, advocated medical libraries and a museum, finally established in 1827, when Sir William Burnett installed Dr Scott as lecturer and librarian at Haslar with a museum curator. Courses of lectures were held until 1871, with naval medical officers attending the new Army medical school, until a naval medical school was established in Haslar in 1881.

The influence of this long period of medical education was reflected in the calibre of the doctors it produced. The health and welfare of convicts during voyages to Australia were transformed by the appointment of Surgeon-Superintendents. The antislavery patrols of the West African Squadron were possible only because of the preventive measures practised by its surgeons, who contributed materially to knowledge of tropical diseases. Nineteenth-century polar expeditions produced the surgeon-naturalist, typified by Sir John Richardson, who made valuable contributions himself and collaborated closely with *Darwin, *Hooker, and *Huxley. Sir Thomas Spencer *Wells dramatically reduced operative mortality in his London hospital by introducing naval standards of hygiene and ventilation.

The modern medical service. Alexander

Turnbull, Inspector-General at Haslar in 1897, deserves the credit for courageous initiatives which ultimately provided the highly professional service of the 20th c. His influence in the Durnsford Committee resulted in the transfer of the medical school to the Royal Naval College at Greenwich in 1912, where access to College departments and to patients with tropical diseases at the Dreadnought Hospital stimulated research, notably that of Sheldon Dudley into the epidemiology and prophylaxis of *diphtheria, and that of Rainsford on *typhoid vaccine. On the outbreak of the Second World War, the school moved to Clevedon in Somerset and, after the war, to Monkton House, Alverstoke, Gosport.

The increasing number and complexity of maritime medical specialties during the 1960s required rapid expansion of research and training facilities. To meet this need, a new *Institute of Naval Medicine was developed on the Alverstoke site in 1969. with responsibility for postgraduate training and research vested in a Surgeon Rear-Admiral who became the first Dean of Naval Medicine. Training in the various maritime specialties is co-ordinated by a Director of Studies in collaboration with the professor of naval hygiene, who is responsible for training and research in naval occupational medicine, and with the professors of naval medicine and surgery, who hold joint appointments with their respective Royal Colleges and with the Institute and Haslar Hospital. They control research and postgraduate training in naval hospitals, which now offer naval medical officers a wide spectrum of clinical experience as there is also a 50 per cent intake of civilian patients. A Director of Medical Staff Training in Haslar co-ordinates the training of medical ratings, including that of state-registered and state-enrolled nurses in conjunction with QARNNS tutors. The Institute team of doctors, physiologists, physicists, psychologists, chemists, and statisticians provides operational support for the fleet. This includes radiological and environmental safety surveillance, radiochemical analysis, mobile mass miniature radiography, the investigation of factors affecting men in relation to their working environment, and control of toxicological and biological hazards in ships and dockyards. Mobile units are immediately available in case of diving and radiation accidents, and for control of epidemics. Research is supervised by Clinical and Environmental Working Parties of medical staff, university consultants, and representatives of the Royal Naval Personnel Committee of the *Medical Research Council. Projects relate to diving, the submarine atmosphere, nuclear radiation, anthropometry, noise, vibration, motion sickness, performance under stress, and survival in extreme conditions. Clinical research centres upon diseases with a high incidence in seamen, such as renal and gastroenterological conditions. The Institute's medical research unit in Devonport dockyard undertakes epidemiological studies in industrial diseases, and dental requirements are

met by a Director of Dental Training and Research. Collaboration with similar American, Canadian, and French institutes has proved to be mutually beneficial and cost-effective.

The increasing diversity of maritime medicine led to reorganization of the Medical Director-General's department in 1973 under Directors of Personnel and Logistics, Health and Research, and Naval Dental Services, with the Matron-in-Chief responsible for nursing services. The medical service was restructured in 1975, with the Dean of Naval Medicine co-ordinating research and training, the Surgeon Rear-Admiral (Naval Hospitals) responsible for clinical standards and practice, and the Surgeon Rear-Admiral (Ships and Establishments) overseeing general practice, the occupational health service in dockyards, and command staff officers who act as community physicians. Emphasis upon triservice collaboration gained impetus from the Defence Medical Services Inquiry Committee's recommendations in 1973. Consultant Approval Boards, the Armed Forces Medical Advisory Board, triservice schools for physiotherapists, radiographers, laboratory technicians, and *dental hygienists and a triservice Directorate of Medical Policy and Plans are examples of a continuing trend. From 1985 a Defence Medical Services Department has been established under a single (triservice) Director-General. (See also ARMY, BRITISH: MEDICAL SERVICES; AIR FORCE, ROYAL: MEDICAL SERVICES.)   J. WATT

References

Allison, R. S. (1943). *Sea Diseases*. London.
Allison, R. S. (1979). *The Surgeon Probationers*. Belfast.
Blane, Sir G. (1785). *Observations on the Diseases Incident to Seamen*. London.
Blane, Sir G. (1815). Statements of the comparative health of the Navy. *Transactions of the Medico-Chirurgical Society*, **6**, 490–573.
Clowes, Sir W. L. (1897–1903). *The Royal Navy. A History from the Earliest Times to the Present*. 7 vols. London.
Cockburn, W. (1696). *An Account of the Nature, Causes, Symptoms and Cure of the Distempers that are incident to Seafaring People. With observations on the Diet of Sea-Men in His Majesty's Navy*. London.
Cotton MSS, Galba, BIII, fol. 154 (formerly 136). British Library. London.
Exchequer Accounts, 56(10), 1513. Public Record Office. London.
Keevil, J. J. (1957–8). *Medicine and the Navy*. Vols 1 and 2, Edinburgh and London.
Lind, J. (1753). *A Treatise of the Scurvy*. Edinburgh.
Lind, J. (1757). *An Essay on the Most Effectual Means of Preserving the Health of Seamen*. London.
Lind, J. (1768). *An Essay on Diseases Incidental to Europeans in Hot Climates*. London.
Lloyd, C. and Coulter, J. L. S. (1961–3). *Medicine and the Navy*. Vols 3 and 4, Edinburgh and London.
Ministry of Defence (1973). *Report of the Defence Medical Services Inquiry Committee*. London.
Oppenheim, M. (1896). *History of the Administration of the Royal Navy, and of Merchant Shipping in Relation to the Navy*. Vol. 1. London.
Parliamentary Papers (1866). *Report of the Milne Committee on Medical Officers*, 60, 85. British Library. London.

Parliamentary Papers. (1884). *Report on Sick Berth and Nursing Staff*, 17, 99. British Library. London.
Parliamentary Papers (1899). *Report on the Training of Medical Officers*, 55, 593. British Library. London.
Sloane MSS 1047. British Library. London.
Statistical Report on the Health of the Navy 1830–1836 (1840–1). London.
Turnbull, A. (1903). *History of the Medical Department*. MSS, Haslar Library.
Woodall, J. (1617). *The Surgeon's Mate*. London.

NECROBIOSIS is the formation of circumscribed degenerative lesions of skin *collagen, seen particularly in diabetic patients.

NECROLOGY. A death roll, an obituary notice, or a history of the dead.

NECROMANCY is the prophesying of future events by supposed communication with the spirits of the dead.

NECROPHILIA is a pathological liking for dead bodies, or a sexual perversion involving intercourse with corpses.

NECROPSY. Synonym for *autopsy.

NECROSIS. Death of tissue.

NECROSIS, AVASCULAR. *Necrosis due to failure of blood supply.

NEEDLE. Any slender sharp metal instrument for puncturing or suturing; or when hollow, for injecting or aspirating.

NEGATIVISM is pathological resistance to suggestion; in pronounced cases the patient does the opposite of what he is asked to do. The same term is sometimes used to denote an abnormal state in which a patient consistently does what he ought not to do (with food, faeces, etc.).

NEGLIGENCE is an act or state of being neglectful, of duty, dress, cleanliness, etc. See also PROFESSIONAL NEGLIGENCE; LAW AND MEDICINE IN THE UK; LAW AND MEDICINE IN THE USA.

NEGRI, ADELCHI (1876–1912). Italian pathologist, MD Pavia (1900). While assistant to *Golgi, Negri discovered the *rabies corpuscles (Negri bodies) in the pyramidal cells of *Ammon's horn in the brains of animals dying of rabies. They are recognized as pathognomonic of this disease. Negri died of pulmonary *tuberculosis aged 35.

NEGUS, SIR VICTOR EWINGS (1887–1974). See OTOLARYNGOLOGY.

NEISSER, ALBERT LUDWIG SIEGMUND (1855–1916). German dermatologist and bacteriologist, MD Breslau (1877). Neisser discovered the bacterial cause of *gonorrhoea, since named *Neisseria gonorrhoeae*. This was in 1879 when pelvic infections and vaginal discharges were not understood. He also investigated *syphilis and worked with his friend Paul *Ehrlich on the use of arsenicals; he strongly advocated the therapeutic value of mercurials, which help prevent the worst manifestations of *neurosyphilis. In 1880 he identified *Mycobacterium leprae* which Hansen had seen in 1873 but had not thought to be the cause of leprosy. He was associated with von *Wassermann in devising his serological test for syphilis.

NEISSERIA is a genus of aerobic gram-negative *diplococci which includes the important pathogens of *gonorrhoea (*Neisseria gonorrhoeae*) and *meningococcal meningitis (*N. meningitidis*).

NÉLATON, AUGUSTE (1807–73). French surgeon, MD Paris (1836). In 1851 Nélaton became professor of surgery at the Hôpital S. Louis. Nélaton, who was surgeon to Napoleon III, was highly regarded as a skilled, wise, and knowledgeable surgeon of unimpeachable integrity and unwavering courtesy. He introduced the rubber *catheter (1860) and was one of the first to use the electrocautery. He popularized *ovariotomy in France and invented a bullet-seeking probe which was first used on Garibaldi at Aspromonte in 1862. A line joining the anterior superior iliac spine and the ischial tuberosity is still commonly called Nélaton's line.

NEMATODE. Any member of the large phylum Nematoda, which consists of roundworms, threadworms, and eelworms, many though not all being endoparasitic in plants and animals. Those of medical importance include *Ascaris, *Strongyloides, *Ancylostoma, *Toxocara, *Trichinella (the agent of *trichiniasis), the several species causing *filariasis, and some others.

NEOMYCIN. A member of the *aminoglycoside group of antibiotics with similar characteristics to the others, except that it is considered too toxic to be administered parenterally. Its use is therefore confined to topical application in infections of the skin and mucous membranes, and to sterilization of the intestine prior to bowel surgery or in hepatic failure.

NEONATE. An infant during the first four weeks of life.

NEOPLASM. Any tumour or new growth, whether or not malignant. See ONCOLOGY.

NEOSTIGMINE is a synthetic quaternary ammonium compound with cholinergic effects, of value in the treatment of *myasthenia gravis and other conditions. It is an *anticholinesterase, that is it acts by inhibiting the enzyme which destroys *acetylcholine.

NEPHELOMETRY is the optical measurement of turbidity in suspensions by means of light scattering.

NEPHRECTOMY is the surgical removal of a kidney.

NEPHRITIS is any inflammation of kidney tissue. When otherwise unqualified, nephritis is usually taken to mean one of that group of disorders collectively known as glomerulonephritis. See NEPHROLOGY.

NEPHROGRAPHY is the radiographic visualization of the kidneys, on plain X-ray films or with the assistance of *pyelography, *arteriography, or *computed transaxial tomography.

NEPHROLITHIASIS. The presence of *calculi within the kidney and upper urinary tract.

NEPHROLOGIST. A specialist in diseases of the kidney.

NEPHROLOGY

Terminology. Etymologically, 'nephrology' should mean 'knowledge of the kidney'—no more and no less. But as the term is actually used, it is virtually synonymous with 'medical diseases of the kidneys'. This usage implies two important exclusions: first, the structure and function of the kidneys except in so far as they relate to the manifestations of renal disease; and secondly, those disorders of the kidney which are commonly referred to surgeons, thus entering the realm of urology, together of course with disorders of the urinary tract which conveys *urine from the kidneys to the outer world. On the other hand, nephrology is not an island within the medical domain: it is therefore not possible to give a coherent account of it without touching on related matters, such as general disorders which may affect the kidney; the effects of renal disease on other systems of the body; and—even more generally—the relationship between kidney disease and that failure to preserve normal body composition which is one of the hallmarks of renal insufficiency.

Historical aspects. The recognition of nephrology as a particular specialty within medicine is comparatively recent, say within the past 20–30 years. Let us leave the causes of this specialization until later; this section will outline the growth of knowledge of renal disease up to the present date.

Individual manifestations of renal disease, such as *haematuria, *dropsy, and uraemic coma, have been observed, even if not recognized, from the earliest times; the particular association between small shrunken kidneys and chronic illness was known both to Greek and to Arab medicine. Among the dark sayings in the *Hippocratic writing we come on 'Colourless urine is bad'; but we cannot tell whether this is the 'badness' of chronic renal failure, or that of *diabetes mellitus.

The ancients were greatly handicapped by their adherence to the theory of the four *humours, and by the lack of chemical methodology, so that they were neither predisposed nor competent to explore the more mundane chemical dimension which is so important in the study of renal disease. In the 17th and 18th c., however, systematic observation of disease in individual patients was encouraged by *Sydenham and *Boerhaave; modern chemical ideas began to be developed, and appropriate methods devised; and the attitudes of the enlightened weakened the hold of authority. Clinically, associations of symptoms were beginning to be more clearly recognized—the association of acute nephritis with scarlatina (*scarlet fever); of dropsy with coagulable urine; and of chronic illness and early death with contracted kidneys. Chemically, analysis had advanced to the stage where it was possible for *Bostock to show that the presence of *albumin in the urine could be matched by a deficiency of albumin in the blood, and that in chronic renal failure there was an excess of *urea in the blood.

By the start of the 19th c. the more sinister forms of renal disease were familiar not only to doctors, but to the educated layman. For example, Sir Walter Scott shortly before his death in 1832 confided to his journal that: 'within these three days I have passed (you may alter the vowel A to the vowel I) a formidable quantity of blood. When a man makes blood instead of water, he is tempted to think of the possibility of his soon making earth.'

The time was thus ripe for the contribution of Richard *Bright of *Guy's Hospital, a contribution so remarkable as to have linked his name forever with that most characteristic of renal diseases, glomerulonephritis (Bright's disease; see below). The quality of the advance made by Bright can be fully assessed only if we consider the difficulty inherent in the study of a disease, or more accurately a group of diseases, which may appear either with dramatic suddenness as haematuria or dropsy, or on the other hand may not be detected until the kidneys have totally failed; which may last for only a few weeks, or for upwards of 20 years; whose outcome ranges from complete recovery to irreversible renal failure; and in which the kidneys after death are most commonly shrunken, but may on the other hand be enlarged. Richard Bright himself summarized his endeavour as 'to connect accurate and faithful observations after death with symptoms displayed during life', in consequence of which saying he has sometimes been described as the pioneer of clinicopathological correlation. This is both more and less than the truth. Of course, Bright was preceded by *Vesalius in the matter of clinicopathological correlation, but he added to it his own very particular contribution—of making, recording, and reporting detailed observations on patients, some of whom were followed for many years. This was Bright's essential contribution, but it was also enhanced by his collaboration with John Bostock's chemical studies. Bright established a framework of the natural history of glomerulonephritis, to build on which has been one of the major strands of clinical nephrology, using Bright's method of long-term observation, and correlation with pathological findings. It is perhaps not too much to claim that, at the broad-brush level, Bright's picture is incomplete in only two respects. The first of these was the connection between chronic renal disease on the one hand, and a liability to cardiac (heart) failure and to *apoplexy on the other; Bright was, of course, well aware of the clinical associations and of the enlargement of the heart, but the connecting link of high *blood pressure had to await recognition until *Mahomed had devised a method of measuring it.

The second, possibly even more important, missing piece in Bright's scheme was the chemical consequences of renal failure. Bostock had, it is true, become aware of the raised blood urea, but this is only one facet of the biochemical catastrophe which is induced by failure of kidney function. As already hinted, it is illogical to dissociate what the kidneys fail to do in disease from what they can do in health: biochemical functional studies join clinicopathological correlation as the second great strand in clinical nephrology. The root of the matter was enunciated by Claude *Bernard in his dictum 'la fixité du milieu interne est la condition de la vie libre'. Or, less dramatically, the health of an organism depends on the composition of the body fluids being maintained within fairly narrow limits. Now, this cannot be achieved solely by tipping out waste products—it is an injustice to the kidneys to call them merely 'organs of excretion'. Just as important, they are 'organs of regulation', keeping stable both the amount of body fluid, and its concentrations of sodium, potassium, hydrogen ions, and their associated anions. This is what W. B. *Cannon described as the *homeostatic function of the kidneys: studies of the composition of body fluid in health and disease have been closely linked with the development of nephrology. In laying the foundations of clinical chemistry, *Folin, *Peters, and van *Slyke laid one of the bases of clinical nephrology.

To take a convenient landmark, by the end of the Second World War, much information had accumulated on the natural history of the various forms of renal disease, and on the biochemical correlates of altered renal function. Methods of determining renal function, both in general and in respect of particular constituents, were available. There was, however, one major handicap to clinicopathological correlation—only end-stage renal disease was available for pathological studies; and of course we had no means of substituting for kidneys which had failed, although we were able to correct some of the biochemical distortions in piecemeal fashion. Before describing the 'nephrological revolution' based on renal *biopsy

and on *haemodialysis, it is necessary to give a broad picture of the content of nephrology.

The content of nephrology. Like other organs of the body, the kidneys are liable to infection, to tumours, to degenerative processes including those of ageing, and to disturbance of their circulation; they may also be specially vulnerable to those toxic agents which they excrete in concentrated solution. Such disorders are approached by the physicians on general lines: for the purposes of this article I shall concentrate on two conditions which are peculiar to the kidney—glomerulonephritis and pyelonephritis (see below).

Glomerulonephritis. To make the account of this condition at all intelligible, it is necessary to indicate the function of the glomeruli, and to outline the varied consequences of their impairment; and to emphasize that we are not dealing with a single entity, such as measles, but with a group of disorders which represent a comparatively small number of responses to a very large number of causative agents and more than one process.

Each of our kidneys contains about a million functional units, each of them consisting of a glomerulus and a tubule. The glomerulus consists of a branching tuft of *capillaries, lying within a capsule from which the tubule drains. Small though they are, the kidneys receive about a fifth of the cardiac output, virtually all of which passes through the glomeruli, which constitute a filter which allows the passage of water and salts, but normally prevents the passage of blood cells and of *protein. This process of filtration produces rather more than 100 ml of fluid each minute, an amount many times greater than the final volume of urine. The tubules greatly concentrate the urine, and also adjust its composition to the needs of the body in various subtle ways. When the glomeruli are involved in disease, the selective permeability may be lost in varying degree, so that the filtrate and, in due course, the urine may contain blood cells and protein. Visible blood in the urine is usually a manifestation of *acute glomerular disease: protein in the urine, constantly present in the acute phase, may persist as a chronic phenomenon, and may or may not be accompanied by blood cells detectable by microscopy, but not so abundant as to colour the urine. If the amount of protein being lost in the urine is massive, say 5 g or more daily, and persistent, the proteins in the blood *plasma become depleted. Plasma proteins normally hold fluid within the capillaries by their *osmotic pressure: when they are depleted, fluid may leak into the tissues, producing clinical *oedema, manifest as a swelling which can readily be indented by the finger—'pitting oedema'. If the disease process affecting the glomeruli is persistent, leading to their replacement by fibrous tissue, the manifestations of abnormal glomerular permeability tend to disappear, only to be replaced by manifestations of inadequate filtration. The raw material for urine is, as it were, being cut off at source, leading to retention of many metabolites, of which urea and creatinine are commonly measured, not as being specially toxic in themselves, but as convenient indicators of excretory renal failure. Like many other organs of the body, the kidneys have a substantial reserve of function, with the consequence that glomerular function may be largely lost without the patient being aware of it. This condition of 'latent nephritis' may of course be revealed by the detection of protein in the urine, followed by quantitative assessment of renal function. When glomerular function falls to 10 per cent or less, symptoms begin to appear, perhaps vaguely at first, with lethargy and headaches. As the condition progresses, it seems as if every system of the body is affected, with indigestion, bone pains, *anaemia, drowsiness, and ultimately *coma testifying to the severity of the biochemical distortions. Some of the complex biochemical changes may represent compensatory adaptations, but may later become autonomous, adding to the clinical misery instead of correcting it. But the primacy of the filtration impairment in producing these changes is shown by the extent to which they can be corrected by *dialysis, which in essence substitutes for filtration. Admittedly, dialysis has to be continued indefinitely, and not all patients are restored to glowing health: there is also a suggestion that a successful *transplant is even more advantageous than long-term dialysis. The fact remains that many thousands of patients are alive on dialysis who would otherwise be dead.

Even the above sketchy account of the consequences of altered glomerular function has indicated the great variety of clinical pictures which can be produced by glomerular disease: however, it is not on that basis that I venture the assertion that glomerulonephritis is a group of disorders, and not a single entity. That case rests on diversity of causation, and on diversity of pathogenesis.

As regards causation (or aetiology), the stereotype of acute glomerulonephritis is an illness which follows a *streptococcal infection after an interval of around 10–20 days, and which is characterized by scanty blood-stained urine, puffiness of the face, and a modest rise of blood pressure and blood urea. Recovery after a variable period, often only a week or two, is the rule; however, a variety of exceptional consequences may lead to chronic *proteinuria, or to chronic renal failure. It is increasingly being recognized that there are many causal agents which can lead to the same clinical picture of 'acute nephritis'. In addition to *antigens from certain strains of streptococci (but not from other strains), these include other bacterial antigens; viral antigens; parasitic antigens, foreign serum, drugs, and endogenous antigens from tumours or damaged cells. Moreover, the same clinical features may appear, not as an isolated renal phenomenon, but as part of a general immunological disorder such as *systemic lupus or *polyarteritis nodosa.

It is likely that the majority of these varied antigens produce their effects by the formation of antigen–antibody complexes, with the antigen in slight excess, but this is not the sole mechanism underlying 'acute nephritis': a very similar clinical picture can be produced by *antibodies directed against capillary *endothelium. I think it can be claimed that the long-acknowledged clinical diversity of glomerular nephritis may, in part at least, be related to a great diversity of causal antigens, and at any rate some diversity in the mechanisms producing the glomerular damage. It can further be stated, without going into detail, that the microscopic appearances of the affected glomeruli are also very variable: for example, in patients with the nephrotic syndrome (heavy proteinuria leading to oedema) the glomeruli may appear normal; they may show considerable thickening of the capillary walls (membranous changes); or they may be stuffed with inflammatory cells (proliferative changes).

This is not a textbook, and I have not attempted to describe the many different ways in which glomerulonephritis may reveal itself. The protean variety of symptoms makes it a great mimic of other diseases; so examination of the urine, especially for albumin or more rarely blood cells, is therefore an important part of any routine examination. (For an excellent detailed account of the natural history of the condition, see Cameron, 1979.)

Pyelonephritis. Strictly speaking, the term *pyelitis should denote infection of the renal pelvis—the cavity within the kidney which collects urine from the assembly of tubules, and then drains into the *ureter *en route* to the *urinary bladder and *urethra. However, while infection may very rarely be limited to the pelvis, without involving the renal substance, and may even cause local pain and some general symptoms of infection, nevertheless, for serious renal damage to occur the renal substance must clearly be involved (pyelonephritis). Involvement of the renal substance is demonstrable by the presence of inflammatory cells in the acute stages, and by patchy coarse *scarring of the kidneys in the chronic stage. The patchiness of the scarring is important in distinguishing pyelonephritis from the diffuse involvement of the kidneys in glomerulonephritis; even more strikingly, pyelonephritis may affect only one kidney, belying the term 'doppelseitige Nierenkrankheit' applied to it by the great German nephrologist Franz *Volhard. Unfortunately, patchy scarring is not unique to pyelonephritis, but may also occur in patients who have taken large doses of *analgesics for long periods, or—more rarely—in patients with patchy arterial disease impairing the blood supply to parts of the kidney. This makes it difficult to estimate the extent to which true pyelonephritis is responsible for end-stage renal failure. A recent estimate from the European Dialysis and Transplant Association, quoted by Asscher (1980) in his monograph on urinary infection, credits (or should it be debits?) some 20 per cent of cases of end-stage renal failure to pyelonephritis, a figure which may be compared with 50 per cent attributed to glomerulonephritis, the remaining 30 per cent being attributable to a whole range of other conditions. Some murkiness is inherent in these retrospective attributions, given that in the course of their failure the kidneys may have lost any appearances which might give a clue to the original cause of trouble. In addition, acute episodes of illness, whether of acute nephritis or of acute urinary infection, may be either silent at the time, or forgotten some years later.

How does infection reach the kidney? In the past, there has been argument over the rival claims of infection ascending the urinary tract, and of infection reaching the kidneys by the bloodstream or even the lymphatics. It is now believed that the overwhelming majority of episodes of urinary infection are due to organisms which have ascended the urinary passages, and not to blood-borne infection. A number of observations support this belief. Of urinary infections seen in the community, more than 90 per cent are due to the organism *Escherichia coli (E.coli)*; even in the more selected population seen in hospital practice, about half the infections are due to *E. coli*. This organism is a characteristic inhabitant of the lower *bowel, from which it can be carried to the opening of the urethra. Contamination of the skin between these two orifices has been demonstrated, the organism being of the same type as that found in the bowel and in the urinary tract of the same patient. Spread in this way is more likely in infancy, where the area is swathed in napkins (diapers); and in women than in men, for obvious anatomical reasons. The higher incidence of urinary infection in infancy, and in the female, gives circumstantial evidence for the validity of this method of spread. Not surprisingly, infection of the lower urinary tract (often known as '*cystitis') is commoner than that of the upper urinary tract ('pyelitis' or 'pyelonephritis'), which again is consistent with ascending infection. However, when there is difficulty in voiding urine, as occurs in infants and children, and also in some elderly men, the likelihood of renal involvement is increased, as organisms grow better in stagnant urine and can also ascend a dilated urinary tract more readily.

Urinary infection may be silent, revealed only by bacteriological examination of the urine. In infants, it may present as fever and vomiting, with no local symptoms. In adults, the typical patient is a woman who suddenly feels shivery, notices that she passes urine more frequently, and with some burning pain; the urine itself may be cloudy, or even blood-stained. If the upper urinary tract is involved, the general feeling of illness may be more severe, and there may be pain in one or both loins. Even though such symptoms may clear up, they do call for medical advice; repeated attacks require bacteriological examination, so that a sensible choice of *antibiotic can be made.

There are, of course, many other disorders which affect the kidney, and some which are peculiar to it, such as *polycystic renal disease, and specific disorders of the tubules which can cause a variety of metabolic derangements. I have chosen to deal with the two conditions which make up the greater part of the work of the nephrologist, and which account for the majority of patients with renal disease. In the remainder of this article, I consider the link between renal and general medicine; and the factors which have led to the comparatively recent emergence of nephrology as a medical specialty.

Nephrology in context. There are a number of reasons why physicians concerned with renal disease have felt the need to retain close links with general medicine. Renal disease can manifest itself in patterns which readily mimic disease of other systems of the body; the kidneys can be the victims of a number of multisystem diseases; the progress of renal disease is bound up with the degree of *hypertension which accompanies it; and there is the close relationship between renal function and the status of body fluid.

Renal mimicry can be exemplified by breathlessness simulating respiratory or cardiac disease; by bone pain simulating locomotor disease; by haemorrhages simulating a coagulation disorder; by vomiting and diarrhoea giving a false suspicion of disease of the alimentary tract; and by headache, confusional states, and coma, which may be wrongly attributed to primary brain disease.

Conversely, a number of general diseases may involve the kidneys, and in some of these at least it is the renal involvement which contributes largely to the fatal outcome. For example, in patients with systemic lupus, it is very largely the extent of renal involvement which determines the outcome. Renal involvement is also of considerable importance in *diabetes mellitus, in the *collagen disorders, in *scleroderma, in *gout, in *amyloid disease, in *myelomatosis, and so on.

Of particular importance is the two-way relationship between renal disease and hypertension. Interference with the blood supply to the kidney (renal *ischaemia) leads to an increase in the output of *renin from the kidney, which in turn produces an increase in circulating *angiotensin, a potent hypertensive agent. On the other hand, pre-existing hypertension can itself damage the kidney, through its effect on blood vessels. A number of patients have died from 'malignant hypertension', in which very high levels of blood pressure caused severe and even fatal renal damage; the central role of the level of blood pressure is demonstrable by the beneficial effect of lowering the blood pressure by the potent hypotensive agents which are now available.

In the brief outline of the natural history of glomerulonephritis, I indicated that in some phases of the disease there is retention of salt (sodium chloride) and water, leading to oedema. In some uncommon forms of renal disease there are, on the other hand, inappropriate losses of salt, and also at times of potassium. In these situations the kidney can be looked on as the culprit, responsible for distortion of body fluid. It may also, however, be the victim of *electrolyte disturbances arising elsewhere, most commonly through fluid loss by vomiting or diarrhoea, but also from *endocrine disease or from excessive *sweating. Severe salt depletion leads to a fall in plasma volume and in cardiac output; the renal circulation is prejudiced, leading to inadequate formation of urine, and retention of urea and other waste products. Potassium depletion can also lead to renal damage, with visible abnormalities in the tubule cells. Occasionally, when impaired renal function and disordered body fluid coexist, it may be difficult to discern which is the primary disturbance: such a situation calls forth all the resources of the general physician, although occasionally the key may be found by looking in the urine for evidence of what the kidneys are actually doing. For example, renal losses of sodium or potassium show up in the urine, whereas alimentary losses are associated with a scanty urinary output of these substances.

Nephrology as a specialty. The rapid growth of medical knowledge is in part the fruit of specialization, and also a potent cause of further specialization. The advancement of knowledge almost always requires a degree of concentration on a narrow focus, to the inevitable neglect of large areas of possible interest. In turn, the accumulation of knowledge so gained soon carries it beyond the total comprehension of any one person. Of course, the generalist doctor must always remain of great importance, lest patients fall into the hands of the wrong specialist. I see specialization in general terms as inevitable, but what are the particular factors which may lead to the crystallization of a new specialty? I believe that this commonly happens when important new and exacting techniques of investigation develop, or when special forms of treatment, again requiring particular expertise, are discovered. In the particular case of nephrology, I believe that both these things happened, and at around the same time, in the 1950s.

In the area of investigation there has, of course, been a steady development for the past half century in biochemical, bacteriological, and radiological methods of studying renal disease; however, for practical purposes we had to wait until after the patient's death to see what was actually going on in the kidney. During the 1950s, renal physicians throughout the world began to practise needle biopsy of the kidney, and to study the tissues so obtained by improved staining methods in thin sections, by electron microscopy, and by immunohistology—special methods capable of revealing immune mechanisms of damage. These exacting techniques have greatly increased the interest in, and knowledge of, renal disease.

As faith without works is dead, so accessions of theoretical knowledge must be supplemented by demonstrably useful procedures if they are to make a major impact. This was provided in the case of nephrology by the advent of the Scribner *shunt, which allows repeated access to the circulation, and so the possibility of maintaining the composition of body fluid near to normal by repeated haemodialysis. This provided for the first time a practicable 'medical' treatment for end-stage renal failure; it removed much of the anxiety from the treatment of acute renal failure due to *shock or haemorrhage; and it also greatly increased the applicability of the 'surgical' approach by renal *transplantation, since it could maintain life during episodes of absent renal function or of *rejection. There have been important further developments, such as subcutaneous shunts with a lesser risk of infection; improved dialysers; and techniques of continuous ambulatory peritoneal dialysis and of haemodialysis in the home, both of which can relieve the strain on hospital facilities.

One advantage of the emergence of physicians specializing in renal disease is that they are now more readily identifiable collaborators with surgeons who are specialists in urology or in transplantation. Similar collaborations are already established in *cardiology and in *gastroenterology. These linkages have the effect of confirming specialization according to the system of the body, and, more important, of bringing different insights to bear on the same problems. Nephrology can now be regarded as an established specialty, though one retaining strong links with general medicine through a common interest in multisystem disorders, the causes and consequences of hypertension, and the disorders of body fluid. See also UROLOGICAL SURGERY.

D. BLACK

References
Asscher, A. W. (1980). *The Challenge of Urinary Tract Infections.* London and New York.
Cameron, J. S. (1979). The natural history of glomerulonephritis. In Black, D. and Jones, N. F. (eds), *Renal Disease*, Ch. 12. 4th edn, Oxford.

NEPHRON. See RENAL TUBULE.

NEPHROSIS is, strictly, any disease of the kidney; it is commonly used synonymously with *nephrotic syndrome.

NEPHROTIC SYNDROME is a syndrome of *oedema, *albuminuria, and hypoalbuminaemia resulting from increased permeability of the renal glomerular basement membrane to *protein. See NEPHROLOGY.

NEPHROTOXIC describes an agent that is poisonous to kidney tissue.

NERVE CELL. See NEURONE.

NERVE FIBRES are the individual components of

nerves; each fibre consists of a fine threadlike process (an *axon or a *dendrite) of a nerve cell (*neurone) surrounded, in the case of larger fibres, by a sheath of *myelin. Each axon or motor (efferent) fibre conducts impulses away from its own cell body, and does so independently of other fibres in the nerve. Dendrites (sensory or afferent fibres) conduct towards their cell body. The myelin sheath, when present, provides high resistance insulation from tissue fluids and enables greater conduction speeds.

NERVE GAS. One of a group of volatile liquids which are severely toxic by virtue of their anti-cholinesterase action, that is they inhibit the enzyme *cholinesterase which normally inactivates the neurotransmitter substance *acetylcholine. Hence acetylcholine accumulates in excess, and prevents normal neuromuscular function.

NERVES are bundles of sensory and/or motor nerve fibres with connective tissue and blood vessels, each nerve running in a common sheath of connective tissue. Within a nerve each nerve fibre conducts impulses independently of its fellows.

NERVOUS BREAKDOWN is an imprecise term denoting any acute and incapacitating emotional or mental disturbance.

NERVOUSNESS is a state of undue excitability, irritability, or restlessness.

NERVOUS SYSTEM. The *central nervous system (*brain and *spinal cord) and the peripheral *nerves considered together, including the *autonomic nervous system.

NERVOUS SYSTEM, CENTRAL. See CENTRAL NERVOUS SYSTEM.

NERVOUS SYSTEM, PERIPHERAL. The neural elements of the body (see NEURONE) and their supporting tissues considered collectively, excluding those contained in the *brain and *spinal cord and also excluding the *autonomic nervous system.

NESTORIAN MEDICINE. The Nestorian Christians were followers of *Nestorius, Patriarch of Constantinople, who in AD 431 was denounced by the Council of Ephesus for his heresy (that Christ had two distinct natures, divine and human). The doctrine, however, continued to flourish in Syria and the East, and the Nestorians, debarred from eminence in Church and State, devoted themselves particularly to medicine. The medical school and hospitals at Edessa (Urfa, the 'Athens of Syria') were taken over, and a school of medicine was established which for a time rivalled that of Alexandria. Despite the success of Nestorian practitioners, they were eventually expelled from the empire in 489 by Emperor Zaro at the instigation of the orthodox Bishop Cyril. The Nestorians then removed to Persia, where they established further medical schools, the most famous being that at Jundishapur. Here the most liberal-minded of the Christians came together with remains of Greek free thought and the ancient knowledge of the East—Hindu physicians were to be found among the professors at Jundishapur. For two centuries the Nestorians translated Greek medical texts into Arabic, thus contributing to the immense flowering of Arabian medicine in the 7th c. and long afterwards.

NESTORIUS (*fl.* 5th c. AD) Nestorius was born at Germanicia in Syria Euphratensis and entered a monastery at Antioch. He became Patriarch of Constantinople in 428, where he preached a denial of Mary as the mother of God in Jesus, which he thought diminished the divinity of Jesus. Others believed that this heresy made Jesus simply human. He thus highlighted the problems of the nature of Christ. Cyril, Patriarch of Alexandria, brought about his downfall partly on theological and partly on political grounds at the Council of Ephesus in 431. Nestorius was sent back to his monastery at Antioch. In 435 his books were condemned and in 436 he was finally banished to the Libyan Desert, where he died some time later. There is still a sect of Nestorians who follow his pure or adulterated religious doctrines.

NETTLE RASH is the familiar rash which occurs when *histamine is released on pricking the skin by the hairs of the nettle, indistinguishable from that of *urticaria. See ALLERGY.

NEURALGIA is any pain originating in a nerve (all pain is, of course, conducted by nerves).

NEURAL TUBE DEFECT is a congenital anomaly resulting from defective development of part of the posterior wall of the spinal canal or the vault of the skull. See SPINA BIFIDA; ANENCEPHALY.

NEURASTHENIA is a term, now obsolete, introduced by G. M. Beard in 1867 to describe a condition he believed was due to exhaustion of nerve cells, the major manifestations of which were fatiguability and weakness combined with a variety of other ill-defined symptoms. Neurasthenia is not now regarded as a precise diagnosis.

NEURECTOMY is the surgical excision of part of a *nerve.

NEURILEMMA. A thin outer membrane which encloses the *axon, and the *myelin sheath when one is present, of individual peripheral nerve fibres. The neurilemma is also called the sheath of *Schwann.

NEURINOMA. A *tumour arising from the outer sheath of a peripheral *nerve fibre (the sheath of

*Schwann or neurilemma), also known as a neurilemmoma, schwannoma, or neurofibroma.

NEURITIS is inflammation of a nerve or nerves. The term is sometimes loosely used to embrace other non-inflammatory lesions of the peripheral nervous system which would more properly be termed '*neuropathy'.

NEUROANATOMY is the anatomy of the *nervous system.

NEUROCHEMISTRY is the chemical physiology of nervous tissue.

NEURODERMATITIS is any skin disorder thought to be due to or aggravated by mental or emotional factors; the term is sometimes used more specifically to denote *atopic *eczema (atopic dermatitis).

NEUROENDOCRINOLOGY is the study of the interactions between the *nervous system and the *endocrine organs, of which the most important is that between the *pituitary gland and the *hypothalamic region of the brain.

NEUROEPIDEMIOLOGY is the *epidemiology of diseases of the nervous system.

NEUROFIBROMA. A tumour arising from the *Schwann cells of peripheral or cranial nerves.

NEUROFIBROMATOSIS is a genetically determined disorder, inherited as an autosomal *dominant characteristic, of which the major manifestations are multiple tumours attached to peripheral nerves (neurofibromas) and pigmented skin patches ('café au lait' spots). Neurofibromatosis is also known as von *Recklinghausen's disease.

NEUROGENETIC is a synonym for (the preferable) 'neurogenic', meaning either originating in the nervous system or giving rise to nervous tissue.

NEUROGLIA is the supporting tissue of the *central nervous system, analogous to *connective tissue elsewhere. Two components are recognized: macroglia, of ectodermal origin like other neural tissue, the cells of which (astrocytes and oligodendrocytes) are concerned with *myelin formation and various metabolic functions; and microglia, containing mesodermal cells similar to *macrophages.

NEUROLEPTIC. One of the group of drugs used to modify the manifestations of *psychoses, known alternatively as 'major tranquillizers' or 'antipsychotics'. See TRANQUILLIZERS.

NEUROLOGIST. A physician specializing in diseases of the nervous system.

NEUROLOGY AND THE NEUROLOGICAL SCIENCES

The term 'neurology' was first used in 1681 by Thomas *Willis to indicate the 'Doctrine of the Nerves', expressly excluding any consideration of the *brain and *spinal cord. The Greek root 'neuro' (meaning bowstring, sinew, or tendon) was chosen by Willis to describe the cranial, spinal, and autonomic *nerve fibres. Not until a century later did the word neurology begin to take on a far wider significance.

Neurology is a discipline for which it is still difficult to devise a wholly satisfactory definition. Broadly speaking, neurology represents that aspect of human biology which is concerned with the *nervous system, its structure and functions, and more especially with the morphological and clinical results of its injuries and disorders. In ordinary parlance, a neurologist is a physician whose special concern is with the diagnosis and treatment of disorders of the nervous system.

Here exists a certain ambivalence, for in many respects there is an overlap with the province of *psychiatry. Neurologists are often called upon to see patients with *neuroses, *hysterical disorders, mild *depressions, and particularly the *dementias. The last-named are highly relevant to a neurologist, for dementia implies some sort of structural alteration in the brain. Another important territory shared by both neurologists and psychiatrists embraces those derangements that follow head injuries. Forensic issues, too, such as the extent of physical and mental disability, and the degree of legal competency, for example testamentary capacity (ability to make a valid will), again fall within the ambit of either a neurologist or a psychiatrist, depending largely upon personal experience and interest.

Some maladies are undisputed neurological problems, even though an underlying lesion of the nervous system is not obvious. The *muscular dystrophies, diseases involving skeletal muscle, belong here, as do the *tics and habit spasms, currently spoken of as *Gilles de la Tourette's syndrome; disorders of sleep such as *narcolepsy; and also the various craft or occupational '*palsies'. Likewise, there are conditions ordinarily handled by a psychiatrist despite a gross derangement of nervous function and behaviour; such conditions include the lowest grades of *mental subnormality; many aberrations of senescence (old age); some manifestations of psychiatric treatment, for example *electroconvulsive therapy; and the symptomatology of *alcoholism and drug *addiction.

Perhaps in clinical practice the neurologist faces his gravest responsibility when confronted by the determination of the end-point of the vital process, an issue which turns upon the detection of the moment of *brain death.

Of necessity, neurology embraces *morphology, for neuroanatomy is a branch both of anatomy and of histology. Closely allied is the scholar who concentrates upon the changes visible to the naked eye and under the microscope, which are caused by disease of the nervous system. In this way, *neuropathology straddles the disciplines of *morbid anatomy and of neurology.

Many academic physiologists choose to concentrate upon the important and expanding domain of *neurophysiology. Preoccupation with the electrical activity of the brain and peripheral nerves leapt ahead with the work of Caton, *Berger, and *Adrian and led to the introduction of such valuable diagnostic tools as *electroencephalography (EEG), *electromyography (EMG), the measurement of conduction along nerve fibres, and that of sensory evoked potentials recorded from the brain (and sometimes over the spinal cord) during somatic, visual, and auditory stimulation (see NEUROPHYSIOLOGY, CLINICAL).

*Biochemistry nowadays plays such an important part in neurological diagnosis and in the understanding of the nature and mechanism of certain nervous diseases, that *neurochemistry has become an important entity in its own right, and one of great promise. So many new chemical transmitter substances, involved in the transmission of nerve impulses from one neurone to another, other than *acetylcholine, *serotonin, and *dopamine have been discovered, that drugs which modify their effects are now the basis of the new science of *neuropharmacology.

Exact aids to diagnosis began with the introduction of *ophthalmoscopy, and then of *lumbar puncture in 1885 by Corning. Additional techniques have now diversified to such an extent as to justify the isolation of a number of subspecialties, one of which is *neuroradiology. Of the present contrast techniques designed to facilitate imaging of various structures, *myelography came first, followed by carotid and vertebral *angiography which visualized the vascular tree supplied by these vessels and anticipated the vascular radio-opaque procedures applicable elsewhere in the body (see RADIOLOGY). For many years air studies, used to outline the cavities or *ventricles of the brain (ventriculography, air encephalography), played an important, if potentially traumatic, part in diagnosis, fortunately now largely rendered unnecessary since the introduction of *computerized (axial) tomographic scanning of the brain (CT or CAT scan). This latter procedure is invaluable, for it rapidly and painlessly reveals with precision the contours of the *cerebral hemispheres; the size, shape, and position of the ventricles; and the presence of focal lesions, whether *ischaemic, *cystic, or *neoplastic. Recently *nuclear magnetic resonance (NMR) has added yet another dimension.

It is a conventional criticism of neurology that, although representing a refinement of clinical expertise in diagnosis, it remains powerless to alleviate or cure. This reproach is certainly no longer appropriate for many of the infective disorders, and neuropharmacology has transformed

the treatment of *migraine, *epilepsy, and *Parkinson's disease, for example. Nor does it apply to some of the surgical procedures of today, shown by the all-important discipline of *neurosurgery, that aspect of neurology which utilizes operative methods of intervention to treat neurological disorders.

The training of a neurosurgeon varies to some extent from one country to another. In the UK it usually transpires that a junior doctor elects to specialize in surgery rather than in medicine, and after taking the obligatory higher diploma qualifying him as a fellow of one of the Royal Colleges of Surgeons, proceeds to serve an apprenticeship in both neurology and neurosurgery. In other countries the procedure may be different. An experienced neurologist may decide to focus his interests upon the surgical methods of treatment, the steps taken to acquire operative technique not always being the same. In the past it has happened that the lack of an experienced surgical colleague has induced a neurological physician to embark upon surgical interventions. The examples of Otto Foerster in Breslau, and Clovis Vincent in Paris, come to mind. Antonio Egas *Moniz of Lisbon occupied a niche that was in many ways unique.

Certain of the nervous disorders that are susceptible to surgical relief fall within the province of *orthopaedics as well as that of neurosurgery, although the frontier is neither sharp nor invariable: examples are the treatment of *sciatica due to disc lesions (see PROLAPSED INTERVETEBRAL DISC); the complications of cervical *spondylosis; peripheral nerve injuries; even the traumatic *paraplegias provide instances of collaboration between neurosurgeons and orthopaedists. Sympathectomy (interruption of the *sympathetic nervous pathways) is another procedure shared by neurological and general surgeons.

At this point it may be appropriate to mention what has been referred to as 'psychosurgery'. Originally this consisted of the practice of *leucotomy, also known as lobotomy, whereby a surgical section of the white matter of the frontal *lobes on one side or on both was carried out in certain cases of obstinate *psychosis, or in some victims of intractable pain. The effect, roughly speaking, was a change in *personality, sometimes for the better. Over the years, various modifications were made, reducing the area of destruction or limiting it to one side of the brain. Still later, psychosurgery embraced destruction by stereotaxic surgery of certain deep structures of the brain, notably the amygdaloid bodies. The heyday of psychosurgery is over since the introduction of many new *psychotropic drugs and at present it is rarely carried out in neuropsychiatric practice.

From what has been said, it is not surprising that the training and the special concern of neurologists have varied from country to country. On the continent of Europe, and particularly in pre-war Germany and Austria, neurology and psychiatry were closely allied disciplines, to their mutual advantage; this liaison does not apply to the same extent today.

At a later date, academic psychologists appeared on the scene: their principal interest lay in the mode of operation of the brain, thus allying them with neurologists whose practice brought them in touch with patients whose symptoms were of a more abstract character. Faculties such as thinking, learning, memory, communication, calculation, spatial conceptions, time-sense, notions as to the body image (*image de soi, Körperschema*), made up *cognition, and became topics of research shared by neurologists and psychologists alike. The expression 'higher nervous activity' (or HNA) became popular and led to the growth of *neuropsychology. In this way it was hoped to probe the nature of some of the subtle and more abstruse symptoms demonstrable at the bedside. Likewise, neurologists, who had for over a century been interested in patients who had suffered impaired *language as the result of brain damage, pointed out the mutual advantage which would accrue from collaboration with academic linguists. The point was taken, and in this way arose the active discipline of *psycholinguistics.

Towards the end of the first half of the 20th c., neurology underwent a considerable change in identity. It has now entered what is sometimes referred to as the 'scientific era' of diagnosis. Before the outbreak of the Second World War, neurology relied upon the work of a comparatively few highly gifted individuals who employed sensitive techniques of history-taking, and scrupulous clinical examination in considerable detail, allied with a flair for shrewd diagnostic assessment. Today the task of a neurologist is different and less demanding: ancillary aids lead to greater speed and possibly greater accuracy in localization, at the same time giving promise of unravelling the pathophysiology of nervous function. Post-war pharmaceutical and neurosurgical refinements have done a great deal to remove from neurology the slur of therapeutic impotence. As in many other disciplines of medicine, teamwork has replaced academic stardom.

It has been a natural consequence that the expressions 'neuroscience' or 'neurological science' are now showing signs of ousting the term 'neurology'. The former designations have the advantage of combining clinical, pathological, anatomical, surgical, and physiological considerations of what are included under 'neurology'.

Thus, the present-day neurologist will find that in his practice he is often called upon to elucidate the causes of headache, which is often due to nervous tension, sometimes to migraine, or rarely to an intracranial *tumour. He will often be required to diagnose and manage cerebral vascular accidents or so-called '*strokes', whether due to infarction (death of tissue due to loss of blood supply) resulting from *embolism or *thrombosis of cerebral arteries or to *haemorrhage into or over the surface of the brain. He must also be expert in recognizing the causes of attacks of loss of consciousness (which may be due to epilepsy or to fainting attacks (syncope)) and in treating these, usually with the aid of drugs; disabling attacks of giddiness (vertigo) also fall within his province. Toxic and infective disorders affecting the nervous system such as *meningitis, *encephalitis, and *encephalomyelitis, whether due to bacteria, viruses, or other causes, also come within his ambit; and in recent years the knowledge that *autoimmunity is responsible for many conditions which affect the central nervous system and/or peripheral nerves (such as some varieties of polyneuropathy) has become increasingly apparent. One common and as yet mysterious crippling disease of the nervous system is *multiple sclerosis, which sometimes runs a relapsing and remitting course but is sometimes remorselessly progressive and in which areas of degeneration with loss of the *myelin covering of nerve fibres within the nervous system (demyelination) may be widespread in the optic nerves, brain, and spinal cord, giving rise, for example, to temporary blindness in one eye (retrobulbar *neuritis) and variable weakness or paralysis in the limbs, often with sensory impairment. *Syphilis of the nervous system (much less common than it was) is also a neurological problem, as are many degenerative diseases including the so-called hereditary *ataxias in which various combinations of deafness, ataxia, paralysis, loss of sensation, and weakness and wasting of muscles may occur and may be due to dominant or recessive *genes. There are also many diseases of the peripheral nerves and muscles (the *neuromuscular disorders) which are commonly investigated and treated by neurologists, as are the large number of developmental and acquired conditions involving the bones of the skull and spine, the intervertebral discs, and the meningeal coverings of the nervous system, which may interfere with the function of the brain or spinal cord, or of the nerves and nerve roots which leave and enter these structures.

The foregoing remarks do not exhaust the topic of the 'growing edges' of neurology. Neurogenetics, neuroepidemiology, veterinary neurology, developmental and paediatric neurology are also to be included among the young and vigorous offshoots that have seeded from multidisciplinary origins.

Localization of function within the brain. The concept of *localization of function* within the cerebral hemispheres was late to arrive in neurological thinking. At first the brain was regarded as an organ which acted as a whole, like the liver or spleen. This opinion was firmly stated as late as 1776–84 by *Cullen in his *Practice of Physick*. *Aristotle had long before looked upon the brain as a structure, the purpose of which was to cool the blood. Later there grew up a less holistic attitude, but for centuries attention was attracted by the lateral ventricles. At first excretory functions were ascribed to these cavities. Later, the Dominican savant *Albertus Magnus, and also Bernard Gordon (c. 1303) of Montpellier made a threefold division of function of the ventricles from before backwards, wherein they consigned various faculties of the mind. How lofty or how lowly the functions were of these cavities continued to be a matter of debate for centuries. Reisch of Baligen in his *Margarita philosophica* (or 'Pearl of philosophy') asserted in 1503 that there were three communicating ventricles, the foremost of which was concerned with 'common sense' (or, better, the sensorium); the middle with cogitation or 'phantasia'; and the hindmost with memory. This tripartite hypothesis aroused scorn from Andreas *Vesalius. William *Harvey, a somewhat intolerant genius, was even more scathing, and referred to Piccolomini as one who would 'mix up the more divine of faculties with the excrements, and localize the soul in the jakes' (or privy). M. *Malpighi reflected that

at one time with some religious awe . . . we worshipped the ventricles and . . . we believed that there were different seats for imagination, memory and other senses. Since eventually, however, the ventricles have been dismissed from this lofty service to become a pair of snuffers, or, so to speak, the sewage drain of excretions, the sinuous white matter of the brain struck our imagination, whose imagined wonderful powers gave fill to our expectations.

That certain areas of the *cerebral cortex and the subjacent white matter might have specific functional import was foreshadowed by *Prochaska in 1784. Franz Josef *Gall did most to establish the doctrine of cerebral localization. He put forward a two-pronged hypothesis: first, he correlated unusual talent or personality traits with overdevelopment of different circumscribed areas of the brain; secondly, he believed that such cortical areas were detectable because of bony prominences in the overlying cranial vault. Later he collaborated with Johann Gaspar Spurzheim and isolated 26 'organs' which he associated with various 'propensities, sentiments, and intellectual faculties'. Each 'organ' comprised a cerebral region of pulpy and fibrous material (i.e. grey and white matter), its volume reflecting the extent of the corresponding propensity. The diversity of cortical development could be gauged by palpating the skull ('phrenology'). These 'propensities' did not correspond to contemporary group factors that make up cognition, but to attributes such as conjugality, sublimity, vitativeness, bibativeness, philoprogentiveness, and so on. Later the 26 organs increased to 35. It is interesting to recall, however, that probably the first of the 'organs' which Gall identified, was the one concerned with language. This faculty was located by him in the most forward portions of the frontal lobe. Unusual facility in speaking was linked with overdevelopment of these areas, which in the living subject betrayed itself by pressure on the orbits and hence by an undue prominence of the eyeballs.

Gall's doctrine aroused considerable interest and at the same time, controversy. Phrenological societies were established in many parts of the world; in the UK there were at one time no fewer than 29 such bodies. In Edinburgh, Gall's teachings were held in even higher esteem, especially as the distinguished Combe brothers were strong advocates. On one occasion they were summoned to Windsor to examine the bumps of the young Prince of Wales, whose tardy academic achievement was causing concern. Sympathetic interest was also displayed in London for a time by *Abernethy, Bentley *Todd, Herbert Spencer, and *Wakely, the influential editor of the *Lancet*. Charles *Bell, *Bastian, and many others were, however, antagonistic.

Although phrenology faded from the medico-scientific scene, it served a useful and enduring purpose. During the first half of the 19th c. the belief steadily mounted that the faculty of language was closely associated with the frontal lobes of the brain. This opinion originated in the teaching of Gall, and in France was strongly supported by the authoritarian dean of the faculty of medicine, Jean Baptiste *Bouillaud. In 1864 at the newly constituted Société d'Anthropologie, a Dr Auburtin delivered a seriously reasoned paper on the role of the frontal lobes in speech. The lecture was listened to with special interest by the secretary of the Society, Paul *Broca, a general surgeon of promise. Two days before the meeting there had been admitted to the Hôpital Bicêtre under the care of Broca a mentally deficient patient who some years previously had become hemiplegic and speechless. His immediate problem, however, was a gangrenous leg from which he died. At autopsy a longstanding ischaemic scar was found in the left cerebral hemisphere involving, among other regions, the second and third frontal gyri. Not until a month later, when a second case came to his notice which was similar in both its clinical and anatomical features, did the Anthropological Society evince interest. Other patients with speech loss were thereupon referred to Broca and in every fatal case, despite a modest protest from *Charcot, post-mortem examination was said to reveal a lesion in the frontal area. In this way Broca unwittingly found himself hailed as the discoverer of the 'centre du langage'.

It should be noted that Gall did not recognize any anatomical or physiological differences between the two hemispheres; to him the cortical organs were bilaterally symmetrical. Such a viewpoint also applied, at first, to Broca. It was not until three years later, by which time he had witnessed 'very many autopsies', that he realized that in every one the pathological lesion had been unilateral, and always left-sided. Moreover, in cases where the lesion was in the *right* frontal area, the patient during his lifetime had not been bereft of speech. Later still it became realized that an important principle of 'cerebral *dominance' was involved and that there was a linkage with the question of handedness or manual preference. In left-handed persons the so-called speech centre was mainly (though perhaps not entirely) right-sided in situation, and in such cases the right half of the brain could therefore be regarded as 'dominant'.

The recognition that the two halves of the brain are not physiological facsimiles, and probably not even anatomical mirror opposites, raises the question of the convolutional patterning. To discuss this matter it is again necessary to consider the history.

Since the days of *Erasistratus of Chios the convolutions (or gyri) of the brain had been regarded as endowed with no more morphological consistency than the disposition of the coils of the small bowel; hence the term 'enteroid processes' which prevailed over the centuries. Even Thomas Willis, the 'father of neurology', saw no plan or significance in the arrangement of the 'cracklings and turnings and windings' of the gyri, although he recognized the brain stem as 'the King's High-way, leading from the metropolis into many Provinces of the Nervous System'. A little later we find even such a great physician as Thomas *Sydenham impressed with the discrepancy between form and function in the brain. Thus he wrote 'yet a diligent contemplation of its structure will tell us how so coarse a substance (a mere pulp, and that not over nicely wrought) should subserve so noble an end'.

That the gyral layout was more or less haphazard was a belief which prevailed until the work of *Vicq d'Azyr and of von *Soemmerring. These were pioneers in tracing meaning and consistency in the fissures and convolutions of the brain. Thereafter, most of these structures became endowed with names and thus arose the idea of 'lobes' of the brain. We now begin to hear of the frontal, parietal, temporal, and occipital lobes. Sometimes these were areas delimited by certain particularly deep clefts or sulci. At other times a simpler topography was preferred, and the four principal cerebral lobes were looked upon merely as those areas of the cortex which underlay the frontal, parietal, temporal, and occipital bones of the skull respectively.

It is now realized that the convolutional patterning is not as undeviating as many 19th c. anatomists believed, especially when secondary and tertiary gyri are considered. Furthermore, the left and the right halves of the brain may betray subtle convolutional differences. Whether this asymmetry is meaningful, we are not yet sure. The best-known instance is the sulcus lunatus which, when present, is more often found in the left hemisphere, indicating to some anatomists that such a half of the brain was the dominant one in that particular case.

Yet another morphological system of differentiation developed early in the present century, as the outcome of microscopical study of the cortex. The grey matter was already known to be made up of various types of cells arranged in a laminated pattern. It was found that such a consistent variegation of cellular structure existed between various parts of the cortex, that it was possible to identify a veritable parquetry. Certain regions were conspicuous because of the presence of larger neurones including the giant nerve cells that are associated with the name of the Russian anatomist V. A. Betz, and from which originate the principal nerve tracts for the transmission of voluntary movement. Other and more extensive areas were found to be particularly rich in small granular cells, and were known as the koniocortex or 'dusty' zones. Roughly speaking, these correspond with what was considered to be the sensory or receptor areas of the brain. At the very back of the brain the grey matter became known as the 'striate area' because of two conspicuous white bands running tangentially and in close parallel formation. This anatomical feature had been noted, but not understood, by Gennari of Parma in 1782; it was later rediscovered by J. G. F. Baillarger. Nowadays the 'white line of Gennari' is recognized as the end-station of the tracts which transmit visual impressions. In this way there grew up the doctrine of cerebral cytoarchitectonics (definition and delimitation of the architecture and distribution of cortical cells) which many neurologists used to try to divide the cortex of the brain into structurofunctional units reflecting perhaps a type of neo-phrenology. Such histological studies were initiated by A. W. Campbell (1905) followed by Elliot *Smith (1907), and considerably elaborated by von Economo, C. and O. Vogt, and especially by K. Brodmann. The last-named constructed a mosaic-like brain map comprising 50 areas, each of which was numerically demarcated.

Although by analogy with the giant-cell cortex and the striate and konic cortical areas, it is tempting to assign strict functional autonomy to each and every one of these 50 areas, it would be rash to do so. Such, indeed, had been the practice adopted by many neurologists, especially in German-speaking countries. Certain discrepancies were overlooked. For example, although skilled microscopists claimed to be able to pin-point which particular region of the cortex was under view, they would have been at a loss to assert which side of the brain they were scrutinizing, although clinicians were well aware that the two halves of the brain were by no means functionally equipotential. Little wonder that neurologists in the UK were lukewarm in their acceptance of the relationship between brain area and function. Their doubts became confirmed by the criticisms of Percival Bailey and von Bonin (1946) and by the iconoclasm of F. M. R. *Walshe, who wrote 'the cytoarchitectonic schemes of areation of the cortex are to an important degree artificial and unreliable'.

Clinicians were not slow to isolate symptoms and signs which they regarded as specific of focal disease or injury of the various lobes. Year by year these have become increasingly elaborate, and yet there was something artificial—even naïve—about correlations of this kind. In the preface to the book *Parietal Lobes* written in 1953, Critchley asserted that, while this was the first monograph dedicated to this subject, it would probably also be the last. He felt not that this book represented the ultimate and categorical work on the topic, but that there was something fundamentally artificial about such a materialistic localization.

Meanwhile the mediaeval reluctance to discern any fixity of arrangement in the bowel-like semblance of the cerebral convolutions, gradually yielded to a more or less firmly established patterning. Certain fissures or sulci were observed to be deeper, and presumably more important, than others. Two in particular became associated with the names of *Rolando and of *Sylvius, respectively. Between them a certain topography seemed evident, and justified labelling. In this way anatomists gradually agreed upon circumscribed pre- and post-central, supramarginal, angular, and cingulate gyri.

The demise of the Gall–Spurzheim way of thinking was slowly replaced over the latter half of the 19th c. by a new school of localizationists. Some concepts were more plausible than others. That the corticospinal or pyramidal tract takes origin, at least in part, from the Betz cells of the pre-Rolandic cortex, and that this constitutes the principal inception of the effector pathways of willed movements, was difficult to deny, although whether this is the sole and immutable motor pathway is another matter, and one which is still argued. To take another example, and to correlate—as many neurologists still do—a small lesion within the parietal cortex of the dominant hemisphere with the assembly of four apparently unrelated symptoms is a big step, and to label such a clinical quadruped as Gerstmann's syndrome is to venture even further. But this 'cartographic' way of thinking is but one example of a prediction made by Arthur *Keith, namely that 'the day will come when we shall be able to estimate the functional value of every convolution of the brain'. Keith was a palaeontologist of international repute, but not a neurologist.

There were some enthusiasts such as Kleist of Frankfurt (b. 1879) who went to extremes and regarded the cerebral cortex as a mosaic, each tessera being undeviating in placement and in purpose. The clinical picture was looked upon as the specific and predictable outcome of malfunction of its own particular regional representation. This ultramaterialistic view possessed a certain attraction, for it was easy to teach and it constituted a target for the diagnostic skill of the clinician. Many other neurologists carried such rigid clinico-anatomical linkages even further.

However, even in the mid 19th c. there was an almost Kantian reaction against such dogmatism. While the perceptions of simple sense data are subserved by focal groups of neurones (nerve cells), other qualities of cerebral activity, such as cognition, memory and language, are more likely to be mediated by extensive areas of the brain, involving both hemispheres in all probability. It was argued that the brain was the organ of thought and of personality, and that no two human beings could be regarded as identical in their cerebral potential, or, consequently, in the way that they behaved when function was impaired. To a dynamic thinking neurologist, a circumscribed lesion of the brain represents merely the hole in a bagel or doughnut. The clinical aftermath must be due to the workings of tissues that are intact, for dead cells are inactive. Localized lesions of the brain might result in manifestations bearing a certain similarity from person to person but certainly no identity. The behaviour of a brain-damaged person in a test situation represents what a particular individual with a focal lesion is trying to achieve with those remnants of his nervous system that are intact, at a particular time and place, in the abnormal context of an artificial set of circumstances.

Among the pioneers of this organismic mode of thinking were Hughlings *Jackson, von *Monakow, Arnold *Pick, Pierre *Marie, Henry *Head, Walter Riese, F. M. R. Walshe, and many others. They never ceased to protest against the fallacy of aligning the localization of sign-producing lesions with the localization of a function. It would be wiser (they said) to avoid as far as possible the term 'localization' and to speak of a 'specialization' of a function.

Riese said that there never will be a cerebral localization of productive thought, since what is really productive and creative in the human mind resists even the most generous and universal localization. Since it is a coming-into-being of what did not exist before, it cannot be correlated with existing material.

While it is largely, if not universally, agreed that relatively simple sense data are 'represented' in small areas of the cerebral cortex, for example vision around the calcarine fissure, hearing in Heschl's gyri, tactile discrimination in the post-central convolutions, two observations are necessary: (i) in the case of audition and sight, both hemispheres are engaged, and (ii) the regions concerned represent but a fraction of the surface grey matter of the brain. Certainly, destruction of these regions will be followed by such losses of function as blindness, deafness, and subtle sensory impairment. There is, however, an odd characteristic about these patients, namely unawareness or even denial of the obvious loss of function. These brain-damaged patients behave quite differently from those whose dim vision, deafness, or anaesthesia is brought about by disease at a peripheral level of the nervous system. This was first observed by Seneca, who wrote in a letter to Lucilius:

You remember Harpaste my wife's nannie who has been pensioned off and lives in our home—this silly woman has suddenly become blind. Now it sounds unbelievable but I can assure you its true—she doesn't know she's blind. She keeps asking the servants to change her rooms because they are so dark.

In neurological practice it is commoner to find

cases where defects are qualitatively incomplete. Thus one patient may be able to see, but not identify, whatever he is looking at, whether it be the face of someone familiar to him, or the nature of the objects lying around him. Yet the moment the friend speaks, he knows immediately who is there; and if he handles the article before him he at once recognizes what it is. In another case, although with his hand he can feel touches with a feather or the point of a pin, the patient—with his eyelids closed—may not be able to recognize objects put into his hand. With phenomena such as these, neurologists speak of central *amaurosis (blindness), prosopagnosia (inability to recognize faces), visual object agnosia (inability to recognize objects visually), astereognosis (inability to recognize the feel and shape of objects by touch). Those neurologists who are topographically minded have no doubt as to where the lesion lies: those belonging to the holistic or more dynamically minded are not so confident. The matter is still more debatable when the problem is one of *aphasia or dysphasia, or impaired speech from brain disease. To ascribe the failure to find a word to a circumscribed lesion of the brain is one thing, but it does not explain the fact that the patient inconsistently misnames objects, calling a knife a spoon one moment, a fork perhaps a little later, and after a pause he comes out with the correct word. Misnaming is not a wholly negative symptom and cannot be the product of nerve cells that are dead. Some structure must be actively operating somewhere in the brain outside the area of what Jackson called 'dirt in the brain'. In his own words, 'Softened brain is no brain; so far as function, good or bad, is concerned, it is nothing at all.'

To a confirmed localizationist, no problem exists. The patient fumbles for words, uses wrong words, is unable to name articles shown him. He has a dysphasia. The CT scan demonstrates a limited mass of new growth in the left fronto-temporal area. One less materialist would be thinking along different lines. Here perhaps is another patient with much the same sort of dysphasia, but the lesion lies elsewhere in the left hemisphere. Yet another patient may have a lesion shown on the CT scan to be a tumour of the same size and in exactly the same region as in the first case, but the clinical pattern of the language disorder appears to be quite different.

This second paradox is so common as indeed to be habitual. It calls for some attempt at explanation. It is probable that the pattern of an aphasia depends upon factors other than anatomical ones. Was the lesion an abrupt one, as in the case of trauma or embolus? Or is the aphasia due to a slow-expanding space-occupying lesion? The age of the patient plays an important part, especially in prognosis. What of the patient himself, his intellectual calibre and his educational status? What was his previous facility with spoken and written words? Was he an illiterate, or was he a master of the spoken word or a professional writer? Was he by chance a bilingual; or a master of several languages in addition to his mother tongue?

Neurologists who are not shackled by the concept of wholly topographical lesions are interested in the subtle phenomena which may characterize a brain-damaged patient, irrespective of the site of the lesion. These constitute what is called the *Grundstörung*, the constituents of which are manifold. Organic repression is one aspect, whereby the patient seems unaware of, or unmoved by, the symptoms of his brain defect. An extreme variant is the denial syndrome. K. Goldstein strongly emphasized that a victim of a brain lesion lives in a shrunken milieu. If he ventures beyond the limits of his capacity he is apt to experience a distressing catastrophic reaction. Unconsciously, the patient so modifies his behaviour and his life-style that he dwells contentedly within his restricted environment, thus avoiding the emotional trauma of malperformance, if not actual failure.

The development of neurological thinking as to consciousness and self-awareness. Certain neurological syndromes were recognized and described thousands of years ago. For example, we can discern references to the complications of head injury in the Egyptian *Edwin Smith papyrus; the author described the sequelae and their prognosis. Accounts of conditions such as epilepsy, loss of speech, lethargy, palsy, and headaches are to be found in the writings of *Hippocrates, *Aristotle, and *Galen. *Aretaeus, early in the 3rd c. AD, clearly elucidated migraine. Tremor was mentioned by *Celsus in his *De medicina*.

Nevertheless, no cogent hypotheses were forthcoming as to the quintessential nature and purpose of the nervous system, and indeed the structures subserving cognition and emotional life were for many centuries a matter of dispute. At times the seat of the 'soul' or the 'vital spirit' was localized within the liver or the spleen, or even the circulating bloodstream. In some communities no location was particularized, and for many hundreds of years medical thinking did not rid itself of the Galenic *humoral doctrine. On the whole, however, it was the heart which was regarded as the principal organ, despite the occasional voice raised in support of the brain. By the 17th c. the dilemma was still unresolved. *Descartes was in no doubt that the brain was all-important and had pin-pointed consciousness in the *pineal body. William Harvey, however, was uncertain about the whole business, while his neighbour and contemporary William Shakespeare was asking 'Tell me where is fancy bred, or in the heart or in the head?'

As emphasized by J. G. Frazer, primitive belief was animist in attitude, and savage man postulated an indwelling and immortal soul that extended to the surrounding fauna and flora. The soul and its attributes could be assimilated by ingesting the flesh of an animal or by ceremonial cannibalism. Other primordial peoples opined that man possessed more than one soul, four in the case of the Hidatsa Indians, seven were postulated by the Borneo Dyaks, and no fewer than 30 by the natives of Laos.

The word 'soul' was introduced into medical parlance by the Greek philosopher Plotinus, and for centuries it was applied to the vital principle, otherwise designated as consciousness, ego-aware-ness, cognition, or common sensibility. Anatom-ical nomenclature was often employed in a purely figurative sense to denote ideas that were highly abstract and obscure. Misunderstandings escalated when Sanskrit or Hebrew terms had to be rendered into Greek and thence into Latin, and later still into the vernacular.

Some theologians and many metaphysicians were universalists and rejected the belief that the soul occupied any delimited habitat. Kant (1724–1804) declared that he had no reason to believe that the indivisible self could be imprisoned in a micro-scopic region of the brain, the soul being everywhere throughout the body, and in its entirety in each of its parts.

A few medical men like *Stahl and Unzer shared this view. Eventually, however, the term 'soul' dropped out of medical nomenclature and was probably last used by Munk in 1877 when he spoke of *Seelenblindheit* in decorticated dogs.

While questions of brain function had for cen-turies been a *casus belli* among the scholars, yet another argument was taking place relating to the peripheral nervous system. This dispute concerned the mechanism by which the nerves transmitted the vital spirit throughout the body. A related question was whether the nerve trunks were solid structures or hollow. Galen certainly looked upon them as tubular in nature, and pointed to the appearance of the cross-sectioned optic nerves. He was, no doubt, led astray by the focally placed central artery of the retina, so obvious to the naked eye. But the belief that peripheral nerves were ducts was held for a considerable period prior to Galen. Vesalius was probably the first to cast doubt upon this viewpoint, and the problem arose as to whether it was possible for the vital spirit to be transmitted along solid nerve trunks in the same way that light passes through air. The question remained unsolved. It is said that John *Locke once attended a tedious and wordy discussion among medical pundits as to whether or not the filaments of the nerves were traversed by a fluid substance. Finally Locke objected that perhaps the question was merely one of terminology, and that a clear definition was needed of the word 'liquor'. Somewhat taken aback, the learned men pondered and eventually realized that they were more or less in agreement that *some* fluid or subtle matter passed through the conduits of the nerves, but whether or not it was to be called 'liquor' was really not important. The riddle was not entirely solved thereby, for even as late as 1839 we find *Schwann admitting that he was not sure whether the nervous fibre was really hollow, or not.

The teaching and practice of neurology. It fol-lows from what has been written that a luxuriant blossoming of clinical neurology took place about 1860. By coincidence, the harvest occurred independently in two sites, namely London and Paris.

In the UK for many years a number of general physicians had been particularly interested in diseases of the nervous system. Outstanding among these was Thomas Willis who occupied the chair of natural philosophy at Oxford. His clinical case notes were lucid and detailed and their perusal shows that Willis anticipated the discovery of several clinical rarities, as for example myasthenia, narcolepsy, Ekbom's syndrome, and very likely developmental *dyslexia.

Next in time was Robert Bentley *Todd who became physician to *King's College Hospital, and for a time was its dean. He wrote extensively upon neurological topics and, in fact, many regard him as the first to describe locomotor ataxia or *tabes dorsalis. His premature death prevented his appointment to the National Hospital for the Paralysed and Epileptic (now the *National Hospital for Nervous Diseases), Queen Square, London. This was a philanthropic institution founded in 1860 to meet the needs of a neglected section of the sick poor of London. Two con-sultants were elected, namely Ramskill and *Brown-Séquard. Soon the staff was augmented by other notables such as Hughlings Jackson, the Nestor of British neurology; William *Gowers, David *Ferrier, Charlton Bastian, Thomas Buzzard, among others. Special advisers were Wil-liam *Fergusson, the royal surgeon, followed by that dominating figure, Victor *Horsley. Neuro-ophthalmological problems were attended to by Marcus Gunn, and *laryngeal complications by Felix *Semon.

The prestige attained by this hospital and its staff made it a teaching centre of world repute, and the traditions were carried on by some distinguished figures such as H. Tooth, Ormerod, Buzzard, Col-lier, Risien Russell, Gordon *Holmes, Kinnier *Wilson, Adie, G. Riddoch, C. P. *Symonds, Russell *Brain, and F. M. R. *Walshe. Other famous neurologists had originally trained at Queen Square. Neurosurgery was exemplified by N. Dott, H. *Cairns, and G. *Jefferson. Although Henry *Head was never associated with the National Hospital, he collaborated with Holmes in clinical research in its wards. Until the end of the First World War, most of the staff were general physicians and also held appointments in under-graduate hospitals.

The first true department of 'pure' neurology in the UK was established in 1918–19. With the end of the First World War, it became the policy of the rebuilt King's College Hospital (which had served solely as a military hospital since 1914), to establish 'special departments' in such disciplines as orthopaedics, laryngology, urology, diabetes, and also neurology. Personal invitations were extended to selected physicians and surgeons in England and Scotland to accept these appointments. In the case of neurology the invitation went to Kinnier Wilson, then an assistant physician at the Westminster Hospital.

Meanwhile, across the Channel, neurology was developing rather differently. J. M. *Charcot already a well-known physician, was offered by the University of Paris in 1862 a special departmental chair in 'les maladies du système nerveux'. He chose to ensconce this department in the old and rather decrepit *Salpêtrière. It was here that Dr Philippe *Pinel in 1795 had ordered the inmates to be unshackled.

As a brilliant and histrionic teacher, Charcot attracted numerous medical disciples not only from Paris but from elsewhere in France and abroad. The Clinique Charcot at the Salpêtrière comprised a large number of beds for female patients, many being incurable. The chronically sick became 'reposantes' and were allowed to live out their days in the hospital. Charcot was therefore in a unique position to observe the long-term stages of many progressive maladies and, from the opportunities afforded through autopsy, was enabled to bring to light important clinicopathological correlations.

After Charcot's death in 1893 the chair in neurology passed successively to F. Raymond, J. J. *Dejerine, Pierre Marie, G. Guillain, and Th. Alajouanine. The last-named was the final holder of this chair in the true sense, for after his retirement, drastic changes took place in structure and organization at the Salpêtrière. The former 'cité grise' as it was often called, became transformed into a well-equipped, modernized hospital, complete with every technical facility.

The Charcot school of neurology afforded succour to one half only of the population of Paris, for by a curious piece of administrative thinking, neurologically sick males were excluded. They were, however, accommodated in various allied hospitals. In such hospitals were located the clinics of A. *Trousseau, Jean *Lhermitte, Charles Foix, J. F. *Babinski, and André-Thomas. G. B. A. *Duchenne occupied a special category. Lacking any department or clinic of his own, he served as a perpetual clinical assistant to a series of complaisant and friendly heads of neurological departments. Being experienced in the newly introduced practice of electrical stimulation of muscles and nerves, his advice was welcomed. He was a close personal friend, as well as protégé of Charcot.

The lustre of the French neurologists was further exemplified by Barré of Strasbourg, René *Leriche, *Brissaud, Crouzon, Souques, Clovis Vincent, J. J. Martel, Raymond Garcin, Mollaret, Bourguignon, J. J. Roussy, *Landouzy, and very many others.

Something distinctive stamps the neurology of France, something which derives from the temperament of its inimitable innovators. Brilliant as clinical observers, they were also highly articulate. Notional thinking was not their forte. Without

exception, each was a man of unusual culture and aesthesis, an artist in the practice of medicine.

This concentration upon the Franco-British role in the early days of neurology does less than justice to the pioneers in the USA and Germany. American contributions were pre-eminent in the territory of surgery. C. H. Frazier was an early exponent and in 1899 devised the operation of cordotomy for the relief of intractable pain. W. E. *Dandy introduced ventriculography and other radiodiagnostic methods into neurosurgery. Harvey *Cushing revolutionized neurosurgical technique by instigating a slow, punctilious, and bloodless methodology that was widely adopted. The outstanding American clinical neurologist of the last century was Silas Weir *Mitchell. He wrote an account of peripheral nerve injuries based on his experiences in the Civil War. *Huntington, a general practitioner in New York State, described the hereditary *chorea known by his name (1872). Others distinguished in this branch of medicine were J. J. Putnam and C. L. *Dana who published the first textbook of neurology in America in 1892. German-speaking neurologists who made notable contributions include *Friedreich, *Romberg, *Erb, *Wernicke, von Economo, and *Oppenheim.

Organized neurological teaching naturally stimulated the appearance of textbooks upon the subject. An early representative was A Treatise on Nervous Disorders in two volumes which appeared in 1820 and 1824 respectively. The author was John Cooke, physician to the London Hospital. Better known is the Manual of Nervous Diseases of Man written by M. H. Romberg of Berlin and originally published in serial form between 1840 and 1846; it was later translated into English. A modern reader might well find the drive to classify in these books excessive and unorthodox but the volumes are wide-ranging in content. A smaller and more readable book was that published in 1854 by Robert Bentley Todd. It comprised a series of essays entitled On Paralysis, Certain Diseases of the Nervous System, etc. A year later the modest but lucid monograph by the young Russell Reynolds, under the title The Diagnosis of Diseases of the Brain, Spinal Cord, Nerves, and their Appendages made its appearance. These publications eventually became overshadowed by a work of far greater import, namely the Manual of Diseases of the Nervous System by William *Gowers. This comprehensive work appeared in two volumes, published in 1886 and 1888 respectively; an American edition appeared in 1888. Gowers produced the clearest, and at the same time most comprehensive, account of clinical neurology, based largely upon his own considerable experience. The author was not only an uncannily shrewd observer, but he was obsessional, and took and retained notes upon the cases which had come under his care. Being also a competent artist, he illustrated his text with no fewer than 341 sketches of his own. The information contained within these two volumes was so vast that, even today, young neurologists who think that they have stumbled upon a novel syndrome or a new physical sign, are advised to consult the 'bible of neurology' before hurrying into print. Gowers was a master of simple yet elegant prose which was unambiguous and jargon-free. The *Manual* continues to be consulted for it is still an emporium of neurological lore.

Contemporary neuroscience. Modern thinking as to the nature of brain function has benefited particularly from an increasing knowledge of neurophysiology and of neuroanatomy. Chandler Brooks has clearly described the evolution of our present ideas upon this subject as being derived from at least six advances in our growing knowledge of brain anatomy, as follows:

1. The development of the cellular theory based upon the work of *Bichat in 1802, Turpin in 1826, and *Schleiden and *Schwann in 1838.
2. The related neurone theory, which evolved naturally from (1). *His, Forel, and *Ramon y Cajal were in the vanguard of this work but it was Willis who had suggested the term 'neurone' while *Waldeyer-Hartz spoke of the Neurone Theory.
3. The concept of functional units, for example the motor unit. Here again Cajal was an instigator followed by *Sherrington and his pupils, notably Eccles.
4. The amplification of work concerning the *reflex pathway. Ideas in this area originated with Jean *Fernel followed by Willis, Descartes, Robert Whytt, Prochaska, Alexander Walker, Charles *Bell, Herbert Mayo, and *Magendie.
5. The discovery of the *synapse. Here Sherrington, Hild, Cajal, Gowers, and de No were responsible for important ideas.
6. Finally, the concept of a cell membrane possessing important anatomical, physical and chemical properties. Early workers on this topic were Brederman and Cremer.

Chandler Brooks went on to assert that modern views concerning functional processes within the central nervous system have taken origin from five major discoveries, namely:

1. The irritability or *excitability, excitation and response, and the associated adaptability of living tissue.
2. *Inhibition, that is those processes opposed to excitation.
3. Integration or the control of response by regulated opposition of excitation and inhibition.
4. The concept of feedback (as in the way in which sensory input modulates movement).
5. The principle of cephalization (the increasing importance, in evolution, of the brain and its increasing specialization).

Within the last few years and even since these concepts were formalized, knowledge has continued to expand explosively. Among numerous examples one can include but a few: the discovery that *dopamine is the *neurotransmitter in certain cell pathways of the *extrapyramidal system and the consequent introduction of its precursor, *levodopa, as an effective treatment for *parkinsonism; the elucidation of specific inherited enzyme defects as the cause of some diseases of the nervous system, such as *Wilson's disease and *Refsum's disease, with the consequent introduction of effective treatment; the discovery that the brain elaborates its own endogenous analgesic substances known as *endorphins with consequential elucidation of many mechanisms subserving pain; the discovery of many new *peptides released from the *hypothalamus which have *endocrine effects upon the *pituitary and other organs; increasing knowledge relating to the many classes of *receptors on cell bodies in the nervous system, in the autonomic nervous system and in voluntary muscle. Many more examples could be cited but these indicate something of the excitement of modern neuroscience and raise considerable hopes that many so-called degenerative nervous diseases, some inherited, will become treatable as a result of sound biochemical and pharmacological evidence about their causation, within the next few decades.

The foregoing paragraphs illustrate patchily the painful steps which culminated logically in the present scientific era of neurology. Not for a moment must it be imagined that the table has been set and that the 'banquet of the brain' is ready. Not all of our most cherished ideas are by any means rigidly ordained. Yesterday's heresy has at times become acceptable, while contemporary beliefs may at any moment be rudely shaken. The neurosciences are not yet sacrosanct.

To quote Wechsler upon the development of neurology.

but the story is by no means ended; in truth it has but just begun. Knowledge of the structure of the nervous system is indeed very far from complete; its functions are but dimly understood. Neurophysiology is an infant just beginning to toddle and walk; biochemistry and biophysics of the nervous system are not even fledglings out of their shells. They are mistaken who think that there can be ultimate understanding of mental processes without fundamental knowledge of the structure and function of the brain. Adventure still beckons to the pioneer in neurology, and glory and honour no less than inner rewards await the coming investigators. It is trenching neither on folly nor prophecy to venture the profession has a great future.

M. CRITCHLEY

Further reading

Brooks, McC. (1973). Current developments in thought and the past evolution of ideas concerning integrative function. In *The History and Philosophy of Knowledge of the Brain and its Functions*. Amsterdam.

Cooper, I. S. (1982). Sir Victor Horsley: Father of modern neurological surgery. In Rose, F. C. and Bynum, W. E. (eds), *Historical Aspects of the Neurosciences*. New York.

Critchley, M. (1949). *Sir William Gowers: an appreciation*. London.

Critchley, M. (1964). The origins of 'Aphasiology'. *Scottish Medical Journal*, **9**, 231–42.

Critchley, M. (1965). Neurology's debt to F. J. Gall (1758–1828). *British Medical Journal*, **ii**, 775–81.

Critchley, M. (1967). *Migraine; from Cappadocia to Queen Square. Perspectives in Migraine*. London.

DeJong, R. N. (1982). *A History of American Neurology*. New York.

Dewhurst, K. (1982). Thomas Willis and the foundation of British neurology. In Rose, F. C. and Bynum, W. E. (eds), *Historical Aspects of the Neurosciences*. New York.

Goldstein, K. (1939). *The Organism*. New York.

Gooddy, W. (1982). Charles Edward Brown-Séquard. In Rose, F. C. and Bynum, W. E. (eds), *Historical Aspects of the Neurosciences*. New York.

Guillain, G. (1955). *J. M. Charcot 1825–1893*. Paris.

Haymaker, W. (ed.) (1953). *The Founders of Neurology*. Springfield, Illinois.

Janz, D. (1969). *Die Epilepsien*. Stuttgart.

Lyons, J. B. (1982). The neurology of Robert Bentley Todd. In Rose, F. C. and Bynum, W. E. (eds), *Historical Aspects of the Neurosciences*. New York.

Spillane, J. D. (1981). *The Doctrine of the Nerves*. Oxford.

Wechsler, I. S. (1950). *The Neurologist's Point of View*. New York.

NEUROMA. A *tumour arising from nervous tissue, usually from elements of the *neuroglia.

NEUROMUSCULAR DISEASE

Introduction. There are three forms of muscle in the human body. The heart is composed of cardiac muscle; there is smooth, unstriated or involuntary muscle in the wall of the stomach and intestine. But much of our body weight is made up by voluntary or skeletal muscle which is under the control of the will; there are hundreds of individual muscles which control movements of the eyes, face, mouth and throat, trunk, and limbs. Voluntary movement is initiated in the motor cortex of the *brain, from which impulses travel downwards through the *brainstem and *spinal cord in the upper motor *neurones of the pyramidal or corticospinal tract; these impulses then excite activity in the anterior horn cells of the spinal cord grey matter, from which arise the motor roots and *nerves which constitute the final common path of motor activity. One such cell and its nerve fibre or *axon is called a lower motor neurone. The motor nerve fibres are each covered with a sheath of *myelin, regularly interrupted at so-called nodes of Ranvier; the myelin sheath is formed and enveloped by specialized cells called Schwann cells. Impulses arising in the anterior horn cells travel down motor roots and peripheral nerves to reach the neuromuscular junction or motor end-plate (where a nerve fibre joins a muscle). Release of the chemical substance, *acetylcholine, at this junction, if adequate in amount, initiates a muscle action potential, which in turn leads to contraction of muscle fibres and hence to movement. The so-called motor unit of voluntary activity consists of one anterior horn cell, its nerve fibre (axon) and the group of muscle fibres which it supplies or innervates. Each motor unit contains many muscle fibres but under normal conditions these cannot contract singly. Firing of one anterior horn cell causes virtually simultaneous contraction of all of the muscle fibres

which it supplies, and this produces a motor unit action potential which can be recorded electrically (see NEUROPHYSIOLOGY, CLINICAL). Each muscle fibre is in turn made up of many *myofibrils as well as *nuclei, specialized *cytoplasm called sarcoplasm, and other *organelles including *mitochondria. The myofibrils are largely made up of thick filaments of a *protein called myosin and thin filaments of one called actin: these filaments interdigitate and slide upon one another so that the myofibril and, in consequence, the muscle fibre shortens when it contracts. Myosin filaments are attached to prominent Z bands which occur at regular intervals throughout each muscle fibre, or myofibre, producing a striped or striated appearance. Each muscle fibre is covered by a *membrane called the sarcolemma, which is made up of an outer basement membrane and an inner plasma membrane.

The neuromuscular diseases are those which involve the motor unit (Fig. 1). The primary patho-

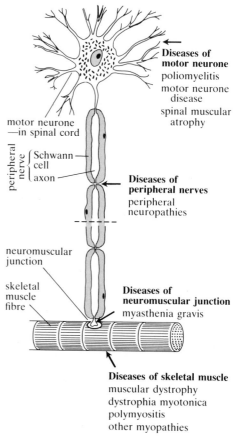

motor neurone
—in spinal cord

peripheral nerve { Schwann cell
axon

neuromuscular junction

skeletal muscle fibre

Diseases of motor neurone
poliomyelitis
motor neurone disease
spinal muscular atrophy

Diseases of peripheral nerves
peripheral neuropathies

Diseases of neuromuscular junction
myasthenia gravis

Diseases of skeletal muscle
muscular dystrophy
dystrophia myotonica
polymyositis
other myopathies

Fig. 1. A diagrammatic representation of the lower motor neurone, neuromuscular junction, and voluntary muscle, and of some of the commoner diseases which affect this neuromuscular system

logical process responsible may lie in the anterior horn cells, in the motor roots or nerves, at the neuromuscular junctions, or in the muscles themselves. Viruses such as that of *poliomyelitis may attack the anterior horn cells (or the motor nuclei of the cranial nerves which are functionally similar but which give origin to nerves innervating muscles of the head and neck). The degenerative diseases which affect these structures are generally known as the motor neurone diseases or spinal muscular atrophies; those which affect the peripheral nerves are known as the *neuropathies, and those which primarily affect muscle are collectively known as the *myopathies.

Disease or death of anterior horn cells or division of their axons, either in a spinal motor root or in a peripheral nerve, causes denervation or loss of the nerve supply to a muscle. In consequence, the muscle can no longer contract: it is paralysed and subsequently wastes progressively. Thus total denervation gives *paralysis: partial denervation gives weakness; the wasting is called denervation *atrophy. Diseases of the neuromuscular junction such as *myasthenia gravis, in which neuromuscular transmission between nerve and muscle is impaired, give weakness usually without wasting but are characterized by fatiguability (weakness which increases progressively following repeated contraction). Many of the primary myopathies like the *muscular dystrophies cause increasing weakness and wasting which go hand in hand, but many metabolic myopathies due to specific biochemical abnormalities are now recognized in which, by contrast, weakness is often much more severe than wasting.

History. Although Thomas *Willis is credited with the earliest description of myasthenia gravis in 1672, it was not until the 19th c. that attempts were first made to distinguish between the many different diseases which cause progressive muscular weakness and wasting. Aran in 1850 described patients with what appears to have been *motor neurone disease, and Meryon in 1852 reported granular degeneration of skeletal muscles. (For the references quoted in this section, see Walton, 1981.) *Duchenne in 1868 and *Gowers in 1879 identified and described the pseudohypertrophic form of muscular dystrophy now called the Duchenne type, while *Erb in 1884 reported muscular dystrophy limited to the scapulohumeral muscles, *Landouzy and *Dejerine (1884) described the facioscapulohumeral variety, and Leyden (1876) and *Möbius (1879) a pelvifemoral variety. *Hutchinson in 1879 and Fuchs in 1890 reported myopathy affecting specifically the external *ocular muscles. *Oppenheim (1900) described severe infantile hypotonia present from birth, while Werdnig (1891) and Hoffmann (1897) reported cases of severe spinal muscular atrophy arising in infancy. The first clear-cut reports of dystrophia myotonica or myotonic dystrophy came from Steinert (1909) and Batten and Gibb (1909),

while paramyotonia congenita was described by Eulenburg (1886) and myotonia congenita by Thomsen (1876). Adult motor neurone disease, first described by Aran in 1850, was later described by Duchenne (1860) and by *Charcot and Joffroy (1869).

Diagnostic methods. Diagnosis of the neuromuscular diseases depends in the first instance upon analysis of the clinical history of the illness and the family history and upon physical examination to detect wasting and/or weakness of the individual muscles at rest and during movement. Methods are available for assessing the strength of most muscles in the human body and of eliciting tendon and other *reflexes (tendon jerks), as well as measuring the ability to perceive different types of *sensation. Clinical differential diagnosis is essentially dependent upon recognizing different patterns of involvement of nerves and muscles.

Several hundred neuromuscular diseases are now recognized and, in many of these, special biochemical or other tests may be needed in addition to clinical examination in order to elucidate the nature of the disease. The three principal investigations of value in diagnosis are, first, estimation in blood samples of *enzymes such as creatine kinase. In many myopathies, like the muscular dystrophies, creatine kinase leaks out of damaged muscle cells, probably due to a defect in the fibre membrane, and is greatly increased in the circulating blood. Lesser increases are common in the motor neurone diseases and spinal muscular atrophies.

Electrophysiological methods, including measurement of nerve conduction velocity, are also important. The rate of *conduction of the nerve impulse is generally unimpaired in the motor neurone diseases and spinal atrophies, although the amplitude (height) of the muscle action potential evoked by nerve stimulation is reduced in proportion to the severity of the weakness and wasting. In many neuropathies, however, and especially in those which affect predominantly the myelin sheath covering the nerve fibres (demyelinating neuropathies) the rate of conduction is markedly slowed. By contrast, when the disease process primarily affects the axon, the rate of conduction may be normal but the amplitude of the nerve action potential is markedly reduced. These techniques are of greatest help in investigating the neuropathies. Similarly, the measurement of the size of the recurring muscle action potential produced by repetitive supramaximal stimulation of a peripheral nerve often helps to assess neuromuscular transmission and thus assists in the diagnosis of myasthenia gravis. *Electromyography, too, is an invaluable diagnostic technique; it involves inserting a needle electrode into a muscle with amplification of the electrical activity so recorded, both at rest and during contraction, and visualization on a cathode ray *oscilloscope. The sound of the activity recorded, amplified in a loudspeaker, is also helpful. *Myotonia gives spontaneous activity on needle insertion, which is virtually diagnostic. Denervation may cause spontaneous activity of single muscle fibres (fibrillation). During muscular contraction, in denervating diseases the surviving motor units are generally normal or large but reduced in number, whereas in primary myopathies the motor units are small, of low amplitude and short duration, or broken up and polyphasic. (See also NEUROPHYSIOLOGY, CLINICAL.)

Perhaps of greatest diagnostic value is muscle *biopsy. This involves removing, either by needle or by an open surgical technique following incision in the skin, a sample of muscle which can then be studied biochemically and microscopically. In some neuromuscular diseases specific abnormalities are seen in sections appropriately stained and examined under the light microscope. Thus the muscular dystrophies, for example, are characterized generally by death or necrosis of scattered muscle fibres followed by digestion or phagocytosis and by the presence of abortive regenerative activity with random variation in size and shape of the muscle fibres, fibre splitting, and central nuclei (not normally present in adult muscle). The spinal muscular atrophies and other denervating diseases tend, by contrast, to give uniform atrophy of small (or sometimes large) groups of muscle fibres, often angulated and containing dark pyknotic (dense) nuclei, which lie alongside fibres with intact nerve supply which look relatively normal. In some chronic spinal muscular atrophies, secondary myopathic change can develop, causing difficulty in diagnosis. In *polymyositis and other inflammatory myopathies, necrosis of muscle fibres is often accompanied by perivascular and interstitial infiltration with inflammatory cells. Within the last 25 years, histochemistry (a method of staining muscle fibres to demonstrate their enzymatic content) and electron microscopy have added new dimensions to biopsy diagnosis. Thus histochemistry has shown that human muscle consists of two major fibre types which are randomly distributed in a chequerboard pattern: type I fibres depend upon *aerobic metabolism, correspond to the red or slow fibres of animal muscle, and have a high concentration of oxidative enzymes, while type II fibres correspond to the fast white fibres of animal muscle, have a high concentration of *glycogen, and depend upon *anaerobic metabolism. Diseases like the mitochondrial myopathies and lipid storage diseases mainly affect type I fibres; in some floppy infants there is a disproportion in size and number between the fibre types; disuse causes selective atrophy of type II fibres; and, after denervation, motor nerve fibres arising from as yet unaffected anterior horn cells may sprout and grow down into the muscle, adopting or reinnervating previously denervated fibres. Such reinnervation can convert type I to type II fibres and vice versa. In consequence, in chronic spinal muscular atrophies, histochemistry may demonstrate large areas of fibres of uniform histochemical type (fibre type grouping). Electron microscopy has contributed particularly to diagnosis by demonstrating many hitherto unsuspected morphological abnormalities in skeletal muscle, especially in some of the congenital, non-progressive myopathies which can cause the so-called *floppy infant syndrome (see below); it has also clarified the ultrastructural substrate of some of the metabolic myopathies.

Motor neurone disease. This condition, also called motor system disease, is a progressive, degenerative disorder of unknown cause which produces signs due to disease of both the upper and lower motor neurones. The lower motor neurone lesions produce weakness and wasting of muscles in the head, neck, and limbs, while involvement of upper motor neurones causes *spasticity or increased tone (resistance to stretch) in the limbs. When the condition begins with weakness and wasting in limb muscles of relatively slow progression, it is often called progressive muscular atrophy; when it begins with increased tone (spasticity) in the extremities, and weakness and wasting with *fasciculation of muscles appears late, it is called amyotrophic lateral sclerosis; while if it begins by affecting muscles of speech and swallowing, spreading to the limbs later, with spasticity in addition, it is called progressive bulbar palsy. The term 'amyotrophic lateral sclerosis' is often used in the USA to identify all varieties of the disease, while 'motor neurone disease' is preferred in the UK. Although the effects of the condition may be modified by appropriate appliances, and temporary improvement in swallowing, for example, may occasionally be produced by surgical means, the disease is usually remorselessly progressive and is often fatal within 2–5 years or rarely 10 or more years after the onset; patients usually die from *respiratory infection. Symptomatic drug treatment can temporarily reduce spasticity, but no drug has any influence upon the course of the disease. In the UK and in the USA the condition is usually sporadic, although it occasionally affects more than one member of a family. The *familial type is very rare in Western countries and even the sporadic variety, which usually begins in middle or late adult life, is relatively uncommon. However, in the Chamorro people, who live in the Mariana group of islands in the Pacific, a form of motor neurone disease, sometimes associated with parkinsonism and dementia (see PARKINSONISM–DEMENTIA COMPLEX), is a common cause of death. It is still uncertain whether this Western Pacific form is genetically determined or is caused by some unidentified environmental factor, although the latter seems increasingly likely.

Spinal muscular atrophy. Whereas both the upper and lower motor neurones are involved in motor neurone disease, there are several varieties of spinal muscular atrophy occurring in infancy, childhood, and adult life, affecting selectively the anterior horn cells of the spinal cord; very occasionally, motor nuclei of the cranial nerves are also affected, giving difficulty with speech and swallowing, less often impairment of ocular movement or facial weakness. Most forms of spinal muscular atrophy are genetically determined and of autosomal *recessive inheritance, although some families have shown dominant inheritance, and very rarely the condition is *X-linked. Werdnig–Hoffmann disease (the severe infantile form) begins shortly before birth or just afterwards, causing diffuse muscular weakness and hypotonia; it leads to progressive paralysis with grave respiratory insufficiency and ultimately infection, with death before the end of the first year of life, or less often, in the second year. Milder varieties commonly producing localized, restricted or more diffuse weakness of limb and trunk muscles, may begin in later infancy, childhood, adolescence, or adult life. The relatively benign variety which begins in late childhood or adolescence is often called the Kugelberg–Welander syndrome or pseudomyopathic spinal muscular atrophy, as it resembles muscular dystrophy (see below). Adult forms of this condition, which closely mimic limb-girdle and facioscapulohumeral muscular dystrophy, are much commoner than was once recognized.

The neuropathies. Within the spinal canal, the posterior roots carry sensory information into the spinal cord and the anterior roots carry motor impulses which leave it. These two combine into spinal nerves at each segment of the spinal column and leave by the intervertebral foramina where they may be compressed by *prolapsed intervertebral discs, often giving upper limb pain when this occurs in the neck or *sciatica when it occurs in the lumbar region of the *spine. Many spinal nerves in the cervical region (the neck) come together to form the brachial plexus; those in the dorsal region leave the spinal canal to form intercostal nerves (which lie between the ribs), while in the lumbar and sacral region they form the lumbosacral plexus. From the plexuses, peripheral nerves arise, most containing both motor fibres concerned with initiating and controlling movement, as well as sensory fibres conveying centrally feeling from the joints, muscles, skin, and other structures. Although small cutaneous nerves which carry feeling from the skin are purely sensory, most peripheral nerves are mixed, containing both sensory and motor fibres.

The term 'neuropathy' embraces all pathological processes involving peripheral nerves. Traumatic neuropathies are those disorders in which peripheral nerves are damaged by physical injury, while the compression neuropathies are processes in which peripheral nerves are compressed by an abnormal anatomical structure, often, for instance, as a result of disease in a joint or in other organs. Thus the ulnar nerve, which passes behind the humerus at the inner side of the elbow (the 'funny bone') can be chronically irritated at this point where it passes between two parts of a muscle called the flexor carpi ulnaris (the cubital tunnel syndrome). This process gives tingling and pins and needles in the little and ring fingers and sometimes wasting of the small hand muscles. Similarly, compression of the median nerve in the carpal tunnel at the wrist, due to swelling of flexor tendon sheaths resulting from overuse, can give tingling and pins and needles which frequently waken the patient from sleep at night and which involve particularly the thumb, the index and middle fingers, and often the ring finger.

When the blood vessels which carry blood to peripheral nerves (the vasa nervorum) are affected by disease, the function of several such nerves may become defective through loss of blood supply (mononeuritis multiplex). This can occur in *diabetes mellitus due to hardening of the arteries (*atherosclerosis) but is more often seen in inflammatory arterial disease, such as *polyarteritis nodosa or other so-called *connective tissue diseases, and in infections like *leprosy.

There are, however, many inflammatory and metabolic diseases which affect peripheral nerves more diffusely, which are called 'the polyneuropathies'. Sometimes, as mentioned above, the myelin sheaths of the peripheral nerves are damaged primarily and the axons only secondarily (the demyelinating polyneuropathies): in other cases, it is the axons which are affected primarily and the myelin sheaths secondarily (the axonal neuropathies). However, in almost all forms of neuropathy, except those which are transient, both the axon and the myelin sheath ultimately suffer to some extent. A common acute or subacute demyelinating neuropathy is the so-called *Guillain–Barré syndrome in which, in severe cases, there is often progressive weakness with tingling and pins and needles in the extremities, developing rapidly over a few days, sometimes leading to paralysis of all four limbs and even of the respiratory muscles, requiring assisted respiration. Usually motor weakness is more severe than sensory impairment, although in occasional cases there is ascending loss of sensation. Subacute cases occur in which weakness affects particularly the proximal limb muscles, at least at first, and there may be no loss of sensation; conduction velocity in peripheral nerves is almost invariably reduced and the protein content of the *cerebrospinal fluid is raised. In most cases, provided that serious complications such as respiratory weakness can be prevented or controlled, recovery is ultimately complete. *Steroid drugs are of no value in acute cases but may help in those which are subacute. A form of steroid-responsive, subacute, demyelinating neuropathy which can ultimately give hypertrophy (or enlargement) of peripheral nerves, due to Schwann cell proliferation, has been described.

In fact the potential causes of polyneuropathy are legion. Thus deficiency of *vitamin B_1, either nutritional or secondary to chronic *alcoholism, or due to heavy metal poisons (lead, arsenic, gold, etc.) which are competitive *inhibitors of this vitamin, can cause a severe axonal neuropathy which is often predominantly sensory at the outset but which later involves motor nerves. *Uraemia, as in chronic renal failure, also causes an axonal neuropathy, while the neuropathy which often complicates diabetes mellitus of juvenile onset involves both myelin and axons. Many drugs can also cause polyneuropathy. One is *isoniazid, particularly in those (about half the population) who acetylate this drug slowly; isoniazid neuropathy is due to competitive inhibition of *vitamin B_6 (pyridoxine) and can usually be prevented, especially in rapid acetylators, by giving vitamin B_6 to patients (such as those with *tuberculosis) who need that drug. Vitamin B_{12} deficiency in *pernicious anaemia also produces a predominantly sensory polyneuropathy as one of its manifestations.

There are also many forms of genetically determined polyneuropathy, some predominantly motor and some mixed motor and sensory (including peroneal muscular atrophy or Charcot–Marie–Tooth disease, a very benign condition in which muscular weakness and wasting is generally limited to muscles below the knees and those of the hands). Various forms of *hereditary sensory neuropathy which may cause perforating *ulcers of the feet or other 'trophic' changes (usually due to repeated unnoticed minor injury) in the extremities, have also been described. Similar changes sometimes occur in neuropathy due to leprosy. Polyneuropathy is also a common non-metastatic complication of *malignant disease. Thus in middle or late life, all patients presenting with an unexplained polyneuropathy deserve investigation to make sure they do not have unsuspected *cancer. In some patients the polyneuropathy associated with malignant disease is also accompanied by myopathy, and the condition is then more properly referred to as a 'neuromyopathy'.

The muscular dystrophies. The muscular dystrophies are a group of primary, degenerative myopathies, all of which, so far as is known, are genetically determined. There are rare forms which appear to be limited to the external ocular muscles (ocular myopathy and the even less common oculopharyngeal variety). Very rarely, too, dystrophy can affect predominantly the distal muscles of the limbs (distal myopathy). However, the commonest varieties are, first, the so-called Duchenne and Becker *X-linked varieties, secondly the autosomal *recessive limb-girdle type, and thirdly the autosomal *dominant facioscapulohumeral form. Typically in all the muscular dystrophies the primary degenerative process affects the muscle fibres and no primary abnormality can be identified in the motor nerves supplying them.

The Duchenne type, being X-linked, affects only boys, save for the exceptionally rare cases of females involved either because of chromosomal translocation or because they have only one X chromosome (see GENETICS). Some are late in walking and do not do so until 18–20 months of age. All affected boys begin, by about the age of three, to have difficulty in walking, with frequent falling, clumsiness in running, difficulty in climbing stairs, and subsequently difficulty in rising from the floor. Enlargement of calf muscles and sometimes of others is common, but there is selective wasting and weakness in upper and lower limb muscles in a consistent pattern. Most patients are confined to a wheelchair by the age of 10 and relatively few survive beyond the age of 20. Although the longevity and quality of life in such patients has been improved by care and attention to posture and by methods used to prevent deformity, no effective treatment for the disease has yet been discovered. Death is either due to respiratory infection or to the involvement of heart muscle.

Current research is concerned particularly with identifying the position on the X chromosome at which the Duchenne gene lies and with subsequent isolation of it. Whether this will ultimately lead to effective treatment is still uncertain, but recent work on the role of *calcium in the muscle fibres of such patients suggests at least the possibility that drugs may become available within the next 10 years which may have at least some beneficial influence upon the disease. In the meantime, prevention is dependent upon techniques now available for the detection of female *carriers who are likely to pass the disease on to their sons. While the Duchenne gene is one of those with the highest *mutation rate in human genetics (approximately one-third of all cases are due to mutation) it is important in a sister of a dystrophic boy to use techniques such as estimation of creatine kinase or *myoglobin in the blood *serum in order to determine whether or not she is a carrier. If she is, then half her sons will be affected by the disease and half her daughters will be carriers. Once a carrier is detected, it is at present possible only to recommend either that she does not reproduce, or that if she wishes to have a family, she should at 14 weeks of pregnancy undergo *amniocentesis to identify the sex of the unborn child; subsequently she may then decide to have an abortion if the fetus is male. While the technique of *fetoscopy may yet help to identify the affected male fetus, making possible selective abortion only of affected males, no totally reliable method of antenatal diagnosis yet exists. Isolation of the Duchenne gene will provide such a method.

The Becker variety of muscular dystrophy, like Duchenne dystrophy, is also X-linked but is more benign and of later onset. Usually, affected individuals walk until they are 15–25 years of age. Many are then confined to wheelchairs but live until the age of 50 years, or later.

The limb-girdle variety may begin either with selective involvement of shoulder girdle muscles (the scapulohumeral form) or in the pelvic girdle muscles (the pelvifemoral form), spreading to the other group later. While it is now known that many patients previously diagnosed as having limb-girdle muscular dystrophy are suffering from spinal muscular atrophy or from some form of metabolic myopathy, a form of limb-girdle dystrophy does certainly exist and runs a much more benign course than the Duchenne type, often leading to a wheelchair existence in middle life, and death before the normal age. By contrast, the facioscapulohumeral variety, of dominant inheritance, is severe in some affected individuals but exceptionally mild in others, who are called abortive cases as they may go through life without recognizing that they have the disease in a mild and restricted form. In this condition there is difficulty in closing the eyes, in pursing the lips, and in whistling. In the upper limbs there is selective involvement of scapulohumeral muscles, as in limb-girdle cases, while in the lower limbs the anterior tibial muscles which elevate (dorsiflex) the feet are the first to be affected. Many patients survive to a normal age. Even this facioscapulohumeral variety may sometimes be mimicked by spinal muscular atrophy or by metabolic myopathies such as mitochondrial myopathy (see below).

Myotonic disorders. Myotonia is a phenomenon of delayed relaxation of muscle in which, after the patient is asked to relax, there is an after-contraction which can be recorded electrically. For example, the patient being asked to open the hand after gripping an object may be unable to do so quickly, and the fingers uncoil only slowly. Similarly, a tap on the tongue or on a limb may produce a dimple which disappears slowly. Sometimes myotonia is generalized throughout the musculature from birth and no other disability develops. In this condition (myotonia congenita) the prognosis is excellent, but the myotonia, which is much worse in cold weather, may restrict movement. Such individuals often force themselves to exercise early in the day to 'wear off' the myotonia. In many families, myotonia congenita is dominantly inherited (Thomsen's disease). However, there is also a recessively inherited variety of myotonia congenita which comes on later in childhood and is also benign. Myotonia may be relieved by drugs such as *quinine, procaine amide, or *phenytoin, but the response in different cases is variable.

By contrast, dystrophia myotonica (also called myotonia atrophica or Steinert's disease) is a disease in which myotonia is often limited to the muscles of the hands and may indeed be clinically unobtrusive or detectable only by electromyography. In such cases, however, facial weakness, *cataracts, weakness of the sternomastoid muscles in the neck, and distal wasting and weakness of limb muscles develop usually in adolescence or early adult life. There is often frontal baldness and *testicular atrophy in the male or *infertility in the female. In some families there is mental retardation or else progressive *dementia with enlargement of the *ventricles of the brain. This condition is progressive and disabling and uninfluenced by treatment; most patients die before the normal age. Infants of mothers with myotonic dystrophy may be very 'floppy' or hypotonic at birth and often show marked developmental delay before developing the typical manifestations of myotonic dystrophy in adolescence.

Inflammatory myopathy. While virus diseases of skeletal muscle such as *Bornholm disease (an acute form of muscle pain or *myositis with fever, which causes difficulty in breathing and pain around the chest wall and *diaphragm lasting for a few days, and which is due to the *coxsackie A3 virus) are seen from time to time, and while *influenzal myositis (in Western countries) or pyogenic myositis due to the *staphylococcus (in tropical countries) are other forms of inflammatory myopathy which occasionally occur, the commonest form of inflammatory myopathy seen in Western countries is polymyositis. In this condition—an *autoimmune disease in which *lymphocytes circulating in the blood became sensitized against skeletal muscle and may invade and damage it—there is often but not invariably muscle pain and tenderness along with diffuse, non-selective weakness of the proximal muscles of the limbs. In some cases there is difficulty in swallowing and inflammation of the skin, when the condition is often referred to as *dermatomyositis. This condition can occur at any age from childhood until late life, but in middle and late life it often complicates malignant disease in the lung or elsewhere. The serum creatine kinase activity is often modestly raised and a muscle biopsy usually demonstrates not only destruction of muscle fibres but also inflammatory cell infiltration. Treatment with drugs such as *prednisone and *immunosuppressive agents like *azathioprine is successful in most cases, but not as much so in patients who have associated malignant disease which determines the *prognosis.

Infestation with Trichinella spiralis (trichinosis, or *trichiniasis), due to eating contaminated pork can mimic polymyositis as it causes diffuse muscle pain. *Polymyalgia rheumatica, a disease of the elderly, causes diffuse muscle pain and tenderness which restricts movement but there is no weakness, the erythrocyte sedimentation rate is greatly raised, and the response to steroid drugs is immediate.

Myasthenia gravis. Myasthenia gravis is another autoimmune disease in which circulating *antibodies form in the blood against the acetylcholine *receptor which lies on the surface of the muscle fibres and with which acetylcholine (released from nerve endings at the motor end-plate) combines. This circulating antibody coats the receptors and prevents acetylcholine so released from having its full effect; in consequence the muscles are weak and excessively fatiguable in that repeated contraction causes increasing weakness. Typically the condition, which is commoner in females but can begin at any age, affects the external ocular muscles, often with drooping of the eyelids coming on towards the end of the day, with or without double vision (diplopia). Often there is difficulty in speaking and swallowing and in chewing (chewing difficulty increasing during a meal is almost diagnostic) and variable weakness of limb muscles without wasting also often occurs, always being accentuated by exercise. A rare variety (often called the myasthenic-myopathic syndrome or the Lambert–Eaton syndrome) is seen particularly in patients with malignant disease, in whom weakness increases at first after exercise but as exertion continues muscle power actually increases. In such cases the tendon reflexes are usually absent, while in true myasthenia gravis they are usually present or even brisk.

The diagnosis of myasthenia gravis is usually confirmed by estimation of circulating antibodies in the blood and clinically by an intravenous injection of edrophonium hydrochloride (Tensilon) which dramatically reverses, if only for a few seconds or minutes, the muscular weakness. This drug inhibits cholinesterase, the enzyme which breaks down acetylcholine at the end-plate. More sustained benefit can be produced by other longer-acting anticholinesterases such as pyridostigmine, but this treatment is essentially symptomatic. It is much more effective in the long term to remove surgically the *thymus gland which produces the white blood cells or T-*lymphocytes, which, by interacting with B-lymphocytes from other tissues, have a major role in producing the antibodies. Steroid drugs and immunosuppressants also have an important role in treatment. In an acute emergency, plasmapheresis, a technique of removing the patient's blood *plasma and of replacing it with plasma which does not contain antibodies, can be of remarkable temporary benefit.

The floppy infant syndrome. The condition of benign congenital hypotonia was mentioned above. However, there are many forms of benign congenital myopathy of variable severity and rate of progression which may be associated with specific structural abnormalities in skeletal muscle fibres. Thus, for example, myotubular or centronuclear myopathy is a condition in which immature fetal myotubes with central nuclei appear to persist into extrauterine life. The affected infants are often limp and floppy and show marked motor developmental delay; there is usually involvement of external ocular muscles, giving a *squint. Sometimes maturation does not occur, but often there is progressive improvement.

A variable clinical course is also seen in patients with central core disease, in which many muscle fibres, often of uniform histochemical type, contain what seem to be non-functioning central cores. The cause of this condition is unknown but usually it is relatively benign and non-progressive.

The same is often true of nemaline myopathy, in which the protein of the Z band of many muscle fibres seems to be abnormal and often breaks up to

give rod-like structures which accumulate beneath the plasma membrane of the affected fibres; these rods have been called nemaline rods after the Greek 'nemo' meaning thread. Some patients with nemaline myopathy have long spidery fingers and other features suggestive of *arachnodactyly, but this is not invariable and the course and prognosis is unpredictable.

Many other morphological abnormalities, often identified only with the electron microscope, have been seen in floppy infants showing motor developmental delay and non-progressive muscular weakness. One such is fibre type disproportion, in which there is a marked disproportion in the relative sizes of the type I and type II fibres in the muscles of the affected infants, but there are a great many others which cannot be mentioned in a short review.

Metabolic and endocrine myopathies. Weakness of proximal limb muscles is often seen in patients with increased *thyroid activity (*thyrotoxicosis) but improves as the latter condition is treated. By contrast, diminished thyroid activity (*myxoedema) can cause slowness of muscular contraction and relaxation, sometimes with muscular enlargement (Hoffman's syndrome). Increasingly severe muscular pain arising during exercise, eventually preventing further movement, is seen in *McArdle's disease due to deficiency of the muscle enzyme phosphorylase; this causes *glycogen to accumulate in skeletal muscle as it cannot be broken down properly. Within recent years many other enzymatic defects affecting muscle glycogen breakdown have been discovered which have similar effects; phosphofructokinase deficiency is one such. In all these conditions the muscle contains excess glycogen and its ability to break down glycogen and to produce one of its principal waste products, lactate, in venous blood is greatly impaired and can be recognized by a simple test.

Other metabolic disorders of muscle include the so-called familial periodic paralyses of dominant inheritance, in which episodes of diffuse muscular weakness can be precipitated by exertion or by a heavy *carbohydrate meal. In some the attacks of weakness are accompanied by a rise in the serum *potassium (the hyperkaelaemic variety), in others by a fall (the hypokalaemic variety). Despite this variation in the biochemical accompaniments of the attacks, they can often be prevented in each type by treatment with drugs which promote the excretion of potassium such as *acetazolamide.

Recently identified, too, have been a number of muscle disorders associated with abnormalities of *fat metabolism. Thus an inherited deficiency of carnitine (a building block essential for *fatty acid metabolism) can result in excess storage of neutral fat in skeletal muscle, giving marked muscle weakness. Sometimes the weakness is improved by giving oral carnitine.

Finally, among the many metabolic myopathies now recognized there are several diseases which can sometimes mimic clinically the limb-girdle or facioscapulohumeral muscular dystrophies and in which abnormal mitochondria can be identified, both by biochemical and morphological studies. The mitochondria may be increased in number or abnormal in size and shape, often containing large crystalline inclusions. Many different systemic and intramuscular biochemical abnormalities have been identified in such cases. Some have also shown *retinal pigmentation and *ataxia or unsteadiness of gait due to abnormal mitochondria in the cerebellum of the brain (the Kearns–Sayre syndrome). Deficiencies of several enzymes of the cytochrome electron transport chain have now been recognized in many patients with mitochondrial myopathy, and knowledge is extending rapidly. Effective treatment may well be discovered for some of these conditions within the next few years.

Conclusions. This review of neuromuscular disorders is perforce superficial and limited in scope, but is intended to give the reader an indication of the complexity of diagnosis and management in a specialized field which was thought to be relatively simple only a few years ago.   J. N. WALTON

Reference
Walton, J. N. (ed.) (1981). *Disorders of Voluntary Muscle*. 4th edn, Edinburgh.

Further reading
Bradley, W. G. (1974). *Disorders of Peripheral Nerves*. Oxford.
Harper, P. S. (1979). *Myotonic Dystrophy*. Philadelphia.
Mastaglia, F. L. and Walton, J. N. (eds) (1982). *Skeletal Muscle Pathology*. Edinburgh.
Rowland, L. P. (ed.) (1982). *Human Motor Neuron Diseases*. New York.
Walton, J. N. and Adams, R. D. (1958). *Polymyositis*. Edinburgh.

NEURONE (NEURON). A *nerve cell, comprising a cell body with several short processes (dendrites) and one long one (the axon) which together with its sheath forms a *nerve fibre. Neurones are responsible for receiving and transmitting nervous impulses.

NEUROPATHOLOGY is the study of the structure and morphology of diseases of the nervous system.

NEUROPATHY is any pathological condition affecting the peripheral nervous system, motor, sensory, or autonomic. Common causes include *diabetes mellitus, *alcoholism, *malnutrition, *genetic abnormality, *carcinomatosis, and mechanical pressure on nerves; but there are many others. See NEUROMUSCULAR DISEASE.

NEUROPHARMACOLOGY is the study of the action of drugs on the *nervous system.

NEUROPHYSIOLOGY, CLINICAL

Introduction. Clinical neurophysiology embraces three major areas. The brain produces electrical activity with small fluctuations in voltage which can be recorded through the intact scalp, amplified, and displayed (usually as an ink trace on moving paper); the study of such activity is termed electroencephalography (EEG). Needle electrodes can be inserted through the skin into voluntary muscles (or, less usefully, surface electrodes can be applied to the skin overlying them) in order to record the electrical activity occurring at rest and during activity. The study of these changes in electrical potential (as displayed on a cathode-ray oscilloscope and as sound via a loudspeaker) constitute electromyography (EMG). Closely allied is the study of the behaviour of peripheral *nerves, both motor and sensory, when they are excited by an electrical stimulus. The excitation of certain sensory pathways, usually those of the visual, auditory, and somatosensory systems, is associated with consistent but often very small electrical responses which, through the use of special averaging techniques, may be identified despite the presence of the often higher-voltage ongoing cerebral activity. This third group of responses studied in clinical neurophysiology are referred to as 'evoked responses'. Within these broad divisions there are numerous more specialized subdivisions which will receive brief mention.

History. *Galvani in 1791 described 'animal electricity' based upon experiments on the excitation of frogs' legs. Within 50 years, the electrical nature of the nerve impulse had been demonstrated by *Dubois-Reymond (1848). Richard Caton demonstrated waxing and waning potentials occurring continually between two electrodes on the surface of the exposed *cerebral cortex. These potentials were unrelated to the heart rate or to breathing in the experimental animal. Although Caton established many factors which influenced cerebral activity in experimental animals, application of this work to man had to await Berger (1929) who, among other things, described the posteriorly situated symmetrical rhythmical activity appearing in man when the eyes are shut—the alpha rhythm of the EEG. Unfortunately Berger's work was virtually ignored and not generally accepted until in 1934 *Adrian and Matthews, using a valve amplification system, confirmed the feasibility of recording the human EEG.

Although the fact that voluntary muscular activity produced electric signals had long been known, it was not until 1912 that Piper made extensive studies of the human surface EMG. The introduction by Adrian and Bronk (1929) of the concentric needle electrode made it possible to study the activity of single motor units (i.e. that group of muscle fibres within a muscle under the control of a single motor neurone in the spinal cord) (see NEUROMUSCULAR DISEASE).

The velocity at which an impulse propagates along a human peripheral nerve was first demonstrated by *Helmholtz (1850). In 1944 it was established that the velocity of conduction was slowed in nerves regenerating after injury. The numerous peripheral nerve injuries of the Second World War provided an impetus to further studies. Initial studies were of the relatively large electrical responses obtained from muscles when their motor nerves were stimulated by electrical means.

Responses recorded directly from nerves are much smaller than those obtained from muscle; a surface-recorded muscle response is often between 10–12 mV in amplitude, while a similar response derived from nerve may only be 10–20 μV. At the time when nerve potentials in man were first studied, the amplitude of the signals recorded approximated to those of the 'noise' levels of the equipment then used and Dawson and Scott (1949) described a simple photographic technique for extracting the signal from 'noise'. Subsequently the use of electronic averaging and vast improvements in instrumentation have allowed the relatively rapid recognition of signals of only a fraction of a microvolt in amplitude.

The development of evoked response measurement from brain and spinal cord using surface electrode recording has been a direct result of the availability of averaging techniques. In many individuals the response of the visual cortex to brief flashes of higher luminance can be seen despite ongoing electrical activity of the brain, as recorded in the EEG. In others, the ongoing activity which constitutes 'noise' in this particular case, exceeds the amplitude of the signal in which we are interested and averaging of many responses may be necessary in order to obtain reproducible results. This is especially so in studying the response of the brain's auditory system to 'clicks' delivered in order to record auditory evoked responses. The auditory system is controlled by a lower part of the brain called the '*brainstem' and the initial signals generated in the auditory brainstem structures in response to the clicks are extremely small. These responses were recorded and fully described as recently as 1971 by Jewitt and Williston (see Halliday, 1982).

Electroencephalography. Electroencephalograms (EEGs) are usually recorded by a trained technician and interpreted by a clinical neurophysiologist. The electroencephalograph, the machine used to make the recording, may have 8, 16, or 20 channels in order to be able to record simultaneously from many areas of the scalp (Fig. 1). The electrodes are positioned in an orderly fashion according to a particular pattern (or montage). For each channel of write-out (usually ink on moving paper) activity between an adjacent pair of electrodes (bipolar) may be displayed, or the potential difference between a single electrode and a remote reference (monopolar) may be recorded. A straightforward out-patient record may take an hour, including placement and removal of the electrodes as well as recording. Relaxation on the patient's part is vital: muscle and movement artefacts readily obscure cerebral activity.

Overbreathing for three minutes provokes alterations in the record, and especially in children, may assist in the diagnosis of *epilepsy; photic stimulation (brief flashes of intense luminance) is also often helpful. The electrical activity of the brain alters profoundly in *sleep (Fig. 2) and either drugged or natural sleep may be deliberately induced to gain further information. The EEG is altered by changes in the conscious level, whether these have a metabolic or structural cause. Localized lesions such as brain *tumours or *infarcts may produce localized EEG abnormalities and certain wave forms have an association with various forms of epilepsy (Figs. 3 and 4). Apart from sedatives, drugs which cause cortical excitation have been used to provoke abnormality in a search for the cause of epilepsy in certain patients. As electrical activity from the inferior and medial parts of the brain is poorly recorded from the scalp, special EEG electrodes such as nasopharyngeal or sphenoidal needles inserted beneath the base of the skull may be used to record signals generated in these structures.

An hour-long EEG is a small sample of cerebral

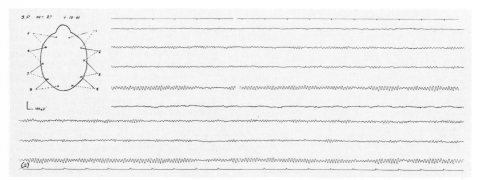

Fig. 1. An 8-channel EEG recording demonstrating rhythmical activity at 8–12 Hz in the posterior region of the head on both sides. The activity is much more evident when the eyes are shut as here and almost disappears when they are open; it is the normal alpha rhythm

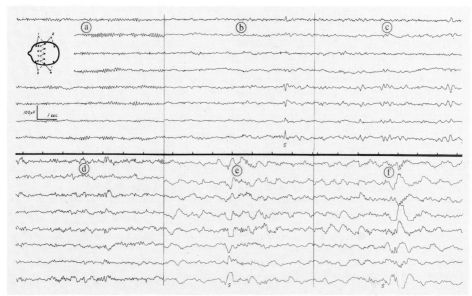

Fig. 2. Serial EEG recordings demonstrating the stages of drowsiness and sleep in a normal man aged 20 years. (a) Early drowsiness; the EEG shows a normal alpha rhythm. (b) Light (stage 1) sleep; the record is of low voltage with mixed frequencies, and a sharp wave is seen at the vertex in response to a sound stimulus at S. (c) Light sleep with dominant slow activity in the theta range at about 5 Hz. (d) Stage 2 sleep; the record shows increasing slow activity and so-called sleep spindles begin to appear. (e) and (f) Stages 3 and 4 of sleep; the record shows increasing irregular delta activity and so-called K complexes are seen in response to the sound stimulus at S. (Reproduced by courtesy from Kiloh, L. G., McComas, A. J., Osselton, J. W., and Upton, A. R. M. (1981). *Clinical Electroencephalography.* 4th edn, London.)

activity taken under artificial conditions. Telemetry is a technique involving radio transmission which allows the subject freedom of movement and of activity while the EEG is being continuously recorded, and ambulatory recording on cassette tape over 24-hour periods is now possible, thus increasing the prospect of detecting transient disturbances of cerebral activity. Analysis of such records by the clinical neurophysiologist was initially visual: the frequency, amplitude, and functional behaviour of the various rhythmical and non-rhythmical fluctuations of potential were com-

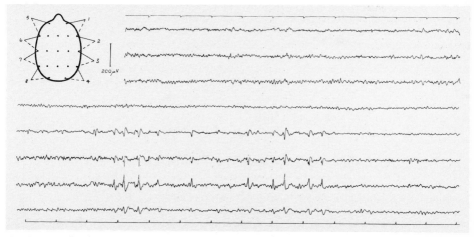

Fig. 3. A recording demonstrating focal spike discharges arising in the left mid-temporal region against a background of almost normal activity. This appearance seen in an EEG recording between attacks is the so-called interseizure pattern characteristic of temporal lobe (complex partial) epilepsy occurring in a man of 30 years of age. (Reproduced by courtesy from Kiloh, L. G., McComas, A. J., Osselton, J. W., and Upton, A. R. M. (1981). *Clinical Electroencephalography.* 4th edn, London.)

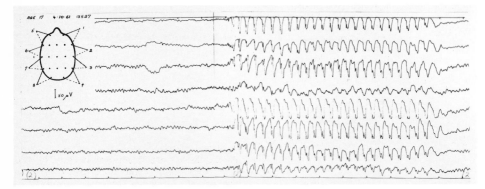

Fig. 4. Generalized bilaterally synchronous and symmetrical 3-per-second spike and wave discharge occurring spontaneously in a girl aged 17 years and associated with a clinical attack of petit mal (an absence seizure)

pared between the two *cerebral hemispheres and against the doctor's knowledge of similar recordings previously studied. The availability of various techniques of automatic analysis has varied in different countries over the years. The current widespread availability of microcomputers has given further impetus to automation.

In certain specialized centres, often those concerned with the surgical relief of intractable epilepsy, recordings are made from electrodes applied to the exposed surface of the brain at operation (electrocorticography). In some such cases, implanted or indwelling electrodes may have been inserted into various parts of the brain at various depths and recordings made from them over a prolonged period (depth electrode recording). This method allows direct recording from certain collections of nerve cells (nuclei) situated in the depths of the brain.

The EEG may provide useful prognostic information when cerebral symptoms develop in neonates and premature babies as some forms of degenerative and/or metabolic brain disease give characteristic appearances. The localization of lesions in this group of patients is less important than correlations between the EEG and the behavioural state of the patient. Other variables such as *respiration, the *electrocardiogram, and eye movements can be recorded simultaneously (polygraphically), together with a more limited number of EEG channels than are normally employed in adults.

Electromyography. The insertion of a concentric needle electrode into a patient's muscle is uncomfortable and contraction of the muscle with the needle *in situ* is more uncomfortable. The clinical neurophysiologist, in carrying out EMG studies, has the responsibility of assessing the patient's clinical problem and of solving or elucidating it by the examination of as few muscles as will give a reliable answer. Serial examinations of the same patient may be required.

Abnormal activity recorded from relaxed muscle may indicate some loss of nerve supply to the muscle (denervation) or else the presence of abnormally excitable muscle fibres in the myotonic group of disorders (see NEUROMUSCULAR DISEASE). Denervation gives repetitive small short-duration potentials (fibrillation); *myotonia gives bizarre repetitive high-frequency discharges, producing a noise like a 'dive-bomber' in the loudspeaker. On gentle contraction of the muscle the concentric needle will record action potentials from single motor units. After partial denervation, motor unit potentials are fewer than normal but are large or normal in configuration. An electronic device, the delay-line, allows such potentials to be 'frozen' on the cathode-ray oscilloscope, and their configuration can then be analysed either qualitatively or quantitatively. In primary muscle disease, the effect of the disease on the motor units is different from that seen when their nerve supply is disordered; the potentials are small, of short duration or 'broken up' (polyphasic). The pattern of electrical activity (called the interference pattern) produced by a maximum voluntary contraction is also analysed (Fig. 5). 'Single fibre' needle electrodes have a much smaller recording surface and record action potentials produced by single muscle fibres. The variability in time in the firing of two adjacent muscle fibres from the same motor unit is referred to as 'jitter'. Present in normal individuals, it is increased in active disease of muscle and nerve but is most abnormal in disorders of impulse transmission from nerve to muscle, for example in *myasthenia gravis.

The micro-organization of fibres of the motor unit may also be examined with this needle, while the recently introduced techniques of 'Macro EMG' and 'Scanning EMG' allow assessment of the size and organization of the motor units in the muscle as a whole.

A technique of stimulating the motor nerve and recording the tiny all-or-none increments in amplitude of the initial electrical responses of the muscle thus stimulated at low stimulus intensity was introduced by McComas. The magnitude of

Fig. 5. This series of illustrations (a–f) illustrates some of the contrasting findings revealed in EMG recordings obtained with a concentric needle electrode from the muscles of a normal subject and from muscles affected by primary muscle disease (myopathy) and by a neurogenic disorder causing partial denervation. (Reproduced from Barwick, D. D. (1981). Clinical electromyography. In Walton, J. N., *Disorders of Voluntary Muscle*, ch. 28. 4th edn, Edinburgh.)

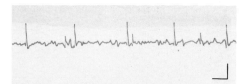

(a) Normal volitional activity on weak contraction. Calibration: 20 ms; 500 μV

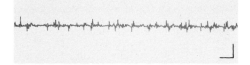

(b) Excessive recruitment of low-voltage short-duration potentials on weak contraction in myopathy. Calibration: 20 ms; 500 μV

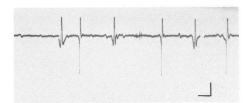

(c) Reduced recruitment of large units on weak contraction in neuropathy. Calibration: 20 ms; 500 μV

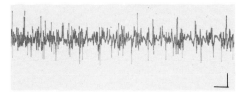

(d) Normal recruitment on forceful contraction. Calibration: 25 ms; 500 μV

(e) Very full recruitment on full volitional contraction of a weak muscle in myopathy. Calibration: 25 ms; 500 μV

(f) Reduced recruitment on full volitional contraction of a weak muscle in chronic neurogenic disease. Calibrations: 25 ms; 500 μV

these individual increments is compared with that of the response to supramaximal stimulation; it is thus possible to estimate the total number of functioning motor units within the muscle and to study variations occurring in different diseases.

Studies of nerve conduction. Motor *conduction velocity (Fig. 6) is measured by stimulating a motor nerve with a supramaximal brief electric shock at two points along its length while recording the response from electrodes placed over a muscle supplied by the nerve. The oscilloscope is triggered by the stimulus and the two latencies (in time) from the shock to the onset of the response are measured, together with the distance between the sites of stimulation and thus the velocity is readily calculated. Sensory conduction (Fig. 7) is measured by applying a sensory stimulus to, say, a

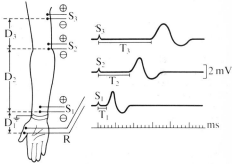

Fig. 6. A diagrammatic representation of the technique of measuring maximum motor conduction velocity in the median nerve. Recordings of the evoked muscle potential are made at R with surface electrodes, the proximal electrode being placed over a muscle of the thenar eminence (the abductor pollicis brevis), the distal electrode over its tendon. The nerve to the muscle is excited by brief (0.1 – 0.2 ms) rectangular pulses at points S_1, S_2, and S_3. The responses are recorded on a cathode ray oscilloscope in the form of waves seen to the right, preceded at S by the artefact produced by the actual stimulus. The interval between the stimulus and response is indicated by distances T_1, T_2, and T_3, depending upon the successive points of stimulation of the nerve. The maximum conduction velocity (CV) in motor fibres in the forearm is calculated by CV (m/s) = $D_2/(T_2-T_1)$. (Reproduced by courtesy from Bradley, W. G. (1974). *Disorders of Peripheral Nerve*. Oxford.)

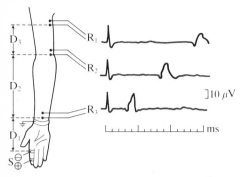

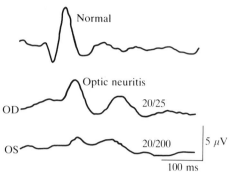

Fig. 7. A diagrammatic representation of the technique for measuring the maximum sensory conduction velocity in the median nerve using orthodromic stimulation. Stimuli are delivered to the sensory nerves of the digit through ring electrodes. Recordings are then made of the volley of impulses which pass up the nerve using electrodes placed over the skin over its course at R_3, R_2, and R_1. The responses are shown on the right. Since the amplitude of the recorded signal is low, averaging of a number of successive stimuli may be necessary. The further away from the stimulus site the recording is made, the smaller the response becomes because of increasing desynchronization in sensory fibres which conduct at different rates. (Reproduced by courtesy from Bradley, W. G. (1974). *Disorders of Peripheral Nerve*. Oxford.)

Fig. 8. Visual evoked potentials produced by stimulation with a pattern reversal method obtained from a 12-year-old boy recovering from bilateral optic neuritis. OD = right eye with improving vision and an acuity of 20/25; OS = left eye with residual markedly impaired visual acuity of 20/200. The potentials recorded from the two affected eyes are compared with a normal recording above. Note that the difference in acuity in the two eyes is reflected in the difference in the amplitude of the evoked potential, but that the peak latency is equally abnormal in both eyes. (Reproduced by courtesy from Aminoff, M. J. (ed.) (1980). *Electrodiagnosis in Clinical Neurology*. Edinburgh.)

ring around a finger and measuring conduction centripetally.

Multiple sites of stimulation may allow the velocity in various segments of nerves to be measured. Local compressive lesions of nerve (as of the ulnar nerve at the elbow) may slow conduction in the affected segment. Diffuse disease of nerves (neuropathies) may affect the *myelin sheath around the nerve (demyelination) when conduction velocity is severely slowed, or may preferentially affect the *axon (the nerve fibre), when conduction is relatively normal but the amplitude of the evoked response is usually reduced. Other neuropathies may be mixed axonal and demyelinating. Knowledge of the type of neuropathy present greatly aids the search for its cause.

Evoked responses. Although it is possible to stimulate electrically many sensory systems, clinical neurophysiology is mainly concerned with three.

Visual evoked responses. When a visual event occurs in a person's visual field, there is an associated electrical change in the visual cortex in the occipital lobe. Changing visual patterns rather than 'flashes' are now widely utilized as stimuli and the responses of the visual cortex are recorded with surface electrodes on the scalp at the back of the head overlying that area of cortex and are averaged electrically (Fig. 8). Segments of the visual fields of individual eyes can be stimulated if necessary.

In *multiple sclerosis, there may be abnormalities of the response even in the absence of clinical signs of disease in the visual pathway and this is helpful in diagnosis. Other disorders of these pathways may also be detected with the technique. A simultaneous recording with an electrode on the conjunctiva allows the registration of the electroretinogram and abnormalities of this are found in some retinal disorders.

Auditory brainstem responses. When a series of auditory stimuli ('clicks') are delivered to the ear and the electrical responses recorded between an electrode at the scalp vertex and at the ear lobe are averaged, a series of tiny waves (only one-hundredth of the amplitude of the ongoing EEG) can be detected. This series of waves represent the successive excitation of the acoustic nerve and of parts of the auditory pathways in the brainstem. The technique may detect lesions of the eighth nerve and thus helps in diagnosing the cause of deafness; the responses may be abnormal in multiple sclerosis or with tumours of the brainstem. In *coma caused by drugs, the responses are still detectable but they are absent if coma is the result of destructive brainstem lesions. The prognosis in comatose states may be helped by this test.

Somatosensory responses. When brief electric shocks are applied to a sensory nerve or to a mixed nerve in a limb, a response can be recorded over the sensory cortex contralateral to the stimulated limb. As with other evoked responses, the wave form can be recorded from surface electrodes on the scalp in a variety of positions. Different components of the response are affected by movement of parts of the body and by siting the electrodes in different regions of the head.

The upward passage of the sensory impulse may

also be followed when stimuli are applied to the leg by recording from electrodes placed over the spinal cord on the surface of the skin at several sites.

It has been found that cortical sensory responses may disappear in the presence of a lesion at any level of the sensory system from the peripheral nerve to the somatosensory cortex. Delayed responses are likely when multiple sclerosis is the causative disease. If a lesion affects the somatosensory cortex itself, the latency of the response may be normal but the wave form is altered.

Abnormally large responses may be seen in rare forms of epilepsy (e.g. myoclonic epilepsy) and in some rare neurological diseases of infancy and early childhood.

Many other more specialized techniques of clinical neurophysiological recording are available, including, for example, the electrical recording of eye movements whether occurring spontaneously or induced (*electronystagmography, electrooculography) but space limitations do not allow their detailed consideration here.

D. D. BARWICK

Further reading

Aminoff, M. J. (ed.) (1980). *Electrodiagnosis in Clinical Neurology*. London, Edinburgh, and New York.

Brazier, M. A. B. (1968). *The Electrical Activity of the Nervous System*. 3rd edn, London.

Halliday, A. M. (ed.) (1982). *Evoked Potentials in Clinical Testing*. London.

Kiloh, L. G., McComas, A. J., Osselton, J. W. and Upton, A. R. M. (1981). *Clinical Electroencephalography*. 4th edn, London.

Lenman, J. A. R. and Ritchie, A. E. (1983). *Clinical Electromyography*. 3rd edn, London.

NEUROPSYCHIATRY is that branch of medicine the practitioners of which are skilled in the disciplines both of *neurology and *psychiatry.

NEUROPSYCHOLOGY is the study of the psychological effects of organic brain disease.

NEURORADIOLOGY is the *radiology of the *nervous system.

NEUROSIS is one of a group of psychological disorders, also known as 'psychoneuroses', distinguished from the *psychoses by retention of insight, contact with environment, and sense of reality. The neuroses may be regarded as a quantitative exaggeration of normal reactions to events and situations (such as anxiety, sadness and fear) not qualitatively different from them. See PSYCHIATRY.

NEUROSURGERY

History. Although surgeons had treated head injuries throughout the ages, modern neurosurgery was not possible until the latter half of the 19th c. with the introduction of anaesthesia in 1846 and of Listerian *antiseptic and eventually *aseptic surgery from 1867. During that same remarkably

fruitful 50 years the bases of *neurophysiology and neurological localization were being laid. Hughlings *Jackson had written *Epileptiform Seizures (unilateral) after an Injury to the Head* in 1863, a *Note on Regional Palsy and Spasm* in 1867, and *A Study of Convulsions* in 1870. From 1861 onwards Paul *Broca presented his views on localization of speech function and in 1876 David *Ferrier's monograph on *The Functions of the Brain* appeared. The first surgeon to apply such principles of cerebral localization was that great surgical innovator Sir William *Macewen of Glasgow. His paper of 1881 was entitled 'Intracranial lesions—illustrating some points in connexion with the localization of cerebral affections, and the advantages of antiseptic trephining' and it is this which establishes his priority in the surgery of the brain. In 1888 at the Annual Meeting of the British Medical Association in Glasgow, Macewen reported 10 cases of intracranial operations, seven of them prior to Godlee's famous operation of 1884. Case 3 (1879) 'Case in which the Symptoms exhibited pointed to Lesion in the Frontal Lobe', proved to be a *tumour of the *dura. It was probably a *meningioma and was the first intracranial tumour to be removed surgically.

It is impossible not to make brief mention of Macewen's experience of the surgery of *cerebral abscess, the results of which, as given in his *Pyogenic Diseases of the Brain and Spinal Cord* (1893) are still unrivalled, despite the use of *antibiotics and radiological aids to localization. The explanation of this extraordinary paradox is twofold. The first reason, the selection of cases, is a fairly negative one. His success with the otogenic cases (see OTOLARYNGOLOGY) is to be found in the fact that being a truly general surgeon (a group long past) and well acquainted with the anatomy of the ear he was able simultaneously to eradicate the source of infection, an essential factor often not achieved in the intervening years, responsibility then being shared between otologist and neurosurgeon.

The development of neurosurgery continued in London through the efforts of Sir Victor *Horsley whose life embraced the surprising combination of fashionable consulting surgeon, active experimental physiologist, and pioneer neurosurgeon. If, as has been suggested above, Macewen's interest in the surgery of the brain had been motivated by the early discoveries in neurological localization, Horsley's preparation was based on his own extensive and continuing physiological experimentation. Horsley's interest in the surgical treatment of *epilepsy and in *pituitary tumours is therefore not surprising. He operated on 10 cases in 1886, his first year as surgeon at The *National Hospital for Nervous Diseases, as it is now known, in Queen Square. Two of these were *gliomas and two were *tuberculomas. One patient had a subcortical *haematoma and one had excision of bone for local headache. Four suffered from *Jacksonian epilepsy and cortical *scars with surrounding cortex were excised. In the same year (1886) at the BMA

Annual Meeting in Brighton, Horsley presented three of the patients operated on for epilepsy. The only death amongst these first 10 was in a patient with a cerebellar tuberculoma who died 19 days after operation. In 1888, with Sir William *Gowers, he published an account of the first correct localization and removal of a *spinal tumour, with recovery from *paraplegia. Horsley died in 1916 on army service in Mesopotamia. He established neurological surgery and in considering his contributions to science and medicine it is of interest to remember his intense, and sometimes bitter, participation in current debates on the evils of *alcohol, the ill-treatment of suffragettes, in defence of *vivisection, and in BMA politics at a time when feelings were roused even more than that preceding 1948.

However, Victor Horsley's surgical technique, although very dextrous and gentle, was based on that of his immediate predecessors of the pre-anaesthetic era in which speed was a primary consideration. The introduction of a more deliberate meticulous technique was one of the most valuable contributions made by Harvey *Cushing, a technique derived from his teacher, *Halsted, which remains the basis of modern neurosurgery. First at the *Johns Hopkins Hospital in Baltimore and, after the First World War, in Boston at the Peter Bent Brigham Hospital, Cushing rapidly and most effectively expanded the range and success of neurosurgery. He and his associates introduced appropriate instruments and such aids as suction and the Bovie *diathermy machine. The disorders of the pituitary were an early interest and in 1912 he published his first book, *The Pituitary Body*. Cushing's extensive experience and detailed accounts of *endocrine disturbances entitle him to be regarded as a founder of endocrinology. Similarly, one of the milestones in the development of neuropathology was the publication with Percival Bailey in 1926 of *A Classification of the Tumours of the Glioma Group on a Histogenetic Basis with a Correlated Study of Prognosis*. Bailey's classification of the gliomas related to a recession to different *embryological cell types was based on his study of Cushing's 2000 histologically verified cases. Cushing wrote widely on many aspects of neurological surgery, including *The Acoustic Neuromas* (1917) and, with Louise Eisenhardt, *The Meningiomas* (1938). In addition to devising a new surgical technique, Cushing established a school of surgery which spread across the world and embodied a special philosophy for the care of this group of patients and the organization of the departments in which they are treated. Thus in the 1920s surgeons began to specialize in the surgical treatment of certain conditions affecting the *central nervous system.

Initially localization was achieved by the assessment of neurological signs and symptoms—a fallible system even in the best hands, as shown by the not infrequent writings on the subject of false localizing signs. It was not until 1910 or thereabouts that the first useful X-rays became available and subsequently, by recognition of abnormal *calcification or changes in the bones of the skull, neurosurgeons made use of this new investigative tool. In 1918 Walter *Dandy, the most inventive of Cushing's pupils, described 'Ventriculography following the injection of air into the cerebral ventricles' in the *Annals of Surgery* and in the following year in the *American Journal of Roentgenology*. Because of the very significant improvement in the localization of intracranial space-occupying lesions by *ventriculography and its subsequent refinements, neurosurgery advanced rapidly and the specialized branch of neuroradiology developed. The degree of certainty provided by the expert neuroradiologist proved an enormous assistance and encouragement to the neurosurgeon and later, with the introduction of cerebral *angiography by Egas *Moniz and *Almeida Lima in 1931, an entirely new dimension appeared with the demonstration of vascular lesions and eventually of the dynamics of the cerebral circulation. In the UK developments of precise techniques of neuroradiology should first be attributed to Edward Twining of Manchester and subsequently to James Bull of London, who was a disciple of the great Stockholm radiologist, Erik Lysholm.

Psychosurgery. Moniz and Lima, in 1935 in Lisbon, were also responsible for the introduction of *psychosurgery by performing the first frontal *leucotomy. Moniz received the Nobel prize in 1949 for his contribution to psychiatry and worldwide thousands of patients were submitted to psychosurgical procedures, many obtaining striking benefit. For a variety of reasons, pharmacological, social, and even political, psychosurgery is now under a cloud and has in many countries been almost abandoned.

Epilepsy. The emotional impact of epilepsy may have been partly responsible for the early and continuing attempts at surgical treatment. Thus, Horsley's early interest has already been mentioned and in 1930 Foerster and *Penfield wrote on 'The structural basis of traumatic epilepsy and results of radical operation'. At the Montreal Neurological Institute *Penfield, with Jasper, his neurophysiological colleague, subsequently explored the human brain in patients undergoing surgery under *local anaesthesia, in the course of the investigation and surgical treatment of epilepsy. Not only did this work, over many decades, establish criteria for the selection of that very small proportion of epileptics suitable for surgical treatment, it also added significantly to knowledge of cerebral function.

Aneurysms (Figs 1 and 2). Of recent years the surgery of *subarachnoid haemorrhage due to cerebral *aneurysms and *angiomas has become an increasing interest in neurosurgical circles and it can now be said that the favourable results obtained make it the treatment of choice, at the

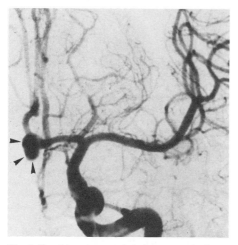

Fig. 1. Carotid angiogram. Anterior communicating artery aneurysm

earliest opportunity, of this common and very hazardous condition. The surgery of subarachnoid haemorrhage illustrates some of the important developments in the subject. The first of these is the essential radiological contribution, already referred to. Next in importance, without doubt, are the highly skilled techniques of the neuroanaesthetist in controlling intracranial and blood pressure. Of importance also have been the introduction of special instrumentation and particularly of the operating microscope, the latter by Reardon Donaghy of Burlington, Vermont, and popularized by Yasargil of Zurich. It is surprising, in retrospect, that the operating microscope had not been used by neurosurgeons earlier, as it had been been by otologists (see OTOLARYNGOLOGY) for many years. There are obvious advantages in improved illumination and vision and in magnification, which in turn lead to modification of the operator's control of movement. The microscope also has great merits in teaching. It is possible for the assistant to have a view identical with that of the operator, which with the aid of television monitoring

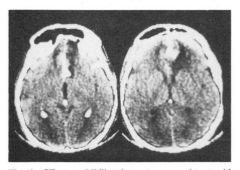

Fig. 2. CT scan. Midline haematoma consistent with subarachnoid haemorrhage from an anterior communicating aneurysm

apparatus can be shared with students or can be preserved on videotape.

The function of surgery in this condition is largely prophylactic. In a few cases, by the removal of a haematoma or drainage of a resultant communicating *hydrocephalus, primary treatment is directed to the consequences of the haemorrhage. In the great majority of cases the object is to prevent re-bleeding and this is usually achieved by occluding the 'neck' of the aneurysm by one of the many specially designed metal clips. The original clips for dealing with bleeding cerebral vessels were fine V-shaped pieces of metal which were squeezed shut by a special applicator and could not readily be reopened. They were introduced by McKenzie and subsequently modified by Olivecrona and Norlén. Sometimes the force used to close such clips resulted in tearing of the aneurysm or of the vessel giving rise to it. This could lead to catastrophe as such vessels are frequently important cerebral end-arteries (providing the sole blood supply to a part of the brain). This hazard was reduced with the use of spring-loaded clips, which are self closing as the applicator is released. These were devised and first used by W. B. Scoville about 20 years ago and are now available in a very wide range of shapes and sizes. The importance of meticulous dissection of the neck of the aneurysm from arachnoidal adhesions and small perforating arteries became increasingly recognized with the use of the operating microscope. It is this which, with improved anaesthesia, should be credited with the enormous improvement in the results of aneurysm surgery during recent years.

Previously two other techniques had been frequently employed—proximal arterial ligation (occlusion by *ligature) and investment of certain aneurysms with muscle, muslin, or a plastic or rubberoid solution. Cervical *carotid ligation, either common or internal, held the field for many years for aneurysms of the internal carotid artery and of its bifurcation. Similarly, clipping of the anterior cerebral artery was employed in the treatment of anterior communicating aneurysms. There is no doubt that in suitably selected cases these procedures were successful in reducing the risk of re-bleeding. They carried the risk of *hemiplegia (due to *infarction) and great ingenuity was used to circumvent this. With the passage of time it also became apparent that some of these patients developed contralateral aneurysms, possibly due to the changes in blood flow following proximal ligation. These operations are now rarely indicated, except occasionally in the treatment of certain very difficult aneurysms of the ophthalmic artery at its origin from the internal carotid. A few aneurysms at the trifurcation of the middle cerebral artery are still treated by investment by some surgeons.

In the 1950s and 1960s the use of induced *hypothermia during anaesthesia became increasingly popular. By reducing the *oxygen requirements of cerebral cells a bloodless field could be obtained by the use of temporary clips and hypotension and much improved operating conditions resulted. However, disappointingly, the overall results of surgery did not improve, there were risks inherent in the method which outweighed its benefits and fairly rapidly it was completely abandoned.

In addition to the purely operative problems of aneurysm surgery, the main factor responsible for success is in the timing of surgery. This is the resultant of three separate but interacting elements, namely the patient's clinical condition, spasm of cerebral arteries, and the risk of re-bleeding. Depending on the severity of the haemorrhage, resulting from spasm of adjacent cerebral arteries or actual destruction of tissue by the haemorrhage, the patient may be judged fit to withstand the additional trauma of angiography and craniotomy (opening the skull) almost immediately, that is within a day or two, or it may be necessary to wait for a longer period until the level of consciousness and general clinical condition have stabilized at a satisfactory level. Sometimes this is never achieved and the patient's condition gradually deteriorates or there is a further, perhaps fatal, haemorrhage. As has been indicated, much of this clinical deterioration, possibly involving a much lowered level of consciousness and specific neurological deficits, is due to spasm, contraction of associated cerebral arteries leading to local *ischaemia, which may vary from day to day and often recovers completely. The causes of cerebral spasm and the search for an antidote have given rise to considerable research activity. What appears definite is that the responsible agent is derived from the breakdown of blood in the subarachnoid space a few days after the haemorrhage following a short period of spasm at the time of the ictus (onset). It is at the moment, therefore, being suggested by a number of neurosurgeons that patients who are in good clinical condition should be treated surgically before the onset of 'secondary' spasm. In any case the peak re-bleeding period during the second week after a haemorrhage must be seriously regarded. Ideally, therefore, patients would be operated on in the first week, the fit ones in the early days of the week and others delayed as necessary but with the increasing threat of re-bleeding in the second and third weeks. To illustrate the risk of re-bleeding in this condition it is known that 55 per cent will re-bleed in the first year after a subarachnoid haemorrhage, most in the first month, with a peak in the second week; the risk continues for the rest of life at a rate of about 3 per cent per annum. Re-bleeding is associated with an increasing risk of death or serious neurological deficit. However, the timing of treatment is not entirely in the control of the neurosurgeon, as almost all patients are first admitted to hospital elsewhere.

There is still some controversy regarding the use of hypotensive (blood-pressure lowering) and anti-fibrinolytic (clot-promoting) drugs during the interval between the haemorrhage and operation. It would be appropriate to continue to treat a patient already known to be suffering from *hypertension but it would be quite mistaken to reduce the hypertension which commonly follows subarachnoid haemorrhage and probably represents a response to cerebral spasm. Arterial *hypotension, under the control of the anaesthetist is, of course, frequently induced at operation during dissection of the aneurysm. The rationale for the use of anti-fibrinolytic agents, such as epsilon amino-caproic acid, in the hope of preventing re-bleeding before operation is undertaken, by inhibiting lysis of the *clot blocking the aneurysmal rupture, is sound enough but the results of *clinical trials have proved difficult to evaluate. Probably at least half the neurosurgeons in the UK use some preparation for this purpose despite the moderate increase of ischaemic complications incurred thereby. The mortality following aneurysmal subarachnoid haemorrhage has been indicated above. Excluding patients regarded as moribund, in good hands a surgical mortality of between 5 per cent and 10 per cent is now achieved with a corresponding reduction in morbidy.

Cerebral ischaemia and arterial *stenosis. The surgical contribution to the treatment of the commoner degenerative cerebrovascular diseases is limited to the occasional evacuation of a haematoma in a reasonably accessible situation with a view to improving neurological recovery rather than in the hope of saving life. For almost 30 years in the treatment of transient ischaemic attacks *endarterectomy has been done at the common carotid bifurcation (see VASCULAR SURGERY). During the past decade, with the use of the operating microscope, more inaccessible carotid stenotic lesions and similar conditions have been treated in increasing numbers by *anastomosis between a branch of the external carotid artery (usually the superficial temporal) through a small craniectomy (a hole in the skull) to a branch of the middle cerebral artery. Less frequently anastomosis has also been made between the occipital artery and a branch of the vertebral artery for posterior circulation ischaemic attacks. There has been a great deal of investigation devoted to the problems of the cerebral circulation in studies of the distribution of cerebral blood flow and the consequences of its disturbance in disease. Much of this has been made possible in the clinical setting by *radioisotope studies giving simultaneous flow patterns of different parts of the cerebral circulation. In animal studies the autoregulatory ability of the cerebral circulation and its responses to chemical and other influences have been demonstrated.

Cerebral tumours (Figs 3, 4 and 5). The treatment of *cerebral tumours has been foremost in neurosurgical activity from the start. It cannot, however, be claimed that much progress has been made as far as the *gliomas, the true tumours of

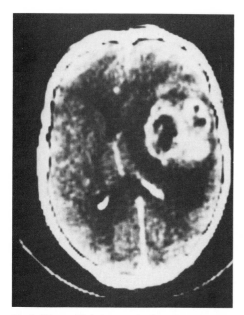

Fig. 3. CT scan. Right frontoparietal, partly cystic, partly solid glioma

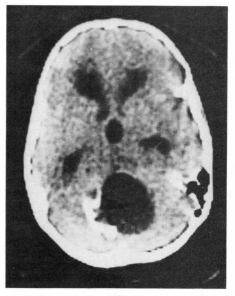

Fig. 5. CT scan. Partly calcified cystic cerebellar astrocytoma in a child with hydrocephalus

brain tissue, are concerned. The management of these fairly common tumours remains the same as it has been for some decades, consisting of neurological recognition, radiological localization, and internal decompression, that is removal of as much tumour tissue as possible without causing further neurological deficit. The value of *radiotherapy, despite a number of elaborately controlled trials,

still remains obscure. The paradox is that with or without radiotherapy, after internal decompression, patients with the most malignant gliomas, theoretically the most radio-sensitive, survive for no more than nine months or a year, while the well-differentiated gliomas may permit survival for many years. Prognosis predicted by the neuropathologist based on the histological appearances of *mitotic activity and cell de-differentiation is absolute. In other words, the more primitive the cell, the more mitotic figures present, the more malignant the tumour. It is no exaggeration to say that, with one exception—the cystic cerebellar *astrocytoma of childhood—a patient harbouring a glioma will, despite surgery and radiotherapy, sooner or later die of it. The *cytotoxic drugs, *vincristine and others, have shown no improvement in the depressing progress of the gliomas. In the past few years Thomas of Queen Square and others have persisted in studies of the immunological responses of these tumours and there is reason to believe that this approach rather than surgery may lead to their control. What has improved beyond all expectation is the radiological localization and recognition of intracranial tumours by the invention in 1973 of *computerized axial tomography by Hounsfield, which after 50 years replaced ventriculography and substituted much more in its place. The CT scanner has undoubtedly altered the practice of medical and surgical neurology. It is difficult to imagine the changes which will follow the next major radiological development, the wider introduction of *nuclear magnetic resonance, for by this non-invasive technique not only structure but function also can be studied in the brain.

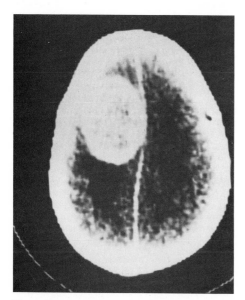

Fig. 4. CT scan. Left frontal parasagittal meningioma

The other intracranial tumours, apart from metastatic tumours, arise from structures adjacent to the brain and produce their effects by local pressure as well as eventually causing an elevation of intracranial pressure. The tumours arising from the dura, the *meningiomas, which constitute about 15 per cent of intracranial tumours, roughly a third of the number of gliomas, are the most common and, being almost always benign and usually presenting only moderate technical difficulty, are the neurosurgeon's favourite tumour. Unfortunately, this is not always the case, as the common situation of these tumours close to and sometimes involving large venous sinuses leads to their incomplete removal and subsequent recurrence—something which occurs more frequently than would be suspected from their macroscopic and microscopic appearances. A small group of meningiomas recur more than once, showing progressively malignant features and are eventually classified as *sarcomas.

Some of the cranial nerves (the VIIIth, IInd, Vth, and VIIth) give rise to tumours, of which the acoustic *neuroma, or schwannoma, is the most celebrated with an incidence of about 8 per cent among intracranial tumours. The acoustic neuroma, being a benign tumour most awkwardly situated in the cerebello-pontine angle, has always presented a challenge to the skill of the surgeon. Cushing described their clinical presentation and in the light of his experience at that time (1917) felt that total removal was impossible. Thereafter, with improvements of technique, the risks of *posterior fossa surgery decreased, although 40 years later a mortality rate of 14 per cent following total removal was quite acceptable. At the same time loss of the facial nerve was regarded as inevitable. The cause of these unfortunate consequences and the severe *cerebellar and *brainstem disturbances which often accompanied them is to be attributed, for the most part, to the delay in recognition of the condition until the tumours had assumed large, almost surgically impossible, dimensions. Twenty-five years ago it was a great rarity to be presented with an acoustic neuroma less than 3 cm in diameter and many were much larger than this, accompanied by *papilloedema and extending upwards through the tentorial hiatus. The successful treatment of this benign tumour is dependent upon its size when presented to the neurosurgeon and it was not until unilateral deafness ceased to be regarded as part of the normal ageing process that otologists, such as Hallpike in the UK and House in the USA, devised tests to identify the small (1 cm diameter) acoustic neuroma. Latterly the CT scanner has also helped with the visualization of small tumours. Even so the proportion of small to large acoustic neuromas remains much more favourable in North America as indicated by House and others. One can only conclude that a socio-economic element is involved. However, the result of this improvement in early diagnosis is that mortality is now very low indeed and neurosurgeons are concerned principally with the integrity of the facial nerve and even with preservation of hearing. Again the operating microscope has made an important contribution.

Pituitary tumours (Fig. 6). The treatment of pituitary tumours has developed to a considerable extent in the past 20 years, due principally to the reintroduction of the trans-sphenoidal approach. This method was first described in the early years of the 20th c. by Oscar Hirsch, a Viennese immigrant to the USA, who continued to use it and to describe his operative results for nearly 50 years. Cushing used the trans-sphenoidal approach in his earlier pituitary operations before he changed to the cranial transfrontal approach. This was the operation in vogue with most neurosurgeons up to fairly recently; it was a logical choice as the prime indication for surgery was the relief of *optic chiasmatic compression caused by suprasellar extension of the tumour. Attempts to influence the endocrine effects of the secreting *adenomas were ineffective at this stage. However, certain surgeons continued to use the trans-sphenoidal operation in some cases, when, for instance, the patient's general condition was thought to be too poor for craniotomy. Thus Norman Dott in Edinburgh, who had learnt the operation from Cushing, taught Gerard Guiot of Paris who in turn passed on this technique to Jules Hardy of Montreal who trained with him. Hardy developed the technical side of the operation and some appropriate radiological aids but his most important contribution has been in the treatment of the endocrine aspects of the pituitary adenomas. The basis of this part of his work was the recognition of the occurrence of microadenomas (tiny tumours) responsible for the endocrine effects of hyperprolactinaemia and *Cushing's disease as well as the larger adenomas giving rise to *acromegaly and *gigantism. Thus a new era opened in endocrinology. Although usually the surgeon can be confident of the complete removal of microadenomas this is not the case with the usual type of adenoma and here, or where there is any suggestion of invasion, radiotherapy is invaluable in the prevention of recurrence. Mention should also be made of the powerful new ergot derivative, *bromocriptine, which was first used in the treatment of acromegaly with varying success, depending apparently upon the proportion of *prolactin-producing cells. The dramatic effect of this drug in rapidly reducing the size of the large *prolactinomas has been demonstrated on a number of occasions by improvement in visual fields and by radiological studies. It is an expensive drug and its long-term effects are not known. It may be that its proper use will prove to be in preparation for operation of some of the large adenomas.

Spinal tumours. The diagnosis of spinal tumours leading to *spinal cord compression is not infrequently delayed, particularly with the often abrupt paraplegia due to *vertebral collapse from *metastatic infiltration leading to vascular occlu-

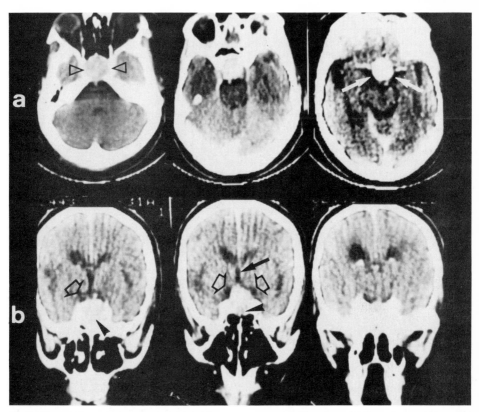

Fig. 6. CT scan. Chromophobe adenoma. (a) Axial scans: tumour outlined by arrows. (b) Coronal scans: a suprasellar extension is shown and the relationship of the tumour to the third ventricle (black arrow)

sion and transverse *myelitis. It is doubtful if surgery is justified in such cases. If detected by the presence of local pain and radiological changes at an earlier stage, radiotherapy is probably the best course. The benign tumours, *neurofibromas and meningiomas, fare much better, even when they present with signs of compression just short of paraplegia. Sometimes, the neurofibroma takes the form of a 'dumb-bell' tumour, passing through an enlarged vertebral *foramen into the chest. The correct management is to remove the intraspinal portion first to safeguard the cord and to hand over to the thoracic surgeon when the patient has recovered from the first operation. The intrinsic tumours of the spinal cord can be decompressed and partially removed and some, in particular the *ependymomas, are radio-sensitive to a most satisfactory degree. The spinal angiomas are associated with special problems which have been dealt with in the UK in the extensive series of cases by Logue of Queen Square and Shepherd of Derby.

The important topic of *prolapsed lumbar intervertebral disc is probably shared about equally with orthopaedic surgeons. The equally important *degenerative conditions of the cervical spine are more usually treated by the neurosurgeon.

Head injuries (Fig. 7). The treatment of the head-injured patient has always been the concern of neurosurgeons. In the Second World War Hugh *Cairns of Oxford directed the treatment of military head injuries in masterly fashion. He made

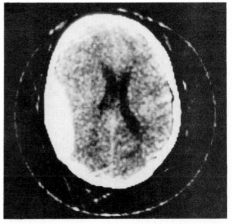

Fig. 7. CT scan. Left extradural haematoma

many contributions to the development of neurological surgery and in company with three other pioneers, Geoffrey *Jefferson of Manchester, Norman Dott of Edinburgh, and Adams McConnell of Dublin, established the subject in the UK and trained the next generation of neurosurgeons preparatory to the expansion of neurosurgery at the inception of the *National Health Service. However, of the 300 000 head-injured patients admitted annually to UK hospitals only a very small minority are ever seen by a neurosurgeon. The method of selection of patients varies, but in general the primary care hospital or department (see SURGERY OF TRAUMA) transfers patients thought to require specialized neurosurgical investigation and treatment for *cerebral compression due to haematomas, compound or depressed skull *fractures, and, less urgently, persisting *cerebrospinal fluid (CSF) leakage. There has recently been much discussion about the criteria of selection of patients both for initial admission for observation and for subsequent transfer. A similar argument continues about the necessity of primary skull X-rays in all cases. Much of the epidemiology of head injury has been the work of Jennett and Teasdale and their colleagues in Glasgow and one of their important contributions has been the development of a Coma Scale to express a simple clinical assessment of the degree of cerebral injury and an Outcome Scale to provide comparable indicators of the results of treatment. These scales have been widely adopted and, amongst other virtues, permit evaluation of methods of treatment of serious head injuries previously not possible. In addition, these and related studies have revealed weaknesses and delays in the referral system to neurosurgical departments, most striking in relation to that group who 'talked on admission but died'. This has led to criticisms of the number of beds available for the treatment of head injuries, controversy about the availability of CT scanning facilities outside neurosurgical departments and discussions about which specialty should be responsible for the care of the head-injured patient in the primary hospital. These are questions not yet answered and unlikely to be resolved in the prevailing financial climate.

The neurosurgeon and pain. This topic is dealt with in detail by Bonica (see PAIN). In intractable pain the injection or division of sensory nerves, the division of pain fibres in the spinal cord (spinothalamic tractotomy), and stereotaxic surgery (see below) are among the methods used by neurosurgeons.

Stereotaxic surgery. One of the most ingenious instruments ever invented was the *stereotaxic instrument devised by R. H. Clarke for Victor Horsley at the turn of the century for use in their animal experiments on the functions of the cerebellum and brain stem. The object of the instrument was to permit stimulation or destruction of deeply situated nuclei or tracts by an *electrode or similar device with minimal disturbance to more superficial structures. Atlases consisting of coronal and sagittal sections of the brains of the cat and monkey were prepared and from them co-ordinates in three planes were transferred to the rectilinear instrument which carried the electrode and was attached to the animal's skull along what was known as Reid's base line. Although Clarke wrote of his expectations of the use of the instrument in human surgery and described its possible applications, 40 years passed before this occurred through the efforts of Spiegel and Wycis in Philadelphia. The stereotaxic system as applied to humans was dependent upon the use of ventriculography combined with specially designed brain atlases, based on those originally produced by Clarke and Henderson. Throughout the world a number of neurosurgeons made stereotaxy their special interest and many different instruments and modifications appeared, eventually with the aid of localization by sophisticated neurophysiological recordings. The *dyskinesias (movement disorders), principally *parkinsonism, formed the predominant interest in stereotaxic surgery and in this major contributions were made by Irving Cooper of New York. Before the introduction of the *levodopa preparations stereotaxic thalamic lesions provided the most effective treatment for Parkinson's disease and comprised at least 80 per cent of stereotaxic operations. In the 20 years from the late 1950s thousands of patients were relieved of the *tremor of this condition, in some *rigidity was reduced but *bradykinesia and the more generalized disturbances were little affected. The complication rate of surgery, even in this elderly group, was eventually less than 1 per cent. With the use of *levodopa the operations performed for parkinsonism have diminished to less than 10 per cent of the previous rate. A reduction of this degree is excessive, as drug treatment (benefiting the generalized effects of the disease) and surgery (the only certain method of controlling severe tremor) are in many cases complementary. There is also increasing awareness of an 'escape' phenomenon after drug treatment for a number of years and it seems likely, therefore, that there will be a gradual return to an increased use of stereotaxic surgery in parkinsonism, at present a method of treatment receiving no mention at all in the writings of certain distinguished physicians.

Modern stereotaxic surgery requires the availability of a wide range of neurophysiological equipment and expertise and probably patients will now be referred to a few centres for the treatment of such conditions as the dyskinesias, certain chronic pain problems, and, increasingly rarely, for the surgical treatment of psychiatric disorders.

An important adaptation of his stereotaxic system has been made by Leksell of Stockholm— stereotaxic radio-surgery. By this method, highly collimated beams of *radiation from cobalt sources (see RADIO-COBALT UNIT) pass through a small accurately defined stereotaxic target. The technique has been successfully applied in the treatment of certain deeply situated tumours and small angiomas and its value is regarded as sufficiently established to have led the Department of Health to finance a special unit for the purpose at Sheffield under David Forster.

Congenital abnormalities. Among the numerous congenital abnormalities of the central nervous system three can be considered of general neurosurgical interest, namely: (i) *hydrocephalus; (ii) spinal dysraphism (see below), and *spina bifida; and (iii) the *Arnold–Chiari malformation and *syringomyelia. Apart from attempts to control hydrocephalus by excision of parts of the *choroid plexus as practised by Scarff many years ago (on the basis of overproduction of CSF), practically all other methods have depended on the use of artificial drainage systems. Torkildsen's procedure of ventriculocisternostomy, using a soft rubber *catheter (inserted between a lateral ventricle and the cisterna magna), was often very effective in the relief of hydrocephalus due to stenosis of the aqueduct of Sylvius. However, it was not until the production of unidirectional valved systems (shunts) made of biologically inert modern plastic materials that satisfactory methods of treatment of hydrocephalus were established. Names such as Spitz-Holter and Pudenz are prominent and many firms on both sides of the Atlantic are engaged in what has become a considerable industry. As might be expected, there are many complications and many reoperations in helping these patients through childhood. Obviously tubes need to be replaced to keep pace with growth but there has also been a considerable incidence of infection, particularly with the earlier, ventriculoatrial (from cerebral ventricle to cardiac atrium) shunts. More recently ventriculoperitoneal (from ventricle to peritoneal cavity) shunts introduced by Raimondi of Chicago have been favoured, with reports of lower complication rates and it also seems likely that the valve mechanisms have improved. There is reason to believe that in some hydrocephalic children there is simply a delay in the development of structures responsible for the absorption of CSF and that after a few years they become independent of artificial drainage.

Spinal dysraphism refers to a variety of congenital abnormalities affecting the lower spinal cord and *cauda equina such as dermal sinus, intraspinal *lipoma, various constricting bands impairing nerve root function, and the gross splitting of the cord in diastematomyelia. A large group of such patients have been treated and studied in detail by Lassman and James of Newcastle and Till at *Great Ormond Street Hospital in London. These children present usually with minor disturbance of function in a leg or in *sphincter control. *Myelographic studies demonstrate the lesion and there is usually no difficulty in deciding on surgical treatment to prevent progression. In some cases, particularly with the lipomas, opinion is still divided and further study is necessary.

The term 'spina bifida' is usually used to indicate a grosser defect, apparent at birth, which may or may not be accompanied by serious neurological defects affecting the legs and sphincters. This latter group has provoked serious ethical questions. For a fairly lengthy period in the mid 1960s neurosurgeons and paediatric surgeons operated on all infants with spina bifida within 24 hours of birth, irrespective of the degree of neurological disability. This was in the nature of a trial of the proposition that early closure of the defect would not only decrease morbidity and mortality but would lead to neurological improvement in some cases. Eventually many of those engaged in this exercise remained unconvinced and the present practice in most centres is to operate on fewer such infants as determined by fairly strict criteria of neurological function. General agreement on such complex ethical problems is not forthcoming (see also ETHICAL ISSUES IN MEDICAL PRACTICE; RELIGION, PHILOSOPHY, AND ETHICS).

More than 20 years ago Gardner of Cleveland suggested that the great majority of patients suffering from the clinical syndrome of *syringomyelia had hydromyelia (a dilated central canal of the spinal cord) associated with a minor degree of the Arnold–Chiari malformation. Subsequent radiological studies and surgical exploration have proved this to be true, but why this was unknown to pathologists remains a mystery. The remaining cases of syringomyelia are due to tumours or vascular abnormalities of the spinal cord. Following Gardner's example a number of neurosurgeons have operated on such patients by performing posterior fossa and upper cervical decompression of the herniated *cerebellar tonsils. The results of surgery are related to the clinical presentation and to its extent and duration. Not surprisingly the least affected patients have shown the most striking benefit. Some patients present clinically with signs of compression of the cord and other structures at the foramen magnum and these have shown more improvement than those with a more spinal 'syringomyelic' presentation, for whom not much more than a halt in further deterioration can be expected. There are three groups of patients in which a procedure to drain the syrinx, such as syringoperitoneal shunt, is indicated. These are: (i) cases showing severe *arachnoiditis at the foramen magnum, which can usually be recognized radiologically, which cannot be satisfactorily decompressed and may be made worse, comprising about 15 per cent of the whole group; (ii) a very small group of post-traumatic paraplegic patients, about 3 per cent, who develop syringomyelia; (iii) the occasional syringomyelic patient whose condition continues to deteriorate after decompression of the Arnold–Chiari malformation.

Conclusion. In 50 years neurosurgery has progressed far in some respects and hardly at all in others. The distribution of neurosurgeons throughout the countries of the world is very uneven. In the UK there are not many more than 100, supported by a relatively large number of assistants and closely associated with a strong body of medical neurologists and neuroradiologists. In the USA there are about 3000 board-certified neurosurgeons and others practising neurosurgery as well. On the continent of Europe numbers vary from country to country but generally are much closer to the numbers in the UK than to those in the USA. In the Third World neurosurgeons are rare. There are neurosurgical societies in many countries. The Society of British Neurological Surgeons was founded by Geoffrey Jefferson and other interested parties in 1926, being preceded by the establishment of the senior American Society of Neurological Surgeons in 1920. The national societies are incorporated in the World Federation of Neurosurgical Societies and the European Association of Neurosurgical Societies which organize teaching and hold regular international meetings.   J. HANKINSON

Further reading
Bowman, A. K. (1942). *The Life and Teaching of Sir William Macewen.* London.
Fulton, J. F. (1946). *Harvey Cushing. A Biography.* Springfield, Illinois.
Jefferson, Sir G. (1960). *Selected Papers.* London.
Northfield, D. W. C. (1973). *The Surgery of the Central Nervous System.* London.
Paget, S. (1919). *Victor Horsley.* London.
Sachs, E. (1952). *The History and Development of Neurological Surgery.* London.
Walker, A. E. (1967). *A History of Neurological Surgery.* New York.

NEUROSYPHILIS is *syphilis affecting the central nervous system, the chief clinical varieties being *meningovascular syphilis, *tabes dorsalis, and *general paralysis of the insane, though the distinctions are not always clear-cut. The latter two are manifestations of late (quaternary) syphilis.

NEUROTOXIC describes any agent which is toxic to nervous tissue.

NEUROTOXIN. Any substance which is poisonous or destructive to nervous tissue.

NEUROTRANSMITTERS are chemical substances released in minute amount at the endings of *nerve fibres in response to arrival of a nerve impulse; in the case of a *synapse, the neurotransmitter diffuses across the synaptic cleft to bind with *receptors on the postsynaptic cell membrane and initiate excitation of the postsynaptic cell. At other types of nerve ending, it similarly causes excitation of the adjacent effector organ. A number of substances which can act as neurotransmitters have been identified, the best known of which are *adrenaline, *noradrenaline, *acetylcholine, and *dopamine.

NEUTRINO. A stable elementary particle with no electric charge or rest mass but with a magnetic moment of one-half unit spin.

NEUTRON. An elementary particle that is a constituent of all atomic nuclei except that of normal hydrogen. The neutron has no electric charge and a mass only very slightly greater than that of the *proton. Outside a nucleus, a neutron decays with a half-life of 12 minutes into a proton, an *electron, and an *anti-neutrino.

NEUTROPHILS are *granulocytes (polymorphonuclear leucocytes) with fine neutral-staining granules. See HAEMATOLOGY.

NEW ENGLAND JOURNAL OF MEDICINE. See MEDICAL JOURNALS.

NEWTON, SIR ISAAC (1642–1727). British scientist. Newton was born at Woolsthorpe, Lincolnshire, England. He was one of the great scientists of all time, epitomizing the revolutionizing of thought in the 17th c. The understanding of the physical world was a necessary prelude to that of the world of life, which includes medicine. His thought was influenced by *Descartes, one of the most seminal philosophers of science. Newton's contributions were to optics, to mechanics and astronomy, and to mathematics. He analysed light into its component colours and believed that it consisted of particles emanating from its source. He invented calculus before Leibniz, who independently discovered it. He is especially remembered for his enunciation of the laws of motion and the law of gravity. These explained much of the behaviour of the material world, and occurrences in orbits of astronomical bodies. His most famous work is that called *Philosophiae naturalis principia mathematica* (Mathematical Principles of Natural Philosophy) published in 1687.

In very early life Newton was separated from his mother, which may have explained some curious personality traits. He was very secretive (he published reluctantly and kept much of his research for himself alone) and indulged in controversial polemics, especially with Robert *Hooke, when his views and opinions were questioned. He was a fellow of Trinity College, Cambridge in 1667, Lucasian professor of mathematics in that university in 1669, fellow of the *Royal Society in 1672 (it was founded in 1660) and later its president. In 1696 he was made Warden of the Royal Mint and moved to London, when his scientific contributions ended.

NIACIN is one of the vitamins of the B group (vitamin B_3), deficiency of which results in the syndrome of *pellagra. Niacin is a mixture of nicotinic acid and nicotinamide, into which nicotinic acid is converted in the body. Nicotinamide is required for the synthesis of an important *coenzyme, nicotinamide adenine dinucleotide (NAD), which plays a vital role in energy formation and storage. Niacin is widely available in the diet and is not destroyed by cooking or standing; niacin deficiency is rarely encountered under Western conditions except in cases of chronic *alcoholism and intestinal *malabsorption. Elsewhere it tends to be associated with a maize-dependent diet.

NICHOLAS OF CUSA (also known as Nicolaus Cusanus and Nikolaus von Cusa) (1401–64). German scholar, churchman, and cardinal. Though his importance was mainly theological, Nicholas made a significant contribution to mediaeval science through the emphasis he placed on experimental knowledge and mathematics, including applied science and diagnostic medicine. His recorded careful experiment showing that a growing plant absorbs something of mass from the air is regarded as the first formal biological experiment and the first experimental proof that air has mass.

NICOLAS, JOSEPH GUILLAUME MARIE (1868–1960). French dermatologist. With *Favre Nicolas described a sexually transmitted disease in which the lymph glands in the groin (inguinal region) enlarge and subsequently break down to discharge in multiple sinuses on the skin. Originally named after these two men, it is now known as *lymphogranuloma venereum.

NICOTINAMIDE. See NIACIN.

NICOTINE is a natural alkaloid, first isolated from the leaves of the *tobacco plant *Nicotiana tabacum* in 1828. It has complex pharmacological actions, the major component of which is transient stimulation followed by more persistent depression of all autonomic ganglia.

Nicotine has no therapeutic application. Its medical importance lies in its great toxicity and in its presence in tobacco. That nicotine makes a major contribution to the addictive properties of tobacco (including *snuff as well as that smoked in cigarettes, cigars, and pipes) is now well established. It is less clear to what extent it is an aetiological agent in the serious chronic diseases associated with tobacco smoking, that is lung *cancer, other cancers, chronic pulmonary disease, *coronary heart disease, peripheral vascular disease, and deleterious effects on fetal growth. The other toxic components of tobacco smoke, particularly tar and *carbon monoxide, are the major factors in these conditions. Hence the widespread, and not entirely unsuccessful, use of nicotine-containing chewing gum (and snuff) in substitution for cigarette-smoking, which is by far the most dangerous form of tobacco use.

NICOTINIC ACID. See NIACIN.

NIGHT BLINDNESS, also known as nyctalopia, is a manifestation of *vitamin A deficiency. Vitamin A, or retinol, is essential for the proper functioning of the retinal receptors known as *rods, which are responsible for vision in dim light (see OPHTHALMOLOGY).

NIGHTINGALE, FLORENCE (1820–1910). British pioneer of nursing. Born of rich and cultured parents in the city after which she was named, she experienced a call to serve God when she was 17. After some years of doubt she became convinced that her vocation was to nurse. Family resistance was overcome with difficulty. In 1853, after a visit to the Institute of Protestant Deaconesses at Kaiserworth, she was appointed Superintendent of the Hospital for Invalid Gentlewomen in Harley Street, London. Her success there inspired Sidney Herbert, the Secretary at War, to ask her to organize the nursing services in the Army hospitals in the Crimea, where the appalling conditions had recently been revealed in articles in *The Times.* She established herself and her 38 nurses at *Scutari where 5000 sick and wounded came under her care. In February 1855 the death rate of soldiers admitted to the hospital was 42 per cent; by June of that year it had fallen to 2 per cent. Miss Nightingale became a legendary figure and on her return to England a fund which reached £50 000 was raised which she used to establish in 1860 an institute for the training of nurses at *St Thomas's Hospital, London.

Thereafter she took no part in public life, seldom leaving her sickroom from which nevertheless there issued a stream of reports and recommendations dealing with sanitary reform in army and civilian life. Universally recognized as the founder of modern nursing, Florence Nightingale was the first woman to be awarded the newly established Order of Merit in 1907. (See also NURSING IN THE UK; ARMY, BRITISH: MEDICAL SERVICES.)

NIGHT TERRORS, also known as *pavor nocturnus,* are a sleep disturbance of young children characterized by a state of terror suddenly interrupting normal sleep and accompanied by screaming, shouting, or groaning. The episode is usually followed by a return to sleep without a period of wakefulness. The child subsequently has complete amnesia for the event, distinguishing *pavor nocturnus* from the more familiar nightmare. It is sometimes regarded as a symptom of cerebral dysfunction. See also SLEEP.

NIGHT VISION. See OPHTHALMOLOGY.

NITROFURANTOIN is an antibacterial drug effective against many organisms causing urinary tract infection, which is the only indication for its use.

NITROGEN is the invisible and almost inert gaseous element (relative atomic mass 14.0067, atomic number 7, symbol N) which comprises about 80 per cent of atmospheric air. As an essential constituent of *nucleic acids and *proteins, nitrogen is vital to all living organisms. It has a particular medical importance in the pathogenesis of *decompression sickness.

NITROGEN MUSTARD. See ALKYLATING AGENTS.

NITROUS OXIDE, laughing gas, or nitrogen monoxide (N_2O), was suggested as an anaesthetic agent by Sir Humphry *Davy in 1800 and successfully used in 1844 by Horace *Wells, a dentist of Hartford, Connecticut. Nitrous oxide remains a valuable inhalational general analgesic and anaesthetic. See ANAESTHESIA.

NITS are the ova or eggs of lice, particularly of the head louse, *Pediculus capitis.* Nits are easily recognized as small rounded bodies firmly adherent to the hair shafts.

NOBEL PRIZES FOR PHYSIOLOGY OR MEDICINE, 1901–84

1901	Emil von Behring (Germany)	Diphtheria antiserum
1902	Ronald Ross (UK)	Mosquito and malaria
1903	Niels Ryberg Finsen (Finland)	Ultraviolet light in lupus vulgaris
1904	Ivan Petrovich Pavlov (Russia)	Conditioned reflex
1905	Robert Koch (Germany)	Tuberculosis
1906	Camillo Golgi (Italy) and Santiago Ramon y Cajal (Spain)	Structure of nervous tissue
1907	Charles Louis Alphonse Laveran (France)	Malarial parasite
1908	Paul Ehrlich (Germany)	Immunity
	Élie Metchnikoff (France)	Phagocytosis
1909	Theodor Kocher (Switzerland)	Thyroid disease
1910	Albrecht Kossel (Germany)	Bases of nucleic acid
1911	Allvar Gullstrand (Sweden)	Physical properties of lens
1912	Alexis Carrel (USA)	Vascular suture
1913	Charles Richet (France)	Anaphylaxis
1914	Robert Bárány (Austria)	Vestibular apparatus
1915	No award	
1916	No award	
1917	No award	
1918	No award	
1919	Jules Bordet (Belgium)	Lysis by complement
1920	August Krogh (Denmark)	Contractility of capillaries
1921	No award	
1922	Archibald Vivian Hill (UK)	Production of heat in muscles
	Otto Meyerhof (Germany)	Lactic acid metabolism
1923	Frederick Grant Banting and John James Richard Macleod (Canada)	Insulin
1924	Willem Einthoven (Netherlands)	Electrocardiography
1925	No award	
1926	Johannes Fibiger (Denmark)	Discovery of the *Spiroptera* carcinoma
1927	Julius Wagner-Jauregg (Austria)	Malaria treatment of dementia paralytica
1928	Charles Nicolle (France)	Transmission of typhus fever by the louse
1929	Christiaan Eijkman (Netherlands)	Discovery of the antineuritic vitamin
	Frederick Gowland Hopkins (UK)	Discovery of growth-stimulating vitamins
1930	Karl Landsteiner (Austria)	Human blood groups
1931	Otto Warburg (Germany)	Intracellular respiration
1932	Charles Sherrington and Edgar Douglas Adrian (UK)	Function of neurones
1933	Thomas Hunt Morgan (USA)	Function of chromosomes
1934	George Hoyt Whipple, George Richards Minot, and William Parry Murphy (USA)	Liver treatment of pernicious anaemia
1935	Hans Spemann (Germany)	Embryonic development
1936	Henry Dale (UK) and Otto Loewi (Austria)	Chemical transmission of nerve impulses
1937	Albert Szent-Györgyi (Hungary)	Studies on vitamin C
1938	Corneille Heymans (Belgium)	Respiratory reflexes
1939	Gerhard Domagk (Germany)	Antibacterial action of sulphonamide
1940	No award	
1941	No award	

1942	No award	
1943	Henrik Dam (Denmark)	Discovery of vitamin K
	Edward A. Doisy (USA)	Chemical structure of vitamin K
1944	Joseph Erlanger and Herbert Spencer Gasser (USA)	Studies of single nerve fibres
1945	Alexander Fleming, Ernst Boris Chain, and Howard Walter Florey (UK)	Antibacterial action of penicillin
1946	Hermann Joseph Muller (USA)	X-ray induced mutations
1947	Bernardo Alberto Houssay (Argentina)	Role of anterior pituitary in carbohydrate metabolism
	Carl F. Cori and Gerty T. Cori (USA)	Carbohydrate metabolism
1948	Paul Müller (Switzerland)	DDT as an arthropod poison
1949	Walter Rudolf Hess (Switzerland)	Hypothalamus and autonomic function
	Antonio Egas Moniz (Portugal)	Prefrontal lobotomy
1950	Edward Calvin Kendall, Philip Showalter Hench (USA), and Tadeus Reichstein (Switzerland)	Adrenal hormones
1951	Max Theiler (USA)	Yellow fever vaccine
1952	Selman Abraham Waksman (USA)	Discovery of streptomycin for tuberculosis
1953	Hans Adolf Krebs (UK)	Citric acid cycle
	Fritz Albert Lipmann (USA)	Coenzyme A in intermediary metabolism
1954	John F. Enders, Frederick C. Robbins, and Thomas H. Weller (USA)	Poliovirus in tissue culture
1955	Hugo Theorell (Sweden)	Oxidizing enzymes
1956	André Fédéric Cournand, Dickinson Woodruff Richards (USA), and Werner Forssmann (Germany)	Cardiac catheterization
1957	Daniel Bovet (Italy)	Synthetic vasoactive drugs
1958	George Wells Beadle and Edward Lawrie Tatum (USA)	One gene–one enzyme concept
	Joshua Lederberg (USA)	Bacterial genetics
1959	Severo Ochoa and Arthur Kornberg (USA)	Biological synthesis of the nucleic acids
1960	Frank Macfarlane Burnet (Australia) and Peter Brian Medawar (UK)	Acquired immunological tolerance
1961	Georg von Békésy (USA)	Physiology of the cochlea
1962	Francis Harry Compton Crick, Maurice Hugh Frederick Wilkins, and James Dewey Watson (UK)	Molecular structure of DNA
1963	John Carew Eccles (Australia), Alan Lloyd Hodgkin, and Andrew Fielding Huxley (UK)	Ionic mechanisms affecting nerve cell membrane
1964	Konrad E. Bloch (USA) and Feodor Lynen (Germany)	Metabolism of cholesterol and fatty acids
1965	Francois Jacob, André Lwoff and Jacques Monod (France)	Genetic control of synthesis of viruses and enzymes
1966	Francis Peyton Rous (USA)	Cancer-producing virus
	Charles B. Huggins (USA)	Hormonal treatment of cancer
1967	Ragnar Granit (Sweden), H. Keffer Hartline, and George Wald (USA)	Chemical and physiological processes in the eye
1968	Robert W. Holley, H. Gobind Khorana, and Marshall W. Nirenberg (USA)	How genes control cell function
1969	Max Delbrück, Alfred Hershey, and Salvador Luria (USA)	Use of phage in studies of inheritance
1970	Julius Axelrod (USA), Bernard Katz (UK), and Ulf von Euler (Sweden)	Chemical mediators of nerve transmission
1971	Earl W. Sutherland, Jr (USA)	Mechanism of hormone action: cyclic AMP

1972	Gerald M. Edelman (USA) and Rodney R. Porter (UK)	Structure of immunoglobulins
1973	Nikolas Tinbergen (UK), Konrad Z. Lorenz, and Karl von Frisch (Germany)	Studies of animal behaviour, instinct
1974	Christian de Duve (Belgium), Albert Claude, and George E. Palade (USA)	Cell biology
1975	David Baltimore, Renato Dulbecco, and Howard M. Temin (USA)	Interaction of tumour viruses and nucleic acids in cells
1976	Baruch S. Blumberg (USA)	Discovery of hepatitis B virus
	D. Carlton Gajdusek (USA)	Slow-acting viruses
1977	Rosalyn Yalow (USA)	Radioimmunoassay
	Roger Guillemin and Andrew Schally (USA)	Isolation of hypophyseal peptides
1978	Werner Arber (Switzerland), Hamilton Smith, and Daniel Nathans (USA)	Restriction endonucleases
1979	Allan MacLeod Cormack (USA) and Godfrey Newbold Hounsfield (UK)	Computer-assisted tomography
1980	George Snell, Baruj Benacerraf (USA), and Jean Dausset (France)	Immunogenetics: the histocompatibility complex
1981	Roger Sperry (USA)	Cerebral hemispheric function
	David Hubel and Torsten Wiesel (USA)	Mechanisms of vision
1982	Sune Bergström, Bengt Samuelsson (Sweden), and John Vane (UK)	Prostaglandins and biologically related substances
1983	Barbara McClintock (USA)	Mobile genetic elements
1984	Niels Jerne (Switzerland)	Concept of the 'network theory' of the immune system
	Cesar Milstein and Georges Koehler (UK)	Production of monoclonal antibodies

Note: The nation listed refers to the site of the prize-winning work, not the birthplace of the scientist.

NOCARDIOSIS is a subacute or chronic suppurative infection of the lungs which may spread to the central nervous system or other body sites, more likely to occur and taking a severer course in immunocompromised patients. It is due to an aerobic gram-positive filamentous bacterium *Nocardia asteroides* commonly present in soil.

NODE. Any small mass of differentiated tissue.

NODULE. A small palpable mass.

NOGUCHI, HIDEYO (1876–1928). American bacteriologist and immunologist, born in Japan, MD Tokyo University (1897). Noguchi joined Simon *Flexner in the department of pathology at the University of Pennsylvania, then moved with Flexner in 1904 to the newly opened *Rockefeller Institute in New York. He continued to be affiliated with that institution until his death in 1928, which resulted from *yellow fever in West Africa while he was carrying out experiments regarding the aetiology of that disease. He and Flexner confirmed that *Treponema pallidum* is the cause of *syphilis, and Noguchi later demonstrated the organism in brain tissue from a patient with *dementia paralytica. In Peru he discovered that a species of *Bartonella* is the cause of *Oroya fever. He also recovered *Leptospira icterohaemorrhagica* from cases clinically diagnosed as yellow fever, and thought this to be the cause of the disease.

NOISE is defined, medically speaking, as sound of intensity sufficient to disturb and/or discomfort the listener. Excessive noise can cause transient or permanent deafness. For example, young people habitually exposed in discotheques, etc. to amplified sound of 85 to 100 *decibels (dB) for long periods suffer impairment of hearing acuity (a whisper is up to 30 dB, a normal voice 30 to 50 dB, a shout about 100 dB). Any noise of 80 dB or more is likely to produce deafness if exposure is prolonged indefinitely. Limits can be set for maximum permissible noise emission in a stated period (e.g. 90 dB in a shift of 8 hours in a working environment). Residents in the vicinity of a motorway should not be exposed to more than 70 dB.

In the UK control of noise emission is provided for under Part III of the Control of Pollution Act 1974, which replaced the Noise Abatement Act 1960. Noise control is largely the responsibility of local authorities, the Department of the Environment being the relevant department of central government.

NOMA is an infective gangrenous ulceration of the mouth, occurring chiefly in children with severe malnutrition.

NOMENCLATURE OF DISEASE. See CLASSIFICATION.

NON-ACCIDENTAL INJURY. See SURGERY OF TRAUMA; FORENSIC MEDICINE.

NON-SPECIFIC URETHRITIS is now one of the commonest sexually transmitted diseases, often abbreviated to NSU (or NGU, for non-gonococcal urethritis). Almost half the cases are caused by the agent of *trachoma (Chlamydia trachomatis)*, a small proportion by that of *trichomoniasis, and the remainder probably by an organism known as *Ureaplasma urealyticum* which is often non-pathogenic. See also VENEREOLOGY.

NOORDEN, CARL HARKO VON (1858–1944). German physician, MD Leipzig (1881). Professor of medicine in Berlin, Frankfurt, and Vienna before finally returning to Frankfurt in 1913. Noorden was a leading authority on metabolic disease. He devised a dietary regimen for the treatment of *diabetes mellitus which was widely used.

NORADRENALINE (NOREPINEPHRINE), one of the *catecholamines, is the major *neurotransmitter of the *sympathetic nervous system; it is released at the terminals of the postganglionic fibres, and by the adrenal medulla. Its effects are mainly alpha-adrenergic (see ADRENERGIC BLOCKADE), and it is a powerful elevator of arterial pressure. Noradrenaline is known in the USA as norepinephrine. See also ADRENALINE; ADRENAL GLAND.

NOREPINEPHRINE. See NORADRENALINE.

NORTRYPTILINE is one of the tricyclic group of *antidepressant drugs.

NOSOCOMIAL INFECTION is an infection acquired in hospital (for which 'nosocome' is an obsolete term).

NOSOLOGY is the nomenclature and *classification of diseases.

NOSTRADAMUS, MICHAEL (Notrèdame, Michel de) (1503–66). French physician and astrologer. Nostradamus studied medicine at Montpellier and remained in the town during the epidemic of *plague, which won him enough popular approval to force an unwilling faculty to accept him. He later practised at Agen, Aix-en-Province, and Salon, but after marrying a rich wife in 1547, turned from orthodox medicine to astrology and casting of horoscopes.

NOSTRUM. A quack remedy (literally 'our own').

NOTHNAGEL, HERMANN KARL WILHELM (1841–1905). German physician, MD Berlin (1863). Trained at the Friedrich-Wilhelm Institute, Nothnagel served as an army medical officer in Berlin. He became professor of medicine in Freiburg-im-Bresgau (1872), Jena (1874), and finally in Vienna (1882). The leading clinician of his day, he was a general physician with an interest in gastrointestinal disease, but also an excellent neurologist. He is remembered by his description of unilateral *oculomotor paralysis associated with ipsilateral cerebellar *ataxia in lesions of the superior cerebellar peduncle of the brain (Nothnagel's syndrome).

NOTIFIABLE DISEASE. See NOTIFICATION OF DISEASE.

NOTIFICATION OF BIRTHS AND DEATHS. See REGISTRATION ACT 1836; REGISTRARS OF BIRTHS AND DEATHS; REGISTRAR GENERAL; OFFICE OF POPULATION, CENSUSES, AND SURVEYS.

NOTIFICATION OF DISEASE. Most countries require notification of certain communicable diseases to local or central government health authorities. Six such conditions are internationally notifiable to the *World Health Organization: these are *plague, *yellow fever, *smallpox, *cholera, louse-born *relapsing fever, and louse-borne *typhus. A further 20 or so are notifiable in the UK, and about twice that number in the USA. In the UK certain occupational diseases and all cases of *cancer are also notified and registered. Some countries make provision for any condition to be temporarily or regionally notifiable.

NOVOCAINE is a proprietary name for the local anaesthetic agent *procaine.

NOVY, FREDERICK GEORGE (1864–1957). American microbiologist, M.Sc. University of Michigan (1887), MD (1891). Novy spent his entire career at the University of Michigan. He worked with V. C. *Vaughan, attempting to correlate manifestations of certain infections with products of bacterial growth. Then he visited *Koch's laboratory and the *Pasteur Institute. On returning to Michigan he qualified for the MD in 1891, and the following year he was appointed professor of bacteriology there, one of the first Americans to hold such a title. He studied anaerobic bacteria, and described a *Clostridium, later called *Clostridium novyi*. Later he developed culture media for *protozoans, *trypanosomes, and *leishmanii. He also discovered the causative agent of American *relapsing fever.

NOXA. Any agent harmful to the body (plural noxae).

NSAID is the acronym for *n*on-steroidal *a*nti-*i*nflammatory *d*rug. NSAIDs, most of which are also analgesic, are used in the treatment of musculoskeletal disorders; *acetylsalicylic acid (aspirin) is the prototype. A large number of compounds is now available; some of the more commonly used are listed in PHARMACOLOGY (Table 6).

NUCLEAR MAGNETIC RESONANCE IMAGING—A NEW DIAGNOSTIC TECHNIQUE

Introduction. Magnetite, a stony oxide of iron (Fe_3O_4) is found quite commonly in many parts of the world. It attracts small pieces of iron and when rubbed on iron objects the latter acquire magnetic properties. These facts were recorded in Greek and Roman writings as well as Chinese literature over 2000 years ago.

When the discovery was made that a freely suspended piece of magnetized iron or magnetite would point north is not clear. The earliest known reference to this use of magnetite in European literature was in 1185, but by the 13th and 14th c. its use was not uncommon. The English name for magnetite—loadstone (or lodestone)—probably means 'leading stone' and follows the custom of calling the Pole Star the lodestar or leading star. Among the ancients the loadstone was regarded as an object of profound mystery and awe. In addition to its navigational uses it was used for the treatment of many ailments and as a contraceptive—perhaps the first applications of magnetism in medicine!

In 1600 Queen Elizabeth I's physician, William *Gilbert, first enunciated the hypothesis that a compass points north because the Earth itself is a large magnet, and another London medical practitioner, Gowin Knight, made major contributions to magnetic compass design during the 1700s.

Following the demonstration of electromagnetism by Oersted, Ampère, and *Faraday in the early 19th c., patent electromagnetic machines were used to administer *electric shocks for therapeutic purposes. These were on sale up to the onset of the Second World War. Magnets had also been used in medicine for the extraction of iron-containing foreign bodies since the First World War.

Nuclear magnetic resonance (NMR), which is a phenomenon in which particular atomic nuclei respond to the application of certain magnetic fields by absorbing or emitting electromagnetic radiation, was first demonstrated by Bloch, Hansen, and Packard (1946) and by Purcell, Torrey, and Pound (1946). Its medical application was pioneered by Erik Odeblad, a Swedish physicist. During the 1950s and 1960s he studied the NMR properties of red blood cells, the tissue and fluids of eye, gingival tissues, vaginal epithelium, cervical mucus, and the process of ovulation (Odeblad and Lindstrom, 1955; Odeblad, 1966). In the early 1970s other workers showed abnormal NMR properties of animal and human *tumours examined *in vitro*.

The first published NMR image was produced by Paul Lauterbur in 1973 and soon afterwards small groups of physicists and engineers at the Universities of Aberdeen and Nottingham began development of imaging systems. Live human images followed in 1977 and clinical images of the brain first appeared in 1980 (Hawkes *et al.*, 1980).

At the present time there are more than a dozen groups involved in the clinical evaluation of NMR imaging systems. Although clinical experience remains small, this technique appears likely to play a significant part in clinical diagnosis.

Basic principles. Nuclear magnetic resonance has been widely used in analytic chemistry for the last four decades. The nuclei of some atoms behave like tiny spinning magnets. When these atoms are exposed to static magnetic fields, their magnetization is preferentially aligned in the direction of the static magnetic field, producing a net nuclear magnetization (Fig. 1). When these atoms are exposed to an additional magnetic field oscillating at the spin frequency of each nucleus, the nuclear magnetization can be rotated from its original orientation through any given angle. Following this perturbation the magnetization returns to its original position, during which time a small electrical signal can be detected in a surrounding coil. The rate at which the magnetization returns to its original position is described by two relaxation times,

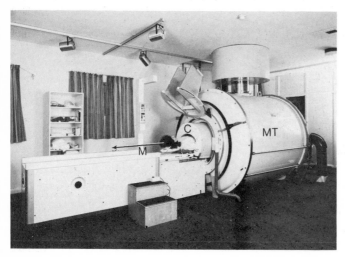

Fig. 1. An NMR machine. The patient lies within the magnet (MT) surrounded by a coil (C). The static magnetic field induces a longitudinal magnetization (M) in the patient. We wish to thank Dr Ian Young and his team from Picker International and the General Electric Company who designed and built this NMR machine and from which all the following images were obtained

T_1 and T_2. T_1 describes recovery in the direction of the external static field and T_2 describes recovery perpendicular to this field. Relaxation in the direction of the magnetic field (T_1) depends on interaction between *protons and the surrounding nuclei and molecules, whereas relaxation in the transverse direction (T_2) depends on interactions of nuclei with one another. Both T_1 and T_2 are sensitive parameters of the local nuclear and molecular environment.

Imaging systems use pulse sequences to produce images with varying dependence on these image parameters, as well as on proton density (Table 1).

Table 1. NMR pulse sequences and their basic image parameters

Pulse sequences	Principal image parameters
Repeated free induction decay (RFID)	Proton density
Inversion-recovery (IR)	Proton density T_1
Spin-echo (SE)	Proton density T_2

There is no known hazard associated with NMR imaging as performed at present (Budinger, 1981), but guidelines have been provided by the National Radiological Protection Board to avoid theoretical hazards due to heating effects and switching of magnetic fields. More detailed accounts of NMR imaging are available elsewhere (Pykett *et al.*, 1982; Partain *et al.*, 1983).

The brain. For a variety of reasons initial clinical attention has focused on NMR examination of the brain (Bailes *et al.*, 1982; Bydder *et al.*, 1982). A high level of grey–white matter contrast is available, providing anatomical detail which is not

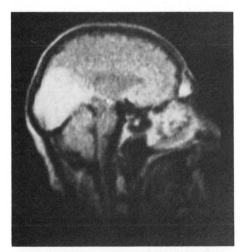

Fig. 2. Brain infarction: sagittal (SE) scan. The infarcted occipital lobe appears lighter (long T_2) than the rest of the brain

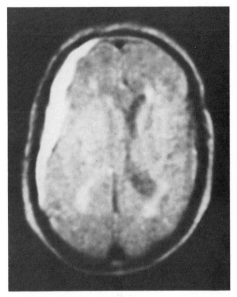

Fig. 3. Subdural haematoma: SE scan. The haematoma (light area) is displacing the brain and has effaced the adjacent lateral ventricle

available with other imaging techniques. Imaging is also available in all three planes and, unlike X-ray computed *tomography (CT), artefact from bone is not a problem.

In cerebral *infarction an increase in T_1 and T_2 is seen. This produces a dark area on T_1-dependent inversion recovery (IR) scans and a light area on T_2-dependent spin echo (SE) scans (Fig. 2). Unlike CT, a central area of liquefaction is seen with *haemorrhage, and subdural *haematomas are demonstrated unobscured by artefact (Fig. 3).

NMR images are also sensitive to flow. This can be manifest either as an increased signal from blood flowing into the section of the brain being scanned at any one moment (usually called the 'slice'), or absence of signal from blood flowing out of the slice. As a result it is possible to demonstrate occlusion of blood vessels, as well as abnormal blood flow in arteriovenous malformations.

In infections, T_2-dependent sequences are of particular interest. Those sequences are very sensitive to the presence of cerebral *oedema. Although the changes are not specific, the sequences illustrate them with a high degree of clarity.

Similarly, in demyelinating diseases such as *multiple sclerosis, abnormal periventricular lesions are well demonstrated, at least in part because of the presence of cerebral oedema (Fig. 4). Evolution of these lesions with time is also well shown.

Periventricular oedema is well seen. This can be of value in distinguishing *ventricular enlargement due to pressure effects, from that resulting from

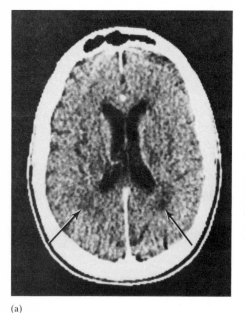

(a)

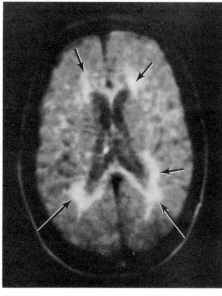

(b)

Fig. 4. Multiple sclerosis. Contrast-enhanced CT (a) and SE (b) scans. Two areas of abnormality are seen on the CT scan. These are also seen on the SE scan (large arrows) as well as other smaller areas of involvement (small arrows)

*atrophy of the brain. Since the treatment of the former condition may involve a ventricular *shunt, the distinction is important.

Tumours mostly display an increase in T_1 and T_2 (Fig. 5), and malignant tumours usually show a greater increase than benign tumours, although this is not always so. Benign tumours show much less surrounding oedema than malignant tumours and, with the latter group, there may be difficulty in defining the margin between tumour and oedema. Mass effects from tumours are very well demonstrated. The high level of grey–white contrast provides a series of interfaces which can be used to assess asymmetry or displacement.

Atrophic change is shown in a similar way to X-ray CT, except that cerebellar atrophy is seen more clearly in the absence of bone artefact within the posterior fossa.

The examination of children is of particular interest (Levene *et al.*, 1982). The high level of grey–white matter contrast enables the process of *myelination to be seen. There is a rapid phase of myelination during the first two years of life, followed by a slower phase continuing into the second decade of life. Delays in this process have been recognized following intraventricular haemorrhage and other conditions. A variety of other abnormalities including brain changes in *cerebral palsy have also been seen *in vivo* for the first time with NMR. The lack of hazard is also important in repeat examinations in this age group.

The thorax. Structures in the *mediastinum can be clearly seen and the flow dependence of signals

from moving blood enables the great vessels to be distinguished from mediastinal masses.

Heart images may be synchronized to the *electrocardiograph so that signal is collected only during one 10–30 ms phase of the cardiac cycle (Fig. 6). This period can be varied to cover both *systole and *diastole. Vascular structure and flow

Fig. 5. Intrinsic brainstem tumour. Contrast-enhanced CT scan (a), IR (b), and sagittal SE (c) scans. Minimal abnormality is seen on the CT scan, but the tumour is well seen on an IR scan, where it appears dark, as well as on the SE scan, where it appears light

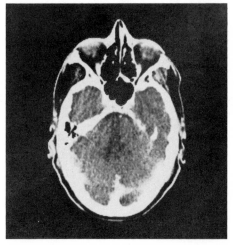

(a)

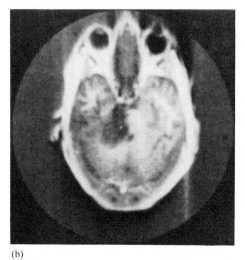

(b)

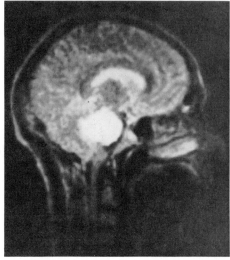

(c)

changes can also be identified, although the clinical usefulness of NMR images of the heart remains to be determined. Blood vessels can be seen in the thorax and *atheromatous plaques have been identified.

The abdomen and pelvis. The *liver and *spleen are readily seen (Smith *et al.*, 1981; Doyle *et al.*, 1982). A variety of different pathological changes has been demonstrated in the liver (Fig. 7). These include primary and secondary tumours, infective changes, *cysts, dilated *bile ducts, and *cirrhosis. Abnormalities have been seen in cirrhosis where no change has been seen with other techniques, although the clinical application of NMR findings is not as obvious as in the brain. X-ray tomo-

graphy, *ultrasound, *biopsy, and *liver function tests all provide valuable alternative diagnostic techniques.

The cortex and medulla of the kidney are seen without the need for intravenous contrast. Loss of this distinction is seen with increasing urea concentration. Whether this is a primary or secondary change is not clear at present.

Anatomical detail within the retroperitoneum and pelvis is well shown, particularly with coronal and sagittal imaging. In CT many soft-tissue tumours have similar X-ray attenuation to the surrounding muscle and other organs and so are recognized by the presence of a mass, displacements, and asymmetry. In addition to these changes, soft tissue tumours usually show a change

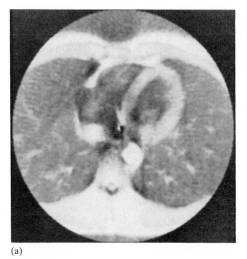

(a)

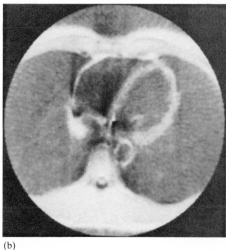

(b)

Fig. 6. Normal heart in systole (a) and diastole (b): IR scans. The heart appears contracted in (a) and more dilated in (b)

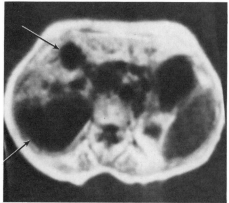

Fig. 7. Liver metastases: IR scan. Multiple metastases are seen (arrows)

in relaxation time with NMR, enabling the abnormal tissue to be recognized in its own right.

Future developments. It is now possible to make a strong case for the clinical efficacy of NMR imaging of the brain, but much more work will be required to assess the value of NMR imaging in the remainder of the body.

Animal experiments have shown that it is possible to image ^{23}Na as well as protons; this ability to trace the movement of sodium may prove to be a useful technique for observing shifts of extracellular water. Another recent development of importance is the use of organic paramagnetic contrast agents such as nitroxide-stable free radicals which shorten T_1 and T_2 (Brasch *et al.*, 1983). These agents may serve as useful indicators of breakdown in the blood–brain barrier; probably, too, it will be possible to attach them to metabolites or chemicals of interest, in order to study the behaviour of the latter, although much more work will be required to assess the toxicity of this group of compounds.

Undoubtedly, proton NMR images will improve in quality over the next few years but equally important is the possibility of producing a 'cheap' NMR scanner. Unlike CT machines, NMR scanners do not require X-ray tubes, solid state detectors, or a moving gantry. With the decrease in price of computers and improvements in the quality of resistive magnets a relatively cheap NMR machine appears to be a realistic possibility. If such a machine is eventually developed it would in large measure overcome one of the outstanding problems with NMR imaging systems—their high cost.

G. M. BYDDER
R. E. STEINER

References

Bailes, D. R., Young, I. R., Thomas, D. J., Straughan, K., Bydder, G. M. and Steiner, R. E. (1982). NMR imaging of the brain using spin-echo sequences. *Clinical Radiology,* **33,** 395–414.

Bloch, F., Hansen, W. W. and Packard, M. E. (1946). Nuclear induction. *Physics Review,* **69,** 127.

Brasch, R. C., Nitecki, D. E., London, D., Toser, T. N., Doemeny, J., Tuck, L. D. and Wolff, S. (1983). Evaluation of nitroxide stable free radicals for contrast enhancement in NMR imaging. *Magnetic Resonance in Medicine,* Society of Magnetic Resonance in Medicine, Annual Meeting, 1982, supplement 1, 25.

Budinger, T. F. (1981). Nuclear magnetic resonance (NMR) *in vivo* studies: known thresholds for health effects. *Journal of Computer Assisted Tomography,* **5,** 800–11.

Bydder, G. M., Steiner, R. E., Young, I. R., Hall, A. S., Thomas, D. J., Marshall, J., Pallis, C. A. and Legg, N. J. (1982). Clinical NMR imaging of the brain: 140 cases. *American Journal of Roentgenology,* **139,** 215–36.

Doyle, F. H., Pennock, J. M., Banks, L. M., McDonnell, M. J., Bydder, G. M., Steiner, R. E., Young, I. R., Clarke, G. J., Pasmore, T. and Gilderdale, D. J. (1982). Nuclear magnetic resonance (NMR) imaging of the liver: initial experience. *American Journal of Radiology,* **138,** 193–200.

Hawkes, R. C., Holland, G. N., Moore, W. S. and Worthington, B. S. (1980). Nuclear magnetic resonance (NMR) tomography of the brain: a preliminary clinical assessment with demonstration of pathology. *Journal of Computer Assisted Tomography,* **4,** 577–86.

Lauterbur, P. C. (1973). Image formation by induced local interactions: examples employing nuclear magnetic resonance. *Nature,* **242,** 190–1.

Levene, M. I., Whitelaw, A., Dubowitz, V., Bydder, G. M., Steiner, R. E., Randell, C P. and Young, I. R. (1982). Nuclear magnetic resonance imaging of the brain in children. *British Medical Journal,* **285,** 774–6.

Odeblad, E. (1966). Micro-NMR in high permanent magnetic fields. *Acta Obstetrica et Gynecologica Scandinavica,* **55,** Supplement 2, 1–188.

Odeblad, E. and Lindstrom, G. (1955). Some preliminary observations on proton magnetic resonance in biologic samples. *Acta Radiologica,* **43,** 469–75.

Partain, C. L., James, A. E., Rollo, F. D. and Price, R. R. (eds) (1983). *Nuclear Magnetic Resonance (NMR) Imaging.* Philadelphia.

Purcell, E. M., Torrey, H. C. and Pound, R. V. (1946). Resonance absorption by nuclear magnetic movements in a solid. *Physics Review,* **69,** 37.

Pykett, I. L., Newhouse, J. H., Buonanno, F. S., Brady, T. J., Goldman, M. R., Kistler, J. P. and Pohost, G. M. (1982). Principles of nuclear magnetic resonance imaging. *Radiology,* **143,** 157–68.

Smith, F. W., Mallard, J. R., Reid, A. and Hutchinson, J. M. S. (1981). Nuclear magnetic resonance tomographic imaging in liver disease. *Lancet,* **i,** 963–6.

NUCLEAR MEDICINE

Introduction. About one patient in three hospitalized in a modern hospital will have a diagnostic procedure performed in which a radioactive tracer has an essential role. For example, the *haemodynamic response of the heart may be assessed during exercise in the diagnosis of *coronary heart disease (Fig. 1); decreased blood flow to the lungs may indicate the presence of pulmonary *embolism (Figs. 2a, b); or the *plasma level of thyroid hormone (*thyroxine) may be a sign of *hyperthyroidism.

The use of radioactive tracers in diagnostic and therapeutic medicine became so widespread that in 1971 such work was recognized as a medical spe-

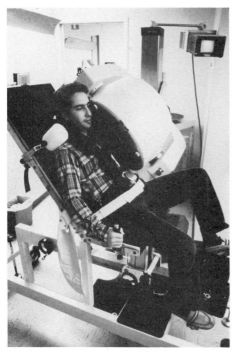

Fig. 1. A scintillation camera is used to image the blood within a patient's heart as he exercises on a bicycle

examine both the site and rate of important biological processes and detect abnormalities as regions of dysfunction. If the first principle of nuclear medicine is the tracer principle, the second is the 'homogeneity principle' which states that the function of many body organs is relatively homogeneous. Disease may first manifest itself as a region of focal dysfunction that may occur before the overall function of the organ has become impaired. This often results in earlier diagnosis.

The approach of the nuclear physician can be called that of applied physiology and biochemistry. The physician-physiologist-biochemist makes direct measurement of regional function. He considers his diagnoses as working hypotheses—as means of predicting the future and planning optimum care of the patient. His physiological and biochemical measurements often provide the essential information for decision-making. For example, they may tell how much and how severely the lung is involved by *cancer, and to what extent residual function will be altered by possible surgery. They may even help define new and useful disease categories. An example of the latter was the finding in the early 1940s of increased thyroidal function in *thyrotoxicosis and decreased function in *myxoedema. Many saw these discoveries as forerunners of a whole series of diseases manifested by abnormally increased or decreased function. This did not happen and it is interesting to wonder why not. There are two probable reasons: (i) most of the research effort was directed to the study of elements rather than molecules and the thyroid is unusual in its concentrating an ionic element, such as *iodine; and (ii) nuclear medicine turned in the direction of providing structural rather than functional information. In the 1950s Cassen and his associates at the University of California, Los Angeles (UCLA) used newly developed *scintillation counters to print pictures of the spatial distribution of radioactive iodine

cialty by the *American Medical Association through the establishment of the American Board of Nuclear Medicine.

What is it about nuclear medicine procedures that makes them so useful in medicine? Their single greatest value is that they give us the unique ability to apply the tracer concept in man himself—that is, to track the course of labelled molecules or cells as they travel through the body. We can

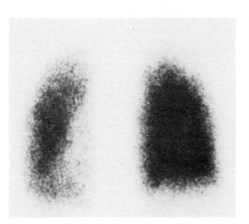

(a)

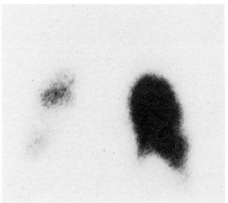

(b)

Fig. 2. (a) The distribution of blood flow to the lungs of a normal person. (b) The distribution of blood flow in the lungs of a patient with pulmonary embolism. There are several areas of decreased blood flow. (Both viewed from rear)

within the thyroid gland. This led to the concept of medical radioisotope scanning, defined as the visualization of an internal organ by mapping the spatial distribution of a radioactive tracer within the body. As in contrast radiography, such as *cholecystography and *urography, a physiological concentrating mechanism was used to concentrate the material. With radioisotope scanning, however, it is not necessary to achieve the high concentration necessary to produce opacity to *X-rays. The relative concentration in the organ with respect to its surroundings is what is important, rather than simply the absolute concentration. Within a few years of the commercial development of a moving detector scanner of the type invented by Cassen, scanning procedures were developed for the detection of brain *tumours (brain scan), for the differentiation of *pericardial effusion (fluid in the membrane covering the heart) from cardiac dilatation, for the differentiation of masses in the *mediastinum which are vascular (made up of, or heavily supplied with, blood vessels) and those which are not, and for renal, splenic, and hepatic scanning, as well as for the study of the thyroid. In 1962, with the commercial development of the scintillation camera invented by Anger in 1958, it became possible to study the heart and the regional circulation of the brain, kidneys, and other organs.

Even in the 1960s physiological studies were developed. In 1963 scanning techniques were used to demonstrate the distribution of *pulmonary arterial blood flow and soon thereafter to reveal regional impairment of *ventilation with the radioactive gas xenon-133. The early 1970s, however, were a turning point for nuclear medicine, bringing to mind Whitehead's statement: 'It is a well-founded historical generalization that the last thing to be discovered in any science is what the science is really about.'

A most important consequence of the invention of the tracer principle by *Hevesy in 1912 was his subsequent elucidation of the dynamic state of body constituents. This principle is an extension of the principle of the constancy of the internal environment first proposed by Claude *Bernard, who pointed out that the concentration of chemical constituents in body fluids is usually kept within a very narrow range and disturbances of these concentrations result in disease. This concept of the constancy of the internal environment, or *homeostasis, has been one of the foundations of modern medicine. Hevesy extended this concept by introducing the concept of the dynamic state.

The story of the development of techniques and methods for the practical use of radioisotopes is the story of the accomplishments of Georg Hevesy. In 1913 with Paneth, he used the lead *isotope radium D as a tracer for lead in the determination of the solubilities of lead sulphide and lead chromate in water. Ten years later he used thorium D (another isotope of lead) to trace the movement of lead in beans. In 1924, working with a dermatologist who

was interested in bismuth salts for the treatment of *syphilis, he studied the distribution of bismuth (radium E) in rabbits. In 1931 he used radium D to determine the lead content of a number of rocks, thereby introducing the concept of the isotope dilution technique. In 1934, after the discovery of deuterium by Urey, Hevesy obtained some heavy water from Urey and used it to measure the mean lifetime of water in the human body and the speed of exchange of water between the body of the goldfish and its environment. In 1935 Hevesy and his co-workers used phosphorus-32 to study the metabolism of phosphorus in rats and man.

In 1936 Hevesy began to receive phosphorus-32 from Ernest Lawrence, who invented the *cyclotron in Berkeley, California. Short-lived isotopes such as potassium-42 and sodium-24 began to be produced for the first time. In 1935 Chiewitz and Hevesy submitted a letter to the editor of *Nature* in which they said 'our results strongly support the view that the formation of bones is a dynamic process. The bone is continuously taking up phosphorus atoms which are partly or wholly lost again and are replaced by other phosphorus atoms.' These classic experiments were extended by Schoenheimer, who pointed out that the apparent stability and constancy of the body is the result of delicate balances among innumerable chemical reactions occurring simultaneously. Even before Hevesy's experiments with phosphorus-32, sodium-24, and potassium-42, Blumgart and his co-workers in Boston carried out the first clinical studies with radioactive isotopes. Over 50 years ago they published their first results of injecting solutions of radon salts intravenously, monitoring the time of arrival of the tracer in the opposite arm as a measure of the velocity of the circulation in normal persons and in patients with a variety of heart diseases. These experiments were done 14 years before radioiodine was first used to study the metabolic activity of the thyroid gland.

In his Nobel lecture Hevesy stated:

The application of isotopic indicators opens new lines of approach not only to the solution of known problems but also by directing our attention to trains of thought not previously considered. Isotopic indicators open the only way to determine the rate, place, and sequence of formation of many molecular constituents of the living organism. The very existence of such methods was instrumental in opening new trains of thought in demonstrating the dynamicity of metabolic processes in concentrating our interest on the problem of velocity of fundamental biological processes.

Applications. To understand the impact of the tracer principle in biology and medicine we need to look at the status of biomedical research prior to the development of radioactive tracer methods. Before such a development, the only method for studying the biochemistry of the body was to measure the way in which various elements and compounds were assimilated, distributed throughout the tissues, converted into other compounds, and finally eliminated from the body. In order to observe the manner in which a living organism metabolized an element, it was necessary to administer sufficient to produce a detectable increase of the amount in the body. Such procedures frequently disturbed the normal chemistry and physiology of the organism and the data obtained did not present a true picture. Secondly, with the stable tracers it was not possible to distinguish the administered substance from the naturally occurring substance. The use of radioactive tracers eliminated many of these problems.

The initial experiments of pioneers, such as Hertz, Hamilton, and co-workers, were concerned with the study of elements, for example, phosphorus and iodine. They carried out extensive investigations of the unique capability of the thyroid gland to accumulate radioiodine in relatively large quantities. The thyroid gland can concentrate the iodine it receives from the blood by a factor of 10 000. Although other organs were found to be capable of the selective uptake of certain elements, none approached the capacity of the thyroid. It was not surprising that radioiodine was accepted eagerly as a new research tool by thyroid physiologists.

Hertz and his associates first demonstrated in 1940 the rapidity with which iodine is accumulated in the thyroid of rabbits. These observations were confirmed in patients with hyperthyroidism by Hamilton and Soley, who measured the accumulation of radioiodine by placing a Geiger counter against the neck. Normal persons and patients with hyperthyroidism, non-toxic *goitre, and hypothyroidism were studied with the aid of this technique. In collaboration with colleagues, including I. Chaikoff, they conducted a detailed series of experiments in animals that elucidated knowledge of the intermediary metabolism of iodine. They also began to use radioiodine to suppress the function of normal thyroid tissue in rabbits and dogs.

The chemical basis of nuclear medicine. In his *Introduction to the Study of Experimental Medicine,* Claude Bernard wrote that physiologists make use of 'instruments and procedures borrowed from physics and chemistry in order to study and measure the diverse vital phenomena whose laws they seek to discover'. In all physiological investigations, 'the grand principle is not to stop until one has reached the physico-chemical explanation for the phenomena one is studying'.

Since the mid-19th c., the relationship between vital phenomena and chemical processes has been well established. Neither chemistry nor physiology alone is adequate to define and solve biological problems. In 1842 with the publication of *Lehrbuch der physiologischen Chemie,* Lehmann provided an organized view of a new discipline, physiological chemistry.

According to this new science, the beginning of the investigation was the study of the properties and reactions of the chemical substances making up the body. The next step was to determine the 'topography' of these substances, that is, their distribution within the fluids, tissues, and organs of the body. Then one began to investigate the processes in which the substances were involved. Before the use of stable or radioactive tracers this could be done only by comparing the material entering the body with the end-products leaving it. A deeper understanding required studies in living animals. These early physiologists and chemists, and physiological chemists, foresaw a future science whose whole purpose would be to study the chemical phenomena of life.

Albert Einstein said that we cannot see nature directly: we see it only in light of questions that we ask. This is the point of view from which we use instruments to view nature. Equally important to improved perception are the ways in which we organize knowledge, package our information, and encode the information, our conceptualization of the physiological or pathological processes. For example, *the particular medium that we use in medical imaging affects our concept of reality.* We must combine our 'ever-more-perfect eyes' with 'ever-more-perfect brains' to permit us to process effectively the large amount of information that now confronts us.

The use of radioactive tracers—nuclear medicine—has made possible an improvement in perception and conceptualization of disease in ways that we never dreamed of only a few decades ago. Nuclear imaging provides us with symbolic representations of patterns and changes in the spatial and temporal distribution of the chemicals that make up living organisms. To picture a biological system, including man, at a single instant in time is inadequate: we must also concern ourselves with the perception of events that occur one after the other; motion and change are the essence of physiology. Limiting our perception to static patterns is equivalent to assuming that nothing ever happens. Therefore our images must be concerned with time, with the order of events and their duration, with the periodicity of body processes, such as the beating of the heart, the emptying of the gall bladder, and so forth.

Whenever we look at a medical image we should ask ourselves what we are really looking at, what types of things we are perceiving within the patient's body. Are we looking at the distribution of X-ray densities, as in *computerized axial tomography, or at the spatial and temporal distribution of chemical substances within the body, as in nuclear medicine imaging, or at the distribution of body surfaces that reflect sound waves, as in *ultrasonics? Our perception of the patient can be thought of as extending all the way from feeling the contours of our patient's face to the most sophisticated use of the electromagnetic spectrum as sources of information about the patient's bodily structure and function. Year after year we devise more precise instruments with which to observe our patients. Yet when we look at the resultant images, we are sad to see that the pictures are still fuzzy and we need to continue our best efforts. We seem to be running after a goal which fades away every time we come within sight of it. This is the paradox of knowledge and should not surprise us. There is no God's-eye view of our patients, or at least we are not permitted to see it.

Nevertheless our new images can affect the practice of medicine profoundly. One of the major concepts of disease is that of abnormal cellular function, advanced by pathologists such as Rudolph *Virchow in 1858. For a long time clinical medicine was practised primarily from the viewpoint of pathology, supplemented by knowledge obtained in pathophysiological experiments in animals. The most important imaging device was the *microscope: the most important diagnostic test was the *biopsy. The goal of the master clinicians at the turn of the century was to be able to predict correctly the pathological findings at postmortem examination. More than any other discipline, pathology linked the anatomical sciences to the clinical practice of medicine. But even the greatest pathologists of that time realized the limitations of a purely anatomical point of view. *Rokitansky, who personally performed tens of thousands of autopsies, said, 'Observation and investigation of the living body requires an experimental pathology to establish the conditions surrounding the origin, existence and involution of the anatomical disturbances that pathology discovers.' After the advances in pathological anatomy, bacteriological, viral, haematological, biochemical, and physiological measurements were incorporated into the practice of clinical medicine, extending our eyes by *spectrophotometry, *immunofluorescence microscopy, and a host of other special tests. The concept of the constancy of the internal environment has been added to the concept of the cellular basis of disease.

We are progressively improving our means of perceiving the dynamic state of body constituents. These new techniques permit us to view our patients' bodies as a symphony of processes, not as simply static structures. Measurements of temporal changes and patterns—the very essence of human physiology—are becoming commonplace.

Technetium-99m. About 75–85 per cent of the examinations of patients with radioactive tracers in modern medical practice involve the use of this radionuclide. Together with the scintillation camera and the computer, technetium-99m has been a major factor in the current practice of nuclear medicine. Its potential use in medicine was proposed by Richards in 1960 but its actual use awaited the work of Harper in 1962. There are several reasons for its widespread use: (i) its short *half-life and mode of radioactive decay keep the radiation dose to the patient low; (ii) it is readily available as a daughter product of the radionuclide, molybdenum-99, with a 67-hour half-life;

(iii) it forms chemically stable complexes with a wide variety of molecules.

In aqueous solution, technetium assumes the stable chemical form of the pertechnetate ion (TcO_4^-). When reduced to lower oxidation states, technetium forms complexes with many molecules, but no truly covalent bonds.

In some cases, labelling a cell or molecule does not affect significantly the previous biochemical behaviour of the labelled substance. Examples are technetium-99m labelled red blood cells, albumin, phosphates, and colloids. In others, the biochemical behaviour is greatly affected by complexing technetium with the molecule. Several generalizations seem warranted: first, most technetium-99m complexes are rapidly excreted by the kidneys or liver when injected intravenously; a notable exception is the accumulation of phosphate complexes in bone. Secondly, fat solubility is a major determinant in whether excretion will be hepatic or renal.

Research directed at development of useful technetium-99m complexes falls into two major categories: (i) labelled drugs, and (ii) labelled substrates, such as *amino acids and *fatty acids.

Considerable effort is being devoted to attempts to label drugs or substrates that react with plasma membrane or intracellular binding sites. The approach involves attaching the technetium-99m atom in a way that does not affect the structural configuration of the molecule that is required for binding to the receptor site. In most cases, this is not possible, and the part of the molecule binding technetium is the same as that reacting with the binding site. One approach is to try to develop

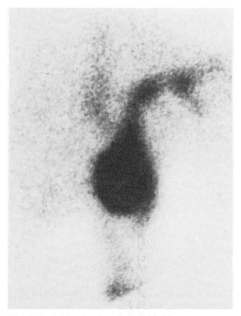

Fig. 3. An image showing the gall bladder

analogues with a technetium-complexing group that is remote from the essential binding group. This approach often results in renal excretion of the complexes without significant uptake by the target binding site. A striking exception is technetium-99m iminodiacetic acid (HIDA) developed as an analogue of the drug, lidocaine (lignocaine), for imaging the myocardium but found useful for the study of the biliary system, because of its rapid hepatic excretion (Fig. 3).

Radiopharmaceuticals. Most radioactive drugs are administered to provide diagnostic information rather than to produce a therapeutic effect, although the use of radioactive iodine to suppress thyroid function is an important exception. In diagnostic studies, information about the patient is encoded in *gamma rays, a type of electromagnetic radiation that has the ability to penetrate the tissues of the body and be detected and measured with imaging devices, such as the Anger scintillation camera, or with 'probe' devices, such as the nuclear stethoscope cardiac probe, which is used to monitor cardiac function. In the case of therapeutic administration, the gamma rays transfer energy to the cells being irradiated in order to decrease their function or kill them, as in the case of cancer therapy. In diagnostic studies, the goal is to maximize the number of photons being recorded while minimizing the associated radiation dose to the patient. From the viewpoint of minimizing the latter, the shortest possible half-life which would permit measurement of the diagnostic information is desired.

Most biochemicals and drugs that we wish to study consist largely of carbon, hydrogen, nitrogen, oxygen, sulphur and phosphorus. Hydrogen, sulphur, and phosphorus have no suitable gamma-emitting isotopes. Carbon-11, nitrogen-13, and oxygen-15 decay by emitting *positrons which combine with electrons to emit two 511-keV photons in almost exactly opposite directions. Their production requires the ready availability of a particle accelerator, usually a *cyclotron, and is limited to a few centres.

After selection of the biochemical substance of interest, the next step is to incorporate the tracer of interest without altering the biological behaviour of the substance. Recently it has been possible to incorporate a radioactive atom, such as technetium-99m, to produce a chemical structure that has the desired structural configuration. For example, technetium-99m has been incorporated into a compound in which two positive charges are separated by 100–120 nanometre units, a structural specificity possessed by drugs with *curare-like activity.

More readily available radionuclides than the positron-emitting nuclides are the radiohalogens (^{18}F, ^{125}I, ^{123}I, and ^{131}I) and the metals (^{99m}Tc, ^{67}Ga, ^{111}In, and ^{113m}In). In a sense these radionuclides, being more readily available, extend the demonstrated successes of positron-emitting

nuclides because they do not require a cyclotron to be available at the site of the studies.

An example is ^{123}I-ω-hepatadecanoic acid, which has been used to study fatty acid metabolism in the heart. Studies of carbon-11 palmitic acid or bromine-75 fatty acids that require a cyclotron are useful for *positron emission tomography, whereas the iodinated fatty acid could be used with the type of scintillation camera available in nearly every hospital.

Another mechanism of labelling fatty acids is that of bio-isosterism. Isosteres are compounds that have similar electronic and steric configuration, often with similar biological properties. One of the earliest applications of this approach was the development of ^{75}Se-selenomethionine as an analogue of methionine for studies of the pancreas by Blau and Bender in 1961. A more recent example is the development of ^{133}I-iodohexadecanoic acid as an oleic acid analogue, used in cardiac studies.

Many attempts have been made to label receptor-specific molecules with radioactive metals such as ^{99m}Tc, ^{67}Ga, ^{111}In, and ^{113}In. The metals are complexed by the receptor-specific compound to form a radioactive metal complex. Although the resulting complexes have at times proved useful, they have lost their receptor-binding ability.

Instruments. Advances in the field of nuclear medicine have been along three lines: better chemicals, better instruments, and better quantification. The latter two are related. With the introduction of *tomography, quantification can be improved significantly. In the past an example of the usefulness of quantification was the measurement of increased or decreased uptake of iodine by the thyroid to indicate hyper- or hypo-function of this organ, respectively. Although abnormally increased or decreased organ function may be found in other endocrine organs, nuclear techniques have not been as successfully applied, partly because of the absence of suitable tracers but also because of problems of quantification of organs less optimally located than the thyroid.

The use of the focused collimator, introduced by Newell in the mid-1950s, was a step in the direction of tomography, but the principle of tomography developed only recently to a more advanced state. It is likely that tomography will prove to be very valuable in the study of the major regulatory system of the body, the brain. Beyond doubt, hyper- and hypoactive states exist in the various major systems, such as the adrenergic, cholinergic, dopaminergic, serotonergic transmitter systems, and others (see NEUROTRANSMITTERS).

Tomography in nuclear medicine is of two types: single photon emission computed tomography (SPECT) and positron emission computed tomography (PECT). The latter permits more accurate quantification, but the former provides significant improvement over planar imaging, where the three-dimensional distribution of radioactivity is projected on to a single plane.

Positron tomography has made possible measurement of regional glucose metabolism in regions of the brain, such as the frontal lobes, auditory cortex, striatum, thalamus, and visual cortex. It has been possible to show the biochemical events related to the psychological processes of vision and hearing, a major achievement in the history of psychology and philosophy. It is perhaps in the study of the brain that both SPECT and PECT will have their greatest impact. A most important recent accomplishment has been the finding that it is possible to demonstrate by imaging dopamine, serotonin, and opiate receptors in the living human brain.   H. N. WAGNER

Further reading

Anger, H. O. (1953). A multiple scintillation counter *in vivo* scanner. *American Journal of Roentgenology*, **70**, 605.

Berger, H. J. and Zaret, B. L. (1981). Nuclear cardiology. *New England Journal of Medicine*. **305**, 799–807 and 855–65.

Blahd, W. H. (1971). *Nuclear Medicine*. 2nd edn, New York.

Blumgart, H. L. and Weiss, S. (1927). Studies on the velocity of blood flow. VII. The pulmonary circulation time in normal resting individuals. *Journal of Clinical Investigation*, **4**, 399.

Gottschalk, A. and Potchen, E. J. (1976). *Diagnostic Nuclear Medicine*. Baltimore.

Hamilton, J. G. (1942). The use of radioactive tracers in biology and medicine. *Radiology, 39*, 541–72.

Hevesy, G. (1946). Some applications of isotopic indicators. In *Les Prix Nobel en 1940–1944*, 95–127. Stockholm.

Rocha, A. F. G. and Harbert, J. C. (1979). *Textbook of Nuclear Medicine: Clinical Applications*. Philadelphia.

Wagner, H. N. *et al.* (1983). Imaging dopamine receptors in the living human brain by positron tomography. *Science, 221*, 1264.

Wong, D. F. *et al.* (1984). Effects of age on dopamine and serotonin receptors measured by positron tomography in the living human brain. *Science, 226*, 1393.

NUCLEAR SEXING. Determination of genetic sex by examining the nuclei of somatic cells, usually in a stained smear from the buccal mucosa. In normal females a large proportion of nuclei show a small stainable body (Barr body) lying in close relationship to the nuclear membrane. This is a condensed mass of chromatin representing one of the two X *chromosomes in an inactive form. In males, who have only one X chromosome, Barr bodies are absent and the smear is said to be 'chromatin negative'.

NUCLEIC ACIDS are naturally occurring compounds present in the *chromosomes or *ribosomes of most cells and responsible either for storing genetic information or translating it into the structure of proteins. See RIBONUCLEIC ACID (RNA); DEOXYRIBONUCLEIC ACID (DNA).

NUCLEOLUS. A small dense body distinguishable within the nucleus of most cells, concerned with the synthesis of ribosomal ribonucleic acid. See CELL.

NUCLEOPROTEINS are compounds consisting of a *nucleic acid in combination with a *protein.

NUCLEUS. The cell nucleus is a membrane-bounded body found within the *cytoplasm of most biological cells, of both plants and animals (termed *eukaryotic* on that account). It contains the *chromosomes. In the non-dividing cell, the nucleus is spherical or ovoid by light microscopy and usually appears homogeneous except for one or more denser bodies termed nucleoli and granules of heterochromatin; when fixed it contains a darkly staining basophilic network. At the onset of mitosis or meiosis, the chromosomes separate out and become visible. See CELL.

NUDISM is the cult and practice of going unclothed.

NUFFIELD, LORD. See MORRIS, WILLIAM.

NUFFIELD PROVINCIAL HOSPITALS TRUST. Founded by Lord Nuffield in 1940, the Trust's original purposes were defined as 'the co-ordination on a regional basis of hospital, medical, and associated health services throughout the provinces; the making of financial provision for the creation, carrying on, or extension of such hospital, medical, and associated health services as are necessary for such co-ordination; and the promotion of improved organization and efficient development of hospital, medical, and associated health services throughout the provinces' (provinces being taken to mean outside the Metropolitan Police District of London). Since the foundation of the *National Health Service in 1948 led to the effective regionalization of the health services in the UK, the main purpose of the Trust has been to assist the development and improvement of hospital and other health services generally and the encouragement of health services research, interpreted in the widest sense. The making of grants has been a major function, usually though not invariably to university departments. More recently, the adoption of an 'institute' role in relation to intelligence and policy exploration has resulted in a programme of seminars, lectures, and conferences associated with a series of Trust publications. The Trust has also established a number of working groups in areas within its field of interest.

NUISANCES REMOVAL ACT 1848. This early public health enactment in the UK was repealed by Section 69 of the Sanitary Act 1860. Both have been superseded by subsequent legislation.

NURSE-PRACTITIONER. A qualified nurse whose role in the provision of primary health care has been enlarged beyond that traditionally assigned to the nursing profession and embraces functions normally carried out by medical practitioners, for example the making of diagnoses and the prescribing of medicaments. See NURSING IN THE USA.

NURSES ACTS 1943–1969. Following the original UK Nurses Registration Act of 1919, a series of Nurses Acts were passed in 1943, 1949, 1957, 1961, 1964, and 1969. Their provisions included the enrolment of assistant nurses, reconstitution of the General Nursing Council, reorganization of the Register of Nurses to include male nurses, financial support for training and the inspecting of training schools, evaluation of nurses trained outside the UK, and abolition of the annual retention fee.

NURSES AGENCY ACT 1957. This UK Act introduced regulation of agencies for the supply of nurses. Persons carrying on such an agency are required to be licensed annually by the appropriate local authority. The licensing authority may inspect records and premises of agencies. Selection of nurses to be provided for each particular case must be made by or under the supervision of a registered nurse or general medical practitioner, and prescribed records must be kept. Any person supplied with a nurse must be advised in writing as to the qualifications of the nurse. The Act prescribed penalties for contraventions of its provisions.

NURSING HOME ACT 1975. This UK Act consolidated previous legislation concerning nursing homes contained in the *Public Health Act 1936 and the *Mental Health Act 1959. A nursing home is defined as any premises used or intended to be used for the reception and provision of nursing for persons suffering from any sickness, injury, or infirmity but excluding NHS hospitals. Maternity homes are included, and mental nursing homes are also defined. Powers of registration, control, and inspection of nursing homes had already been conferred on the Secretary of State for Health and Social Services under the provisions of the *National Health Service (Reorganization) Act 1973.

NURSING HOMES. Small private hospitals.

NURSING IN THE ARMED SERVICES. See ARMY, BRITISH; NAVY, ROYAL; AIR FORCE, ROYAL; ARMED FORCES OF THE USA: MEDICAL SERVICES.

NURSING IN THE UK. The clerk of the *Society of Apothecaries, giving evidence in 1904 to a Select Committee on Registration of Nurses, said:

Speaking for myself, I never saw such a thing as a nurse inside my house. Now, my boy has hardly anything the matter with him before in comes a nurse the first thing, before we can say Jack Robinson. We were able to get on perfectly well in those days. I think there is a good deal of unnecessary fuss made these days about illness.

This was perhaps the last date on which an educated middle-class man could have made such a statement; a century earlier most such men would have felt, like him, that nurses were unnecessary. From the time of Christ, care of the sick, feeding the hungry, clothing the destitute, and visiting those in prison had been seen as the duty of everybody, not the task of a specialized worker. The emergence of nursing as a role for a trained skilled person occurred during the second half of the 19th c., as the result of the combined action of a great outburst of scientific and medical discoveries, and of the social pressures resulting from the Industrial Revolution and its related events.

Throughout the centuries, the women in a household cared for the sick of their family, just as they fed and clothed them in health. The care of the indigent and homeless sick devolved mostly on the religious communities until the Reformation. The nursing historian finds much of interest in these times, but it is hard to recognize our predecessors, and this account will be confined to the present century and the last.

Florence *Nightingale wrote in 1892 (*Nightingale Papers*, vol. CLXIV, p. 27, British Museum):

There comes a crisis in the lives of all social movements. This has come in the case of nursing in about thirty years. For nursing was born but about thirty years ago. Before it did not exist, though sickness is as old as the world.

She was alluding to the establishment of the first nurse-training school at *St Thomas's Hospital in 1860. She recognized that there was a body of nursing knowledge, manual skills, and ethical principles that could be taught, and she had the charisma, following her work in the Crimean War, to induce people to believe her. Moreover, she showed in her *Notes on Nursing* that nursing knowledge could be objectively defined, and derived from scientific rules.

At one time, men could be divided into landed gentry, merchants and shopkeepers, and 'others'. The Industrial Revolution saw the rise of a prosperous middle class of manufacturers who began to look for professional advancement for their children. Medicine started to attract numbers of applicants, all able to pay for hospital experience, and doctors now found it necessary to divide beds among themselves for teaching purposes. In the first half of the 19th c. hospitals in London and the big provincial cities had so many medical students that there was no need of nurses, except as unskilled attendants. One effect of this sudden rise of medical training was that acute medicine and surgery provided all the 'interesting' cases and 'good teaching material', and the chronic sick, the enfeebled aged, and the psychiatrically ill were not wanted in the voluntary hospitals. This has had very far-reaching effects, felt today on the structure of the *National Health Service, and the lack of esteem felt for some specialties like *geriatric care, in which the need is very great.

Intrinsically, there was no reason to think of nursing work as suitable for women but not for men. It needs tenderness, devotion, and resolution, as they were needed in hospitals in the 19th c., but men are not deficient in any of those qualities. There were, however, two important facts: firstly that nursing was always seen as part of domestic household work; secondly, as Josephine Butler noticed in 1866 (*Education and Employment of Women,* London, 1866, p. 3) that there were at that time 2.5 million women, mostly spinsters and widows, seeking means of support through work.

Working-class women might hope to find employment in factories where, although they were badly paid and overworked, they met outside their homes, and learned the facts of industrial life. Middle-class women could be governesses, often working only for their keep, or clerks working a 60-hour week for 12 shillings. A few were trying to gain registration as doctors, many were beginning to realize that without a vote women had no political power. When during the Crimean War (1854–6) Florence Nightingale showed that there was work which intelligent women could do in hospital, so enthusiastic was the response that by the 1890s more women wanted to nurse than could be trained.

Miss Nightingale wrote to Benjamin Jowett in 1889, 'When very many years ago I planned a future, my one idea was not organising a hospital but organising a religion'. Thus the shape of nursing in the UK for nearly three-quarters of a century was fashioned by a great pioneer and by the social trends of Victorian England. Nurses were to be women, and they were dedicated to their work; they were therefore doubly vulnerable to economic exploitation, and remained so until the middle of the 20th c.

Our feelings and ideas about pre-Nightingale nursing derive from two sources. One is fiction, and it is surprising how powerful is the image of Sairey *Gamp, and of the women whom Scrooge saw quarrelling over his clothes after his 'death'. The other is fact. For instance, *St Bartholomew's Hospital, London, has continuous records from 1549, and from the accounts of the governors' meetings one can picture the work of the sisters (charge-nurses) who lived in a room off their wards, gave simple care, fetched the patient's food from the buttery, and in early times washed their ward linen and spent their 'spare' time in spinning. A lot of kindly unpretentious care went on, and in times of plague and pestilence, heroism was shown.

Miss Nightingale's new recruits and their contemporaries left many accounts of what they found when they first arrived on the hospital scene. The 'new' nurses were, not unnaturally, rather disdainful and disapproving about those whom they were replacing. Their predecessors might have been forgiven for some of the ways in which they maintained their fortitude in the days before *anaesthetics and *antiseptics. A sister wrote in 1902 about the conditions when she entered the first school at St Bartholomew's Hospital in 1877.

Drunkenness was very common among the staff nurses, who were chiefly of the charwoman type, frequently of bad character, with little or no education, and few of them with even an elementary knowledge of nursing. . . . One woman I remember who came some little time after I did, and under whom I worked, had been a lady's maid, and had never done a day's nursing. She was, however, of a decidedly superior class to any of the others. . . . Nursing, as you understand it now, was utterly unknown. Patients were not nursed, they were attended to, more or less. . . . The work was very hard—lockers, locker boards and tables of course to scrub every day. No, we did not as a rule scrub the floors, though I have scrubbed the front ward of Matthew on a special occasion before 6 a.m. . . . The patients had their beds made once a day, the bad ones had their sheets drawn at night . . . then you thought nothing of having fourteen or fifteen poultices to change. All wounds of course suppurated, and required poulticing two or three times a day . . . the thermometers in use then were very much longer than those in use now, and had to be read while in position, as they ran down at once when removed from the mouth or armpit. They cost 12/6d each. The sisters and nurses never used a thermometer, the dressers and clerks took the temperatures when required.

This, then, was the nursing scene in 1877. Infection, both medical and surgical, was rife. The nurse's role was underdeveloped and she worked for long hours at hard work with little reward. Light was, however, breaking on the hospital scene. Anaesthesia had arrived to relieve the lot of the patients and of surgeons; the nature of infections like *typhoid and *cholera began to be understood. Doctors were now able to cure; they no longer had time to use those long thermometers. The nurse stopped scrubbing the floor, and began to undertake different tasks. She acquired her role by taking over duties delegated from the doctor, and so became the servant of the doctor rather than of the patient. This relationship was facilitated by the fact that doctors were men and nurses were women, and adopted readily the Victorian mode of dependency. Even today there are many parts of the world, including some Western European countries, in which doctors head nursing organizations and formulate their policies. A century was to pass before nurses were to feel that though there are many areas of medicine and surgery in which their responsibilities are secondary to those of the doctor, they have a distinct and separate professional role in detecting, defining, and filling patients' needs.

State registration. Nursing in the 1880s and 1890s involved much physical as well as mental stress. *Streptococcal infections were still dangerous, so *scarlet fever, *nephritis, and *rheumatic fever afflicted them. Septic fingers were painful and disabling, *diphtheria and *tuberculosis were still fatal diseases. Chronic foot pain was a common cause of drop-out until working hours became reasonable a century later.

Yet these women found time in all their hardships not only to upgrade the care in hospitals, but to dream of professionalism. They thought and talked about the content of nursing, how long nurse-training should be, how to establish higher education (was it possible that there might one day be university degrees in nursing?) Above all they thought about statutory training and state registration of nurses.

Miss Nightingale had little use for registration until, late in her life, she recognized it as inevitable. If a nurse lived in a home, under supervision and moral guidance, she would be a worthy practitioner of her art. She still thought of nursing as a kind of religious life for spinsters: when they married, they left nursing. Mrs Bedford Fenwick, the great proponent of registration and professionalism, throughout a long life wrote, spoke, and worked unceasingly, seeking support, helping to promote bills, and finally living to see state registration attained in 1919, and to be the first nurse on the register of the *General Nursing Council (GNC).

The USA. The history of nursing in the USA has many similarities to that of the UK. In 1777 George Washington had ordered that women be recruited to help nurse the troops, but these had mainly engaged in cooking for the sick. Just as the Crimean War had shown the need for nurses, so did the Civil War (1861–5) with the added trauma that the battles were fought on their own soil, between their own husbands and brothers.

Louisa May Alcott, the author of *Little Women*, nursed during the Civil War, and in *Hospital Sketches* (1863), described her work.

Up at 6, dress by gaslight. Till noon I trot, trot, giving out rations, cutting up food for helpless 'boys', washing faces, teaching my assistants how beds are made or floors are swept, dressing wounds. At 12 comes dinner for patients, and afterwards letter writing for them.

Religious orders of all denominations played a big part in field hospital nursing, and in 1861 Dorothea Dix was appointed Superintendent of the Female Nurses of the Army to recruit and train nurses.

From earliest days American nurses have striven to uphold and emphasize the intellectual component of nursing, and the universities have supported them in their aims. In 1907 Mary Nutting was appointed to the Faculty of Teachers' College, as the first professor of nursing in the world.

The USA produces large numbers of articulate and intelligent nurses to lead the profession. Their nursing literature is the most extensive in the world, the amount of research they undertake is commendable. Perhaps the most admirable feature of American nurses as far as the UK is concerned is their ability to innovate and experiment, to criticize and evaluate their own work, and not to be afraid to abandon an unproductive theory. See also NURSING IN THE USA AND CANADA.

Overseas nursing. By the close of the 19th c. British nurses were being appointed to work for the government in the (then) British colonies, now mostly independent countries. Until State Registration in 1919 these nurses had no agreed

corpus of nursing knowledge to teach, and some could do no more than impart what they had learnt at home. It was possible to hear African students describing how they would give a bed-bath, and beginning 'First close the nearby windows', as if they had been in Liverpool or Glasgow.

The overseas nurses had to adapt not only to climatic extremes and diseases they had never known before, but to social systems that hardly envisaged nursing. It seemed unnatural to some cultures to cherish the diseased and sickly, and the physical care involved in nursing was a task for menials, not for the educated. Women in many societies could not nurse men, so male students had to be recruited. Mission hospitals and mission nurses contributed together with colleagues in the Overseas Nursing Association to the growth of indigenous nursing patterns. Hong Kong was the first 'colony' to obtain reciprocal registration with the GNC in 1935. Great advances were made between the First and Second World Wars, and many people came to train in the UK, and returned to train others.

At the turn of the century British nurses were showing their colleagues overseas their ideas of care. Eighty years later these nurses of the Third World may have things to teach us. They did not have to struggle through the pre-anaesthetic, pre-antibiotic era, or to fight the battle for professional recognition. Developing countries may believe that prestigious hospital buildings for the sick are an out-of-place export from older societies, and that their resources can be more profitably used on *immunization, *health education, *dietetics, and *antenatal and *midwifery services. In such services nurses have a key role, and British nurses may yet learn from them how nursing skills are best deployed. At the 1981 Congress of the International Council of Nurses a Kenyan nurse, Eunice Kiereini, was elected president.

The turn of the century. By the end of the 19th c. the new nurse of Florence Nightingale's ideals had displaced the pre-Crimean one as the model. Work and thought was taking place on many fronts (Fig. 1). Hospitals and their matrons (nurses in charge of hospitals) were deeply concerned with the length of nurses' training and had a vested interest in making it lengthy, since the pay of the probationer was minute, and if she formed a major part of the work force, this was to the advantage of impecunious hospitals. The period of training successively rose from one to two and then to three years. This was the limit of acceptability, except in the case of the fashionable teaching hospitals, which were able to ask a fourth year as a staff nurse (registered nurse, junior to the sister in charge of a ward) at a low salary.

Many organizations were formed to further the aim of state registration, but nurses were also concerned with the activities of colleagues abroad, the struggle for votes for women in the UK, and the formulation of their own role and the best means of

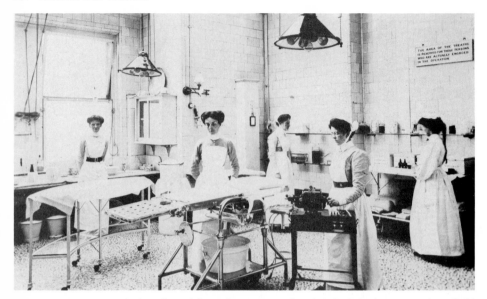

Fig. 1. The coming of anaesthetics and asepsis began the emergence of a technical role for the nurse, as shown in this photograph of an operating theatre at St Bartholomew's Hospital. (Reproduced by permission of the Medical Illustration Department, St Bartholomew's Hospital, London)

educating them for it. Mrs Bedford Fenwick was not only an international as well as a national protagonist of registration, but keenly interested in educational techniques. In the *Nursing Record,* which she edited and mostly wrote for nearly half a century, she began to give book prizes for and to publish the 'case study' as a means of encouraging nurses to observe their patients and their illnesses, and to record the results of care. This still remains, as the nursing case study, an important tool of education, and an abiding element in nursing journals. She said at the International Council of Nurses in 1907:

To enumerate our most pressing needs; we require preliminary education before entering hospital wards; we need postgraduate education to keep us in the running; we need special instruction as teachers to fit us for the responsible positions of sisters and superintendents; we need a state-constituted board to examine and maintain discipline in our ranks, and we must have legal status to protect our legal rights and to ensure us ample professional autonomy.

All her aims have now been realized, but the first decade of the 20th c. was a time of increasing anxiety as the shadow of approaching war inhibited action in many spheres. We have many accounts of what was happening to bedside nurses in the closed world of hospital wards and nurses' homes. The work still kept the dual aspect of domestic work and personal care (Fig. 2). One of the exhibits at a World Fair in Chicago in 1894 was

the Ward Toilet Basket: a brown plate basket divided in the middle and lined with red American cloth, and having also a loose cover of the same; on the one side fits a plasmon powder box and a covered glass bottle for recti-

fied spirit, a brush and comb, nail brush, small tooth comb, scissors and soap case; on the other is placed a dusting brush, whisk brush for mattress, dusters, and a bottle of that invaluable liquid, Sharpe's Metal Polish.

This account shows that the nurse's role as a domestic and personal attendant had changed little in 20 years, but the nurse had a deep feeling for that role, however limited the medical and pharmacological resources of aid remained. This account was written by a lady who began to train in 1916, and whose career led her to head Lady Minto's Indian Nursing Service, and see the independence of India in 1947. She says of her probationer days

Life was hard. Cleaning and washing patients, making beds, giving bedpans, and then cleaning again . . . lockers, brasses, mackintoshes, spittoons. Very seldom were we probationers allowed contact with anything interesting or instructive. Many fell by the way, as often as not because of the ward sisters' stinging sarcasm. Medical students suffered in the same way, but they were in the wards each day for a short time only.

With our long hours on duty, one particular patient depended so much on the personal touch of the individual nurse. We really did see them through their illness, which I think made our job so absorbingly interesting. We were at their bedside each day for ten to thirteen hours . . . and for twelve hours on night duty . . . we became part and parcel of their sufferings.

Treatments included saline infusions, bread, linseed and kaolin poultices, and mustard plasters. I have seen cupping done to relieve congestion and have myself applied leeches.

Lest indeed it should be thought that skilled sustained personal attention was not likely to be curative, this same lady relates how in 1923 in India she was sent to nurse an engineer's wife with

Fig. 2. Nursing as a vocation. The sister in the early 20th c. divided her life between the patients in her ward and her sitting room which led off it. (Reproduced by permission of the Medical Illustration Department, St Bartholomew's Hospital, London)

blackwater fever at a small coalfield in the hills. She went up to the bungalow in a coalbucket, together with the coffin which it was thought her patient would need very soon. A week later the nurse triumphantly sent the coffin down again empty.

She describes in her account of her training a sad feature of ward life, the verbal harshness inflicted on junior staff by those above them. It is alluded to in most nursing reports of the time, and was not entirely extinct at the beginning of the Second World War. The multiple levels of senior grade now seen did not exist. Matron was in sole command, and the ward sisters were directly responsible to her and her assistant; then came the staff nurses. The warm and lovely name of home sister was often belied by the nature of these ladies, who ruled the nurses' home with frosty discipline. Rooms were inspected daily, and their owners had to conform to rules about the number of articles and photographs that could be displayed. Rooms were commonly unheated, electric fires and radios were not allowed.

In the wards probationers (student nurses) worked under continual blame and criticism. It was as if training had to be made as rigorous as possible, so that only the strongest survived. It is sometimes said that this was the result of rule by elderly spinsters, but this is a simplistic view. Medical

students were managed in much the same way by the consultants: ward rounds were often painful occasions, when learners were held up to ridicule in front of their patients. Perhaps it was a feature of an age in which parents sent their sons to boarding schools knowing that they would be bullied and caned, but believing it would make men of them.

This relation with seniors had to be borne in surroundings of pain and death, so what induced young women to support it? The challenge to endure is quite a powerful one, and patients always appreciated their nurses. Juniors had great camaraderie among themselves, and this warmth was especially evident among those who joined on the same day. Nurses of a 'set' often remained friends for life, and appeared to enjoy recounting stories of the hardships they had endured. They called each other by their surnames, as girls at that time did at university, in imitation of men. Curiously enough, some of them who came a generation later to look at the schools of nursing where their daughters were training, asked, 'Do you think that patients are as well looked after as they used to be, now that nurses have so much done for them?'

First World War and after. The effect of the First World War on nursing was tremendous. Nurses were needed in unprecedented numbers, and the Voluntary Aid Detachment (VAD) founded by the British *Red Cross met part of the demand. Male nurses working in mental hospitals left to join the services, and many nurses in general hospitals left to care for casualties. There were two million casualties on the Western Front alone, mostly adult men, so that there were very many spinsters and widows who would have to earn their living after the war.

During the war women had proved themselves in many fields. The vote could no longer be withheld from them, and the nurses' demand for state registration had to be granted, to try to bring some order into their ranks.

The College of Nursing had been founded in 1916 to further nursing interests, and survives today as the Royal College of Nursing (RCN), the main professional body concerned with educational policy, ethical standards, and conditions of service. In 1920 the General Nursing Council was established to compose a syllabus for instruction and examinations, and to compile a register of trained nurses.

A young profession can, of course, always be criticized with hindsight. If control could have been retained by nurses it would have brought professional benefits. Now the government had established the registering body, and the interests of government then and now have been in manning the hospitals for the National Health Service (NHS) at the lowest capital and running cost.

The twenties were a time of inflation, depression, and unemployment. This meant that it was easier to recruit student nurses: it was not, however, easy to retain them; the wastage rate remained at about one-third in general hospitals, and much higher in mental hospitals. Successive reports speak of long hours, low pay, ancient buildings, and harsh discipline. Tuberculosis was still an active threat to young nurses.

Nurses in the thirties were aware of the social trends towards a welfare state, and to more state control of individuals, but they were busy with their own internal problems of registration, curriculum development, and education. Those nurses who were working then in larger general and teaching hospitals remember them as a time of stability in a world that was about to explode.

Hours were still long and pay low, but the nursing role was well established: it was to give comfort; the patient always came first. Nurses did not run unless there was a fire or *haemorrhage. Such axioms were not thought of as clichés, but as truths that were to be followed. Pride in one's training school was felt, and rather parochial quips exchanged about 'rival' institutions, for example St Thomas's for a lady, Guy's for a flirt, Bart's for a nurse.

'Good nursing' might still save lives for which no medical cure existed. *Diabetes now was treated by *insulin, but lobar *pneumonia patients still underwent a long dangerous illness culminating in a crisis, through which nurses might hope to bring them. Healthy young men who had a *hernia operation stayed in bed until their stitches were removed. A drug called *prontosil had been discovered which could cure infections, so we heard. *Blood transfusion was becoming common, so surgical *shock was retreating. Lung surgery was becoming safer, and heart surgery would soon be feasible.

One of the most disturbing things nurses had to learn at this time was that comfortable bed-rest might be lethal, and that nursing care which encouraged immobility was a disservice. Venous *thrombosis and pulmonary *embolism, as well as many other less dangerous but very uncomfortable results, were attributed to bed-rest. Early mobility for patients made nurses question their clinical practices in many fields.

The Second World War and after. The Emergency Hospital Service was set up in 1938; one of its functions was to supply the increase in numbers of nurses that war would entail. Heavy civilian casualties were expected from bombing, although fortunately it was a year before bombing became intense. The Armed Services wanted another 4000 trained nurses. An endeavour was made to speed recruitment, and to reduce the needs of the civilian hospitals by the rather simple method of discharging the patients. A Civil Nursing Reserve was established: apart from trained people who had left nursing, it was composed of assistants with some experience but no qualifications, and orderlies with mainly domestic experience. The government found itself the employer of a very large number of nurses.

In 1941 it was recommended that all hospitals should pay the same salaries as those of the Reserve, and they would receive central reimbursement. Movement towards a National Health Service had taken a big step forward.

Recruitment remained difficult all through the war, and civilian hospitals had a particularly hard time. In 1944 it was decided to direct nurses to priority areas, but the opening of the Second Front in the summer changed the picture, and in 1945 came peace.

During the war women had won advancement in many fields of employment, as well as sharing the hardships of the battlefield and the prisoner-of-war camps. An enormous field of work had been opened up to women, and in the years of full employment they had no difficulty in finding skilled work. Nursing had lost its old appeal of being the major field of employment for women. It was now seen as an area of low pay, hard work in Victorian premises, and women were no longer eager to tolerate such conditions.

In an endeavour to fill vacancies, more auxiliaries and students were recruited, so that the ratio of untrained and trained staff altered for the worse. The age of entry was lowered in the hope that there were many young people who went elsewhere because they were too young to nurse. Headmistresses now saw nursing as an occupation for the under-educated and were unwilling to help intelligent candidates to nurse.

The inauguration of the NHS in 1946 should have been a time of hope. A free health service was to be one of the bases of the new caring society, but nurses and doctors were depressed and anxious. Assistant nurses were now a statutory grade, working for enrolment with the GNC. One-year 'crash' courses for people with war-time nursing experience abounded. 'Cadet' schemes for children leaving school were legion, in the hope that bridging the gap between school and hospital would keep up numbers. All these tended to make worse the serious imbalance between untrained and trained staff. Those who qualified and remained in nursing were promoted early and without training to posts of responsibility. In some areas the number of patients awaiting admission was high and the staff meagre.

A change was coming, too, in the traditional role of the nurse. *Antibiotics and *renal dialysis and other technical procedures were coming into common use. People began to be cured, and the quality of nursing care became of less obvious importance to the outcome of an illness, if not to the well-being of people during that illness.

Suggestions and proposals for the ailments of the nursing profession were not lacking. Doctors, the general press, political parties, trade unions, nursing journals, the RCN, and the GNC all took part. Many thought that more money for staff would solve all problems, others that the harsh attitudes that prevailed must be cured. Some wanted the training lengthened, some shortened. All wanted the syllabus reorganized, but not all in the same direction. Everyone agreed that many students were unequal academically to the demands of the syllabus, and their eventual failure was traumatic to them and discouraged recruitment, but if they were not recruited, there was no one to do the work. Matrons went on recruiting missions to Africa, the West Indies, and Asia in search of potential students, pupils, and auxiliaries, and tutors found that they must teach English as well as nursing. Overseas men and women who became State Registered would have a qualification recognized at home, but others would not, which caused ill feeling. Patients and nurses had no understanding of each other's cultural background, and little of their language.

Statistics of the time are not very reliable, but an estimate in the 1960s was that 35 per cent of the nursing force came from overseas. Wastage in 1961 was 39 per cent overall, and another source of loss to the service was the number of registered nurses who went to the USA, Canada, and Australia, where conditions were better and salaries higher. This still further increased the imbalance between trained staff and learners.

In 1962 the GNC was able to reintroduce the educational entrance test, which prevented the recruitment of inadequate people who could be used for their services for a year or two and then discarded. Nurses themselves began to express their need for an education to afford them professional status, and financial reward sufficient to ensure that the nurse did not have to abandon the work that he/she was trained for in order to gain an adequate living.

Changes taking place in the population were to have a profound effect on the task of the nurse, but this was not yet mirrored in the syllabus. The birth rate had fallen, people lived longer, and old people had problems finding a place in the small houses in which their children lived. About a third of hospital admissions were for mental disease or handicap, but neither of these facts was reflected as yet in the nurse-training syllabus, which was still based on the 'acute hospital'. Perhaps this is the time to take a brief look at the nursing services for psychiatric patients.

Psychiatric nurses. The plight of the mentally ill has varied considerably down the centuries, but has never been less than sad. When England consisted predominantly of small rural communities, a certain amount of eccentricity of behaviour or lack of endowment could be tolerated within the community. With the coming of the Industrial Revolution and the growth of cities, the insane were confined in institutions. Since derangement of behaviour was a common sign of insanity, the uninformed spectator often felt that this could be altered if the patient so wished, and if he did not he was either perverse or possessed. Fear led to brutality, and those who tended the insane were custodians rather than nurses. There are some great humanitarian names in the history of lunacy, but until the close of the 19th c. the mentally ill were confined to secure institutions in the country, out of sight and often out of most people's mind.

The hospitals were built very much to a pattern, standing in large grounds with a water tower as a conspicuous feature. Doctors and nurses were isolated from the rest of medicine, and male and female nurses married and lived in tied cottages around the grounds. The inmates, some of whom were confined for quite trivial reasons were there for long periods, often for life. The philosophy was to provide a safe quiet life for the inmates. As a medical specialty, psychiatry was not held in great esteem by other doctors, and those who practised it often showed little interest in nursing.

Outbursts of rage and violence were handled by isolating the patient in a padded cell. These remained in use until the 1940s, and there were psychiatric doctors and nurses who defended their use, believing that segregating the violent prevented the spread of excitement to other patients, and allowed a sobering-up period.

As the mid-century approached, the wind of change began blowing through psychiatric hospitals, and the cure of some kinds of mental disease seemed possible. *Syphilis, which had caused *general paralysis of the insane, could be cured by *penicillin. Insulin therapy began to be used for *schizophrenia; *electroconvulsive therapy was used for *depressive psychoses. Many psychiatrists began to believe in a physical cause for mental illness, and hence in physical cure. *Vitamin administration was popular, brain surgery arrived, and most important of all were the new drugs.

Many of these treatments did not survive long in favour, but they brought a new feeling of hope. Perhaps it was the personal attention lavished on the patient receiving treatment that brought relief of symptoms. Nurses now felt that their skills could influence outcome, and that they had a real curative function.

The Royal Medico-Psychological Association had been conducting examinations for nurses since 1891, and in 1951 the GNC took over. The Minister would not allow the council to impose an educational test for mental nurse students until 1964, so wastage from psychiatric hospitals remained high in spite of increasing awareness of the possibilities of the nursing role. Morale among psychiatric nurses was not high. Recruitment was poor, and nurses feared that the GNC might close the mental register, as had happened to the nurses trained to look after patients with infectious fevers. The Minister had announced his plans for district general hospitals with psychiatric units. The nurses saw that general hospitals would attract the less seriously ill and the most medically 'interesting' cases, and the mental hospitals would be left in the country with the chronic residue. Although syphilis was disappearing, psychoses due to alcoholism and drug abuse were on the increase. People were living longer, so there were more psychogeriatric admissions, such as patients suffering from *senile dementia.

The movement of people in and out of mental hospitals meant that the public became more aware of what constituted nursing and medical practice, and were more critical. The media began to pay attention to this field, and found that sometimes hospital authorities were more concerned with denials of malpractice and protecting staff from criticism than with protecting patients. 'Revelations' and accounts of abuses led to public enquiries, and although these may apply only to small numbers, they still occur.

There is no way in which we can condone callousness or cruelty, but it is necessary to think how or why it can happen. Mental hospitals are still physically isolated, and many are Victorian and depressing. It is not, however, in the worst premises that one finds the worst care: much devoted and admirable nursing is carried out under very inhibiting conditions. The nature of the work is such that most people would find it too hard for them. The habits and behaviour of some of the mentally sick are bizarre. Many nurses feel that some of their patients ought to be in prison rather than in a mental hospital (and many prison officers,

conversely, think that some of their inmates ought to be in hospital).

Looking at staff/patient ratios and the facilities available in mental hospitals, one finds that the acute and admission wards are much better provided for than are the chronic ones, where patient dependency is high. Staff still form a closed community, group loyalty to colleagues is high, and there is unwillingness to report minor incidents which, if unchecked, may lead to bad practices.

Openness on the part of everyone in mental hospitals can do nothing but good. Visitors should be welcome, complaints and criticisms dealt with promptly and without rancour. If doctors see themselves as leaders in the clinical situation they should assume the responsibilities that go with the role, co-operating with and helping the nurses to a view of the importance of the curative possibilities of their own function that will be for the good of patients and staff as well.

The general public is urged to adopt a helpful and healthy attitude to the mentally afflicted and their nurses. A recovered depressive writes (*Guardian,* 2 May 1982): 'Mental illness has always been socially unacceptable in Britain. It is a taboo subject. . . . I have felt keenly the mediaeval cruelty with which people view mental illness.' Mental nurses notice with pain when they are shopping in the local town that ex-patients with whom they had a good relationship now pass them without speaking. These nurses are doing on our behalf, and for our relatives, work that most people could not do; they deserve our support and esteem.

Men as nurses. In mediaeval times the homeless sick were tended by the religious orders, some of which were especially concerned with such work. Men were cared for by the monks, women by the nuns. After the dissolution of the monasteries, such care as there was became the responsibility of the laity. The order of *St John of Jerusalem still keeps today its tradition of care for the sick and injured that it has retained through the centuries.

When Florence Nightingale led her regiment of women into hospitals, these were only occupied by attendants. Women were in desperate need of work and the ability to earn a living, just as medical advances increased the scope of work available: they were not going to surrender this area of work to men without a struggle and they conducted with determination for many years a campaign against them. In this they were assisted by several circumstances. The two most important were that nursing was so badly paid that men who could gain a better reward would want to do so. The second was that nursing had the image of being a female occupation, and to compete with women for work did not seem to most men a male role.

There is, of course, no reason why men should not display devotion and tenderness. If we think of paediatric nursing, people are fathers as well as mothers. Once one has accepted that at bedside level men and women can contribute equally, doubts about the role of men in nursing disappear. Obviously they can also be managers, administrators, and professors.

There were many psychological pressures on men. When they first became heads of hospitals there was no other title for them than that of matron. The University of London kept the name of their teaching award as the Sister Tutor's Diploma until the 1970s, holding that women had never objected to being called 'bachelors' and 'masters', and that the male tutors should not object to being 'sisters'.

In 1939 there were 120 male students in general nursing, and only seven training schools accepted them. In 1949 there were 2400 male students. The increase was chiefly on account of the work done by male nurses during the war. Many who had nursed in the services had found a vocation, and wanted to be registered nurses. Up to now, men had not made nursing a primary choice, but times were changing.

In 1947 the Queen's Institute started to accept men as students for district nursing, and from 1961 they were able to train as health visitors. In 1960 the Royal College of Nursing had its charter amended in order to enable it to accept male nurses as members.

The last bastion of female exclusiveness to fall was midwifery, and a few men have qualified. While it does not at the moment seem likely that they will ever be very numerous, no one finds it odd that men should become *obstetricians, and it is natural that some men should want to be midwives.

In 1980 men formed about one-sixth of the nursing force. One important social fact influencing their distribution is that men do not have their service interrupted when children arrive, and those who seek promotion tend to have a more straightforward path than married women. There is, therefore, a fair proportion of men seeking promotion away from bedside nursing.

The part played by men in securing more realistic salary scales should be recorded. They have always formed an important element in mental nursing where union organization was strongest. They spoke with a united voice, represented themselves as heads of families, and rejected the popular view that as nurses worked for love they did not need financial reward.

The part of a prophet is an unrewarding one, and there are many factors such as unemployment levels, salaries, and central funds available for health staff, as well as vocational views, that will influence the number of men in nursing. However, at present there does not seem to be a marked tendency to a change in numbers.

Role of the nurse. Medical and scientific advances in the second half of the 20th c. have given the nurse marvellous opportunities in care (Fig. 3), but have also presented her with acute practical and ethical problems of which her predecessors could not have dreamed. The student nurse

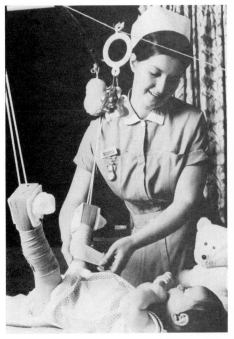

Fig. 3. Nursing as a vocation. Giving skilled personal care remains highly rewarding today. (British Official Photograph; Crown Copyright Reserved)

must today have experience not only in her training hospital, but in the elements of psychiatric nursing, midwifery, community services, and the care of the old. When she is registered or enrolled she can take certificates in a variety of specialties, and can consider whether she works not just in hospitals, but with the armed services, in occupational health, with a primary care team, the prisoner service, overseas nursing, or in the community. If she chooses the last, she can be a *health visitor, a *district nurse, a midwife, or work in a *family planning clinic.

The work of the district (community) nurse has changed in content and method. People live longer, to suffer more *degenerative diseases; in many areas there are large immigrant populations with pressing problems, especially among the women. Some diseases disappear, some make sporadic reappearances; some problems, like baby-battering, come increasingly to attention. Patients no longer bake their dressing in the oven; the nurse no longer does her rounds on a bicycle. Nurses increasingly work as a part of a team with general practitioners and health visitors, and the ability to consult with fellow professionals is a stimulus to maintain standards and increase knowledge.

The hospital nurse is in charge of her environment, and the patient comes as a client. The district nurse is in a different position: she can enter a patient's home only at his invitation, and if her services and attitudes are not acceptable she can be refused admission. She has, however, unrivalled opportunities to give total care. She sees the patient's life style, his social problems, and those of his family and relatives. A very great deal of the nursing in the UK is done by relatives in the home, and many of these need the support of the nurse over technical procedures, and advice and teaching on how to cope with problems. She can see the need for help from the social workers or the health visitor, and knows when it is advisable for the doctor to call.

Some classes of work decline: for instance, delivery in the home becomes increasingly uncommon; but the work of the psychiatric community nurse is seen to be increasing in value, as discharge of patients to their homes becomes more frequent. The nurse can see that medication is regular, and give advice to the relatives as to how to react.

Reorganization. The hospital ward is the centre in which nurses mostly learn their art and science, and is where the general public most often meets nurses. The ward sister was traditionally the linch-pin in this important setting, and up to the Second World War she stayed in her post for years, often living in a bed-sitting-room attached to the ward, and devoting her life to her ward. Consultants depended on her clinical judgement, and she was the stable element on the ward team, often at great personal sacrifice. She had no nursing superior but Matron.

Social circumstances after the war were making such sisters scarcer and the advent of an increasingly shorter working week, and its implications for a 24-hour service made her former role impossible. In 1963 the Salmon Committee was set up, which was to occasion the disappearance of this traditional figure, and to cause the biggest upset among nurses since 1920. Brian Abel-Smith spoke about nursing embarking on registration with its military heritage showing in its language, its religious tradition conveyed in its sentiments, and its humble ancestry revealed in its uniform. The implementation of Salmon was to produce a marked rise in its military aspect.

The Salmon Report, published in 1966, dealt with the structure of the hospital nursing service from ward sister upwards, and how administration and management were to be formulated. Sisters were now to be nursing officers of both sexes, nursing officers managed a group of wards, senior nursing officers co-ordinated their work and were responsible to a principal nursing officer. After a brief trial in a few places, in 1967 the Board of Prices and Incomes recommended that the Salmon structure be implemented.

The results were painful in many ways. People who liked bedside nursing saw that pay and pension prospects demanded that they move up the promotion ladder. Matrons disappeared: unit officers took on management positions without formal training. Senior nurses had to reapply for their own re-named positions, and sometimes found themselves rejected after years of performing their duties apparently to everyone's satisfaction. In 1979 came a major health service reorganization which produced nursing posts at District, Area, and Regional levels. There were more vacancies than there were adequately prepared nurses to fill them, and the same applied to the medical and financial officers who made up the management teams.

The 1970s were a time of crumbling attitudes and beliefs, and awakening of economic awareness. Hospitals had been built in the belief that there would always be a supply of low-paid workers to move goods by hand, and of student nurses to do the lion's share of the nursing. Now everyone was working shorter hours, earning bonuses and over-time money, and union activity in hospitals was increasing. Although one must regret the loss of some of the erstwhile attitudes, the good old days were not always good for nurses. They no longer fill matron's inkwells, or put buttons on the consultants' white coats. They have many problems still to solve: one is how to bring pressure to bear for salary rises when they cannot bring themselves to take industrial action. Another is how to maintain morale in the face of recurrent reorganization. The last was in 1981, when again senior nurses have been losing posts which they had previously held. Recession has brought scarcity of money in the Health Service, which means that nurse managers have to deal with severe limitation of resources.

The bedside nurse today. While morale is not high among senior nurses, it is perhaps possible to perceive at the basic clinical level an air of hope and of independent self-awareness as professional nurses that is quite new. During the last 25 years nurses have seen an immense change in all aspects of medical and surgical care, and very important questions were asked as techniques like renal dialysis, positive pressure ventilation, and cardiac monitoring became available (Fig. 4). The nurse had to ask herself whether her task was to tend mechanical appliances or to give traditional nursing care to a patient while a technician looked after the machines. There is no doubt what the lay public feels. Recently, the British Broadcasting Corporation were making a nursing programme of a patient after open heart surgery, and the cameras were moving over many marvellous appliances. A nurse appeared, and bending over her apparently unconscious patient spoke clearly and gently to her while moistening her lips and tongue. The electricians watching all exclaimed, 'Ah! there's a real nurse!'

Cardiac resuscitation in its early stages caused much anxiety and heart searching for nurses, and also for the medical staff. If it was ineffective, we felt defeated: if it was successful, we sometimes found we had restored a life of handicap. Once the technique was routine, patients approaching their end might have their life prolonged for a few days at the expense of destroying the peace and quiet

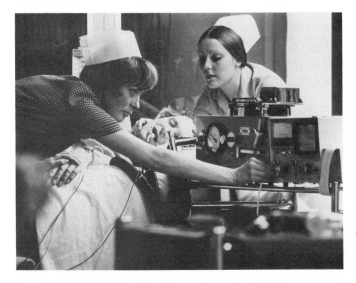

Fig. 4. The modern nurse is a trained professional, able to offer technical as well as personal care. (British Official Photograph; Crown Copyright Reserved)

that everyone deserves. Similar fears and queries arose when donor kidneys first came into demand for kidney transplants.

With experience, together with good communication with doctors, improving methods and understanding, such problems are resolved and the previous anxieties are allayed; nevertheless, new ones constantly arise. At the moment, the appropriate care for the handicapped newborn causes much discussion. What future problems lie ahead we cannot foresee, but it is inevitable that they will come.

Nurses cannot surrender their consciences to medical orders, and are morally and legally responsible for their actions and decisions. Perhaps it is this approach to professional maturity that has made nurses ask what their real function is, and to find an answer in the rather pedantically named Nursing Process.

Once nurses used to be asked in state examinations, 'What are the signs, symptoms, and treatment of (e.g.) diabetes mellitus?' Today this would seem strange: diseases occur only when they are manifested in people, and it is people, not diseases, for whom we care. When someone comes into hospital, nurses assess from a written nursing history what are the problems which the nurse can possibly solve; set a series of goals we may hope to reach for him; use in attaining these goals, the very best nursing care we can give; review these goals and our methods of reaching them; and afterwards assess how successful we were in attaining them. The amount of teaching and learning that goes on is considerable.

It is not only in general hospitals that this ambition to formulate and give the best and most personal care is pursued. In psychiatric and mental deficiency hospitals, and in the community, the same kind of movement is going on to increase the quality of care and hence the level of professional

satisfaction. Perhaps we can hope that the winds of administrative change will blow less frequently for a few years, and that the grades that at present are going through a difficult and discouraging stage will find more satisfaction.

Professional preparation. When the first schools of nursing were established in the 19th c., the ways in which candidates were to be prepared for their work had to be considered. Only a few pioneers spoke of nursing education: most spoke of training, and incorporated that word in the name of the school.

The nurses received their instruction mostly from the doctors, learning tasks that had been delegated to them by doctors, such as bandaging, applying splints and poultices, giving medicine, and taking temperatures. Sisters in the early days had no real knowledge they could pass on, but as they began to be replaced by the new 'trained' nurses, the sister became an important source of clinical acumen and task-orientated nursing. Matron or the home sister taught what was called ethics, but was mostly hospital etiquette.

As more and more conditions were understood and became amenable to medical treatment, doctors gave courses of lectures in diseases. These were accounts of signs, symptoms, and treatment of pneumonia or nephritis: they were not accounts of how to manage or nurse people with these diseases, but discussed abstract considerations. Nurse teachers gave lectures and demonstrations on techniques of dealing with symptoms like constipation or fever, but not about the people who suffered from them; these were all grouped under one label, the patient. This attitude was still prevalent when the GNC began to formulate examinations to determine suitability for the state registers.

The practical tests were conducted in the classrooms of schools of nursing, where nurses were asked to lay trays and trolleys showing their knowledge of procedures. Since the syllabus was updated only at intervals, nurses might find their professional competence being tested by questions on *cupping or the application of *leeches, long after these practices were obsolete.

Too much time cannot be given to the stages by which these attitudes and methods became outdated. As nurses gained insight into the uniqueness of their possible role, they refined the methods of evaluating professional competence. On-going assessment of practical skills in giving and planning individual care, knowledge of responsibilities for drug therapy, ability to plan for a group of patients, and for the nurses who give that care, has taken the place of classroom tests. This assessment takes place in the wards and among patients for whom the candidate is working.

The role of the universities in nurse education has been much slower to become established in the UK than in North America, where most universities have a faculty of nursing: after the Second World War the better-known nurse-training schools in the UK were able to attract candidates with educational attainments that would have enabled them to enter university. It was hard that intelligent women should have to choose between an academic education, and work which they had a deep desire to undertake. The GNC began to approve courses shared between a university and a school of nursing, which would lead to a degree and to state registration as a nurse. The number of applicants for these courses was an indication of the desire for advanced education by nurses, and demand for places has continued. Apart from the number of courses based in schools of nursing, there are professors of nursing in universities in England, Scotland, and Wales.

There are also now opportunities to take a Master's degree or a Doctorate (e.g. Ph.D.) in many universities. Some of these are taught degrees that offer clinical nursing as a specialty. When nursing degrees were established, some objected that graduate nurses would speedily desert clinical nursing for administration. This has not proved to be the case: many people who want to gain degrees as well as nursing qualifications have clinical nursing in hospital or the community as their primary interest. Another important point to notice is that when the Open University was established, a large number of nurses, including some very senior ones, enrolled for part-time degrees, and had a very high level of success, in spite of the length of study involved.

Looking to the future. Facts do not speak for themselves: they indicate the beliefs, inclinations, and interests of the author who selected them from an enormous amount of relevant material. The major legislative and statutory changes in nursing are mentioned only marginally because good accounts exist elsewhere.

Looking at nurses around the world, one sees that their work, reward, and status is influenced by many factors: by the structure of society; by views on women's work and position; by the gross national product; by the resources available for the health services; by whether the country is northern or southern, industrial or agricultural; by the life expectancy; and by the nature of the health problems to be attacked. Developed countries that have conquered the major infections are struggling with illness caused by the environment and the machines they have created, and by problems like smoking, alcohol, and drug abuse.

One notices the cyclical nature of some of the solutions to nursing questions, and that these become important in different countries at different times. It may be that student nurses are put into hospital wards to learn their craft with no preliminary training; 50 years later it seems important that they all be given introductory training in a school. In another 50 years' time, nurses think of a 'new' idea, that teaching ought to begin at the bedside where the student's main interests lie. In the 1930s it was thought imperative to introduce the grade of enrolled nurse for those who needed a simplified kind of training. Today it is being widely suggested that a single grade be reintroduced. All countries are concerned about providing medical care by the state for those unable to pay for it themselves, and about the relation between state care and private medicine; none are sure how hospitals should be planned, or what is the best size.

In spite of the many variables and imponderables, there has been remarkable unanimity among nurses about the nature of their function, and although their ideas on how best to fulfil this aim alter over the years, this is the statement most often quoted about them:

The unique function of the nurse is to assist the individual, sick or well, in the performance of those activities contributing to health or its recovery (or to peaceful death) that he would perform unaided if he had the necessary strength, in such a way as to help him gain independence as rapidly as possible.

This aspect of her work, this part of her function, she initiates and controls; of this she is master. In addition, she helps the patient to carry out the therapeutic plan as initiated by the physicians. She also, as a member of a medical team, helps other members as they in turn help her, to plan and carry out the total programme whether it be for the improvement of health, or the recovery from illness, or support in death.

(Henderson, 1966)

WINIFRED E. HECTOR

Reference
Henderson, V. (1966). *The Nature of Nursing.* New York.

Further reading
Abel-Smith, B. (1960). *A History of the Nursing Profession.* London.
Baly, M. E. (1980). *Nursing and Social Change.* 2nd edn, London.
Baly, M. E., Robottom, B., Clark, J. and Chapple, M. (1981). *A New Approach to District Nursing.* London.

Bendall, E. R. D. and Raybould, E. (1969). *A History of the General Nursing Council, 1919–1969*. London.

Glossary

GNC. General Nursing Council (there were formerly separate Councils for England and Wales; for Scotland; and for Northern Ireland). The statutory body, established in 1919, to register trained nurses, recognize training schools, and conduct national examinations (see UKCC below).

Categories of registered nurses until 1983 were:

SRN. State registered nurse (general)

RMN. Registered mental nurse

RNMS. Registered nurse for the mentally subnormal

RSCN. Registered sick children's nurse

Student nurse. Someone training for one of the registers.

SEN. State enrolled nurse. Training for the Roll is shorter and less academic than that for the Register.

UKCC. In 1983 the United Kingdom Central Council for Nurses, Midwives and Health Visitors replaced the General Nursing Councils, the Central Midwives' Board, and the Council for the Education and Training of Health Visitors.

SCM. State Certified Midwife. A trained midwife recognized by the Central Midwives' Board.

Auxiliary nurse, or nursing assistant. These have no statutory recognition and receive in-service training in tasks in hospital wards and departments. They maintain a good environment, and undertake simple bedside care.

District or community nurse. A registered or enrolled nurse who works outside the hospital, and is usually employed by the Local Health Authority.

RNT. Registered nurse tutor. A state registered nurse who undergoes further training in order to become a teacher of student nurses.

Health Visitor. A registered nurse who has passed a recognized academic course in health teaching and relevant subjects. The health visitor gives advice in the home on the prevention of illness and accidents, diet, immunization, and family problems, especially for the very young and the old.

Ward sister/charge nurse. The nurse responsible for devising and delivering nursing care to a group of patients, and supervising the nurses, students, and pupils who work in the unit. The head nurse is the American counterpart of the ward sister.

NURSING IN THE USA AND CANADA

Introduction. This brief article documents the development of North American nursing towards fulfilling its role as a primary health profession and an academic discipline. An attempt has been made to present developments which pertain generally with regard to nursing practice, education, and research in Canada and in the USA, and to note major differences between the two countries. Since nursing in Canada is influenced by provincial and territorial as well as federal laws and policies, and in the USA, by jurisdiction of the several states, as well as federal laws and policies, generalizations do not pertain universally within each country. No attempt has been made to identify all of these differences.

All helping professions have emerged in response to human needs and all have followed a similar course of development. Throughout history, social groups have perceived their own need for particular kinds of assistance in order to attain goals to which they aspired and those they believed to be valued by and valuable for all human beings. They then gave sanction to the development of identifiable fields of work, populated by those whose propensities for providing services set them apart as practitioners of particular crafts.

Originally, practitioners (e.g. the clergy, physicians, lawyers, teachers, apothecaries) possessed meagre knowledge that they acquired through personal experience; later, accumulated knowledge, skills, and wisdom were transmitted from masters to apprentice learners in each vocation. Still later in the development of helping occupations, technical training programmes were established through which to transmit to neophytes-in-training the advances in science that rationalized the skills they employed in their respective fields of work. Eventually, professions emerged when the several occupations spawned their own investigators and scholars who identified, discovered, and structured, each within its own unique perspective, the respective bodies of knowledge judged to be fundamental to professional practices. Those bodies of knowledge were eventually recognized as bona fide academic disciplines which were continuously advanced, refined, and restructured in accordance with the new insights gained by scientists and other scholars in each profession. Nursing is accepted as a profession and is slowly becoming recognized as an academic discipline.

The preparation of professionals is surely the responsibility of universities, for it is there that research and scholarship abound. Recognition of human needs for specific caring services together with recognition of the need of practitioners for extensive professional knowledge, skills, and values have thus been central to the emergence of all health professions, among them nursing. Nursing's system of education in North America is undergoing remarkable change and its scholarly work is developing rapidly.

It was Florence *Nightingale who, in 1860, clearly articulated the essence of nursing practice, set forth principles that were essential in developing sound programmes of pre-service nursing education, and identified the focus of and approaches to systematic enquiry through which nursing's body of knowledge could be extended. She saw clearly the complementary nature of the work of nurses and doctors. She noted that doctors are properly concerned with detecting, diagnosing, and treating human ills, whereas nurses are concerned with helping people attain, retain, or regain their health—'putting patients (human beings) in the best possible condition for nature to act upon them'. She thereby defined the practice domain of the professional 'nurse' as that of appraising human health assets and potentials (innate health-seeking mechanisms and learned behaviours) and of judiciously using nursing strategies (compensatory, supporting, sustaining, teaching, motivating) that help those they serve to achieve function, comfort, general health, and independence in executing their own health and therapeutic regimens. When death is imminent, nurses must assist in preserving peace and dignity.

In 1860, Nightingale observed that nature's laws of health were then all but unknown, thus indicating an appropriate focus for future fundamental research in nursing. She proposed also that nurses, through systematic observation and careful record-keeping, should define those nursing actions that are effective in helping persons to attain or be restored to health. Her concepts of nursing and nursing research and the educational principles she espoused have influenced remarkably the development of North American nursing as a profession and discipline up to the present day.

Nursing practice. Prior to the establishment of nursing schools based upon Nightingale's principles, nursing practice in North America was the responsibility of wives and mothers in their own homes and of orders of religious sisters and deaconesses in hospitals operated by them (Canadian Nurses' Association, 1968; Kalish and Kalish, 1978). The latter group were prepared through apprentice training and were motivated by the ideals of selfless service and charity. Patients in secular hospitals, in contrast, had to depend upon workers who neither subscribed to those ideals nor had the benefit of such training. The care they provided was often deplorable.

In Canada, it was the missionaries who recognized society's need for nursing care and who often called upon nuns to provide it. The need for particular institutions to take responsibility for providing preparation for nurses whose work could complement that of physicians was noted in the famed Shattuck report to the legislators of Massachusetts in 1850 (Kalish and Kalish, 1978). Subsequently, experiences in the Civil War in the USA demonstrated as vividly as did the Crimean War, the need for well-prepared nurses.

The success of Florence Nightingale during the Crimean War in improving the health of British soldiers and her system of education to prepare British nurses captured the interest of American physicians and lay-women who were eager to improve the care provided for patients in hospitals. North America's first schools of nursing, established on the Nightingale plan, were opened in Connecticut, Massachusetts, and New York in 1873 and in Ontario in 1874. Both Canadian and US trainees availed themselves of opportunities to prepare for a new career in those early schools and in other hospital-based schools that were established in response to demands created by the rapidly growing, westward migrating populations in both countries. The trainees and their teachers quickly demonstrated their worth by markedly improving patient care.

Nursing care and nursing education were largely synonymous in the late 19th and early 20th c. in that trainees and their teachers provided all the care that was available to hospitalized patients:

moreover, students often cared for sick people in their own homes, but the fees were collected by hospitals that soon took over control and operation of nursing schools. Graduates of the early schools often engaged in private duty nursing in patients' homes as that was their only source of employment, unless they established new nursing schools in the many new hospitals that were built.

Nursing leaders' concern for promoting public health led them to establish visiting nurse services as early as 1877 in the US and shortly thereafter in Canada. Visiting nurses provided care and health education for poor and sick people who often lived in deplorable and unhealthy dwellings. As the benefits of care provided for medically indigent sick people in their homes became apparent, so visiting nurse services were extended to individuals and families who could pay for them.

The Victorian Order of Nurses (VON), now celebrating 85 years of service, is Canada's oldest and largest visiting nurse organization. Originally providing a variety of services, including care in hospitals, the VON now provides health appraisals, direct nursing care, and health education for acutely and chronically ill persons in their own homes and in a variety of community settings. Service is given upon referral, on a fee-for-visit basis, based upon ability to pay. The VON is eligible for reimbursement by third-party (often insurance) payers. The agency serves all people and adjusts its programmes and special projects in accordance with community needs.

In the USA, non-profit, voluntary Visiting Nurse Associations (VNAs) provide services comparable to those provided by the VON, each agency serving a defined local community and providing (primarily) service in people's homes. Some agencies provide primary health care for children in selected schools and for workers in some industrial organizations on a contractual basis. Fees are assessed on a per-visit basis and agencies are eligible to receive reimbursement from third-party payers.

Public health nurses have been employed by local health departments from the early 1900s. They participate in health surveillance and screening programmes and routinely provide *immunizations, and child and adult health promotion services for persons who are medically indigent. Health Department nurses work in co-operation with other health professionals in public schools and health clinics. They rarely provide home care, but engage in comprehensive programmes of primary care.

In Canada, the Department of National Health and Welfare and the several Provincial Health Departments exercise general surveillance over the health of citizens and their environments and are responsible for the development of health policies for the nation. The national and provincial nurses provide consultant and advisory services to local health departments.

The National Department's Medical Services

serves as a Health Department for the Yukon and Northwest territories. Nurses in that department receive special training and provide emergency and maternity care in outpost nursing stations and health centres, provide public health services, care for patients in hospitals that were built for the Indians, and give nursing care in the homes of those they serve, sometimes travelling by planes, boats, dog sleds, snowmobiles, and snowshoes. They annually join the Department's mobile health teams who carry out medical and health care services to persons in remote areas during the summer season.

The United States Public Health Service and counterpart State Health Departments develop health policy and programmes, based upon needs in the nation and respective states. These Health Departments are caretakers of the public health, although other governmental agencies also have some responsibility for various aspects of health policies. Nurses provide specific consultant and advisory services, often within programmes. Public health department nurses operate at local, state, and national levels, with those at local levels providing direct services (e.g. health teaching, child health appraisals, immunizations, and diagnostic screening programmes). Nurses at state and federal levels serve as advisers and consultants, administer particular programmes, and participate in recommending health policies.

The notion that the nurse's role should include helping families prepare for new members began during the 1920s, a time when pregnancy and childbirth were viewed as essentially normal processes and when some mothers were served by untrained midwives, sometimes with unfortunate or disastrous results. Before the rise of the medical specialty of obstetrics and gynaecology, registered nurses enrolled for postgraduate preparation which equipped them for careers as nurse-midwives, responsible for prenatal, intrapartum, postpartum, and infant care of persons experiencing normal pregnancies. A comparative study of outcomes of care provided by physicians and trained nurse-midwives demonstrated, in 1930, that care provided by the midwives was as good as, or superior to, that provided by doctors (New York Academy of Medicine, 1933).

Nurse-midwifery services have been sustained in areas in the USA that are under-served by physicians. With growth in the number of medical specialists in obstetrics, however, nurse-midwifery services declined, until recently when families seeking to have family-centred natural childbirth experiences have again sought the services of nurse-midwives. The popularity of these services is not uniform among physicians, nurses, and families needing maternity services, in spite of evidence that nurse-midwife providers report excellent results with regard to the well-being of persons served, family satisfaction, and costs (Diers, 1982).

Nursing care of patients experiencing stress and mental illnesses and those manifesting behavioural aberrations became noteworthy when care, in contrast to isolation and incarceration, became accepted in North America. Following the First World War, new therapies (electroconvulsive therapy, brain surgery, psychoanalysis) required that nurses learn new strategies and approaches. After the Second World War, additional psychotherapies, based upon various behavioural theories, required that nurses develop more and different approaches to the promotion of the mental health of those cared for in acute and long-term care settings and in mental health clinics. Psychiatric/mental health nursing became an integral part of the repertoire of all registered nurses, beginning in the mid-1940s.

Prolongation of the lives of North Americans has led thoughtful nurses to recognize that enlightened health (nursing) care of *geriatric citizens, including those living in retirement centres and in nursing homes, can be effective in promoting their independence, preventing debilitating conditions, and stimulating practices that promote health and ensure an acceptable quality of life. Although that goal is still not achieved universally, the beneficial outcome of good nursing care for elderly citizens is clear.

Currently, in both Canada and the USA, most registered nurses serve in hospitals. In these institutions, care is growing ever more complex because of advances in knowledge and its translation into new and often heroic medical techniques of diagnosis and treatment. Patients in nursing homes, too, are sometimes more gravely ill because of hospital regulations requiring effective use of acute hospital facilities, and the numerous chronic diseases that often accompany old age. Nursing care is demanding and requires that nurses be knowledgeable, skilful, humane, and well able to collaborate with doctors and other health professionals in the planning and execution of programmes of effective patient care.

Whereas nursing care in hospitals was originally provided by nurses who served groups of patients for whom they planned and provided complete care, hospitals soon organized their nursing services according to the industrial model, employing the so-called functional method of nurse assignment. Nursing care of all patients on a given unit was then divided among registered nurses, practical nurses (called nursing assistants in Canada), and aides, each responsible for specific functions (e.g. taking temperatures, administering treatments, recording). Such functional assignments often prevented nurses from getting to know patients, from appraising their needs properly, fulfilling their nursing requirements, and evaluating the outcome; they brought frustration and discouragement for professionals who sought to fulfil the nurse's role and to derive satisfaction from its execution.

Functional assignments gave way eventually to 'team assignments', with registered nurses ostensibly serving as team leaders responsible for appraising the nursing care requirements of a given group of patients and assigning the nursing care needed to members of the team, made up of other RNs and nursing assistants of various kinds. Team nursing was recommended as making effective use of the (varied) talents of nursing team members, was cost-effective, and permitted professionals to guide and direct the nursing care provided for patients. In fact, shortage of professional nurses meant that non-professional staff were required to serve as team leaders and to give nursing care while the professionals managed the nursing divisions, executed treatments that were ordered for patients, and carried out numerous clerical functions. 'Team' nursing proved to be little better than 'functional' nursing and nurses wishing to give professional service achieved little job satisfaction. Meanwhile, medical procedures and technologies of care were becoming increasingly complex.

Numerous types of *intensive care units (e.g. premature infant care, renal, cardiac, surgical) were developed in order to make effective use of expensive equipment and to provide constant surveillance of patients whose conditions required it. Nurses had to become highly specialized technicians as well as professional care givers; increasingly the phenomenon of mental exhaustion ('burn out') was experienced.

Enlightened nursing administrators reacted by developing plans for professionals to serve a limited number of patients (the number determined by their care needs) as their 'primary' nurse. Under that plan, each patient is assigned a primary nurse whose responsibility it is to appraise his nursing care needs, plan and execute his care, be responsible for it throughout the 24-hour day and throughout his hospital stay, and plan for his discharge. 'Associate' nurses relieve the primary nurse for time off duty, but are required to carry out the plan of care delineated by him/her at all times. Services to the primary nurse are provided by assisting personnel so that professionals can give complete care and derive satisfaction from it. Additionally, clinical specialist nurses are available with whom generalist nursing practitioners can consult in order to give highly sophisticated care. Indeed, grouping of patients makes it possible for highly skilled nursing specialists to give care to patients, to share their expertise with other nurses, and to develop mentor relationships with both students and staff. Studies have shown that primary nursing results in high-quality nursing care for patients, enhances patient satisfaction, reduces nursing staff turnover, and is cost-effective. It is also highly demanding and requires that nurses master a vast range of professional knowledge, that they are highly skilled, and that they are independently accountable for care to the persons they serve, as well as to the institutions in which they work. Clearly, they must receive high quality professional education through which to develop such professional proficiency.

This review of nursing practice shows that the fundamental principles of good nursing practice are now recognized and their benefits are valued; moreover it demonstrates the stability of fundamental objectives of nursing—to promote the health of persons of all ages, sick and essentially well, in order that they will become independent in executing their own health and therapeutic regimens (Kelly, 1981). What has changed with time is the growing groups of persons served, the complexities of their care needs, and the amount of knowledge, skill, and wisdom that nurses must acquire.

Specialization in nursing. Acceleration in the development of nursing specialties has been steady since the mid-1940s. At present, specialist nurses serve as practitioners, consultants, and teachers, giving care to particular populations (e.g. *paediatric, geriatric), persons afflicted with particular diseases and having bodily system disorders (e.g. *oncology, *neurological, *orthopaedic patients), and particular aggregates (e.g. workers needing *occupational health nursing services, families needing nurse-midwifery services).

Regulation of the nursing profession. Nursing practice is regulated in North America through systems which register individual practitioners who have demonstrated eligibility and competence to practice. Such registration procedures are authorized by provincial, territorial, and state laws.

The procedures are different in Canada from those in the USA. With the exception of one province (Ontario) and one territory (Yukon) registration is the statutory responsibility of the provincial and territorial nurses' association whose members also set standards for practice and education, excercise disciplinary sanctions, and approve nursing schools. In Ontario, those responsibilities reside with the College of Nurses of Ontario. The Canadian Nurses' Association is responsible for preparing the nurse registration examination for purchase by the professional societies who administer it and set the passing scores (marks) for the several provinces. Certificates of registration (RN) are renewed annually by payment of a fee, thereby making initial registration by examination a life-long permit to practise, except in some provinces that require proof of recent work experience. Transfer of registration from one locale to another is not difficult, inasmuch as the registration procedure is uniform throughout Canada. In four Canadian jurisdictions, the registration procedure is, in fact, a licence, inasmuch as the laws both define practice (and prevent other than RNs from practising) and protect use of the title 'RN'. In eight jurisdictions, the laws are permissive, protecting only the title.

In the USA, responsibility for setting standards for nursing practice and nursing education, for authorizing nursing schools, and for disciplinary action regarding individual RNs, resides in the several State Boards of Nursing whose members are appointed by each state's chief executive. In most states the majority of members are registered nurses or a combination of registered and practical nurses, serving with lay representatives of the public and members of other health professions. Board members serve for specific staggered terms; sometimes their appointments are made upon recommendations of State Nurses' Associations. Political considerations often determine members of Boards, which vary in size, in composition, and in qualifications specified in the state statutes. Some states have two Nursing Boards to govern practical and professional nurse registration.

Most states allege that they have mandatory laws, a few are still permissive. In fact, the exclusionary clauses and failure to restrict nursing practice to registered nurses make the claim of mandatory laws invalid.

A Council of State Boards (made up of 50 elected presidents and executives appointed by the several board members) is responsible for determining the subject matter about which registered nurses are examined and from which testing agency the examination is purchased. Each State Board sets its own passing score for the examination, determines its procedures for disciplinary action, and selects its means for monitoring and determining the adequacy and currency of practitioners' knowledge and skills.

Numerous modifications have been made in registration procedures and requirements, and in nurse practice acts and regulations that guide practice and education. A few states register 'advanced' practitioners. Variations in the state regulations have tended to make interstate movement of nurses increasingly difficult, even though all registered nurses take the same examination at the time of its annual or twice-yearly administration.

A major change was introduced in nursing in 1965 when in Canada and in the USA there was seen to be an inadequate supply of physicians, particularly in isolated areas and in inner cities, wherein particular populations were under-served in relation to health and medical care. That circumstance provided an opportunity for Ford, a public health nursing academician, and Silver, a medical academic colleague, to introduce an educational programme for nurses that marked the beginning of what is known as the 'nurse-practitioner movement' in the USA.

Ford described the opportunity presented by the paucity of medical services as one in which she sought to test an 'advanced' clinical role for community health nurses in the health care of children. The 'paediatric public health nurse practitioner', as originally envisaged, was to be prepared in a graduate programme of study and was to be competent to make clinical judgements and management plans based upon a health history and a clinical data base. Health appraisals and plans for care were to be based upon information gained through developmental histories, records of past and current health problems, psychosocial appraisals, and physical examinations of persons served. The nurses so prepared were to be independent practitioners, accountable to persons served, colleagues of other health professionals, and exemplars of the nurse-professional's role (Ford, 1982). Some nurses viewed the nurse-practitioner as one who was prepared for and demonstrated a new 'expanded' role for nurses: other nurses saw the functions delineated as those which represent primary nursing care, which has long been an integral part of the nurse-professional's role.

Physicians, in general, envisaged the 'nurse-practitioner' (the title was promptly shortened) as a physician's assistant, responsible to him for practice decisions and outcomes, and a practitioner whose post-registered nurse preparation should be under medical direction and supervision. That misconception led to compromise of the original plan and to the institution of short-term training programmes leading to certificates that were offered under the aegis of medical schools and hospitals, with trainees under the tutelage of physicians, some nurses, and later, nurse-practitioners who had graduated from the early programmes.

Registered nurses who had completed from two to six years of pre-service preparation in nursing and who had varying amounts of nursing experience, were admitted to those programmes, graduated, and were eligible for certification as nurse-practitioners (NPs). Many of those graduates functioned as surrogates for physicians to whom they were responsible, providing primary medical and health care in under-served areas, at the direction of physicians and with their services eligible for reimbursement from third-party payers—if their practices were supervised by physicians. Several studies were reported, comparing physicians and nurse-practitioners with regard to the primary care functions performed, patient outcomes, satisfaction of persons served, and costs and income derived from services. Generally, the studies demonstrated that primary care provided was similar from physicians and from NPs, and that patient satisfaction was comparable; cost and income data demonstrated mixed findings (Jones, 1980). These studies were conducted both in Canada and in the USA.

Federal and private funding for demonstration projects, for training programmes, and for evaluations was available in both Canada and in the USA. In the USA such funding has been a major factor in this sustained 'movement'. Nurse-practitioner programmes operated by nursing schools were originally of two kinds. Relatively short postgraduate programmes of continuing education were open to registered nurses holding associate, baccalaureate, and higher degrees and to those graduated from diploma programmes. They led to the award of certificates and made those who had completed the training eligible for certification as nurse-practitioners. Graduate (specialty) programmes that were operated by nursing schools restricted admissions to registered nurses who fulfilled admission criteria for graduate study in nursing; they led to master's degrees. In general, focus in these programmes was on preparing primary care practitioners and could be in numerous specialties, for example a paediatric nurse-practitioner, geriatric nurse-practitioner, nurse-anaesthetist practitioner. Some such programmes prepared candidates for teaching as well as for practice. Graduates were eligible for certification as nurse-practitioners (DHEW, 1980). Many such graduate programmes continue.

Shortly after the nurse-practitioner movement began, several state boards of nursing in the USA were asked to modify nurse practice laws and to alter practice regulations, as it was alleged that nurse-practitioners' 'expanded role' was not adequately covered under existing legal definitions of nursing practice. It was doubtful if these views were valid, unless nurse-practitioners were independently engaged in making differential medical diagnoses and in prescribing medicaments—functions that are explicitly denied to nurses in several nurse practice laws. In fact, NPs usually function within strict limits under physicians' supervision. None the less, some state boards did effect changes in laws and regulations, sometimes with collaboration from members of medical boards in the same states in order to authorize 'expanded' (not clearly defined) functions. In at least one state, NPs are now authorized to prescribe selected medicaments.

The 'nurse-practitioner movement' did not develop in Canada. Early programmes and related evaluations were funded by the National Department of Health and Welfare, but nurses and physicians have not sought to continue them. Instead, preparation for primary health (nursing) care is routinely a part of all first professional and advanced degree programmes in nursing. Training of nurses who function in the outposts comes under the aegis of the Department of Health and Welfare, with responsibility delegated to faculties at Dalhousie University and the University of Alberta.

In both Canada and in the USA some opposition to nurse-practitioners has been forthcoming from physicians who perceive threats to their traditional responsibility for providing primary medical care, especially since projects indicate that an adequate supply or surplus of physicians will be experienced within the current decade. In the USA, some nurse-midwives, nurse-practitioners, and nurse-anaesthetists have been challenged with respect to the legitimacy and legality of their practices by some medical societies and state medical boards. The challenge is to nurses' right to engage in primary health care. It derives, seemingly, from the perception held by some physicians that primary medical care is, in fact, primary health care and, therefore, the exclusive prerogative of physicians. Nurses in North America generally reject that concept, since the essence of their practice and that for which they are prepared is promotion of the health of those they serve.

Nursing education. Developments in nursing education have been comparable in Canada and in the USA. In both countries, nursing schools were originally operated in accordance with Nightingale's sound educational principles. In both countries, those schools soon became departments of hospitals. Initially they were apprentice training programmes, with meagre, unorganized, and quite incidental didactic preparation being secondary to trainees' work experiences in hospital wards, and sometimes, in patients' homes.

Over the years, hospital-based programmes leading to diplomas have been lengthened and strengthened by raising admission standards for applicants, enhancing faculty qualifications, increasing the amount and scope of the preclinical science content, strengthening the component of nursing science and arts, and establishing affiliations to ensure that students would have well-rounded, clinical programmes. Some schools have established affiliations with colleges whose faculties teach the science courses: some schools have included communication skills and some humanities courses in their curricula. Faculties in many hospital-controlled schools continue to claim that they offer programmes of professional study: others state that they aim to prepare nursing technicians.

Since the numbers of diploma programmes in nursing have been steadily declining in North America, over the past three decades, the propagation of graduates from those schools is also decreasing. The largest proportion of nurses now practising, however, had their initial preparation for nursing in diploma programmes.

In both North American countries, nursing's professional societies have taken the official view that all nursing personnel should be prepared in their respective nation's system of post-secondary education (e.g. universities), rather than in service (e.g. hospital) agencies. In Canada, following a major study of nursing schools in 1930 the report recommended that nursing education should be incorporated into the Canadian system of general education and be subsidized by government funds. In the USA, the first major study of nursing and nursing education was published in 1923; it was then recommended that professionals be prepared in universities. Similar recommendations have emanated from numerous subsequent studies of nursing and nursing education.

In 1946, an experimental nursing education project in Windsor, Ontario, demonstrated that an independent school of nursing could prepare a skilled clinical nurse in two, rather than three years, if the school had control of the learning opportunities provided.

In 1951, Montag demonstrated in the USA that it was possible to prepare nursing technicians capable of carrying out nursing procedures safely and effectively for selected patients, when they have the supervision and surveillance of professionals—in two-year programmes of study operated by community colleges and technical institutes (Montag, 1951). Thereafter, nursing programmes operating under the aegis of those institutions flourished in the USA. They led to associate in arts or associate in science degrees and graduates were eligible to take the examination designed for certifying registered nurses. If successful, they practised as registered nurses.

In 1965 the American Nurses' Association took the official position that the nation's system of education should change—to have the baccalaureate degree representing minimal preparation for entry into professional practice and the associate degree representing minimal preparation for entry into technical nursing practice. That transition is under way, although quite slowly.

Transfer of responsibility for nursing education to Canadian post-secondary institutions began in 1966, in Saskatchewan, when responsibility was vested in the province's department of education, transferred from the department of health. Since then, other provinces have made similar transfers. By 1978, a report demonstrated that only 25 diploma programmes were still operated by hospitals. All others, now two years in length, are operated by post-secondary institutions, including community colleges and technical institutes. Graduates of diploma programmes are eligible for registration and award of the RN certificate upon passing the Canadian examination for registration.

Numerous recommendations made by nursing educators, since the beginning of the current century, have proposed that universities take responsibility for preparing professionals for the field. In 1909, the University of Minnesota opened a basic nursing programme which initially did not lead to an academic degree. The first programme leading to a baccalaureate in nursing degree was offered by the University of Cincinnati, in 1916. In 1919, the University of British Columbia opened Canada's first baccalaureate programme in nursing.

First professional degree programmes in nursing are now offered by colleges and universities in all Canadian provinces and in all of the USA. Most of them are four to five years in length, combine liberal and professional study, and lead to baccalaureate degrees. In Canada, the professional society has endorsed the notion (in 1978) that primary as well as acute and long-term care should be an integral part of all first professional degree programmes in nursing. That society is now developing a statement on minimal educational preparation required for professional nursing practice.

In the USA, concurrence among most major professional nursing societies has been obtained (1982) to the effect that entry into professional nursing practice requires, at a minimum, completion of a programme of professional study leading to a baccalaureate in nursing degree. Since control of nursing and basic nursing education in the USA rests with the several state boards of nursing, it is not known when the US system of nursing education will change to reflect that position. In the interim, nursing service agencies are making changes in their employment practices that may hasten the introduction of that change. Additionally, registered nurses graduated from diploma and associate degree programmes are seeking higher education opportunities and new candidates for nursing education, in increasing proportions, are seeking entry into first professional degree programmes offered by universities. Most of those programmes in both Canada and the USA accommodate registered nurses, or offer programmes designed specifically for them.

In the recent past, several nursing educators have set forth the notion that the relentlessly escalating complexity of nursing practice and the importance of the decisions nurses make and the care they give in primary, acute, and long-term care settings require that nursing practitioners should be mature, well-educated, career-committed, service-oriented persons who are provided with demanding programmes of professional study that are based upon a broad liberal education at college level. Such programmes are now available in both Canada and the USA. For example, McGill University, Province of Quebec, offers a three-year, first professional degree programme in nursing that leads to the M.Sc. (Applied) degree; Case Western Reserve University in Ohio offers a three-year first professional degree programme which culminates in the award of the ND degree.

Nursing preparation at advanced levels, designed to equip nurses for leadership positions, began in 1898 at Teachers' College, Columbia University. That programme offered instruction in pedagogy and in science for the preparation of teachers and in hospital economics and administration for those seeking to become superintendents of nursing. Preparation for clinical specialty nursing practice began when hospitals offered postgraduate courses of a few months' duration. Today, North American nurses receive preparation for specialty nursing practice, teaching, administration, and research in selected universities whose graduate nursing faculties offer programmes leading to master's and doctoral degrees.

In both Canada and the USA, nursing's clinical specialists are prepared through programmes that combine advanced professional science with selected experiences in clinical specialty practice under the tutelage of nursing leaders who are themselves scholars and practitioners. Some, but not all, programmes include graduate preparation in the science and art of education or the science and art of administration. Most clinical specialty programmes lead to the master's degree, although in the USA some doctoral programmes also provide preparation in clinical specialties, in education, and in administration. Although some preparation for scientific enquiry is included in most master's level programmes and some require the completion of an independent study and the preparation of a thesis, it is generally believed that preparation of the independent investigator/scholar requires doctoral study.

Whereas only a few years ago, master's level preparation was looked upon as a terminal degree for nurses, that circumstance no longer prevails. Beginning in the 1950s, nurses in increasing numbers began to seek doctoral degrees. Initially, many or most of them from both Canada and the USA enrolled in programmes in Education leading to Ed.D. and Ph.D. degrees; but it was not long before they enrolled in programmes in the basic disciplines as well. Several funding sources have enhanced nurses' opportunities for such advanced study, thereby quite remarkably and quickly increasing the numbers of nurses who have completed requirements for a variety of doctoral degrees.

During the 1960s and in rapidly accelerating numbers in the 1970s, nursing faculties in the USA were approved for and began offering programmes leading to professional doctorates in nursing (DNS; D.N.Sc.; DSN) and research doctorates (Ph.D.) as well. These programmes have accommodated nurses from Canada and the USA and those from other countries, too. Currently, approximately 25 doctoral programmes in nursing are offered through selected US university graduate schools. Nursing faculties in those programmes offer preparation for specialty nursing practice in a variety of fields, preparation for administration in nursing schools and in health care agencies, and for research in nursing. By far the greatest number of doctoral programmes in nursing lead to Ph.D. degrees.

Plans began in Canada to offer doctoral programmes of study in nursing with a national seminar on the subject, held in 1978. Since then, plans have gone steadily forward and such programmes are in various stages of planning and development. A conjoint doctoral programme in which nurses are enrolled and in which the graduate nursing faculty participates is now operative at the University of Toronto.

This review of developments in nursing education in North America demonstrates the nurse's growing commitment to scholarly endeavours through which to enhance nursing's development as a learned profession and a respected academic discipline.

Research. Although nursing's research direction was set by Florence Nightingale in the mid-1880s, a century passed before significant numbers of North American nurses committed themselves to careers that included scientific enquiry. The profession's need relative to research development was to train a cadre of nurses whose academic preparation would equip and motivate them to engage in systematic enquiry.

Before the 1950s, a few nurses completed doctoral study in the basic disciplines and thereafter, engaged in research. Usually their investigations were designed to advance knowledge in the disciplines in which they had completed doctoral study, rather than to conduct enquiries that would advance nursing knowledge. Nurses who did engage in investigation of nursing problems were primarily those who sought to document nursing's history; to obtain trend data about nursing, nurses, nursing schools, and nursing agencies; to ascertain the relative value of particular nursing procedures (e.g. the efficacy of face masks/various sterilizing procedures in reducing air/equipment contamination); or to review the characteristics of nursing students, practitioners, and leaders. Often those studies were carried out or directed by investigators prepared in disciplines other than nursing. An occasional nurse did, however, design and conduct research that advanced knowledge fundamental to nursing practice. Classic examples are Doris Schwartz's demonstration of the value of nursing care in the reduction of the frequency with which hospitalized patients required sedatives and Gwen T. Wills's documentation of the mutual withdrawal behaviour manifested by hospitalized patients and by hospital staff members who were ostensibly helping them cope with mental health problems.

By the mid 20th c., nursing leaders in Canada and the USA, with the support of their respective professional societies, nursing research advocates in governmental agencies, and faculties in higher education institutions, were successful in obtaining financial support (initially often provided by nurses themselves) to underwrite support of research training for nurses and support of nursing research.

In 1952, nursing's first journal devoted exclusively to publication of research reports (*Nursing Research*) was launched in the USA. Early in the 1960s, the Canadian Nurses' Association transformed its library into a national library service and the library became a repository for nursing archival materials and for reports of nursing research. In both countries, the official journals of the National Nurses' Associations as well as other nursing specialty journals (clinical nursing, nursing administration, and nursing education) increasingly serve as means for communicating findings from nursing investigators' work. In 1968 McGill University's School of Nursing launched a new refereed journal (*Nursing Papers/Perspectives in Nursing*) devoted to publication, in both English and French, of scholarly treatises related to nursing practice, education, administration, and research. Since 1978 three new research journals (*Advances in Nursing Science, Research in Nursing and Health,* and *Western Journal of Nursing Research*) have begun publication in the USA and the official journal of Sigma Theta Tau (*Image*) has devoted its space primarily to reports of scholarly enquiries. All of those journals have increased in size and/or frequency of issues, and in numbers of subscribers, all indicative of the growth in the scholarly productivity and research interests of North American nurses.

In the late 1950s and for the following decade, research development grants, provided on a competitive basis to qualifying university nursing schools in the USA through the Division of Nursing of the United States Public Health Service, made funds available to underwrite projects designed to enhance faculty competence in the conduct of research and to support pilot investigations. Meanwhile, in both Canada and the USA, increasing numbers of nurses enrolled for doctoral study in the basic disciplines (in both countries) and in nursing (in the USA). Fellowships, scholarships, bursaries, and low-interest loans from several sources enlarged the opportunities provided for North American nurses to pursue education at the highest level of scholarship. Many nurses combined full- and part-time employment with full- and part-time study in order to attain their academic goals.

In 1955 the American Nurses' Foundation (ANF) was established to serve as the research arm of the ANA and to receive and award grant funds in support of nursing research. The ANF and the national and local chapters of US nursing's national honour society, Sigma Theta Tau, annually provide research grants on a competitive basis to nursing investigators. In both countries, federal, provincial/state, and some university as well as other local funds are available to nursing investigators who compete with others seeking support for their scholarly endeavours. Although such funds are not always extensive or adequate in amount to underwrite meritorious projects, they have given impetus to the conduct of research by nurses as well as by other members of the scientific community. Nurses have demonstrated their ability to be successful in such competition for research funds.

In the mid-1960s, federal funds became available to selected university schools of nursing in the USA to enlarge opportunities for nurses to study in fulfilment of requirements for Ph.D. degrees in relevant basic disciplines. Those nurse-scientist training grants made it possible for trainees to receive research preparation in a related discipline and at the same time, to continue their involvement in nursing. The ultimate goal was to have those trainees investigate nursing problems, advance knowledge of particular relevance to nurses, and following their academic preparation, make their professional/scholarly contributions to nursing as a developing academic discipline.

Prior to termination of the nurse-scientist grant mechanism, several universities had developed doctoral programmes in nursing in the USA. In 1978 Canadian nurses, with sponsorship of the Canadian Nurses' Association, the Canadian Nurses' Foundation, and the Canadian Association of University Schools of Nursing, and with funds provided by the W. K. Kellogg Foundation, conducted a national seminar on doctoral preparation

for Canadian nurses. That seminar, and an earlier one held in the USA under sponsorship of the Division of Nursing of the United States Public Health Service, provided opportunities for North American nurses to address and resolve some important issues concerning preparation of nursing research workers and to set directions for the future. There is little question that Canadian universities will support the development of doctoral programmes in nursing, just as have universities in the USA. Currently, one conjoint programme is operative and another is being developed.

Nursing research is flourishing in Canada as well as in the USA. Support for research derives from federal, provincial, and local sources. At the national level, nursing investigators compete for funds available through the National Health Research Development Program and the Canadian Nurses' Foundation. At the provincial level, funding amounts are variable, but since 1980 have been available in British Columbia, Manitoba, Ontario, and Saskatchewan. In 1982, by Ministerial Order, the Alberta Foundation for Nursing Research was created, with public funding of 1 000 000 dollars (over a five-year period) to support nursing research in Alberta. The Foundation is administered by a Board of Directors of nurses and lay people responsible for developing research priorities and mechanisms for awarding grants. Foundations and voluntary organizations in Canada, as in the USA, provide funds in support of nursing research (Canadian Nurses' Association, 1981).

Professional nursing societies in both North American countries, regional nursing organizations, honour societies, and selected research-orientated university nursing schools now regularly sponsor research conferences. Additionally, several university schools of nursing have developed research centres and institutes in which faculty and pre- and post-doctoral students work together in the design and conduct of nursing investigations. By the late 1970s specific university centres were becoming known for the research interests and productivity of their associated scientists, theorists, and philosophers. In several, perhaps most, of those research centres, nursing investigators collaborate with other nursing scholars as well as with scholars in other disciplines in the conduct of research in which they have a mutual and complementary interest.

In Canada and in the USA there are growing numbers of health care agencies that are supportive of nursing as well as medical research and in some of them, nursing and medical investigators are colleagues in the design and conduct of investigations. The nature of such research is diverse.

A small group of nursing scholars have developed paradigms and conceptual frameworks that give focus to nursing investigations and are of heuristic value in the generation of promising hypothetical and theoretical notions about phenomena that are of particular concern to nurses. Several have produced articles and books dealing with concept clarification, theory development, and research design; others have designed, developed, tested, and demonstrated the utility, validity, and reliability of new research instruments.

In sum, within the past three decades nursing research and nursing's scholarly productivity in North America have grown quite remarkably in both quantity and quality. In contrast, it has taken more than a century for nursing to emerge through the stages of being a craft, a vocation, essentially a technology, and finally, a full-fledged profession. Nursing, in the 1980s, is becoming recognized in North America as a primary health profession and a bona fide academic discipline.

ROZELLA M. SCHLOTFELDT

References

Canadian Nurses' Association (1968). *The Leaf and the Lamp*. Ottawa.

Canadian Nurses' Association (1981). *The Development of Nursing Research in Canada: A Background Paper*. Ottawa.

DHEW Publication No. HRA80-2 (1980). *Longitudinal Study of Nurse Practitioners III*. Hyattsville, Maryland.

Diers, D. (1982). Future of nurse-midwives in American health care. In Aiken, L. (ed.), *Nursing in the 1980s*, 267–94. Philadelphia.

Ford, L. (1982). The contributions of nurse practitioners to American health care. In Aiken, L. (ed.), *Nursing in the 1980s*, 231–47. Philadelphia.

Kalish, P. and Kalish, B. (1978). *The Advance of American Nursing*. Boston.

Kelly, L. (1981). *Dimensions of Professional Nursing*. 4th edn, New York.

Jones, P. (1980). *Nurses in Canadian Primary Health Care Settings*. Toronto.

Montag, M. (1951). *The Education of Nursing Technicians*. New York.

New York Academy of Medicine (1933). *Maternal Mortality in New York City*. New York.

Nightingale, F. (1860). *Notes on Nursing*. London.

NUTRITION

The scope of nutrition. The subject of nutrition deals with biological processes whereby an organism ingests, digests, absorbs, transports, utilizes, stores, or otherwise disposes of food substances in health and disease. These processes involve phenomena of catabolism (degradation), anabolism (synthesis and transformation), detoxification, and excretion of constituents of foods (including beverages). They generate energy essential for maintaining basic physiological functions, physical activity, and temperature regulation; they replace and repair tissues and sustain growth, including that occurring during the reproductive interlude of pregnancy and *lactation.

All materials, except molecular *oxygen, required for these functions are normally provided by ingested foodstuffs, including the building blocks (or their precursors) of *tissues, *hormones, *enzymes, and other metabolic regulators. Those entities of which sufficient quantities cannot be biosynthesized by the organism to sustain these biological processes must be exogenously supplied. They are recognized as 'essential nutrients', e.g. essential *amino acids, essential *fatty acids, essential inorganic elements (including '*trace elements'), water, and sources of *energy. The macronutrients (*fat, *carbohydrate, *alcohol, and *protein) are the sources of energy.

Foodstuffs contain countless chemically identifiable substances other than nutrients which may or may not have biological significance for the consuming organism. Such naturally occurring substances range from pigments to pharmacologically active constituents such as *goitrogens, *oestrogens, lathyrogens (see LATHYRISM), *haemagglutinins, *stimulants and depressants, antienzymes, natural *radioactivity, and a host of other 'naturally occurring toxicants', to inert non-digestible residues. They include those important compounds that excite the chemical senses of taste and smell as well as incidental products of plant and animal metabolism or of processing (e.g. congeners in fermented beverages). Most of these are present in such trace amounts that they are identifiable only by highly sensitive analytical techniques. Foods are infinitely more complex in content and biological effect than the precisely compounded simple mixtures of relatively pure nutrients that constitute the solutions often used in hospital for *total parenteral nutrition (TPN).

The complexity of substances ingested as food is compounded by the cultural and sociopsychological, even political, influences that determine the acceptability of particular foods within a society and an individual's 'likes or dislikes'. Too often the public confuses the science of nutrition with the diverse circumstances or events—economic, technological, political, climatic, geographical, etc.— that determine availability or acceptability of foodstuffs.

Similarly, there frequently is but limited professional comprehension of the scientific scope of nutrition because of preoccupation with a particular medical need—feeding the infant, especially those born prematurely, the patient with an *inborn error of metabolism, *obesity, hyperlipidaemia (i.e. excess *lipid in the blood), *hypertension, a *malabsorption syndrome or a surgically compromised gastrointestinal absorptive capacity, as when a portion of the stomach or intestine is removed, *nephrectomy, and so on. Successful management of any of these over a long period demands knowledge and appreciation of the multiple biological aspects of foods and of the quantitative nutrient requirements of the individual.

The nature of nutritional diseases. Diseases of which the aetiologies are most directly relatable to foods are those due to deficient or excessive intakes or those due to food-contained *toxins. Early medical observers recognized these relationships of food to disease, sometimes with seemingly intuitive perception. Thus *Hippocrates, whom *Garrison regarded as 'the greatest of all physicians', wrote:

Growing bodies have the most innate heat; they therefore require the most food, for otherwise their bodies are wasted. In older persons the heat is feeble, and they therefore require little fuel, as it were, to the flame, for it would be extinguished by much.

Persons who are naturally very fat are apt to die earlier than those who are slender.

. . . but then it is no less mistake, nor one that injures a man less, provided a deficient diet, or one consisted of weaker things, than what are proper, be administered. For, in the constitution of man, abstinence may enervate, weaken and kill. And there are many other ills, different from those of repletion, but no less dreadful, arising from deficiency of food . . .

*Celsus, in the first Latin treatise on medicine, *De re medicina*, devoted four of his eight books to diseases treated by diet and regimen. He introduced the subject of food with

. . . we come to those which nourish, namely food and drink. Now these are of general assistance not only in diseases of all kinds but in preserving health as well, and an acquaintance with the properties of all is of importance, in the first place that those in health may know how to make use of them, then as we follow on to the treatment of diseases, we can state the species of aliments to be consumed. . . .

Malnutrition and deficiency diseases. Diseases of various aetiologies may be (and often are) nutrition-related or altered by diet. Those syndromes for which factors relating to the quality or quantity of foodstuffs are either causative or curative are properly regarded as diseases of malnutrition (i.e. bad or faulty nutrition). Subjects who are malnourished may show signs of gross underfeeding (*starvation, as in famine), of lack of a specific essential dietary nutrient (as in the classic deficiency syndromes of *scurvy, *pellagra, or *beriberi), of ingestion of grossly excessive quantities of some nutrient (energy: obesity; *carotene: yellowing of the skin; *fluorine: mottled enamel; *vitamin D: abnormal calcification). Ingestion of unusual amounts of food substances that contain a naturally occurring toxic constituent may produce a food-related disease such as lathyrism, a crippling paralysis of the lower limbs due to consumption of the seeds of *Lathyrus sativus* during periods of famine. Such food-related toxic syndromes and other types of food-related diseases, including unusual reactions to foods, and the property of some essential food constituents as 'risk factors' for individuals with predisposition to particular diseases, are not considered to be primarily states of malnutrition, certainly not deficiency diseases. They may under certain circumstances lead to malnutrition. Food-carried bacterial infections or *parasitic infestations or *mycotoxins, although food-related, are problems of food sanitation or hygiene.

Deficiency diseases may be of simple dietary origin resulting from omission from the diet of foodstuffs that are sources of an essential nutrient. Thus, failure to eat fruits and vegetables, major sources of *vitamin C, can result in scurvy. Deficiency diseases may also be conditioned in pathogenesis, that is they may result from some abnormality that renders unavailable a nutrient that is consumed in the diet or from an abnormality that greatly increases the amount of the nutrient required by the individual. Various medical abnormalities may decrease the absorption of a nutrient from the gastrointestinal tract. Pathological processes that decrease the absorption of fat also alter the absorption of fat-soluble factors and may result in manifest deficiencies of fat-soluble vitamins such as *vitamin A, vitamin D, or *vitamin K. *Pernicious *anaemia results from failure of the gastric mucosa to secrete the '*intrinsic factor' which is necessary for absorption of vitamin B_{12} from the gastrointestinal tract; hence, vitamin B_{12} ingested in the food is unabsorbed and the individual becomes deficient, manifesting anaemia and other evidences of vitamin B_{12} deficiency. A deficiency of this vitamin may also result from a strictly *vegetarian diet because vitamin B_{12} is supplied by animal foodstuffs. In such instances the deficiency is one of simple dietary lack. A common example of an increased requirement of an essential nutrient is that of *iron due to the chronic excessive loss of blood through gastrointestinal bleeding or *menorrhagia. The resulting loss of iron (as *haemoglobin) in the red blood cells may increase the requirement beyond the level that can be obtained from the usual diet meeting the Recommended Dietary Allowances. Emotional or psychiatrically based disturbances (e.g. *anorexia nervosa, *bulimia, food phobias) may also result in malnutrition.

Many of the classic deficiency diseases were recognized earlier by physicians as being food-related. The specific nutrients, a lack of which causes the syndromes have, however, been identified only during the 20th c. In some instances (e.g. *iodine and endemic *goitre; iron in *chlorosis or anaemia) the therapeutic value of the missing substance was known prior to appreciation of the aetiological relationship to dietary intake. Evidence for direct relationship between a particular nutrient and a deficiency syndrome has gradually evolved, sometimes through the study of the foods known to be related to the syndrome in man (vitamin C), sometimes from the study of the chemical content of human tissues (iodine), and in some instances from observations or experiments initially in lower animals and later identification of a corresponding syndrome in the human (vitamin K). In all instances, the elucidation of the nature of the essential nutrient and of its metabolic role(s) have depended heavily upon experimental studies in laboratory animals at some stage of developing knowledge.

Current understanding of malnutrition makes possible accurate clinical diagnoses, including identification of specific nutrient deficiencies through laboratory procedures. The most widely recognized well-established syndromes of malnutrition and their characteristic features are summarized in Table 1.

Table 1. Characteristic features of well-recognized vitamin or mineral deficiency diseases

Deficiency disease	Nutrient deficient	Clinical characteristics
Scurvy	Vitamin C (ascorbic acid)	Perifollicular petechiae; swollen, red gums that bleed easily; lassitude, general weakness; haemorrhage in the joints; loosening of the teeth; plasma vitamin C virtually undetectable.
Beriberi	Vitamin B_1 (thiamine)	Peripheral neuritis; loss of deep tendon reflexes (especially lower extremities); oedema; cardiac enlargement (right-sided); bradycardia; increased pulse pressure; low erythrocyte transketolase activity; low urinary thiamine.
Wernicke–Korsakoff syndrome	Vitamin B_1	History of alcoholism; disorientation, confusion; ataxia, severe loss of memory; confabulation; abnormally low erythrocyte transketolase.
Ariboflavinosis	Riboflavin	Lesions at corners of mouth (angular stomatitis or cheilosis); photophobia with pericorneal injection; seborrhoeic dermatitis; glossitis; increased *in vitro* stimulation of erythrocyte glutathione reductase activity by flavin adenine dinucleotide.
Pellagra	Niacin (nicotinic acid, nicotinamide) (or the precursor amino acid, tryptophan)	Symmetrical dermatitis of exposed surfaces of hands, arms, lower extremities, face, and neck; diarrhoea; glossitis, anxiety, hallucinations, dementia; low urinary N-methyl-nicotinamide.
Tropical sprue Macrocytic anaemia of infants Pernicious anaemia of pregnancy	Folic acid	Steatorrhea (sprue); glossitis; macrocytic anaemia; weakness; weight-loss, debility; low levels of folate in blood serum and erythrocytes.
Anaemia of vegetarians	Vitamin B_{12}	History of strict vegetarianism; weakness; macrocytic anaemia; glossitis; megaloblastic changes in bone marrow; low levels of serum vitamin B_{12}.
Pernicious anaemia	Conditioned deficiency of vitamin B_{12}	Macrocytic anaemia; megaloblastic marrow; glossitis; peripheral neuritis; evidence of spinal cord degeneration; atrophy of gastric mucosa; gastric achlorhydria; lack of gastric 'intrinsic' factor and decreased absorption of labelled vitamin B_{12}; low levels of serum vitamin B_{12}.
Convulsive seizures in infants	Vitamin B_6 (pyridoxine, pyridoxal, pyridoxamine)	Convulsive seizures in infants; convulsions in deprived adults; neuropathy of lower extremities in older subjects under treatment with isoniazid; cheilosis and seborrhoeic dermatitis; low levels of pyridoxal phosphate in plasma or whole blood.
Xerophthalmia	Vitamin A (retinol; precursor, carotene)	Night blindness; corneal dryness, dullness; corneal ulceration, degeneration, perforation; conjunctival Bitot spots; blindness; low serum vitamin A levels; defective dark adaptation.
Rickets and oesteomalacia	Vitamin D (various forms; exposure to ultraviolet irradiation sunlight)	Defective calcification of bones; enlarged epiphyses with uncalcified cartilage; enlargement (beading) of costochondral junction of ribs; bowing of legs in young children; in adults bone deformations due to softening and stress; pseudo-fractures; characteristic changes in bones on X-ray; elevated alkaline phosphatase activity and low concentration of 25-OH-D in plasma.
Hypoprothrombinaemia (haemorrhagic disease of the newborn; hypoprothrombinaemia associated with biliary obstruction or malabsorption)	Vitamin K	Haemorrhagic tendency, bleeding; low level of prothrombin in plasma; prolonged blood clotting time; in adults associated with defective gastrointestinal absorption (biliary obstruction, sprue, other cause of steatorrhoea, or liver disease) or with anticoagulant therapy.

Deficiency disease	Nutrient deficient	Clinical characteristics
Microcytic hypochromic anaemia	Iron	Lassitude, weakness, pallor, other general symptoms of anaemias; history of diet deficient in iron in infants and children; in adults usually associated with chronic blood loss; low blood haemoglobin; red blood cells pale, small, low in haemoglobin; low level of iron in serum, increased levels of iron-binding protein transferrin.
Dwarfism, sexual infantilism of adolescence	Zinc	Growth failure; delayed sexual maturation of adolescents; impairment of wound healing; low levels of zinc in plasma and in red blood cells.
Acrodermatitis enteropathica	Genetically conditioned zinc deficiency	In weanling infants; severe skin rash around body orifices; diarrhoea; failure to thrive; skin infections; death; responds to zinc or zinc picolinate.
Endemic goitre	Iodine	Enlargement and hypertrophy of the thyroid gland; usual onset girls 12–18 years, boys 9–13 years of age; endemic in iodine-deficient geographic areas; persists throughout life; secondary thyrotoxicosis may develop as may carcinoma; low urinary excretion of iodine; increased uptake of labelled iodine by thyroid.
Cretinism	Iodine	In endemic goitre areas; iodine-deficient mothers may produce offspring who are mentally retarded, becoming dwarfed, with empty, expressionless faces, saddle nosed, with widely set eyes, drooling, open mouth, with or without thyroid enlargement.

Scientific delineation of nutritional requirements. It is not surprising in retrospect that the simple dietary deficiency, scurvy, was early noted to be food-related. Signs of scurvy appear after from 6 weeks to 3 months of depletion, and vanish dramatically following administration of an antiscorbutic food.

Many early writers convincingly recorded the efficacy of vegetables, fresh fruits, especially berries, cherries, oranges, lemons, as antiscorbutics. In *The Surgeon's Mate*, the first text for ship surgeons on long oceanic voyages (1617) John *Woodall emphasized the role of antiscorbutic foods in the cure and prevention of scurvy. He wrote:

> . . . The use of the juice of lemons is a precious medicine and well tried, being sound and good, let it have the chief place, for it will deserve it . . .

Bachstrom in 1734 observed

> . . . and where a person, either through neglect or necessity, do refrain for a considerable time from eating the fresh fruits of the earth, and greens, no age, no climate or soil are exempt from its [scurvy] attack.

He thus set forth the deficiency nature of scurvy, even rating the efficacy of antiscorbutics: fruits most efficacious and roots and fresh herbs less so. The subsequent publication, however, of *Lind's treatise on the scurvy (1753) was a landmark in both experimental nutrition and clinical investigation. Lind's remarkable literature review, his nicety of experimental design, clarity and acuteness of recorded observations with unerring correctness of interpretative conclusions combined to produce a classic treatise that deserves to be considered as initiating the modern scientific era of

nutrition and of clinical investigation (see NAVY, ROYAL: MEDICAL SERVICES).

The direct aetiological role of food in some diseases gradually came to be appreciated. The state of knowledge a century ago was well summarized by Hirsch (1885). He grouped together as 'chronic disorders of nutrition' chlorosis, scurvy, beriberi—all now clearly established deficiency syndromes—but was understandably ambivalent as to the aetiological role of diet in *diabetes and *gout. Some examples of significant discoveries are chronologically listed in Table 2. Only within the present century has it been possible chemically to identify most essential nutrients, a deficiency of which produce diseases.

Table 2. Chronology of some events in the development and application of the science of nutrition

c. 25 AD. *Celsus, in the first Latin treatise on medicine classified foodstuffs and emphasized their role in maintaining health.

1542. A Dyetary of Health by Andrew *Boorde, one of the first publications in English, described factors affecting the health of man and the part played by diet.

1554. Chlorosis described by Johann Lange.

1611. *Woodall, in *Surgeon's Mate,* recommended citrus fruit for protection against scurvy on sea voyages.

1614. Sanctorius (see SANTORIO) published his studies of body weight, food, and excreta; first metabolic balance studies.

1642. Beriberi described by Jacob Bontius, in posthumous publication of his notebooks.

1645. Rickets described by Daniel Whistler; *Inaugural Medical Disputation on the Children's Disease of the English which the inhabitants idiomatically call The Ricketts,* published in Latin at Leiden.

1650. Classic description of rickets made by Francis *Glisson: *De rachitide* (English translation, 1651).

Table 2 (*cont.*)

1652. First coffee house opened in London; tea and chocolate introduced. Garden for vegetables and a hospital established at the Cape of Good Hope for protection of sailors from scurvy.

1730. Pellagra described by Gaspar Casal and called 'mal de la rosa'.

1734. Bachstrom coined the term 'antiscorbutic'.

1747. First controlled human dietary experiment by James Lind showed citrus fruits cured scurvy.

1753. Publication of treatise on scurvy by James Lind.

1770. William Stark died as a result of dietary experiments ments on himself.

1771. Frapolli described and named pellagra. *Spallanzani began experiments of digestion in animals and man.

1772–5. Sailors on historic voyages with Captain James Cook remained free from scurvy.

1780. Spallanzani provided experimental evidence that digestion was not fermentation but was chemical action of gastric juice. First patent granted for drying vegetables.

1789. First measurements of human energy metabolism by respiration made by *Lavoisier and Seguin.

1796. Lemon juice officially introduced in British Navy as a prophylactic against scurvy. *Jenner introduced vaccination against smallpox.

1803. Gastric digestion shown to be a chemical process by J. R. Young (Pennsylvania).

1810–23. Chemistry of animal fats investigated by Chevreul.

1810. Cystic oxide (later named cystine) isolated from urinary calculus by *Wollaston; first amino acid discovered. Maize believed cause of pellagra according to Marzari. Nicholas Appert patented his process for canning food.

1814. Fats shown to be composed of fatty acids and glycerol (Chevreul).

1816. Nitrogen-containing compounds shown by *Magendie to be essential in the diet of dogs.

1821. First chemical analysis of an American food (Indian corn, maize) published by John Gorham of Harvard University. Scientific principles of cookery established by Fredrick Accum, chemist, in his book *Culinary Chemistry*. First canning factory established in USA (Underwood in Boston).

1833. Experiments and Observations on the Gastric Juice and the Physiology of Digestion by William B. *Beaumont reported 238 observations and experiments on Alexis St Martin.

1834. Patent for ice-making machine issued to Jacob Perkins.

1835. Beriberi described in a treatise by John Grant Malcolmson.

1838. 'Protein' introduced as a term by Mulder (at the suggestion of Berzelius).

1839. First nitrogen balance studies in animals (cow and horse) made by Boussingault.

1840. Exophthalmic goitre described by *Basedow.

1849. Pernicious anaemia described by *Addison.

1850–2. Iodine used for goitre prophylaxis by Chatin in France.

1854. Difference in nutritive value of proteins (cereal seeds and legumes) shown by Lawes and Gilbert at Rothamsted, England.

1853–6. Florence *Nightingale fed sick soldiers during Crimean War.

1857. Relationship between nitrogen excretion and protein intake demonstrated by *Voit.

1861. Calorimeter for measurement of basal metabolism built by *Pettenkofer and Voit.

1862. Minimum dietary standards for survival of the unemployed poor prepared by Edward Smith for the Privy Council of England.

1863. Nitrogen metabolism investigated by W. S. Savory using rats as laboratory experimental animals.

1867. Iron believed to be a dietary essential by Boussingault; he analysed food for iron and calculated iron content of diets.

1875. Infantile scurvy described by Cheadle.

1876. Concept of essential amino acids introduced by Th. Escher.

1877. *Pavlov began classic studies on digestion in dogs.

1880. Lunin in Bunge's laboratory showed mice failed to survive on purified diet (synthetic milk diet).

1883. Heat production per unit of body surface area shown to be the same for all warm-blooded animals (Rubner). Scurvy in infants distinguished from rickets and treated by fruit juice, potato, and fresh meat juice by *Barlow.

1885. Large-scale controlled dietary experiments in the diet of sailors of the Japanese navy by K. Takaki prevented beriberi.

1889. Milk found deficient in iron by Bunge.

1890. Geographic distribution of rickets found by Palm to be related to amount of sunlight.

1894. Law of conservation of energy demonstrated by Rubner to be true in nutrition. US Congress appropriated $10 000 for investigation of nutritive value of human foods by US Department of Agriculture. The Pennsylvania Hospital hired its first dietitian.

1895. Iodine discovered in the thyroid gland by Baumann.

1896. Publication of *Chemical Composition of American Food Materials* by *Atwater and Bryant, USDA Bulletin 28 (revised many times), the basic reference on food composition for 44 years.

1897. *Eijkman published his work on causes of beriberi.

1902. Alkaptonuria identified as a hereditary disease of metabolism by Archibald *Garrod. Pellagra reported in the USA. The term dietitian began to be used in hospitals.

1904. Atwater and *Benedict designed a respiration calorimeter for human nutrition studies.

1906. Identification of tryptophan as an essential amino acid made by *Hopkins and Willcock. Concept of unknown accessory food factors introduced by F. G. Hopkins. Experimental evidence showed that differences in nutritive value of proteins are related to amino acid composition. Pure Food and Drug Act passed by US Congress largely through efforts of Harvey W. Wiley.

1907. Scurvy produced in guinea pigs by experimental diet by Holst and Frölich.

1909. Inborn Errors of Metabolism published by Archibald Garrod. Karl Thomas introduced the term 'biological value of proteins' and developed a method for its determination.

1910. Goitre in trout prevented by iodine (Marine and Lenhart).

1912. Funk coined the term 'vitamine'.

1913. Discovery of a fat-soluble accessory food factor.

1914. *Goldberger assigned to study pellagra by US Public Health Service.

1916. 'Fat-soluble A' and 'water-soluble B' were names given to accessory factors discovered by McCollum and Davis, and Osborne and Mendel.

1917. Marine and Kimball demonstrated prophylactic value of iodine for simple goitre in schoolchildren.

1918. Experimental rickets in dogs shown by E. *Mellanby to be due to lack of a fat-soluble vitamin.

1919. Rickets cured by exposure to quartz mercury vapour lamp (Huldchinsky).

1919–22. Water-soluble B factor shown to be more than one factor.

1920. 'Vitamine' changed to 'vitamin' on the recommendation of Drummond. *Whipple demonstrated haemoglobin regeneration in dogs fed raw liver. Vitamin A activity of carotenoids demonstrated by Steenbock.

1921–4. Blindness in children shown to be result of lack of vitamin A.

1921. Alfred Hess treated rickets by exposure to sunlight.

1922–4. Vitamin E discovered by Evans and Bishop.

1922. McCollum identified vitamin D in cod-liver oil. Methionine discovered by Mueller.

1924. Iodization of table salt begun in Michigan. Antirachitic properties in food produced by irradiation; discovered independently by A. Hess and H. Steenbock.

1926. Crystals of vitamin B_1 isolated by Jansen and Donath. *Minot and Murphy successfully used liver (in large daily amounts) in treatment of pernicious anaemia.

1928. Goitrogenic effect of cabbage demonstrated in rabbits. Synthesis of vitamin B found in rumen of cow. Hexuronic acid isolated from adrenal cortex by Szent-Gyorgyi. Copper found to be essential for haemoglobin regeneration in rats. Black tongue produced experimentally in dogs and shown to be similar to human pellagra.

1929. Polyunsaturated fatty acids, linoleic and linolenic acids, found essential for rat growth by Burr. Castle showed that beef contained an 'extrinsic factor' and normal gastric juice an 'intrinsic factor' which given together caused red blood cell formation in pernicious anaemia patients.

1930. Conversion of carotene to vitamin A *in vivo* demonstrated by T. Moore.

1931. Manganese and magnesium shown to be essential nutrients for the rat. High fluorine content of drinking water identified as cause of mottled enamel of teeth. Anaemia factor postulated by Wills when megaloblastic anaemia of pregnancy responded to liver or yeast extracts.

1932. Crystalline vitamin C prepared from lemon juice by King and Waugh. Crystalline vitamin D, calciferol, prepared. The first flavoprotein discovered by *Warburg.

1933–9. Pantothenic acid identified and isolated.

1933. *Kwashiorkor identified as a nutritional disease by Cicely Williams in Africa. Riboflavin identified as part of vitamin B_2 and isolated as pure yellow crystals from milk. Titration with 2,6-dichlorophenolindophenol developed by Tillmans for quantitative determination of vitamin C.

1934. Dynamic state of body fats demonstrated by use of deuterium incorporated into fatty acids and fed to mice (Schoenheimer). *Phenylketonuria discovered by Asbjorn Folling of Oslo. Rat *acrodynia factor named vitamin B_6. Zinc found to be an essential nutrient for rats. Vitamin K discovered by Dam of Copenhagen.

1935. Threonine discovered as an essential dietary amino acid.

1936. Thiamine synthesized by Williams and Cline. Pure vitamin E isolated from unsaponifiable fraction of wheat germ oil and named tocopherol.

1937. Nicotinic acid identified by Elvehjem and co-workers as the curative factor for the black tongue in dogs.

1938. Vitamin B_6 obtained in crystalline form. Absorption of iron shown to be dependent on need, and iron stores regulated by intake (McCance and Widdowson). Classification of amino acids as essential and non-essential by W. C. Rose. First description of riboflavin deficiency in man made by Sebrell. Tryptophan found to be effective in preventing pellagra in swine. Radioactive iron used in haemoglobin-regeneration studies by Whip-

ple. Curative factor for nutritional anaemia of monkey designated as vitamin M by Day *et al.*

1939. *Choline shown to be a lipotropic factor.

1940. Classic experiment on development of scurvy in man on a vitamin C-free diet performed by Crandon and Lund.

1941. Folic acid proposed as term for a growth factor for bacteria by Mitchell, Snell, and R. J. Williams. First standards for enrichment of wheat flour established in USA; modified in 1943. First table of Recommended Dietary Allowances prepared by the Food and Nutrition Committee of the National Research Council, USA.

1944–6. Ancel Keys and co-workers performed classic studies on effects on young men of experimentally induced semi-starvation and methods of dietary rehabilitation.

1945. Pteroylglutamic acid synthesized.

1947–9. Evidence found for conversion of tryptophan to niacin in man.

1947. Vitamin B_{12} identified.

1948–9. Crystalline vitamin B_{12} isolated from liver concentrates and shown to contain cobalt.

1948. Fluoridation of some community water supplies began in USA.

1953. Molybdenum found in the essential enzyme, xanthine dehydrogenase. Vitamin B_6 shown to be essential for infants.

1954–5. Amino acid requirements of young men determined by W. C. Rose

1955. Parakeratosis identified as zinc deficiency. Low phenylalanine diets used in treatment of phenylketonuria. Ubiquinone, or coenzyme Q, isolated. Vitamin B_{12} structure determined and named cyanocobalamin. Phenylalanine and threonine requirement of infants determined. Diets devoid of wheat *gluten gave favourable response in coeliac disease. Thyroidal uptake of ^{131}I used to detect subclinical iodine deficiency states.

1956. Quantitative amino acid requirements of young women determined by Leverton.

1957. Selenium demonstrated to be an essential trace element for warm-blooded animals.

1959. Chromium, trivalent form, found to be an essential trace element for man.

1963. Zinc deficiency in man reported by Prasad and others.

1968. 25-hydroxycholecalciferol identified by DeLuca as an active metabolic form of vitamin D_3.

1971. 1,25-dihydroxycholecalciferol isolated as a metabolically active form of vitamin D_3 and showed hormone-like action.

1973. Deficiency of carnitine associated with lipid storage myopathy.

1975. Retinal degeneration associated with taurine deficiency in cats.

1979. Selenium reported effective in preventing Keshan disease.

Source: Adapted from E. Neige Todhunter (1976), *Nutrition Reviews,* **34,** (12) 353–65.

Knowledge of human requirements is now sufficient that purified formulations of nutrients can confidently be prepared for indefinite maintenance of individuals, even though there remains uncertainty concerning the exact quantitative requirements of some essentials, especially those more recently demonstrated essential nutrients required in only micro-micro quantities, e.g. selenium (Se) and chromium (Cr). For practical planning one does not aim simply to fulfil the

Table 3. Food and Nutrition Board, National Academy of Sciences–National Research Council Recommended Daily Dietary Allowances[a] (Revised 1980). Designed for the maintenance of good nutrition of practically all healthy people in the USA

	Age (years)	Weight (kg)	(lb)	Height (cm)	(in)	Protein (g)	Water-soluble vitamins						
							Vita-min C (mg)	Thia-min (mg)	Ribo-flavin (mg)	Niacin (mg NE)[b]	Vita-min B$_6$ (mg)	Fola-cin (μg)[c]	Vita-min B$_{12}$ (μg)[d]
Infants	0.0–0.5	6	13	61	24	kg×2.2	35	0.3	0.4	6	0.3	30	0.5
	0.5–1.0	9	20	71	28	kg×2.0	35	0.5	0.6	8	0.6	45	1.5
Children	1–3	13	29	90	35	23	45	0.7	0.8	9	0.9	100	2.0
	4–6	20	44	112	44	30	45	0.9	1.0	11	1.3	200	2.5
	7–10	28	62	132	52	34	45	1.2	1.4	16	1.6	300	3.0
Males	11–14	45	99	157	62	45	50	1.4	1.6	18	1.8	400	3.0
	15–18	66	145	176	69	56	60	1.4	1.7	18	2.0	400	3.0
	19–22	70	154	178	70	56	60	1.5	1.7	19	2.2	400	3.0
	23–50	70	154	178	70	56	60	1.4	1.6	18	2.2	400	3.0
	51+	70	154	178	70	56	60	1.2	1.4	16	2.2	400	3.0
Females	11–14	46	101	157	62	46	50	1.1	1.3	15	1.8	400	3.0
	15–18	55	120	163	64	46	60	1.1	1.3	14	2.0	400	3.0
	19–22	55	120	163	64	44	60	1.1	1.3	14	2.0	400	3.0
	23–50	55	120	163	64	44	60	1.0	1.2	13	2.0	400	3.0
	51+	55	120	163	64	44	60	1.0	1.2	13	2.0	400	3.0
Pregnant						+30	+20	+0.4	+0.3	+2	+0.6	+400	+1.0
Lactating						+20	+40	+0.5	+0.5	+5	+0.5	+100	+1.0

		Fat-soluble vitamins			Minerals					
		Vita-min A (μg RE)[e]	Vita-min D (μg)[f]	Vita-min E (mg α-TE)[g]	Cal-cium (mg)	Phos-phorus (mg)	Mag-nesium (mg)	Iron (mg)	Zinc (mg)	Iodine (μg)
Infants	0.0–0.5	420	10	3	360	240	50	10	3	40
	0.5–1.0	400	10	4	540	360	70	15	5	50
Children	1–3	400	10	5	800	800	150	15	10	70
	4–6	500	10	6	800	800	200	10	10	90
	7–10	700	10	7	800	800	250	10	10	120
Males	11–14	1000	10	8	1200	1200	350	18	15	150
	15–18	1000	10	10	1200	1200	400	18	15	150
	19–22	1000	7.5	10	800	800	350	10	15	150
	23–50	1000	5	10	800	800	350	10	15	150
	51+	1000	5	10	800	800	350	10	15	150
Females	11–14	800	10	8	1200	1200	300	18	15	150
	15–18	800	10	8	1200	1200	300	18	15	150
	19–22	800	7.5	8	800	800	300	18	15	150
	23–50	800	5	8	800	800	300	18	15	150
	51+	800	5	8	800	800	300	10	15	150
Pregnant		+200	+5	+2	+400	+400	+150	h	+5	+25
Lactating		+400	+5	+3	+400	+400	+150	h	+10	+50

[a] The allowances are intended to provide for individual variations among most normal persons as they live in the United States under usual environmental stresses. Diets should be based on a variety of common foods in order to provide other nutrients for which human requirements have been less well defined.

[b] 1 NE (niacin equivalent) is equal to 1 mg of niacin or 60 mg of dietary tryptophan.

[c] The folacin allowances refer to dietary sources as determined by *Lactobacillus casei* assay after treatment with enzymes (conjugases) to make polyglutamyl forms of the vitamin available to the test organism.

[d] The recommended dietary allowance for vitamin B$_{12}$ in infants is based on average concentration of the vitamin in human milk. The allowances after weaning are based on energy intake (as recommended by the American Academy of Pediatrics) and consideration of other factors, such as intestinal absorption.

[e] Retinol equivalents. 1 retinol equivalent = 1 μg retinol or 6 μg β-carotene.

[f] As cholecalciferol. 10 μg cholecalciferol = 400 IU of vitamin D.

[g] α-tocopherol equivalents. 1 mg d-α-tocopherol = 1 α-TE.

[h] The increased requirement during pregnancy cannot be met by the iron content of habitual American diets nor by the existing iron stores of many women, therefore the use of 30–60 mg of supplemental iron is recommended. Iron needs during lactation are not substantially different from those of nonpregnant women, but continued supplementation of the mother for 2–3 months after parturition is advisable in order to replenish stores depleted by pregnancy.

Source: Committee on Dietary Allowances, Food and Nutrition Board (1980). *Recommended Dietary Allowances.* 9th revised edn, Washington, DC.

minimal requirements of an essential nutrient (i.e. just the quantity that will prevent detectable deficiency manifestations). The widely used guide for planning is the Recommended Dietary Allowances (RDA) of the Food and Nutrition Board, National Academy of Sciences, National Research Council (NAS–NRC) (Table 3). These standards 'are the levels of intake of essential nutrients considered, in the judgment of the Committee on Dietary Allowances of the Food & Nutrition Board on the basis of available scientific knowledge, to be adequate to meet the known nutritional needs of practically all healthy persons'.

These allowances are composite judgements by competent scientists who weigh the accumulated knowledge concerning each nutrient in order to arrive at the best approximation. The varied types of evidence that must be sought and reviewed in processing the data used to reach such an approximation include:

nutrient content of foodstuffs;

precursors, if any, and efficiency of their conversion;

active forms and metabolites;

nutrient intakes of individuals and of population groups in relation to: (i) laboratory assessments of nutrient levels in blood, tissues, and excreta; and (ii) clinical observations of nutritional state;

clinical, dietary, and laboratory studies of subjects with deficiency syndromes spontaneously occurring, experimentally induced, or conditioned, and therapeutic response of such subjects to quantitatively administered nutrients;

nutrient balance studies where these are applicable;

evidence concerning absorption, bioavailability,

Table 4. Estimated safe and adequate daily dietary intakes of selected vitamins and minerals [a]

	Age (years)	Vitamins		
		Vitamin K (μg)	Biotin (μg)	Pantothenic acid (mg)
Infants	0–0.5	12	35	2
	0.5–1	10–20	50	3
Children and adolescents	1–3	15–30	65	3
	4–6	20–40	85	3–4
	7–10	30–60	120	4–5
	11+	50–100	100–200	4–7
Adults		70–140	100–200	4–7

	Age (years)	Trace elements[b]					
(mg)		Copper (mg)	Manganese (mg)	Fluoride (mg)	Chromium (mg)	Selenium (mg)	Molybdenum (mg)
Infants	0–0.5	0.5–0.7	0.5–0.7	0.1–0.5	0.01–0.04	0.01–0.04	0.03–0.06
	0.5–1	0.7–1.0	0.7–1.0	0.2–1.0	0.02–0.06	0.02–0.06	0.04–0.08
Children	1–3	1.0–1.5	1.0–1.5	0.5–1.5	0.02–0.08	0.02–0.08	0.05–0.1
and	4–6	1.5–2.0	1.5–2.0	1.0–2.5	0.03–0.12	0.03–0.12	0.06–0.15
adolescents	7–10	2.0–2.5	2.0–3.0	1.5–2.5	0.05–0.2	0.05–0.2	0.10–0.3
	11+	2.0–3.0	2.5–5.0	1.5–2.5	0.05–0.2	0.05–0.2	0.15–0.5
Adults		2.0–3.0	2.5–5.0	1.5–4.0	0.05–0.2	0.05–0.2	0.15–0.5

	Age (years)	Electrolytes		
		Sodium (mg)	Potassium (mg)	Chloride (mg)
Infants	0–0.5	115–350	350–925	275–700
	0.5–1	250–750	425–1275	400–1200
Children	1–3	325–975	550–1650	500–1500
and	4–6	450–1350	775–2325	700–2100
adolescents	7–10	600–1800	1000–3000	925–2775
	11+	900–2700	1525–4575	1400–4200
Adults		1100–3300	1875–5625	1700–5100

[a]Because there is less information on which to base allowances, these figures are not given in Table 3 and are provided here in the form of ranges of recommended intakes.
[b]Since the toxic levels for many trace elements may be only several times usual intakes, the upper levels for the trace elements given in this table should not be habitually exceeded.
Source: Committee on Dietary Allowances, Food and Nutrition Board (1980). *Recommended Dietary Allowances.* 9th revised edn, Washington, DC.

excretion, total body content, biological half-life, turnover rate of the nutrient;

evidence concerning toxic levels of the nutrient.

The nature and extent of data available on a particular nutrient vary and new studies accumulate at differing rates. Hence the RDAs are revised at approximately 5-year intervals. The first edition (1941) contained proposed quantitative standards for *calories, protein, calcium, iron, vitamins A and D, and thiamine, riboflavin, niacin, and ascorbic acid (10 nutrients). Although the need was then recognized to consider other members of the vitamin B complex, no specific values could be given for daily allowances of these. The ninth (1980) edition includes recommended allowances for 17 nutrients (Table 3) and for an additional 12 selected vitamins and minerals, 'Estimated Safe and Adequate Daily Dietary Intakes' (Table 4).

Not to be confused with the RDAs are the USRDAs promulgated by the US *Food and Drug Administration for use in nutrition labelling of food products. These standards are based upon the RDAs but are simplified estimates of allowances which combine age and sex categories of nutrient allowances into single ones for adults and for children. In so doing the largest allowance from the RDA table has been used and hence the USRDA overstates the allowances set by the NAS–NRC.

Differences between estimated allowances, requirements, or standards from nation to nation are due to: (i) different criteria adopted in defining the intent of the 'standard'; (ii) the different information available at the time of development of the respective recommendations; (iii) variation in weight accorded to particular data by respective committees.

Dietary fibre. The tough threadlike supporting structures of plants and of many animal tissues are commonly termed '*fibre'. Related terms used to designate such constituents have included 'unavailable carbohydrates' and 'roughage'. These chemically differing structural components vary both qualitatively and quantitatively with the foodstuff, with its variety, age, and method of processing. Chemically they range from complex carbohydrates, polysaccharides including celluloses and hemicelluloses, to lignin, pectic substances, gums, and other polymeric materials. Earlier analytical methods did not distinguish between these components. Such distinction is, however, biologically important because of the different biological properties and influences on the gastrointestinal tract of each category.

The differing biological effects of those materials grouped under the term 'fibre' include effects on *stool weight (bulk), on serum *cholesterol level, and on gastrointestinal absorption (bioavailability) of specific nutrients and metabolites. 'Fibre' resists *digestion (degradation) by intestinal enzymes and other digesting juices. In passing through the gastrointestinal tract it may exert a sponge-like action to retain water, act as an agent influencing a

cation exchange by adsorbing *bile salts, adsorbing or binding *zinc or other inorganic nutrients and reducing their bioavailability, or similarly binding toxic materials. Dietary fibre may directly influence faecal bulk through its ability to bind water; it may alter faecal bulk indirectly through influencing bacterial growth and metabolism in the *colon.

The specificity of the chemically distinct constituents loosely grouped together as 'fibre' for these complex physiological effects remains to be identified. The resultant effects on health cannot be precisely specified, but some seem reasonably clear:

stool weight is increased, left-sided colonic stasis is reduced, colonic tension of *constipation and of *diverticular disease is lessened;

some types of dietary fibre reduce the postprandial rise in *blood sugar, altering the *insulin needs of certain diabetics;

some fibre increases the excretion of bile acids and may reduce the level of cholesterol in the serum, suggesting a beneficial effect on *coronary heart disease incidence.

Epidemiological associations postulated between high-fibre diets and a decreased incidence of many gastrointestinal conditions including *haemorrhoids, *appendicitis, *cancer of the colon, *diverticulitis, *colitis, and *Crohn's disease remain circumstantial. The multiple differences in environmental and biological characteristics of the populations studied obscure any conclusive relationships.

Fibre is not regarded as an essential nutrient, but as a component of the diet that may be beneficial to health. The amount and type of dietary fibre that will be maximally desirable in the human diet cannot yet be estimated; the usual intake by different populations has not yet been sufficiently well documented.

Diet therapy in disease. The use of food and of diet in therapy was clearly advocated by the ancients, indeed it was repeatedly mentioned in texts and inscriptions in ancient Egypt. Examples of recognized and valid specifics such as those cited here for scurvy are numerous. However, much advocated diet therapy was without justification and, in retrospect, merely part of the polypharmacy that characterizes medical efforts in many ages when specific agents are not known. In modern times, before the age of *chemotherapy, *sulphonamides, and the *antibiotics, true therapeutic specifics consisted of *digitalis, *quinine, *arsenicals and *mercury for *syphilis, *thyroid extract, insulin, and a longer list of nutritional specifics. These latter included: protein for protein-energy malnutrition and protein-deficiency *oedema; vitamin C-containing foods and preparations for scurvy; *cod-liver oil and its concentrates for *rickets; antipellagra foodstuffs and concentrates (especially *yeast); sources of vitamin B_1 or thiamine for beriberi; iron for nutritional deficiency anaemia; iodine to prevent and treat goitre; liver extract therapy (source of vitamin B_{12}) for pernicious anaemia; fish-liver oils and other sources of vitamin A for *night blindness and *xerophthalmia due to vitamin A deficiency; and crude liver, yeast, and related concentrates as sources of an emerging factor now known to be folic acid for the treatment of *sprue.

A host of 'therapeutic diets' were being used for many medical and surgical conditions. Only a few of these were based upon well-established currently acceptable evidence. In fact, in 1941, the distinguished metabolic scientist Eugene F. DuBois wrote 'if we can eliminate a large number of worthless, special diets, the time and money that is saved can be employed in making the fewer diets better'. Today, sound principles of diet therapy exist, permitting good management of many of the *inborn errors of metabolism and of other metabolic disorders such as various types of hyperlipidemia, hypertension, non-insulin-dependent diabetes, promotion of surgical rehabilitation, malabsorption syndromes, and weight control. Rehabilitation can be greatly expedited through well-planned utilization of scientifically sound enteral and parenteral nutrition and, in selective cases, total parenteral nutrition (TPN), even maintaining patients well for very long periods.

Despite these remarkable advances, a plethora of dietary misinformation and food faddism plagues both the public and the medical profession. It is promoted by self-serving unscrupulous entrepreneurs, pseudo-scientists, mystics, cults, and charlatans. (See FRINGE MEDICINE, ETC.; HEALTH FOODS.)

Additionally, through soundly conceived procedures for evaluation, some 'time-honoured' and deeply ingrained concepts that have resulted in dietary prohibitions are being corrected. During the past decade, there has been a remarkable assembly of evidence that supports the view that moderate consumption of alcoholic beverages is beneficial in reduction of risk of cardiovascular disease. Objective examination of the evidence pertaining to the effect of *caffeine on health indicates that despite the fact that acutely administered caffeine increases *blood pressure, plasma *renin activity, and secretion of *hydrochloric acid by the stomach, the chronic consumption of caffeine by normal subjects has no effect on blood pressure, plasma *catecholamines, plasma renin activity, serum cholesterol, blood glucose, or urine production. Furthermore, 'the consumption of coffee or caffeine-containing beverages does not appear to be associated with myocardial infarction, lower urinary tract, renal, or pancreatic cancer; teratogenicity; or fibrocystic breast disease' (Curatolo and Robertson, 1983).

The result of the better scientific basis for nutritional therapy and its application is vastly improved care of patients, more pleasant and acceptable regimens for many patients, and remarkably sustained productiveness for some previously totally incapacitated individuals.

Unusual reactions to food (*food allergy and *food idiosyncrasy). Individuals may react adversely to a particular food or ingredient: the types of reactions vary and the terms used to define the nature of the reactions are often widely confused. Psychologically based food aversions are frequently mistakenly considered to be physiologically caused. The true adverse food reactions may be: (i) of idiosyncratic, metabolic, pharmacological, or toxic nature without involvement of the *immune system of the body; or (ii) they may represent a *hypersensitivity or allergy resulting from immune system involvement. Clinically, symptoms may present promptly after ingestion of the offending food or be delayed for hours to days.

Immediate allergic hypersensitivity to food may appear as transitory swelling and itching of the lips, mouth, or *pharynx, as nausea, abdominal discomfort, vomiting, or diarrhoea, with or without *urticaria (patchy itching and oedema of the skin). *Asthmatic symptoms occur more frequently in children than adults. True *anaphylactic reactions may be life-threatening.

The most common offending foods include nuts, peanuts, egg, milk, shellfish, fish—all foods of high nutrient density. Hence, when these have been implicated the diet must be carefully planned to ensure maintenance of nutrient intake consistent with needs, particularly when the food of the young child is altered. Fortunately, in food-protein gastroenteropathy of infants and children their sensitivity to milk or to soy protein decreases or often disappears as they age, so that they tolerate the food later in life. Allergic reactions due to sensitivity to food proteins may be altered by preparation (processing) of food, because of the sensitivity of some allergenic proteins to heat or other treatment.

A gastrointestinal sensitivity to the cereal (wheat, oats, rye, barley) protein, gluten, produces in susceptible persons a malabsorption syndrome resembling the folic acid deficiency disease of sprue. Diarrhoea, malabsorption of fat (steatorrhoea), bloating, and weight loss occur. The symptoms are relieved by removing the offending cereal from the diet.

Gastrointestinal symptoms attributable to specific sugars in foods are not immune-system related, but result from the level of activity of gastrointestinal enzymes. Symptoms of abdominal discomfort, diarrhoea, distension, and *flatulence following intake of milk or of milk sugar (lactose) arise because there is insufficient gastrointestinal lactase to hydrolyse the ingested disaccharide *lactose into *galactose and *glucose, and there is consequently *fermentation of the lactose by the microflora of the gut. The enzyme lactase is normally present in all young, but it decreases with age at differing rates. It may also decrease or disappear temporarily in the young child with a febrile illness or with severe malnutrition such as protein-energy malnutrition (e.g. *kwashiorkor). Less significant decreases occur with age among northern peoples or Caucasians, an earlier or greater decrease among those of Oriental or African origin. There results, therefore, a varying quantitative intolerance to lactose-containing milk. So-called lactose intolerance is rarely due to complete absence of the enzyme; accordingly, most children and adults, even among non-milk-drinking populations, may tolerate milk in servings of 150–200 ml.

Impairment of digestion of other disaccharides due to absence of the splitting enzyme is rarer than is 'lactase deficiency'. The absence from the human intestine of enzymes to split the oligosaccharides raffinose and stachyose, coupled with the presence in the *ileum and colon of microflora that utilize these sugars to produce volumes of gas—carbon dioxide, methane, hydrogen—accounts for the *flatus-producing property of beans, onions, soy, cabbage. These foods contain the oligosaccharides and are often avoided because of the individual's belief that he or she has an unusual 'sensitivity' to such foods.

Examples of other types of unpleasant reactions to foods are such reactions as the so-called '*Chinese restaurant syndrome' and the hypertensive reaction to *tyramine-containing cheese (especially Cheddar) in hypertensive persons under therapy with *monoamine oxidase-inhibiting drugs (MAOIs). Some red (Italian) wines and the yeast hydrolysate, Marmite, as well as liver and the meat of some game birds, are also reported to contain tyramine; Marmite also contains *histamine. The Chinese restaurant syndrome, so named because the symptoms initially were described as being experienced by a person shortly after he started to eat a meal in a Chinese restaurant, is a reaction to the ingestion of a highly concentrated flavour enhancer, monosodium glutamate (MSG). The transitory sensations described are those of 'burning', 'tightness', and/or 'numbness' of the upper chest, neck, and face. In some instances dizziness, chest pain, headache, and nausea have been described. Subsequent studies show that the symptoms can be produced in about one-third of all persons upon ingestion of a concentrated beverage containing very large quantities (5g) of MSG; that the symptoms appear to be sensations derived from a response of receptors in the gastrointestinal tract (oesophagus), not due to effects on the brain; and that more usual concentrations of the flavouring agent (of the order of 0.75 per cent) are highly unlikely to produce any reaction even in 'sensitive' individuals. Such understanding of the nature of food idiosyncracies permits avoidance of discomforts that may sometimes be experienced and at the same time avoids unnecessarily restrictive regimens that may reduce the appeal or nutritional contribution of wholesome foods.

Food toxins. For the 'toxic diseases' of 'trembles' (milk sickness), *ergotism, and 'endemic colic' (lead colic) the evidence of relationship to foods was accepted by Hirsch (1885) who, however, favoured for *pellagra the maize toxin hypothesis. It is now established that a wide variety of intoxications affecting man and other animal species may result from naturally occurring toxicants in commonly used foodstuffs, and many of the causative toxicants have been identified. Some examples cited in the initial report of the Food Protection Committee, NAS–NRC, are as follows:

The solanine alkaloids of the potato have caused many cases of poisoning in man, especially under circumstances of unusual consumption involving the sprouts, eyes, and skin. Exposure of freshly harvested potatoes to sunlight increases the solanine content, and a level of more than 0.1 per cent of the alkaloid has been considered to render the potato unfit for human consumption. A factor in buckwheat is responsible for fagopyrism, a form of photosensitization. This has not been a problem in man, but cattle develop the syndrome, which is characterized by an inflammation of the eyes, nose, and ears when buckwheat is included in their forage. Photosensitization has been reported from the handling of parsnips. Naringen, a glycoside present in unripe grapefruit, is irritating to the gastrointestinal tract. Lycopene, an aliphatic hydrocarbon related to carotene, accumulates in the liver and has caused illness in man as a result of the chronic consumption of large quantities of tomato juice. Phytates in cereals tend to reduce the assimilation of calcium from the diet. Prunes contain derivatives of hydroxyphenylisation that have potent laxative activity by virtue of their gastrointestinal irritant properties. Certain purines and pyrimidines have been reported to promote the atherogenic activity of an atherogenic diet in experimental animals. Outbreaks of honey poisoning have been reported in the United States and Europe. The honey became poisonous when bees collected the nectar from certain plants, e.g., mountain laurel, rhododendron, oleander, and azalea, that contain highly toxic cardioactive glycosides. Disulfiram, a chemical substance known to interfere with the normal metabolism of alcohol, has been reported to be present in an edible mushroom, 'inky cap' (*Coprinus atramentarius*). Several cases of acute illness have resulted from the drinking of an alcoholic beverage following the consumption of this mushroom. It has been reported that both the white and the yolk of the hen's egg are carcinogenic when fed to mice.

Grossly excessive intake of any of the essential nutrients can prove toxic. Many cases of illness and death have resulted from ill-advised toxic amounts of vitamin A or vitamin D, excess therapeutic iron or iodine, excessive intakes of selenium, fluorine, and of other essential nutrients.

The significance of the nearly ubiquitous presence of such naturally occurring toxicants in foods deserves comment. Widely used, highly valuable foodstuffs are considered safe, not because of the absence of potentially toxic substances, but because the quantities of these substances present are insufficient to produce harm under ordinary circumstances of preparation and patterns of consumption. The dictum of Paracelsus holds 'Was ist das nit gifft ist? Alle ding sind gifft und nichts ohn gifft/Allein die dosis macht das ein ding kein gift ist' or as simply translated by Wayland J. Hayes, Jr, 'Dosage alone determines poisoning'. (See also POISONING.)

Food and nutrition as risk factors. Nutritional influences may alter the pathogenesis, course, or complications of diseases. Since the observations of Hippocrates concerning 'persons naturally very fat' the association of obesity with increased mortality has been recognized and much evidence has now accumulated that obesity is a risk factor that increases both illness and death from diabetes and cardiovascular disease. Such nutritional risk factors are not considered to be primary aetiological agents in the sense that a deficiency of vitamin A causes night blindness and xerophthalmia or that an excessive intake of fluorine produces mottled dental enamel and, if sufficiently in excess, the bone changes of fluorosis.

Present-day widespread concern among the

Table 5. 1983 Metropolitan height and weight tables

Men

| Height | | Small | Medium | Large |
feet	inches	frame	frame	frame
5	2	128–134	131–141	138–150
5	3	130–136	133–143	140–153
5	4	132–138	135–145	142–156
5	5	134–140	137–148	144–160
5	6	136–142	139–151	146–164
5	7	138–145	142–154	149–168
5	8	140–148	145–157	152–172
5	9	142–151	148–160	155–176
5	10	144–154	151–163	158–180
5	11	146–157	154–166	161–184
6	0	149–160	157–170	164–188
6	1	152–164	160–174	168–192
6	2	155–168	164–178	172–197
6	3	158–172	167–182	176–202
6	4	162–176	171–187	181–207

Women

| Height | | Small | Medium | Large |
feet	inches	frame	frame	frame
4	10	102–111	109–121	118–131
4	11	103–113	111–123	120–134
5	0	104–115	113–126	122–137
5	1	106–118	115–129	125–140
5	2	108–121	118–132	128–143
5	3	111–124	121–135	131–147
5	4	114–127	124–138	134–151
5	5	117–130	127–141	137–155
5	6	120–133	130–144	140–159
5	7	123–136	133–147	143–163
5	8	126–139	136–150	146–167
5	9	129–142	139–153	149–170
5	10	132–145	142–156	152–173
5	11	135–148	145–159	155–176
6	0	138–151	148–162	158–179

Note: Weights at ages 25–59 based on lowest mortality. Weight in pounds according to frame (in indoor clothing weighing 5 lbs, shoes with 1 inch heels (men); 3lbs, shoes with 1 inch heels (women).
Sources of basic data: 1979 Build Study, Society of Actuaries and Association of Life Insurance Medical Directors of America, 1980.

Table 6. Metric conversion of the 1983 Metropolitan height and weight tables with height in metres and weight in kilograms

Men

Height metres	Small frame	Medium frame	Large frame
1.57	58.0–61.0	59.5–64.0	62.5–68.0
1.60	59.0–61.5	60.5–65.0	63.5–69.5
1.63	60.0–62.5	61.0–66.0	64.5–71.0
1.65	61.5–63.5	62.0–67.0	65.5–72.5
1.68	61.5–64.5	63.0–68.5	66.0–74.5
1.70	62.5–66.0	64.5–70.0	67.5–76.2
1.73	63.5–67.0	66.0–71.0	69.0–78.0
1.75	64.5–68.5	67.0–72.5	70.5–80.0
1.78	65.5–70.0	68.5–74.0	71.5–81.5
1.80	66.0–71.0	70.0–75.5	73.0–83.5
1.83	67.5–72.5	71.5–77.0	74.5–85.5
1.85	69.0–74.5	72.5–80.0	76.0–87.0
1.88	70.5–76.0	74.5–81.0	78.0–89.5
1.90	71.5–78.0	76.0–82.5	80.0–91.5
1.93	73.5–80.0	77.5–85.0	82.0–94.0

Women

Height metres	Small frame	Medium frame	Large frame
1.47	46.0–50.5	49.5–55.0	53.5–59.5
1.50	46.5–51.5	50.5–56.0	54.5–61.0
1.52	47.0–52.0	51.0–57.0	55.5–62.0
1.55	48.0–53.5	52.0–58.5	56.5–63.5
1.57	49.0–55.0	53.5–60.0	58.0–65.0
1.60	50.0–56.0	55.0–61.0	59.5–66.5
1.63	51.5–57.5	56.0–62.5	60.5–68.5
1.65	53.0–59.0	57.5–64.0	62.0–70.5
1.68	54.5–60.5	59.0–65.5	63.5–72.0
1.70	56.0–61.5	60.5–66.5	65.0–74.0
1.73	57.0–63.0	61.5–68.0	66.0–76.0
1.75	58.5–64.5	63.0–69.5	67.5–77.0
1.78	60.0–66.0	64.5–71.0	69.0–78.5
1.80	61.0–67.0	66.0–72.0	70.5–80.0

public for 'slimming' seems somewhat incongruous with the more detailed analyses of many long-term investigations of obesity, cardiovascular disease, and mortality. Studies have recently resulted in an upward revision of the weight considered compatible with best health, although they have confirmed that extremes of overweight (and of underweight) are associated with increased risks of mortality. Long-used tables of 'optimal weight' based on life insurance company data have recently been revised and reflect this same trend (Table 5). The public preoccupation with 'slimming' is probably due more to current society's views relating to cosmetic appeal and the 'keep-fit' cult than to health effects.

The concern of the public for a given food and nutrition-related risk factor appears to be especially great during the early stage of development of scientific information about the significance, if any, of the suspected risk. An example is the attention given to the question whether foods may be a source of significant cancer-causing substances—a hypothesis addressed repeatedly by official and non-official national and international agencies during the 1970s and 1980s. The principles involved here exemplify those that apply in assessing other dietary risk factors.

Under special experimental circumstances many substances commonly consumed, even basic foods, may accelerate the formation and growth of neoplasms, or exhibit biological properties in common with a known carcinogen in some rodent test-species. These properties are attributed even to some essential nutrients and normal metabolites. Determining whether these phenomena have significance for human food practices requires an understanding of nutritional *toxicology permitting sound scientific judgements as to the relevance of the experimental dosage level to the potential human intake and the similarities or differences in absorption, metabolism, turn-over rates, excretion, and storage between the experimental species and man. Especially pertinent is the constancy of intake of the material under experimental feeding conditions compared with (or contrasted with) the expected exposure of free-living humans, whose varied food supply differs from season to season and from year to year throughout life.

Experimental animal studies further reveal that other substances in commonly consumed foodstuffs—for example cabbage, Brussels sprouts, tea, coffee—inhibit chemically induced carcinogenesis. Many vegetables and other edible plant materials are found to contain inhibitors. These inhibitors fall into three categories: (i) those that prevent the formation of carcinogens from precursors (e.g. ascorbic acid, α-tocopherol); (ii) 'blocking agents' that prevent carcinogenic agents from reaching or reacting with critical target sites; and (iii) inhibitors that act subsequent to exposure to carcinogenic agents (e.g. retinoids, inhibition of synthesis of *prostaglandins, and some protein inhibitors).

To illustrate further the complexity of interpreting the practical significance for man of experimental evidence concerning dietary risk factors, one can cite the identification of an increasing series of potent mutagenic compounds formed during cooking. Mutagens often, but not always, prove to be carcinogenic in animal tests. The mutagenic substances increase with longer cooking (broiling) of meats and fish. The carcinogenic potential of these substances for experimental animals and for man remains to be defined. The implication for interpretation of benefit/risk of health effects of cooked foods, of common heat-labile infections and of safe basic sources of essential nutrients similarly remains unresolved. Those with simplistic answers are either naïve or knaves!

Evaluation of much longer-studied dietary risk factors is illustrated by hypertension. While reduction of sodium intake is useful in treatment of hypertension, the case is weak for the claim that the usual average intake level of dietary sodium is a risk factor in the induction of hypertension in the normotensive healthy individual. Similarly, the hypothesis that a deficient intake of potassium is

causative remains unconvincing, and so too is evidence relating to *polyunsaturated fats, calcium intake, and excessive alcohol intake as factors that influence the initiation of hypertension.

It is obvious that guidance concerning a healthful dietary regimen for healthy individuals (i.e. those without a confirmed allergy or idiosyncrasy to a particular foodstuff) cannot, indeed must not, be naïvely construed to 'avoid' any single postulated risk factor. One does well to be guided by the advice of Celsus:

> A man in health, who is both vigorous and his own master, should be under no obligatory rules. . . . His kind of life should afford him variety. It is well to avoid no kind of food in common use; to attend at times a banquet, at times to hold aloof; to eat more than sufficient at one time, at another no more. . . .

Such advice for variety, moderation, and enjoyment of food is fully consistent with current scientific knowledge and with the recognized nutritional benefits of including representatives of each category of foodstuffs in one's daily diet to assure a nutrient intake adequate to meet needs of optimal health.   W. J. DARBY

Further reading

Committee on Diet, Nutrition, and Cancer, National Research Council (1982). *Diet, Nutrition, and Cancer*. Washington, DC.

Committee on Dietary Allowances, Food and Nutrition Board, (1980). *Recommended Dietary Allowances*. 9th revised edn, Washington, DC.

Coon, J. M. (1966). Discussion in Food Protection Committee, Food and Nutrition Board. *Toxicants Occurring Naturally in Foods*. Washington, DC.

Curatolo, P. W. and Robertson, D. (1983). The health consequences of caffeine. *Annals of Internal Medicine*, **98**, (part 1), 641–53.

Darby, W. J., Broquist, H. P. and Olson, R. E. (eds) (1982–4). *Annual Review of Nutrition*, vols 1–4. Palo Alto, California.

Dustan, H. P. (1983). Nutrition and hypertension. *Annals of Internal Medicine*, **98**, (part 1), 660–2.

Food Protection Committee, Food and Nutrition Board (1973), *Toxicants Occurring Naturally in Foods*. 2nd edn, Washington, DC.

Fregley, M. J. and Kare, M. R. (1982). *The Role of Salt in Cardiovascular Hypertension*. New York and London.

Goodhart, R. S. and Shils, M. E. (1980). *Modern Nutrition in Health and Disease*. 6th edn, Philadelphia.

Hathcock, J. N. (1982). *Nutritional Toxicology*, vol. 1. New York and London.

Herbert, V. (1980). *Nutrition Cultism; Facts and Fiction*. Philadelphia.

Herbert, V. and Barrett, S. (1981). *Vitamins and Health Foods: The Great American Hustle*. Philadelphia.

Hirsch, A. (1885). *Handbook of Geographical and Historical Pathology* (Creighton translation from the 2nd German edn), vol. 2. London.

Hollingsworth, D. F. (1983). Dietary standards. In *Nutrition Reviews, Present Knowledge in Nutrition*. 5th edn, Washington, DC.

Irwin, M. Isabel (1980). *Nutrition Requirements of Man: A Conspectus of Research*. Washington, DC.

Keys, A. (1980). Overweight, obesity, coronary heart disease and mortality. *Nutrition Reviews*, **38**, 297–307.

Lusk, G. (1938). *Nutrition*. New York.

McCarron, D. A. and Kotchen, T. A. (1983). Nutrition and blood pressure control. *Annals of Internal Medicine*, **98**, (part 2), 697–890.

McCollum, E. V. (1957). *A History of Nutrition*. Boston.

Marshall, C. W. (1983). *Vitamins and Minerals: Help or Harm?* Philadelphia.

Nutrition Reviews (1984). *Present Knowledge in Nutrition*. 5th edn, Washington, DC.

Pyke, M. (1968). *Food and Society*, London.

Sugimura, T. (1982). Tumor initiators and promoters associated with ordinary foods (The Ernst W. Bertner Memorial Award Lecture). In Arnott, M. S., van Eys, J. and Wang, Y.-M. (eds), *Molecular Interrelations of Nutrition and Cancer*. New York.

Watt, J., Freeman, E. J. and Bynum, W. F. (1981). *Starving Sailors: The Influence of Nutrition upon Naval and Maritime History*. National Maritime Museum, Greenwich.

World Health Organization (1960). *Endemic Goitre*, WHO Monograph Series No. 44. Geneva.

NUTTALL, GEORGE HENRY FALKINER (1862–1937). Anglo-American bacteriologist, MD California (1884), FRS (1904). After studies in Baltimore and Göttingen, Nuttall was appointed lecturer in bacteriology at Cambridge in 1900, becoming the first Quick professor of biology in 1906. He carried out important researches on *immunology, *parasitology, and *insects as vectors of disease. He founded the *Journal of Hygiene* in 1901 and *Parasitology* in 1908.

NYCTALOPIA is a synonym for *night blindness.

NYMPHOMANIA is intense sexual excitement in the female, indiscriminately directed at any male (or, in 'inverted nymphomania', at any female) and unrelieved by *orgasm. Nymphomania is a rare episodic state which may have an organic basis (e.g. drug *psychosis, *encephalitis, neurological temporal lobe lesions) and is to be distinguished from female hypersexuality which is simply one end of a normal distribution curve.

NYSTAGMUS is a rapid *tremor of the eyeballs independent of normal ocular movements. Nystagmus is classified according to its direction (horizontal, vertical, rotatory), character (e.g. oscillatory, phasic), and any precipitating factors.

NYSTATIN is an *antibiotic agent obtained from the mould *Streptomyces noursei*. It is active against a number of *yeasts and *fungi but is used mainly against *Candida infections, by topical application to the skin and mucous membranes. It is ineffective by mouth and is too toxic for parenteral use. The name derives from New York State, where it was developed.

O

OBESITY is a condition of excess body fat. The weight/height² index (body mass index or BMI) is a better indication of obesity than body weight alone in adult men and women (but not children). Obesity is usually arbitrarily defined as existing when body weight exceeds 120 per cent of ideal weight; expressed as BMI in kg/m² of body surface this value is 27 for men and 25 for women. Alternatively reference can be made to the widely available Metropolitan Life Insurance Company Tables which provide guidelines for acceptable weight ranges at different heights (see NUTRITION).

Whatever definition is used, obesity is very prevalent among Western populations, particularly in the middle-aged. There is no doubt that it is an important health hazard and carries an increased risk of premature death. It has been estimated that life expectation diminishes by about 2 per cent for each kg of body weight above normal. Among the major associations of obesity are *coronary heart disease, *hypertension, *diabetes mellitus, *osteoarthrosis of weight-bearing joints, several forms of *cancer (colon, rectum, and prostate in men; breast, uterus, and cervix in women; and some less common cancers) and *gall bladder disease. Liability to *varicose veins, menstrual abnormalities, and respiratory disorders is also increased, and surgical operations carry a greater than normal risk.

OBJECTIVE. In an optical system such as a *microscope, the objective is the lens or complex of lenses that is nearest the object being examined.

OBSCENITY is that which is filthy, disgusting, or offensive to the senses or the sensibilities. Obscenity is notoriously difficult to define except in a specific cultural context. According to current English statute, material 'shall be deemed to be obscene if its effect . . . is, if taken as a whole, such as to tend to deprave and corrupt persons who are likely . . . to read, see or hear the matter contained or embodied in it'.

OBSESSION. A pathologically persistent or recurrent idea, which may be emotionally generated and which sometimes motivates towards irrational action.

OBSTETRIC FORCEPS. Any of a variety of instruments designed to assist in the extraction of the fetal head during childbirth. See OBSTETRICS.

OBSTETRICIAN. A physician specializing in the medical care of pregnancy and childbirth. See OBSTETRICS.

OBSTETRICS is the science, art, and craft concerned with reproduction in the female, and overlaps greatly with *gynaecology. In all societies throughout time the processes of reproduction are common enough, as the rising population of the world bears witness. Yet they are normally hidden from public sight by moral custom as well as by the internal nature of the processes from fertilization to birth. This hidden quality has led to much mystery and superstition, reinforced by religious attitudes. Until recently all of these have tended to hold back understanding and the development of obstetric care. Midwifery, until the 20th c., was essentially a simple craft practised by women to help their parturient sisters. It has now, however, become more than this since obstetrics has made its impact on practice.

Despite the private nature of midwifery, through the centuries there must have arisen awareness of *morning sickness, increased micturition (passage of urine), swelling of the breasts, enlargement of the abdomen and fetal movement ('*quickening') as symptoms and signs of pregnancy. Their causes have been speculated on for generations. But it is a measure of ignorance that in some primitive societies today the relationship between sexual intercourse and pregnancy is not known. Many areas of ignorance have taken centuries to dispel.

Terrifying and inexplicable aspects must always have been obvious, such as abortion, bleeding in pregnancy and immediately after birth, stillbirths, abnormal babies, deaths soon after birth, twins, swelling of the limbs and face, fits and death of the mother. And in labour there were those unfortunates who simply could not deliver the baby and so died together with the fetus.

It is to be realized that these horrors have always been relatively few, and perhaps the more dramatic because of that. But they seemed to strike without rhyme or reason and could not be foretold. Antenatal care, for instance, is a product only of the 20th c. Before then all was assumed to be well with the pregnant woman until something went sadly wrong, and then there was so little that could be done to spare her and her baby. The apprehension surrounding pregnancy and birth can now scarcely be imagined. The only refuge was in prayer, and acceptance of the will of God. Meanwhile all sorts of useless nostrums were applied which now seem little more than lucky charms.

Modern women and their obstetricians and midwives are the inheritors of centuries-old tradition in which progress and changes of attitude have been slow, halting and erratic. It is the purpose here to trace some of them.

Labour and disproportion. The dramatic event of reproduction is labour, leading to delivery of the baby. The suffering woman can be seen to need help. The recurrent uterine contractions are painful as they force open the cervix (neck of the womb) during the first stage of labour, and as they contribute to the expulsion of the baby during the second stage. The physical effort can be seen to be enormous as the baby is driven through the birth canal. This consists, from above downwards, of the uterus, cervix, vagina, and perineum (the so-called soft parts) surrounded at the lower end by the bony ring of the pelvis (hard parts) (Fig. 1). The perineum is the thick wedge of tissue between the back of the vagina and the front of the anus, the base of the wedge being the skin in that situation. It is enormously stretched as the baby's head distends the vulval orifice just prior to delivery, and it may tear, lacerating skin, vaginal wall, and the muscle between them.

In normal labours, which are the vast majority, the baby's head is bent forward with the chin on the breastbone, in an attitude of flexion. This presents the smallest cross-section of the head to the hollow cylinder of the birth canal. The top of the head, the vertex, is then said to present (Fig. 2). This is most favourable for easy delivery. It is a helpful analogy

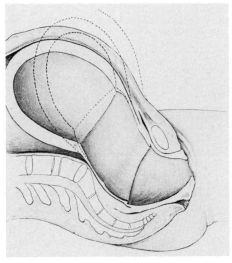

Fig. 1. The birth canal at the end of labour, with baby and placenta removed. It shows upper and lower segments of the uterus and the distended vagina just before expulsion of the baby. The uterus rises to the shape of the dotted line during contractions in labour.

All illustrations in this article are reproduced with permission from Clayton, S. G. and Pinker, G. D. (eds), (1972), *Obstetrics by Ten Teachers*, 12th edn, London, unless otherwise stated. There is now a 13th edn. (1980)

to think of the progress of the head like that of a ball negotiating a netball (or basketball) ring with the net being made of some rigid material. If the ball is round (as in the vertex presentation) there will be little difficulty. If the ball is egg-shaped or slightly square, and its long diameters present to the ring and net, then there may be difficulty; and, of course, sometimes the ball is made too big or the ring too small. All these problems can arise during labour, and the emphasis is always on the head, since this is the broadest part of the baby. If the head can negotiate the birth canal, then the body and limbs will do so too.

If the baby's chin lifts off the chest as the head is gradually extended, the cross-section presented to the birth canal increases, and the point on the head which presents moves forwards from the vertex to the crown and to the brow (Fig. 3), and ultimately extension may be so complete that it is the face (Fig. 4) which comes first. All these malpresentations can cause great difficulty in labour and may make delivery impossible without intervention. If, however, the pelvis is large enough and the head small enough, then delivery may still be possible without help. Unfortunately in times past pelves were often too small because of malnutrition during the growing period of a woman. When there is disproportion in size, whether relative as with extended heads, or absolute because the head is too big or the pelvis too small, then in past centuries the labour was obstructed, the baby died and so did the mother later. The baby died of asphyxia as its blood supply through the placenta failed, or because of brain damage and bleeding into it as a result of the tight squeezing of the head.

In about 3 per cent of cases it is not the head of the baby which presents during labour, but the bottom or breech (Fig. 5), and rather more rarely the baby may lie transversely (Fig. 6) across the mother's abdomen, when the hand, arm and chest present. Delivery is then impossible without help. With breech presentation, delivery is usually possible and may be spontaneous. However, the head of the baby then comes last through the birth canal and, again, if there is disproportion the baby will die. In addition, once the body is born, the blood supply to the baby is cut off and with the face inside the vagina it cannot breathe, so that if delivery is not reasonably rapidly effected the baby will die of asphyxia. However, the slight merit of breech presentation in earlier times was that the obstetrician could put a hand into the birth canal and pull on the leg or legs; he could apply traction and withdraw the baby. This is not possible, without instruments, when the head presents. The hand can be inserted but there is nothing on the baby to grasp, and it is physically impossible to get two hands into the pelvis alongside the head. In the transverse lie, pulling on the hand or any part of the upper limb simply compounds the difficulties. Nevertheless, Soranus of Ephesus, who practised in Rome in the 2nd c. AD, found that in transverse lie it might be possible to push up the chest and head, to grasp a leg and to convert the presentation to that of breech. This is the operation of internal version. To be successful, enough liquor (water) must remain round the baby and the uterus must be fairly relaxed. Without these conditions the uterus may be ruptured and the patient will die of haemorrhage or of later infection.

The next step was to try internal version on those in whom the head presented and was stuck without chance of delivery. As before, the head is pushed up, the baby turned and a leg grasped and pulled down. If the cervix is not fully open and the pulling is too hard, then it may be torn with dire consequences. Internal version and traction are there-

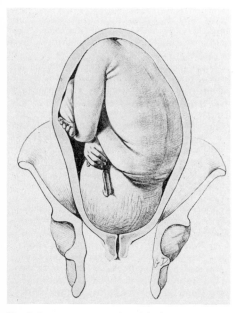

Fig. 2. A common presentation of the fetus at the end of pregnancy with the back to the left of the mother and the head over the cervix

Fig. 3. The partly extended head, giving a brow presentation. Nearly always needs obstetric help for delivery

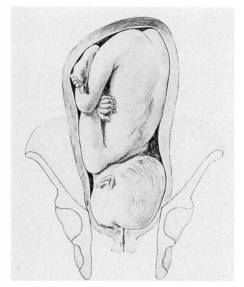

Fig. 4. The fully extended head, giving a face presentation. Delivery may be easy, or may need obstetric help

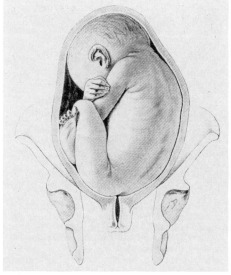

Fig. 5. Breech presentation, which needs obstetric help in delivery

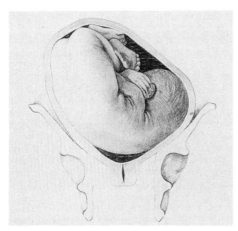

Fig. 6. Transverse lie, with the shoulder presenting. Delivery is not possible until this is corrected

fore far from ideal and the baby often dies. However, in early days the object was to save the mother: at least version gave her a chance when, without it, she would certainly have died undelivered.

Internal version was not widely used and after Soranus midwifery went into a dark age, for the religions of the time kept women more or less in subjection, looking upon them as chattels and sources of sin. Learning tended to be in the hands of a celibate clergy, whose medical sources were mainly the writings of *Galen, who was dogmatic, often wrong, and had little to say about midwifery. 'In sorrow shalt thou bring forth' is no text for bringing succour to childbearing women.

Internal version was not reintroduced until the 16th c. by Ambroise *Paré, who was more famous as a military surgeon. He also advocated the use of the birth stool, which is a chair in which the front is cut away so that the seat is U-shaped (Fig. 7). This allows egress of the baby while the birth attendant

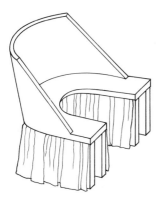

Fig. 7. The birth stool shown in Jacob Rueff's *De conceptu et generatione hominis* (1587). Redrawn from Graham, H. (1950), *Eternal Eve*, London, p. 86

kneels in front of the seated parturient to receive the baby. He thought, like Soranus, that the pelvic bones will separate during labour, so enlarging the birth canal. The belief was unfortunate and wrong, for it means that there can be no concept of disproportion.

The Renaissance in medicine was associated with the publication of *De humani corporis fabrica* by Andreas *Vesalius in 1543; this is the foundation of modern anatomy. He was followed in the chair at Padua by Gabriel *Falloppius (Fallopio), eponymously remembered by the Fallopian tube. This marks an interest in, and the development of the understanding of, female pelvic anatomy, leading to better concepts of disproportion.

By 1701 Hendrik van *Deventer of Holland had extended work on the pelvic bones and recognized disproportion, although he had the extraordinary notion that the sacrum and coccyx swung backwards during labour. However, he scouted the idea of separation of the pelvic bones, and made classifications of variations in size and shape of the pelvis. His teachings spread and the scene was set for the diffusion of knowledge of the obstetric forceps later in the 18th c. This was the next major advance in the management of disproportion: indeed a good claim can be made for the belief that these are the most beneficent instruments ever devised. In about $2\frac{1}{2}$ centuries they must have saved hundreds of thousands, possibly millions, of lives and prevented untold suffering.

Obstetric forceps (Fig. 8). It must have been harrowing to watch a woman in labour quite unable to deliver her baby, whose scalp hair might be visible at the vulva; she would slowly deteriorate and die. Yet the hands can do nothing for only one can be inserted into the pelvis and it cannot gain purchase and traction on anything. Pushing on the abdomen exhausts the woman further and achieves nothing except perhaps rupture of the uterus with a quicker death. Levers made of metal were tried. They were broad and curved on the flat, the object being for the end to be hooked over the occiput of the baby (the bony prominence at the nape of the neck), then using the underside of the pubic arch as a fulcrum, the head was to be prised out. Damage to mother and baby could be severe. It is to be suspected that often it did not work as hoped. A horrible though justifiable alternative was to destroy the baby with scissors and bone crushers to reduce its size. This too could cause much damage to the mother, and might even kill her if left so late that she was already exhausted.

The fillet was a complicated system of leather loops. The intention was to slip it over prominent parts of the fetal head so that traction could be applied. Similar to the lever was the vectis: this had a broad blade whose centre was cut away in a fenestration, perhaps to make it lighter. The blade was tapered into the handle and was also bent over at its end. This was intended to hook over the occiput, which was pulled on directly rather than

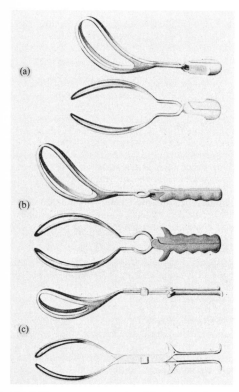

Fig. 8. Three common varieties of the obstetric forceps. There are many others. Note the curves to fit (a) the baby's head and (b) to conform with the curve of the birth canal

being levered out. This might avoid damage to the mother. This instrument is important since two of them placed together look extraordinarily like the modern forceps. Palfyn of Ghent in 1721 showed his 'mains de fer' which were like two vectis blades placed in opposition to each other and parallel.

The *Chamberlen family must be credited with what now would be called the breakthrough in the design of an effective forceps. Theirs is a remarkable story. William was a Huguenot Protestant working in Paris at about the same time as *Paré. He fled to England during the massacre of St Bartholomew's Day in 1572. He practised in London in midwifery and seems then to have been using forceps, though their design was kept a close secret within the family. It was then normal to keep medical advances, or supposed advances, to oneself in order to enhance one's practice. In this William was followed by his two sons, Peter the Elder and Peter the Younger. The metal forceps were prevented from clinking by binding them in leather. They were kept in a large box carried into the parturient's room, taken out under her clothes and bedclothes, used and restored to their box without anyone seeing them.

The Chamberlens often fell foul of the medical establishment, for they were brash braggarts and entrepreneurs, but they must have attained some position since Peter the Elder was *accoucheur to the Royal Household and he handed this post on to his nephew Peter III, who attended Henrietta Maria, wife of Charles I, in one of her confinements. Peter III had a son Hugh I, whose son was Hugh II, the first to divulge the family secret. How knowledge of the forceps became more public is not known, but Peter the Elder retired to Woodham Mortimer Hall in Essex after the execution of Charles I. He died there in 1683 and his wife hid some of his instruments under the floorboards of the attic, where they remained until discovered in 1813.

The unusual thing is that three Essex doctors, Edmund Chapman, William Giffard, and Benjamin Pugh, all living within a few miles of Woodham Mortimer, all used and wrote about the obstetric forceps in the third and fourth decades of the 18th c. How they came to know of the instrument, they did not disclose. The features of the forceps that matter were: (i) that they had each blade inserted into the pelvis separately on each side of the head; (ii) that they crossed over each other at a lock held by a removable pin, rather like scissors. This meant that on gripping the handles the pressure on the head could be increased to obtain more effective traction. This idea had been used before with a fixed pin, but this would not work since the blades have to be opened so widely to embrace the head that they cannot be got into the pelvis. Then Chapman in 1733 and 1735 found that when he lost the pin the operation was easier and just as effective. He also illustrated that the blades he used were curved not only to fit the head but also to fit the curve of the pelvis.

The knowledge of the forceps brought William *Smellie to London from his native Lanarkshire. He practised in and around Leicester Square and set up a school of midwifery. He showed towering common sense, knowledge, and experience in his *Treatise on the Theory and Practice of Midwifery* of 1752 and became known as the Master of British Midwifery. He wrote on many aspects of his subject (see MEDICAL BOOKS AND LIBRARIES): in particular, his rules for the use of the forceps are still applied today. In 1754 he published a *Set of Anatomical Tables*, depicting with remarkable accuracy the anatomy of women in labour. Unfortunately he ran into vitriolic opposition from local midwives, the most polemical being Elizabeth Nihell, married to a surgeon-apothecary, both of them practising from the Haymarket. It was the forceps which brought men into the field of midwifery and that was resented, and often still is, by women.

One of William Smellie's pupils was William *Hunter, also of Lanark. He became the most fashionable obstetrician (man-midwife then) of his day. He was more than just this, however, for he studied anatomy and published a superb *Anatomy* of the *Human Gravid Uterus* in 1774. The famous John *Hunter was William's brother and ten years his junior, but it was almost certainly William's influence that brought John to London and partly inspired him to his brilliant career in anatomy and surgery.

In Paris and in Germany there were masters of midwifery too: it was essentially knowledge of the forceps and their use that made them so. An advance made by Étienne Tarnier in the 1860s was that of axis-traction with the forceps. Before his time the forceps were especially helpful where the fetal head was well down in the pelvis. However, with disproportion the head may never fully enter the pelvic brim—this is known as the high head. If the forceps are applied to it there is great difficulty in pulling in the right direction since the birth canal is curved with the concavity forwards. Tarnier devised a system where the pull was always in conformity with the curve. The operation is not without dangers to the mother when the head is high: it is now seldom, if ever, done because Caesarean section has been substituted for it.

Since the beginning there have been many slight variants on the essential nature of the forceps, but little real change. The late 19th c. saw patterns devised by Barnes and Neville in London and by *Simpson and Milne-Murray in Scotland. The 20th c. brought two—those of Kielland in 1916 and of Wrigley in 1935.

Kielland practised in Oslo. His forceps design was radically different from previous ones in that the planes of the blades were set back from that of the handles and were less curved to fit the pelvis, and in addition the lock was made to slide, so that one blade could be further advanced within the pelvis than the other, which is not possible when the lock is fixed. These modifications solved two problems. It is normally safe to deliver the baby by forceps only when the occiput is to the front of the mother's pelvis, to emerge from under the pubic arch (Fig. 9). Often when a labour is not progressing the occiput is to the side of the pelvis. If ordinary forceps are then applied, one blade is over the occiput and the other over the face, and this may deform the baby's head and damage it. Ordinary forceps must only be placed on the sides of the fetal head running near the ears. When the occiput is not at the front, one hand has to be put into the pelvis and the head rotated until the anterior position is obtained, when the forceps can be applied. Kielland's forceps, however, can be applied properly on to the baby's head whatever its position. The sliding lock allows this and also the correction of any tilt (asynclitism) on the head. This can then be followed by rotating the head with the forceps so that the occiput comes to the front. In other words, the rotation is done with the instrument rather than the hand. This is much easier but potentially more dangerous to the mother so that a great deal of skill is needed.

Wrigley's forceps are classic in design, but are light and have had the handles reduced to almost

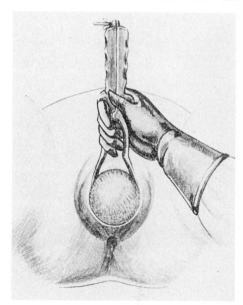

Fig. 9. Forceps in place to extract the head

vestigial proportions. This prevents their use deeply in the pelvis for the high head and they can be used only for a head which is low down and near to delivery. They cause little if any damage and so are suitable for the tyro.

In the USA, Barton introduced a forceps in 1924 to deal in a different way with the problem of the head with the occiput to the side. Piper devised forceps in 1929 to aid the delivery of the after-coming head in breech delivery.

In the 1950s Malmström of Sweden perfected a technique of vacuum extraction of the baby. The instrument became known later as the ventouse. A metal cup is applied to the fetal scalp and air is evacuated by a pump. This is done slowly so that the scalp can be drawn up into the cup, and it also swells with oedema. A firm purchase is established and then traction can be applied, to pull the baby's head out of the pelvis. It can be very effective when the head is low in the pelvis: it can be applied whatever the position, and as the pull increases the occiput will often rotate naturally to come to the front. It can also be applied in the first stage of labour before the cervix is fully dilated, when forceps are much too dangerous. However, the ventouse too can similarly be dangerous and so is seldom recommended in such cases. The idea of the vacuum extractor was not new with Malmström but he was the first to make it effective. It is widely used in Europe and many countries where obstetric skill is at a premium, but less so in the USA.

Episiotomy (Fig. 10). This is the operation of making a deliberate surgical cut in the perineum to remove obstruction by firm muscle, to prevent a tear extending backwards into the rectum and anus, and to speed up delivery. In forceps

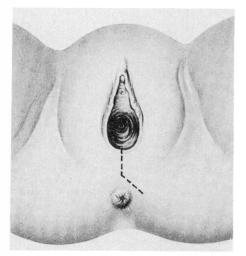

Fig. 10. Episiotomy. The dotted line shows a form of incision of the skin and underlying muscle to enlarge the outlet of the birth canal

deliveries it is almost always done. Fielding Ould of Dublin in *A Treatise on Midwifery* of 1741 drew attention to its value and it has become widely used everywhere. When done at the right time, just before delivery, it can make things easier for mother and baby. Now local anaesthesia is used, but for about two centuries that was not possible. The wound is repaired by suturing after the birth of the placenta (after-birth). When suturing was not common the women's legs were tied together in the hope of giving rest to the healing parts. For a few days after delivery episiotomies are painful and they may give rise to discomfort on intercourse for long afterwards. On the other hand, they may prevent extensive tears causing rectovaginal *fistula, with consequent faecal incontinence, and they may diminish the incidence of uterovaginal *prolapse. That they can be used too much, and that results are not always entirely satisfactory, is certain.

Induction of labour. In disproportion between the size of the fetal head and the maternal pelvis, a possible answer is to diminish the size of the head or alternatively to enlarge the pelvis. If pregnancies can be interrupted before full term then the babies and their heads are smaller. Denman of the *Middlesex Hospital, London, advocated the early induction of labour in certain cases in *An Introduction to the Practice of Midwifery* in 1794; it became widely used in England. Its drawbacks are that although it might prevent the problems of disproportion, not all women go into labour when the membranes are ruptured artificially through the cervix to let out the liquor amnii (amniotic fluid), and this may lead to serious infection endangering both mother and baby; in addition, if an error of judgement is made over the size

of the baby, it may be so small (premature) that it cannot survive apart from its mother. The operation is not now much used for the purposes of preventing disproportion, but may play a large part in other conditions, as will be seen later.

Symphysiotomy and pubiotomy. Enlargement of the pelvis to overcome disproportion can be achieved by surgically cutting through the joint holding the pubic bones together, or alternatively the pubic bones can be sawn through. By separating the thighs carefully the pelvic cavity can be opened up. However, this disrupts the sacroiliac joints leading to postural and walking problems later, and the operations may damage the bladder and urethra. These operations are not now performed, except perhaps in extreme cases in backward countries.

Caesarean section. In the 7th c. BC, Numa Pompilius promulgated the *Lex Caesarea* which ruled that if a pregnant woman died the baby should be removed from the womb and buried separately. There is some evidence that removal of the baby through a surgical incision in the abdomen and uterus was attempted several millennia before this in India with the object of delivering a live child. The first well-attested case of Caesarean section in Europe was that of Jacob Nüfer, a Swiss sow-gelder, who in 1500 performed a section on his own wife after doctors had been unable to do anything for her. He used his own instruments and his knowledge derived from his trade. Both mother and baby survived and Frau Nüfer had several successful pregnancies later. The operation was done without benefit of anaesthesia, as was the case for several centuries subsequently, although various forms of opiates and alcohol were freely used in an effort to diminish pain.

The operation was a last despairing resort, since the mortality for both mother and baby was so high. Nevertheless, it had a place, as even Smellie, a cautious humane man, allowed. The problems to be solved were those of haemorrhage at the time of operation and after, infection afterwards, anaesthesia, and suturing of the wounds in the uterus and abdominal wall. These were not all solved until well into the 20th c.

The first operations inevitably involved a quick slash through the abdominal wall, centred on the navel and to one or other side of it, and carrying this incision on through the uterine wall, which can bleed profusely. The baby is hauled out by the legs, the uterus contracts vigorously and the placenta and membranes are extruded or can be pulled out by the hand. The fluid (liquor amnii) escapes all over the abdominal cavity, and if it has become infected because of a long labour this is carried into the *peritoneum, causing the dreaded complication of peritonitis. The incision through the upper muscular part of the uterus is known as the classic Caesarean section.

A reduction in the dreadful mortality was achieved by Porro of Pavia (1876). After delivery he removed the upper part of the uterus and sutured the lower stump into the abdominal wound. This excised a potent source of infection and allowed drainage of the potentially infected area. The popularity of this operation was short-lived, since it took away the uterus. Preserving this organ depended on suturing the wound in it and this was not done with any regularity until the 1880s. It was at about this time, too, that *chloroform, introduced in about 1847 by *Simpson, became more widely used.

The next step in developing the operation came from Frank of Germany in 1906. He put the incision in the uterus low down near the bladder in the so-called lower segment Caesarean section; the incision was also transversely placed. The merits of this are that the uterine wound is isolated behind a flap of peritoneum, thus often preventing spread of infection into the general peritoneal cavity, and the tension on the wound is less than that made in the upper segment, so that healing more easily occurs. Many other anatomical variants have been tried, but now it is the lower segment operation which is almost universally performed. Until the last 20 years or so, however, the abdominal incision was still made vertically, running down from the navel. Now the Pfannenstiel incision, running across the abdomen just above the symphysis pubis, is the one favoured, for it is cosmetically more attractive.

Apart from operative technique, infection was much diminished after *Lister introduced *antisepsis towards the end of the 19th c., and this was quickly followed by *asepsis as understanding of *bacteriology grew at about the same time. *Chemotherapy and *antibiotics were products of the 1930s and 1940s and subsequently, and were given a fillip in development by the Second World War and the frequency of wounding. *Blood transfusion also improved as a consequence of war, and the same is true of *anaesthesia. All were quickly pressed into service in obstetrics, so that all operations, especially Caesarean section, became much safer. Now as many as 10 per cent or even more deliveries are effected by section. Its safety has solved the problems, to a large extent, of disproportion, of bleeding in late pregnancy, of difficult labour where forceps are inappropriate and potentially dangerous, of imminent fits, of failure to go into labour after induction, of maternal distress in labour and of a variety of conditions which may threaten the life and integrity of the fetus. It may be that it is too frequently used, for there are still some disadvantages in it, and it should not therefore be performed purely for convenience; nevertheless, properly used, it has saved thousands of lives of mothers and babies and has prevented much serious distress and morbidity. It must rank with the forceps operation as one of the greatest medical advances of all time, for the amount of suffering, potential and actual, which it has relieved. Its success depends on a long thread of history and the contributions of many in several different fields.

Infection has been the scourge and killer of childbearing women for centuries. Immediately after birth there is a raw, slightly bleeding surface where the placenta has been in the uterus, and there may be lacerations of the genital tract, or wounds in the abdomen and uterus after Caesarean section. All are very prone to infection, and in addition so are the urinary tract and the breasts as they begin to produce milk. In 1795 Alexander Gordon of Aberdeen recognized that infection could be carried from one patient to another by midwives and doctors. In 1843 Oliver Wendell *Holmes in America proclaimed '*The Contagiousness of Puerperal Fever*'. In Vienna *Semmelweiss (1861) wrote of the patterns of the disease which he had seen, in particular that students and doctors attending post-mortem examinations of patients dying of *puerperal fever might carry it directly to the labouring women whom they next delivered.

Light was not to be cast on to this problem, however, until the rise of bacteriology, especially in the hands of *Pasteur and *Koch. In 1879 Pasteur reported the presence of *streptococci (*microbes en chainettes*) in the blood and lochia (discharge from the uterus after birth, which continues for many days) of women suffering from puerperal fever.

Lister seized on these ideas and in surgery introduced the *carbolic (acid) spray. This was taken up in midwifery too, and it is of interest that Lister was called in to the General Lying-in Hospital, York Road, Lambeth, London, to help there when the hospital had to be closed because of an epidemic of puerperal fever which killed many patients. He remained consulting surgeon to the hospital and ultimately became its president. His influence on midwifery practice was therefore direct. The notion of antisepsis was enlarged and extended by that of asepsis, preventing as far as possible the access of noxious organisms to any susceptible site. Antisepsis, asepsis, and *sterilization of equipment are now bedrock principles of surgery and obstetrics.

It is obviously better to prevent infection, but the advent of the *sulphonamides in the 1930s and of *penicillin in the 1940s brought many swift cures in those afflicted with puerperal fever. The change was almost miraculous: patients who a year or two previously would have died, or would have undergone weeks and months of suffering, were cured virtually overnight. The range of antibiotics is increasing rapidly so that, although puerperal infection is still to be feared, it has been largely overcome.

Haemorrhage. Immediately after the birth of the baby the placenta separates from the uterine wall, which has a rich blood supply. Very severe bleeding can then occur in what is called postpartum haemorrhage. Much blood may be lost and the woman may die. The normal control of the bleeding is by the vigorous contraction of the uterine muscle, followed by clotting to seal off the open mouths of small and large blood vessels. The essential, therefore, is to give the uterus every opportunity to contract and to make it do so if it cannot do so normally. Sometimes the uterus will respond to rubbing gently with the hand on the abdomen. When it is hard it can be squeezed (*Credé of Leipzig, 1853) to expel clots and the placenta, which in the cavity of the uterus can impair contractions. Once the uterus is empty, *ergot preparations can be given which pharmacologically make uterine muscle contract strongly. An alternative is for the accoucheur to pass the whole hand through the vagina into the uterus and remove the placenta manually. The danger of this is the introduction of infection and the possible perforation of the uterus; it is never lightly undertaken. A further alternative is to pull on the *umbilical cord whose end lies outside the vulva and is attached above to the placenta. This fell into desuetude because if the uterus is not firmly contracted the whole organ may be turned inside out (inversion) which causes extreme shock.

In the 1940s, however, the management of the third stage of labour and the control of haemorrhage became simplified. *Ergometrine had been isolated from crude preparations of ergot and was shown to be an active principle in making the uterus contract. Chassar Moir (1943) popularized its use by *intravenous injection before the delivery of the placenta. Before this time it was thought to be dangerous to give ergot until the placenta had been delivered. The immediate result of this change was to reduce postpartum haemorrhage from around 10 per cent to about 3 per cent. Later still, *oxytocin, the hormone of the posterior pituitary gland which causes uterine contractions, was isolated and then synthesized for therapeutic use. In combination with ergometrine it is ideal for administration just before delivery of the placenta and postpartum haemorrhage is now a comparative rarity.

When haemorrhage of any kind occurs, its worst ravages in death and prolonged illness can now be offset entirely by blood transfusion. The relatively free use of this technique obtained a fillip from the Second World War, for it is invaluable in all forms of trauma.

Bleeding from the genital tract before the 28th week of pregnancy is classed as *abortion (miscarriage): after the 28th week it is called antepartum haemorrhage. It is nearly always caused by premature separation of the placenta from the uterine wall. If the placenta, for quite unknown reasons, should be situated in the lower part of the uterus (a condition known as placenta praevia) bleeding of some degree is inevitable. This is because the lower segment has to stretch to allow the baby to come through the birth canal. The placenta is inelastic and so is sheared from part of its attachment with consequent bleeding. It is now relatively easily dealt with by Caesarean section performed at the right time. The obstetrician's hand may be forced by the severity of the bleeding and then the baby may be small and very premature. This is undesirable, so it is more usual, if the bleeding is not too severe (which it rarely is at first), to allow the pregnancy to run on under close supervision in hospital until the baby is sufficiently grown and mature and then to do the section. Only if the bleeding is dangerous is the section done before this. Prior to the safety of Caesarean section, the only recourse was to try to press on the placenta by applying toothed forceps to the baby's scalp and attaching a weight to their handles, or in the case of a breech presentation pulling a leg down out of the cervix and applying a weight to it. This has great dangers for mother and child.

The other major form of antepartum haemorrhage is known as accidental, or more recently abruptio placentae. Here the placenta is in the upper part of the uterus, and yet suddenly separates from the uterine wall. There are all degrees of separation, from very slight with some pain and tightness (indicating contraction) of the uterus, to massive almost total separation with very severe pain, a very hard uterus and a great deal of internal bleeding with slight loss visible at the vulva. With more than one-third separation the fetus dies of asphyxia. Pain must be relieved with the more powerful *analgesics: blood transfusion is needed to replace blood lost from the circulation. If the baby is alive, Caesarean section may be best: if the baby is dead, then labour may be induced. This last was not realized to be the best treatment until the 1950s. Before then conservative treatment was in vogue, awaiting the natural onset of labour. This was because it was thought that the uterus was more or less paralysed and would not contract. This reason was invoked to explain the very common occurrence of postpartum haemorrhage after delivery. In fact this has now been shown to be caused by disturbance of the blood clotting mechanisms. The advanced technology and science of blood clotting have made this discovery possible and the condition rationally treatable.

Another matter of slow recognition, shortly afterwards in the 1960s, was that the total renal failure (anuria) which often followed abruptio placentae was mainly due to inadequate blood transfusion because estimates of blood loss were inexact. This was rectified, partly through knowledge gained from military surgery and from other branches of surgery where more massive operations were being undertaken.

The problem of haemorrhage has now largely been solved, thanks to pharmacology, to safer surgical intervention, and to freely available blood transfusion.

Antenatal care. When things go wrong in pregnancy, something, however ineffective, has always had to be done. J. W. Ballantyne of Edinburgh is credited with the idea of investigating the pathology of pregnancy by close supervision and observation with a view to prevention and correction of abnormalities found. To this end, in 1902 Ballantyne had a bed in the Edinburgh Royal Infirmary; later he had more. His primary intention seems to have been to try to prevent fetal abnormality. This grand aim was not then possible and did not become so until the 1940s. However, he soon shifted his attention to the problems occurring in the mother. The next step was to have out-patient clinics which mothers attended, rather than just in-patient beds. Such prenatal clinics were introduced in Adelaide in 1910, in Sydney in 1912, and in Edinburgh in 1915. In 1911 a clinic was started in Boston, USA.

The natural history of pregnancy, therefore, became more widely known. This consolidated much of the knowledge obtained over previous centuries. The combination of out-patient care to define at-risk patients with in-patient care to minimize the risks has been crucial in the philosophy and practice of prenatal care. Disorders discovered early so that they can be treated forthwith, or the foreseeing of potential disaster and averting it, are the cornerstones of the philosophy.

In the early months of pregnancy the sometimes excessive vomiting (hyperemesis gravidarum) can be checked and treated psychologically, with drugs, and with replacement of *electrolytes, long before it has progressed to serious illness and death. The various forms of abortion (miscarriage) can be slowed down in progress, or accelerated, and their serious sequels of haemorrhage and infection overcome. In addition, early in pregnancy it may be possible to foresee whether there may be the likelihood of disproportion in labour. This is done by clinical assessment of the interior of the pelvis by manual examination. This can be refined by direct X-ray measurement in which definite dimensions can be given to diameters of the pelvis. Caldwell and Molloy in the USA were especially notable pioneers among many others. This X-ray *pelvimetry was widely practised until the potential dangers of X-rays, especially to the fetus, were recognized. Now it is much restricted, but may still be of immense value in certain cases. In this prognosis for the successful outcome of pregnancy and labour, Dugald Baird of Aberdeen emphasized, over many decades dating from the 1950s mainly, the importance of assessment of the patient's height, age, social class, and parity (the number of babies she has had previously). Height is an index of previous nutrition, especially in the growth period. Women of small stature may have small pelves, perhaps distorted by *vitamin D deficiency, and they suffer an increased risk of disproportion.

Social class, as defined by the Registrar-General according to the type of work done by a woman's husband or consort, is correlated with income, with nutrition and standard of housing and the whole life-style. In all senses (economic, medical, and many more) of the term, social class I is better off than social class V and the unmarried, and there is a gradient running down through classes II, III, and IV. These social and economic factors express themselves, too, in reproductive success: social class I fares better in every respect than do the other classes, in order. A concerted effort on the part of the obstetric services to help those disadvantaged who are small, of higher age groups, who have too many children, and are of low social class, with all that that implies in education, housing, and nutrition, undoubtedly improves reproductive success. This is measured in terms of maternal deaths and *morbidity, and fetal and neonatal deaths, and morbidity. But this is relatively short term: in the long term, some of the best results for successful childbearing and child-rearing will come from political, social, and economic action to improve the well-being of women throughout their lives so that at all times they are of good physique, well nourished, decently housed, hygienic, and well educated. Obstetric problems will then be at a minimum.

Later in pregnancy, problems of bleeding can be recognized early and their worst effects prevented. If there are malpresentations these can sometimes be corrected by simple manual means and perhaps induction of labour. Caesarean section can be freely used to avoid many dire consequences of disorder, for often this ends as soon as the pregnancy does. This is especially so with pre-eclampsia (formerly called toxaemia of pregnancy), which is a disorder peculiar to pregnancy and characterized by raised blood pressure, oedema (swelling in the tissue spaces) and protein in the urine. It can be the precursor of fits (eclampsia) which, if not controlled, may lead on to the death of both mother and fetus. One of the great successes of antenatal care has been in the recognition of this in its early stages by routine measurement of the blood pressure and testing for the other signs too. Treatment can then be instituted and delivery effected at the right time so that mother and fetus are saved. An interesting point is that success has come from empirical methods only, since the cause of the disease is still quite unknown.

Antenatal care has eliminated the ravages of congenital *syphilis and has minimized the worst effects of disease in the mother such as *diabetes, cardiac and renal diseases, and many others. The skills of physicians, surgeons, obstetricians, paediatricians, and pathologists can all be brought to bear at appropriate times in this crucial period of a woman's life and that of her fetus.

Sonar (*ultrasound), introduced and perfected by Ian Donald of Glasgow, has been a major technological advance. Without danger it allows scanning of the pelvic organs throughout pregnancy. It has improved the accuracy of management of abortion and it can measure the size of the fetal head and body, identify some abnormalities in the fetus, show where the placenta is in the uterus, diagnose twins (Fig. 11), other multiple pregnancies, and accurately count the fetal heart rate. It is a safe and powerful diagnostic

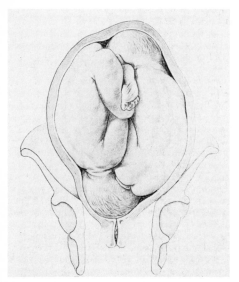

Fig. 11. Twins. They often fit together like this but there are all possible combinations of head or breech presentation

tool, the limitations of which have not yet been reached. It is widely used now in other disciplines too.

The second half of the 20th c. Purely obstetric techniques such as forceps, Caesarean section, mechanical induction of labour, episiotomy, internal version, embryotomy, delivery of the baby and placenta, and antenatal care were all established by the end of the Second World War. They were essentially clinical and manipulative and could be encompassed by one educated and trained person. The war, however, give a fillip to physics (particularly electronics), chemistry, biology, engineering, and in medicine to pharmaceuticals, anaesthesia, blood transfusion, and surgical techniques. Science and technology exploded, and they still increase their territory in all branches of medicine. The old ogres of obstetrics, namely disproportion, haemorrhage, infection, pre-eclampsia and eclampsia, malpresentations and malpositions of the fetus, and pain, were controlled if not entirely overcome in every case. Inevitably the centres of attention changed: the territory that had been conquered still had to be held, but there was still more to be taken. The remarkable *Confidential Reports into Maternal Mortality in the UK,* which are issued triennially, show that the careful application of knowledge already accumulated by everybody concerned with childbirth does reduce the numbers of deaths of mothers and probably of fetuses and newborns. Regrettably, however, some disasters still occur because of human failings in patients, midwives, and doctors. Careful attention to clinical detail by all the health professions is still vitally important. Science and technology do not sweep away this necessity, nor will they compensate for its

lack. The maintenance and improvement of clinical, scientific, and technological standards is a function of educational and academic bodies such as the Royal College of Obstetricians and Gynaecologists, the Royal College of Midwives, universities, the *Central Midwives' Board, and many others, as well as individual practitioners. None of these should be forgotten in the contributions they make to the welfare of childbearing women and their families. They help to hold the line and push it forward.

With many physical dangers overcome, attention switched to the psychology of childbirth, mainly under the impetus of women's groups and enlightened doctors. As early as 1933, Grantly Dick Read emphasized the value of *natural childbirth in psychological well-being. Many others have taken up the theme in many parts of the world. There have been notable changes in attitude of the professionals as a result of these movements, and the ambience of hospitals has improved (husbands are often present at delivery; lighting is less harsh; the surroundings are quieter), although there is still much to be done. General practitioners have urged the psychological value of the management of childbirth in small units where the mother may be close to home. Some have advocated a return to more deliveries at home. There had been a move towards having all deliveries in hospital under consultant care in the 1950s and 1960s: this was because statistics had shown that it was physically safer to have babies there rather than in small general practitioner hospitals or at home. This is changing again with a slow move back to these places. But the domiciliary services have very much dwindled and may not recover, and higher standards of physical care are now demanded both by the public and the professions. Moreover, conditions of work for doctors and midwives have changed, so that they are not expected to be available 24 hours a day, every day. This, of course, has affected hospitals too, so that teamwork is essential. Critics point to the way that this breaks a beneficial psychological bond built up between a woman and one attendant, but work patterns have to be accepted as doing this.

The other rapidly developed centre of attention has been the fetus and newborn. The change was probably not fully possible until mothers were much safer than they had been, although babies had always been vastly important in the philosophy of obstetrics as the proper end of the reproductive process. Nevertheless, there is now a newer freedom to look to the concerns of the fetus and baby.

Until the middle of the 20th c., congenital abnormalities (see TERATOLOGY) were assumed to be due to *genetic causes and therefore (in the state of knowledge then) irremediable. Then in 1941 Gregg of Sydney, an ophthalmologist, noted a connection between congenital cataract and the occurrence of German measles (*rubella) early in pregnancy. All subsequent evidence bore out the correctness of this observation, and other abnormalities were found to be due to rubella infection. This proved that intranatal infection was a cause of fetal anomaly. By advanced laboratory techniques, rubella infection in pregnancy can now be diagnosed, and if the embryo and fetus are at risk of abnormality the pregnancy can be terminated with the agreement of the parents. Alternatively, and very much better, women can be *immunized against rubella before they become pregnant and their subsequent babies are then protected from harm.

As well as certain infections being harmful to the fetus, it has now been realized that many drugs given to the pregnant mother can cause damage. This was highlighted by the *thalidomide tragedy, when mothers given this drug bore babies with severe limb deformities. Other drugs can also cause ill effects and this has led to even greater care in prescribing. Testing of new drugs before marketing is now very strict and always includes investigation of the possibilities of causing fetal growth and developmental abnormalities. X-rays, too, are used with increased caution because of these possible effects.

A further disorder that sprang to light in the mid-century was erythroblastosis. This is due to *rhesus-factor incompatibility between the blood of the mother and her fetus so that she produces *antibodies which destroy fetal red blood cells and cause *anaemia. This can cause death *in utero* or can make the baby very ill at birth. The possibility of this happening can be forecast by taking samples of the mother's blood to demonstrate the antibodies. These facts have been known for some time and now, thanks to the brilliant work of Cyril Clarke in the UK, the production of antibodies by the mother, and their effects in the fetus and newborn, can be suppressed. Preventive injections of antisera (anti-D) into Rh-negative mothers likely to be sensitized by fetal red cells passing into their circulations have all but eliminated this disorder. Before this form of prevention was available, other methods of treatment were used. The first was to remove the blood from the newborn's circulation and replace it with transfused blood (exchange transfusion); this cured the anaemia and removed the offending antibodies. The next step was to try to do this while the fetus was still *in utero* (intrauterine transfusion), the object then being to try to correct the anaemia until the baby could be born some time later. It was found that this could be done by introducing the transfused blood into the peritoneal (abdominal) cavity of the fetus by a hollow needle passed through the maternal abdominal wall and uterus. More recently still, a form of telescope (fetoscope) has been introduced into the uterine cavity which allows the fetus to be seen, and also the blood vessels of the placenta. Needles can sometimes be introduced into these vessels so that a transfusion can be directly given into the fetal circulation, or other therapeutic substances can be injected. Just looking at the fetus in this way is called *fetoscopy and may allow early diagnosis of some surface abnormalities.

Invasion of the amniotic cavity by needles to withdraw fluid has become increasingly common; this is called *amniocentesis. Cells shed from the fetal skin and lungs can be seen microscopically and certain genetic abnormalities diagnosed, especially *Down's syndrome. Pregnancy can then be terminated to avoid the birth of an abnormal baby. Certain diseases of genetic type are linked to only one sex (*X-linked diseases). Examining the cells can determine sex and, if the baby should be at risk, a termination can be offered. Abnormal chemical substances can also be found, or there may be *enzymes not normally present in the liquor. Their presence may suggest that termination might be best, or may alert the paediatrician to problems which he can deal with at birth or shortly after. With very small babies which are prone to respiratory distress after birth, this can be foreseen and even prevented by treatment of the mother if the likelihood of the disorder is demonstrated by analysis of the liquor.

Antenatal care at regular intervals should give the opportunity for the woman to establish rapport with her obstetrician and midwives so that she may become receptive to health education for herself and her baby. Advice should be given on the potentially harmful effects of alcohol and tobacco and advice can be given about diet and hygiene, all with a view to inculcating a healthier life-style for the woman and her family. The doctor–patient relationship in pregnancy is of precious and unique significance on both sides. It can be used to great effect for the benefit of both parties. The *Health Education Council and other voluntary bodies also give useful advice to pregnant women.

Labour. This, too, has not escaped the attention of medical technology. *Oxytocin and *prostaglandins may be used to start or reinforce uterine contractions. This is done for inducing labour or speeding up a slow labour, perhaps combined with rupturing the membranes round the baby to let out the amniotic fluid (liquor amnii) and make the uterus contract more strongly. *Salbutamol and alcohol and other test substances have been used to slow down or stop uterine contractions, especially in premature labour, so that the fetus shall not be expelled too much before its due time and so be weakly and too small. These various accelerators and brakes are frequently, but not universally, successful. There is little doubt that future research will find other more useful chemical substances.

Many electronic machines have been devised to measure electrical impulses in the uterine wall, to measure the strength of uterine contractions and the pressures being exerted within its cavity. There are also instruments for measuring the rate of the fetal heart and its responses to the contractions of labour. They can show when the fetus may be at risk, and this can be confirmed by taking a very small sample of blood from the fetal scalp, where it is accessible through the opening cervix, so that the gases it contains may be analysed. These may show that the baby should be delivered immediately, perhaps by Caesarean section.

These various monitoring machines and interventions have sometimes caused criticism, especially from feminist groups. They point to the normality of most labours and blame obstetricians for interfering too much. Their complaints are often justified for they can be used too often and without due thought and medical indication. On the other hand, doctors can point to times when these inventions have helped them to save lives. The technology in the labour room needs to be controlled and not be allowed to run riot. The exact indications for its use have not been fully worked out and agreed on. This is an urgent task, since the emotional experience of childbirth is now realized to be very important. Unbridled, careless, unthinking use of technology, almost as a routine, is to be deplored as likely to destroy the precious values of childbearing.

Similar anxieties have been expressed about the use of various methods of pain relief in labour. The drugs used have included *tranquillizers, soporifics, and analgesics, ranging from *codeine through to *pethidine and *morphine. Properly employed they can be very helpful, but they can be overprescribed and impair the woman's perception of her own experience. Many now object to this and lay much emphasis on their own psychological preparation for childbirth, which may eschew drugs of all kinds. Both sides of the argument can, unfortunately, be taken to extremes. Each woman, with her doctor's help, must be her own judge. There is not, and need not be, a universal pattern to suit everyone. The full circumstances of labour cannot be foreseen and it is up to the obstetrician to supply the appropriate remedies when things are not as they should be, but he must be sure of his ground and his reasons before counselling interventions and monitorings of any kind.

In addition to drugs for pain relief given by mouth or by injection there are in use many anaesthetic methods. The oldest is gas (*nitrous oxide) and air and this has been improved by substituting oxygen for air. The aim is to give rapid brief relief of pain, especially towards the end of the first stage of labour when the cervix is near the limits of stretching. Trilene, too, like gas and oxygen may be self-administered. An anaesthetist may sometimes give other substances by *inhalation, or alternatively he may induce epidural anaesthesia by an injection of local anaesthetic around the *spinal cord. This numbs the lower half of the body and removes virtually all the pain of labour, although the woman herself remains fully aware of what is happening. Of course this needs the insertion of a needle into the back or near the tail-bone. A tiny *catheter can be left in place and through this further injections of anaesthetic can be made. Injections of local anaesthetic have been used round the cervix to dull the pain of dilatation, but they are little used nowadays. Local anaesthetics are very frequently injected, however, into the perineum and round the vulva and its main nerve supply (pudendal block) in order to cut down the pain of distension of that area as the fetal head is being born, or for the performance of episiotomy, or the application of forceps.

Babies at birth are now cared for by paediatricians (see PAEDIATRICS), a large part of whose work nowadays is in neonatalogy (diagnosis and treatment of disorders of the newborn infant). Over the past few decades they have become very skilled in the management of the large variety of disorders which may afflict the newborn. In particular there has been the recognition that some babies are born before their time (premature) and some have grown poorly within the uterus despite there being an apparently adequate amount of time (small-for-dates); these need different forms of management. Now they can often be recognized before birth by obstetrical clinical methods and by estimations of the hormone outputs of the placenta. These give an assessment of whether the placenta is functioning well or badly, and whether the baby is at risk or not. This may well determine whether birth should be expedited, either by induction of labour or by Caesarean section. The skill of the paediatrician has made it possible for the obstetrician to do Caesarean section ever earlier in pregnancy, with much improved chances of survival of the baby. The combined skills of the paediatrician and obstetrician have greatly improved prognosis.

The historical pattern. The historical pattern of the development of obstetrics is that of almost no scientific and medical progress until the 18th c. when forceps were first widely used. Other operations were developing but were risky, especially Caesarean section. The 19th c. saw hints of understanding of pre-eclampsia, with proteinuria and raised blood pressure being recognized. Bacteriology, antisepsis, and chloroform came towards the end of the century. The 20th c. brought antenatal care, chemotherapy, antibiotics, anaesthesia, blood transfusion—the last two with greater variety, expertise, and knowledge. Specialization increased, demanding high educational standards for practitioners to acquire, update, and put new knowledge into practice. At the same time research increased, aided by so many other disciplines. Now the psychological components of childbearing are prominent and there is wider understanding and control of uterine contractions, of the placenta in its manifold functions, and of the fetus and the newborn. Intervention in the uterine environment, both indirect and direct, has become possible and is used more and more. The aim of obstetric care is to aid the process of childbearing to produce always a healthy mother and a healthy baby. Until that is done, the striving for perfection will go on, using obstetric knowledge and skills and pressing into service those of any other relevant discipline.   P. RHODES

Further reading

Graham, H. (1950). *Eternal Eve*. London.
Guthrie, D. (1945). *A History of Medicine*. London.
Johnstone, R. W. (1952). *William Smellie*. Edinburgh.
Kerr, M., Johnstone, R. W. and Phillips, M. H. (1954) *Historical Review of British Obstetrics and Gynaecology 1800–1950*. Edinburgh and London.
Radcliffe, W. (1947). *The Secret Instrument*. London.
Rhodes, P. (1985). *An Outline History of Medicine*. London.
Simpson, M. (1972). *Simpson the Obstetrician*. London.
Speert, H. (1958). *Obstetric and Gynecologic Milestones*. New York.
Spencer, H. R. (1927). *The History of British Midwifery from 1650 to 1800*. London.
Thomas, H. (1935). *Classical Contributions to Obstetrics and Gynecology*. Springfield, Illinois.

OBSTRUCTIVE JAUNDICE is *jaundice due to obstruction to the flow of *bile, for example obstruction of the biliary tract by *gallstones, *carcinoma of the head of the *pancreas, or a large variety of other possible causes operating within or outside the liver. Since the *bilirubin reabsorbed into the blood is of the soluble conjugated form, it is excreted by the kidney causing dark urine. At the same time, the stools are pale due to lack of bile pigment in the faeces.

OCCIPITAL LOBE. The hindmost part of each *cerebral hemisphere, the cortex of which contains the primary receptive area for the sense of vision.

OCCIPUT. The posterior projection of the head.

OCCLUSION is the closure, obstruction, or blocking off of an opening, passage, or cavity.

OCCULTISM is the doctrine and practice of the ancient and mediaeval reputed sciences involving secret and mysterious agencies, or their modern equivalents, such as magic, alchemy, astrology, theosophy, etc.

OCCUPATIONAL CRAMP is a form of occupational *neurosis in which muscular spasm occurs in groups of muscles involved in a particular occupational task when an attempt is made to undertake that task, although the same muscles function normally under other circumstances. Writer's cramp is the best known example. (Stoker's cramp is due to salt depletion and does not come under this heading.)

OCCUPATIONAL DISEASES OF FARM WORKERS. Agricultural workers, by virtue of their occupation, are exposed to a greater variety of infective and parasitic agents than is the general population. They may therefore be at greater risk of contracting such conditions as *brucellosis, *glanders, *erysipeloid, *ringworm, *orf, *cowpox, *tetanus, *hydatid disease, etc. An allergen associated with mouldy hay accounts for the condition known as '*farmer's lung'. See also OCCUPATIONAL MEDICINE.

OCCUPATIONAL MEDICINE

From industrial disease to occupational health. Occupational medicine is that branch of medicine concerned with the effects of work on health and the effects of health on the ability to work. It is essentially a discipline in *preventive medicine, a part of more general *environmental medicine, and closely related to both *community and general medicine. The evolution of the concept of occupational health initially from observations on industrial disease can be traced from antiquity.

Historical development. Occupation has always exerted a profound influence on the pattern of life and health of mankind. This influence has been traced from prehistoric times to the present day by Hunter (1978). Socrates referred to the mechanical arts as carrying a social stigma which damage the bodies of those who work at them, this physical deterioration resulting also in 'deterioration of the soul'. *Hippocrates in *Airs, Waters and Places* made observations on the effects of environment on health and the quality of life but did not focus specifically on the occupational environment. However, Hippocrates in 370 BC described severe *colic in a worker who extracted metals, and may have been the first to have recognized *lead as the cause of this symptom.

Cinnabar, the red sulphide of *mercury, had been mined in Almaden, Spain, since Phoenician times and was used by the Romans as a durable pigment, together with red lead and other metallic compounds to decorate buildings. Metallic mercury, the quicksilver of *Aristotle, was also recovered from the same mines. *Pliny in the 1st c. AD described mercury poisoning as a disease of slaves, for the mines contaminated with mercury vapour were too unhealthy for Roman citizens to work in. Pliny also described workers with lead oxides used as pigments tying up their faces in loose bags to avoid inhaling the poisonous dust.

The Middle Ages saw the development of metalliferous mining in Central Europe. The rich veins of silver at Joachimsthal led to the minting of the silver Joachimsthaler, later corrupted in English to dollar (Hunter, 1978). In *De re metallica*, published in 1556 and ably translated into English by a past president of the USA and his wife (Hoover and Hoover, 1912) a classical scholar, Georgius Agricola, gave a detailed description of the mining, smelting, and refining of gold and silver in this region. Agricola described the methods employed for ventilation, and illustrated primitive methods of personal protection in a series of woodcuts. He described mining accidents and major disasters in mines, later to become all too familiar. He described also the harmful effects of dry dust inhalation giving rise to difficulty in breathing and destruction of the lungs. In the mines of the Carpathian mountains, Agricola commented, may be found women who had married seven husbands, all of whom had died prematurely. A little later, *Paracelsus, a Swiss physician, wrote on the occupational diseases of mine workers, smelter workers, and metallurgists, giving a detailed description of mercurialism.

It is, however, Bernardino *Ramazzini who is generally acknowledged as the father of occupational medicine. His *De morbis artificum diatriba*, published in 1700, related to the history of occupational medicine as William *Harvey's *De motu cordis* related to that of physiology (Sigerist, 1936). Ramazzini practised as professor of medicine in the newly restored University of Modena and in his later years held the chair of medicine in Padua. Ramazzini superseded the medical practice of 2000 years by adding one important question—'What is your occupation?'—to Hippocratic history-taking (Farrington, 1941–3). He described in his treatise 54 different occupations associated with particular diseases and included a description of the ill effects on surgeons of rubbing into the skin mercurial ointments in the treatment of *syphilis, of the diseases of the mirror-makers of Venice, and a chapter on the diseases of learned men. Ramazzini is commemorated today in the American and European Ramazzini Societies, in the Collegium Ramazzini, and in particular in the University of Occupational and Environmental Health in Keio, Japan, which houses a statue of this widely cultured personality who was both physician and epidemiologist.

Technological progress in the 18th c. led to the complex changes in the pattern of life and the environment aptly termed the Industrial Revolution, which the UK pioneered. There are many literary works, epitomized by those of Charles Dickens, which describe the insanitary and polluted condition of the new towns and the working conditions in mine and factory. Epidemics of *typhus were known as factory fever, *cholera was rife, and *tuberculosis common. The father of industrial medicine in the UK was a Leeds physician, Charles Turner *Thackrah, who in his short life published in 1831 *The Effects of the Principal Arts, Trades and Professions, and of Civic States and Habits of Living, on Health and Longevity, with Suggestions for Removal of Many of the Agents which Produce Disease and Shorten the Duration of Life*. Thackrah was a contemporary of *Addison, *Bright, and the poet *Keats at *Guy's Hospital in London where they trained, and later was the founder of what grew into the Leeds University School of Medicine. He wrote on the dust diseases of the lungs of miners and the grinders of metals using sandstone wheels, the fork-grinders of Sheffield dying before the age of 40. In his observations on the common association of silica dust inhalation (see SILICOSIS) with tuberculosis, to give rise to lethal silico-tuberculosis, Thackrah antedated the current concern in developing countries where occupational exposures interact with *endemic disease and *malnutrition to give rise to more severe disease.

It was not, however, industrial disease which acted as the stimulus to reform in the 19th c. The observations of Edwin *Chadwick into the relationship between environmental conditions and ill health and the work of John *Snow on the mode of transmission of cholera led to increasing public concern about the environment and the campaign for clean water, approached only in significance for public health by the campaign for clean air a century later. Reform of the squalid conditions in the working environment was initiated again, not by industrial disease, but by public awareness of the outrageous exploitation of child labour in mines, factories, and mills. The untiring efforts of Robert Owen, Lord Shaftesbury, and others imbued with the humanitarian spirit, kindled public awareness and led to eventual legislation. The first effective *Factory Act of 1833, entitled *An Act to Regulate the Labour of Children in the Mills and Factories of the United Kingdom*, set the minimum age for employment at nine years, prohibited night work for those below 18 years and restricted work to 12 hours a day. The Act was effective because it established a Factory Inspectorate to ensure that the age requirements were heeded. The Factory Act of 1844 led to the appointment of certifying surgeons for the purpose of examining young persons prior to employment.

The scandal of the climbing boys who swept the chimneys, immortalized in English literature, was finally brought to an end in 1875, when Lord Shaftesbury introduced a Bill requiring chimney sweeps to hold a work licence. One hundred years previously, Percivall *Pott, surgeon to *St Bartholomew's Hospital, London, by means of pertinent epidemiological observations, linked scrotal *cancer to ingrained soot in the skin. Percivall Pott's observations provided the first evidence for an environmental cause for cancer. His work was followed by that of Butlin who in 1892 showed that pitch, tar, and mineral oil also caused cancer of the skin, opening the road to work on experimental carcinogenesis.

At the beginning of the 20th c. industrial disease was common in the UK. In particular, lead was widely used in industries in which women and children were employed indiscriminately and poisoning claimed many lives annually. Thomas Legge, appointed first medical inspector of factories in 1898, pioneered work on the prevention of *lead poisoning and was instrumental in the introduction of the notification system for lead poisoning and certain other industrial diseases. As a result of his work, lead poisoning, responsible for nearly 4000 notified cases with over 100 deaths annually in the early 1900s, steadily declined in frequency despite increasing lead consumption. The four aphorisms of Sir Thomas Legge, author of *Public Health in European Capitals* and of *Lead Poisoning and Lead Absorption* are still relevant and widely quoted (see LEGGE, THOMAS).

Notification of certain industrial diseases, while likely to be incomplete, was effective in reducing their incidence as it enabled attention to be drawn to the work site for control measures to be instituted. In addition to these notifiable diseases now reported to the Health and Safety Executive (see HEALTH AND SAFETY AT WORK ACT 1974) there are a larger number of occupational diseases prescribed by the Department of Health and Social Security for the purpose of giving financial benefit to workers shown to have contracted them in scheduled occupations. The old *Workmen's Compensation Acts have now been superseded by the *Social Security (Industrial Injuries) (Prescribed Diseases) Regulations 1975.*

While frank industrial disease has been progressively declining in incidence in the UK over the years, subclinical effects, manifested by biochemical or other measurable changes whose significance is not always apparent, are seen more frequently. Such is not the case, however, in all parts of the world. In developing countries undergoing rapid industrialization, gross occupational disease may be seen on a scale not seen in the UK since the days of the Industrial Revolution.

Although the classic industrial diseases have declined in incidence in the UK and other industrialized countries, it should be noted that none has been eradicated. Furthermore, new industrial diseases have developed, related to modern technologies, unknown even a century ago.

*X-rays were discovered in 1895 and *radium isolated in 1898 but the physicists working with newly discovered *ionizing radiation knew nothing of its biological effects. The first case of skin cancer resulting from X-irradiation was reported in 1902, and by 1922 100 radiologists were estimated to have died from their occupational exposures. Pierre *Curie experienced radium *dermatitis and both Marie *Curie and her daughter died of *leukaemia. In the early days, radium salts were used in the production of luminous dials. In a New Jersey factory between 1916 and 1923, girls pointed their brushes, dipped in radioactive paint, between their lips, ingesting the toxic material, resulting in death from aplastic *anaemia and bone *sarcoma some years later. More recently radiation sickness and deaths have occurred following accidental exposure to fission products in nuclear energy establishments.

Asbestos has been used in industry on a greatly increasing scale since about 1890, becoming invaluable in modern technology. The first case of interstitial pulmonary fibrosis, or *asbestosis, was probably described in 1907. The association between asbestosis and *bronchogenic carcinoma was recognized in 1935 and subsequent epidemiological studies have shown a greatly increased risk from bronchial carcinoma following combined asbestos exposure and cigarette *smoking. In 1960, an association was recognized between exposure to crocidolite or blue asbestos and a hitherto rare malignant disease, *mesothelioma of *pleura or *peritoneum, in the communities clustered round the asbestos mines in Cape Province, South Africa. Subsequent enquiry has revealed a high mortality

from mesothelioma following exposure to crocidolite, in particular in asbestos laggers, boilermen, and ship repairers in the UK, North America, and elsewhere. Amosite, or brown asbestos, has more recently also been shown to give rise to mesothelioma. As mesothelioma may develop 40 years or more after initial exposure to asbestos, and as it was not recognized until 1960, the mortality from this condition, currently rising, is expected to continue to rise at least until the end of the century.

Four cases of a rare and highly malignant tumour, haemangiosarcoma of the liver, were reported in 1974 in men engaged on the polymerization of *vinyl chloride from one plant in North America. Subsequent investigation led to the discovery of similar cases in men with heavy past exposure to vinyl chloride monomer in the UK and elsewhere. Following the institution of effective control measures, exposure has been drastically reduced and it is hoped that few further cases will occur.

These three examples, ionizing radiation, asbestos, and vinyl chloride, illustrate the hazard resulting from the introduction of new materials and processes into industry. Technological development makes it likely that new occupational diseases will occur in the future, to minimize which an effective monitoring system for new chemicals and processes, and constant vigilance by both clinician and epidemiologist, is required.

Contemporary occupational practice. The end of the Second World War saw the founding of the *World Health Organization (WHO) and the start of the internationally integrated programme which led to the eradication of *smallpox. In 1950, a joint International Labour Organization (ILO)/WHO committee defined occupational health as:

the promotion and maintenance of the highest degree of physical, mental and social well-being of workers in all occupations; the prevention among workers of departures from health caused by their working conditions; the protection of workers in their employment from risks resulting from factors adverse to health; the placing and maintenance of the worker in an occupational environment adapted to his physiological equipment and, to summarize, the adaptation of work to man and of each man to his job.

This definition advances the concept of occupational health beyond the prevention of occupational disease, and introduces the promotion of positive health and the concept of fitting the job to the worker. A full account of current occupational health practice is given by Schilling (1981), and recent advances in this field have been described by McDonald (1981) and Harrington (1984).

The aims and functions of an occupational health service originally drawn up by the ILO and endorsed by the Council of Europe in 1972 specified:

1. The protection of workers against the health hazards of work;

2. The adaptation of the job to suit the workers' health status; and

3. A contribution to the establishment and maintenance of the highest degree of physical and mental well-being in the workforce.

Occupational health in the UK. The *National Health Service (NHS) in the UK originally did not include occupational health services, which came initially under the jurisdiction of the Ministry of Labour, later the Department of Employment. The reorganization of the NHS in 1982 still excluded occupational health. Independently from the NHS, the larger privately controlled industries and the publicly controlled organizations, like the National Coal Board, British Rail, and the Post Office, developed their own non-statutory occupational health services for their employees. In several areas, health services for groups of small factories were organized on a co-operative basis, initially with grants from the Nuffield Foundation. However, many of the smaller plants, where the worst working conditions may be found had (and still have) minimal cover by general practitioners with part-time appointments in industry, or no cover at all. In the earlier years of the NHS, statutory requirements were supervised by Medical Inspectors of Factories under the jurisdiction of the Ministry of Labour, as established following the appointment of the first medical inspector in 1898. During the first half of the 20th c., successive legislation on matters related to health and safety built a cumbersome legal edifice which still had many inadequacies and omissions.

The report of the Committee of Enquiry on Safety and Health at Work was followed by a new broadly-based enabling act, the *Health and Safety at Work, etc., Act of 1974, aimed at covering all persons at work. The Act brought within its jurisdiction for the first time people working in hospitals and schools, and included the control of processes which may affect the health and safety of the general public, such as emissions into the atmosphere, the discharge of toxic substances into waterways and on land, and the transport and storage of potentially dangerous materials. The Employment Medical Advisory Service (EMAS) which superseded the old medical inspectorate of factories was established by a separate Act in the preceding year.

The Health and Safety at Work, etc., Act set up the Health and Safety Commission (HSC) answerable to the Secretary of State of the Department of Employment. The Commission is a tripartite body representing trade unions, employers, and local authorities. The operational arm, the Health and Safety Executive (HSE), is responsible for implementing the advisory functions of the Commission and for enforcing the statutory provisions. The old Inspectorates of Factories, Mines and Quarries, Alkali and Clean Air, etc., have been transferred to the Executive, with powers to issue improvement or prohibition notices to require action to be taken against dangerous processes.

EMAS forms the medical arm of the HSE, and currently comprises about 120 doctors and nurses organized on a regional basis. EMAS is responsible for advising the HSE, doctors, employers, workers, and unions on health matters related to employment. More specifically, its responsibilities include: (i) the performance of medical examinations of young people identified as necessary by the *School Medical Service and giving advice; (ii) statutory medical examinations (e.g. of lead workers); (iii) investigation of notifiable industrial diseases and gassing accidents; (iv) giving advice to physicians, employers, and trade unions; (v) performance of surveys on existing hazards and for the identification of new hazards.

One survey performed by EMAS gave a broad overall picture of occupational health services in the UK and produced a discussion document on the aims and functions of occupational health services (HSC, 1977). A more recent document (HSE, 1982) gives guidance on the establishment and scope of occupational health services. The principal functions identified are: (i) prevention of accidents and ill health; (ii) treatment of accidents and ill health occurring at work; and (iii) the promotion, maintenance, and restoration of health. Under this third heading is included the general health surveillance of the workforce and the resettlement of sick and injured workers. The multidisciplinary nature of the occupational health service is illustrated with reference to the role not only of the medical practitioner but also of the occupational health nurse, the occupational hygienist, the first-aider, and of safety representatives.

While the Health and Safety at Work, etc., Act is directed primarily to protect persons at work, it is also designed to protect the general public from risks to health or safety resulting from the activities of persons at work. Important and innovative features of the Act are the placing of the onus of responsibility on the employer to ensure, as far as is reasonably practicable, the health, safety, and welfare of his employees and also of persons not in his employ with access to his premises. Furthermore, the employee has a duty to take reasonable care and to co-operate with others to ensure that the required measures are complied with.

Despite the progress made by the Health and Safety at Work, etc., Act, in ensuring occupational health cover for all employees, occupational health services in the UK remain inadequate and uncoordinated. The structure described above has remained essentially unchanged since the early days of the NHS. That is, the larger companies and nationalized industries tend to have full occupational health services; many companies with 500 persons or less may have a full-time nurse with a part-time doctor and a designated safety officer. Some companies employ a part-time doctor to carry out statutory examinations and others may have no provision for occupational health cover at all. The group occupational health services have a valuable role but have had problems as a result of the recent economic depression. To illustrate the extent of this anomalous situation, the largest employer in the UK, the Department of Health and Social Security, has no integrated health service for NHS staff, despite the many physical, chemical, microbiological, and psychological hazards which may be found in NHS premises. The provision of occupational health and hygiene in the UK at the present time has been reviewed by a House of Lords Select Committee (1983) who gave their recommendations for services, research, and training.

While most physicians with full-time appointments in occupational health services will have received appropriate training for their posts, many doctors with part-time appointments, general practitioners in particular, have no occupational health training at all. Occupational medicine is now an accredited specialty in the UK and the other countries of the European Economic Community. A Diploma in Industrial Health (DIH) is granted by some UK universities, and a Master of Science degree in occupational medicine is awarded by the *London School of Hygiene and Tropical Medicine of the University of London. In 1978, the Faculty of Occupational Medicine was established at the Royal College of Physicians, London, now responsible for academic standards. The faculty awards an associateship (AFOM) and a membership (MFOM) by examination and a fellowship (FFOM) by election. Candidates for the AFOM are required to have completed two years in approved full-time posts or part-time *pro rata* to become eligible.

The Royal College of Nursing awards the Occupational Health Nursing Certificate (OHNC) to nurses who have completed two years' post-registration experience in nursing, following a full-time course of 6½ months' duration or part-time for 18 months. About 200 certificates are awarded annually. Training for a career in occupational hygiene is provided at undergraduate level at Aston University, Birmingham, and the South Bank Polytechnic, London. A Master of Science degree is awarded by London, Manchester, and Newcastle Universities following one-year full-time postgraduate courses. A professional qualification can also be obtained under the British Examining and Registration Board in Occupational Hygiene (BERBOH) appointed jointly by the British Occupational Hygiene Society and the Institute of Occupational Hygienists.

Occupational health in other countries. As in the UK, occupational health services have developed separately from mainstream medicine in most Western European countries. However, the Council of the European Community has issued a directive on the protection of workers from the risks related to exposure to chemical, physical, and biological agents at work (Council of the European Community, 1980). A series of individual directives has been planned, aimed at establishing in the first instance limit values for occupational exposure to a number of chemical agents and to asbestos, and for the appropriate health surveillance of workers. The directive on lead will become operative in the UK in 1986. Occupational health is co-ordinated through the Health and Safety Directorate, Directorate-General V of the Commission of the European Communities centred in Luxemburg, although research is the priority of Directorate-General XII in Brussels. Occupational health guidelines for chemical risk have been defined under the EEC's Environmental Chemical Data and Information Network (ECDIN). These guidelines advise on pre-employment examination and investigation, periodic medical examination, and biological monitoring procedures, giving action levels where these are available (Council of the European Community, 1983).

Occupational health in the Scandinavian countries is highly organized at national level. The Institute of Occupational Health in Finland, with one central and six regional centres, employs over 500 persons engaged on an extensive programme of multidisciplinary research related to occupational health.

In the USSR occupational health and hygiene are fully integrated in the general medical care system.

In the USA the federal agencies responsible for occupational health are the Occupational Safety and Health Administration (OSHA) and the National Institute for Occupational Safety and Health (NIOSH), the former answerable to the Department of Labor, and the latter to the Department of Health through the Center for Disease Control of the US Public Health Service. These organizations liaise with the broader-based US Environmental Protection Agency, in particular through its office of Health and Environmental Assessment in Washington. The American Conference of Governmental Industrial Hygienists (ACGIH) have produced a listing of levels of airborne substances known as Threshold Limit Values (TLVs) below which it is believed that most workers may be repeatedly exposed without adverse effect. These levels have been adopted by many countries, including the Health and Safety Executive in the UK (HSE, 1984).

In the developing countries, many of which are undergoing rapid industrialization, the importance of occupational health is becoming increasingly realized. There has been exploitation of cheap labour in certain cases by multinational companies in areas where control measures for worker health and safety could not be readily enforced. The problems of occupational exposure to chemical and physical hazards are compounded by pre-existing malnutrition and a high incidence of infectious disease. Occupational health services in such situations are often combined with *primary health care delivery to the worker and to his family and may be much more cost-effective when organized in this way.

The role of international agencies. The World Health Organization (WHO) has had, since its inception, a major role in the field of occupational health. A global medium-term programme for workers' health covering the period 1984–9 aims at the development of occupational health programmes as an integral part of health service infrastructure. Further work is planned on the integration of occupational health services with primary health care delivery. Emphasis is being placed on 'work-related diseases' rather than purely occupational diseases, and studies are planned on psychosocial hazards, reproductive hazards, and the application of *ergonomics to health promotion. The application of occupational health and safety programmes to agricultural workers through the primary health care system is also receiving priority. WHO has produced, among other publications, a series of monographs on environmental health criteria through its International Programme for Chemical Safety, and a series of reference monographs on chemical carcinogenesis through the International Agency for Research on Cancer (IARC) (e.g. 1979) centred in Lyon, France. In addition to the activities of the WHO Central Office of Occupational Health within the Division of Non-Communicable Diseases in Geneva and the activities of IARC in Lyon, the WHO Regional Office in Copenhagen has produced a series of reports as for example, on occupational health hazards in hospitals (WHO, 1983a) and on women and occupational health risks (WHO, 1983b).

The International Labour Organization, also based in Geneva, is best known to occupational physicians through its occupational safety and health series of publications, in particular through the *ILO/UC International Classification of Radiographs of the Pneumoconioses*, whose standard films are widely used in epidemiological studies on an international basis.

The interaction between occupational health and general environmental health, and more generally between industrial activity and the conservation of the environment, can be well illustrated by reference to the activities of the International Register of Potentially Toxic Chemicals of the United Nations Environment Programme (UNEP). The programme is currently producing a listing of environmentally dangerous chemicals and processes of global significance for distribution to world governments following submission to the governing council of UNEP in 1984. This listing includes the metals lead, mercury, and cadmium, carbon dioxide, oxides of nitrogen, sulphur dioxide and its derivatives, and what has been termed the injudicious use of pesticides, which still gives rise to poisoning on a large scale in many parts of the world.   G. KAZANTZIS

References

Commission of the European Community (1983). *Occupational Health Guidelines for Chemical Risk.* Luxemburg.

Council of the European Community (1980). Council directive. *Official Journal of the European Communities.* **23**, 8–13.

Farrington, B. (1941–3). The hand in healing. A study in Greek medicine from Hippocrates to Ramazzini. *Proceedings of the Royal Institution of Great Britain*, **32**, 60–91.

Harrington, J. M. (ed.) (1984). *Recent Advances in Occupational Health*, no. 2. London.

Health and Safety Commission (1977). *Occupational Health Services: The Way Ahead.* London.

Health and Safety Executive (1982). *Guidelines for Occupational Health Services.* London.

Health and Safety Executive (1984). *Control of Substances Hazardous to Health (COSHH) 'Control Limits', EH/40/84.* London.

Hoover, H. C. and Hoover, L. H. (eds.) (1912). *Georgius Agricola: De re metallica* (translated from the first Latin edn. of 1556).

House of Lords Select Committee on Science and Technology (1983). *Occupational Health and Hygiene Services.* London.

Hunter, D. (1978). *The Diseases of Occupations.* 6th edn, London.

International Agency for Research on Cancer (1979). *IARC Monographs on the Evaluation of the Carcinogenic Risk of Chemicals to Humans.* IARC Monographs, Vols 1–20, Supplement 1. Lyon, France.

McDonald, J. C. (1981). *Recent Advances in Occupational Health.* London.

Schilling, R. S. F. (1981). *Occupational Health Practice.* 2nd edn, London.

Sigerist, H. E. (1936). Carpenter Lecture: Historical background to industrial and occupational diseases. *Bulletin of the New York Academy of Medicine*, **12**, 597–609.

World Health Organization (1983a). *Occupational Hazards in Hospitals.* Copenhagen.

World Health Organization (1983b). *Women and Occupational Health Risks.* Copenhagen.

OCCUPATIONAL NURSING. See OCCUPATIONAL MEDICINE.

OCCUPATIONAL PHYSICIAN. A physician specializing in the health of the working population and in diseases associated with occupational environments. See OCCUPATIONAL MEDICINE.

OCCUPATIONAL THERAPISTS. Occupational therapy is defined by the American Occupational Therapy Association as a method of treatment for the sick or injured by means of purposeful occupation. The goals are to arouse interest, courage, and confidence; to exercise mind and body in healthy activity; to overcome disability; and to re-establish capacity for industrial and social usefulness. Occupational therapists have traditionally taught handicrafts, but the scope has been widened to include physical exercises, games, music, and household and industrial skills.

OCHSNER, ALTON (1896–1981). American surgeon, MD Washington University (1920). After internship and residency in the USA, Ochsner spent three years in postgraduate study in European clinics; then he returned to posts at Northwestern University and the University of Wisconsin, before moving to Tulane University, where he was chairman of the department of surgery until 1961. He headed the Ochsner Clinic in New Orleans (similar to the Mayo, Crile, and Lahey Clinics elsewhere in the USA). He contributed to knowledge of surgery in both abdominal and thoracic areas, and was active in national and international surgical societies.

OCULAR. Pertaining to the eye.

OCULIST. A specialist in diseases of the eye; an ophthalmologist. See OPHTHALMOLOGY.

OCULOMOTOR PARALYSIS. The oculomotor (or IIIrd cranial) nerve supplies all the extrinsic muscles of the eye, that is those responsible for eye movements, with the exception of the superior oblique muscle (supplied by the trochlear or IVth cranial nerve) and the lateral rectus (supplied by the abducens or VIth cranial nerve). When a lesion affects the oculomotor nerve alone, the paralysed eye is deviated laterally and downwards and there is loss of upward, downward, and medial movement; in addition, there is complete *ptosis with *mydriasis and loss of *pupil reactivity.

OD is a hypothetical force (also known as the odylic force) postulated by von Reichenbach (1788–1869), said to permeate all nature and to manifest itself in certain individuals of sensitive temperament; it has been invoked to explain the phenomena of *mesmerism and animal magnetism.

ODONTOLOGY is the scientific study of the teeth.

ODOURS. Awareness of odours is often useful in medicine, as it is in daily life. Characteristic smells on the breath occur after the use of tobacco, alcohol, and cannabis, the stale odour of acetaldehyde being a delayed sign of alcohol indulgence. Volatile drugs such as paraldehyde and various anaesthetic agents are usually obvious; the sweetish smell of acetone may indicate ketosis due to diabetes or starvation; lead poisoning is said to confer a metallic odour on the breath (*halitus saturninus*), and poisoning with arsenic, selenium, phosphorus, and tellurium can be suggested by a smell akin to that of garlic; *foetor hepaticus* is a musty smell characteristic of severe liver disease with encephalopathy thought to be due to the presence of mercaptans in the expired air; foul-smelling breath (*foetor oris* or halitosis) can occur in apparently healthy individuals but also results from sepsis of teeth, gums, sinuses, and respiratory tract.

O'DWYER, JOSEPH (1841–98). See OTO-LARYNGOLOGY.

OEDEMA is the presence of excess fluid in the tissue spaces. A sufficient accumulation in the subcutaneous tissues causes visible swelling of the part concerned. The fact that this is due to excess extracellular fluid and not to any other cause is confirmed by the characteristic sign of 'pitting on pressure'; firm pressure with a finger or thumb maintained for at least five seconds causes a depression in the swollen area which takes some minutes to disappear after pressure is removed.

Oedema may be localized, due to local vascular causes such as venous or lymphatic obstruction, or generalized, which implies overall body retention of fluid and electrolytes. The latter occurs, for example, in some forms of heart and kidney disorder, though there are many other causes. The distribution of oedema fluid is influenced by hydrostatic factors. It thus tends to accumulate in the relatively lax tissues under the skin, and especially in dependent parts of the body (feet, ankles, and lower legs in the ambulant patient; over the sacral and pelvic regions in those confined to bed).

OEDIPUS COMPLEX is the term for the complex of a child's emotions associated with a subconscious desire for the parent of the opposite sex, which, if not resolved, may according to Freudian theory lead to feelings of guilt and difficulty in forming normal sexual relationships.

OESOPHAGOSCOPY is *endoscopy of the oesophagus.

OESOPHAGUS. The gullet, that part of the alimentary tract which connects the *pharynx with the *stomach; it consists of a musculomembranous tube running downwards through the *mediastinum and passing through the *diaphragm.

OESTROGEN. Any substance, natural or synthetic, which produces changes in the female sexual organs similar to those produced by oestradiol, the natural *hormone of the vertebrate *ovary. The main actions of oestrogens are: development of female *secondary sexual characteristics; stimulation of vaginal cornification, myometrial hypertrophy, and endometrial hyperplasia (which may be followed by withdrawal bleeding); and inhibition of *follicle-stimulating hormone secretion by the anterior *pituitary gland, suppressing ovulation. Oestrogens are also produced by the *placenta, and in small amounts by the *adrenal cortex and the *testis. Indications for their therapeutic use include: oral *contraception; *menopausal symptoms and *osteoporosis; certain cases of breast and prostate *cancer; certain cases of *dysmenorrhoea and *menorrhagia; and inhibition of *lactation.

OESTRUS. The brief period (usually one or two days) during which female non-human mammals evidence sexual desire and are receptive to copulation. Oestrus, which coincides with *ovulation, is part of a physiological cycle characteristic of sexually mature female mammals (the oestrous cycle), of which *menstruation may be regarded as a variant.

OFFICE OF POPULATION, CENSUSES AND SURVEYS (OPCS). This UK government department, which incorporates the General Register Office, is responsible for the regulation of civil marriages, the registration of births, marriages, and deaths in England and Wales, and control of the registration services; the analysis of vital medical and demographic statistics and publication of reports thereon; the periodic census of the population; research into the attitude and circumstances of the general public or of particular groups of individuals. The director of the OPCS is also *Registrar-General for England and Wales.

OIL. Any greasy liquid which is insoluble in water and soluble in *alcohol and *ether. Mineral oils are mixtures of various *hydrocarbons, while animal and vegetable oils are simple *lipids, mixtures of fatty acid glycerides distinguished from fats only by their liquidity.

OINTMENT. Any greasy water-insoluble preparation, usually containing medicinal substances. The commonest base is some mixture of liquid, soft, and hard paraffins.

OKEN, LORENZ (or Okenfuss) (1779–1851). German physician and naturalist. MD Freiburg (1804). In 1832 after brief appointments at several universities Oken became attached to Zurich. He was a leader of the semi-mystical school of nature-philosophy and is said to have combined great originality of thought with much ineptitude. He was the first to organize scientific congresses outside the university framework.

OLD AGE. See AGEING; GERIATRIC MEDICINE; GERONTOLOGY.

OLD MOORE'S ALMANAC was the best known of the early English almanacs published by the Stationer's Company. Francis *Moore was a physician, astrologer, and schoolmaster who published the almanac, containing weather predictions, in order to promote the sale of his pills. The first number was completed in July 1700 and contained predictions for 1701. The front cover of the edition for 1791, in the possession of W. Foulsham & Co. Ltd, carries a twopenny duty stamp and reads:

Vox Stellarum: or, a Loyal Almanack for the Year of Human Redemption M,DCC,XCI. Being the Third after Bissextile or Leap-Year. In which are contained All things fitting for such a Work; as, a Table of Terms and their Returns; The Full, Changes, and Quarters of the Moon; The Rising, Southing, and Setting of the Seven Stars, and other Fixed Stars of Note; the Moon's Age, and a Tide Table fitted to the same; The Rising and Setting of the Sun; the Rising, Southing and Setting of the Moon; Mutual Aspects, Monthly Observations; and many other Things, useful and profitable.

There are a number of present versions, containing many predictions besides the weather. One edition, widely available in newsagents and corner-shops, is priced at 25 pence; that of 1791 cost 'ten pence, stitched'.

OLD VIENNA SCHOOL. The 'old Vienna school' of medicine was established about the middle of the 18th c. by two able physicians, van *Swieten and de Haen, both of whom had been trained in Holland. Hospitals and clinics were established, and the *Allgemeines Krankenhaus, Vienna's famous general hospital, was founded in 1784. This hospital alone was dealing with 14 000 patients a year by the end of the century, when the great sanitarian Johan Peter *Frank was the director. Joseph Leopold *Auenbrugger was a young physician at this time when he published his pamphlet describing his invention of *percussion for elucidating obscure diseases of the chest. During the first quarter of the 19th c., while clinical medicine was reaching new heights in London and Paris, the Vienna school lapsed into a period of relative inactivity, until reinvigorated by the work of *Rokitansky and *Skoda.

OLFACTION is the sense of smell.

OLFACTOMETER. An instrument for measuring the acuity of *olfaction.

OLIGODENDROGLIA is one of the component elements of *neuroglia, the supporting tissue of the nervous system; its cells (oligodendrocytes) are responsible for the formation of *myelin in the white matter of the brain and spinal cord.

OLIGOPHRENIA. Mental subnormality; arrested mental development.

OLIGURIA is the passage of abnormally small quantities of *urine.

OMBUDSMAN. The appointment in the UK of an ombudsman, more formally known as the Health Service Commissioner, was provided for under the *National Health Service (Reorganization) Act 1973. His function is to investigate complaints arising primarily from administrative failure or error, and not those involving clinical matters or family practitioners for which an established system for dealing with complaints already existed. The responsibilities of the Commissioner, whose security of tenure can only be disturbed by Parliament, extends to Wales and Scotland with offices and representation in those countries. Of cases investigated and reported on, most have so far involved waiting-list errors, inadequate records, and inadequate information given to patients' parents or relatives. Many have resulted from faults which were easily remediable.

OMENTUM. A loose fold of *peritoneum, associated with a variable amount of *adipose tissue, which hangs down from the *stomach and *colon within the abdominal cavity.

ONANISM is the extravaginal depositing of semen (see Genesis 38:9), as in *masturbation or *coitus interruptus.

ONCHOCERCIASIS is infestation with the adult worms and microfilariae of the *nematode parasite *Onchocerca volvulus*. It is endemic in tropical communities living within a few kilometres of fast-flowing water, the breeding environment required by the blackfly (*Simulium damnosum*), which is the vector of the disease. The important and tragic complication of onchocerciasis is loss of vision as a result of microfilarial invasion of the eye ('river blindness').

ONCOGENES are viral *genes, that is segments of *deoxyribonucleic acid (DNA), thought to be capable of inducing malignant transformation in cells.

ONCOLOGIST. A physician, surgeon, or therapeutic radiologist who specializes in the diagnosis and treatment of cancer. See ONCOLOGY; RADIOTHERAPY.

ONCOLOGY (NEOPLASTIC DISEASES). Cancer is defined by the *American Heritage Dictionary* (1969) as 'Any of various malignant neoplasms that manifest invasiveness and a tendency to metastasize to new sites', and by the *Concise Oxford Dictionary* (1976) as 'Condition in which there is malignant tumour from uncontrolled growth of tissue, tending to spread and to recur when removed'. A tumour or new growth (neoplasm) can be benign, in which case it displaces and compresses but does not invade and destroy normal tissue, or malignant, when it will invade and destroy normal structures and often spreads by the blood or lymphatic systems to other tissues or organs. Such a malignant growth is popularly known as a cancer.

Early history. Cancer was known to the ancients, and dreaded then as it is now. The English word comes from the Greek word for crab, introduced by *Hippocrates some 500 years before the Christian era, because of its presumed resemblance to the crab. *Galen, writing in about AD 200, accepted the Hippocratic concept of cancer as a manifestation of an imbalance of the four *humours of which the body was considered to be composed. The humours were biological counterparts of the four elements of *Empedocles: air, fire, earth, and water. These, in combinations, produced the qualities of heat, cold, wetness, and dryness. The four body humours were blood, phlegm, yellow bile, and black bile. When they were in proper and harmonious proportions, there was health: disease resulted from deviations of the humours in quantity or in balance. Cancer was a manifestation of an excess of black bile, or melanchole. Cancer is, indeed, a melancholy disease.

This ancient humoral form of holistic medicine persisted in Europe until the 15th c. The concept, however, became ever more elaborate by the introduction of abnormal as well as normal humours. Scirrus, or *scar, became the name for cancers presenting as hard swellings or indurations, and were separated from the later ulcerated stages. Cancer was included with a variety of other *ulcers, *carbuncles, *furuncles, and masses such as *buboes and *aneurysms, all designated as 'tumours contrary to nature'. The complete confusion resulted in elaborate listings of over 200 diseases and lesions attributed to abnormalities or excesses of black bile, of which but few could have been cancerous.

By the 17th c. the black bile theory of cancer was replaced by the *iatrochemical hypothesis introduced by *Paracelsus, in which balances of humours were substituted by balances of chemicals, plus a heavy component of mysticism. Cancer was related to an excess of *arsenic. Two other theories of cancer were also introduced. One was based on the involvement of *lymph nodes by cancer. Turning cause and effect around, cancer was attributed to coagulation of lymph and resultant stasis and irritation. The other theory was that cancer was contagious, a concept that has lingered into the present.

During the long stretch of European history from 500 BC to AD 1700, the treatment of cancer was a combination of crude surgery, *cauterization, a variety of salves containing escharotics (scar-forming corrosive agents) such as arsenic, plus the mandatory *blood-letting and *purging, to which were added *herbal and other preparations of magical or symbolic significance. Cancer of the lip, skin, and of the female breast were described in surgical texts because they were accessible and approachable. But cancers of the stomach and of the uterus were also known to Hippocrates. Cancer of the uterus was clearly described by *Aetius of Amidia during the 6th c., and cancer of the rectum was familiar to John of *Arderne in the 14th c.

The 18th century. The history of cancer turns from speculation and confusion to empirical description and *classification during the 18th c. Gendron in 1700 published a slim book on cancer that eschewed causative hypotheses and described cancer arising locally as a hard growing mass, which penetrated deeper tissues by 'filaments', and finally ulcerated or spread. He concluded that only localized cancers that were removed completely with their extensions were curable, something that was well known to Hippocrates.

The rise of gross (macroscopic, as distinct from microscopic) pathology, then known as morbid anatomy, is usually dated from *Morgagni's great work of 1761, which included unequivocal descriptions of cancer of many internal organs. The London school of John *Hunter produced *Baillie's illustrated *Atlas of Pathology* in 1793, and the Paris school introduced *Bichat's concept of tissues rather than organs as the basis of pathological lesions. Gross observations on many autopsies, and meticulous descriptions of individual types of cancer, led to several simple classifications. Neoplastic diseases were now clearly identified and separated from inflammatory and other pathological processes.

During the 18th c., dubbed the Age of Reason in European history, there were several other seminal events in oncology. The first medical facilities for cancer were established, the one in France for charitable reasons and because there was fear that cancer was contagious, and the one in London for the purpose of studying the disease, as well as a charity. Percivall *Pott in 1775 described chimney sweeps' cancer of the scrotum, the first clear example of an occupational cancer (see OCCUPATIONAL MEDICINE). Also recorded were suspicions that cancer of the breast was associated with celibacy, and that cancers of the lip and nose were initiated by *tobacco smoking. Attempts were even made to transfer cancer between individuals, and from man to dog; neither was successful.

Treatment was still limited to surgical extirpation of accessible lesions, but the cautery was now retired. Wider resections for cancer, to include regional lymph nodes, was recommended by the French school of surgeons headed by *Petit. John Hunter was more conservative and recommended restricting surgery to tumours that were movable and without enlargement of the regional lymphatic nodes.

The 19th century. By the early 19th c. gross pathology and surgical treatment of cancer reached the limits of knowledge available at the time. The great medical events of the century came in 1838, when microscopic pathology was introduced, in 1846, when *anaesthesia was discovered, and in 1867, when *antiseptic and *aseptic surgery dawned. These events, of course, belong to all of medicine, and cancer patients were but one class of the beneficiaries.

Johannes *Müller was the pioneer who looked through the then new achromatic microscope at tumours and other tissues of man and animals collected in European museums of pathology. He recognized that tumours were composed of *cells, and that tumour cells resembled embryonic cells. This magnificent accomplishment, made on crudely teased-out unstained specimens, and recorded in a single, un-Germanically slim volume, revolutionized the understanding of neoplastic growth. Müller and his students, among whom were *Schwann, *Schleiden, *Virchow, and *Cohnheim, founded cellular pathology. Interchanges of ideas and arguments among them played a large part in evolving observations that led to the greater understanding of cancer cell formation, growth, and spread (histogenesis). Essential to progress in this field were ever-improved micro-scopes, and methods of tissue preparation for microscopic examination (see PATHOLOGY).

Rudolf Virchow placed microscopic pathology in the centre of biomedical research, and led German medical science to world pre-eminence. He did not do so well for oncology, holding to the belief that cancer arose from connective tissue, in a way denying his own aphorism of cell continuity. But the histogenesis of cancers arising from epithelial and non-epithelial cells was firmly established by other illustrious German pathologists, including von *Recklinghausen, Remak, and others.

Knowledge regarding the morphological appearance of tumours and the relation of appearance to clinical outcome was fairly complete by the beginning of the 20th c. Histopathology was now the final arbiter of the diagnosis, histogenesis, and prognosis in cancer. Morphology, of course, had to be correlated with the clinical features of cancer, especially recurrence, metastasis (spread), and lethality.

With better and more secure diagnosis, classifications of cancer were developed using the primary site and the type of cellular origin as the criteria. *Leukaemia and *lymphomas became included among neoplastic diseases. Cancer was now recorded more frequently in death certificates and in regional vital report compilations. Standard classifications and reporting systems were developed in England, and the first international classification of the causes of death was adopted in 1900. It was now possible to study cancer as it afflicted different populations, extending the limited records previously gathered in a few larger cities in Europe.

Clinical and *epidemiological observations related a number of environmental exposures to the development of cancer during the industrial revolution of the 19th c. Chronic contact with shale oil, coal distillates, and petroleum products were added to soot as causes of skin cancer. An inordinate prevalence of lung cancer among the miners of the Black Forest was described in 1879, probably the first internal cancer associated with occupation. Aniline dye industry workers were shown in 1895 to develop cancer of the urinary bladder. An *iatrogenic cancer of the skin, due to long-term ingestion of potassium arsenite as a tonic, was recorded by 1887.

During the Victorian era, with the British Empire extending over the globe, British physicians added to the list several environmental cancers among native populations. From India came reports of cancer of the abdominal wall among Kangri natives, who warmed themselves with baskets of live coal carried under their clothes. From Egypt, a causal relationship was suggested between urinary bladder cancer and infestation by *Schistosoma haematobium* flukes (see BILHARZIASIS).

The 20th century. By the beginning of the 20th

c., therefore, there were many examples of cancer in which causal environmental factors were clearly defined. European clinicians, however, considered that these situations were limited to occupational groups and to natives of distant lands.

An important source of information about cancer was a systematic gathering of tumours among animals. Pathological museums of veterinary as well as of human material were established in many capital cities of Europe. Veterinary specimens were obtained from domesticated animals and from abattoirs. Collections were extended to specimens from many species gathered around the world. It was evident that neoplastic diseases in animals and in man were similar, and that they were widely distributed among many species of the animal kingdom.

Anaesthesia and Listerian antiseptic surgery allowed surgical invasion of all body cavities. More extensive removals (resections) of internal cancers were developed in the surgical centres; *Billroth of Vienna typified the period. Pathology collections grew and statistics on the occurrence of cancer in hospital patients now included observations on the end-results of treatment. Hospitals gradually evolved from charitable sanctuaries to centres in the vanguard of medical advances.

Surgeons recognized the inadequacies of their skills in the face of advanced disseminated neoplastic disease. A few pioneers began to urge public education aimed at reducing the delay in the treatment of cancer. Such delays were due not only to the fear of surgery and the grave outlook, but to the fact that cancer was considered to be shameful, particularly as it afflicted the breast and uterus of women. Slowly these societal attitudes began to change.

In the biomedical sciences, the latter part of the 19th c. belongs to *bacteriology, invented by *Pasteur and expanded by *Koch. The techniques of bacteriology were applied to cancer, and the medical literature between 1880 and 1910 is replete with claims of isolation of a wide variety of microorganisms as the cause of cancer. These were false starts in the study of cancer: nevertheless, the investigations stimulated interest and expanded facilities for further work.

At the turn of the 19th to the 20th c. occurred three major scientific advances that influenced all sciences, including medicine. These were, first, the discovery of ionizing radiation, as X-rays by *Roentgen in 1895 and as radioactivity by the *Curies in 1899. Second, filterable *viruses as disease-causing agents were demonstrated by Ivanowsky in 1894 and by Beijerinck in 1899, both using tobacco mosaic disease as their material. And, third, in 1901 three botanists rediscovered *Mendel's 1866 contribution to the mechanism of heredity, ushering in *genetics as a new discipline.

Cancer research. The experimental period of oncology also can be dated to the first years of the 20th c., with transplanted tumours in rats and mice as its primary material. The first successful transplantation of tumours was performed by Novinsky, a veterinarian in St Petersburg in 1877, but his work was neglected. The extensive investigations of Jensen, a veterinarian in Denmark, on transplantations of tumours in mice that he published in 1903 marks the start of experimental cancer research.

During the next decade arose cancer research units in Europe, the USA, and Japan. Among the most prestigious were the *Imperial Cancer Research Fund laboratories in London, the *Rockefeller Institute in New York, the *Pasteur Institute in Paris, and the Tokyo Imperial University. Professional cancer organizations were initiated, with the Berlin Cancer Committee being established in 1900, and the American Association for Cancer Research in 1907. Special cancer journals began publication, the German *Zeitschrift für Krebsforschung* in 1904, the Japanese *Gann* in 1907, and the American *Journal of Cancer Research* in 1916.

Cancer attracted public as well as professional interest. The American Society for the Control of Cancer was founded in 1913, primarily for the education of the public and earlier detection of cancer among women. This was reorganized in 1944 as the American Cancer Society (ACS), with expanded objectives that included legislative stimulus for the support of cancer research. Professional and public interest culminated in the National Cancer Act of 1937, which expressed in law the intent of the USA to control cancer through research. The scope of this legislation was broadened by the National Cancer Plan of 1971. The budgets for cancer research activities rose from less than $1 000 000 before 1940 to over $1 000 000 000 four decades later. The level of activities was also expanded in many European countries and in Japan following their recovery after the Second World War.

The world-wide attack on cancer during the first 80 years of the 20th c. can be divided into several major phases that emanated from seminal discoveries which provided new insights and approaches, as well as new materials and techniques. Among these phases the following are historical and noteworthy.

Transplantable tumours in mice and rats were the first laboratory material for cancer research. Particular interest was focused on the fact that animals implanted with tumours were immune to further implants if the original tumours regressed or if the tumour was excised. Hopes for an immunological solution of cancer were dissipated by the limitation of the induced *immunity to the specific tumour. The approach fell into disrepute, to re-emerge when genetics and cellular immunity were better understood—with the help of transplanted tumours.

Studies on the biology of transplanted tumours in rodents indicated that viable cells were necessary for successful *grafts. The resultant growths were derived from the transplanted cells, whereas the vascular and nutritive sources came from the host. The requirement of cells for transplantation became dogma. Cell-free transmissions of chicken leukaemia, achieved by Ellermann and Bang of Denmark in 1908, and of chicken sarcoma, achieved by Peyton *Rous of New York in 1911, were rejected as exceptions. Nevertheless, the two leading hypotheses regarding the aetiology of cancer were that it was due to viruses, or to somatic *mutation.

Mammalian genetics, developed by William Castle at Harvard University, found an important application in cancer research. It led to the development of *homozygous mouse strains that allowed work on genetically defined animals. Breast cancer was shown to aggregate among females of certain mouse families, and to be related to reproduction and to *ovarian function.

Chemical carcinogenesis was opened up as a laboratory research field by Yamagiwa of Japan, a student of Virchow and first professor of pathology in Tokyo. In 1915 he and Ichikawa produced cancers of the ears of rabbits by repeated applications of coal tar. The active chemicals, polycyclic aromatic hydrocarbons such as *benz(a)pyrene, were identified by 1930 by a London group under E. L. Kennaway. *Oestrogenic steroids were isolated during the same period, and were shown to produce cancers of the breast and other *hormone-dependent end organs in mice. The chemical relationship between the oestrogens and the polycyclic aromatic hydrocarbons suggested that cancer could be the result of an *inborn error of *cholesterol metabolism. The implication that specific cancers might normally be caused by such chemicals only was, however, refuted by Yoshida's description of hepatocarcinomas in rats fed azo dyes.

Thousands of compounds, many being analogues of known carcinogens, were added to the list of cancer-causing chemicals. Many chemical carcinogens required metabolic conversion into the actual proximal carcinogens. Many chemicals defined as carcinogens produced mutations in bacterial or animal systems, indicating that their action involved changes in the genetic material of the cells. *Ionizing radiation also was carcinogenic and mutagenic, as was the *ultraviolet radiation portion of the spectrum that produced skin cancers in man and animals.

Biochemical investigations on cancer tissue were stimulated by *Warburg's discovery that tumours resembled embryonic tissue in their anerobic glycolysis (breakdown of glycogen to glucose in the absence of oxygen). This reversion of tumours toward embryonic behaviour was also manifested by the elaboration of *proteins characteristic of the fetal stage of development.

Epidemiologists such as Doll in the UK and others in the USA established during the 1950s that the pandemic of lung cancer being experienced in the Western world was due to tobacco smoking, especially in the form of cigarettes. Other human carcinogenic situations were defined, such as the industrial exposures to asbestos leading to *mesothelioma, and *vinyl chloride producing angiosarcoma of the liver. Exposure to ionizing radiation produced myelocytic leukaemia among survivors of the Hiroshima atomic bomb disaster (SEE RADIATION INJURY), and increased the occurrence of *thyroid and other cancers. Oestrogens given in large doses during pregnancy produced cancer of the *vagina in the offspring, and cancer of the *endometrium in women who used them for protracted periods following *menopause. A strong *synergism was defined between asbestos and tobacco smoking, leading to a high risk of lung cancer among individuals exposed to both agents.

Host factors in the induction and growth of neoplasms were explored in animals and in man. The genetic component influenced both, but was related to specific neoplasms and conditions; phenotypes rather than genotypes. Hereditary neoplasms in man included retinoblastoma, multiple *polyposis of the colon, and preneoplastic states such as *xeroderma pigmentosum, *neurofibromatosis, and *Down's syndrome. Relatives of individuals with some such syndromes, such as *ataxia-telangiectasia, were shown by Swift to have a higher risk of cancer than the general population. Families with many cancers had a higher risk of developing additional cancers than families without such a history. This effect, of obvious public health import, could be attributed to sharing habits or to the environment as well as to heredity.

Nutritional factors in carcinogenesis were adduced from statistical studies on human populations and from animal studies. Unnecessary calories, and excessive fats and meat in the diet, were related to a higher occurrence of cancer. Religious groups on modest diets and eschewing tobacco and alcohol had one-third less cancer than the general population of the USA. The addition of retinoids, antioxidants, or selenium to the diet decreased the appearance of spontaneous and induced cancers in experimental animals. Formal field trials to test these hypotheses are being planned by the US National Cancer Institute.

The hormonal milieu of the host, and exogenous hormones, influenced the appearance of cancers of hormone end-organs, such as the breast and *prostate. Immunodeficiency, in experimental animals and in tissue recipients in whom rejection was inhibited by drugs invented for cancer chemotherapy, was shown to increase the occurrence of neoplasms, especially of lymphoid origin.

Chemotherapy of cancer (*antineoplastic chemotherapy) attempted empirically since antiquity, became a major research field during the 1940s. George Beatson's report on 1896, on the amelioration of advanced breast cancer by ovariectomy, was extended with exogenous oestrogens and *androgens. Charles *Huggins in 1941 showed beneficial effects of *castration and of oestrogens on advanced prostatic carcinoma. *Alkylating chemicals, analogues of the deadly *mustard gas designed for chemical warfare, were found to shrink lymphatic tissue and tumours derived therefrom. Anti-folic acid compounds, such as *methotrexate, were demonstrated by Sidney Farber to have therapeutic effects against acute leukaemia of children.

The dream of curative systemic therapy for disseminated cancer became reality when methotrexate was used against *choriocarcinoma of women. Chemotherapy by multiple drugs converted disseminated *Hodgkin's disease from a universally fatal affliction to one that was curable in most patients. Leukaemia and several other neoplasms of children also yielded to chemotherapy combined with surgery and radiation (radiotherapy). Over 20 drugs comprised the armamentarium against cancer by 1980, including alkylating agents, *antimetabolites, derivatives of micro-organisms, and platinum complexes.

Surgical procedures, facilitated by blood replacement (transfusion), control of *shock, and *antibiotics, became more extensive following the experiences of the Second World War. Statistical analyses of the results, however, did not verify significant improvements by heroic surgery (that involving hazardous and massive removal of tissue). Less extensive resections were substituted: even the classic radical Halsted mastectomy was modified to more limited procedures.

Radiotherapy, first in the form of radium, was quickly applied to cancer after its discovery, but more as an escharotic (scar-forming) agent than as a new form of energy. French and German radiobiologists worked out the doses and schedules for external delivery of X-rays. Radiation, by 1930, joined surgery as the second modality by which cures could be achieved in some patients with cancer.

The totality of clinical management, including diagnosis of smaller lesions by radiological and *ultrasound visualization, was finally reflected in better survival among patients with cancer. From less than 30 per cent five-year survival during the 1930s, the proportion rose to 45 per cent by 1980. This improvement, however, was more than compensated for by increased total mortality, attributable primarily to the self-imposed tobacco-caused cancer of the lung.

The possibility of viral and immunological causes of cancer, rejected for many years, forcibly re-entered the research arena during the 1950s. Among the key discoveries that forced the reconsideration were the Bittner mammary tumour virus of mice, transmitted through the milk of the mother. The finding emerged from mammalian genetic research at the Jackson Laboratory in Bar Harbor, Maine, where it was shown that mammary tumours in mice were transmitted extrachromosomally. A kidney tumour in frogs was concluded to be of viral origin. Skin cancers in domestic rabbits were produced by the Shope virus from

papillomas of wild rabbits. Finally, Ludwig Gross demonstrated cell-free transmission of leukaemia to newborn mice. A wide spectrum of tumours was induced in several species by a mouse virus (*polyoma) grown in tissue culture by Sarah Stewart and Bernice Eddy. Polyoma virus overcame the dogma of tumour and species specificity that was derived from previously accepted oncoviruses.

Tumour immunity also had a resurgence by 1960, through the discovery and verification of tumour transplantation *antigens. There was now no doubt that some tumours produced specific antigens that elicited a cellular type of reaction.

Viruses of both the *deoxyribonucleic acid (DNA) and *ribonucleic acid (RNA) type thus caused a number of cancers in animals, especially neoplasms of the leukaemia–lymphoma complex in chickens, cats, and cattle. In chickens and in cats some forms of the disease behaved as a classic infection with horizontal transmission (transmission from case to case as distinct from vertical transmission from one generation to the next). *Vaccines were achieved for a form of chicken lymphoma, and were being developed for feline and bovine leukaemia.

In man, a herpes-like DNA virus, the *Epstein–Barr agent (EBV), was isolated from African paediatric *lymphoma, and was shown to be causally related not only to that disease but to nasopharyngeal carcinoma endemic in China, and to *infectious mononucleosis (glandular fever). A form of leukaemia was also found to be associated with a retrovirus. *Hepatitis B virus (HBV) was associated with hepatocarcinoma, and a vaccine against it was developed. An immunological association was adduced between cancers of the cervix and of the penis, and *Herpes hominis* 2 virus (HHV2). The neoplastic entities related to viruses in man required environmental triggers, such as recurrent *malaria in the African lymphoma, and hepatotoxins such as *aflatoxin in the case of hepatocarcinoma. A peculiar outbreak of *Kaposi's sarcoma among homosexual men in the UK and the USA also appeared to be transmissible as an infection.

Molecular biology has been the cutting edge of all biomedical research, including cancer, for the past several decades. Cancer, in turn, has provided much material for advances in molecular biology. *Tissue culture, started by *Carrel and Burrows in 1911, developed as an arm of cancer research into the production of mammalian cell *clones, and of cell hybrids between species. The simplified bundles of genetic nucleic acids represented by oncogenic viruses allowed the discovery of enzymes which split such molecules at specific sites. Temin and Baltimore simultaneously discovered reverse transcriptase, illuminating the mechanism by which single-stranded RNA entities can enter and replicate DNA.

The interlink between genetics and virology became even closer with the discoveries of genes that travelled between chromosomes, and of the separation of viral genomes, called *oncogenes, from human tumours. Cancer could now be described as a viral genetic infection, or as an infectious gene.

Segments of DNA from several human tumours have been reported to produce *in vitro* transformation of mouse cells, and to become incorporated into the mouse DNA. This represents the isolation and transfer of human oncogenes.

The technology emanating from molecular biology that is already available, in the form of recombinant DNA and *monoclonal antibodies (see IMMUNOLOGY) from hybridomas, allows the prediction of subsequent steps in the research on cancer.

The control of many forms of cancer may well be achieved by scientific research before the close of the 20th c.   M. B. SHIMKIN

Further reading

Anonymous (1982). *Decade of Discovery: Advances in Cancer Research, 1971–1981*. Bethesda, Maryland.
Burchenal, J. H. and Oettgen, H. F. (eds) (1981). *Cancer. Achievements, Challenges and Prospects for the 1980s*. New York.
Frederickson, D. S. (1981). Biomedical research in the 1980s. *New England Journal of Medicine*, **304**, 509–17.
Rather, L. J. (1978). *The Genesis of Cancer*. Baltimore.
Shimkin, M. B. (1977). *Contrary to Nature, an Illustrated History of Cancer*. Washington, DC.
Shimkin, M. B. (1981). *Some Classics of Experimental Oncology*. Washington, DC.

ONYCHIA is infection of the matrix of a finger- or toe-nail.

OOCYTE. Ovarian cell, precursor of the *ovum.

OOPHORECTOMY is the surgical removal of one or both *ovaries.

OPENING SNAP. A discrete short high-frequency sound heard on cardiac *auscultation following shortly after the second heart sound, associated with mitral valve opening at the beginning of *diastole. An audible opening snap at or near the apex of the heart is a characteristic sign of *mitral stenosis.

OPERATING THEATRE. A room designed and equipped for the purpose of carrying out surgical operations, usually with anterooms for anaesthetic induction, recovery, surgical and nursing staff, etc.

OPERATING THEATRE ATTENDANTS. Ancillary staff attached to operating theatres; theatre orderlies.

OPERATION. Any surgical procedure.

OPHTHALMIA. Any severe inflammatory condition of the eye. Ophthalmia neonatorum refers to acute purulent conjunctivitis developing in infants within a few days of birth as a result of direct infection from the mother's birth canal, due for example to *gonorrhoea.

OPHTHALMOLOGIST. A medically qualified specialist in diseases of the eye; an oculist. See OPHTHALMOLOGY.

OPHTHALMOLOGY

Introduction. One of the deep-rooted fears of reflective man is that he should lose his sight and live in a dark world unable to find food and shelter and without the ability to protect himself. This is the reason for the concern which even a trivial eye injury or illness may arouse in us today, and why the earliest medical writings contain numerous references to diseases of the eye and the efforts of the ancients to alleviate them.

The eye conditions prevalent in the dry and dusty lands of the Middle East, where the earliest literate peoples lived, are those of the lids and the membranes covering the eye, the so-called external diseases. Some, like *styes and lid *cysts, are quite trivial: others are more severe, and these include corneal *ulceration and *trachoma which may lead to partial or complete blindness. Early records, such as the *Ebers papyrus (c. 1550 BC) indicate that these and many other external conditions were recognized and that there were specific treatments for some of them. However, this lore was in the hands of the priests and it was only under their direction that a class of skilled hand-workers undertook surgical operations.

It was not until the age of *Hippocrates that medicine was released from the shackles of priesthood and the supernatural. The first step, and a very faltering one, was to determine the anatomy of the interior of the eye.

The anatomy of the eye. In the 4th c. BC *Aristotle dissected the eyes of apes and other animals and concluded rightly that the eyeball is essentially a sphere composed of three concentric layers (Fig. 1). There is an outer tough protective layer called the sclera on account of its hardness (the Greek word for hard is *skléros*), and the cornea which is the smaller front part of it, no less tough but perfectly transparent. The middle layer is composed almost entirely of blood vessels; this is the choroid. The innermost layer is the retina. It is formed of thin friable and transparent tissue and

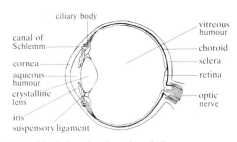

Fig. 1. Vertical section through eyeball

was not recognized for centuries as the key tissue that it is.

*Galen in the 2nd c. AD investigated the transparent jelly-like materials which occupy the centre of the globe and mistakenly credited the crystalline lens, by virtue of its position in the centre of the sphere, as being the actual organ of sight. Galen knew nothing of the function of the vitreous humour occupying the globe behind the lens or for that matter the aqueous humour in front of it; both had to wait for the advent of modern techniques for their functions to be elucidated.

Galen recognized the optic nerve or 'stalk' of the eye and also the chiasm or partial crossing of the optic nerve fibres lying under the brain itself. Nothing was known of the nervous pathways known as the optic tracts and radiations which pass to the occipital cortex at the back of the brain, where light impulses from the retina are interpreted and stored in the memory.

The fundus of the eye. Just over 100 years ago, and still aged less than 30 years at the time, the great German physicist Hermann von *Helmholtz invented his 'eye mirror', forerunner of the present-day oculist's *ophthalmoscope, which enables him to view the interior of the eye. The picture he sees is in brilliant colour and magnified some 20 times (Fig. 2). The most striking feature is the optic disc or commencement of the optic nerve with the blood vessels of the retina radiating from it. The uniform red 'eye-ground' is due to the *capillary network of the choroid showing through the transparent retina. The macula, a little smaller than the disc and situated to its outer side, is the seat of the most acute sense of form and colour.

The normal anatomy and the numerous pathological changes in the smaller blood vessels can be seen in the fundus more clearly and conveniently than elsewhere in the body. In the last two decades these observations have been extended by photography, and even greater magnification of selected areas of the retinal circulation can be made by fluorescein *angiography (Novotny and Alvis, 1961). In this technique the dye *fluorescein is injected into the circulation and photographed on cine-film during its passage through the retina and choroid. Even when the fundus is obscured, for

example by blood, it is possible by means of *ultrasound to obtain accurate information regarding the position of structures such as the lens and retina.

The refraction of the eye. *The dioptric system of the eye.* The fact that the image of a luminous external object is formed on the retina was proved as long ago as 1625 by Scheiner. He experimented with the eyes of recently slaughtered animals and on carefully cutting away the sclera and choroid from the rear of the eyeball he actually saw, on the retina, a minute inverted picture of the outside world.

All the transparent structures of the eye are involved in this refraction or bending of the rays of light which is necessary to form an image on the retina: the dioptric system. The principal agent in refraction is the cornea, which is equal in strength to a +40 dioptre convex lens. The crystalline lens is responsible for a further one-third of the refraction.

Refractive errors and accommodation. Hypermetropia, myopia, and astigmatism are anomalies of refraction rather than ocular diseases. Their optics and their correction are shown in Fig. 3(a)–(e). The common form of astigmatism is due to a faulty contour of the front surface of the cornea which, instead of being symmetrically curved like a watchglass, is more curved in one meridian than in the other; like the contour of the back of a spoon. The result is that it is impossible to get a point focus of a distant object on the retina as, in fact, the name of the condition suggests (a = without, stigma = a point). If, for example, the vertical lines of the object are brought to a line focus the horizontal are out of focus and vice versa. The condition can be corrected by spectacle lenses of cylindrical form as these lenses refract in one meridian without affecting the other. This applies to both convex or concave cylindrical lenses. The same correction is valid in the less common condition where the astigmatism is due to tilting of the crystalline lens. The focusing of near objects on the retina is brought about by alteration in the shape and therefore of the power of the crystalline lens; this is called accommodation and the mechanism was explained by Helmholtz. The lens (seen in section in Fig. 1) is convex and elastic and attached to the ring of the ciliary processes (Fig. 4) by the suspensory ligament. When the ring is slackened as the ciliary muscle contracts in accommodation, the lens becomes more convex and its refractive power is increased. In middle life the lens loses its elasticity and focusing of near objects is no longer possible except with the aid of correcting lenses (presbyopia).

Spectacle lenses. Most refractive errors can be corrected by spectacle lenses ('glasses'). There is endless argument among scholars as to the origin of spectacles and other correcting lenses. It is said, for example, that Nero had a huge emerald with a concave depression which enabled him to over-

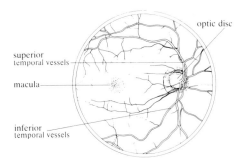

Fig. 2. Ophthalmoscopic view of right fundus

Fig. 3. (a) Emmetropia (the ideal state). Parallel rays of light from a distant object are refracted by the cornea and lens and form a sharp image exactly on the retina. (b) Hypermetropia. Because of a shorter globe or insufficient refraction by the cornea and lens, parallel rays of light do not come to a focus on the retina and the image is blurred. (c) Correction of hypermetropia. A convex spectacle lens is placed in front of the eye and this augments the convergence of parallel rays, which are now brought to an exact focus on the retina. (d) Myopia. Because of a lengthening of the globe or, less commonly, excessive refraction by the cornea and lens, parallel rays of light come to a focus in front of the retina and the image is blurred. (e) Correction of myopia. A concave spectacle lens is placed in front of the eye and this diverges parallel rays so that they are brought to an exact focus on the retina.

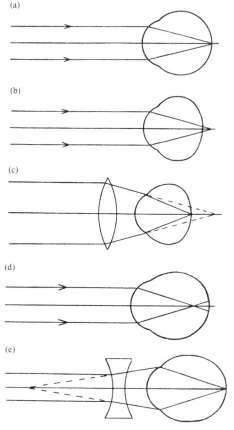

(a)

(b)

(c)

(d)

(e)

come his myopia and enjoy the bloodspilling of the arena. There seems little doubt that in the 13th and 14th c. glasses were used to overcome presbyopia and there is evidence of this in the writings of Della Spina of Pisa who died in 1313 and Roger *Bacon of Oxford. Myopia, then, is correctable by minus (concave) lenses and hypermetropia and presbyopia by plus (convex) lenses. In the common form of astigmatism, where the two principal meridians are 90° apart, cylindrical lenses are used to correct the error.

Contact lenses. In the early 19th c. Thomas *Young, a sufferer from myopia and astigmatism, demonstrated on his own eyes that it was possible to neutralize the effect of the corneal curvature by immersing the eye in water. Sir John Herschel the astronomer suggested in 1827 that refractive errors could be treated by enclosing the patient's cornea by a light 'shell' the front surface of which could be ground to any required curvature, and which just cleared the cornea. The interval between the back of the shell and front of the cornea was to be filled with saline, which, having the same refractive index as the cornea itself, would neutralize any defects (such as irregular astigmatism) the shell might have. This was a theoretical concept and it was not until some 60 years later that A. E. Fick actually made the first contact lenses on this principle. They were supported on the sclera ('haptic' lenses) and in most cases were extremely uncomfortable; they were therefore tolerated only when a marked improvement in vision was obtained. It was not until the 1950s that 'corneal' contact lenses, floating on the tear film, were developed: the greatly increased tolerance made their wearing a practical proposition for even minor errors.

The physiology of vision. One of the marvels of nature is the manner in which our eyes reveal the world around us. Helmholtz, in one of his 'popular lectures', said: 'It is by the eye alone that we know the countless shining worlds that fill immeasurable space, the distant landscapes of our own earth, and all the varieties of sunlight that reveal them, the wealth of form and colours among flowers, the strong and happy life that moves in animals.' How then, do rays of light impinging on the retina bring about the perceptions, memories, and philosophical concepts which we all share?

The reception, transmission, and interpretation of visual impulses. Rays of light from external objects pass through the dioptric system of the eye and form images on the retina. This delicate transparent membrane has two main nervous components. First, the sensory receptors—the rods and cones—form part of the posterior retina and here the light impulses impinge. This causes electric impulses to be set up and these pass along the second group of nervous elements—the transmitting nerve fibres—which make an infinite number of connections with adjacent nerve cells and finally leave the eye in the optic nerves to the *mid-brain where, in our reptilian ancestors, there were centres of vision to perceive images from these impulses. In man, however, they merely form a nervous relay system and the impulses pass on in the optic chiasm, the optic tracts, and radiations in the substance of the brain until they reach the occipital cortex where they are finally converted into sensations of sight. In the optic chiasm, half the nerve fibres, from the nasal halves of both retinae, cross the midline and those from the temporal halves do not. Thus the fibres in the left optic tract and radiation, travelling to the left occipital cortex, come from the nasal half of the right retina and the temporal half of the left, thus carrying impulses from the right halves of the visual field of each eye. Interruption of that pathway would thus cause blindness in the right half field, known as a *hemianopia. The occipital centres are connected with other, mostly unknown, areas of the brain where the visual images are stored in the memory to be compared with earlier ones and are so interpreted in the light of experience.

The rods and cones. The central and peripheral areas of the retina show a striking contrast in their sensitivity to light, colour, and form. This is due to two kinds of light-sensitive receptors in the retina, known because of their shape as rods and cones.

The cones are elements shaped like little rockets. They are most numerous in the macular area where they greatly outnumber the rods; in fact in the centre of the macula itself is a small area called the fovea which is entirely composed of cones. Cones are sensitive to details of form and colour and are used in conditions of good illumination. They are of three types and each responds to one of the three primary colours, red, green, and blue. Different colour shades are perceived by using a mixture of these three types of cones, rather as a painter mixes colours on a palette. Bleaching, by light, of the pigment *rhodopsin (or visual purple) is just one of the complex mechanisms which takes place when light falls on the rods and cones.

The rods are cigar-shaped cells and are most numerous in the peripheral parts of the retina. They are sensitive to movement and are used particularly in conditions of reduced illumination (twilight vision). On a starlit night, for example, it is the function of the rods to pick up the relatively infrequent light signals from the landscape by using the more peripheral parts of the retina. There is little or no colour in low illumination and as there are few rods in the macular area there is a scotoma or shadow right at the centre of the object being regarded.

Adaptation. On passing from an area where the illumination is good, such as a well-lit room, to the darkness outside, the eye 'adapts'—that is it becomes accustomed to the dark. Both the vision, and thus the ability to move about, gradually increase until after about half an hour the retina is fully adapted to the new conditions (dark-adapted). Conversely, on passing from a poorly illuminated area to a well-lit one there is a sudden blinding dazzle for a few seconds as the eye, in this case, adapts to light. In about 3–4 minutes the eye again sees colour and detail.

The fields of vision. The visual field of each eye is the whole panorama which can be seen surrounding the object (fixation-spot) which is being observed. The inner (nasal) portions of the fields overlap and the outer (temporal) fields allow us to see directly sideways to the left and right. The central area of the field, served by the macula,

extends only 3 or 4 degrees from the fixation point; away from this, the visual acuity drops off sharply towards the periphery. There are therefore two elements to a visual field, just as there are in the retina—a central and a peripheral—and they are intimately linked. The peripheral field supplies the broad outline, and the central the detail. Any movement or object of interest is picked up by the rods of the peripheral retina: this causes reflex movements of the eyes, so that the macular areas are brought to bear on the area of interest, which can then be examined minutely by the macular cones. It is often found that, in conditions of disease, one or other part of the field is selectively attacked.

The intraocular circulation. *Retinal and choroidal vascular systems.* In the interior of the eye there are two independent vascular systems: the retinal and the choroidal.

The retinal circulation consists of the arteries and veins with their smaller branches, which are seen with the ophthalmoscope radiating from the optic disc (Fig. 2). These vessels supply the inner transmitting layers of the retina. The choroidal circulation, which surrounds the outer layers of the retina like a mantle, is a much richer vascular network consisting of wide intercommunicating channels which supply the outer third of the retina. This includes the rods and cones, which need a rich supply of oxygen.

The choroidal circulation is continuous with that of the ciliary body and iris and the combined structures are often referred to as the uveal tract.

The intraocular fluid. The interior of the globe is permeated by a watery fluid which is formed by a process of filtration and secretion by the ciliary processes (see below): in the anterior chamber, the space between the cornea and the crystalline lens, it circulates freely and is known as the aqueous. The intraocular fluid also percolates the vitreous (Fig. 1) and, very slowly, the lens. This slow and steady flow of fluid allows the exchange of oxygen and waste products of metabolism to take place in the transparent structures which do not have their own blood supply.

A further function of the intraocular fluid is the maintenance of the pressure inside the eye. The eyeball, like the tyre of a car, needs a positive pressure inside it to maintain its spherical shape. In the eye the pressure is maintained by a balance between the amount of intraocular fluid which is produced and the rate at which it flows out of the eye through minute pores, the trabeculum, into the canal of Schlemm and from thence into the general circulation. There are many ways in which this equilibrium can be disturbed.

If the pressure rises above the normal 16–22 mm of mercury the eye is said to be glaucomatous (see below) and if it falls too low and the globe loses its spherical shape, the eye is said to be hypotonic.

Disorders of the retina. The retina is the key structure of the eye. Failure of its blood supply is the most frequent cause of loss of vision. The failure may be due to disease of the retinal vessels themselves or to partial or complete closure of the vessels of the choroid. Sometimes the neural elements of the retina may fail, often from hereditary conditions, and they are sometimes poisoned by toxins and drugs.

Diabetic retinopathy is a good example of disease of the retinal vessels themselves, and is the most common cause of blindness under the age of 65. *Diabetes causes vascular lesions in many parts of the body and the retinae are particularly vulnerable.

There are two forms of diabetic retinopathy. In the proliferative type, which is characteristic of juvenile or insulin-dependent diabetes, pathological 'new-formed' vessels sprout from the normal retinal vessels and, as they are thin-walled and weak, they are very prone to rupture and cause recurrent bleeding: this leads to the formation of opaque bands and membranes in the retina and vitreous and may eventually lead to retinal detachment and blindness.

Maturity-onset diabetics suffer from a more benign condition, simple diabetic retinopathy. Here the walls of the capillary vessels, particularly those lying to the outer side of the macula, become weaker and leak. The first sign of the condition is the appearance of small round red spots—retinal microaneurysms—which are formed by localized ballooning of the walls of minute capillary vessels. Later, the capillaries start to break and small retinal haemorrhages occur; or *plasma leaks into the surrounding retina. Finally, making up the characteristic ophthalmoscopic picture, yellowish-white plaques of *lipid exudates, often in the form of rings, are deposited in the retina. If the macula itself is involved in these changes, a drop in the visual acuity always occurs.

Both types of diabetic retinopathy are amenable to treatment by photocoagulation (usually with a *laser beam). In the proliferative disease the dangerous new vessels can be eradicated directly and they can also be made to regress by ablating large areas of the peripheral retina. In simple retinopathy the sites of leakage can be found by angiography and obliterated by laser.

Macular degeneration. A common cause of loss of vision in people over the age of 65 is a *degenerative change at the macula; the condition usually occurs in both eyes. Patients frequently notice a kinking of straight lines and later a distortion of the form of objects. Over a period of 1–5 years a completely blind area, or scotoma, develops at the centre of the visual field and this prevents any vision requiring detail. The peripheral field, however, is unaffected. Both the retina and choroid are involved to varying degrees, so the fundus picture is also variable. Sometimes the changes consist of a few small patches of pigment disturbance at the macula: in other cases, fluid leaks from weakened choroidal capillaries to form raised whitish patches between the choroid and pigment epithelium of the retina. Yet again there may be actual bleeding from these degenerate capillaries, and there may be treatable by laser. In the majority of eyes, however, there is the ultimate formation of a central patch of defunct functionless retina.

Patients who find that there is an obvious deterioration in their vision naturally assume that they are suffering from a progressive condition and fear that they will eventually become completely blind. It is therefore highly important to reassure them that the peripheral vision will remain and that they will be able to get about unaided and attend to toilet and other personal affairs without the assistance of others.

Other vascular diseases. Many other diseases of the blood vessels or blood cells bring about changes in the fundus and these are often of diagnostic importance. *Hypertension, *arteriosclerosis, temporal *arteritis and a rare condition causing inflammation around retinal veins, called Eales's disease, cause generalized or localized narrowing of the retinal vessels, which may lead to vascular occlusions or intraocular haemorrhages. Diseases of the blood cells themselves, such as *sickle-cell haemoglobin C disease, macrocytic *anaemia, and the *leukaemias, have typical retinal signs.

The retinal neural tissue itself is highly vulnerable. A common *familial condition is retinitis pigmentosa. There is a progressive degeneration of the retinal rods, which results in failure of dark adaptation, leading to progressive field loss and eventual blindness in the fourth or fifth decade.

Retinal detachment. This is caused by intraocular fluid separating the neural layers of the retina from the pigment cells, following the development of holes or tears in the former. These holes may be caused by trauma (see below), high (severe) myopia, and degeneration of the retina. Detachment may also follow the contracture of *connective tissue formed after bleeding into the vitreous (see below), and may be caused by malignant *melanoma, a growth of the choroid. Following the pioneer work of Jules Gonin of Lausanne earlier this century, the surgical treatment of detachment carries a high chance of success. Gonin insisted on meticulous care in ophthalmoscopic examination in order to locate every hole and to seal it by *cautery. This is now done by laser or by cryotherapy (freezing).

Toxins and drugs. The neural tissue of the retina may be damaged by the use of tobacco (usually of the strong pipe variety, rarely cigarettes) or by *methanol ingestion. Iatrogenic (drug-induced) blindness from macular dystrophy may follow prolonged treatment with *chloroquine or *ethambutol. It is usual, therefore, to monitor the visual acuities and central fields when these drugs are being administered.

Disorders of the cornea and lens. As light passes

through the eye to the retina, little energy is lost: this is because it passes through four perfectly transparent structures, namely the cornea, the aqueous, the crystalline lens, and the vitreous.

The cornea is one of nature's masterpieces which was developed in fishes 400 million years ago and has not been improved on since. It is only 0.6 mm thick at its centre and is extremely tough. Its main bulk is formed by the substantia propria. Here the *collagen fibres run in interlacing bundles of fibrils in basket-work pattern; the absolute regularity of this creates the transparency.

The cornea is a dehydrated tissue. This is due to the activity of the front layer of the cornea (the epithelium) and the back layer (the endothelium) which remove fluid from the central layers. *Oedema results in a thickened opaque cornea. Other causes of corneal opacity are ulcers of the epithelium, inflammation of the substantia propria (deep *keratitis), and degenerative conditions of the cornea. All these conditions usually result in scarring, but the collagen fibres used in the repair no longer have their regular arrangement and a localized grey opacity is formed. If this is central, a marked loss of vision results. This can be alleviated by corneal grafting. This was first shown to have a place in ocular therapy by Filatov in Odessa and Tudor-Thomas in Cardiff: in principle, grafting comprises the removal of a disc of cornea containing the opaque scar and replacement with a disc of similar size from a cadaver cornea. Improvements in surgical techniques and tissue typing have greatly improved results, and a clear graft can now be expected in some 75 per cent of cases.

The crystalline lens, cataract. Like the cornea, the crystalline lens (Fig. 1) owes its transparency to the very regular arrangement of its component fibres. These are laid down like the layers of an onion, so that the earliest, formed in fetal life, remain in the centre (lens nucleus) and the more recently formed layers lie nearest to the surface (lens cortex). The whole lens is enveloped in an elastic cover, the capsule. Any opacity, large or small, in the nucleus, cortex, or capsule is known as a cataract. They are usually classified by their mode of origin. Those present at birth (congenital cataracts) may be caused by virus infections (notably *rubella) infecting the mother during the first 3–12 weeks of fetal life and others are familial. Traumatic cataract is dealt with below. *Endocrine diseases such as diabetes often result in cataract. So-called senile cataract is by far the most common and is caused by a lack of oxygen inside the eye as the blood supply of the choroid and retina gradually fail with age.

World-wide, cataract is the greatest single cause of blindness and, moreover, of blindness which can be treated. The usual symptom is a gradual loss of vision in a white painless eye. The diagnosis is easily made with the ophthalmoscope as the lens opacities are clearly seen silhouetted against the red fundus background. The treatment is surgical

but operation is not necessarily indicated when the condition is diagnosed: it is often many years before cataracts have advanced sufficiently to impair vision, and much depends on the visual requirements, occupation, and interests of the patient. The operation of couching of cataract, possibly invented by the ancient Babylonians and still carried out in remote places today, is performed by introducing a thin sharp knife into the eye in front of the lens, which is then depressed backwards into the lower part of the vitreous where it no longer obscures vision. Modern cataract techniques owe their origin to the 18th c. French oculist Daviel who made an incision about half an inch long along the lower margin of the cornea and, aided by a small scoop, expressed the cataractous lens through it and out of the eye. Essentially the same operation for removal of cataract has been practised since but, with the advent of the operating *microscope and finer instrumentation, surgery has now reached near-perfection. The most significant advance in the past two decades, pioneered by Harold Ridley of London, has been the substitution of the cataracterous lens by an acrylic insert (prosthesis).

Glaucoma, the condition of raised intraocular pressure (see above) occurs in many pathological conditions (secondary glaucomas); two of these are iritis and hyphaema (see below). In addition there are two primary glaucomas which are due to 'built-in' defects in the eyes themselves rather than being caused by other eye diseases. They are known as open angle (chronic simple) glaucoma and closed (narrow) angle or angle closure glaucoma. The angle which differentiates the two types is that formed where the back surface of the cornea and the front surface of the iris meet. This is often known as the filtration angle because it is here that the trabeculum is situated (Fig. 4).

Open angle glaucoma. In these eyes the contour of the filtration angle is exactly the same as in the normal eye. The defect lies in the pores of the trabeculum which in these people become narrower with age. The raised pressure, usually some 5–15 mm of mercury above normal, is usually not apparent until middle life. The condition sometimes runs in families. The raised pressure

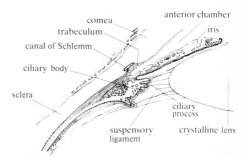

Fig. 4. The angle of the anterior chamber magnified 25 times

acts on the optic disc which is the weakest part of the eye. This is forced backwards, giving a very typical ophthalmoscopic appearance known as cupping; cases are very frequently diagnosed on routine examination for glasses. As the cupping increases, the disc capillaries become obliterated and the disc itself becomes white (glaucomatous atrophy); at this stage the vision is seriously affected.

Milder degrees of open angle glaucoma respond well to medical treatment such as pilocarpine drops which open up the drainage channels or 1.0 per cent *adrenaline and 0.5 per cent timolol which reduce the production of aqueous. In the more severe cases which cannot be controlled by these means, surgery is indicated. Most procedures aim at short-circuiting the trabeculum and draining the aqueous under the conjunctiva. Encouraging results involving the use of lasers are currently under trial (laser trabeculotomy).

Angle closure. The built-in defect, which again is familial and often occurs in middle life, is a flattening in the curve of the cornea. This results in the lens being much nearer to the cornea than in the normal eye and, as age increases and the lens becomes larger, the filtration angle becomes increasingly narrow. Two effects may follow. In the first place, adhesions form between the back of the cornea and the front of the iris (chronic angle-closure glaucoma). The response to treatment, and prognosis if untreated, is much as in open angle glaucoma described above. The second effect is that a condition may arise in which there is periodic closure of the angle when the periphery of the iris comes into contact with the cornea. This gives rise to sudden attacks of pressure which may be as high as 50 or 60 mm of mercury (acute angle closure glaucoma). The attacks may be brought on by pupil dilatation caused by darkness or emotion and they give rise to the symptom of 'haloes', spectral coloured 'rainbow' rings around lights. There may be many of these sub-acute glaucoma attacks in one or both eyes, all resolving spontaneously, but an occasion is likely to arise when the blockage becomes fixed and the pressure rises still further. There is then the danger of strangulation of the blood supply of the eye, and blindness. The condition of acute angle closure is heralded by severe pain and the vision rapidly fails. The raised pressure causes a haziness of the cornea, the globe is congested, the anterior chamber is markedly shallow, and the pupil dilated. This is a major medical emergency. The secretion of aqueous is stopped by the administration of *acetazolamide and the pupil constricted by *miotics. When the pressure is reduced and the eye is quiet, the operation of iridectomy is performed and this effectively prevents recurrence.

Inflammations of the globe. The 'red eye' is a common diagnostic problem; it may be a trivial affair or one leading to blindness. There are four possible causes.

Conjunctivitis. Inflammation of the conjunctiva, the delicate membrane which covers the exposed part of the eyeball, is caused by bacterial or viral infections, or by allergy. The redness is most marked in the areas covered by the lids and is brick-red in colour (conjunctival congestion). In the infective forms it is often accompanied by a discharge. There is no loss of vision and no pain although there may be a gritty feeling. The condition is usually not serious and responds rapidly to *antibiotic drops (but see below on trachoma).

Keratitis in the ulcerative and deep forms has already been described (see above). In the acute stages there is a localized opacity corresponding to the area of cornea involved and a dusky purple congestion of the sclera around the cornea (ciliary congestion).

Iritis. The uveal tract is composed of the iris in front, the ciliary body and the choroid behind. The three are closely linked by the same vascular network so that inflammation centred in one part may easily involve the two others. There are many causes, most being endogenous (not due to any external cause) and including *toxoplasmosis, *sarcoidosis, *focal infections, and *herpetic conditions. It may also be associated with *arthritis as in *Still's disease of children, *Reiter's syndrome, and *ankylosing spondylitis. In iritis there is ciliary congestion surrounding the cornea which shows a generalized haze. The pupil is small and tends to be stuck to the lens capsule behind it, causing secondary glaucoma. The most important measure in the acute stages is to dilate the pupils with *mydriatics to prevent pupil adhesions and to lessen the inflammatory effects by administration of local *steroids.

Acute glaucoma. An acute attack of closed angle glaucoma has been described (see above); there is usually more pain and loss of vision than in other forms of red eye but the ciliary congestion is often masked by oedema. The important diagnostic sign is that in this condition the pupil is always dilated, whereas in the other three conditions it is small.

Injuries to the eye. Two types of injury must be considered, penetrating and non-penetrating.

Non-penetrating injuries. Contusions caused by blunt objects are the most common eye injuries. In anatomical order from skin to optic nerve, the most important are as follows: (i) *fractures of the facial bones including 'blow-out' fractures of the orbital floor (the orbit is the bony cavity within the skull, in which the eye is enclosed) are often masked by bruising of the lids; (ii) corneal abrasions, in which the delicate epithelium is stripped off the surface, cause extreme pain but heal readily on padding the eye; (iii) iris tears result in bleeding into the anterior chamber (called hyphaema) and secondary glaucoma, a dangerous complication caused by blockage of the pores of the trabeculum by red cells; (iv) the crystalline lens may be displaced and later, a cataract may develop; (v) retinal tears may result in the immediate formation of a vitreous

countries is served by the International Agency for the Prevention of Blindness (director Sir John Wilson), British Commonwealth Society for the Blind (Haywards Heath, Sussex UK), and by the World Health Organization and others.

Aids for the blind. *Low vision aids* What the blind ask of the sighted is that they should be helped towards their independence, free of patronage. There is a world of difference between a totally blind person and one who is able to find his way unaided, and yet another who is able to decipher a letter, however slowly. The partially sighted can often be helped by the use of magnifying devices, usually referred to as low vision aids (LVA) sometimes to the extent of holding down a job in competition with the sighted.

The simple hand-held magnifying glass is a boon to many, but this leaves only one hand free and so is useless as an aid for occupations like sewing. This difficulty can be overcome by fitting 'telescopic' lenses on to reading glasses, focused either for near vision or for distance such as a television screen. The field of vision is, however, very limited, so telescopic lenses cannot be worn for walking about. A greatly enhanced magnification can be obtained by using closed circuit television (CCTV) and this enables a few words or even a single letter to occupy the entire screen. Reading for pleasure tends to be laborious but such a device is invaluable when reading for information; it will enable a musician to check a score, for example, or a housewife to look up a recipe. This kind of apparatus, once found only in the schools for the partially sighted, is now widely available.

Communication by sound. For the blind, radio is one of the greatest boons. In the USA there are many regular daily transmissions on special wavelengths reserved for the blind: in the UK the weekly programme 'In Touch' serves similar functions. These programmes are usually presented by blind or partially-sighted announcers, and keep the blind in touch with news items of special interest to them and to the many sighted listeners who care for them.

Talking Book Services are now highly developed in Europe and the USA. A wide selection of titles is available on easy-play cassette recorders. The cassettes are sent post-free in most countries and, in the UK particularly, there is an excellent volunteer organization which maintains and repairs the sets. In addition, educational authorities provide cassettes which cover many courses of study at all levels.

One of the most recent and useful devices to enable the blind to convert print into sound is the so-called reading machine invented in the USA and marketed as the Kurzwell reading machine. This machine scans ordinary newsprint and converts it into sound, the speed being selected by the listener. It cannot decipher handwriting and any print which is to be read must be absolutely clear; already the quality of the sound is acceptable and will doubtless be improved in time.

Guide dogs. Music has always been a vocation of the blind, and the patron saint of blind musicians is St Hervé. He was born in the Dark Ages towards the end of the 5th c. in Brittany and became blind in early childhood. Renowned for his piety as for his musical attainments, he travelled widely in France, guided always by his dog.

The instinct to pilot is highly developed in dogs which hunt in packs, alsatians, labradors, and collies in particular. However, it is only in the last 50 years or so that organizations like Seeing Eye, Inc. of the USA, and subsequently in many other countries in the developed world, to train both the blind person and the dog into a working partnership have been formed. This is done at special 'schools' and takes about a fortnight for animal and man to get adjusted to one another. An important factor is that there should be a similarity in temperament; an attempt to match a timid blind person with a dog that needs firm handling is courting trouble!

Communication by touch. Many of the gadgets and aids to living among the sighted have been discovered by the blind themselves; and none is more helpful and universally used than the Braille script. Louis Braille was born at Coupvrey some 23 miles from Paris. When he was a very small boy he was blinded by sympathetic ophthalmia, being struck in the eye while playing with an awl in his father's leather shop. Of exceptional intellect, he became a teacher and later a full professor at a school in Paris. Braille developed the method of reading and writing by touch from an idea of an army officer Charles Barbier. Barbier was interested in the military aspects—the possibility of passing messages silently and in darkness—but when his attention was drawn to the method, Louis Braille immediately saw its potential as a means of communication for the blind. He simplified and improved the code which consists of a 'cell' of six embossed dots set in two parallel lines of three. Thus letters, numerals, and punctuation marks all had their distinctive position in the 'cell'. Reading and writing were thus made possible for the blind and for 150 years braille has been their chief means of communication. Only recently have electronic devices, in part, superseded it.

Louis Braille died of a chronic chest complaint at Coupvrey, at the early age of 43. He was interred at the local cemetery, but later his remains were removed to the Pantheon to lie among the illustrious dead of France. Except for his hands—the hands which have guided countless numbers of the blind to freedom—they rest at Coupvrey.

J. H. DOBREE

References

Kupfer, C. (1980). Tomorrow's blind population. In Wilson, J. (ed.), *World Blindness and its Prevention*, 32–5. Oxford.

Novotny, H. R. and Alvis, D. L. (1961). Method of photographing fluorescence in circulating blood in the human retina. *Circulation*, **24**, 82.

Wilson, J. (ed.) (1980). *World Blindness and its Prevention.* Oxford.

Further reading

Davson, H. (1980). *Physiology of the Eye.* 4th edn, Edinburgh.

Dobree, J. H. and Boulter, E. (1982). *Blindness and Visual Handicap: the Facts.* Oxford.

Michaelson, I. C. (1980). *Textbook of Diseases of the Fundus of the Eye.* 3rd edn, Edinburgh.

Roper-Hall, M. J. (1980). *Stallard's Eye Surgery.* 6th edn, Bristol.

Rose, F. C. (1976). *Medical Ophthalmology.* St Louis.

OPHTHALMOPLEGIA is paralysis of one or more of the muscles of the eye.

OPHTHALMOPLEGIC MIGRAINE is a variety of severe *migraine, in which *oculomotor paralysis develops during the course of the attack. It is postulated that the oculomotor nerve is compressed by swelling of or around the internal *carotid artery.

OPHTHALMOSCOPE. An instrument which enables inspection of the interior of the eye.

OPIATE is an imprecise term often employed to mean any drug or mixture of drugs which is either *hypnotic or *addictive, whether or not derived from or related to the *opium alkaloids.

OPIE, EUGENE LINDSAY (1873–1971). American pathologist, MD Johns Hopkins (1893). After several years as junior pathologist under W. H. *Welch, he moved to New York as one of the original members of the *Rockefeller Institute. Later he became head of the department of pathology at Washington University, St Louis, University of Pennsylvania, and Cornell Medical College. On retirement from these he returned to the Rockefeller Institute, where he continued his research in experimental pathology until an advanced age. In the long course of his professional life he made important contributions to knowledge in several fields, including *tuberculosis, *pancreatic dysfunction, and the processes of pyogenic and granulomatous inflammation.

OPISTHOTONOS is spasm of the extensor muscles throughout the length of the body, which then rests on the *occiput and the heels with the back arched. Opisthotonos typically occurs in *tetanus and *strychnine poisoning.

OPIUM is an extract of the capsules of the opium poppy (*Papaver somniferum*). It is the source of the narcotic, analgesic, and addictive opium alkaloids, which include *morphine, *codeine, *papaverine, *apomorphine, thebaine, and about 15 others.

OPPENHEIM, HERMANN (1858–1919). German neurologist, MD Berlin (1881). From 1883 to 1891 Oppenheim worked at the neurological clinic of the *Charité. In the latter year he established a private clinic and in 1893 was granted the title of professor. He described *amyotonia congenita (Oppenheim's disease, 1900), and an alternative method of evoking the plantar reflex (Oppenheim's reflex, 1902).

OPPORTUNISTIC INFECTION describes infection by micro-organisms whose normally low pathogenicity is enhanced by depression of the host's humoral or cellular immune defences, such as occurs in immune deficiency syndromes and the administration of immunosuppressive drugs. The systemic *mycoses, such as *aspergillosis and systemic *candidiasis, *toxoplasmosis, *cytomegalovirus infection, and *pneumocystis pneumonia are examples. See IMMUNOLOGY.

OPSONIZATION is the process whereby bacteria or other particles are coated with an *antibody protein or a component of the *complement system (substances known in this context as opsonins) and thus rendered susceptible to *phagocytosis by polymorphonuclear *leucocytes or *macrophages.

OPTIC ATROPHY. Primary optic atrophy is the abnormal ophthalmoscopic appearance of the *optic disc resulting from degeneration, demyelination, or compression of the fibres of the optic nerve. The disc shows a white pallor with sharply demarcated edges and reduced vascularity; the lamina cribrosa and the physiological cup are prominent. Particularly when *multiple sclerosis is the cause, the pallor may be more obvious in the temporal halves of each disc.

It is usually possible to distinguish this appearance from that of secondary optic atrophy, which is a sequel of long-standing *papilloedema. In this case the pallor is more grey, and the lamina cribrosa and disc margins are poorly demarcated.

OPTIC CHIASM is the X-shaped formation presented by the two *optic nerves at the point of crossing (decussation) of the fibres from the inner halves of the retinae.

OPTIC DISC. The head (or commencement) of the *optic nerve in the centre of the *retina, as seen on ophthalmoscopic examination of the optic fundus with the instrument directed a little inwards from the axis of the eye. It is a well demarcated, round or slightly oval, pale area with the blood vessels of the retina radiating outwards from its centre. Inspection of the optic disc is an essential part of routine physical examination. Abnormalities of diagnostic significance include *optic atrophy and *papilloedema. See also OPHTHALMOLOGY.

OPTIC FUNDUS. The interior aspect of the back (fundus) of the eye, as seen magnified some 20 times on ophthalmoscopic examination. The *optic disc, the *macula, and the retinal blood vessels radiating outwards from the centre of the disc are the most obvious features, displayed against the red background of the choroid (the vascular coat of the eye) seen through the transparent *retina. See also OPHTHALMOLOGY.

OPTICIAN. One who supplies spectacles. In the UK, an ophthalmic optician tests sight, prescribes glasses, and supplies them. A dispensing optician does not test sight, but supplies glasses to the prescription of others. See GENERAL OPHTHALMIC SERVICES.

OPTIC NERVE. The IInd cranial nerve, consisting of *nerve fibres conveying impulses from the light-sensitive *receptors (rods and cones) of the *retina. The optic nerve runs backwards from the eye to meet its fellow from the opposite side at the *optic chiasm, a point of *decussation; here the fibres deriving from the inner half of each retina cross over to join the uncrossed fibres of the outer halves, forming right and left optic tracts. Thus while each optic nerve consists of fibres from the eye of the same side, the right optic tract carries fibres from the right halves of both eyes (representing the left visual field), and vice versa. See also OPHTHALMOLOGY.

OPTICS is the study of light.

ORAL PHASE is a psychoanalytical term for the earliest stage of psychosexual development, occupying approximately the first year of life, during which pleasure is obtained by oral activities. It is succeeded by the anal phase.

ORBIT. The bony cavity occupied by the eyeball and its appendages, formed by the apposition of eight of the skull bones.

ORCHIDECTOMY is the excision of one or both *testes.

ORCHITIS is inflammation of the *testes.

ORF is a contagious pustular dermatitis of sheep, a virus infection to which goats are also susceptible. The lesions occur on hairless areas, particularly around the mouth and hooves. It can be transmitted to man, when it usually takes the form of a single maculopapule on the hand or arm; this becomes vesicular (forms a blister) and harmlessly resolves.

ORGAN. Any multicellular part of an animal or plant which forms a separate structural and functional unit, for example liver, kidney, lung, etc.

ORGANELLE. A persistent structure with specialized function forming part of a cell, for example a mitochondrion, liposome, ribosome, centriole, flagellum, etc. (see CELL). An organelle in a cell is analogous to an organ in a whole organism.

ORGANISM. Any living animal, plant, fungus, bacterium, or virus.

ORGANIZER. Any part of an *embryo which performs an induction on another part, that is which influences its differentiation.

ORGANOTHERAPY is the treatment of disease by administration of extracts of animal organs, usually *endocrine glands, now replaced by the use of pure *hormones.

ORGASM is the culmination or climax of sexual intercourse, arousing an intensely pleasurable sensation in both sexes, and accompanied in the male by ejaculation of *semen.

ORIBASIUS, (?325–?403). Byzantine physician. Oribasius was born in Pergamum but trained in Alexandria. He was made physician to the Emperor Julian the Apostate and on his orders wrote an anthology of the writings of the leading Greek physicians and surgeons. He had little originality but wrote well on dietetics and paediatrics. He did much to establish the authority of *Galen and his book *Synagogae medicae* was widely used in the Latin West and by the Arabs.

ORIENTAL SORE. One of the several names for cutaneous *leishmaniasis.

ORIGIN OF SPECIES, THE, is the classic work of Charles *Darwin, published in 1859, in which he proposed *natural selection as the main mechanism of evolution. The full title was *On the Origin of Species by means of Natural Selection, or the Preservation of Favoured Races in the Struggle for Life.*

ORNITHOSIS. See PSITTACOSIS.

OROYA FEVER is a bacterial infection characterized by fever and *haemolytic anaemia, confined to certain parts of South America. The causative organism is a small gram-negative bacillus *Bartonella bacilliformis*, transmitted by species of biting *sandfly, particularly *Phlebotomus verrucarum*.

ORTHODIAGRAM. An undistorted *X-ray silhouette made by tracing the outline of an organ or structure on a fluoroscopic screen.

ORTHODONTICS is the branch of *dentistry concerned with the correction of irregularities of the teeth and jaws.

ORTHOPAEDICS

This article on orthopaedics is divided into three parts: firstly, the definition as it has evolved from the first use of the word until today; secondly, a description of the kinds of abnormalities it encompasses; and thirdly, a historical account of three conditions and their treatment. The three conditions, *scoliosis, *fracture of the neck of the *femur, and osteogenic *sarcoma, have been chosen as examples of the evolution of diagnostic and therapeutic advances.

Orthopaedics as a defined branch of medicine is a term attributed to Nicholas Andry, who first used it in a book written in 1741. Whitman (1896) wrote that 'Andry is sometimes called the father of the specialty, and there appears to be a very general misapprehension as to the object and scope of his book . . . (which) was what might be called a nursery guide . . . intended only for parents and nurses.'

Development of the specialty. In English the word first appears in a prospectus of the *Royal National Orthopaedic Hospital in 1840, according to the *Oxford English Dictionary*. However, it appears to have been used even earlier in the USA in the designation of the Boston Orthopedic Institution in 1837. It originally referred to what its Greek roots imply, namely, a concern with developmental abnormalities. It was defined in the first edition of the *Oxford English Dictionary* (begun 1857 but published in 1888) as 'relating to or concerned with the cure of deformities in children or bodily deformities in general'. Thus, it was during the interval between 1840 and 1857, or perhaps as late as 1888, that the definition was broadened to include bodily deformities of adults as well as those of children.

At about the same time, there were two developments that allowed general surgical practice to evolve in the modern manner, namely, the discoveries of *asepsis and of *anaesthesia. They transformed the meaning of the term orthopaedics to emphasize the surgical methods of treatment. Some definitions of recent date define orthopaedics as a purely surgical specialty.

Most of the physical abnormalities that today fall into the province of the orthopaedic surgeon have existed for as long as records exist, but despite prehistoric evidence that deformities, injuries, and infections of bones existed then, as they still do, that evidence and evidence that those abnormalities were treated in demonstrable ways, does no more than reveal the material basis for the evolution of what is now meant by orthopaedics.

The term now designates a specialty in medicine and properly its generally accepted use should date back to the time when medical specialization began. In English-speaking countries at least, doctors began to specialize about 100 years ago. The situation then developed where groups of doctors restricted their practice largely or exclusively to one specialty, and those doctors were subsequently called specialists.

For orthopaedics in the UK, 1898 was the year when the first attempts were made to establish a formal group, called the British Orthopaedic Society, consisting of orthopaedic surgeons (orthopedists in the USA). There were 40 original members of that society, but it was short-lived and it was only after the First World War that a viable association was formed, starting in 1918. Sir Harry Platt has described the formation of the British Orthopaedic Association, which was founded in 1918 and is still extant.

In the USA the first orthopaedic society, the American Orthopedic Association, was founded in 1887, membership being highly restricted. The larger organization, the American Academy of Orthopedic Surgeons, was founded in 1933 and includes nearly all American doctors certified by the National Board of Orthopedic Surgery and practising orthopaedics.

Definition. The various organizations mentioned defined in their by-laws what the term orthopaedics means and their definitions go somewhat thus:

The medical specialty that includes the investigation, preservation, restoration and development of the form and function of the extremities, spine, and associated structures by medical, surgical and physical methods.

It is evident that this definition differs considerably from dictionary definitions, for example: 'that branch of surgery which is specially concerned with the preservation and restoration of the function of the skeletal system, its articulations, and associated structures', or 'a surgical specialty in which diseases of the bones and joints as well as body deformities have a prominent part'. Inasmuch as the purpose of this article is to portray orthopaedics as it is now practised, and to draw the broad outlines of how that practice evolved, some explanation of the variation in modern definitions becomes germane to the account that follows. The dictionary definitions omit perhaps the most important category of lesions treated by orthopaedic surgeons, namely those due to *trauma, which include fractures, articular or ligamentous injuries, injuries to *tendons, and the aftermath of all these injuries. The definitions offered by the orthopaedic societies tend to include much more. The societies are obviously attempting to include in their definitions all of the professional activities covered by their members. In that process, the definition embraces at least one medical specialty that does not belong—rheumatology—whereas much research activity in fields as diverse as engineering, metallurgy, polymer chemistry, and even pharmacology, would fit the orthopaedic designation as defined. It may well be true that the word orthopaedic is undergoing gradual change to a more general context, as in the lay usage (orthopaedic shoes or mattresses) or in its use to describe collaborative efforts (British Orthopaedic Engineering Society, Orthopaedic Research Society). The adoption of the word by laymen is not as modern as one might think. The *Oxford English Dictionary* cites a quotation in 1863, 'There cobblers lecture on orthopedy because they cannot sell their shoes.'

Historical evolution. Many who are interested in

the historical or even prehistorical origins of orthopaedic lesions turn to palaeontology. The obvious reason is that the mineral in bones can retain the morphological characteristics of the original bones of the person or animal, and of most of the abnormalities that might affect such bones. No soft tissue can survive for centuries or even millennia and so palaeopathology is concerned mainly with bony residues. Apart from bones with lesions of interest mainly to anthropologists, such as *trephine holes in the *cranium and bones from which inferences can be drawn about height, weight, posture, etc., specimens, including those from mummies, have been and are being discovered that reveal characteristic lesions of interest to orthopaedics, namely *amputations; fractures that have united or that have not united; deformities as a result of injuries; infections, including those possibly *syphilitic, or *leprous, or *tuberculous; *Paget's disease; developmental anomalies; etc.

Students of art history will find many allusions to paintings, sculpture, and other depictions in which there are representations of what may well be lesions such as old *poliomyelitis, scoliosis, *kyphosis, *dwarfism, etc. In the ancient writings of Egyptians, Indians, Chinese, Greeks, and Romans, there are passages that describe actual lesions and there are also accounts of what therapeutic measures then were appropriate. They sometimes include drawings that show the manipulative techniques used for fractures or *dislocations, the *splints to be used, etc.

However, between the 1st and 18th c., despite the continually augmented body of written works, in many parts of the world the status of orthopaedics as currently defined did not change very much. Until the advent of the surgical prerequisites of anaesthesia and asepsis, orthopaedic surgical procedures were done infrequently. They were always simple, and resorted to when other measures, mostly mechanical, failed. They were done by people whom one would regard today as special craftsmen, like bonesetters, or individuals skilful in the devising of splints or traction devices, but who also, in general, would treat patients for any ailment whatsoever. Many such individuals were churchmen, as they were in Greek and Roman times. Some of them were trained in hospitals, as in the Middle Eastern or European centres, but many were untrained self-styled healers.

The names of many doctors of outstanding general reputation are cited in the writings of those 17 centuries, but only here and there is a subject specifically orthopaedic in character referred to, and then in scant detail. Contributing to the scarcity of writings on orthopaedic subjects, in the Middle Ages particularly, was the fact that the physicians, as a group, were usually those who had some training and an elevated status in society. Few physicians as such existed then, and not only were they generally unavailable to the populace,

but also they mostly concerned themselves with matters that would tend to exclude orthopaedics—drugs, blood-letting, etc., and not wounds, fractures and abscesses. Those were generally cared for by surgeons or barbers (see BARBER-SURGEONS) that is, individuals much lower in the social scale who were often illiterate.

Between the Middle Ages and the emergence of doctors who regarded themselves as orthopaedic surgeons, in the last two decades of the 19th c., history records the names of only a few doctors who made important contributions to what is now called orthopaedics. Usually they devised treatments for one condition or another, for example William *Little publicized *tenotomy of the *Achilles tendon for clubfoot (talipes), and for spastic or paralytic equinus, even though first *Stromeyer and later *Delpech were usually given credit for this. Venel, who established in Switzerland the first orthopaedic institute, deserves mention as also does John *Hunter, who by feeding madder to pigs revealed the pattern of growth of the bones. Non-surgical, mechanical treatment, by manipulation, traction, and splinting was the order of the day: pioneers in that field were *Scarpa, who devised an apparatus for correction of clubfoot; Mathysen, who first advocated *plaster of Paris *casts and splints; and Hugh Owen *Thomas, who decried the forcible traction manipulation that was being practised, and advocated gentleness in treatment, and rest for the affected part.

Although the specialty of orthopaedics can thus be said to have begun, the surgical side of the specialty was far outweighed by the mechanical. In the last two decades of the 19th c., and perhaps for two decades thereafter, orthopaedists were mostly occupied with splints, *braces and *callipers, or with mechanical apparatus for traction, manipulation or immobilization, or for gradual correction of deformities by the external application of pressure.

During those several decades, there were many outstanding practitioners whose contributions to the development of surgical orthopaedic treatment are well recorded in the journals devoted to orthopaedic surgery. Those published in the USA and the UK record mostly the achievement of practitioners in the English-speaking countries and one journal, which dates back to 1889, and which for many decades has been a collaborative effort from all English-speaking countries is the *Journal of Bone and Joint Surgery*. In one issue, published in 1950, there is not only a summary of those achievements, but also an overview of the work done on the European continent up to 1950. Inasmuch as hundreds of men are cited and bibliographies of nearly 1000 articles and books are listed, it is apparent that single individuals and achievements or even a sample cannot be selected from this cohort for special mention, without doing many others an injustice. Surprisingly, there is no readily available book written recently on the subject of the history of orthopaedics or of orthopaedic surgery. There have been sporadic attempts to collect classic articles or accounts (cf. Bick and the series in the journal, *Clinical Orthopedics and Related Research,* volumes 1 until the present, in which one article per issue is included about a classic description (Bick, 1976)). Shands's collection of bibliographies of those American orthopaedic surgeons who made their mark in the late 19th and early 20th c. may also be cited (Shands, 1970).

There have been a few historical reviews that attempt a description of notable advances in knowledge concerning the many conditions that may be called orthopaedics, but here, too, the diversity of the clinical spectrum makes it impractical to delineate all or even most of the conditions. To compound the problem, new entities have been annexed to the specialty when it was found that they were amenable to orthopaedic methods of treatment. Some well-known conditions came to be newly recognized as groups of entities to be treated in different ways (as in the example below of scoliosis). In another of the examples treated at length below, fracture of the neck of the femur, which was considered to be one entity, now has been recognized as several, divisible according to anatomy as well as to prognosis, and especially to treatment, as will become evident.

Some modern advances. In order to portray the advances in orthopaedic knowledge during the period since its origins, which we have defined as beginning in 1875, three entities will be described: they are idiopathic adolescent scoliosis, sub-capital fracture of the head of the femur, and osteogenic sarcoma.

Scoliosis (lateral curvature of the *spine), has been recognized since antiquity. However, the idiopathic adolescent type, now to be considered, was not segregated from those scolioses that are now recognized as being caused by other known diseases that destroy or alter the bony tissues of the spine asymmetrically, so that a curvature can result in the chronic stage. There are also diseases that weaken or paralyse the paraspinal muscles asymmetrically, with the result that unbalanced muscle contraction forces the spinal column into a curve in the coronal plane. Examples of such bony lesions are some cases of tuberculosis, or other infections, some *tumours, some fractures, *neurofibromatosis, etc. Examples of the muscular group include some *myopathies, e.g. *muscular dystrophy, and some *neuropathies that cause paralysis or muscular imbalance, for example anterior *poliomyelitis, *cerebral palsy, spinal muscular atrophy, etc. *Congenital anomalies, such as hemivertebrae, *spinal dysraphism, diastematomyelia, and *meningomyelocoele, also contribute to the list of causes of scoliosis, and while the pathogenesis of such anomalies is usually not known, and they are therefore termed idiopathic, the scolioses they cause are distinct from idiopathic adolescent scoliosis, where no anomalies of development have been identified.

Both patients and doctors often recognized adolescent scoliosis, and its broad clinical characteristics, long before most of the other causes of scoliosis became known, but all too frequently it was confused with the effects of tuberculosis of the spine (*Pott's disease) or other spinal lesions.

The orthopaedic treatment used before the surgical era consisted of bracing, and in some instances, bed-rest. These alternatives were still the therapeutic mainstays long after the first decade of the 20th c. Ingenious combinations were developed of turnbuckles and hinges, wooden and then metal frames, usually combined with leather straps, lining, and padding. The only surgical measure that was used in treatment (and rarely used at that time) was section of the attachment of some of the muscles thought to cause or aggravate the curve (e.g. the latissimus dorsi).

The discovery of roentgenography (X-rays) allowed a better definition of the severity and character of curves and some refinement in diagnosis as to aetiology. With check X-rays, the therapist could appreciate the effects he was achieving by applying forces in bracing and he could quantify the results of his treatment over time.

It was only during the decade of 1920–30 that the X-ray came into such common use that it permitted surgeons to apply the surgical techniques of *arthrodesis with bone grafting, to maintain the correction of curves which had previously been obtained by the mechanical devices that were then available, including plaster casts as well as braces. *Grafts, for arthrodesis of other joints than in the spine, had previously been described by Ollier and others long before 1890, and surgical arthrodesis, to correct deformities that centred upon a joint, was also well known. As applied to the spine, the combination of these two surgical techniques, superimposed on the mechanical preoperative correction of curves and followed by postoperative maintenance of correction by a cast or a brace, was delayed until two prerequisites to the successful performance of *spinal fusion could be met—anaesthesia that could be prolonged for hours, and development of intravenous therapy to meet the patients' needs for large amount of fluids (including *blood transfusions).

During the 1920s and 1930s these technical developments were improved to the extent that spinal fusion for scoliosis became a standard operation, but even so, the curves could not be fully or even half corrected, and when the deformity was extensive and the spinal joints were not very flexible, the degree of correction left much to be desired. Furthermore, the recumbency in a cast after the operation usually lasted many months, and often a year in bed was prescribed as part of the operative programme.

A number of mechanical devices were described during the decades 1940–60 to improve the correction and to shorten the period of morbidity: none were very effective until Harrington in the 1960s perfected his apparatus to the point where it represented a considerable improvement in the quality of the results, and a considerable reduction in morbidity. Harrington's device consists of a system of hooks and rods, such that when the hooks are engaged at selected sites in the spinal column, they allow the rods on which the hooks are threaded to span a pair of hooks and the intervening spinal segments can be ratcheted apart. In that way, effective localized traction can be applied, and maintained on the concave side of a curve and the lateral curve satisfactorily reduced. The apparatus also can supply compression on the convex side, by means of screws on threaded rods. Other devices using similar principles are also being developed (e.g. that of Luque). Concomitantly with Harrington, Perry and Nickel were developing methods of skeletal traction that were much more efficient than the hinged or turnbuckle cast previously used, and the method of intermittent, non-skeletal traction of Cotrel. Their method involved fixation to the skull, with screws, of a metal ring, called a halo, and fixation of pins to either the iliac bones or the femora so that between the halo and the pins, rods could be inserted to exert forceful traction and correction of the spinal curves.

Meanwhile, beginning in 1964, the advantages of an anterior approach attracted attention. One of the objectives of correction of a scoliosis is to reduce or eliminate its rotational components, because the lateral displacements of the affected vertebrae are usually accompanied by rotation of the vertebrae and, most conspicuously, of the vertebral bodies. With the posterior approach, the rotational deformity is not well corrected as a rule. Dwyer devised a system consisting of a cable that passed through a series of devices attached to the bodies of the affected vertebrae. When the cable was pulled taut, a massive correction could be applied to the engaged vertebrae, correcting their rotational as well as their lateral displacement. The devices in question then allow the secure fixation of each vertebra to the taut cable. Improvements on Dwyer's system are being brought out (e.g. Zielke).

In many of the developed countries, notably the English-speaking and Scandinavian countries, the improvements in medical services to the public, particularly in the last 50 years, have had a strong part to play in diagnosis and treatment of adolescent idiopathic scoliosis. As the deformity came to be recognized earlier, and treated earlier, many more patients were treated effectively, non-operatively for the most part, and fewer (relatively speaking) had to have operations. When they did, the curves were less severe and therefore more easily corrected to an acceptable degree.

It is not yet evident what practical implications will be drawn from the extensive studies that have been, and are being, mounted with respect to this condition. The character of various kinds of curves is being studied with engineering techniques that include measurement or computation of forces and angles and displacements and strengths of the various skeletal elements and of the muscles. In the not-too-distant future we may see therapeutic forces being applied by cyclic electrical stimuli to the spinal muscles, a clinical experiment which is even now under way.

Fracture of the neck of the femur, which for decades has been called a 'problem' fracture, even now is responsible for a large proportion of care rendered by orthopaedists. It represents such a large commitment of physicians and facilities because it occurs so commonly in older patients, usually in women. It constitutes, and has always constituted, a problem because its treatment does not correspond strictly to the treatment in principle of most other fractures.

It is doubtful whether this fracture, or, more rigorously, this category of fractures, would have been diagnosed with accuracy in any significant number of cases until radiographs were easily obtained, and were of adequate quality. It has already been remarked above how X-rays of the spine, that might be obtainable for a sporadic patient just before 1900, and in the ensuing two decades, had a role in diagnosis and treatment. So it was with fractures of the hip. Prior to 1900, the diagnosis of fracture of the hip was made commonly, and the dire consequences were realized. The diagnosis was based on the sudden onset of the symptoms and signs, after a fall or accident. The dire consequences were recorded in mortality figures because perhaps more than one in four patients died within a month or two of the accident.

It will be convenient to confine the discussion here only to that fracture of the neck of the femur that is subcapital, and to omit any consideration of more distal fractures. Several advantages follow. The subcapital lesion more aptly epitomizes many recent developments in orthopaedic surgery than do the other fractures of the neck of the femur; transcervical, intertrochanteric, comminuted, etc. The other fractures have a better prognosis, in general. They also present other kinds of clinical problems, most of which can be lumped under one heading, that of fixation of the fracture fragments, whereas the subcapital fracture presents not only that problem (in a purer form than the others) but also the problem of diagnosis of bone vascularity, in a population at high risk.

To set the stage, let us first describe what the usual course of events would be, with a subcapital fracture coming under treatment about 1875. There was then no dearth of textbooks on fractures and all mentioned fracture of the femoral neck. Most distinguished between an intracapsular and extracapsular break, but inasmuch as the diagnosis was reached *in vivo* without X-rays and the signs and symptoms for the two varieties were identical, that distinction was one made only post-mortem.

The medical writings of the period show that usually a surgeon (a general surgeon) would diagnose and treat the patient. No particular interest was paid to the condition by those who considered themselves orthopaedists. In the *Transactions of the American Orthopedic Association*, perhaps the earliest journal devoted to the specialty, the first 1000 articles (1889–1912) contain only 33 on hip fractures, and many of these wrongly included slipped epiphysis.

The treatment that might be rendered by the surgeon was conservative, consisting either of bed rest alone, bed rest with traction, or application of a splint of some kind. Much discussion appeared on whether manipulation of the fragments was of value. It is difficult to imagine the thought processes of a manipulating doctor, who could have had no good idea of the nature of the fracture fragments, of how they were orientated, and of what their position might be after applying any particular manoeuvre.

Before 1900, there are scattered reports of attempts at surgical treatment, with what would now be called open reduction and internal fixation. The reduction was usually accomplished by manipulating the distal fragment, with the fracture under observation. The fixation device was commonly a peg of bone (usually beef bone), but in some cases ivory was used and in others metal pins. Since so much modern orthopaedics depends on the use of metal devices (prostheses) implanted in the body, much has been written about early use of metal for orthopaedics and for other surgical purposes. Venable and Stuck (1947) propose 1775 as the year when a fracture was first wired (with a brass wire) and they cite other internal uses of metal (e.g. a gold plate to replace part of the cranium; iron, bronze, or silver sutures to fix fractures). One cannot read their account, and any others describing the circumstances of practice in the 19th c., without concluding that such experimental treatment was rarely successful. A typical report, remarkable because it contains an illustration of a good radiograph of a reduced subcapital fracture of the hip, with a silver nail (apparently rounded and headless) holding the fragments, was published in 1899, but few details were given on how long it was before the patient walked, etc.

The detailed step-by-step account of how the modern pin fixation method of treatment of a subcapital fracture of the neck of the femur developed to its current status need not be systematically reviewed. Suffice it to say that, by 1900, most of the conceptual and technological prerequisites had been developed, even though they may not have been commonly in use. There were three major developments, two technological and one conceptual, that remained to be worked out. One already alluded to was the development of the X-ray capability to the point where the fracture fragments could not only be visualized, but visualized quickly and in an operating theatre. The surgeon had to have the capability to perform a closed reduction of the fracture, and then he had to have an adequate array of 'hardware' in order to fix the fragments—a nail, and perhaps also a plate attached to the nail, inserted from the side, without having to uncover the fracture fragments in order to have a full view of the siting of the fixation apparatus. The technological developments therefore involved not only the X-ray tube, and machine, but also the visualization process: some of the technical requirements were the X-ray tube with a rotating anode, film to replace glass plates, the fluoroscopic screen, and more recently the image intensifier.

The second technological development that had to be considered concerned the fixation device. Even by 1900 it was common knowledge that nails or pins or wires made out of any of the materials that had been tried, would usually prove so irritating to the tissues that they would cause suppuration. The materials that were least irritating—boiled beef bone, ivory, silver, gold, in that order of 'inertness'—were not strong enough. Most nails now in use are made of one of a specific group of stainless steels or of cobalt chromium alloys, specially devised for minimal reactivity with tissue. The development of these two groups of alloys, begun about 1910, did not reach a practical level of usefulness for the 'hip nail' until about 1930. The ensuing half-century is studded with reports of advances in the composition and design of the nails, and the techniques of their fabrication that were developed to avoid specific weaknesses and breakage, but none of them deserves special mention.

The third development, that we have called conceptual, relates to the determination of whether the fracture had so decreased the supply of blood to the proximal fragment as to preclude the success of any treatment designed to allow the fracture fragments to unite. It was already known in 1880 that the blood vessels to the proximal fragment were in jeopardy from the fracture, and also from any manipulation, but that idea could not influence treatment by nail fixation, *vis-à-vis* treatment as soon after the injury as possible by the alternative method that has been developed—a prosthetic replacement of the femoral head, thus obviating the need for a blood supply. The goal of being able to assess reliably the viability of the femoral head has not yet been reached, but touching briefly on some of the investigative efforts of recent years will serve to highlight some research that might be called orthopaedic.

Radiological determination of necrosis of the femoral head, as revealed by intensification of the mineral content or lack of absorption of the bony substance, has been recognized as long as good radiographs have been available, but those changes cannot be demonstrated early enough after an injury to be included in considerations of early treatment (say, within a month of the injury). Attempts to show, by radiographic methods like radiodensitometry, the earliest evidence of *necrosis, have not been successful. Measuring how much blood would drip from the proximal fragment, as impaled on a special nail, was one early method suggested, and was used prior to the actual fixation process. It was used purely as an aid to prognosis, because, at the time, prosthetic replacement was not an option. The method, crude as it was, proved unreliable: other ways, using injected *radioisotopes as indicators of blood flow, were suggested for the purpose and were developed to a considerable degree. The first radioisotope that was tried, radiophosphate (1935), has been followed by a succession of other elements, the most recent and popular being technetium, the first element that was made artificially (1937), and which is produced in large quantities in the fission products of uranium. At present, the use of this material would be considered routine practice for an orthopaedic surgeon treating a patient with a subcapital fracture of the femoral neck, so that he may first decide whether his patient is one who should undergo the nailing procedure, provided that the femoral head has retained its blood supply. The contraindications might be advanced age, or other conditions that add risk to the prolonged morbidity from nailing versus replacement. The technetium scan would thus be performed on younger or healthier patients, and if no uptake of technetium was seen in the femoral head, a prosthetic replacement would be the treatment of choice, despite the other findings favourable to nailing.

It should be realized that the above schedule of treatment depends on a large body of data concerning patients treated mostly since about 1950, during which time orthopaedic surgeons have taken over from the general surgeon the treatment of fractures.

The orthopaedic surgeon now is generally conceded to be the specialist most capable of, and most engaged in, the treatment of fractures of the appendicular and axial skeleton. At present, orthopaedic surgeons are acknowledged as appropriate therapists for all fractures from the cervical spine to the toes, and even now, social developments are under way in which centres for the treatment of the victims of accidents have given rise to superspecialists (accident surgeons) who are not properly called orthopaedic surgeons in that they treat only traumatic cases and not the other categories within the specialty (see also SURGERY OF TRAUMA).

The alternative treatment for subcapital fractures of the femoral neck—prosthetic replacement—now comes up for discussion. Conceptually, the procedure derives from the idea of *arthroplasty, and that idea had already been formulated long before 1875. To interpose some material between the acetabulum of the pelvis and the head of the femurs is a logical extension of the earlier basic effort at arthroplasty that consisted of reshaping the articulating surfaces. The materials that were tried included fascia, pig bladder, skin, and sometimes manufactured fabrics; even as late

as 1940 the same idea was reflected in the use of membranes made of Cellophane, and then of other polymers, draped over the reshaped femoral head. The idea that the femoral head might be replaced by a solid object found expression in the report of Hey Groves, in 1926, who used ivory. After Smith Peterson's development of cup arthroplasty, it was only logical for metal to replace the ivory, as in Moore's hemiarthroplasty (1943); that would be an extension of the concept, given the metallurgical advances already mentioned that were then evident. That operation, still being done on occasion for subcapital fractures of the neck of the femur, is not as durable as is total hip replacement, the development of which will now be summarized.

Although as early as 1938, a model of a total hip replacement was being worked on by Wiles, the succession of devices of McKee and others all yielded indifferent success until *Charnley, in 1960, hit upon the two ideas that are the foundation of the modern successful total hip replacement. One of those ideas is having the articular surface of the acetabulum replaced by a minimally reactive polymer, and his choice was polyethylene, while the femoral prosthetic component, replacing the femoral head, including the articular surface and the neck of the femur, is made of a minimally reactive metal, and his choice was stainless steel. His other idea was to obtain firm fixation of each component to the bone, by polymerizing, *in situ*, polymethyl methacrylate, as a cement, or more strictly a grout. Since 1960 literally dozens of devices have been designed and used, most of which represent modifications based on the concepts just described. Modifications of the materials include use of a ceramic instead of the metal, or porous metal to allow ingrowth of bone and thus avoid the complications that have attended the use of the 'cement'. It has become apparent that, in spite of many important improvements in the technique of instillation of the cement, it is one of the most vulnerable parts of the implant. Ways to circumvent its use are even now under investigation. One of the most ingenious is the use of a spongework of wires, attached to the surface of the stem of the femoral component, that fits into the remains of the femur, in its medullary cavity. The spongework, being springy, can be driven into the cavity, where it establishes firm pressure on the walls so as to fix the device in place. The interstices of the sponge allow the bone to deposit and stabilize the fixation, during the period of healing.

With the two treatments that have been described (nail fixation and prosthetic replacement) there has been a dramatic change in prognosis for the patient with subcapital fracture of the femoral neck. The common consequences evident about 25 years ago (prolonged morbidity and high mortality) are now uncommon. No longer is there prolonged recumbency or high mortality in the first two months after the injury. And while the ranks of the elderly and infirm population in nursing homes and other types of facilities for custodial care still include large numbers of patients who have had fractures of the neck of the femur, many suffer their injury in such establishments, after having been admitted for other diseases. The expectation now is for a patient who has had a subcapital fracture of the neck of the femur, who is not otherwise infirm, to resume the level of activity that was evident prior to the fracture, in the large majority of cases.

The development of total hip arthroplasty, summarized above, represents the application of but a small fraction of the research that has been, and is being, pursued. A small selection of topics will indicate the directions of investigation. An entirely new professional, the bioengineer, has emerged during the last 25 years, and institutes have been established for the purpose of applying engineering techniques to medical problems (biomedical engineering). Hip disease continues to be a major beneficiary of the effort. Some of the special fields that are represented are lubrication, wear, polymer chemistry, failure analysis, motion analysis, stress distribution analysis, powder metallurgy, and corrosion chemistry.

Because of the special vulnerability of patients undergoing total hip arthroplasty to complications of infection and *thrombophlebitis, the research efforts include exploration of *antibiotic *prophylaxis (as, for instance, incorporation of an antibiotic drug in a polymethylmethacrylate cement) and the use of *anticoagulants such as *aspirin, *warfarin, *dextran, and *heparin, intra-operatively and postoperatively.

Osteogenic sarcoma, or osteosarcoma, is the most common primary malignant tumour of bones and has been recognized as a malignant lesion for centuries. About 1875, that recognition in an individual patient would have been delayed until the tumefaction was grossly apparent. Where amputation was feasible, that treatment was used, and the general surgeon rather than the orthopaedic surgeon had in his repertory several techniques applicable according to the level of the lesion. Radiographic developments allowed earlier diagnosis and, perhaps, a better choice of a level to amputate, but little more in the way of either diagnosis or treatment. The development of radiation therapy did not have much bearing on this tumour, as it had on many others, because it was soon discovered that osteosarcoma was not particularly responsive to radiation therapy.

Major refinements in diagnosis have been developed for this variety of cancer since, on the basis of biological behaviour, other varieties of bone cancer, secondary as well as primary, have also been identified. Until the last half-century, however, those refinements in diagnosis hardly concerned the surgeons, because only one option in treatment was available once the X-ray and clinical data suggested the diagnosis, and when histological examination of a *biopsy specimen showed the characteristic patterns. The status of knowledge concerning osteosarcoma just after the Second World War was that, even if treated early by amputation, only about 10 per cent of patients would survive. As early as 1929, however, it was known that exposure to *radium and in particular ingestion of radium, would elicit the development of an osteosarcoma. While this fact was of little relevance to clinical practice then, or even now, except where individuals are exposed to massive irradiation, it constitutes the original observation on which extensive orthopaedic research has been built during the last 30 years. It deserves mention because of its importance relative to nuclear energy, atomic weapons, and contamination of the food or the environment with *radioactive materials. An example of the research is the epidemiology of osteosarcoma relative to determined levels of radiation, either from naturally occurring substances, or from cosmic rays, or from radiation produced by human activities (bomb tests, dumping of radioactive wastes, siting of facilities that emit radiation).

During the last two decades, orthopaedic surgeons, who had essentially acquired responsibility for bone tumours, even as they did over fractures at about the same time (1940–50), have developed a collaboration with oncologists in the treatment of patients with osteosarcoma. Several types of chemotherapy, usually developed for other varieties of malignancy (*antineoplastic chemotherapy), proved to be exceptionally effective for osteosarcoma, and, at present, the survival rate, instead of being 10 per cent or less, has been estimated at 50 per cent or more. This dramatic improvement in results has to be taken short of face value because of the possibility that results that seem good now may well deteriorate with time, as late recurrences of tumours or *metastases develop.

However, the common experience of having patients survive who have had amputations, has furnished a stimulus to orthopaedic surgeons to develop methods for ablating tumours without amputation, and several types of clinical research at present are directed at that goal. They attempt to replace the cancerous tissue with an internal prosthesis: a massive *allograft in some cases; a custom-made metal or metal-and-polymer substitute for the bone or joint that has been removed, in others.

A word, too, should be said for developments in external prostheses where there is no alternative to amputation. The bioengineers have been able to apply much that was learned in industrial and space technology, to the development of better prostheses, even to use of motorized elements, under control from electrical stimuli derived from the patient's own remaining musculature, proximal to the site of amputation.

Finally, mention should be made of research regarding osteosarcoma that attempts to probe the pathogenesis of the malignancy. The results of *immunological studies of patients with osteosarcoma, and of patients who have had massive allografts, as well as animal models, suggest that in osteosarcoma there may be found an aetiological mechanism (apart from excessive radiation) that offers even better therapeutic opportunities than present-day chemotherapy and ablation.

Present scope of orthopaedic surgery. Today, the practice of orthopaedic surgery, especially in the developed countries, is undergoing important changes. In a decade or so, what is now being written of its scope may not be apposite. Some of the major changes depend on the organization of medical services as they are distributed in the population, for example the establishment of accident hospitals as in Birmingham, England, Vienna, Austria, and various cities in Sweden, Switzerland, West Germany, and the USA. Other changes depend on narrowing the area of specialization of sizeable groups of orthopaedic surgeons. Those groups include specialists in the orthopaedic conditions of children, and specialists in the treatment of conditions involving hands. The former treat such conditions as scoliosis, club foot, *congenital hip dislocation and other anomalies, and *neuromuscular disorders, whereas the latter are concerned with the mounting number of industrial accidents, the common disabilities from arthritis involving the fingers, etc. As mentioned above with regard to replacement arthroplasty of hips that are destroyed, or cannot function because of localized lesions that are painful, the hand surgeon today will replace joints in the hand with either metal or polymeric substitutes. That type of operation is done so frequently that it may well qualify as standard therapy, despite the fact that new models of joints, and even of small bones, continue to be devised.

However, most orthopaedic surgeons are not so specialized, and the scope of their practice usually encompasses most of the lesions and diseases mentioned; most of them will do all or most of what may be called standard operations. Nearly all those in active surgical centres, and especially those who started practice in the last decade or so, will do total hip arthroplasty procedures, and many will now regard the same replacement therapy for other joints (knee, elbow, shoulder, and ankle) as too specialized for their level of skill. However, the bulk of their work is concerned with four broad subjects, namely backache, fractures, problems related to the feet, and what is now called 'sports medicine' (see SPORT AND MEDICINE). Only the first two will be discussed, briefly.

Backache represents a major diagnostic and therapeutic concern, and in addition it has important industrial and economic implications. The spectrum of lesions that affect the back includes arthritis, *gout, and other systemic or disseminated conditions, but it also includes *prolapsed intervertebral disc, spinal *stenosis, and even lowly ligamentous strains and *sprains; the symptom that all of these may have in common is backache. That symptom also characterizes many non-orthopaedic lesions involving one organ or another, or, perhaps, in *psychosomatic cases, no organ at all. Given the all-too-common incidence, the large number of possible aetiological lesions, the inordinate number of diagnostic tests that may be required, and the different types of therapy to go with each distinctive lesion, it is nevertheless true that the cause of many backaches cannot be diagnosed, and in such patients the therapy prescribed by the orthopaedic surgeon along standard principles, based on anatomical and biomechanical considerations, may be ineffective. For such cases patients frequently seek the help of other therapists, for example *cheiropractors, *osteopaths, psychotherapists, and others.

Fractures, which formerly were treated by general surgeons as well as orthopaedic surgeons, are now almost exclusively treated by the latter. More and more of them are being treated surgically, that is by operative reduction of the displacement and fixation of the fragments, instead of the older, more conservative manipulative reduction and immobilization of the part in a plaster cast. The reasons for this are complex and include economic as well as technical considerations: these include, for example, the expense of hospitalization or prolonged periods of unemployment. Road accidents causing fractures are so common that treatment of the injured patient, and of those who have sequelae of fractures, may represent a large fraction of an orthopaedic practice.

J. COHEN

References
Bick, E. M. (1976). *Classics of Orthopedics.* London.
Shands, A. R. (1970). *The Early Orthopedic Surgeons of America.* St Louis.
Venable, C. S. and Stuck, W. G. (1947). *The Internal Fixation of Fractures.* Springfield, Illinois.
Whitman, R. (1896). Presidential address. *Transactions of the American Orthopedic Association,* 19 May.

Further reading
Beasley, A. W. (1982). The origins of orthopedics. *Journal of the Royal Society of Medicine,* **75,** 648–55.
Brothwell, D. and Sandison, A. T. (1967). *Diseases in Antiquity.* Illinois.
Browne, E. G. (1921). *Arabian Medicine.* Cambridge.
Jarcho, S. (1965). *Human Paleontology.* New Haven.
Keith, A. (1919). *Menders of the Maimed.* Philadelphia.
Lyons, A. S. and Petrocelli, R. J. (1978). *Medicine, An Illustrated History.* New York.
Riesman, D. (1936). *The Story of Medicine in the Middle Ages.* New York.
Rogers, W. A., et al. (1950). The twentieth century—The background of half a century of progress. *Journal of Bone and Joint Surgery,* **32B,** 451–740.
Williams, D. F. and Roaf, R. (1973). *Implants in Surgery.* Philadelphia.
Wong, K. C. and Wu, L. T. (1976). *History of Chinese Medicine.* New York.

ORTHOPAEDIC SURGEON. One who specializes in the surgery of the skeletal system, its articulations, and its associated structures. See ORTHOPAEDICS.

ORTHOPNOEA is the inability to breathe easily except when sitting upright.

ORTHOPTICS is the remedial training of the eye muscles. See also OPHTHALMOLOGY.

ORTOLFF OF BAVARIA (*fl.* 15th c.). A successful writer of medical books living in Wurzburg, Ortolff is best known for his *Artzneibuch* (1477) a popular textbook of medicine. In *c.*1500 he published *Frauenbüchlein oder wie sich die schwangern Frauen halten sollen,* a guide for pregnant women.

OSCILLOGRAPH. Any instrument for recording electrical variations (oscillations).

OSCILLOSCOPE. A cathode ray tube which displays electrical variations.

OSLER, SIR WILLIAM BT (1849–1919). Anglo-Canadian physician, MD McGill (1872), FRCP (1883), FRS (1898). Born in Ontario, the son of a clergyman who had emigrated from Falmouth, Cornwall, Osler began his medical training at Toronto, moving to Montreal where he graduated MD McGill in 1872. After touring the European medical centres for two years he returned to Canada as professor of the Institutes of Medicine in *McGill University, becoming physician to the *Montreal General Hospital in 1878. His reputation grew so rapidly that after six years he was invited to take the chair of medicine in the University of Pennsylvania and five years later to become the foundation professor and physician at the *Johns Hopkins University Hospital at Baltimore.

During his 15 years in this post he influenced medical teaching throughout the USA, combining the bed-side methods of the English school with the laboratory associations of the German. Here too he wrote his work *The Principles and Practice of Medicine* (1892) which is now in its 20th edition and has been the model for all later textbooks.

In 1904 he moved to the more peaceful atmosphere of the Regius chair of medicine at Oxford, where his antiquarian and literary tastes had leisure in which to develop. His success in the UK was no less than it had been in the USA. He expanded the preclinical departments at Oxford and helped to overcome the University's traditional suspicions of 'the sciences'. He was largely responsible for founding the Association of Physicians of Great Britain and Ireland and the *Quarterly Journal of Medicine.* In 1911 he received a baronetcy.

At the time of his death the *Lancet* obituary described him as 'the greatest personality in the medical world'. His influence upon the teaching and practice of medicine in the USA and the UK is incalculable, but he was also an outstanding clinical observer. He was among the first to study the *platelets (1874), to describe *hereditary haemorrhagic telangiectasia (Osler–Rendu–Weber disease, 1901), *polycythaemia vera (Vaquez–Osler's disease, 1903), and *infective endocarditis (*Osler's nodes, 1909). The biography of Osler written by *Cushing is one of the great medical biographies of all time.

OSLER'S NODES are painful pea-sized nodules in the pads of the fingers and toes which appear and disappear (after hours or a day or two) during the course of *infective endocarditis, of which diagnosis they are strongly suggestive. They have been thought to be the result of an immunological vasculitic reaction, but recent studies suggest that *Osler's own view that they represent minute *emboli from the infected heart valves was correct.

OSMOLALITY (OSMOLARITY) is the number of osmotically effective (see OSMOSIS) dissolved particles per unit quantity of a solution, expressed either as (milli)osmols per kilogram of solvent (osmolality) or as (milli)osmols per litre of solution (osmolarity). The osmol is the standard unit of osmotic pressure, being equal to the gram molecular weight divided by the number of particles or ions into which a substance dissociates in solution.

OSMOSIS is the flow of water (or other solvent) through a semipermeable membrane, that is one which will permit passage of the solvent but not of the substance dissolved. When solutions of different strength are separated by such a membrane, solvent will flow from the weaker to the stronger until they are of equal molecular concentration. The pressure which must be applied to the stronger solution in order to prevent such flow is termed the osmotic pressure.

OSSICLE. Any small bone, but particularly those of the *middle ear.

OSSIFICATION is the formation of new bone, which normally takes place in pre-existing *cartilage or fibrous tissue.

OSTEITIS is inflammation of bone.

OSTEITIS DEFORMANS is a synonym for *Paget's disease of bone.

OSTEITIS FIBROSA CYSTICA is the name given to the radiological and pathological changes in bone structure characteristic of *hyperparathyroidism, sometimes also known as von *Recklinghausen's disease of bone.

OSTEOARTHRITIS. See OSTEOARTHROSIS.

OSTEOARTHROSIS is a chronic degenerative non-inflammatory condition of joints frequently known also as 'osteoarthritis'. Some degree of osteoarthrosis is almost universal in older age groups and may be regarded as the inevitable result of the wear-and-tear of a lifetime; when severe, however, it is an important cause of disability. Genetic factors probably influence the rate and degree of degenerative change, as do abnormal stresses on joints, for example the weight-bearing joints in *obesity.

OSTEOCHONDRITIS is literally, inflammation of bone and cartilage; in practice, it is applied to a heterogeneous group of conditions associated with *necrosis of these tissues (also known as osteochondrosis).

OSTEOGENESIS IMPERFECTA is a genetic condition, usually transmitted as an autosomal *dominant characteristic, in which the bones are abnormally brittle and fragile, and repeated fractures give rise to skeletal deformities. In one of the two main varieties, known as osteogenesis imperfecta congenita, the fractures begin *in utero* and the baby is born with deformities; in these cases, another characteristic finding is a blue discoloration of the *sclera (white) of the eye. In the other, osteogenesis imperfecta tarda, the appearance of fractures is delayed until the child begins to walk. The condition, the pathophysiological mechanism of which is not fully understood, is also known as fragilitas ossium.

OSTEOLOGY is the study and knowledge of bones.

OSTEOMA. A non-malignant *tumour of bone.

OSTEOMALACIA is softening of the bone due to inadequate absorption and utilization of *calcium, the usual cause being deficiency of *vitamin D. Osteomalacia is the adult equivalent of *rickets in childhood.

OSTEOMYELITIS is inflammation of bone involving the *marrow, usually due to a pus-forming *staphylococcal or *streptococcal infection. Osteomyelitis is now a less common and much less dangerous condition than it was before the advent of *antibiotic therapy.

OSTEOPATHY is a system of therapy founded by an American country practitioner named Andrew Taylor Still (1828–1917) based on the manipulation of skeletal structures. Still's original hypothesis, that all diseases were explicable on the basis of faulty structural relationships and would therefore yield to physical manipulation, has little credence today; but modern osteopaths justifiably claim some success in the treatment of certain painful conditions involving bones and joints. See FRINGE MEDICINE, ETC.

OSTEOPETROSIS, also known as Albers–Schonberg or marble bone disease, is a rare genetically determined disorder of bone function in which there is a failure of normal bone resorption, so that it becomes excessively dense. In the severe or malignant form of the condition, the bone marrow and its blood-forming tissue are obliterated and cranial deformities appear in early childhood. Milder syndromes occur in which the dense bone (which is more brittle than normal) is detected on X-ray following a fracture, or in which the presentation is with *osteomyelitis.

OSTEOPOROSIS is the loss of bone tissue resulting in thinning and weakening of bony structures. The cardinal manifestations are decreased radiographic density, back pain, vertebral collapse, and liability to limb fractures. The commonest cause is old age (senile or postmenopausal osteoporosis), but there is a long and heterogeneous list of other conditions which may be complicated by osteoporosis, many of which are associated with hormonal imbalance; they include *thyrotoxicosis, *acromegaly, *hyperadrenalism and treatment with *corticosteroids, *hypogonadism in either sex, total and prolonged immobilization, *rheumatoid arthritis, and a number of others. Occasionally no cause can be found.

OSTEOTOMY is the surgical cutting of bone.

OTITIS is inflammation of part of the ear, as in otitis externa, otitis media, and otitis interna. See OTOLARYNGOLOGY.

OTOLARYNGOLOGY (sometimes also called otorhinolaryngology, or ear, nose, and throat surgery), as a specialty in its own right has existed for barely 100 years. This seems remarkable when it is appreciated that diseases of the ears, nose, and throat are among the commonest causes of morbidity in man. The reason for this relatively late emergence will be discussed later.

Anatomically, the area exposed to disease involves the portals of entry for food and air and encompasses the organs of *taste and *smell, of *balance and *hearing, and of *speech. The eye and orbit are closely related anatomically and disease in that area may also present to the otolaryngologist. Obviously, disease in these important organs can alter the whole pattern of a person's existence: for example, failure to develop speech, in a child of normal intelligence, because of congenital deafness (*deaf mutism) is a severe psychological, social, and educational handicap. About one in 10 000 live births produce children with impaired hearing; this may be considered as relatively rare.

Childhood is a period when *immunity to common infections is developed as a result of exposure to both endemic and epidemic infections. The incidence of inflammatory disease of the respiratory tract is therefore particularly high in childhood and is part of the wider process of developing immunity, which in turn is part of the general process of maturation. Many such infections are of viral origin. Some confer life-long, others only a temporary immunity. Thus, at any stage of life a common cold may predispose to a more severe bacterial secondary infection such as *sinusitis, *laryngitis, *bronchitis, or *otitis media.

Because man is a gregarious animal, the transfer of infectious respiratory disease from person to person dates from the first formation of tribes. In the past, many children must have perished from respiratory infections or their complications before immunity could be developed.

In the last 250 years the formation of even larger conurbations and the increasing sophistication of patterns of social behaviour, combined with increasing scientific knowledge and technical expertise, have led to a modification of man's environment. Many of these modifications have not been to his advantage biologically: examples include *atmospheric pollution, and *hypersensitivity to drugs, food, and other chemicals. Where these are introduced through the alimentary or respiratory tracts, severe adverse reactions can result. Technological advance in one field may bring with it dangers in another. Thus, the use of asbestos to protect against the risk of fire has saved many lives: on the other hand *asbestosis has taken its toll of life, too, and recently it has been discovered that asbestos may play a part in the causation of cancer of the *larynx.

Increasing scientific knowledge has led to a better understanding of the disease process and to the development of powerful therapeutic agents capable of modifying this process; it has also produced a better standard of health and hygiene. This has resulted in an increase in the population, a reduction in neonatal deaths, and an increased life expectancy. Today's physician is therefore called upon to deal with a fourth category of disease, associated with the processes of *degeneration: as far as the otolaryngologist is concerned, he has to deal with degeneration in the organs of hearing and balance. At the extremes of age, therefore, impaired hearing may lead to psychological problems due to social deprivation, and in the case of the elderly it may be complicated by a sense of insecurity of balance and posture.

Towards the middle of the 18th c. the pattern of life in the UK underwent a fundamental change associated with the Industrial Revolution. Until that time the economy was basically agrarian and therefore healthy. With the aggregation of the population into larger communities, disease could spread more widely. Deplorable housing, and little or no sanitation, favoured the rapid spread of disease and such conditions certainly allowed respiratory disease to prosper. Complications were common and the remedies available were non-specific and, for the most part, ineffective. If man, woman, or child were to survive the onslaught of disease they had to rely on immunity developed early in life, combined with the body's natural defences. The *exanthemata, in particular *scarlet fever and *measles, as well as *whooping cough, caused permanent damage to the lining of the respiratory tract. The condition was often aggravated by secondary bacterial infection leading to further destruction of tissue and irreversible changes. So it is that the diseases of the ears, nose, and throat which gave rise to serious handicap among the urban community between the middle of the 18th c. and the first quarter of the 20th c. were deafness with or without suppuration from the ears, failure to develop normal anatomy due to nasal obstruction, *syphilis, *tuberculosis, and cancer.

Not only was there no really effective treatment for these diseases, but there was also the practical difficulty of examining the patient. Because the organs to be inspected were all situated deep below the body surface it was very difficult to deliver sufficient light to the affected site to obtain an adequate view. However, in 1854 this was overcome by Manoel Garcia, a singing teacher who invented the first reflecting head mirror. With this instrument, which is in effect a concave mirror with a hole in the centre through which the observer looks, it is possible to shine a reflected light into the ear canal, the nasal cavities and, using a second mirror at the back of the throat, into the space behind the nose and also into the larynx and *pharynx. This invention made possible the foundation of a special discipline of oto-laryngology; the instrument was used initially not only to make a diagnosis, but also to provide the light needed to carry out operative procedures. It is still used in many clinics today but its use in the operating theatre has been superseded by the development of the electric headlamp.

History. Modern medicine is based on the three fundamental disciplines of anatomy, physiology, and pathology and this is also true of otolaryngology. By the end of the 16th c. *Vesalius, *Eustachio, and *Falloppius had determined the anatomy of the auditory apparatus, the soft *palate, and the *cranial nerves.

It became clear that sound entering the ear via the ear canal (external auditory meatus) reaches the ear-drum or *tympanic membrane. This sound causes the membrane to vibrate and the vibration to be transmitted across the middle ear (which communicates with the back of the throat or nasopharynx via the *Eustachian tube) through a chain of three tiny bones (the auditory ossicles); the last of these, the stapes, has a round 'foot' which fits into an oval bony window where it comes into contact with the membrane of the inner ear. The inner ear, enclosed within the petrous *temporal bone of the skull, has two main parts, both confined by membranes and both filled with fluid. One, the cochlear apparatus (so called from the Greek kochlias, a snail, because it forms a spiral like a shell) is the organ of hearing. Vibrations transmitted to the fluid in the *cochlea are recorded by the sensitive cells of the organ of *Corti, which then initiate nerve impulses which are conveyed by the auditory or acoustic nerve to the brain, where the sound is finally recorded and interpreted. The second major structure in the internal ear is the *labyrinth, consisting of three *semicircular canals, each of which lies in a different plane of space, and two other cavities called the utricle and saccule. The labyrinth is the principal organ of balance. Movement of fluid within it on a change in head position produces nerve impulses which travel in the labyrinthine nerve with the auditory nerve to the brainstem. Repetitive movement of this fluid can cause *motion sickness; sudden or severe movements or disease of the labyrinth can cause *giddiness or *vertigo. Thus excessive fluid (hydrops) in the labyrinth can cause recurrent severe attacks of vertigo in the condition commonly called *Ménière's disease. Just as the functions of the conducting apparatus of the middle ear and of the cochlea and auditory nerve can be tested in patients complaining of deafness by *audiometry (see below), there are also tests of labyrinthine function which are commonly used in clinical practice. It is known, for example, that warm or cold water injected into the external auditory meatus will in the normal individual produce a *reflex, giving repetitive to-and-fro movement of the eyes (*nystagmus),. a sign which often accompanies attacks of vertigo. The duration of this nystagmus can be measured; these caloric tests using warm and cold water are commonly used not only to assess labyrinthine function but also to test brainstem reflexes, as in the diagnosis of *brain death.

Thus, even though it had not been possible to make much headway in the examination and treatment of the patient, progress had been made in the fields of structure and function. From the late 18th c, the detailed anatomy of the ear had been known and theories now began to proliferate as to how the ear actually converted the sound waves into a message which could be interpreted by the brain. Two main theories were advanced, one by *Helmholtz and one by *Rutherford. Initially, they were considered to be mutually exclusive, for Helmholtz maintained that particular areas of the cochlea responded to particular frequencies, whereas Rutherford felt that the basement membrane vibrated uniformly in all its parts and that the amplitude of the vibration represented the intensity of the signal. Both of these theories have been attacked and defended over the years and they have been modified. Present explanations of the function are centred round cochlear hydrodynamics.

The contribution of science and technology to development in otolaryngology. The difficulties confronting the specialist wishing to examine the ears, nose, and throat have been touched upon above. Great progress was made following the introduction of the head mirror by Garcia. However, it is just as necessary to make accurate measurements in testing hearing as it is in testing vision. Until 50 years ago the otologist judged hearing by using a conversational or whispered voice, in order to determine the amplitude or loudness which was required for the patient to hear accurately. Tuning forks were used to distinguish between the two main classes of deafness: these are conductive (attributable to a disorder in the sound-wave transmitting system) and sensorineural (attributable to disorders of the hearing organ or of the neural pathways). Clearly, such methods were insufficiently accurate. However, it was necessary to wait until the valve amplifier was developed before the first accurate audiometer, capable of varying both pitch and amplitude, could be produced. The technique is invaluable, for example, in diagnosing occupational deafness, in which the ability to perceive certain tones is impaired by continual exposure to loud noise. In Ménière's disease, hearing acuity may improve with increasing loudness of the stimulus (loudness recruitment). However, standard audiometry has the disadvantage that it depends upon the patient's subjective response and patients vary in their reliability. Furthermore, it is of no use in assessing the hearing of young children who cannot understand subjective audiometry instructions. Nevertheless, the development of an objective electronic test had to await the development of a small computer combined with the audiometer. With this device, the signal can be applied repetitively to the patient several thousand times and the cochlear, brainstem, or cortical potentials are recorded from the skin of the head and are fed into an analogue computer and averaged. This has proved to be an invaluable instrument for objective measurement in children or in exceptionally difficult cases. Electrical evoked response audiometry, as it has been named by Hallowell Davis, is still only in the early stages of development. Similar techniques are available for the assessment of the patient with vertigo and this has led to the development in the UK, in the USA and in many other countries, of a subspecialty called neuro-otology or audiological medicine.

The rapid strides that have been made in the last 30 years in the field of *electronics have led to the development of much more sophisticated *hearing aids than had previously been available. Whereas in 1948 at the inception of the *National Health Service in the UK the aids which were available without charge were large and heavy and required two bulky batteries to power them, the aids currently available are worn behind the ear and supplied with a small plastic insert for the ear canal. The response curve of both the aid and the ear piece (receiver) can be varied to some extent in order to match the pattern of the patient's hearing loss. In the commercial field even more sophistication and variety is available. However, because a hearing aid can only provide amplification, albeit modified in respect of frequency bands, it is found to be more satisfactory for the patient with conductive deafness rather than the sufferer from sensorineural deafness. This is because the latter may have additional problems with the neural pathways and central connections, such as 'recruitment' which may be defined as an increased sensitivity to small changes in amplitude. In the elderly patient, slowing down in the rate of cerebration may lead to confusion when efforts are made to offset the hearing loss by amplification. Audiological physicians therefore deal not only with the investigation of the deaf and vertiginous patient, they also prescribe hearing aids and advise about auditory rehabilitation.

One aspect of the specialty which has benefited enormously from technological advance is the field of *endoscopy—the examination of internal organs by looking down a lighted tube which has been passed into the internal cavities. The early instruments designed for the purpose were provided with very small electric bulbs which gave inadequate light and burned out rapidly. The original instruments were hollow and the inspection was carried out by the naked eye. In due course magnifying telescopes were added which helped by providing a larger image of the distant site, but it was not until the development of *fibre-optics that a cable and light carrier could be designed which enabled a much stronger 'cold' light to be introduced into the depths of the lung, larynx, and oesophagus. The introduction by Hopkins of solid rod lenses into telescopes gave an added benefit by allowing a greater angle of view and a considerable increase in the depth of focus. The improved lighting system in conjunction with the better optical system has meant that it is now possible to take electronic flash photographs of the clinical findings in colour. This is a great help both in teaching and for the patients' records. Further advances are being made all the time and it is now possible to pass flexible fibre-optic endoscopes into patients, often under local anaesthesia, and to obtain a satisfactory view of the affected organ. Furthermore, it is often possible to carry out minor operative procedures using specially designed instruments which are passed along a separate channel in the tube wall.

The introduction in 1952 of the first Zeiss operating *microscope revolutionized the techniques of operative surgery. Originally the instrument was introduced to help in the *microsurgery of the ear, usually for the surgical procedures designed for the relief of conductive deafness. However, after only a brief experience of using the microscope, it became clear that it had a part to play not only in otology but also in laryngology and rhinology. Currently most otolaryngologists use the microscope both in the out-patient department and in the operating theatre. By the use of the microscope it has been possible to develop new techniques and new safer approaches not only to the ear and the larynx but also to the pituitary fossa and the posterior cranial fossa for the removal of tumours in these sites. About 10 years after the otolaryngologists began to use the microscope it was taken up by other surgeons. It is now used by vascular surgeons, plastic surgeons, neurosurgeons,

orthopaedic surgeons, and ophthalmic surgeons.

A recent development in microsurgery has been the fitting of an argon and carbon dioxide *laser to the microscope and to endoscopes. The otolaryngologist uses only the carbon dioxide laser. By combining magnification and laser it is possible to carry out a very accurate destruction of *tumours, usually benign tumours, in sites where access is difficult.

Another important development has been the use of *ultrasonic destruction of the labyrinth, sparing the cochlea, in the treatment of Ménière's disease.

The introduction of effective drugs. Modern otolaryngology owes more than most specialties to the introduction of powerful new drugs which have specific actions in the management of disease. The major crises which occurred in the specialty before the introduction of *sulphonamide therapy in the 1930s were attributable to secondary bacterial infections caused by the *streptococcus, the *pneumococcus, and the *staphylococcus, which complicated primary respiratory viral infections. All ear inflammations were looked upon as potentially very serious because of the risk that the patient might develop complications such as *mastoiditis, which in turn could lead to *meningitis, *cerebral abscesses, or *septicaemia, leading to *pyaemia and death. The introduction of sulphonamides brought about a dramatic improvement in the situation and with the introduction of *penicillin in 1942 there was a further marked reduction in the incidence of mastoiditis and its complications. Over the past 40 years many *antibiotics have been developed and have proved to be successful in dealing with some of the most virulent organisms. However, these advances have not been achieved without cost: resistant strains of organisms (see MICROBIOLOGY) have evolved which have rendered some antibiotics ineffective; other antibiotics, which have been very effective in dealing with overwhelming infections in some organs, have had very serious toxic effects upon others. The inner ear is particularly susceptible to the *aminoglycoside group of drugs and cases of permanent total deafness have been recorded resulting from their use.

Another group of drugs which has proved very helpful in the management of diseases commonly encountered by the otolaryngologist are the *antihistamines. These have been particularly helpful in managing allergic rhinitis of the seasonal type (hay fever) and also in the control of the symptom of giddiness (vertigo) associated with labyrinthine irritation. The last 20 years have witnessed the introduction of cytotoxic agents which have had a most beneficial effect in the control of certain *malignant diseases. Some groups of malignant tumours that previously had a very poor prognosis because of the rapidity of their growth, can now be controlled by the use of cytotoxic drugs (*antineoplastic chemotherapy) combined in some cases with *radiotherapy. Tumours in this category include the *lymphomas and some of the malignant embryomata commonly seen in childhood.

The changing patterns of disease. The nature of the work in any specialty changes with advances in knowledge of pathology and therapeutics. The last century has seen remarkable progress in the field of otolaryngology. One hundred years ago the main problems were the necrotizing infections which often produced fatal complications. Chronic infections such as tuberculosis and syphilis were relatively common: indeed, tuberculosis of the larynx was seen regularly in the out-patient clinic until about 25 years ago. It then virtually disappeared in the UK until the arrival of the immigrant population from the continents of Africa and Asia. One hundred years ago, laryngeal cancer was common but was then seen mainly in men. With the change in *smoking habits, many more cases are now being seen in women. Laryngeal cancer has always been a malignant tumour with a favourable prognosis. Whereas 100 years ago the only treatment available for such a patient was surgery, in the UK today most patients with laryngeal cancer are treated primarily with radiotherapy. Surgery is reserved for those cases that are not controlled with radiotherapy or in whom the growth recurs after radiotherapy.

Twenty years ago, much of the general otolaryngologist's work was taken up with the surgical treatment of the child with recurrent infections of the upper respiratory tract. In the UK over 300 000 children a year had their *tonsils and *adenoids removed. However, it is now appreciated that recurrent upper respiratory inflammation is one way in which the immature body develops immunity to infection. Much of the surgeon's time today is taken up in explaining to the worried parent what is happening, thus avoiding unnecessary surgical intervention. There is still much upper respiratory infection in childhood requiring treatment but the type of treatment advised has changed. The family doctor treats all cases of acute otitis media with antibiotics and many of these children recover completely, but there are still some who develop residual middle ear effusions. This may necessitate the insertion of middle ear 'ventilation' tubes (*grommets) in order to equalize air pressure on either side of the tympanic membrane and to allow resolution and absorption of the exudate. There is still a possibility of residual deafness in cases which remain untreated.

Conductive deafness has always been a challenge to the otolaryngologist because it appears to be amenable to surgical correction. From the earliest days of the specialty attempts were made to correct conductive deafness due to *otosclerosis. In this disease the stapes becomes fixed in the oval window by new bone formation. Early operative attempts to relieve this included the total removal of the stapes; these often ended in disaster. However, before the First World War some suc-

cess was achieved by a 'fenestration operation' in which the focus of disease was short-circuited by the creation of a new pathway for sound waves through the lateral semicircular canal. In the late 1930s Julius Lempert in New York perfected the operation and brought relief from their deafness to many people. Nevertheless, the operation had the disadvantage that a cavity was created within the ear and these cavities frequently produced unpleasant discharge. A further major advance occurred when Samuel Rosen introduced his 'stapes mobilization' procedure. This gave excellent short-term benefit, but unhappily the stapes tended to become fixed again as the disease progressed. The current procedure of choice is removal of the stapes (stapedectomy) in which the bone, or part of it, is removed and replaced with a *prosthesis made of wire or Teflon combined with vein, fat, connective tissue, or gelatin sponge. The long-term results are good but there are still patients in whom the hearing deteriorates again after a period of years.

Although most major cancers of the head and neck are handled in the first instance by chemotherapy or radiotherapy there is one site where these two modes of treatment do not offer significant advantages over surgery. Post-cricoid carcinoma (cancer of the upper end of the gullet or oesophagus) commonly seen among middle-aged women has always proved to be a great challenge to the surgeon. The nature of the disease is such that distant spread of the disease occurs late but, provided that the local growth can be excised, there is a good outlook. Until recent years the difficulty has been to excise an adequate margin of tissue around the growth. However, over the past 15 years, it has become possible to excise the whole tumour, together with the oesophagus, and to bring up the stomach through the thorax to be united with the cut end of the pharynx. The operation has proved to have great advantages for the patient because it does away with long stays in hospital and multistage repair procedures, and allows feeding to be started early; this is an important consideration for patients who have often been on the verge of starvation for many months preoperatively. The five-year survival rate for this condition has been improved considerably by the use of this procedure.

With the arrival of the operating microscope, operating in a confined space became both easier and safer. Operations which had formerly been considered to be too dangerous or too difficult now became possible. Alternative approaches to intracranial diseases were worked out and were found to have less morbidity: examples of these have included the transphenoidal approach (through the nose) to the *pituitary gland for the removal of tumours, and the translabyrinthine approach to the posterior cranial fossa for the removal of small laterally placed acoustic neurinomas (benign growths on the auditory nerve). The more traditional approach to the pituitary by craniotomy (opening the skull) entailed a considerably longer stay in hospital and greater morbidity postoperatively. Although it is possible for the otologist to carry out the translabyrinthine approach to the internal auditory meatus on his own, most otologists carry out this procedure in co-operation with a neurosurgeon because, even with modern imaging techniques, it is often difficult to assess accurately the size of the tumour to be removed; the services of the neurosurgeon may be needed to deal with a larger tumour.

The operating microscope has revolutionized the management of the chronically discharging ear. It is now used routinely in the out-patient department for determining the extent of the disease and for carrying out cleaning under magnification. This has reduced the number of cases requiring operative surgery. The microscope has enabled more precise excision of the diseased tissue and has made possible reconstructive procedures for the repair of the sound-conducting apparatus, which fall into two categories: in the first, the patient's own tissue is used to construct a partial or a complete sound-wave transmitting system; more recently, cadaver material taken from previously healthy ears and preserved in a *tissue bank has been used. The nature and the extent of the operation depends upon the degree of destruction but when there has already been considerable damage to the chain of ossicles it is often easier, and gives a better result, to replace them as a complete chain attached to the donor ear drum. This type of operation is called tympanoplasty and ranges from a simple patching procedure of the tympanic membrane in order to close a perforation, to a complete replacement of the sound-conducting mechanism.

Recent developments in the specialty. The past 20 years have seen further specialization within the specialty. Not only have otolaryngologists specialized in audiological medicine, but surgeons have tended, in large centres, to confine their interests to one particular field or one particular age group. Consequently there are now those who specialize in head and neck *oncology and those who practise only otological surgery. In the other category of those who restrict their practice to a limited age group are those who have made a particular study of the diseases which commonly present in childhood. Paediatric otolaryngology (as it is called) began in Eastern Europe shortly before the Second World War but it has now become recognized throughout the developed world as an independent subspecialty. The advantage which is claimed for such subspecialization is that it provides better care for the patient because of the increased experience which the surgeon has gained in his chosen field. However, it would be wrong to suppose that all that was required was the will to make a change. All of these new developments owe much to the very considerable advances which have been made in the field of *anaesthesia. Better monitoring of the patient during surgery has

improved the chances of survival from major procedures. Controlled *hypotension has greatly facilitated microsurgery of the ear and combined *local and general anaesthesia for endoscopic examinations has allowed adequate time for the examination of very small infants and for the repair of some of the major abnormalities which are encountered.

Some of the people who have established the specialty of otolaryngology. It is never possible to be totally objective in selecting those whose contributions to a particular field have been of great importance. There are some individuals who would be accepted by all as having made outstanding contributions. An attempt will be made to include many of these. Their names are arranged in chronological order rather than in order of merit.

Prosper Ménière (1799–1862), a French physician, published an account of a female patient with labyrinthine vertigo which he demonstrated was due to disease of the ear and not, as had been thought previously, to intracranial disease.

Joseph Toynbee (1815–66) has been called the 'Father of British Otology'. His book *Diseases of the Ear* was published in 1860. He introduced into England the aural *speculum for the examination of the ear. He was the first otologist to describe otosclerosis.

Rudolf *Virchow (1821–1902) of Berlin was the histopathologist who had the greatest influence in promoting knowledge of otolaryngological pathology.

Christian Theodor *Billroth (1829–94) was the first surgeon to remove a cancerous larynx, in 1873. He was also the first surgeon to resect the oesophagus.

Adam *Politzer (1835–1920) taught otology in Vienna. He was born in Hungary and studied in Vienna where he opened the first aural clinic in 1873 with Gruber. His attainments as a linguist enabled him to teach in five languages and he made important contributions to our knowledge of the anatomy and pathology of the ear.

Sir W. Morrell *Mackenzie (1837–92), one of the founders of British otolaryngology, founded the Golden Square Hospital for Diseases of the Ears, Nose and Throat. He achieved a world-wide reputation as a laryngologist and published *Growths in the Larynx* in 1870 and later *Diseases of the Nose and Throat* in 1880–4. In 1887 he advised on the management of Crown Prince Frederick of Prussia who was thought to be suffering from cancer of the larynx. No evidence of cancer was found in three biopsies by *Virchow, but even so the patient died of laryngeal cancer.

Joseph P. O'Dwyer (1841–98) of Cleveland, Ohio, in 1895 introduced *intubation of the larynx for respiratory difficulty, mainly for the management of laryngeal *diphtheria.

Friedrich Bezold (1842–1908) was the first surgeon to give a clear account of the surgical pathology of mastoiditis.

Sir William *Macewen (1848–1924) of Glasgow was a general surgeon. He carried out many operations for the drainage of brain abscesses and his results were superior to any others until the advent of antibiotics. His pioneer work *Pyogenic Diseases of the Brain* was published in 1893.

Sir Felix *Semon (1849–1921) was born of German parents, came to England to study under Morrell Mackenzie and became a naturalized British subject. Semon made many contributions to academic laryngology and was the propounder of Semon's law, which stated that in a progressive destructive lesion of the motor nerve supplying the intrinsic muscles of the larynx, abduction of the vocal cords is affected before adduction. He acquired an international reputation as a laryngologist.

Sir Charles Ballance (1856–1936). Ballance was an English surgeon who established the management of intracranial complications of middle ear suppuration on a sound surgical basis. He also made major contributions to mastoid surgery.

Markus Hajek (1862–1941) was a Hungarian by birth, who studied and practised in Vienna and made considerable contributions to rhinology and laryngology as head of the Viennese school.

Chevalier *Jackson Sr of Philadelphia USA (1865–1958) was the pioneer laryngologist and endoscopist in America. He achieved world-wide acclaim for his ability as a surgeon and for his careful preservation of records of many patients by accurate drawings of the clinical findings.

Edmund P Fowler Sr (1872–1966), together with R. L. Wegel, published the first audiograms—charts which plotted the patient's hearing by frequency and intensity compared with a norm.

Robert *Bárány (1876–1936). Bárány was born in Vienna and later moved to Uppsala. He won the Nobel prize for physiology and medicine in 1914 for clarifying understanding of the vestibular apparatus.

Wilhelm Brunings (1876–1958) of Jena made great contributions to the advancement of proximal light endoscopy.

Sir Victor Ewings Negus (1887–1974) was an English laryngologist who prepared a definitive account of the *Comparative Anatomy of the Larynx* (1949), which was a condensation of a much larger work on the larynx published in 1928.

Julius Lempert (1890–1962) of New York City, perfected the fenestration operation for otosclerosis and made significant contributions to the techniques of modern mastoid surgery. Although he was to live to see many of his ideas about the management of otosclerosis superseded, his contribution to microsurgical techniques in the ear have won a permanent place in the history of the specialty.

Georg von Békésey (1899–1972), was a winner of the Nobel prize for physiology and medicine in 1961 although he was primarily a physicist. He worked in his native Hungary and later in Sweden and the USA. He made outstanding contributions

to otology, auditory physiology, and psychoacoustics.   R. PRACY

Further reading
Ballantyne, J. and Groves, J. (eds) (1979). *Scott-Brown's Diseases of the Ear, Nose and Throat*, Vols 1–4. London.
Hinchcliffe, R. and Harrison, D. (eds) (1976). *Scientific Foundations of Otolaryngology*. London.
Maran, A. G. D. and Stell, P. M. (eds) (1979). *Clinical Otolaryngology*. Oxford.
Scott Stevenson, R. and Guthrie D. (1949). *A History of Otolaryngology*, Edinburgh.
Snow, J. B. (ed.) (1980). *Controversy in Otolaryngology*. Philadelphia.

OTOLOGIST. A physician or surgeon specializing in conditions affecting the ear. See OTOLARYNGOLOGY.

OTOLOGY is the branch of medicine dealing with the ear. See OTOLARYNGOLOGY.

OTORHINOLARYNGOLOGIST. A specialist in diseases of the ear, nose, and throat. See OTOLARYNGOLOGY.

OTOSCLEROSIS. A cause of deafness, in which an abnormality, sometimes genetically determined, of the surrounding bone hinders the movement of the *stapes, one of the tiny *ossicles which transmit sound vibrations from the eardrum to the inner ear. Surgical treatment can be of help. See OTOLARYNGOLOGY.

OTOSCOPE. An instrument for facilitating inspection of the external auditory canal and eardrum.

OVARIAN CYST. Benign ovarian cysts may occur at any age, although they are most common between 35 and 55. Often they produce no symptoms at all, and thus may become very large before the patient notices something amiss. Her increasing girth, often put down to simple obesity, may be commented on by friends. Or she may develop pressure symptoms (e.g. breathlessness, indigestion, piles, swelling of the legs, varicose veins) as a result of the sheer size of the tumour. Backache may occur, but frank pain is uncommon, as is menstrual disturbance.

OVARIAN FOLLICLES is an alternative term for *Graafian follicles. See also OVULATION.

OVARIECTOMY is the surgical removal of one or both *ovaries (synonymous with oophorectomy).

OVARIOTOMY is a surgical incision of the *ovary, usually to remove an ovarian tumour; the word is sometimes used synonymously with *oophorectomy.

OVARY. The ovary is the female *gonad, a paired organ situated one at each side of the *uterus below the opening of the *Fallopian tube. During the 30 years or so of female reproductive life, from *menarche to *menopause, ovulation, the production of a single ovum, occurs once a month. Like the male gonad, the ovary in addition to the production of *gametes has an *endocrine function, secreting the *hormones responsible for female *secondary sexual characteristics.

OVERLAYING is the suffocation of an infant by lying on top of it.

OVULATION is the extrusion of an oocyte (egg or ovum) from a *Graafian follicle on to the surface of the *ovary, whence it passes via the *Fallopian tube into the *uterus. Ovulation occurs once a month on about the 15th day of the menstrual cycle throughout the female reproductive period (i.e. from *menarche to *menopause). It is marked by slight *pyrexia and in some women by *mittelschmerz. Maturation of Graafian follicles is under the control of *follicle-stimulating hormone secreted by the anterior *pituitary gland. See also FERTILITY DRUG.

OVUM. The female reproductive cell or *gamete. During the reproductive period of the human female, a single ovum is released from one or other *ovary at monthly intervals on or about the 15th day of each menstrual cycle.

OWEN, SIR RICHARD (1804–92). British physician and naturalist, MRCS (1826), FRS (1839). Owen trained at Edinburgh and later at *St Bartholomew's Hospital, London, where he was appointed lecturer in comparative anatomy in 1829. In 1827 he had become assistant conservator of the *Hunterian museum at the Royal College of Surgeons and in 1836 was advanced to professor of comparative anatomy and physiology. He was made superintendent of the natural history department of the British Museum in 1856. He was created Companion of the Order of the Bath in 1873 and advanced to Knight Commander of the Order of the Bath in 1884. Owen was the leading comparative anatomist of his time in Europe.

OXALATE. Any salt of oxalic acid. Excessive secretion of oxalate in the urine (hyperoxaluria) can result in the formation of calcium oxalate stones in the urinary tract. See UROLOGICAL SURGERY.

OXFAM was started in 1942 as the Oxford Committee for Famine Relief by a few citizens who decided to do something to help hungry children in Greece, which was then under Nazi occupation. From that time it has come to be a household word, distributing over £19 million each year. Its aims are 'To relieve poverty, distress and suffering in any part of the world . . .'. It is essentially a fund-raising and grant-giving body, the money coming from private (often small and multiple) donations and from an immense amount of voluntary work. The employed staff is relatively small.

The policy is to assist personal and local endeavours of the poor to help themselves. In several areas of the world there are field directors: they are approached with projects needing support, and they also seek them out in order to give assistance to agencies working locally and who are therefore most likely to understand the problems. These field directors evaluate the projects and make recommendations to the central committees of Oxfam. Often very small grants may help enormously in such matters as sanitation, the building of latrines, irrigation, and buying seed or implements for agriculture. An Asian village may be transformed by a few hundred pounds assisting it with agriculture, water supply, drainage, hygiene, shelter, and medical supplies. Health education for local people, using them in their turn as teachers, can bring great dividends at low cost. The effectiveness of such programmes is also evaluated by the field directors. A vast range of projects supported for 1983 is published and shows work in 76 countries and in several places within them, and much of it is in support of health care. About 20 per cent of the budget is allotted to this.

Though most of its work is of this kind, Oxfam is also one of the first to receive calls for help when disaster strikes as in famine, drought, flood, earthquakes, and wars, with their terrifying human aftermaths. Then food, blankets, tents, medical supplies, engineers, and doctors are often supplied in very short time. There are standby teams of volunteers for this type of relief.

OXIDATION is the combination of *oxygen with a substance or the removal of *hydrogen from it. The term is also used more generally to signify any reaction in which an atom loses electrons, for example the change of iron from the ferrous (Fe^{2+}) to the ferric (Fe^{3+}) state.

OXIMETER. A photoelectric instrument for measuring the *oxygen saturation of *haemoglobin. The technique of measurement is called oximetry.

OXOSTEROIDS are metabolic products of *hormones, the urinary content of which is derived chiefly from *corticosteroids but partly also from *testosterone; their measurement provides a rough indication of *adrenocortical function.

OXYGEN is a gaseous element (atomic number 8, relative atomic mass 15.9994, symbol O), which is odourless and invisible. Oxygen is the most abundant element in the earth's crust including the seas and the atmosphere; it constitutes 20 per cent by weight of atmospheric air. It is chemically very active; both combustion and *respiration involve combination with oxygen. All known forms of life (except some bacteria) depend on a supply of oxygen to provide energy by metabolism of *glucose or some other nutrient. In man, oxygen is absorbed into the bloodstream through the lungs and transported in combination with *haemoglobin to the tissues. Pure oxygen is of therapeutic value in many situations.

OXYGEN DISSOCIATION CURVE. The sigmoid curve describing the relationship between the partial pressure of *oxygen and the volume in reversible combination with unit mass of *haemoglobin (or the percentage saturation of haemoglobin with oxygen). The shape and position of the curve are influenced by a number of variables, most notably temperature, pH, and $p\mathrm{CO}_2$.

OXYTOCIN is one of the two hormones secreted by the posterior lobe of the *pituitary gland; it initiates *labour at the end of pregnancy, stimulates uterine contraction, and also plays a part in *lactation.

OXYURIS is the *threadworm or pinworm, *Oxyuris* (or *Enterobius*) *vermicularis*.

OZONE is a form of molecular oxygen with three instead of two atoms (symbol O_3). It is very active chemically and a powerful oxidizing agent, sometimes used as a disinfectant. Ordinary air contains only minute amounts; higher concentrations are irritant to the lungs.

P

PABULUM. Food of any kind.

PACCHIONI, ANTONIO (1665–1726). Italian physicist and anatomist. Pacchioni practised in Rome where he was physician to the Ospedale della Consolazione. In 1692 he described the protrusions of *arachnoid membrane now known as *Pacchionian bodies.

PACCHIONIAN BODIES are small granulations associated with the *arachnoid mater of the *meninges, through which the *cerebrospinal fluid is reabsorbed into the venous circulation.

PACEMAKERS. The normal cardiac pacemaker is a collection of cells situated in the wall of the right atrium called the *sinoatrial node; it has a greater inherent rhythmicity than any other part of the *myocardium and it therefore initiates the wave of excitation which produces each contraction of the heart. Artificial pacemakers are electrical devices for providing regular external stimuli in order to maintain an adequate heart rate in patients with *heart block, in whom inherent rhythmicity has partly or completely failed. See also CARDIOLOGY II.

PACING is maintaining the heartbeat by repetitive stimulation of the myocardium with a *pacemaker.

PADUA, in northern Italy, had a university founded there in 1222, the second oldest in Italy. The university was part of the movement which led to the Renaissance, and it had a long tradition in science and medicine. *Galileo was professor of mathematics. Andreas *Vesalius was professor of anatomy in 1537, and his book *De fabrica* marked the beginning of scientific medicine. Gabriel *Falloppius followed Vesalius in the chair. *Fabricius ab Aquapendente taught William *Harvey when he visited, and perhaps gave the Englishman the idea of the valves in veins. Other famous visitors, for whom Padua was an essential part of their studies and itineraries, were Thomas *Vicary, John *Caius, and Sir Thomas *Browne. *Santorio was there and *Fracastoro, and *Morgagni was professor of anatomy in 1721. He might be seen as the founder of pathology, and Bernardino *Ramazzini in 1700 published the first work on *occupational diseases. For two or more centuries the work coming from Padua was seminal and a key to much of the history of medicine during the Renaissance and after.

PAEDERASTY is anal intercourse between a man (the paederast) and a boy.

PAEDIATRICIAN. A physician specializing in children's diseases. See PAEDIATRICS.

PAEDIATRICS. The grand design for the upbringing of children is to cultivate the inherent biological potential of each individual from the beginning of life. In this undertaking the parents or care-givers have the prime responsibility, yet much responsibility rests on society as a whole which provides the opportunity, the material environment, the education, and in no small degree the motivation.

Child health matters and child illness are also the concern of the family and of society, and it is chiefly here that the paediatrician has his contribution to make. How far this interference should penetrate, what are the limits of his responsibility, to what extent the care of children should be 'medicalized', are questions for discussion and review. The answers have certainly changed since paediatrics became a science as well as an art. Only since this change, which happened about a century ago, have paediatrics and paediatricians been generally accorded in the public mind (and in the mind of colleagues) a right to a professional independence separate from general medicine.

What is paediatrics? Paediatrics can be described as the study of all those subjects which concern the paediatrician in carrying out his work as a doctor for children, keenly aware that the child is part of a family. In such a context the paediatrician may be defined as a doctor who specializes in the science and practice of paediatrics. These two statements, which may be criticized as somewhat loose and even not sufficiently serious, do cover not only the extraordinary scientific advances but also the changes in philosophical concepts which have occurred during the last few decades in relation to the needs and the medical care of children. The simple basic observations were that children when sick or when disabled by reason of congenital defect do behave differently from adults similarly affected, and that certain diseases seem to occur in childhood only. The need for different doses of drugs, and the tendency towards recovery were also recognized; and doctors have always seen themselves as experts on infant feeding.

The elaboration of the subject did not start logically with observations on the fetus and then after birth on the newborn baby, the infant, the toddler, the schoolchild, the adolescent, and finally the mature adult developed as far as circumstances allowed to his full potential. Rather, what happened was the reverse. For much of history the child patient, like the child in general, was treated as a miniature adult expected to behave both physiologically and pathologically in the same way as his parents. As the frontiers were pushed back to the earlier years, management based on these ideas was found wanting, especially for those under five years of age. `The newborn baby was always recognized as having its own peculiar problems compounded of the stress and trauma of delivery, the need to adapt to independent extrauterine life, and the presence in some of *congenital abnormalities. Interest in the infant and the newborn led eventually to the concept of antenatal paediatrics, with emphasis on the state of the pregnant woman who is responsible for the intrauterine environment in which the fetus grows (see ANTENATAL DIAGNOSIS).

The build-up of knowledge revealed the importance of development. The acquisition of skills like walking and talking, long called 'milestones', came to be understood as developmental processes evolving slowly according to a constant plan, and interdependent. The concept of milestones was both inappropriate and misleading. The study of the abnormal showed the magnitude of the cloud of ignorance that obscured knowledge about the development of the normal healthy child, and how progress may be helped and how hindered. Much recent research has been devoted successfully to the dissipation of this cloud.

Paediatrics, then, originated from the study of diseases of children. When we learn of the modern high-technology paediatrics which enables a delicate operation to be performed on the fetus while it is still in the womb, it is difficult to appreciate how simple were the beginnings of the subject. The story contains many strands, among them the recent application of science and technology, both growing apace, but including also revolutions in our ways of thinking about children and families and of organizing our society. A stage has been reached in which, on the one hand, a fetus with damaging defects, who until recently would have been accepted even by the sorrowing parents as an inevitable part of reproductive wastage, is now given all available intensive care. In contrast, in the next room a potentially perfectly formed fetus is destroyed through termination of pregnancy, accepted as proper by all the individuals concerned and by the community as a whole. This curious paradox of contemporary Western culture has an important influence on the practice of paediatrics.

History. Because of the prolonged dependency of the human offspring, cultural patterns of many kinds have developed in human societies. These give the majority of parents the confidence to face the awesome responsibilities of discharging their obligations to the new baby through the adoption of routine cultural procedures. The methods have

always covered the care of the normal, with extra measures for dealing with signs and symptoms, that is with appearances and behaviour regarded as not normal. Lists of these abnormal happenings date from the earliest human records. Both in the Egyptian *Ebers Papyrus, dating from the first half of the 16th c. BC, and in the slightly later Berlin Papyrus on mother and child, there are sections on the diseases of infancy. In Indian and Chinese manuscripts and to a lesser extent in the *Talmud*, diseases of children are described and discussed. *Hippocrates in his *Aphorisms,* notably in the fragment 'On Teething', shares responsibility for the kind of list which persisted with relatively little change either in its content or in the accompanying recommendations from classical times down to the middle of the 16th c. AD. This constitutes external rather than internal medicine: sores, rashes, lumps, and bumps seen and felt from the outside without the use of artefacts or any exploration within.

Little remains in the West of this ancient wisdom or of the practices embodied in folk medicine except the aim, which is to rear children successfully so that they are fitted to take their proper places in an orderly society. That such matters should be the concern of a specialist would have surprised the doctors of the early part of the 20th c. It was only then that the idea began to be accepted in the UK that the diseases of children needed the knowledge and skill of a specialist. For the first 50 years he was to be known as a children's specialist and his specialty as 'the diseases of children'.

In other countries, matters had progressed a little more quickly. A private hospital for the treatment of children was opened in Vienna in 1787. Half a century later, public children's hospitals followed in Berlin (1830), St Petersburg (1834), and Vienna (1837), but it was the French who led the way.

After the Revolution, the French government, recognizing that the children of the people needed the best possible medical treatment in order to grow into healthy citizens, founded, in 1802, a hospital for sick children (Hôpital des Enfants Malades) in Paris. The assumption of responsibility by government ensured continuity and sufficient resources to make possible the study of diseases of children. From 1838 to 1843 Barthez and Rilliet published their three-volume work on the diseases of children which remained the bible for doctors for the next 25 years. It was the time of the French pre-eminence in clinical medicine and in physiology.

In contrast, in England such endeavours were left to private charity. In fact a *Foundling Hospital had been opened by Thomas *Coram in London in 1739. Attempts to gather sick children together, so that doctors might learn by experience how to treat them and to compare the success of different treatments, were made by George *Armstrong in 1769 and by John Bunnell Davis in 1815; both proved abortive. It was not until 1852 that Charles *West opened the first British Hospital for Sick Children in *Great Ormond Street. In all these plans, the objective was first and foremost to cut down the high infant and child mortality rates by improving the skill and knowledge of the doctors, but this was by no means the sole objective. Instructions were given to mothers about hygiene and the general care of children and there were opportunities for the training of nurses. However, although the hospitals provided centres in which medical and nursing skills could be fostered, it was soon evident that their contribution to falling death rates would be small. Indeed, hospital admission could itself engender epidemics of *infectious diseases, often fatal. The solution was to be sought and found elsewhere in the better ordering of the public health.

Paediatrics and paediatricians (pediatrics and pediatricians in American usage) had made an earlier and more encouraging start in the USA, where an American Pediatric Society held its first meeting in 1889, the *Archives of Pediatrics* having been founded five years earlier. The members of the former society, like the contributors to the latter journal, were physicians with 'a special interest in the study of diseases in children'. Nevertheless, much time and space were devoted to infant feeding. Hygiene, public health, and child labour were even at that time recognized as appropriate subjects for discussion, but, naturally, the doctors' chief concern was disease. The first American children's hospital was opened in Philadelphia in 1855.

In Austria and in Germany the approach was more academic. The problems of infant nutrition and of infant feeding were joined with studies of the diseases of the newborn and of the early childhood years. The lead which these countries took over France, where modern medicine had found its first home, remained with them until the First World War when it crossed the Atlantic. Abraham *Jacobi, L. Emmett *Holt, Henry Koplik, J. Lewis Smith, William *Osler, not all confining their work to children had, among others, laid firm foundations upon which the next generation of their pupils, too numerous to mention, built the science of paediatrics while not neglecting the art. The culmination came when John Howland (1873–1926) established the first academic department of paediatrics, the Harriet Lane, at *Johns Hopkins Hospital in Baltimore in 1912. The pre-eminence of American paediatricians is generally recognized throughout the world today, although notable paediatric contributions both in medicine and surgery are owed to others. Sweden can claim in Rosen von Rosenstein (1706–73), professor of medicine at Uppsala, the founder of paediatrics as a specialty, by reason of his authorship in 1765 of the first textbook entitled (in English translation) *The Diseases of Children and their Remedies*. National pride in this achievement has inspired Swedish paediatricians who, despite their enthusiasm for machines, have developed important insights into the social aspects of their subject.

Frederic *Still in London and John Thomson (1856–1926) in Edinburgh were the first two British specialists in diseases of children. The others, who acted as physicians in the children's hospitals, were general physicians with a special interest in sick children—and particularly in the recognition of such modifications of adult illnesses as occurred during childhood, in illnesses which seemed mainly or only to affect children, and in malformations deemed to be of congenital origin. Still himself described a children's form of *rheumatoid arthritis in his MD thesis in 1896. *Mental deficiency was a special interest, not in its own right but when it formed one of a collection of congenital defects. Only Thomson in his pamphlet *Opening Doors* (1923) aimed to tell parents what they could do to help their disabled child.

The real function of the children's specialists in those early days remained 'general medicine applied to the special age-group', which began at birth, although many years were to pass before the *obstetricians were won over to relinquish their nominal responsibility for the newborn. When the special age-group ends is still undecided, the onset of *puberty being one obvious determinant. The development of adolescent medicine as a further specialization has only a limited following.

Diseases of children. The children's diseases which at first occupied the most attention of the children's specialists and filled the hospital beds were those due to infection. These were often acute and sometimes either fatal or the cause of handicapping sequelae. Of the chronic infections, *tuberculosis took prime place and as recently as the end of the 1930s about half of the beds in a children's ward in the UK were occupied by children infected with tubercle bacilli.

The most numerous, although not the most serious, infections were the so-called acute specific fevers, epidemics of which swept countries in recognized cycles, disrupting life both through the illness itself and through the *quarantine techniques aimed at limiting spread. These common acute fevers—*diphtheria, *measles, *scarlet fever, *whooping cough, *mumps, and the like—were generally looked on as part of the process of growing up, although adults were also sometimes affected. The sufferers were treated at home by their family doctors or in the special 'fever hospitals' where their care was undertaken by fever experts or, more commonly, by *medical officers of health who, except in the large conurbations, combined this taste of clinical work with mainly administrative duties. The children's specialists were concerned mostly with the complications.

The introduction of effective *immunization against this group of diseases began with diphtheria toxin–antitoxin mixtures with which research workers had been experimenting from the early years of the 20th c. During the 1920s, *clinical trials were being made on selected populations. A major preoccupation was the risk of *serum-sickness, a complication of immunization noted by von *Pirquet in Vienna in 1905 and leading him to his conception of *allergy. The general adoption of active immunization took many years. Its introduction found the general public, and even the doctors, somewhat suspicious despite the century-long experience of *smallpox *vaccination. Protection against *tetanus and, to a lesser degree, against whooping cough became available but it was not until the 1940s that what was being offered in the UK was accepted by the majority as safe and beneficial. These preventable diseases with their toll of death and disability virtually disappeared from the Western world. The success of the immunization programmes has changed the pattern and the needs of medical and surgical care in the West. However, nature abhors a vacuum, and the place formerly occupied by the acute specific fevers in mortality and morbidity tables has been quickly filled by accidents. No doubt the same will happen when the programmes, which depend for their practical application on many changes in society, are adopted in the rest of the world.

The most spectacular of the epidemic diseases, infantile paralysis (acute anterior *poliomyelitis), had seemed to be increasing in parallel with improving standards of hygiene. As late as 1951, periodic epidemics (first noted in 1910) swept the USA and Sweden, inducing the sort of community panic which we associate with the plagues of the Middle Ages and leaving a trail of death and serious motor handicap. Since the introduction of the *Salk vaccine, first described in 1953, these catastrophes have become part of history.

The two important infections which most occupied the children's specialists before the Second World War were acute diarrhoea and vomiting (*gastroenteritis) in infancy and tuberculosis in its manifold forms.

Many babies in the first year of life died from what was called summer diarrhoea but this later began to appear as winter epidemics accompanying outbreaks of acute *respiratory infection. Those affected were seldom breast-fed and seldom from the wealthier section of the population. Often they had been born prematurely and were not thriving when the acute illness began. Sometimes specific bacteria could be identified, more often the cause remained a mystery. Biochemical studies, when they became available, confirmed the clinical impression that it was not the causal agent, whatever that was, so much as the resulting loss of fluid and salts from the vomiting and the diarrhoea that led to metabolic bankruptcy and death. Treatment came to be a battle to replace in correct proportions the water and chemical losses and this time-consuming process kept the medical staff occupied for much of their time by night as well as by day. Looking back at populations where these outbreaks have for the most part died out, improvement in socioeconomic conditions and in general standards of hygiene and nutrition seems likely to have played an important part. Nevertheless, the development of virology has demonstrated that *viruses have a more important role in the aetiology of this condition than bacteria.

The problems posed by tuberculosis were different. *Consumption had been recognized in classical times and tuberculous disease of bone had been diagnosed, with as much certainty as is possible, in the third millennium BC. *Koch identified the tubercle bacillus, publishing his researches in 1882. Infection was spread by coughing and less commonly by drinking infected milk, and by the dawn of paediatrics tuberculosis had established itself as a community as well as a family disease. Certainly, among urban populations almost every child, either as a baby or at some time before maturity, would encounter and be challenged by the tubercle bacillus. Some babies succumbed: others overcame the challenge, becoming sensitized, so that their response to further almost inevitable encounters led to an altered reaction; this, through the results of his tuberculin test, confirmed von Pirquet in his belief in his concept of allergy.

A whole system of special clinics and dispensaries was aimed at first at treatment of the individual patient. Later, mass *radiography led to early case-finding, better segregation of open cases (patients with bacilli in their *sputum) and a reduction in the sources of infection. Grandfather coughing by the fireside was removed and his opportunities were lessened for infecting his grandchildren. The discovery of an effective *antibiotic (*streptomycin) by *Waksman in 1944 provided the final touch. It would be unwise to suppose that tuberculosis has been permanently defeated; it could return. It would find a community of susceptible people of all ages, with disastrous results. Similarly, mutations may enable bacteria to develop resistance to antibiotics. For the present, bacteria are largely defeated and viruses may, through *interferon, be facing a similar fate.

Although these astonishing successes neither originated in children's hospitals, nor directly involved paediatrics, they greatly influenced the health of children. At the same time, further researches had put into the doctors' hands other antibiotics so that the treatment of most non-viral infections could be safely undertaken at home by family doctors or, if in hospital, within a much shorter time and with less resulting debility. These advances, with the reduction in tuberculosis, effective treatment of *meningitis, the virtual disappearance of acute gastroenteritis, *osteomyelitis, and *rheumatic fever with its tendency to cause *valvular disease of the heart, reduced the demand for hospital beds and therefore for the hospital paediatrician practising general medicine.

Meanwhile, many new diagnoses became available. Some diseases, like *cystic fibrosis of the pancreas, could be recognized on clinical grounds once the original observers had defined the history of symptoms and the accompanying physical signs;

other diagnoses depended on laboratory findings. Chromosome studies helped in the classification of the mentally handicapped, in identifying modes of inheritance and in elucidating, for example, the nature of *Down's syndrome (mongolism). The demonstration of an extra chromosome added to the certainty of diagnosis and ruled out the idea of some environmental fault arising during fetal life. By means of *amniocentesis, the birth of an affected baby can now be confidently predicted. If this can be done early enough, birth can be prevented by termination of the pregnancy. Microchemistry and modern laboratory techniques have increased biochemical knowledge. *Chromatography and *electrophoresis have revealed the mechanisms underlying many diseases, including diseases of the *blood, and have brought to light many '*inborn errors of metabolism'. Archibald *Garrod, who introduced this concept, himself realized that variant metabolic pathways did not necessarily produce illness or pathological changes in the tissues, unless the variant system was challenged, for example by the need to metabolize a drug.

Improvements in *radiology, especially image intensification, have allowed more to be seen with less exposure to *ionizing radiation while *computerized axial tomography (the CT scan) and the use of *ultrasound have, like other non-invasive techniques, brought new dimensions to diagnosis.

The multiplication of powerful drugs and biological preparations has enabled the paediatrician and his patient to benefit from these laboratory-dependent diagnoses, which would otherwise be no more than arid academic exercises. Nevertheless, the possibilities for preventive measures have come into the foreground. Identification of serious fetal abnormalities, both anatomical, as in *spina bifida (myelomeningocele), and metabolic, as in some inborn enzyme deficiencies, has led to that extreme form of prevention, the termination of the pregnancy and of fetal life itself. In other diseases, screening tests of the newborn may lead to dietary regulation (in *galactosaemia) or substitution therapy (in *hypothyroidism) so that the secondary effects of the primary defect can be lessened if not entirely prevented. Tissue typing (see HLA) has already led to the early recognition of vulnerable children in diabetic families. The future development of preventive paediatrics seems assured.

Neonatal paediatrics. For half of this century the newborn baby remained for the most part under the care of the obstetricians and the *midwives. With the establishment of the *National Health Service (NHS), an increasing number of paediatricians spread their services country-wide for the first time. The children's specialist had previously been summoned only when something went seriously wrong, and too often too late to be effective.

The newborn baby, deprived of specialist care, presented another difficulty. Ignorance of normal physiology and special pathology was virtually complete: the baby was expected to behave in both like a miniature adult. The relatively common difficulty in starting to breathe was likened to suffocation after drowning and techniques were adopted that would then be appropriate in such circumstances. Only slowly did the idea dawn of development, of realizing that the newborn baby's lungs were being called on to expand for the first time (as with many other functions) and that the failure to establish a function in the first place was an entirely different process from the interruption of a function long established. This applied no less to many vital metabolic processes, coming into action for the first time after birth with some elements still immature. During this period general medicine was experiencing a great increase in knowledge through technical progress in X-rays, in biochemistry, and in physiology and pathology in general. Unfortunately, many of the laboratory methods were not suitable for small children or babies because of the large quantity of blood required for various analyses.

Since the 1960s, the care of the newborn (neonatology) has been one of the most rapidly developing subspecialties of paediatrics. This was first made possible by advances in microchemistry, enabling biochemical data to be obtained from small samples of blood. The main impetus for this work came from Usher in Montreal who described unexpected alterations in babies' acid–base balance (1961). Discovering how to correct these when respiratory difficulties also arose opened up the field of the normal physiology of the newborn. As long as babies were seen as miniature adults and their special pathological responses and needs remained unrecognized, scientific treatment or indeed effective treatment was almost impossible.

This breakthrough has been followed by much excellent and careful research. Special apparatus for monitoring the vital functions and the reactions of the newborn have now been devised and are available in all properly equipped maternity centres. Following the virtual elimination of infection from the nurseries by the careful use of antibiotics, new methods have allowed the survival to healthy childhood of many babies previously regarded as doomed.

Interest and expertise in the care of the newborn inevitably led to interest in the fetus. Could some newborn problems or even some congenital abnormalities (that is, abnormalities discovered at birth) have their origins in damage acquired in the womb? Antenatal paediatrics was pioneered by Leonard Parsons (1879–1950) who discussed the vigour and growth of the baby and its *immunity against infective disease in a lecture in 1946. The danger of maternal *rubella to the fetus had been recognized five years earlier by Gregg in Australia; the hazards involved damage to the eye, the heart, and the brain. The rubella problem should be eliminated by the immunization of schoolgirls as now widely practised in the UK and USA.

An example of the immaturity of a metabolic

system is provided by blood (*rhesus) incompatibility between mother and fetus, which can kill the fetus or produce severe *anaemia. Incompletely metabolized pigment derived from *haemoglobin stresses the immature excretion pathway because, in the first few days of its life, the newborn baby's liver cannot fully metabolize this pigment. The excess of pigment from the breakdown of red blood corpuscles due to incompatibility between maternal and fetal blood (*haemolytic disease of the newborn) is deposited in and permanently damages centres at the base of the brain (*kernicterus). At first the elaborate procedure of washing out the haemolysing antibodies by exchange transfusion of suitable blood was used to prevent the damage. The protection with anti-D *immunoglobulin of women (immediately after the birth of a first child) against sensitization, now widely available, has brought haemolytic disease of the newborn under control in both theory and practice.

The knowledge of the possible damage to the newborn arising from intrauterine events led to a temporary hope that other congenital defects, and particularly mental handicap, could be preventable. The observations and researches on *phenylketonuria, a condition attributable to a deficiency of the enzyme which breaks down *phenylalanine, strengthened this hope when it was shown in that condition that an 'exclusion' diet (low in phenylalanine) could improve the baby's intelligence. However, these expectations in the main have found only modest realization.

The nursery for *intensive care has now shed its frills and ribbons and has replaced them with a frightening array of sophisticated equipment. One of the problems begotten by new techniques is, as ever, that of deciding when to apply them. Starting from the seemingly fatal case in which they provide a 'last hope', they tend to gather a momentum which ends, accompanied by attempts at prediction, in an attempt at prevention. Because of the insuperable difficulty inherent in predictive methods, the end result, while saving some babies from disaster, is the 'prevention' in some cases of events that would not have happened. This would not matter if all interventions were completely safe and not too costly: however, neither condition can claim to be fulfilled.

Several complications result. First, there is the constantly recurring ethical problem of when to employ high technology and, if its success is not immediately apparent, at what point to end it. The second is the production of iatrogenic (treatment-induced) disease. Not to be ignored is the emotional effect of decision-making and outcome upon the various people concerned, including the patient; this can be devastating.

Ethical dilemmas. The realization that these are unavoidable concomitants of technical advances has brought a new dimension into paediatrics and a response, not only from the parents but also from the law, as well as from the public at large. These problems come particularly to the fore in deciding, for example, whether to treat actively a severely malformed infant. This ethical dilemma can never have a satisfactory outcome, for the paediatrician any more than for parents or baby. Its influence on paediatric practice can only be to warp judgement and to introduce considerations over and above the best interests of the baby who is the patient. In the end, the judgement of what those interests are, rests on a human decision. Of necessity the decision cannot be the baby's. Should the parents take decisions which, whatever they are, may lead to feelings of guilt for the rest of their lives? Is a lawyer, a judge, an independent social worker or a committee of experts more likely to find the answer than the paediatrician and the social worker involved with the family? These problems await solution. Meanwhile, they cast a deep shadow over the practice of paediatrics. (See ETHICAL ISSUES IN MEDICAL PRACTICE; RELIGION, PHILOSOPHY, AND ETHICS.)

Iatrogenic disease. Iatrogenic disease, 'a harmful' disorder unwittingly induced in the patient by the inappropriate use of drugs or other forms of management and treatment', has always to be kept in mind when new drugs or apparatus come into use. Two examples serve as illustrations of how this happens. After the Second World War, the efficiency of the *incubators used in the care of premature babies increased, so that whereas the earlier models had not produced high oxygen atmospheres, now they could reach 90 per cent. It had been traditional to give an oxygen supplement to the premature baby whether or not he had breathing difficulties, in the hope of improving the chances of survival. No scientific basis existed for this practice and certainly no one would have prescribed the newly available high oxygen concentration. Suddenly in the 1940s an 'epidemic' occurred in the USA and in the UK of babies, with an eye condition in which damaged tissue behind the lens (*retrolental fibroplasia) caused seriously impaired eyesight or total blindness. Norman Ashton and his colleagues at the Institute of Ophthalmology, London, in 1953 showed how high oxygen atmospheres can cause these eye changes in kittens: the dangers of high oxygen, once recognized, could be avoided.

The public were made more sharply aware of the vulnerability of the fetus by the drug *thalidomide, excellent as a mild nocturnal hypnotic for the treatment of *morning sickness during the early weeks of pregnancy, the time at which it could produce the maximum damage for the developing fetus.

The thalidomide episode, which involved the most notorious of iatrogenic conditions so far described, revealed in an unforgettable way the subtle dangers of the modern therapeutic explosion. From the therapeutic nihilism of the early days of the 20th c., medicine has moved to a polypharmacy aimed against suffering which used to be borne with courage but is now seen as 'unnecessary'. The limbless population of thalidomide children, now entering their third decade, should serve as a reminder that the astonishing range of powerful, effective, and scientifically produced therapeutic agents have the capacity to harm as well as cure. This too, like ethical dilemmas, must be borne constantly in mind in the practice both of obstetrics and of paediatrics.

Infant feeding. Besides diseases, the early child specialists were greatly concerned with *infant feeding, devising special formulae and recommending their own modifications of cow's milk. The results were judged by careful inspection of the baby's napkins (diapers). Such stool-gazing extended to the making of coloured wax models representing the results of different kinds of indigestion. Some of the formulae, very precisely elaborated, would have required standardized measures more likely to be found in the laboratory than in the kitchen. The principle was that the baby would adapt itself to the requirement of the formulae, the prescribed quantities, and the prescribed timetable. It was only in the aftermath of the Second World War that the focus of attention was transferred from the stools to the baby. The important place allotted to the 'pleasure principle' by adults in their own habits did the good service to their babies of replacing rigidity by 'on demand' feeding.

A large body of beliefs about the feeding, hygiene, clothing, and general care of babies and children had been handed down from generation to generation. Such beliefs and the habits derived from them are deeply entrenched and difficult to change, even among sophisticated people. The dangers are less in the West than in countries like Africa where, for example, Dr Cicely Williams found that feeding methods were responsible for chronic ill health and, all too often, death. It would be good to be able to say that practices introduced from the West have always been improvements. Certainly, artificial feeds manufactured under the best conditions are an improvement on home-made thin gruels and other substitutes for breast feeding. However, when, with high-pressure salesmanship, such milks of convenience compete with breast feeding, the bottle with its danger of introducing acute gastroenteritis becomes a deadly instrument.

Paediatricians who are aware of this danger are also aware of the tragic amount of *malnutrition that affects children in the developing world, both from ignorance of nutritional needs and inability to provide for them. In India, where large families and small incomes abound, the National Integrated Child Development Service seeks in some degree to provide a remedy. Faced with the size and extent of the problem, the paediatrician in the Western World is tempted to take refuge in academic medicine. One of the anxieties, otherwise, is how to reconcile efforts to lower infant and child mortality rates with the knowledge that one result of success will be to increase the competition for already insufficient food supplies. Paediatric improvements on their own can do no more than shift the tragedies of death and sickness from one point in the life cycle to another.

Paediatric surgery. During the years when the medical treatment of children was advancing, the surgeons had not been idle. *Orthopaedic surgery, which dates from Robert Owen at the end of the 19th c., and the surgery of accidents, together with the surgery of tonsils, adenoids, and the middle ear, have always contained a large paediatric element. The relatively small amount of acute surgery needed for children in their middle years seemed to be satisfactorily included within general surgical practice. The surgeon does not operate alone: his opportunities and his successes depend on the services of skilled anaesthetists and the scientific regulation of body fluids; recent increases in knowledge in both these fields have benefited children no less than adults.

Within the abdomen lie those internal organs most accessible to the surgeon. Newborn babies with lethal congenital defects causing intestinal obstruction were the first to benefit from the new skills. The relieving operations remained within the competence of many general surgeons, given the assistance of interested anaesthetists, and working with paediatricians and paediatric nurses.

The turning point, which led to the establishment of a number of paediatric surgical departments and professorships in the UK in the 1960s, was the decision to apply comprehensive treatment to newborn babies with spina bifida (myelomeningocele). The total treatment called for the services of the neurosurgeon, the urogenital, and the orthopaedic surgeon. Paediatric surgeons, practising a new specialty, soon mastered the necessary techniques.

After the abdomen, the chest (see CARDIOTHORACIC SURGERY). Taussig and *Blalock in Baltimore, in the 1940s, recognized that the lives of some '*blue' babies could be saved and prolonged by reconstructive techniques. An abnormal heart with abnormal great blood vessels entering and leaving it, which can support the single body circulation (systemic) in the fetus, may not be able to manage the new situation at birth when the second or pulmonary circulation is needed for respiration. The use of ultrasound and studies of the dynamics of the circulation by cardiac catheterization have allowed the greater precision in diagnosis which is essential before operation. A gradual and steady improvement in all techniques has increased the safety of such cardiac surgery at ever-earlier ages. Babies with congenital heart defects which, unless rectified, are incompatible with extrauterine survival, can now benefit from advances both in diagnosis and in surgery.

Children with handicaps. The change that followed the redirection of paediatrics from the study of children's diseases to the study of child health would doubtless be included as part of the 'medicalization' of the health of the community imputed by Illich and his disciples to self-interest. At the time, in the 1950s and 1960s, liberation from the preoccupation with acute infective disease struck the practising paediatrician differently. Now he had time to attend to chronic illness, and especially to exercise his compassion on children with handicaps. These handicaps could be physical, for example in *cerebral palsy, or mental, where his earlier contribution had been limited to making or confirming the diagnosis. All handicaps produce emotional stresses which, if unresolved, can stand in the way of progress. It did not take long before the paediatrician recognized the effect, sometimes devastating, always dangerous, which the birth and the continued presence of severely disabled children could have on parents and siblings. The need for counselling has strengthened the link between paediatricians and medical social workers.

One good result of the thalidomide episode has been a greater concern with other handicapping conditions. Readers of the *Beveridge Report (1942) will have been impressed by his confidence in *rehabilitation and the contribution that it should make to the health and efficiency of the nation. Sickness absence from work, in particular, should greatly diminish. In the late 1930s rehabilitation was being promoted by the establishment of special centres and hospital departments. The war, with its wounded, gave an added impetus which was reinforced by the increase in road traffic and road accidents. The first application of the rehabilitation techniques to paediatrics was in the management of spastic children (cerebral palsy). Some time elapsed before a fundamental difference between rehabilitation of children and that of adults was appreciated. As observed above in connection with the expansion of the lungs at birth, a function being performed for the first time is by no means the same as restoring a previously successful function. Children need 'habilitation', not rehabilitation. There is a further consideration: the baby progresses into childhood through a programme of development, so that what happens today is greatly influenced by what happened yesterday. The baby has to gain control of the neck muscles before it holds up its head, of its head before it can sit, of sitting before standing, or standing before walking. Each baby has a time-related programme of development. The delay in reaching one stage not only delays the next, but makes its accomplishment more difficult. Problems of movement show the relationships most clearly, but, as will be discussed below, both emotional and intellectual development share this problem with motor development, with the additional handicap that in these a stage missed may not be replaceable.

During and after the thalidomide episode, attention focused on the baby born with spina bifida (myelomeningocele). This shorthand label covers a multiplicity of handicaps for which a number of surgical techniques have been devised, some adapted from the treatment of other conditions. For example, transplanting muscles to compensate for those paralysed by poliomyelitis found an application for the lower limbs of children paralysed by the nerve defect. Serious problems in the kidneys and the urogenital tract used to cause death during adolescence from failure of that system. Chronic infection, which contributed largely to the damage, can now be kept under control with antimicrobial treatment, while the urinary tract obstructions and other structural abnormalities can be helped by modern surgical techniques. The management of babies born with these defects can serve to illustrate many of the problems and difficulties to which the modern technical facilities have given rise.

That something is wrong is evident at birth. That something may be going to be wrong at birth can often be predicted by testing the amniotic fluid (amniocentesis) at a stage early enough for termination of pregnancy to be possible. After the birth, an assessment can be made of the extent of the difficulties, which can involve not only the spine and the spinal cord, but the brain itself (obstructive *hydrocephalus), the hip joints and the lower limbs, and the kidneys and the urogenital tract. With experience, the doctors can give a prediction of the likely extent of the paralysis and of the complications, together with a suggestion as to what kind and number of surgical operations may be suffered during infancy and childhood. The probable quality of the child's life can then be assessed. What is less predictable is how much of the ensuing emotional stress each parent will stand and what the effect will be on the marriage (or the partnership).

Parents today are often well-informed about these kinds of medical and surgical problems as one result of publicity in the *media, especially television programmes. Nevertheless, they remain biologically unchanged and still suffer all the traditional pangs of guilt at having created a handicapped abnormal baby. Subconsciously they mourn the normal healthy baby whom they had planned, while at the same time they have to accept and love the imperfectly formed baby that they have. They have also to face all the hard work, emotional and physical, that lies ahead. Relationships within the family can never be the same again and it is small wonder that marriages break. On the other hand, some parents, who were not really happy about the prospect of a new baby, rally to support the handicapped one so that the need to work together and the feeling of responsibility strengthen and mature the parents themselves and serve to cement the relationship.

All of these possibilities must be in the mind of the paediatrician and must help to guide the advice and explanation that he gives to parents about the management of a baby born with severe congenital abnormalities. The quality of the child's life is not the sole factor: the probable effect on the whole family of caring for the child is also important.

It must be proper for the views and wishes of parents to be included in the assessment after full discussion. Whether they should be paramount is a proposition as debatable as whether paramountcy should be attached to a right of every baby under all circumstances to be given the chance to live. Certainly, no decision must be imposed on the parents. The temptation to act by rule of thumb must be resisted by all concerned. Experience in practice raises doubt about the wisdom of some recent court decisions which appear to support the view that a doctor has a duty always to apply all available life-saving measures whatever the circumstances or predictable outcome. The surgeon cannot be compelled even by the court to operate against his better judgement. The paediatrician seems, for the time being, to have no such right in law to refuse.

However the matter is viewed, the birth of a handicapped baby is a tragedy: it is not, however, a defeat, but the start of a battle which has to be won.

The child with a mental handicap. Paediatrics as practised has played only a minor part in supplying the needs of mentally handicapped children other than in diagnosis, yet their numbers alone, not taking into account the distress that they can cause to the family, qualifies them for more serious paediatric attention. Underlying the solution to their problems is the recognition that these problems fall into two well-defined groups with differing needs both as regards management and possible prevention.

Mild mental handicap is in one sense an artefact. Because the distribution of *intelligence as measured by IQ follows a Gaussian curve, some 2 per cent of the child population inevitably fall into the group with an IQ of 20–70 (2–3 standard deviations below the mean of 100). Such children are usually physically normal and present no recognizable brain lesions. Their childhood problems are chiefly educational and only those who need special education are recognized. Their numbers are probably in the region of 140 000 in a school population in England and Wales aged 5–14 years. Insufficient language stimulation in early infancy is an important causative factor. Since most are to be found in the lower social classes, prevention is social and cultural rather than medical. Better-informed parents, and programmes like Headstart in the USA, should be of value. Most of the children, if given encouragement can, as adults, live socially and economically independent lives.

Children with severe mental handicaps are less numerous (some 50 000 in England and Wales, 0–14 years), are found in all social classes, and usually have some neurological lesion. Mongol children (with *Down's syndrome) have until now contributed about one-quarter (1.5 per 1000 births). Other chromosomal abnormalities, birth trauma leading to cerebral palsy, enzyme deficiencies, congenital abnormalities of brain development, and damage from abuse are also causes. In some cases the child's intelligence is less severely affected and this brings him into the mild mental handicap group as far as education is concerned. The majority remain dependent for life. Without willing and competent parents or substitute caregivers, institutional life is necessary; this is especially the case when the child has a physical handicap as well.

For all these children, with mild as well as severe mental handicap, the quality of care in the early years, if not for the whole of childhood, is critical. Institutions are seen, not as repositories for children too difficult to handle outside, but as having a vital therapeutic role. Although there may be no medical treatment in the form of drugs or operations, there is much training and teaching to be done. When, through rejection and neglect, the mental handicap is compounded with emotional disturbance, the person may become unmanageable.

A relatively recent concentration on thoroughgoing assessment in special clinics during infancy is leading to the earlier recognition of handicaps. The benefit from this considerable expenditure of trained personnel and money is the prevention of many secondary problems and difficulties. In the UK, local authorities have statutory responsibilities including the provision of appropriate education and specially trained teachers. Social workers and psychologists have a large part to play. One hoped-for future development is the more positive inclusion of mentally handicapped children in general paediatrics. The current consensus of opinion that as many children with severe mental handicap as possible should be cared for at home has made this more important. Unfortunately, sufficient supporting services in the community have not yet been provided.

Children with behaviour problems. Child *psychiatry stands apart from paediatrics. The necessary technical skills both for understanding and for treatment are acquired only through a lengthy training. It cannot be denied that the work of *Freud and the concepts that lie behind *psychoanalysis were viewed with suspicion and scepticism for many years by doctors in general and by paediatricians no less. Bitter disputes between the different psychiatric schools did not help. The explanations in these psychiatric terms of human behaviour, including the behaviour of the doctor himself, are not always acceptable and are often met with strong resistance. Such opposition remains in the minds of many doctors. Nevertheless, child psychiatry has established an essential place in child health, a place which is likely to get larger in the future.

Child guidance. The movement towards helping to correct the maladjustments of children through specialized Child Guidance Clinics began in the

USA in the 1920s. The resulting separation of psychiatry from paediatrics proper was strongly opposed by paediatricians specializing in neurology, who believed that paediatricians should acquire psychiatric knowledge and skills and use it themselves. This kind of demarcation dispute has not yet been settled. Lack of time and opportunity make it well-nigh impossible to combine the two trainings, a problem that arises with most of the specializations within a specialty. D. W. *Winnicott practised for some years in London in the double role, but in time this became impossible and he ended purely as a child psychiatrist, with an influence world-wide. The training of workers from the UK began at the New York Child Guidance Clinic in 1928 and these pioneers were able to start the movement in the UK on their return. Some clinics were associated with local education authorities and some with hospitals.

An element of chance determines the most appropriate place of referral. Tolerance of deviant behaviour varies among parents and teachers. The deviant behaviour itself may be obviously emotional, like *depression, withdrawal, or *anxiety. Not eating or sleeping, stomach-ache, bilious attacks, and wetting and soiling are 'medical' and call for a doctor. Midway come fidgeting, nail-biting, thumb-sucking, stuttering. Truanting and stealing may attract the attention of the police. What directs the way in which the child reveals his inner emotional tensions is not fully understood; meanwhile, the need for several approaches seems to be justified.

In practice, child psychiatrists are unlikely ever to be sufficiently numerous to help all the children with emotionally induced disorders of behaviour; nor should they be needed. Some conditions such as *neurosis, *psychosis, antisocial and conduct disorders do need their expertise, but behaviour disorders which are found mainly in families seeking help, should be within the competence of general practitioners and paediatricians, and should be given greater emphasis in medical training.

The emotional disturbances that follow handicaps could be diminished, if not prevented, if the children's needs were fully assessed and the parents better informed about those needs. Schools, too, must improve their recognition of handicaps to learning. The sense of failure that produces low self-esteem in the child has a powerful and sometimes disastrous effect on character and on the development of intelligence, and may seriously distort personality. The misunderstanding of children who have difficulty in learning to read, write, and spell, and who may be labelled 'mentally handicapped', can lead either to withdrawal into hopeless apathy or to aggressive and disruptive behaviour. Such a fate still awaits too many *dyslexic children. That such mishandling plays a part in the incidence of delinquency and deviant behaviour cannot be denied.

Recently, attention has been focused on counselling needs, not only for parents grappling with chronic illness or handicap and with bereavement, including *stillbirth, but also for doctors, nurses, and social workers when they become (as they should) emotionally involved with their work. The movement away from the attitude of 'us' (the professionals) and 'them' (the patients), which characterized practice in the early years of the century, has been one of the most important factors in humanizing paediatrics and striking the balance between the art and the science.

Fresh orientations. The historic medical preoccupation with epidemic and infective disease has left a deep impression on medical thinking about the nature of disease and of the problems which it sets for doctors. This medical model begins with the clinical recognition of a syndrome or a disease. From the latter part of the 19th c. after the work of *Pasteur and *Koch, specific agents, mainly bacterial, were attached to many of these 'diseases' as prime causes; this allowed certainty of diagnosis. Observation of a sufficiently large sample of affected patients forms the basis for predicting the likely outcome, the prognosis. The discovery of the causative agent can lead to specific treatment by the use of a drug which attacks, neutralizes, or destroys the agent. There is now a specific disease, a specific cause, and a specific treatment: what remains is the search for a method of prevention. Public health measures and some form of immunization often provide the answer. One drawback is that concentration on bacteria reduces the importance of the patient.

The results of applying these methods to infective diseases have been outstandingly successful, bringing them virtually under control. Since bacteria themselves are not entirely passive agents and have the ability to develop drug resistance, it is unwise to assume that the chapter on infective disease is closed; the profligate use of antibiotics serves only to hasten the day when that chapter will need to be reopened. Encouraged by success, doctors tend to favour this medical model, even when it is inappropriate.

Non-accidental injury and child neglect. Child abuse and neglect are more common than was once recognized. The authoritative description of the *battered child syndrome by Kempe and his colleagues in Denver in 1962 drew attention to the fact that injuries, including some serious enough to cause death, could be inflicted on babies and children by their own parents or care-givers. Scepticism was the normal reaction both of doctors, other professionals including lawyers, and of the public at large. However, the observations had been carefully made and, slowly, the truth of Kempe's claims has come to be recognized the world over.

The validity of a syndrome depends first on the fact that the evidence is consistent and recognizable; there was no doubt that this was the case. The medical model assumes a causative agent, a natural history to be observed leading to prognosis, a treatment to be devised and, finally, the possibility of prevention. Unfortunately, in the nature of child abuse and neglect such an approach does not and cannot work. Nevertheless, charitable persons with money to spend are saying that child abuse is the major *disease* of childhood and that research must be funded so that a *cure* is found. Meanwhile, much research time and money are consumed in sharpening up the diagnostic criteria, studying the predictive evidence which points to parental vulnerability, attempting to construct a prognostic framework and planning methods of treatment or prevention. All of this needs the skills of other professionals.

The physical battering which brings the family for help and *does* need medical treatment is now recognized as only part of a much larger problem. The emotional stresses associated with the injuries are regarded as due to more than the pain and the fear that they produce. Rejection, lack of love and caring in the relationship, is even more damaging to the child than the trauma, short of death or brain damage. The physical injury reveals to the outside world the tragedy within the family of emotional tensions leading to abuse. The fundamental problem is the failure of the adults to adapt to the responsibility of caring properly for the dependent child. Among the many reasons are a disturbed or distorted personality and unbearable socio-economic stresses. Concentration on the medical model leads to neglect of the wider issues which are involved.

The new paediatrics is thus drawn outside the purely clinical areas of children's diseases. There is a choice: the paediatrician's contribution could be limited to making the diagnosis of child abuse and neglect after finding in the child the results of physical, emotional, or mental stress or damage; the management of the family (for what is needed is management, once the wounds and fractures have been treated) could then be left for other professionals. That there is sometimes a case for individual, family, and group psychotherapy cannot be disputed, although it is available too seldom.

Community paediatrics. Part of the answer lies in the community, in socioeconomic stresses, and in an absence of neighbourliness. One of the directions in which paediatrics could develop would be in studying the needs of families and demonstrating to the authorities the effects of deprivations upon the growth and development of the children, so that some urgency is attached to finding and providing solutions. Housing, income, employment, and schooling may all be implicated.

Specializing in child health, in contrast to diseases of children, requires paediatricians to involve themselves in community affairs. The medical model of disease in its historic form will not serve. Defining the objectives of community child health, devising methods of work, and agreeing areas of responsibility are problems that demand solution in the future. (See also COMMUNITY MEDICINE.)

Much depends on the community's attitude towards children. Despite honeyed words at election times, no government yet has seriously considered child welfare as a priority. The French, and to some extent the Scandinavian countries, have come nearest to it. The children, of course, cannot themselves benefit directly. Their biological dependence on care-givers, whether natural parents or of another kind, ensures that help reaches them indirectly through the family.

The children's progress from the total dependence on the environment within the mother's womb, through nursery, school, and apprenticeship, provides plenty of scope for stresses of all kinds, yet it is becoming more and more clear that what is fundamental to the personality of the child is what happens during the early years, with the perhaps surprising importance of the early days after birth. There is now a whole literature on the bonding of affection between mother and baby and the likely consequence of its failure to become established.

Children in hospital. One area in which improvements have taken place is in the management of children in hospital. The children's needs differ from those of the adults for whom hospitals were originally planned and built. As long ago as 1815 John Bunnell Davis, a London physician particularly interested in the care of sick children, opposed the idea of in-patient beds for children when he was planning his dispensary. He believed that babies and young children in hospital would die of infection or from a 'broken heart' due to separation from mother; the reality of Davis's fears was confirmed later (see MATERNAL DEPRIVATION). Ward infection remains a danger, although the modification of building design and a greater knowledge of how infection spreads have diminished that risk, while antibiotics have minimized the risk to life and health.

The emotional stress, Davis's 'broken heart', took almost a century and a half to become generally recognized. In children's hospitals and wards, parental visiting was originally strictly limited if not prohibited. Only in the early 1950s and 1960s the example set by James *Spence in Newcastle upon Tyne began to be followed and parents in a few forward-looking centres were encouraged to visit and even to move into hospital with their child, at least until he or she had settled down. Schoolteachers for the older and 'play-ladies' for the younger patients were employed. Other centres continued to wave the red flags of danger of introducing infection and of making the child unhappy (he often cried for a while after parents left). It took the National Association for the Welfare of Children in Hospital (NAWCH, founded in 1961) to spread the wisdom country-wide, a difficult task made somewhat easier by the retirement or disappearance of the old opponents both among nursing and medical staff, but one which is still incomplete.

The better understanding of the emotional needs of children and of the importance of strengthening rather than damaging family bonds, lay at the root of these changes. Paediatrics can fairly claim to have been the prime mover in the general humanizing of the hospital scene. The children's ward, used as little as possible, should provide an alternative environment to home life with ploys to make hospital admission a pleasure and an educational experience.

In the future the infants should, as far as possible, be nursed by their parents, leaving the medical treatments for the nurses. The nurses themselves, like the doctors, need training in normal child behaviour and how to handle the behavioural problems which naturally follow the stress of illness and its treatment in a strange environment. Better planning of out-patient services should lessen the need for hospital beds for children.

The need to humanize the management of maternity in obstetric departments illustrates the limitations of the medical model. This, properly, concentrates on complications and their prevention and has lowered morbidity and mortality rates: the limitation has been that the emotional needs of the whole family were dangerously neglected. Mothers have at last realized the value to their health and happiness of making choices and taking responsibility themselves. Their demand to be allowed to make informed choices is bringing about important changes.

The future. Is it possible to predict the future of paediatrics? The application of scientific methods of diagnosis and the high technology available for modern treatments have revolutionzed the subject within the last four decades. The importance of research is taken for granted in this communication. Immunization and the use of antibiotics have removed from the forefront the infective diseases which had engaged medical attention for centuries. The time released has been spent on chronic illness and handicaps. The prevention of infections remains important but the prevention of handicap is an even more important task in relation to human suffering. To discharge this task, attention has been focused on prediction, especially antenatally, which can lead to prevention of the potentially deleterious effect of the defect or to termination of pregnancy. The paediatrician, therefore, faces ethical and moral problems which hitherto he has been left to solve on behalf of the community. This relative independence in decision-making is under threat and this is a conflict yet to be resolved.

The pampered populations of the Western world can still afford to spend time on these arguments which surround the fate of individual children. Meanwhile, hordes of children in the rest of the world are condemned to undernutrition, infectious disease, exploitation in labour under conditions hazardous to health, prostitution, and other forms of abuse and neglect. Improved obstetric and neonatal care removes one check on population growth, and so would the abolition of epidemics, famine, and war; how then can children's food requirements be assured without artificial population control? Here is another problem affecting child health, with a large ethical component.

It can be argued that the effects on the community of the improvements in child health for which sufficient knowledge already exists are not the concern of paediatrics. Sticking to his traditional last, the future paediatrician will be faced with more and more refinements in diagnosis. Developments in tissue typing may show differences in the liability to certain diseases, which in turn could concentrate prediction and prevention on vulnerable children. Organ *transplants including *bone marrow transplants should increase life expectancy for babies with congenital defects of organs, metabolic and hormonal deficiencies, and cancer.

A better understanding of family dynamics could diminish the risks of delinquency and abuse of alcohol, drugs, and sex in adolescence. Education in the way in which the human body develops physically, mentally, and emotionally should play an important part. *Mens sana in corpore sano* remains an ideal. Whatever the temptation, the practising paediatrician must never forget the beautifully designed natural defences of the human body, nor the fact that emotional stress is not the same as emotional damage. Sometimes both physical and emotional stress are necessary for the optimal development of the human being.

A. WHITE FRANKLIN

Further reading

American Academy of Pediatrics (1971). *Lengthening Shadows*. New York.

Ashton, N., Ward, B. and Serpell, G. (1953). Role of oxygen in the genesis of retrolental fibroplasia. *British Journal of Ophthalmology*, **37**, 513–20.

Beveridge, Sir W. (1942). *Social Insurance and Allied Services*, Cmnd. 6404. London.

Cameron, H. C. (1955). *The British Paediatric Association 1928–1952*. London.

Court, S. D. M. (1976). *Fit for the Future*, Cmnd. 6684. London.

Faber, H. K. and McIntosh, R. (1966). *History of the American Pediatric Society 1889–1965*. New York.

Neale, V. (1970). *The British Paediatric Association 1952–1968*. London.

Usher, R. (1961). The respiratory distress syndrome of prematurity. *Pediatric Clinics of North America*, **8**, 525–38.

PAEDOPHILIA is the sexual orientation of adults towards children.

PAGET, SIR JAMES, BT (1814–99). British surgeon, MRCS (1836), FRS (1851). Paget was born in Great Yarmouth, the eighth of 17 children. His father, a prosperous shipowner and brewer, was Mayor of Yarmouth but later fell upon hard times. At the age of 16 James Paget was apprenticed to a local surgeon, Charles Costerton. During his apprenticeship he and his brother Charles, published *The Natural History of Yarmouth* (1834). In 1834 he enrolled at *St Bartholomew's Hospital, London, where Costerton had trained. During his time as a student, he discovered and described *Trichinella spiralis*. He was admitted as a member of the Royal College of Surgeons in 1836, but as he could not afford the fees for a surgical pupillage he was unable to serve as a house surgeon. In his early years he was forced to support himself by teaching, editing, and writing. He was appointed curator of the pathological museum at St Bartholomew's Hospital in 1837, and lecturer in anatomy and physiology in 1843. He was elected surgeon to the Finsbury dispensary in 1841 and in 1843 he became one of the original fellows of the Royal College of Surgeons and accepted the post of warden of the residential college for students at St Bartholomew's. Three years later he was elected assistant surgeon in spite of objections that he had neither been a surgical pupil nor a house surgeon. In 1861 he was advanced to full surgeon. He was elected president of the Royal College of Surgeons in 1875 and vice-chancellor of the University of London in 1883. His service to the royal family began as early as 1858 as surgeon-extraordinary to the Queen and the Prince of Wales. In 1867 he became sergeant-surgeon-extraordinary, and in 1877 sergeant-surgeon. He received a baronetcy in 1871 when he retired from St Bartholomew's, after a serious illness.

Paget catalogued the pathological museums at St Bartholomew's Hospital and at the Royal College of Surgeons and in doing so acquired a knowledge of *pathology unrivalled by any other surgeon. For many years he was the leader in his branch of the profession in London, although renowned for his teaching and his diagnostic ability rather than his operative expertise. His name is still attached to a number of disorders. He was the first to describe *fibrosarcoma of the abdominal wall (*Paget's recurrent fibroid, 1851); a superficial *necrosis of bone (Paget's quiet necrosis, 1870); an eczematoid cancerous lesion of the nipple (*Paget's disease of the nipple, 1874): and osteitis deformans (*Paget's disease of bone, 1876).

PAGET'S DISEASE OF BONE is a not uncommon skeletal disorder, particularly in later life, of unknown aetiology. There is patchy increase in bone vascularity accompanied by uncoordinated bone resorption (osteolysis) and new bone formation (osteosclerosis). Bone pain, weakness, deformity, and pathological fractures may result; there are characteristic X-ray changes and elevation of the serum *alkaline phosphatase level is usual. The condition, also known as osteitis deformans, has in recent years been shown to respond to treatment with *calcitonin.

PAGET'S DISEASE OF THE NIPPLE is a condition presenting as an apparent superficial inflam-

mation of the nipple region in middle-aged women but due to underlying cancer of the breast, usually an *adenocarcinoma of the ducts.

PAGET'S RECURRENT FIBROID is a *fibrosarcoma recurring in scar tissue following earlier removal.

PAIN has been a major concern of mankind since its origins and the subject of ubiquitous efforts to understand and control it. This article is devoted to a brief overview of the concepts and treatment of pain throughout the ages. The material will be presented in four parts: (i) a historical review from primitive times to the 19th c.; (ii) the theories evolved in the latter half of the 19th and the 20th c.; (iii) advances in pain research made during recent decades; and (iv) current modalities available for the effective treatment of acute and chronic pain. Detailed accounts can be found in the references.

Historical perspectives. Pain is as old as mankind and perhaps even older; there is reason to believe that it is inherent in any life linked with consciousness (Fülop-Miller, 1938; Bonica, 1953). Certainly there is evidence that man has always been afflicted with this evil, for as the records of every race are examined, one finds testimonials to the omnipresence of pain. On Babylonian clay tablets, in papyri written in the days of the pyramid builders, in Persian leathern documents, in inscriptions from Mycenae, on parchment rolls from Troy, down through the ages in every civilization, in every culture, are found prayers, exorcisms, and incantations bearing testimony to the prevalence of pain. The unearthing of prehistoric human skeletons added millions of years to man's recorded history of several millennia, and with it our knowledge of pain has been thrust back into the dark chasm of time, back into the aeons; for many of these bones were indelibly stamped with signs of painful diseases, giving us evidence of how early were the beginnings of man's *via dolorosa*. Thus wrote the French surgeon Daetigus: 'Were we to imagine ourselves suspended in timeless space over an abyss out of which the sounds of revolving earth rose to our ears, we would hear naught but an elemental roar of pain uttered as with one voice by suffering mankind' (Fülop-Miller, 1938).

Pain has been one of the greatest factors to affect the course of human events, for scarcely any man has escaped its throes. As classical authors relate the lives of heroes, as mediaeval chroniclers tell the legends of saints, and as biographers write of philosophers, artists, soldiers, inventors, scientists, and reformers, invariably one chapter of these biographies is entitled 'Pain'. The emotional and physical consequences of chronic pain have been emphasized repeatedly by scientists, writers, and poets. Milton wrote (in *Paradise Lost*, Book VI):

. . . pain is perfect misery, the worst
Of evils, and excessive, overturns
All patience.

It is natural that from its beginning mankind should have attempted to understand the nature of pain and to make attempts to control it.

Prehistoric times. Primitive humans had no difficulty in understanding pain associated with injury but they were mystified by pain caused by disease (Keele, 1957). They treated pain from injury by rubbing (massaging) the part or exposing it to the cold water of streams or lakes, the heat of the sun, and later that of fire. Pressure, too was used to benumb the part and thus lessen the pain, and probably in time primitive men learned that pressure over certain regions (nerves) had a more pronounced effect, though they did not know why (Bonica, 1953).

The cause of painful disease was linked with intrusion of certain objects or evil spirits into the body, and treatment consisted of extracting the intruding objects or making efforts to ward off, appease, or frighten away the pain demons with pain ornaments—rings worn in the ears and nose, talismans, amulets, and similar charms. Above all, conjurations, spells, and words of might (magic) were used by the injured man, enabling him to put the pain demons to flight.

When primitive people could not relieve their own suffering they called on the head of the family who, according to *anthropologists, in prehistoric times was the woman—the Great Mother—who acted as priestess and sorceress in one. Even in the subsequent patriarchal state, woman remained pre-eminent as healer, as evidenced by the sibyls and pythonesses of the ancients and the blonde Agamede of the Greeks, which are classical examples of women who wielded exclusive power of exorcizing the demons of illness and pain. Gradually, however, her duties of banishing pain were taken over by the *medicine man, conjuror, or shaman of the tribe who, having no maternal instinct and having the same shape as other men of the village, had to rely on the art of conjuring. It was therefore necessary for him to change his shape by dressing as an antidemon and to make his house a special 'medicine hut' where he muttered incantations and fought and wrestled with the invisible pain demons. Later he also administered pain-relieving *herbs.

Ancient concepts. The ancient Egyptians and Babylonians believed that painful afflictions other than wounds were caused by religious influences of their gods, or spirits of the dead, which usually arrived in darkness and entered the body through the nostril or the ear. Several papyri contain descriptions of headaches, toothaches, and other face and head pains (Macht, 1915; Tainter, 1948; Sigerist, 1951). The Egyptians considered the *heart and the blood vessels, not the *brain, to be the organs responsible for pain.

In ancient India, the earliest concepts of pain and other medical knowledge were attributed to the god Indra. Buddha, about 500 BC, attributed the universality of pain in life to the frustration of desires: 'Birth is attended with pain, decay is painful, disease is painful, death is painful. Union with the unpleasant is painful; painful is separation from the pleasant and any craving that is unsatisfied, that, too, is painful' (Keele, 1957). Although recognizing pain as a sensation, Buddhist and Hindu thought in general attached far more significance to the emotional level of the experience. Like the Egyptians, the Hindus believed that pain was experienced in the heart.

In ancient China, medical practice was codified in the *Nei Ching,* the Chinese canon of medicine, traced back to the time of Huang Ti, who lived about 2600 BC (Bonica, 1979). The ancient Chinese believed that heat produced pain by injuring the spirit, whereas cold injured the body and caused swellings. Pain was thought to appear when the vessels containing blood and air were obstructed. The rationale for the relief of pain by the Chinese treatment of *acupuncture of one of the 365 suitable points of the body may be explained by their belief that: 'when the evil is a recent guest in the body, it does not yet have a fixed abode and can be expelled. In order to do so, it is brought forward where it can be met and detained, and then, by means of draining (by acupuncture) disease is brought to an immediate end' (Bonica, 1979).

The ancient Greeks were intensely interested in the nature of sensory data and the sense organs of the body found a prominent place in their physiological speculations. Pythagoras (566–497 BC), the first great Greek thinker, who travelled widely to Egypt, Babylon, and India, apparently stimulated his disciple *Alcmaeon to carry out intensive study of the senses (Keele, 1957). Alcmaeon, without apparent precedent, produced the idea that the brain, not the heart, was the centre for sensation and reason. Despite the support of Democritus, Anaxagoras, and Plato, this view did not gain widespread acceptance, due in part to the opposition of *Empedocles and above all *Aristotle, for whom the heart constituted the *sensorium commune.* Plato (427–347 BC) believed that sensation in man resulted from the movement of atoms communicating through the brain to the soul. He believed that pain may arise not only from peripheral stimulations but as an emotional experience in the soul. Aristotle believed that pain was an increased sensitivity of the sense of touch caused by excess of vital heat. Like touch, pain arose in end-organs of the flesh and was conveyed by blood to the heart. He denied that the brain played any part in sensation, emotion, and intellect, but, like the others, he believed that pain was felt in the heart as a 'quale'—a quality of the soul, a state of feeling, the experience opposite to pleasure, and the epitome of unpleasantness.

Soon after Aristotle's death, his successor Theophrastus (372–287 BC) cast doubt on Aristotelian physiology and Straton (340–260 BC), who succeeded Theophrastus reintroduced the concept that the sensation of pain is perceived in the brain. Moreover, *Herophilus and

*Erasistratus of Alexandria provided anatomical evidence that the brain is part of the *central nervous system and the nerves attached to the neuraxis (brain and *spinal cord) are of two kinds: those for movement and those for feeling (Keele, 1957). Despite this, and much subsequent evidence which emerged, the teachings of Aristotle and other Greek philosophers on pain were accepted by the ancient Romans and remained 'truth' for the ensuing 2000 years.

Ancient remedies. With the transition of man's idea of the cause of pain from evil spirits to punishment inflicted by an offended deity, the method of relieving pain changed also, and the medicine man was replaced by the priest, servant of the gods (Bonica, 1953). Together with the natural remedies, the priest relied on prayers, usually made at the shrines of the deities—whether these shrines were the ziggurats of the Babylonians and Assyrians, the pyramids of the Pharaohs, the pillared temples of the Greeks, or the teocallis of the Aztecs. In holy ecstasy, the priests besought deities to enlighten them of the offence committed by the sufferer smitten with a painful illness, using charms and sacrifices to propitiate the immortals. With sacrifices duly made, the gods were ready at times to listen to the supplications of the priests and perhaps to grant relief. Classical medicine was based on such belief and even Hippocrates believed that 'Divinum est opus sedare dolorum' (divine is the work to subdue pain).

In addition to prayer, priests used natural remedies consisting mostly of herbs. The origin of the medicinal use of herbs is lost in the mists of antiquity (Macht, 1915). We are told in the *Rig-Veda* of the ancient Hindus that 'such herbs come to us from the most ancient times, three eras before the gods were born'. It is most probable that before they were used by priests as adjuvants to prayers, herbs were used by primitive man who, experimenting with various plants as foods, discovered that some of them were efficacious in assuaging pain. Their use was gradually taken over by the medicine man, who surrounded his knowledge of the mystic herbal concoctions handed down to him by sorcerers and magicians with mystery, incantations, and rituals. The latter were, and continued to be, indispensable psychotherapeutic adjuvants to the *prescriptions concocted by early physicians.

The use of *analgesic drugs derived from plant life was prominent in all ancient cultures. The earliest records relate legends of pain-relieving effects of such plants as the *poppy, *mandragora, hemp (*cannabis), and *henbane. The Babylonian clay tablets from Nippur (2250 BC) contain the first written record of the use of analgesics (Macht, 1915). The *Ebers papyrus of the 16th c. BC describes the use of *opium, prescribed for Ra's headaches (Tainter, 1948). The ancient Egyptians were also highly skilled in *trephining of the skull for treatment of headache and facial pain and they, as

well as the Babylonians and Assyrians, used exercise, heat, cold, and massage extensively.

*Aesculapius, the Greek god of medicine, was said to have used a potion made from herbs called *nepenthe* to produce relief of pain. Theophrastus wrote a detailed report of the use of opium for pain relief. The works of such famous physicians as *Hippocrates, *Dioscorides, *Pliny, Pien Ch'iao, and *Hua T'o contain many references on the use of drugs for the relief of pain (Bonica, 1953). Among the earlier references on the use of pain-relieving drugs are those found in the writings of Homer, the Greek poet, who described in his *Odyssey* that Ulysses and his comrades were treated by Helen of Troy, daughter of Zeus, who 'cast into the wine whereof they drank, a drug to lull pain and anger and bring forgetfulness to every sorrow'. In Homer's *Iliad* (Book XI, lines 963–7), Eurypylus, wounded in battle, makes the following requests of Patroclus, the physician (Bonica, 1953):

With lukewarm water wash the gore away
With healing balms the raging smart allay
Such as sage Chiron, sire of pharmacy
Once taught Achilles, and Achilles thee.

Patroclus complied with his request and:

Cut out the biting shaft and from the wound
With tepid water cleansed the clotted blood;
Then pounded in his hands, the root applied
Astringent, anodyne, which all his pain allayed;
The wound was dried and stanched the blood.

*Celsus, in his *De medicina,* written during the 1st c. AD, mentions one of the first references to analgesic pills (Bonica, 1953). At about the same time lived Pliny the Elder, Scribonius Largus, and Dioscorides, a Greek army surgeon in the services of Nero, all of whom wrote extensively on the preparation and use of mandragora, opium, henbane, hemp, and other drugs for the relief of pain. Largus and Dioscorides also advocated *electrotherapy, in the form of shocks from torpedo fish, for *neuralgia and headache and probably also practised surgical methods for the relief of pain. *Galen in the 2nd c. AD rescued the work of Herophilus and Erasistratus which had been ignored by the Romans and carried out extensive studies of his own that re-established the physiological importance of the peripheral and central nervous system in pain. He also wrote a book on pain as a diagnostic symptom and spoke enthusiastically of the analgesic effects of opium and mandragora.

The Middle Ages and the Renaissance. As the ignorance and superstition of the Dark Ages settled over Europe after the fall of Rome, the works of Galen, Herophilus, and Erasistratus and other ancient Greeks and Romans virtually disappeared, but the Aristotelian concept survived. During this period, the centre of medicine shifted to Arabia, where *Avicenna in the 11th c. codified all available medical knowledge including the cause and mechanisms of 15 different varieties of pain (Bonica, 1979). Avicenna appears to have been the first to suggest that pain was a separate and distinct sense and suggested exercise, heat, and massage in addition to the use of opium and other drugs for the relief of pain.

The Renaissance fostered a great scientific spirit to encourage many remarkable advances in chemistry, physics, physiology, and anatomy, but especially understanding of the nervous system by such outstanding men as *Mondini, *Eustachios, da *Vinci, *Vesalius, *Varolio, and others, all of whom considered pain as a sensory event carried by the nerves of touch and experienced in the brain. Despite evidence to the contrary, the Aristotelian concept of pain as a passion of the soul felt in the heart and a doctrine of the five senses still prevailed. Thus, William *Harvey, who in 1628 discovered the circulation, still believed that the heart was the site where pain was felt.

In contrast, *Descartes, Harvey's contemporary, adhered to Galenic physiology and considered the brain to be the seat of sensation and motor function. In his book, *L'homme* (*Man*) published in 1664 (14 years after his death), Descartes described the conduction of sensation including pain

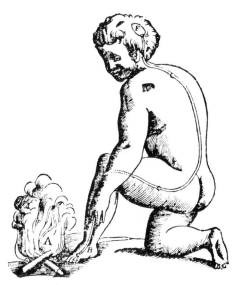

Fig. 1. Descartes' (1664) concept of the pain pathway. He writes: 'If for example fire (*A*) comes near the foot (*B*), the minute particles of this fire, which as you know move with great velocity, have the power to set in motion the spot of the skin of the foot which they touch, and by this means pulling upon the delicate thread (*cc*) which is attached to the spot of the skin, they open up at the same instant the pore (*d. e.*) against which the delicate thread ends, just as by pulling at one end of a rope makes to strike at the same instant a bell which hangs at the other end.' (Reproduced by permission from Melzack, R. and Wall, P. D. (1965). Pain mechanisms: a new theory. *Science*, **150**, 971–9. Copyright 1965 by the American Association for the Advancement of Science.)

via 'delicate threads' contained in nerves which connected the tissues to the brain (Melzack and Wall, 1983). Peripheral stimulation by burning, for example, caused minute particles of fire to pull on the delicate cord just like pulling at the end of a rope to strike a bell (Fig. 1). This was the precursor of the specificity theory that was introduced two centuries later.

During the Middle Ages and Renaissance, there were virtually no advances in pain therapy. Thus we find that *Paracelsus in the 16th c. still advocated the use of opium and other natural herbs and such physical therapeutic methods as electrotherapy, massage, and exercise. During the latter part of the Middle Ages, the somniferant sponge, which was a sea sponge saturated with a concoction of opium, hyoscine (scopolamine), mandragora, and juices of other plants, became quite popular in Europe. Unfortunately, the effects of the sponge were unpredictable and occasionally sleep progressed to death.

The 18th and 19th centuries. The 18th c. was ushered in with the same concepts on the nature of pain and the same methods for its control as had been advocated for the previous two millennia. Fortunately, however, during the 18th c. several developments took place pertaining to pain and its control. For one thing, great progress was made in the knowledge of the anatomy and physiology of various parts of the *sympathetic and central nervous system by *Willis, *Borelli, Winslow, *Malpighi, von *Haller, and others (Keele, 1957). During the last part of this period (1794), Erasmus *Darwin, grandfather of Charles *Darwin, wrote that pain was a phase of unpleasantness and said that pain resulted 'whenever the sensorial motions are stronger than usual. . . . A great excess of light . . . of pressure or distention . . . of heat . . . of cold produces pain.' He thus anticipated the intensive theory of pain that was introduced several decades later. During the latter part of the 18th c., the new era of *analgesia was initiated with Joseph *Priestley's discovery of *nitrous oxide and the subsequent observation made by Sir Humphry *Davy of the analgesic properties of this gas.

The scientific study of sensation in general and pain in particular in the modern sense really began in the first half of the 19th c. when physiology emerged as an experimental science. This era was initiated in part by the publications of *Bell and *Magendie who demonstrated with animal experiments that the function of the dorsal roots of spinal nerves is sensory and that of the ventral roots is motor. The impetus to the scientific study of pain was further enhanced by the writings of Johannes *Müller who presented *The Doctrine of Specific Nerve Energies,* which stated that the brain received information about external objects and body structures only by way of the sensory nerves, and the sensory nerves for each of the five senses carried a particular form of energy specific for each sensation. Müller recognized only the five classical senses, with the sense of touch incorporating for him all of the qualities of experience that we derive from stimulation of the body. Müller's concept, then, was that of a straight-through system from the sensory organ to the brain centre responsible for the sensation.

Pain theories. During the ensuing century anatomical, physiological, and histological studies were done that prompted the formulation of two physiological theories of pain—the specificity theory and the intensive theory. These theories were formulated statements or hypotheses, based on observations and reasoning, presenting the principles which underlie the phenomenon or experience we call pain.

The specificity (or sensory) theory stated that pain was a specific sensation with its own sensory apparatus independent of touch and other senses. This theory, which, as previously mentioned, had been first suggested by Avicenna and later by Descartes, was definitely formulated by *Schiff in 1858 after his analgesic experiments in animals (Dallenbach, 1939; Bonica, 1979). Noting the effects of various incisions in the spinal cord, he found that pain and touch were independent: section of the grey matter of the spinal cord eliminated pain but not touch, and a cut through the posterior white matter caused touch to be lost, but pain was unaffected. The theory was supported by later experiments of Blix in 1882 and Goldscheider in 1884 who discovered separate spots for warmth, cold, and touch in the skin. A decade later, von Frey extended these studies to map out pain and touch spots, but he also did histological examination of skin intended to identify specific end-organs responsible for each sensation. On the basis of his findings and some imaginative deductions, von Frey expanded Müller's concept of the sense of touch to four major cutaneous modalities: touch, warmth, cold, and pain. Von Frey's theory, which dealt with receptors only, prompted others to believe that pain is subserved by specific fibres from the receptors to spinal cord and by specific pain pathways in the neuraxis. Experiments were carried out in peripheral nerves to show that there is a one-to-one relationship between receptor type, fibre size, and quality of experience. Other animal experiments suggested that the anterolateral quadrant of the spinal cord was critically important for pain sensation, a concept that was reinforced by Spiller's observation of analgesia with pathological lesions of this part of the cord and the early results with section of the spinothalamic tract by Spiller and Martin to produce analgesia in the contralateral lower half of the body.

The intensive theory, which was first anticipated by Darwin and subsequently suggested by *Henle and others in the 1880s, was explicitly formulated by *Erb in 1874, who maintained that every sensory stimulus was capable of producing pain if it reached sufficient intensity (Bonica, 1953; Melzack and Wall, 1983). This theory received subsequent support from Blix and Goldscheider, both of whom had abandoned the specificity theory. In 1894 Goldscheider fully developed the theory that stimulus intensity and central summation were the critical determinants of pain. This was the first variant of the intensive theory which was to be followed by other theories called 'patterned' and 'summation' theories, all of which proposed that the particular pattern of nerve impulses that evoked pain were produced by the summation of the sensory input from skin into the neuraxis (spinal cord and brain).

Thus, by the end of the 19th c., there existed three conflicting concepts on the nature of pain. The specificity theory and the intensive theory, which were in opposition to each other, were embraced by physiologists and a few psychologists. These two theories opposed the traditional Aristotelian concept that pain was an affective quality, which at this time was being supported by most philosophers and psychologists, especially H. R. Marshall in America. During the decade between 1886 and 1895, there were proponents of each of these three theories who became involved in unprecedented and intensely fierce controversies. In an attempt to reconcile the views of physiologists with those of philosophers and psychologists, Strong in 1895 suggested that pain consisted of the original sensation and the psychic reaction or displeasure provoked by the sensation. This concept was later embraced by others, including *Sherrington, who believed that pain was composed of both sensory and affective (feeling) dimensions.

During the first five decades of the 20th c., research on pain continued and the published data acquired were used to support either the specificity theory or the intensive theory, or a modification of these. The intense controversy between von Frey and Goldscheider continued until the late 1920s and each rallied supporters. Livingston in 1943 proposed his own theory of central summation in support of the intensive theory. He suggested that the intensive stimulation resulting from nerve and tissue damage activates fibres that project to internuncial (connecting) *neurone pools in the spinal cord, creating abnormal reverberatory activity in closed self-exciting neurone loops. This prolonged abnormal activity bombards the spinal cord transmission (T) cells which project to brain mechanisms that underlie pain perception. The abnormal internuncial activity also spreads to lateral and ventral horn cells in the spinal cord, activating the *autonomic nervous system and motor system, respectively, producing vasoconstriction, increased work of the heart, and skeletal muscle spasm. These, in turn, produce further abnormal input, thereby creating a 'vicious circle'. Brain activities such as fear and anxiety evoked by pain also feed into and maintain the abnormal internuncial pool activity (Fig 2). Other workers, including Ranson, Bishop, and Wolff and their co-workers, supported the specificity theory. Thus, the controversy con-

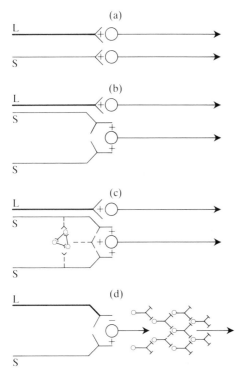

Fig. 2. Schematic representation of conceptual models of pain mechanisms. (a) The *specificity theory* espoused by von Frey, who believed that large fibres (L) transmitted touch and small fibres (S) mediated pain impulses in separate, specific, straight-through pathways to touch and pain centres in the brain. (b) The *summation theory* first espoused by Goldscheider, who believed that convergence of small fibres on to a dorsal horn produced pain and that touch was transmitted by large fibres. (c) Livingston's *conceptual model of reverberatory circuits* involved in chronic pathological pain states in which nociceptive impulses initiate prolonged activity in the self-exciting chain of neurones and bombard dorsal horn cells, which then transmit abnormally patterned volleys of nerve impulses to the brain and also to anterior and anterolateral horn cells that become involved in abnormal reflexes leading to skeletal muscle spasm and sympathetic hyperactivity. (d) The *interaction theory* proposed by Noordenbos, who believes that large fibres inhibit (−) and small fibres excite (+) central transmission neurones, which project to a multi-synaptic system that leads to the brain. Part of this theory was incorporated into the Melzack–Wall theory depicted in Figure 3. (Modified from Melzack, R. and Wall, P. D. (1970), Psycho-physiology of pain. *International Aesthesiology Clinics*, **8**, 3–34.)

tinued, but by mid-century the theory of the philosophers had been wholly discarded and the specificity theory had prevailed and became taught universally.

The duality of pain theory. To take into account the psychological factors that had been shown to influence pain and consolidate these with the specificity theory, Wolff, Hardy, and Goodell in the 1940s reintroduced the concept of the duality of pain that had been proposed by Strong and Sherrington and called it the 'fourth theory of pain'. They believed that pain can be separated into two components: the perception of pain and the reaction to pain. The perception of pain, like the perception of other sensations (such as temperature and touch) is a neurophysiological process, which has special structural, functional, and perceptual properties and is accomplished by means of 'relatively simple and primitive' neural receptive and conductive mechanisms. The reaction to pain, on the other hand, is a complex physiopsychological process involving the cognitive functions of the individual and is influenced by past experience, culture, and various psychological factors that produce great variation in the 'reaction pain threshold'. This concept assumes a one-to-one relationship between the intensity of the stimulus and pain perception and relegates the reaction to pain as a secondary response consequent to the sensation achieved in a straight-through push-button or alarm system fashion.

The sensory interaction theory. In 1959 Noordenbos proposed the sensory intearaction theory which derived from Goldschneider's original concept and also from subsequent proposals by Head, Bishop, and others, suggesting the existence of two systems involving transmission of pain and other sensory information: a slow system which involves the unmyelinated and thinly *myelinated fibres and a fast system which involves the large myelinated fibres. He proposed that the small-diameter slowly conducting somatic afferent fibres and small visceral afferents project into the cells in the dorsal horn of the spinal cord and the summation of inputs from the small fibres produces the neural patterns that are transmitted to the brain to produce pain. The large-diameter fast-acting fibres inhibit transmission of impulses from the small fibres and prevent summation from occurring. Diseases that produce a selective loss of large fibres bring about a loss of inhibition and thereby increase the probability of summation and of normal pain phenomena. He further proposed that one of the ascending systems that transmit pain signals is the short-axon multisynaptic system in the core of the spinal cord. Fig. 2 is a schematic presentation of the conceptual models of pain mechanisms presented until that time.

The Melzack–Wall theory. New data acquired during the preceding decade led Melzack and Wall in the early 1960s to reappraise the specificity and intensive theories. They concluded that the specificity theory is strongly supported by physiological evidence of specialization of the nervous system, but its psychological assumption that sensation is achieved via a fixed direct-line communication from the skin to the brain in a straight-through 'push-button' fashion is its great weakness. The scientific evidence failed to support the assumption of a one-to-one relationship between the intensity of the stimulus and pain perception but instead suggested that the amount and quality of pain perceived is determined by many physiological and psychological variables. Similarly, the intensive theory is strongly supported by the evidence on central summation and input control but is weakened by ignoring peripheral specificity. The scientific evidence suggests that pain is not due to neural activity that resides exclusively in nociceptive pathways which are traditionally considered to be specific for pain, but rather is a result of activity in several interacting neural systems, each with its own specialized function. As a result of these considerations, Melzack and Wall published their own theory in 1965 that took into account the evidence of physiological specialization, central summation, patterning, modulation of input, and the influence of psychological factors.

The original Melzack–Wall theory of pain is illustrated in Fig 3. As noted, impulses evoked by peripheral stimulation are transmitted to three systems: the cells in the substantia gelatinosa (an area of the posterior horn of grey matter in the spinal cord close to the entry of posterior root fibres), the dorsal column fibres that project toward the brain, and the spinal cord transmission (T) cells that mediate information to the brain. The theory is based on the following propositions: (i) the transmission of nerve impulses from afferent fibres to the spinal cord T cells is modulated by a spinal gating mechanism in the dorsal horn; (ii) the spinal gating mechanism is influenced by the relative amount of activity in large-(L) and small-diameter (S) fibres; activity in large fibres tends to inhibit transmission (close the gate) while small

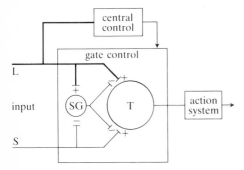

Fig. 3. Schematic diagram of the gate-control theory of pain (Mark I): L, the large-diameter fibres; S, the small-diameter fibres. The fibres project to the substantia gelatinosa (SG) and first central transmission (T) cells. The inhibitory effect exerted by SG on the afferent fibre terminals is increased by activity in L fibres and decreased by activity in S fibres. The central control trigger is represented by a line running from the large-fibre system to the central control mechanisms; these mechanisms, in turn, project back to the gate-control system. The T cells project to the action system. +, excitation, −, inhibition. (Reproduced by permission from Melzack, R. and Wall, P. D. (1965). Pain mechanisms: a new theory. *Science*, **150**, 971–9. Copyright 1965 by the American Association for the Advancement of Science.)

fibre activity tends to facilitate transmission (open the gate); (iii) the spinal gating mechanism is influenced by nerve impulses that descend from the brain; (iv) a specialized system of large-diameter rapidly conducting fibres, labelled the central control 'trigger', activates selective cognitive processes that then influence by way of descending fibres the modulating properties of the spinal gating mechanisms. This system carries precise information about the nature and location of the stimulus and conducts so rapidly that it may not only 'set' the receptivity of cortical neurons for subsequent afferent volleys but may, by way of the descending fibres, influence the sensory input at the gate control system and at various other levels of the neuraxis. This rapid transmission makes it possible for the brain to identify, evaluate, localize, and selectively modulate the sensory input before the action system is activated; (iv) when the output of the spinal cord transmission (T cell) exceeds a critical level, it activates the action system—those neural areas that underline complex sequential patterns of behaviour and experience characteristics of pain.

The Melzack–Casey theory. Three years later Melzack and Casey expanded the theory by taking into account subsequently acquired new knowledge derived from physiological and behavioural studies that further emphasize the motivational, affective, and cognitive aspects of the pain experience. These pertain to neural systems beyond the gate and involve interaction of the neospinothalamic and palaeospinothalamic projecting systems and neocortical processes. They suggested that the neospinothalamic projecting system in the brain serves to process sensory discriminative information about the location, intensity, and duration of the stimulus, while impulses that pass through the palaeospinothalamic tract and paramedial ascending system activate reticular limbic structures that provoke the powerful motivational and aversive drive and unpleasant affect that triggers the organ into action. Neocortical higher central nervous system processes, such as the evaluation of the input in terms of past experience, exert control over both activities in both discriminative and motivational systems. These three categories of neural activity interact with one another to provide perceptual information, the motivational tendency toward escape or attack, and cognitive information based on an analysis of multimodal information, past experience, and probability of outcome of different response strategies. All three forms of activity influence motor mechanisms responsible for the complex pattern of overt responses that characterize pain. In 1982, Melzack and Wall modified their theory to take into account information recently acquired that will be mentioned in the next section.

Despite the deficiencies which the Melzack–Wall and the Melzack–Casey models of pain may have, they have proved to be among the most important developments in this field. In addition to providing the most comprehensive formulation of pain mechanisms, the theories have stimulated much physiological and psychological research and have provoked the development of new approaches to pain therapy based on the prediction that pain may be reduced by electrical stimulation of peripheral nerve fibres (electroanaesthesia). Interest in pain research has also been markedly enhanced by the International Association for the Study of Pain (IASP) and the journal *Pain*. IASP is the first multidisciplinary international organization, the members of which include the foremost pain scientists and pain therapists representing virtually every biomedical science and clinical disciplines from four dozen countries. Through its sponsorship of the journal *Pain*, which publishes original research and reviews of a multidisciplinary nature, and its triennial world congresses on pain, and through the publication of the congress proceedings and its national chapters, IASP has helped the exchange and diffusion of new information and has helped to improve the quality and quantity of research and pain therapy (Bonica *et al.*, 1979, 1983).

Recent advances in pain research. During the past two decades, more new knowledge has been acquired on the anatomical, neurophysiological, biochemical, and psychological substrates of acute and chronic pain than in preceding history. This new information makes it crystal clear that transmission of pain signals produced by tissue damage caused by disease or injury involves a vast array of nerve pathways and biochemical compounds and is modulated by input from the periphery, by activity in the spinal cord, and by powerful descending inhibitory and excitatory systems which bring signals from the brain and brainstem. The anatomical substrates are depicted in Fig. 4, while the physiological, biochemical, and psychological substrates are summarized below.

Tissue-damaging or noxious stimuli caused by injury or disease activate specialized high-threshold receptors called nociceptors which are endings of small myelinated (A delta) and unmyelinated (C) fibres that supply the skin, muscle, viscera, and other 'pain-sensitive' body tissues. Some of these nociceptor-afferent units are activated only by noxious mechanical stimuli, others by noxious heat, and still others respond to all types of noxious stimulation including chemical agents liberated by cells damaged by injury, *inflammation, or *ischaemia (as occurs in heart disease) (Bonica, 1979). These nociceptor-afferent units, acting as transducers, convert the stimuli into nociceptive impulses (pain messages) that are promptly transmitted to the central nervous system. Nociceptive impulses from the entire body below the head are transmitted via fibres which synapse with interneurones or second-order neurones in the dorsal horn of the spinal cord, while impulses from the head are transmitted via fibres in cranial nerves V, VII, IX, and X which synapse with neurones in the trigeminal sensory nucleus caudalis.

On reaching the spinal cord dorsal horn or nucleus caudalis, some primary peripheral nociceptive afferents terminate and make direct or indirect contact with cells in the superficial part of these structures (laminae I and II) and send collaterals that terminate deeper (lamina V) while others terminate more medially (laminae VII and VIII) (Bonica, 1979). Some of these cells in the dorsal horn are known as nociceptive-specific because they receive input exclusively from high-threshold peripheral afferents, while others are known as 'wide-dynamic range' neurones because they receive input from low-threshold fibres concerned with touch sensation and also from nociceptive afferents, so that they are able to respond with increasingly higher frequency of impulse discharge to touch, pressure, and noxious stimuli. The convergence of visceral high-threshold afferents and low-threshold afferents from the skin supplied by the same spinal cord segments on lamina V neurones are said to provide the neural basis for the phenomenon of referred pain associated with visceral and deep somatic disorders.

In addition to making synaptic contact and receiving input from primary nociceptive afferents, these dorsal horn neurones also receive input from the large myelinated peripheral afferents, from the short-axon interneurones of the substantia gelatinosa and also receive synaptic input from the terminals of supraspinal, descending neural control systems. Thus it is obvious that the dorsal horn and nucleus caudalis, which traditionally were considered to be simple relay stations, are very complex structures containing a large number and many varieties of neurones and synaptic (contact) arrangements that permit not only reception and transmission, but a high degree of sensory processing including local abstraction, integration, selection, and appropriate dispersion of sensory impulses. This complex form of local processing is achieved through the phenomena of central convergence, central summation, excitation, and inhibition coming from the periphery, from local and segmental interneurones, and from the brain and brainstem. These processes involve the liberation of putative excitatory *neurotransmitters including substance P and *somatostatin, and through the liberation of the endogenous opioid *peptide called encephalin, and other inhibitory neurotransmitters. These very complex interactions determine the transmission and modulation of nociceptive information.

After being subjected to these modulating influences in the dorsal horn, some of the nociceptive impulses pass through internuncial neurones to the anterior and anterolateral horn cells where they stimulate motor neurones that supply the skeletal muscles and sympathetic neurones that supply blood vessels, viscera, and sweat glands.

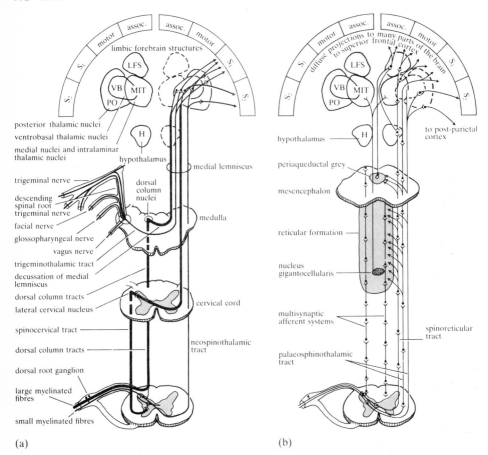

Fig. 4. The conducting somatosensory projection pathways in the neuraxis and brain. (a) *The lateral rapidly conducting pathways* consisting of the neospinothalamic tract, the trigeminothalamic tract, the dorsal column–lemniscal pathway, and the dorsolateral tract (of Morin). Note that the neospinothalamic tract and trigeminospinothalamic tracts receive input from small myelinated peripheral afferents, while the dorsal column–lemniscal system is composed of the central branches of large myelinated primary afferents coming from the periphery. The trigeminothalamic tract receives input from small myelinated primary afferents, which are part of the trigeminal, facial, glossopharyngeal, and vagus nerves. All of these fast conducting fibres project to the ventrobasal and posterior thalamic nuclei without synapse. (b) *The medial slowly conducting pathways* consisting of the palaeospinothalamic and spinoreticular tracts and the multisynaptic afferent systems. All of these pathways are composed of very thin, slowly conducting fibres which project to the reticular formation, the periaqueductal grey, the hypothalamus, and the medial and intralaminar thalamic nuclei where they synapse with neurones that connect with the limbic forebrain structures and with diffuse projections to many other parts of the brain. The nucleus gigantocellularis also sends fibres to these structures while the periaqueductal grey sends input to the limbic forebrain structures and sends descending fibres to the spinal cord which have a modulating (inhibitory) action on transmission of pain messages from the body to the brain. (Modified from Bonica, J. J. (1977). Acute and chronic pain. *Archives of Surgery*, **112**, 750.)

These are involved in segmental reflex (automatic) responses consisting of skeletal muscle spasm, and often increase cardiac output and blood pressure. Other nociceptive impulses are transmitted to neurones, the axons of which make up the spinothalamic tract and other ascending systems; the impulses are thus conveyed to the brainstem and the brain to provoke suprasegmental reflex and cortical responses. Suprasegmental reflex (autonomic) responses consist of stimulation of respiration, of circulation, and of release of

*adrenaline and other endocrine substances involved in the stress response.

It has long been known that the spinothalamic tract transmits pain messages from below the head, and that the trigeminothalamic tract transmits those from the head. However, evidence acquired during the past two decades indicates that the latter system also transmits other sensory information and is composed of two parts that have different anatomical, physiological, and functional characteristics: the neospinotrigeminothalamic tract and the palaeospinotrigeminothalamic tracts. Recent evidence also suggests that several other ascending systems participate in transmission of pain signals: on the basis of their anatomical and functional characteristics, these and the spinothalamic tracts have been grouped into two major systems—the medial system and the lateral system (Fig. 4).

The lateral system includes the neo-spinothalamic and trigeminothalamic tracts, the spinocervical tract, and the dorsal column post-synaptic system. This group is composed of long thick fibres that conduct rapidly, have a discrete somatotopic organization, and make connection with the ventrobasal thalamus and posterior thalamic nuclei where they synapse with another relay of fibres that project to the somatosensory cortex. The evidence suggests that the lateral system is concerned with rapid transmission of phasic discriminative information about the onset of injury, its precise location, its intensity, and its duration, and can quickly bring about responses that prevent further damage.

The *medial system* is composed of the palaeospinothalamic, palaeotrigeminothalamic, spinoreticular, and propriospinal systems. The palaeospinothalamic, palaeotrigeminothalamic, and spinoreticular fibres consist of a few long, and many short, thin fibres that are not somatically organized and which pass medially to project to the reticular formation, the periaqueductal grey matter, the hypothalamus, and the medial and intrathalamic nuclei where they synapse with neurones that connect with the limbic forebrain structures and with diffuse projections to many other parts of the brain. The multisynaptic proprio-spinal system also consists of very short thin fibres that ascend throughout the cord in the grey matter (in contrast to the ventrolateral tracts which lie in the white matter) and project to unknown desti-nations in the brain. Because of the thinness of the fibres, their multisynaptic nature, and the lack of somatotopic organization, impulses passing through this system are much slower in reaching the brain than are those said to transmit tonic information about the state of the organism. These impulses signal the actual presence of peripheral damage and continue to send messages as long as the wound is susceptible to re-injury.

Modulation of nociception and pain. One of the most exciting areas of recent research concerns the various neural, biochemical, and psychophysiolo-gical mechanisms that participate in the modula-tion of nociceptive information from tissues to the brain (Bonica et al., 1979, 1983). In the peripheral system, injury or inflammation causes the libera-tion of pain-producing substances and/or damages nerves and thus lowers the threshold of the noci-ceptive afferent units so that innocuous stimulation (light touch) produces pain. On the other hand, innocuous stimulation of the skin by rubbing, by application of cold, and by transcutaneous electri-cal stimulation, in some way impairs the trans-mission of nociceptive impulses from the periphery to the central nervous system. Nociceptive trans-mission in the dorsal horn is also affected by the activity and interactions of local interneurones in supraspinal and descending systems.

In 1968, it was noted that electrical stimulation of the lateral periaqueductal grey (PAG) and periventricular grey (PVG) matter of the midbrain produced a profound analgesia (loss of pain perception) without apparently interfering with motor function or with the animal's response to other sensory stimuli. A series of brilliant experi-ments by many workers during the ensuing decade have shown: (i) that this phenomenon, known as stimulation-produced analgesia or SPA, often outlasts stimulation by many seconds or minutes; (ii) that SPA inhibits the activity of dorsal horn neurones involved in nociception but not those concerned with other sensations; (iii) that the effects of SPA are partly or wholly diminished by administration of naloxone, a morphine antagon-ist; and (iv) that injection of very small amounts of *morphine directly into PAG produced analgesia, indicating that a major action of morphine is to activate descending inhibitory neurones in the brainstem.

These studies were paralleled by the discovery of opiate receptors on nerve cells, whose structure was such that a morphine molecule fitted into them like a key into a lock. This led to the quest for, and identification of, endogenously produced sub-stances which were called *endorphins (endo-genous morphine-like substances) and encephalins (opioid substances in the brain). As a result of these and other studies, it was found that SPA produced impulses that descend in the dorsolateral funiculus and make contact with and stimulate a variety of short-axon interneurones in the substan-tia gelatinosa at every level of the spinal cord. Some of these interneurones contain encephalin which inhibits transmission of nociceptive informa-tion by preventing the release of substance P, the neurotransmitter that permits the transfer of noci-ceptive impulses from one nerve to another. This descending modulating system has input from the cerebral, limbic system, and other structures which are known to be involved in the psychological dimension of pain. More recent studies have sug-gested that there are other descending inhibitory systems that do not involve opioids. The data acquired to date make it perfectly clear that there are a number of mechanisms of pain inhibition, some involving spinal mechanisms; others involv-ing supraspinal mechanisms; some involving opi-oids and some not; and some involving centrifugal control on spinal nociceptive systems and some not. In addition to changing drastically our con-ceptualization of pain mechanisms, the new data have had a major impact on the development of new modalities for relief of pain. Figure 5 depicts the latest schema of the Melzack–Wall theory of pain, with inclusion of the pain-inhibitory systems and other recent facts.

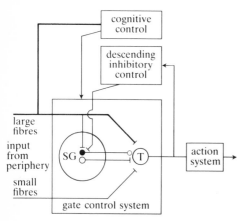

Fig. 5. The gate-control theory: Mark II. The new model includes excitatory (white circle) and inhibitory (black circle) links from the substantia gelatinosa (SG) to the transmission (T) cells as well as descending inhibitory control from brainstem systems. The round knob at the end of the inhibitory link implies that its actions may be presynaptic, postsynaptic, or both. All connections are excitatory, except the inhibitory link from SG to T cell. (Modified from Melzack, R. and Wall, P. D. (1983). *The Mechanism of Pain.* New York.)

Psychological factors. Another very productive series of recent studies, carried out by psychologists, psychiatrists, and behavioural scientists, has helped to emphasize the importance of learning, personality, culture, and the environment in influencing the patient's pain behaviour, and to clarify the psychodynamics of *anxiety, *depression, *hypochondriasis, and other emotional and affective consequences of acute and chronic pain. These studies also have provided impressive evidence that the medical model is not sufficient to explain the abnormal illness behaviour manifested by some patients with chronic pain and requires the inclusion of a behavioural model. This emphasis on chronic pain behaviour resulting primarily from reinforcing environmental influences or so-called operant pain mechanisms has had a favourable impact on the management of some patients with chronic pain. Moreover, these studies have demonstrated clearly that patients with pain which is attributable primarily to emotional problems describe pain in the same way as those in whom the pain results from nociceptive input from pathological processes.

Brain mechanisms. Nociceptive impulses that reach the highest parts of the brain activate very complex systems concerned with integration and perception, or recognition of the sensation of pain. Simultaneously cognitive, analytical, judgemental, and memory processes interpret the type, quality, and meaning of the pain within the framework of the individual's learning, personality, culture, ethnic background, past experience, motivation in their personal influences, and the psychological condition of the individual at the time that the pain

is perceived. These highly complex interactions of sensory motivational and cognitive processes that produce pain sensation act on the autonomic and somatic motor systems and initiate psychodynamic mechanisms of anxiety, apprehension, and fear, and collectively produce the complex physiological, psychological, and behavioural responses that characterize the multidimensional pain experience.

Current therapies for pain. The best therapy for pain is to remove the cause by medical, surgical, or physical means but, unfortunately, in many instances the cause cannot be eliminated and the pain itself must be treated. For effective therapy, it is necessary to differentiate acute pain from chronic non-malignant pain, and these should be considered as different from cancer pain. Acute pain is usually associated with acute disease or injury and usually lasts from several hours to a number of days, depending on the course of the disorder. Chronic pain is defined as pain that persists beyond the usual course of an acute disease, or beyond a reasonable time for an injury to heal, or is caused by a chronic disease and/or psychopathology. Cancer-related pain is usually chronic but it may be acute, such as that associated with fracture of a long bone due to a secondary deposit of cancer in the bone.

Analysis of past results reveals that some patients with acute pain and many with chronic pain were not relieved effectively. This has happened for two important reasons: (i) gaps in knowledge of basic mechanisms resulted in the use of the wrong therapy; and/or (ii) that the available knowledge and therapies were not properly applied because physicians were not taught the basic principles of pain management. Moreover, some chronic pain syndromes involve such a complex array of physical, psychological, emotional, and social factors that it is difficult (if not impossible) for a single physician to treat them effectively. The usual consultation carried out in the isolation of each specialist's office and the consequent fragmented reports by each consultant so commonly seen in traditional medicine have been found to be inefficient, often leading to wrong diagnosis and/or therapy.

The acquisition of much new knowledge and recent clinical experience have changed our concepts and approaches to the diagnosis and therapy of chronic pain. Some of these have been mentioned and will be elaborated in the discussion of specific therapies. Two important advances in chronic pain therapy have been the activation of many multidisciplinary pain clinics/centres and an increasing number of hospices for the treatment of terminally ill patients. The multidisciplinary approach is based on the concept developed by Bonica in the 1940s that complex pain problems could be managed most effectively by a team of specialists from different disciplines, each member contributing his/her individualized knowledge and skills to the common goal of making a correct diagnosis and devising and applying the most effective therapeutic strategies which often involve more than one modality. The members of these teams interact closely, work together, and discuss each pain problem face to face at the daily conferences. The hospice concept, first put into practice by Cicely Saunders in the 1960s, includes effective relief of pain and other symptoms, emotional support to the patient and family, and other strategies to allow the patient to live the last few weeks or months of life fully and to die with the greatest possible dignity, whether in the hospital or in the home (see DEATH, DYING, AND THE HOSPICE MOVEMENT).

Currently, the various therapies that are available to use for acute and chronic pain can be grouped into six categories (listed in the order of frequency of use and efficacy): (i) drugs to produce systemic analgesia and other effects; (ii) neurostimulation techniques; (iii) physical therapies; (iv) regional analgesia; (v) psychological analgesia; and (vi) destructive neurosurgical procedures. Each of these will be considered briefly. For more comprehensive discussion the reader is referred to other sources (Bonica, 1953; Keele, 1957).

Drug therapy. The modern era of the pharmacological pain control began in 1806 when Sertürner reported isolation of morphine from opium (Macht, 1915). Some two decades later, Leroux isolated salicin, and Wohler reported the synthesis of *urea which paved the way for the development of synthetic systemic analgesics by chemical synthesis (Tainter, 1948). These led to the development of derivatives of salicin and other compounds, and finally in 1899 Dreser produced *acetylsalicylic acid which was marketed as aspirin. During the 20th c., even greater progress was made in the development of *narcotic and non-narcotic analgesics. These included semisynthetic derivatives of morphine such as diacetylmorphine (heroin), hydromorphone (Dilaudid®), and oxymorphone (Numorphan®); later, wholly synthetic narcotic analgesics were developed, of which pethidine or meperidine (Methadine®) was the first. Subsequently, methadone (Dolophine®) and morphinan were synthesized and from these a large ber of derivatives that constitute important synthetic opioids were developed. In addition to non-narcotic and narcotic analgesics, another heterogenous group of drugs (usually labelled adjuvants) are used in conjunction with one or both of the other classes. These drugs constitute the most frequently used method for the relief of pain because they are readily available, inexpensive, simple to administer, and if properly used are reasonably effective in relieving various types of pain.

1. *Non-narcotic analgesics.* The efficacy of aspirin and other non-narcotic analgesics in relieving headache, arthritic pain, muscular pain, and mild to moderate pain caused by other conditions has been appreciated for nearly a century. Because in some individuals aspirin and other aspirin-like drugs produce adverse *side-effects such as *dyspepsia, gastrointestinal bleeding, and *allergic reactions, a number of new compounds have been marketed in recent years. Although these produce a lesser incidence of side-effects, they are no more effective in relieving pain and are much more expensive. Therefore, aspirin remains the best all-round non-narcotic analgesic available at present. Most of these agents are now called non-steroidal anti-inflammatory drugs (NSAID) and have the propensity to produce analgesia and reduce *fever and, except for acetaminophen (*paracetamol, Tylenol®), they have an anti-inflammatory action. Recent studies have revealed that most of these drugs produce analgesia by inhibiting the synthesis of *prostaglandins, which are pain-producing substances that are synthesized in injured or inflamed tissues and which sensitize nociceptors. During the past decade, NSAIDs have been found to be especially effective in relieving severe bone pain due to cancer metastases (which produce prostaglandins) and to have some antitumour effects. Moreover, these drugs have been shown to potentiate the analgesic action of narcotics and are often given in combination with *codeine to relieve moderate pain or with morphine or other potent narcotics for the relief of severe pain. For acute pain NSAIDs are given as needed, but for chronic pain they should be given at fixed intervals to achieve and sustain effective analgesia for prolonged periods.

2. *Narcotics.* Morphine is the best potent narcotic to treat severe pain and has long been considered to be the standard of reference against which all other narcotics are compared. Given by mouth or by injection it produces pain relief for 3–5 hours. There are currently some two dozen narcotics in use, some of which are semi-synthetic derivatives of morphine and other wholly synthetic compounds. Extensive clinical trials have shown that equivalent analgesic doses of various narcotics administered to the general population produce a similar incidence of side-effects, although some patients may be more sensitive to one or more of the side-effects than the general population. Adverse side-effects include constipation, excessive sedation, confusion, nausea and vomiting, and depression of respiration and circulation. Moreover, all potent narcotics cause *tolerance and physical dependence, both of which are normal pharmacological responses to prolonged narcotic administration. Tolerance is characterized by progressive resistance to the analgesic effects and other actions of the drug, while physical dependence is characterized by the development of the abstinence syndrome on prompt withdrawal of the drug. Unfortunately, these pharmacological responses are often confused with *addiction or psychological dependence which is characterized by an abnormal behaviour pattern of drug abuse, by craving of a drug for other than pain relief, by

becoming overwhelmingly involved in the procurement and use of the drug, and by the tendency to relapse after withdrawal.

The fear of tolerance, physical dependence, and addiction has caused many physicians and nurses to prescribe and/or administer narcotics in insufficient doses; consequently, severe pain often persisted. Indeed, some patients have received only one-third to one-quarter of the amount required to relieve severe pain. In some instances, the fear of addiction has caused patients not to take the prescribed doses. That these are not valid reasons for underdosing narcotics has been clearly demonstrated by laboratory and clinical studies. For one thing, addiction rarely occurs in patients receiving narcotics for pain relief, even for as long as several months: the psychological profiles of these patients differ from those of the drug abusers. For another, physical dependence does not occur in patients with acute pain given these drugs for several days; it requires 3–4 weeks of regular administration before clinically relevant physical dependence occurs. In patients with severe pain due to metastatic advanced or terminal cancer, and who are likely to require narcotic therapy until death, addiction and physical dependence should not be considered to be valid reasons for not giving adequate amounts of these drugs. On the other hand, potent narcotics should not be prescribed for patients with chronic non-malignant pain who are likely to live for years, because these patients do develop tolerance and physical dependence and become confused by chronic narcotic therapy.

In recent years, partial narcotic agonists/antagonists have been introduced such as pentazocine (Talwin®, Fortral®), butorphanol (Stadol®), nalbuphine (Nubain®), and more recently buprenorphine (Buprendrex®, Temgesic®) because these drugs are associated with a lower rate of tolerance and physical dependence; unfortunately, they have the disadvantage of producing *hallucinations and restlessness in many patients.

For therapy of acute postoperative pain, post-traumatic pain, and the pain of acute myocardial infarction or other acute visceral disease, narcotics are given intramuscularly or intravenously as they are needed. However, for cancer pain they should be given by mouth and in ample doses, administered at fixed time intervals beginning with a lower dose and raising the dose until effective analgesia is achieved and sustained.

3. *Adjuvant drugs* that are currently in use include: (i) *antidepressants: amitriptyline (Elavil®, Endep®, Tryptizol®) and doxepin (Sinequan®), which produce an analgesic effect, decrease insomnia, and in high doses decrease the depression that is often a consequence of chronic pain; (ii) *antihistamines (hydroxyzine), which *potentiate the analgesic effects of narcotics; (iii) *anticonvulsants: carbamazepine (Tegretol®) and phenytoin (Dilantin®, Epanutin®), which are effective in treating *trigeminal neuralgia, postherpetic *neur-algia, and other deafferentation pain syndromes; and (iv) *corticosteroids, which are potent anti-inflammatory agents that prevent the release of prostaglandins, stimulate appetite, and elevate mood and are thus very useful in relieving severe pain caused by cancer infiltration of the brachial or lumbosacral nerve plexus or soft-tissue infiltration.

Neurostimulation techniques. The publication of the Melzack–Wall theory of pain and the information on intrinsic analgesic mechanisms prompted the introduction and ever-increasing use of electrical stimulation applied to the skin, to peripheral nerves, to the spinal cord, and to deep parts of the brain (Melzack and Wall, 1983). Transcutaneous electrical stimulation (TENS), electroacupuncture, and even manual acupuncture by stimulating peripheral nerves or nerve-endings in some way produce pain inhibition at the dorsal horn and/or activate some of the supraspinal descending inhibitory systems. TENS has been used for the relief of postoperative and post-traumatic pain, and even labour pain, and for a variety of chronic pain syndromes including cancer. The results in many thousands of patients suggest that this method produces significant short-term relief in 70–80 per cent of the patients and long-term relief in 15–30 per cent of the patients. Therefore, it seems most useful in treating acute pain but should also be tried in the treatment of various chronic pain syndromes. The results have been similar with peripheral nerve stimulation which entails the implantation of an electrode on one of the major nerves supplying the upper or lower limb, such as the sciatic nerve.

In the late 1960s and early 1970s stimulation of the spinal cord was achieved via an operation (*laminectomy) and implantation of the electrode over the spinal cord, known as dorsal column stimulation (DCS). However, in recent years the technique has been refined to avoid surgery: the electrode is placed on the dura mater covering the spinal cord through a large needle which is introduced through the intact skin and advanced until its bevel (point) is in the epidural space, from which follows the long title of 'percutaneously implanted spinal cord epidural stimulation' (PISCES). Published reports suggest that with this procedure there is a significant short-term improvement in 70–80 per cent and long-term relief in 35–40 per cent of the patients. Spinal stimulation is preferentially effective for the treatment of pain due to nerve injuries but is not effective in relieving very severe pain, especially that of visceral origin.

Deep brain stimulation is achieved by *stereotactic placement of a stimulating electrode into the thalamus or hypothalamus, or more recently into the periaqueductal or periventricular grey matter, usually with patients under local anaesthesia (Melzack and Wall, 1983). Accurate placement of the electrode is achieved by means of a stereotactic apparatus, X-ray control, and a trial stimulation for 1–2 weeks before the wires are stitched into the scalp and are connected to an induction receiver and external transmitter that allow self-stimulation by the patient for pain control. These techniques have been used mostly for patients with advanced cancer pain, although some have used it for non-malignant chronic pain. The published data suggest that about 40–55 per cent of the patients derived excellent pain relief, about 20–30 per cent derived 50–75 per cent relief, while the rest derived no benefit. The data suggest that SPA is more effective in patients with cancer pain due to persistent peripheral nociceptive stimulation and is ineffective in deafferentation pain.

Regional analgesia. The development and widespread use of general and regional *anaesthesia were two milestones in man's continuous struggle to control pain achieved in the 19th c. Stimulated by Davy's observation of the analgesic properties of nitrous oxide, a number of individuals studied this gas and *ether as an anaesthetic and these efforts culminated in the first public demonstration of the efficacy of ether to produce general anaesthesia for surgery at the *Massachusetts General Hospital in Boston on 16 October 1846 by William T. G. *Morton. This epochal event, which Sir William *Osler later described as 'medicine's greatest single gift to suffering humanity', was followed by the widespread use of ether and later *chloroform. Although little progress was made in the ensuing six decades, in the early part of the 20th c. physicians began to develop the specialty of anaesthesia. The progressive growth in the number of specialists was paralleled by an impressive gain in knowledge of body functions and advances in agents and techniques and apparatus for their administration. The introduction of endotracheal anaesthesia in the early 1920s and the advent of artificial (controlled) *ventilation made possible the first intrathoracic operation for the removal of a lung. The introduction of *curare, the old South American arrow poison, into anaesthetic practice in 1942, and subsequently other muscle relaxants, revolutionized general anaesthesia because it permitted the use of a much lower concentration of the anaesthetic and better operating conditions. With these and other advances, the anaesthetist has been able to maintain ventilation, circulation, and other vital functions as normally as possible, not only during the operation but before and after surgery. This type of total anaesthetic care has had a major impact on surgical practice and it has been critical to the success of open heart surgery, longer brain operations, organ transplantation, radical operations for cancer, and surgery in the critically ill, very old, and in very small infants.

*Regional anaesthesia for the control of surgical and non-surgical pain was also developed in the latter half of the 19th c. This was made possible by the development of the needle and *syringe in 1845–55, and the isolation of *cocaine at that time, with the subsequent demonstrations of its analgesic properties, which culminated in the use of cocaine for surgery of the eye by Karl Koller in 1884. Koller's report was received with great enthusiasm and provoked prompt widespread application of the method because it held the promise of producing anaesthesia locally without the deleterious effects on vital organs inherent in general anaesthesia, as administered at the time. This was followed by the development of techniques to inject cocaine, and later other local anaesthetics, into tissues and virtually every major nerve in the body to produce 'regional' anaesthesia. Although these procedures were first developed for surgical anaesthesia, it was not long before some physicians began to realize the value of the method in the control of intractable non-surgical pain. During the 20th c. analgesia limited to the painful part, achieved with local anaesthetics or neurolytic agents, has been used widely for the treatment of acute and chronic painful conditions unrelated to a surgical operation. Recently acquired knowledge has prompted the application of narcotics into the spinal canal to produce regional analgesia for the relief of acute and chronic pain, including cancer pain.

Regional analgesia with local anaesthetics. Local anaesthetics act by stabilizing the membrane of nerve fibres, and thus prevent transmission of nociceptive and other impulses for periods ranging from minutes to hours, and even days, depending on the local anaesthetic and technique used. Because the thinner the nerve fibre the greater its susceptibility to local anaesthetic, it is possible to block preferentially the A delta and C fibres involved in pain without significant interference with muscle function and touch sensation; hence the term regional analgesia. By using higher concentrations, one can produce loss of motor function and even touch sensation—a condition called regional anaesthesia. Regional analgesia may be used as a diagnostic, prognostic and/or therapeutic measure (Bonica, 1953).

1. *Diagnostic blocks* with local anaesthetics properly applied are very useful in : (i) helping to ascertain specific nociceptive pathways; (ii) helping to define the mechanisms of pain; and (iii) aiding in differential diagnosis of the site of nociceptive input. For example, in a patient with pain in the low back and lower limb from *prolapsed intervertebral disc, it is essential to determine which nerve root is involved, and this can be achieved precisely by selective paravertebral block. Similarly, if after adequate examination there is still doubt whether pain in the abdomen is caused by visceral disease or by a disorder in the abdominal wall, block of intercostal nerves will relieve the latter and not the former, whereas block of the coeliac plexus (which contains the pain fibres from the viscera) relieves visceral pain but not abdominal wall pain.

2. *Prognostic blocks* are useful to predict the analgesic efficacy and side-effects of neurolytic blocks or neurosurgical operations and also afford

the patient an opportunity to experience the numbness and other side-effects that follow the long-term procedure.

3. *Therapeutic blocks* with local anaesthetics are used to provide patients with prompt relief of severe excruciating pain for hours or days, and occasionally for longer periods. For example, continuous segmental epidural block of the affected spinal segments produces complete relief of postoperative pain, post-traumatic pain, the excruciating pain of a herniated disc, or severe cancer pain for a number of days or even a couple of weeks. Moreover, a series of local anaesthetic blocks often relieves pain associated with myofascial syndromes and muscle spasm, the pain of *causalgia and other reflex sympathetic *dystrophies and, occasionally, *phantom limb pain and other chronic pain syndromes. It has long been known that, in these conditions, the relief of pain and the associated symptomatology outlasts the pharmacological effects of the drug, and usually with each subsequent block the relief lasts for a progressively longer period and eventually it does not return. It has been suggested that the blocks stop the sensory input that bombards the spinal transmission cells and thus bring about a cessation of self-sustaining activity of the neurone loops in the neuraxis that are responsible for some chronic pain states. Furthermore, the relief of pain permits the use of the body, allowing the patient to carry out normal motor activities, and these in turn would produce patterned inputs, particularly from muscles that would contain a high proportion of active large fibres which further close the gate and delay the recurrence of pain. In addition, the motor impulses that descend from the brain to the spinal cord are accompanied by inhibitory descending control impulses which would reduce the sensory input during movement.

Intraspinal narcotics. The recently acquired knowledge on opiate receptors led to animal studies that clearly demonstrated that the injection of small amounts of morphine or other narcotics into the subarachnoid or epidural space produced block of nociceptive impulses from a region of the body without blocking other somatosensory, somatomotor, or sympathetic functions (Bonica *et al.*, 1983). These findings promptly led to the use of intraspinal narcotics to produce regional analgesia in patients with severe acute and chronic pain, including cancer pain. In contrast to the duration of 3–4 hours achieved with intramuscular injection of morphine, subarachnoid or epidural injection of this drug produces pain relief for 16–24 hours. To achieve the relief for several days or weeks, a very small plastic catheter is introduced into the subarachnoid or epidural space through a special needle, the needle is then removed and the catheter taped to the patient's body. Usually 0.5–1 mg of morphine injected into the subarachnoid space or 6–8 mg diluted in 6–8 mg saline injected into the epidural space every 18–24 hours provides effective pain relief. In patients with cancer or other chronic pain syndromes that require prolonged administration, continuous implantable infusion systems are used to avoid the risk of infection inherent in repeated injections. A silastic catheter is placed with its tip at the appropriate level of the epidural space, the catheter is then tunnelled under the skin so that its proximal end is in the front part of the body and it is then connected to an implanted infusion plant reservoir which can be refilled percutaneously every 10–15 days.

As with all other techniques, this procedure is associated with certain adverse side-effects, the most important of which is respiratory depression, but fortunately the incidence is very low. Other side-effects include diffuse pruritus (itching), urinary retention, nausea and vomiting, and development of tolerance. Tolerance can be minimized by avoiding injection of large amounts and, if it develops, injection of one or two doses of local anaesthetics in some way eliminates it.

Regional analgesia with neurolytic agents. Regional analgesia with neurolytic blocks achieved by the injection of alcohol or *phenol involves the intentional destruction of a nerve or nerves for a period of time, to produce interruption of nociceptive pathways for weeks, months or sometimes permanently, depending on the site of the injection. Neurolytic agents completely destroy nerve cell bodies or their connections to the central nervous system, and consequently these are not able to regenerate and the interruption is permanent: conversely, if the agent is injected into the nerve distal to the cell body, the nerve is capable of regeneration and, after several months, the pain returns and a neuroma has formed which may itself produce pain. On the basis of these facts, in the past neurolytic agents have been injected into the subarachnoid space of the spinal canal to destroy the dorsal sensory rootlets proximal to the cell bodies or into the gasserian ganglion to destroy many or all of the cell bodies of the trigeminal nerve; only in rare cases have they been used to destroy peripheral nerves.

In the past these procedures have been used primarily for patients with cancer pain, but also in patients with non-malignant chronic pain. However, the recently acquired information that loss of peripheral sensory input produces long-term abnormal activity in dorsal horn and other parts of the central nervous system dictates that neurolytic blocks should not be used in patients with non-malignant chronic pain. Moreover, the recent advent of refined neurosurgical procedures, neurostimulation techniques, and psychological methods has decreased the indication for neurolytic blocks, even in cancer pain. Nevertheless, several neurolytic procedures remain useful, particularly in patients with severe advanced cancer pain who have a short life expectancy, are poor risks for major neurosurgical procedures, and cannot be relieved adequately with narcotics.

1. *Subarachnoid neurolysis* entails the injection of alcohol or phenol into the subarachnoid space to achieve chemical sensory rhizotomy (destruction of sensory rootlets) and has been used successfully for the treatment of severe pain of advanced cancer in many thousands of patients (Bonica, 1953; White and Sweet, 1969). Pain relief usually lasts for several months and sometimes even longer, although not infrequently it is necessary to do several blocks to achieve complete destruction of the rootlets. Available data suggest that this procedure produces complete relief in about 50–60 per cent of cancer patients, partial relief in about 20–25 per cent, and no relief in the rest. This procedure is particularly useful in relieving severe pain in the trunk, because one can achieve good analgesia without significant adverse side-effects. On the other hand, even when expertly carried out, subarachnoid neurolysis of the rootlets of the upper or lower limb will result in transient muscle weakness in 15–20 per cent of patients and in 3–5 per cent of these the weakness is prolonged. Moreover, if the block is done for pain in the pelvis or lower limb, there is transient bladder and/or rectal sphincter dysfunction in 20–25 per cent of the patients due to interruption of the autonomic nerves, and this persists in 5–7 per cent.

2. *Neurolytic block of the trigeminal sensory root or gasserian ganglion* has been used for many years to relieve effectively severe trigeminal neuralgia and cancer pain in the anterior two-thirds of the head. Although the reintroduction of thermo-coagulation of these structures has decreased the need for neurolytic block (White and Sweet, 1969), there is still a definite place for these procedures in managing severe pain due to advanced or terminal cancer, particularly in localities where the neurosurgical technique is not available and there are physicians skilled in the block procedure.

3. *Coeliac plexus block.* The same may be said of coeliac plexus block achieved with either 50 per cent alcohol or 7–10 per cent aqueous phenol to relieve severe pain caused by cancer of the pancreas, stomach, or other abdominal viscera. Both of these neurolytic procedures produce complete, or almost complete, relief of pain in 75–80 per cent of patients until their death. For the reason mentioned above, neurolytic blocks of spinal nerves should not be carried out except in patients with severe excruciating pain not amenable to narcotics, and in whom neurosurgery is contraindicated.

4. *Neuroadenolysis of the *pituitary gland* (NALP), developed by Moricca of Rome, has been found to be effective in relieving severe diffuse cancer pain in various parts of the body. This procedure entails the introduction of a needle through the nose and through the sphenoid bone under X-ray control until its tip is in the centre of the sella turcica which contains the pituitary gland. Slow injection of small increments of absolute alcohol results in complete relief in about 50–60 per cent of the patients, partial relief in another 25–35 per cent, and no relief in the rest. Adverse side-effects include transient *diabetes insipidus in about 60 per cent of the patients, rhinorrhoea (leakage of *cerebrospinal fluid into the nose) for 1 to 2 days, and diplopia (double vision) in 2–3 per cent of the patients.

Physical therapies. The large variety of physical therapeutic techniques that have been used for centuries remain an important method of pain relief. One or more of these procedures is usually combined with other modalities. The following is a partial list: (i) manual therapy in the form of massage or manipulation; (ii) exercise; (iii) mechanical therapy in the form of traction or compression; (iv) superficial and deep heat; (v) application of cold in the form of ice packs or ice massage or the use of vapocoolant sprays. These procedures are used for mild to moderate pain caused by musculoskeletal disorders. Despite the widespread use of these modalities, their mechanism of pain-relieving action is not known. It has been suggested that most of these procedures produce an increase in blood flow to the painful part and this enhances the elimination of pain-producing substances and repair of damaged tissue. However, Melzack and Wall (1983) believe that the most plausible hypothesis is that these procedures produce sensory inputs that ultimately inhibit pain signals by closing the gate. This effect may be achieved either by activation of large fibres by gentle stimulation which produces inhibition at segmental levels, or by strong stimulation of small fibres which project nociceptive signals to the brain stem, which in turn sends messages to the spinal cord through descending inhibitory mechanisms that close the gate. Various procedures in physical medicine may be explained by either or both mechanisms.

Psychological techniques. The recent knowledge acquired by psychological and behavioural studies has led to the development and widespread use of a number of techniques for the psychological control of pain. These include: psychophysiological procedures such as progressive muscular *relaxation and *biofeedback; operant or external contingency managing approaches; hypnotic suggestion techniques; the use of strategems to distract attention or change the meaning of the pain; social modelling techniques; and a variety of other cognitive-behavioural interventions. Data from numerous reports suggest that all of these techniques have some value in the treatment of pain in some patients but there are meagre data from controlled clinical trials (Bonica *et al.*, 1983; Melzack and Wall, 1983).

1. *Progressive muscle relaxation training* has been used widely to relax tense muscles believed to cause pain, and beneficial results have been reported in patients with tension headache, *migraine headache, low back pain, postoperative pain, temporomandibular joint dysfunction syndrome, and phantom limb pain. It has been suggested that this technique reduces pain not only by

decreasing muscle tension but also by decreasing arousal and the consequent release of *catecholamine, and increase in blood pressure, heart rate, and metabolism, all of which are responses to psychological *stress and when present feed into the nervous system to produce pain directly or indirectly by facilitating activity in neurone pools that project pain signals to the brain.

2. *Biofeedback* has been used widely to treat a variety of painful disorders on the assumption that: (i) a physiological disorder underlies the pain; and (ii) the patient can be taught to control and correct the underlying disorder when given feedback. Techniques currently used include: (i) *electromyographic (EMG) feedback to reduce muscle tension; (ii) skin temperature feedback intended to decrease dilatation of extracranial vessels which is thought to be the cause of migraine headache; and (iii) *electroencephalogram (EEG) feedback to help the subject produce alpha brain activity, a relaxed state thought to be incompatible with pain. These techniques have been used primarily to treat tension headache, migraine headache, low back pain, and a few other types of chronic pain syndrome, with variable success. Indeed, several reports indicate that biofeedback is not superior to less expensive, less instrument-orientated treatment such as relaxation training. It has been suggested that biofeedback is a useful vehicle for distraction of attention, relaxation, suggestion, and providing the patient with a sense of control of his pain.

3. *Operant conditioning* strategies for the treatment of chronic pain behaviour are based on the well-established psychological principles that complex patterns of behaviour are subject to the influence of, or under the control of, learning factors and to a considerable degree are governed by consequences in the environment. Fordyce was the first to suggest that in some patients chronic pain behaviour is a learning process which may or may not be initiated by a major or even minor injury. In such patients, the pain behaviour (complaint of pain, stopping work, lying in bed) is reinforced by favourable consequences or reactions on the part of those important to the patient, and by those in the work environment. Thus, a husband who for years has been inattentive to his wife becomes solicitous and concerned and gives special attention when she sustains an injury, the patient is allowed time out from work, gets sympathy from friends and physicians, and is given medicines. All these and other factors are favourable consequences that reinforce a pain behaviour. In such a patient, chronic pain behaviour continues as long as the consequences are favourable and eventually becomes independent of the underlying pathology and persists even after the original pathogenic factor is gone. Under such conditions, a pain habit that is real and is readily accounted for by learning *conditioning has developed.

The major therapeutic strategies are: (i) to place the patient in a controlled environment where the positive pain behaviour reinforcers are precisely identified; (ii) to decrease pain behaviour by withdrawal of positive reinforcers by ignoring pain complaint and other pain behaviours and at the same time complimenting 'well' behaviour; (iii) to decrease progressively analgesics and other drug intake (detoxification programme); (iv) to encourage increased physical activity and other types of 'well' behaviour by such positive reinforcements as complimenting and encouraging the improvement in exercise, walking, and other physical activities; and (v) to maintain the gain brought about by behaviour change in the treatment programme by modifying the consequences of pain behaviour and 'well' behaviour at home and work. Several workers have reported improvement as measured by increased activity, marked decrease or elimination of drug intake, return to some form of work, and in other ways leading normal lives in 60–70 per cent of the patients at follow-up which has ranged from 6 months to 7 years. While such results are very encouraging, it is important to realize that: (i) this obtains for a highly selected group which in one case consisted of 30 per cent of all patients referred to the programme and, of these, two-thirds achieved significant improvement; (ii) while the pain behaviour is decreased or eliminated, many patients continue to feel pain but they are simply conditioned not to manifest it overtly; and (iii) the programme as originally proposed entails hospitalization for 6–8 weeks and is very costly. To minimize the cost, some clinicians conduct the programme on an outpatient basis. In any case, since most of the patients managed with the operant conditioning programme have been disabled for many years and have cost society large amounts of money, the cost/benefit ratio is still favourable, even when only 20 per cent of the patients are rehabilitated.

4. *Hypnosis.* Although *hypnosis for the relief of pain has been used since ancient times and a number of isolated reports of hypnosis as an effective method of relieving pain were published during the last half of the 19th and the first half of the 20th c., its acceptance as an ethical form of medical practice and the legitimate subject for scientific study are recent developments (Melzack and Wall, 1983). During the past three decades a number of scientists have studied its phenomena and many clinicians have reported its successful use in managing patients with a variety of pain syndromes. The advantage of the technique is that it reduces or eliminates pain without unpleasant or destructive side-effects, and, by reducing emotional stress and by teaching autohypnosis, it can create life-enhancing attitudes in the patient. The disadvantage of the technique is that it requires the service of an experienced hypnotherapist, it is time-consuming and only about 15–20 per cent can achieve sufficient hypnotic depth to get complete relief of pain. To use this method effectively, it is necessary to determine the hypnotic susceptibility

of the patient, and his/her willingness to be hypnotized and ability to concentrate, and to develop rapport between patient and therapist so that the patient has no fear of hypnosis and has absolute confidence in the therapist.

5. *Other cognitive-behavioural techniques* aim to correct faulty conditions (attitudes, beliefs, and expectations) underlying emotional and behavioural disturbances. With these procedures, patients learn to identify distorted beliefs and to substitute more positive thoughts, and are taught specific cognitive skills such as imagery, focused attention, distraction, relabelling sensation, relaxation, and other strategies for coping with pain. These processes aim to increase the patient's awareness of events that aggravate the pain, and actions that reduce it, so that the patent may better avoid or deal more effectively with pain-increasing events and use pain-relieving actions. A variety of cognitive-behavioural procedures have been subjected to clinical trial and although the results are encouraging, the precise role of these procedures for relieving pain is not known and will require controlled clinical trials in patients with specific pain syndromes.

Neurosurgical operations. The studies that led to the wide acceptance of the specificity theory in the 19th c. suggested that in patients with severe intractable pain (the cause of which could not be eliminated), surgical section of the sensory pathways should provide permanent relief (Bonica, 1953; White and Sweet, 1969). During the last part of the 19th c., procedures were developed to cut sensory pathways in peripheral spinal or cranial nerves (neurotomy), those that supply viscera contained in sympathetic nerves (sympathectomy) and, later, section of the sensory roots (rhizotomy) of spinal or cranial nerves or section of the spinothalamic tract in the thoracic region (spinothalamic tractotomy or cordotomy). During the first half of the 20th c., techniques of sectioning the spinothalamic tract at high levels in the cord, medulla, the midbrain, and surgical lesions of the thalamus were developed, refined, and used for various pain syndromes. In the late 1940s psychosurgical procedures entailing operation upon various parts of the brain, known as prefrontal lobotomy or leucotomy, were introduced as a means of diminishing the affective aspect (suffering) associated with pain. All of these operations produce side-effects and other disadvantages which, together with recently acquired knowledge, has prompted the abandonment of neurotomy and sympathectomy, the restriction of rhizotomy and spinothalamic tractotomy, and the introduction of new and less destructive techniques. The role of these procedures will be briefly summarized.

1. *Rhizotomy.* Spinal dorsal rhizotomy is used only in highly selective patients, with very severe pain involving one or a few spinal segments in the thorax and abdomen and in the perineum. This procedure is rarely, if ever, indicated for the relief of extremity pain because a section of all of the roots supplying the limb produces extensive loss of sensory input (deafferentation) with loss of proprioception and consequently results in a virtually useless limb. To avoid this problem, recently 'selective posterior rhizotomy' has been introduced; with the aid of an operating microscope it is feasible to section only the fine afferent fibres in the lateral division of the dorsal root leaving intact the larger afferents that mediate touch in the medial division. In any case, this procedure should be reserved for patients with advanced cancer because it is now known that chronic deafferentation produces long-term abnormal function in the central nervous system which may result in deafferentation pain.

2. *Cranial sensory rhizotomy.* Section of the sensory root of the trigeminal nerve is still being done for the relief of severe excruciating trigeminal neuralgia not relieved by drugs or other less destructive operations, and is also used for severe excruciating pain in the anterior two-thirds of the head, caused by advanced cancer. In patients with cancer that involves other cranial nerves and the upper neck, section of the sensory roots of cranial nerves V, VII, IX and X and of the upper two or three cervical nerves is carried out through an open operation (posterior craniotomy). The disadvantages of this operation are: (i) it requires a major operation and produces loss of all sensation; (ii) it is often followed by very uncomfortable sensations (paraesthesiae); and (iii) it carries the risk of *corneal ulcers due to loss of the corneal *reflex.

3. *Percutaneous differential thermal rhizotomy.* These disadvantages have prompted the reintroduction and refinement of percutaneous differential thermal rhizotomy of the roots of the ganglion of the fifth cranial nerve (White and Sweet, 1969). This procedure is performed with local anaesthesia using a needle electrode that is introduced through the face and made to pass through the foramen ovale until its point is in the ganglion or root of the nerve; then a radiofrequency stimulus is applied to permit differential thermocoagulation with continuous monitoring of the patient to achieve the desired degree of analgesia. Since the unmyelinated and small myelinated nociceptive fibres are more sensitive to the destructive effects of heat, these fibres can be destroyed preferentially while sparing touch sensation. Properly carried out, this procedure produces complete short-term pain relief in 80–90 per cent of the patients and long-term relief in 50–60 per cent of the patients. A similar technique of percutaneous differential radiofrequency rhizotomy of the glossopharyngeal nerve for the relief of severe excruciating pain in the throat has recently been described.

4. *Spinothalamic tractotomy.* Section of the spinothalamic tract in the upper thoracic spinal cord has been used for more than half a century, and in the hands of a skilled neurosurgeon it produces almost complete pain relief in the lower

part of the body in 75–90 per cent of the patients. Unfortunately, the pain relief lasts only some 12–16 months and rarely longer, despite the fact that the interruption produced by the lesion is permanent. This suggests that the nervous system finds other pathways for transmission of pain signals and that this procedure should be reserved only for patients with cancer who are predicted to live less than 12–18 months. Because the standard procedure requires a major operation to expose the cord (laminectomy) and is thus associated with a mortality rate of 5–10 per cent and morbidity in 15–20 per cent of the patients, it has virtually been replaced by percutaneous cervical cordotomy.

5. *Percutaneous cervical cordotomy* entails the introduction of a needle through the skin and the deeper tissues in the upper neck (previously anaesthetized with a local anaesthetic): the needle is then passed through the intervertebral space and advanced until its point is in the anterolateral part of the spinal cord. A precise location of the needle is ascertained by a stimulating technique which produces pain, tingling, and other signs; then a radiofrequency stimulus is applied in increments until there is ample analgesia in the contralateral half of the body. The procedure has the advantage of being a relatively minor operation with an extremely low operative and postoperative mortality and very low incidence of complications, while at the same time it produces good pain relief in 75–90 per cent of the patients for periods of several months. Because of these advantages, it has replaced not only open cordotomy but also subarachnoid alcohol or phenol blocks in those centres where a skilled operator is available. Unfortunately, only a relatively small number of persons are skilled enough to carry out percutaneous cordotomy.

Section of the spinothalamic tract in the medulla is infrequently used because it carries a high risk of mortality and complications. On the other hand, section of the descending trigeminal tract in the medulla interrupts the sensory fibres of cranial nerves V, VII, IX, and X and is highly effective in relieving pain in the face and the anterior two-thirds of the head. The major disadvantage is that it requires a craniotomy.

6. *Cranial stereotactic operations.* Mesencephalic tractotomy carried out under stereotactic control with local anaesthesia interrupts the ascending systems in the midbrain and produces effective pain relief for 6–12 months. Lesions made surgically in the hypothalamus and thalamus have also been shown to produce relief of severe cancer pain for periods of 6–12 months and therefore are indicated in patients with advanced cancer in whom other procedures are not available. Unfortunately, only a few surgeons throughout the world have the skill to carry out these procedures.

7. *Psychosurgery.* Prefrontal lobotomy, as originally proposed, produced pain relief but this was accompanied by severe apathy and mental confusion and loss of affect. To diminish the side-effects, White and Sweet (1969) introduced gradual bilateral coagulation of the medial frontal white matter, achieved by implanting electrodes. This graduated lesion causes patients to be free from concern about pain or death. Another operation to achieve these objectives is cingulotomy, but this also produces affective changes, although to a much lesser degree than lobotomy. These operations should be reserved for patients with severe excruciating intolerable cancer pain who have only a few months to live.　　　　　J. J. BONICA

References
Bonica, J. J. (1953). *The Management of Pain.* Philadelphia.
Bonica, J. J. (1979). Introduction. *Association for Research in Nervous and Mental Disease,* **58,** 1–17.
Bonica, J. J., Liebeskind, J. C. and Albe-Fessard, D. (eds) (1979). *Advances in Pain Research and Therapy,* Vol. 3. New York.
Bonica, J. J., Lindblom, U. and Iggo, A. (eds) (1983). *Advances in Pain Research and Therapy,* Vol. 5. New York.
Dallenbach, K. M. (1939). Pain: History and present status. *American Journal of Psychology,* **52,** 331–47.
Fülop-Miller, R. (1938). *Triumph Over Pain* (translated by Eden and Cedar Paul). New York.
Keele, K. D. (1957). *Anatomies of Pain,* Springfield, Illinois.
Macht, D. I. (1915). The history of opium and some of its preparations and alkaloids. *Journal of the American Medical Association,* **64,** 477.
Melzack, R. and Wall, P. D. (1965). Pain mechanisms: A new theory. *Science,* **150,** 971–9.
Melzack, R. and Wall, P. D. (1983). *The Challenge of Pain.* New York.
Sigerist, H. E. (1951). *A History of Medicine,* Vol. 1. New York.
Tainter, M. L. (1948). Pain. *Annals of the New York Academy of Science,* **51,** 3.
White, J. C. and Sweet, W. H. (1969). *Pain and the Neurosurgeon. A Forty-Year Experience.* Springfield, Illinois.

PALAEOPATHOLOGY is the study of disease in ancient peoples, as deduced from examination of osseous remains, mummies, and other evidence such as ancient writings.

PALATE. The partition separating the oral and nasal cavities; it comprises a bony portion in front (the hard palate) and a fleshy portion behind (the soft palate). The latter is drawn up during swallowing to occlude the back of the nose.

PALLIATIVE THERAPY is treatment undertaken with the objective of relieving symptoms, particularly when these are painful or in some other way distressing, but in the knowledge that it will not affect the outcome of the disease.

PALMER, WILLIAM (1824–56). British physician and poisoner, MRCS (1846). Palmer was trained at *St Bartholomew's Hospital London and practised in Rugeley, Staffordshire. He was found guilty on circumstantial evidence of poisoning his wife in 1854, and his brother and his friend

James Parsons Cook in 1855. He was believed to have murdered 13 persons in all.

PALMISTRY is fortune-telling from inspection of the pattern of creases in the palm.

PALPATION is the act of examining by means of touch.

PALPITATION is subjective awareness of the beat of the heart, usually as an unpleasant thumping sensation in the chest or at the root of the neck. It occurs in normal subjects when the force of the beat is abruptly increased, as by emotion or on lying down in bed. *Extrasystoles often cause palpitation, as may other disturbances of cardiac rhythm.

PALSY. Paralysis.

PALUDRINE® is a proprietary name for *progunil, a drug used in the prevention and treatment of *malaria.

PANCREAS. A large elongated glandular structure situated transversely at the back of the abdominal cavity, behind the stomach. Its function is primarily digestive; its secretion, the pancreatic juice, contains a variety of digestive *enzymes and passes into the *duodenum via the pancreatic duct. The pancreas also has an endocrine function, secreting *hormones directly into the blood stream. These hormones are elaborated by cells scattered throughout the gland, in clusters called the '*islets of Langerhans', and are chiefly concerned with the regulation of *carbohydrate metabolism; they include *insulin, *glucagon, and *somatostatin.

PANCREATITIS is inflammation of the *pancreas.

PANDEMIC. An epidemic of intercontinental or world-wide proportions. See EPIDEMIOLOGY.

PANEL PRACTICE is a general medical practice which provided advice and treatment to insured wage-earners under the terms of the *National Health Insurance Act 1911, implemented in 1913.

PANNICULITIS is inflammation of the subcutaneous layer of fatty tissue.

PANNUS. A layer of *granulation tissue which develops over the *synovial membrane of joints in *rheumatoid arthritis and which contributes to their immobilization; also, a layer of granulation tissues infiltrating the *cornea in *trachoma and obscuring vision.

PANTOTHENIC ACID is a member of the water-soluble *vitamin B complex, an essential component of the human diet as part of the *coenzyme A molecule. It is, however, so widely available in foodstuffs that spontaneous deficiency is not known to occur.

PAPANICOLAOU, GEORGE NICHOLAS (1883–1962). American pathologist, MD University of Athens. Papanicolaou was born in Greece; he began scientific work in the fields of oceanography and physiology in Monaco. He moved to New York City in 1913, where he joined the department of pathology at Cornell Medical College. His best known work was on the exfoliative *cytology of the *vagina and the uterine *cervix. He demonstrated changes in vaginal epithelium at different phases of the menstrual cycle, and developed a cytological test for malignant change in the uterine cervical epithelium. This test has been widely employed for early detection of malignant change, and is often referred to as the 'Pap smear' (see CERVICAL SMEAR).

PAPAVERINE is one of the *opium alkaloids, but with a pharmacological action quite different from that of *morphine; its major effect is to relax involuntary muscle, and it has been used mainly as an *antispasmodic in ischaemic conditions due to arterial spasm.

PAPILLA. Any small nipple-like protuberance.

PAPILLOEDEMA is oedematous swelling of the *optic disc, due to raised intracranial pressure compressing the *optic nerve; the cause is usually a space-occupying lesion such as a tumour inside the skull, but papilloedema may also result from malignant *hypertension or from *thrombosis of the central vein of the *retina.

PAPILLOMA. A small wart-like benign *tumour derived from *epithelium.

PAPOVAVIRUS. A group of small *deoxyribonucleic acid (DNA) *viruses, many of which have the capacity to cause *tumours in animals (e.g. *papilloma, *polyoma, *sarcoma, *warts).

PAPPENHEIM, ARTUR (1870–1916). German haematologist, MD Berlin (1895). After working in the Cancer Institute in Berlin from 1906 to 1909 Pappenheim was given the title of professor in 1912. One of the leading young haematologists, he founded the journal *Folia haematologica* (1904), and published a superlative *Atlas der menschlichen Blutzellen* (1905–12). He invented the specific stain for *plasma cells (Unna–Pappenheim stain). He died of *typhus contracted on active service.

PAPULE. A pimple; a small circumscribed lump on the skin.

PAPWORTH VILLAGE COLONY. A village settlement for patients with stable *tuberculosis founded in 1916 by Pendrill Charles Varrier-Jones and later moved to Papworth in Cambridgeshire. It comprised residential cottages, workshops, and a sanatorium and hospital; it enabled such patients to live a relatively normal working and family life while remaining under strict medical supervision. It may be regarded as the forerunner of the modern *rehabilitation centre.

PARA-AMINOSALICYLIC ACID (PAS) is an antibacterial agent formerly used in the treatment of *tuberculosis but now replaced in drug combination regimens by agents that are more effective, less toxic, and easier to take, such as *ethambutol.

PARACELSUS, THEOPHRASTUS PHILIPPUS AUREOLUS BOMBASTUS VON HOHEN-HEIM (1493–1541). Swiss physician. Paracelsus, always known by this assumed name, was taught by his father, a cultivated physician. He later attended several universities and may have received the MD Ferrara, although this is not known for certain. He began practice in Strasbourg but in 1527 was appointed town physician and professor of medicine in Basle. He so outraged his colleagues by burning the works of *Galen and *Avicenna and by admitting *barber-surgeons to his lectures, which were delivered in the vernacular, that he was forced to flee in 1528. Thereafter he wandered through Central Europe as an itinerant practitioner vigorously propounding his iconoclastic doctrine. He died, it is said, in a drunken brawl in Salzburg at the age of 48. Paracelsus has been called the 'Luther of medicine'. Coarse-fibred but violently articulate, he defied the authority of Galen and Avicenna, condemning all medical teaching not based on experience. In so doing he opened the door to the renaissance of medical thought. An able doctor and a competent chemist, he introduced *laudanum, *sulphur, lead, and *mercury into Western therapeutics and popularized tinctures and salts. He associated *cretinism with endemic *goitre and distinguished mental defect from acquired mental illness.

PARACENTESIS is the release of fluid accumulated in a body cavity (e.g. *pleural, *peritoneal) by puncturing and draining through a needle or tube.

PARACETAMOL is one of the two most important non-narcotic *analgesic drugs in current use, the other being *aspirin. Paracetamol, also known under the trade name of Panadol® in the UK and known as acetaminophen in the USA, is less irritant to the stomach than aspirin and is often prescribed for that reason. Unlike aspirin, it has no significant anti-inflammatory action. The chief disadvantage of paracetamol is the danger of overdosage, which can cause serious liver damage.

PARAESTHESIAE are abnormal skin sensations variously described as tingling, prickling, burning, or 'like pins and needles'.

PARAGONIMIASIS is infestation with a hermaphroditic *fluke (trematode worm) of the genus *Paragonimus* (e.g. *P. westermani, P. uterobilateralis*), which inhabits the lungs and occasionally other tissues of various mammals including man. Lung flukes have a remarkable life-cycle, requiring two intermediate hosts, the first being (as in the case of other trematodes like *bilharzia) an appropriate freshwater snail, the second a freshwater crustacean (crayfish or crab). Human infestation is acquired by eating inadequately cooked crabs or crayfish, and must be differentiated in diagnosis from other chronic lung diseases, particularly *tuberculosis.

PARA-INFLUENZA VIRUS is one of a group of viruses, in which four distinct types have been recognized, belonging to the family of *paramyxoviruses. Para-influenza virus is a common cause of respiratory infections, ranging from the common *cold to *pneumonia; type 2 is particularly associated with *croup in children.

PARALDEHYDE is a rapidly acting and powerful *sedative drug, which occurs as a liquid with an unpleasant smell and taste. It is for this reason administered rectally or by parenteral injection. It is particularly useful for controlling situations in which there is acute mental disturbance, and is relatively safe.

PARALYSIS is loss of function in a muscle or group of muscles.

PARALYSIS AGITANS is idiopathic or primary parkinsonism, also known as Parkinson's disease. It is one of the commonest neurological conditions, particularly in the elderly among whom its prevalence is about 0.5 per cent. The manifestations are those of *parkinsonism. The aetiology is unknown.

PARALYTIC SHELLFISH POISONING. See RED TIDE.

PARAMEDICAL describes non-medical personnel engaged in tasks of an ancillary or supportive medical nature.

PARAMYOCLONUS MULTIPLEX is a form of progressive *myoclonus in which the repetitive sudden involuntary contractions of muscle groups occur first in the shoulder girdle and later spread to involve the muscles of the trunk, limbs, face, and neck. It is now more often known as hereditary essential myoclonus.

PARAMYXOVIRUS. A group of single-stranded *ribonucleic acid (RNA) viruses which includes the *para-influenza, *mumps, *measles, canine distemper, and *rinderpest viruses.

PARANASAL SINUSES are the cavities, lined with

mucous membrane and containing air, which communicate with the nasal cavity; they are the ethmoidal, maxillary, frontal, and sphenoidal sinuses.

PARANOIA in its pure form is a rare variety of *schizophrenia, commonest in men over the age of 30. The patient builds up an increasingly elaborate delusional system which may have its origin in some genuine grievance but which is beyond all bounds of reality. The delusions of persecution (and of grandeur, often also present) may, however, long remain concealed from others if not openly expressed, since the patient may appear mentally normal in all other respects; even to the extent that homicidal attempts may be the first manifestation. Certain political assassinations have been explained on this basis. Paranoid reactions also occur in *depression, *alcoholism, and *senile dementia.

PARAPARESIS is partial *paralysis of the lower half of the body.

*PARAPHIMOSIS. Strangulation of the glans of the *penis by a retracted tight foreskin (*prepuce).

PARAPHRENIA is a form of *schizophrenia occurring in later adult life and more commonly in women characterized by wildly improbable delusions of persecution (cf. *paranoia).

PARAPLEGIA is *paralysis of the lower half of the body.

PARAPSYCHOLOGY is the study of *extrasensory perception and allied phenomena (clairvoyance, telepathy, etc.) which appear to transcend natural laws.

PARAQUAT is a highly toxic bipyridyl contact herbicide used in various proprietary weedkiller preparations (e.g. Gramaxone, Weedol). It is very irritant externally and can cause corneal damage if it gets into the eye; ingested, even a small amount is lethal. Liver, kidney, and lung are all severely affected; the liver and kidney may recover, but the damage to the lung is irreversible. The lesson that stands out from a review of paraquat deaths in the UK is that paraquat solutions should never be decanted into soft-drink bottles.

PARASITE. An organism living in or on another and obtaining food from it; a parasite may or may not harm its host, but confers no benefit upon it. Parasites of man include bacteria, viruses, fungi, protozoa, and metazoa (multicellular organisms), notably worms. See PARASITOLOGY.

PARASITOLOGY is the scientific discipline dealing with the association of two organisms. The word 'parasite' is derived from Greek; it means 'situated beside'. Parasite was used in ancient Greece to describe people who ate beside or at tables of others. In spite of this 'social' background of the word, scientists started to use it in a specific way: parasites are defined as organisms residing on or within another living organism. Parasites may, therefore, be organisms that are either animals or plants, including a diversity of species such as bacteria, yeasts, fungi, algae, viruses, protozoa, helminths, and arthropods. From a biological point of view parasitology may be defined as that branch of ecology in which one organism constitutes the living environment of another. This broad definition of parasites is not, however, the one that is in common use currently. From the medical point of view parasitism and potential harm to the host have become synonymous. This distinction is important to differentiate living together in harmony (*symbiosis) where there is no unilateral or mutual metabolic dependency between the two organisms involved, from 'parasitism' where such dependency is an essential feature. Furthermore, parasitism represents a subgroup of symbiosis; there are thousands of species that use the symbiotic way of life and only some of these may cause disease in man, animals, or plants. Further restriction of the domain of parasitology occurred at one point between the 17th and 19th c. Parasitology became the science dealing with zooparasites, that is organisms that belong to the animal kingdom. In contrast, parasites such as bacteria, viruses, and fungi that have been classified as of plant origin are dealt with in the discipline of *microbiology.

History. The history of parasitology does not give a clear idea of the development of the field. Anthony van *Leeuwenhoek has been credited with seeing the first *protozoon using a simple microscope. Between 1674 and 1716 he described many free-living protozoa and also the first parasitic protozoan, *Eimeria stiedai*. The description of the first human parasitic protozoon was made in 1681 by van Leeuwenhoek; he found *Giardia lamblia* in his own *diarrhoeic stools. The major discoveries of parasitic protozoa were, however, delayed for more than a century. During the 19th c. the *trypanosomes, *amoebae, and *malaria parasites were described. *Worms or *flukes, on the other hand, comprised almost all known parasites until the 1870s. In retrospect, evidence for several worm infections have been found in ancient Egyptian *mummies (1210–1000 BC) reflecting the long-standing relationship between man and parasites. The famous *Ebers papyrus of 1550 BC (Fig. 1) indicates that in Ancient Egypt at least four worm infections were recognized including *Ascaris lumbricoides, *Taenia saginata, Dracunculus medinesis (*guinea worm), and Schistosoma haematobium (*bilharzia) (Fig. 2). The papyrus also includes information on arthropods such as *fleas, *flies, and *lice. More recently, evidence was obtained from examining tissue sections of ancient Egyptian mummies that *Trichinella spiralis existed as an infection during that period. Worms also were

Fig. 1. Description of a urinary tract related syndrome included in the Ebers papyrus. The discharge from the penis refers to haematuria, a characteristic feature of schistosomiasis haematobium

mentioned by Assyrian, Babylonian, and Greek physicians. The two most prominent historical discoveries of worms occurred in 1379 (*Fasciola hepatica*) and in 1558 (*Cysticercus cellulosae*) but it was not until the 18th and first half of the 19th c. that many species of worms and arthropods were identified and classified. The latter part of the 19th c. and early 20th c. witnessed consolidation of the discoveries of many human parasites in general, identification of their life cycle, and recognition of their related disease syndromes.

Parasitology as a science is now undergoing a fundamental change because of the major bio-

Fig. 2. Photomicrograph of a liver section from 'Nakht', a mummy of a 14-year-old ancient Egyptian. The body was found in Thebes; it was buried approximately 3000 years ago. In spite of the dried soft tissue structures, two *Schistosoma haematobium* eggs with the characteristic terminal spine can be seen. (Reproduced by courtesy of Dr Peter K. Lewin, Department of Pediatrics and Pathology, Hospital for Sick Children, Toronto)

medical revolution that led to important discoveries in *molecular biology and *biochemistry. These tools are now being applied to the study of human parasites; the day may be close when we shall see molecular biology paving the way for the development of antiparasitic *vaccines and new methods of controlling these infections.

Zooparasites are widely spread in the animal kingdom; parasitic members have been described in every major phylum. Among the protozoa, several species of amoebae, flagellates, and ciliates and all of the sporozoa are parasitic. Metazoa include species that are common parasites of marine invertebrates. Parasitic representatives of the helminths, flat- and round-worms, are numerous. In addition arthropods are represented by many parasitic species or they may be involved in disease transmission as *vectors.

Biology of parasites. The three major groups of organisms now recognized as falling within the scope of parasitology are protozoa, helminths, and arthropods. They vary greatly in many biological characteristics and this raises several questions about why they were originally lumped together. Historically there is no justification for including protozoa, helminths, and arthropods in a single group, except that they are all zooparasites. Biologically, however, they are quite different; protozoa are unicellular organisms that are microscopic in size and that share with other micro-organisms such as bacteria and viruses the capability of dividing and multiplying within their mammalian *host. In contrast, worms are multicellular, all adults can be seen by the naked eye and may reach huge dimensions, for example some tapeworms which may reach 10 m in length. Furthermore, worms generally cannot multiply within the mammalian host; to increase the worm population in a specific host, re-exposure must occur. The third group of zooparasites, the arthropods, represent again a heterogenous collection of vectors of disease which may be bacterial, viral, or protozoan or they themselves may parasitize mammalian hosts causing varying degrees of discomfort or disease.

The heterogeneity of animal species included in the discipline of parasitology resulted in a continuing controversy because of marked differences in their biology. Recently the term microparasites has been introduced to include viruses, bacteria, and protozoa. They are all small in size, have high rates of direct reproduction within the host and result typically in a short duration of infection. Macroparasites, on the other hand, include worms and arthropods, are larger, have much longer generation time as multiplication in the host usually does not occur, and produce infections that tend to be prolonged. This basic differentiation between protozoa, helminths, and arthropods is not only biologically relevant but must be appreciated in order to understand their transmission and population dynamics, and eventually to design rational control programmes.

Parasites originated from their free-living ancestors; they evolved along with their hosts. Consequently certain groups of parasites are limited to specific groups of hosts. This evolutionary relationship between parasites and their hosts may give certain valuable information about the relationship between different groups of hosts. For example, the moderately evolved monogenetic trematodes parasitize only fish while the highly evolved digenetic trematodes are found not only in fish but more commonly in higher vertebrates. Furthermore, the more advanced digenetic trematodes tend to occur in the highest host groups. Similarly, as evolution progressed in different host groups, parasites specific for that group evolved.

Parasites may need more than one group of hosts. A definitive host is the one that harbours the adult stage of a parasite while the larval forms are located in an intermediate host. Some parasites may have more than one intermediate host. A vector is an arthropod, mollusc or other agent which transmits the parasite from one vertebrate host to another. If parasite development occurs within the vector it is called biological to differentiate it from mechanical vectors, where parasites are simply passively transmitted.

The field of parasitology is full of definitions and descriptive terminology including the types of parasites, hosts, and the relationship between parasites and their hosts. Although helpful in some particular circumstances, they will not be reviewed in this discussion because of their limited usefulness in general.

Host–parasite relationship. Entry of a specific parasite into a specific host is called infection. The outcome of such a process determines the survival of the parasite and the occurrence of untoward effects, e.g. disease. Parasites invade their hosts through skin or mucous membranes, or by ingestion, or they may be transmitted through the placenta from the mother during the process of birth, or by blood transfusion. Upon entry into the host, parasites may die or be killed, or may go through the host unchanged; in both cases no major pathological consequences of infection can be detected in the host. Alternatively, parasites may survive within the host or may proceed to develop and multiply. In both circumstances disease may occur. It is, therefore, important to differentiate between infection and disease due to zooparasites. The aetiology of disease due to parasite invasion of mammalian hosts is almost always multifactorial; both parasite and host contribute to a delicate balance that may either arrest infection or lead to pathological sequelae. Parasites result in disease because of their specific physiological or nutritional needs; disease may also occur because of mechanical destruction of host tissues. The host in turn attempts to reject the foreign invader using a multiplicity of immunological and non-immunological mechanisms. A by-product of some of these host responses is a chain of immunopathological reactions that ultimately results in significant morbidity.

The host–parasite relationship is a dynamic process; the host uses several natural (innate) and acquired protective mechanisms. The complex structure of zooparasites in contrast to bacteria and viruses poses a significant challenge to host immune responses. Furthermore, not all of these responses are protective. In fact, protective *immunity is the exception rather than the rule following a specific parasitic infection. Successful survival of parasites has dictated that several mechanisms of evasion of host protective mechanisms have been developed to ensure their propagation. Parasites evade their host's immune responses either by simple mechanisms such as intracellular location or by more elaborate processes involving changing their *antigenic structure or altering the host responses in a way that favours their survival.

Clinical significance. Zooparasites constitute a major group of the infectious diseases of man and animals. Their prevalence and intensity have not been drastically changed in most of the developing world. The major parasitic protozoan and helminthic infections of man and their estimated prevalence and the main endemic areas are summarized in Table 1. The burden of illness from these infections is staggering and the available methods of control are limited. Table 2 summarizes major arthropods that are medically significant because they act as vectors for parasitic or other infections. Other parasitic insects include *Siphonaptera,* the fleas; *Mellophaga*, the biting lice, and *Anoplura*, the sucking lice.

The prevalence, intensity, and clinical significance of parasitic infections vary in different parts of the world. They are generally more prevalent in warm climates, in less developed areas, and in the socially deprived sections of any given society. Environmental and economic factors are prominent among those responsible for endemicity of parasitic infections in many parts of the world. Attempts to control the major parasitic infections have yet to demonstrate the effectiveness of any given strategy. In the 1940s and 1950s vector control and *chemotherapy were thought to be the effective measures against the spread of malaria. Short-term successes were achieved but soon drug resistance developed in the mosquito vectors and in the parasite. Newer tools, whether chemotherapeutic or immunological, are therefore urgently needed to bring about containment of these major health problems. Furthermore, their close relationship to socioeconomic development and the role of cultural factors must be taken into consideration in formulating control strategies.

A. A. F. MAHMOUD

Further reading
Andersen, R. M. and May, R. M. (1982). The population

Table 1. Major parasitic infections of man

	Species	Disease	Estimated prevalence (millions)	Major endemic areas
Protozoa	*Plasmodium falciparum* P. vivax P. ovale P. malariae	*Malaria	800	Latin America, Africa, Asia
	*Entamoeba histolytica	*Amoebiasis	Ubiquitous	World-wide
	Trypanosoma gambiense } T. rhodesiense	African *sleeping sickness	20–40	Tropical Africa
	T. cruzi	South American *trypanosomiasis *Chagas' disease	40	Central and South America
	Leishmania donovani L. tropica	*Kala azar Cutaneous *leish-maniasis	10–20	Latin America, Africa, Asia
	L. mexicana } L. braziliensis	Mucocutaneous leishmaniasis		
	Toxoplasma gondii	*Toxoplasmosis	Ubiquitous	World-wide
Helminth	Ascaris lumbicoides	*Ascariasis	1000	World-wide
	Necator americanus } Ancylostoma duodenale	*Hookworm disease	750	World-wide
	Schistosoma haematobium } S. mansoni S. japonicum	Schistosomiasis (*bilharziasis)	200–300	South America, Caribbean, Africa, Asia
	Wuchereria bancrofti } Brugi malayi	Lymphatic *filariasis	200–300	South America, Africa, Asia
	Onchocerca volvulus	River blindness (*onchocerciasis)	50	Central America, West Africa
	*Taenia solium } T. saginata	Taeniasis	?	World-wide

Table 2. Major arthropod vectors of human parasitic diseases

Class	Genus	Aetiological agent
Crustacea	Diaptomus	Diphyllobothrium latum
	Cyclops	Dracunculus medinensis
Insecta	*Anopheles	Plasmodia
	Triatoma Rhodnius	Trypanosoma cruzi
	*Culex	Wuchereria bancrofti
	Phlebotomus	Leishmania
	Simulium	Onchocerca volvulus
	Glossina	Trypanosoma

dynamics and control of human helminth infections. *Nature*, **297**, 557–63.

Cohen, S. and Warren, K. S. (eds) (1982). *Immunology of Parasitic Infections*. 2nd edn, Oxford.

Schmidt, G. D. and Roberts, L. S. (eds) (1981). *Foundations of Parasitology*, 1–795. 2nd edn, St Louis.

Warren, K. S. and Mahmoud, A. A. F. (eds) (1983). *Tropical and Geographical Medicine*. New York

PARASYMPATHETIC NERVOUS SYSTEM. Part of the *autonomic nervous system, which regulates the involuntary activity of glands, smooth muscle, and cardiac muscle. The parasympathetic system derives from the cranial and sacral parts of the neuraxis (cf. the *sympathetic system which is associated with the thoracic and lumbar segments). The nerves involved are the IIIrd, VIIth, IXth, and Xth *cranial nerves (known also as the oculomotor, facial, glossopharyngeal, and vagus nerves respectively) and the second, third, and fourth sacral nerves. The effects produced by stimulation of these parasympathetic fibres include: visual accommodation by constricting the pupil and focusing the lens; salivary secretion; slowing the heart and decreasing its force of contraction; decreasing pulmonary ventilation; increasing digestive activity; emptying the bladder and rectum; and penile erection.

PARATHYROIDS. The *endocrine organs controlling *calcium homeostasis. The parathyroid glands are small yellowish bodies attached to the posterior surface of the *thyroid gland; there are usually four in all, arranged in two pairs, but the number is variable. The glands secrete the hormone parathormone. The essential function of parathormone is to counteract any tendency of the blood calcium to fall. It thus promotes the release of calcium from bone, enhances absorption of calcium from the gastrointestinal tract, promotes renal tubular reabsorption of calcium, and increases renal phosphate and bicarbonate excretion.

PARATYPHOID FEVERS are a group of enteric fevers allied to *typhoid fever but generally milder. They are due to infection with species of *Salmonella* other than *Salmonella typhi*.

PARAVACCINIA VIRUSES are the putative agents, non-bacterial and non-vaccinial, of skin rashes occasionally associated with *vaccination.

PARÉ, AMBROISE (?1510–90). French surgeon. After working as a barber-surgeon's assistant, at the age of 19 Paré moved to Paris as a resident surgical student at the *Hôtel-Dieu. In 1536 he became a master *barber-surgeon and joined the army. He served intermittently for the next 30 years. In 1552 he was appointed *chirurgien ordinaire* to Henry II and continued as *premier chirurgien* throughout the three following reigns. He acquired a reputation for skill, judgement, and probity both in the court and the army. Probably the greatest surgeon of the 16th c., Paré revolutionized the treatment of wounds, abandoning the use of the cautery for simple dressings. He recommended ligature of the vessels, devised many types of *prosthesis, and advocated *massage. The son of an artisan, he knew no Latin and wrote in the vernacular, but in spite of this and the opposition of the professors of the Sorbonne, he was elected to the Collège de S. Côme in 1554. His great reputation was founded as much on his transparent honesty and compassionate character as on his undeniable surgical skill.

PAREGORIC is a camphorated tincture of *opium, an old remedy for diarrhoea (consisting of powdered opium, anise oil, benzoic acid, camphor, ethanol, and glycerin).

PARENCHYMA is the distinctive tissue characteristic of an organ and responsible for its functioning.

PARESIS. Partial *paralysis.

PARINAUD, HENRI (1844–1905). French ophthalmologist. Parinaud described *conjunctivitis due to contact with animals and an *ophthalmoplegia due to paralysis of the external rectus muscle of one eye with spasm of the internal rectus of the other.

PARITY is the condition of having borne children (e.g. nulliparous, multiparous, etc.).

PARK, MUNGO (1771–1806). British physician and explorer. Park trained in Edinburgh and in 1791 became a surgeon in the mercantile marine. His first exploration of the Niger was from 1794 to 1797, when he returned to England and gained some renown by his book *Travels in the Interior Districts of Africa* (1799). In 1801 he set up in practice in Peebles, but in 1805 accepted an invitation to organize another expedition to find the source of the Niger. He was killed with all his companions by natives at Boussa.

PARK, WILLIAM HALLOCK (1863–1939). American bacteriologist and public health authority, MD Columbia (1886). Most of Park's professional career was devoted to bacteriological studies, in laboratories at *Bellevue Hospital or in the New York City Public Health Department, of which he became director. He was an early worker in the manufacture and use of *diphtheria *antitoxin, and an influential authority in determining policy aimed at control of *tuberculosis, diphtheria, and *poliomyelitis.

PARKINSON, JAMES (?1775–1824). British physician and palaeontologist. Parkinson practised in Hoxton where he recorded the first recognized case of fatal perforative *appendicitis in 1812, and published in 1817 *An Essay on the Shaking Palsy* (*Parkinson's disease). He was an original observer with radical political views. He collected fossils and wrote a three-volume work *Organic Remains of a Former World* (1804–11).

PARKINSON, JOHN (1885–1976). English physician, MD (1901), FRCP (1923), Kt (1948). A Lancastrian from Manchester Grammar School, Parkinson's medical training was at the London Hospital, where he worked with Sir James *Mackenzie. He wrote widely on cardiac disease, and was a founder of *cardiology in the UK, being physician to the cardiac department at the London Hospital and president of the Cardiac Society. He kept a footing in general medicine, and was a notable president of the Association of Physicians in 1950.

PARKINSONISM is a characteristic constellation of neurological signs due to disease or degeneration of the *basal ganglia of the brain (often referred to as the 'extrapyramidal' motor system), particularly of that part known as the substantia nigra. The condition is associated with a reduction in the *dopamine content of nigral *neurones and is often alleviated by the administration of the dopamine precursor *levodopa or by one of its analogues. The four major features of the syndrome are: muscular rigidity, bradykinesia (paucity and slowness of voluntary movement), a slow tremor at rest (especially of the arms and hands), and postural deformities. The patient's appearance, with a mask-like face, a short shuffling gait, and a 'pill-rolling' tremor of the hands, is familiar and unmistakable.

Parkinsonism may be divided into three main groups: the first is idiopathic or primary parkinsonism, also known as Parkinson's disease or paralysis agitans; in the second group, parkinsonism is the result of a known aetiological agent, such as *encephalitis lethargica (pandemics of which occurred between 1919 and 1926), intoxication with *manganese or certain drugs (particularly neuroleptic agents such as *phenothiazines); and the third group comprises a few more widespread degenerations of the central nervous system (including cerebral vascular disease) in which parkinsonism is only one part of the clinical picture, along with, for example, *dementia, cerebellar *ataxia, *ophthalmoplegia, etc.

PARKINSONISM–DEMENTIA COMPLEX is a syndrome characterized by three main features: memory impairment, progressing to severe *dementia; urinary *incontinence; and gait abnormalities resembling those of *parkinsonism. Radiologically there is evidence of dilatation of the cerebral ventricles; the condition may result from occult (or normal pressure) *hydrocephalus, and can be ascribed to *cerebrospinal fluid outflow obstruction. The association of dementia with features resembling those of parkinsonism also occurs in patients with widespread degenerative central nervous system changes due, for example, to arteriopathy. A variety of progressive parkinsonism with dementia believed to be due to to an unidentified environmental agent occurs in the Chamorro people of the Pacific Mariana islands.

PARKINSON'S DISEASE is idiopathic or primary parkinsonism, also known as paralysis agitans. See PARKINSONISM.

PARONYCHIA is pyogenic infection of the nail folds.

PAROSMIA is any disturbance of the sense of smell.

PAROTID. The largest of the three pairs of *salivary glands, situated below and in front of the ears.

PAROTITIS is inflammation of one or both *parotid glands, the commonest cause of which is infection with the *mumps virus.

PAROXYSM. A temporary but violent attack, for example of coughing.

PAROXYSMAL HAEMOGLOBINURIA is the excretion of free *haemoglobin in the urine following episodes of intravascular *haemolysis; haemoglobin is released into the plasma and passes into the glomerular filtrate. In the condition known as paroxysmal nocturnal haemoglobinuria (the Marchiafava–Micheli syndrome), red blood cell destruction occurs usually though not invariably at night and is due to the action of activated *complement on an abnormal population of red cells. The phenomenon may be demonstrated in vitro by various methods of activating complement, for example by acidifying the serum (Ham's test). The cause of this condition is unknown, but evidence of general bone marrow depression is often present. *Phlebothrombosis, especially involving the hepatic and mesenteric veins, is a common complication. Among a number of other varieties of paroxysmal haemoglobinuria are those precipitated by exposure to cold (due to a complement-fixing antibody often associated with a viral or syphilitic infection) and by prolonged or vigorous exercise ('march' haemoglobinuria, due to mechanical damage to red cells).

PAROXYSMAL NOCTURNAL DYSPNOEA is paroxysmal breathing difficulty due to episodic failure of the left ventricle with consequent pulmonary congestion and oedema, formerly known as *cardiac asthma. The nocturnal incidence of the symptom, which is related to *orthopnoea, is due to the patient, having gone to sleep propped up on pillows, slipping down into full recumbency during the course of the night. He awakes gasping for breath and usually seeks relief by sitting on the side of the bed with the legs dependent; so intense may be the feeling of suffocation that he rushes to open a window and leans out to breathe. The symptom is characteristic of conditions which put a burden on the left ventricle, such as arterial *hypertension and aortic *valve disease.

PARR, THOMAS (?1483–1635). Born at Winnington, Shropshire, he acquired fame as 'Old Parr' and claimed to have 'done penance in a white sheet' for begetting a bastard when he was aged 105. He was taken to London by the Earl of Arundel and presented to the King. He died of the unaccustomed rich diet. William *Harvey carried out a post-mortem examination.

PARRAN, THOMAS (1892–1968). See PUBLIC HEALTH IN THE USA.

PARRY, CALEB HILLIER (1755–1822). British physician, MD Edinburgh (1778), LRCP (1778), FRS (1800). Parry practised in Bath where he became physician to the General Hospital and interested himself also in agriculture and husbandry. He was an acute clinical observer and the first to describe *exophthalmic goitre (1786), *facial hemiatrophy (1814), and *megacolon (1825, posthumously).

PARTHENOGENESIS is the development of an unfertilized *ovum into an individual (parthenos = virgin). Parthenogenesis occurs normally in some plants and animals, in which conventional sexual reproduction (providing the genetic recombination desirable for evolutionary purposes) takes place at other times. The phenomenon may be induced artificially in ova which are not normally partheno-genetic, including those of some mammals, by various techniques (cooling, pricking, acid treatment, etc.).

PARTICLE. A minute mass of matter. Elementary particles are the basic units of which atoms, and all matter, are composed. There are three types of stable particle (*protons, *electrons, and *neutrinos), which combine with *neutrons to form stable atoms; but many other short-lived particles are known, and these also play an essential part in the structure of matter.

PARTNERSHIPS are a long-established feature of *general medical practice in many countries. They have increased greatly in number in the UK since the inception of the *National Health Service. In 1983 more than 80 per cent of family doctors were working in partnerships.

PARTURITION is the process of childbirth. See LABOUR.

PARVOVIRUS. A group of very small single-stranded *deoxyribonucleic acid (DNA) *viruses widely distributed in vertebrates.

PAS is an acronym representing both *para-aminosalicylic acid and *periodic acid–Schiff.

PASSAGE (usually with French pronunciation) means the process of passing micro-organisms through a number of successive hosts or cultures, either in order to maintain them or with the objective of modifying their virulence.

PASTE. A semiliquid medicinal preparation intended for external application. Pastes usually contain a high proportion of finely powdered solids such as zinc oxide and starch and are fairly stiff; they are useful for circumscribed lesions such as those which may occur in *psoriasis and chronic *eczema.

PASTEUR, LOUIS (1822–95). French chemist and microbiologist. Pasteur was born in Dôle, Jura, the son of a tanner. The family moved to Arbois in 1827 where he received his early schooling, acquiring the *Baccalauréat è Sciences* in 1840 and being admitted to the Ecole Normale in 1843. Here he investigated the optical properties of racemic acid and showed it to consist of equal parts of dextro- and laevo-rotatory tartaric acid. He became *docteur ès sciences* in 1847 and was appointed professor of physics at Dijon in 1848 moving to the chair of chemistry at Strasbourg the next year. In 1857 he was made director of scientific studies at the École Normale. Meanwhile he had shown that fermentation in wine, beer, and milk was due to micro-organisms (see MICROBIOLOGY) which were not

spontaneously generated but normally abounded in the atmosphere (1864). It was this work which inspired *Lister to introduce *antiseptic methods in surgery in 1865. Pasteur was called by the government to investigate the disease of silkworms which was bringing ruin to the French silk industry. By 1868 he was able to show that there were two distinct microbial diseases, and how the diseased stock could be detected early and the infection prevented. By this time he had become professor of chemistry at the Sorbonne. In 1865 he sustained a stroke resulting in a left hemiparesis. He recovered sufficiently to return to work. In 1873 he was elected to the Académie Française. His interest in pathology grew and in 1877 he identified the causes of *anthrax and fowl cholera and developed protective *vaccination against them. His celebrated studies in *rabies began in 1882 when he showed that the *virus was present in the nervous tissue of affected animals and that it became attenuated when such tissue was exposed to heat. Injections of the heated material would then protect animals against infection. On 6 July 1885 he successfully applied this preventive method to a nine-year-old boy, Joseph Meister, the first patient to receive it.

Pasteur died peacefully at Villeneuve-l'Étang on 28 September 1895, a selfless and venerated scientist who had contributed more to the advancement of medicine and surgery than any member of the medical profession.

PASTEURELLA. A genus of micro-organisms causing disease in domestic animals including birds (canaries, fowl, ducklings, and geese). The causative agent of *plague, *Yersinia pestis*, was formerly known as *Pasteurella pestis*.

PASTEUR INSTITUTE, THE, in Paris, was founded in the lifetime of Louis *Pasteur, and he was its first director. In 1885 he administered *rabies vaccine to a person for the first time. In 1886 the results were so good that he advocated that an institute should be founded against rabies. Money poured in and the Institute began in 1888. Pasteur attracted many top-class scientists and set up five departments: for microbe research in general; applied to hygiene; for microbial morphology; for microbe technology; and for rabies. Among the first five researchers were *Roux and *Metchnikoff. Other now world famous names from the Institute were *Yersin, *Bordet, Nicolle, d'Hérelle, *Calmette, *Guérin, *Laveran, Bovet, Jacob, Lwoff, and Monod, eight of whom won *Nobel prizes in physiology or medicine.

Now the Institute is a private state-approved foundation, which helps generate total intellectual freedom. There are eight departments: bacteriology and mycology; ecology; virology; immunology; molecular biochemistry and genetics; molecular biology; experimental physiopathology; and a clinical department. The hospital facilities were started in 1900 and it is private and non-profit-making. The Institute was instrumental in assisting the Institut du Radium to apply Marie *Curie's discoveries to medicine. There is an intensive teaching programme for about 250 students and 350 trainees from many parts of the world. The influence of the Institute spreads far beyond its walls, not only through its students, but because there are Pasteur Institutes in Lille and Lyon, and also throughout the world, which although independent have associations with the Paris one. Several of them are in developing parts of the world, and this is in the Pasteur tradition of help, especially in public hygiene and sanitation and control of infection. There are many co-operative research ventures in these fields of operation. It is regrettable that the vast contributions to knowledge and humanity begun by one man and carried on by his distinguished successors cannot be fully documented here. The Institute has an unrivalled record of continuing distinction. (See also RESEARCH INSTITUTES.)

PASTEURIZATION is partial sterilization by heating, particularly of milk, to a temperature and for a period of time which is sufficient to destroy most pathogenic *bacteria (though not their spores). Thirty minutes at 60 °C is usual; 15 seconds at 72 °C is also employed.

PATELLA. The knee cap, the sesamoid bone embedded in the common tendon of the extensor thigh muscles (quadriceps femoris).

PATHOGEN. Any agent of disease, but particularly a disease-producing micro-organism.

PATHOGENESIS. The mode of production or development of a disease; the developing pathological process.

PATHOGNOMY is knowledge of the clinical manifestations of diseases.

PATHOLOGICAL ANATOMY is a synonym for *morbid anatomy.

PATHOLOGIST. A specialist in *pathology, the branch of medical science concerned with the disordered structure and function of cells, tissues, and organs in disease.

PATHOLOGY is that branch of the biological sciences which is concerned with the nature of disease and its causes, and the effects of those diseases on the structure and function of body organs and tissues. In its widest sense therefore it covers all aspects of causation and effects of abnormalities of function and structure which result from any agent which produces damaging effects on the body, whether those agents be genetically determined and result in inherited disease, or are physical, chemical, microbial, or virological; thus the study of pathology ranges from the effects of

inheritance of abnormal *genes such as occurs in some *inborn errors of metabolism, to the widespread effects of the immediate burns of an atomic explosion, to the more distant effects on the blood-forming organs, and the eventual production of cancer of various kinds which are the late result of irradiation, through to the ever-growing knowledge of the effects of virus disease on almost every organ of the body.

Introduction. Almost every seriously damaging genetically determined or external agent of physical, chemical, or microbial nature produces changes in function which are largely mediated by disturbances of chemical mechanisms within the body, often through abnormalities of one or many of the numerous intracellular *enzyme systems. Although such changes are included in the broad definition of pathology their study is now undertaken largely by biochemists, and the subject of *biochemistry and biochemists is dealt with elsewhere in this volume. Similarly, the effects of damaging agents of any kind on the blood-forming organs and the therapy of the disorders that are produced by such effects are now studied by a further special branch of pathology called *haematology, the specialist concerned with this branch being known as a haematologist. Other disciplines which until recent times were commonly grouped under pathology, and which are still frequently housed in the same building, are *microbiology, concerned with the study and investigation of *bacteria and their effects on the body, *virology, often regarded as a special subgroup of the latter but concerned with rather different techniques and with the effects of virus infections, and *cytology, concerned with the examination and interpretation of the normal and abnormal cells which become separated from the surface of the body or of its organs or from secretory tissues of the body during health and disease. Under the term pathology this article deals with the oldest of the disciplines included under this heading, namely that which is concerned with the study of the gross and microscopic effects of disease processes.

History. As Esmond Long says in his very readable *History of Pathology,* 'The first pathologist was the first man to reason with uncommon care upon the physical ailments inflicting him' and this stage was presumably reached many years before the survival of written records on medical treatises. Nevertheless the records of anatomical treatises are said to go back as far as 4000 BC and Egyptian papyri dating from the 17th–15th c. BC record much detail of traumatic bone and head injury, tumours, parasitic infections, and the methods and instrumentation for dealing with many diseases (see EBERS PAPYRUS; EDWIN SMITH PAPYRUS). The Egyptian custom, which lasted for 5000 years, of *embalming their dead must have resulted in considerable knowledge of the appearance, if not the correct interpretation, of diseased internal organs and indeed examination of mummified remains from that era has confirmed the presence of bone diseases, infective and degenerative, as well as pulmonary, renal, and liver disorders entirely similar to those found at the present time. Throughout this time medicine and its interpretation was intimately linked with theology (see RELIGION, PHILOSOPHY, AND ETHICS), a tradition only broken by members of the Hippocratic school of the 5th and 4th c. BC where the first attempts at a mechanistic explanation of disease began and dominated medical thinking for centuries (see HIPPOCRATES). In this concept disease was largely attributed to changes in body fluids or *humours, and anomalies or imbalances of the four principal defined humours resulted in all the forms of diseases known. The description of the various disorders defined by this school, including particularly those relating to *inflammation (either occurring naturally or within wounds) and to *tumours (both benign and malignant) were well described and often well correlated with the clinical conditions which accompanied them, but the humoral interpretations were not seriously challenged until the Renaissance and continued to affect thinking almost to the present century. Good anatomicopathological descriptions were made on specialized subjects which remained for a time uncluttered by explanations involving the humoral hypothesis, the most important and lasting of these being the work and writings of *Galen whose life spanned the last three-quarters of the 2nd c. BC. His theoretical explanations of pathological change involved an even greater extension of the humoral hypothesis but his direct observations and some of his conclusions were startlingly accurate. Thus he recognized the presence of *pus in the *urine as a sign of internal inflammation involving the bladder and kidneys. Through dissection and experimentation on animals he correctly interpreted the role of the kidneys in urinary excretion and the formation of renal *calculi; he associated the pain of *renal colic with the passage of *stones and some of his observations on malignant tumours and their occurrence and spread were broadly accurate. All, however, were interpreted as developments resulting from humoral changes of which those involving black bile, in particular, resulted in most malignant growths.

Over the next 1000 years only occasional investigators and writers on pathological topics contributed significant new knowledge. The next major advance in understanding of disease processes began with the dissection of the dead, possibly introduced originally for judicial reasons, which probably began in the late 13th or early 14th c., a process long prohibited as a desecration and much inhibited after its prohibition by Papal decree (see also ANATOMY). Despite this the Italian school, from the 13th to the 16th c. probably made the greatest progress in anatomical dissection and pathological description, and Antonio Benivieni, a physician practising in Florence in the late 15th c.,

performed a number of *autopsies, apparently having first obtained permission from the patients' relatives. These post-mortem examinations, performed with the objective of identifying the diseased parts, identified cancer of the stomach, *gallstones, and cases of intestinal obstruction. Many other observations were made which are now difficult to interpret and which were unlikely to have been associated with the clinical symptoms which led to death. The 16th c. saw the dissection of the human dead becoming a more common practice throughout Europe, and the production of pathological descriptions mostly in works on medicine, but occasionally as separate volumes on pathology. The dissection of executed criminals was frequent, a practice not likely to lead to much advancement of the knowledge of disease but which at least produced increasing knowledge of the normal appearances of the internal organs against which abnormalities could be more accurately judged and described.

Throughout the 16th and 17th c., pathological anatomy became established in Western Europe, particularly in Italy, Germany, France, and Switzerland through relatively accurate descriptions of many of the disorders which affect the intestinal canal, the lungs, heart, and other solid viscera. Johann Jacob Wepfer of Schaffhausen in the late 17th c. accurately described cerebral haemorrhage as the causation of *stroke and on his own death was autopsied and an accurate drawing of his *aorta preserved. The 17th c. was a time of blossoming of anatomical studies in England. Thomas *Willis of London described the *circle of Willis, the circle of vessels at the base of the brain which supplies that organ with blood. Francis *Glisson gave a detailed description of the anatomy of the liver and, more importantly, Marcello *Malpighi of Bologna and Pisa, who was one of the founder-users of the *microscope, gave accurate descriptions of *capillaries and *red blood cells and the minute structure of the lungs, spleen, and kidneys. The microscope was used around the end of the 17th c. in Holland and about the same time by Robert *Hooke of London whose major contribution lay in his initial description of many of the cellular and histological features of human tissue. Malpighi himself was again autopsied by a colleague who gave helpful descriptions of his abnormal organs but even then interpreted the changes according to a version of the old humoral pathology. During the 17th c., pathological anatomy made great strides on the basis of many thousands of post-mortem examinations. In addition, the examination of specimens removed from patients by surgical procedures had become a regular practice used by leading surgeons, and records exist of findings both in surgical specimens and autopsies of the disorders present in many distinguished people at that time, including a good many royal personages. In many ways the basis of modern pathology was founded at about this time by *Morgagni. He performed numerous post-mortem examinations, recorded his findings in great detail and attempted to correlate these with the detailed clinical symptoms and signs shown by the patients during life. He described strokes, gave detailed descriptions of *aneurysms, of ruptured hearts, of vegetative *endocarditis, and also gave a clear account of lobar *pneumonia, a subject never specifically recognized before then; he accompanied this with an accurate account of its clinical presentation and course leading to death. Although much of what he found was misinterpreted, and was still overlaid in explanation by a fanciful extension of humoral theory, he nevertheless greatly extended knowledge of pathological anatomy and set a high standard for the actual performance of the autopsy and the accurate description of the findings. The 18th c. in England also saw the extensive development of detailed pathological texts, that of Matthew *Baillie of the late 18th c. being in great demand and running through several editions and translations. *Bright, *Addison, and *Hodgkin all made contributions which have kept their names alive in medicine today; Hodgkin was a professional pathologist who retired in 1837 from medical practice when he failed to gain the promotion he regarded as his prerogative in the hospital.

This period of the first half of the 19th c. also produced major contributions from other British physicians and surgeons interested in pathology such as Matthew Baillie and John *Hunter and from French physicians with similar enthusiasm for the subject such as Xavier *Bichat and René *Laennec. *Rokitansky worked in Vienna for almost 40 years until 1866 and developed the art of post-mortem examination into what it later became in the 20th c. His clinicopathological correlations extended not only to the association of symptoms and signs with abnormal organ appearances but to explanations of the *aetiology of disease and the functional derangements which had been found. His basic doctrine, which involved the concept of a primitive fluid substance from which formed elements were derived was, however, merely a variation of the humoral hypothesis and proved to be contemporary with a loudly and fiercely stated opposing view, expressed by Rudolf *Virchow who was probably the greatest contributor to the history of pathology. Not content with following the scrupulous post-mortem method of Rokitansky, which had led to numerous and accurate descriptions of diseased organs and their relationship to clinical disease, Virchow developed the use of the microscope in order to lay the foundations of cellular pathology (studies of the effects of disease upon cells) and applied analytical chemistry to studies of the body tissues. Final editions of his books contained descriptions, drawings, and diagrams and explanations of the spread and development of pathological processes which stand the test of much modern theory. He had, of course, the advantage of seeing the emergence of new knowledge of infectious lesions and of their relationship to the micro-organisms which were then being isolated and their presence and significance comprehended. Nevertheless Virchow's contribution remains that upon which most modern pathological thinking has developed; thus it is not too great a leap in time to move from mention of his contribution to descriptions of present-day pathology.

Present-day pathology—organization. *Diagnostic pathology services*. Justification for starting an account of modern pathology with a description of the diagnostic services which are mostly situated within hospitals in all parts of the world, is that they employ most trained people working in pathology and deal with most pathological material; further, the work of laboratories within hospitals is essential to the accurate *diagnosis and treatment of patients under a Westernized system of medicine. Many pathologists have had experience in more basic branches of the biological sciences during their training or during an earlier period of work in experimental or research pathology.

The modern pathology department in a major hospital is a large and complex building containing many thousands of square feet of laboratories, either incompletely or sometimes completely, divided into the various major specialties previously mentioned; frequently a complex of laboratories, often called an institute of pathology, contains sections of morbid anatomy and histopathology (with which the rest of this article will be concerned), haematology, *blood transfusion, chemical pathology, microbiology, virology, and cytology; some laboratories also include a division of *immunology, a rapidly growing discipline of major importance for the further understanding and development of pathology. Occasionally the complex includes a section of *genetics and/or cellular or *molecular biology. Many have their own out-patient department where patients referred by hospital staff or general practitioners directly to doctors working in the various laboratory disciplines may be examined and investigated. This practice is becoming increasingly common, particularly in relation to haematology and immunology, but all the disciplines involved may from time to time make use of the facility.

The internal organization of such pathology departments varies. In small hospitals the building is usually a single unit, and two or three pathologists specializing in morbid anatomy and surgical *histology, in haematology, microbiology, biochemistry, and cytology supervise all the disciplines within the laboratory, with the help of non-medical scientists and trained medical laboratory technologists. Administratively, many small departments have a single pathologist nominated either indefinitely or for a period of several years as the person in administrative charge. In teaching institutions or large acute hospitals, the large complex of buildings which forms the laboratories will merely be connected structurally but will have their own internal arrangements for clerical and out-patient services and will run as separate units closely related to other pathological disciplines in their geographical siting. Occasionally, and particularly where specific units have reached national and international distinction and are committed to extensive research, the buildings for morbid anatomy, haematology, microbiology, etc. will be separate and scattered more widely over a site. This arrangement carries the great disadvantage of the need to duplicate engineering and technical facilities, and inhibits that association between members of the several disciplines upon which much fruitful theoretical and practical discussion and consultation about individual patients often depends.

The department of morbid anatomy and surgical histology within a laboratory serving a hospital complex of 700–1000 or so beds will, if not involved in teaching, frequently have three or four medically qualified pathologists and a total staff of 15–25, including clerical staff and technologists. A teaching unit may well have twice as many such staff, especially if it is a centre for training pathologists, when the staff may well consist of 10–15 senior pathologists, usually each with a special interest in some particular topic and an equal or even greater number of young, recently qualified doctors undergoing training in one or more of the laboratory disciplines. To this complement are added scientists, usually drawn from other branches of the biological sciences and engaged in research programmes, and a technical staff which may vary in size from 20 to 50 people. Buildings for such staff are often very large, an average department with non-teaching responsibilities for a hospital of 800–1000 beds having a minimum of some 300–400 m² of laboratory space with autopsy room and body-storage facilities, specimen and chemical storage, museum preparation, demonstration, instrument conservation, seminar rooms, and photographic facilities in addition (see ILLUSTRATION AND PHOTOGRAPHY). An undergraduate teaching department, with the additional facilities required for students and research, frequently extends to 1000–2000 m² of laboratory and office space.

The principal work of a routine non-teaching department is the diagnosis of the disease processes present in surgical specimens removed from patients (surgical histology) and the performance of post-mortem examinations for the diagnosis of causes of death and other lesions in patients dying in the hospital and of patients who have been seen as out-patients and who die outside hospital. In many laboratories, particularly in the UK, numerous post-mortem examinations are performed on subjects who have died suddenly or by non-natural means outside the hospital, these latter being done for *coroner's enquiries, although in many countries, separate autopsy facilities outside hospitals exist for this work. Specially selected

and trained pathologists attached to general hospital departments or teaching hospitals have recognition in the UK by the Home Office, and are frequently referred to in the Press as Home Office pathologists; they perform post-mortem examinations on deaths with criminal implications, therefore acting as forensic or medicolegal pathologists (see FORENSIC MEDICINE). In addition, in many non-teaching hospitals, pathologists and technical staff are engaged on research projects, on the development of new methods, on the defining of detailed changes to be found in patients who exhibit rare or previously unknown clinical syndromes, and in regular teaching or clinicopathological discussion with other members of staff. For these purposes, material obtained through surgical procedures or post-mortems are demonstrated, with particular emphasis on unusual or difficult cases and on those which might have been affected by earlier diagnosis or more appropriate therapy. Such demonstrations are of value to clinicians, radiologists and pathologists in other disciplines, but the pathologists themselves also learn from their clinical and radiological colleagues.

Post-mortem examination (autopsy). The performance of autopsies on patients in whom there is doubt as to the precise cause of death or of some features of the disease, as well as on many patients in whom it is felt certain that accurate diagnosis has been made in life, is an important monitor of the quality of clinical practice in hospital. The modern tendency, almost throughout the world, is for the numbers of routine autopsies performed on patients dying in hospital, in whom it is felt a satisfactory diagnosis and cause of death has been established, to reduce in number. This is unfortunate since almost every well-conducted post-mortem examination reveals features which were unsuspected by the clinician, or variations from what was confidently thought to have been present. Furthermore, even during the routine treatment of fatal illnesses, complications will arise, either as a result of therapy and/or the disease process itself, which may be of future importance when apparently similar cases occur. It is, furthermore, crucial for pathologists and clinicians in training, including radiologists, to see autopsy material from cases which have or have not produced evidence of abnormality within the systems investigated. A comparison, for instance, of radiological findings in the lungs with the appearance of these organs at autopsy is of major benefit to training and monitoring in radiology; the demonstration of cerebral or cardiac lesions in patients who have had complicated investigations, carried out to provide accurate information about the functioning of these organs during life should invariably, if death occurs, be checked by post-mortem examination. Only by such continuous post-mortem monitoring of clinical investigation and performance is the standard of many clinical procedures kept at a high level and the learning process continued throughout the life of the hospital staff.

The method of performing a post-mortem examination varies only little in trained hands. The aim is to examine in detail all the internal organs, to ascertain the cause of death and to note all abnormalities present whether or not they are related to the primary disease; to sample, for further investigation, any organ which appears to be diseased; to retain for further investigation any other material (blood, stomach contents, *cerebrospinal fluid) should this appear necessary or desirable. Clearly, to achieve this the abdominal and thoracic cavities need to be opened, and for examination of the brain and spinal cord, part of the skull and spinal column has to be removed. The skin incisions and bone removals are performed in such a way that suturing leaves the body with no evidence (beyond sutured incisions) of the procedure. Except in medicolegal cases (where removal of wounds or broken bones or finger nails, for example, may be necessary for the purposes of presenting evidence), no deformation of the body, and in particular of the face, should take place.

An experienced pathologist can tell a great deal about the disease processes in the various organs of the body at the post-mortem itself. Many changes within the heart, lungs, kidneys, liver, alimentary tract, brain, and other organs are sufficiently characteristic to allow a firm diagnosis to be made on examination of the gross specimens. As examples, deformation of a heart *valve may lead to a confident diagnosis of rheumatic heart disease, a condition for which many valve replacements are performed (see CARDIOTHORACIC SURGERY); the state of the coronary arteries can be examined in detail and the site of *coronary thrombosis or severe narrowing of the coronary arteries due to *atheroma can be identified and related to the state of the heart wall and the position of any damage which may have resulted from deprivation of blood supply. Destruction of the heart wall (or *myocardium) usually called an infarct (infarction is *necrosis of tissue due to loss of blood supply or *ischaemia), is the commonest cause of the sudden heart attack which kills so many middle-aged men throughout Western civilization. Similarly, many tumours or *ulcerations in the alimentary tract can be diagnosed post-mortem and specific lung infections can be suspected by their characteristic appearance; similarly, many conditions of the brain and spinal cord or the kidneys can be precisely identified. No post-mortem examination is complete without the examination of all parts and all systems of the body. It is insufficient to limit the autopsy to the elucidation of the cause of death, or to the examination of those organs thought to be diseased. Unfortunately inadequate autopsies are frequent in practice; this results in the non-recording of many associated or unassociated abnormalities within other body organs. This renders useless, or even misleading, retrospective surveys of post-mortem examinations seeking for correlations or new facts such as complications of drug therapy, and leaves gaps or inaccuracies in knowledge which a properly conducted post-mortem examination is intended to remedy.

No autopsy is complete without histological verification of at least the principal findings, and in many cases it is necessary to examine samples of many tissues which have appeared normal but which on histological examination may prove to be diseased. Therefore at the end of the autopsy, samples of tissue should be removed from all the major organs and from any special tissues such as nerve or muscles if it is thought they might have been affected by the disease process; these are preserved for later processing and examination by microscopy.

In relation to specimens sent for examination after removal from patients in surgical procedures, the histological examination assumes paramount importance. With some surgically removed specimens such as breast, large bowel, kidney or stomach, where ulceration or infection or tumour formation has occurred, it is commonly possible for the experienced pathologist to diagnose the nature of the lesion and define its extent. The situation is never left at this: microscopic spread of tumours may have occurred which can be detected only by sampling the tissues known to be susceptible to such spread; the establishment of the benign or malignant properties of a tumour can be ascertained with certainty only by microscopic examination.

Preparation of tissues for microscopic examination. The procedure which is usually undertaken to prepare tissues for microscopic examination will now be briefly described. Many variations of this simple description are in use as refinements, or because some tissues process better with somewhat different techniques, or because one will eventually be attempting to identify some specific chemical substance or enzyme within the tissue concerned; however, the basic principles remain the same and are as follows.

The examination of human or animal or plant material under a standard microscope in order to define the relationships of the various cells to each other and to find possible abnormalities, requires an extremely thin strip of tissue to be prepared through which light can be transmitted. The average thickness attempted for these tissue slices (referred to as sections) lies between 2 and 8 micrometre (μm) (1 micrometre = 1000th of a millimetre). The relatively soft and pliable tissues of most organs of the body (as can be felt on oneself by squeezing the arms or legs), cannot in the fresh state be accurately cut into thin sections. Furthermore, to see the individual constituents such as the nucleus, the nucleolus, the cytoplasm, and cell membrane (see CELL) it is preferable to have them coloured by different dyes to produce a contrasting appearance between the different elements. Very limited dye staining can be done on fresh or recently living tissue without chemical processing. The principle, therefore, of histological processing is that the cellular state of the tissue at the time of its removal by the surgeon or pathologist is treated chemically in such a way that the final microscopic appearance is as close to that of the living state as can be achieved. A further highly desirable aim is that the sections can be permanently stored, because back reference to them is often necessary.

Almost all procedures start with the removal from the surgical specimen (or the organ being sampled) of a portion of tissue about 2–2.5 cm^2 in area and 3–4 mm thick. The site from which this tissue is taken is chosen with care by an experienced person, for it is quite clear that to take material from the wrong site, and thus to miss the diseased tissue, could have catastrophic results. All specimens must be accurately identified and that identification must stay with the tissue throughout the processing procedure. Mistakes in identification or labelling of specimens can have serious results for the patient as well as severe medicolegal consequences for the pathologist. From a surgical specimen of bowel or breast, many blocks of tissue may be taken: in a suspected cancer of the colon, many areas of the bowel wall may need to be examined to determine the extent of the malignant process; and many lymph nodes and blood vessels, particularly the draining veins, will need to be sectioned at specified intervals from the original growth to determine the extent of the spread. All this information is vital to the surgeon and his decisions on further therapy. The tissue blocks removed from the surgical or post-mortem specimen, are then fixed in a material (a fixative) which not only preserves the cellular structure but stops further enzymic action which would result in putrefaction or autolysis of the tissue. Many substances may be used for this purpose. Four per cent formaldehyde solution (or 10 per cent formalin) is the commonest in use but ethanol, picric acid, mercuric chloride usually with formalin, and many other fixatives are employed. The poisonous nature of all these materials relates largely to their potency for destroying the chemical processes of the cell: mercuric chloride is a fixative which produces great clarity in the appearance of cell structures, but it also corrodes metals severely and is a dangerous poison, a few grams of which will cause rapid death in humans.

This initial process of killing the enzymic processes of the tissues and usually of altering or denaturing the *proteins of the cell is known as *fixation and is necessary for the production of good permanent preparations for microscopy. The period of fixation varies from several hours to a few days according to the type of tissue, the size of the tissue block, and the type of fixative. The aim of the later stages of processing after fixation is its replacement by material which will enable extremely thin sections to be cut with a sharp knife. After fixation, therefore, the tissue is dehydrated by the removal of water from the block through the use of increasing strengths of alcohol or of some other dehydrating fluid. Gradual dehydration causes less distortion of the tissue than rapid processing. The alcohol is then replaced by a chemical which mixes with wax or some other plastic substance which will permeate the tissue and give it a consistency suitable for the preparation of thin sections without disintegration or splitting. Fat solvents such as chloroform or toluene are commonly chosen for this process, so that the tissue block, infiltrated with alcohol, spends a further few hours or days in several changes of solvent until the alcohol is completely replaced by solvent. The tissue block is now ready to be infiltrated with wax which is soluble in the solvent. If paraffin wax is used, infiltration takes place at a temperature just above its melting point; after infiltration by the tissue in one or more changes of liquid wax the block of tissue is removed from the wax and allowed to cool. The wax solidifies and one then has the original tissue entirely embedded in and infiltrated by wax. Extremely thin slices (usually 5–6 μm thick) of tissue are then cut from the waxed block by the use of a special cutting instrument known as a microtome, which is essentially an extremely sharp knife with a mechanism for advancing the tissue block against the edge of the knife at known intervals so that sections of known thickness can be cut from it. The thin waxed sections are floated on hot water to melt the wax and spread or flatten out the section; the section is then picked off on to a thin plate of glass (known as a slide) and usually measuring approximately 8 by 2.5 cm. The wax is once more removed from the section by solvent, the solvent removed by alcohol and the alcohol removed by decreasing the alcoholic concentrations until eventually the tissue is once more infiltrated by water, a state in which staining of the cell constituents by water-soluble dyes is possible. Many variations in the later parts of the processing procedure are performed according to the thickness of the sections desired and the type of staining which is to be done, the latter being determined by what parts of the cell system it is particularly desirable to demonstrate. In many instances a number of different staining procedures are applied to different sections from the same block, and many stains are known which demonstrate particular features of a cellular system.

Until 20 years ago, when automated procedures developed, the processing of tissue from receipt of the specimen to microscopy frequently took approximately 10 days, so that patients and clinicians waited that period of time for a histological report. Other, more rapid methods were available, but over the past 20 years apparatus which automatically transfers the tissues from one fluid to another at defined intervals and at the same time keeps the tissues gently but persistently rotating through the fluid so that interchange of the various chemicals takes place continuously, has reduced the whole of the process to 24–36 hours. Histological results are therefore now available within 2–3 days after removal of tissue from patients, thus giving the clinician much earlier information on the precise diagnosis and enabling earlier therapy to start or earlier discharge of the patient from hospital to occur and, very importantly, enabling a statement to be made to the patient within a much shorter time of the operation.

Variations in embedding materials carry advantages under some circumstances: ester wax (a mixture of sterates and polyethylene glycol), allows sections 1–3 μm thick to be cut with less contraction of tissue than that which occurs through the higher temperatures required of paraffin wax; cellulose nitrate (celloidin) embedding (see below on Neuropathology) shrinks tissues less than wax, produces good cohesion between tissue layers, and permits large undistorted sections of brain (in particular) to be cut at thicknesses up to 25–30 μm. Any variation to one part of the processing procedure will necessitate variations in the other constituents and parts of the process.

Histological material taken from post-mortem examinations goes through an identical process, although in most laboratories the surgical tissues are given priority, with those obtained from autopsies going through the processing machines and being cut and prepared for histological examination at a less urgent pace.

Several other methods of preparing tissues for microscopy are available and some methods are essentially different in various parts of the procedure because of the nature of the material being processed. Bone, for instance, is usually decalcified and has to be if it is to be sectioned after embedding in wax like ordinary soft tissue. Decalcification usually takes place in a weak acidic solution, usually of formic acid, and according to the size and density of the bone to be softened by removal of calcium the process can be achieved in a few days or weeks. Undecalcified bone can be sectioned but requires special techniques (see below on Osteopathology).

In addition to operative specimens in which whole or parts of organs such as kidney or breast or stomach may be removed containing abnormalities which require accurate diagnosis, many small samples of tissue are removed from patients for the sole purpose of diagnosis, a procedure known as 'diagnostic *biopsy'. The size of the tissue 'biopsy' varies greatly and in recent years a special cutting needle rather than surgical incision has frequently been employed. Small samples of tissue obtained by excision or by needle biopsy form a major part of the diagnostic work of a surgical histology department. Material frequently removed includes that readily available from or through the surface of the body such as biopsies of skin, lymph nodes, superficial tumours, and infections and lesions within the mouth and nasal cavity. Additionally, biopsies of the alimentary, respiratory, and urinary tract (particularly the bladder) and the cervix and the body of the uterus are frequent sources of small fragments of tissue on which diagnosis is required.

Material from these organs is obtained by the insertion of rigid or flexible instruments through which incision of the organ is possible. The alimentary tract is accessible through the use of such a flexible tube known as a fibre-optoscope (see FIBRE-OPTICS) through which the surgeon can see the lining of the organ and can, if desired, remove a small fragment of any tissue which arouses suspicion. Small fragments of the uterine cervix or body can be obtained by scraping or cutting from the exposed surface; to reach the uterine body, dilatation of the cervical canal is followed by curettage of the lining of the uterine body (endometrium) with a special curved cutting instrument. Biopsies of solid internal organs such as liver, kidney, and lung and of skeletal muscle can be obtained by large biopsy needles introduced through the skin under local anaesthesia. Such small fragments of tissue in the laboratory need great care in identification, labelling, and processing and great skill in their sectioning since failure to obtain satisfactory sections can lead to total loss of diagnosable material. Naturally, tissue encased in bone such as brain or spinal cord has to be biopsied after removal of bone for access; loss or damage or poor fixation or sectioning of such material is a matter of serious consequence and has to be avoided at all costs.

Tissue staining is a device for making microscopic structures more clearly visible than they are when unstained. In diagnostic pathology and in much research, the stained sections are thin enough to transmit normal daylight or, nowadays, light from a variable-intensity light source built into the microscope. Much the commonest combination of stains used is haematoxylin and eosin. Haematoxylin is a natural dye extracted from the Mexican dogwood tree; in modified form it stains nuclei clearly and dark blue in colour, and is also used for staining of myelin and neuroglia in the central nervous system, elastin and reticulin fibres, and skeletal muscle striations. Eosin is a synthetic dye prepared from fluorescin which stains cell cytoplasm and most supporting structures of normal organs and blood cells, various shades of red to yellow, thus presenting a sharp contrast to the components stained by the haematoxylin. Many methods of colouring the components of cells and their secretions and supporting structures have been devised using different natural and synthetic dyes. Many synthetic dyes are derived from benzene, itself a colourless substance, but readily converted to a coloured compound by changing its chemical configuration. These chemical colour-bearing configurations are called chromophores and the compounds which contain them are known as chromogens. The three main groups of chromophores derived from benzene are the quinonoid dyes (thianin, methylene blue, neutral red, basic and acid fucsin, aniline blue, eosin, haematein), the azo-dyes (Congo red and trypan blue), and nitro-dyes (picric acid and aurantin), these constituting the bulk of the different dyes used in routine and research histology.

The staining of tissues involves a number of different processes, the majority using natural and synthetic dyes originally developed for textile dyeing, although now the development and production of biological stains alone is a large industry. The action of many dyes depends upon their ionization in solution; a so-called basic dye yields cationic or positively-charged dye ions and negatively-charged colourless ions; and acidic dye yields anionic or negatively-charged coloured dye ions. Neutral dyes are made by the interaction of basic and acidic dyes and have a coloured dye in both parts of the molecule. Basic dyes stain or combine with acidic tissue components such as nuclei, and acidic dyes with basic components such as cytoplasm. Some staining procedures work by elective solubility: that is to say the dye has a greater affinity for the tissue component (fat) than the vehicle (alcohol) in which it is in solution.

Other stains depend upon reactions of colourless substances with tissue components, which result in the production of a coloured dye or a coloured chemical product which is not a dye; the latter method is the basis of many histochemical procedures. A further important group of methods utilizes the capacity of some tissue components to reduce metallic compounds with the deposition of the metal rendering that component sharply defined and (normally) black. Metallic impregnation, as this procedure is called, mostly involves the reduction of ammoniacal silver, the deposited silver demonstrating different tissue components, reticulin fibrils, basement membranes, nerve fibres, various pigments, fungi, etc. by variations in the ammoniacal silver nitrate and the conditions of the reaction.

Histochemistry is not to be sharply separated from other staining techniques; it uses known chemical reactions for the identification of particular substances or groups of substances in tissues and has been in existence for 150 years. In some procedures the end-product is a coloured dye which has been converted from a colourless solution by a chemical constituent in the tissue. The detection of aldehydes in tissues involves such a procedure and conclusions about the basic chemistry can be deduced from the method used to release the aldehydes.

In most instances the coloured end-substance is not a dye, but a specific chemical produced by a modification of a well-known chemical reaction. Thus ferric iron in tissues which usually results from previous haemorrhage, is identified by its combination with colourless potassium ferrocyanide to produce a deep blue deposit in the section which is potassium ferric ferrocyanide (Prussian blue). Methods exist for the detection of many metals and other inorganic compounds, but procedures in common use identify a range of *carbohydrates and mucosubstances, *proteins and *amino acids, *lipids, *lipoproteins and proteolipids, and an ever-increasing number of *enzymes.

Enzyme histochemistry adapts the properties of enzymes to produce a coloured product at the site of enzyme action in the tissues. In most techniques the chemical substance on which the enzyme is known to act (the substrate) is applied to the tissues and the reaction product (of enzyme action on the substrate) is demonstrated by the use of a second chemical reaction, or a dye technique. In most techniques the two stages take place consecutively, but some methods combine the substrate with a dye-forming salt so that a colour reaction occurs simultaneously with the enzyme action. A few methods involve the conversion of a coloured soluble substrate to an insoluble precipitate.

The majority of methods are best performed on frozen cryostat sections of fresh material, and all attempts to estimate variations in the concentration of enzymes (quantitative enzyme histochemistry) require such conditions, since fixation and post-mortem change may rapidly destroy or diminish enzyme activity, or permit the diffusion of the enzyme from its original site. Many enzymes may, however, be detected in post-mortem tissues, and some even after considerable periods of fixation. Rigid control of the conditions of the procedures is always necessary, and sections under investigation should always be compared with the results on tissues known to contain the enzyme and treated simultaneously under the same conditions. Further controls using an inhibitor of the specific enzyme being sought should always be used to avoid the possibility of false positive reactions due to the presence of other substances in the tissues.

Methods have been designed for the detection of many enzymes: phosphatases, esterases, lipases, oxidases and peroxidases, dehydrogenases and diaphorases represent some of those in more common use. The techniques are more commonly used in research, but are important in diagnostic pathology. Thus the detection of acid phosphatase in a secondary adenocarcinomatous deposit may confirm its origin in a *prostatic carcinoma. The investigation of muscle disease by the histological examination of a small piece of surgically removed muscle should always involve the identification of the changes in the principal muscle fibre types, the latter being classified by their histochemical properties. The specific diagnosis of the inherited or *inborn errors of metabolism may be made by the demonstration of the absence of activity of a specific enzyme in the relevant tissues, or by the deposition of abnormal products in the tissues resulting from defective enzymic activity.

Immunohistology (immunohistochemistry) is employed for the demonstration of *antigens and *antibodies in tissues and is probably, with *electron microscopy, the most significant development in histological technique in the past

40 years. Direct and specific staining of these substances is not possible, so that the methods employed involve the use of markers through which specific antibody–antigen reactions become visible. The original technique of A. H. Coons and his co-workers localized specific substances in tissues by the use of antibodies conjugated with a fluorescent dye (the direct method); the site of the latter produced a brilliant fluorescence on ultraviolet irradiation. A more sensitive procedure was later developed (indirect method) in which the primary, unlabelled antibody is first applied to the section. The site of the antibody–antigen reaction is then detected by applying a second, labelled antibody, this being raised to the immunoglobin of the animal in which the first antibody was raised. Again the marker may be a fluorescent dye, but the use of an enzymic label (usually peroxidase) has widespread application in histology, since it can frequently be applied successfully to formalin-fixed material which is unsuitable for fluorescent techniques and the preparations are permanent, while the results are visible with a standard light microscope. Any substance against which a pure antibody can be raised can be demonstrated in tissues by this technique. In practice, considerable experience is needed in performing the procedures and in interpreting the results because non-specific fluorescence is often present and background staining may occur in the peroxidase procedure.

Many antibodies are now available commercially. They require precise testing against known positive controls to determine the best conditions for demonstration of the antigen, particularly the optimum dilution of the antibody, and for evidence of cross-reaction against other antigens.

Mono-specific antibodies can now be produced by obtaining antibodies produced by clones derived from a single cell (*monoclonal antibodies). The time-consuming process involved in separating off the individual cell which is producing the desired antibody (see IMMUNOLOGY) is justified by the ability, after successful *cloning, to continue to produce a pure antibody free from cross-reactivity. It seems possible to produce antibodies against most biological substances, including many, such as *peptides, which are not immunogenic *per se*. An ever-increasing number of highly sensitive antibodies are becoming available which will demonstrate the presence of specific substances not previously detectable by any histological technique. Thus, *hormones secreted by the alimentary tract, pancreas, thyroid, ovary, testicle, and pituitary can be specifically identified, and specific chemical substances, including enzymes, can be similarly detected. As a research tool the methods are proving of immense value. As a single example, within the central nervous system, whilst histochemical methods for detecting some *neurotransmitters are in use, the availability of pure antibody for use on formalin-fixed and paraffin-embedded material allows specific

neurotransmitter cell systems to be identified, studied, and mapped with great accuracy.

The value of immunohistology to research of many different kinds can hardly be overestimated. Its role in routine histological diagnosis is more limited, although growing steadily. The identification of some viral and fungus infections is possible and occasionally best made by immunohistology; malignant and benign infiltrations of lymphomatous type may be distinguished. Metastatic tumours, such as thyroid carcinomas, may be positively identified by the demonstration of thyroglobulin; the detection of human chorionic gonadotrophin in metastases from gestational, ovarian, or testicular growths may allow a firm diagnosis so that highly effective tumour chemotherapy can be given early in the disease. Many other tumour markers detectable by immunohistology exist, as do markers of other disorders of immunological origin; it has to be said, however, that most such disorders are readily diagnosed by their distinguishing histological features and the use of immunohistology is frequently only an expensive, though beautiful, confirmatory icing on the cake.

The field in which its use is absolutely necessary for routine purposes is in the diagnosis of kidney disease, particularly in the accurate identification of the various forms of *glomerulonephritis (see below on Nephropathology). The diagnosis of a number of skin disorders with characteristic patterns of immunoglobin deposition and complement-fixing antibodies is also more certain than histological procedures alone.

Autoradiography is a method used for demonstrating radioactive materials in tissues, whether they are naturally occurring or have been introduced as *radioisotopes as part of an experimental procedure. The site of the radioactive material is demonstrated by the property of the radiation emitted to reduce silver salts in a photographic emulsion; if the latter is applied to tissue sections, the location of the labelled substance within the tissue can be identified by the position of the black grains visible on light microscopy; and the precise subcellular structures involved may be identified by electron microscopy. Isotopes of carbon (^{14}C), hydrogen (tritium, ^{3}H), and iodine (^{131}I) are in common experimental use. The technique has many important applications: tracing of the cellular pathways of specifically labelled compounds in metabolic processes; identification of the site of action of labelled drugs and their subsequent breakdown; the study of cell turnover in normal and *neoplastic tissue by the use of tritiated thymidine which is incorporated into dividing cells and permits accurate and ready estimation of *mitotic activity. Grain counting under precisely controlled conditions is the basis of quantitative autoradiography.

Quantitative histology. Methods for the precise estimation of the volume, shape, and number of the various tissue components within organs constitutes the basis of this technique, which is now being applied to the different elements of almost every organ and to the changes produced by many diseases. The qualitative descriptions of cell size (large-sized, medium, or small), number (many, few), etc. has long been regarded as unsatisfactory, but the time-consuming nature of quantitative procedures, the difficulty of obtaining and measuring adequate samples, the contraction of tissue during fixation, processing, and staining, all add difficulties to quantitative procedures (morphometry), which are nevertheless essential for progress in understanding of many disorders. The techniques used vary from various manual methods, such as counting by eye the numbers of nerve cells in a particular part of the brain, or measuring the diameter of muscle fibres in cross-section by use of an eye-piece micrometer, and the performance of similar methods on photographs, to the use of computerized particle-analysing apparatus in the counting and measuring of many features automatically. Most of the latter procedures, although more rapid than manual methods, require great care and supervision if the results are to be credible, since the apparatus, unmodified or uncorrected by human intervention, cannot distinguish, for example, overlapping cells from single larger structures. The application of the various methods evolved for the actual procedures and the extrapolation of the results of sampling procedures to whole organs or systems is infinite.

Many experimental and observational research projects involve quantitative histology: the changes in tissues following drug therapy and the understanding of lung, brain, and muscle disease are a few of the many examples which may be quoted to illustrate the importance of this attempt to be more precise and scientific in histological analysis. Some routine diagnoses also necessitate quantitative analysis; the diagnosis of metabolic bone disease (see below on Osteopathology) and certain muscle disorders are examples in which morphometry is essential.

Some microscopic techniques in use in pathology (see also MICROSCOPE). *Fluorescent microscopy.* This method has assumed great importance, particularly in research, in the last 10 years because of the development of immunofluorescent techniques for the demonstration of antigens and antibodies in tissue and serum. Fluorescence in biological specimens depends upon the emission of rays of different and longer wavelength when illuminated by light of particular wavelengths. The illumination in fluorescent microscopy is usually ultraviolet light, and in fluorescent specimens light rays of longer wavelength but within the spectrum of visible light are given off and are seen as various colours against a black background. In addition to its frequent use in immunofluorescent techniques, fluorescence is greatly used in research; when it is combined with fluorochrome dye procedures the identification of

bacteria, fungi, tissue components and heavy metals in sections is possible.

Some substances within tissues show primary or natural (or auto-) fluorescence. These include substances such as riboflavin, vitamin A, and elastic fibres but in most research and diagnostic procedures secondary fluorescence is produced by the combination of a fluorochrome dye such as thioflavin T which interacts with substances in the tissues. Thus tubercle bacilli can be demonstrated brilliantly and quickly when combined with auramine so that their detection even in small numbers within a tissue or a smear can be very rapid. A further advantage of fluorescent techniques is that they are able to detect very low concentrations of particular tissue components because even when present in small amounts, visible fluorescence is produced. Its most important use is, however, within the technique of immunofluorescence both in diagnostic and research procedures.

Stereoscopic microscopy. The stereoscopic dissecting microscope is in common use. It consists of a pair of low-power microscopes set at an angle of around 15 degrees with which it is possible to examine specimens under low magnification by transmitted or incident light; this gives a large depth of focus and stereoscopic qualities. The whole surface of a specimen can be examined by moving it around and dissection of any particular part is easy. Its commonest use is for the identification of tissue when its origin is in doubt, for selection of particular parts of tissue for processing, and for orientation of small specimens prior to processing and paraffin embedding, so that the sections are cut in the desired plane. Examination in this way of small fragments of mucosa from the bowel, particularly the jejunum when this is suspected of being atrophic, is particularly useful for diagnosis and orientation before cutting.

Polarized light microscopy (polariscopy). This instrument depends on the ability of prisms of calcite (Nicol prisms) or polaroid to transmit light which is vibrating in a single plane. Two prisms set at right angles to each other in the beam of light cut out all light from the microscope, but material which is birefringent or doubly refractile (anisotropic) placed between the prisms in the beam of light, causes the birefringent object to be brightly visible against a dark background. Human tissues which are anisotropic are striated muscle fibres, bone matrix, and collagen, but cholesterol and talc crystals share the same property. The rapid identification of the latter two substances in human tissues and the verification of bone matrix and *amyloid are probably the most frequent uses of this technique in pathology.

Dark ground microscopy enables visualization of certain objects through their capacity to diffract or deflect indirect light into the microscope tube. The desired optical effect is produced by using a paraboloid condenser, in direct contact with the lower surface of the microscope slide (with a layer of cedar wood oil between) and with light totally prevented from reaching the microscope viewing tube by a circular black disc covering the centre of the lower surface of the condenser. Light passing through the outer condenser is reflected through the specimen at an angle which prevents its entering the microscope unless it is deflected or diffracted by particulate matter; the latter then appears brilliantly illuminated against a black background. Its most frequent use is for the detection of living organisms in fresh specimens, rather than the examination of histological material; it has been in use for decades in the examination of tissue fluids for *spirochaetes (particularly that causing *syphilis) and for the detection of *trypanosomes, *amoebae, *Trichomonas vaginalis* (see TRICHO-MONIASIS) and other micro-organisms.

Electron microscopy enables the details of tissues to be seen with clarity at magnifications of 100 000–150 000 times. The resolution of particles of 0.5 nm (5Å) (compared with 0.2 μm by light microscopy) is obtainable and satisfactory resolution of two objects separated by as little as 0.1 nm (1Å) is possible. Its introduction into pathology has had effects in all disciplines and in histology it has resolved numerous previously speculative or totally unknown aspects of normal and abnormal cell structure, by the visualization of subcellular particles and has revolutionized the interpretation of many long-recognized light microscopic changes. Its influence and use in research has been much greater than its effects on routine pathology, partly because of the expense of the instrument itself, and the time-consuming nature of the processing, section cutting, and examination of the material and of the subsequent photography, and partly because most diagnostic histopathology can be successfully performed without recourse to electron microscopy. Research into the pathology of almost any disorder makes electron microscopy highly desirable and frequently essential; its use in routine laboratories is much more limited, but the diagnosis of some tumours may be resolved by its use; some inherited and acquired metabolic disorders of the nervous system and other organs produce diagnostic appearances, but the diagnosis of renal disease is the example, above all others, where availability of the technique is essential (see below on Nephropathology). Biopsy material is highly desirable for electron microscopy, but, despite the rapid degenerative changes in subcellular structures after death, much information has been gathered by the use of tissue obtained post-mortem.

Tissues for electron microscopy are fixed in glutaraldehyde or osmium tetroxide rather than in standard histological fixatives which frequently give poor results with numerous artefacts. The very small fragments (usually less than 1 mm³) are embedded in methacrylate or epoxy resin and extremely thin sections (around 0.06 μm) are cut

on an ultramicrotome using a low-power microscope for visualization of the minute block and sections. Glass or diamond knives are required for this task. Staining of sections is not by dyes or coloured solutions, but contrast in density within the tissues is enhanced by the use of heavy metal salts such as lead citrate or uranyl acetate. The adaptation of histochemical and autoradiographic techniques has enabled the precise location of chemical processes at subcellular level to be ascertained.

Both transmission and scanning electron microscopy are in use in research, the latter enabling tissue surfaces to be examined in detail with remarkable three-dimensional images resulting. Only transmission electron microscopy is so far of use in routine diagnosis and with the exception of centres for renal disease, only laboratories pursuing research projects as well as routine histopathology justify the acquisition of the apparatus and technical expertise at this time.

Rapid frozen sections. The surgeon may require a histological diagnosis during an operative procedure principally to decide whether or not the operation should proceed further; to submit the tissue for routine diagnosis would involve a delay of two or three days and clearly would necessitate termination of the operation with the possibility that a further operation will be needed when the histological report is available. To avoid this, methods have been developed for the rapid sectioning of tissue. For many years this was done by rapid fixation of the tissue in a heated fixative such as formaldehyde, followed by freezing of a small block of tissue using carbon dioxide gas and cutting of the frozen block on a sharp knife in a manner similar to that employed in cutting a paraffin block. By this technique sections some 8 μm thick and often of poor quality were obtainable but it was common for a reasonably certain diagnosis to be made within 10–15 minutes of the specimen being removed from the patient. Artefactual distortion of tissue made diagnosis less certain, particularly in early or very small lesions and it sometimes proved impossible to make even a provisional diagnosis. In the past 20 years much more satisfactory sections have been obtained with speed and without rapid fixation of tissue by taking a small piece of the unfixed material, freezing it with carbon dioxide gas and then cutting it in an enclosed freezing chamber (the whole apparatus being known as a cryostat) in which both the knife employed for cutting and the tissue are held at the same temperature of roughly −15 °C. Under these circumstances when both tissue and knife have the same temperature, sections of 4–6 μm thick can be readily obtained and after a few moments of post-section fixation these can be stained rapidly using the standard dyes; in many instances a certain diagnosis can be made within a few minutes of removal of tissue from the patient.

To achieve the most rapid sections and

diagnosis, the apparatus may be set up in a room immediately adjacent to the surgical operating theatre. It is necessary under these circumstances to have an expert technician and diagnostic histopathologist available adjacent to the theatre, and the waste of time involved in the latter arrangement has meant that in most hospitals, the cryostat is placed in the general histopathology laboratory with urgent transport of the material from theatre to laboratory, and an immediate telephone call back to the surgeon giving the diagnosis. This method, although highly satisfactory for the purpose of immediate diagnosis, must still be followed by the routine processing and preparation of diagnostic slides both for the purpose of checking the diagnosis made on the cryostat-sectioned material and for the preparation of permanent sections which can be stored and referred to later if necessary. One other disadvantage of the procedure is that since the material is cut without fixation, infected tissue containing living micro-organisms may contaminate the cryostat itself; the latter must then be sterilized, a tedious and time-consuming procedure which may put the instrument out of use for 24–48 hours. The danger is of course particularly great if the sectioned material contains tubercle bacilli or other dangerous organisms capable of surviving at low temperature.

One other method of rapid diagnosis frequently used during surgical procedures is to take a small fragment of removed tissue and to smear it or squash it on to a glass slide (tissue smears or tissue squash preparation). This, in some staining techniques, is then rapidly air-dried, stained, and examined; in others it is rapidly fixed (fixation of a thin layer of tissue smeared on to a slide is very rapid because the fixative immediately reaches the cells) and then staining of the section follows. By microscopic examination of the cells a diagnosis may be possible within 5–6 minutes of the specimen being received in the laboratory. Since one is looking only at cells from the tissue this method constitutes a cytological diagnosis (see below) and in experienced hands carries a very high degree of accuracy, particularly in relation to the distinction between benign and malignant tumours. One of its most frequent uses is for the diagnosis of *cerebral tumours: some pathologists prefer to see smears, rather than sections of the tissue cut on the cryostat, because with cerebral tumours the latter method can produce difficulties owing to the difference in appearance which sections from cerebral tumours often assume in cryostat sections compared with that in standard processed material.

In addition to their use for rapid diagnosis, frozen sections are often employed for the demonstration of special substances within cells; the use of fixatives, as earlier stated, destroys many chemical processes.

Cytology. Most pathology laboratories now have a department dealing purely with cytology, that is with the examination of cells which become detached or are deliberately removed from the surfaces or linings of body cavities or hollow organs such as the bladder of stomach. By simple fixation and staining techniques, microscopic examination of the exfoliated cells may reveal abnormalities or variations which have major diagnostic implications. The specialty has assumed great importance because of the possibility of making the early diagnosis of malignant lesions without operative or, in some instances, invasive procedures of any kind. Thus cancer of the bladder or kidney may be diagnosed from the examination of the cells in the urine. The common and serious condition of cancer of the uterine cervix can be diagnosed at an early stage by the examination of the cells that can be scraped from the surface of the cervix, a simple and rapid procedure (the Papanicalaou test) performed without anaesthetic and requiring negligible special facilities. Indeed, in this organ and in some others, changes which precede malignant tumour development (pre-malignant cytological changes) are frequently diagnosable and the removal of the precancerous areas can then be simply performed, with considerable guarantee of total cure. A further great advantage of cytological procedures is the fact that the few abnormal cells (which may be missed in a biopsy) may be found amongst the thousands which can be examined from the whole surface of, for instance, the cervix of the uterus. The method therefore has the great value of providing evidence of early malignant disease within superficial epithelium and, in theory, could the necessary cell surfaces be reached, the early diagnosis of cancer within most organs could be made by this method. Thus cancer of the stomach has been diagnosed early on many occasions by obtaining cells from the lining of the stomach by a technique which involves the patient swallowing a narrow flexible tube either for washing or scraping or removing small fragments of the surface epithelium. Cancer of the colon can be diagnosed by similar procedures or by washing thoroughly the internal surface of the colon, but the vast amount of fluid which results from washing such a large organ presents formidable difficulties in concentrating the specimen, often contaminated with faeces, and in visualizing the cells. Nevertheless, the development of instruments (flexible *endoscopes) for visualizing the colon at a great distance from the anus has allowed the development of techniques for removing surface epithelium from suspected areas of large bowel. Carcinoma of the lung, the commonest of the lethal cancers in males in the Western world can also be diagnosed by finding malignant cells in the sputum. The problem here is to obtain specimens sufficiently early in the course of the disease and then to identify the exact site of the growth within the bronchi or major passages of the lungs so as to begin treatment before the cancer has spread too far for effective surgery. Pathology departments are undoubtedly the proper places for developing cytological diagnostic techniques; a consultant cytologist should have broad general training in pathology since control of the accuracy of cytological diagnosis depends upon comparison of the cytological preparations and diagnoses with the preparations and diagnoses which are made on the surgical specimens removed later.

Specialized histopathology. Advances in medicine generally have been so great over the past 40 years that it is quite impossible for any clinician within medicine or surgery to be conversant with all aspects of the subject. In consequence, many specialties have arisen in clinical medicine which have required the development of similar detailed knowledge and of new techniques within the laboratory to produce diagnostic facilities comparable in complexity with those available in the clinical field. Thus, within large pathology departments, particularly within teaching hospitals to which difficult specimens may be referred from elsewhere, histopathologists with special interests, diagnostic skills, and the knowledge of the special techniques required for modern diagnosis have developed sections or departments devoted to the investigation of particular body systems or organs. A few of these, as illustrations of specialized histopathology, will now be described.

Neuropathology is concerned with disorders of the central and peripheral nervous system and also, usually with disorders of skeletal or voluntary muscle, many of which are associated with diseases of the central nervous system (CNS). The necessity for specialized knowledge and techniques in this field has been recognized for over 100 years and neuropathologists form the oldest-established of all the special histopathology groups. The reasons for specialization in this field are several.

The brain, by comparison with any other organ of the body, is highly complicated anatomically and physiologically, and morphologically it varies very greatly in different parts. This is in total contrast to, for instance, the liver or kidney where the organization of the tissues is similar throughout the whole normal organ and considerable knowledge of the normal structure and many of the techniques needed for diagnosis of the diseases which involve those organs may be acquired during training as a general histopathologist. Knowledge of the detailed structure of the CNS, that is the brain and spinal cord and the peripheral nerves and muscles, takes longer to acquire and many of the disorders which occur within this system are not paralleled by similar disorders within the other general organs of the body. In consequence pathologists, highly trained and skilled in the diagnosis of disorders of the remainder of the body, may have considerable difficulty in interpreting the findings produced by some disorders of the CNS.

The techniques for demonstrating various constituents of the CNS also vary considerably from those used in general histopathology; many staining procedures are shared with general histopathology but some of the complex and more difficult procedures are confined to use with the nervous system.

Furthermore, the emphasis in neuropathology is very much more on the detailed study of post-mortem material, particularly of the changes in the brain, with much less time being spent on the diagnosis of material removed surgically than is the case in general histopathology. Although a study of biopsies from the CNS is largely conducted by similar methods to those used on standard surgical histological material, the study of the brain and spinal cord removed at post-mortem examination is performed rather differently, partly because of the necessity to correlate neuroanatomical abnormalities with the patients' symptomatology and disease state, but also because it is impossible to obtain entirely satisfactory preparations of central nervous tissue with preservation of neuroanatomical relationships without prolonged fixation of the brain by comparison with other organs. Thus the usual procedure after autopsy is to fix the brain by suspending it in a large quantity of 10 per cent formol saline for a minimum of 3–4 weeks before cutting it into numerous slices for detailed study of its different parts, and for selecting material for histological examination. Success within this specialty therefore requires not only a considerable knowledge of anatomy and physiology of the central nervous system, but also a degree of patience and obsessional attention to detail which many pathologists find uncongenial, as they do the need to spend so much time on post-mortem material rather than on the diagnosis of biopsies. Specialization in this field is so great that many neuropathologists acquire a more detailed knowledge of the structure and function and diseases of particular parts of the brain or become expert in research into a small group of related disorders, or in some instances, even into one particular disorder, such as *multiple sclerosis. Many people working in neuropathology, apart from performing the routine diagnostic work relating to surgical biopsies and post-mortem diagnostic work and the demonstration and teaching which is associated with it, spend much of their lives studying one or a small group of related neuropathological conditions.

Some of the technical procedures used in neuropathology, as in other specialized histological fields, require extra training and skill on the part of technical staff. The staining of nerve cells and their processes, and of the so-called supporting tissues of the central nervous system, the *glial cells, necessitates particular fixation, processing, and staining techniques, some of which are inconsistent or occasionally unsatisfactory even in highly skilled hands and may be deleteriously affected by prolonged delay between death and post-mortem examination. This particularly applies to some of the silver impregnation techniques which are used for demonstrating nerve cell processes and, as with every other organ, to the electron-microscopic demonstration of the fine details of cell structure or to histochemical procedures. A further unusual feature of neuropathology is the frequent necessity to prepare very large sections. Large sections of other organs may be needed to demonstrate continuity and distribution of abnormalities within, for instance, kidney or bladder or breast. Sections up to 12 cm across and involving half or even whole sections of brain may be needed to demonstrate the extent and distribution of a pathological process and in particular the different anatomical structures within the brain which that process involves. Many laboratories use a form of cellulose nitrate, usually celloidin or low viscosity nitrocellulose (LVN) in place of paraffin wax for embedding brain slices before sectioning. This procedure enables large sections to be cut and stained without disintegration. The sections for this purpose are usually 20–50 μm thick, although with LVN thin sections are possible. Celloidin embedding takes several weeks and greatly increases the time between post-mortem examination and the availability of tissue sections. For this reason and because celloidin embedding involves some fire and toxicity hazards, the method has been replaced in many laboratories by the use of compounds consisting of purified paraffin wax and plastic polymers from which large intact sections can be produced with the same facility as after celloidin embedding.

Neuropathology, because of its extra training needs and because of what many pathologists see as disadvantages or uncongenial aspects of the work, is a subject in which specially skilled pathologists are in short supply throughout the world. Mostly they are associated with neurology and neurosurgical departments and, less frequently, with psychiatric units or hospitals. Luckily, neurologists and in some instances psychiatrists, particularly in Western Europe, fill some of the needs in this specialty by undergoing a period of study in a neuropathology department and then organizing and running their own laboratories, usually for the study of one particular disorder or a particular group of disorders. This is not unique to neuropathology in that clinicians working in other highly specialized fields still contribute materially to the advancement of knowledge in pathology by running specialized laboratories, but neuropathology is perhaps a subject, more than any other, to which neurologists and psychiatrists have contributed, and although to a more limited extent than in the past, still contribute to the advancement of the subject.

Osteopathology. Histopathologists specializing in osteopathology are much less common than neuropathologists, but they are needed because of the rarity with which certain tumours of the bones develop and the necessity therefore for some pathologists to acquire special knowledge of bone tumours for their accurate diagnosis, and because of the difficulties that are involved in the preparation of bone for histopathological study. Some bone tumours present diagnostic difficulty not only because of their rarity but because they have an essentially benign course and are closely similar histopathologically to some malignant bone tumours; the correct differentiation is essential for prognosis and therapy. In addition some rare tumour-like conditions of bone actually result from metabolic disturbances, particularly those produced by the *parathyroid gland which may be primarily disordered or diseased as a secondary consequence of chronic renal disease; much experience may be needed in this difficult field.

The technical difficulties of dealing with extremely hard bone have been previously mentioned; although this is usually readily overcome in the small fragments presented for biopsy diagnosis, it may nevertheless present a formidable problem in the detailed examination of large specimens or of samples of bone which have been removed for the confirmation or elimination of metabolic bone disorders, particularly those associated with abnormalities of calcium metabolism such as *osteoporosis or *osteomalacia. Diagnosis of the latter disorders involves a detailed knowledge of normal bone structure at different ages throughout life and frequently requires quantitative estimations of the different elements within bone tissue, particularly of the total mass of bone compared to marrow cavity, and the quantitative relationship between calcified bone and uncalcified osteoid, the latter being the term which refers to the tissue from which calcified bone is normally formed. Examination of decalcified bone gives unreliable results and the production of good sections of undecalcified bone is difficult. Dense cortical bone or teeth may require sawing and then manual grinding to achieve usable thin sections. Cancellous bone can usually be cut using a heavy microtome and knife after embedding in resin or by a special technique following double embedding in cellulose nitrate–paraffin wax material.

Osteopathologists tend to be associated with large teaching hospital departments. Bone biopsy specimens are frequently referred to them by general histopathologists, and indeed, they usually provide a collecting and cataloguing centre for bone tumours from a wide area, thus accumulating knowledge of the incidence and behaviour of bone tumours. The establishment of bone registries and research interest within the field of bone tumours and joint or metabolic bone disease, is an important role of the specialist osteopathologist.

Nephropathology (renal pathology). The widespread special study and increased knowledge of renal disorders has largely arisen in the last 20 years with the development of the technique of percutaneous kidney biopsy and of haemodialysis and renal transplantation for chronic renal failure, and through advances in immunochemistry and electron microscopy. Therapeutic advances have necessitated the accurate diagnosis and a better understanding of the natural history and causation of the diseases which cause chronic renal failure. It has been known for over 150 years that the first symptoms which finally lead to *renal failure may occur months or years before or may totally escape notice, but it was only with the introduction of renal biopsy by the insertion of a long cutting needle into the kidney through the skin of the loin (percutaneous renal biopsy) that precise diagnosis became possible. Repeated biopsies have enabled the natural history of the diseases and their response to treatment to be followed. Kidney biopsy is now a common procedure and the examination and diagnosis of the narrow columns of kidney tissue, which measure roughly 1 mm × 1 cm, requires special techniques and expert interpretation.

Many cases of renal failure in early and middle adult life are due to glomerulonephritis or chronic renal infection of microbial type (chronic *pyelonephritis): the former term is applied to a group of diseases, in most of which antigen–antibody complexes are deposited within the tissues of the renal *glomerulus; the size and appearance of the deposits, the various *immunoglobulins and components of *complement involved coupled with the histological and electron-microscopic appearances, usually enable a precise diagnosis of the type of glomerulonephritis to be made. From this, prognosis may be predicted and the most helpful therapy devised. The renal glomerulus, of which several million exist in each kidney, is a small collection of ramifying membrane-covered capillaries within a bag-like capsule (the epithelial cells of which extend over the capillaries) through which fluid is filtered off from the blood into the glomerular space; from there the fluid passes into the tubules of the kidney for various corrective absorptions and secretions to take place before arriving in the large kidney passages as fully formed urine; from there it proceeds down the ureter to the bladder. In people with various forms of glomerulonephritis the filtration unit of the kidney, the glomerulus, is progressively damaged at varying rates according to the type of nephritis, and its filtration capacity diminishes, until, when the process reaches a life-threatening stage, most of the glomeruli have ceased to act as effective filters and renal function is dependent upon the few which remain, many of them already being in an abnormal state. Much disturbance of kidney tubule function has also usually developed by this stage. The diagnosis of the precise form of glomerulonephritis, particularly early in the disease process, can only be made by applying some or all of the above-mentioned techniques to renal biopsy specimens and almost inevitably is best performed in centres where a nephropathologist works. Many other diseases affect the kidneys: tumours; specific infections such as *tuberculosis; *diabetes which produces a special form of glomerular destruction; many drugs; incompatible *blood transfusion; all may produce renal changes which are readily diagnosed on histological examination and most of which lead to renal failure.

Apart from diagnosing the original condition and determining the stage of renal destruction, renal biopsy may also be required after renal *transplantation, particularly if transplant *rejection is suspected. It is now possible to judge the latter to some extent from examination of urine and blood but the precise stage and cause of the rejection procedure is again best determined by renal biopsy. Nephropathology has therefore become an essential part of the diagnosis and control and management of patients with serious renal disease and is an essential technical and diagnostic aid for any team which deals with patients in chronic renal failure, especially those likely to need renal transplantation. The actual histological techniques can be rapidly acquired by competent laboratory technologists, but the interpretation of the light- and electron-microscopic appearances and the development of immunofluorescent techniques requires considerable training and experience. Electron-microscopic examination and photography of the multiple minute sections of renal tissue may take many hours to complete. The whole procedure is extremely time-consuming and dealing with 5–6 cases a week may be a full-time occupation for a nephropathologist with one or two technologists.

Other specialized fields of pathology. Forensic and paediatric pathology are two other well-known specialized fields. Most general pathologists can deal adequately with much of the work arising from children, but the development of clinical techniques which have made the survival of premature babies possible has led to the need for special knowledge and study of such infants and the specialty of perinatal pathology is rapidly developing, although skilled practitioners are scarce at this time.

Many other pathologists develop special knowledge and expertise in the diagnosis of the disorders of the different systems of the body and quite a number come to spend the greater part of their time in such disciplines. Most such specialist pathologists work in teaching hospitals or research institutes. In large pathology departments many pathologists spend most of their time in one subspecialty while contributing to the general diagnostic work and to the supervision or performance of the post-mortem examinations. Hospitals exist which deal with disorders of special organs, such as the eye, skin, ears, or female genital tract, and pathologists working there inevitably develop diagnostic and technical skills denied to general pathologists and act as reference centres, and occasionally as diagnostic centres for several hospitals which deal with only occasional cases. Pathologists working in the few hospitals which specialize solely in eye disorders obtain a unique experience and knowledge of the pathology of the eye. Producing first-class sections of the enucleated eye is difficult and requires special techniques, so that many such specimens are not tackled by routine departments but are sent to an ophthalmic pathologist. The study of diseases of the inner ear, where the hearing apparatus is embedded in dense bone, is another field in which very few pathologists have expert knowledge and sufficient experience to make a profitable study of disease states; indeed otopathology hardly exists in many countries and there is a great need to train small numbers of pathologists to work in that subject.

Most other subspecialties of pathology have arisen in those disciplines in which the diagnostic procedures normally take place at a reasonable and often high level of accuracy in the general pathology department. The great majority of general pathologists report on and diagnose large numbers of skin biopsies, gynaecological specimens, lymph nodes, biopsies from the liver or alimentary tract or breast, and quite commonly on biopsies from bone lesions. Their diagnostic ability enables them to deal with tumours from any part of the body. Nevertheless, some pathologists justifiably claim to be specialist hepatopathologists (specializing in diseases of the liver) or breast pathologists (specially skilled in the diagnosis and contributing to the management of tumours and other diseases of the breast). Pathologists with specialist knowledge in even small corners of pathology are of great value, since they become the reference point for unusual and difficult material and act as second opinions and educators for general pathologists in cases of unusual difficulty.

Experimental pathology. Pathologists working in hospital laboratories contribute greatly to research in pathology through special investigations of material obtained from patients or through observations made post-mortem. The side-effects of drugs on human tissues, variations which occur in particular disease states, the identification of enzyme defects, immunological abnormalities, the identification and classification of sub-varieties of particular disorders, the detailed natural history of the changes in the tissues in certain disorders, are all being continuously re-examined with the newer diagnostic laboratory tools, and knowledge increases year by year. Many pathologists engaged in such observational research also hold grants to enable them to pursue experimental work related to their observational studies, such grants coming from bodies such as the *Medical Research Council, the *Cancer Research Campaign, the *Wellcome Trust and many more for studies which are impossible to pursue on humans but which are vital for understanding, and commonly for advance in therapy.

Experimental pathology inevitably involves the techniques previously described but also a wide range of other techniques, some of which involve animal experimentation but many of which do not. Tissue culture, for instance, is the growth in artificial media of cells obtained from organs of the body or from circulating blood, and is a field of much profitable research in relation to human disease. The culture of malignant cells obtained from human tumours allows study of the speed of their growth, the methods whereby they may be induced to develop into more normal tissues and the effects of possible therapeutic agents upon them. The identification of the cells of origin of tumours which has proved impossible by histological procedures, is not infrequently obtained through tissue culture. The production of hormones and enzymes from growing cells is also studied in this way. Indeed, many pathologists now contribute to and collaborate effectively in work on cell biology, molecular biology, and *deoxyribonucleic acid (DNA) recombinant technology.

Many techniques of experimental pathology utilize major advances in chemistry and electron microscopy. Following elucidation of the histological features of unusual or apparently new conditions (or even conditions which have been studied for decades) much more information may be obtained by the use of cell-fraction analysis. In this technique, cells are broken down into their various constituents, so that, for instance, cell membranes may be separated and their chemical characteristics and enzyme properties determined; the products of subcellular particles such as mitochondria may then be studied in isolation. This intermingling of chemical or microbiological with histological techniques is a much-used and often profitable form of multi-disciplinary research with which almost all large research groups are involved.

Pathologists are frequently involved in multidisciplinary research which originates in other fields. Thus the development of surgical procedures intended for use on patients is frequently designed and tested in animals and assessment of the degree of success in terms of healing and restoration of function and structure may involve several disciplines, including pathology. All of the many thousands of drugs developed each year for the possible treatment of human disorders have to be tested rigorously on animals for effectiveness against similar conditions but particularly for the detection of toxic side-effects: these are determined by clinical observation of the animals during life and by post-mortem examination with detailed histological examination of all the organs. (See also EXPERIMENTAL METHOD.)

Naturally the greater part of experimental pathological research in any place is directed towards the subject in which the pathologist or group of pathologists or, not uncommonly, a whole institute, may be concerned. Thus a group interested in disorders of muscle inevitably includes one or more workers whose main contribution will be in the histopathology of the changes found in the patients or animals being investigated, in the tissue culture of the muscle obtained from patients or animals with similar disorders, in the electron microscopy of disorders whose fine cellular detail has not been conclusively decided, in observations on muscle following therapy and indeed in some aspect of many of the experiments being conducted. In institutes devoted to cancer research, pathologists are involved in the precise identification of any human disorder being specially studied, in its natural history, in the progressive morphological changes which lead to the final development of malignant tumours, in experiments in which attempts are being made to induce that particular type of tumour by the means which are suspected to be involved in human tumours, and in the assessment of therapy on humans and animals.

Many diseases in humans are paralleled by similar disorders in animals and the search for and identification of animal models of human disease is an important part of experimental pathology in which many veterinary pathologists have an important role. Naturally occurring diseases in animals have been identified which are either identical or similar to important human disorders and these lead to combined investigations between veterinary and human pathologists. The study of multiple sclerosis, of dementing processes, and the various forms of muscular dystrophy have all involved the painstaking attempt to identify or produce disorders in animals of an identical kind, since only through such identification can detailed study of the development of such conditions and their causation be determined by experimental procedures. Even after many decades the study of multiple sclerosis is hampered by the lack of a naturally occurring identical disorder in animals and by the failure to produce, by experimental procedures, an identical condition in any laboratory animal. A form of *encephalomyelitis closely related to multiple sclerosis has been a model for the study of this disorder in experimental animals but nothing precisely the same as the human disease has so far been produced. It should go without saying and without any imputation of cruelty or misuse that many animal experiments are necessary if disorders, incompletely understood and treated at this time, are ever to be dealt with successfully in humans. In the treatment of cancers, particularly the *leukaemias and diseases of the lymph nodes such as *Hodgkin's disease, immensely successful strides have been made in the last 20 years; much progress would have been impossible had the *chemotherapeutic agents which now deal successfully with many patients with such diseases not been extensively tested on animals. More basic information, furthermore, would never be available without animal studies; thus the effects of undernutrition on the development of the brain have been established by careful feeding experiments on animals and the precise time during pregnancy at which certain nutritional elements have particularly important roles can be determined only by such means. The chemical processes involved in disease states may be traced by the use of radioactive chemicals; the use of such radio-labelled substances is often only permissible in experimental animals. The testing of the origin

of particular cancers, in which human epidemiological studies suggest that specific toxins may be involved, study of the development of atheroma and vascular thrombosis for the better understanding of coronary artery disease and the development of stroke, again requires animal experimentation for the elucidation of details of the process; studies of numerous other human disorders have similar limitations and cannot possibly be obtained by observation or experiment on human subjects.

Thus many experiments on animals in all fields related to medicine develop as a result of questions which are raised by the study of patients. Many involve the solution of practical problems, such as the development of new surgical procedures or the testing of the efficacy of drugs. Many other experiments involve attempts to elucidate the basic changes which precede or are involved in the development of the disease process and the identification of the causative agent, whether this be chemical, physical, microbial, virological, or genetic. Thus experimental pathology in all its forms almost inevitably and continuously mirrors the progress being made in the study of human disease. Clearly, for humane reasons, close watch is kept on the type and variety of experiments and of the reasons for doing them, but without the availability of various forms of experimental pathology, some of which do not involve animals in any case, present knowledge of disease processes and their development, consequences, and therapy would be far more defective than at this time and would continue to be so.   B. E. TOMLINSON

Further reading
Anderson, J. R. (ed.) (1982). *Muir's Textbook of Pathology.* London.
Drury, R. A. B. and Wallington E. A. (1980). *Carleton's Histological Technique.* Oxford.
Long, E. R. (1928). *A History of Pathology.* Baltimore.
Tausig, M. J. (1979). *Processes in Pathology—an Introduction for Students of Medicine.* Oxford.

PATHOLOGY TECHNICIANS. See TECHNICIANS; PATHOLOGY.

PATHOPHYSIOLOGY is the physiology of disordered function.

PATIENTS. Earlier usage of the word 'patient' to mean any suffering or sick person is now obsolete, the term now being restricted to one under the care of a medical attendant.

PATIENTS' ASSOCIATION, THE, was started in 1963 in the UK because of anxieties about patients in the *National Health Service (NHS) possibly being used without their informed consent in medical experiments, and as the results of the *thalidomide tragedy came to light. There has always been concern that the near monopoly of health care of the NHS in the UK could lead to an overemphasis on the welfare of the providers to the relative neglect of those for whom they should care. Patients' rights to care, consideration, courtesy, and good facilities may be swamped by health professionals' interests, and organizations to further these. There is good evidence that this can occur through ignorance and insensitivity. The Patients' Association attempts to prevent and remedy these proper causes of complaint. It is a voluntary body which relies on subscriptions from its members and it aims to 'represent and further the interest of patients: give help and advice to individuals: acquire and spread information about patients' interests: promote understanding and goodwill between patients and everyone in medical practice and related activities'. It has had success in focusing attention upon a potentially neglected group whose rights and interests should never be ignored. It promotes its aims by using all organs of the *media, advising individuals who feel they have legitimate complaints, and by making suggestions for improvements and innovations to health institutions of all kinds. The patient's voice is no longer overwhelmed by strident ones from other quarters.

PATIENTS, NOTABLE (ILLNESSES OF THE FAMOUS). Illness afflicts nearly everyone at some time, unless he/she is cut off in the prime by traumatic accident. Few escape illness entirely, even if it is only terminal, after a previously healthy life. But the major fascination of disease in the famous is when it is relatively prolonged. The question then arises as to whether it contributed to, or changed, the character of the sufferer. It is the effect of the malady on behaviour that is intriguing, since the famous achieve their fame because of the influence they have on the affairs of mankind. If they had not been ill, would that influence have been exercised in a different way? Would it have been greater or less, more malign or more benign, more creative or less?

Problems of interpretation. There is a special fascination in trying to answer these questions since almost any conclusion must, in the nature of things, be untestable. It is a game of speculation in which anyone can win. It is a sphere of 'wingy mysteries' and 'airy subtleties' in Sir Thomas *Browne's happy phraseology. In the remoter past the particular illness in a famous person often has to be a matter of guesswork. The insights and presuppositions of past ages were often very different from our own. The words used for medical conditions may have changed their meanings, often greatly. For instance there are now recognized to be many causes of fits or convulsions, yet in the past they might all have been called *epilepsy. Similarly, any enlargement of the abdomen was referred to as dropsy, which, if it is used at all today, has been restricted to *ascites (excessive fluid in the peritoneum), and even this has multiple causes. For over 1000 years ideas of *pathology were couched in terms of the four *humours—white bile, black bile, blood, and phlegm. This was the basis of a concept which has

been entirely discarded: the words and ideas do not mean the same now as then.

Another problem in interpretation is that disease in its various manifestations is not understood by historians and critics trying to appreciate the lives of their subjects, just as doctors writing of illness in the famous do not fully understand the political or artistic contributions of individuals. None of these experts in their fields has full insight into different yet contingent ones. Nevertheless, despite the drawbacks, and inevitable errors in interpretation, the subject of illness in the notable has endless fascination. In addition, there is still another possibility of mistake in that we can only know something of what the person did, together with his illness. There is no knowing what he/she would have done without the affliction.

Very few examples of illness in the famous can be given here. They can only be pointers to further interesting studies in the influence of disease on human history. That disease has had effects is undoubted, especially in epidemics which have afflicted large populations, as in the *Black Death of the 14th c., and which have affected the outcome of battle campaigns. The role in individuals is more uncertain and harder to trace, since similar diseases have different effects on different people, and their effects on the course of history or their place in culture may not be agreed by all.

Psychopaths? Was Caligula mad? Historians disagree. He certainly showed very strange, sadistic, and unpredictable behaviour, and claimed divinity. It may be that that was not unusual at the time, but if it were, how much did it contribute to his own downfall and to the ultimate decline of the Roman Empire? The successors of Caligula, Claudius I and Nero, might also in some contexts be declared insane, yet their behaviour might have been dictated by the times in which they lived. Extravagant beliefs in one's own divinity now may seem psychotic, but the idea of the divine right of kings only finally expired in England at the end of the Stuart dynasty, in the late 17th c.

Perhaps it is power that corrupts and makes those who wield it psychopaths in our eyes. There are many possible examples in mediaeval times, including the Borgia popes and Torquemada of the Spanish Inquisition. The historical line of psychopaths in authority is far from extinct. Hitler, Mussolini, and Stalin spring to mind, as do many of the dictators in the world's news of today. To libertarians these men (very rarely women) were mentally sick and unbalanced, yet their influence on individuals and peoples was vast.

Physical diseases. Away from psychological illness there is the apparently safer scientific ground of physical demonstrable disease. Even here, however, there is room for much variety in interpretation. All behaviour in thought and/or action is essentially of psychological origin: it is therefore the effect of physical disease on mental function that is of interest. Christopher Columbus and his sailors are credited with bringing *syphilis to Europe from the New World in the 1490s. Columbus himself may have been suffering from the disease on his second voyage in 1494, and there is some evidence that he may have had *rheumatoid arthritis too, for he found it difficult to write sometimes. But later still he heard voices from heaven, and this may have been due to the final stages of syphilis—*general paralysis of the insane. Lord Randolph Churchill, father of Sir Winston, also suffered from this disease.

The physical deformity of Richard III caused him to be called Crookback, suggesting abnormality of the spine. Recent suggestions (Rhodes, 1977) however, are that he did not have a hunchback but some relatively slight maldevelopment in the right shoulder region, called Sprengel's deformity. Doubts have been cast, too, on whether he was quite such a villain as earlier writers made him out to be. Perhaps it is too easy to ascribe a warped mind to a distorted body.

Royal Families. There seems little doubt that Alexander the Great and Julius Caesar suffered from epilepsy. In Britain, syphilis was invoked as the cause of much of the trouble which afflicted Henry VIII. He was promiscuous enough to have contracted the disease, and his queens were astonishingly infertile. Anne Boleyn suffered stillbirths after the birth of the daughter who was to become Elizabeth I, and this can be characteristic of syphilis in childbearing women. Her failure to produce a male heir was among the reasons for her execution. King Henry had an ulcer on his leg, too, and this can be a sign of syphilis. However there is dispute about its site, and if it was in the lower third it is more likely to have been due to *varicose veins, for he was a big, overweight man. Another suggestion is that he may have suffered from *amyloid disease, but this explains less about him than does the possibility of syphilis. It may be, too, that his successor Edward VI suffered from congenital syphilis, although his portraits do not suggest this; he was so pale and sickly that he might have had *leukaemia. His half-sister Mary Tudor undoubtedly had an *ovarian cyst, from which she died, so it was probably cancerous. It was her death that brought Elizabeth to the throne for her glorious reign. The reason for her childlessness remains obscure, and she probably used her marriageability for diplomatic purposes, playing suitors off against one another. But in fact she menstruated rarely and possibly not at all, so she might have had congenital absence of the *uterus in the disorder of testicular feminization. She probably availed herself of the opportunity to become pregnant with the Earls of Leicester and Essex and others, and at one time she was medically examined (probably perfunctorily by modern standards) for a statement to be issued that she was capable of bearing children.

Many political upheavals have been occasioned by infertility, unsuccessful pregnancy, or failure to produce a male heir. One such was the end of the House of Stuart in the 18th c. when Queen Anne had fourteen miscarriages and no live issue; this brought the House of Hanover to the British throne. Some of their number, probably especially George III, may have suffered from *porphyria. This is an *inborn error of metabolism of genetic origin, with many possible clinical manifestations; it is thought that George III's madness may have been caused by it. Another genetic disorder, *haemophilia, has plagued many ruling houses, especially those of Spain and Russia, but also that of Britain. Queen Victoria was probably a carrier of the gene causing the disease, which affects males only. It expresses itself as bleeding, after even minor trauma, which will not stop. It cripples by bleeding into joints, particularly the knees.

Art and science. Illness in other than rulers has intriguing aspects too. Florence *Nightingale, the founder of modern nursing, retired to her bed with what must have been *neurosis or more probably *hysteria, since she lived to a ripe old age; but perhaps it was this, in part, which drove her to achieve so much. Charles *Darwin was also a chronic invalid after his exploratory voyages, the findings of which led to the theory of evolution. Perhaps the illness, maybe due to some infection which he contracted in South America (perhaps *Chagas' disease), was responsible for his physical lethargy. Without it he might not have had the time for contemplation, writing, and thought which gave rise to conclusions which have revolutionized scientific and much other thought.

In the creative arts, special examples spring to mind: Beethoven was deaf, and Milton went blind. How far did these conditions contribute to their genius? Each had produced masterpieces before his affliction crept up on him, but nothing could stop them in their creativity, except final extinction. It is a matter of wonder for the ordinary mortal that the musician could hear sounds, and the poet see words long after the primary faculties of hearing and seeing had departed. Whether these losses contributed to their achievement or not must ever be ground for debate and opinion.

Charlotte Brontë in the 19th c. suffered from *depression and homesickness of severe degree. She was upset by the deaths of several close members of her family, and she had an intense inner life, as shown in her novels. Her sexual imagery, though couched in delicate terms as befitted the age and the daughter of a parson, was strong. Her repressed feelings may have been responsible for the disease which killed her—excessive vomiting of pregnancy (*hyperemesis gravidarum) which may often have a neurotic basis.

Charlotte's brother Branwell died as a result of *opium poisoning and *alcoholism, probably with superadded pulmonary *tuberculosis. This brings to mind De Quincey and his *Confessions of an English Opium Eater,* with its visions expressed in limpid prose. Samuel Taylor Coleridge was another who indulged in opium. Was his poem *Kubla Khan* a vision seen under its influence? Perhaps it scarcely matters when the poem is read as a thing of beauty. Inspiration and creation are unfathomable, though it seems they can be aided by drugs and alcohol. The latter was certainly an influence on Dylan Thomas, Brendan Behan, and Eugene O'Neill in their contributions to literature.

In painting there have been many discussions about how eye mechanisms and disorders may affect the artist's vision and so his pictures: *astigmatism might distort perspective; *colour blindness could determine the pigments used by a particular painter. Yet the expression on canvas is that of the inner man, who may, for quite different reasons than the state of his eyes, discard more mundane perspectives and colours. Perhaps van Gogh is the most illustrious painter with an identified illness, which was depression severe enough to make him slice off part of his ear, and ultimately commit suicide (see ART AND MEDICINE).

Statesmen. In modern times there have arisen many anxieties about the health of public figures, especially politicians and statesmen. There was the famous Yalta Conference towards the end of the Second World War, attended by Roosevelt from the USA, Stalin from Russia, and Churchill from the UK. Churchill had already suffered from *pneumonia and heart disease when in North Africa, and probably had had a slight *stroke a little before the Conference. Roosevelt was ageing and had suffered from the effects of *poliomyelitis for many years. Stalin probably suffered from high *blood pressure and cerebral *arteriosclerosis. He certainly had some irascible outbursts, perhaps inexplicable on other grounds. Yet the fortunes of the Western world were in the hands of these ageing, sick, or potentially sick men. Sir Anthony Eden (later Lord Avon), who was Prime Minister of the UK, had his political career cut short by surgical mishaps consequent on *gall-bladder disease. Press reports frequently suggested that President John F. Kennedy of the USA had *Addison's disease, and certainly he had chronic low *back pain. M. Pompidou, former President of France, was widely thought to be taking *steroids for some complaint when he was in power.

The world's statesmen tend to be elderly, at which time some degree of cerebral arteriosclerosis is almost inevitable, and they are likely to suffer from a variety of *degenerative diseases, particularly *arthritis. The pains of this, and the impaired blood supply to the brain, may well distort judgement and lead to impatience and rigidity of ideas. There are, at present, no means of getting rid of some of these sick men who cling to power and who may use it irrationally because of their illnesses. One of the problems is that degenerative disease may come on so gradually and insidiously that neither the sufferer nor those around him realize what has happened, and that judgement and memory may be impaired by organic disease; there

is also the tendency to protect and cover up the deficiencies of leaders for fear of loss of confidence by the public at large. This is a potentially very serious matter which ought to gain the attention of politicians, civil servants, and perhaps the medical profession.

For the reasons stated earlier, it is not possible to explain the behaviour of notable people purely in terms of the diseases from which they may or may not have suffered. One can only be sure that such diseases must have played their part in shaping the character of the person for good or ill. Character is essentially expressed in psychological terms in thought and in action. Inevitably, therefore, it is the possible effects of physical disorder on psychology, or of psychiatric disorder *per se* which claims most attention. It is the boundary between the normal and the psychopath where the interest lies, and it is often a boundary difficult to draw, especially with the inadequate information which we have in medical terms. More important and less striking is the range of degenerative slow onset disease, which may affect the famous and infamous, and which may cause behaviour to change in subtle ways which may be inapparent and yet which might affect the lives of many. These may be a cause of decline in the creativity of the artist and in the decision-making ability of rulers. Notable persons are just as much heir to the weaknesses of the body and mind as all the rest: they may rise above them and use them as strengths, or they may succumb and fade, helping to raise or dash the hopes of their more mundane audiences.   P. RHODES

Reference
Rhodes, D. L. (1977). The deformity of Richard III. *British Medical Journal*, ii, 1650.

Further reading
Bett, W. R. (1952). *The Infirmities of Genius*. London.
Dewhurst, Sir J. (1980). *Royal Confinements*. London.
Kemble, J. (1933). *Idols and Invalids*. London.
Rhodes, P. (1971). Virgin Queen. *British Medical Journal*, ii, 244.
Rhodes, P. (1972). The illnesses of the Brontë family. *Brontë Society Transactions*, **16**, (2), 101.
Scott Stevenson, R. (1962). *Famous Illnesses in History*. London.

PATRICIDE is the killing of one's father.

PAUL OF AEGINA (*fl.* AD 640). Greek physician. The details of Paul's life are few. He is known to have visited Rome, but he studied and practised in Alexandria, remaining there after the Arab invasion in 640. He compiled the *Epitomae medicinae libri septem,* a medical encyclopaedia much of which was drawn from Pribasius. It was extensively quoted by the Arabs. His writings support *Galen, but give clear and original descriptions of surgical procedures. His *materia medica* comes from *Dioscorides.

PAUL, JOHN RODMAN (1893–1971). American

physician and epidemiologist, MD Johns Hopkins (1919). After postgraduate training in pathology and clinical medicine at *Johns Hopkins, Paul became director of the Ayer Clinical Laboratories at the Pennsylvania Hospital (1922–28) after which he moved to Yale where he spent the remainder of his professional life. He devoted much attention to the *epidemiology of infections within families and school groups. His studies on various expressions of *streptococcal infections at different age periods did much to clarify the association of β haemolytic streptococcal infection and development of *rheumatic fever. In the course of these studies he and Bunnell discovered the development of heterophile *antibodies in patients with *infectious mononucleosis (for some time called the Paul–Bunnell test). Later he and associates conducted studies of acute *poliomyelitis, showing the enteric and viraemic early phases of the infection. Later he developed the technique of 'serological epidemiology', that is testing sera for specific antibodies in samples obtained from various age and population groups from different parts of the world.

PAUL–BUNNELL TEST. A test for the presence in serum of the sheep erythrocyte *agglutinins (heterophil antibodies) characteristic of *infectious mononucleosis.

PAVLOV, IVAN PETROVICH (1849–1936). Russian physiologist, MD St Petersburg (1879). After working with *Heidenhain and with *Ludwig, in 1890 Pavlov became professor of pharmacology at the Military Medical Academy and director of the Experimental Medical Institute in St Petersburg. His early work was on the circulation and control of blood pressure but he soon turned to the physiology of digestion where his skill as an animal operator enabled him to make notable advances. For this work he was awarded the Nobel prize in 1904. The latter part of his working life was occupied by his researches on '*conditioned reflexes', the field for which he is now particularly remembered.

PEARL, RAYMOND (1879–1940). American biostatistician, Ph.D. University of Michigan (1902). After research in biology at the University of Michigan, the University of Pennsylvania, and the Maine Agricultural Station, Pearl moved to *Johns Hopkins as professor of biometry. He is looked upon as a pioneer in statistical treatment of biological phenomena, including human fertility, population changes, and mortality.

PEARSON, KARL (1857–1936). British biologist and mathematician, BA Cambridge (1879), FRS (1896). Pearson was appointed Goldsmid professor of applied mathematics and mechanics in London in 1884, and in 1891 became Gresham professor of geometry. Thereafter he became increasingly interested in *biometry and *eugenics. In 1911 he was made the first Galton professor of eugenics. He founded the journal *Biometrika* in 1901 and was an influential teacher of *statistics and biometry.

PECTORILOQUY is the transmission of the spoken voice through the chest wall, which can be assessed by both *palpation and by *auscultation. When even a whisper is loud and clearly articulated as heard through the stethoscope, the sign of 'whispering pectoriloquy' is said to be present; it suggests abnormally increased sound conductivity between bronchi and surface due, for example, to consolidation of the intervening lung *parenchyma (as in lobar *pneumonia).

PEDICULUS CAPITIS, the head louse, is a species closely related to the *body louse but whose habitat is restricted to the hair of the head; unlike the body louse, it is not known to be a vector of disease. Infestation with head lice, common under institutional conditions, is nevertheless of great nuisance value as well as socially distressing. The active parasites are easily recognized with the naked eye, as are the eggs or nits which are firmly adherent to hair shafts.

PEDICULUS CORPORIS. See BODY LOUSE.

PEDICULUS PUBIS. See CRAB LOUSE.

PEDIGREE ANALYSIS is the study of the blood relatives of a patient with a particular disease in order to determine whether it is likely to be of genetic origin and, if so, the likely pattern of inheritance (e.g. autosomal dominant, autosomal recessive, sex-linked recessive, polygenic, etc.). Pedigree analysis to be reliable requires observation (preferably direct) of sufficient members (preferably all) of several successive generations of the family concerned; and partial as well as complete expressions of the abnormality must be sought. In pedigree investigation the original patient is usually known as the index case, the proband, or the propositus. See GENETICS.

PEDODONTIST. A dentist specializing in the dental care of children. See DENTISTRY.

PEDUNCLE. A stalk or stem; any stem-like structure serving as attachment, for example of a tumour.

PELIOSIS RHEUMATICA. Henoch–Schönlein (allergic or vascular) purpura associated with non-migratory polyarthritis, chiefly of the knees and ankles; it is also known as Schönlein's disease or purpura rheumatica.

PELLAGRA is the deficiency syndrome resulting from lack of *niacin in the diet, niacin (or vitamin B_3) being the generic term for nicotinic acid and its physiologically active amide nicotinamide. The cardinal manifestations, often accompanied by those due to deficiency of other dietary components, are thickness, roughening, and pigmentation of exposed skin areas (pellagra = 'rough skin'), inflammation of the tongue, diarrhoea, and various mental disturbances leading to *dementia. Pellagra is rarely encountered under conditions of Western civilization except when secondary to *alcoholism, intestinal *malabsorption, or one or two rarer conditions. Elsewhere it is associated particularly with maize-dependent diets.

PELVIMETRY is the measurement of the dimensions of the *pelvis, of particular importance in *obstetrics.

PELVIS. The lower part of the trunk of the body, comprising the region bounded by the two hip bones and the sacral and coccygeal portions of the spine.

PEMOLINE is a weak central nervous system *stimulant.

PEMPHIGUS is a descriptive term for skin diseases characterized by prominent blister formation.

PENFIELD, WILDER GRAVES (1891–1976). Canadian neurosurgeon, MD Johns Hopkins (1918). Born in the USA and later naturalized Canadian. Penfield received his surgical training in New York City; he moved to Montreal in 1928 to become surgeon to the *Royal Victoria Hospital and first director of the Montreal Neurological Institute. In the course of craniotomies performed under local anaesthesia, for treatment of focal *epilepsy or for removal of *tumours, he was able to add important information to knowledge of areas of cortical function (see NEUROSURGERY).

PENICILLAMINE is a *chelating agent, used in the treatment of heavy metal poisoning and other conditions where chelation is desired. It has also been used in the treatment of *rheumatoid arthritis. Penicillamine is an *amino acid obtained from the hydrolysis of *penicillins.

PENICILLIN was the first of the *antibiotics (1941), for which the 1945 Nobel prize was awarded to *Fleming, *Florey, and *Chain. The name is now a generic term for a large number of derivatives of 6-amino-penicillanic acid obtained naturally or semisynthetically from the moulds *Penicillium* and *Aspergillus* (the original penicillin G was from *Penicillium notatum*). They exert their antibacterial action by interfering with the synthesis of an essential component of bacterial cell walls known as peptidoglycan; there is no action against cells of host tissues except in a few individuals with a specific *allergy to the penicillin molecule. Collectively, the penicillins have a wide spectrum of activity against micro-organisms: it includes particularly those which are gram-positive (staphylococci, streptococci, pneumococci) but also some which are gram-negative (meningococci, gonococci); and some *spirochaetes (including that responsible for *syphilis), some *clostridia, and some *fungi. Antibacterial spectra vary between different penicillins.

PENIS. The male external organ of micturition and copulation, developmentally homologous with the female *clitoris. (Phallus is not an exact synonym, being reserved for the erect penis.)

PENNSYLVANIA, THE MEDICAL COLLEGE OF, was founded in 1850 as the Female Medical College of Pennsylvania. Among the Quakers of Philadelphia women were accepted more as the equals of men than in most other societies. Many male Quaker doctors were more willing to take women as apprentices—the pattern of medical education of the time—than other contemporaries. However, as in Europe, women still found difficulty in obtaining degrees from medical institutions. A benefactor of Philadelphia was found in William Mullen. With the aid of Joseph S. Longshore the Female Medical College was started. An Act of incorporation was granted in 1850 by the Legislature with very little opposition. Forty women began medical studies in the first year. The College was thus in the forefront of the fight for women to become full members of the medical profession. The Civil War temporarily closed the College, but then, under a succession of able deans, it flourished. The earliest was Ann Preston who insisted on the founding of The Women's Hospital in 1861, to provide clinical facilities for education. This came into being because of male opposition to women attending the practice of other hospitals in Philadelphia. By 1867 the name was changed to that of The Women's Medical College of Pennsylvania. Slowly the institution progressed through familiar phases of expansion and dissension, as in similar enterprises elsewhere. Pavilion Hospital was opened in 1904. In 1913 the hospital and College were alongside one another, though the College later moved to a new site on Henry Avenue. The First World War and its aftermath brought financial problems and so did the requirement of the *American Medical Association, in its role of setting standards of medical education, in 1935 that there should be six full-time professors. On both occasions a great benefactor was found in Mrs James Starr Jr, wife of a philanthropist. Ultimately the fight for medical education for women was won and in 1969 the name was changed again to that of The Medical College of Pennsylvania. Men were then admitted to its courses, to its staff, and to the offices of dean and president. (See also WOMEN IN MEDICINE II.)

PEPPER, WILLIAM (1843–98). American physician, MD Pennsylvania (1864). Pepper remained in Philadelphia, and became professor of medicine and dean at the medical school of the University of Pennsylvania, making substantial contributions to its development. He wrote extensively on clinical medicine, and was a leader in the founding of several American medical societies. He persuaded William *Osler to move to Pennsylvania from McGill (before Osler went on to *Johns Hopkins).

PEPSIN is one of the important enzymes of *digestion, secreted by the *stomach and responsible for breaking down *proteins into *polypeptides.

PEPTIC ULCER is ulceration of the stomach, lower oesophagus, or first part of the duodenum, that is those parts of the gastrointestinal tract subjected to the action of the *hydrochloric acid and *pepsin secreted by the stomach. Peptic ulcer is exceedingly common; between 10 and 20 per cent of the population develop an ulcer at some time in their lives. Duodenal ulcers are commoner than those in the stomach (gastric ulcers), although this ratio varies between different populations. Men are more often affected than women, particularly in the case of duodenal ulcer. Symptoms vary in severity, and in any case tend to be remittent. Chief among them is periodic epigastric pain which at its worst can be quite disabling. The major complications are haemorrhage, perforation into the peritoneal cavity, and obstruction at the outlet of the stomach (pyloric stenosis). The causation of peptic ulcer is not well understood and is probably complex. Mental and emotional stress is usually held to play a part, and it is known that genetic factors are also important.

PEPTIDE. A compound of two or more *amino acids linked together by peptide bonds; a peptide bond (—CO.NH—) is formed from the union of the carboxyl group (COOH) of one amino acid with the amino group (NH_2) of another, water (H_2O) being lost in the process. Peptides are classified according to the number of amino acid residues (or cores) they contain, for example dipeptides, octapeptides, polypeptides, etc.

PERCEPTION. Appreciation of a sensory stimulus.

PERCIVAL, THOMAS (1740–1804). British health reformer, MD London (1765). Percival holds an important place in epidemiology for his analysis of *bills of mortality from 1772–6, and for his *Code of Medical Ethics* published privately in 1794, and later in 1803. His intellectual forebears were *Pringle and *Lind, whose concerns were health in the army and navy respectively, and he paved the way for *Southwood Smith and Edwin *Chadwick, the great health reform pioneers.

PERCUSSION is a standard method of physical examination whereby the resonance of structures lying beneath the body surface is assessed by striking it to elicit a sound. The usual technique is to lay one hand on the surface with the fingers separated, and to tap the middle phalanx of the middle finger with the tip of the other middle finger.

PERFUSION is the blood flow through an organ, tissue, or part.

PERGAMUM was the capital city of an ancient kingdom in Asia Minor (alternative spelling Pergamon). Pergamum is famous for the school of sculpture which flourished there in the 3rd and 2nd c. BC; for the early Church which was founded there in the 1st c. AD; and for having been the birthplace of *Galen in AD 131.

PERIARTERITIS is inflammation of the outer arterial wall and of the tissues immediately surrounding it. 'Periarteritis nodosa' was formerly used for the condition of which the preferred designation is now '*polyarteritis nodosa'.

PERIARTERITIS NODOSA is the term formerly used for polyarteritis nodosa. See POLYARTERITIS.

PERIARTHRITIS is inflammation of the tissues immediately surrounding a joint.

PERICARDIAL EFFUSION is the accumulation of fluid within the *pericardium, which may accompany *pericarditis or occur as part of generalized fluid retention. Rapid or large accumulations cause *tamponade.

PERICARDITIS is inflammation of the *pericardium, which may be involved in a variety of pathological processes, infective and otherwise. Pericarditis may be incidental to some other major illness (*coronary thrombosis, *renal failure, *carcinoma, *trauma, etc.) or may present *sui generis*. When the latter is the case, the commonest aetiologies are *rheumatic fever, *virus infection, and *tuberculosis.

PERICARDIUM. The fibroserous membrane enclosing the heart; like the serous membranes of the *pleura and the *peritoneum, it has parietal and visceral layers which move against each other and which are separated by a potential space.

PERIMETRY is the measurement of the field of peripheral vision.

PERINEUM. The surface area of the pelvic outlet, comprising the region between the external *genitalia in front and the *anal orifice behind.

PERIOD. Any interval of time. The more precise physical definition is the constant time interval between recurrences of a periodic (regularly repetitive) function.

PERIODIC ACID–SCHIFF REACTION. A histological staining technique for revealing the presence of *glycogen, neutral *polysaccharides, and *glycoproteins in tissue sections. The section is treated first with periodic acid and then with Schiff's reagent (a fuchsin stain for detecting *aldehydes).

PERIODIC DISEASE is a syndrome of unknown aetiology characterized by various combinations of fever, joint pain, oedema, vomiting, and abdominal pain. The symptom complex recurs and subsides at regular intervals in individuals who otherwise appear to remain perfectly healthy.

PERIODIC RESPIRATION is any pattern of breathing in which a period of hyperventilation alternates with one of hypoventilation and/or apnoea. *Cheyne–Stokes respiration is the most familiar type.

PERIODONTICS. See DENTISTRY IN THE UK; DENTISTRY IN THE USA.

PERIODONTIST. See DENTISTRY IN THE UK; DENTISTRY IN THE USA.

PERIODONTITIS is inflammation of the tissues surrounding and supporting the teeth, a major cause of dental trouble and tooth loss. See DENTISTRY.

PERIOSTEUM. The thin sheath of specialized connective tissue carrying blood vessels and nerves which envelops all bones. Its integrity is essential for new bone formation in adult life and therefore for the healing of fractures.

PERIPHERAL VASCULAR RESISTANCE. The overall resistance offered to blood flow in the periphery of the blood vascular system, which is determined by the state of contraction or relaxation of the *arterioles. The peripheral vascular resistance may be roughly assessed as the ratio of the mean arterial blood pressure to the total peripheral blood flow (normally identical to the *cardiac output). In arterial *hypertension, it follows that if the cardiac output is normal, the total peripheral vascular resistance must be abnormally raised.

PERISTALSIS. The wavelike contractions of involuntary muscle which continually pass along the long axis of tubular organs, notably the *gastrointestinal tract, propelling the contents in a forward direction.

PERITONEAL DIALYSIS. See RENAL DIALYSIS.

PERITONEOSCOPY is synonymous with *laparoscopy.

PERITONEUM. The serous membrane of the abdomen, consisting of a parietal layer lining the abdominal and pelvic walls continuous with a visceral layer which encloses each abdominal structure. The layers are mobile relative to each other, and a potential space exists between them (the peritoneal cavity).

PERMEABILITY. A structure is said to be permeable to a substance if it allows that substance to pass through it.

PERNICIOUS ANAEMIA is *megaloblastic anaemia due to impaired absorption of *cyanocobalamin (vitamin B_{12}), caused in turn by a gastric defect in which there is *achlorhydria (an important diagnostic feature), and the *gastric juice is also deficient in 'intrinsic factor', a protein substance which promotes B_{12} absorption. The aetiology is unknown, but it seems likely that *autoimmunity plays a part in the pathogenesis. The essential features are those of severe and progressive anaemia; the red blood cells are abnormally large (macrocytosis), so that the mean corpuscular volume (MCV) is elevated. Neurological symptoms may develop, due to *neuropathy or to degeneration of the lateral and posterior columns of the spinal cord (subacute combined degeneration of the spinal cord). Pernicious anaemia (or Addisonian anaemia as it is also called, *Addison having described the condition in 1849) was almost invariably fatal until the classic discovery by *Minot and Murphy (1926) of the effect of feeding liver, a landmark which led ultimately to the identification of vitamin B_{12}.

PERSEVERATION is the persistent repetition of words or actions despite the patient's efforts to say or do something else. See LANGUAGE, COGNITION, AND HIGHER CEREBRAL FUNCTION.

PERSONA is the term used by *Jung to signify the set of attitudes adopted by an individual to fit the role he perceives for himself in society; in other words, the 'persona' is the personality displayed to the world, as opposed to the inner or unconscious personality, which Jung termed the 'anima'.

PERSONALITY is an inclusive term used to indicate the totality of behavioural, attitudinal, intellectual, and emotional characteristics of an individual.

PERSPIRATION. Sweat, *sweating.

PERTUSSIS is a synonym for whooping cough. Pertussis is a highly contagious infection of the respiratory tract with a marked predilection for infants and young children, usually conferring lifelong immunity. It is caused by the bacterium *Bordetella pertussis*, formerly known as *Haemophilus pertussis*. The common name derives from the characteristic inspiratory whoop which follows the prolonged and distressing spasms of coughing.

Whooping cough is a dangerous as well as an unpleasant disease; serious complications can occur during the acute illness, which has a significant mortality, and it leaves some patients with a lifelong legacy of crippling respiratory disability. Active *immunization effectively reduces both frequency and severity. This should be initiated at the age of about two months, and requires three spaced injections; it is usually combined in a triple vaccine protecting also against *diphtheria and *tetanus.

PERTUSSIS VACCINATION. Active immunization against whooping cough using a killed suspension of *Bordetella pertussis*. See PERTUSSIS.

PERUVIAN BARK is a synonym for cinchona bark (Jesuit's bark, etc.). See QUININE.

PERVERSION. Deviant sexual behaviour, that is other than normal sexual intercourse. Many such deviations are no longer regarded as either pathological or socially unacceptable and the less pejorative term 'sexual deviance' is often preferred.

PES CAVUS. Increased concavity of the longitudinal arch of the foot.

PESSARY. A vaginal *suppository, or a mechanical device inserted into the *vagina to provide tissue support or to prevent insemination of the *uterus.

PETECHIA. A tiny reddish punctate spot in skin or *mucous membrane due to capillary *haemorrhage.

PETERS, JOHN PUNNETT (1887–1950). American physician. Peters graduated at Yale, but studied medicine at Columbia. He returned to Yale in 1921, and remained there, becoming senior professor in the department of medicine. His scientific interests lay in body fluid and in renal disease, leading to the publication of *Body Water*; but he had wide interests in the application of chemistry to clinical medicine, expressed most fully in his collaboration with van *Slyke, in *Quantitative Clinical Chemistry*. The two volumes, *Methods* and *Interpretation* were indispensable handbooks from their first appearance in 1931. Peters was a liberal in his concern for the general availability of medical care; and in his resistance to McCarthyism, tangibly expressed in his reinstatement by the Supreme Court to the post of consultant to the surgeon-general of the US army, from which he had been dismissed.

PETHIDINE is a synthetic narcotic analgesic with actions similar to but somewhat less potent than those of *morphine; like morphine, it is highly addictive. Its analgesic effect is prompt but short-lived and therefore not suited to the relief of pain due to terminal *malignant disease. It is widely used in *obstetric analgesia, and is the analgesic of choice when intracranial disease is known or suspected. Pethidine is also known as meperidine or Demerol® (in the USA).

PETIT, JEAN LOUIS (1674–1760). French surgeon, MS (1700), FRS (1715). After training in Paris Petit became an army surgeon in 1692. In 1700 he became a master of surgery and left the army to teach anatomy and surgery. He earned a great reputation and was acclaimed as the first surgeon in France. In 1731 he founded L'Académie des Chirurgiens. He was elected a fellow of the Royal Society in 1715 having published the important *L'art de guérir les maladies des os* (1705). Petit invented the screw-tourniquet, undertook the first *mastoidectomy in 1736, and distinguished *cerebral compression from *concussion. The anatomical area bounded by the iliac crest, the latissimus dorsi muscle, and the external oblique muscles is known as Petit's triangle.

PETIT MAL is a specific form of minor *epilepsy, characterized by temporary lapses of consciousness lasting only a few seconds and beginning and ending abruptly; the patient, usually a child or young adult, may be unaware that anything has happened and carry on with whatever he was doing. Attacks may occur only occasionally, or may be up to several scores a day. Petit mal, also known as 'absence seizure' is associated with a characteristic *electroencephalographic (EEG) pattern.

PETRI DISH. A circular flat-bottomed vertical-sided shallow glass dish with a slightly larger glass cover of similar shape, in which micro-organisms are cultured on a nutrient medium.

PETTENKOFER, MAX JOSEF VON (1818–1901). German physician and hygienist, MD Munich (1843). After a short spell on the stage, Pettenkofer turned to medicine studying under *Liebig. He was made professor of dietetics and medical chemistry in Munich in 1847; he moved to the chair of hygiene in 1852. He founded the Institute of Hygiene in Munich in 1879. Although one of the pioneers of hygiene he did not accept that some diseases had a bacterial cause, believing them of chemical origin. To prove his point he drank a pure culture of *Vibrio cholerae* and suffered no ill-effect. In addition to his contribution to public health most of his researches were in the field of *metabolism. In old age he became severely depressed and committed suicide at the age of 83.

PETTY, SIR WILLIAM (1623–87). British physician and political economist, DM Oxford (1649). Petty became a fellow of Brasenose College, Oxford, and professor of anatomy in 1651. In 1652 he was made physician-general to the army in Ireland and surveyed and mapped that country. He was knighted in 1662 and was a founder fellow of the Royal Society. At the end of Cromwell's era of Commonwealth he fell from grace, but later enjoyed the favour of Charles II. A distinguished administrative and financial reformer, Petty was a pioneer political economist who urged the need for statistical data. He was too an ingenious inventor; he designed a double-keeled vessel and tried to install power in a ship.

PFEIFFER, RICHARD FRIEDRICH JOHANNES (1858–1945). German bacteriologist, MD Berlin (1880). Pfeiffer worked with *Koch from 1887 until he became a professor in the Institute of Hygiene in 1894. He moved to the chair of hygiene in Königsberg in 1899 and to that in Breslau in 1909. In 1892 he described the *influenza bacillus (*Haemophilus influenzae*), now known not to be the cause of influenza, and in 1896 *Micrococcus catarrhalis*. He established the life cycle of *Coccidium oviforme* in rabbits in 1892, and in 1894 described *bacteriolysis.

PFLÜGER, EDWARD FRIEDRICH WILHELM (1829–1910). German physiologist, MD Berlin (1855). A pupil of Johannes *Müller Pflüger was made professor of physiology in Bonn in 1859. Although he was an experimental embryologist and an ingenious designer of instruments, most of his research was into *metabolism. He was especially interested in respiratory gaseous exchange and was responsible for the concept of *respiratory quotient.

pH is a measure of *hydrogen ion concentration expressed as its negative logarithm to the base ten. A solution with a pH of 7 is neutral. Solutions with a pH of less than 7 are acidic and those with a pH of more than 7 are alkaline.

PHACOMATOSIS is a term which embraces a number of genetically determined neurological disorders associated with multiple *hamartomas of the skin and eye. They include *neurofibromatosis and *tuberous sclerosis, and are also known as the neurocutaneous syndromes.

PHAEOCHROMOCYTOMA. A *chromaffinoma of the *adrenal medulla or *sympathetic ganglia which secretes excessive quantities of *adrenaline and *noradrenaline, causing episodic or persistent *hypertension.

PHAGOCYTE. Any cell able to ingest foreign materials. Many cells have this property to some degree, but the most intensely phagocytic are the *polymorphs, the *monocytes, and the *macrophages (the 'professional' phagocytes).

PHAGOCYTOSIS is the process by which a *phagocyte engulfs into its cytoplasm other cells, bacteria, or other particulate matter by flowing all around the foreign object, forming a vacuole.

PHALLUS. The erect *penis; a word used most often in the context of its ancient symbolism.

PHANTOM LIMB. An illusion of the presence of an amputated limb, which may be associated with pain, aches, or *paraesthesiae referred to the absent part.

PHARMACEUTICAL INDUSTRY. The pharmaceutical industry in the 1980s has three outstanding characteristics: it is highly successful; it is completely international; and it is centrally dependent on its research and innovation. Understandably, these three characteristics are closely interlinked. First, the world-wide growth of the industry since the 1940s has resulted from its major role in the discovery and development of the vast majority of modern medicines in use today (Schwartzman, 1976). In turn, the cost of the research involved is such that new medicines must be sold in all countries if this initial investment is to be recovered. And the risks of failure in research are such that high returns are necessary to attract this investment in the first place. However, the very success of the industry, and the central role which its discoveries play in the practice of medicine, have given rise to economic and ethical difficulties. The growth of the modern industry, its organization, and activities, and the controversial issues which surround it will be discussed briefly in this article.

Historical background. The antecedents of the present-day industry are extremely ancient and very varied. For example, in the UK the first pharmaceutical manufacturing organization was established by the Worshipful *Society of Apothecaries of London in 1671. Between 1702 and 1805 this laboratory had the monopoly of the supply of medicines to the Royal Navy, and it also supplied the army, the East India Company, and the colonies for many years (Haines, 1976).

During the 19th c., many individual pharmacists turned to large-scale manufacture to supplement their own local dispensing activities. They produced standard preparations of bulk substances and they manufactured specially formulated preparations from these ingredients of natural origin. By the end of the 19th c. several of these manufacturers had established large international businesses. Only a few of them, however, have survived the transition from this traditional pattern of manufacturing in the last century to become established as research-based manufacturers of synthetic pharmaceutical chemicals in the latter part of the 20th c. Most of the others either went out of business or were absorbed by the survivors; their traditional medicaments based on naturally occurring drugs had been superseded by modern specific synthetic remedies originating from the new industry's research laboratories.

In addition to the traditional 19th c. wholesale pharmaceutical manufacturers, other companies with chemical manufacturing experience started to diversify into pharmaceuticals in the 1900s. In particular, the continental dyestuff producers entered the pharmaceutical industry because of the early chemical connection between dyestuffs and *antibacterial compounds. Later, some of the manufacturers of 19th c. 'patent medicines' also started to invest in research to develop new medicinal chemicals. Then, in the 1940s, large chemical companies, particularly in the USA, which had *fermentation expertise started to manufacture *antibiotics. Finally, other very large international chemical combines joined companies from this multiplicity of backgrounds to complete the formation of the international industry as it exists in the 1980s. Interestingly, however, some of the most recent recruits to the industry are very small high-technology companies with an expertise in molecular biology, whose significance will be discussed later in the article.

Present structure. The industry, having grown from such diverse roots, is itself still very varied. The main central core of the industry focuses on the development, manufacture, and marketing of new *prescription medicines. There are between one and two hundred principal international companies making up this sector of the industry, with several hundred more with smaller research facilities or which concentrate on formulating existing medicinal chemicals into new preparations.

In addition, there is an important sector of the industry which produces medicines based on older established active ingredients, and which advertises them under brand names direct to the public. Thirdly, there are the manufacturers of so-called 'generic' medicines—preparations sold under their official *pharmacopoeial names. These again are based on well-established chemical ingredients, and are made available for prescription in cases where the doctor has not specified a particular manufacturer's brand. The sales of these generic preparations represent only about 10 per cent of the total sales of prescription medicines. This is partly because doctors prefer to prescribe under the brand name; but, more importantly, it is because all new medicaments, which are still protected by patents, are available only in branded form (Office of Health Economics, 1976). This, again, is discussed later.

These three main groups of manufacturers—of branded prescription medicines, nationally advertised medicines, and 'generic' preparations —show a considerable degree of overlap, with the same companies often involved in all three types of business. It should also be pointed out that over a period of years the medicines manufactured by the 'generic' companies will originally have been developed as innovations within the research-based sector of the industry. Hence the seminal role of research for the industry as a whole. In addition, there are the manufacturers of *herbal remedies and *health foods, and of specialist products such as medicinal *gases, who do not form part of the pharmaceutical industry as it is generally defined.

As far as the research-based innovative core of the pharmaceutical industry is concerned, there is a very striking international geographical pattern. Throughout the 1960s and 1970s, and in the early 1980s, only five countries in the world have dominated the scene. These are the UK, France, West Germany, Switzerland, and the USA. According to a British National Economic Development Office study in 1973, these were the countries responsible for the largest number of new pharmaceutical chemical entities between 1958 and 1970 (National Economic Development Office, 1973). The USA had produced 204; Switzerland, 54; the UK, 51; West Germany, 35; and France, 23. In terms of international trade, these five countries again dominate the picture. In 1980 their net balance of trade ranged from $1217 million (£529 million) each for the UK and the USA to $796 million (£346 million) for France. No other country in the world achieved significantly more than $100 million (say £50 million) in a positive balance of trade for pharmaceuticals; most countries are net importers (National Economic Development Office, 1983).

The absence of the Eastern European countries from the list of major pharmaceutical innovators is often a source of comment. Many people believe that they spend substantially on pharmaceutical research, but that the central state control of their economy has inhibited their success. The other possibility is that—like countries such as Australia and Canada which function with an overt 'cheap drug' policy—they have deliberately decided to be 'free-riders', taking advantage of the pharmaceutical discoveries in Western Europe and the USA, without contributing to the cost of pharmaceutical research.

There is likely to be one major change in the international pattern of the pharmaceutical industry in the 1980s and 1990s. This is the development of the Japanese industry. Already in 1980 the Japanese companies were the third largest spenders on pharmaceutical research in the world. The US companies spent £655 million ($1506 million), West Germany £425 million ($978 million), and Japan £360 million ($800 million). Switzerland, the UK, and France came fourth, fifth, and sixth, with £312 million ($718 million), £280 million ($644 million), and £216 million ($497 million) respectively (Teeling Smith, 1983). In terms of the 100 leading pharmaceutical products on the world markets, Japan had ousted France from fifth place in the same year. There seems little doubt that the Japanese pharmaceutical industry plans to follow the example of its motor car, motor cycle, and electronics industries in penetrating deeply into world markets.

The role of research. The figures quoted above indicate the magnitude of the research investment in the pharmaceutical industry. It is now generally believed that it costs on average about £50 million to develop one successful new medicine (National Economic Development Office, 1981).

With such large sums of money at stake, it is

important to understand the process of pharmaceutical innovation in the industry today. There are broadly three approaches, which to some extent overlap. The first is to screen compounds from a wide variety of sources for potential pharmacological activity. For example, a company may take compounds occurring in nature (such as salicylic acid), modify them, and then see what pharmacological actions the new compounds have on animals; or a company manufacturing synthetic agricultural chemicals may randomly test these to see if they have any pharmacological activity. Second, more specifically, a company may take a new compound with a known pharmacological action and then modify it chemically to see how its activity is affected.

This process is sometimes disparagingly dismissed as leading to unnecessary 'me-too' medicaments. However, often the molecular variations are important therapeutic advances. Even if the new molecular modification does not represent a broadly based pharmacological advance, it may still be important for a minority of patients. For them it may be more effective than the original innovation, or it may have fewer side-effects and be better tolerated. In addition, it is at this stage that an element of serendipity creeps into the process of pharmaceutical innovation. For example, in France a random evaluation of compounds known to be effective as *antihistamines led to the discovery of their important *psychotropic properties. The first *tranquillizers were developed in this way.

However, the third broad approach to pharmaceutical innovation appears on theoretical grounds to be the most scientific, although it is not always the most effective in practice. This is the specific synthesis of compounds which are expected from a scientific hypothesis to have a particular pharmacological action. The use of *para-aminosalicylic acid (PAS; sodium aminosalicylate) in the treatment of *tuberculosis was an example of this theoretical approach. It was known that the TB bacteria fed on para-aminobenzoic acid, and it was postulated that if they could be given sufficient PAS to feed on instead they would 'starve to death' through lack of their essential para-aminobenzoic acid. This proved to be the case. More recently, the industry development of the adrenergic *betablockers for heart disease and hypertension and the discovery of the histamine $*H_2$-receptor antagonists for the treatment of *peptic ulcers are both examples of this third more rational approach to pharmaceutical research.

Once a 'product candidate' has been identified and synthesized as a result of one of these three approaches, there starts the very long and painstaking task of testing the chemical compound for any warning signs of toxicity and for its pharmacological effectiveness first in human volunteers and then in patients. This whole process is now estimated on average to take about 10 years between the first synthesis (and patenting) of the compound and its eventual marketing in the form of a pharmaceutical preparation. The great majority of hopeful new approaches fail in this latter testing stage, either because the chemical does not live up to its early promise as an effective treatment, or because it proves toxic to some species of animal, or because it causes untoward adverse *side-effects during *clinical trials in man. This is an important aspect of the element of risk which justifies the higher than average returns from the few medicines which do eventually reach the market. There is also, of course, the risk that serious adverse effects may becomes apparent after the medicine has been put on the market. Apart from the seriousness for the patients and prescribers, this again is a commercial catastrophe for the manufacturer, who will usually have to discontinue selling the product.

Economic factors. This raises the question of the economic environment which is necessary to support the pharmaceutical industry's investment in research. It is now generally accepted economic theory that any industry which is based on innovation must be protected from the unfettered forces of pure price competition (Chamberlin, 1933). The mechanism for providing this protection is through patents and the use of brand names. These give the innovator the exclusive right to sell his innovation for the period of the patent life, and continue to give him some protection from imitators through the use of the brand name after the patent has expired. Incidentally, the brand name can itself give an important incentive to innovation in cases where no patent protection is available because the new medicine is based on an already known chemical. This was the case, for example, with the analgesic *paracetamol and with L-dopa (*levodopa) for the treatment of *Parkinson's disease. Neither of these compounds could be patented and the companies which marketed them were dependent on brand names to get an economic return for the work involved in testing and manufacturing the preparations.

In the UK and the rest of Europe, patents give the innovator 20 years of exclusivity to sell the new medicine. In the USA, the period is 17 years. However, as has already been pointed out, about 10 years of this period are taken up with the development and testing of the medicine. Thus in the UK, Japan, and the USA there have been moves to try to get the period of patent protection to run from a later date—for example, when the medicine is first tested in man rather than when it was first synthesized. As a result it is possible to get up to five years' extension of patent life under a new US law. In Europe, however, patents still give only a relatively short period in which the innovator can try to recover his investment (National Economic Development Office, 1981).

The use of brand names in prescribing has recently been a controversial issue. Clearly brand names are intended to give the original pharmaceutical manufacturer some extra financial return, beyond that obtainable under patent, so branded prescription medicines are more expensive than the 'generic' alternatives produced by other companies once the patent has expired. In addition, brand names guarantee the reliable source of the medicine and ensure that the patient receives exactly the same formulation each time the medicine is dispensed. Medicines dispensed under their generic name may have significant variations in their pharmacological action even when they contain exactly the same amount of active chemical ingredient. These variations arise from differences in the method of formulation of the medicine by different manufacturers, all of which will nevertheless comply with the official standards set out in the pharmacopoeia. The use of the specific manufacturer's brand name in prescribing and dispensing avoids this risk of variation as the medicine will in this case invariably be manufactured in exactly the same way. On the other hand, the prescribing or dispensing of the cheaper unbranded medicines can save either the health service or the patient money. This raises the whole question of the appropriate profitability of pharmaceutical companies and the balance between a natural desire to have a 'cheap drug bill' and the importance of continuing to finance industrial pharmaceutical research.

Most countries in Europe have some sort of comprehensive health service under which medicines are provided free or at nominal cost (Vaizey, 1982). The USA is to a large extent an exceptional case in that the patient still usually pays directly the full cost of the medicines prescribed for him. In the case of non-prescribed nationally advertised medicines, of course, in all countries the patient pays the full price for the medicine which he purchases.

Under the European health services, a variety of measures have been taken to try to reduce the cost of the pharmaceutical service. Perhaps the best balanced and most sophisticated of the arrangements has existed in the UK, where under the Pharmaceutical Price Regulation Scheme each manufacturer negotiates annually with the Department of Health and Social Security over the appropriate level of prices and profit for all its sales to the British *National Health Service (NHS). This Scheme has specifically tried to strike a balance between the reasonableness of prices for the NHS and the need to encourage investment in continuing pharmaceutical research in the British industry. The Scheme is renegotiated at regular intervals to try to ensure that this proper balance is still being achieved.

On the other hand, West Germany has tried to limit pharmaceutical costs by restricting doctors' prescribing freedom, and countries such as Belgium, France, and Italy have had much stricter control on the individual prices of prescription medicines. The UK government has also now introduced substantial limitation on doctors' choice of medicines under the NHS, in addition to its price control scheme. In general, there continues to be a debate on the best method of getting pharmaceuticals as cheaply as possible, without at the same time inhibiting the pharmaceutical industry's ability to invest in continuing and increasingly expensive research. However, as has already been hinted, there is an unfortunate desire for some countries which do not themselves have a strong research-based industry merely to want to pay the lowest possible prices for their medicines.

Safety of medicines. Apart from economic considerations, an important aspect of the development of the pharmaceutical industry over the past 20 years has been the effort devoted to trying to make medicines as safe as possible. In 1961 the *thalidomide disaster focused world-wide attention on the ability of medicines to do harm as well as good. Ironically, medicines before that date had often been very toxic compounds with the risk of serious adverse reactions. For example, *strychnine and *arsenic were still in the pharmacopoeias in the early part of the 20th c., and medicines such as *amidopyrine, amethocaine, *phenylbutazone, and *chloramphenicol were known causes of fatal reactions in some cases in the 1950s.

Nevertheless, since 1961 much stricter government controls have been introduced in all countries to try to prevent any adverse effects occurring with medicines. These have not, however, been fully effective. For example, practolol caused serious adverse effects in the 1970s and benoxaprofen was withdrawn from the market in the 1980s because of deaths in elderly patients who had received the medicine. In general, the most effective way to reduce these inevitable risks lies within the pharmaceutical industry itself—which in economic terms has most to lose from therapeutic disasters. Government can only provide a second line of defence, which will avoid deliberate irresponsibility or a gross error of judgement on the part of a company, but which cannot guarantee safety. The pharmaceutical manufacturers need continually to emphasize that they cannot develop absolutely safe medicines. Like any form of therapy, medication can involve risks. There is much discussion at the moment as to how patients can most appropriately be compensated if a medicine does indeed harm them (see LAW AND MEDICINE IN THE UK; LAW AND MEDICINE IN THE USA). This is a very difficult subject in which both government and the industry are involved (see GOVERNMENT AND MEDICINE IN THE UK).

Before concluding this article, two special subjects are worth mentioning. The first is the role of the pharmaceutical industry in the Third World and the second is the prospect of future progress for the industry in its contribution to therapeutics.

The Third World. In the Third World there are overwhelming medical problems. These stem from a shortage of medical personnel and facilities, and from a serious maldistribution of these scarce resources between the privileged urban areas and the neglected rural districts. It has been suggested that the inappropriate marketing of medicines and even of medicinal foods (e.g. infant foodstuffs) by the industry has added to these problems, and pharmaceutical manufacturers are very sensitive to these criticisms. The industry has, therefore, introduced recently a Code of Marketing Practice to apply to Third World countries. This is similar to, but less stringent than, similar Codes of Practice which have been operated for many years in some developed countries such as the UK. The intention is to ensure that medicines are never advertised for inappropriate indications or without due attention being paid to their possible risks.

More positively, the pharmaceutical industry is trying to step up its research programme into methods of preventing or curing the specifically Third World health problems such as *malaria and *onchocerciasis. It is also discussing with the *World Health Organization (WHO) how certain basic medicines can be made available at very low prices for the least developed countries. Finally, the industry is co-operating with WHO in training pharmaceutical personnel for the Third World.

Prospects for the future. Returning to the Western World, and looking to the future, there seem to be tremendous prospects for advances over the next 20 years from pharmaceutical industry research (Wells, 1983). These advances, like progress in the past, will come from an effective collaboration between academic medical scientists and the pharmaceutical industry. The former very often produce the basic knowledge from which pharmaceutical progress can develop. The latter have the resources and the expertise to convert this basic knowledge into new therapeutic substances.

One important area for such co-operation is in relation to *molecular biology and *genetic engineering. The fundamental understanding of the chemistry within the human cell which has emerged in the past 30 years is now reaching a stage where it is likely to lead to treatments for virus diseases, many more cancers, and autoimmune disorders. Another important area is in brain biochemistry, where there are prospects of effective therapy for schizophrenia and possibly for senile dementia and the addictive diseases, such as alcoholism.

Thus, in conclusion, the modern international pharmaceutical industry, which dates only from the 1940s, seems to have a flourishing future ahead of it. There are economic problems which it must overcome, such as some countries' obsessional desire to obtain 'cheap drugs'. But on the whole, the prescription medicine manufacturers have a good relationship with their immediate 'customers', the medical profession. As the predominant source of most of the new medicines in the past 40 years and as the probable source of all important pharmacological advances in the next 40, the pharmaceutical industry has on balance

indeed made, and should continue to make, a very strong, positive, and beneficial contribution to the progress of medicine.　　　　G. TEELING SMITH

References
Chamberlin, E. H. (1933). *The Theory of Monopolistic Competition; A Re-Orientation of the Theory of Value.* Cambridge, Mass.
Haines, G. (1976). *The Grains and Threepenn'orths of Pharmacy. Pharmacy in New South Wales 1788–1976.* Kilmore, Australia.
National Economic Development Office (1973). *Innovative Activity in the Pharmaceutical Industry.* London.
National Economic Development Office (1981). *Research and Development Costs, Patents and Regulatory Controls; a consultative document.* London.
National Economic Development Office (1983). *Pharmaceuticals Industry; Report by the Pharmaceutical Sector Working Party.* London.
Office of Health Economics (1976). *Brand Names in Prescribing.* London.
Schwartzman, D. (1976). *Innovation in the Pharmaceutical Industry.* Baltimore and London.
Teeling Smith, G. (1983). *The Future for Pharmaceuticals; the Potential, the Pattern and the Problems.* London.
Vaizey, J. (1982). *Ill in Europe.* London.
Wells, N. E. J. (ed.) (1983). *The Second Pharmacological Revolution.* London.

Further reading
Bezold, C. (1981). *The Future of Pharmaceuticals; the changing Environment for New Drugs.* New York and Chichester.
Chain, E. B. (1963). Academic and industrial contributions to drug research. *Nature,* **200,** 441.
Chien, R. I. (ed.) (1979). *Issues in Pharmaceutical Economics.* Lexington, Massachusetts.
Cooper, M. H. (1966). *Prices and Profits in the Pharmaceutical Industry.* Oxford.
Reekie, W. D. and Weber, M. H. (1979). *Profits, Politics and Drugs.* London.
Tishler, M. (1973). Drug discovery—background and foreground. *Clinical Pharmacology and Therapeutics,* **14,** 479.

PHARMACEUTICAL SOCIETY OF GREAT BRITAIN. The professional body for the pharmaceutical profession in the UK. The Council of the Society is responsible for publishing the *British Pharmaceutical Codex* (now the *Pharmaceutical Codex*). See PHARMACY ACTS 1852, 1868, 1954; PHARMACY AND PHARMACISTS.

PHARMACIST. A druggist, pharmaceutical chemist, or (formerly) an *apothecary, that is a person qualified and licensed to make up prescriptions and to dispense medicinal substances. See PHARMACY AND PHARMACISTS.

PHARMACOGENETICS is the study of genetically determined variation in individual responses to drugs.

PHARMACOLOGY, CLINICAL PHARMACOLOGY, AND THERAPEUTICS

Introduction. Therapeutics is the branch of medicine concerned with the treatment of disease. Rational therapeutics uses chemicals to counteract, or reverse, the effects of those pathological processes which cause disease and is based on the disciplines of pharmacology, clinical pharmacology, and toxicology. Pharmacology is the scientific study of the effects of chemical substances on living systems and the chemicals which pharmacologists investigate include normal constituents of the body, compounds extracted from other animals or plants, as well as substances synthesized by chemists. The biological systems studied by pharmacologists range from microbiological organisms, parts of cells, intact cells, and organs, to whole animals.

Clinical pharmacologists investigate the effects of drugs in man, and are especially involved in studying those actions which might lead to therapeutic benefits or adverse effects. Clinical pharmacologists make a particular study of the way in which man (especially patients with disease) absorb, metabolize, and excrete drugs because these processes are important determinants of the rate and extent of drug action. Furthermore, clinical pharmacologists have a special interest in evaluating the efficacy and safety of drugs during their clinical use. Toxicology is the study of poisons or potential poisons. Toxicologists are not only involved with the potential adverse effects of drugs but also with the possible toxicity of household and industrial chemicals, food additives, pesticides, herbicides, other environmental pollutants, and cosmetics.

The nomenclature and classification of drugs is the source of considerable national, international, and professional confusion. Like any chemical, drugs have strict scientific names (e.g. N-acetyl para-aminophenol, *acetylsalicylic acid) but these are usually too cumbersome for everyday clinical use. When a chemical is to be used as a drug the Pharmacopoeial Commission assigns a 'trivial' name which is chosen for its relative simplicity, its resemblance to the scientific name, and its chemical origins. These names, such as *paracetamol for N-acetyl para-aminophenol, and aspirin for acetylsalicylic acid, are known as 'generic' or 'non-proprietary' names. The pharmaceutical company which sells a drug, frequently does so under a 'proprietary' or 'brand' name which is a registered trade mark and the property of the company. A drug will have only one 'generic' name, but may have several different 'brand' names: thus, Panadol, Panasorb, and Calpol are all brand names of products containing paracetamol. (See PHARMACEUTICAL INDUSTRY.)

Drugs are classified in one of three ways. The therapeutic class describes the condition, or symptom, for which the drug is used (e.g. oral contraceptives, *analgesics, antidiabetic agents, or *anticonvulsant drugs). Many drugs, however, are useful in a wide range of disorders, or form subcategories within a single therapeutic class, and are classified on the basis of their pharmacological actions (e.g. *diuretics, *antihistamines). Within a therapeutic or pharmacological class, drugs may be further classified according to their chemical family (e.g. tricyclic *antidepressants, thiazide diuretics, or *phenothiazine antipsychotics).

Historical development of pharmacology and therapeutics. For thousands of years rational therapeutics has been based upon either logic or empiricism. Where physicians have claimed knowledge of the cause of a particular disease, and where they have believed that a drug could reverse the pathological process, they have applied the remedy—'logically'—as a treatment or cure. Alternatively, where by chance a remedy has been empirically observed to exert a favourable outcome in patients with a particular disease, other patients with the same condition have been given the drug in the anticipation that they too will derive benefit. These general principles still apply today. To be valid, however, they require an accurate *diagnosis of the patient's condition, a precise knowledge of the pathological process which is causing it, as well as a detailed understanding of the pharmacological and toxicological properties of the proposed remedy.

Until recently many of the remedies used in medicine were at best useless, and at worst harmful. Before the last century most of the theories which attempted to explain the origins of disease were hopelessly inadequate, and knowledge of the way in which drugs produced their biological effects was scanty. Inevitably, the 'logical' use of medicines to attempt to reverse an erroneously conceived underlying pathological process with a chemical of ill-defined properties usually failed. The empirical approach also suffered from serious defects because the natural history of many conditions was so poorly understood that spontaneous remissions were frequently mistaken for therapeutic successes. Moreover, clinical methods were too primitive to enable accurate diagnoses to be made. Consequently, when a single remedy was used in the treatment of several indistinguishable disorders, most patients would derive little benefit even if the drug really was effective in one of these conditions.

Pharmacology and therapeutics of ancient civilizations. In the ancient world, products derived from animal, vegetable, and mineral sources were used for two pharmacological purposes—to attempt to cure disease, and to poison animal or human enemies. Primitive man in widely separated countries readily discovered the virtues of *opium, *hashish, *cinchona, *tobacco, and podophyllin; and he also developed fatal arrow poisons such as *curare, ouabain, and *veratrine.

The civilizations of ancient China, India, and Egypt possessed extensive *pharmacopoeias which included many hundreds of medicinal preparations. A large proportion were of little real value (apart from a *placebo effect) and some were undoubtedly harmful. However, they also included substances with pharmacological properties which have survived until the present day.

Thus, the Ancient Egyptians knew of the *emetic properties of copper salts and squill, the *purgative action of *castor oil, and the analgesic and *hypnotic effects of opium.

Pharmacology and therapeutics of Greece and Rome. European medicine began with the early Greek classical period and centred around *Hippocrates (460–370 BC). Although Hippocrates was not an experimentalist, he set standards of clinical description and ethics that have survived to the present day. In therapeutics, Hippocrates believed 'do good, or at least do no harm' and was largely concerned with assisting natural recuperation. Although he was acquainted with many drugs, his scheme of treatment was usually confined to such simple expedients as fresh air, good diet, and massage, and he largely rejected the nonsensical remedies of his predecessors. During the later Greek classical period, the school of empiricism culminated in the development of quasi-experimental pharmacology and toxicology. King Mithridates of Pontius (120–63 BC) studied the art of giving and taking poisons and is reputed to have attempted to *immunize himself against poisoning with the blood of ducks fed toxic substances, as well as to have tried to prepare a 'universal antidote' (*mithridaticum).

The pharmacology and therapeutics of the Graeco-Roman period is dominated by Aurelius Cornelius *Celsus, Pedacius *Dioscorides, and *Galen. Celsus, who lived in the reign of Tiberius Caesar, was not a physician but a man of letters who compiled encyclopaedic treatises on medicine and agriculture. His volume on drugs, which served as a handbook of therapeutics, included a classified list of medicines, and a description of pharmaceutical methods. Dioscorides, a Greek army surgeon in the service of Nero, wrote an authoritative account of medical botany which was used for over 1600 years. Galen, probably the most famous Greek physician after Hippocrates, instituted an elaborate system of polypharmacy based on mixtures derived from plants. The adjective 'galenical' describing such products, is still used today. Between the fall of the Roman Empire and the Renaissance, the work of Dioscorides and Galen continued to dominate pharmacology and therapeutics. Arabian physicians made some additions, and their descriptions of the preparation of drugs became the standard authority during the Middle Ages.

Renaissance and post-Renaissance pharmacology and therapeutics. The great advances in medical sciences which occurred during the 16th and 17th c. were not paralleled by substantial progress in pharmacology and therapeutics. The most notable Renaissance pharmacologist was Aureolus Theophrastus Bombastus von Hohenheim (1493–1541) who was more popularly known as *Paracelsus. As well as being an able physician, Paracelsus was a skilled chemist who rejected *alchemy for chemical therapeutics, and who incorporated opium, mercury, lead, sulphur, arsenic, and potassium sulphate in his pharmacopoeia. He popularized *tinctures, using alcoholic extracts of plants in an effort to separate their therapeutic and toxic components. In general, however, there was virtually no attempt to investigate, or validate, the wide variety of remedies available. The first edition of the *London Pharmacopoeia* (1618) contained 1960 treatments including foxes' lungs, powders of precious stones, human saliva and sweat, dried sexual organs, and even animal excreta. The editions of 1650 and 1677 were little better. Johann *Glauber (1604–68), a skilled analytical chemist, was almost alone in advocating the use of pure chemical preparations instead of animal products of dubious origin.

The 18th c. was marked by the beginnings of a more scientific and rational approach to therapeutics. The disappearance of some of the more outrageous remedies advocated previously, as well as the introduction of several active and useful drugs, was due to the influence of such physicians as Hans *Sloane (1660–1753), Richard *Mead (1673–1754), William *Heberden (1710–1801), and the pioneering work of William *Withering (1741–99). Withering, a Birmingham physician and medical botanist, learned from an old Shropshire lady of the virtues of the foxglove (*Digitalis purpurea*) in *heart failure. He performed a series of clinical studies with the drug—a crude preparation of *digitalis glycosides—which culminated in the publication of his pharmacological classic *Account of the Foxglove* in 1785. Digoxin and digitoxin, two active cardiac glycosides, are widely used today: but their therapeutic properties, and adverse effects, were carefully recorded by Withering 200 years ago. (See also HERBAL REMEDIES, ETC.)

The emergence of modern pharmacology and therapeutics. The extraordinary advances in pharmacology and therapeutics which have occurred during the past 200 years are in stark contrast to the slender progress during the preceding 3000 years. The development of chemistry during the 19th c. encouraged the isolation and synthesis of a range of novel compounds in pure form whilst a better understanding of *physiology and *biochemistry provided pharmacologists with a framework for studying the action of chemicals on living systems. Moreover, the development of *pathology and knowledge of the aetiology and pathogenesis of disease encouraged pharmacologists and physicians to seek ways of reversing disease processes by chemical means.

The advances in chemistry which began during the early 19th c. largely arose from the work of Friederich Wöhler (1800–82) who not only undertook the first synthesis of an organic chemical substance (urea) but also synthesized *morphine and salicin. He also demonstrated (1824) that ingested foreign chemicals can undergo metabolism within the body, and showed that benzoic acid taken with food appears in the urine as hippuric acid. By the end of the 19th c. a considerable range of synthetic chemical substances, some of which are used today, became available as therapeutic remedies. They included *chloral (a hypnotic), *cocaine (a local anaesthetic), *ephedrine (a bronchodilator), and *heroin (similar to morphine).

François *Magendie (1783–1855), a French physiologist, is often regarded as the founder of modern experimental pharmacology. Magendie attempted to explain biological phenomena in terms of physics and chemistry, and regarded pathology as 'the physiology of the sick man'. His pharmacological investigations included studies of *bromides and *iodides, *strychnine (showing its action on the *spinal cord), morphine, veratrine, and *emetine. His pupil Claude *Bernard (1813–78), although primarily a physiologist, also experimented in a systematic manner with drugs and poisons, investigating the pharmacological properties of curare, and showing that *carbon monoxide produces its deleterious effect by displacing *oxygen from *haemoglobin. The first university chairs of pharmacology were established in Europe and North America during the latter part of the 19th c., when the subject became an integral part of the undergraduate medical curriculum.

The work of Magendie and Bernard was followed by important conceptual advances in understanding the mechanisms of drug action. Alexander Crum Brown and John Frazer showed (1869) that relatively small changes in the chemical structure of drugs such as morphine and strychnine produced compounds with very different pharmacological properties. They speculated that a relationship exists between the pharmacological activity of a substance, and its chemical structure. Such 'structure–activity' relationships form the basis of much of modern medicinal chemistry, since many compounds are now known to owe their biological activities to certain structural groups. Nine years later, J. N. *Langley put forward the hypothesis that tissues might contain a specific 'receptor substance' for drugs, and this concept was extended by the German pharmacologist Paul *Ehrlich. The increasingly scientific approach to clinical pharmacology and therapeutics was typified by Thomas Lauder *Brunton (1844–1916). An Edinburgh graduate, who ultimately became physician at *St Bartholomew's Hospital, Brunton pioneered the application of the physiological findings of pharmacology to internal medicine, and he can reasonably be regarded as an early clinical pharmacologist. His most memorable achievement was the introduction of nitrites and nitrates (e.g. *amyl nitrite, *glyceryl trinitrate) for the treatment of *angina pectoris, which he devised on physiological and pharmacological grounds, and which are still widely used today (Table 2). (All Tables will be found at the end of this entry.)

During the present century pharmacology and clinical pharmacology have developed along four main lines. First, studies of the mechanisms of drug action—particularly the recognition and identification of 'drug receptors'—have achieved increasing prominence with important consequences not only in enhancing knowledge of how drugs act, but also in providing the stimulus for new drug discovery. Secondly, the identification of the endogenous chemicals involved in a variety of physiological and pathological processes—from *neurotransmitters to mediators of *inflammation—has allowed the development of both synthetic analogues and antagonists. This, too, has had major applications in the search for novel treatments of disease. Thirdly, it has become increasingly recognized that the study of drugs in isolated tissues and experimental animals is an insufficient basis for their therapeutic use, and that careful studies of their action and fate in human volunteers and patients is essential. Finally, the use of randomized controlled *clinical trials, rather than anecdotal case-histories, to study the efficacy of drugs has provided a solid scientific basis for therapeutics. The post-war emergence of clinical pharmacology (out of basic pharmacology and clinical medicine) has been as important as the development of pharmacology (from chemistry and physiology) in the last century.

Basis of drug action. There are four fundamental mechanisms by which chemicals produce pharmacological effects—binding to specific receptors, chemical neutralization or incorporation, interactions with cell *membranes, and physical effects.

Specific receptors. Many drugs, as well as naturally occurring substances, produce their effects by interacting with specific and discrete parts of cells. Receptors are large molecules (usually *proteins) which bear recognition sites for specific chemicals known as 'ligands'. The binding of a ligand to its receptor initiates a train of events resulting in a characteristic response such as muscular contraction or glandular secretion. *Agonists* are ligands which usually mimic the action of a naturally occurring hormone or neurotransmitter, and examples include *salbutamol and terbutaline (Table 3), the opioids such as *codeine and morphine (Table 4), and steroids (Table 8). By contrast, *antagonist* ligands bind to specific receptors without stimulating the tissue. They produce their effects by displacing naturally occurring agonists and thus prevent the latter's actions. In the absence of agonist stimulation, antagonists are usually devoid of biological activity. Examples of drug receptor antagonists include the anti-ulcer drugs *cimetidine and *ranitidine (Table 1), the antihypertensive drug prazosin (Table 2), and the antipsychotic agents *chlorpromazine, *haloperidol, and flupenthixol (Table 4).

Although the existence of specific receptors has been suspected for nearly a century it is only in recent years that they have been isolated and characterized. Several different types of receptor can be identified.

1. *Neurotransmitter receptors.* Within both the central and peripheral nervous system, communication between nerve cells, and between nerves and muscle, is achieved by chemical means. When an impulse reaches the end of a nerve fibre, a specific chemical (neurotransmitter) is released which diffuses across the so-called 'synaptic cleft' (*synapse) to an adjacent nerve or muscle cell. The neurotransmitter then interacts with its specific receptor lying within the postsynaptic nerve or muscle cell membrane, producing stimulation. The most important neurotransmitters are *noradrenaline, *acetylcholine, *dopamine, *gamma-aminobutyric acid (GABA) and *enkephalin. They are all agonists and their effects are terminated either by destruction by specific *enzymes situated close to the receptor (e.g. acetylcholinesterase for acetylcholine, GABA transaminase for GABA), or by 're-uptake' into the presynaptic *neurone via a specific transport mechanism (e.g. noradrenaline).

One of the most important observations in modern pharmacology is that receptors which are specific to a particular neurotransmitter may also be tissue-specific, or functionally specific. Thus, cardiac cholinergic receptors differ from those in voluntary muscle, despite the fact that receptors in both organs are stimulated by the same neurotransmitter (acetylcholine). Similarly, noradrenergic receptors producing constriction of blood vessels (alpha-noradrenergic receptors), are different from those in the heart and lungs (beta-noradrenergic receptors). Indeed, cardiac beta-noradrenoceptors (so-called $beta_1$-receptors) are different from those in the lungs ($beta_2$-receptors). Subpopulations of dopaminergic receptors and encephalinergic receptors have also been described. This has permitted the development of synthetic agonists and antagonists which are specific for particular tissues.

2. *Hormone receptors.* Many hormones, including sex steroids and *insulin (Table 8), exert their effect via specific receptors. In many instances pure preparations of naturally occurring hormones are valuable therapeutic agents and examples include *cortisol, *thyroxine, and insulin. Some hormones, however, are so rapidly metabolized in the body that they are largely ineffective unless given by intravenous infusion. Synthetic analogues, which retain the chemical configuration required for agonist activity but which are more resistant to metabolism within the body, have achieved wide clinical use. This particularly applies to the synthetic *oestrogens and *progestogens used in combined oral contraceptive preparations (Table 8).

Synthetic hormone antagonists to oestrogens and androgens have recently become available for the treatment of hormone-dependent *cancers. The oestrogen antagonist *tamoxifen is valuable in the treatment of certain forms of *breast cancer, while the androgen antagonist *cyproterone acetate is being increasingly used for cancer of the *prostate in men.

3. *Enzyme inhibitors.* The formation and breakdown of most body components is catalysed by proteins known as enzymes. An enzyme usually displays a high degree of specificity for a particular metabolic reaction, and contains an 'active site' which mediates its catalytic action. Many important therapeutic agents are enzyme inhibitors: these drugs bind to the enzymes 'active sites' and thus prevent their normal action. Because of the high specificity of most enzymes, it is frequently possible to achieve comparable specificity of drug action.

Inhibition of the formation of a biologically active substance within the body provides the basis for the action of aspirin and the other so-called 'non-steroidal anti-inflammatory drugs' (Table 6). These drugs all inhibit the formation of a family of chemicals known as *prostaglandins which are formed within cells from arachidonic acid. Certain prostaglandins participate in inflammatory reactions which cause fever and pain. The non-steroidal anti-inflammatory drugs—by inhibiting their synthesis—thus inhibit the production of their anti-inflammatory, *antipyretic, and analgesic effects.

4. *Transport receptors.* The transport of certain substances across cell membranes is mediated by specific 'pumps' contained within the cell wall. A number of drugs inhibit these transport systems which thus represent their receptor sites. *Cardiac glycosides (Table 2) act by inhibiting the enzyme *adenosine triphosphatase (which provides the energy to exchange sodium and potassium across the walls of heart muscle cells) and, as described above, tricyclic *antidepressants (Table 4) act on the presynaptic transport receptors at noradrenergic synapses.

Chemical neutralization or incorporation. Some drugs exert their effects either by chemical neutralization, or by incorporation into critical cell molecules.

1. *Chemical neutralization.* The simplest form of chemical neutralization occurs when alkalis are used to treat symptoms due to excess gastric acid. Alkali mixtures containing sodium bicarbonate, magnesium bicarbonate, or aluminium hydroxide (Table 1) will neutralize hydrochloric acid within the stomach and relieve the pain of *peptic ulceration.

2. *Chemical incorporation.* Some of the most effective anti-cancer drugs produce their effects by undergoing incorporation into molecules which are critical to efficient *cell division. Since cancer cells are distinguished by their uncontrolled and rapid cell turnover, they are preferentially affected by these classes of drugs. However, other rapidly dividing, normal cells in the body may also be affected, resulting in serious adverse reactions, including loss of hair, sterility, and depression of bone marrow function. *Alkylating agents (Table

7) all possess the property of forming strong (covalent) linkages with the primary genetic material *deoxyribonucleic acid (DNA), producing a major distortion of function in cell division. *Antimetabolites (Table 7) are chemical analogues of the *purine and *pyrimidine bases which are essential components of DNA. They are incorporated enzymatically into DNA (so-called 'lethal' synthesis) where they miscode genetic information and cause cell death.

Membrane interactions. Several drugs, including both general and local *anaesthetics, appear to act within nerve cell membranes by a non-receptor mechanism. Volatile general anaesthetics such as *ether, *chloroform, *halothane, and *nitrous oxide are a diverse group of chemicals with similar pharmacological properties. It is believed that they dissolve in the cell membranes of nervous tissue and thereby alter their function. However, the precise molecular basis for their action is obscure. Local anaesthetics, such as lignocaine, block conduction along nerve fibres by dissolving in the fibre membranes but, again, the details of their actions are poorly understood.

Physical effects. Many commonly used therapeutic agents produce their effects by a purely physical action. Despite the relative simplicity of this mechanism, such drugs retain an important place in therapeutics. Thus, substances which passively alter the volume and consistency of *faeces (Table 1) are used to treat disorders of the bowel; blood and blood substitutes restore the circulating blood volume after *haemorrhage or fluid loss; and osmotic diuretics, such as mannitol, increase urine flow by reducing water reabsorption in the renal tubules.

Drug handling. Drugs may be administered either locally or systemically. Local administration is intended to confine a drug to the diseased organ or tissue, and topical skin preparations, nose drops, or vaginal *pessaries are typical examples. After so-called 'systemic administration' either orally (by mouth), or parenterally (by injection), drugs reach their intended site of action via the blood stream: they will also, however, inevitably reach other tissues where they may cause unwanted effects. In recent years it has become apparent that the intensity and duration of effect of many drugs depends on their handling within the body which, in turn, is regulated by the processes of drug absorption, distribution, and elimination.

Absorption. Most drugs are given orally and must pass through the stomach before undergoing absorption in the upper small *intestine. Conditions which delay gastric emptying such as food, fear, pain, nausea, and fever will delay both the absorption and therapeutic effects of a drug. Intestinal absorption of most drugs occurs by simple diffusion across the mucosal lining of the gut. Drugs which, for physicochemical reasons, do not readily diffuse across the *mucosa will be retained in the intestinal tract and excreted in the faeces.

Such drugs will not, therefore, reach the circulation, and must be given by injection if a systemic effect is required. On the other hand, non-absorbable *antibiotics can be effective in the treatment of intestinal infections.

Drug molecules which cross the lining of the gut must pass through the liver before reaching the systemic circulation. Some drugs are so avidly metabolized within the cells lining the gastrointestinal tract, or by the liver, that only a small fraction of an oral dose is available to exert a systemic effect. With glyceryl trinitrate (Table 7) this fraction is so minute that no systemic effect is observed: however, sucking a tablet of glyceryl trinitrate under the tongue avoids 'presystemic' destruction because the blood draining the mouth by-passes the liver and flows directly into the main circulation.

Distribution. Once drugs reach the blood stream they are distributed, to a greater or lesser extent, to various tissues and organs. The degree to which drugs penetrate individual organs and cells is governed by many factors including the chemical properties of the drug, the structural characteristics of the tissue, and its blood supply. Even within the blood, many drugs are loosely bound to red blood corpuscles or plasma protein which can therefore act as a 'reservoir'. Penetration of drugs into the brain is restricted by 'tight junctions' between cells lining the cerebral blood vessels, and only those compounds which are sufficiently soluble to dissolve in the *lipid membrane of this so-called 'blood–brain barrier' are capable of producing pharmacological effects within the *central nervous system.

The principles governing drug distribution are put to practical use both in selecting drugs for individual patients, and in the development of new drugs. Thus, the selection of an antibiotic appropriate for treating bacterial *meningitis is determined (at least in part) by its capacity to cross the blood–brain barrier. In the context of new drug development, the recent introduction of two new histamine₁-antagonists (terfenadine and astemizole), which do not cross the blood–brain barrier and are thus devoid of the *sedating effect of their predecessors, offer substantial hope to sufferers from *hay fever.

Elimination. Once drugs have been absorbed into the systemic circulation, various physiological and biochemical processes act to eliminate them from the body. The rate of drug elimination is usually expressed as an 'elimination half-life' which represents the time taken for the blood concentration to fall by half. Biological half-lives vary from the very short (2–3 minutes in the case of insulin), to the very long (several hundred hours in the case of some benzodiazepines).

Elimination half-lives are important determinants of the intensity and duration of drug action. Hypnotics with long half-lives, for example, will persist until the following morning after a bed-time dose and may cause 'hangover' effects. Thus after taking nitrazepam (Table 4), which has a half-life of 24 hours, only 25 per cent of the dose will have been eliminated from the body by the following morning and 50 per cent will still be present at bed-time the next evening. When drugs are given repeatedly accumulation will occur unless the dosage interval is less than at least three or four times longer than the half-life. In the treatment of many chronic conditions this may, of course, be highly desirable. Accumulation continues for a period corresponding to approximately five half-lives before plateauing to reach a 'steady state', and the longer the half-life the higher the steady state level of drug in the blood. Since, broadly speaking, steady state drug levels in the blood correlate with those in tissues and with the magnitude of drug effects, long half-lives tend to cause more intense and persistent pharmacological actions.

Drugs are eliminated from the body either by renal excretion, or by metabolism.

1. *Renal excretion.* Some drugs are excreted in unchanged form by the kidneys, but the rate of renal elimination varies for different drugs. The *penicillins (Table 5), for example, have half-lives of 60 and 90 minutes, whereas digoxin (Table 2) has a half-life of 30–40 hours. However, provided that renal function is normal, the rate of renal excretion of a particular drug shows little variation between individuals.

In the presence of renal disease, however, renal drug excretion rates fall and half-lives become longer. Consequently, higher blood levels and more intense pharmacological effects (including adverse reactions) may occur. It is therefore necessary to reduce the dosages of drugs undergoing renal excretion, if toxicity is to be avoided, in patients with disordered kidney function. The immature kidney of the newborn infant, and the 'normal' decline in renal function which occurs with advancing years, also renders the very young and the elderly susceptible to drug toxicity if conventional adult dosages (even allowing for difference in body weight) are given. Fortunately, kidney function can be reasonably well predicted from simple blood tests, and drug toxicity due to 'relative overdosage' of renally excreted drugs in the newborn, the elderly, and the patient with kidney disease, is largely avoidable.

2. *Metabolism.* The majority of drugs used in clinical practice undergo metabolism in the liver before their degradation products (drug metabolites) can be excreted in the urine. Often these metabolites are pharmacologically inactive, and drug metabolism is therefore frequently regarded as a detoxification mechanism. In recent years, however, it has become apparent that some drugs are themselves biologically inactive, and that their pharmacological effects are produced by their metabolites. Furthermore, in an increasing number of instances drug metabolites have been shown to possess a similar pharmacological profile to that of their parent drug, or even to cause toxic adverse effects.

A wide variety of drug metabolic pathways have developed during evolution—probably as a protection against toxins in food and the environment in general. The detailed metabolic fate of a particular drug may therefore be extremely complex, and drug metabolites themselves often undergo further biotransformation before they can be excreted by the kidneys. Despite this, it is usually possible to identify a drug's 'major' metabolic pathway and its corresponding metabolite. Clinical pharmacology and therapeutics, however, remain bedevilled by two major problems—differences between individuals in rates of drug metabolism, and differences between species in both rates *and* routes of drug metabolism.

During the past 25 years it has been apparent that, even amongst healthy individuals, there are marked interpersonal variations in the rates at which people metabolize drugs via specific pathways of biotransformation. This is partly due to genetic factors, and partly due to environmental influences which we face in everyday living. Although the relative importance of nature and nurture differs for different metabolic pathways, the therapeutic consequences are similar. Individuals who are 'slow' metabolizers of a particular drug will have longer drug half-lives, higher 'steady state' blood drug levels and greater risks of suffering toxicity; 'rapid' metabolizers will have shorter half-lives, lower blood levels, and greater risks of therapeutic failure.

The genetic control of drug metabolism varies qualitatively for different pathways, and quantitatively for different races. Known environmental factors influencing individual pathways include cigarette smoking, alcohol, exposure to certain environmental pollutants (e.g. pesticides), *other* drugs taken at the same time (e.g. oral contraceptives), certain foods (e.g. brassica vegetables), and the relative proportions of dietary protein and carbohydrate. Add to this the obvious effects of liver disease, the less obvious effects of cardiac, respiratory, and renal disease, and changes attributable to gender and age, and it becomes clear that the ability of any one individual to metabolize a particular drug can be difficult to predict, particularly when he is ill. Where the margin between therapeutic failure (due to a relative underdosage) and toxicity (due to relative overdosage) is large, such differences may be important only for a few individuals lying at the extremes of rapid and slow metabolism. Where the margin of safety is small, special steps must be taken to ensure therapeutic efficacy or safety.

Species differences in the rates and routes of drug metabolism have special implications for the testing of new drugs. Preclinical toxicity tests are usually carried out in mice, rats, hamsters, rabbits, dogs, and occasionally monkeys. Small animals usually have much more rapid rates of drug metabolism than humans, and at equivalent weight-for-weight doses they usually achieve much lower blood levels than are seen in patients. Moreover, species differences in routes of drug metabolism mean that pharmacologically active metabolites formed in man may not be present in animals. It is for these reasons that, in theory, animal toxicity tests are performed at much higher doses than would be expected to be used in patients, and in species whose metabolic pattern most closely resembles that of man. In practice these criteria are often difficult, if not impossible, to apply and this is one of the many reasons why new drugs may produce unexpected adverse effects despite 'adequate' preclinical toxicity studies.

Scientific basis of therapeutics. *Efficacy.* Until about 1950, most therapeutic remedies were introduced into clinical practice on the basis of anecdotal evidence. The effects in a few patients would be observed and if apparent benefit occurred, others with the same disease would then be treated. This approach to the demonstration of efficacy of a new, or established, remedy is now regarded as hopelessly unreliable and has been responsible, over several thousand years, for the adoption of much useless treatment. First, the natural progression of most disease is extraordinarily variable: even patients with lethal forms of cancer may quite spontaneously have prolonged periods of remission; patients with less life-threatening conditions (including many psychiatric, neurological, rheumatic, dermatological, and cardiac disorders) also have long remissions, or the disease may even show a spontaneous arrest; furthermore, many everyday illnesses such as the common infectious diseases of childhood or musculo-skeletal injuries, usually recover without (or despite) medical intervention. Under these circumstances the apparent demonstration of recovery, remission, or reduction of symptoms in a few patients forms no basis for the scientific proof of efficacy. Second, the demonstration in the laboratory that a particular drug has pharmacological properties which are likely to be useful in certain diseases, is no reason for assuming therapeutic efficacy, even though it might represent a valid reason for careful clinical studies: not only may man fail to respond in the same way as laboratory animals, but he may also experience severe adverse effects which outweigh the drug's benefits. Third, drugs are often used in conjunction with other therapeutic manoeuvres such as bedrest, nursing care, physiotherapy, or other drugs: comparisons between patients treated with a new drug, and previous experience (often referred to as 'historical' controls), can readily be confounded by such changing factors. Furthermore, the psychological effects of using a new drug are so profound, in both patient and doctor, that unintentional bias on the part of both parties may lead to erroneous conclusions. Patients with primarily subjective symptoms such as anxiety, depression, pain, insomnia, and nausea often show some improvement even when given tablets or capsules containing no active pharmacological ingredient: this so-called 'placebo' response does not mean that the particular symptoms are non-existent, or over-played, but are a demonstration of the power of the optimistic psyche to influence subjective sensations.

The randomized controlled *clinical trial is a technique for examining efficacy which aims to eliminate all these sources of bias. Its evolution over the past 30 years owes much to the late Sir Ronald *Fisher and to Sir Austen Bradford Hill, and represents a most important advance in medical science. Its principles have been used not only to evaluate the efficacy of drugs and other therapeutic manoeuvres (surgery, physiotherapy) but also in the fields of *public health, education, social sciences, and even the penal system. The technique is as follows: patients with a particular disorder, and who are reasonably homogeneous (i.e. alike in relevant characteristics), are randomly allocated to two (or more) treatment groups. One group receives the particular drug under study, and other groups receive either no drug, a placebo, or a comparative drug. The outcome in the patients in each group is then compared statistically, and likelihood of any difference occurring as a result of chance is calculated: if the probability of a difference occurring by chance is less than 1 in 20, then the 'null' hypothesis (i.e. that there is *no* difference between treatments) is usually rejected. If further analysis of the study shows flaws, then this conclusion may be revised: for example, subsequent examination of the patients' records may show that, fortuitously, those with less severe forms of the disease were—despite 'random' allocation—allocated to one treatment group.

Various additional measures are frequently adopted in randomized controlled trials to eliminate confounding factors. Very often, and especially where subjectivity by the patient or investigator might introduce bias, the patient and the doctor are kept ignorant of the treatment group to which the former has been randomly allocated. This so-called 'double-blind' technique can be undertaken by ensuring that the patients in the control group receive a drug, or placebo, that is similar in appearance, smell, and taste to that given to the test group. A further refinement, often adopted in studying the efficacy of a drug which produces symptomatic relief of a chronic disorder (e.g. arthritis or high blood pressure), is the 'cross-over trial'. In this technique, the patient is treated with both the test drug and, on a separate occasion, the control drug. Thus, patients act as their own controls, but the method is obviously ethically inapplicable in circumstances where a cure resulting from the use of the drug is highly probable.

Ideally a randomized controlled trial should use a placebo as the control treatment. This not only allows a smaller number of patients to be studied (because the difference in response between the groups is likely to be larger) but also allows a more accurate estimate to be made of adverse effects. In circumstances where no effective form of alternative treatment is available, there can be no moral or ethical objection to the use of a placebo provided that patients have freely given their consent to participate. Where effective alternatives are already available, then the control group is normally treated with a comparative drug. The fact that in one randomized controlled trial, the difference between the test group and the control group is 'statistically significant', does not necessarily prove that the new treatment is effective, because even in the absence of bias, any conclusion is based on an assessment of probabilities. It is customary, therefore, for new drugs to be assessed by several independent clinical trials. When the aim of a trial is to show that the test drug is as effective as an established remedy, the statistical technique is to calculate the probability of no difference and this requires much larger numbers of patients within each group. Finally, it is important to appreciate that although a new drug may be *statistically* better than placebo, this result may not be *clinically* significant: in the case of a new drug for *obesity, an average weight loss of 1 kg (2.2 lb) over 3 months compared with a placebo may be statistically significant, but is of little clinical relevance as the amount of weight lost over so long a period would be regarded as inadequate.

Adverse reactions. Unwanted and unintended effects of drugs given at normal therapeutic doses are known as adverse reactions (often inaccurately described as side-effects). All drugs will produce, at least in some individuals, adverse reactions which can be classified into one of two types.

1. *Type A reactions* are augmented pharmacological effects which are exaggerated, but otherwise predictable responses. They are usually manifestations of pharmacological effects which are observed when larger than normal doses are given. Examples include low blood pressure (hypotension) resulting from the use of antihypertensive agents, hangover effects from hypnotics, or constipation with opioid analgesics. They occur either because of enhanced sensitivity of the particular tissue or organ at which the drug acts, or because the individual displays unusual 'handling' of the drug. Individuals who eliminate the drug slowly will be at particular risk.

Type A reactions are usually common, predictable from the known pharmacology of the drug, reproducible in animals, and are rarely dangerous. Although they usually disappear when the drug is stopped, they are not necessarily an indication to withdraw the drug altogether—merely that the dose should be reduced.

2. *Type B reactions* are bizarre responses that are unrelated to the drugs' known pharmacological properties. They are often unpredictable, and can rarely be reproduced in experimental animals. Typical examples include *rashes with antibiotics,

and the oculomucocutaneous reactions to practolol. They are not apparently dose-dependent, are often serious, and are usually an indication to stop the drug completely.

The principal difficulty posed by adverse drug reactions, both in an individual patient and in the community at large, is their prediction and detection. Type A reactions, to which patients with impaired drug elimination rates are particularly susceptible, can often be anticipated from animal and human pharmacological studies. With the exception of drugs undergoing predominantly renal excretion and for a few well-characterized genetically controlled pathways of drug metabolism, prediction in individual patients can be very difficult. Furthermore, some Type A reactions produce signs and symptoms which are similar to those of the underlying disorder (e.g. digoxin and cardiac arrhythmias), or may be similar to those of another common condition (e.g. non-steroidal anti-inflammatory drugs and gastric upsets). A careful history from the patient, a detailed knowledge of the properties of the drug, and measurement (when feasible) of blood levels, may help. Positive responses to withdrawal and subsequent rechallenge are usually regarded as diagnostic, but these measures are often impractical. Type B reactions, which are often more serious, pose a greater problem because there are rarely specific tests for distinguishing drug-induced from other forms of those manifestations. If there have been previous published reports of an association between a particular drug and a suspected reaction, then the possibility of a drug-related aetiology can be more easily considered. As with Type A reactions, however, the distinction between drug-induced and naturally occurring disease may be difficult. Once this aetiology is suspected, it may be possible to obtain some confirmatory evidence from the effects of withdrawal, although certain Type B reactions persist for long periods. Rechallenge with the drug is rarely justifiable.

Common adverse reactions, occurring more often than once in 500 patients, are usually recognized during early clinical trials. Indeed, safety evaluation has now become an important and integral component of clinical trials for efficacy because it is possible in this setting to adopt objective criteria for their detection. Thus, investigators will record the frequency of any adverse clinical events in both the test and control groups: a statistically significant increase in the frequency of particular symptoms or abnormal laboratory tests amongst patients treated with the test drug strongly suggest an adverse reaction. In this manner, it is possible to identify previously unsuspected adverse reactions and to obtain some estimate of their frequency.

Reactions occurring more rarely are extremely difficult to recognize. For statistical reasons, if a reaction occurs once in 1000 treated patients, 3000 of these treated patients would have to be observed to be 95 per cent certain of seeing the reaction in one. If the potential reaction is indistinguishable from a common naturally occurring disorder, then the number of subjects required could run into tens of thousands. Several techniques have been devised to solve this problem. In the wake of the *thalidomide tragedy, the UK Committee on the Safety of Medicines set up a spontaneous reporting system whereby all doctors are asked to inform the Committee, in strict confidence, about any suspected adverse reaction they encounter. Although it has generated useful information, this method is uncontrolled and can lead to bias: consequently, other methods are usually necessary to confirm or refute an association between drugs and suspected adverse reactions. A method which has proved to be particularly valuable once such a hypothesis has been generated, is the 'case-control' study. In this, the frequency of takers of a drug amongst patients with a particular condition are compared with the frequency of takers of the same drug in patients who do not suffer from the condition. The technique can be quick and effective, as was the case with the association between blood clotting and the oral contraceptive pill. The most powerful technique, however, is the cohort study where a large group of patients starting treatment with a drug are followed for months or years. This approach can not only confirm suspected adverse reactions and recognize previously unsuspected reactions, but can also estimate their incidence. Against this are the considerable logistic problems that arise in identifying the appropriate patients and arranging for their long-term follow-up. A study of oral contraceptives organized by the Royal College of General Practitioners is an outstanding example of the value of this technique.

It is axiomatic in modern therapeutics that patients should, on average, be better off taking a drug than not. It follows that a drug should be given to treat a particular condition only if it has been shown to be effective. Furthermore, the benefits should have been shown to outweigh the risks. In the treatment of lethal or life-threatening conditions, relatively straightforward clinical trials can demonstrate a favourable ratio between these two, but in many situations the benefit–risk ratio is much more difficult to establish. In the case of drugs used to relieve the symptoms of arthritis, the severity of the disease will inevitably influence the degree of risk which patients would be prepared to accept. For drugs which merely provide symptomatic relief for self-limiting conditions (e.g. a common *cold or a *sprained ankle) the degree of acceptable risk is likely to be very small.

In the UK at the time a new drug is marketed for widespread use the benefit–risk ratio will have been carefully considered by the Committee on the Safety of Medicines and found to be favourable. Where it is found to be unfavourable, the drug is refused a marketing licence. For reasons discussed above, this decision is in many respects a provisional one and, with time, the assessment may change. Thus, rare but important adverse effects may appear when many thousands of patients are treated, as some adverse effects may manifest themselves only after many years of continuous use, or safer drugs may become available. Where the benefit–risk ratio appears to become unfavourable, the Committee on the Safety of Medicines may recommend changes in the terms under which the drug can be marketed, or may recommend to the Secretary of State for Health that its licence be revoked or suspended.

Prescribing. When a doctor prescribes a drug for a particular patient, three separate aspects have to be considered: which drug and for how long; the dose and frequency of dosing; and what monitoring is required to optimize efficacy and minimize toxicity.

The drug. Having decided to recommend drug therapy to a patient, the choice of which particular compound to prescribe will depend on the patient's disorder, its severity, the way in which the drug is handled, its potential adverse effects, and its compatibility with other medicines that the patient may be taking.

The dose and dosage interval. From the previous discussion it should be clear that the dosage and the frequency of dosing (the dosage interval) are important determinants of the response to drug therapy. The dosage interval is mainly governed by a drug's elimination half-life: for compounds with short half-lives short dosage intervals will be required, while longer dosage intervals are appropriate for drugs with long half-lives. It is now generally appreciated that patients can remember to take drugs once or twice daily with reasonable accuracy, but that with more frequent dosing patients become increasingly forgetful. Considerable efforts are therefore made to use once- or twice-daily dosing regimens—either by selecting drugs with longer half-lives, or by prescribing sustained release preparations of those with shorter half-lives. Even so, it is necessary for some drugs (e.g. many antibiotics) to be given three or four times daily.

The effective dose depends on a variety of factors. For a few drugs, the therapeutic and toxic doses are so widely separated out that a 'standard' dose can be defined. For many drugs, however, interpersonal variation renders the concept of a standard dose quite unacceptable. For such drugs, two options are available. When the clinical condition is urgent, the doctor may feel it necessary to risk Type A adverse reactions in favour of guaranteed therapeutic success and will therefore initiate treatment with a relatively high dose: where the clinical problem is less urgent, then it is usual to start treatment with a low dose and to increase it in the light of the patient's response.

Monitoring drug treatment. When patients are prescribed regular drug treatment it is mandatory that careful monitoring—both for efficacy and safety—are undertaken. Lack of efficacy may be due to an erroneous diagnosis and thus inappropriate drug therapy, or it may be due to relative underdosage for the particular individual. Evidence of an adverse reaction to the drug may be an indication for lowering the dosage, or withdrawing the drug altogether.

Drug therapy can be monitored by three methods. Obviously the most important method relies on the the patient's subjective symptoms. In many instances, however, drugs are given to correct biochemical or physiological abnormalities (e.g. *diabetes mellitus, *hypertension) which do not give rise to symptoms, and with some drugs, the earliest laboratory manifestations of toxicity may be subclinical. In both these circumstances, monitoring can be most effectively achieved by measurement of the appropriate pharmacological effect (e.g. *blood sugar in diabetes or *blood pressure in hypertension). Finally, it is becoming increasingly possible to monitor blood levels of particular drugs in order to optimize therapeutic efficacy and minimize toxicity. This technique is expected to be more widely used in the future.

Development of new drugs. When promising new drugs have been synthesized by medicinal chemists, they undergo both preclinical and clinical evaluation before becoming widely available.

Preclinical studies. Before new chemicals are given to man, they undergo careful laboratory tests. These include detailed studies of their effects on isolated animal organs and tissues, as well as their actions in intact animals. New drugs are also subjected to detailed toxicological studies in experimental animals after single doses, and during prolonged administration for up to two years or more. At the end of these studies, the animals' major organs are removed for microscopic examination and other analytical tests. Depending on the proposed clinical use, special tests (e.g. reproductive toxicity (see TERATOLOGY), carcinogenicity) may also be undertaken. If the results of these investigations are judged to be satisfactory, human studies may be undertaken.

Clinical studies. Clinical studies with new drugs are divided into three phases:

The first phase involves the administration of single doses to patients or, more often, volunteers. The aim of this is to confirm that the drug has the pharmacological effect in man that has been anticipated in animals, to study how it is handled in humans, and to assess the likely tolerance of patients who will be exposed to it. In the first human experiments it is usual to start with a very small dose, and then gradually to increase it until the estimated therapeutic dose has been reached.

The aim of the second phase is to investigate, usually by means of randomized controlled trials, the efficacy of the drug in the particular disorder for which it has been designed. These studies are accompanied by an evaluation of its safety: this not only involves general safety monitoring, but may also include more detailed investigations of those organs which have been shown to be especially vulnerable in experimental animals.

The final premarketing phase is designed to investigate the new drug's performance when given to larger numbers of patients, and when compared with existing remedies. Again, this study includes assessment of both safety and efficacy. If the appropriate national regulatory authority is satisfied that the new drug is effective, and that its safety in relation to efficacy seems appropriate, then the pharmaceutical manufacturer concerned may be permitted to market it.

Postmarketing studies. Once a new drug has been marketed both the manufacturer and the medical profession will continue to study its actions. Sometimes clinical experience with it will either suggest new uses, or an association with unexpected adverse effects. In the case of the latter, two particular problems may arise: first, the drug may on rare occasions produce serious reactions which were not seen during animal tests, and which could not have been detected in the relatively small numbers of patients (usually 1000 to 3000) who participate in the premarketing studies; secondly, some adverse effects may become apparent only after several years of continuous use and, again, may not be predicted from animal tests or in relatively short clinical trials (usually 3–6 months). It has been argued that premarketing trials of new drugs should be much more stringent, involving more patients treated for longer periods of time. However, such a step would inevitably lengthen the development time for new drugs and would deprive many patients of their benefits. In the opinion of the author, it is more appropriate for new drugs to be subjected to more careful postmarketing studies.

Conclusions. Modern drugs have had a major impact on contemporary medicine. Advances since 1945 (only 17 out of 110 drugs shown in Tables 1–8, which are admittedly selective and incomplete, were available before this date) have resulted in the availability of effective treatments for a wide variety of disorders resulting either in cure or a substantial improvement in the quality of life. These developments have occurred as a result of a better understanding of medicinal chemistry, pharmacology, and clinical pharmacology. Overall, the positive features of modern drugs have far outweighed the negative ones (adverse reactions). In some instances, however, this has not been the case and current research is being directed towards producing safer remedies. We must also hope that future research will result in the development of effective treatment for patients to whom we cannot, at present, offer anything of much value. Recent biochemical and pharmacological advances in identifying new neurotransmitters (e.g. certain brain peptides) and chemical mediators (e.g. lipoxygenase products of arachidonic acid) should provide a useful stimulus.   M. D. RAWLINS

Table 1. Some drugs used in the treatment of gastrointestinal disorders

Therapeutic class	Pharmacological class	Drugs	
		Generic name	Brand names (UK examples)
Anti-ulcer agent	Antacid	Aluminium hydroxide	Aludrox
Anti-ulcer agent	Antacid	Magnesium trisilicate	
Anti-ulcer agent	Histamine (H_2) antagonist	Cimetidine	Tagamet
Anti-ulcer agent	Histamine (H_2) antagonist	Ranitidine	Zantac
Anti-ulcer agent	Mucosal protective	Tripotassium dicitratobismuthate	De-Nol
Anti-ulcer agent	Mucosal protective	Sucralfate	Antepsin
Antidiarrhoeal	Adsorbent	Kaolin	Kaopectin
Antidiarrhoeal	Opioid	Codeine phosphate	
Antidiarrhoeal	Opioid	Diphenoxylate	Lomotil
Antidiarrhoeal	Opioid	Loperamide	Imodium
Laxative	Bulking agent	Ispaghula husk	Isogel Metamucil
Laxative	Stimulant	Bisacodyl	Dulcolax
Laxative	Stimulant	Cascara	
Laxative	Stimulant	Senna	Senokot
Laxative	Stool softener	Dioctyl sodium sulphosuccinate	Dioctyl
Laxative	Osmotic laxative	Lactulose	Duphalac

Table 2. Some drugs used in the treatment of cardiovascular disorders

Therapeutic class	Pharmacological/Chemical class	Drugs	
		Generic name	Brand names (UK examples)
Anti-arrhythmic	Local anaesthetic	Lignocaine Disopyramide	Xylocard Rythmodan
Anti-arrhythmic	Calcium antagonist	Verapamil	Cordilox
Antihypertensive	Centrally acting	Methyldopa Clonidine	Aldomet Catapres
Antihypertensive	Adrenergic nerve blocker	Debrisoquine	Declinax
		Guanethidine	Ismelin
Antihypertensive	Alpha-adrenoceptor antagonist	Prazosin	Hypovase
Antihypertensive	Peripheral vasodilator	Hydralazine	Apresolin
Anti-anginal	Nitrate	Glyceryl trinitrate	Sustac
Anti-anginal	Nitrate	Isosorbide dinitrate	Cedocard
Anti-anginal	Calcium antagonist	Nifedipine	Adalat
—	Beta-noradrenoceptor antagonist	Propranolol Oxprenolol Atenolol	Inderal Trasicor Tenormin
—	Diuretic	Bendrofluazide	Aprinox
—	Diuretic	Frusemide	Lasix
—	Diuretic	Spironolactone	Aldactone
—	Cardiac glycoside	Digoxin	Lanoxin
—	Anticoagulant	Heparin Warfarin	Hepsal Marovan

Table 3. Some drugs used in the treatment of respiratory disorders

Therapeutic class	Pharmacological class	Drug Generic name	Brand names (UK examples)
Bronchodilator	Beta-adrenoreceptor agonist	Salbutamol Terbutaline	Ventolin Bricanyl
Bronchodilator	Cholinergic antagonist	Ipratoprium bromide	Atrovent
Bronchodilator	Phosphodiesterase inhibitor	Theophylline	
Bronchodilator	Inhaled corticosteroid	Betamethasone valerate	Bextasol
Bronchodilator	Mast cell stabilizer	Sodium cromoglycate	Intal
Antitussive	Opioid	Pholcodine	Sancos

Table 4. Some drugs used in the treatment of central nervous system disorders

Therapeutic class	Pharmacological/chemical class	Drugs Generic	Brand names (UK examples)
Hypnotic	Benzodiazepine	Nitrazepam	Mogadon
Hypnotic	Benzodiazepine	Flurazepam	Dalmane
Anxiolytic	Benzodiazepine	Diazepam	Valium
Anxiolytic	Benzodiazepine	Chlordiazepoxide	Librium
Anxiolytic	Benzodiazepine	Lorazepam	Ativan
Antipsychotic	Dopamine antagonist	Chlorpromazine	Largactil
Antipsychotic	Dopamine antagonist	Haloperidol	Haldol
Antipsychotic	Dopamine antagonist	Flupenthixol	Depixol
Antidepressant	Tricyclic drug	Amitriptyline	Tryptizol
Antidepressant	Tricyclic drug	Imipramine	Tofranil
Antidepressent	Tricyclic drug	Dothiepin	Prothiaden
Antidepressant	Monoamine oxidase inhibitor	Phenelzine	Nardil
Antiemetic	Cholinergic antagonist	Hyoscine	
Antiemetic	Histamine (H_1) antagonist	Cinnarizine Cyclizine	Stugeron Valoid
Antiemetic	Dopamine antagonist	Prochlorperazine Metoclopramide	Stemetil Maxolon
Analgesic	Prostaglandin synthetase inhibitor	Aspirin Ibuprofen Mefenamic acid	Solprin Brufen Ponstan
Analgesic	Opioid	Codeine Dihydrocodeine Pethidine Morphine Papaveretum	DF118 Omnopon
Anticonvulsant	Barbiturate	Phenobarbitone	
Anticonvulsant	Hydantoin	Phenytoin	Epanutin
Anticonvulsant	Iminostilbene	Carbamazepine	Tegretol
Anticonvulsant	GABA transaminase inhibitor	Valproate	Epilim
Antiparkinsonian	Dopamine precursor	Levodopa	Sinemet Madopar
Antiparkinsonian	Cholinergic antagonist	Ophenadrine	Artane

Table 5. Some drugs used in the treatment of infections

Therapeutic class	Pharmacological/chemical class	Drugs	
		Generic name	Brand name (UK examples)
Antibacterial	Penicillins	Benzylpenicillin Ampicillin Flucloxacillin	Crystopen Penbritin Floxapen
Antibacterial	Cephalosporins	Cephaloridine Cefuroxime	Ceporin Zinacef
Antibacterial	Tetracyclines	Oxytetracycline	Imperacin
Antibacterial	Aminoglycosides	Gentamicin	Genticin
Antibacterial	Sulphonamides	Sulphamethoxazole	
Antituberculous		Isoniazid Rifampicin	Rimifon Rifadin
Antilepromatous		Dapsone	
Antifungal agent		Miconazole	Manistat
Antifungal agent		Nystatin	
Antiviral agent		Idoxuridine	Herpid
Antiviral agent		Acyclovir	Zovirax
Antiprotozoal agent	Antimalarials	Primaquin	
Antiprotozoal agent	Antimalarials	Proguanil	Paludrine
Antiprotozoal agent	Antimalarials	Pyrimethamine	Daraprim
Antiprotozoal agent	Amoebicides and trichomonacides	Metronidazole	Flagyl
Antihelmintic	Schistosomicides	Praziquantel Oxamniquine	Bittricide Mansil
Antihelmintic	Ascaricides	Piperazine Thiabendazole	Antepar Mintezol
Antihelmintic	Filariacides	Diethylcarbamazine	Banocide

Table 6. Some drugs used in the treatment of musculo-skeletal disorders

Therapeutic class	Pharmacological/chemical class	Drugs	
		Generic Name	Brand names (UK examples)
Non-steroidal anti-inflammatory	Salicylate	Aspirin	Solprin
Non-steroidal anti-inflammatory	Propionic acid derivative	Ibuprofen Flurbiprofen	Brufen Froben
Non-steroidal anti-inflammatory	Acetic acid derivative	Diclofenac Fenclofenac	Voltarol Flenac
Non-steroidal anti-inflammatory	Indolacetic acid derivative	Indomethacin	Indocid
Non-steroidal anti-inflammatory	Oxicam	Piroxicam	Feldene
Antirheumatic	Gold salt	Aurothiomalate	Myocrisin
Antirheumatic	Chelating agent	Penicillamine	Distamine
Antirheumatic	Immunosuppressive agent	Azathioprine	Imuran
Antigout	Xanthine oxidase inhibitor	Allopurinol	Zyloric

Table 7. Some drugs used in the treatment of malignant disease

Pharmacological/chemical class	Drugs		
	Generic name		Brand names (UK examples)
Alkylating agent	Busulphan		Myleran
	Cyclophosphamide		Endoxana
	Melphalan		Alkeran
Cytotoxic antibiotic	Doxorubicin		Adriamycin
	Bleomycin		
Antimetabolite	Methotrexate		
	Mercaptopurine		Purinethol
Vinca alkaloids	Vincristine		Oncovin
	Vinblastine		Velbe

Table 8. Some drugs used in the treatment of endocrine disorders

Therapeutic class	Pharmacological/chemical class	Drugs	
		Generic name	Brand names (UK examples)
Antidiabetic	Insulin	Neutral insulin	Actrapid
		Insulin zinc suspension	Monotard
Antidiabetic	Sulphonylurea	Chlorpropramide	Diabenese
		Glibenclamide	Daonil
Antidiabetic	Biguanides	Metformin	Glucophage
Antithyroid		Carbimazole	Neomercazole
Steroids	Glucocorticoids	Prednisolone	Prednesol
		Cortisone	Cortisyl
Steroids	Oestrogens	Ethinyloestradiol	
		Mestranol	
Steroids	Progestogens	Norethisterone	
		Medroxyprogesterone	
Steroids	Androgens	Testosterone	
		Methyltestosterone	

Further reading

Avery, G. S. (1982). *Drug Treatment.* Sydney.
British National Formulary (1984). British Medical Association & The Pharmaceutical Society of Great Britain, London.
Davies, D. M. (1981). *Textbook of Adverse Drug Reactions.* 2nd edn, Oxford.
Dukes, M. N. G. (1980). *Meyla's Side Effects of Drugs.* Amsterdam.
Gilman, A. G., Goodman, L. S. and Gilman, A. (1980). *The Pharmacological Basis of Therapeutics.* London and New York.
Laurence, D. R. and Bennett, P. N. (1980). *Clinical Pharmacology.* Edinburgh.
Laurence, D. R. and Black, J. M. (1978). *The Medicines You Take.* London.
Martindale, W. (1982). *The Extra Pharmacopoeia.* London.

PHARMACOPOEIA. A compilation of recognized drugs, giving data relevant to preparation, recognition, standards of purity, dosage, storage, and labelling. See also BRITISH PHARMACOPOEIA; NATIONAL FORMULARY (USA); NATIONAL FORMULARY, BRITISH.

PHARMACOPOEIA COMMISSION. A body set up under the *Medicines Act 1968 charged with the responsibility, under the authority of the Health Ministers, of preparing new editions of and amendments to the *British Pharmacopoeia* (previously the responsibility of the *General Medical Council).

PHARMACY ACTS 1852, 1868, 1954. These UK statutes are analogous to the *Medical Acts. They concern the education, qualification, standards, conduct, and control of the pharmaceutical profession and the powers and duties conferred on the professional body for pharmacy, the *Pharmaceutical Society of Great Britain. See PHARMACY AND PHARMACISTS.

PHARMACY AND PHARMACISTS. The history of pharmacy in the UK is inseparable from that of the *apothecaries who were the predecessors of the pharmacists in the practice of the profession.

The 1904 edition of the *Oxford English Dictionary* gives four definitions of the word pharmacy:

1. 'A medicine or a medicinal potion' (this use is said to be obsolete and rare);
2. 'The use or administration of drugs or medicines' (which is said to be now chiefly poetic or rhetorical, or as a vague extension of the next sense);
3. 'The art or practice of collecting, preparing, and dispensing drugs, especially for medicinal purposes; the occupation of a druggist or pharmaceutical chemist' (the leading current sense);
4. 'A place where medicines are prepared or dispensed; a drug store or dispensary'.

A pharmacist is defined as 'A person skilled or engaged in pharmacy; a druggist or pharmaceutical chemist'.

To be legally recognized as a pharmacist a person must have an appropriate pharmaceutical qualification and his name must be in the *Register of Pharmaceutical Chemists*.

There has been controversy about the origin of the title pharmacist but most authorities now believe that it is derived from the Greek word (*pharmacon*) meaning a remedy but which can also mean a poison or dye.

The Latin title Societas Pharmaceutica was used for the Society of Apothecaries of London in the 17th and 18th c. and some form of the word pharmacist was used for the apothecary in Latin documents for several centuries both in the UK and on the continent of Europe, showing that the words were regarded as synonymous.

The 1881 edition of the *Oxford English Dictionary* defines the apothecary as:

1. orig. One who kept a store or shop of non-perishable commodities, spices, drugs, comfits, preserves etc. (This passed at an early period into the next; in 1617 the Apothecaries' Company of London was separated from the Grocers'.)
2. spec. The earliest name for: One who made and sold drugs for medicinal purposes—the business now (since about 1800) conducted by a druggist or pharmaceutical chemist.

From about 1700 apothecaries gradually took a place as general medical practitioners, and the modern apothecary holds this status legally, by examination and licence of the Apothecaries' Company; but in popular usage the term is archaic.

Some form of the word apothecary has been used to describe the practitioner of pharmacy in many countries and is still the usual name in Scandinavia, Germany, Austria, Holland, German-speaking Switzerland, Poland, the Soviet Union, and Bulgaria. In other countries, notably the UK, France, Italy, Portugal, Spain, and the USA, the title apothecary, although formerly used, has been replaced by some form of the word pharmacist and the older title is rarely, if ever, encountered except in a historical context. In colonies and independent countries of colonial origin, usage has always followed the trend in the parent country.

In some countries, such as England and Wales and Ireland, the reason for the change is obvious since in those countries the apothecaries, as a profession, changed from the practice of pharmacy to that of medicine, but in others the cause is less apparent.

In France the old title of *apothicaire* was once a proud one but during the 17th and 18th c. the French apothecaries were the target of much ridicule from writers such as Molière and cartoonists like Daumier because it was customary for them to administer *clysters or *enemas to members of the Royal family, the services, and the aristocracy. The satire was not aimed at the apothecaries but inevitably affected them and they changed their title to *pharmacien*. The revolution perpetuated the change since the revolutionaries associated the old title with feudalism and the new one with Greek democracy. The Napoleonic conquests probably influenced a similar change in countries then occupied by the French.

In the USA the title apothecary is being revived for pharmacists dealing only with drugs, medicines, and closely related health products. It is also sometimes used for their pharmacies. The American College of Apothecaries is an organization of pharmacists who pledge themselves to conduct only professional pharmacies.

These changes of title have been discussed by Whittet (1962–72) in a series of articles under the general title 'From Apothecary to Pharmacist.' Several papers have been published on the origins of the titles apothecary and pharmacist and these were summarized by Whittet (1962). In contrast to the controversy about that of pharmacist there appears to be general agreement that the word apothecary originated from the Greek word ἀποθήκα (*apotheka*; storehouse) from ἀποτίθημι (*apotithemi;* to lay aside) which became *apotheca* in Latin and apothecary in English.

Historical development of pharmacy. *Ancient times.* Pharmacy, the art of the apothecary, is one of the oldest professions in the world. Prescriptions containing drugs that are still in use have been found at Nippur, a city of ancient Sumeria, on clay tablets which are believed to date from about 2700 BC. The famous *Ebers papyrus, mentioning many drugs and medicines, was probably written in about 1550 BC. There are numerous references to the apothecary in the Old Testament of the Bible, many of which were quoted by Wootton (1910). The earliest is that in Exodus 30:25, where the holy anointing oil is prescribed to be made 'after the art of the apothecary' and, in the same chapter v.29 the ingredients of incense are ordered to be made into a confection 'after the art of the apothecary, tempered together.' In II Chronicles 16:14 the apothecaries' art is mentioned in the preparation of sweet odours and divers kinds of spices for the burial of King Asa.

Nehemiah 3:8 records that 'Hananiah, the son of one of the apothecaries' worked on the repair of the walls of Jerusalem by the side of Haraiah of the goldsmiths. This suggests that in Jerusalem there were city trade guilds like those which were common in mediaeval Britain and which still exist in several cities such as London and Chester.

In Ecclesiastes 10:1, we find the passage 'Dead flies cause the ointment of the apothecary to send forth a stinking odour'. This is said to be a proverb meaning that a little folly spoils a reputation for wisdom. From it also comes the expression 'a fly in the ointment'. In several instances in the Revised Version of the Bible the word apothecary has been replaced by 'perfumer'.

In the Apocrypha, however, there is a well-known passage referring to the apothecary in which it is obvious that a practitioner of pharmacy is intended.

In Ecclesiasticus 38:3–8 we find:

The Lord hath created medicines out of the earth;
And he that is wise will not abhor them.
Was not the water made sweet with wood,
That the virtue thereof might be known?
And he hath given men skill,
That he might be honoured in his marvellous works.
With such doth he heal men and taketh away their pains.
Of such doth the apothecary make a confection;
And of his works there is no end;
And from him is peace over all the earth.

In some modern versions of the Bible the word apothecary has usually been replaced by pharmacist.

In the 7th c. the Holy Places of Christendom came under attack, first by the Persians and later by Muhammad and his followers, including the Saracens and later the Ottoman Turks. There followed about 850 years of sporadic fighting between the Christians and the Muslims. These wars were known as the Crusades. A hostel for pilgrims to the Holy Places was set up as early as AD 600. Among the Crusaders were the Knights Hospitallers, founded at about the end of the 11th c. and formally recognized in 1113; their duty was to care for the sick and wounded. They became known as the Order of *St John of Jerusalem; members of the Order established numerous hostels and hospitals in the Holy Land, of which one is said to have survived the Saracen reconquest. After their expulsion from the Holy Land the Hospitallers established themselves in Cyprus (1291–1310), Rhodes (1310–1522), and finally in Malta (1530–1798). It seems likely that their hospitals included pharmacies. There is a mention of a well-equipped pharmacy in the Order's hospital at Rhodes (Renwick, 1958).

Much information about the Holy Infirmary at Malta has been given by Cassar (1965). Many beautiful specimens of apothecaries' drug jars and other equipment from the Infirmary are in the Malta Museum and there are a few in the Museum of the British Order at St John's Gate, Clerkenwell, London.

The various editions of Kremers' *History of Pharmacy* (Kremers, 1940; Kremers and Urdang, 1951; Sonnedecker, 1963, 1976) give useful and interesting outlines of the development of pharmacy from its earliest antecedents in Babylon, Assyria, Egypt, Greece, and Rome, through the Middle Ages in Europe and the Arab world, to the rise of professional pharmacy in representative countries of Europe—Italy, France, Germany, the UK, and Spain. Pharmacy in the USA is also discussed in considerable detail and many examples are given of discoveries and other contributions to science and to society by pharmacists of many countries.

The development of pharmacy in the UK. Because of its contacts with so many parts of the world through the first and second British Empires and the Commonwealth which developed from the latter, British pharmacy has had a world-wide influence. The development of pharmacy in the UK, especially in England and Wales, will therefore be discussed in some detail. Similarities and differences between British and European continental pharmacy will be described as will those between the four main countries of the UK, England, Wales, Scotland, and Ireland.

In Saxon England and in the early Norman period there was no difference between physician, apothecary, and surgeon, the practitioner known as a 'leech' performing the functions of all three. During the later Norman period the trade in drugs and spices was handled by the mercers, a title which originally meant a merchant who dealt in small wares.

Pepperers and spicers. In the latter part of the 12th c. this trade passed to the pepperers and spicers. The former were first mentioned as a guild in a Pipe Roll of 1179/80. (The Pipe Rolls were accounts of payments to the Crown.) The entry was under a Latin heading which meant 'Amercement [fine] of adulterine guilds in the city'. The guilds were called adulterine because they had not purchased the right of association from the Crown. The Pepperers' Guild must, therefore, have been founded some time before 1180. Pepperers and spicers dealt with the same types of commodities, known as 'spicery', a term which embraced not only spices, crude drugs, and prepared medicines, but also many other products such as sugar, alum, and dried fruits. The history of the pepperers and spicers has been discussed by Trease (1957, 1964), Whittet (1968), and Matthews (1962, 1980). It seems likely that the apothecaries formed an autonomous specialized section of the Pepperers' Guild as there are references to Wardens of the Apothecaries as early as 1328.

In 1345 the pepperers and spicers founded the Fraternity of St Anthony which was restricted to pepperers, spicers, and apothecaries and in 1373 changed its title to the Grocers' Company. The apothecaries remained a section of these guilds until they finally seceded in 1617.

The encroachment of the apothecaries into medicine gradually increased and from about the reign of Henry VIII in the early 16th c. there began a long struggle between the apothecaries and the physicians about the extent to which the former could prescribe for and treat patients as well as dispense medicines and sell drugs and medicines.

Numerous apothecaries, both London and provincial, were granted Episcopal Licences to practise medicine and/or surgery, for example, George Haughton of London (medicine, c.1634), Job Weale of Kingston upon Thames, a member of the London Society (medicine, 1637), William Dove of Devon (medicine and surgery, 1580), Nicholas Tripe of Ashburton (apothecary, surgery, and *man-midwifery, 1747), Toby Parnell of Congleton, Cheshire (surgery, 1663).

The apothecaries. The apothecaries were discontented at being under the domination of the grocers, whom they regarded as being inferior in knowledge and skill, so they made determined efforts to gain their independence.

In 1617 they were given a Charter by King James VI of Scotland who had become James I of England in 1603. This established them as a City guild or Livery Company under the title of the Worshipful Society of Apothecaries of London. The Charter gave the apothecaries control of pharmacy in 'the City of London, Liberties and Suburbs thereof and within seven miles of the City' and it was not until 1815 that the Society's powers extended throughout England and Wales.

In the provinces the apothecaries were not numerous enough to form separate guilds so they joined those of other occupations such as the mercers or merchants, grocers or *barbersurgeons. There are also numerous examples of members of the London Society practising in the provinces and of the sons of provincial apothecaries being apprentices to London apothecaries. No doubt many of these returned to practise in the provinces. The position of the apothecaries in provincial guilds has been described by Whittet (1964).

After the grant of their Charter the London apothecaries increased in numbers and influence and some members began to devote more of their time to medicine rather than to pharmacy. They greatly strengthened their position as medical practitioners during the Great *Plague (bubonic plague) of 1664–6 when most of the physicians, who were the attendants of the rich, went with the Court to Oxford. Many of those who remained died and a few fled. Almost all of the apothecaries remained in London and treated the victims of the epidemic (Whittet, 1971).

From the time of the Plague until the end of the 17th c. the apothecaries encroached more and more on medicine although many continued to practise pharmacy and some practised both.

Eventually, in 1703, the College of Physicians brought a case against a London apothecary, William Rose for practising medicine by treating a patient without the supervision of a physician. He was convicted but when he appealed to the House of Lords (the final arbitrator of British law) the conviction was annulled (Bayles, 1940).

From then onwards the apothecaries practised quite openly both medicine and pharmacy until the *Apothecaries Act of 1815 gave the Society of Apothecaries complete control of the general practice of medicine and of the education concerned with it. The Society retained those powers until the setting up of the *General Medical Council in 1858 following the *Medical Act of that year.

The Society of Apothecaries is now a medical body and its Licence in Medicine and Surgery (LMSSA) is a registrable medical qualification. The Society also awards postgraduate diplomas in industrial health, medical jurisprudence, venereology, history of medicine, and philosophy of medicine, and for pharmacy technicians. The Society founded a faculty of the history of medicine and pharmacy in 1959. Philosophy was added to the title in 1973. The faculty organizes a series of eponymous lectures in the history and philosophy of medicine and pharmacy. Accounts of the history of the Society of Apothecaries have been given by Barratt (1905), Wall, Cameron, and Underwood (1963), and Copeman (1967).

The chemists and druggists and pharmacists. Although the apothecaries dominated pharmacy before the 18th c. there is evidence that both chemists and druggists were engaged in the preparation and sale of drugs and medicines for at least 250 years before the foundation of the *Pharmaceutical Society of Great Britain in 1841.

Chemists probably developed from the *alchemists, one of whose aims was to discover the elixir of life, and from the followers of *Paracelsus, the 16th c. Swiss physician and chemist who advocated the use of chemical remedies, especially minerals.

The druggists were members of the Grocers' Company who dealt mainly with *herbal remedies, usually in the raw or unprepared state.

Many variants of the word 'pharmacist' were used in the 16th and 17th c., most frequently to describe apothecaries but sometimes also for chemists and druggists. The old spelling of the title was chymist.

There is now ample evidence that there was less distinction between apothecary, chemist, druggist, and pharmacist than was previously believed, especially in the provinces.

During the 18th and early 19th c., as the apothecaries tended to devote more and more of their time to the practice of medicine, the chemists and druggists took over their pharmaceutical functions. Moreover, those apothecaries still practising pharmacy frequently described themselves as 'Apothecary and Druggist' and sometimes only as 'Druggist' or 'Chemist and Druggist'.

An attempt to make a General Pharmaceutical Association was made in 1795 but the organization did not last long. Finally in 1841 a large group of chemists and druggists combined with the apothecaries still practising pharmacy to form the

Pharmaceutical Society of Great Britain which became the examining body for practitioners of pharmacy in the UK.

In Scotland the apothecaries were mainly associated with the surgeons. The early Edinburgh apothecaries appear to have been members of the Barber-Surgeons' Guild founded in 1505, which was given powers in 1621 to inspect drugs and destroy defective ones. There were also 'simple apothecaries' or 'pharmatians' who did not practise surgery and who, in 1682, came under the protection of the Royal College of Physicians of Edinburgh.

In 1778 when the Royal College of Surgeons of Edinburgh received its Charter the apothecaries and barbers were separated from the surgeons. Towards the end of the 18th c. druggists appear to have become numerous and they joined with the simple apothecaries to form the Society of Druggist-Apothecaries which was granted a Royal Charter. That Society became incorporated in the Pharmaceutical Society of Great Britain in 1841.

In Glasgow the Faculty of Physicians and Surgeons (now the Royal College of Physicians and Surgeons of Glasgow) was established in 1599 by the Royal Charter of James VI and that body controlled the practice of medicine, surgery, and pharmacy in the West of Scotland.

When the Pharmaceutical Society of Great Britain was founded in 1841, it took control of pharmacy throughout Scotland as well as in England and Wales (Whittet, 1962–72).

In Ireland the apothecaries were incorporated by a Charter of James II dated 1687 into the Barber-Surgeons' Guild of St Mary Magdalen, which had received its first Charter from Henry VI in 1446.

In 1745 George II granted the apothecaries a Charter giving them independence as the Guild of St Luke. The Irish apothecaries also began to practise medicine and the Licentiate of the Apothecaries' Hall of Dublin was recognized as a registrable medical qualification by the General Medical Council in 1859. In 1875 the Pharmaceutical Society of Ireland was founded to take over control of pharmacy in that country.

On the separation of the Irish Republic from the UK the Pharmaceutical Society of Northern Ireland was founded in 1925 and became the registering body in that province (Whittet, 1962–72).

Development of pharmacy in Commonwealth countries. In general, pharmacy in Commonwealth and in former British Empire or Commonwealth countries has developed on similar lines to those in the UK. In most of the English-speaking countries except the USA, the title most used by the public for the practitioner of pharmacy is 'chemist'. This leads to confusion with other persons with chemical qualifications working in other branches of chemistry. The title chemist is restricted to registered pharmacists in the UK *only* in connection with the sale of goods by retail. The Royal Society of Chemistry, the professional body of chemists, as distinct from pharmaceutical chemists or pharmacists, has introduced the title 'Chartered Chemist' for the higher grades of its membership. Many pharmacists, however, also belong to that Society.

Matthews (1962) has described the foundation and development of several Commonwealth pharmaceutical societies. Histories of pharmacy in two major Commonwealth countries have recently been published—Australia (Haines, 1976), and New Zealand (Combes, 1981).

Development of pharmacy in other European countries. In most European countries the apothecary or pharmacist developed from the pepperers and spicers in a manner similar to that in the UK and there also chemical remedies came into use. Many of these countries also had apothecaries' guilds but in none of them did they change from pharmacy to medicine.

In the independent countries derived from other empires (e.g. those of France, Holland, Portugal, and Spain) pharmacy has usually followed the pattern of that in the former colonial power.

Community or general practice pharmacy. There are considerable variations in the style of community pharmacy (also called general practice or retail pharmacy) in the various European countries. In Scandinavia, Austria, and the Eastern Bloc countries, pharmacies tend to be restricted to purely professional activities, dealing only in medicine and medical, surgical, and allied health products, whereas in others such as the UK many para-pharmaceutical and even non-pharmaceutical items are sold. In the UK it has become the custom for pharmacists to supply cosmetics and photographic materials, both of which were originally developed by pharmacists. Some of the branches of the large pharmaceutical chains have become general stores but the dispensing of medicines is kept separate and remains a professional activity.

Pharmacies have been nationalized in the Eastern Bloc countries and in Sweden. In most European countries there is control and restriction of the opening and siting of pharmacies which also have a monopoly of the supply of medicines. These conditions do not apply in the UK or in Germany.

Health services are now in operation in many countries and have had a profound effect on the practice of pharmacy. There are many differences in these and in the methods of payment for services (Wertheimer, 1977).

In contrast to the position in the USA the title 'drug store' is not used in the UK for a pharmacy, where the former title means a shop owned and run by a non-pharmacist which sells proprietary medicines available by law for sale other than from pharmacies (General Sales List preparations), medical and surgical sundries, health products, foods, disinfectants, etc. Somewhat similar premises exist in continental Europe (e.g. droguerie (France), drogeria (Germany), drogheria (Italy), drogueria (Spain), etc.). Although the types of products sold in these shops vary from one country to another, none is under the direct control of a pharmacist. In some countries, however, a pharmacist may own one in addition to a pharmacy. American-type drug stores, under that title, exist in some European cities (e.g. Paris and Geneva).

Hospital pharmacy. The history of pharmacy in British hospitals has been described by Whittet (1965) who also dealt in detail with that of *University College Hospital and of its forerunner the London University Dispensary (Whittet, 1953 and 1962).

There is ample evidence that hospitals in the sense of houses of healing were attached to mediaeval monasteries in continental Europe and in the UK, but, unfortunately, in the latter, due to the dissolution of the monasteries in the 16th c. no pharmacies and very few records remain. Although those monastic infirmaries were mainly for the treatment of sick monks they also cared for sick pilgrims and for some of the local sick. Several famous British hospitals, notably the Royal Hospital of *St Bartholomew, *St Thomas's, and the *Bethlem Hospitals were ecclesiastical foundations.

The terms 'apothecarius' and 'apotheca' were in use from ancient times but, before the 12th c. it cannot be assumed that they referred to the apothecary and to his store in the pharmaceutical sense. Some records of English monasteries of the 12th and 14th c. undoubtedly refer to pharmaceutical apothecaries and it seems probable that there were monk-apothecaries attached to the larger monastic infirmaries. These persons probably tended the herb gardens which were attached to many monasteries (see also HERBAL REMEDIES ETC.). The three ancient London hospitals mentioned above all had apothecaries from at least the 16th c.

In the UK hospital apothecaries followed the general trend (Whittet, 1979) and, after a transitional period during which they practised both pharmacy and medicine they became what are now the Resident Medical Officers.

The apothecaries' change from pharmacy to medicine occurred later in hospitals than in community pharmacy, usually in about the middle of the 19th c. By that time the Pharmaceutical Society had been founded and the majority of the larger hospitals appointed pharmacists, although a few employed apothecaries' assistants known as dispensers. The latter title was also incorrectly used for registered pharmacists in hospitals for some years. It should not now be so used as it implies an unqualified person. It is now recognized that no hospital should be entirely without the services of a pharmacist.

Most hospitals in the UK now belong to the *National Health Service (NHS) and their pharmaceutical services have been the subject of several

studies which have led to some degree of standardization. In 1955 the report of a committee chaired by Sir Hugh Linstead was published. It defined the duties of hospital pharmacists as:

1. To be responsible for the provision, nature and quality of drugs, medicinal preparations, dressings, chemicals and pharmaceutical sundries;
2. To ensure that during their storage in hospital, the potency and quality of all these items are maintained;
3. To obtain the equipment necessary for the efficient and economical working of the pharmaceutical department;
4. To make preparations to be used in dispensing prescriptions; to prepare other products for medical or surgical use; and to devise formulae to meet special needs;
5. To dispense prescriptions;
6. To investigate pharmaceutical problems arising in the use of medicaments;
7. To assist in the development of new methods of treatment;
8. To promote economy in the use of medical supplies;
9. To assist in efficient prescribing by advising upon the nature and properties of medicaments and upon the selection of the most suitable substances and the form in which they should be prescribed;
10. To instruct or advise on the instruction of those whose duties involve the handling of the material provided by the Department;
11. To provide all necessary facilities for pharmaceutical students to obtain a comprehensive training in every aspect of the Department's work.

In 1968 the report of a committee chaired by Sir Noel Hall was published. It recommended that the hospital pharmaceutical services should be organized in larger units and that pharmacists should play a greater part in their administration. The services were therefore reorganized into Regions and Areas, and Regional and Area Pharmacists were appointed.

In 1974 the National Health Services Reorganization Act came into force (see NATIONAL HEALTH SERVICE). Its aim was to integrate the community, hospital, and local authority health services. Regional, Area, and District Health Authorities were established throughout England and most appointed Pharmaceutical Officers. The Regional and Area Pharmaceutical Officers had additional duties such as responsibility for the pharmaceutical services of former local authority clinics and for coordinating the community pharmaceutical services with those of the hospitals.

District Pharmaceutical Officers were also appointed. These were pharmacists in charge of hospital pharmacies who were given additional responsibilities for organizing the pharmaceutical services of districts. The boundaries of the latter were usually determined by local considerations such as geography, population distribution, and communications.

The arrangements in Scotland, Wales, and Northern Ireland were very similar except that there were no Regional Authorities or Officers and some of the duties of the latter were undertaken by the Chief Pharmacist of the respective central departments and others by Area Officers or, in the case of Scotland by the Chief Administrative Pharmaceutical Officers of the Health Boards.

In a further reorganization of the NHS which took place in 1982 the Areas were abolished and the duties of their Officers were shared between the Regional and District Officers. The appointment of these pharmaceutical officers allowed the pharmaceutical services to be rationalized. Several specialized subjects such as manufacturing, quality control, radiopharmaceuticals, and information services were developed on a regional basis. Central and peripheral advisory committees were appointed to advise the various health authorities.

Until recently, in some hospitals, much manufacturing was undertaken with the intention of producing cheaper products than those available from industry. It was also common for attempts to be made to copy popular proprietary medicines. With the introduction of potent new medicaments which were not available as the pure drug, and with the increasing complexity of such modern medicaments, hospital pharmacists began to examine their manufacturing programmes more critically and, apart from preparing simple *infusion fluids and preparations not available commercially, often restricted their activities to what is mainly bulk dispensing.

That trend was accelerated by the *Medicines Act of 1968 (Whittet, 1972a). Although NHS hospitals, as Crown property, are legally exempt from its requirements, they are nevertheless being applied administratively.

Clinical or ward pharmacy. Probably the most significant development in hospital pharmaceutical practice in recent years has been a steady movement towards a special interest in patients and in all aspects of the administration of drugs to them including their pharmacological and therapeutic effects and pharmacokinetics. This change of interest has resulted in pharmacists visiting the wards to advise on the choice of medicaments and their use to the best advantage of patients, leading to the development of what is now known as 'ward pharmacy' or 'clinical pharmacy', the extent and scope of which varies considerably in different hospitals. The pharmacist is often able to give invaluable advice about drug interactions and side-effects.

Another subject of special concern to pharmacists is the effect of formulation on the action of drugs, now known as 'biopharmaceutics'. Faulty formulation may result in preparations being devoid of pharmacological activity and different formulations may have different degrees of activity. The term 'bioavailability' has been coined for the study of the release of active ingredients from solid dosage forms such as tablets and capsules.

The development of clinical pharmacy has been accompanied by the establishment of information services which provide specialized pharmacological and pharmaceutical knowledge for the use of medical, pharmaceutical, and nursing staffs.

Clinical pharmacy is still a developing subject and seems likely to have a profound effect on the practice of pharmacy, especially in hospitals (Lawson and Richards, 1982).

Health centre pharmacy. The premises from which general practitioners of medicine carry out their practices in the UK are usually called 'surgeries', whilst those of specialists are called 'consulting rooms'. Recently, many practitioners have formed partnerships or larger groups and now practise from larger premises. Pharmacists are not employed in group practices, however, and medicines are supplied from them only in rural areas.

Health centres, on the other hand, vary in size from those employing only a few doctors to what are virtually miniature hospitals with accessory departments such as radiology, pathology, etc. These premises belong to the NHS and are administered by the local Health Authority but the medical staffs are independent practitioners in contract with the Health Service.

Most health centres do not have pharmacies, and patients, except in rural areas, are given prescriptions to be dispensed in community pharmacies.

In a few there are pharmacies under the control of full-time NHS pharmacists, while in others, pharmacies have been established by consortia of local pharmacists who may employ pharmacists to manage them. This arrangement is that generally favoured by the Pharmaceutical Society and by most of the profession (Whittet, 1972b).

Manufacturing pharmacy. There has been a pharmaceutical industry in the UK since 1671 when the Society of Apothecaries of London established in its Hall a laboratory which remained active until 1922. A laboratory was established at the Apothecaries' Hall of Dublin in 1792. Numerous pharmaceutical manufacturing firms developed from the pharmacies of apothecaries.

Pharmaceutical education. In the early days pharmaceutical education was by means of apprenticeship to a practitioner, usually, in later years, accompanied by lectures and/or demonstrations.

A School of Pharmacy was founded by the Pharmaceutical Society of Great Britain in 1842, within a year of the foundation of the Society (Wallis, 1964). The School of Pharmacy later became affiliated to London University and eventually formed a constituent college called the School of Pharmacy of London University, as did the School of Pharmacy of Chelsea College, formerly Chelsea Polytechnic.

The following English universities award degrees in pharmacy: Aston in Birmingham (B.Sc.); Bath (B.Pharm.); Bradford (B.Pharm.); London (B.Pharm.); Manchester (B.Sc.); and Nottingham (B.Pharm).

In Scotland, Heriot-Watt University of Edinburgh and Strathclyde University of Glasgow award the degree of B.Sc. in Pharmacy while the University of Wales in Cardiff awards a Bachelor of Pharmacy degree. Queen's University of Belfast in Northern Ireland also awards a B.Sc. in pharmacy.

The following British Polytechnics award the degree of B.Sc. in Pharmacy through the Council for National Academic Awards: Robert Gordon's Institute, Aberdeen; Brighton, Leicester, Liverpool, Portsmouth, and Sunderland.

Persons obtaining a degree in pharmacy must register with the appropriate registering body before being allowed to practise in community pharmacy or in NHS hospitals. Registration is not essential for work in the pharmaceutical industry but many persons with pharmaceutical degrees working in that industry do register as pharmacists.

Registration with the Pharmaceutical Society of Great Britain includes membership of that Society (MPS). Fellowship (FPS) was awarded to holders of the former Pharmaceutical Chemist diplomas; it is now awarded either for research work approved by a committee of the Society or, in the case of those who have been on the Register of Pharmacists for 20 years, as a mark of distinction on the recommendation of the Panel of Fellows.

Persons obtaining the degree in pharmacy of Queen's University, Belfast, are entitled to register as pharmacists in Northern Ireland, becoming members of the Pharmaceutical Society of Northern Ireland (MPSNI). Under a reciprocal agreement they may also become members of the Pharmaceutical Society of Great Britain. The Northern Ireland Society also awards a fellowship.

Several British universities award degrees of Master of Pharmacy, Philosophy, or Science in pharmaceutical subjects either by research or by course work.

The schools or departments of pharmacy may be independent faculties of pharmacy or pharmaceutical sciences or may be autonomous divisions of faculties of medicine or science. Many pharmacists now obtain the degree of D.Phil. or Ph.D. through research while a few proceed to the degree of D.Sc. based upon published research.

Up to the present time no British university awards the degree of Doctor of Pharmacy, but this is available from several American universities either after a qualifying examination or for achievement in specialized subjects such as clinical pharmacy.

In the Republic of Ireland the Department of Pharmacy of Trinity College of the National University of Ireland in Dublin awards a degree in pharmacy (B.Sc.). Registration with the Pharmaceutical Society of Ireland entitles the graduate to membership of that Society (MPSI) which also awards a fellowship. Higher degrees in pharmaceutical and related subjects are also awarded by the National University of Ireland.

The College of Pharmacy Practice. In 1981 the Council of the Pharmaceutical Society of Great Britain decided to found a College of Pharmacy Practice with the following objects:

1. To promote and maintain a high standard of practice;
2. To advance education and training in all pharmaceutical disciplines and at all levels;
3. To establish standards for vocational training;
4. To advance knowledge of the application of pharmacy in total health care;
5. To conduct, promote, and facilitate research into the practice of pharmacy and to publish the results of those endeavours.

Founder membership was open to senior pharmacists with appropriate qualifications and experience and about 500 persons accepted such membership. There are also about 100 student members. The College is, at present, an autonomous body attached to the Pharmaceutical Society but may become independent.

Pharmacy technicians. During the period when apothecaries were in charge of hospital pharmacies, semi-trained assistants were employed for simple dispensing and other routine duties. They were known as apothecaries' or dispensing assistants or as dispensers. The titles elaboratory man, elaboratorian, and drugman were formerly used. Such persons are now usually called pharmacy assistants or aides.

The Apothecaries Act of 1815 directed the Society of Apothecaries to institute an examination to test the fitness of 'assistants to apothecaries in compounding and dispensing medicines'. Holders of that certificate were employed by 'dispensing doctors', hospitals, and by community pharmacies. The Society of Apothecaries has continued to award a certificate, the regulations for which are kept continually under revision to make its holders assistants to pharmacists and the title has been changed to that of dispensing technician. In addition, some other pharmaceutical organizations founded in 1965 the Pharmacy Assistants Training Board which arranged for the City and Guilds Institute of London to examine for and award a Certificate for Pharmacy Technicians. The Scottish Association for National Certificates and Diplomas also awards a Certificate.

Recently Business and Technician Education Councils have been set up in England and Wales and in Scotland and have drawn up syllabuses for a Pharmacy Technician Certificate (now called the B/TEC Certificate) which will be of a higher standard than any of the former ones.

The Society of Apothecaries certificate syllabus has been revised to make it equivalent to Part I of the B/TEC Certificate. It seems likely that most technicians both in hospital and community pharmacy will take one or other of these certificates. It is possible that the title 'technician' will ultimately be restricted to holders of the B/TEC certificate.

Pharmaceutical education abroad. Pharmaceutical education in Commonwealth countries has generally followed that in the UK, but standards vary in the different countries from university degrees equivalent to British ones to diplomas not much more advanced than those of pharmacy technicians. The Commonwealth Pharmaceutical Association is attempting to help member countries to raise the standards of the poorer qualifications.

The UK has agreements with Australia and New Zealand for the mutual recognition of pharmaceutical qualifications (Matthews, 1962). Other persons wishing to practise in the UK may submit evidence of their qualifications to the Pharmaceutical Society which has a committee to assess the applicants' fitness to practise here. The committee may require them to undergo further study and to spend some time in gaining practical experience of British pharmacy.

Many interesting developments have originated from the USA. A recent one is the adoption by about 15 of the states of the title 'pharmacy doctor' (PD) for all of their pharmacists irrespective of whether they hold doctors' degrees.

Negotiations are in progress for the promulgation of a Directive of the European Economic Community for the mutual recognition of pharmaceutical qualifications throughout the Community, which at present includes Belgium, Denmark, France, Germany, Greece, Holland, Italy, Ireland, Luxemburg, and the UK; Spain and Portugal are about to join.

Pharmaceutical organizations. *The Pharmaceutical Society of Great Britain.* As well as being the registering body for pharmacists the Society is the professional organization which controls educational standards and has a disciplinary committee to maintain and control professional standards. Through its Department of Pharmaceutical Sciences it undertakes research into the formulation, stability, bioavailability, and other properties of medicines and does testing for the Department of Health and other bodies.

Through the Pharmaceutical Press the Society publishes the weekly *Pharmaceutical Journal,* the monthly *Journal of Pharmacy and Pharmacology,* the *Pharmaceutical Codex,* the *Extra Pharmacopoeia* (Martindale), and several other books. It also arranges scientific and professional meetings and an annual conference.

The National Pharmaceutical Association. As a professional body the Pharmaceutical Society is precluded from taking a direct interest in negotiations about pharmacists' terms of services and related subjects. In the early 1920s the National Pharmaceutical Union (now Association) was established to deal with such matters. This body represents the interests of most community pharmacists in the UK and also organizes insurance and legal defence services for its members. Similar bodies exist in Northern Ireland and the Irish Republic.

Associated with, but independent of, these organizations are committees which negotiate with the Departments of Health the terms of service and remuneration of community pharmacists, for example the Pharmaceutical Services Negotiating Committee (England and Wales) and the Pharmaceutical General Council (Scotland).

The Guild of Hospital Pharmacists. Pharmacists took over from apothecaries the control of pharmacy in hospitals towards the end of the 19th c. and found the need for a body to represent their special interests. A Public Dispensers' Association was founded in 1897 and later became the Public Pharmacists' Association. In 1923 that organization joined with the pharmacists of the Hospital Officers' Association to form the Guild of Public Pharmacists, later the Guild of Hospital Pharmacists. In 1974 the Guild merged with a trade union, the Association of Scientific, Technical and Managerial Staffs—a very controversial decision in view of that union's radical views.

From 1936 the Guild published a journal, the *Public Pharmacist,* later the *Journal of Hospital Pharmacy,* now replaced by the *Proceedings of the Guild of Hospital Pharmacists.*

The British Society for the History of Pharmacy. In 1952 the Pharmaceutical Society established a History of Pharmacy Committee which became in 1967 the British Society for the History of Pharmacy. This organizes several evening meetings per year in London and an annual weekend conference in various provincial centres. It publishes a newsletter, *The Pharmaceutical Historian,* three or four times a year.

The Institute of Pharmacy Management International. This body, founded in 1964, has several overseas branches, especially in the Commonwealth. It is primarily concerned with the organizational and managerial aspects of pharmacy, and awards diplomas of membership and fellowship as well as publishing a journal.

The British Pharmaceutical Conference. Shortly after the foundation of the Pharmaceutical Society a group of pharmacists began to attend annual meetings of the British Association for the Advancement of Science and at that of 1863 they founded the British Pharmaceutical Conference. This meets annually for an exchange of reports and views on scientific and professional matters. The Conference eventually became part of the Pharmaceutical Society, the president of which becomes president of the Conference also.

Miscellaneous specialist groups. Numerous specialist groups within pharmacy have formed societies or similar organizations to discuss their particular subjects, for example clinical pharmacists, information pharmacists, radiopharmacists, rural pharmacists, and those engaged in quality assurance and regulatory affairs, drug research and drug dependence. These bodies organize meetings and symposia on their special subjects.

The pharmaceutical division of the Department of Health and Social Security (DHSS). A few individual pharmacists were employed in the Ministry of Health (now the DHSS) before the establishment of the NHS but the office of Chief Pharmacist was not created until 1947 when Harold Davis was appointed. He was responsible for many developments in the organization of pharmaceutical services resulting from the *National Health Service Act of 1946 and also played a prominent part in the foundation of the European Pharmacopoeia Commission.

Davis retired in 1967 and was succeeded by T. Douglas Whittet who was closely involved with the Medicines Act of 1968 and its implementation, including the appointment of the Medicines Inspectorate and the pharmaceutical staff of the Licensing Authority. Whittet retired in 1978 and was succeeded by B. A. Wills. There are now about 100 pharmacists and allied staff in the Department and they are involved in virtually all aspects of pharmacy. There are Chief Pharmacists in the Scottish Home and Health Department and the Department of Health and Social Services of Northern Ireland, and a Pharmaceutical Adviser works at the Welsh Office.

Pharmacy in the armed services. As early as the 13th c. the royal apothecaries often accompanied the King on his military campaigns. When Charles I reorganized the army in 1660 medical officers were appointed on a regimental basis and apothecaries, dispensers, and clerks were engaged for the hospitals. They were warrant officers but ranked as ensigns for quarters and allowances.

In 1661 the post of apothecary-general was created and that officer, together with the physician-general, and surgeon-general, formed the Army Medical Board.

By 1856 the apothecaries had become medical men and from then onwards the army trained its own dispensers in the Army (now Services) School of Dispensing. During the two World Wars pharmacists served in the Royal Army Medical Corps with the rank of sergeant-dispenser. In recent years some commissioned pharmacists have been recruited but there are still army dispensers with a training equivalent to that of civilian pharmacy technicians.

The Royal Navy has always recruited either apothecaries or pharmacists with the appropriate qualifications. There, too, the apothecaries became medical officers and from 1872 dispensers who were qualified as pharmacists were appointed. The title became pharmacist in 1916. Naval pharmacists hold civilian appointments in peacetime but are commissioned officers in wartime. The Navy also employs technicians known as sick-berth attendants.

The Royal Air Force employs dispensers like those of the army and formerly had a training school for them. They are now trained at the Services School of Dispensing at Colchester. A few commissioned pharmacists have been appointed to the Royal Air Force.

Pharmacopoeias. Most developed countries have published *pharmacopoeias, the purpose of which is to lay down standards for drugs and their preparations. Among the principal national ones are the British, French, German, Spanish, and US pharmacopoeias (Urdang, 1946a, 1951).

The *British Pharmacopoeia (BP), the first edition of which was published in 1864, developed from the London, Edinburgh, and Dublin Pharmacopoeias, the first editions of which appeared in 1617, 1699, and 1793 respectively.

In recent years the Scandinavian countries, Denmark, Finland, Iceland, Norway, and Sweden collaborated to produce the Nordic Pharmacopoeia.

The *World Health Organization produced the International Pharmacopoeia in 1951, a second edition in 1956, and a third in 1967. It was not, however, binding on any country and represented a set of recommended standards.

The European Pharmacopoeia. A very important development has been the production of the European Pharmacopoeia. In 1964 the six original European Economic Community (EEC) countries, Belgium, France, Germany, Holland, Italy, and Luxemburg, together with Switzerland and the UK, formed the European Pharmacopoeia Commission which has published several volumes of the European Pharmacopoeia, the first volume of which appeared in 1969. The following countries have now joined the Commission: Austria, Denmark, Iceland, Ireland, Norway, and Sweden, while Finland and Portugal send observers to the Commission's meetings. Greece has joined and Spain is likely to join the EEC in the near future and they will presumably also join the Commission.

The participating countries are pledged to adopt the standards of the European Pharmacopoeia as their official standards. As the pharmacopoeias of France, the UK, and Holland are used in their former colonial territories the European Pharmacopoeia is likely to have a world-wide influence but it will be many years before it becomes comprehensive enough to replace those of individual countries.

Other pharmaceutical compendia. The British Pharmaceutical Codex. The *British Pharmaceutical Codex (BPC) has been published by the Pharmaceutical Society at irregular intervals since 1907. It is a complementary volume to the British Pharmacopoeia; it contains information on the action and uses of drugs in addition to analytical and formulary data. For many years the BPC was much more comprehensive than the BP as it described most available drugs whereas the BP included only a selected representation of each group of drugs. The Codex was the first publication to lay down standards for surgical dressings, *sutures and similar products, *antisera, *vaccines and related substances, and preparations of human *blood products.

When the British Pharmacopoeia Commission was taken over by the DHSS as a result of the

Medicines Act of 1968, the Commission became a statutory committee under that Act. It decided that the *BP* should become the sole book of standards for medicinal and related products and for their preparations.

The edition of the *Codex* published in 1980 was, therefore, called the *Pharmaceutical Codex* and was somewhat different from earlier editions. It is now a reference book about the chemical and physical properties of drugs and medical, surgical, and related products together with information on their action and/or uses, with data about preparations and pharmaceutical aids.

The British Veterinary Codex. With the introduction of many new drugs for the treatment of animals the Council of the Pharmaceutical Society set up a Veterinary Codex Committee in 1950; this produced the first edition of the *British Veterinary Codex* in 1953 with a *Supplement* in 1959. Responsibility for that publication was also taken over by the British Pharmacopoeia Commission under the Medicines Act. The Commission thus became the body to establish standards for both human and animal medicines.

The Extra Pharmacopoeia (Martindale). William *Martindale, chief pharmacist and lecturer in pharmacy of University College Hospital, London, collected information about medicines for the benefit of hospital staff and students and also assisted in preparing a regular feature in the *Pharmaceutical Journal* entitled 'Dispensing Memoranda'. These formed the basis of the *Extra Pharmacopoeia* which he first published in 1893. That work has now become one of the most popular and useful reference books on drugs and medicines; it is widely known as 'Martindale', thus immortalizing the name of its founder. It is now published by the Pharmaceutical Press and has reached 29 editions, and has an associated computer information service.

The British National Formulary (BNF). The *British National Formulary* developed from the *National Formulary for National Health Insurance Purposes* first published in 1927. The latter was gradually enlarged and became the *National (War) Formulary* in 1941. After the war a Joint Formulary Committee (of the British Medical Association and the Pharmaceutical Society) was established to produce a standard prescribers' formulary for use in the NHS. The first edition of the *BNF* was published in 1949. It and subsequent editions contained much information about the actions and uses of drugs. In the late 1970s it was decided to publish the *BNF* in a new form arranged on the basis of the pharmacological and therapeutic actions of drugs and their preparations in order to make the book primarily a handbook for prescribers. The first edition in the new style appeared in 1981 and the formulary is to be revised every six months.

The dental formulary. A formulary containing the drugs and preparations available for prescribing by dentists under the NHS is prepared by a subcommittee of the Joint Formulary Committee and, like the *BNF*, is published by the Pharmaceutical Press.

Other pharmaceutical literature. Numerous textbooks devoted to the various pharmaceutical subjects are published in the UK. In addition to the journals already mentioned there is an independent weekly one entitled the *Chemist and Druggist*, first published in 1859. The *Chemist and Druggist Diary* is a useful reference book which is published annually. There are also periodicals on specialized subjects such as clinical pharmacy, pharmacology, and clinical pharmacology.

Legal controls in pharmacy. The earliest legal controls were concerned with the distribution of poisons and later of psychoactive (*psychotropic) drugs capable of abuse with serious social consequences. With the introduction of so many new potent drugs, recent legislation has tended to control medicines as such to ensure their safe use and optimum effectiveness. For example, the British *Medicines Act of 1968 is concerned with the quality, safety, and efficacy of medicines and related products and with their distribution.

Other legislation is concerned with the training and qualifications of pharmacists, with the purity of drugs, and with the protection of the public from faulty and dangerous drugs. Legislation in the UK was discussed by Matthews (1962) and in the USA by Kremers (1940), Kremers and Urdang (1951), and Sonnedecker (1963, 1976). The prevention of drug adulteration in 19th c. UK was the subject of a book by Stieb (1966) and the historical aspects of medicinal drug control were discussed at a conference in 1966 (Blake, 1970).

International pharmacy. Over the past 30 years there has been considerable international collaboration within pharmacy between governments, official pharmaceutical bodies, and individual pharmacists.

A pharmaceutical committee of the Council of Europe (Partial Agreement) has existed for many years. It consists of representatives of the governments of Austria, Belgium, Denmark, France, West Germany, Holland, Ireland, Italy, Luxemburg, Switzerland, and the UK. It meets twice a year to discuss pharmaceutical subjects. The European Pharmacopoeia Commission arose out of that Committee but is now independent of it.

In 1966 the European Free Trade Association (EFTA) set up a working party to discuss the trade in pharmaceuticals and this resulted in the establishment in 1970 of a Convention on the Mutual Recognition of Pharmaceutical Inspections. When the UK and Denmark left EFTA to join the EEC the Convention became an independent one and several other countries have now joined it. The secretariat of EFTA arranges 'workshops' and joint inspections in connection with the Convention.

There are several committees affecting pharmacy in the EEC, for example the Pharmaceutical Committee and the Committee on Proprietary Medicines.

There is no pharmaceutical committee of the World Health Organization but there are several expert committees and working parties concerned with various aspects of drugs and with the *International Pharmacopoeia*. There is also a chief pharmaceutical officer at WHO headquarters in Geneva.

The International Pharmaceutical Federation, commonly called FIP from the initials of its French title (*Fédération Internationale Pharmaceutique*), was founded in 1912 and has grown in strength and influence since the Second World War, but has recently been weakened by the withdrawal of the American Pharmaceutical Association. An equivalent International Pharmaceutical Students Federation was founded in 1942.

There are regional organizations in the Americas (The Pan-American Congress of Pharmacy and Biochemistry) and in Asia (The Federation of Asian Pharmaceutical Associations). Kremers (1940), Kremers and Urdang (1951) and Sonnedecker (1963, 1976) have outlined international trends.

A Commonwealth Pharmaceutical Association was founded in 1969, the inaugural meeting being held in London. Commonwealth Pharmaceutical Conferences have been held in Melbourne (1972), Bombay (1977), and Trinidad (1982).

Outstanding apothecaries and pharmacists. Many apothecaries and pharmacists have made outstanding contributions to the sciences, especially to botany and chemistry, and several have gained great fame. Their part in society has been described by Urdang (1946b) and by Matthews (1981), while Whittet has outlined their contributions to pure food and drugs (1960a), botany (1974), plant chemistry (1973a), and analysis (1973b). Whittet has also described the work of many who gained fellowship of the *Royal Society for their contributions to the sciences (Whittet, 1960b).

Pharmaceutical antiques. Pharmaceutical containers such as apothecaries' drug jars and various types of equipment such as pill tiles, mortars and pestles, carboys, and trade tokens are now highly valued antiques. Recent books on the subject have been published by Matthews (1971), on apothecaries' jars by Drey (1978), and medical ceramics and glass by Crellin (1969) and by Crellin and Scott (1972). A series of papers on apothecaries' tokens by Whittet (1982) has appeared in the *Pharmaceutical Journal* and is continuing.   T. D. WHITTET

References

Barratt, C. H. R. (1905). *The History of the Society of Apothecaries*. London.

Bayles, H. (1940). The Rose Case. *Chemist and Druggist*, **132**, 473–4 and **133**, 8–9.

Blake, J. B. (ed.) 1970). *Safeguarding the Public. Historical Aspects of Medicinal Drug Control*. Baltimore and London.

Cassar, P. (1965). *Medical History of Malta*. London.

Combes, R. (1981). *Pharmacy in New Zealand*. Wellington.

Copeman, W. S. C. (1967). *The Apothecaries 1917–1967*. London.

Crellin, J. K. (1969). *Medical Ceramics*. London.

Crellin, J. K. and Scott, J. R. (1972). *Glass and British Pharmacy, 1600–1900*. London.

Drey, R. E. A. (1978). *Apothecary Jars*. London and Boston.

European Free Trade Association (1970). *Convention for the Mutual Recognition of Inspections in Respect of the Manufacture of Pharmaceutical Products*. Geneva.

Haines, G. (1976). *The Grains and Threepenn'orths of Pharmacy. Pharmacy in N.S.W. 1788–1976*. Kilmore, Australia.

Hall, Sir N. (1970). *Report of the Working Party on the Hospital Phaemaceutical Service. The Noel Hall Report*. London.

Kremers, E. (1940). *History of Pharmacy*. Philadelphia, London, and Montreal.

Kremers, E. and Urdang, G. (1951). *History of Pharmacy*. 2nd edn, Philadelphia, London, and Montreal.

Lawson, D. H. and Richards, R. M. E. (1982). *Clinical Pharmacy and Hospital Drug Management*. London.

Linstead, Sir H. (1955). *Report of the Sub-Committee on the Hospital Pharmaceutical Services. The Linstead Report*. London.

Matthews, L. G. (1962). *History of Pharmacy in Britain*. Edinburgh and London.

Matthews, L. G. (1971). *Antiques of the Pharmacy*. London.

Matthews, L. G. (1980). *The Pepperers, Spicers and Apothecaries of London during the Thirteenth and Fourteenth Centuries*. London.

Matthews, L. G. (1981). *Pharmacists in the Wider World*. London.

Renwick, E. D. (1958). *A Short History of the Order of St. John*, p. 26. London.

Sonnedecker, G. (1963). *Kremers and Urdang's History of Pharmacy*. 3rd edn, Philadelphia, London, and Montreal.

Sonnedecker, G. (1976). *Kremers and Urdang's History of Pharmacy*. 4th edn, Philadelphia, London, and Montreal.

Stieb, E. H. (1966). *Drug Adulteration. Detection and Control in Nineteenth Century Britain*. Madison.

Trease, G. E. (1957). The 'Spicer-Apothecary' of the Middle Ages. *Future Pharmacist*, Summer 1957, 54–8.

Trease, G. E. (1964). *Pharmacy in History*. London.

Urdang, G. (1946a). Pharmacopoeias as witnesses of world history. *Journal of the History of Medicine and Allied Sciences*, **1**, 46–70.

Urdang, G. (1946b). *Pharmacy's Part in Society*. Madison.

Urdang, G. (1951). The Development of Pharmacopoeias. *Bulletin of the World Health Organization*, **4**, 577–603.

Wall, C., Cameron, H. C. and Underwood, E. A. (1963). *History of the Worshipful Society of Apothecaries of London, Volume 1 1617–1815*. London.

Wallis, T. E. (1964). *The History of the School of Pharmacy, University of London*. London.

Wertheimer, A. I. (ed.) (1977). *Proceedings of the International Conference on Drug and Pharmaceutical Services Remuneration*. Washington, DC.

Whittet, T. D. (1953). A history of pharmacy at University College Hospital. *Chemist and Druggist*, **159**, 519, 644 and 670; **160**, 17 and 43.

Whittet, T. D. (1960a). Some contributions of pharmacy

to pure food and drugs. *Chemist and Druggist*, **174**, 378 and 441.

Whittet, T. D. (1960b). Pharmaceutical fellows of the Royal Society. *Pharmaceutical Journal*, **185**, 79.

Whittet, T. D. (1962). London's University Dispensary. Forerunner of University College Hospital. *Chemist and Druggist*, **178**, 217.

Whittet, T. D. (1962–72). From apothecary to pharmacist. A study of changes of title. *Chemist and Druggist*, **177–98.**

Whittet, T. D. (1964). The apothecary in provincial gilds. *Medical History*, **8**, 245.

Whittet, T. D. (1965). History of pharmacy in British hospitals. In Poynter, F. N. L. (ed.), *Evolution of Pharmacy in Britain*. 17–44.

Whittet, T. D. (1968). Pepperers, spicers and grocers. Forerunners of the apothecaries. *Proceedings of the Royal Society of Medicine*, **61**, 801.

Whittet, T. D. (1971). *The Apothecaries in the Great Plague of London of 1665*. Epsom, Surrey.

Whittet, T. D. (1972a). The Medicines Act of 1968. *Chemische Rundschau*, 7 June.

Whittet, T. D. (1972b). The effect of Health Centres on general practice pharmacy. *Pharmaceutical Journal*, **208**, 223.

Whittet, T. D. (1973a). Some contributions of pharmacists to plant chemistry. *Australian Journal of Hospital Pharmacy*, **3**, 13–20.

Whittet, T. D. (1973b). Some contributions of pharmacists to analysis. *Pharmaceutical Journal*, **211**, 536–42.

Whittet, T. D. (1974). Some contributions of British pharmacists to botany, *Pharmaceutical Journal*, **212**, 97–104.

Whittet, T. D. (1979). The transition from apothecary to pharmacist in British hospitals. *American Journal of Hospital Pharmacy*, **36**, 492–7.

Whittet, T. D. (1982). A survey of apothecaries' tokens including some previously unrecognised specimens. *Pharmaceutical Journal*, **228**, 719–24 (continuing).

Wootton, A. C. (1910). *Chronicles of Pharmacy, London*, **1**, 46–76.

PHARMACY AND POISONS ACT 1933. This UK Act, together with the subsequent Poisons List Order and Rules 1966–8, established control of the practice of pharmacy and the sale and supply of 'poisons'. Under the Act, a Poisons Board was created with authority to draw up a Poisons List. The List recognizes two classes of substance: those used in medical, dental, and veterinary practice and restricted to sale by registered pharmacists; and those in common domestic use, which may be sold by persons registered by local authorities. Restrictions on sale and supply vary with the nature of the substances, and certain exemptions are made. Subsequent relevant legislation was contained in the Pharmacy and Medicines Act 1941, the *Medicines Act 1968, and the *Poisons Act 1972. See PHARMACY AND PHARMACISTS.

PHARYNGITIS is inflammation of the *pharynx.

PHARYNGOSCOPY is the visual examination of the *pharynx.

PHARYNX. The cavity lying behind the nose and mouth and providing the passage of communication from them to the *larynx and the *oesophagus respectively; it is thus a channel both for respiratory gases and for food and drink, common to the respiratory and alimentary tracts. The pharynx, which has a muscular wall lined internally with mucous membrane, is usually divided into three zones: the nasopharynx (above the level of the soft *palate); the oropharynx (between the palate and the upper edge of the *epiglottis); and the hypopharynx (below the upper edge of the epiglottis).

PHASE CONTRAST is a technique of microscopy which allows structural boundaries to be visualized without special staining, based on the utilization of phase differences of reflected and transmitted light waves passing through and around the objects under study. See MICROSCOPE.

PHENACETIN is an aspirin-like *analgesic and *antipyretic drug (*p*-ethoxyacetanilide, also known as acetophenetidin) which, though it was widely used for many years after its introduction (in 1887), is no longer recommended; taken over long periods, it can cause serious damage to the kidneys (so-called analgesic nephropathy). *Paracetamol is now the preferred alternative to *aspirin.

PHENELZINE is one of the monoamide oxidase inhibitor group of *antidepressant drugs.

PHENINDIONE is one of the oral *anticoagulants, also known under the proprietary name of Dindevan®. Because of occasional hypersensitivity reactions, the *coumarin group of drugs (e.g. *warfarin sodium) is usually preferred.

PHENOBARBITONE is a long-acting *barbiturate, the main remaining use of which is in the control of *epilepsy.

PHENOCOPY. A characteristic, indistinguishable from one which is normally genetically determined, produced by environmental causes.

PHENOL (C_6H_5OH), formerly known as carbolic acid, is a powerful *antiseptic with a characteristic smell which is poisonous when ingested. See also LISTER.

PHENOLPHTHALEIN. See LAXATIVES.

PHENOME is a term used in classification systems to denote a group of organisms related by *phenotype.

PHENOTHIAZINE is the parent compound of a number of drugs, of which the prototype is *chloropromazine, used primarily for the treatment of *psychoses. The phenothiazine derivatives belong to that group of drugs known variously as major *tranquillizers, antipsychotics, or neuroleptics.

PHENOTYPE. The sum of the observed characteristics of an individual, whether of genetic or environmental origin. See GENETICS.

PHENTOLAMINE is an alpha-adrenergic blocking agent, the main use of which is in the diagnosis and management of suspected or established *phaeochromocytoma.

PHENYLBUTAZONE is a potent *non-steroidal anti-inflammatory drug (NSAID) which was extensively used in the treatment of rheumatic disorders, being particularly effective in *gout and *ankylosing spondylitis. It has, however, various serious side-effects; of the adverse reactions reported, blood *dyscrasias (aplastic anaemia, agranulocytosis, thrombocytopenia) are the most important and have caused a number of fatalities. In the UK the drug was therefore withdrawn from general use in March 1984. Its use is now restricted to ankylosing spondylitis and its supply limited to hospitals only.

PHENYLKETONURIA is a genetically determined inability to metabolize L-phenylalanine, which unless detected and treated soon after birth results in mental retardation. See INBORN ERRORS OF METABOLISM.

PHENYTOIN is a drug widely used in the control of *epilepsy, also known under the proprietary name Epanutin® or Dilantin®.

PHILIP, SIR ROBERT WILLIAM (1857–1939). British physician. MD Edinburgh (1887), FRCP Edinburgh (1887). Philip was appointed lecturer in chest disease to the *Edinburgh Royal Infirmary in 1890 and physician to the Royal Victoria Hospital for Consumption in 1894, becoming professor of *tuberculosis in 1917. He opened the first tuberculosis dispensary in the world in Edinburgh in 1887 and the first in London in Paddington in 1909. He was knighted in 1913, president of the Royal College of Physicians of Edinburgh from 1918 to 1923, and president of the British Medical Association in 1927. Philip was a brilliant organizer and administrator who founded the tuberculosis service.

PHILOSOPHER'S STONE. A putative object or mineral substance capable of effecting the transmutation of base metals into gold. It was the ultimate goal of *alchemy and the quest for it chief among the preoccupations of alchemists ('philosophers'). Some felt that the stone, when found, would also prove to have the power to cure all diseases and to prolong life indefinitely.

PHIMOSIS. A *prepuce, of which the orifice is too small to permit retraction over the glans penis, the usual justification for *circumcision other than that performed on religious or tribal grounds.

PHIPPS, HENRY (1839–1930). American philanthropist. Phipps made money out of a variety of enterprises, especially iron and steel manufacture with the *Carnegies. He took a special interest in *tuberculosis. He founded the Phipps Institute at the University of Pennsylvania (see RESEARCH INSTITUTES) and a psychiatric clinic at *Johns Hopkins Hospital, Baltimore.

PHLEBECTOMY is the surgical excision of part or all of a vein.

PHLEBITIS is inflammation of a vein, which may be due to trauma or infection, or which may follow *thrombosis within the vein. In either case, since inflammation of the vein wall favours secondary thrombosis, the condition is usually one of 'thrombophlebitis'. The alternative term 'phlebothrombosis' tends to be reserved for cases of venous thrombosis without signs of inflammation.

PHLEBOGRAPHY is the radiographic visualization of veins after filling them with a radio-opaque material.

PHLEBOTHROMBOSIS is venous thrombosis without obvious inflammation. See PHLEBITIS.

PHLEBOTOMUS. See SANDFLY.

PHLEBOTOMY is synonymous with *venesection.

PHLEGM was one of the four *humours of early medical science; in modern lay usage, it is equivalent to *sputum.

PHLEGMON. See CELLULITIS.

PHLOGISTON was the supposed principle of combustion, postulated by *Stahl at the beginning of the 18th c. to be present in all combustible substances and to be liberated during the process of combustion.

PHLS. See PUBLIC HEALTH LABORATORY SERVICE.

PHOBIA. A pathological fear of a particular class of objects or situations unrelated or disproportionate to any threat it presents. Common phobias are fear of heights, open spaces (agoraphobia), enclosed spaces (claustrophobia), cancer, snakes, syphilis, and very many others. Phobias when disabling may require psychiatric attention.

PHOCOMELIA is a severe congenital anomaly in which the limbs fail to develop, so that the hands and feet may be directly attached to the body. See THALIDOMIDE.

PHONATION is the production of voice sounds.

PHONETICS is the study of voice, vocal sounds, spoken language, and pronunciation.

PHONOCARDIOGRAPHY is the recording of the sounds generated by the action of the heart.

PHOSGENE is carbonyl chloride ($COCl_2$), a colourless poisonous gas with a smell of musty hay. See CHEMICAL WARFARE.

PHOSPHATASE is the term for a large group of *enzymes, widely distributed throughout the body, which split *phosphate from its organic compounds (esters).

PHOSPHATE. Any salt or ester of phosphoric acid (H_3PO_4).

PHOSPHENE is a visual sensation appearing with the eyes shut, not due to the penetration of external light.

PHOSPHORYLATION is the introduction of a phosphate group into an organic molecule.

PHOTOCHEMOTHERAPY is treatment with drugs which induce sensitivity to light, particularly natural or artificial ultraviolet radiation. For example, members of the psoralen group of drugs are used in combination with long-wave ultraviolet radiation (the combination known for short as PUVA) in the treatment of *psoriasis.

PHOTOMETER. An instrument for measuring luminous intensity, usually by comparing two light sources.

PHOTOMICROGRAPHY is photography with the aid of a *microscope. Photographs so obtained are called photomicrographs.

PHOTOPHOBIA is intolerance of bright light.

PHOTOSENSITIVITY is abnormal sensitivity of the skin to light, particularly sunlight.

PHOTOSYNTHESIS is the process, on which all forms of life (except certain bacteria) depend, by which green plants utilize the energy of sunlight to synthesize carbohydrate from atmospheric carbon dioxide and water. Chemically the reaction is a complex one and not fully understood; the presence of *chlorophyll, however, is essential.

PHRENIC NERVE. A long nerve which arises in the neck from the cervical plexus, from where it runs downwards to enter the thorax and traverse the length of the *mediastinum to reach the *diaphragm. It carries sensory fibres from the pleura, pericardium, and peritoneum and makes connections with the sympathetic plexuses; but its chief importance is that it provides the motor innervation of the diaphragm, right and left phrenic nerves supplying the respective hemidiaphragms.

PHRENOLOGY is a pseudoscience which purports to relate mental development and mental faculties to the external configuration of the skull. See NEUROLOGY.

PHTHISIS is an archaic term for pulmonary *tuberculosis.

PHYCOMYCOSIS is a broad term covering infection with a variety of fungal species that is almost always 'opportunistic', that is occurring in individuals whose immune defences (see IMMUNOLOGY) have been compromised by pre-existing disease or exposure to immunosuppressive agents.

PHYSIC is an archaic term approximating to *internal medicine, that is the medicine practised by physicians in the UK and by internists in the USA.

PHYSICAL EXAMINATION is ordinarily taken to mean examination of the patient using the examiner's five senses aided only by the portable tools of his trade such as *stethoscope, tendon hammer, *ophthalmoscope, etc., and excluding special investigative techniques like lumbar puncture, blood biochemistry, radiography, electrocardiography, etc.

PHYSICIAN. In the UK, one who practises internal medicine or one of its subspecialties, as distinct from surgery and obstetrics; in the USA, any qualified medical practitioner.

PHYSICIANS TO THE SOVEREIGN. See ROYAL MEDICAL HOUSEHOLD.

PHYSICK, PHILIP SYNG (1768–1837). American surgeon, MD Edinburgh (1792). Physick returned to Philadelphia, where he soon became a leading surgeon; indeed he has sometimes been called the father of American surgery. He was responsible for developing many practical procedures and technical devices useful for the practice of surgery in the pre-anaesthetic era. Among these were methods for dealing with fractures and dislocations, amputations, design of instruments for removal of bladder stone, absorbable suture materials, and curved suturing needles (see also SURGERY).

PHYSICS, MEDICAL (AND SOME CONTRIBUTIONS OF ELECTRONICS AND ENGINEERING TO MEDICINE).

   Introduction. Historically, the specialty of medical physics was introduced and developed in support of *radiotherapy, establishing an enduring and highly productive collaboration that continues to flourish. However, it soon became apparent that the broad spectrum of physical sciences, including not only physics but also electronic and mechanical engineering, mathematics, and computing, could make contributions in many other fields of medicine as well. This article is intended to illustrate briefly just some of the fields in which progress has been made as a result of excellent collaboration between medicine and the physical sciences and, it is hoped, to act as a stimulus to still greater fulfilment of that potential.

Radiation physics. Nowadays, the expertise of radiation physics frequently encompasses radiotherapy physics, in which developments continue, diagnostic radiology physics, and radiation protection. Despite some obvious overlap, each aspect is sufficiently different to merit separate consideration.

Radiotherapy physics. The classic inputs of medical physics to all aspects of radiotherapy include dosimetry, treatment planning, and often a responsibility for the calibration and correct functioning of treatment machines as well as for the sealed radioactive sources used for treatment. Fundamental theoretical and empirical work has established an excellent basis for dosimetry and planning, and inevitably, continues as more modern and powerful machines, such as the linear accelerator illustrated in Figure 1, are introduced for routine teletherapy and, in some centres, where the usefulness of *neutrons or *pions is under investigation. Even the production of moulds (Fig. 2), for maintaining the correct alignment of the tumour within the beam, has progressed with the introduction of new vacuum-forming techniques as well as new materials.

Radiology physics. Since medical use of *radiation represents the greatest exposure of the population to man-made sources, it is appropriate that increasing attention is being given to the wide range of *X-ray examinations in order to minimize radiation exposure and to ensure quality control. In many regions of the UK, collaborative programmes of investigation are now well established and have been extended to include more recent developments such as *computerized axial tomography (CAT), *nuclear magnetic resonance (NMR), and digital radiography (see RADIOLOGY). In these latter fields, there is a general realization that the quantitative nature of the data used to generate the images permits the extraction of considerably more information relating to body composition, metabolism, and function. Although work in this field is still at a relatively early stage, it has considerable potential.

Radiation protection of the patient and of the staff in medicine has long been practised with respect to ionizing radiation. However, over recent years it has been necessary to include the increasing use of non-ionizing radiation, particularly ultrasound (see below), ultraviolet rays,

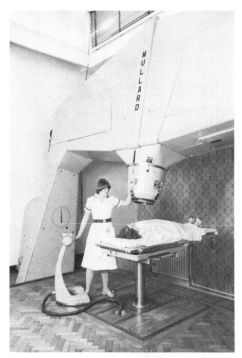

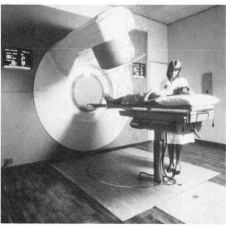

Fig. 1. The Mullard 4 MV linear accelerator (top), installed at Newcastle General Hospital in 1953, was one of the earliest megavoltage accelerators. It was replaced after 27 years of service, having given over 18 000 full courses of treatment involving nearly 300 000 patient attendances, by the more modern machine shown below. (Reproduced by courtesy of Philips)

microwaves, and laser radiation. These modalities require different methods of dosimetry, calibration, and radiation protection. A further recent development relating to radiation protection within the National Health Service in the UK concerns community health, as it may be influenced by environmental discharges of radio-

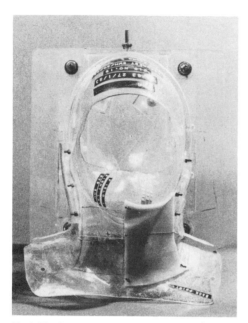

Fig. 2. The shell illustrated was used for the treatment of a larynx on a cobalt-60 teletherapy machine. Due to the patient's asymmetrical neck, the left-hand side of the shell required an additional 3 mm of wax in order to produce a symmetrical dose distribution

active materials from major nuclear installations. In one Region at least, appropriate District Health Authorities have representatives on the Local Liaison Committee and the environmental and emergency subcommittees of major plants and are expected to provide authoritative medical advice to other local bodies as well as to the general public.

Radioisotopes. The wide-ranging applications of *radioisotopes in medicine bear further testimony to excellent collaboration, where apart from radio-

therapy they are employed in an ever-increasing number of imaging and non-imaging diagnostic tests. (See also NUCLEAR MEDICINE.)

Radioisotope imaging. Although radioisotope images are generally inferior in anatomical detail to those obtained by CAT or NMR, they are unique in simultaneously demonstrating metabolism and function. The resolution of modern *gamma cameras approaches the best theoretically attainable. Recent developments include dynamic imaging and emission computerized axial tomography (ECAT), based on computer processing of data, as well as the production of new radiopharmaceuticals.

Dynamic studies are now common for renal, liver, and lung function, cerebral and cardiac blood flow and in gastrointestinal investigations. Quantitative data are provided, which are extremely use-

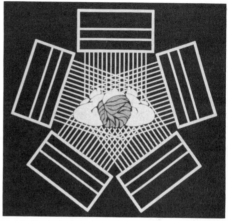

Fig. 3. The principles of Emission Computerized Axial Tomography (ECAT) are illustrated in which a gamma camera is rotated about the patient to produce cross-sectional images of the distribution of an administered radiopharmaceutical.

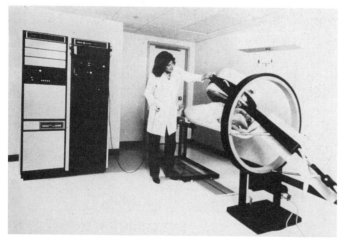

Fig. 4. A modern gamma camera with ECAT facilities. (Reproduced by courtesy of International General Electric)

ful clinically and can often provide a differential diagnosis.

Gamma cameras with ECAT facilities are now available commercially from several manufacturers and the clinical usefulness of the technique is being evaluated and extended more widely. As illustrated in Figure 3, the method is analogous to that of CAT with the detector rotating around the relevant area of the body, but, in this case measuring gamma rays emitted from the administered radiopharmaceutical rather than X-rays transmitted through the body. A cross-sectional image showing distribution in that region is then computed. Work is proceeding, especially in medical physics departments, on three-dimensional display of the tomographic images with 'rotation' of the image and 'peeling' of layers to detect otherwise hidden abnormalities. Figure 4 shows a typical commercial ECAT gamma camera system.

There have also been exciting developments in the range of radiopharmaceuticals available for imaging, including *monoclonal antibodies. Table 1 summarizes some of those currently in general use. Bearing in mind the potential impact of other modalities, one major company has made an assessment of future trends both in the types of clinical examinations and of the principal radiopharmaceuticals expected to be in use during this decade, as illustrated in Table 2.

Non-imaging applications. Studies of organ function, measurement of blood flow in, for example, muscle and brain, and the detection of *thrombi do not necessitate imaging and are well-established procedures using relatively simple equipment for external counting of an administered radiopharmaceutical. More recent developments primarily concern the examination of body composition and metabolism in which whole-body radioactivity counters can have a significant role. In contrast to conventional counters employing a shielded room with some 10 cm of lead or 15 cm of steel in the walls, floor, and ceiling, housing the detectors and the patient (temporarily), 'shadow-shield' counters have been designed and often constructed in-house giving comparable performance. Absorption and retention of a radioactive tracer such as iron-59, labelled *vitamin B_{12}, calcium-49, or zinc-69m can be determined directly by measuring radioactive emission from the patient shortly after administration (100 per cent) and when faecal excretion is complete, following an oral dose, or at appropriate intervals following a parenteral dose. The uncertainty and unpleasantness of excreta collection and assay is avoided and even blood losses can be quantified on an out-patient basis. If the whole-

Table 1. Some substances used to image various organs

Organ	Radiopharmaceutical
Brain	Technetium-99m pertechnetate (TcO_4)
CSF	Indium-111 diethylene triamine penta acetic acid (DTPA)
Thyroid	Technetium-99m (TcO_4)
	Iodine-123 iodide
Lung	Technetium-99m HSA microspheres (20 μm)
	Xenon-133 gas
Heart	Thallium-201 chloride
	Technetium-99m red cells
Liver	Technetium-99m colloid
Spleen	Technetium-99m heat denatured red cells
Pancreas	Selenium-75 selenomethionine
Kidney	Technetium-99m glucoheptonate
	Technetium-99m dimercapto-succinic acid (DMSA)
	Technetium-99m DTPA
Adrenal	Selenium-75 selenocholesterol
Bone	Technetium-99m methyl diphosphonate (MDP)
Abscess	Indium-111 white cells
	Gallium-67 citrate
GI tract	Technetium-99m (TcO_4), colloid, various 'meals'
Lymphatic system	Technetium-99m colloid

Table 2. Nuclear procedures performed, in millions: actual and predicted

Procedures (USA)	1976	1979	1981	1982	1985	1990
Brain	2.2	1.3	1.1	1.0	1.2	1.3
Lung perfusion	0.8	0.7	0.6	0.6	0.6	0.6
Lung ventilation	0.1	0.3	0.5	0.5	0.5	0.5
Thyroid uptake	0.3	0.2	0.1	0.1	0.1	0.1
Thyroid scan	0.6	0.5	0.4	0.3	0.2	0.2
Bone	0.8	1.2	1.6	1.8	2.2	2.7
Liver and spleen	1.2	1.3	1.3	1.3	1.3	1.3
Kidney	0.1	0.1	0.1	0.1	0.1	0.1
Soft tissue	0.07	0.1	0.14	0.15	0.2	0.2
Cardiac	0.06	0.3	0.6	0.9	1.3	2.0
Monoclonal antibodies						1.0
Total	6.3	6.0	6.5	6.8	7.7	10.0

Note: The predicted increase in procedures by 1990 will be due to bone, cardiac, and monoclonal imaging. Procedures of brain imaging have become less frequent due to the advent of CAT scanning.

Fig. 5(a). The equipment developed to produce the ultrasound beam plots in Fig. 5(b). The dark disc is a piezoelectric film hydrophone, in which the central 1 mm² area actually measures the acoustic pressure. This is scanned within the water-filled tank by stepping motors under computer control. The transducer under test is mounted outside the tank, the beam being transmitted through a thin plastic window. The tank walls are normally lined with sound-absorbing material, omitted here for clarity

Fig. 5(b). *Below left.* A transverse plot of the pressure distribution in the focal plane of a 19 mm diameter, 3.5 MHz transducer, focused at a range of 100 mm. Scale marks represent 10 mm intervals and contours represent 6 dB intervals. *Below right.* A longitudinal plot of pressure distribution from the same transducer. Note the scale compression in the direction of the beam axis

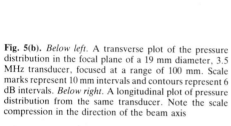

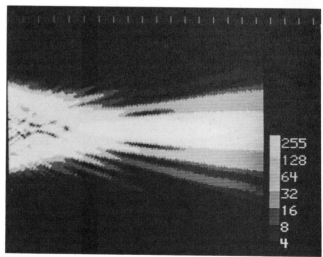

body counter is sufficiently sensitive, total body potassium can be measured directly by detecting gamma rays from the naturally occurring radioisotope potassium-40. Other elements can also be measured after or during exposure of the body or some relevant part of it to a small dose of neutrons which induce transient radioactivity. Using this procedure of *in vivo* activation analysis, calcium, phosphorus, nitrogen, sodium, chlorine, oxygen, hydrogen, and carbon as well as potassium have been measured in the total body, while iodine, calcium, phosphorus, cadmium, iron, and copper have been determined in various body organs or regions.

Ultrasound. Ultrasound is now well established

in medicine for diagnosis and for treatment, having become the method of choice for many examinations. Despite this already impressive progress, the modality remains capable of yet more exciting and useful developments.

As a result of the rapid and continuing improvement in the image quality of real-time scanners, B-scanners as such could become obsolete, their facilities being incorporated into hybrid machines using gantry-mounted real-time scanners. At least one medical physics department is working on a new method, real-time C-scanning, combining the high resolution capability of strong focusing and the clinical advantages of real-time viewing.

A water-immersed scanning gantry in which the patient is coupled to the scanner by means of a polythene window has been developed by an Australian group and is now available commercially, while, in the USA, a transmission system using lenses is being developed with the subject partially immersed in a water bath. Both systems can provide excellent images.

Increasingly, microcomputers and microprocessors are being coupled to scanners for quantitation of images, such as area and volume determination of, for example, the head and thorax of the *fetus. More sophisticated computing is being applied in several centres to the problems of tissue identification, for which there is significant promise.

A further area of rapid development and intensive investigation involves the use of doppler-shifted ultrasound for measuring blood velocity and velocity profiles.

Ultrasound has been used for some years in treatment: at relatively low frequency and power levels for *physiotherapy and at high intensities, with focusing so that surrounding tissue is exposed to only low intensities, in *Ménière's disease, for example. It has also been used in *neurosurgery to produce isolated tissue lesions, to destroy *pituitary function and in *otolaryngology to treat *papillomata of the larynx. Recently, commercial equipment has become available which is suitable for treating primary or secondary *malignant disease of the spine.

The measurement of power levels is obviously important and, in evaluating transducers, beam profiles must be determined. Instrumentation has been devised for this purpose. A beam plotting system produced recently incorporates a microcomputer both for controlling the movements of the pressure-measuring hydrophone and for storing and processing the measured data. A typical beam plot is shown in Figure 5.

See also ULTRASONICS.

Computing in one form or another now contributes to many clinical specialties and almost every facet of medical physics and bioengineering, to which some allusion has already been made.

Substantial minicomputers are commonly the workhorses for the preparation of sophisticated treatment plans for individual patients in radiotherapy. Through programming expertise, the machine can be used, often simultaneously, for other tasks such as the storage, retrieval, and manipulation of patient data including clinical trials, the generation of elegant graphics, and multi-user applications. As well as being dedicated data processing and controlling machines for such imaging equipment as CAT and NMR scanners, digital radiography, and gamma cameras, minicomputers are in use for analysing an increasing range of physiological signals, 24-hour *electrocardiograms (ECGs) being a well-known example.

Microcomputers (and microprocessors) are now being interfaced to, or are integral parts of, a wide spectrum of clinical instrumentation, as described below. However, technological developments are rapidly blurring the distinction between mini- and microcomputers. Microcomputers employing faster 16-bit processors and more suitable for the use of high-level languages are now available with the promise of even greater computing power per unit cost. There will be considerable capability for intercommunication among machines, with the opportunity to share the more expensive peripherals as increasing use is made of dedicated systems in preference to a shared central computer. Although the ability to write computer programs is now much more widespread, those able to program efficiently and professionally are far fewer. A major need for expertise in hardware support, as in the design and construction of computer interfaces, and also in software support, is likely to increase. (See also COMPUTERS IN CLINICAL MEDICINE; COMPUTERS IN MEDICAL ADMINISTRATION, ETC.)

Clinical instrumentation and physiological measurements. The development of instrumentation and physiological measurements, usually in response to a specific clinical need, is now an integral part of collaborative modern medicine.

In terms of major equipment, it is important to recall the substantial part played by hospital and university departments of medical physics or physics in the realization of, for example, NMR and its applications to medicine, together with current investigations of the potential use of electrical impedance variations in tissue (applied potential tomography) for imaging.

At a more modest level, but not necessarily of lesser clinical importance, a great variety of equipment is being developed to solve particular problems. By way of illustration, a few examples are presented relating to several different clinical specialties.

For cardiological investigations (see CARDIOLOGY II), a mobile electrophysiology laboratory, housing in a single unit all that is required for the investigation of problems of cardiac rhythm and conduction, has been constructed. It contains sensing amplifiers, displays, timing indicators, and stimulators. A hand-held mapping probe, which can be easily sterilized, has been built for use in surgical approaches to *arrhythmia management. Electrical mapping of the heart can be effected during open-heart surgery, enabling unwanted electrical pathways in the heart to be identified and surgically cut. The system is illustrated in Figure 6.

Intracranial pressure (ICP) monitoring in the management of head injuries and severe neurological disorders generates a volume of data that is difficult to assimilate for immediate application. However, microprocessor-based systems have now been developed which effectively provide on-line collection and analysis of patient data. The systems, which can include a monitor routine that will support a remote terminal and allow self-checking diagnosis to be run, simplifying calibration and fault detection procedures, represent a

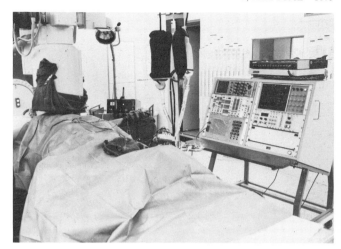

Fig. 6. A mobile electro-physiology laboratory for electrical mapping of the heart during open-heart surgery

low-cost solution to the problem of condensing ICP data.

One example of many devices used in caring for *neonates concerns a portable heart-rate monitor. The baby's ECG signal, which is continuously sampled, is electronically processed in a small portable battery-powered digital monitor to derive the instantaneous heart rate. The heart rate is shown on a liquid crystal display. Alarms are incorporated not only for high and low rates but also for faulty leads and battery status.

Electrophysiological measurement equipment for *ophthalmology and *audiology has been developed to a new level of sophistication, often based on computer or microprocessor systems for the processing and analysis of the data. Evoked response testing can now have a fuller role in each field.

In *obstetrics and *gynaecology, a low-power telemetry system has been produced in which a small two-channel transmitter is worn on a belt around the abdomen of the patient who is near to or in labour. Using the dilatation of the cervix, a scalp *electrode can safely be attached to the baby's head and also a small pressure sensor tube is inserted beyond the baby and into the womb. These sensor signals are amplified and converted into digital code before transmission to the receiver. The telemetry system has an operating range that allows the patient to move freely about a ward, while simultaneously allowing medical staff to monitor the progress of labour and the health of the unborn child.

A 12-channel multi-purpose optical turbidity instrument to determine the growth of *bacteria has been produced using only one light source, a *laser, and one photodetector. This allows the accuracy and stability of the system to be easily controlled. A special arrangement of spinning prisms and fibre-optic cables is used to distribute light sequentially to, and collect light from, 12 standard one-inch sample tubes housed in a black

anodized aluminium block. The whole assembly is temperature-controlled and is enclosed in a gas-tight structure, allowing a choice of atmospheres under which measurements can be performed. A microprocessor manages and controls the system and has been programmed to correct automatically for variation in the optical transmission of the test tubes and ageing of both the photodetector and light source. Information from an ongoing experiment is displayed on a TV monitor screen, as well as being stored in memory. The latter allows statistical calculations to be performed at the conclusion of a run. A graphical printer is used to output the data and construct the appropriate graphs. The equipment is shown in Figure 7.

A new electroplexy system for *electroconvulsion therapy has been devised enabling a threshold to be established for the minimum amount of electrical energy required to produce a convulsion in the individual patient and providing subsequent treatment at just above the threshold.

Bioengineering and technical aids for the handicapped. In the present context, bioengineering

Fig. 7. A 12-channel multi-purpose optical turbidity instrument for determining the growth of bacteria, using a laser and single photodetector

concerns the application of expertise in mechanical engineering to medicine (excluding equipment maintenance). At some centres, a 'technical aids for the handicapped' service has been established under the wing of bioengineering even though some of the new devices developed may draw heavily (or even exclusively) on skills in electronics.

Bioengineers have made major contributions in many fields such as the development of artificial limbs, joints, and organs (see REHABILITATION; ORTHOPAEDICS). Biomaterials, their tissue compatibility, and applications continue to be explored, as with carbon fibre. Studies of the mechanics of tissue and of locomotion have led to improved understanding of conditions like bedsores or, using gait analysis techniques, have provided guidance for the orthopaedic surgeon. However, since these aspects are already widely reported in the literature, attention will be focused on the 'low technology' applied to the innovation or improvement of technical aids for the handicapped.

Many aids for the handicapped cannot be produced commercially because of the frequent need to tailor the equipment to the intended user but, even when an aid can be standardized, the quantity requirement is often so small that manufacturers find production costs prohibitive. As some examples may illustrate, devices developed may be invaluable to the clients concerned.

A wheelchair head controller has been devised for a severely handicapped child whose total movement was restricted to some movement of the head. By an appropriate arrangement of levers and microswitches coupled to a relay control system, the child is able to control the chair, gaining an important degree of mobility and independence. The controller is shown in Figure 8.

Based on low-cost commercial microcomputers, a system has been produced providing environmental control for the severely disabled by use of a single switch. The scope of the computer has been exploited as a communications system with a facility also to draw pictures, to generate multichoice examination papers, to generate games that allow assessment of the client (often a

Fig. 9. An expanded keyboard, fitted with a transparent guard and armrest having a finger hole above each key, for a calculator used by a student with limb tremor

child), and even to permit music to be composed and played back.

Conversely, the miniaturization of modern calculators made their use impossible by a student with limb tremor and a modification has been made to produce a substantially expanded keyboard, fitted with a transparent guard and armrest having finger holes above each key. The device is shown in Figure 9.

A voice level indicator has also been developed for a profoundly deaf person unable to judge his vocal power during speech. The signal from a small microphone attached to the lapel is fed to an LED display of intensity worn like a wristwatch, as illustrated in Figure 10.

Many devices have been produced for use in the homes of patients, particularly the elderly, including an aid for getting into and out of the bath and a

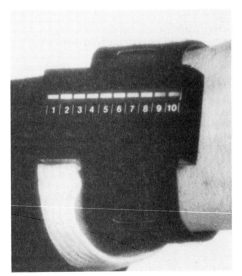

Fig. 10. A voice level indicator, operated from a small lapel-worn microphone, enabling a profoundly deaf person to judge his vocal power during speech

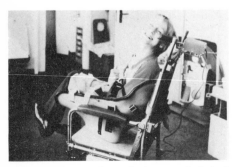

Fig. 8. A head-operated controller for a motorized wheelchair of a handicapped, but delighted, child

mobile trolley of adjustable height for transporting dishes between the oven, table and sink, to quote but a few examples.

Conclusions. The human body can be described in technological terms as a machine controlled by the world's most sophisticated, largely self-programmable, microcomputer. It is able to move in any direction with a forward speed of up to more than 32 km/h (20 m.p.h.) on land and lesser speeds in water. Control can be effected through self-adjusting binoculars and by audible or tactile signals. The system is powered by a variety of fuels fed through a multiconvertor, partly self-regulating, carburettor. The machine is largely waterproof and semi-immersible. It can self-replicate and, to a very large extent, repair itself. Although no guarantee is provided, the equipment has an expected lifetime of 70 years or more. However, in the event of malfunction, diagnosis of the problem (and ideally its rectification) should be achieved without 'lifting the bonnet'. Furthermore, no manuals relating to construction, function, or repair are provided. In these circumstances, the need for interdisciplinary collaboration is obvious. The substantial strides already made as a result of co-operation between clinicians and physical scientists are only outlined briefly here but they may form a basis and catalyst for greater fulfillment of the enormous potential that remains.   K. BODDY

PHYSIOGNOMY. The face or countenance, particularly viewed as an index to mind or character.

PHYSIOLOGIST. A scientist who studies the functions of living organisms; in the medical context, one concerned with the normal functions of the human organism. See PHYSIOLOGY.

PHYSIOLOGY

Introduction. Physiology, as the term was first used and as is most appropriate in this volume, is the study of the functions of the human body. A less restricted definition is the study of the processes involved in the function of all living organisms. With the growth of new biological sciences, many human functions are included in other sciences. The immune reactions of man are often handled by *microbiologists, as the subject was first raised by studying the reaction of man to bacteria, although now a major new discipline of *immunology has emerged, the processes which give individuality to man will undoubtedly receive more attention in the future, within what is usually considered to be human physiology. The chemical reactions of the body are now largely dealt with in *biochemistry and *molecular biology, although these overlap with much of physiology. Thus, accounts of the molecular basis of muscular contraction generally appear, with some variation in emphasis, in textbooks of biochemistry, molecular biology, and physiology, not to mention general biology.

Another reason why physiology has meant more than human studies is that much knowledge based on experiment could not be directly obtained from human study, but was derived from work in other organisms and was found to apply to man. Studies of the effects of disease and injury have always complemented the findings of direct experimentation; the vital role of the *heart to life must have been known to early man through hunting, long before warfare confirmed the notion, and before ritual extirpation of the heart was practised by many primitive people. *Hippocrates observed the crossed 'representation' of the *brain in a patient with skull *abscesses, and since then human illness has been a fertile source for direct observation of human physiology. Beginning with *Galen, or more correctly with Galen's predecessors in Alexandria whose work reaches us almost exclusively through Galen, evidence gathered from other organisms was a most fruitful source of fundamental physiological knowledge. Galen used the pig and many other mammals and birds, while *Harvey made his observations on man, snakes, and invertebrates. Beginning with *Pasteur, the *micro-organisms were found to yield invaluable information and studies of *yeasts, colon *bacilli, etc., have each made a major contribution to human physiology. How well they have served can best be illustrated by two examples. The very first physiological experiment was suggested by *Erasistratus, a predecessor of Galen at Alexandria, who, in trying to answer the question of whether the *pulse was caused by active propagation of an impulse in the *artery or by purely passive transmission of a pulse wave, proposed to substitute an inert tube for a section of an artery and to see whether or not the pulse continued beyond it. Erasistratus and Galen and others who later tried the experiment had so much difficulty with haemorrhage and clotting that the experiment was not successfully performed. Harvey recounted the case of a patient in whom a long segment of a leg artery was transformed by disease into a rigid calcified tube, but who nevertheless had a peripheral pulse, strongly suggesting that the arterial pulse is not transmitted by active propagation in the vessel wall. Since Harvey's time, this has been the opinion of physiologists, supported by much confirmatory evidence such as that of *Poiseuille based upon the science of hydraulics, which he founded. Not until occluded arteries were replaced by dacron *grafts was the experiment of Erasistatus adequately performed, and the pulse wave was found to be propagated through the inert tube. The direct evidence in man came hundreds of years after this view had been accepted generally.

Another example is more recent. It was Harvey's view that the heart functions as a pump, and the accepted view since has been that it has no other function, but this remained unproved until recent attempts were made to test the ability of mechanical pumps to maintain life. This has now been amply proved, first in animal experiments, later in man. The fact that a human patient survived on a pump for 112 days offered the first direct evidence in man to support a basic tenet of human physiology postulated 350 years earlier.

This view of human physiology as a part of the larger physiology of all life is a most important advance since it was first accepted as a formal discipline. Before then it was a subject for discourse between physician and philosopher, and even earlier had first appeared in rudimentary form in folk knowledge. The first actual textbook of physiology in which this title was used for the science was Jean *Fernel's *Seven Books of Physiology,* published in 1554. It was written as the Renaissance came to Paris, and as the errors, obscurities, and imperfections of the old Greek literature reaching Europe by translation and retranslation in Aramaic, Persian, and Arabic became apparent; it corrected the erroneous idea held by many students that they needed only to study the original and uncorrupted texts to attain perfect and complete knowledge. This knowledge motivated *Vesalius, who at much the same time began to study the original texts of Galen's *anatomy. Vesalius must be given credit for seeing and seizing one advantage denied to Fernel: that of checking findings by actual dissection, which enabled him to found modern human anatomy with his magnificent textbook of 1543. Fernel failed to accept that the experiment was the foundation of physiology, so this view had to wait until Harvey. Nevertheless, Fernel's book is of interest as the first organized textbook of physiology, containing a summary of views that had persisted in a more and more systematized form for at least 1500 years. Although it may seem totally without any application to modern physiology or to science in general, it was the background out of which modern science and scientific physiology developed.

Jean Fernel and ancient physiology. *The unity of life and nature.* Ancient and primitive people recognized that the life of plants and of animals was characterized by the same features of birth, growth, reproduction, and death, despite many structural and functional differences; the observation that even Neanderthal man buried his dead on a bed of flowers bears this out. At a later stage it seemed as if living things were produced from or by the earth so that a continuum was seen from the non-living to the living world; various expressions such as 'earth to earth and dust to dust' persist from those times. *Aristotle expressed this in his 'ladder of life' which began in the non-living world and extended upward to the plants through the various animal species to man. Although Aristotle called this a *ladder,* he pointed out that each upward step was often unclear and that transitions between non-living and living, from plant to animal, and from successive stages of animal development to man were often difficult to distinguish.

Thus a continuum rather than a stepwise progression of nature was proposed, including living and non-living nature, plants and animals, and 'lower' and 'higher' animals leading to man. Hence, the phenomena of life could be studied via the common tools of science. The instruments and principles of chemistry and physics were each appropriate in the study of plant and animal function, and the fact that over the centuries this has proved more and more to be the case demonstrates the inherent good sense of the very earliest thinkers. It explains the mutual assistance the sciences afford each other; while the more basic sciences are often even more helpful to the applied, there have been classic examples of the reverse. One such was the study by *Galvani which gave the impetus to subsequent experiments on electricity through his discovery of the generation of an electric current by the junction of dissimilar metals.

The four elements. This is why Fernel began his physiology with the four elements, air, fire, earth, and water. The list, including two pairs of opposing polarities, fire and water, and air and earth, seemed to represent a Mesopotamian rather than an Egyptian influence; but there was no unanimity among Grecian philosophers about the stature of all four as basic elements. Some reduced all to a single primary element and considered water or fire as fundamental, but nearly all those who postulated a single element thought in terms of an interchange from it to the other three. Fire must have been a powerful force as it was encountered in nature, and was adapted to human use; the Greeks used it for heating, cooking, firing of pottery, and for great mysteries such as the reduction of metals like copper or tin, and glass-making. The relation of the sun to fire was recognized and the sun was often worshipped as the source of life. Water was equally important in Egypt and Mesopotamia but especially in Egypt, where the unusual regularity of the flooding of the Nile gave rise to a Nilotic year long before an astronomical year was established. The relation of air and breathing to life was well known and the relation of air to fire, as in the bellows in metallurgy, was another everyday experience. By Galen's time, a relationship between the influence of air on life and on fire had been accepted.

The temperaments. These were closely attached to the elements and as the mixture of the latter varied, they also varied, thus producing the varying temperaments of the individual and his parts. Fernel defined the harmony and the concert of the principal qualities in this mixture. The four temperaments were again a pair of opposites, hot and cold, and wet and dry arranged two to each element and each shared by two elements. Thus air was hot and moist, fire was hot and dry, earth was dry and cold, and water was cold and moist. On the balance of temperament depended the nature of the species and the health of the individual. In relating plants to animals all plants were cold and all animals warm, but comparing animals, the lion was warm and man was cold. In comparison with the ant, however, man was warm. Each part of the human body had its own temperament: blood was always warm, as were the spirits, heart, and liver; the brain was cold, along with the spinal cord and tendons. During the first few years of life the temperament was generally hot and moist, the next stage was hot and dry, the third stage was dry and cold and, in the last days, cold and moist. Nevertheless, each individual's own natural temperament might overbalance the effect of age or other influences. For centuries, balance of temperament was used as a guide to therapy, and all medicines were classed as heating or cooling, moistening or drying.

The humours. These were often associated with temperaments as the four humours were each connected with a pair of temperaments. The four humours—blood, yellow bile, black bile, and phlegm—were roughly equated to the four elements. Blood, like fire, was hot and moist; black bile, like earth, was cold and dry; phlegm, like water was cold and wet, while yellow bile, like air, was warm and moist. It was thus proper to speak of a choleric individual when yellow bile predominated and of sanguine, melancholy, or phlegmatic temperaments when one of the other three was in excess.

Natural heat and the spirits. All living things lived by virtue of natural heat, not the same as elemental heat, which had its source in an occult and hidden principle. It was found in plants and animals, cold-blooded and warm-blooded, and was the primary instrument of all functions. It was greatest during childhood and youth, when it was associated with much humidity, and lessened in old age, being linked with increasing dryness. It varied with the seasons, being greatest in winter when the cold weather repelled it to the interior of the body and less in the summer when the pores of the skin opened and let it escape.

All parts of the body received veins, arteries, and nerves, depending upon them for nutrition and warmth. The veins brought a constant supply of the natural spirits supplying materials for day-to-day nourishment, being concocted first in the stomach and then made in the liver. This was why the liver was more liberally supplied with heat than other organs; it was the 'cooker' of the body. Some natural spirit carried in the venous blood reached the heart by the vena cava and after elaboration in the right ventricle was transported across the interventricular septum through narrow channels to the left ventricle where, after tempering by air from the lungs, it was endowed with heat and became the vital spirit which was then distributed throughout the body by the arteries. The part that was transported to the brain was for the third time elaborated in the *rete mirabile* (a complex of tiny blood vessels) and thereafter transported to the cerebral ventricles by the choroid plexus where, with the admixture of other nutriments and air, and by conversion, it became the animal spirit

appropriate for all nervous functions such as movement and sensation.

The faculties of the soul. To Fernel, as to the ancients, the soul was very obscure, the principal cause of the body's functions. *Sherrington describes it in this usage as life-soul and Fernel spoke of the soul as everything that gave the body life and vital actions. Since philosophers had defined the soul by life and as they distinguished several kinds of life, they also recognized several kinds of soul. Plants had only a natural soul, animals a sensitive soul, and man an intelligent or rational soul.

The natural faculties, common to plants and animals, were nutrition, growth, and reproduction. While growth and generation were limited, nutrition was constant throughout life. The nutritive faculty repaired that lost, by converting food into the substance of the body. The nutritive faculty had four auxiliary faculties; the attractive, the retentive, the concoctive or alterative, and the expulsive. This was most clearly seen in the digestive system, but all parts had the same faculties. The several parts of the body attracted their own special nutritive needs from the blood: the heart attracted blood and spirits, the kidney, liver, spleen, etc. their specific secretions. When the alterative, retentive, and absorptive faculties had run their course, the final expulsive factor came into play and the waste products were expelled. Appetite and aversion were parts of the attractive and expulsive factors and not separate faculties.

The animal was endowed with yet other faculties, including first the whole gamut of sensations beginning with those such as touch and ending with the special sensations of sight, hearing, olfaction, and taste that were reported to the common sensorium in the brain; here also were located other faculties such as discernment, memory, imagination, and desire. Finally, the animal was endowed with the faculty of movement by which it approached the desirable object or fled from danger.

The mind with its intelligence was queen of all parts of the soul and it was through this that man surpassed the animals. Intelligence was simple, incorporeal, separate, immortal, and eternal. Here Fernel got into difficulties in connecting this, the rational soul, with the operation of the brain and with the more primitive natural and sentient souls. In effect, the human soul directed all the body's functions.

Form and function—division of labour—and the sympathy between parts. Galen taught the close association of form and function. He could not, of course, examine structure closely enough to be able to see that, at the molecular level, structure and function are virtually inseparable and, in fact, identical.

The separate bodily parts were recognized as semi-independent and adapted for specialized purposes for the benefit of the whole organism just as workers in a society each work in a specialized way for the whole and each receives sustenance from the whole.

Co-ordination of the many separate activities was not always clear; the nervous system was obviously involved. In addition there were other unknown mechanisms like sympathy. Such a sympathy existed between the breast and the uterus, for instance, accounting for the enlargement of the breasts in pregnancy.

Fernel, like all those before him, was preoccupied with drawing an orderly systematic physiology from Galen and set aside all experimental work. Only in a few places did he express new or different opinions and it is difficult to judge whether these were based on observations of his own, the observations of others, or upon the logic of his theoretical constraints. He advised his readers to insert their fingers into an animal heart to test its heat, and correctly associated contraction of the heart with the pulse wave; he recognized that an enclosed body of air diminished in volume when a candle was burned inside it; however he did not acknowledge that Galen and his predecessors in Alexandria introduced physiological experiment and that his experiments on the origin of the phrenic nerve, on the function of the recurrent laryngeal nerve, and on the separate identity of motor and sensory nerves were the foundations of physiology.

Harvey and the circulation. *Reintroduction of the experimental method.* From Galen to Harvey practically a millennium and a half passed with almost no physiological experimentation. There was a thin thread of continuity constituted by such unique spirits as *Nicholas of Cusa who had an unusual opportunity of reading old manuscripts from the decaying libraries of the mediaeval monasteries and cathedrals of Germany. One such manuscript extant in but a few copies, by an otherwise unknown writer named Markelinos, reported that *Herophilus routinely determined the heart rate in his patients using a clepsydra (a time-measuring device worked by flow of water). Cusa may have seen that manuscript or one like it, for in the fourth book on the use of the balance in his famous work *The Idiot*, he too measured the heart rate with a clepsydra, and went on to recommend study of the specific gravity of urine and of blood and other variables of man. His ideas suggest his influence on later workers and the slow transition from the old world to the present day. He recommended that bodies of equal size and shape be let fall from a high tower and their time of fall be measured with a clepsydra. While this suggestion probably derived from Aristotle, who thought that the rate of fall of bodies in air was like the sinking of bodies in water and was related to their specific gravity, this was probably the stimulus to *Galileo's work on falling bodies. In both Cusa's hypothetical and Galileo's actual experiment, timing was by a clepsydra. Later, Galileo discovered the laws of the pendulum and showed that the pulse beat could be expressed objectively in the length of a pendulum swinging in time with the pulse. *Santorio may have derived his measurement of the pulse rate from Galileo, but his observation of the respiratory/heart-rate relationship was his own. Van *Helmont almost certainly got the idea of measuring the specific gravity of urine from Cusa and also the idea of growing a willow tree in an iron pot for several years, adding nothing but water and concluding that the total weight of the new growth had come from water. This and the similar experiment by Robert *Boyle were originally suggested by Cusa. It is interesting to note that Cusa, Galileo, and Boyle even used the dialogue as the form of some of their most important writings.

Of course Galileo, Sanctorius, van Helmont, and Boyle did much more than follow Cusa's suggestions, but in doing so they uncovered new phenomena which in time led to the discovery of more new phenomena. As Francis Bacon predicted, national and international institutions were later established which carried these central themes through the years and the generations.

Thus, Harvey was not the first of the new biological and medical thinkers, but he was certainly one of the first. Moreover, he had advantages denied his predecessors. Essentially all the necessary information about the circulation was available to Galen. He knew, for instance that all the blood could be drained from an animal either via the veins or via the arteries, and this led him to believe that there were interconnections in the lungs and in the periphery as well as in the interventricular septum. He knew that the blood vessels contained only blood, that the heart had expulsive power and that it had valves. Bellows were everywhere and the function of valves was well known. Water pumps were known and in Galen's own home town for many years the *windkessel* was in use in fire pumps to give a constant flow, even though the action of the single-stroke pump was intermittent. Still, these facts may not have been completely obvious to Galen: in the coastal cities of his experience, the main way water moved was by canal and as often as not the canals were filled in the morning and emptied at night or in tidal areas regulated by the tide. Even in Rome the water supply was by aqueduct with a pitch of no more than six or eight inches in a mile. Pipes were in use but almost exclusively by those wishing to steal water.

Things were different for Harvey: pumps were everywhere, powered by windmills or water-wheels, and water systems were being installed in many cities. Harvey may have seen the first system installed in London, where water was pumped from the Thames by a water-wheel and distributed to the houses of its subscribers by a piping system. Then too, Harvey had both at Cambridge and at Padua the example of Vesalius who had shown through human anatomy that the greatest heritage from Galen was experimentation and not reliance on a textbook account that forced things into a system which Galen himself had put forward tentatively and not as established truth.

But there was more to this than the times and circumstances and Harvey's undoubted genius —something that caught his attention and forced him to think about the circulation. Robert Boyle says that, in their only meeting, Harvey told him that the original stimulus came from his professor of anatomy at Padua whose favourite subject was his own discovery: that of the *valves in the veins. For two decades *Fabricius had been writing and lecturing about these valves, and had shown that they were one-way structures that freely let pass a probe in one direction but arrested it in the other. They could readily be seen in the living man as small knots in the forearm veins when they were engorged by application of a *tourniquet of 'middling tightness' which as we now know impedes venous return but not arterial flow into the arm. Of all the thousands of students taught by Fabricius, only Harvey seems to have reached the obvious conclusion that even Fabricius had missed, namely the direction of the flow of blood in the veins. This led to one of the simplest and most elegant experiments of physiology. A valve is located somewhere in the arm on a single stretch of vein and with one finger the vein is occluded an inch or two peripherally. Another finger strokes the blood centrally and blood passes freely out of the vein toward the heart. If one now attempts to cause a reflux of blood from the well-filled vein past the valve and toward the periphery, this is impossible because of the valve, and the short empty segment remains collapsed, only to become filled again as the occlusion is relieved and the segment is filled from the periphery. It is, therefore, evident that the flow of the blood in the veins is from the periphery to the heart and there cannot be any flow in the reverse direction. Now this experiment can be kept up endlessly, and one can thus calculate the amount of blood transmitted to the heart by a single vein. If the segment is considered to hold 0.5 ml of blood, and the operation takes 2 seconds per cycle, then 15 ml of blood is transmitted to the heart in 1 minute and about 900 ml in 1 hour, over 20 litres in 1 day. This amount of blood cannot possibly be generated de novo in the periphery and must come somehow from the arteries. In fact, if the tourniquet is tightened sufficiently to stop the pulse the experiment fails.

With this start, Harvey continued to trace the course of the blood in a series of simple yet decisive experiments, first to the right heart, then through the pulmonary arteries, with reflux prevented by the valves of the atrioventricular junction and at the pulmonary artery. Thus there was no escape except across the lung to the pulmonary vein and into the left heart. From the left ventricle because of valves at the atrioventricular junction and at the base of the aorta, blood could go nowhere except into the aorta and then back to the veins. Harvey never saw the *capillaries which join the arteries to the veins, but postulated their presence and in due

time they were seen with the *microscope. To watch the arterial, venous, and capillary circulation in a web of a frog's foot, or in a tadpole tail, is still a moving, satisfying, and simple experiment, which, like Harvey's first, has been repeated by generations of physiologists and medical students.

Harvey's work set the record straight and raised questions that continue to interest us today. Harvey noticed that the right heart was found only in animals with lungs and forthrightly stated that it was made for the lungs. Very soon Richard *Lower showed that the change in colour from venous to arterial blood was due to aeration in the lungs and that this could be accomplished simply by passing a stream of air through the lungs without the alternate inspiration and expiration by which aeration is normally accomplished. Lower even produced an 'artificial lung' as a pulmonary bypass in which blood was spread out in a thin sheet on the bottom of a vessel that connected the right heart to the left heart. Thus the basic function of the lungs became clear and much of the mystery attributed to the blood in the lungs was removed. We are reminded of two more experiments of Lower's when racehorse owners or dog fanciers speak of blood lines in their animals, or when we speak of warm- or cold-hearted people, or receive a cordial welcome: in one, he was able to maintain life in a dog for some time by infusing a replacement fluid into the circulation while blood was withdrawn at another site; blood did not therefore serve a mystic purpose, but it was simply a biochemical fluid. The other experiment was not so clearly Lower's (or his alone), but was a part of his time, and that was *blood transfusion. These experiments followed the introduction of the *syringe as a means of giving intravenous injections of drugs (partly due to Christopher *Wren). They first took place from one animal to the other of the same species but rapidly ended up with the transfusion of sheep's or calves' blood to humans. There were probably four transfusions of blood in Paris and even in Oxford Lower transfused sheep's blood into a foolish divinity student. This was going too far and the practice was quickly suspended, but later transfusion was to become a common surgical procedure and only a few religious zealots still believe that blood is anything but a simple physiological fluid.

Lavoisier and combustion. The virtual disappearance of physiological experimentation between Galen and Harvey does not mean that experimentation in other fields disappeared. The metallurgists continued to work and iron works in Roman times were of real importance. Mechanical devices were developed to serve the shipping industry and in fact Rome was almost on the very brink of an industrial revolution. Gold was highly prized and extensive mining and refining installations existed. It was known that exposing an impure mass of gold and silver to a reducing flame in a coating of lead foil freed the mass of everything but the gold and silver, while cupelating the same sample with antimony got rid of the silver as well and left pure gold. Antimony thus became known as the 'sovereign remedy' and soon found its way into medicine. Much interest in gold was focused on making it go as far as possible by preparing gold leaf or alloys, while retaining its characteristic appearance. A favourite method was to fabricate the desired object from an alloy of silver and gold and then to immerse it in sea water which dissolved the superficial layer of silver and left a thin layer of pure gold on the outside. After burnishing, it resembled a pure gold object. A vessel suspected of being so alloyed was a problem presented to Archimedes, who solved it by discovering specific gravity. The lens or burning glass was known to the Greeks and by the 12th or 13th c. biconvex eye glasses were in use, principally for *presbyopia. One can well imagine the revolution in rug-making, weaving, and other occupations such as the scholarly professions which demanded clear and close vision, that had formerly to be given up between the ages of 40 or 50, but now could be pursued 20 to 35 years longer. The Byzantines had invented Greek fire (a combustible compound used to set fire to enemy ships) which implies that they may have known how to make a petroleum distillate. Hence there must have been many people who knew what could be done with fire and how to make vessels and tubings from glass and were curious about what fire could do. Two things favoured their endeavour. First was the idea of the *quintessence*. Fire, air, water, and earth were the basic elements but they were philosophical abstractions and beyond experimental attack. Later generations gave real substance to them by trying to select an actual substance as the actual *quintessence* of the element. Thus, it was agreed that sulphur was the quintessence of fire because it burned completely, leaving no ash, and must therefore consist of nothing more than the element of fire. One can readily see why mercury or quicksilver was selected as the quintessence of water. Salt, possibly saltpetre, became the quintessence of earth and finally van Helmont coined the word gas as the quintessence of air. Van Helmont recognized that there were many species of gas and his gas-sylvester is recognizable to us as *carbon dioxide. Thus the chemists of the times worked with real substances and the search for the basic element became a matter of experiment. By the invention of the word gas with many varieties that he and others soon produced, van Helmont raised the possibility that air might not be the single element it had always been thought to be; this prepared the way for acceptance of the view that it is a mixture of two principal gases with traces of other rare gases. The theory of the ancients that all substances came from original elements led to the hope that by some fortunate chemical means a base metal might be converted into gold, and generations of *alchemists sought to succeed in the conversion or in discovering the mythical *philosopher's stone which would turn base metal into gold and cure all diseases. Although alchemy attracted many *quacks and swindlers, the alchemists learned much about chemistry and fire, and in time became chemists with less ambitious but more attainable goals.

Three observations or experiments led to our present understanding of the nature of combustion. They were: (i) the gain in mass of metals or other substances after calcination or oxidation (see below); (ii) the reduction in the volume of air enclosed over water when a candle is permitted to burn itself out in the confined space; and (iii) the discovery of gunpowder.

The gain in weight of calcined substances. Galen himself noted that when lead sheets were stored in a cellar, they gained in mass, showing himself to be a true lover of learning and not simply a very good physician. Robert Boyle made the same observation when phosphorus was burned and wondered if some substance passed through the glass and into the material. Jean Rey learned from his pharmacist of the gain in mass of tin when it was calcined by prolonged heating in the melted state in an open pot. He postulated on common-sense grounds that the gain in mass came from the air, the only medium in intimate contact with the tin.

When *Lavoisier learned of the discovery of *oxygen from Joseph *Priestley he carried out Jean Rey's experiment properly by placing the tin in a large flask and then sealing it so that the tin was exposed only to the air in the flask. When after the usual prolonged heating an amount of the metallic tin was converted to a calx, the whole assembly had not gained mass. When the sealed vessel opened a hissing sound was heard, air rushed into the flask, and the whole gained in mass. There was indeed something in air that had combined with the metal. Recognition that combustion and calcination represented oxidation or the chemical combination of the substance with oxygen, was the beginning of the new chemistry.

The diminution of air by combustion. This observation was first made about the time of Galen and repeatedly after then until *Mayow. It was not possible until glassware was available and in sufficient size and shape—illustrating the clear relationship between science and technology. A candle in its holder was set up in the centre of a vessel of water and the candle lighted. A second vessel was inverted over the candle making certain that a water seal was established with a margin of safety to accommodate the expansion of air by the heat of the flame. In due time the candle would go out and, when the temperature had stabilized, the water level in the vessel covering the candle had risen, indicating a diminution of the air volume by about one-fifth. We now know that the carbon dioxide formed by the combustion of the candle in the oxygen of the air readily dissolved in water and was therefore removed and the oxygen used up in the combustion was wholly removed from the confined air which was therefore reduced in volume.

This experiment was repeated by many alchemists and at last by Mayow who came very close to understanding the nature of combustion. If he did not, at least he was followed by those of the Oxford School, including Robert *Hooke, Stephen *Hales and Priestley, leading to Lavoisier, who defined combustion as we now know it.

Mayow was primarily responsible for another experiment that also measured the amount of oxygen in air and showed that he was an original worker. He arranged a small dish of nitric acid on a stand in a basin of water covered by a bell jar with a water seal as in the candle experiment. A string passing around a pulley in the bell jar and to the outside around the open end of the bell jar held some iron filings suspended over the acid. The iron filings were let fall into the nitric acid and caused the liberation of a brownish gas. The brownish colour soon disappeared and, as it did, the volume of the air in the bell jar diminished. We now know that the iron and nitric acid interacted to form nitric oxide which then reacted with the oxygen to form nitrogen dioxide, which was readily soluble in water. This again removed the oxygen from the air, and in the hands of later workers like Fontana and Ingenhous became the principal method for measuring the oxygen content of samples of gas.

Gunpowder. Just who discovered gunpowder and where is still a matter of dispute, but knowledge of it came to Europe from the East, and India is the most likely source as saltpetre is commonly found there. India was the world source of saltpetre (potassium nitrate) before discovery of the Chilean nitrate beds. Although Chilean saltpetre is sodium nitrate, it is easily converted into potassium nitrate.

The composition of gunpowder is simple. It contains two combustible substances, carbon and sulphur, and an appropriate amount of saltpetre. The mixture readily explodes when exposed to a flame or ignited by a spark; this can take place when the package of explosive is under water or confined in a closed space behind a rifle or cannon ball or, as Robert Boyle showed, in a vacuum. The fact that saltpetre supplied something like air in the combustion of carbon and sulphur must have been vaguely recognized by many involved in early experiences with gunpowder, but it remained for Mayow and Hooke to talk of something common to both the saltpetre and air in that both supported combustion by supplying 'nitro-aerial' particles.

Combustion in the living organism. When Lavoisier went on to show that combustion was nothing other than oxidation of carbon and hydrogen in the substance to carbon dioxide and water, he proceeded with other studies of importance in relation to the history of oxygen and its role in combustion. He was the first to express the formula $C + O_2 = CO_2$ and heat with specific proportions of each so that by knowing one variable all the others could be calculated. After making the first calorimeter, Lavoisier measured the heat produced by recording the quantity of ice melted in its jacket. He found that whether the substrate was burned or whether a living animal was studied, for equal amounts of oxygen consumed, equal amounts of heat were produced. He later realized that in animal metabolism certain amounts of hydrogen were also oxidized to water. Lavoisier carried out similar studies of human calorimetry and came to the same conclusion.

The dependence of Lavoisier on the past was illustrated by his errors as well as by his successes. His greatest error consisted in thinking that oxygen was responsible for acidity. This came directly from Hooke and Mayow, who wrote of the acid nature of nitro-aerial spirits. Even in Haller's *First Lines of Physiology* of 1786, it was asked whether the use of the lungs was not to absorb a nitre of the air into the blood, and it went on to say that there is certainly a kind of volatile acid in the air.

Lavoisier then concluded that human metabolism is nothing more than a slow combustion of carbon and hydrogen, no different from the combustion of the same substances *in vitro*. The flame of life was, in the last analysis, nothing more than the burning of a candle. How this was accomplished without flame, without high internal heat, and with requisite slowness was the work of the next 150 years and depended largely on the next great forward step in anatomy and physiology which defined the living unit, the *cell.

The new physiology. *The cell doctrine* (see also CELL). By the 14th c., glass of the requisite transparency was being made, as were lenses for glasses to correct presbyopia, while concave lenses were first mentioned a century later by Nicholas of Cusa. When a concave and a convex lens were lined up at proper distances one had on the one hand the telescope which Galileo exploited so well, and on the other the compound microscope. Robert Hooke was one of the first to explore the potential of this new tool in his *Micrographia*. Examining a piece of cork, he found it to be made of countless tiny compartments about a million to a square inch, each one of which was a little box or cell. The further development of the compound microscope enabled later workers to see the same basic structures in both plants and animals and to state the general principles of the cell doctrine which are:

1. There occur both in plant life and animal life organisms that can in truth be called individuals because they consist of a single cell only.

2. Every plant or animal developed in any higher degree is an aggregate of fully individualized independent separate beings, the cells themselves.

3. Each cell leads a double life; an independent one pertaining to its own development alone and another, which can be called its social function, having to do with an adaptation or exaggeration of some basic function to serve the organism as a whole. Multicellular organisms might therefore be thought of as a society of cells with the same sort of

division of labour that takes place in our complex society.

4. The fundamental power of the organism reflects in the last analysis the fundamental powers of the individual cells. The most general statement of these powers resolves itself into the carrying out of chemical changes within the cell or in the surrounding fluids which may be designated as metabolic phenomena or *metabolism*.

Irritability. Another doctrine that had developed independently, quickly recognized as adapting readily to the cell doctrine, was the doctrine of *irritability* or the ability of a cell to respond to a stimulus by an appropriate response. A single-cell organism responds to a potentially harmful stimulus by avoidance, to the presence of food by moving towards it; these are but the first of a series of responses aimed at individual and species survival. In multicellular organisms there are countless stimulus–response sequences by which the life of the organism is maintained. Rudolph *Virchow made the cell doctrine and irritability the central themes of modern *pathology in his *Cellular Pathology*, which saw pathology as being the study of the response of cells to harmful stimuli. While the doctrine of irritability soon failed as a central theme of more than one general system of medicine, it did provide a way of looking at physiological events as purely physical-chemical chains of events not requiring intervention of a 'soul', 'mind', 'archeus', or of some other metaphysical factor incapable of physiological definition.

The cell doctrine was thus a most important generalization of modern biology and a worthy counterpart of Lavoisier's new chemistry. Both were essential to the development of modern physiology. Its first fruits were *histology and pathology, then *microbiology, *embryology, *genetics, and more recently cell biology. All of these pertain to the physiology of the cell and have served as principal stimuli to advances in medicine in the last 100 years. Ehrlich concluded that the cell doctrine is the axis around which the modern science of life revolves. This may be true in broad outline but other advances in science and technology played their part. The new instruments of physics were rapidly applied to physiological study: it is hard, for instance, to imagine that progress could have occurred in physiology without the electrical stimulators that begin to be available between the third and fourth decades of the 19th c. The discovery of surgical *anaesthesia gave the physiologist a way to work without causing pain in his experimental subjects, and the advent of aseptic surgery permitted a new and wider range of chronic experimentation.

The internal environment. Pondering on the ability of seeds to withstand storage for many years in a dry environment, and for many *protozoa and small metazoa, such as rotifers, to survive prolonged desiccation by encystment, Claude *Bernard concluded that life was a balance between the environment and the vital chemical actions by which it was maintained. Even some mammals had periods when bodily activity was generally suppressed, as in hibernation of marmots and dormice. The hibernation of bears is perhaps more commonly recognized today, although Bernard did not mention it. Some animals are inactivated by heat, and aestivate rather than hibernate. From this Bernard concluded that life requires a certain state of the environment, including water, oxygen, and temperature and foodstuffs without the presence of excess body wastes. In considering how most multicellular organisms maintain their central integrity in an environment in which lesser organisms die or enter a form of suspended life, Bernard planned some early experiments of his own. Measuring the *blood sugar of dogs fed in various ways, largely on bread, or meal, or meat, or a mixture of them, he found that the blood sugar remained constant, because of the presence of animal starch or *glycogen in the liver. When the supply of *carbohydrate was high, glucose was converted to glycogen and stored in the liver but when at some later time dietary carbohydrate was deficient, glycogen was broken down to maintain the blood glucose. Thus, in more highly organized animals the blood formed the immediate environment of the individual cells and allowed the animal to be relatively free of the influence of the ambient or external environment (see also HOMEOSTASIS). As he wrote,

I believe I was the first to insist on this: that there are really two environments for the animal; one the *external environment* in which the organism is placed and the *internal environment* in which the elements of the tissues live. Life does not run its course within the external environment, atmospheric air for the aerial being, fresh or salt water for the aquatic animals, but within the *fluid internal environment* formed by the circulating organic liquid that surrounds and bathes all of the anatomical elements of the tissues; this is in the lymph or plasma, the liquid portion of the blood which in the higher animals perfuses the tissues and constitutes the ensemble of all the interstitial fluids. It is the expression of all the local nutritions and is the source and confluence of all the elementary exchanges. A complex organism must be considered as an association of *simple beings* which are the anatomical elements which live in the fluid internal environment.

The constancy of the internal environment is the condition for free and independent life. The mechanism that makes it possible is that which assures the maintenance within the internal environment of all the conditions necessary for the life of the elements.

The cell doctrine, together with Lavoisier's new chemistry, were certainly the major causes of the subsequent revolution in physiology. Only a quarter of a century after Lavoisier's death, Wohler made *urea from ammonium cyanate. This was the first preparation of a substance that was formerly produced only by a living organism, and became part of the growing evidence that although the processes in the living organism may not be the same as those of *in vitro* chemistry, they are chemical nevertheless.

Maintenance of the internal environment. About 60 per cent of the body weight is water, and a third of this (20 per cent of body weight) lies outside the cell. This is the fluid from which cells derive their nourishment and into which they discharge the products of their metabolism. It is strictly comparable to the watery environment of the monocell except that when the monocell finds its surroundings unfavourable it moves on to a more favourable environment. In the multicellular organism this translation is impossible; it is the environment, or part of it, that moves past the cell and then past processing stations which purify it of toxic substances and replace the nutritive substances that have been used up. Three important stations are: (i) the gastrointestinal tract which supplies food, water, and *vitamins; (ii) the lungs which add oxygen and eliminate excess carbon dioxide; and (iii) the kidneys which selectively retain or reject crystalloids.

The part of the extracellular fluid that circulates is the blood *plasma, which differs from the intercellular or interstitial fluid only in containing: (i) red blood cells to increase its ability to transport oxygen and carbon dioxide; (ii) *protein to achieve a proper distribution of water between the blood and the interstitial fluids; (iii) a clotting mechanism that serves as a protection against haemorrhage, as well as *white cells and immune proteins which give the organism its own individuality and protect it from attack by micro-organisms.

The cardiovascular system. In fulfilling its functions and maintaining a constant internal environment the whole system has but one purpose, that of maintaining capillary perfusion, for it is only at the capillaries that exchange between the blood and interstitial fluid takes place. There are over a billion capillaries throughout the body, all supplied by the ramifications of a single vessel, the *aorta; the cross-sectional area of the whole of the capillary system is nearly a thousand times that of the aorta. Hence, the flow velocity of blood in the capillaries is about one-thousandth that in the aorta, which means that the blood is in the capillaries for only 1 second. Since the arm-to-arm circulation time is about 20 seconds and somewhat more than twice as much in the leg in man, it means that the greatest time is spent in distributing blood in the arteries and returning it in the veins; with each complete circulation about 1 second will be spent in the lung capillaries and another second in the systemic capillaries.

Even today the three most common examinations of the heart and circulation are: (i) the examination of the *pulse; (ii) *auscultation of the heart sounds; and (iii) the determination of the *blood pressure. Herophilus, a predecessor of Galen in Alexandria, was reported by a later writer to have carried with him a clepsydra which could be calibrated to fit the age of the patient and the pulse was counted during the time it took to sink. A count in excess of normal was taken to indicate fever. In 1450 Nicholas of Cusa proposed a variation; the mass of water emerging from a clepsydra was measured during the time it took to count 100 beats. Both methods were of value only to the one physician who did the examination because each clepsydra was different. Only when Galileo came to understand the constancy of the pendulum was it possible to obtain universally applicable data and Sanctorius made several models of *pulsilogum* in which a pendulum made of a weight on a cord was adjusted in length until it was synchronized with the pulse. It was less useful than it might have been because there was no direct expression of counts per time interval; this was impossible at the time because there was as yet no clear definition of a minute or at least no accurate means of measuring it. Kepler was probably the first to express the pulse rate in counts per minute (he said 60) and as watches came into use this measurement became a routine.

The heart acts in reality as two pumps, each double, that on the right serving the pulmonary circulation and that on the left, the systemic circulation. The atria or auricles help to fill the ventricle but they are not essential, as shown by the fact that auricular fibrillation is not inconsistent with life; the essential chambers are the two ventricles. If they act as pumps with a closed system of distribution and collection, then the usual rules of haemodynamics ought to apply. One of the oldest laws of hydraulics is that water in a static system will rise to the height of the source; this is exactly how Stephen Hales carried out his experiment, inserting a glass tube into an artery of a horse and determining how high the blood would then rise. In his first experiment it was 8 ft 3 in (about 2.5 m), but varied as much as 4 in (10.5 cm) with each heart beat and with each breath by as much as a foot (0.3 m). Almost a century later the open tube was exchanged for a mercury *manometer and shortly thereafter *Ludwig placed a float with a stem and writing stylus on the open end of the manometer so that the blood pressure could write itself out on a revolving drum surrounded by smoked paper, and this could later be varnished to make a permanent record of the changes the blood pressure underwent. (He thus introduced the idea of recording physiological events, one of the principal tools of physiological progress.) Records of blood pressure so made showed pulsatile variations described by Ludwig—a slight variation with each beat and a larger variation with each breath. Interpreting the results was made difficult by the knowledge that both the mass of blood and the mass of mercury imposed an inertia on the system which made the results so obtained represent only the *mean* blood pressure, thus obscuring any rapid changes. The answer lay in developing instrumentation with a faster response time; this had the material effect of reducing sensitivity so that a completely satisfactory system was constructed only after the advent of electronic amplification. Even before then, however, manometers such as those of Hamilton were made with a stiff metal membrane displacing a mirror and deflecting a beam of light, and gave reliable records. They showed that although the heart beat was intermittent, the blood pressure had a constant factor, the *diastolic pressure, on which was superimposed the *systolic factor. The flow of blood into the capillaries and back to the heart was thus essentially constant. The reason had been known to the hydraulic technicians of the Alexandrian era: it was the air-chamber or *windkessel* effect (employed especially in fire engines) to ensure a constant stream of water even though a single pump with an intermittent output was employed. If an air chamber was placed on the output side of the pump, part of the output would enter it and compress the air while the other part of the water passed out in a jet from the nozzle. Then while the pump was on its upstroke the water in the air chamber would be forced out by the compressed air, thereby converting an intermittent output of the pump into a constant outflow at the nozzle. The heart is an intermittent pump ejecting blood only during contraction (systole) and filling and waiting for an instant of time (diastole) for a new stimulus to beat. During systole some blood flows out of the arteriolar system into the capillaries while the rest is stored in the aorta and large arteries which stretch and accommodate it under the greater pressure. Then during diastole the blood is ejected into the capillary and the pressure in the aorta and great vessels falls. Thus there is never a time when there is no pressure in the great vessels, so that there is always some capillary propulsion. Two values of blood pressure are therefore important; the systolic blood pressure, which is mainly a measure of the amount of blood ejected by the heart during systole, and the diastolic pressure, which is mainly related to the state of the small arteries called *arterioles, which by their contraction or relaxation determine how fast blood leaves the arteriolar tree.

This direct method of measuring blood pressure from a needle in an artery is not as difficult as it once was, especially with recent improvements in techniques. Yet good medical practice dictates that everyone should have his or her blood pressure determined whenever visiting a doctor and, when in hospital, every few hours or even more often. No invasive method could be applied as often, and hence indirect methods are needed. These all involve the use of an occlusive pneumatic cuff placed around an arm or leg. Pressure in the cuff is applied uniformly to the tissues and the arteries of the limb and when it reaches and exceeds systolic pressure, blood flow in the limb is cut off. Determination of the systolic pressure is thus easy and requires no more than palpation of the artery. Diastolic pressure is another matter. When an aneroid manometer was employed that showed the variations transmitted to the cuff from the artery it was found that the point of maximum oscillation of the manometer was generally close to the diastolic

pressure and to accept this is a common European practice. American and British practice, which still uses the mercury manometer, to which the oscillometric method is not well adapted, still follows the ausculatory method of *Korotkoff, the Russian physician who heard a series of sounds with a *stethoscope applied to the artery just distal to the cuff. There is silence when cuff pressure is greater than the systolic pressure and sounds begin as pressure falls below systolic pressure and jets of blood emerge below the cuff. As pressure in the cuff falls, an evolution takes place in the quality of sounds until, when the cuff pressure reaches diastolic pressure, there is a sudden reduction in the loudness of the sound. Despite variables that result from the cuff size and difficulties in obtaining a clear diastolic reading, the method is so readily available and well documented from millions of determinations that it is an indispensable clinical tool. It was not used in America until *Cushing introduced it as a routine procedure in surgery in 1906 and our knowledge of *hypertension in man is no older than this. If we consider the effect it has had on the care of human disease, this indirect method is probably physiology's greatest contribution to medicine.

Heart sounds. This is the third of the three basic determinations that established cardiology as a medical specialty, namely, auscultation of the chest and recognition of the heart sounds.

Harvey was possibly aware of the heart sounds, for in his lecture notes from 1616 he wrote as follows: 'It is certain from the structure of the heart that the blood is perpetually carried across through the lungs into the aorta as by the two clacks of a water bellows to raise water.' It is interesting to note that while the first part of the sentence was in Latin, as indeed was the set of notes, the last part was in English. Perhaps he did this to take advantage of the double meaning of 'clacks', meaning both the sounds made by the flap valve of a bellows and the valves themselves. Thus it may be that Harvey knew the heart sounds and considered them of valvular origin. He did not mention the bellows-pump analogy in *De motu cordis*, and none of his students followed up the idea (if one existed); it was another 200 years before the subject came up again.

By 1818 physical diagnosis was well advanced in Paris hospitals and direct auscultation was in use in many. Listening to the chest of an obese young lady, *Laennec became impatient with direct auscultation; rolled up some sheets of paper into a hollow cylinder to make the first stethoscope, finding that it dramatically improved the quality of auscultation. Making a more durable model of wood he went on to studies on the auscultation of the thorax, and the stethoscope rapidly became the instrument most commonly carried by doctors and the badge of the profession.

Laennec heard the two major heart sounds as we hear them today: a first rather dull and prolonged sound and the second immediately after and without an interval and resembling the noise made by a valve or a whip, or the yapping of a dog, and of lesser duration than the first. Finding the first sound isochronous with the aortic pulse he correctly assigned the first sound to ventricular systole, but then mistakenly attributed the second to the oncoming atrial beat of the next cardiac cycle, thus making the heart sounds the products of two successive systoles. In time the correct assignment was worked out by other workers, the first sound indicating the onset of systole, principally caused by the closure of the atrioventricular valves, and the second coming with the end of ventricular systole and the closure of the aortic valves. A third sound is sometimes heard during the period of rapid filling as well as an atrial sound heard best during total atrioventricular block.

Properties of cardiac muscle. A number of discoveries about the heart served as models applicable to other systems and showed how a mechanism employed at one site can be modified for use in another. Here we can mention: (i) the refractory period; (ii) the myogenic origin and conduction of the heart beat; (iii) the double innervation of the heart; (iv) the importance of the composition of the extracellular fluid; and (v) the *electrocardiogram.

The heart was recognized to respond to electrical stimuli soon after skeletal muscle and nerve were found to be responsive, and *Bowditch, working in Ludwig's laboratory, noted that the heart did not always respond to each of a series of stimuli. Marey, recording the heart directly, found that it became unresponsive to stimuli as systole began and recovered its irritability only at the end of systole. It was he who called the interval of unresponsiveness the *refractory period.* Carlson later showed that the greater part of this period was *absolutely* refractory and was followed by a period when the heart responded only to a stronger than usual stimulus; this he called the *relative refractory period.* Finally, *Adrian showed that, following the relative refractory period, the heart showed a short interval when a stimulus of less than usual strength would evoke a response; this was the *supernormal period.* When in the 20th c. it became possible to study *axons and other irritable tissues, the same three phases again came to light.

For a long time it was thought that cardiac muscle, like skeletal muscle, depended for its contraction on its nerve supply, but this became less and less likely since cutting the *vagus nerve, thought to be its main nerve supply, did not cause cardiac arrest in the way that cutting the nerve to a skeletal muscle caused *paralysis. When it became possible to construct a primitive generator that would deliver a series of shocks, the device came into the hands of the brothers *Weber, one of whom (a physicist) provided the stimulator while the other (a physiologist) was aware of the lack of knowledge about the influence of the vagus. When this nerve was stimulated in a frog the heart beat

slowed or even stopped. This was also quickly confirmed in mammals, and brought about an immense revolution in physiology for until then nerves were thought to be able only to *excite* and not as, the vagus clearly did, to *inhibit.* Vagal stimulation was later shown to weaken the force of atrial contraction, to shorten the atrial refractory period, to shorten the atrial monophasic action current, and to delay or suspend conduction across the atrioventricular bridge. The influence on ventricular contraction was minimal.

This was followed by numerous studies involving stimulation of every accessible visceral nerve. A nerve going to the heart from the stellate ganglion in the root of the neck was found to have the opposite effect on the heart. It increased the heart rate (hence its name the *accelerans*), it facilitated conduction across the atrioventricular bridge, and also increased the force of ventricular contraction (the positive inotropic effect). There is evidence that the increased ejection per beat during exercise is mainly due to this effect.

It was then found that many visceral organs had such a double innervation, one set of nerves *exciting* and the other set of nerves *inhibiting* their activity: thus the *pupil is constricted by the third nerve and dilated by the *sympathetic; the *bronchi are constricted by the vagus and dilated by the sympathetic; intestinal motility is inhibited by the sympathetic and increased by the vagus; contraction of the *bladder is mediated by *parasympathetic nerves and inhibited by the sympathetic.

During the above studies it was found that the nerves to the heart could be cut without interrupting the rhythmic beat. There were, however, in the heart, collections of nerve cells in the sinoatrial region and near the atrioventricular junction. Throughout the 19th c. it was thought that peripheral ganglia could be the centres for *reflexes that took place within viscera without requiring the presence of the *central nervous system. The idea was primarily that of *Bichat and explains why the double system of visceral innervation is still called the *autonomic* system. Throughout most of the 19th c., workers still subscribed to the view of a local neurogenic origin of the heart beat and neurogenic conduction from atrium to ventricle and within each chamber. In the late 19th and early 20th c., much work showed that the neurogenic view could not be supported and that the heart generated and transmitted impulses within the atria, across the atrioventricular bridge, and throughout the ventricles solely by the action of its muscle fibres. Thus the heart in the chick embryo begins to beat before any nerve fibres grow into it. Later work detected a node of modified muscle cells at the strategic sinoatrial region which acts as a pacemaker and another node at the atrioventricular junction (atrioventricular node) which acts to carry the impulse across to the ventricles. Thus we can conclude that the heart operates purely by myogenic action and that the nervous system is present to regulate that activity. We come to the second conclusion that in acting as a *pacemaker and as a conducting medium, heart tissue acts exactly as does nervous tissue through the propagation of electrical impulses.

Richard Lower chose well when he used beer as a perfusion solution by which he maintained life in a dog even when most of the blood had been replaced by beer. Beer at that time was not only osmotically active but no doubt contained sodium, potassium, and carbon dioxide in significant amounts. When later Stephen Hales injected plain water into the pulmonary artery he noticed that a watery fluid appeared in the bronchi and that there was general swelling of the tissues. It was not until near the end of the 19th c. that *Ringer began studies of the effects of *ions in a heart perfusion solution which showed that not only is the osmotic pressure of a perfusion solution important but also its molecular composition. An isotonic solution of sodium chloride would not maintain the beat of a perfused frog's heart, but the addition of calcium to the perfusate brought back the beat though in time it caused the heart to stop in systole. Potassium added while the heart was still beating permitted relaxation and if an excess were added it stopped the heart in diastole. The effects of potassium to relax and calcium to increase the force of contraction seemed to be more related to the relative proportions of potassium and calcium rather than absolute concentrations. These results have been confirmed by later studies and the role of these principal ions, sodium, potassium, and calcium, has been more fully elucidated.

Sodium, in a concentration of close to 140 mEq/l of plasma is largely responsible for the osmotic pressure of the extracellular fluid. It also initiates the action potential in nerves and in the heart. It is also associated with calcium in maintaining cardiac contractility in a reciprocal way when the osmotic pressure is maintained by sucrose. Lowering the concentration of sodium has the same effect as increasing that of calcium. Potassium present at only 4 mEq/l can affect the resting potential of both nerve and muscle because this factor is regulated by the ratio of intracellular potassium (about 150 mg/l) to the extracellular concentration of the ion. Calcium is important for two reasons: it affects the irritability of nerve and muscle and acts as the excitation–contraction coupler in muscle contraction. In the heart the special role of calcium seems to be to prolong the monophasic action current by an inward flow across the membrane.

Recognition of the electrical activity of the heart came soon after the discovery of such activity in skeletal muscle and nerve. It began with the observation by *Kölliker and *Müller that, when the nerve of a frog muscle preparation was draped over the frog ventricle, the muscle preparation always contracted at least once with each heart beat and frequently twice. Matteucci then demonstrated the action potential of skeletal muscle. The experiment succeeded even better when a mammalian heart was used. Kölliker and Müller concluded that the action current of the heart stimulated the nerve lying upon it. Diaphragmatic contractions synchronous with the heart beat may similarly be seen in experimental animals because the phrenic nerve is stimulated by the action current of the heart. As *galvanometers increased in sensitivity, but not in frequency response, the rheotome (a 19th c. instrument used to plot the time–voltage course of a complex electrical wave) was used to sample the potential at several points along the cardiac cycle, and a typical double potential was mapped out.

Development of the capillary electrometer as a recording device permitted the first direct recording of the heart beat (of the exposed atrium) by Marey, and soon afterwards the electrocardiogram (ECG) in man was recorded, particularly by *Waller. The special meaning of the double wave form in the ECG was worked out by Burdon-Sanderson who showed that the duration of electrical negativity was far longer than the intraventricular conduction time and hence the first phase of the ECG portrayed the conduction of the impulse over the ventricle and the second phase, the recovery from the impulse.

The first really satisfactory instrument for recording the ECG in man was constructed early in the 20th c. by *Einthoven, based on an instrument devised by Ader for recording telegraphic messages. Here the requirements were: (i) a high response frequency that gives rapidly repetitive responses to stimuli of increasing frequency (so the maximum number of messages could be sent); and (ii) maximum sensitivity because of attenuation of the signal. Ader solved his problem by reducing the moving coil, as for instance, in the D'Arsonval galvanometer, to a single microscopically fine wire placed between the very close pole pieces of a powerful magnet. The magnet was drilled to accommodate a powerful projecting microscope which cast the shadow of this 'string' upon a camera slit that in turn focused the shadow on a moving strip of photographic paper. Einthoven's ECG followed Ader's instrument faithfully except that the moving string was made even smaller by drawing out quartz to a diameter of 6–10 μm and gilding it to make it a conductor. The magnetic gap was made very small and the image projected over a metre or more to obtain maximal optical magnification consistent with an adequate intensity of light. This instrument revealed what have come to be the familiar P-QRS-T waves of the ECG. From its earliest use in medicine the ECG has proved to be of value in the diagnosis of the *arrhythmias, such as auricular and ventricular *fibrillation, blocks of the impulse conduction at the atrioventricular and bundle branches, and in failure of nutrition such as cardiac *infarction. If anything the ECG has become even more important in recent years because more and more can be done in such conditions and the diagnosis becomes more and more critical.

Digestion and metabolism. That gastrointestinal activity involves three main processes, namely motility, digestion, and absorption, must have been appreciated from the earliest stages of human history. At one time it was thought that digestion itself was simply a process of extreme trituration, grinding the food so fine that it became impalpable and entered the blood directly. There was always an alternative thought, that the process was more like *fermentation with which people had long been acquainted in brewing and wine-making. But the greatest stimulus to new work came from the observations William *Beaumont made on his patient, Alexis St Martin, who developed a gastric *fistula after an accidental gunshot wound and provided a unique opportunity for study of gastric secretion. Soon thereafter Payen and Persoz observed that from an aqueous extract of *yeast they could obtain a heat-labile substance which converted starch into glucose. They called their product diastase (now called *amylase) and it was the first of the *enzymes to be discovered, using the general term later given to these substances by Kühne. A year later *Schwann discovered *pepsin in gastric juice and subsequently Berzelius used the word catalysis to describe agents that accelerated both organic and inorganic processes. He predicted that men would find in living plants and animals thousands of catalytic processes taking place between the tissues and the fluids. Bertholin in 1860 extracted an enzyme from yeast which converted sucrose into glucose and postulated that the living cells produce many enzymes by which the chemical work of the body is carried out. When in 1897 Edward Buchner was able by high pressure to extract a series of enzymes from yeast, it became possible to carry out the entire sequence of alcoholic fermentation from starch to alcohol and carbon dioxide without the presence of a living cell. Since then, we have learned how important are enzymes in practically all chemical reactions of the cell, having a central role in metabolism, genetics, and cell biology.

Meanwhile the list of digestive enzymes has grown in parallel with our knowledge of food substances, so that we now know that proteins are broken down to amino acids, starches and sugars into hexoses (glucose, fructose, and galactose) and fats into their components of fatty acids and glycerol.

Here may be mentioned the *vitamins, because they are ingested with food and, unless they are present, a diet adequate in calories, protein, carbohydrate, and minerals, fails to maintain health. Most act as *coenzymes or essential ingredients in enzymes or are otherwise essential components in a metabolic chain. Some of them have been associated with human disease in a dramatic way. *Scurvy was first described by Jacques Cartier in an account of his second voyage to Canada in 1535. Here nearly all of his men suffered from various degrees of scurvy, with softening of the gums, loss of the teeth, mucocutaneous haemorrhage and

weakness; some died of it. Indians living nearby also suffered from the disease: they showed Cartier how to cure his men with an infusion of leaves and branches of a local evergreen. Soon the juices of the citrus fruit were found to contain an antiscorbutic factor (*vitamin C) and its prophylactic use has practically eliminated scurvy. Next to be observed on a large scale was *rickets, a disease of bone development seen particularly in children. Though *Glisson had described rickets in the 17th c., it was not until much later that *cod liver oil and sunshine, providing *vitamin D, were recognized as curative or prophylactic. Much later *beriberi was recognized as another disease that could be cured by small dietary additions and it was recognized that it was clearly a deficiency disease (of *vitamin B_1). Scurvy and rickets were then also shown to be deficiency diseases and their associated vitamins were sought. (For the chemical nature of the vitamins and their role see NUTRITION.) Not all vitamins are necessary for all mammals, which can synthesize some without the need for external sources. It is interesting that vitamin C or *ascorbic acid is synthesized in all animals but man and the guinea pig.

The observations of Beaumont on Alexis St Martin stimulated workers to produce similar fistulas in experimental animals and in order to prevent food contamination, pouches were formed opening to the outside but closed off from direct communication with the rest of the stomach. Of the various workers who began such studies, apparently only one, Ivan *Pavlov, kept the nerve supply from the vagus nerve intact. He also introduced the technique of sham feeding so that the animal could eat normally but the food would pass to the outside through exteriorization of the *oesophagus and did not enter the stomach. With either preparation, teasing the animal with food would cause a copious flow of gastric juice and if the animal were then permitted to eat, an even greater flow of gastric juice would occur. When the same experiment was carried out after denervation of the stomach or the pouch, there would be no secretion. In addition, when a bell heralding food was rung, gastric secretion also occurred—a *conditioned reflex. While this was not the first work to demonstrate nervous control over so-called vegetative or autonomic functions, it was the first demonstration of nervous control of gastric secretion and was accepted as explaining enzyme release during digestion. Indeed, in the 19th c. a concept of a universal nervism placed all regulation in the hands of the nervous system.

In 1902 *Bayliss and *Starling proposed another medium of control. Papers had recently appeared showing that injection of acid into the duodenum still evoked secretion of pancreatic fluid after denervation. Bayliss and Starling ground up some duodenal mucosa in an acid solution and after filtration injected the crude extract. They were rewarded by an increase in the flow of *bicarbonate-rich pancreatic fluid. They reasoned that the acid gastric contents entering the duodenum caused release of a substance they called *secretin which passed into the venous circulation of the *duodenum via the mucosal capillaries and reached the *pancreas again via the circulation. These experiments were significant in two ways: they pointed out a second mechanism for the control of secretion, and they led to the subsequent discovery of *gastrin secreted by the gastric antral mucosa which increases primarily gastric acid and pepsin secretion. Cholecystokinin-pancreozymin, which stimulates *gall-bladder contraction and the secretion of enzyme-rich pancreatic fluid, is a third similar substance. Other substances have been identified, such as enterogasterone, which inhibits acid formation after the stomach has emptied, villikinin, which increases intestinal motility, and endocrinin, which increases the secretion of intestinal juices. The other important result of this experiment was that all materials secreted into the bloodstream which influenced distant organs were classified as *hormones, the Greek for 'I excite' (see also ENDOCRINOLOGY).

Gastrointestinal motility. It has long been known, perhaps first to priests who made predictions based on the shape that intestines assumed when thrown into water, that for a short time after death the intestine shows increased motility. This would suggest that there is partial inhibition of motility during life by some agent, that is quickly eliminated after death. This was confirmed when, in the middle of the 19th c., repetitive stimulation had become a common instrument in physiological laboratories. When the splanchnic nerve was thus stimulated, motility was reduced or inhibited. When the vagus was stimulated, motility increased. This confirmed that the viscera receive a double innervation via the vagus or other parasympathetic nerves and via the sympathetic, and that inhibition and excitation both take place peripherally. It was found subsequently that even after total denervation the elementary motion of the gastrointestinal tract continued, and it became clear that the gastrointestinal tract has its own intrinsic property of motility and that its nervous control is only regulatory.

Classic studies of gastrointestinal motility were made by Cannon, who mixed *barium salts with the food of conscious non-drugged cats and was thus able to see intestinal motions as they appeared on the fluorescent screen of his primitive *X-ray equipment. He was then able to see: (i) the segmentation that mixes the food and applies it closely to the wall of the gut for optimum exposure to digestive juices and for absorption; and (ii) the shorter or longer runs of *peristalsis (recurrent wave-like contraction) by which food is eventually propelled through the stomach to the colon. What causes the contraction is apparently a spontaneous depolarization that begins in the longitudinal muscles and produces a burst of action potentials or a second depolarization that evokes muscular contraction. There is thus a rough similarity to the heart in which the first event is a partial depolarization or pacemaker potential that sets up the propagated action potential.

A second type of motility involves the intestinal villi. The musculature throws the mucosa into folds or plications which change constantly, increasing the absorptive surface and ensuring that the contact of villi and food is constantly changing. The villi are themselves in constant motion with the same effect.

Absorption, once considered as a passive process largely dependent upon concentration, turns out to be more complicated. Not only water but also hexoses and amino acids seem to be associated with sodium absorption. The disaccharides, maltose, sucrose, and lactose are split into their component monosaccharides in the cells rather than in the lumen of the intestine as once thought. Fat is emulsified and then reduced to micelles by bile salts and these are rapidly admitted to the cell by its lipid-permeable membrane. Within the cell they meet enzymes which can convert them back to triglycerides, invest them with a protein coat, and extrude them as chylomicrons into the extracellular space, where they find their way into the lymph vessels, then into the thoracic duct, and finally into the venous blood. There they join some of the fat that entered the cell as short-chain fatty acids, avoided the chylomicron process, and entered the portal vein directly.

The respiratory system. The pulmonary circuit is a low-pressure circuit as far as both arterial and capillary blood pressure are concerned. Pulmonary artery pressure is but a fraction of systemic arterial pressure, being only 25 mmHg against a systemic pressure of 120 mmHg. Diastolic pressure is about 10 mmHg instead of 80. Capillary pressure is about 10 mmHg. The osmotic pressure of the plasma is close to 25 mmHg so that water will tend always to flow from tissue spaces into the blood, so that the alveolar or air sacs in the lungs will be 'dry', and the thin membrane, two cells thick, between the lumen of the *alveoli and the blood of the lung capillaries, will be optimal for the ready passage of oxygen into the blood and the passage of carbon dioxide out of the blood into the alveoli.

At a baby's first breath, the thorax expands and the lungs fill with air. Thereafter lung volume is smaller than that of the thorax and they are held expanded by the adhesion of the lung pleura to the thoracic wall pleura by means of a thin fluid layer separating them, providing along with adhesion for a sliding contact which allows conformity of the two surfaces as the thorax changes its shape with each breath. The lungs therefore act as elastic bags that increase in volume during inspiration only to diminish in size during expiration. Part of the elasticity that brings the lungs back to their expiratory volume rests in the tissues themselves, but more is due to the surface tension of the fluid layer lining the alveoli.

The motive power for breathing is the alternate contraction and relaxation of respiratory muscles which are ordinary skeletal muscles like those of the limbs, and are served by the same kind of motor nerve with its neurones in the ventral horn and its motor fibre emerging from the anterior root. They differ only in their central control that makes them discharge periodically, controlling the rhythm of breathing in an unbroken sequence throughout life. The first problem in respiration was where in the central nervous system is this rhythm generated and what is its mechanism? Ordinary breathing is largely accomplished by inspiratory muscles only, with a natural recoil of the lungs when these muscles relax, being the main cause of expiration. But when breathing is increased, as during exercise, true active expiratory muscles are brought into play. Talking, coughing, sneezing, and singing require active expiration; this is why patients with transection of the spinal cord in the lower cervical segments can breathe because their phrenic nerves are still intact, but cannot talk or cough because the phrenic innervates a purely inspiratory muscle.

The answer to the first question came first. Following Galen in making serial sections of the spinal cord and brainstem in animals, *Legallois found that spontaneous breathing continued even when all the brain was removed above the *medulla. When the medulla was removed the animal stopped breathing, but could be maintained 'alive' by artificial respiration. Soon afterwards *Flourens located what he called the 'vital node' in the floor of the fourth ventricle at the obex, and all subsequent work has confirmed this general localization. In the 1930s Pitts, Magoun, and Ransom stimulated this area in the cat and found a more caudal area which functioned as an inspiratory centre and a more rostral area that acted as an expiratory centre.

There are three fundamentally different mechanisms that might account for the rhythm of breathing. All are probably partly valid and all centre upon the spontaneous capability of the inspiratory centre. It could be: (i) spontaneously quiescent and activated only reflexively; (ii) spontaneously continuous in its discharge and in nature only inhibited reflexively; and (iii) intrinsically periodic in its discharge but accessible to many reflexes that regulate it according to the situation of the moment.

The first theory, that of Gesell, considers the respiratory centre as a highly complex reflex centre. According to him a completely deafferented respiratory centre would be silent, and would discharge only when enough excitation comes from the multitude of afferents that end upon it. Such a situation would be seen when breathing in an atmosphere of low oxygen. The reflex discharge from most afferents would then be cut off, except that from the oxygen receptors in the *carotid body, which fire at an increased rate and maintain breathing. Such a situation might exist during anaesthesia or in atmospheres low in oxygen, as in balloon or aircraft flight at high altitudes. If at this moment the lungs were flooded with a high concentration of oxygen, the reflex drive of the oxygen lack is abruptly shut off before other reflex drives have time to recover, and *apnoea results. The evidence supporting this theory is largely anecdotal, however.

The second theory introduced one of the most useful and universal theories of physiological regulation, that of 'feedback', which in technology is even older. Hero of Alexandria made a device by which a coin in a slot would start wine flowing into a flask and when the correct amount had entered, the flow would automatically stop. Much later, Drebbel equipped a furnace with a device in which a thermometer was mounted horizontally on a pivot which tipped over when the requisite heat was reached and lowered a damper on the air intake. The idea of negative (and positive) feedback was thus by no means new when first applied to physiology by *Hering and *Breuer in the mid-19th c. They arranged a tracheal cannula inserted into an anaesthetized animal so that air flow in and out of the lungs could be interrupted at any time. When this was done, it was seen that whatever phase respiration was in at the time of occlusion continued much longer than normally. When the vagus nerves were cut, the respiratory cycle was unaffected by stopping the air flow. This led to the conclusion that inflation of the lungs stimulated receptors which reflexly inhibited inspiration and induced expiration. This led to the realization that many physiological phenomena are monitored similarly and that negative feedback is common in physiology.

Shortly thereafter Markwald asked why the experiments of Hering and Breuer did not produce a more lasting continuation of inspiration when air inflow was stopped and approached the problem like Legallois by making more and more caudal sections of the brainstem and then by cutting the vagi to interrupt the Hering–Breuer reflex. He found that cutting the vagi had no effect until a section was made somewhere in the middle of the *pons, when *vagotomy was followed by prolonged inspiration. He then argued that the basic output of the respiratory centre was a constant inspiratory effort which was interrupted by either the Hering–Breuer reflex or a pontine centre, or a combination of both.

Markwald's idea was confirmed and amplified by Lumsden who named the upper pontine centre the pneumotaxic centre. He came to the conclusion that the medullary centre was not the true respiratory centre at all, and downgraded it as the gasping centre. As long as the lower pons and the vagi were intact, breathing was normal, but when they were cut, breathing ceased in inspiration (apneusis). He therefore postulated the presence of a third component of respiratory control, a lower pontine apneustic centre. This meant a transposition of normal respiratory control from the medulla to the pons, with the apneustic centre potentially discharging continually, and with this constant discharge being segmented by feedback circuits via lung inflation and the Hering–Breuer reflex, and by the pneumotaxic centre.

The third theory made the discharge from the inspiratory centre purely spontaneous and intrinsic and this is the view held today. Even so, it is difficult to be sure of the contributions from other centres and other reflexes in the minute-to-minute regulation of respiration. Oxygen deficiency acts via receptors in the carotid bodies: carbon dioxide excess via central receptors in the rostral and lateral parts of the ventral surface of the medulla; both have their influence on breathing via nervous connections. Panting is produced as part of the heat-control mechanism in the hypothalamus and coughing and sneezing are protective reflexes from the respiratory tract. Some people sneeze when suddenly exposed to bright light, a phenomenon known to Galen. Voluntary effort can produce a greater volume of ventilation than any other factor, and the changes in respiration during talking, singing, crying, etc. bear witness to a very important cortical control. It must be emphasized that the various centres scattered through the medulla and the pons are in fact only semi-specialized regions of the diffuse reticular formation.

The 100th anniversary of the invention of the balloon emphasizes the quantitative aspects of man's dependence on oxygen, for with the first high-altitude flights it was realized that there was an upper limit to man's ability to maintain an adequate oxygen content in his blood. The problem was emphasized as aircraft attained higher and higher altitudes and finally as space travel began. At all levels air contains about 20 per cent oxygen but the concentration of oxygen depends on this factor plus the prevailing atmospheric pressure which at sea level is 760 mmHg. The partial pressure of oxygen at sea level is thus about 150 mmHg and that in the arterial blood about 100 mmHg. At an altitude somewhere above 3500 m (or about 12 000 ft), atmospheric pressure has fallen to 500 mmHg and it therefore becomes impossible to maintain a normal body oxygen, and at higher levels it becomes harder and harder to maintain life. Even with acclimatization, human beings do not live above 5500 m (or about 16 000 ft). If one breathes pure oxygen, there is still an upper limit beyond which it is impossible to assure an adequate concentration of oxygen in the blood; this point is reached at about 14 500 m (40 000 ft). This is met by pressurizing the passenger space of aircraft to maintain a near-normal interior pressure and hence a normal oxygen content. This involves the risk of explosive decompression. Apparently the Russian space vehicles, at least at the beginning, were pressurized with air at atmospheric pressure while the American vehicles were pressurized with pure oxygen at less than atmospheric pressure. (See also AEROSPACE MEDICINE.)

Other problems beset attempts to dive to greater and greater depths. Because of the weight of water,

pressure increases by approximately one atmosphere for every 10 m (33 ft) of descent. During the dive, the tension of oxygen rises with the increased atmospheric pressure and is treated by reducing the original chemical concentration of the gas. As deeper dives are made, the work of breathing increases. Substituting helium for nitrogen in the breathing mixture avoids the intoxication resulting from excessive concentrations of nitrogen.

It is on emerging from a dive that another danger must be avoided. At high pressures both oxygen and nitrogen enter solution in the tissues. The oxygen is used in tissue metabolism but the nitrogen remains inert and as the pressure diminishes on emergence from the dive there is a danger of bubble formation due to its release in all tissues: in the nervous system they may cause paralysis; in the joints, pains; and in the blood, interference with circulation to the brain, heart, and lungs. The only way to prevent *decompression sickness (caisson disease, 'the bends') is to follow faithfully a prescribed routine of gradual ascent to allow time for the nitrogen elimination. Much effort has been expended in making tables showing the most efficient way to decompress, but on deep dives, the time spent in decompression seriously reduces that which can be spent at depths and serious consideration has been given to providing submerged habitats in which the diver will spend considerable time and emerge only once after several days of submergence. (See also ENVIRONMENT AND DISEASE.)

The kidneys. Water is regulated at its intake site by the gastrointestinal tract and on the output side by the kidneys. Although its characteristic structure, the *glomerulus, was described in the last half of the 17th c., *Bowman is credited with a full description of the renal unit two centuries later. Roughly, there are two essential structures, the glomerulus and the tubule. The first is a tuft of capillaries surrounded by a capsule (Bowman's) which opens into the tubular system. The arteriole entering the glomerulus is larger than that leaving it and there are but two layers of cells between the blood in the capillaries and the lumen of the capsule; so numerous are the units and so many the glomeruli that the total surface exposed between capillaries and capsules is about 1.5 m². The tubule issuing from the capsule is at first convoluted, then assumes a loop shape, and after going through another convolution enters the collecting duct which passes down through the pyramid of the kidney and empties into its pelvis. There are two kinds of loops called the loops of *Henle. The cortical (surface) glomeruli have a short loop of Henle and the distal convoluted tubular system is more superficially situated; they comprise about 85 per cent of the renal units. The units from the medulla (interior) have long loops of Henle which pass down through the inner medulla almost to the pelvis; these units are about 15 per cent of the whole number.

This structure is essential to the proper functioning of the organ. The structure of the glomeruli suggests that here a process of filtration occurs. The discrepancy in size of the afferent and efferent arterioles is such that the blood pressure in the capillary tufts must be higher than in the usual systemic capillary, and such is the case with blood pressures around 60–70 mmHg instead of the 25 mmHg of the systemic capillary. It was not until the third decade of the 20th c. that actual filtration was demonstrated by A. N. *Richards, who punctured the Bowman's capsule of a frog kidney under a microscope and showed that the glomerular fluid was an ultrafiltrate of the plasma containing all its constituents except the plasma proteins. A disturbing finding that the fluid in some early experiments contained no glucose was quickly put to rest by the observation that the frogs had been kept into the winter and had no detectable blood glucose. When frogs were tested that had a blood glucose it turned up in the glomerular filtrate.

Measurement of the glomerular filtration rate (GFR) is owed to Homer Smith who reasoned that if one could find a substance that is excreted only by filtration and is neither secreted nor reabsorbed by the tubules, one could calculate how much plasma was 'cleared' of that substance and would then know the glomerular flow. This was obtained by determining the plasma concentration of the substance and the amount appearing in the urine in any unit of time. Such a substance turned out to be inulin, a polymer of fructose with a molecular weight of about 5000. The 'clearance' of this substance in man is about 125 ml/min.

Out of this emerges a very impressive corollary. If 125 ml of glomerular filtrate are formed in a minute, some 180 litres are formed in a day, while 1–2 litres of urine reach the bladder. It is obvious that most of the water is reabsorbed. This glomerular filtrate contains glucose at a concentration like that in the plasma, say 80 mg/100 ml, yet none appears in the urine. It too must be reabsorbed. Micropuncture of the tubules demonstrates that absorption occurs in the proximal tubule and in the collecting duct.

This information facilitates another experiment in order to explain why sugar appears in the urine in *diabetes mellitus. Glucose is administered to establish several successively higher concentrations of blood glucose and at each the amount of glucose presented to the tubules for reabsorption is calculated. At each level of blood sugar the output of glucose is measured. No matter what the blood level may be, the output of glucose is always about 375 mg of glucose per minute less than that reaching the tubules via the glomeruli. This is called the transport maximum for the tubules (TM). Glucose appears in the urine only when more sugar reaches the tubules than they can reabsorb. Other substances reabsorbed include Na^+, K^+, PO_4^{2-}, and amino acids. Most of them are reabsorbed in the proximal tubules with the exception of Na^+, which is absorbed mainly in the ascending limb loop of Henle. Hydrogen ions are secreted by the proximal and distal tubules.

Some substances must be secreted, such as derivatives of hippuric acid, complexes of *iodine, or *penicillin, none of which participate in normal metabolism, and a few that are present as part of normal metabolic processes, such as the metabolic products of *serotonin. The reason for interest in the substances that are secreted becomes obvious when the clearance of one of these substances is determined. The clearance of para-aminohippuric acid (PAH) is about 600 ml a minute which means that 600 ml of plasma are cleared of their content of PAH in a minute. Allowing for the red blood cells, we get a figure a little over 1 litre/min as a minimum figure for blood flow through the kidneys. This means that something between one-quarter and one-fifth of the cardiac output at rest passes through the kidneys.

Water reabsorption from the glomerular filtrate is the main mechanism for control of the osmotic pressure of body fluids. When water is scarce a very concentrated urine is produced. In man this can be as high as 1800 mosmol/l in contrast to a value of 300 mosmol/l in the body fluids. The dog can concentrate its urine to about 2500 mosmol/l, the usual laboratory rat to 3000 mosmol/l, and desert mammals can concentrate their urine even more. On the other hand when water is plentiful and is drunk freely, the urine may become hypotonic (diluted). When *alcohol is consumed a diuresis is produced above that caused by the volume of fluid taken in so that the net result may be *dehydration.

The ability of the kidney to produce hypotonic and hypertonic urine and, by so doing, to regulate the output of water appears to depend upon the counter-current distribution established by the closely applied descending and ascending branches of the loop of Henle, plus the ability of the ascending loop to reabsorb sodium. This establishes a gradient of osmotic pressure with the cortical tubular urine hypotonic and the inner glomerular urine more and more hypertonic as the pelvis is approached. The same gradient is established in the interstitial fluid surrounding the tubules. The permeability of the collecting ducts to water is regulated by a hormone of the posterior *pituitary lobe, itself under control of osmoreceptors in the *hypothalamus, long known as pitressin because of its blood-pressure-increasing effect, but now more correctly known as the *antidiuretic hormone (ADH). If the body is well hydrated, there is little or no production of ADH, the collecting duct has little permeability to water, and the urine is hypotonic. If the water supply is limited and the osmolarity of the fluids surrounding osmoreceptors in the hypothalamus is high, nerve cells are excited, ADH is produced, water passes out of the collecting duct, and the urine is concentrated.

The locus and mechanism of oxidation. Although Lavoisier recognized that the net result of animal metabolism was an oxidation of carbon and hydrogen producing heat, he knew nothing about the cell as the physiological unit of the organism. He inclined to the view that oxidation might take place in the lungs where oxygen would have the first contact with the living organism. We could imagine that the products of cellular metabolism might be brought to the lungs for oxidative restoration as Lavoisier suggested. If this were true the blood leaving the lungs ought to be warmer than that entering them. Several workers recognized this and saw that experimental confirmation would depend upon measurement of the temperature of mixed venous blood. This was acomplished first by Claude Bernard through simultaneous catheterization of the right and left ventricles in sheep. He found that the blood in the left ventricle was cooler than in the right and that therefore the blood had been cooled by its passage through the lungs. By contrast, blood left various other organs warmer than it entered, indicating that the cells all over the body were the source of heat and therefore the site of oxidation. The two centuries that followed were devoted first to testing whether Lavoisier was correct in concluding that the animal metabolism did indeed involve net oxidation of the carbon and hydrogen. This involved the realization that foods were of three kinds, carbohydrates, fats, and proteins. Determining the caloric value of each gave agreement about the *in vitro* and *in vivo* heat production of carbohydrates and fats. The heat production of protein was less only because it was incompletely metabolized in the body; when the *in vitro* heat of the incompletely metabolized residue was subtracted from the total *in vitro* heat production there was agreement between the *in vitro* and the *in vivo* results.

The larger question of how oxidation takes place *in vivo* without the high temperature of *in vitro* oxidation took longer to resolve. It began with the discovery of enzymes that facilitate chemical reactions in the body. The invertase of yeast, and pepsin of gastric juice, were discovered in 1834 and 1835. Thereafter new digestive enzymes were recognized more rapidly and towards the end of the 19th c. it was recognized that intracellular enzymes could also be extracted and studied. The last 40 years have confirmed that oxidation is a function of cells, that it takes place largely in the *mitochondria, and that after preliminary anaerobic breakdown of hexose all foodstuffs enter a common metabolic pool that oxidizes them by a series of enzyme-facilitated steps. The oxidative mechanism is coupled to the energy-expending mechanisms by the conversion of ADP to ATP (see BIOCHEMISTRY) which then migrates to the site of energy expenditure within the cell. The ubiquitousness of this metabolic pathway, even in yeasts and other unicellular organisms, strikingly confirms the ancient view of the interrelations of living organisms. The arrangement of enzymes in the mitochondria and the order of the citric acid cycle give ample evidence that even at a molecular level there is a close relationship of structure and function.

Integration—nervous and hormonal. *Electrophysiology.* The invention of the Leyden jar was a great advance in the physics of electricity as it allowed a slow build-up of an electrical charge and then its rapid discharge, delivering a substantial shock. It was therefore important in physiology as workers quickly found that it would stimulate nerves and muscles so well that it was generally concluded that the nervous system must operate by electricity and that the 'animal spirits' of Galen were electrical fluid. In trying to prove this hypothesis, Galvani made two discoveries of outstanding merit. He showed that nerve or muscle could be stimulated by contact with two dissimilar metals which were touching each other at their other end. No experiment attracted more attention or was repeated more often. Galvani thought that the metallic arc set free the electricity in muscle and that this electrical discharge stimulated the muscle to contract. The physicist Volta thought otherwise; by making a pile of alternate zinc and copper cells he was able to multiply the electricity to a point where the instrument gave off sparks and clearly produced electricity without requiring the frog nerve-muscle preparation used by Galvani. Although he did not demonstrate animal electricity, Galvani initiated our knowledge of current electricity, the foundation of the modern electrical age. He continued his experiments in search of a contraction produced without metals and found it when he looped the nerve of his frog nerve-muscle preparation over a muscle that had been injured. Each time the testing nerve made contact with both the injured and uninjured surfaces of the muscle, the testing muscle contracted. Galvani by this experiment had discovered what is now called the injury current. This arises because all excitable tissues—skeletal, cardiac, and smooth muscle, as well as nerves—are electrically charged, the inside being negative by about 100 mV to the outside. Injury alters this polarity and hence an injury current passes between the injured and non-injured surface.

The technique of testing for current using a frog nerve (the rheoscopic frog preparation) became an early galvanometer as no instrument could demonstrate small voltages. When Matteucci looped the nerve of his rheoscopic preparation over the muscle of another nerve-muscle preparation and that muscle was stimulated to contract, the rheoscopic muscle also contracted. This was due to the 'action current', a potential developed whenever a nerve or muscle become physiologically active.

Although the importance of electricity in nerve and muscle was thus confirmed, the way in which it related to normal function was not clear. The first experimental evidence came from *Helmholtz, who modified an ingenious method newly invented for measuring the velocity of a projectile. His method allowed him to measure the time from the moment of nerve stimulation to that of the muscular response; he measured the latencies from two locations of stimulating electrodes, one as close to the muscle as possible and the other as far away from the muscle as possible. The only difference was thus the conduction time between the near and distant points, which worked out at about 30 m/s for the frog motor nerve studied. A few years later Bernstein showed that the action potential of nerve is propagated along at the same rate as that determined by Helmholtz. Thus one may think of nerve conduction as explicable through a resting potential which alters during activity to give an action potential, which in turn stimulates adjacent resting tissue with subsequent self-propagation of the action potential along the nerve.

Modern work completely confirms this view. All irritable tissues maintain a difference in resting potential with the inside negative to the outside. This is in part due to the high concentration of potassium and chloride inside the cell and their relatively low concentration in the extracellular fluid. The result is a membrane polarization with an array of positive charges on its outside and an equal array of negative charges on the inside.

It was once thought that the impulse was due to a simple depolarization caused by disappearance of the potassium potential. Now we know that there is also a reverse potential due to the opening of the sodium channels by which a sodium polarization temporarily replaces the potassium potential. As sodium is in higher concentration outside the cell, it is of opposite polarity so the net action potential, the motive force of conduction, is about 130 mV.

Junctional transmission. An exotic drug that came early to Europe from America was the arrow and dart poison of the natives in the Amazon basin, mainly extracted from a plant known as *curare (curara).* Some reached Claude Bernard in the middle of the 19th c. It was known that the drug had to enter the circulation to be effective, and that it caused muscular paralysis and death by paralysing the respiratory muscles. Claude Bernard showed that the drug did not interrupt nerve conduction nor transmission in the spinal cord nor yet muscle contraction: he concluded that there was only one vulnerable location, the discontinuity between nerve and muscle, the neuromuscular junction.

Soon after *Loewi had shown that the effect of the vagus upon the heart is due to release of a chemical transmitter liberated by nerve endings and had identified this as *acetylcholine, *Dale found that this substance was present in many tissues and organs. Its mode of action at vagal endings was shown by all parasympathetic endings. It was blocked by *atropine and was similar in action to *muscarine (hence the muscarinic effect). In another mode of action, the nicotinic, it is also the transmitter at the neuromuscular junction. Here it depolarizes the muscle membrane locally,

creating an end-plate potential. If this reaches a critical level it sets up a propagated impulse (an action potential) in the muscle. This in turn liberates calcium from stores in the *sarcoplasmic reticulum and the calcium binds to a contraction-inhibiting protein. The actual contraction is then produced by sliding upon one another of the orderly interdigitated molecules of myosin and actin which are responsible for the cross-striations of skeletal and cardiac muscle. (See also NEUROMUSCULAR DISEASE.)

The processes involved in the operation of the nervous system both centrally and peripherally are therefore: (i) the initiation of nerve impulses by stimuli. This process involves depolarization to a critical level, when a runaway increase in sodium conduction occurs and a propagated disturbance begins. Depending on the structure involved, one stimulus only may be sufficient as in the contraction of a muscle fibre produced by a quantum of acetylcholine liberated at the motor end-plate; or perhaps a hundred or more may be needed at a synapse upon a motor neurone where summation of separate subliminal stimuli is usual; (ii) conduction of a propagated impulse in the axon; (iii) liberation of a chemical transmitter in the region of discontinuity between one cell and another (the synapse). Acetylcholine and noradrenaline are the main transmitters outside the nervous system. They both act within the central nervous system (CNS) but there are many other transmitters such as *dopamine, *serotonin, glycine, *gamma-aminobutyric acid (GABA), and glutamic acid. The transmitter in turn produces a post-synaptic potential to continue activation within the nervous system or to act finally on an end-organ like skeletal, cardiac, or smooth muscle or a gland.

Inhibition. The vagus inhibits the heart by hyperpolarization; this reduces the frequency and amplitude of pacemaker potentials. This also happens in postsynaptic inhibition within the CNS where the hyperpolarization due to increased potassium permeability moves the resting potential away from the firing level. Presynaptic inhibition also occurs when inhibitory fibres end on synapses: they depolarize the synaptic ending and reduce the output of transmitter so that it fails to excite the postsynaptic membrane.

Integration. Integration of the activity of the whole nervous system is based on: (i) the fundamental neurone doctrine which holds that the functional unit of all nervous activity is the nerve cell or neurone which establishes relationships with other neurones only by contract or contiguity and never by physical continuity; (ii) there are only three kinds of neurones, namely (a) an afferent neurone conducting information into the CNS from many receptors, (b) an effector neurone forming the last link between the CNS and the organ innervated, and (c) internuncial neurones forming more and more complicated communication pathways between the first two. In man the *cerebellum and *cerebrum contain vast and complex internuncial pathways.

The segmental level: the reflex. There is a vast array of afferent neurones activated by many external receptors which determine the type of sensation to which a particular afferent responds: in skin are receptors for touch, pain, heat, cold, etc., within muscle are receptors for tension; within the viscera are receptors for pain, pressure, etc., the arteries have receptors for blood pressure, and the head is equipped with receptors for body position, acceleration, and distance receptors for hearing, sight, and olfaction. Probably all receptors excite the afferent fibre by generating a local potential like an end-plate potential or excitatory postsynaptic potential and impulses are sent by the appropriate segmental afferent to the spinal cord or *brainstem, evoking an appropriate reflex response. The muscle spindles respond to passive stretch of muscle and evoke its contraction. This is the simplest reflex and requires only afferent and efferent neurones and a single synapse. The flexor withdrawal reflex of a limb causes contraction of flexor muscles in response to a potentially harmful stimulus and requires at least one internuncial neurone and two synapses. As shown by *Bell and *Magendie, all sensory (afferent) fibres enter the CNS system via dorsal roots and all motor (efferent) fibres leave via ventral roots. The dorsal and ventral (anterior) roots combine to form spinal nerves which leave the spine at each segmental level, and then combine into peripheral nerves. The motor system supplying skeletal muscles is strictly segmental, the motor neurone lies within the central nervous system, and each muscle fibre receives one terminal nerve fibre only, which excites it. Viscera, like smooth and cardiac muscle, glands, etc. have a double innervation with nerves of a very different character, on the one hand excitatory and on the other inhibitory, thus tending to be regulatory. This double system is characterized by migration of the efferent neurones outside the CNS to ganglia, once thought to be independent reflex centres, giving the name autonomic to this system. It has two subdivisions, the sympathetic, with a restricted outflow in the thoracolumbar segments and its ganglia close to the spinal cord, and a more or less antagonistic system, the parasympathetic with a craniosacral outflow and more peripheral ganglia, usually in or near to the organs innervated.

The reticular system. The internuncial cells of the segmental system of the spinal cord and brainstem fulfil another function. They form an intercommunicating, co-ordinating system, within the spinal cord and brainstem through which the first level of integration and control is achieved. In the medulla are centres for the control of the circulation, heart, and respiration, for coughing, sneezing, and vomiting. There is also a reticular centre that can inhibit spinal reflexes and can regulate the central effect of afferent impulses by imposing inhibition at the first synapse on the path from the segmental to higher levels. More rostrally in the brainstem is a reticular activating centre which can augment spinal reflexes. Centrally, this part of the system acts as an activator, responsible for consciousness and alertness.

Palaeocortex—the limbic system. Forming a part of each cerebral lobe is a zone of cortical tissue called the limbic system because it more or less forms the limb of the *cerebral hemispheres. It is associated with the amygdaloid, hippocampal, and septal nuclei. With its main efferent connections in the hypothalamus it subserves hunger, thirst, sexual behaviour, fear, anger, and motivation. The hypothalamus contains neurones that bypass the usual arrangements dependent on afferent organs for originating nervous responses. There are cells in the supraoptic nuclei of the hypothalamus that respond to increased osmotic pressure of the blood by causing the release of antidiuretic hormone from the posterior lobe of the pituitary. There are also cells activated by blood temperature which activate heat-controlling mechanisms, and others respond to blood glucose to regulate hunger and satiety. Other parts of the hypothalamus respond to various hormones in feedback inhibition of the hypothalamic–pituitary axis which caused their secretion in the first place.

The neocortex. The principal difference in man's nervous system from that of animals is the size of the neocortex; this seems to account for major differences in man's behaviour. It is linked to the brainstem and spinal segments by long fibre tracts that surround and bypass the multineuronal short axon relays of the reticular substance; whereas in that system it is hard to distinguish ascending and descending pathways the neocortex has specific input and output tracts. Because of the eyes, where the lens causes an inverted and reversed retinal image of the environment, the cortical representation of the visual field in the occipital lobe of the brain is crossed and inverted. This is probably why all other sensory inputs are represented in the same crossed and inverted fashion, and why motor output has followed the same pattern. Thus the left side of the body is represented on the right side of the brain with the feet at the top and the head at the bottom. Since the long fibre tracts are much like electrical wiring, such incoming fibres fall into place beside those entering earlier, and cortical localization is topographical, that is central representation reproduces bodily relationships. Thus in the *thalamus where afferent fibres come together before going on to the cortex, the outline of the body can be followed from the mouth to the tail. In the sensory and adjacent motor cortex, the animal is similarly represented, appropriately outlining an animal or man, with the feet in the central sulcus, the back directed forward, with the tail at the top and the head at the bottom. The shape of this animal in miniature is influenced by the extent of representation of each part. In all animals the face has a predominant representation and in man the mouth and hand distort the diagram or homunculus.

The neurophysiology of psychological processes. The techniques of physiological study have long been applied in *psychological studies, and promise to elucidate the physiology of behaviour. If electrodes are implanted anywhere in the animal brain from the amygdaloid nuclei through the hypothalamus and connected to a bar that an animal depresses to give itself an electrical stimulus to that part of the brain evoking pleasure or reward, the animal soon learns to operate that self-stimulating system almost to the exclusion of everything else.

Recent work has concerned the ability of the higher primates, the chimpanzee, the orang-utan, and gorilla to think in abstraction. This has been frustrated in the past by the inability of the animals to vocalize adequately. Recently some animals have been taught to communicate by standard American sign language. The conclusions to be drawn from these studies are still debatable but they have revealed a greater richness of mental behaviour than was suspected. Man is the only animal that has handedness and speech, and both are usually located in the left cerebral cortex. The reason for this is uncertain but hemisphere specialization is a reality, the left hemisphere controlling skilled movements as in writing and speech, and being the hemisphere of factual knowledge. The right hemisphere is more apparently concerned with artistic abilities. (See also LANGUAGE, COGNITION, AND HIGHER CEREBRAL FUNCTION.)

Hormones. If we look upon the cell as the origin of all multicellular organisms, then we may conclude that specialization or division of labour among the cells of the body results from accentuation or evolution of a property to be found in primitive unicellular organisms. Thus all cells have a communication system whereby a local stimulus is appreciated by the whole cell. But in the nervous system this becomes a special role of neurones where impulses are conducted over neuronal processes for long distances. A single afferent fibre may extend from the toe to the medulla—a distance in man of over a metre.

It is not therefore surprising to find substances similar to *somatostatin, *adrenocorticotrophic hormone (ACTH), β-endorphin, cholecystokinin, *glucagon, *catecholamines, serotonin, acetylcholine, and *steroids in protozoa, and to find that in these primitive organisms *adrenaline stimulates *adenyl cyclase and is blocked by *propranolol. Nor is it surprising to find that hormones can be produced by cells other than those that are their primary sources. Many brain *peptides are found also in non-neural tissue, as, for example, somatostatin in the islet cells of the pancreas (see ISLETS OF LANGERHANS) and in some pancreatic tumours; also the receptor and post-receptor events of cerebral catecholamine action are faithfully reproduced in liver cells. ACTH is found not only in the pituitary but also in normal placenta, the adrenal medulla, and in the fetal lung. In the guinea pig a porcine-like or rat-like *insulin is found in the brain and other extra-pancreatic tissues. The hormones are thus chemicals similar to if not identical with those manufactured by very primitive cells; in the vertebrate they are diverted to special purposes and are preponderantly though not exclusively manufactured by special tissues. The recent discovery of natural *morphine-like substances, the *endorphins, indicates how closely interrelated are human and primitive cells.

Despite what would seem compelling inferences to be drawn from blood-borne deficiencies deriving from the ancient practice of castration (i.e. removing the testes apparently removed something important from the blood) the 19th c. was so dominated by the doctrine of the nervous control that hormonal–humoral control was neglected until the end of the century. Three discoveries then came together to introduce the idea of hormonal control. First was the discovery of the metabolic control exerted by the *thyroid gland through its secretion of *thyroxine. Then came that of the hypertensive effect of the *adrenal medullary hormone, adrenaline, and the discovery of secretin, which was secreted into the blood by the cells of the pyloric *mucosa, causing the secretion of a watery basic fluid by the pancreas. Bayliss and Starling introduced the name hormone for this new class of chemical substances which were secreted by glands of internal secretion and had an action on distant organs. Later came the discovery of insulin, of the *glucocorticoids and mineralocorticoids of the adrenal cortex, and the *parathyroid hormone that acts as a calcium-modifying hormone. The principal male secondary sex characteristics appear to depend on *testosterone produced in the *testes while those of females are in part due to the secretion of *oestrogens secreted by the *ovaries. The female *menstrual cycle is a two-stage affair divided at the time of *ovulation and preparation of the *endometrium; the first stage ends in ovulation which is largely oestrogenic and the second stage is both oestrogenic and progestogenic.

Pregnancy continues the production of oestrogen and progesterone from the ovary in response to *gonadotropins from the *placenta and in humans the placenta also secretes oestrogens and *progesterones, especially in the last two trimesters.

The pituitary. The success of Oliver and Schäfer in extracting adrenaline led others to study organ extracts and an extract of the pituitary gland was also found to raise blood pressure. It was named pitressin or *vasopressin and was found to be produced by the posterior lobe of the pituitary. In man it acts as a hormone regulating water output by the kidneys and is now named after this function, as the *antidiuretic hormone (ADH). Also found in the posterior lobe is a uterus-contracting hormone, *oxytocin. It plays a part in the uterine contractions during *labour, in uterine cramps during *menstruation, and in the contractions that help to transport *sperm into the *Fallopian tubes. It also stimulates the smooth muscle of the breasts and by a reflex involved in the act of breast feeding it is responsible for milk flow.

Attention was drawn to the anterior pituitary lobe and its production of growth hormone (GH), by the observation of increased growth in individuals with some pituitary *adenomas (tumours that continue to secrete the normal hormone). If increased activity starts before the cessation of growth, it produces *gigantism. If it develops after bony epiphyseal union, it produces an overgrowth of terminal bones and viscera, *acromegaly.

Five other hormones of the anterior pituitary have since been discovered: the thyroid-stimulating hormone (TSH, thyrotrophin); a hormone stimulating the adrenal cortex, adrenocorticotrophic hormone (ACTH); a hormone stimulating follicular growth in the female and spermatogenesis in the male, *follicle-stimulating hormone (FSH); a hormone stimulating ovulation and *corpus luteum production in the female with the production of oestrogen and progesterone, and testosterone production in the male, *luteinizing hormone (LH); and a hormone stimulating the production of milk, known as *prolactin.

The hypothalamic–pituitary axis. The posterior lobe of the pituitary develops as an outgrowth of the nervous system and has a nerve supply from the hypothalamus by which hormonal secretion is regulated. The anterior lobe, by contrast, has no significant nervous connection. It does, however, have a rich portal venous system with capillary networks connecting with the hypothalamus. It was the discovery of this portal system that stimulated subsequent work revealing the important hormonal link between the hypothalamus and anterior pituitary. Geoffrey Harris showed that anterior pituitary malfunction could be produced by blocking the portal circulation, and confirmed that hypothalamic control of the anterior pituitary is hormonal. Guillemin and Shally were responsible for the first extraction, chemical identification, and synthesis of hypothalamic hormones. There are factors releasing thyrotrophin (thyrotrophin-releasing factor or TRF), corticotrophin (CRF), growth hormone (GHRF), follicle-stimulating hormone (FRF), and luteinizing hormone (LRF) and probably also a prolactin-releasing factor (PRF).

Integration is not therefore the province of any one system: in reality integration is a result of basic properties of the individual cells that comprise the body, and of their interaction.

Physiology and medicine. It was Galen's hope that physiology would become the handmaiden of medicine and that experiment would be the guide to diagnosis and therapy. He expected too much, too soon, but in one instance gave us an almost perfect model. He was called to see a young man who had been thrown from his chariot, had landed on his neck, and was paralysed from the neck down. He could breathe, but could not talk; his doctors had poulticed the paralysed parts. Galen had carried out perhaps the best of his experimental work on the nervous system and had shown that the nerves to the limbs came off the spinal cord and that as successively higher sections were made in the cord, successively higher muscle groups were paralysed. The only exception to this rule was in the origin of the phrenic nerve which, although it innervated the diaphragm (the muscle separating the thorax and abdomen), arose in the mid-cervical part of the spinal cord. Galen thus understood how injury to the lower cervical cord could cause complete paralysis from the arms down. The patient could still breathe with his diaphragm yet could not talk as the diaphragm is a muscle of inspiration only and could not provide the motive power for vocalization. He ordered the poultices to be removed from the limbs and to be placed instead over the neck and back; the patient recovered. Although the therapy was probably of no avail and the patient may have recovered spontaneously, nevertheless this case stands as an example in which an experiment may have guided therapy.

The like did not happen again until the beginning of the modern era in 19th c. medicine. In 1883 Theodor *Kocher reported on several children in whom he had used the new Listerian method to perform total *thyroidectomy because of respiratory difficulties caused by retrosternal *goitre. Later he admitted that the surgical triumph had become a disaster: the children had stopped growing, their skins had become thick and dry, hair scanty and dry, and there was a growing mental and physical dullness. He named the condition cachexia thyrostrumipriva and remarked how similar it seemed to the condition long known in Switzerland as *cretinism. The results were discussed at the London Clinical Society at which it was concluded that the condition known in England as *myxoedema, cretinism, and cachexia thyrostrumipriva were probably identical and attributable to a loss of functioning thyroid gland. Soon George Murray showed that fresh or dried thyroid gland was an adequate replacement, and patients who had been incompetent for years because of myxoedema were restored to normal physical and mental lives.

This was the beginning of physiological medicine: soon the association of simple goitre with iodine deficiency made possible its virtual elimination by iodination of salt. *Hyperthyroidism was soon recognized but for many years its treatment was partial removal of the gland. After the Second World War, compounds like *thiouracil were discovered which blocked some stages in the biosynthesis of thyroid hormone.

The second great physiological discovery was that of *insulin in the early 1920s. Although in the 19th c. von Mehring and Minkowski had shown that removing the pancreas caused *hyperglycaemia and *glycosuria in dogs, attempted isolation of a hormone was unsuccessful for many years because it was inactivated by the protein-digesting enzymes of the pancreas, trypsin, and chymotrypsin. *Banting and *Best inactivated the synthesis of these enzymes by ligating the pancreatic duct, and allowing time for the cells which produced them to atrophy, so that the hormone was preserved during extraction. Since about 3 per cent of the population is diabetic, this was indeed a great medical discovery. However, insulin has not cured diabetes and there are aspects of diabetes as a disease that insulin does not control. Nevertheless, great progress has been made in all types of hormonal replacement therapy especially since the slight structural differences between human and non-human protein hormones have been recognized and synthesis in commercial amounts of human hormones has become possible (see GENETIC ENGINEERING).

Replacement therapy is not the only medical use of many hormones. Thus adrenaline finds a place in medicine in the therapy of *asthma and acute *allergic disorders. The *catecholamines based on adrenaline and noradrenaline may influence a host of functions of the parent hormones, ranging from reduction of secretion in the nasal passages to increase in mental alertness and reduction in appetite. The discovery of *hydrocortisone, the predominant glucocorticoid of the adrenal cortex, and of several natural and synthetic products with the same action, made possible complete hormone replacement in *Addison's disease, and in the adrenogenital syndrome. However, the *glucocorticoids and their anti-inflammatory effect are also of use in asthma, acute allergies, *serum sickness, *myasthenia gravis, *dermatomyositis, and the connective tissue diseases involving immune reactions. The feedback inhibition of pituitary gonadotropins by oestrogens and progesterones, probably via the hypothalamic-releasing factor (HRF), has made possible the development of oral *contraceptives ('the Pill') with the most far-reaching social repercussions of any medical discovery.

There is no longer any scientific reason why dietary deficiencies should occur. The avitaminoses have practically disappeared and scurvy, rickets, beriberi, and *pellagra are now rarely seen, except in alcoholics.

Quite apart from global understanding of a large and complex disease entity, fully as important and at times more universally applicable have been more restricted understandings. Once Ringer had shown the value of a balanced salt solution, the practice of maintaining the volume and composition of the internal environment by intravenous or other injection of fluids became possible and is now a routine procedure. The electrocardiogram and electroencephalogram, which started as physiological tools, are now in routine use for the information they can give in the diseases of the heart and brain.

The idea that *toxins exert their influence on cells through molecular attachment of a non-toxic part of the molecule to a *receptor on the cell membrane was central to the doctrine of immunity as developed by Paul *Ehrlich. However, many such receptors are important in the normal metabolism of the cell and are used by toxins because of some similarity in their molecular structure to the normal transmitter to which the receptor responds. In fact some substances, especially hormones such as catecholamines, glucagon, vasopressin, ACTH, LH, TSH, and TRF, do not enter the cell, but combination with the receptor releases *cyclic AMP which acts as a second messenger within the cell to produce the change associated with each hormone. When it was discovered that the adrenal medulla produces two hormones, adrenaline and noradrenaline, it was found that while both substances increased the rate and force of contraction of the heart, noradrenaline caused more contraction of arterioles. The difference seemed to be explained by the existence of two catecholamine receptors, one an alpha-receptor causing constriction of visceral arteries along with other effects and the other a beta-receptor causing increase in cardiac rate and force of contraction. Soon blocking agents were discovered for both receptors and it was found that the *beta-blocking agents were invaluable in the treatment of hypertension. This one class of drug may alone be responsible for the decline now seen in the mortality from heart disease.

*Histamine is a simple chemical compound derived from the amino acid histidine by simple decarboxylation; it is found in many cells and is released during inflammatory and allergic processes. *Antihistaminic drugs began to appear soon after the Second World War and have been of great value. In 1938 Babkin proposed that histamine might have a role in the release of gastric acid, but much opinion was against the proposal because histamine is usually released in reactions involved in damage, injury and inflammation and because most antihistaminic drugs had no effect on gastric acid secretion. It was finally recognized that there is more than one histamine receptor: H_1, which is that for histamine's action in inflammation and allergy, and another, H_2 involved in its action to produce secretion of gastric acid. Blocking agents for the *H_2 receptors have been prepared and have found instant success as *antacids in *peptic ulcer control; within a few years they have come to be among the most prescribed drugs in many countries.

Conclusion. Paul Ehrlich wrote in his Nobel lecture of 1908 about the cell doctrine, the concept around which the whole of the modern science of life revolves:

It is, I think, a generally acknowledged and undisputed fact that everything which happens in the body, assimilation and dissimilation, must ultimately be attributed to the cells alone, and furthermore that the cells of different organs are differentiated from each other in a specific way and only perform their different functions by means of this differentiation.

Now, at this moment, the time has come to penetrate into *more subtle chemism* of cell life and to break down the concept *of a unit* into a *great number* of individual and specific and *partial* functions. But what happens in the cell is chiefly of a *chemical* nature and since the configuration of chemical structures lies beyond the limits of the eye's perception we shall have to find other methods of investigation for this. This approach is not only of great importance for the *real* understanding of the life processes, but also the basis for a truly rational use of medical substances.

This is indeed what has happened in the intervening years.   H. E. HOFF

Further reading

Beaumont, W. (1959). *Experiences and Observations on the Gastric Juice and the Physiology of Digestion.* Facsim. of original 1833 edn. New York.

Bell, G. H., Emslie-Smith, D. and Paterson, C. R. (1980). *Textbook of Physiology.* 10th edn, Edinburgh.

Brooks, C. McC. and Cranefield, P. F. (1959). *The Historical Development of Physiological Thought.* New York.

Dibner, B. (1952) *Galvani–Volta: A Controversy that Led to the Discovery of Useful Electricity.* Norwalk, Connecticut.

Fabricius, Hieronymus ab Aquapendente (ed. Franklin, K. J.) (1933). *De venarum ostiolis 1603 of Hieronymus Fabricius ab Aquapendente (1533–1603).* Facsim. edn. Springfield, Illinois.

Foster, Sir M. (1907). *Lectures on the History of Physiology during the 16th, 17th and 18th centuries. Delivered as the Lane Lectures at the Cooper Medical School in San Francisco, 1906.* New York.

Fulton, J. F. (1966). *Selected Readings in the History of Physiology* (completed by L. G. Wilson). 2nd. edn, Springfield, Illinois.

Galvani, L. (trans. Green, R. M.) (1933). *Commentary on the Effect of Electricity on Muscular Motion.* Cambridge, Massachusetts.

Hales, S. (ed. Cournand, A.) (1964). *Statistical Essays.* Facsim. edn. New York.

Hall, T. S. (1969). *History of General Physiology: 600 B.C. to A.D. 1900,* 2 vols. Chicago.

Harvey, W. (1928). *An Anatomical Disquisition on the Motion of the Heart and Blood in Animals.* London and Toronto.

Harvey, William (ed. Franklin, K. J.) (1957). *Movement of the Heart and Blood in Animals.* Oxford.

Harvey, William (ed. Franklin, K. J.) (1958). *The Circulation of the Blood. Two Anatomical Essays by William Harvey Together with Nine Letters Written by Him.* Oxford.

Harvey, William (trans. O'Malley, C. D., Poynter, F. N. L. and Russel, F. K.) (1961). *Lectures on the Whole of Anatomy.* Berkeley, California.

Harvey, William (ed. Franklin, K. J.) (1963). *The Circulation of the Blood and Other Writings.* London and New York.

Harvey, William (ed. Whitteridge, G.) (1964). *Anatomical lectures: Prelectationes anatomie universalis de musculis.* Edinburgh.

Hodgkin, A. L., Huxley, A. F., Feldberg, W. A. H., *et al.* (1977). *The Pursuit of Nature: Informal Essays on the History of Physiology.* Cambridge.

Laennec, R. T. H. (trans. Forbes, J.) (1962). *A Treatise on Disease of the Chest.* Facsim. of London 1821 edn. New York.

Langley, L. L. (1973). *Homeostasis: Origins of the Concept.* Strandsburg, Pennsylvania.

Lower, Richard (ed. Franklin, K. J.) (1932). *De corde* (London, 1669). Oxford.

Marckwald, M. (trans. Haig, T. A.) (1888). *The Movements of Respiration and their Innervation in the Rabbit. With a Supplement on the Reaction of Respiration to Degeneration and on the Question of the Existence of Respiratory Centres in the Spinal Cord.* Glasgow.

Needham, J. and Baldwin, E. (eds) (1949). *Hopkins and Biochemistry: 1861–1947; papers concerning Sir Frederick Gowland Hopkins with a selection of his addresses and a bibliography of his publications.* Cambridge.

Nobelstiftelsen (1964). *Physiology or Medicine.* Nobel lectures, including presentation speeches and laureates' biographies; vol. 1 1901–21, vol.2 1922–41, vol.3, 1942–62, vol.4 1963–70. Amsterdam.

Partington, J. R. (1961–70). *A History of Chemistry,* 4 vols. London and New York.

Rothschuh, K. E. (trans. and ed. Risse, G. B.) (1973). *History of Physiology.* New York.

Schwann, T. (trans. Smith, H.) (1847). *Microscopical Researches into the Accordance in Structure and Growth of Animals and Plants.* London. (Includes Scheiden, M. J., Contributions to phytogenesis, pp. 229–68).

Sherrington, Sir C. S. (1940). *Man on His Nature.* (The Gifford Lectures, Edinburgh of 1937–8). Cambridge.

Singer, C. (1959). *A History of Biology.* 3rd edn, London and New York.

Stirling, W. (1966). *Some Apostles of Physiology: being an Account of their Lives and Labours, Labours that have Contributed to the Advancement of the Healing Art as well as to the Prevention of Disease.* Reprint, London.

Virchow, R. (trans. Change, F.) (1860). *Cellular Pathology as based upon Physiological and Pathological Histology.* 2nd edn, London. (Also published 1971, New York.)

Wright, Sampson (ed. Keele, C. A., Neele, E., and Joels, N.) (1982). *Applied Physiology.* 13th edn, Oxford.

PHYSIOTHERAPIST. A person trained and qualified in *physiotherapy.

PHYSIOTHERAPY is treatment by physical methods such as exercise, massage, muscular re-education, heat, electrical stimulation, etc. Physiotherapy is one of the recognized professions ancillary to medicine, and in the UK it is under the control of the Chartered Society of Physiotherapy. The attentions of a skilled physiotherapist can be of inestimable value in a wide variety of disorders, particularly those involving muscles, ligaments, bones, joints, muscles, and nerves.

PHYSOSTIGMINE. See ESERINE.

PIA MATER. The innermost of the three *meninges, which envelops the *brain and *spinal cord.

PICA is an appetite perversion characterized by a craving for particular, often bizarre, articles of diet. Children with pica sometimes attempt to eat material or articles that could not be regarded as food. Pica is not uncommon in pregnancy.

PICK, ARNOLD (1851–1924). Czech neuropsychiatrist, MD Vienna (1875). Appointed professor of neurology and psychiatry in the German University of Prague in 1886, Pick published many papers on the pathological anatomy of cerebral diseases. He described presenile *dementia with focal cerebral atrophy (Pick's disease, 1892).

PICK, LUDWIG (1868–1935). German pathologist, MD Leipzig (1893). Pick was awarded the title of professor of pathological anatomy in Berlin in 1909, and he became full professor in 1921. He described the *sphingomyelin storage disorder (Niemann–Pick disease, 1927).

PICKERING, SIR GEORGE WHITE (1904–80). British physician, MD Cambridge (1955), FRCP (1938), FRS (1960). Pickering worked with Sir Thomas *Lewis and became professor of medicine at *St Mary's Hospital in London in 1939, moving to the regius chair at Oxford in 1956. In 1968 he was elected Master of Pembroke College, Oxford. His interests were mainly in cardiovascular disease and his book *High Blood Pressure* (1955) was widely acclaimed. He did much to encourage continuing education in medicine by advocating the building of postgraduate centres.

PICKLES, WILLIAM NORMAN (1885–1969). British general practitioner, LMSSA (1909), MB BS London (1910), MD London (1918), FRCP (1963). The first president of the College of General Practitioners (see GENERAL MEDICAL PRACTICE), Pickles practised for 53 years in the village of Aysgarth, Wensleydale, Yorkshire. His book, *Epidemiology in a Country Practice* threw original light on the spread of infection in a rural district. 'Rural districts, where the population is thin and the lines of intercourse few and always easily traced, offer opportunities which are not to be met with in the crowded haunts of large towns.' He knew everyone in Aysgarth and, with his wife, kept meticulous records. There is an admirable quality of simplicity in his research methods and writing. His book survives as a classic. 'There is something in country practice which breeds content.'

PICKWICKIAN SYNDROME. The syndrome of *obesity, *cyanosis due to *hypoventilation, and somnolence. Other features are excessive eating, fatiguability, breathlessness, carbon dioxide retention, secondary *polycythaemia, pulmonary hypertension, and eventually *cor pulmonale. The syndrome is named with reference to Mr Wardle's boy Joe, in *The Posthumous Papers of the Pickwick Club* by Charles Dickens, published in 1837.

PIGMENTATION is abnormal coloration of skin or mucous membranes due to the deposition of a pigmented substance. In many cases this is dark brown and due to *melanin (melanoderma), which is responsible for normal skin pigmentation; increased activity of the melanocytes (see SKIN)

may be due to local factors such as irritation or may be generalized as a result of increased secretion of *melanocyte-stimulating hormone (MSH) by the anterior pituitary. Thus patchy or diffuse melanoderma can occur in very many conditions, including sunburn, pregnancy, menopause, old age, Addison's disease, multiple neurofibromatosis, pediculosis ('vagabond's disease'), malaria, pellagra, diabetes mellitus, carcinomatosis, and others, as well as in a number of primary skin diseases. Pigmentation may also be due to iron-containing derivatives of *haemoglobin, such as haemosiderin; this type is seen following skin and subcutaneous haemorrhages, and in *haemochromatosis or 'bronzed diabetes'. Other metals which may be deposited in the skin causing pigmentation include silver (argyria), bismuth, and mercury.

PIKE'S PEAK is a mountain in Colorado (4298 m) where much physiological work on the effects of exposure to high altitude was carried out, for example, the studies of J. S. *Haldane in 1912 on acclimatization. See ENVIRONMENT AND DISEASE.

PILES. See HAEMORRHOIDS.

PILL, THE. When not otherwise qualified, the contraceptive pill. See CONTRACEPTION.

PILLS are small spherical or ovoid masses, designed to be swallowed, used for the administration of pharmaceutical agents. The active substance (or substances) is mixed with a vehicle, the excipient, to confer cohesion and firmness. 'Pill' is sometimes loosely used synonymously with *tablet.

PILOCARPINE is an *alkaloid with cholinergic effects, used in *ophthalmology to cause *miosis in the treatment of *glaucoma.

PINCUS, GREGORY (1903–67). American biologist and endocrinologist, Sc.D. Harvard (1927). Pincus was on the faculty of several Boston universities before becoming director of the Worcester (Massachusetts) Foundation for Experimental Biology. His main interest was in the properties of the steroid *hormones, especially in connection with function of the *gonads. He made fundamental contributions to the development of *contraceptive methods, using oral* steroid preparations.

PINEAL. The pineal body, a small structure protruding from the centre of the brain derived embryologically from the *ependyma of the third ventricle. Though its tissue is rich in various *neurotransmitter substances and it is innervated by postganglionic *sympathetic fibres, it is not known to have any precise function in man. In animals, it is concerned with *gonadal function, with *circadian rhythms, and with variations in skin *pigmentation.

PINEALOMA. A rare *tumour, sometimes a true neoplasm of pineal *parenchyma, more often a *teratoma, sometimes with other cellular elements predominant. Precocious puberty is an occasional association.

PINEL, PHILIPPE (1745–1826). French physician, MD Toulouse (1773). Pinel supported himself by translations until in 1793 he was given charge of the insane at the Hospice de Bicêtre and in 1795 at the *Salpêtrière. At both he instituted a new era in *psychiatry by his strenuous opposition to violent methods of treatment, and by insisting that the chains of all patients be removed. He made an attempt to devise a Linnaean *classification of diseases in his *Nosologie philosophique* (1789).

PINK DISEASE. See ACRODYNIA.

PINK EYE. Acute *conjunctivitis.

PINNA. The external and visible part of the ear.

PINTA is a skin disease of tropical South America, disfiguring but with little effect on general health. It is caused by a *spirochaete (*Treponema carateum*) closely related to those which cause *syphilis and *yaws.

PINWORM. See THREADWORM.

PION. A pi-meson, one of the group of unstable elementary particles known as mesons which have a mass intermediate between that of electrons and protons.

PIORRY, PIERRE ADOLPHE (1794–1879). French physician, MD Paris (1816). Piorry's medical studies were interrupted in order to serve as a dresser with the army in Spain. He later worked with *Broussais and *Magendie; he was appointed to the chair of internal pathology at the Faculté in 1840 and to that of medicine at the Charité in 1846. He invented the '*pleximeter' and wrote *Traité sur la percussion médiate* (1828) on its use.

PIPE SMOKING is a less dangerous method of *smoking tobacco than cigarettes, probably because less inhalation of smoke occurs in life-long pipe smokers who are in any case often relatively light smokers. Another factor may be the lower temperature of combustion in the bowl of a pipe. The mortality rate of pipe smokers is higher than that of non-smokers but the increase is small compared with that for cigarette smokers. However, cigarette smokers who change to pipe-smoking as an alternative to giving up smoking altogether may not improve their health and life prospects very much, since an established inhalation habit is usually transferred to other methods of smoking.

PIROGOFF, NIKOLAI IVANOVICH (1810–81). Russian surgeon, MD Dorpat (1832). After training in Moscow Pirogoff studied and graduated in Germany. He was made professor of surgery in Dorpat in 1836 and in St Petersburg in 1840. Pirogoff was in charge of the medical services during the Crimean war and served at Sebastopol in 1854. One of the most important figures in Russian medicine he was a medical educationalist and a supporter of women's role in medicine. A skilled surgeon he is known for his osteoplastic amputation of the foot (Pirogoff's amputation, 1854) and for his attempt to induce *anaesthesia by administering *ether rectally (1847).

PIRQUET, CLEMENS FREIHERR VON (1874–1929). Austrian paediatrician of Vienna. Pirquet described a test for *tuberculosis in which the surface of the skin is scarified through two drops of old tuberculin, an *antigen. A positive result is when after 24–48 hours the site of the scratches shows a red inflamed papule with a central areola. This test confirmed previous tuberculous infection, but did not determine whether the disease was active. Pirquet was one of the founders of the study of *allergy.

PITCAIRN, DAVID (1749–1809). British physician, MD Cambridge (1784), FRCP (1785), FRS (1782). Pitcairn followed his uncle, William Pitcairn, as physician to *St Bartholomew's Hospital, London, in 1780. He was the first to note that lesions of the heart valves followed *rheumatic fever. His father, Major Pitcairn, was killed at Bunker Hill in 1775 and his brother Robert, was the first to sight Pitcairn Island on 2 July 1767 which was thus given his name.

PITCAIRNE, ARCHIBALD (1652–1713). British physician, MD Rheims (1680), MD Aberdeen (1699), FRCS Edinburgh (1701). Pitcairne was a founder fellow of the Royal College of Physicians of Edinburgh and one of the Edinburgh medical school. He served as professor of physic in Leiden in 1692 and 1693. After this he practised in Edinburgh. Pitcairne was a controversial figure, an ardent Jacobite, and an anti-presbyterian.

PITCH is that quality of a sound which is determined by the frequency of vibration of a sound source; a high frequency produces a sound of high pitch.

PITUITA. Secretions of *mucus; *phlegm.

PITUITARY GLAND. The pituitary gland, or hypophysis, is located at the base of the brain, attached by a stalk to the *hypothalamus. It is the most complex of the endocrine glands, having a number of functions including the control of several other glands ('the leader of the endocrine orchestra'). It has two major components, the anterior lobe or adenohypophysis and the posterior lobe or neurohypophysis.

The anterior lobe which is itself regulated by the

hypothalamus secretes a number of important hormones. These include the following seven: growth hormone (somatotropin or GH) which is essential for normal growth and also influences carbohydrate metabolism; *prolactin (lactogenic hormone), which regulates the secretion of milk; *adrenocorticotrophic hormone (ACTH) which controls the secretion of hormones from the adrenal cortex; two *gonadotrophic hormones, one of which (*follicle-stimulating hormone or FSH) controls the formation of ova by the ovary in the female and sperms by the testis in the male, and the other (*luteinizing hormone or LH) the secretion of sex hormones by the gonads; *melanocyte-stimulating hormone (MSH) which controls the pigment-producing cells of the skin; and *thyrotrophic hormone (TSH), which stimulates thyroid gland activity.

The neurohypophysis stores and releases two hormones: *oxytocin, which initiates labour at the end of pregnancy, stimulates uterine contraction, and also plays a part in lactation; and *antidiuretic hormone (ADH), which stimulates renal retention of water and has a blood-pressure-raising effect.

PITYRIASIS is any skin disease characterized by the formation and shedding of branny scales.

PLACEBO. A treatment known to be without effect given to a patient either merely to please him or her, or else to serve as a 'control' treatment in comparison with a potentially effective substance or method which is being subjected to *clinical trial. In the latter case, the aim is to eliminate the 'placebo effect', that is the improvement which many patients exhibit merely because they are taking or undergoing something which they believe will do them good.

PLACENTA. The placenta unites the mammalian *fetus to the maternal *uterus and serves as its organ of respiration, nutrition, and excretion. The placenta, which is developed from fetal tissue, is in close contact with the maternal blood circulation so that diffusion of oxygen and nutrients (but not cells or particulate matter) can occur in one direction and of carbon dioxide and urea in the other. It contains a dense network of fetal blood vessels which communicates with the remainder of the fetal circulation by means of the umbilical arteries and vein. The placenta also acts as a maternal endocrine organ, producing *hormones (*gonadotrophin, *oestrogen, *progesterone) necessary for the maintenance of pregnancy. The placenta is extruded shortly after the birth of the infant (the 'afterbirth'), at which stage it weighs about 0.6 kg and is discoid in shape, about 2 cm thick and 16 cm in diameter.

PLACENTA PRAEVIA is an abnormally situated *placenta, lying across or adjacent to the opening of the *uterus. It is a cause of haemorrhage in late

pregnancy or during labour, and may necessitate *Caesarean section.

PLAGUE is a severe *bacterial infection due to the organism *Yersinia pestis* (formerly known as *Pasteurella pestis*). It is endemic in parts of South-East Asia and Africa, and occurs sporadically elsewhere. Primarily a disease of wild rodents, transmission to man usually occurs as a result of the bite of a *rat flea, causing the clinical variety known as bubonic plague in which regional *lymphadenitis (bubo) is prominent. When the condition becomes septicaemic and pneumonic, person-to-person transmission occurs by droplet infection. Untreated, the mortality rate of plague is high; but it responds well to early *antibiotic therapy. See also BLACK DEATH.

PLANIGRAPHY is the radiographic visualization of structures in a single plane of the body, as in *tomography.

PLANIMETER. A mechanical integrating instrument which measures surface areas utilizing a movable tracing arm.

PLANTALGIA is pain in the sole of the foot.

PLAQUE, DENTAL. See DENTISTRY.

PLASMA is the liquid which together with the suspended cells comprises blood. *Serum is plasma without *fibrinogen, after the latter has been removed by the clotting process. See HAEMATOLOGY.

PLASMA CELL. A B-*lymphocyte in its most active antibody-secreting form. See IMMUNOLOGY.

PLASMAPHERESIS is the technique of whole body *plasma exchange, the plasma being replaced with fresh frozen plasma or some other osmotically appropriate fluid.

PLASMID. An extrachromosomal genetic element existing and replicating autonomously in the cytoplasm of a cell. Bacterial plasmids are closed loops of *deoxyribonucleic acid (DNA) consisting of only a few *genes, capable, for example, of conferring antibiotic resistance on the host cell; they are utilized in *genetic engineering.

PLASMODIUM is the genus of *protozoal parasites which includes the causative organisms of *malaria.

PLASTER is fabric coated with an adhesive substance for application to the skin, for protective and medicinal purposes. See also PLASTER OF PARIS.

PLASTER OF PARIS is made from powdered calcium sulphate ($CaSO_4.\frac{1}{2}H_2O$), obtained by heating gypsum, or hydrated calcium sulphate

(CaSO$_4$.2H$_2$O), to 120–30 °C so that it loses three-quarters of its water of crystallization. On mixing with water, plaster of Paris sets and rapidly hardens. It is particularly useful for making casts and bandages for purposes of immobilization.

PLASTIC AND MAXILLOFACIAL SURGERY

History. Plastic surgery is not a new medical specialty. Indeed, if a specialty in medicine is defined as a limited field of medicine engaged in exclusively by its practitioners, plastic surgery goes back to ancient times.

In the Egyptian papyri (see EBERS PAPYRUS and EDWIN SMITH PAPYRUS), there are descriptions of individual physicians who concerned themselves with the treatment of fractures of the facial bones and with war injuries and accidents involving the soft tissues. A review of their methods of repair offers interesting reading for students of medicine (Gnudi and Webster, 1950).

In India in the 13th and 14th c. it was common practice to punish convicted criminals by amputations or mutilations of body parts. A frequent punishment for adultery was amputation of the nose. As a result a considerable demand sprang up throughout the country for artisans who might be skilled in the surgical replacement of the human nose. The law of supply and demand soon produced a group of specialists in what we would now call plastic surgery.

In the Hindu religion institutional law prevented Hindus who belong to the highest levels of the Caste system from touching human blood. It was, therefore, left to the lowly tile makers of the seventh caste to develop the necessary surgical skills for rebuilding the nose. Over a period of many generations, these skills were developed and passed down from father to son, unknown to the Western world of medicine.

In 1794 two British physicians travelling in India were invited to witness one of these nasal reconstructions, performed in the foothills of Mahvatta. The patient was held to the ground by four strong men as the surgeon quickly cut free most of the skin from his forehead, leaving it attached only by a small bridge at the medial eyebrow region. The skin was then turned, folded, and roughly shaped into the form of the nose before being fastened to the newly incised skin around the edges of the healed nasal defect. Crude stitches and thorns were used to fasten the new nose into position and the patient's forehead was then allowed to heal over a period of weeks. The slip of skin remaining between the eyes was divided 25 days later. When this dramatic operation was reported subsequently by the visitors, in the *Gentleman's Magazine* (1794) in London, it met with disbelief and ridicule. Only some years later was the validity of the report established and we, to this day, use and know this basic technique of transferring the forehead skin to reconstruct the nose as the 'Indian method of rhinoplasty'.

Plastic surgery is sometimes defined as 'that branch of medicine which seeks to correct congenital or acquired deformities in order to improve function, appearance, or both'. It deals with defects both of the integument and of the underlying musculoskeletal framework. Although it is chiefly concerned with deformities involving the face, and the head and neck region, it also includes the treatment of deformities of the hands and feet, of body contours, and of the external genitalia.

The noun, person, is derived from the Latin 'persona' which signified the facial mask that actors wore and then, secondarily, the meaning was applied to the role played by the actor or the personage he represented in the play. The word has gradually become synonymous with the idea of an individual person. Since every human face is different, we have come to associate our individuality primarily with our faces. Indeed, we recognize each other by our faces, and each of us has difficulty in separating our identity from our facial self-image. For that reason, physicians have come to recognize the enormous importance of dealing with deformities, great and small. Deformities inhibit function by making an individual feel that his image is inadequate. The word, plastic, basically means 'form', and it is the form of the human face and body that primarily concerns the plastic surgeon. The plastic surgeon tries to give a part of the body better 'form' as well as improved function.

*Aristotle, in his treatise, *On the Parts of Animals*, stated, 'Art indeed consists in the conception of the result to be produced before its realization in the material'. That ability is a quality much needed by the plastic surgeon. It is a quality that should distinguish the artist from the technician. In 1798 Desavit first used the term 'plastique' in a medical paper, and in 1838 Zeis published the first *Handbuch der plastischen Chirurgie*. It is of note that plastic surgery was entirely reconstructive in nature until the 20th c. In recent decades, the reliability and safety of this branch of surgery were advanced to such a degree that elective cosmetic or aesthetic surgery now is highly reliable and extremely popular. The basic principles of aesthetic surgery and reconstructive surgery are interwoven; the only clear distinction between the two is that aesthetic surgery is performed for deformities of a lesser degree. Such deformities might often be accepted as within the range of 'normal' by laymen. Thus, in one sense, the surgeon is attempting, in the case of aesthetic surgery, to make improvements within the narrow range of normal anatomy. Such surgery always carries some risk and should not be undertaken unless the person's sense of deformity is producing significant emotional problems which might lead to inhibitions that could significantly affect the patient's behaviour and personal relationships —inhibitions often eliminated by appropriate surgery.

During the 8th c. AD Arabian scholars, with the

rise of Islam, provided Arabic translations of the work of the famed Indian practitioner Sushruta. Thus, Europeans—in particular Italians, including the Branca family of Sicily and Gaspare *Tagliacozzi of Bologna—became familiar with ancient methods of plastic surgery that had been developed on the subcontinent of India (Gnudi and Webster, 1950).

Between the years 1530 and 1600, southern Europe and the Italian peninsula endured an extraordinary amount of violence and bloodshed. As has been the case in more modern times, warfare always stimulates the development of further skills in plastic surgery. During this period, Gaspare Tagliacozzi (Fig. 1) published his treatise in 1597 entitled *De curtorum chirurgia per insitioneum.* This great work established him as the first modern plastic surgeon. He described the use of flaps of skin and fat taken from the upper arm to reconstruct the nose. He employed a technique of delaying (or outlining) a flap with a preliminary operation to make it safer at the time of transfer. (Later developments allowed flaps to be taken from the neck, for example to close a defect in the lip; Figs. 2 and 3.) Tagliacozzi, like William Harvey, was ridiculed and persecuted for his medical 'heresies'. Following his death there was a decline in all science and medicine, including the practice of plastic surgery, throughout Europe, and this lasted during the 17th and 18th c. In these dark times, surgeons reported the mythical use of reparative tissue taken from a slave or person other

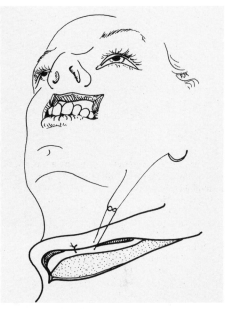

Fig. 2. This illustrates a patient who has a loss of the upper lip, secondary to its removal for cancer. The tube flap is being raised on this patient's anterior neck. Two parallel incisions approximately 5 cm apart and 16 cm in length have been made down to the level of the underlying platysma muscle. The two edges of the skin flap lying between these incisions are brought together on the underside with a series of sutures, as indicated. This creates a cylindrical tube of skin still attached to the neck at each end. The remaining skin of the neck may be drawn together beneath this elevated tube with an additional row of sutures. At the first operation, this flap is not transferred to the lip since the complete division of one end of the attachment to the neck would result in skin necrosis of that end, due to inadequate blood supply. The raising and creating of the tube at this first stage is called a 'delay' operation, which allows progressive improvement in the circulation to occur over the next three-week period. At the end of that time, it becomes safe to divide one end of the tube and to transfer it into the defect in the lip

Fig. 1. A wooden statue of Gaspare Tagliacozzi, the father of modern plastic surgery, at the University of Bologna. He is holding a model of the human nose and contemplates the problem of its reproduction

than the patient and used for *grafting. They even believed that this tissue would in turn die whenever the donor suffered a similar fate.

Little progress in plastic surgery was made until 1794 when the letter from India was published in the *Gentleman's Magazine* in London, detailing the rebuilding of the nose for Cowasjee, a bullock driver with the English army in the war of 1792. Joseph Carpue, a noted English surgeon, intrigued by this story of surgery in India, devoted the next 20 years of his life to confirming the details and methods that were used. Finally, he attempted the operation himself in 1814. His patient had been an officer in the Egyptian army who had been treated for *syphilis by the use of *mercury. This medication, apparently, caused the loss of his nose.

In an operation, lasting 37 minutes, Carpue raised the forehead skin as a flap and inserted it

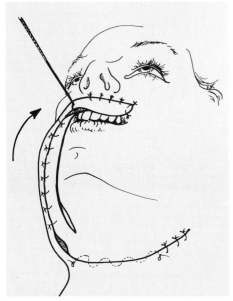

Fig. 3. The second stage in the transfer of the tube pedicle flap from the neck into the lip. One of the pedicles (that one on the left side of the neck) has been divided and the remaining defect in the neck closed with further sutures. This end of the tube is then carried upwards and placed into the defect in the upper lip in an appropriate fashion to restore the missing tissue. It is sutured into position and an additional period of three weeks or longer will be necessary before the remaining attachment to the neck can be divided to allow the final fitting of the flap into the patient's right cheek. For many years, this creation of the tube flap has been a time-honoured way of transferring tissue in plastic surgery. The closure of the skin edges to create the tube avoids leaving a raw area and thus prevents drainage, infection, and other troublesome problems that would otherwise occur. The Russian surgeon, Filatov, is generally credited with introducing the tube flap. Many Western surgeons have improved and added to the technique

into incisions in the patient's face around the defect caused by the missing nose. This operation and a second one performed by Carpue in 1815 marked the introduction of major reconstructive plastic surgery into Western medicine (Carpue, 1816).

During the 19th c. several other European surgeons made important contributions to the specialty of plastic surgery. These included von Graefe and his publication of *Rhinoplastik* in 1818 in Germany (Figs. 4 and 5). His younger contemporary, Dieffenbach (1845), ingeniously extended the principles of nasal reconstruction to many other types of defects involving the face and lips.

In France, *Dupuytren (1832) developed in 1832 new methods for treating *burns and for relieving severe *contractures of the hands. At the same time von *Langenbeck was making major contributions to the closure of congenital clefts of the *palate in children. In 1851, *Velpeau's *Operative*

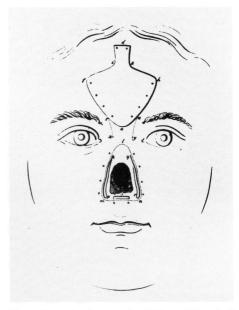

Fig. 4. Illustration from von Graefe's book. *Rhinoplastik* (1818), shows his diagram on the forehead to outline the shape of the skin needed to rebuild the nose

Surgery described a number of new reconstructive procedures introduced by the American surgeons, Pancoast and Mutter of Philadelphia, as well as Mott, Post, and Buck (see Fig. 6).

In December, 1869, Reverdin (1870), an intern working in the department of Guyon, presented a patient before the Imperial Society of Surgery of Paris. This represented the first demonstration of

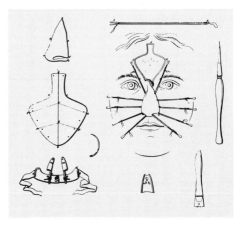

Fig. 5. The forehead flap has been transferred into the nasal defect. Small fish-tailed wooden sticks are used to allow daily tightening and loosening of the stitches. The lower left-hand corner pictures a splint to maintain the nostril air passages during the healing period. This is a modification of the ancient Indian method of rhinoplasty described in Susruta

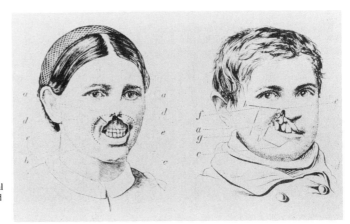

Fig. 6. Gurdon Buck illustrates his early use of local skin flaps from the cheeks and lips to repair full-thickness defects about the mouth

free skin grafting in modern medicine. Claude *Bernard, at that meeting, called attention to the importance of these 'epidermik grafts'. Ollier (1872) and *Thiersch (1874) published extensions and developments of this technique to show that larger grafts, including grafts containing *dermis as well as *epidermis, could also be used. In England, Wolfe *et al.* (1876) first described the use of a full-thickness skin graft for the treatment of eyelid deformities.

Early plastic surgery in the USA and the UK. In the USA, the first specialization in plastic surgery appears to have developed as a result of the stimulation by William Stewart *Halsted, the first professor of surgery at the *Johns Hopkins University School of Medicine. He encouraged one of his younger associates, John Staige Davis, to limit his practice to plastic surgery. In 1919 Davis published the first textbook in English on plastic surgery, entitled *Plastic Surgery—Its Principles and Practice*. Even today, it is used by plastic surgeons in planning operations involving the transfer of flaps of local tissue to repair defects.

At the beginning of the First World War, Davis, and Morestin of France, were the only two recognized specialists in plastic surgery among the allied forces. Trench warfare in France produced a staggering number of maxillofacial wounds and few military surgeons knew how to deal with these. Morestin, a native of Martinique, conducted an active plastic surgery programme at the military hospital of Val-de-Grâce in Paris (Morestin, 1915). He died prematurely in the great influenza epidemic in 1917 but not before he had interested a British surgeon, Harold *Gillies, in the field of plastic surgery. Gillies subsequently established a military plastic surgery centre at the Queen Mary Hospital in Sidcup, Kent. At this hospital, many young surgeons including Kilner and *McIndoe, Ferris Smith of the USA, Waldron and Risdon of Canada, and Pickerill of Australia, learned the operative methods and skills of handling patients with severe war injuries.

During that war, Kazanjian, a dental surgeon from Harvard, was working at Etaples near Boulogne; he applied his knowledge of prosthetic dentistry to the early treatment of gunshot wounds of the jaws and perfected new methods of *splinting jaw fractures associated with massive loss of bone. He developed principles that were still in use 60 years later (Kazanjian, 1974). When the USA entered the war in 1917, Surgeon-General *Gorgas organized a section on oral and plastic surgery for the US military forces. Vilray P. Blair of St Louis headed that section and chose Robert H. Ivy as his assistant. Five years earlier, Blair had published a classic book entitled *Surgery and Diseases of the Mouth and Jaws* (1912). Blair devised the wartime system of training two-man teams, composed of a general surgeon and a dental surgeon, in plastic techniques with short courses of instruction. These teams were then assigned to military hospitals where patients with major face and jaw injuries could be concentrated. This worked well (Ivy, 1918).

During and after the First World War, the programmes of national medical meetings began to include papers concerned with plastic surgery for war veterans who returned home still deformed. These described new possibilities for plastic surgery (Filatov, 1917). For the first time, citizens in many countries began to see significant numbers of the war-wounded on the streets and in the neighbourhoods, attempting to re-enter civilian life. Laymen began to appreciate the role of plastic surgeons in health care.

In the 1920s and 1930s, John S. Davis and Vilray P. Blair in the USA, and Harold Gillies in the UK were leaders in the developing specialty of plastic surgery. Each made important and original contributions applying plastic surgical principles to the deformities of civilian life. Gillies (1920) helped to pioneer the development of the tube pedicle flap (in which a flap of skin, still with its blood supply, was fashioned into a tube and attached to another part of the body, being detached from its original attachment only when it had 'taken' in its new environment (see Figs. 2 and 3), while Blair and his associate, Barrett Brown developed the technique of cutting and using large split-thickness skin grafts to resurface the wounds of patients with major burns (Blair and Brown, 1929). Earl Padgett (1939) and George Hood, an engineer, developed the first mechanical dermatome that could be used for taking large sheets of split-thickness skin grafts. This instrument made it possible for surgeons with a modest amount of training in plastic surgery to take skin grafts of adequate quality for covering large skin defects. During the Second World War, this device saved many lives and limbs.

During the period between the First and Second World Wars, cosmetic or aesthetic plastic surgery was beginning to develop. A German surgeon Joseph (1928) was developing the modern method of corrective rhinoplasty (reshaping of the nose), permitting the operation to be carried out by means of incisions entirely within the nose. At the same time in France, Passot and Noel were developing the first rather limited procedures that led to our present methods of facelifting to correct the sagging tissues of the ageing face.

Although facelifting is considered to be the major type of cosmetic surgery by the lay public, the use of cosmetic surgery to correct the body image in other ways is rapidly spreading. Women with very small or very large breast development are seeking correction of excessive deformity in either direction. Body contouring in the form of removal of large folds of skin and fat from the abdomen or upper legs has proved increasingly effective. Even skeletal alterations involving reshaping of the bony skull, correcting the abnormally small or the abnormally large lower jaw and chin, straightening the curved spine, or elongating the excessively short neck have become acceptable and common procedures. Even patients who are excessively tall or excessively short may now have modest (up to four inches in change) corrections made in height. The follow-up studies on such patients indicate remarkably valuable and enduring effects on their living effectiveness. All of this would suggest that cosmetic surgery will probably increase rather than decrease in the years ahead.

In 1937 Vilray Blair and 12 other senior American plastic surgeons established the American Board of Plastic Surgery. For the first time, a serious effort to broaden and standardize the training of all plastic surgeons was launched. At the end of the Second World War, only 200 American surgeons could meet the qualifications for certification by the American Board of Plastic Surgery. Even in 1951, only two 'full-time' academic plastic surgeons had been appointed to head plastic surgery divisions in American medical schools (Robert McCormack at the University of Rochester in New York and Milton Edgerton at the Johns Hopkins University in Baltimore, Maryland). During the ensuing 30 years, 4000 additional plastic surgeons received Board qualified training, and 87 American medical schools now have recognized divisions in plastic surgery. In several of them plastic surgery has been given full departmental status. England, Scotland, and Ireland also established postgraduate training programmes for plastic surgeons in major medical centres.

Much of the exciting recent growth in the specialty came about as a result of the Second World War and the lessons learned in the centres for treatment of the war-injured. These plastic surgery hospitals were created to repair the thousands of injured hands and faces of soldiers, sailors, and pilots. One of the largest American centres was the Valley Forge General Hospital at Phoenixville, Pennsylvania. Here, the chief of the plastic surgery section, Barrett Brown and his associate, Bradford Cannon, trained a corps of young general surgeons in the newest methods of general reconstructive surgery. The medical officers who worked at this hospital and at other military plastic centres returned to civilian life in the late 1940s, and began to apply the newly learned wartime plastic surgical techniques to civilian problems such as cancer of the head and neck, industrial and automobile injuries, aesthetic and body contour surgery, and correction of deformities caused by conditions such as *arthritis and *stroke.

During the years just before the Second World War, Sterling Bunnell, Alan Kanavel, and Sumner L. Koch pioneered advances in surgery of the hand in the USA. Their efforts were complemented by Frederick Wood-Jones in the UK and Marc Iselin (1962) in France. Principles that were developed in significant measure by these pioneers were improved greatly as a result of the experience of military surgeons during the Second World War. As a result of their wartime experiences in England, Rank and Wakefield returned to Australia to establish a division of hand and plastic surgery and Penn opened a hospital in South Africa for a similar purpose.

Important advances had been made during the Second World War in the management of the injured hand. For the first time, hand surgery became a major part of the work of plastic surgeons throughout the world. Since the Second World War, it has been evident that complex hand surgery is best performed by a surgeon trained in the detailed anatomy and physiology of the upper extremity, who has the surgical skills to reconstruct all injured tissues including skin, tendons, nerves, bones, joints, and blood vessels. By the end of the Second World War, the scope of plastic surgery had been defined. In the 1950s William Littler inspired many young plastic surgeons to become serious students of surgery of the hand. In the 1960s Paul Brand, working in Vellore, India, demonstrated that the hand and facial deformities of *leprosy could be greatly ameliorated by plastic surgical techniques.

Following the Second World War, new medical centres sprang up to recognize the specialty of plastic surgery in many countries in Europe. Burian established a department of plastic surgery at Charles University in Prague in 1948. In Vienna, Eiselsberg, Pichler, and Esser also developed the specialty. In Germany, Schuchardt established a plastic clinic in Hamburg to treat soldiers who had been injured on the Russian front while Wassmund, in Berlin, carried on the work originally started by Axhausen.

In France, surgeons who had been trained in the UK and in the USA immediately following the Second World War established the French School of Plastic Surgery under the leadership of Morel-Fatio and Claude Dufourmentel. At this same time in South America, plastic surgery was being developed and demonstrated by Marino and Malbec. This world-wide activity led to the founding of the International Association of Plastic Surgeons. Its first Congress was held in 1955 in Stockholm at the invitation of Tord Skoog.

The specialty of plastic surgery in Japan developed as a result of the leadership of Ohmori. This was partly as a result of the stimulus he received from Bradford Cannon (of Valley Forge Hospital fame), while observing the latter's work at the *Massachusetts General Hospital in 1952.

The present day. Today plastic surgery includes not only those traditional fields relating to reconstructions of the nose and maxillofacial surgery to correct fractures and deformities of the facial bones and jaws, but also includes the treatment of patients needing complex reconstructions of the hand, or repair of *paraplegic pressure sores, or grafting of wounds resulting from *frostbite and major thermal burns. Other plastic surgery patients require the preparation of soft tissues for *orthopaedic surgery or for the repair of peripheral nerves. In the 1950s and 1960s, plastic surgeons began to make substantial contributions to the treatment of head and neck malignancy by developing methods of reconstruction of the face and jaws. These procedures were designed to help patients regain the abilities to talk, swallow, breathe, and control saliva. They were combined with large excisions for cancers of the tongue, jaws, throat, or salivary glands.

The broadening scope of plastic surgery required diversified training of its practitioners. The plastic surgeon could not afford to work in isolation but needed contact with surgeons in many other fields from whom he might draw principles needed for the planning and execution of reconstructive operations in almost any part of the body. This was recognized by the American Board of Plastic Surgery in its insistence on a period of training in general surgery prior to entering additional years of training in plastic surgery.

In the UK, during the Battle of Britain, large specialty hospitals similar to those in the USA for plastic surgery and jaw reconstruction were organized (Clarkson, 1966). In addition the work of McIndoe in treating severely burned airmen received increasing recognition. The efficiency of these concentrated and highly specialized wartime plastic surgery hospitals in both the USA and the UK was apparent to all who witnessed the results obtained. Unfortunately, this valuable lesson was later ignored during the conflicts in Korea and in Vietnam—to the detriment of the injured soldiers.

Today, a division or department of plastic surgery has an important academic role in almost every large medical centre throughout the USA. Plastic surgeons are involved not only in generalized and major reconstructive surgery throughout the body, but also in basic research including the fields of wound healing, tissue *transplantation, biology of *implantation of synthetic materials, *genetics, human *embryology and development, speech pathology and, most recently, research involving the new fields of *microsurgery and craniofacial surgery.

The field of microsurgery did not develop until it was realized that the neuromuscular system of man was capable of great manual skill—even when objects were magnified to 40 or 60 times normal dimensions. It is now clear that if the microsurgeon can clearly *see* the tiny artery, vein, or nerve, he is quite capable of *holding* his instrument, hands, and sutures sufficiently steady to place them with great accuracy. It is not uncommon for the microsurgeons to place 10 or 12 separate sutures around the circumference of an artery of no more than 0.5–1 mm total outside diameter. Once this capability was demonstrated, the world of reconstruction of small structures began to unfold. Although it has been a subspecialty pioneered by plastic surgeons, microsurgery is now becoming a part of the technical armamentarium of many other special fields of surgery. Without this new capability, we would not be able to return amputated fingers to the hands of workers, replace the avulsed hair-bearing scalp, or move important structures from one part of the body to the other by means of re-establishing the microcirculation in the new site. Microsurgery is on the threshold of even greater wonders.

Similarly, craniofacial surgery has made possible the correction of severe deformities due to birth defects that require repositioning of the *cranium, *orbits, and facial bones. Craniofacial surgery became a reality with the establishment of multidisciplinary teams of plastic surgeons, neurosurgeons, and ophthalmic surgeons. It became possible to translocate and reposition the human eye without loss of vision, once methods permitting exposure of the brain and its protection during surgery were developed. These techniques were pioneered by Tessier (1967) in France and by Edgerton (1970) and Converse (1972) in the USA in the late 1960s and early 1970s.

Unfortunately, the public perception of the plastic surgeon is that of an individual concerned primarily with aesthetic or cosmetic surgery and the correction of relatively minor deformities, such as are associated with the ageing face. This, despite the fact that the plastic surgeon of today is required to complete a seven-year period of postgraduate residency training and is expected to master a great variety of surgical procedures concerned with repair of skin, tendons, nerves, bone, and blood vessels throughout the body.

At present, many 'plastic' operations are performed by surgeons trained in other surgical specialties. But when a given reconstructive or aesthetic operation may be performed, not only better, but more safely and more efficiently, without increasing the medical cost, then it is in the interest of the patient and society that he be treated by a specialist in plastic surgery (Edgerton, 1974).

Because of rapid progress and technical developments, plastic surgery has developed one of the most ambitious and far-reaching postgraduate educational programmes within medicine. As is true in many medical specialties of the 1980s, continuing education is required throughout the entire professional career in order to keep abreast of technical advances in the field.

Aesthetic surgery is an important subdivision of general plastic surgery. The primary goal of treatment is improvement in the emotional health and self-image of the patient. When properly selected, these patients show enormous psychological and vocational gains following operation. The lay public has come to appreciate the value of these procedures and, hence, the demand for aesthetic surgery continues to increase.

Pope Pius XIII stated, in 1958, 'If we consider physical beauty in its Christian light, and if we respect the condition set by our moral teachings, then aesthetic surgery is not in contradiction to the will of God, in that it restores the perfection of that greatest work of creation, Man' (Wilflingseder, 1975).   M. T. EDGERTON

References

Blair, V. P. (1912). *Surgery and Diseases of the Mouth and Jaws*. St Louis, Missouri.

Blair, V. P. and Brown, J. B. (1929). Use and uses of large split skin grafts of intermediate thickness. *Surgery, Gynecology and Obstetrics*, **49**, 82.

Carpue, J. C. (1816). *An Account of Two Successful Operations for Restoring a Lost Nose from the Integuments of the Forehead*. London.

Clarkson, P. (1966). Sir Harold Gillies. *British Medical Journal*, **ii**, 641.

Converse, J. M. (1972). *Reconstructive Plastic Surgery*. 2nd edn, Philadelphia.

Davis, J. S. (1919). *Plastic Surgery—Its Principles and Practice*. Philadelphia, Pennsylvania.

Dieffenbach, J. F. (1845). *Die operative Chirurgie*. Leipzig.

Dupuytren, G. (1832). *Leçons orales de clinique chirurgical faites à l'Hôtel-Dieu de Paris*. Paris.

Edgerton, M. T. (1974). The role of plastic surgery in academic medicine. Presidential address. *Journal of Plastic and Reconstructive Surgery*, **54**, 523.

Edgerton, M. T., Udvarhelyi, G. B. and Knox, D. L. (1970). The surgical correction of ocular hypertelorism. *Annals of Surgery*, **172**, 473.

Filatov, V. P. (1917). Plastic à tige ronde. *Vestnik oftal*, No. 5.

Gentleman's Magazine (1794). A communication to the editor, Mr Urban, signed B.L. and dated 9 Oct. 1794. London.

Gillies, H. D. (1920). *Plastic Surgery of the Face*. London.

Gnudi, M. T. and Webster, J. P. (1950). *The Life and Times of Gasparo Tagliacozzi*. New York.

Graefe, C. F., von (1818). *Rhinoplastik; oder, Die kunst den verlust der Nase organisch zu ersetzen in ihren früheren Verhältnissen erforscht und durch neue Verfahrungsweisen zur hölherne Volkommenheit gefördert*. Berlin.

Iselin, M. (1962). La plastie en Z rectifiés. *Annals of Chirurgie Plastic*, **7**, 295.

Ivy, R. H. (1918). War injuries of the face and jaws. *Surgery, Gynecology and Obstetrics*, **27**, 101.

Joseph, J. (1928). Nasenplastik und sonstige Gesichtsplastik nebst einem Anhang uber Mammaplastik. *Ein Atlas und Lehrbuch*. Berlin.

Kazanjian, V. H. and Converse, J. M. (1974). *The Surgical Treatment of Facial Injuries*. 3rd edn, Baltimore, Maryland.

Morestin, H. (1915). La reduction graduelle des difformités tégumentaires. Reprinted in *Bulletin Memorial Société Chirurgie*, **41**, 1233.

Ollier, L. (1872). Greffles cutanée ou autoplastique. *Bulletin Academie Medicine*, **1**, 243.

Padgett, E. C. (1939). Skin grafting in severe burns. *American Journal of Surgery*, **43**, 626.

Reverdin, J. L. (1870). Greffes épidermiques; expérience faite dans les service de M. le docteur Guyon. *Bulletin Société Impériale Chirurgie*.

Tagliacozzi, G. (1597). *De curtorum chirurgia per insitioneum*. Venice.

Tessier, P., Guiot, G., Rougeria, J., Delbet, J. P. and Pastoriza, J. (1967). Osteotomies cranio-naso-orbitalfaciales. *Annales Chirurgie Plastic*, **12**, 103.

Thiersch, C. (1874). Ueber die feineren anatomischen Veranderungen bei Aufheilung von Haut auf Granulationen. *Archivs Klinique Chirurgie*, **17**, 318.

Wilflingseder, G. (1975). Personal communication.

Wolfe, D., Bellucci, R. J. and Eggston, A. A. (1876). A new method of performing plastic operations. *Medical Times and Gazette*, **1**, 608.

Zeis, E. (1838). *Handbuch der Plastischen Chirurgie*. Berlin.

PLATELETS are the smallest cellular elements of the blood, minute non-nucleated fragments (also called thrombocytes) formed from larger bone-marrow cells (megakaryocytes). Platelets play an important role in blood coagulation and in certain immunological reactions. See HAEMATOLOGY.

PLATT, ROBERT (Baron Platt of Grindleford, life peer, 1967) (1900–78). English physician, MD Sheffield (1923), FRCP (1935). Platt trained in Sheffield, and became a busy consultant in that city, with a special interest in diseases of the kidney. This career was interrupted by the Second World War, in which he rose to the rank of Brigadier. He then became the first full-time professor of medicine in Manchester, and soon attained a national reputation as an outstanding clinician, and an adviser on medical education and research, and even on hospital staffing. He was president of the Royal College of Physicians of London from 1957 to 1962, during which time the College became much more active in postgraduate education, and the decision was taken to acquire premises which would enable it to fulfil this task—the result being the building designed by Denys Lasdun on the east side of Regent's Park. It was also during his presidency that the College set up a committee 'to report on the question of *smoking and *atmospheric pollution in relation to carcinoma of the lung and other illnesses'; the publication of the report on *Smoking and Health* in 1962 was a landmark in creating public awareness of the dangers of smoking.

PLEOCYTOSIS is an increase in the number of cells in the *cerebrospinal fluid.

PLEOMORPHISM. Occurrence in a number of different forms.

PLETHORA. Congestion with blood.

PLETHYSMOGRAPHY is the recording of changes in the total volume of an organ or part, often used as a measure of blood flow through it (e.g. finger plethysmography).

PLEURA. The serous membrane lining the interior of the thoracic cavity (parietal layer) and enveloping the lung (visceral or pulmonary layer). The layers are continuous with each other and move against each other as the lung expands and contracts during breathing. They enclose a potential space known as the pleural cavity.

PLEURAL CAVITY. The potential space enclosed by the visceral and parietal layers of the *pleura.

PLEURAL EFFUSION is an accumulation of fluid within the *pleural cavity. See also PLEURISY.

PLEURISY is inflammation of the *pleura. In dry pleurisy, the inflamed surfaces move against each other causing a characteristic sharp pain on breathing, and on *auscultation a pleural friction rub can often be heard. These manifestations disappear when fluid accumulates in the pleural cavity (pleural effusion); the chief signs are then a marked impairment of resonance on *percussion and diminution of breath sounds on *auscultation.

PLEURODYNIA is pleural pain, often used synonymously with *Bornholm disease.

PLEXIMETER. The object which is tapped during examination by *percussion; this is usually the middle phalanx of the examiner's middle finger (the pleximeter finger) but sometimes a small plate pleximeter is substituted.

PLEXUS. Any network of vessels or nerves.

PLINY THE ELDER(Gaius Plinius Secundus) (*c.* AD 23–79). Roman natural historian. Pliny served in the army and later as a proconsul in Spain and Africa. He wrote an encyclopaedic natural history, *Naturalis historia*, in 37 volumes. Books XX–

XXXII deal with medicine. He died from exposure to fumes due to the eruption of Vesuvius.

PLOMBAGE is the surgical *occlusion with inert material (plombe) of a cavity in the body, for example in bone, or in the thorax round a collapsed lung.

PLUMBISM. *Lead poisoning.

PNEUMA was a supposed all-pervading vital principle which was central to a Graeco-Roman theory of medicine widely accepted during the 1st c. BC and AD. Pneuma was carried around the body in the nerves and underwent changes in particular organs; at death it left to rejoin a universal stockpile. The doctrine of pneuma was promulgated by *Erasistratus among others.

PNEUMATISM is a school of medical practice based on the theory of *pneuma.

PNEUMATURIA is the passage of air or other gas in the urine.

PNEUMOCOCCUS is a gram-positive diplococcus, the official name of which is now *Streptococcus pneumoniae*. A facultative anaerobe, it is responsible for the vast majority of cases of lobar *pneumonia, many other types of bacterial pneumonia, and a variety of serious infections elsewhere in the body, including meningitis.

PNEUMOCONIOSIS is a lung disease produced by the inhalation and pulmonary deposition of dusts, of occupational or other environmental origin. The extent of interference with lung function depends on the nature and size of the dust particles and the pulmonary reaction to them. Thus some pneumoconioses are relatively innocuous, such as those due to carbon particles (anthracosis) and to iron dust (siderosis). Others, like *silicosis and *asbestosis are much more serious. See OCCUPATIONAL MEDICINE.

PNEUMOCYSTIS is a genus of micro-organisms thought to be *protozoa but of which the life-cycle has not been established with certainty. *Pneumocystis carinii* is the causative agent of a life-threatening form of *pneumonia (pneumocystosis) which characteristically occurs as an *opportunistic infection in patients with congenital immunodeficiencies and those under treatment with immunosuppressive agents; it has been reported in as many as 50 per cent of patients with the *acquired immune deficiency syndrome (AIDS). In healthy subjects, infection with *Pneumocystis* probably occurs but is asymptomatic.

PNEUMOENCEPHALOGRAPHY is the *radiographic demonstration of *brain structures through visualization of the cerebral ventricles and subarachnoid space after replacement of *cerebrospinal fluid with air or other gas.

PNEUMOMEDIASTINUM is the presence of air in the *mediastinum, usually due to *trauma involving the bronchial tree (also known as mediastinal *emphysema).

PNEUMONECTOMY is surgical removal of a lung.

PNEUMONIA is inflammation of the parenchyma of the lungs, that is the alveoli and interstitial tissue, due to infection with micro-organisms. The term '*pneumonitis' is almost synonymous, but strictly speaking means inflammation of lung tissue from any cause. Almost any micro-organism can under certain circumstances cause pneumonia, including many species of bacteria, virus, rickettsia, and fungi.

PNEUMONITIS is inflammation of the parenchyma of the lungs from any cause, including chemical and physical agents. The term *pneumonia is sometimes used synonymously but usually implies inflammation due to infection with micro-organisms unless otherwise specified. An alternative usage restricts the meaning of pneumonitis to mild segmental inflammation.

PNEUMOPERITONEUM is the presence of air in the *peritoneal cavity. Artificial pneumoperitoneum is sometimes induced in order to assist *radiological diagnosis; it was formerly a common procedure in the treatment of pulmonary *tuberculosis, to help in immobilization of the lung.

PNEUMOTHORAX is the presence of air in the *pleural cavity. Normally the subatmospheric pressure in the potential pleural cavity keeps the parietal and visceral pleural layers in close apposition. This situation is disturbed if a communication develops between the cavity and the atmosphere, air is sucked in, and the elastic lung collapses; since the respiratory movements of the chest wall can no longer expand it, it ceases to function. If the communication should act as a valve, gas pressure builds up within the cavity, displacing the mediastinal structures to the opposite side and interfering with circulation (tension pneumothorax).

Pneumothorax can result from penetrating chest wounds, from various types of lung disease (particularly *emphysema), and in otherwise healthy subjects probably as a result of minor congenital weaknesses in the lung wall which rupture under strain (spontaneous pneumothorax). An artificial pneumothorax can readily be induced by inserting a hollow needle through the chest wall; this was formerly used as a method of resting the lung in the treatment of pulmonary tuberculosis, and can sometimes be of value in diagnostic *radiology.

PODAGRA. Synonym for *gout.

PODIATRY is the US term for *chiropody.

POIKILODERMA is any variegated or mottled appearance of the skin.

POISEUILLE, JEAN LÉONARD MARIE (1797–1869). French physiologist, D.Sc. Paris (1828). Poiseuille's early career is obscure. Later he became an inspector of schools. He studied the circulation, devised a mercury *sphygmomanometer in 1828, and enunciated his law. This states that the rate of flow of a liquid in a tube is given by the formula: $\pi p r^2 / 8 l \mu$, where p is the pressure of the liquid, r the radius of the tube, l its length, and μ the coefficient of the liquid's viscosity.

POISONING

Historical. Even today, mere mention of the word poisoning is enough to conjure up in the minds of most people ideas of diabolical infamy. No doubt this is due to what they have read about the subject in history. Numerous malefactors in the past set out to achieve their evil ends by using poison to dispose of those who stood in their way. The records over the ages are replete with accounts of this kind. Three millennia before Christ, Menes, the first of the Pharaohs, is reported 'to have cultivated and studied poisonous and medicinal plants and to have accumulated animal, mineral, and vegetable poisons'. Then there is the story, in the *Odyssey* of Homer, wherein Helen is described as discreetly introducing into the wine of Telemachus and Menelaus a drug that acted as a powerful *anodyne. Likewise in Greek legend, Hecate was knowledgeable about *aconite, Medea was familiar with the properties of *colchicum and Hercules is said to have met his end from wearing a shirt after his wife had impregnated it with poison. Again, probably a little more factually in the affairs of Greece, the sentence of judicial homicide on Socrates was implemented by way of the *hemlock cup. Interestingly, *Hippocrates, in his extensive writings, seems to have paid little positive attention to this topic, though he did insist that his students should abjure any trafficking in poisons at all.

About the same era, Mithridates, King of Pontus, probably distinguished himself as the first practising clinical immunologist. To protect himself against his enemies he is reported to have taken a repertoire of poisons, first in tiny doses and then in increasing amounts with the object of establishing in himself what might be regarded as a state of polyvalent *immunity. Whether or not he was successful in these efforts remains questionable, for he is believed ultimately to have died in battle. What he further espoused was a 'universal antidote', to which the name *Mithridaticum came to be applied. Great faith was accorded to this over succeeding centuries, though to judge from what has survived about its recipe it was, in all likelihood, spurious. Then there was the 'Poisons Maiden' of ancient Persia, of whom it was written that: 'It was the belief of many people that it was possible to feed a girl on poisons and thus make her so venomous that a kiss, or act of sexual intercourse, would prove fatal to her lover'. In Roman times deliberate poisoning took on the dimensions almost of an orgy, notably with a vogue for the wives among the aristocracy to dispose conveniently of their husbands by this means. Probably, though, the outstanding exponent at that time was Locusta, the handmaiden to Nero in many senses, who carried out what was tantamount to an extermination programme directed against those to whom her master had taken a dislike. She it was who eliminated Claudius with a dish of toxic *mushrooms.

Women, it seems, displayed a particular penchant for this art. Around the turn of the 15th c. the exploits of Lucretia *Borgia were notorious, along with those of her male kin. Then there was Toffana, in 17th c. Naples, who devised a concoction from the decomposing flesh of a hog, combined with *arsenic, which was purveyed, extraordinarily enough, as a cosmetic and was said to have conferred death in a fairly short space of time on those to whom it was applied.

In France, during the reign of Louis XIV, the toxicological excesses of 'La Voison' came to light, as did those of the Marquise de Brinvillers, of whom it has been written 'She visited the hospitals of Paris . . . in the guise of a Sister of Charity, to experiment upon helpless invalids . . . and while outwardly tender, compassionate and sympathetic, she succeeded in sending a large number to the dead house without incurring suspicion'. In England, the last legal execution by boiling was performed on Margaret Davie in 1542, who had 'pouysoned three households that she dwelled in'.

Still, the male counterparts were not to be outdone. Landru, in France, in the 1920s, sent a whole succession of innocent, if gullible, women to their doom, probably with the aid of cyanide. So the catalogue could be prolonged, indefinitely for sure, but not to the same intensity over latter years. What is so lacking from these historic accounts, for all their lurid colour, is anything that might lend scientific verification to them. After all, confirmation as to the real cause of death by the strict standards of pathology is of relatively recent introduction (see FORENSIC MEDICINE). Postmortem dissection (autopsy) of the body, even for unnatural deaths, was far from routine until little more than a century ago and, in any event, this would have proved far from informative so long as morbid anatomy and histology remained undeveloped as disciplines. No wonder, then, that sudden demise from any cause could be attributed to poisoning, simply on an anecdotal or spiteful basis.

What was more, direct evidence pointing to a toxic aetiology was out of the question until the quantitative, chemical examination of the organs and the tissues became feasible: that had to await the pioneer endeavours of Orfila (a Spaniard whose professional career was spent very largely in France) no earlier than the first half of the 19th c., although at about the same time Alfred Swaine Taylor of *Guy's Hospital, London was advancing this same study in Britain.

Turning to more recent fiction, poisoning has sometimes been chosen by authors as the seminal misdeed upon which to construct their mysteries for inspired detection, although generally, it seems, they prefer shooting or some other form of physical assault. Classical literature, however, has its examples of drama by poisoning, not least the works of Shakespeare. Was it not the Ghost of Hamlet's father who declared: 'Upon my secure hour thy uncle stole, with juice of cursed hebenon in a vial, and in the porches of my ear did pour the leperous distilment?' Not that there are many practising toxicologists today who would be so bold as to expatiate upon the nature and biocidal attributes of the 'cursed hebenon', nor would they single out the otological approach as the chosen route of administration. Even more impressive perhaps, was the immolation of Cleopatra, when she clasped the asp to her bosom and uttered the fateful cry: 'With thy sharp teeth this knot intrinsicate of life at once untie'. Sadly, perhaps, these instances are all too few.

Terminology. The term toxin is derived from the Greek word for an arrow (cf. toxophily) and owes its origin to the device of applying lethal material to the points of such weapons to aggravate the consequences of any wounds so inflicted. Today, toxicology has come to mean the science built upon the study of toxic phenomena in the widest sense.

By contrast, the etymological source of the word poison is shared with that for potion, implying a liquid that is imbibed. Today, poisoning is generally taken to mean the act, or process, by which anything toxic finds its way into a living body, whether via the mouth, through the skin, by inhalation, or by any other route, so as to give rise thereafter to adverse effects.

Analytical toxicology. The last 150 years have seen great progress in the harnessing of precise chemical analysis to the elucidation of death, or injury, by poisoning. Today, with modern techniques and instrumentation, the most minute traces of alien compounds can be detected, not only from tissues and organs post-mortem, but also in biological samples such as *blood and *urine collected during life. The enigma, nevertheless, commonly presents itself as to whether that which is revealed in this way has, after all, acted pathogenically. Arsenic, after all, is an almost ubiquitous element, so the distinction has to be made between what is a natural accompaniment and what is a dangerous excess—or sometimes between what is present from sinister misdeed and that which has gained entry to the body innocently from, say, the regular use of an arsenic-based hair 'tonic'.

Similarly, the majority of drugs can be taken safely enough in therapeutic doses, whereas in excess they may be very damaging. Frequently the resolution of these uncertainties is far from easy, and that is why, for instance, one reads of the conflicting views of so-called 'experts' during the course of legal hearings. This brings into focus the status of analytical toxicology in practice. It emerged, understandably enough, in the realm of forensic science being, as it were, the progeny begotten by analytical chemistry out of forensic pathology. It has been reared, therefore, in the detection of crime and the bringing of miscreants to justice. Only over the last few decades has much emphasis been placed on the toxicological analytical findings in clinical poisoning, as distinct from that inspired homicidally or in the furtherance of allied crimes.

Definitions and explanations. By British law, at least, no explicit legal definition has been accorded to the expression poison. Rather is it regarded, as under the Offences Against the Person Act 1861, as 'any destructing or noxious thing' that may be employed with intent to murder, to enable an indictable offence to be committed, to endanger life or inflict grievous bodily harm, or to injure, aggrieve, or annoy. A wide range of criminal intentions is thereby envisaged in connection with the use of poison and what is inherent in each of these is the malicious intent, or what the lawyers choose to call the *mens rea*. So, notwithstanding the preference in many countries for certain specified substances to be statutorily scheduled as poisons, in order to regulate their manufacture, distribution, sale, and supply, that is not to connote that, on the one hand, these materials are universally harmful nor, on the other hand, that any other compounds not so categorized are necessarily devoid of deleterious effects. *Paracelsus, four centuries or more ago, declared that 'All substances are poisons; there is none which is not a poison. The right dose differentiates a poison and a remedy.'

So now the process of poisoning may be examined more closely. It embodies three components: (i) the poison, or toxin, which may be any substance derived from mineral, plant, animal, or synthetic origin; (ii) its access to a living system, which may be *in vitro*, as in a tissue culture, or *in vivo,* that is a plant or animal of any species, no matter how simple, or how elaborate; and (iii) an adverse response. Without all of these three factors being present, poisoning cannot be said, in fact, to arise, although in the absence of one of them it may be fair then to refer to potential, or suspected, poisoning.

Scrutinizing more closely each of these contributions in turn then, toxicologically speaking, the poison must be identified and, better still, characterized physically and chemically. If the subject is to be treated as a science, then no credence can be given to toxic *humours, *miasmata, and the like, even if such intangible influences are invoked from time to time. Also to be borne in mind is the chance

that the toxic moiety is not always identical with the named chemical, or agent, but may be a function of an impurity, or contaminant, as with dioxin in some chlorinated phenolic compounds. What is more, not merely ambient exposure, but access or penetration of the toxin to the living system must be achieved as well. A child grasping a bottle with unpleasant contents is not, *ipso facto*, obliged to be poisoned from it: that will occur only when the material reaches, say, the alimentary tract from swallowing it. Again, not all chemicals finding their way on to the skin are thereupon absorbed percutaneously: uptake in the quantitative sense must have occurred.

Finally, not merely a reaction, but what can be regarded as an *adverse reaction, must be evinced. Herein can enter an element of moral as well as anatomical or physiological judgement. Thus a *cardiac glycoside, such as digoxin, at certain doses can bring about a beneficial response, whereas in overdoses it can be catastrophic. Characteristically, but not invariably, there is a dose–response correlation which is germane to all toxicological thinking and reasoning. Nowhere is this better exemplified than in the manner in which a person reacts to increasing libations of *ethanol. These quantitative concepts may be invested with some degree of mathematical precision. (See PHARMACOLOGY.)

Whereas toxicity may not be an intrinsic property of a substance, to the extent that its physicochemical features may be defined, it is nevertheless recognized that the inherent capacity for harm varies widely between one compound and another. A small dose of potassium cyanide can kill quickly; a far greater amount of sodium chloride (common salt) is required to be lethal. One method for arriving at an order of toxicity is to determine the lethal dose, for death or survival can usually be well differentiated. But animals vary in size, as they do also between species, between strains, between sexes, and between individuals. What is more, the quantity proving fatal is likely to range more widely still according to the route of administration—oral, dermal, by injection, or by inhalation, etc. So these variables are standardized, as far as they can be. Then, by observing the fate of comparable groups of animals, of the same species, strain, sex, and initial body weight, kept under uniform conditions, but given separate doses of the substance under test, group by group, a graph can be constructed displaying percentage mortality against dose and a figure can thereupon be calculated for what is called the LD_{50}. Descriptively, this is the weight of the substance which, conventionally expressed as so many milligrams per kilogram of body weight, should supposedly kill just 50 per cent of the creatures selected. The answer may extend from a few milligrams at one extreme, for a highly toxic material, to so great an amount at the other extreme for something that is practically innocuous that it is physically impossible to administer sufficient to bring about death. In the end, though, these figures must be viewed as no more than approximate indices or guides. The influence upon them of biological variation can be enormous and the disparity between species can be striking. The guinea-pig, for instance, is very sensitive to *penicillin, whereas for man this compound is almost non-toxic. The object, on so many occasions, is to ascertain how much of some substance or other will do harm to man or, more definitively, how much will kill him. For reasons embracing ethics and the sanctity of human life, direct experiments on *Homo sapiens* must be forsworn. That is why, in such default, the investigator turns to animal experiments. There is then all the uncertainty of trying to extrapolate from these species to man. (See also EXPERIMENTAL METHOD.)

Referring to exposure, this may be a single event—one dose by mouth, one injection, one dermal application, or one phase of inhalation. The ensuring response may be immediate or delayed. Whatever happens, the situation then is that of acute poisoning. At other times the exposure may be continued regularly over a few days, over weeks, or over a few months. Reactions may make their appearance sooner or later. Usually there is an interval during which the prolonged uptake overhauls the excretion. Cumulation of the toxin can thereby arise and any manifestations are those of short-term toxicity. There may be a need for maintaining the dosing daily, or continuously, throughout the normal life-span of the selected species and such a study is that of long-term toxicity. In any of these experiments, with a duration beyond the acute stage, the criteria by which reactions are recognized are not confined to death or survival alone, but also include observations on behaviour, measurement of changes in body weight, biochemical and haematological checks at intervals, and post-mortem appearances, both macroscopic and microscopic. The figure usually sought in this context is the highest daily dose that fails to bring about any changes and this is said to represent the maximum no-effect level.

Expressly in these life-span studies a search may be made for any statistically significant difference in the incidence of *tumours, innocent or (in particular) malignant, between the treated and the untreated, control groups. This affords a pointer to carcinogenicity; in other words, the capacity for causing *cancer. In this respect, the histological nature of the *neoplasms seen may add weight to any conclusions.

Further, specially designed investigations may be embarked upon to determine reproductive toxicity, teratogenicity, neurotoxicity, mutagenesis (the tendency to cause *mutations) and so on, as circumstances may dictate.

Finally, an attempt may be made to reveal how the toxin finds its way into the body, how it becomes distributed throughout the organs and tissues, and the manner in which it is excreted. Likewise, the biochemical mechanism of its action and its biochemical fate when it is subjected to the influence of the metabolic *enzymes within the body may need to be unravelled as well. To these aspects the term metabolism (or toxicokinetics) is generally applied.

The enquiries pursued into the phenomena of poisoning as just described constitute the science of *experimental toxicology*. The findings which thus accrue provide a formal basis upon which can be erected the disciplined practice of *clinical toxicology*, *veterinary toxicology*, *occupational and industrial toxicology*, and *environmental toxicology* in its widest sense, including studies of *food additives, pesticides, cosmetics, toiletries, and household products, together with the possible impact of chemicals in all their diversity upon the surroundings in which man must exist and upon the flora and fauna therein. Legislative force may be imposed to control, or curtail, the dangers for which toxic substances might otherwise be responsible and these statutory measures should be framed with due regard to *regulatory toxicology*. Then, as already explained, whenever a knowledge of poisons, scientifically assembled, is directed to the detection of crime, to the apprehension and conviction of felons, and to the judicial settling of civil disputes, one comes into the realm of *forensic toxicology*.

Fundamental to any form or branch of toxicology is the death, injury, or harm for which a poison may be properly blamed. Apart from this one common feature about its curricular content, toxicology has grown or evolved as a concatenation of physics, chemistry, biochemistry, physiology, pharmacology, pathology, medicine, genetics, mathematics, together with a smattering of other subjects alongside. Few, if any, people can claim mastery of knowledge under all of these headings, so toxicologists tend to become subspecialists. Yet there is still a demand for those who can command an informed appreciation over the whole scene, who are capable of viewing events objectively and who nurture a modicum of wisdom to form balanced judgements, without neglecting the risk–benefit considerations. For nothing in life is of unsullied beneficence, or is totally evil. If man is to survive and to progress he must weigh the pros and cons and take what he has decided to be the most desirable course. Even so he will not evade every single adversity. Indeed, it might be argued that toxicology, in the end, is a school of learning which relies primarily on scientific induction but which, in its utilization and the deductive reasoning so employed, cannot afford to neglect the moral and, some might add, the political implications.

Poisoning in practice. Already it has been noted that, so far as Western civilizations are concerned, wilful poisoning with evil intent is apparently uncommon. The possibility of such offences being committed must never be overlooked and it behoves the doctor, not only as a citizen but more so in his professional capacity, ever to be on the alert for this eventuality. In the fairly recent past, for example, thallium has been the instrument both for wanton murder and for killing to serve political ends. *Paraquat, too, has been the resort of the frustrated paramour. Arsenic, meanwhile, has not been forgotten by the criminally inclined, while various drugs have served the purpose of the wilful killers. Almost any substance can be exploited by those bent upon homicide and, being an unfamiliar happening, murder by poisoning can so easily be missed, unless percipient suspicion is always exercised.

An intended fatal outcome to poisoning is not always attained. Then the offence is one of attempted murder. But the original purpose may not have been to kill at all, only to 'injure, aggrieve, or annoy'. This is when less importance may be attached to the intrinsic toxicity of the agent than to the intention behind it.

Coming to notice over recent years has been that variant of child abuse—'baby battering', (or, as it is now called, 'non-accidental injury')—in which poison takes the place of physical trauma. In desperation, or in sheer malice, adults—usually the parents, although sometimes baby-sitters, nurses, or others—may intentionally give noxious agents to youngsters to hurt them, to harm them, or to kill them. A variety of substances has been utilized in this way—sleeping mixtures, oral antidiabetic drugs, and, astonishingly, ordinary table salt or even domestic coal gas. In the absence of an immediate fatal result, poisoning along these lines may become repetitive or habitual. Recovery while in hospital and relapse upon returning home provides a useful clue. It is for the medical and paramedical personnel, together with the social workers, ever to be on the *qui vive* for this state of affairs, the more so where the domestic background is disturbed. Since prima facie a crime is afoot, the police should be informed. Punitive action against the guilty party, however, seldom affords a satisfactory solution. Social support, unremitting surveillance, and care orders may be more rewarding in the long run.

Another form of criminal poisoning that may be encountered is that in which poisoning is attempted in the furtherance of another offence, for example rape or theft. The culprits concerned, it would seem, are rarely possessed of sufficient toxicological knowledge, or have to hand the most appropriate agents, to carry out their plans with any finesse, so that detection and discovery are commonplace.

If it is so that culpable poisoning, for which some explanations have already been given, is, after all, fairly unusual, then what are the other toxic preoccupations of society today? Paradoxically, the bane of civilization at present could well be the passion with which so large a proportion of the population engages in self-poisoning not only, at times, with drug overdoses, but also with excessive exposure to *tobacco, excess ingestion of *alcohol, etc. The age range of those so inclined, while nominally adult, is seen to cover early adolescence right through to senility. Under primitive conditions it must be assumed that life is uncertain anyway, that survival against natural odds is at a premium, and that the endeavours of most of the people are mobilized towards the preservation of life and not to abdication from it. Self-immolation would be pointless. Not so in those territories where the lifestyle is physically much more secure. Then it is that folk are beset by psychological misgivings, by apathy, and by mental depression. A few of them become so desperate that they choose complete escape by suicide. Many more, however, would seem to be possessed of no firm resolve for finality. Instead, a temporary withdrawal, for example via alcohol, or a suicidal 'gesture' with less than a lethal dose of a drug (parasuicide), suggests itself as sufficient relief, or they guess that a gesture of self-sacrifice will attract to them the sympathy, kindness, and support which they so crave—what the psychiatrists have named a 'cry for help'. Whatever may be the personal motives, the figures show that the incidence of self-poisoning today has reached quite disproportionate levels and has risen to an epidemic magnitude. Without question, in the everyday practice of medicine, the poisoned patients whom the doctor is called upon to treat will, with odd exceptions, all come into this category. And what are the agents to which they turn for these toxicological excursions? Not being too conversant with the pharmacological refinements they show a preference for the drugs which, they assume, will have their main action on the brain. These comprise the *hypnotics, the *sedatives, the *tranquillizers, the *antidepressants, and the *analgesics. Another assurance they gain from this selection is that if these medicaments are beneficial in therapeutic doses and only perilous in substantial overdoses, then somewhere in between there must be a quantity that is demonstrably disturbing without being death-dealing. Towards chemicals, agricultural pesticides, and the repertoire of wares about the home and the garage they are more hesitant for, like shooting, hanging, and drowning, the result might well be all-or-none, which is hardly what they desire. *Carbon monoxide, too, is less conveniently to hand and there have been one or two occasions when the would-be suicide has persisted for more than an hour with the head in the natural gas oven and the tap turned on but not alight, with the mortification of discovering that nothing happened at all—apart from an unexpected, calamitous explosion later from attempting to light a cigarette for solace in the gas-rich atmosphere. Those more enlightened, yet none the less single-minded about suicide, are often astute enough to pursue oblivion by running a motor car in a closed garage and settling in a seat to await the end. Indicative, supposedly, of the indecision of the parasuicides is the readiness with which they partake of, not a single drug, but a mélange, topped up with a modicum of alcohol.

This trend in perverse human behaviour with so many of the population indulging in drug overdoses would be all the more devastating if the mortality accompanying it were of a similarly high order. Clearly this is not so and the death rate for those entering hospital in this condition is ultimately little more than about 1 per cent. The majority of these patients are not seriously ill at all, from the physical point of view, and that accords with their idea at the outset not to kill themselves. By the reverse token, as it were, most of the unfortunate characters who actually succumb to self-poisoning are found dead even before medical care can be summoned to their assistance, or before they reach hospital. Having decided to kill themselves they brook no mistakes and withdraw to a place where they are unlikely to be discovered, such as a locked room, where they write a suicide note, and proceed to swallow an enormous overdose that is sure not to fail. Their counterparts, engaged in just a gesture, by contrast confine themselves to a meagre overdose and stage the incident to call attention to themselves, even to the point of exhibitionism.

Between this type of conduct and accidental poisoning a clear distinction should be drawn. Rarely, it must be admitted, do adults poison themselves by mistake, as for instance when they gulp down a noxious fluid, for example a weedkiller, that has been stupidly decanted into a beer bottle, or when sodium chlorate is mistaken for common salt. The more common accident comes about toxicologically when someone is inadvertently exposed to poisonous fumes—as of carbon monoxide from an internal combustion engine thoughtlessly left running in a confined space, or a domestic gas or paraffin (kerosene) hot-water heater or boiler that is improperly installed or badly functioning, so that complete oxygenation to carbon dioxide does not proceed. Misadventure of a toxic nature can also supervene at work. Chronic poisoning from lead and mercury has been recognized for centuries as, for example, in thermometer makers; fumes, as of cadmium from soldering, of hydrogen sulphide in sewers, of arsine from metals, etc. may pose a threat by inhalation; other chemicals may find their way into the body through the skin, as with some agricultural pesticides. A note of reservation might be entered here, however, insofar as the official mortality statistics of accidental poisoning may be quoted. These summaries are collated from the verdicts of *coroners and similar officials, derived from individual cases. In their proceedings, these arbiters commendably lean towards charity so, if the evidence pointing to suicide is not unassailable, it can be a kindness towards the relatives to reach a verdict of accident, in preference to suicide, with all the odium associated therewith.

There exists, still, another burden of poisoning that is classified as accidental and that involves small children. Indeed, child poisoning has for some years now been accorded considerable publicity—not without good reason. Before the age of about one year there is little chance of a youngster suffering from poisoning, apart from an inadvertent or deliberate act on the part of an adult—to which some explanation has already been devoted—and this, fortunately, is uncommon. Thereafter, though, the infant in the course of its development becomes voluntarily mobile. It begins to explore its surroundings and, advancing through what *Freud entitled the '*oral phase', it begins to put things into its mouth—indiscriminately. In this way and with the assistance of parental guidance, it gradually learns what is acceptable and what is not. To deny it this experience would be to stunt its ascent towards maturity. The trouble is that if, perchance, the materials, or objects, that so find their way into the mouth should be swallowed and if, at the same time they should prove toxic, then a calamity may ensue. As this aspect of the modern scene is one that has excited some anxiety it may be worthwhile to examine the relevant facts, so far as they can be assembled. For England and Wales alone, some 20 000 children are taken into hospital each year because they are believed to have been poisoned. A similar state of affairs seems to obtain in other parts of the Western world. Now if regard is paid to the mortality figures it will be noted that, in the same territory of England and Wales, rather less than 200 children per year are certified as dying from poisoning—a frighteningly large total, in all conscience. But on further subdivision it will be seen that about 150 of these deaths are brought about by carbon monoxide, to which, as it transpires, gas heaters, motor car engines, and other domestic services contribute very little. The principal explanation for this mortality is discovered, strangely enough, to lie with fires, explosions, etc., in which the burning and trauma in themselves are not fatal, whereas post-mortem tests reveal that carbon monoxide liberated at the site of the disaster must have proved to be the lethal agent.

The remaining 50 or so child deaths are brought about from swallowing a variety of medicines, chiefly in what are described as 'solid-dose' forms, that is tablets and capsules, these being left carelessly about the home and within reach, not least in the domain of the grandparents. The particular drugs implicated are those most commonly purchased and most widely prescribed. Until recently, *aspirin occupied a prominent position on the list, although it is gratifying to learn that, following the adoption of child-resistant packaging for products embodying this drug, its pre-eminence in this way no longer holds. Moreover, notwithstanding the agitation engendered by what have been alluded to as the fearsome chemicals to be found today in most homes and gardens, careful surveys have demonstrated that very few household products in fact constitute a toxic menace to small children. There may be strong arguments for insisting upon all medicines being stored in locked cupboards or cabinets, and also for having them packed in child-resistant containers of one pattern or another, but to extend these demands to the rest of the aids to housekeeping might well be as impracticable as it would be superfluous. At the same time the comment might be made that the deaths, however inexcusable, are not the whole story. What about the agony surrounding the rest of the 20 000 who, even if they do not succumb, have undeniably had to be taken into hospital care owing to poisoning? Again, scrutiny of the records will disclose that nearly all of these youngsters are discharged on the day immediately following admission; in other words, they stay in just overnight. Further, from the case reports it can be seen that hardly any of them have needed treatment, that the majority of them have exhibited no symptoms and that those symptoms actually experienced have been of no more than minor severity. The influences that conspire to this scenario thus become obvious. Parents who have been the target for the publicity that has converged upon child poisoning are terrified by the prospect and, on the slightest suspicion regarding their own offspring, they rush for medical help. The hospital is their destination. Among the accident and emergency staff and the paediatricians to whom they turn, the counsel of caution rightly prevails. In so far as the history may be disconcerting and the prognosis unpredictable it is obviously more prudent to take the child into the ward, where it can be under professional observation, than to send it back home where it may suddenly and catastrophically relapse. The psychological repercussions, both for the young patient himself and also on a wider scale socially may be debated, while the logistics may be deplored, but pragmatically, after all, the existing arrangements may serve as unquestionably the best way of solving an awkward problem.

From the preventive angle there is no gainsaying that any measure calculated to avoid the primary incident should be encouraged. This is why there has been the widespread advocacy for child-resistant containers. For the medicinal tablets, capsules, and other 'solid-dose' forms, probably the most effective deterrent, albeit the more expensive, is to have them enclosed in strip, or 'bubble' packs, made of strong plastic, or metal foil. These may not be altogether beyond the manipulative faculties of the child to open, but seldom is the endeavour persistent so, at the worst, no more than a few items are released. Toxic doses consequently are not readily to hand. Alternatively, there are the specially designed, multi-dose, reclosable containers, fashioned so as to thwart the simple-minded child but still falling within the capabilities of the knowing adult. This principle, however, can be defended only so long as the top is always meticulously replaced each time after use—a habit that cannot invariably be guaranteed. Then there are the objections of the older people, not least the grandparents who are enjoying poly-pharmaceutical domiciliary medication, that with their *arthritis and other disabilities these ingenious containers are quite beyond their capacity to open anyway.

Poisoning, through ignorance or carelessness, that is to say accidentally, can befall workers whilst engaged on their rightful duties. This is occupational poisoning (see OCCUPATIONAL MEDICINE). In the acute form this is seen chiefly when toxic fumes or gases are allowed to escape and/or the appropriate respiratory protection is not being worn. Mention has been made previously about cyanides, cadmium fumes, arsine, and hydrogen sulphide in this context. More insidiously, long-term exposure, which may be intensified by poor hygiene in the workplace, may not be recognized by its immediate or acute effects, but only by those that are delayed, when they may be the result of cumulation. There is, in addition, the chance that after a symptomless latent period cancer may emerge. Particular chemicals have been inculpated in this respect, including *benzpyrene, β-naphthylamine, asbestos (see ASBESTOSIS), and *vinyl chloride monomer, among others. As it happens, the confirmed chemical human carcinogens are relatively few in number. What is so demoralizing about them, however, is the realization that they cannot be so indicted until there has already been a series of human casualties and tragedies —what has been reprovingly referred to as 'counting the bodies'. For this reason it has become commonplace now to subject more and more chemicals to experimental carcinogenicity testing in animals, giving priority to the newer compounds for which there is no previous 'track record' occupationally. Whether the findings derived from such studies are altogether dependable for the sake of prediction is arguable. Do the laboratory mouse and rat constitute sound experimental analogues for man? The mouse, as a species, is regarded by some experts as being inclined to respond abnormally to carcinogens. Further, what is sometimes overlooked by the uninitiated is that normal untreated animals are disposed to spontaneous cancers, the more so towards the end of their life span. So a positive, or negative, conclusion can be arrived at only by calculating the significance of the difference in incidence between the treated and the untreated control groups. Hardly ever is there a clear-cut yes-or-no answer. Dosage is another complication. The large quantities of test chemicals forced upon the passive animals in the cage, besides being disproportionately high in relation to what the human exposure may be, can be so toxic generally and so upsetting that any predisposition to cancerous changes may be non-specifically enhanced. This being so, it could be contended that, with all these vagaries, the warnings from the animal experiments could be overheeded to the point of excessive caution. Courage and resolution are nevertheless demanded to put aside what may be no more, in the end, than false alarms. For years men, especially those on the staff of some laboratories, have worked with and in an atmosphere of formaldehyde. Epidemiologically there is no suggestion that thereby they are a greater prey to cancer. Yet many of them have become fearful of this prospect since animals kept continuously in a high atmospheric concentration of this vapour have been demonstrably prone to nasopharyngeal carcinomata. Similarly, women who have opted to have their hair dyed about once a month by the application of colouring agents to the scalp are, together with their hairdressers, being warned that cancer may overtake them from what is to be regarded simply as capitulation to vanity, because mice fed daily on large amounts of these same dyes are found to exhibit more cancers. The reason for quoting these two examples is to emphasize that, for the sake of protecting workers occupationally from all the conceivable carcinogenic dangers from the chemicals that they may be called upon to handle, the decision calls for careful circumspection.

Departing from malignancy but remaining, as might be said, within the factory precincts, the distress can be recalled of the men first employed in the manufacture of synthetic female hormones (*oestrogens). They were not at all delighted to find their breasts enlarging to the contours of their womenfolk, nor were they appeased when they took on many other signs of feminization. Currently causing some unease, too, are the indications that women doctors practising as anaesthetists may experience a greater risk of abortions, presumably from the anaesthetic agents with which they work. There is no limit to the multiplicity of adverse effects toxicologically that might be provoked by the various compounds and materials with which workers must deal occupationally. The fears, moreover, are reinforced by the knowledge that some serious diseases and disabilities have been brought about in this way. Today, more than ever, the specialty of occupational medicine and, within that, of occupational toxicology, is a demanding one from all sides. In the present age, moreover, when medical treatment is founded so largely upon drugs, there has emerged a disturbing awareness of what has been designated, somewhat inaptly, as *iatrogenic disease, which may be more descriptively entitled therapeutic poisoning. This encompasses all the adverse reactions that may beset patients from what is ostensibly the proper prescribing of drugs in medical care, distinguishing this from deliberate overdose. These misadventures can be traced to various origins. Thus there may be errors in the formulation or dispensing of the medicines—that is to say, at the pharmaceutical stage, so that the patient is unwittingly given, and takes, a noxious preparation. A memorable event of this kind came to light about 40 years ago in the USA when a sulphanilamide intended as an anti-infective agent was concocted as an aqueous solution containing ethylene glycol. Out of 353 people who took this mixture, no fewer than 105 died. In a similar category, though not so much medicinally, was the so-called 'ginger jake paralysis', again in the USA, brought about by the casual contamination of ginger extract by neurotoxic cresyl phosphates during manufacture. With the more insistent supervision and quality control that now obtains, both by the producers themselves and at the instance of authority, incidents of this type have fortunately become rare. Then there are what have been described as *idiosyncratic reactions, which are more peculiar to the individual than to the product. Thus some people promptly exhibit the symptoms of *salicylate poisoning even when they have swallowed no more than two tablets (i.e. the recommended dose) of aspirin. Others suffer the distress of 'cinchonism' from the small amount of *quinine in commercial brands of tonic water. Of graver import are the serious disorders of the *bone marrow leading to intractable *anaemia and death which may overtake a few people who are given *chloramphenicol, prescribed as an *antibiotic. The relatively new antidepressant drug, mianserin, may be similarly incriminated. Again *clioquinol, which became a popular remedy for the relief of diarrhoea, was found in Japan to be associated with the distressing condition of *subacute myelo-optic atrophy.

Another phenomenon to be considered under this heading is the cumulation which may ensue from the injudicious administration of some drugs over a period of time, so that their effects are intensified. Classically, *bromides may behave in this way when taken over weeks, or months, as a sedative. Likewise *phenytoin, an accepted agent for the control of *epilepsy, may be harmless enough at certain doses, whereas a slight increase in the amount taken may overwhelm the resources of the body to dispose of it and the consequences are then calamitous.

Overall, it must be borne in mind that virtually no drug is truly specific. Accompanying the principal effect on the body for which it is designed are others as well. *Morphine, besides being an analgesic and a hypnotic, for which purposes it may be excellent, is also constipating, emetic, depressant to the respiration, and addictive—features that are far less desirable. The doctor, when prescribing, must bear the possible side-effects in mind, must decide on his course of action by, as it were, a risk–benefit evaluation and advise the patient accordingly. So while all these complications of medicinal treatment may not apparently conform to the popularly accepted ideas of poisoning, there is no denying that they so qualify by definition, being noxious agents having access to the living body and setting up troublesome responses.

Setting aside veterinary toxicology, still to be noted is environmental toxicology, an all-embracing subject that bids fair to take all the other toxicological specialties under its wing (see ENVIRONMENT AND DISEASE). In the natural order of things, natural surroundings have not been free from deleterious agents. In some parts of the world, notably certain areas of the Andes mountains in South America, arsenic is present at such levels in the soil and in the water that the human population living therein is the subject of chronic arsenicalism to a tragic degree. Similarly in, for example, the Madras region of India, the natural fluoride intake directly from the water is so high as to bring about endemic *fluorosis in the teeth and skeleton. *Cassava root, favoured in the diet of some countries, may contain cyanide that causes tropical ataxic *neuropathy among those who eat it. Elsewhere the fungal contamination of food crops, as of *aflatoxin on groundnuts, may be the reason for cancer in the consumers. In some caves and underground workings, toxic vapours and gases may lurk. What, however, has fostered so much apprehension during this latter half of the 20th c. has been the burgeoning of industry and, more crucially, the vast growth of the synthetic chemical industry, with the creation and distribution of legions of entirely novel compounds and their entry, by one route or another, into the environment as a whole. Spectacular in this manner were the organochlorine insecticides—DDT, aldrin, dieldrin, endrin, etc. These were all very stable compounds, both chemically and biologically, and hence they were very persistent. Applied to plants, they were taken up by animals and so, via the food chain, they came to be concentrated in the raptorial species, interfering with reproduction and leading to death. With their wide dispersion throughout the globe these chemicals were recovered, albeit in minute traces, in creatures such as penguins far away in the Antarctic. Meanwhile it became apparent that very few members of the human population anywhere could boast a complete absence of organo-chlorines from their body fat.

A factory effluent, finding its way into the sea at Minamata Bay in Japan, led to the assimilation of mercury, first by the marine plankton and thence into fish. The inhabitants of the bay, subsisting largely on a fish diet, then became the subjects of an epidemic of serious organo-mercury poisoning (*Minamata disease). Other disquieting outbreaks of this kind have come to notice.

An epidemic of a crippling neuropathy in Morocco was traced to the contamination of what was thought to be edible oil with *tri-ortho-cresyl phosphate, while the toxic pathogenesis of what has been called the 'toxic oil syndrome' in Spain, which made its appearance in 1981, killing over three hundred people and maiming thousands of others, has still not been elucidated. Adequate control to circumvent these calamities is a daunting task, the more so unless the clock is to be turned back and humanity throughout the world reverts to a primitive livelihood. Toxicologically, the whole issue is a challenge, for the mere presence of an alien substance must not be equated automatically with its toxicity. Selenium, for example, may be an element essential to life in small amounts, whereas it is poisonous in excess. The analysts, with their refined equipment and techniques, can nowadays detect and measure substances in the most miniscule concentrations. Toxicology, as pointed out earlier, is pledged to the operation of a dose–response relationship and this must be judicially respected throughout. Deplorably, environmental toxicology finds itself embroiled with politics, so that creeds have a facility for ousting objectivity and reasoning. A polarization has emerged, with the 'defenceless, suffering individual' on the one side and 'the might of the multinational industrial corporations' on the other. This is, indeed, a pabulum on which the sensation-seeking media thrive.

Poisoning clinically—diagnosis and treatment. Wide-ranging though the toxicological controversy may be on a political and social plane, to the practising doctor poisoning normally implies the necessity to treat an acutely ill patient who usually is suffering from a self-administered overdose of drugs or, on occasion, of some other harmful agent. There is then no time to philosophize: the *Hippocratic obligations dictate that the case of the sick person is a priority, as for any medical emergency, putting aside any reluctance that might be engendered because this is, perhaps, the fifteenth time that the person concerned has wilfully taken an overdose.

Contrary to popular belief, the physician in this situation has at his command no comprehensive battery of *antidotes. The place for these is, indeed, very limited, but wherever specific agents do exist—as with *oxygen for carbon monoxide poisoning, naloxone for *opiates, cobalt edetate for *cyanide, methionine for *paracetamol, desferrioxamine for iron salts, etc., these must be mobilized immediately if they are to be effective. Otherwise, the management of the poisoned patient is non-specific and follows the same lines as that for any other medical emergency. No time should be wasted on arriving at a precise diagnosis at the outset, or in dallying to identify the causal agent. Instead, attention is concentrated on maintaining adequate breathing, on taking measures to overcome cardiovascular 'shock' in which the heart's action fails to maintain a sufficient head of *blood pressure in the peripheral arteries, on ensuring that the kidneys function properly and that there is no dearth or surfeit of fluids in the body, on guarding against infection, and generally taking proper care of the subject, especially if he (or she) is comatose. These same principles inform the treatment regimen throughout, whether it be at the stage of first aid, hospital ward care, or that of the intensive therapy unit.

Only in a minority of cases is it helpful to mobilize the resources of the chemical toxicology laboratory for analyses to detect and measure the poison in the blood, urine, etc. Nor should it be routine to endeavour actively to remove the offending agent from the body. The stomach may be emptied by inducing vomiting, or by what is termed 'gastric aspiration and lavage' (in other words, the '*stomach pump'), but such manoeuvres should be decided upon individually and with discrimination, for they may be unnecessary, or even positively contraindicated and dangerous. Other techniques aimed at accelerating the elimination of the toxin, once it has been absorbed by the body and has found its way into the tissues, as by purposefully augmenting the urine flow (forced diuresis), or by means of the artificial kidney (haemodialysis), or by haemoperfusion have only a limited application in carefully defined circumstances.

Clinical experience and critical assessment now, over many years, have demonstrated that with these schemes of management, based primarily on conservative or supportive measures directed at safeguarding the vital processes of the body, the outcome for the poisoned patient is more favourable and less beset by complications than can ever be achieved by more energetic intervention or esoteric procedures.

Where noxious substances are inhaled, instead of being taken orally or injected, the therapeutic approach must be modified. To begin with, further exposure must be curtailed by moving the victim from the contaminated atmosphere, taking care that in this operation the rescuers are not overcome as well. Thereafter, respiration must be maintained, oxygen being added if there is cyanosis. Some harmful gases are essentially irritant and therefore inflame the airways, with fluid then exuding into the air spaces; breathing becomes laboured and wheezy and insufficient air may be inhaled. The tissues are thereby denied their supply of oxygen and the skin and mucosae take on the bluish tinge of *cyanosis. The patient must then be coupled to a mechanical *respirator adjusted to function with what is called 'positive, end-expiratory pressure' ('PEEP'). Corticosteroid drugs are frequently prescribed as an adjunct, although their advantages are not dramatic.

Other gases may pass via the lungs to the tissues of the body, without necessarily irritating the air passages *en route*. Carbon monoxide behaves thus and so does arsine. The task then is to deal with the systemic intoxication, furnishing general support meanwhile and not neglecting the respiration.

The laboratory. As already explained, analytical toxicology owes its origins to forensic medicine. In this context its findings had to be accurate, reliable, and beyond reproach. Seldom do the legal determinations advance at a frantic rate and, accordingly, there was no pressure upon the forensic laboratories promptly to produce the answers. The demands made in hospital, on the other hand, are much more insistent, with patients' lives at stake. In some measure, precision and exactness can yield to urgency, for decisions on patient care cannot be deferred indefinitely. The laboratory service, moreover, must be on call throughout the 24 hours, for poisoning is no respecter of defined working hours. Logistically to organize and maintain hospital laboratory facilities to meet all the

clinical needs has proved to be almost impracticable. The compromise has been to set up one or two major centres, highly equipped and expertly staffed. Because of the distances so projected, special provision has to be made to transport the specimens expeditiously while, in the reverse direction, the results can be telephoned forthwith. It must be appreciated that this is a very specialized organization, expensive to capitalize and costly to run, and should be called upon not as a routine but exclusively when patient care would be embarrassed without guidance from the laboratory and also, possibly, when there may be forensic implications.

Poisons information. There are today in circulation a vast range of chemicals, drugs, pesticides, household products and so on, many of which are potentially toxic. New ones are constantly appearing; commonly they are labelled with uninformative trade names and their toxicity may be obscure. Textual sources of enlightenment being lacking, the policy in many countries has been to organize Poisons Information, or Poisons Control Centres. These must operate day and night throughout the year. They may be staffed by doctors, or by paramedical personnel. Some will handle enquiries only from members of the medical profession; others cater to the public at large. In each centre a comprehensive and up-to-date index is compiled, listing all the products on the market (so far as is known), their composition, their toxicity, the symptoms to which they might give rise, and an outline of treatment. These centres accept no professional responsibility for the care of individual patients, but they can offer guidance to whoever on the spot directly has a duty of care.

Statutory control. Clearly, poisons have an enormous potential for human depredation. Virtually all nations have introduced laws and statutes in order to control the supply and distribution of substances which are poisonous to man. The examples given here relate to mechanisms of legal control now in force in the UK. In an ethically conscious society people must be protected not only against the wilful acts of those resolved upon injuring, or killing, their fellows, but also against the accidental poisoning of the entire population, or of specific groups, or of individuals, therein, because of their occupations, their location, their habits, or the environment more generally. Progressively, over little more than the last hundred years, governments in most countries have introduced legislation to counter any foreseen toxic dangers that may arise. Whereas the controls so enacted vary in detail from one administration to another, the pattern they all follow is much the same, as are their objectives which may be illustrated by reference to the major legal measures that are operative in the UK.

To regulate the sale, supply, distribution, storage, labelling, etc. of toxic substances the *Poisons Act 1972 applies to those which are expressly scheduled thereunder, the selection of these items being devolved upon a representative body of experts constituted under the Act and known collectively as the Poisons Board. The Secretary of State, when putting proposals before Parliament, must pay heed to the recommendations of this Board, which he can reject only by an acceptable explanation to the House.

Under the Food and Drugs Act 1972, regulations are made by the Minister of Agriculture, Fisheries and Food, again subject to Parliament, stipulating *inter alia* the nature and sometimes the maximum quantity of what are called deliberate food additives—preservatives, antioxidants, colouring agents, etc.—that are officially approved for use in the diet. In so doing he is again advised by an independent committee of experts. Furthermore, as a general principle under this Act, food and foodstuffs offered for sale must be fit for human consumption and must not be injurious to health.

Drugs to be regarded in the category of human medicines (and also, as it happens, veterinary medicines as well), whether available solely on prescription or on unrestricted sale to the public, and then either by way only of pharmacists, or more widely through retail outlets, come under the purview of the *Medicines Act 1968. The statutory body advising the Secretary of State for Health and Social Security is then the *Medicines Commission with, answering thereto, an expert *Committee on the Safety of Medicines and another on the Review of Medicines. By these means, exacting obligations are imposed for the pre-marketing testing of drugs, for their *clinical trials, and for the subsequent monitoring of adverse reactions.

For those particular drugs which are addictive, for example, morphine, heroin, cannabis, etc., and which may be exploited on this account, the control is much more rigid and this is exercised under the *Misuse of Drugs Act 1971.

To provide for the safety of workers in relation to their exposure occupationally to toxic materials and, further, to offset the hazards that may befall other members of the population who may be affected incidentally by the toxic effects of industrial and agricultural operations, the *Health and Safety at Work, etc. Act 1974 is on the statute book. Various orders have been made under this heading, not least the Health and Safety (Agriculture) (Poisonous Substances) Regulations 1975, which gives the force of law to the precautions that must be observed for the safe handling of certain designated pesticides, these being singled out on account of their being more harmful occupationally. Otherwise, in the UK the proper handling of these chemicals so as not to imperil the user, the consumer as regards food residues, and the environment as a whole, is effected under the Pesticides Safety Precautions Scheme which has been conducted jointly between government and industry by voluntary agreement. This lays down vigorous demands for pre-marketing testing and unequivocal recommendations for safe usage, as well as continuing surveillance thereafter under commercial conditions. Elsewhere in the world these arrangements have been largely subject to legal dictates, and it is only recently that statutory authority has been given to what have hitherto been voluntary provisions in the UK.

Attention is also directed authoritatively to the consequences of releasing poisonous substances into the air, on to land, or into rivers, with the corresponding risks thereby to inhabitants and other fauna that may come into contact with such discharges. Wanton disposal in this way comes within the terms of the Deposit of Poisonous Waste Act 1972 and the Regulations framed within its enabling clauses. Similar controls formally obtain in many other countries.

Just as the ordinances already cited here in relation to British policy by no means constitute an exhaustive list, so no details have been given regarding the statutory framework in other lands, where the systems may be even more elaborate. Mention should nevertheless be made that the British Consumer Protection Act 1961 is designed to afford protection to the UK population as a whole against the dangers of many goods and services, and similar controls exist in many other countries. What is more, it is in this, as in other such spheres of influence, that international bodies, for example the European Economic Community and the OECD, together with the United Nations through its Environment Programme, the Food and Agriculture Organization, the *World Health Organization, and the International Labour Organization, have become very active in their efforts to mitigate damage from poisoning in its widest sense.

Clearly, there is almost no limit to the restrictions that can be imposed authoritatively to curb or prevent toxic excesses. The extent and manner of so doing, however, is often more at the behest of political pressures than the result of careful scientific and medical evaluation. Regard, it seems, must be paid not only to what experts might decree but also to what the 'man in the street' may feel. No doubt that is why in the UK, while a Royal Commission on Environmental Pollution may pontificate, Parliament must in the end decide. The science of toxicology, too, has its limitations. It is far more competent at curtailing recognized poisoning, or preventing the resurgence of that type of poisoning that has been encountered previously, than ever it is at predicting those novel toxic manifestations that have hitherto never been contemplated. Both the Minamata disaster with mercury in Japan and the toxic oil syndrome that assailed Spain in 1981 exemplify these inadequacies.   R. GOULDING

Further reading

Finkel, A. J. (1982). *Hamilton and Hardy's Industrial Toxicology*. 4th edn, Boston.

Fletcher, W. W. (1974). *The Pest War*. Oxford.

Goulding, R. (1967). One man's meat. *Journal of the Royal College of Surgeons of Ireland*, **3**, 13–23.

Goulding, R. (1984). *Poisoning*. Oxford.

Joull, J., Klaasen, C. D. and Amdur, M. O. (eds) (1980). *Casarett and Doull's Toxicology*. 2nd edn, New York.

Loomis, T. A. (1968). *Essentials of Toxicology*. London.

Matthew, H. and Lawson, A. A. H. (1979). *Treatment of Common Acute Poisonings*. 4th edn, Edinburgh.

Smith, S. (1952). Poisons and poisoners through the ages. *Medico-Legal Journal*, **20**, 153–67.

Vale, J. A. and Meredith, T. J. (eds) (1981). *Poisoning: Diagnosis and Treatment*. London.

POISONOUS FRUITS. See POISONOUS PLANTS.

POISONOUS FUNGI. The ingestion of poisonous fungi is uncommon, but can be deadly dangerous. Most non-edible fungi are merely either unpleasant or uninteresting but are non-toxic or only mildly so. The highly poisonous species are all gill fungi, the commonest (to which about 90 per cent of deaths are attributable) being *Amanita phalloides* (Death Cap), of which one cap may be fatal. Other closely related but much rarer species are *Amanita virosa* (Destroying Angel) and *Amanita verna* (Fool's Mushroom). *Amanita pantherina* (Panther Cap) can cause severe *atropine poisoning, but fatalities are rare. The same applies to the attractive-looking fairy-tale mushroom *Amanita muscaria* (Fly Agaric), which also contains *muscarine. Other species (e.g. *Russula emetica*, some *Gyromitra* spp.) contain thermolabile toxins and are consumed by some after cooking. *Coprinus atramentarius* contains *disulfiram (Antabuse®) and thus causes symptoms of poisoning when ingested with alcoholic drinks.

It must of course always be borne in mind that any species of fungus, including the familiar cultivated and wild mushrooms, may be responsible for food *allergy in susceptible individuals.

POISONOUS PLANTS. Poisoning by plants is uncommon, occurring most often in children. Nevertheless, a large number of plants contain poisonous compounds in their roots, leaves, flowers, seeds, or fruit and may under certain circumstances, for example when used in 'bush tea' infusions, cause toxic syndromes. A comprehensive list is not possible, but they include: the Solanaceae, many of which contain mixtures of alkaloids such as *atropine, *hyoscyamine, *scopolamine, and *nicotine, examples being *Atropa belladonna* (Deadly Nightshade), *Solanum dulcamara* (Woody Nightshade or Bittersweet), *Hyoscyamus niger* (Henbane), *Datura stramonium* (Thorn Apple), *Nicotiana tabacum* (Tobacco), *Capsicum* spp. (e.g. Tabasco), *Scopolia* spp; *Cytisus laburnum* (Laburnum), which contains the neurotoxic alkaloid cytisine, also found in broom and lupin seeds; *Conium maculatum* (Hemlock), which contains coniine, also neurotoxic; *Cicuta virosa* (Water Hemlock or Cowbane), which has caused fatalities by virtue of its highly poisonous cicutoxin; *Oenanthe crocata* (Water Dropwort), which has a similar toxin; *Aconitum napellus* (Monkshood), which contains aconite; *Colchicum*

spp. (Autumn Crocus or Meadow Saffron), which contain *colchicine; *Digitalis purpurea* (Foxglove) and *Nerium oleander* (Oleander), which contain *cardiac glycosides; *Cannabis sativa* (Hemp, Marijuana, etc.), which contains *tetrahydrocannabinol and related compounds; *Senecio longilobus* (Ragwort), once used as an emmenogogue, and *Crotalaria* spp., infusions of which cause hepatic veno-occlusive disease; *Bighia sapida* (Ackee), the unripe fruit of which contains hypoglycine, the causative toxin of Jamaican vomiting sickness; *Lathyrus* spp. (sweet peas) which cause spastic paraplegia (see LATHYRISM); *Argemone mexicana* (Mexican Poppy), a contaminant of mustard oil, which contains sanguinarine and interferes with carbohydrate metabolism causing an 'epidemic dropsy' syndrome resembling acute wet *beriberi; and very many others including the familiar medicinal plants rhubarb, cascara, and senna.

POISONS. See POISONING.

POISONS ACT 1972. This UK Act consolidated the provisions of the *Pharmacy and Poisons Act 1933, in particular those concerning the Poisons Board, 'Poisons' List, and Poisons Rules. Provision was made for amending orders to the List and Rules. Local authorities were required to keep a register of persons entitled to sell non-medicinal poisons, and requirements for such persons were detailed.

POISONS BOARD. A body established under the provisions of the *Pharmacy and Poisons Act 1933. Section 17 of that Act gave the Board authority to draw up a Poisons List classifying substances according to medicinal and non-medicinal use.

POISSON, SIMÉON DENIS (1781–1840). French mathematician. Poisson started medicine but failed to complete his studies. In 1806 he became professor of mathematics at the École Polytechnique in Paris, then moved to astronomy, and finally to pure mechanics in the new Faculté des Sciences in 1809. For medicine his important contribution was the Poisson distribution, still much used in *statistics and *epidemiology.

POLARIZATION. For polarization of nerve and muscle cells, see DEPOLARIZATION. Polarization of light signifies the restriction to one plane of the vibrations of light waves.

POLIOMYELITIS is an acute *virus infection, also known as infantile paralysis, with a world-wide distribution confined to primates. Spread is from person to person, the portal of entry being the gastrointestinal tract. In the vast majority of instances, infection produces either no symptoms at all or only those of an influenza-like illness or febrile digestive upset. A proportion of patients, however, manifest signs of *meningitis and a proportion of these develop the motor paralysis which was the much feared complication of the epidemic disease in communities with good sanitation (and hence a low level of naturally acquired immunity) before the advent of active *immunization programmes. The prevention of paralytic poliomyelitis, with its acute dangers and its frequent legacy of crippling disability, is one of the triumphs of public health and community medicine. In countries which have been able to maintain vaccination campaigns, the disease has been virtually eliminated. See MICROBIOLOGY; INFECTIOUS DISEASES; EPIDEMIOLOGY.

POLIOVIRUS, of which there are three serotypes, is a small non-enveloped RNA virus belonging to the *enterovirus genus. It is the causative agent of *poliomyelitis.

POLITZER, ADAM (1835–1920). Hungarian physician and otologist. Politzer occupied the chair of otology in Vienna. He made contributions to all branches of otology, and lectured fluently in German, French, Italian, and English. He described the cone of light seen in the normal eardrum, and the hearing, on swallowing, of a tuning fork placed centrally on the forehead in only the normal ear. Still in use is his bag used for inflating the middle ear through the *Eustachian tube. See also OTOLARYNGOLOGY.

POLITZERIZATION is the inflation of the middle ear using a soft rubber bag (Politzer bag).

POLLEN is formed of the microspores of seed plants (Gymnospermae and Angiospermae) containing male gametophytes, carried by wind or insects to ovules or stigmas for germination. Many pollens are potent allergens. See ALLERGY.

POLLUTION. Man has always tended to defile the natural environment in which he has evolved, and the rapid progress of science and technology during the 20th c. has brought new assaults on the human ecosystem: examples are radioactive fallout from nuclear weapon testing; river pollution from industrial waste; lead pollution of the atmosphere by the internal combustion engine; persistent contamination of the environment by chlorinated hydrocarbon insecticides such as DDT; noise pollution by jet aircraft; sea and coastal pollution by fuel oil leakage; and very many others. Nearly all are of medical importance.

POLYA, EUGENE JENO ALEXANDER (1876–1944). Hungarian surgeon, MD Budapest (1898). Working as a surgeon in Budapest, Polya was awarded the title of professor of surgery in 1914. In addition to valuable experimental work on *pancreatic *necrosis he devised an operation for *gastrectomy with implantation of the gastric remnant end-to-side into the *jejunum (Polya's operation).

POLYANDRY. Multiple husbands. See POLYGAMY.

POLYARTERITIS is multiple inflammation of arteries. Polyarteritis nodosa (also known as periarteritis nodosa and Kussmaul's disease) is an uncommon but serious disorder of uncertain aetiology in which focal and inflammatory lesions occur in small- and medium-sized arteries throughout the body. It is one of the collagen or connective tissue diseases believed to be due to an autoimmune process. See RHEUMATOLOGY.

POLYARTHRITIS is *arthritis involving a number of joints simultaneously.

POLYARTHROPATHY is any pathological condition affecting more than one joint.

POLYCYSTIC DISEASE is an inherited condition, in which the kidneys show multiple cyst formation with or without similar changes in the liver. There are two forms, which appear to be distinct entities. Childhood polycystic kidney disease (PKD) is relatively rare, and the pattern of inheritance is that of an autosomal *recessive characteristic. Death occurs in childhood or adolescence, from renal failure in younger children, but in adolescents more often from the liver lesions which lead to portal hypertension and liver failure. Adult PKD, on the other hand, is fairly common, accounting for about 5 per cent of all patients treated in *renal dialysis and transplantation units. It is inherited as an autosomal *dominant trait, and since the condition does not become manifest until well into adult life, after the reproductive period, its transmission is assured. The clinical manifestations include pain and swelling in the loins, *haematuria, urinary infections, renal *calculi, *hypertension, and eventually renal failure. In some families, these features may not develop until old age, though the pathogenetic mechanism of this late development is obscure. Genetic counselling must be directed at the children of patients, who have a one in two chance of transmitting the genetic defect to their own offspring and of subsequently becoming affected themselves.

POLYCYTHAEMIA is an increase above normal in the total circulating *red blood cell mass. In many cases, the increase is an adaptive reaction to prolonged shortage of oxygen, as for instance in those who live at high altitudes and in heavy smokers; a similar reaction occurs in various forms of chronic heart and lung disease, and in those patients with congenitally abnormal types of *haemoglobin. Polycythaemia vera is the name applied to a condition in which an increase in red cell mass appears to be primary and purposeless, analogous to the increase in white blood cells that characterizes *leukaemia.

POLYCYTHAEMIA VERA is primary *polycythaemia, also known as polycythaemia rubra vera, erythraemia, and Vaquez–Osler disease.

POLYDACTYLY is a congenital anomaly associated with supernumerary fingers and/or toes.

POLYGAMY is the practice of having more than one spouse concurrently, subdivided into polyandry (several husbands) and polygyny (several wives). Where polygamy is customary it can sometimes be seen to have had some biological, if not ethical, justification.

POLYGENIC describes an inherited characteristic which is controlled by a number of genes, each with a small but additive effect. See GENETICS.

POLYGRAPH. An instrument for simultaneously recording a number of physiological variables, such as arterial pulse and pressure, central venous pulse, respiratory rate, skin conductivity, etc. Polygraphs intended to reveal the physiological concomitants of anxiety and emotion are known as lie-detectors.

POLYMORPH is an abbreviation for polymorphonuclear *leucocyte (neutrophil *granulocyte).

POLYMORPHISM is the occurrence within a species of widely different inherited forms, the rarest of them too common to be maintained by recurrent mutation. See GENETICS.

POLYMYALGIA is pain in several muscles simultaneously. Polymyalgia rheumatica is a specific syndrome of later life associated with pain in the muscles of the limb girdles and generalized muscle stiffness after brief periods of immobility.

POLYMYOSITIS. See DERMATOMYOSITIS; NEUROMUSCULAR DISEASE.

POLYNEURITIS is inflammation of many nerves simultaneously. In practice, it is synonymous with polyneuropathy. See NEUROMUSCULAR DISEASE.

POLYNEUROPATHY. See NEUROMUSCULAR DISEASE.

POLYOMA VIRUS is a tumour-producing virus of the *papovavirus group, endemic in mice.

POLYP. A protrusion of *mucous membrane occurring in the nose and elsewhere.

POLYPEPTIDE. A *peptide containing a number of *amino acid residues.

POLYPHARMACY is a deprecatory term for the simultaneous prescription of a number of medicines.

POLYPOSIS is the occurrence of multiple *polyps,

particularly a genetically determined disorder (polyposis coli) in which multiple adenomatous polyps develop in the *colon and become malignant unless surgically removed.

POLYSACCHARIDE. Any of a large class of naturally occurring complex *carbohydrates whose molecules are derived from the condensation of four or more simple *sugar molecules (monosaccharides). *Starch, *glycogen, and *cellulose are polysaccharides; so are the components of dietary *fibre.

POLYUNSATURATED FATS are *fats containing *fatty acids in which there is more than one double bond between carbon atoms, at which addition can occur. The best dietary sources of polyunsaturated fatty acids are vegetable oils, such as those derived from sesame, soya, sunflower, and corn (maize). The prevailing view that it is desirable to increase the ratio of polyunsaturated fat to saturated (i.e. no double bonds) fat in the human diet is based on evidence that a high intake of saturated fat is associated with a high plasma *cholesterol level, increased blood coagulation indices, and increased morbidity and mortality from the effects of *atherosclerosis, particularly *coronary heart disease. Polyunsaturated fatty acids, on the other hand, have been shown to lower total plasma cholesterol and reduce blood clotting indices.

POMPHOLYX is a recurrent *eczematous condition characterized by small *vesicles on the palms and soles.

PONS. That part of the brainstem which connects the *mid-brain above with the *medulla oblongata below and lies in front of the *cerebellum.

POOR LAW COMMISSION. A body established by the Poor Law Amendment Act 1834 to administer the provisions of that enactment. The Commission had been proposed by Edwin *Chadwick; it had three members, and Chadwick himself was appointed secretary. It remained in existence until the creation of the Poor Law Board in 1847. The powers of the latter were in turn transferred to the *Local Government Board in 1871.

POOR LAWS. A series of enactments which spanned more than 500 years and which provided increasingly comprehensive official arrangements for the relief of poverty, the roots of the present-day social security system of the UK. The Poor Law Act 1388 was passed in the wake of the *Black Death (the pandemic of plague of 1346–50) and was essentially a law against vagrancy, designed to restrict the mobility of labour. Among many later pieces of legislation, two landmarks were the Poor Law Act of 1601, the famous '43rd of Elizabeth', and the great Poor Law Amendment Act 1834, which set the framework of social welfare in the UK for the next 100 years. The poor laws effectively came to an end in 1929 when the Local Government Act disbanded the Poor Law Unions and the *Boards of Guardians (which had administered the workhouses), establishing Public Assistance Committees in their place; local authorities were enabled to take over the poor law infirmaries as municipal hospitals. See also GOVERNMENT AND MEDICINE IN THE UK.

POPPY. Any plant of the genus *Papaver* (which includes the *opium poppy *P.somniferum*) or of the related genera *Meconopsis* and *Glaucium*.

POPULATION. All the inhabitants of a given country or area considered together, or; the number of such inhabitants; more generally, the whole collection of units from which a sample may be drawn. See STATISTICS; EPIDEMIOLOGY.

PORNOGRAPHY was originally the description of the lives and practices of prostitutes. Pornography now has a wider meaning which may be defined as the depicting (verbally or visually) of events calculated to arouse sexual excitement in the reader, listener, or beholder. Pornography flourishes in most modern societies in one form or another, often illegally, but opinion on such matters as its harmfulness or value remains widely polarized.

PORPHYRIA is the term for any condition in which there is excessive production and excretion of porphyrins or their precursors, porphyrins being intermediate compounds formed in the process of synthesis of the principal (in man) respiratory pigment *haem. The biochemistry of the various types of porphyria is complex; most are *inborn errors of metabolism, that is they are due to inherited enzyme deficiencies, though some are acquired due to the ingestion of toxic substances. They are usually classified into erythropoietic and hepatic types, according to whether the main site of abnormal porphyrin production is the *bone marrow or the *liver. The clinical manifestations of the porphyrias are various and diverse; they include cutaneous *photosensitivity and other skin disorders, attacks of acute abdominal pain, and neuropsychiatric abnormalities. The urine may be reddish orange or brown, or may blacken visibly while standing in the light.

PORPHYRINS are a class of naturally occurring pigments derived from pyrrole. They are the basis of respiratory pigments in plants and animals, including *chlorophyll (in which the porphyrin molecule is linked to a magnesium atom) and the *haem of *haemoglobin (where the link is to *iron). See also PORPHYRIA.

PORTAL HYPERTENSION is elevation of pressure in the portal vein, due to obstruction to flow in the small tributaries of the vein within the liver, for example as a result of hepatic *cirrhosis. Among the consequences of portal hypertension are *ascites, *splenomegaly, and varicose dilatation of the venous anastomoses at the junction of the *oesophagus and *stomach, which may lead to severe haemorrhage.

PORTAL VEIN. A short wide venous channel formed by the union of veins draining the *stomach, *intestine, and *spleen that conducts blood (containing the nutrients derived from *digestion) to the *liver.

PORTERS are a group of hospital ancillary staff who undertake a variety of duties as well as gatekeeping, for example the transport of patients between departments.

PORTIER, PAUL-JULES (1866–1962). French immunologist, MD Paris. Portier discovered, together with Charles Robert *Richet, the phenomenon of *anaphylaxis, a term which they introduced to describe hypersensitivity to a foreign substance induced by previous exposure to that substance. The events which led up to their experiments, initially on toxins from jellyfish and sea-anemones, are described in IMMUNOLOGY. The work, which was published in 1902 (*Comptes Rendues de la Société de Biologie, Paris,* **54,** 170) resulted in Richet being awarded the Nobel prize in 1913. Portier was elected a member of the biological sciences section of the *Academie de Médecine in 1929.

PORTWINE STAIN. A bluish-red area on the skin due to a capillary *haemangioma. When on the face, and following the sensory distribution of one of the divisions of the *trigeminal nerve, it is diagnostic of the Sturge–Weber syndrome, in which similar vascular anomalies occur in the underlying *meninges and *cerebral cortex and cause generalized or focal *epilepsy, sometimes with contralateral *hemiplegia, mental retardation, and cerebral calcification on X-ray.

POSITRON. A positive *electron; an elementary particle with the same mass as an electron and an electric charge of equal magnitude but opposite sign. Some unstable nuclides have a deficit of neutrons, and decay by conversion of *protons to *neutrons and positrons, with immediate emission of the positrons as positive beta-particles. Positrons themselves do not decay, but on passing through matter they collide with negative electrons as a result of which both particles are annihilated with the production of two photons of electromagnetic radiation in the form of *gamma rays emitted at an angle of 180° to each other. It is these 180° simultaneous gamma rays which are detected in *positron emission tomography (PET), using positron-emitting isotopes of carbon, oxygen, and nitrogen in labelled compounds injected into the patient.

POSITRON EMISSION TOMOGRAPHY AND RELATED TECHNIQUES

Introduction. The use of *gamma-ray-emitting *radioisotopes to measure regional tissue function offers a unique means of observing focal pathophysiology that occurs in disease. Following the introduction of the tracer into the body, its local tissue content can be detected by monitoring the emitted photons using a suitably collimated radiation detector placed external to the patient. From the magnitude of the recorded signal and its time course, information can be obtained about the physiological pathway being traced. In clinical medicine this principle has been developed extensively and constitutes the basis of *nuclear medicine procedures. It is clear that to exploit fully the opportunities for measuring *in vivo* physiology, gamma-ray-emitting forms of the basic biological elements are needed. However, when one examines what tracers are available in this category we see that they all have short radioactive half-lives $(T_{\frac{1}{2}})$. The longest-lived gamma-ray-emitting forms of oxygen, nitrogen, and carbon, are oxygen-15 (2.1 minutes $T_{\frac{1}{2}}$), nitrogen-13 (10 minutes $T_{\frac{1}{2}}$), and carbon-11 (20.1 minutes $T_{\frac{1}{2}}$) respectively. There is no gamma-emitting form of hydrogen but, for labelling purposes, fluorine-18 (110 minutes $T_{\frac{1}{2}}$) has been used as a hydrogen substitute. It follows, with the exception of fluorine-18, that these radionuclides need to be manufactured at the place of their application. For this, a high-energy radiation beam of charged particles is needed. To produce this, a particle accelerator is used, which usually takes the form of a *cyclotron.

Once the radioisotope is introduced into the body, the problem presents itself of how to measure accurately the tracer's concentration within the tissues. The signal recorded by the externally placed radiation detectors viewing the body will represent a superimposition of information. This follows since the gamma rays will arise from within overlying mixtures of tissues. Using rectilinear scanning of collimated detectors or a *gamma-ray camera, one can obtain a two-dimensional distribution of what is often a complex three-dimensional distribution of physiological mechanisms. Clearly, a *tomographic read-out is needed of the tracer's distribution within the body. Furthermore, in order to extend the measurement of tissue function to its quantitative limit, the tissue's radioisotopic concentration needs to be measured in absolute units. This is a prerequisite of all *in vitro* radionuclide assays in biochemistry studies. In conventional nuclear medicine, such quantitation is exceedingly difficult to achieve. Positron emission tomography is a means of measuring the *in vivo* distribution of the aforementioned short-lived radionuclides. It demonstrates the regional tissue concentration of tracer in *computerized axial tomographic (CAT) distributions. This methodology rests on the fact that when the short-lived isotopes decay, they emit positrons, which are positively charged beta-ray-like particles. These rays travel away from the disintegrating nucleus for no more than a few millimetres and are then captured by negatively charged electrons that are present in matter. The result of this capture is that both the positron and electron concerned annihilate. The net energy of this is expressed by the emission of two gamma rays, each of 511 000 electron-volts in energy. These emerge from the point of annihilation at almost 180 degrees to each other. Consequently, radiating from the tissues containing the radioisotope are pairs of correlated gamma rays. By placing radiation detectors on opposite sides of the body and arranging for them to operate in a coincidence mode, the simultaneous emergence of the two photons can be recorded. From each registered coincidence event, the position of the disintegrating nucleus can be assigned to a line drawn between the two detectors involved. A positron emission tomograph (PET) consists of arrays of coincident detectors placed around the body (Fig. 1). They are so arranged as to collect sufficient angular data from which the tomographic distribution of the tracer can be obtained using computer reconstruction techniques. The reconstruction principles are essentially the same as those present in X-ray CAT. The difference is that in the latter, a photon beam is transmitted through the body and the resulting tomographic read-out represents tissue density.

An important feature of PET is that a correction can be made for distortion in the signal caused by the loss of gamma rays due to some absorption by the tissues themselves. This is achieved by using a transmission scan that is similar to that of X-ray CAT. Thus the response of the PET can, for most geometrical conditions of the body, be calibrated in absolute units of tracer concentration. The combination of the interesting short-lived isotopes of oxygen, nitrogen, carbon, and fluorine and an accurate means of measuring their regional tissue concentration provides a unique non-invasive tool for studying quantitatively regional tissue physiology, biochemistry, and pharmacology. From this combination, examples of techniques that have been developed to measure regional tissue function include blood flow, oxygen, glucose, and amino acid utilization.

The positron emission tomography laboratory. The combined use of the short-lived positron-emitting isotopes and a positron emission tomograph requires a multidisciplinary technical/scientific base. The cost of a minimum-sized cyclotron and shielded room is about £1 000 000. The accelerator needs to be run by at least one engineering/technical person. The production of the short-lived radionuclides and their use for labelling appropriate compounds to be used in *in vivo* tracer studies requires a specialized radiochemistry team. The cost of the specialized PET scanner itself depends on the type of machine. Commercially produced, in 1983 whole body scan-

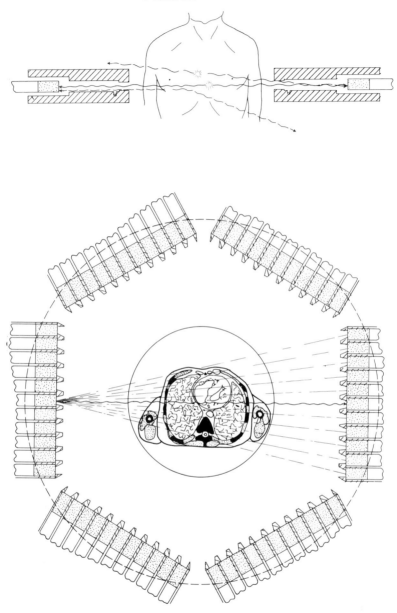

Fig. 1. The physical arrangement of the radiation detector system in a typical positron emission tomographic scanner

ners also cost about £1 000 000. Due consideration needs to be given to the physical performance of this PET scanner. This is usually the responsibility of medical physicists (see PHYSICS, MEDICAL), who also address the problems of modelling the tracer kinetics that underlie the studies being carried out. Each specific application requires committed technical help in performing the clinical measurements themselves. This, not least, is because of the immediate nature of studies being carried out with

isotopes whose half-lives are measured in minutes. In order to derive quantitative data for a parameter of regional tissue, computer data processing is necessary. This requires the service of a computer programmer.

Having itemized the technical/scientific base upon which PET needs to be based, it will be clear that the clinical application of such a tool is not, in the first instance, one of routine clinical diagnostic use. The investment has to be considered as a clinical scientific facility where the aim is to obtain new information about disease and its treatment. The complexity and multidisciplinary nature of the measurements concerned demand that the medical doctors involved need to be committed on a full-time basis to the research procedures. This in turn requires further investment over and above that of the technical/scientific staff base. To maximize the exploitation of such a facility it is highly desirable that it should be based within a research-orientated medical centre. Ideally, this needs to be positioned within an urban area from which an appropriate patient population can be drawn and extended support can be provided by clinical research-orientated medical practitioners. In 1984, of the 33 centres in the world that claim to be active in the PET field, only about 13 are optimally positioned with facilities that approach the criteria itemized above. A further 20 PET centres are projected world-wide over the next few years.

Measurements of regional tissue function using PET. This investigative specialty is relatively new and comparatively few quantitative measurements of regional tissue function have been reported.

Regional tissue blood flow and oxygen utilization are being measured using oxygen-15. Glucose utilization has been measured with both carbon-11-labelled glucose and fluorine-18-labelled deoxyglucose. Blood volume can be measured by tagging red cells (*erythrocytes) with *carbon monoxide labelled with carbon-11 or oxygen-15. Metabolism of the *myocardium has been approached using carbon-11-labelled *fatty acids. The use of carbon-11-labelled amino acids such as methionine and leucine is being pursued to study regional *protein synthesis. Some work has been reported on the use of labelled drugs as a means of determining regional tissue pharmacological kinetics. An example of this is carbon-11-labelled *erythromycin in pneumonia (Wollmer et al. 1982). In addition to the logistical complexity of labelling and using compounds labelled with short half-life isotopes, a major hurdle facing the field is the development of appropriate tracer kinetic models. These are needed in order that data obtained on the tissue's uptake of tracer can be transformed into specific values for the physiological parameters being traced. The restraints on realizing these are compounded by the pathophysiology concerned and by how this may distort the kinetic models worked out for normal physiology. The data output, although often in the form of images of regional tissue function, has to be analysed quantitatively and communicated as such to the scientific community. The analysis and presentation of information, which initially takes the form of large matrices of data points, is proving an intellectual challenge in exploiting the measurements.

Clinical scientific information that has emerged from PET. As a way of illustrating the clinical scientific output of this specialty, selected reports from the various centres are itemized. In *stroke

patients, it has been shown that a state of critical *perfusion persists for about 24 hours after the *ictus (Wise et al., 1983). The data indicate that, within this period, oxygen utilization in the affected area is less reduced than that of blood flow. Studied at later times, metabolism falls further and the tissue tends to a state of excess blood flow sometimes called luxury perfusion. In multi-infarct *dementia and *Alzheimer's presenile or senile dementia, although focal reduction of blood flow and oxygen metabolism are seen, these are matched and there is no indication of a chronic *ischaemia (Frackowiak et al., 1981). In the pre-stroke state, that is in patients with extensive extra-cranial vascular disease, cerebral blood flow and oxygen utilization are often within normal limits; however, regional blood volume tends to increase. This perturbed relationship of flow to volume indicates an attempt by the brain's vasculature to reduce perfusion resistance (Gibbs et al., 1984).

In *schizophrenia, Sheppard et al. (1983) have shown in newly diagnosed unmedicated patients that cortical patterns of oxygen utilization and blood flow are the same as those for normal subjects. Buchsbaum et al. (1982), however, have shown in chronic schizophrenia that a state of frontal hypometabolism exists. Engel et al. (1982a, b) have shown areas of focal glucose hyper- and hypo-utilization in *epileptics for the ictal and interictal phases respectively. Kuhl et al. (1982) have reported decreased basal ganglia glucose utilization in patients with *Huntington's chorea. PET techniques have been used to study the focal change of glucose utilization in the normal brain during a series of controlled stimuli (Phelps et al., 1981). In *gliomas and breast carcinoma it has been shown that the *neoplasms are relatively overperfused in that the fractional extraction of oxygen from the blood is of the order of 20–30 per cent (Ito et al., 1982; Beaney et al., 1984), DiChiro et al. (1982) report that glucose utilization of the glioma tends to correlate with the tumour grade and Rhodes et al. (1983) have shown preferential aerobic glycolysis (glucose breakdown) in these tumours. In ischaemic heart disease, a focal increase of glucose utilization has been reported by Schelbert during exercise-induced *angina. Selwyn and Allan (1981) have shown that, after an angina episode, the focal disturbance of myocardial physiology persists for periods longer than those indicated by symptoms or perturbations in the *ECG. (For more extensive reading on the specific applications the following reviews are recommended: for radiochemistry for PET, see Comar et al. (1982); for brain studies see Phelps et al. (1982) and Frackowiak and Lenzi (1982); and for the myocardium, see Schelbert (1982). Muehllehner and Colsher (1982) have reviewed the instrumental aspects, and overall concepts of PET applications have been discussed by Jones (1980, 1982).

Future applications of PET. Further improvements in spatial accuracy of PET scanners themselves are predicted over the next few years. To date, application has concentrated on studies of tissue energy supply and metabolism together with first-hand observations of the presenting focal pathophysiology in certain diseases. It is clear that the field will evolve into measurements of more complex physiological pathways of which protein synthesis, *receptor binding (Wagner et al., 1983; Syrota et al., 1985), and labelled pharmaceuticals (Leenders et al., 1984) will be part. In addition, the role of research will move from one of observing the pathophysiology to studies of the effect of specific interventions. It is here that an opportunity presents itself for determining objectively the effect of therapeutic regimens. Although the research work itself will continue to be undertaken in relatively few selected centres, the scientific output will be of relevance to many areas of practical clinical medicine. T. JONES

References

Beaney, R. P., Lammertsma, A. A., Jones, T., McKenzie, C. G. and Halnan, K. E. (1984). Positron emission tomograghy for *in vivo* measurement of regional blood flow, oxygen utilisation, and blood volume in patients with breast carcinoma. *Lancet*, **ii**, 131–4.

Buchsbaum, M. J., Ingvar, D. H., Kessler, R., Waters, R. N., Cappelletti, J., Van Kammen, D. P., King, A. C., Johnson, J. L., Manning, R. G., Flynn, R. W., Mann, L. S., Bunney, W. E. and Sokoloff, L. (1982). Cerebral glucography with positron tomography. Use in normal subjects and in patients with schizophrenia. *Archives of Geriatric Psychiatry*, **39**(3), 251–7.

Comar, D., Berridge, M., Maziere, B. and Crouzel, C. (1982). Radiopharmaceutical labelled with positron emitting radioisotopes. In Ell, P. J. and Holman, B. L. (eds), *Computed Emission Tomography*, Oxford.

DiChiro, G., De La Paz, R. L., Brookes, R. A., Sokoloff, L., Kornblith, P. L., Smith, B. N., Patronas, N. J., Kufta, C. V., Kessler, R. M., Johnston, G. S., Manning, R. G. and Wolf, A. P. (1982). Glucose utilisation of cerebral gliomas measured by [18F] fluorodeoxyglucose and positron emission tomography. *Neurology*, **32**, 1323–9.

Engel, J., Kuhl, D. E., Phelps, M. E. and Mazziotta, J. C. (1982a). Interictal cerebral glucose metabolism in partial epilepsy and its relation to EEG changes. *Annals of Neurology*, **12**(6), 510–17.

Engel, J., Brown, W. J., Kuhl, D. E., Phelps, M. E., Mazziotta, J. C. and Crandall, P. H. (1982b). Pathological findings underlying focal temporal lobe hypometabolism in partial epilepsy. *Annals of Neurology*, **12**(6), 518–28.

Frackowiak, R. S. J. and Lenzi, G. L. (1982). Physiological measurement in the brain from potential to practice. In Ell, P. J. and Holman, B. L. (eds), *Computed Emission Tomography*. Oxford.

Frackowiak, R. S. J., Pozzilli, C., Legg, N. J., du Boulay, G. H., Marshall, J., Lenzi, G. L. and Jones, T. (1981). Regional cerebral oxygen supply and utilisation in dementia: A clinical and physiological study with oxygen-15 and positron tomography. *Brain*, **104**, 753–78.

Gibbs, J. M., Wise, R. J. S., Leenders, K. L. and Jones, T. (1984). Evaluation of cerebral perfusion reserve in patients with carotid artery occlusion. *Lancet*, **i**, 310–4.

Ito, M., Lammertsma, A. A., Wise, R. J. S., Bernardi, S., Frackowiak, R. S. J., Heather, J. D., McKenzie, C. G.,

Thomas, D. G. T. and Jones, T. (1982). Measurement of regional cerebral blood flow and oxygen utilisation in patients with cerebral tumours using 15O and positron emission tomography: analytical techniques and preliminary results. *Neuroradiology*, **23**(2), 63–74.

Jones, T. (1980). Positron emission tomography and measurements of regional tissue function in man. *British Medical Bulletin*, **36**, 231–6.

Jones, T. (1982). The applications of positron emission tomography. In Ell, P. J. and Holman, B. L. (eds), *Computed Emission Tomography*. Oxford.

Kuhl, D. E., Phelps, M. E., Markham, C. H., Metter, E. J., Riege, W. H. and Winter, J. (1982). Cerebral metabolism and atrophy in Huntington's disease determined by 18FDG and computed tomographic scan. *Annals of Neurology*, **12**(5), 425–34.

Leenders, K. L., Herold, S., Brooks, D. J., Palmer, A. L., Turton, D., Firnau, G., Garnett, E. S. and Nahmias, C. (1984). Pre-synaptic and post-synaptic dopaminergic system in human brain. *Lancet*, **ii**, 101–11.

Marshall, R. C., Tillish, J. H., Phelps, M. E., Huang, S. C., Carson, R., Henze, E. and Schelbert, H. R. (1983). Identification and differentiation of resting myocardial ischemia and infarction in man with positron computed tomography, 18F-labelled fluorodeoxyglucose and 13N ammonia. *Circulation*, **67**, 766–78.

Muehllehner, G. and Colsher, J. G. (1982). Instrumentation. In Ell, P. J. and Holman, B. L. (eds), *Computed Emission Tomography*. Oxford.

Phelps, M. E., Mazziotta, J. C., Kuhl, D. E., Nuwer, M., Packwood, J., Metter, J. and Engel, J., Jr (1981). Tomographic mapping of human cerebral metabolism: visual stimulation and deprivation. *Neurology*, **31**, 517–29.

Phelps, M. E., Mazziotta, J. C. and Huang, S. C. (1982). Study of cerebral function with positron computed tomography. *Journal of Cerebral Blood Flow and Metabolism*, **2**, 113–62.

Rhodes, C. G., Wise, R. J. S., Gibbs, J. M., Frackowiak, R. S. J., Hatazawa, J., Palmer, A. J., Thomas, D. G. T. and Jones, T. (1983). *In vivo* disturbance of the oxidative metabolism of glucose in human cerebral gliomas. *Annals of Neurology*, **14**, 614–26.

Schelbert, H. R. (1982). The heart. In Ell, P. J. and Holman, B. L. (eds), *Computed Emission Tomography*. Oxford.

Selwyn, A. P. and Allan, R. M. (1981). Radionuclides in cardiology: present and future prospects. In Yu, P. N. and Goodwin, J. F. (eds), *Progress in Cardiology*, Philadelphia.

Sheppard, G., Gruzelier, J., Manchanda, R., Hirsch, S. R., Wise, R., Frackowiak, R. and Jones, T. (1983). 15O positron emission tomographic scanning in predominantly never-treated acute schizophrenic patients. *Lancet*, **ii**, 1448–52.

Syrota, A., Comar, D., Paillotin, G., Davy, J. M., Aumont, M. C., Stulzaft, O. and Maziere, B. (1985). Muscarinic cholinergic receptor in the human heart evidenced under physiological conditions by positron emission tomography. *Proceedings of the National Academy of Science*, in press.

Wagner, H. N., Burns, H. D., Dannals, R. F. et al. (1983). Imaging dopamine receptors in the human brain by positron tomography. *Science*, **221**, 1264–6.

Wise, R. J. S., Bernardi, S., Frackowiak, R. S. J., Legg, N. J. and Jones, T. (1982). Serial observations on the pathophysiology of acute stroke. The transition from ischaemia to infarction as reflected in regional oxygen extraction. *Brain*, **106**, 197–222.

Wollmer, P., Pride, N. B., Rhodes, C. G., Sanders, A.,

Pike, V. W., Palmer, A. J., Silvester, D. J. and Liss, R. H. (1982). Measurement of pulmonary erythromycin concentration in patients with lobar pneumonia by means of positron tomography. *Lancet*, **ii**, 1361–4.

POSTERIOR FOSSA when otherwise unqualified refers to the posterior cranial fossa, the floor of the posterior subdivision of the cranial cavity (which contains the *cerebellum, *pons, and *medulla oblongata).

POSTERIOR ROOT GANGLIA. The *ganglia found on the posterior roots of the *spinal nerves, also known as the spinal ganglia. They contain the cell bodies of the sensory *neurones of the nerves.

POSTGRADUATE AND CONTINUING MEDICAL EDUCATION IN THE UK

The pre-registration year. In order to obtain full *registration with the *General Medical Council (GMC) all doctors qualifying in the UK are required to complete 12 months of *pre-registration experience. This must include a minimum of 4 months' experience in internal medicine and 4 months in surgery. In practice, the year is almost invariably made up of two 6-month appointments, each of which gives general experience in internal medicine or general surgery, or a combination of general and specialized experience, for instance, in general medicine and geriatrics, or general surgery and orthopaedics. Provided that the minimum requirements for medicine and surgery are met, the remaining 4 months during the pre-registration year can now be spent in a wide variety of specialties, including, in some circumstances, *general medical practice.

In each part of the country pre-registration posts are selected and regularly reviewed by the medical school of the university in the region concerned (see MEDICAL EDUCATION IN THE UK AND EUROPE). It is the responsibility of the university to inform the GMC about these posts, so that a comprehensive national list of approved posts may be maintained. The number of posts available in the UK is slightly in excess of the number of medical graduates qualifying each year.

Overseas medical graduates are normally expected to have completed the equivalent of a pre-registration year before entering the UK. They must obtain either full or limited registration from the GMC, according to their eligibility, in order to engage in any form of medical practice in the UK and, therefore, in order to undergo postgraduate training.

Training beyond the pre-registration year. Practically all postgraduate training in the UK takes place within the *National Health Service (NHS). This provides employment for doctors who obtain relevant clinical and laboratory experience while progressing through the training grades.

The grades of appointment for junior hospital doctors are *senior house officer (SHO), *registrar, and *senior registrar. The minimum length of time a doctor would expect to spend in each of these grades is 1 year, 2 years, and 3–4 years respectively. In practice, the time taken for training varies greatly: it depends on personal aims and preferences, success in passing postgraduate examinations, competitiveness of the specialty concerned, and other factors such as changes of career choice.

Although there is an increasing tendency to develop training programmes, or 'rotations' which provide a 2- or 3-year package of training at the SHO/registrar level, it remains true that most of these posts are advertised and filled individually. Doctors may compete for SHO and registrar posts throughout the country and thus construct their own programme of postgraduate training. There is much movement from one region to another, and between specialties. This arrangement clearly has advantages and disadvantages: it is a somewhat uneasy compromise between the benefits of individual freedom with scope for personal initiative, and the demerits of lack of planning with consequent inefficiency and even injustice.

At senior registrar level the linking of posts into training programmes is the general rule, and these usually provide experience in both 'teaching' and 'non-teaching' hospitals. The numbers of senior registrar posts in each specialty are related to the expected numbers of *consultant vacancies, so that once this final stage of training is achieved there is a high probability of obtaining a career appointment in the specialty. Most senior registrar posts are concentrated in, or associated with, teaching centres, while SHO and registrar posts are available in hospitals of all kinds. Postgraduate training in the UK is thus a very widely dispersed activity and this is also becoming increasingly true of undergraduate medical training, since many 'non-teaching' hospitals make a contribution to this. In fact, the terms 'teaching' and 'non-teaching' are becoming somewhat inappropriate.

The fact that most hospitals in the UK have postgraduate trainees confers benefits on both teachers and students, which would not readily be given up. It means, however, that the numbers of SHO and registrar posts available for training are very large in relation to the numbers that would strictly be needed to maintain the future establishment of trained hospital specialists and general practitioners. This creates a career structure problem which has been under discussion for some time. About half the available SHO and registrar posts are occupied by overseas doctors, although their distribution differs between regions and specialties. These doctors make a large contribution to the daily work of the NHS, without necessarily always being at a stage where they should rightly be asked to do so. The recent expansion of the British medical schools will eventually enable the NHS to become self-sufficient in service provision, and this will have major implications for postgraduate training and the place of overseas doctors in the system.

Terminology and concepts. For a career in one of the hospital specialties, a new terminology has emerged since the publication of the report of the Royal Commission on Medical Education in 1968 (*The Todd Report*) relating to 'general professional training' during the SHO and registrar years, and 'higher specialist training' at the senior registrar stage. The meaning of 'general' in this context is not, however, always clear. In most specialties, and particularly perhaps in internal medicine or surgery, it is appropriate to seek 'general' experience in the discipline before aiming to become, for example, an endocrinologist or a urologist. This is different from 'general professional training' as conceived by Todd, which was a period during which young doctors could obtain a broad range of clinical or laboratory experience in a variety of different specialties before becoming committed to a lifetime in one. There are many advantages in this broader view of general professional training, which continues to be discussed. Many doctors have not made a firm career choice by the end of the pre-registration year, and others change their choice during the subsequent few years for various reasons. It is important to provide as much chance as possible for young doctors to sample the work of various specialties before making a definite career decision, and without being disadvantaged in competition with those who make an earlier choice.

'Completion' of training. Over 50 specialties are recognized within the NHS. There are no specialist registers maintained by the GMC, but there is an increasing tendency for individual Royal Colleges and Faculties to certify the 'completion of training' at the end of the senior registrar period. This '*accreditation' is quite distinct from specialist registration as it is understood in other countries; it denotes that a full sequence of 'general professional' and 'higher specialist' training has been undergone, which will normally take a minimum of 6–7 years, and it has significance in the British context because it is intended to indicate eligibility to apply for a consultant (tenured) appointment in the NHS. In the hospital service, only the consultant has independent responsibility for the care of patients. In principle, and from the medico-legal point of view, all other medical staff work under his supervision although, in practice, the delegation of an increasing degree of responsibility to the trainee—particularly at the senior registrar level—is an important part of the 'completion' of his training.

General practice. Postgraduate training for general practice (see GENERAL MEDICAL PRACTICE) consists of 2 years of varied experience in relevant hospital appointments and 1 year as a trainee in general practice. This minimum training is now required by law and has come to be known as 'vocational training'. The hospital component is normally made up of four 6-month SHO appointments in specialties appropriate to general prac-

tice, and including two to be chosen from: general medicine, geriatrics, paediatrics, obstetrics and gynaecology, general surgery or accident and emergency, and psychiatry. This, together with the trainee year in general practice, roughly corresponds to 'general professional training' for the hospital specialties.

Although it is possible to become a principal in general practice immediately on completion of vocational training, it is likely that as time goes by it will become increasingly common to spend a further period comparable to 'higher training', in general practice, before becoming a principal.

Throughout the country, many vocational training schemes are now available which are highly competitive. Doctors selected for these may start immediately after the pre-registration year on a 3-year programme of hospital and general practice appointments which make up the required ('prescribed') experience. Some doctors prefer to seek individual SHO posts for themselves, independently of organized vocational training schemes. Doctors who decide to enter general practice after considering other careers may ask for some or all of their SHO and registrar experience to be recognized, as 'equivalent experience', towards the required training for general practice.

Training for other careers. Schools of public health in the UK do not have a defined postgraduate training function in relation to the NHS. Public health, epidemiology, and medical administration are now incorporated within the broad specialty of *community medicine. Postgraduate training programmes in community medicine begin at registrar level, for doctors who have already obtained experience in a clinical field. The programmes incorporate the registrar and senior registrar phases and lead to appointments as specialist in community medicine, which have the equivalent of consultant status.

The general heading of community medicine is also used to include those doctors who work in community health, for example in school clinics or family planning clinics. These doctors are currently employed as clinical medical officers or senior clinical medical officers, and appropriate training programmes are being developed. However, the future of this work force is under discussion, particularly in relation to the role of the general practitioner and of the specialist paediatrician in *screening and *preventive services for children in the community, so that the organization of postgraduate training programmes in community paediatrics is under active consideration.

Occupational health services are increasingly provided within the NHS, but for the most part specialized medical practice in the field of industrial and *occupational medicine is outside the NHS. Postgraduate training is provided through a number of agencies, including private industry and the nationalized industries. The Royal College of Physicians has a faculty of occupational medicine which makes recommendations about training, and schemes suitable for accreditation are developing at senior registrar level, which often offer experience both in industry and in a university department.

University posts. A feature of the British system is the close relationship and extensive interchange between NHS and university appointments. In the clinical departments of the medical schools, appointments at junior lecturer and lecturer level are available which combine teaching and research responsibilities with clinical experience. Such posts carry honorary NHS grading at SHO, registrar, or senior registrar level depending on the circumstances, and arrangements are made with the various Royal colleges and faculties whereby time spent in such appointments may be counted towards the requirements for training in the specialty concerned. It is thus possible for many doctors who have spent periods of time in a university department to return to the NHS by applying for posts at various levels, including consultant level. Conversely, many applicants for university appointments—including the most senior—come from the NHS since in various ways opportunities are provided during the course of NHS training for doctors to gain experience in teaching and research.

How training is provided. The Royal Colleges and Faculties are primarily responsible for determining postgraduate training requirements in their own specialties. The more important postgraduate examinations, which are virtually essential for progression towards a consultant appointment, are organized and controlled by the Royal Colleges and Faculties. These are independent bodies, entirely separate from the universities, the NHS, and from government or political control. The colleges individually lay down requirements for their examinations. These frequently stipulate minimum periods of time that must be spent in training posts recognized for the purpose. This, in turn, gives the colleges the right to inspect SHO and registrar posts in the NHS to determine their suitability for training purposes. An important means of monitoring the quality of training exists in this way. It may sometimes have been applied too leniently but it gives powerful leverage to the colleges, whose interests are educational, in relation to the NHS authorities which are responsible for providing the necessary resources. Threat of withdrawal of recognition for training is serious: in effect, it means discontinuation of the post, and this not only has implications for the running of the service but influences morale and prestige. There is every incentive, therefore, for the NHS authorities to comply with college recommendations on such matters as the adequacy of library and other educational facilities, and the assurance that trainees will have adequate time for study and attendance at courses. The colleges and faculties appoint visitors to look at posts throughout the country at about 5-yearly intervals. For vocational training in general practice, the Royal College of General Practitioners (RCGP) appoints visitors to look at hospital SHO posts in conjunction with visitors from the college of the hospital specialty concerned, and suitable posts are 'selected', at regional level, for vocational training from among those approved by the colleges responsible for the hospital disciplines. In general practice itself, GP principals who wish to be trainers are carefully selected at regional level and their performance is monitored thereafter. The RCGP appoints visitors to inspect training practices.

Within each NHS region, the Royal Colleges and Faculties appoint regional advisers who act as a link between consultants and general practitioners who are responsible for training, and their parent colleges centrally. In many specialties a consultant is nominated in each district as the college or faculty tutor; he has a general responsibility for the welfare of local trainees, and maintains liaison with the regional adviser.

The actual process of postgraduate training takes various forms. First, and most important, is clinical or laboratory apprenticeship which enables appropriate experience to be obtained. Various forms of secondment can be arranged, to provide experience in a special unit or subspecialty. Similarly, it is possible for a registrar to move to an SHO appointment in a different specialty, for training purposes, and to retain a registrar's salary. Secondly, many kinds of day-release and other part-time courses are arranged, frequently through the initiative and co-operation of university departments. It is an accepted feature of NHS training that time is available for trainees to attend these courses. Thirdly, many activities take place at hospital level, or in general practice, which combine teaching with the monitoring of standards. These take the form of group discussions, case conferences, analysis of complications and deaths, journal clubs, and literature reviews, etc. Fourthly, there is much participation of trainees in nationally or regionally organized conferences and meetings. These may concentrate on the detailed aspects of a particular specialty, or serve to fill potential educational gaps for a wide range of trainees; for example, a number of short courses are now available for senior registrars on the topic of management for clinicians. Participation in these activities is voluntary, but much note is taken of such involvement, and of examination achievements, by college visitors in assessing the viability of a clinical unit for training. Private discussion with trainees is a regular feature of these visits. A wide variety of research opportunities is available during training, including leave of absence to work abroad, and reference has already been made to the interchange with university departments.

Wide provision is made for the postgraduate training of doctors with domestic commitments and those who, through disability or for other reasons, are not able to compete in the normal way for established posts throughout the country. Supernumerary appointments may be provided on a part-time basis at SHO, registrar, or senior registrar level; these are individually planned in regard to their educational content and are subject to approval by the appropriate Royal College or Faculty for examination and accreditation purposes.

An increasing number of overseas doctors come to the UK on a 'sponsorship' basis. This does not necessarily imply financial support, but rather that training requirements are discussed and planned in advance, by arrangement between mutually respected educational sponsors at home and abroad, who are prepared to vouch for the quality of the training, and the calibre of the trainee, respectively. Far too often in the past, overseas doctors have arrived in the UK without any prearranged appointment, without planning of any training programme, and indeed sometimes without any clear view of their future intentions. This has often led to disappointment and frustration, with overseas doctors occupying those posts which are least satisfactory from the training point of view. It is hoped that the increasing use of organized sponsorship arrangements will do much to avoid this problem.

Monitoring. Assessment of the progress of individual trainees is largely in the hands of the consultants or general practitioners with whom they work. In addition, there are regional arrangements discussed in the next section. Since so much of postgraduate training in the UK still depends upon applying for successive jobs there is inevitably a form of continuous assessment, through the interviewing process and the quality of referees' reports. This is coupled, of course, with the need to pass specialist examinations at the appropriate stage.

All forms of medical practice in the UK, including general practice, now require postgraduate training to be satisfactorily completed. This means that if medical unemployment is to be avoided and the best use made of the available doctors, it is a system in which everyone must succeed. Although postgraduate training is competitive, to varying degrees in different specialties, it is being seen increasingly as a process in which trainees are counselled and advised appropriately, rather than rejected and left to their own devices. The Royal Colleges and Faculties again have an important controlling and monitoring influence at the conclusion of training, since appointment committees for all consultant posts include a college representative. He is able to assess whether individual applicants have satisfied the college's criteria for 'completion of training' and is also authorized to comment on the job description for the appointment. This is particularly important since it helps to ensure that sufficient opportunity is available at the consultant level for continuing study, teaching, and

the maintenance of standards through educational awareness.

Co-ordination of arrangements. Over the last 15 years better arrangements have developed for co-ordinating postgraduate medical education. It remains true, however, that so many interests are concerned—the colleges, the universities, the medical profession, the Health Departments (see GOVERNMENT AND MEDICINE IN THE UK), the NHS, and the GMC, that neither the system itself, nor any description of it, can be entirely consistent or coherent.

Centrally, there is a Council for Postgraduate Medical Education (CPME) in England and Wales, with similar councils in Scotland and Northern Ireland. These bodies bring together the relevant interests from the medical and dental professions, the Royal Colleges and universities, and the Health Departments, to provide a forum for discussion and to make recommendations concerning policy. The GMC has observers on these councils. The role of the GMC itself has changed greatly since the Medical Act of 1978 gave to it an overall responsibility for all phases of medical education, and thus extended its remit into the field of postgraduate and continuing education. With this broad concern for educational standards, it is expected that the GMC will stand in the same relationship to the Royal Colleges and Faculties in regard to postgraduate and continuing education, as it does in relation to the medical schools in regard to undergraduate education. Thus postgraduate and continuing education are the joint responsibility of the GMC, the Royal Colleges and Faculties which set down minimum training criteria and maintain standards in their own specialties, the NHS and the universities which jointly provide employment, teaching, and training, the medical profession itself which is responsible for looking to the quality of its own work, and the Health Departments which must achieve the necessary manpower integration between the needs of training and those of providing a service.

Each region of the country has a Regional Postgraduate Committee, which, like the CPME, brings together the interests of the Royal Colleges, through their Regional Advisers, the NHS, the local medical school, and the medical profession. Regional Postgraduate Committees normally have subcommittees concerned with the individual specialties, including general practice, which assume a general responsibility for working towards the best utilization of the training potential of the specialty throughout the region. Co-ordination between specialties, which is an essential element in the concept of general professional training, is an important function of Regional Postgraduate Committees. In each university with a medical school there is a postgraduate dean who functions as the chief executive officer of the Regional Postgraduate Committee in regard to the organization and control of postgraduate and continuing education throughout his region. Monitoring of the progress of trainees, at regional level, is carried out through regional committees, which usually receive annual progress reports from consultants on trainees in post, including supernumerary part-time trainees, so that counselling can be offered where necessary, advice can be given about problems and difficulties that may be arising, and weaknesses in training arrangements can be brought to light. There are usually close links with the Regional Manpower Committee, and this is of great importance since postgraduate training is a fundamental element in medical manpower planning.

Evaluation, continuing education, and assessment of competence. The Royal Colleges of Physicians and the Royal Colleges of Surgeons have for several hundred years brought together specialists in these fields. The formation of independent Royal Colleges for other specialties, including general practice, is more recent. Admission to membership or fellowship of a college has traditionally been by examination, a test of the knowledge and clinical skills to be expected of those who aspire to practise the specialty concerned. Imperfect as such assessments must be, they have served over the years to give some credibility to the concept of competence and its evaluation in the postgraduate field. Outside the college system numerous diplomas—in child health (paediatrics), occupational medicine, tropical medicine, obstetrics, and many other subjects—have served to testify in a similar way to the achievement of some minimum acceptable standard. Hence there has grown up a long tradition of postgraduate examinations which, confusing in their variety and purpose, have nevertheless become embedded in the fabric of British postgraduate training, as well as being highly valued abroad. Although individual universities sometimes offer higher degrees or diplomas, the overriding philosophy in the UK is one of national examinations which provide a commonly accepted benchmark for trainees and practitioners throughout the country.

The colleges and other specialist associations have also played a key part in the arranging and promulgation of courses, meetings, and other educational activities for established practitioners. This and other aspects of continuing medical education have a long history, beginning with the proliferation of journals, congresses, specialist organizations, and local medical societies in which the traditions of British medicine are rich. Discussion of mutual problems and practices between colleagues, and between teachers and students at various levels, has been characteristic of the best in hospital work for a long time but some barriers of tradition have had to be broken down. The greater problems that face single-handed practitioners outside the hospital setting have also had to be faced.

Great impetus was given to continuing education in the UK in the early 1960s, following the initiative of the late Sir George *Pickering and the *Nuffield Provincial Hospitals Trust, by the establishment of postgraduate medical centres in the larger peripheral hospitals. These centres now exist throughout the country, and provide meeting places where general practitioners, hospital doctors, administrators, and other health professionals can come together for educational activities of various kinds, with the support of library and other facilities. Also during the 1960s, the Health Departments began to make specific funds available for continuing education of general practitioners, and much activity has developed from this. Vocational training schemes incorporate regular teaching sessions, study groups, seminars, etc. as part of a structured programme which generates the expectation that such activities will be carried on throughout professional life. Courses are arranged for trainers, and prospective trainers, in general practice. With the growth of group practices, much continuing education within general practice itself takes place in the environment of the practice: the postgraduate centre is the natural locus for those activities which are of joint concern to hospital doctors, general practitioners, community physicians, and other health professionals.

There has always been an implicit recognition of the fact that the true purpose of continuing education is to improve the quality of patient care, through keeping up to date, having the opportunity to compare practice with others, and hence influencing professional standards. The emphasis, therefore, is rightly not on ritual attendance at a specified number of meetings, or on the mass-production of programmes in order to meet an artificially determined requirement, but upon the proper motivation of students and postgraduate trainees, and on the quality and relevance of what is provided for them and by them. Continuing education and 'audit' are not separate exercises, but different aspects of the same process: the setting, evaluation, and improvement of standards is the best exercise in continuing education. Conversely, it is continuing education in every form, from reading the journals to attendance at international congresses, which enable standards to be discussed and set on the right basis.

Continuing education is coming to be seen as an integral part of the process of postgraduate training, since this can never be 'complete', even at the time of retirement. Relicensure is not a feature of the British system and is not, in a formal sense, likely to be so. Mechanisms exist for dealing with doctors whose competence or standards of professional behaviour give serious cause for concern through illness or for any other reason. But repeated specialist examinations or similar tests are too blunt an instrument for the important work that remains to be done on measuring the quality of medical care and assessing the effectiveness of postgraduate and continuing education. The first requirement for this is doctors who are open-minded, and accustomed to think in terms of lifelong learning. They must have a working environment in which this life-long learning is accessible, in a wide variety of forms, and in which there is a reasonable prospect of translating its lessons into better medical care. In this way critical evaluation becomes a normal feature of medical practice and a basic determinant in its change.   J. PARKHOUSE

Further reading
Committee of Enquiry into the Regulation of the Medical Profession (1975). *The Merrison Report*. Cmnd. 6018. London.
Committee of Enquiry set up for the medical profession in the UK (1976). *Competence to Practise. The Alment Report*. London. (Obtainable from: 27 Sussex Place, Regent's Park, London NW1 4RG.)
Council for Postgraduate Medical Education in England and Wales (1981). *Part-time in Medicine*. London. (Obtainable from 7 Marylebone Road, London, NW1 5HH.)
House of Commons Social Services Committee (1980–1). *Fourth Report. Medical Education, with Special Reference to the Number of Doctors and the Career Structure in Hospitals*. London.
Nuffield Provincial Hospitals Trust (1962). Conference on postgraduate medical education. *British Medical Journal*, **1**, 466–7.
Nuffield Provincial Hospitals Trust (1965). Assessment of postgraduate medical education. *British Medical Journal*, **ii**, 557–64.
Pereira Gray, D. J. (1979). *A System of Training for General Practice*. 2nd edn, London.
Royal Commission on Medical Education (1965–8). *The Todd Report*. Cmnd. 3569. London.

POST-MORTEM EXAMINATION is synonymous with *autopsy and necropsy.

POST-MORTEM ROOM ATTENDANTS. Mortuary attendants, with duties in respect of *autopsy examinations.

POSTURE is the general attitude, position, and deportment of the body, normally maintained by unconscious reflex activity.

POTAIN, PIERRE CARL ÉDOUARD (1825–1901). French physician, MD Paris (1853). A professor at the Faculté in 1859, Potain was associated with the Hôpitaux S. Antoine and Necker, succeeding to the chair of pathology in 1876 and of medicine the next year. He is remembered now for his apparatus for aspiration of *pleural effusion. He described an 'air *sphygmomanometer' in 1889.

POTASSIUM is a soft white very reactive element (relative atomic mass 39.102, atomic number 19, symbol K), a member of the alkali metals. Potassium is the main intracellular *cation of most living tissues; chemically it resembles sodium, which is the main extracellular cation. As with sodium, the movement of potassium ions across cell membranes is fundamental to the process of neuromuscular excitation (see DEPOLARIZATION). Because of its physiological importance, depletion of body potassium (hypokalaemia) constitutes a dangerous disturbance of *electrolyte balance which must be corrected by the administration of potassium salts.

POTASSIUM, SERUM. See HYPERKALAEMIA; HYPOKALAEMIA.

POTENCY refers particularly to the strength of medicinal agents, and to the ability to have *orgasm in sexual intercourse (see IMPOTENCE).

POTENTIAL means possible as opposed to actual; it is often an abbreviation of 'potential difference', the electrical equivalent of hydrostatic pressure difference.

POTENTIATION is the promotion of a pharmacological effect by the action of another drug or agent; it is applied similarly to physiological and biochemical effects.

POTOMANIA is a morbid craving for alcoholic drink; it is sometimes used synonymously with *dipsomania.

POTT, PERCIVALL (1714–88). British surgeon, freeman of *Barber-Surgeons' Company (1736), FRS (1764). Pott was elected assistant surgeon to *St Bartholomew's Hospital, London, in 1741 and surgeon in 1749. In 1753 he became a foundation member of the Corporation of Surgeons and its master in 1765. He was the first honorary fellow of the Royal College of Surgeons of Edinburgh (1786). Pott was the leading British surgeon of his day. He forbade the use of the *cautery and is responsible for describing the following eponymic disorders: *Pott's fracture, which he is said to have sustained himself (1750); *Pott's puffy tumour (abscess overlying local osteomyelitis of the skull, 1768); chimney sweep's cancer (epithelioma of scrotum, 1775); and *Pott's disease (tuberculosis of spine, 1779).

POTT'S DISEASE is *tuberculosis of the spine; it is rare now in the USA and the UK, but is still an important complication of tuberculosis elsewhere in the world. The initial site of infection is usually in the anterior part of a vertebral body, spreading from there through the intervertebral disc to an adjacent vertebra. There may be a collapse of bone causing anterior angulation and a characteristic hunchback deformity. The '*cold abscess', which may also spread to structures beyond the spine, can exert pressure on the spinal cord causing weakness or paralysis of sphincters or legs ('Pott's paraplegia'). The ultimate response to antituberculous chemotherapy and immobilization is often good, obviating the need for surgical intervention unless paralysis has occurred.

POTT'S FRACTURE is a serious ankle injury in which the foot is forcibly bent outwards with respect to the lower leg. The outer bone of the leg, the fibula, is fractured above the ankle; the inner side of the ankle is injured, either the lowest part of the tibia being broken off or else the medial ligament is torn. The ankle is then unsupported and may become dislocated.

POTT'S PUFFY TUMOUR is an extradural *abscess resulting from *osteomyelitis of the skull, causing the syndrome of localized headache, tenderness, and *oedema over the affected area.

POUCH OF DOUGLAS. The fold of *peritoneum which dips down between the *rectum and the *uterus.

POULTICE. A hot dressing for application to the skin either for the purpose of *counter-irritation or in order to increase local blood flow.

POUPART, FRANÇOIS (1616–1708). French surgeon and anatomist. He graduated in medicine at Reims, but practised at the *Hôtel-Dieu in Paris. He was a naturalist of distinction and was elected a member of the French Academy of Sciences in 1699. He gave his name to the *inguinal ligament (Poupart's ligament).

POWDERS are mixtures of powdered medicinal substances, sometimes with adjuvants such as diluents and dispersing agents. They may be soluble, dispersible, or effervescent, and are normally intended for oral administration. They are usually mixed with water before administration, except in the case of some veterinary powders which are mixed with the animal's feed. The degree of comminution of powders is expressed by means of a 'sieve number' in millimetres (mm) or micrometres (μm), which is the nominal aperture size of the finest sieve through which the whole of a particular powder will pass.

POWER, SIR D'ARCY (1855–1941). British surgeon and medical historian, BM Oxford (1882), FRCS (1883). Power was elected assistant surgeon to *St Bartholomew's Hospital, London, in 1898 and surgeon in 1904. During the Second World War he commanded the 10th (London) General Hospital (RAMC). He was knighted in 1919. Power was a medical historian, editor, and biographer of great erudition.

POX is a name which has been used for several diseases characterized by 'pocks' or eruptive *pustules on the skin; the term persists only in compound form in common terms, for example *chickenpox, *cowpox, *smallpox, etc. It was also once used as a synonym for *syphilis.

POXVIRUS. A group of related large deoxyribonucleic acid (DNA) *viruses which includes the causative agents of *vaccinia, *smallpox, and a number of animal pox infections.

PRACTICE. See MEDICAL PRACTICE.

PRACTITIONER is a term which denotes a person in possession of qualifications to practise medicine though not necessarily engaged in active medical practice.

PRAUSNITZ, CARL WILHELM (1861–1933). German hygienist and bacteriologist. Prausnitz studied in many German universities. He was appointed professor in Graz, Austria, in 1893. He was a pioneer in all aspects of hygiene and epidemiology, pushing through reforms in food control, sewage, drainage, ventilation, and lighting systems, as well as *infectious disease prevention.

PRAXIS. Practice as distinct from theory; also, a collection of examples for practice. Or, alternatively, skilled voluntary movement, lost in *apraxia.

PRECIPITANT. Any substance or agent responsible for precipitation, whether of a visible deposit in a solution, or of an event such as the sudden onset of a disease.

PRECIPITINS are *antibodies which, when they react with their homologous *antigen, produce a visible aggregate of antigen–antibody complex.

PRECLINICAL EDUCATION. See MEDICAL EDUCATION IN THE UK AND EUROPE; MEDICAL EDUCATION IN THE USA AND CANADA.

PRECOCITY. Premature development.

PREDNISONE is one of the synthetic glucocorticoids (see CORTICOSTEROIDS). Like cortisone, it is an 11-keto compound and is not itself biologically active, requiring *in vivo* conversion to the 11-betahydroxyl compound prednisolone in order to exert its pharmacological effects.

PREGNANCY is the condition of being with child or young, that is having within the body a fertilized *ovum (zygote), a developing *embryo, or a growing *fetus. See OBSTETRICS.

PREGNANCY TEST. There are a number of tests which have been developed for the detection of pregnancy, most of which utilize chemical, *bioassay, or (more recently) *radioimmunoassay techniques for the estimation of *hormone levels in urine or plasma.

PREMATURE BABY. A viable infant born before full term, that is after a gestation period of less than 38 weeks. Prematurity is also defined by reference to birth weight as less than 2.5 kg (5.5 lbs).

PREMATURE BEAT. See ECTOPIC BEATS.

PREMENSTRUAL TENSION is a syndrome

occurring in the few days prior to *menstruation and usually ascribed to salt and water retention associated with the hormonal changes at that time; symptoms vary but often include headache, insomnia, fatiguability, and emotional lability.

PREPUCE. The foreskin, the loose fold of skin that covers the glans penis in uncircumcised men.

PRE-REGISTRATION HOSPITAL APPOINT-MENTS are resident medical and surgical hospital appointments which must be fulfilled by those newly graduated in medicine in order to obtain admission to the UK Medical Register. See MEDI-CAL EDUCATION IN THE UK AND EUROPE; GENERAL MEDICAL COUNCIL; POSTGRADUATE AND CONTINUING MEDICAL EDUCATION.

PRESBYOPIA is the visual impairment resulting from old age. With advancing years, the power of the lens to accommodate in order to focus near objects is gradually lost owing to decreasing elasticity, and corrective spectacles are required for close vision (reading, needlework, etc.). See OPHTHALMOLOGY.

PRESCRIPTIONS are the written directions for the preparation, supply, and administration of medicines. In the UK, a prescription for a controlled drug may not be dispensed by a pharmacist unless the requirements of Regulation 15 of the Misuse of Drugs Regulations 1973 are met. The prescription must be handwritten in ink, or be otherwise indelible, must give the name and address of the patient, the dose and the quantity of the drug to be supplied in both words and figures, and must be signed with the doctor's full signature. Controlled drugs include cocaine, the narcotic analgesics, and amphetamine and related compounds; controlled drugs are identified by the letters CD in the *British National Formulary*. A large number of other drugs are 'prescription only' medicines. These include most of the other potent drugs used in medical practice (e.g. antibiotics, hormones, vaccines, hypnotics, etc.).

PRESENIUM. The period of life preceding old age.

PRESENTATION, in medicine generally, means the complex of symptoms and signs which first manifest the presence of a disease process. In obstetrics, it denotes the particular part of the fetus presented to the birth canal at the onset of labour (see OBSTETRICS).

PREVALENCE is the number of instances of illness or of persons ill, or of any other event such as accidents, in a specified population, without any distinction between new and old cases. The prevalence may be recorded at a stated moment ('point prevalence') or during a given period of time ('period prevalence'). When the term

'prevalence' is used without qualification, it must be taken to mean 'point prevalence'. When prevalence is expressed as 'prevalence rate', the denominator used is the number of persons in the specified population at the given time; or in the case of period prevalence, the average number of persons during the defined period or the estimated number at the mid-point of that period (Hogarth, 1978, *Glossary of Health Care Terminology,* World Health Organization, Copenhagen). See EPIDEMIOLOGY.

PREVENTIVE MEDICINE attempts to control disease by the identification and elimination of causes. Since potentially remediable causes range from such factors as ignorance, poverty, poor sanitation, and maladministration on the one hand to minute gene aberrations on the other, the scope of preventive medicine is virtually boundless. The catalogue of past success, for example the declared elimination of *smallpox in 1980, needs no rehearsal. Emphasis should instead be given to the fact that present knowledge has by no means yet been fully exploited. This applies to many promising and intellectually exciting new developments (e.g. the application of molecular biological techniques to *trophoblast biopsy in early pregnancy) but still more to the mundane matters of *health education with respect to alcohol and tobacco, legislation further to reduce road traffic casualties, fluoridation of drinking water, and very many others. See COMMUNITY MEDICINE.

PRIAPISM is persistent, often painful, penile erection.

PRIAPUS is equivalent to *phallus, from Priapus the Greek and Roman god of procreation.

PRICKLY HEAT is an itchy rash of erythematous papulovesicular type due to obstruction of the ducts of the sweat glands and escape of sweat into the *epidermis. Prickly heat is associated with prolonged excessive heat load.

PRIESTLEY, JOHN GILLIES (1879–1941). English physiologist, MD London (1903). Priestley was born in Yorkshire, and educated at Eton and Oxford, he went on to obtain a medical qualification at *St Bartholomew's Hospital, and to direct the chemical pathology laboratory there. He served with distinction during the First World War, towards the end of which he collaborated with J. S. *Haldane in studying the after-effects of gas poisoning. These two men had already published their classical paper on 'The Regulation of the Lung-Ventilation' (*Journal of Physiology,* **32**, (1905) 224–66), which established the dominant role of *carbon dioxide in determining the depth and frequency of *respiration. In his later years in the physiology laboratory in Oxford, he also worked on the regulatory functions of the kidney; and he prepared the subject index for the first 60 volumes of the *Journal of Physiology,* a task which must arouse the sympathy of any compiler.

PRIESTLEY, JOSEPH (1733–1804). British scientist and theologian, FRS (1766). Priestley was trained for the presbyterian ministry and held numerous posts, but the resentment aroused by his unorthodox opinions persuaded him to emigrate to the USA in 1794. He was also a distinguished chemist discovering 10 new gases including *carbon monoxide, sulphur dioxide, and *nitrous oxide. He noted that air was 'vitiated' by combustion or respiration, but could be 'restored' by growing green-leaved plants in it. He showed that a 'new gas which was better to breathe than common air' was formed on heating nitre (1771) or mercuric oxide (1774). Unable to cast off the phlogiston theory, he called this gas 'dephlogisticated air'. *Lavoisier after conversation with Priestley immediately appreciated its importance and gave it the name of *oxygen.

PRIG, BETSY is a character in Charles Dickens's novel *Martin Chuzzlewit* (1843–4); she is a disreputable old nurse, the friend and professional colleague of Mrs Sarah *Gamp.

PRIMAQUINE is a synthetic antimalarial drug, used particularly in the eradication of benign tertian *malaria after primary treatment with *chloroquine.

PRIMARY HEALTH CARE is a term which is usually employed to mean primary medical care, which is that provided by the general medical practitioner to whom a patient first turns for advice, although it can have a wider connotation embracing services provided by other health professionals. See also GENERAL MEDICAL PRACTICE.

PRIMIDONE is a drug used in the control of most varieties of *epilepsy, also known under the proprietary name Mysoline®.

PRINCIPAL. A partner or established single-handed practitioner (as distinct from an assistant or trainee) in a *general medical practice in the UK.

PRINCIPLES AND PRACTICE OF MEDICINE is the title of the famous textbook of medicine published in 1891 by Dr (later Sir) William *Osler, the Canadian-born physician, who became professor of medicine successively at the universities of *McGill, Pennsylvania, *Johns Hopkins, and Oxford, where he occupied the regius chair. The last edition to be published during Osler's lifetime was the eighth in 1912; the ninth appeared in 1920 shortly after his death. The book was subsequently revised by McCane and later by *Christian up until 1939. It was revived again after the Second World War by Harvey and colleagues from Johns Hopkins and continues. The same title was given to a textbook published in 1952 by Sir Stanley David-son, currently in its 13th edition (1981) as a multi-author work originating primarily from the departments of medicine and therapeutics of the University of Edinburgh.

PRINGLE, SIR JOHN, BT (1707–82). British physician and theologian, MD Leiden (1730). Born in Stitchel, Roxburghshire, Pringle studied at St Andrews, Edinburgh, and Leiden in Holland. He was professor of moral theology in Edinburgh, and combined this with medical practice. In 1742 he was appointed physician to the army commander on the continent. At the battle of Dettingen (1743) in Germany he proposed that military hospitals be sanctuaries, which was accepted by the French commander. This was the forerunner of the idea of the *Red Cross, which was established in 1863. He was present at the battle of Culloden in 1745. In 1752 he published *Observations on the Diseases of the Army,* which helped improve the environment of serving men and military hospitals and their practice. In a paper read at the Royal Society he used the word 'antiseptic' for the first time. He became physician to King George III and president of the Royal Society. He married a daughter of Dr Oliver of Bath whose name is associated with Bath Oliver biscuits.

PRIVATE PRACTICE. See MEDICAL PRACTICE.

PRIVY COUNCIL. Originally the private council of a sovereign with the function of advising on the administration of government. In the UK, the Privy Council is a body of advisers appointed by the sovereign which includes certain members by usage, such as the princes of the blood, the archbishops, and the chief officers of past and present ministries of state. Its functions are now either purely formal or are carried out by committees; and Privy-Councillorship is mainly a personal dignity conferred in recognition of eminent public service.

At present, the Privy Council numbers about 380 members, but is only summoned as a body in order to sign the Proclamation of the accession of a new sovereign or when the sovereign announces an intention to marry. The number normally summoned is four (the Lord President and the ministers chiefly concerned with the particular business), the quorum being three.

Committees of the Council, the most important of which is the Judicial Committee, are responsible *inter alia* for dealing with appeals from the disciplinary bodies concerned with medicine, dentistry, and the professions supplementary to medicine (see GENERAL MEDICAL COUNCIL). Until 1965 the Medical Research Council was responsible to a ministerial Committee of the Privy Council. Thereafter, by virtue of the Science and Technology Act 1965, this function was transferred to the Secretary of State for Education and Science.

PROBANG. A flexible instrument made of

whalebone with a sponge, ball, or button at the end for introduction into the pharynx and oesophagus in order to apply medication, to extract a foreign body, or to push obstructing material down into the stomach. The probang was invented by the Welsh judge Walter Rumsey (1584–1660) who named it provang but his reasons for calling it this are not known.

PROBE. Any surgical instrument used primarily for exploratory purposes; any instrument or method used for exploration (e.g. in biology, genetics, electronics, space research, etc.).

PROBENECID is one of the uricosuric drugs, i.e. substances which, by blocking the renal tubular reabsorption of urate, promote the excretion of *uric acid in the urine. It is of value in the treatment of the hyperuricaemia of *gout. Probenecid also blocks the tubular excretion of certain *antibiotics, notably the *penicillins and *cephalosporins, and may be administered in conjunction with these drugs in order to enable them to achieve a higher blood concentration.

PROCAINE is the earliest (1905) and one of the most successful synthetic local anaesthetic agents, widely used for more than 50 years but now superseded by newer drugs. See LOCAL ANAESTHESIA.

PROCARBAZINE is an antineoplastic drug used chiefly in the treatment of *Hodgkin's disease. Because it has an action like that of *disulfiram, alcoholic drinks should be avoided during its administration.

PROCESS. A projection, prominence, protuberance, outgrowth, extension, etc. of or from the main body of an anatomical structure.

PROCHASKA, GEORG (1749–1820). Czechoslovakian physician and physiologist. Prochaska was professor of anatomy and ophthalmology both at Prague and Vienna. He was one of the first to recognize the integration of function in centres of the brain and showed that movements could be initiated in lower parts of the brain than the *cerebrum.

PROCIDENTIA is a severe degree of *prolapse of the *uterus or *rectum, with most or all of the organ exteriorized.

PROCTITIS is inflammation of the *rectum.

PROCTOLOGIST. A surgeon specializing in anorectal disorders.

PROCTOLOGY. The study of disorders of the anus and rectum.

PROCTOSCOPY is inspection of the *rectum with the assistance of an illuminated *speculum.

PRODROMES are premonitory symptoms or signs heralding the onset of some disease; the word is often used in the Greek form 'prodromata', and also adjectively as 'prodromal'.

PRODUCT LIABILITY. See PHARMACEUTICAL INDUSTRY.

PROFESSIONAL CONFIDENCE is the principle that information obtained by doctors and by extension by their non-medical colleagues during the course of their professional duties shall not be disclosed to others without the consent of the patient concerned, unless there are overriding moral or legal considerations to the contrary. The author of the *Hippocratic Oath enshrined this principle in the following words: 'All that may come to my knowledge in the exercise of my profession or outside of my profession or in daily commerce with men, which ought not to be spread abroad, I will keep secret and will never reveal.' (For a discussion of the practical application of the principle, the reader is referred to D. D. Reid (1977), 'Confidentiality', in A. S. Duncan, G. R. Dunstan, and R. B. Welbourn (eds), *Dictionary of Medical Ethics*, London.)

PROFESSIONAL EXAMINATIONS are those which must be passed for professional qualification.

PROFESSIONAL MALPRACTICE (alternatively 'malpraxis') is a term which embraces all forms of medical misconduct including *professional negligence. It is not confined to, nor does it have the specific English legal connotation of, the latter term. Improper advertising by a medical practitioner, for example, can be described as professional malpractice. It is, however, extensively used in the USA in connection with legal actions involving the unintentional tort of negligence. See LAW AND MEDICINE IN THE UK; LAW AND MEDICINE IN THE USA.

PROFESSIONAL NEGLIGENCE is defined as a failure of the doctor to exercise reasonable skill and care which results in injury to the patient. Under English law, negligence as so defined constitutes a tort or civil wrong (i.e. not a crime), and a civil action is necessary in order for the patient to obtain redress. In England, a judge alone determines liability and the amount of damages to be paid, the former requiring a judgement about the standard of care which can be regarded as reasonable under the particular circumstances and the latter an assessment of an adequate level of compensation for whatever injury has been suffered; in other countries, including Ireland and the USA, a jury is also involved. Proof of negligence requires the existence of a professional duty towards the patient, a breach of that duty, and injury to the patient resulting from that breach. Actions must be brought within three years of the act complained of, or within three years of the plaintiff becoming aware of the harm resulting from it. Some countries, (e.g. Sweden, New Zealand) operate forms of 'no-fault' compensation for patients suffering the consequences of medical accidents. See LAW AND MEDICINE IN THE UK; LAW AND MEDICINE IN THE USA.

PROFESSIONAL PROTECTION SOCIETIES are organizations which, in return for subscription to membership, provide doctors and dentists in the UK and some other countries (e.g. Australia, Canada, France) with indemnity against the results of legal actions involving professional negligence and some other matters, with medicolegal advice, and with legal representation when necessary. Three such organizations, which are not insurance companies, exist in the UK; they are the Medical Defence Union, the Medical Protection Society, and the Medical and Dental Defence Union of Scotland. Elsewhere, for example in other European countries and in the USA, professional liability indemnity is provided by commercial insurance companies; this may be very much more expensive and is a more restricted service than that provided by the protection societies. See LAW AND MEDICINE IN THE UK.

PROFESSIONS SUPPLEMENTARY, AUXILIARY, AND COMPLEMENTARY TO MEDICINE IN THE UK. With the increasing complexity of modern medicine and treatment the number of auxiliary, complementary, and supplementary services that the doctor and his patient require has greatly increased. The *Department of Health and Social Security (DHSS) in the UK now recognizes more than 40 occupations which may be described as paramedical. The more important are:

Artificial kidney technicians
Biochemists
Chiropodists
Clinical psychologists
Dark room technicians
Dental hygienists
Dental surgery assistants
Dental technicians
Dietitians
Electronics technicians
Medical laboratory scientific officers
  (technicians)
Medical photographers
Medical physics technicians
Occupational therapists
Opticians
  ophthalmic
  dispensing
Orthoptists
Pharmacists
Pharmacy technicians
Physicists
Physiological measurement technicians:
  audiology

cardiology
neurophysiology
Physiotherapists
Post-mortem room technicians
Radiographers:
  diagnostic
  therapeutic
Remedial gymnasts
Speech therapists

Paramedical occupations in the UK. Until 1936 no attempt had been made to regulate these occupations nor to identify and register those technicians or practitioners who were proficient. In that year the British Medical Association formed the Board of Registration of Medical Auxiliaries and in 1954 employment in the *National Health Service (NHS) was limited to those registered with the Board. Finally in 1960 a regulatory Bill, the *Professions Supplementary to Medicine Act, became law.

Professions supplementary to medicine. The 1960 Act provided for a number of boards, each of which would be responsible for one of the supplementary professions. The boards were all related to a Council for the Professions Supplementary to Medicine which provided their legal, financial, and administrative framework. Each board was to consist of members of the specific profession in a majority of one, medical practitioners concerned in the specialty, and an educationist. The council was to be made up of a representative of each board, and nominees of the *Royal medical colleges, of the *General Medical Council, of the UK *Health Departments, and of the *Privy Council, one of the last being chairman. Originally there were seven boards representing respectively chiropody, dietetics, medical laboratory technology, occupational therapy, physiotherapy, radiography, and remedial gymnastics. In 1967 they were joined by the orthoptists. The term 'professions supplementary to medicine' must now be held legally to describe only these eight occupations.

The duties of the boards, which are legally autonomous, are to identify and register persons professionally competent in these occupations, to approve the standards of qualification and training, and to enforce professional discipline. Registration is not statutory, but only those practitioners registered by the relevant board are accepted for employment in the NHS. No such restriction applies to private practice. Registration entails observance of a code of conduct which demands that patients are treated only when referred by a doctor, that diagnosis and treatment is limited to what the practitioner has been trained to do, and that he does not represent himself as competent on account of training or experience to treat disease. Approval of the qualifying standard and of the training is the most important of the board's functions. Minimum educational standards before acceptance for training are set by the board, which also approves the course to be followed. In all cases, except for dieticians and medical laboratory technicians, the examining body which grants the qualification is the chief or sole professional institution of the particular specialty. In addition to these duties the professional institutions advance the knowledge and skills of the profession and represent its general and economic interests in society.

In general the educational standards required for entry are similar in all the supplementary professions, consisting of five General Certificate of Education passes at 'O' (ordinary) level or two at 'A' (advanced) level, one of which should be in a science subject. Different colleges and training establishments may have different requirements. An initial registration and annual retention fees are payable. Additional details of the different professions are set out in the following paragraphs.

Chiropodists. The Society of Chiropodists awards the diploma of membership (M.Ch.S) by examination after a three-year course. A fellowship of the society (F.Ch.S) is obtainable by special examination, thesis, or for unusual distinction.

Clinical psychologists. Many clinical psychologists work in the British NHS. All possess a first degree in psychology after three years of study in a university or polytechnic, and a Master's degree (M.Sc.) in clinical psychology usually based upon an additional two-year course. These colleagues are especially concerned with the use of psychometric techniques in the assessment of brain disease and dysfunction but also contribute in many cases to patient care and counselling. Compulsory registration through the British Psychological Society is now under consideration. (See also PSYCHOLOGY.)

Dietitians. Professional qualification is by university degree in dietetics or nutrition followed by practical work or by a postgraduate diploma in dietetics after acquiring a basic science degree. Validation is jointly by the Dietetic Board and the British Dietetics Association.

Medical laboratory scientific officers (MLSOs; formerly known as medical laboratory technicians). The title MLSO is largely confined to scientific officers employed in the hospital service of the UK National Health Service. Individuals fulfilling similar duties in UK universities are still generally known as technicians. The professional qualification required is either the Higher National Diploma or Certificate or a university degree. Both require validation by the Board and the Institute of Medical Laboratory Sciences. Students can enrol with the Institute when training and when qualified become an associate (AIMLS). After two years they can obtain the fellowship (FIMLS) by further examination, thesis, or by acquiring a higher degree. The examination is in one of seven specialized branches of medical laboratory science.

Occupational therapists. The College of Occupational Therapy conducts examinations and grants diplomas in association with the British Association of Occupational Therapists, of which successful candidates may become members.

Orthoptists. The British Orthoptic Council acting jointly with the British Orthoptists' Society are responsible for examinations and for granting diplomas.

Physiotherapists. Examinations are conducted and the diploma (MCSP) awarded to successful candidates by the Chartered Society of Physiotherapy. The Society and the Board together approve training schools.

Radiographers. The College of Radiographers is responsible for the qualifying examinations and for the award of diplomas. There are two basic diplomas, DCR(R) in diagnostic radiology and DCR(T) in radiotherapy. Once a diploma has been gained, the recipient is eligible for membership of the Society of Radiographers. The College also gives post-diploma qualifications in nuclear medicine, in medical ultrasound, a higher diploma, and a teacher's diploma.

Remedial gymnasts. The Society of Remedial Gymnasts is responsible for examination after three years' training at institutions it has approved. It awards its certificate validated by the Board, to successful candidates.

Other paramedical occupations in the UK. Of the other paramedical occupations and professions listed earlier in this article, some are only incidentally of medical concern, such as biochemists, darkroom technicians, electronic technicians, photographers, and physicists. Some do not require a scientific or academic training; the remainder, opticians, pharmacists, and speech therapists are discussed below. Finally, social workers, although employed by the local authority and not by the DHSS, deserve mention because it is frequently difficult to draw a line between social support and medical care. This is particularly true when physical disability, mental defect, or illness complicate the issue. The social worker carries heavy responsibilities, especially when there is suspicion of cruelty or non-accidental injury to children.

Opticians. There are two professional grades of optician. The ophthalmic optician is trained to distinguish between ocular and other cases of visual disability, to test visual acuity, and to prescribe and fit spectacles and contact lenses. This training extends over 4 years: during the first 3 years he (or she) undertakes a full-time degree course at an approved university and for the fourth, he engages in practical work under a qualified ophthalmic optician. Alternatively he may enrol for a 4-year diploma course. At the end of his training his degree is validated by the British College of Ophthalmic Opticians (Optometrists) or he is required to pass the College's examination before registration with the General Optical Council.

The dispensing optician is trained to fit spectacles, contact lenses, and other ophthalmic appliances, but is not permitted to prescribe, nor test sight. Only a doctor or an ophthalmic optician is legally permitted to test sight. Less demanding educational standards are required and the period of training is only 2 years.

Pharmacists. Persons are not permitted to practise as pharmacists in the UK unless registered with the Pharmaceutical Society and holding the Society's diploma of membership (MPS). To achieve this, a degree in pharmacy from one of the schools approved by the Society is required. The course of training lasts 3 years and must be followed by 1 year of practical experience, 6 months of which is spent in a hospital pharmacy or under a pharmacist in general pharmaceutical practice. (See also PHARMACY AND PHARMACISTS.)

Pharmacy assistants work under the supervision of a pharmacist carrying out dispensing, stock-taking, and other work as directed. They undergo training while employed, with part-time study. Certificates of proficiency are awarded after examination by the Society of Apothecaries, the City and Guilds Institute of London, and the Scottish Technical Board.

Speech therapists. The College of Speech Therapists was formed in 1948 by the union of the remedial section of the Association of Teachers of Speech and Drama and the department of speech therapy of the Central School of Speech Training. In 1960 the College declined inclusion among the professions supplementary to medicine because it claimed to be autonomous and concerned as much with education as with medicine. It has been legally incorporated and its functions are to maintain high standards of training, academic knowledge, and ethical conduct in the profession. It is an examining body and confers its licence (LCST) on successful candidates, maintaining a register of its licentiates, and publishing a directory.

Social workers. The Central Council for Education and Training of Social Workers is responsible for approving courses of training, examinations, and for awarding certificates of qualification (CQSW) to successful candidates. There are several programmes of training. Candidates must be aged 22 years or over. The requirements are a degree or diploma in social work followed by an approved postgraduate course of 1 year, or a 4-year university or polytechnic course in social science, the final year being devoted to professional training.   R. BODLEY SCOTT

PROFESSIONS SUPPLEMENTARY TO MEDICINE ACT 1960. This UK Act established a coordinating council to supervise a number of registration boards who register members of the supplementary professions and regulate their professional education and conduct. Candidates for appointment by *National Health Service or local authorities who belong to these professions must appear on the appropriate register. Those covered include chiropodists, dieticians, medical laboratory scientific officers, occupational therapists, physiotherapists, radiographers, remedial gymnasts, and orthoptists. See PROFESSIONS SUPPLEMENTARY, AUXILIARY, AND COMPLEMENTARY TO MEDICINE IN THE UK.

PROFESSORIAL UNITS are hospital units in the various clinical disciplines staffed in whole or in part by doctors, scientists, technicians and (very occasionally) nurses employed by a university, as well as by staff employed by the hospital, of whom one or more is of professorial rank.

PROGERIA is premature senility. One variety, the Hutchinson–Gilford syndrome, is a rare type of *dwarfism of unknown aetiology which confers a characteristic appearance of premature old age and of a 'plucked bird'. It develops early, during the third and fourth year of life, and most patients die in childhood or adolescence (the median age at death is 13 years). Degenerative disturbances, particularly *atherosclerosis with cardiovascular and cerebrovascular manifestations, are common.

Another, unrelated, condition known as Werner's syndrome develops in early adult life. This is inherited as an autosomal *recessive characteristic, but again the fundamental defect is unknown. All the changes of cell senescence occur: there is premature greying, hair loss, hearing loss, teeth loss, *cataracts, *arthritis, *osteoporosis, *diabetes mellitus, and premature *atherosclerosis. A high proportion of affected individuals develop malignant tumours, especially *sarcomas. Werner's syndrome is sometimes called 'adult progeria' to distinguish it from the childhood syndrome.

PROGESTERONE is the body's principal progestational *hormone, that is the hormone which prepares the *endometrium for implantation of the fertilized *ovum. This preparation takes place during the second half of each menstrual cycle throughout the reproductive period of life, under the influence of progesterone secreted by the *corpus luteum formed in the ovarian follicle after *ovulation; if pregnancy supervenes the corpus luteum and progesterone secretion persist. Progesterone ($C_{21}H_{30}O_2$) is also produced by the *adrenal cortex and the *placenta. Because they inhibit ovulation, progestational substances are widely employed in oral *contraceptive formulations.

PROGESTOGENS are natural or synthetic substances with progestational activity.

PROGNATHOUS. Having protruding jaws.

PROGNOSIS is the forecasting, or forecast, of the future course and the ultimate outcome of a disease.

PROGRESSIVE BULBAR PALSY. See MOTOR NEURONE DISEASE; NEUROMUSCULAR DISEASE.

PROGRESSIVE MUSCULAR ATROPHY. See MOTOR NEURONE DISEASE; NEUROMUSCULAR DISEASE.

PROGUANIL is an antimalarial drug used in *prophylaxis (daily dosage) and treatment in areas of British influence but rarely in US practice. Proguanil is also known under the proprietary name of Paludrine®.

PROHIBITION is used to mean the interdiction by law of the manufacture, importation, or sale of alcoholic drinks for common consumption. In the USA, prohibition was enforced between 1920 and 1933, in accordance with the 18th Amendment to the US Constitution. During this period the manufacture and sale of drinks containing more than 0.5 per cent of ethyl alcohol were illegal. Prohibition ended with the 21st Amendment, on 5 December 1933.

PROKARYOTES are cellular organisms without a distinct nucleus or nuclear membrane, whose genetic material is in the form of haploid *deoxyribonucleic acid (DNA) (unpaired chromosomes). Bacteria and blue-green algae are prokaryotes; all other cellular organisms, plant and animal, are *eukaryotes. See CELL.

PROLACTIN is the lactogenic hormone secreted by the anterior lobe of the *pituitary gland which controls the secretion of milk by the *mammary glands of the postpartum female.

PROLACTINOMA. A *pituitary tumour which secretes *prolactin.

PROLAPSE is a falling or slipping down of an organ; when otherwise unqualified, it usually means prolapse of the *uterus, a not uncommon condition in multiparous women in which the uterine cervix descends to or beyond the vaginal orifice and sometimes the whole uterus is extruded. Rectal prolapse through the anus occurs sometimes in children.

PROLAPSED INTERVERTEBRAL DISC, also known as 'prolapsed nucleus pulposus', 'herniated nucleus pulposus', or 'slipped disc' is thought to be the usual cause of acute back pain, particularly in the cervical and lumbar regions, and of radicular or nerve root pain, particularly that which is felt along the distribution of the sciatic nerve (sciatica). Each intervertebral disc is a tough flexible pad lying between the bodies of adjacent vertebrae (see SPINE); it consists of a soft centre, the nucleus pulposus, surrounded by a circular ring of fibrous tissue, the annulus fibrosus. The latter is at its weakest posteriorly, and if some particular strain is put on it, for example by bending, it may allow the nuclear pulposus to bulge backwards. Depending on whether this bulge (or hernia) is in the mid-line or to one or other side of it, it can press on the spinal cord itself or on one or more of the spinal nerve roots. When in the lumbosacral region, lumbago and/or sciatica can result, together with, in many cases, objective evidence of interference with sensory and motor nerve pathways. A similar situation arises not infrequently in the cervical spine. Involvement of the relatively more rigid thoracic spine is less common.

PROLINTANE is a weak central nervous stimulant drug of uncertain therapeutic value sometimes added to vitamin and 'tonic' mixtures.

PRONTOSIL® is the proprietary name for the prototype *sulphonamide introduced in the early 1930s, now no longer in use.

PROPHYLAXIS is the prevention of disease, or the preventive treatment of a recurrent disorder.

PROPRANOLOL is a drug which causes beta-adrenergic blockade (see BETA-BLOCKERS; ADRENERGIC BLOCKADE); it is used in a wide variety of conditions where this pharmacological effect is desired (e.g. *hypertension, *angina, *arrhythmias, *myocardial infarction, *thyrotoxicosis, psychiatric disorders, etc.).

PROPRIETARY MEDICINES. see DRUGS; PHARMACEUTICAL INDUSTRY.

PROPRIOCEPTION is the reception of sensory information by structures (proprioceptors) within the tissues, especially information concerning the movement and sense of position of parts of the body.

PROPTOSIS is forward displacement of the eyeball.

PROSECTOR. One who dissects a body for the purpose of anatomical or pathological demonstration.

PROSTAGLANDINS are a group of related complex *fatty acids found in most human tissues. They may be regarded as local tissue *hormones, sharing some of the characteristics of hormones and of *neurotransmitters. They are subdivided into six types, labelled A to F, the degree of saturation of the side-chain being in each case designated by the subscript 1, 2, or 3 (e.g. PGE_2 etc.). They have many biological effects, possibly by influencing the activity of the enzyme *adenyl cyclase. These include effects on vascular permeability, blood pressure, acid secretion by the stomach, platelet aggregation, body temperature, the action of certain hormones, and uterine contractility. The action of prostaglandin preparations on the pregnant uterus is employed therapeutically to procure abortion and to induce labour.

PROSTATE. A gland of the male reproductive system of mammals, which contributes its secretion (acid phosphatase, citric acid, and proteolytic enzymes) to *semen. It surrounds the neck of the *bladder and the proximal portion of the *urethra. It comprises both muscle and glandular elements. In man it often becomes enlarged as a result of *hyperplasia in middle and old age, causing symptoms of urinary obstruction which require surgical relief. The prostate may also be the site of bacterial infection (prostatitis) and of *carcinoma.

PROSTATECTOMY is surgical removal of the *prostate gland.

PROSTHESIS. An artificial substitute for a body part.

PROSTRATION is a state of helplessness or total exhaustion.

PROTANOPIA is defective colour vision of the dichromatic type (see COLOUR BLINDNESS) in which red and green sensitivity are lacking.

PROTEIN. Any of a class of very complex nitrogenous organic compounds of high molecular weight (18 000–10 000 000) which are of fundamental importance to all living matter. They consist of hundreds or thousands of *amino acids joined together by *peptide linkage into one or more connected *polypeptide chains which in turn are folded in various ways. The precise sequence of amino acids is identical in each molecule of a given protein. This sequence is determined by the sequence of the nucleotides in the nucleic acid of the *chromosomes of the cells in which the protein is synthesized; three nucleotides code for each amino acid, of which about 20 occur in nature.

Most proteins form colloidal solutions in water or dilute salt solutions, except for some with elongated (fibrous) molecules which are insoluble. Proteins are frequently 'conjugated', that is combined with other substances, such as nucleic acids (nucleoprotein), carbohydrates (muco- or glyco-proteins), and fats (lipoproteins).

Only autotrophic organisms (most chlorophyll-containing plants and a few bacteria) can synthesize amino acids and hence proteins from inorganic constituents; all other organisms are heterotrophic and ultimately depend on the synthetic activities of autotrophic organisms.

PROTEIN-ENERGY MALNUTRITION is a self-explanatory term, often abbreviated to PEM, formerly called protein-calorie malnutrition (PCM). It covers the spectrum of undernutrition, including both the extreme clinical expressions known as *marasmus and *kwashiorkor.

PROTEINURIA. See ALBUMINURIA.

PROTEUS is a genus of gram-negative bacilli, species of which are common in faecal material and most of which are not highly pathogenic. *Proteus vulgaris* is a fairly frequent cause of *cystitis and occurs also as a secondary invader in various suppurative infections.

PROTHROMBIN is the precursor *enzyme (also known as factor II) of *thrombin. During the process of blood clotting, thrombin catalyses the conversion of the soluble *fibrinogen into *fibrin. See HAEMATOLOGY.

PROTON. A stable elementary particle of positive electric charge equal to that of the *electron but of opposite sign. Protons, together with the electrically neutral *neutrons of almost equal mass, make up the nucleus of all atoms; in an electrically neutral atom the number of protons in the nucleus (the atomic number) is equal to the number of planetary electrons. A single proton is a hydrogen *ion, that is a normal hydrogen atomic nucleus.

PROTOPLASM is the matter of which all biological cells consist, which in nucleated cells is subdivided into that composing the nucleus (nucleoplasm) and that surrounding the nucleus (cytoplasm). It is a complex watery *colloid, containing protein, lipids, carbohydrates, nucleic acids, and inorganic salts. It is usually taken to exclude large vacuoles, masses of secretion, and ingested material.

PROTOZOA are unicellular animals, comprising the simplest phylum of the animal world. A few are parasitic in man and therefore of medical importance. They include the causative agents of *malaria, *trypanosomiasis, *leishmaniasis, *amoebiasis, *giardiasis, *toxoplasmosis, and *trichomoniasis. See PARASITOLOGY.

PROTOZOOLOGY is the study of *protozoa, and is a branch of zoology.

PROUT, WILLIAM (1785–1850). British physician and chemist, MD Edinburgh (1811), FRCP (1829), FRS (1819). Prout was the first 'chemical physiologist'. He showed that the stomach contained free *hydrochloric acid. The dictum that the relative atomic masses (atomic weights) of all elements are multiples of the relative atomic mass of hydrogen is known as 'Prout's law'.

PROWAZEK, STANISLAUS JOSEF MATHIAS VON (1875–1915). Bohemian protozoologist, Ph.D. Vienna (1899). Prowazek discovered the cause of *trachoma and fowl pest while working as an assistant to *Schaudinn whom he followed at the Institut für Schiffs- und Tropenkrankheiten, Hamburg, in 1906. He died of *typhus investigating an outbreak in a Russian prisoner-of-war camp in

1915. Henrique da Rocha-Lima, who also acquired the disease but recovered, discovered the cause and named it *Rickettsia prowazeki* in his honour and in that of H. T. *Ricketts, who also died investigating it.

PRURITUS is itching, which may be generalized or localized to a particular area (e.g. pruritus vulvae, pruritus ani, etc.). It can have many causes including a large number of primary skin diseases and some systemic disorders such as *diabetes mellitus and *obstructive jaundice.

PSEUDOCHOLINESTERASE is an *enzyme, also known simply as cholinesterase, widely distributed in the body, which inactivates *choline esters. ('True' cholinesterase, which inactivates *acetylcholine is acetylcholinesterase.) About one person in 300 is deficient in pseudocholinesterase and in consequence cannot degrade succinylcholine, a muscle relaxant drug often used as an adjuvant in general *anaesthesia.

PSEUDOGOUT is a joint condition of middle and later ages affecting particularly the knees and hips. It has a tendency to be monarticular and may, like gout, occur in acute and painful attacks. Pseudogout, also known as pyrophosphate arthropathy or chondrocalcinosis, is due to the synovial deposition of crystals of calcium pyrophosphate and other calcium salts.

PSEUDOHERMAPHRODITE. Any case of *intersex other than the rare instances of true *hermaphroditism. Male pseudohermaphrodites are gonadally and genetically male but with female external characteristics; the converse is true of female pseudohermaphrodites.

PSEUDOHYPERTROPHY is a disproportionate enlargement of some groups of muscles which occurs in certain types of *muscular dystrophy and occasionally in other myopathic and neurological disorders, due to infiltration with other tissue elements. See NEUROMUSCULAR DISEASE.

PSEUDOHYPOPARATHYROIDISM is a rare genetic disorder characterized by abnormal resistance of the tissues to the effects of *parathyroid hormone, simulating *hypoparathyroidism.

PSEUDOMONAS is a genus of aerobic gram-negative *bacilli widely distributed in the environment, including hospitals. Most do not cause human disease, but one, *Pseudomonas aeruginosa* (formerly known as *P. pyocyanea*) can be the agent of such diverse infections as *endocarditis, *meningitis, *pneumonia, *otitis, wound and burn sepsis, and various types of *nosocomial (i.e. hospital-acquired) infection. The last is particularly liable to occur in ill patients and, because *Pseudomonas* is resistant to many conventional antibiotics, as a 'superinfection' after other organisms have been cleared. *Pseudomonas mallei* is responsible for *glanders.

PSEUDOTUMOUR CEREBRI is a syndrome characterized by manifestations of increased intracranial pressure (headache, vomiting, and *papilloedema) without true localizing signs or any other evidence of a space-occupying lesion such as a cerebral tumour. The syndrome is due to cerebral *oedema and is now more often known as benign intracranial hypertension. A number of aetiological factors have been identified, but in many cases the condition resolves without any cause having been established. Treatment with *corticosteroids and/or *diuretics may be needed to reduce the pressure.

PSEUDOXANTHOMA ELASTICUM is a rare *recessively inherited disorder of elastic tissue affecting predominantly the skin, eyes, and vascular system. The name derives from the appearance in early adult life of yellowish *macules and *papules in the skin histologically found to be composed of abnormal *elastic tissue.

PSITTACOSIS is an acute respiratory infection, often with *pneumonia, acquired from birds and due to the organism *Chlamydia psittaci.* The reservoir was originally thought to be exclusively in psittacines (the parrot family) but this is now known not to be so and the more accurate term ornithosis is to be preferred.

PSORIASIS is a common chronic relapsing skin disease, the causation of which is unknown but which is strongly influenced by *genetic factors. The essential abnormality appears to be an excessively rapid turnover of cells in the epidermal layer of the skin. The rash consists of scattered red papulosquamous patches with silvery scales which do not usually itch and are characteristically concentrated on the extensor surfaces, that is the elbows, knees, and back. The scalp is often affected but the face rarely so. The nails show two typical signs: a deep linear pitting, and separation of the tip from the bed by yellowish keratin. A proportion of patients develop a condition closely resembling *rheumatoid arthritis (psoriatic arthropathy). Psoriasis is common, affecting between 1 and 2 per cent of the population in the USA and Europe. It is very persistent, though temporary remissions are common, both with and without treatment. Other illnesses, and indeed stress of any kind, can precipitate exacerbations.

PSYCHASTHENIA is an imprecise term—'psychic weakness'—introduced by the French psychiatrist Pierre *Janet. As used by him, it embraced all *neuroses characterized by anxiety, phobias, compulsions, and obsessions.

PSYCHE. The mind.

PSYCHEDELIC is a term used of drugs which cause visual *hallucinations, supposedly 'expanding' consciousness and heightening perception. They may also be psychotomimetic, that is produce mental states resembling *psychosis.

PSYCHIATRIST. A medically qualified specialist in mental disorders. See PSYCHIATRY.

PSYCHIATRY is the branch of medicine concerned with mental disorders. In this article, psychiatry is considered from several points of view. First, there is a brief account of the disorders which are the concern of psychiatry. This is intended to give the reader some familiarity with terms used later in the article. Next comes a review of the historical origins of modern psychiatry. This introduces the reader to a number of aspects of the subject which are discussed further in the next three parts of the article. The first is concerned with psychiatry as a branch of the medical profession, that is with the kind of medical work that psychiatrists undertake and the ways in which they are trained to carry it out. The second considers psychiatry as an academic discipline: it is concerned mainly with research and teaching. The third describes the main kinds of treatment used in psychiatry and the ways in which services are arranged for mentally disordered patients.

Mental disorders. It is not possible to give a complete description of mental disorders here. Instead, a brief account will be given of the common disorders that will be mentioned later in this article. (Further information will be found in brief entries dealing with specific forms of mental illness.) It is usual to divide mental disorders into three groups: mental handicap, personality disorder, and mental illness. These are not mutually exclusive; one person can suffer from more than one disorder, for example personality disorder and mental illness.

Mental handicap (also called mental retardation) is present from the earliest years. It is characterized by abnormally low intelligence although other aspects of psychological development may be involved as well. People with severe mental handicap often have physical handicaps—for example difficulty in walking or controlling the bladder. Mentally handicapped people find it difficult to cope with the ordinary demands of life—in milder cases with shopping and travelling, in severe cases even with dressing and personal hygiene. In the most serious cases the person may be unable to speak or to care for himself in any way, but most mentally handicapped people can live reasonably normal lives provided that they or their families receive some help.

Personality disorders usually become apparent from the teenage years. They may affect any aspect of personality but intelligence is normal. There are many kinds of personality disorder. One is the *psychopathic personality disorder (such people

are sometimes called psychopaths, or sociopaths). People of this kind do not make loving relationships and seem self-centred, heartless, and callous. This lack of feeling often contrasts with a superficial charm. They are also impulsive, and their lives lack a sense of plan or persistent striving for goals. Psychopathic personalities lack guilt, and appear indifferent to the effects of their actions on other people. They make poor parents and some neglect or abuse their children. Another example of a personality disorder is the paranoid type. These people are unduly suspicious and sensitive. They are constantly on the look out for attempts by others to deceive or play tricks on them. They appear secretive, devious, and jealous and have little capacity for enjoyment.

Mental illnesses appear after a period of normal development. They are divided into *neuroses and *psychoses. Although the finer points of this distinction are rather complicated, for the present purposes only two distinguishing features need be mentioned. First, psychoses are generally more severe (they correspond, more or less, to the layman's idea of madness); neuroses are less severe (corresponding to the layman's idea of nervous disorders). Secondly, in psychosis, the person is generally unaware that he is ill (he 'loses insight') while in neuroses he retains this awareness. Each of these two broad classes of mental illness is divided into several further categories. For the present purposes only a few need be considered.

There are three principal groups of psychosis. The first group is called organic (a term that refers to the presence of a structural abnormality in an organ of the body). This kind of psychosis is caused by a known physical disease which either affects the brain directly (e.g. a *cerebral tumour) or indirectly (e.g. toxic products in the blood caused by kidney failure).

When an organic psychosis develops quickly, the patient is muddled and uncertain of his whereabouts (in everyday terms he is delirious). When an organic psychosis develops slowly, the first sign usually is poor memory. This is followed by a gradual decline in all intellectual functions (dementia). In the other two types of psychosis, no physical disease can be discovered. For this reason they are called 'functional' psychoses (functional is a term used in medicine to indicate the absence of organic pathology). The two types are: affective disorders, so called because they are primarily disorders of mood (the word affect is sometimes used as a technical term for mood); and *schizophrenia.

Affective disorders take two forms, *mania and *depression. Some patients experience only the one; others have attacks both of mania and of depression. When the latter occurs, the condition is called *manic-depressive psychosis. A depressive psychosis is much more than ordinary feelings of sadness. The mood is of profound pessimism often accompanied by thoughts of suicide and morbid self-blame. Sleep is disturbed, appetite impaired, and activity reduced. The picture of the manic patient is just the opposite. He is elated (although sometimes irritable as well), overactive, and inappropriately confident in his own abilities. Some manic patients enter into hare-brained business schemes, others squander their money in spending sprees, or commit other serious mistakes in their personal affairs.

Neuroses are also subdivided, according to the most prominent symptom, into anxiety neurosis, obsessional neurosis, and hysteria. Anxiety neuroses are dominated by anxious thoughts and feelings. These are accompanied by the bodily accompaniments of *anxiety: racing heart, dry mouth, sweating, etc. These sensations are familiar to everyone; the patient with a severe anxiety neurosis differs in experiencing feelings bordering on terror. These occur more or less continuously and in circumstances in which there is no objective reason to be afraid. Obsessional neuroses have less in common with ordinary experience. They are characterized by repeated intrusive thoughts concerned with themes that distress the patient. For example, a religious person may have blasphemous thoughts, a prudish person sexual thoughts, and a fastidious person thoughts about contamination with faecal matter. Such ideas are often accompanied by actions to ward off the thoughts: for example, a person with thoughts about contamination may wash his hands repeatedly.

In *hysteria, symptoms characteristic of physical illness occur without any physical cause. For example, the patient cannot move an arm however hard he tries, even though the nerves, muscles, and other structures involved are all healthy. Because hysteria arises from emotional conflict in the unconscious part of the mind, the patient is unaware of the cause.

Psychiatrists also treat some conditions which do not fall neatly into this scheme of classification. They are involved in the treatment of people who have become dependent on alcohol or drugs. They treat disorders of eating such as *anorexia nervosa in which a person, often a teenage girl, engages in relentless attempts to lose weight through extreme dieting, exercise, and other means. Psychiatrists also give help to people who, although not mentally ill, are passing through a period of intense personal difficulties which have caused emotional distress.

Children also suffer mental disorders. In preschool children these usually involve the behaviours which are being established at that time—the establishment of normal patterns of sleeping and eating and control over aggressive feelings. In older children, most psychiatric disorders fall into two main groups: emotional disorders and conduct disorders. The former are characterized mainly by anxiety, unhappiness, and excessive worries; the latter by stealing, truancy, and aggressive behaviour.

These mental disorders are found in every country. Neuroses are more frequent than psychoses. Minor emotional disorders resembling, but less severe than, neuroses are more common still. Thus it has been estimated that about one-sixth of patients attending general practitioners in the UK have a minor emotional disorder either on its own or accompanying physical illness.

Before leaving the subject of mental disorders, it is necessary to refer to the (mistaken) view that mental disorders do not exist; that they are merely medical labels attached to unusual behaviour that the majority of people cannot tolerate. The American writer Szasz has expressed this view in the phrase 'the myth of mental illness'. Three sets of observations support the view that mental illnesses are real entities. The first observation will have been made by any reader who has seen a person suffering from acute schizophrenia or mania: the severity of the disorder and its sudden appearance in a person who has up to that time lived a socially conforming life is exceedingly difficult to reconcile with the idea that mental illness is merely a label attached to unconforming people. The second observation is that identical forms of mental illness occur at the present time in places with widely different social structures (e.g. rural areas of Nigeria, large cities in the USA, and Pacific islands). The third observation is that the forms of mental illness recorded in the medical writings of previous centuries closely resemble those seen today. There are also observations of a more technical kind, such as the finding of biochemical abnormalities in patients with schizophrenia and mania. These also indicate that mental illnesses are more than forms of behaviour that a particular society finds inconvenient. Nevertheless, it is of course true that people can be called mentally ill when they are not. This can happen when a doctor does not examine his patient adequately or fails to use generally agreed criteria for *diagnosis. Thus there have been reports of the detention in hospital in some countries of political dissidents who are mentally healthy.

The development of modern psychiatry. *The ancient world.* The treatment of mental illness has not always been the province of doctors. For long periods of recorded history, mental disorders have been thought of, not as illness but as the result of divine or demonic possession. It is true that Graeco-Roman medical writings contain some references to mental illnesses and that these illnesses were generally regarded by the writers as having bodily causes and requiring medical treatment. However, in the ancient world generally and throughout the Middle Ages, mental illness was more often ascribed to possession by supernatural forces. As such it was not generally thought to be the concern of doctors. Instead many mentally ill people were either given religious help or persecuted as witches.

New beginnings. In the 16th and 17th c. a more scientific approach to mental disorders began to develop. Several doctors wrote about the less severe mental disorders that physicians encountered among their patients. For example, Timothy Bright published a *Treatise on Melancholy* in 1586, Thomas *Willis referred to *melancholia and hysteria in his lectures in 1663 and Thomas *Sydenham wrote about hysteria and *hypochondriasis. However, most doctors had little to do with the care of patients with severe mental illness, and there were hardly any hospital provisions for such treatment. Indeed, until the beginning of the 18th c. the only hospital in England devoted solely to the care of the insane was the *Bethlem Hospital. At this time, most psychotic patients were not treated in hospital, but lived as best they could in the community, often as beggars or vagabonds. Others were in prison.

In the first half of the 18th c. small signs of progress began to appear. In England three other hospitals began to provide for the mentally ill. These were Bethel Hospital (1724) in Norwich, and *Guy's Hospital (1728) and the French Protestant Hospital (1737) in London. In Ireland, a mental hospital was founded in Dublin with money left for this purpose in the will of Jonathan Swift, who died in 1745.

In 1751 St Luke's Hospital was opened in London. The physician to this new hospital was William Battie, a distinguished medical man who served as president of the Royal College of Physicians from 1764 to 1765. He instituted courses of clinical instruction in psychiatry at St Luke's and later published them. His book was the first significant English medical text devoted solely to psychiatric disorders. In the introduction, Battie explained that one of the purposes of the founders of St Luke's was to 'introduce more gentlemen of the faculty to the study and practice of one of the most important of branches of physick'. In his writings, Battie warned against the excessive use of many of the treatments of the day, such as *emetics, *purges, and *blood-letting. He stressed that even severe mental illness often recovers spontaneously if the patient receives good nursing.

Battie's book was followed by other publications which reflected a growing interest among doctors in the problems of mental illness. Meanwhile the interest of the general public in psychiatry was increased by the news of the illnesses of George III, whose first mental disorder occurred in 1788–9. At the same time a small number of psychiatric hospitals were founded by public subscription. Many of these were associated with a general hospital—foreshadowing the arrangements that are thought desirable today. In addition, small private *asylums for the mentally ill (called 'madhouses') flourished in many parts of the country. Some of these mad-houses were supervised by doctors, others by laymen. Although a number were the subject of scandals, many provided efficient and humane care.

Hospital reform. It was not only in the UK that many mentally ill people were being treated in poor conditions. In France the conditions in the mental hospitals of Paris were equally unsatisfactory. In 1793 Philippe *Pinel set out to reform the Bicêtre, a hospital in which many patients were restrained in chains. Pinel released these patients from their chains and instituted a more liberal form of care. He made the important observation that the abnormal behaviour of mentally ill patients can be caused as much by unsuitable treatment as by illness.

In the UK, the pioneer of similar reforms was a layman Quaker philanthropist, William *Tuke. In 1796 he established a new kind of institution in York, calling it The Retreat. In The Retreat restraint was seldom used, neither were any of the harsh physical treatments of the day. Instead, patients were nursed in quiet friendly surroundings in which they could remain until their illness abated. This 'moral' (i.e. psychological) treatment was intended to foster self-control, so reducing the need for external restraint.

Despite the example of The Retreat, the conditions in many hospitals continued to be very unsatisfactory Those in the Bethlem Hospital eventually provoked a public inquiry in 1807. The subsequent report was followed in 1808 by legislation for England and Wales. This legislation allowed each county to provide, at public expense, an asylum for the mentally ill.

Although the County Asylum Act of 1808 encouraged the building of asylums, progress was extremely slow. For this reason, a further Act was passed in 1845, requiring counties to take action. In the new county asylums that resulted from this legislation, patients were at first managed with 'moral' treatment. As time passed, more and more patients were admitted because the public was becoming less willing to tolerate the mentally ill in the community, or pay for their maintenance in *poor-law institutions. The resulting overcrowding led to less satisfactory care and to an increasing use of restraint in inadequately staffed wards. It therefore became necessary to restate the liberal ideas of the earlier pioneers. Between 1835 and 1837 Charlesworth and Hill, working at the Lincoln asylum showed, once again, that mental hospitals could be conducted without the use of restraint. Similar principles were subsequently expounded by John *Conolly in an important book *The Treatment of the Insane without Mechanical Restraints,* published in 1856.

The birth of academic psychiatry. In the early 19th c. the academic study of psychiatric disorders developed most strongly in France and Germany. In France, Pinel published his *Traité de la manie* in 1801. This influential text was followed in 1838 by another important book written by Pinel's pupil *Esquirol. Pinel's book was notable for the quality of the descriptions of disease and for the use of simple statistics of the frequency of various forms of mental illness. However, it was in Germany that psychiatry first became firmly established as a subject for study in the universities. In 1811, J. C. A. Heinroth was appointed to the first chair of 'mental therapy' in Leipzig, a post that was renamed the chair of psychiatry in 1828. In 1865 William *Griesinger was appointed the first professor of psychiatry and neurology in Berlin. He soon developed a university department for the study of mental disorders. Other chairs of psychiatry were established in Göttingen (1866), Heidelberg (1871), Leipzig (1882), and Bonn (also 1882); and in Zurich (1869) and Vienna (1877).

With these academic developments, the study of psychiatric disorder began to flourish in German-speaking countries. Several themes were important. First, the study of the natural course of psychiatric disorder, notably by Kahlbaum and *Kraepelin. It was mainly on the basis of these outcome studies that Kraepelin was able to develop a comprehensive classification of mental illness which is the basis of the schemes in use throughout the world today.

The second theme was concerned with the relationship of psychiatric disorder to brain pathology. Enquiries of this kind were encouraged by the progress being made at the time in identifying the pathological lesions in *neurological disorders. Among similar studies applied to mental disorders, the work of *Meynert and *Wernicke was particularly influential. The discovery of *general paralysis of the insane (GPI) gave encouragement to this line of research. However, the scientific methods of the day were not adequate for such complex problems and further progress was limited.

The third theme was also concerned with the causes of mental disorder. It developed from the work of a Frenchman, Morel, who in 1809 proposed ideas which came to be known as the 'theory of degeneration'. This postulated first that mental illness is inherited, and secondly that it tends to appear in an increasingly more severe form as it is transmitted to successive generations. These ideas flourished for a time. They had the unfortunate effect of encouraging a pessimistic approach to treatment, and gave support to those who wished to remove the mentally ill from society. Partly as a reaction to this approach, the last part of the 19th c. saw an increasing interest in the psychological causes of mental disorder.

The rise of psychoanalysis. The most important step in developing ideas about psychological factors in mental illness was taken by a neurologist. Sigmund *Freud began his professional career as a research worker, changing to the clinical practice of neurology when he was in his late twenties. In his new work, he often saw patients whose symptoms could not be explained as the result of organic disease. Some of these patients had hysteria, and they were particularly difficult to treat. Freud therefore arranged a visit to the clinic of the distinguished French neurologist *Charcot to learn

about his use of *hypnotism in hysteria. When he returned to his practice in Vienna, Freud began to use hypnosis with similar patients. However, he was not a natural hypnotist and began to experiment with an alternative technique of his own. In this, no attempt was made to induce a hypnotic trance; instead, patients simply spoke aloud the thoughts that came into their minds (free association). From this simple beginning, Freud gradually developed the elaborate techniques of *psychoanalysis.

Freud was not content simply to treat patients, he also tried to discover the psychological causes of their conditions. Finding little to help in the textbooks of the time, he set out to develop his own psychological theory. Freud's ideas were complex and ingenious. They were particularly controversial at the time because he referred repeatedly to sexual motives. Freud also stressed the role of the unconscious and irrational parts of the mind, and the effects of childhood experience on the behaviour of adults. None of these ideas was wholly original, but Freud succeeded in welding them together in a novel and imaginative way.

These broad aspects of Freud's theories have had a great influence on the arts and literature, as well as the ways in which ordinary people think about the mind. In psychiatry they were important in directing attention to the importance of psychological factors in mental disorder. In addition, Freud's practical discoveries about the technique of psychoanalysis laid the foundation of modern methods of psychotherapy. These were important contributions to psychiatry. However, the details of Freud's theory were less satisfactory. Despite frequent revisions, the theory has not provided a satisfactory explanation for most mental disorders. Furthermore, the theory was not constructed as a set of scientific hypotheses which could be tested, so that it has not fitted easily with the scientific ideas on which medicine is generally based.

Freud's own contributions were outstanding in their breadth and ingenuity, but several of his colleagues and successors also did important work. Among these, *Jung made the most significant independent contribution. Jung had read some of Freud's papers and decided to apply the ideas to the study of schizophrenia. Before long the two men were collaborating closely, but in 1914 Jung left the psychoanalytical movement because he disagreed strongly with some of Freud's most important ideas, notably his emphasis on sexual motivation. Jung's 'analytic psychology' has not equalled psychoanalysis in its influence on psychiatry and psychology, partly because Jung's writings were often less clear and compelling than those of Freud. Another distinguished Swiss psychiatrist, Eugen *Bleuler resigned from the International Psychoanalytic Association in 1910. Bleuler made important contributions to the understanding of the psychological disorders of schizophrenic patients. His departure from the psychoanalytical circles removed from Freud an important early opportunity to establish psychoanalysis within the universities. It was not until the 1930s, and in America rather than Europe, that this came about.

Not all those who were interested in the psychological cause of mental illness worked with Freud. The most important of the others was the French psychiatrist Pierre *Janet. His theories were less elaborate than those of Freud. Janet recognized an unconscious part of the mind and his theory was also concerned with mental forces. He differed from Freud in seeking the causes of neurosis mainly in contemporary events rather than in the experiences of childhood.

Psychiatry between the wars. Inevitably the First World War interrupted the development of psychiatry. The return of peace marked the beginning of a period of increasing interest in the prevention and treatment of mental disorders. In the UK one of the most important events was the opening of the *Maudsley Hospital. Henry Maudsley had worked as a psychiatrist at the Manchester Lunatic Asylum (Cheadle Royal) before becoming professor of medical jurisprudence at University College, London. Maudsley wrote three important textbooks and was a most influential teacher in his day, but his lasting achievement was an imaginative plan for a new kind of psychiatric hospital concerned with early treatment, teaching, and research. Maudsley gave a substantial endowment which helped to establish the hospital and the associated academic developments.

In the post-war years, gradual progress was made in opening out-patient clinics for the treatment with psychotherapy of the less severe mental disorders. Some of these—the child guidance clinics—were devoted to the care of children. As well as seeking to relieve the immediate problems of these children, it was hoped that treatment in childhood would prevent mental illness in adult life. Unfortunately, these hopes proved to be over-optimistic.

By the 1930s further developments were taking place, notably the introduction of new forms of physical treatment for serious mental disorders. In 1933 Sakel described insulin coma treatment for schizophrenia. In this treatment, injections of *insulin were used to cause a temporary fall in *blood sugar. Repeated treatments of this kind were found to benefit some schizophrenic patients. Subsequently the beneficial effects were shown to be non-specific, probably resulting from increased nursing attention. For this and other reasons, insulin treatment is no longer used.

Another treatment introduced in the 1930s is still in use today. Convulsive treatment for severe states of depression was described in 1938 by Cerletti and Bini. At first a drug, cardiazol, was used to produce the convulsions, but this was soon replaced by electrical stimulation, so that the method became known as *electroconvulsive

treatment (ECT). The new treatment produced dramatic improvement in severe depressive disorders—conditions which, up to that time, often lasted for months or even years and had a significant death rate from suicide or self-starvation.

*Leucotomy was the third treatment to be introduced in the 1930s; the first operation was performed in 1935 by Egas *Moniz. Leucotomy is a form of brain surgery which has the immediate effect of reducing aggressive behaviour, anxiety, severe depression, and obsessional symptoms. Although often effective in these ways, the original operation was often followed by undesirable changes in personality. Although modified operations have largely eliminated these personality changes, they are seldom used today because equal benefit can usually be obtained from drug treatment.

In the 1930s, psychoanalysis was developing in important ways. This development owed much to the migration to the USA of a number of influential German analysts, including Franz Alexander, Erich Fromm, and Karen Horney. These people did two things of note: first, they modified Freud's theories by placing less emphasis on sexual instincts and on the events of early childhood, and more on contemporary social forces; secondly, they began to establish psychoanalysis as an important ingredient of American psychiatry.

The UK also received many psychoanalysts fleeing from Nazi persecution and they, too, were found opportunities to re-establish their work. Nevertheless, psychoanalysis never assumed the dominant place in British psychiatry that it attained in North America. That a more eclectic view prevailed in the UK was, no doubt, partly a reflection of national temperament, but it also reflected the influence of two outstanding teachers. These were D.K. (later Sir David) Henderson of Edinburgh and A.J. (later Sir Aubrey) Lewis of the Maudsley Hospital in London. Both had trained in America with Adolph *Meyer, a Swiss psychiatrist who was professor of psychiatry at Johns Hopkins Medical School. Meyer was an influential teacher who championed an approach to psychiatry which stressed the interplay of psychological, social, and physical causes of mental disorder and discouraged an excessive preoccupation with any one set of theories. These ideas, known as psychobiology, became the mainstay of British psychiatry through the teaching of Henderson and Lewis.

Psychiatry after the Second World War. The post-war period was marked by two important therapeutic advances. The first, which originated in experiences gained from the practice of psychiatry in the armed forces, was the use of social rehabilitation using small and large groups. These methods were increasingly used to treat the schizophrenic patients who were resident in overcrowded mental hospitals. Reforms were introduced which in many ways repeated those of the early 19th c. Locked doors were opened, restrictions removed, and patients encouraged to take more responsibility for themselves. These liberalizing steps were aided in 1952 by the second therapeutic advance: the discovery in France of the beneficial effects of the drug *chlorpromazine. This drug suppresses many of the most troublesome symptoms of schizophrenia, including the overactive and aggressive behaviour which had been the main reason for the restrictions imposed on schizophrenic patients in earlier years. As a result of these two advances in treatment, the number of in-patients in psychiatric hospitals in England and Wales, which had been rising progressively, began to fall. Similar changes took place in other countries as the new methods of treatment were introduced.

The discovery of chlorpromazine was soon followed by the development of other valuable drugs. In the early 1950s, the drug *isoniazid was being used to treat *tuberculosis. Related compounds were tested and one of these—iproniazid—was found to produce euphoria in some patients, although it was less effective as an antitubercular agent (see CHEST MEDICINE). Subsequently iproniazid and similar compounds were used to treat depressive disorders. In 1957 Kuhn found that another drug, imipramine, also had antidepressant properties. Since that time, imipramine and related drugs have transformed the treatment of depressive illness, which can now often be treated in its early stages by family doctors. Soon after this, Cade discovered that *lithium carbonate can prevent relapses of manic-depressive disorders. This new use of a drug to prevent relapses of mental illness was an important milestone.

Another feature of the post-war period was the development of community services designed to enable mentally ill patients to live outside hospital. Such people need help with work and accommodation as well as continuing psychiatric treatment. To provide this help, rehabilitation units, hostels, and sheltered workshops were developed. (They are described later in this article.)

In the UK, one of the most important general features of post-war medicine was the development of a comprehensive system of good general practice. This was becoming well established by the time that the availability of safer and more effective drugs enabled general practitioners to undertake the treatment of many people with the less serious mental disorders, including many who in other countries would be treated by specialists. At the same time, the new policies of treating patients in the community, involved family doctors increasingly in the care of people with chronic mental illness and with the mentally handicapped. Indeed, a survey showed that general practitioners refer to specialists only about one in 20 of the patients who consult them with problems which have an important psychiatric component.

At the same time that patients with minor disorders were being treated more by their family doctors, the care of patients with major forms of mental illness was increasingly undertaken in small psychiatric units attached to general hospitals, rather than in large mental hospitals. However, recurrent shortages of funds for health care held back the ambitious plans for replacing all the old psychiatric hospitals in this way.

While in the UK in the post-war years, psychiatrists were particularly concerned with improving the care of patients with severe mental disorders, psychiatrists in the USA were developing psychoanalytical ideas. In the post-war period, psychoanalysis became strongly represented in the American medical schools and training in psychoanalysis became a general requirement for a successful career in psychiatry. These developments led to good provisions for psychotherapy, and they fostered an interest in less severe psychological problems including those of physically ill people. These were some of the benefits of these developments. However, the extreme reliance on psychoanalysis in the USA also had disadvantages for psychiatry as a whole. One of the problems was that psychoanalysts began to claim too much. The assertions that they could explain a wide range of human behaviour, from physical illnesses such as *asthma to social phenomena such as the behaviour of crowds, led to increasing scepticism on the part of other doctors and informed laymen. Because some laymen wrongly equated psychoanalysis with psychiatry, they became sceptical of the subject as a whole. By the 1970s the influence of psychoanalysis in American psychiatry had begun to wane and it is now one force among many, as it has always been in the UK.

The mentally handicapped. Until the second half of the 19th c. few provisions were made for mentally handicapped people. By the end of the century many of these people were confined in large hospitals in which they were segregated from society, partly with the intention of preventing them from having children. Many of these hospitals were understaffed, and provided insufficient variety and stimulation for their patients. While hospital provisions were often inadequate in this way, arrangements for care in the community were generally lacking and many of the mentally handicapped remained in hospital for the greater part of their lives.

These conditions persisted until well after the Second World War when, as many of the mentally ill were being discharged from hospital, more attention was given to the possibility of discharging mentally handicapped people as well. Gradually, hostels, special schools, and sheltered work were provided. Progress was slow and many hospitals continued to be overcrowded and understaffed. Even today, in many hospitals for the mentally handicapped, hard-pressed staff are attempting to cope with impossible demands.

Developments in psychiatry and the law. The law is concerned with mentally ill and mentally handicapped people in two ways. First, there are provisions concerned with mentally ill offenders whose illness appears to have reduced their responsibility for actions which have broken the law. Those which most often come to public notice are concerned with the killing of another person by someone who is, or is claimed to be, mentally disordered. Secondly, the law defines the circumstances in which mentally disordered or mentally handicapped people can be admitted to hospital and kept there, against their own expressed wishes. In general terms, this is permissible by law when a person is suicidal or dangerous to others as a result of mental illness (or in certain circumstances severe personality disorder or mental handicap). This legislation has two aims: it serves to prevent the improper admission to a psychiatric hospital of a person who does not need to go there; and it ensures that people who do not realize that they are ill receive the treatment they require. It has always been difficult to balance these considerations. In the 19th c. public concern was aroused by reports of cases in which people had been admitted to mental hospitals against their will and without adequate reason. This led to the requirement that all admissions to a mental hospital must be 'certified' by a magistrate. This requirement continued until 1930 by which time it had become apparent that it was preventing the admission to hospital of other people whose illness was in an early stage and who were likely to benefit if they could enter hospital in a more informal way. The *Mental Treatment Act of 1930 allowed the admission of voluntary patients, although it retained the requirement that a magistrate should be involved in the admission to a psychiatric hospital of those who were unwilling to enter.

In 1959 a new *Mental Health Act was introduced in England and Wales. A magistrate was no longer involved in the compulsory admission of patients to a psychiatric hospital: instead, the procedure was usually completed by the nearest relative (or a social worker) and two doctors. By this time, more effective methods of early treatment had reduced substantially the need for compulsory admission. Thus in the 1980s, only a few patients are admitted in this way to a psychiatric ward, the great majority being voluntary admissions carried out with no more formality than entry to a medical or surgical ward. In 1983 a further Mental Health Act came into force requiring, for example, a statutory second opinion prior to the administration of certain forms of treatment in patients incapable of giving informed consent.

Psychiatry as a branch of the medical profession. *The branches of psychiatry.* Psychiatry is now a major medical specialty. In the UK at the end of the 1970s there were about 1500 *consultants practising some branch of psychiatry in the *National Health Service (NHS), that is about 1 in 8 of all consultants. Because the subject is now too large for one person to be expert in all its aspects, several forms of specialization have developed. One is

concerned with the care of the mentally handicapped; all the rest are concerned with mental illness. The latter can be divided into general psychiatry and three 'subspecialties': child and adolescent psychiatry, psychotherapy, and forensic psychiatry. As well as these subspecialties, many psychiatrists develop a special interest in a particular type of practice, for example with the elderly (psychogeriatrics), with people who are dependent on drugs or alcohol, or in rehabilitation.

The work of the psychiatrist. Psychiatrists seldom work on their own. They are usually members of a team which includes nurses, occupational therapists, psychologists, and social workers. In the care of the elderly, the team often includes physiotherapists; and in the case of children, teachers. Psychiatrists work closely both with general practitioners and their team of nurses and health visitors, and with social services departments.

A psychiatrist's work is usually based on an in-patient unit in which severely ill patients can be treated. This may be in a psychiatric hospital or in a general hospital. However, as only a minority of psychiatric patients are now treated in hospital, much of the psychiatrist's time is spent with day-patients or out-patients, seeing patients in the community, or with consultations in general hospitals, general practices, or with the staff of hostels or workshops.

Child psychiatrists generally spend more of their time in out-patient work and less in work with in-patients, than do those who work with adults. They also advise parents, schoolteachers, and the staff of children's homes about the care of individual children and about the management of groups of children. Nowadays child psychiatrists work alongside paediatricians in helping handicapped children and those with serious physical illness.

Forensic psychiatrists treat offenders. They see people who are remanded for psychiatric reports by the courts, advise the courts about matters such as a mentally ill offender's responsibility for his illegal actions, and provide treatment especially for those few mentally ill or mentally handicapped patients who are potentially dangerous.

Psychiatrists specializing in the care of the mentally handicapped are concerned, nowadays, mainly with the mental illnesses and behavioural problems which are more frequent among the mentally handicapped than among people of normal intelligence. They often take the main responsibility for planning the services needed for an individual child and his family, although many of these provisions are the direct responsibility of the educational and social services, and of the family doctor.

Education and training. All psychiatrists have qualified in medicine and many have undertaken a period of general medical work, before starting specialized training in psychiatry lasting about 6 years. During the first 3 years of this training, the trainee usually works in a series of posts in an organized scheme. These posts are chosen to provide wide experience in treating all kinds of psychiatric disorder in people of all ages. At the same time the trainee undertakes a course of academic study, usually organized by one of the university departments of psychiatry. In the UK, at the end of about 3 years the trainee takes an examination for the membership of the Royal College of Psychiatrists. Comparable arrangements exist in other countries, although the details of timing of the professional examinations are not all the same. In the last 3 years of training the future consultant psychiatrist extends his experience and learns to take increasingly greater responsibility by working in approved posts while continuing academic work. In the UK, during the first 3 years of psychiatric training all follow the same syllabus. In the later years the trainee begins to specialize. For example, future child psychiatrists work exclusively with children and their families; those who wish to take a special interest in psychogeriatrics spend at least half their time in the care of the elderly; and future psychotherapists undertake intensive training in this kind of treatment.

At the end of this training, most psychiatrists in the UK apply for a consultant post in the NHS. In many other countries the fully trained psychiatrist enters private practice, often combining this with a part-time hospital appointment. Consultant psychiatrists keep their knowledge up to date by attending postgraduate meetings organized locally or nationally—in the UK by the Royal College of Psychiatrists, by a comparable professional body in other countries.

Some laymen confuse the training of psychiatrists and clinical psychologists. Although the role of the latter is described in the entry on psychology, the main points will be repeated here for the convenience of the reader. Clinical psychologists begin their training with a 3-year degree course in psychology instead of the 5-year medical course, and the subsequent pre-registration year. They then undertake a course in clinical psychology, usually for 2–3 years. Some also obtain a research degree.

Psychiatry as an academic discipline. There are now academic departments of psychiatry in all British universities with medical schools. In this article, academic psychiatry will be considered briefly from four viewpoints: subject matter, methods of enquiry, advances in knowledge, and educational activities.

The subject matter of academic psychiatry is concerned with the description, distribution, causes, and treatment of psychiatric disorders. Effective enquiries into these issues often require information about other matters such as normal psychological functioning, brain physiology, and social influences on human behaviour. For this reason, academic psychiatry is partly concerned

with these matters as well, and some academic psychiatrists have undertaken a course of study in related disciplines such as psychology, or *psychopharmacology. Equally, psychiatrists contribute to the solution of problems in these other fields of knowledge, for example to questions about the ways that drugs act on the brain, or normal personality develops. In addition, psychiatric research teams often include members of one of these cognate disciplines.

So far, consideration has been given to the central subject matter of psychiatry and to related topics on which psychiatrists can claim to have expert knowledge. At times, psychiatrists are asked to give opinions about matters that are outside either of these areas of special knowledge. Their views are sometimes sought on such matters as the behaviour of crowds (e.g. in relation to football hooliganism), and the causes of events in history (so-called psychohistory). Some psychiatrists have welcomed this extension of the traditional boundaries of their subject. However, it is now agreed by most psychiatrists that their knowledge about mental illness does not equip them to give expert opinions about these wider issues. In other words, they are not part of the subject matter of psychiatry, although psychiatrists may have informed views about them in the same way that other educated people have views.

Methods of enquiry. Many different methods of enquiry are used in psychiatric research. In this section, a brief account will be given of clinical, epidemiological, genetic, biochemical, social, and psychological methods.

Clinical observations of patients and of the course of disease are the foundation of psychiatry. Until recently progress in psychiatry was hampered by a lack of reliable ways of describing and quantifying the phenomena of disease. In recent years suitable methods have been developed and, with them, more reliable ways of making diagnoses. This progress has led, in turn, to better studies of the distribution of mental disorders in populations (epidemiology). Epidemiological methods are concerned with the distribution of disease within a society: for example attempted suicide is more common among people who live in areas with overcrowding and poor social amenities.

Studies of the distribution of disease can also be used to investigate the role of *heredity in mental illness. In this case the studies concern people with different degrees of kinship with patients with the illness in question. For example, schizophrenia is considerably more common among the identical *twins of schizophrenic patients than among the non-identical twins of schizophrenics. Because identical twins have the same genes and non-identical twins do not, this suggests that part of the cause of schizophrenia is inherited. An alternative strategy is to study people who have been adopted at birth, and also their biological and adoptive parents. If a condition is inherited, it will be found more often in the biological parents of affected individuals than in the adoptive parents.

*Genetic influences generally act through changes in biochemical mechanisms, and it is reasonable to suppose that in mental disorders these changes take place in the brain. Unfortunately it is very difficult to investigate chemical processes in the human brain in living patients: therefore most of the evidence obtained so far is indirect. One approach is to look for biochemical changes in the blood, in the hope that these reflect those in the brain. Another approach is to identify, in animals, the chemical messengers on which the working of particular parts of the brain depend and then to test these functions in mentally ill people. If a brain mechanism depends on, say, the chemical messenger *dopamine and it is disordered in schizophrenia, this supports the hypothesis that schizophrenia is associated with disordered dopamine mechanisms. In practice, the brain mechanisms for controlling *hormone production are often studied because they can be assessed indirectly by measuring hormones in the blood. A third approach is to study in animals the biochemical changes produced by drugs which are effective in treating a disorder. To return to the previous example, it is known that the drugs used to treat schizophrenia block the chemical messenger, dopamine. This might mean that there is too much dopamine in the brain of schizophrenic patients (although other explanations are possible as well).

Even if a biochemical disorder were to be proved in schizophrenia, this would not explain everything about a schizophrenic patient's condition. For this, psychological and social investigations are needed as well. These have shown, for example, that some of the symptoms of schizophrenia are made worse when the patient is understimulated, while others are made worse when he is stimulated too much. Psychological and social methods are also important for the study of neuroses and personality disorders. For example, knowledge about the ways in which fear responses are learnt by normal children and adults, is relevant to the study of anxiety neuroses.

In the past, the study of neuroses was based mainly on methods and theories derived from psychoanalysis. As noted earlier, these are concerned mainly with the irrational and unconscious parts of the mind, which are not easily investigated with the methods of experimental psychology. Because psychoanalytic theory was developed specifically to explain the phenomena of mental illness, it inevitably appears more relevant than many of the theories derived from experimental psychology which were generally developed to explain normal behaviour. This partly explains the popularity enjoyed by psychoanalytic ideas in the past. However, although these ideas contribute in important ways to an understanding of the psychological experiences of some neurotic individuals, they have proved less useful as general explanations for serious mental disorders such as schizophrenia and manic-depression.

Some recent advances in knowledge. Because psychiatric research is advancing rapidly, it is impossible to review in this article even a small proportion of the recent advances in knowledge. Instead, four representative examples will be given, two concerned with treatment, two with causes.

The most striking progress has been in developing and evaluating new treatments for serious mental disorders. Drugs are now available to reverse the symptoms of depressive disorders, reduce the acute symptoms of schizophrenia, and control mania. It is also possible to prevent many recurrences in schizophrenia, mania, and depressive disorders. These beneficial effects have been demonstrated in rigorous *clinical trials. At the same time, substantial progress has been made in finding out how these drugs work (e.g. the dopamine-blocking effects of drugs used in schizophrenia which were described earlier). This in turn has stimulated fruitful research into the chemical messengers used in different parts of the brain, and the factors which disturb their actions.

Psychological treatments have also advanced. New methods called behaviour therapy have been developed using knowledge and techniques from experimental psychology. Behaviour therapy is particularly valuable for neuroses. Many anxiety neuroses can now be treated in this way without the need for drugs, and for most obsessional neuroses, behaviour therapy is now the best treatment. Methods are being developed for some kinds of depressive disorders, and effective behavioural treatments have also been developed for social difficulties, sexual problems, eating disorders, and a variety of other abnormal behaviours. Like the new drug treatments, these behavioural methods have been tested in clinical trials. Moreover by studying their actions carefully, more has been learnt about psychological processes in health and disease.

New knowledge has also been gained about the causes of mental illness. For example, schizophrenia has been shown to have multiple causes. Genetic factors have been shown to be of major importance, but it has also been demonstrated that stressful life events play an important (and measurable) part in precipitating the illness in predisposed people, and provoking relapses. Some of these stressful events appear to act by increasing emotional arousal, an effect that can be prevented by *tranquillizing drugs. One kind of stressful event has been shown to be particularly likely to increase emotional arousal and provoke relapse: this is the experience of living with a relative who is both emotionally involved with the patient and critical of him.

Important progress has also been made in unravelling the complicated causes of mental illness in the elderly. It used to be supposed that all serious mental diseases in old people were caused by *degenerative changes in the brain. Now it is known that schizophrenia, depressive disorders, and mania all occur in late life and generally respond to the treatments used in younger people. At the same time, the abnormalities in illnesses caused by brain degeneration have become better understood. Structural changes have been studied with the *electron microscope and other methods, and biochemical abnormalities have been identified as well. The latter are particularly important because they are potentially reversible by chemical means (i.e. with drugs) whereas structural changes are more likely to be permanent.

Education. Psychiatrists teach medical students, postgraduate doctors who are training to work in psychiatry and in general practice, psychologists, and social workers. All medical students now receive substantial teaching about the emotional aspects of physical illness and about the diagnosis and treatment of psychiatric disorders. This instruction is an essential foundation for all medical practice. After qualification, those doctors who intend to work as general practitioners usually undertake further training in psychiatry to prepare themselves to treat the many patients who consult their family doctors about disorders with an important emotional component. The training of psychiatrists has been referred to earlier in this article.

Psychiatric treatments and psychiatric services. This section begins with short descriptions of the most important kinds of psychiatric treatment. After this an account is given of the organization of services required to provide these and other treatments for the mentally ill in a community.

Psychiatric treatments can be divided into three groups: physical, psychological, and social. Sometimes a patient requires only one of these, for example psychotherapy, to help with difficulties in personal relationships. More often, a combination is needed: for example, drugs to relieve severe depressive symptoms and psychotherapy directed to emotional problems that might lead to further depression. It is a common misconception that there is an inherent conflict between the prescription of drugs and the use of psychotherapy. On the contrary, a combination is not only compatible in principle but also often necessary in practice.

Physical treatment. This term is used to describe the prescription of drugs, the use of electroconvulsive therapy, and the (rare) use of neurosurgical operations. In practice nowadays, most physical treatment is with drugs.

Drugs that alter psychiatric symptoms are of three kinds: anxiolytic (i.e. reducing anxiety), antidepressant, and antipsychotic (i.e. relieving the symptoms of psychoses). One commonly used drug does not fit into any of these groups: this is lithium carbonate, a substance used to prevent recurrences in manic-depressive illness (a serious mental illness characterized at times by excitement and at other times by severe depression). Each of the main groups of drugs contains many different compounds. Within each group the beneficial effects of the drugs differ only slightly, the main variations being in their unwanted ('side') effects. These psychotropic drugs provide an effective and safe way of controlling the symptoms of illness. Antidepressant and antipsychotic drugs are also used to prevent relapse in some patients.

*Antidepressant drugs have transformed the treatment of depressive disorders. Patients who, in the past, would have remained depressed for months or even years, now usually improve within a few weeks with antidepressant drug treatment. Most of even the severe depressive disorders, which threaten life through suicide or failure to eat and drink, can be treated in this way, although a few require the more rapid action of electroconvulsive therapy (as explained later).

Antipsychotic drugs have also brought about substantial changes in the well-being of schizophrenic patients. Although these drugs do not cure the condition, they calm the patient and reduce the most troublesome symptoms. This action usually makes it possible for patients to engage in a programme of rehabilitation and return to life outside hospital. In some cases the protective effect of drugs has to be continued for many years.

Electroconvulsive therapy (ECT) has already been referred to, when it was explained that it was introduced as a treatment for severe depressive disorders at a time when no other effective treatment was available. Antidepressant drugs have replaced ECT for most purposes, being in general just as effective. However, their beneficial effects do not appear as quickly, and the more rapid effect of ECT is still the best treatment for urgent cases. In addition, a few patients who fail to respond to antidepressant drugs benefit from ECT.

The introduction of *psychosurgery has also been referred to already. Nowadays it is used rarely, and then only for patients suffering from longstanding and very severe obsessional neuroses or severe recurrent depressive disorders, refractory to all other treatment. Modern operations have few adverse effects, but the extent of their benefits is still a matter on which there are genuine differences of opinion and many psychiatrists do not recommend operation at all.

Psychological treatment includes psychotherapy—'talking treatment'—and behaviour therapy in which more attention is given to activities than talk. Psychotherapy can be divided according to its length and intensity, the number and relationship of the people taking part, and the psychological theory on which it is based. Each will be considered in turn.

1. *Psychotherapy.* The longest and most intensive form of psychotherapy is psychoanalysis. This is usually carried out on five days a week for as

much as several years. Psychoanalysis is intended to bring about profound changes in personality. However, it has not been shown beyond doubt that the changes brought about by psychoanalysis are greater than those produced by shorter forms of psychotherapy. Because of this uncertainty, psychoanalysis is not used widely in the UK, and only minimal provisions are made for it within the NHS. In the USA it is more freely available, mainly from private practitioners.

Counselling refers to treatment that is brief and not intensive, often no more than half a dozen sessions each lasting for about half an hour. It is intended to give support at times of personal distress and to aid adjustment to problems. There are many intermediate forms between the extremes of psychoanalysis and counselling. A common type of psychotherapy is given once a week for between 6 and 12 months, depending on the extent and severity of the problems.

In individual psychotherapy, one therapist treats one patient. In small group psychotherapy, one therapist treats about eight patients, generally using a technique in which the interactions between the patients are more important than those between each patient and the therapist. In marital therapy, the therapist treats the partners of a marriage, at least one of whom has emotional problems arising from this relationship. This treatment is sometimes called 'couple therapy' to take account of cases in which the partners are not married. In family therapy, other family members, usually children or grandparents, take part. This treatment is usually for the psychological problems of one or more of the children.

There are many kinds of psychotherapy, each based on a different psychological theory. The best known are the comprehensive theories of Freud and Jung. However, in recent years, treatments have been based on other psychological theories. These include interactional analysis, gestalt therapy, and encounter groups. This confusing array of seemingly contradictory theories suggests either that none can be well founded or alternatively that their shared features are more important than their points of difference. In practice, most psychotherapy carried out by psychiatrists is either founded on the theories of Freud (or less often those of Jung) or on principles derived from accumulated clinical experience. Moreover, even psychotherapists who have undertaken special Freudian (or other) training generally use their special techniques only when carrying out long and intensive treatment. When the treatment is shorter and less intense, there is little difference between the practice of therapists who subscribe to different theoretical schemes.

2. *Behaviour therapy* has altogether different origins. It is based on findings from psychological experimentation concerned with factors that determine normal behaviour. These are combined with empirical discoveries about the ways in which psychiatric symptoms can be modified most effec-

tively in clinical practice. In general, the emphasis is not on discussion of emotions and interpersonal problems, as in psychotherapy, but on actions which the patient can take to overcome his current symptoms and abnormalities of behaviour. Unlike psychotherapy, most behavioural techniques have been evaluated in clinical trials. They have been shown to be effective for symptoms such as *phobias and obsessions which do not generally respond well to psychotherapy. Their use in depressive disorders is still being evaluated. They have a place in child psychiatry and in the training and education of subnormal children and adults.

Social treatment. The term social treatment is used in two ways. First, it refers to methods in which the influences of a social group are used to bring about beneficial changes in patients. The second is to describe attempts to arrange a suitable environment for the patient, for example by finding the work and living conditions which are most likely to be beneficial. Social treatment in either of these senses is to be distinguished from social work which is the name for the various activities of the professional group of social workers. They try to ensure the welfare of people who have social difficulties (especially children and old people); they organize and supervise community resources such as hostels and old people's homes; they arrange the provision of services such as meals-on-wheels for the old; and they provide counselling for people who need this.

One special form of social treatment is called a therapeutic community. This term is used to describe a group of patients who share a common problem such as difficulty in relationships, or drug dependence. These people live together either in a psychiatric ward or a hostel. They take part in common activities and spend much of their day in group discussions. These groups often have 20 or more members. The whole group meets together on some occasions; on others it divides into smaller groups of 8–10 members. The focus of these large and small group discussions is the patients' problems in their relationships with one another. Problems such as inappropriate aggression, social withdrawal, or unwillingness to take responsibility, are among those commonly discussed. Typically the discussion is direct and forceful. Because the patients are resident, it is possible to arouse strong emotional responses in group therapy that might be hazardous in people returning home from outpatient treatment. It is hoped that changes brought about in these problems within the therapeutic community will generalize to everyday life when the patient is discharged.

(Some authors include in social treatment the sheltered work, residential arrangements, and other support services that are described in this article under 'organization of services', below.)

Psychiatric services. In every branch of medicine, the provision of services depends on social conditions as well as clinical considerations. This is particularly true of psychiatry, because the scale and type of provision required for mentally ill people is determined in part by the willingness of a society to tolerate unusual behaviour and to care for its handicapped members. The number of hospital places needed for mentally handicapped people or schizophrenic patients depends crucially on this factor.

The pattern of psychiatric services also varies with the system of health care in a society. In a country such as the USA, in which much health care is privately funded, there is likely to be more emphasis on provision for mild or short-lived illnesses such as neurosis, than for severe or long-lasting conditions such as mental handicap or chronic schizophrenia. Conversely, in a Marxist society, in which minor emotional problems are more likely to be thought of as reflecting defects in the social system than abnormalities of the individual patient, there is likely to be a less generous provision for the treatment of these disorders and more for the psychoses. In developing countries, with limited resources for all kinds of medical care, psychiatric services are usually limited to the treatment of severe psychoses, while the care of neurotic patients is generally in the hands of native healers. Because this article cannot cover all these matters, the following account is largely concerned with psychiatric services in the UK.

The organization of services. Now that much psychiatric treatment is provided outside hospital, steps have to be taken to organize in the community some of the provisions for chronic patients that used to be found only in large hospitals. One way of doing this is in a centre in the community which patients attend by day. Day hospitals can provide most of the forms of treatment available in a psychiatric ward, including psychotherapy, occupational therapy, and the supervision of medication. Moreover, in a day hospital treatment can be arranged to meet the needs of individuals: some attend every day, others only once or twice a week. It is a further advantage of day hospital treatment that patients can maintain links with other family members which would be broken by a long admission to hospital. Because no beds are provided, day hospitals can be sited in ordinary houses in the community, near to patients' homes. Some patients do not need any medical provision but simply occupation, company, and general care. When only these are provided, the institution is called a day centre rather than a day hospital.

Provisions for sheltered work allow patients with chronic mental illness or mental handicap to make use of their remaining abilities. The work is intended to lead to a sense of purpose and provide some financial reward. It is sheltered from the need to work at too great a pace, and complex tasks are usually broken down into simpler stages. Work of this kind can provide companionship and the satisfaction of shared achievement for people who

would otherwise be unoccupied, bored, and unwell.

Although most patients with a persistent psychiatric disorder or mental handicap can live at home or in ordinary lodgings, a few need special accommodation. Some of these people have no family; others have a family but experience difficulties when they live at home. These difficulties arise either because the patient is less well in these surroundings or, occasionally, because his illness seriously affects the health and well-being of another member of the family—for example one of the younger siblings of a mentally handicapped child, or the frail spouse of a demented old person.

Many of the patients who need special accommodation require little supervision: they can live in a 'group home'. This is an ordinary house shared by about six patients who, together, can perform all that is needed for a normal home life—shopping, cooking, gardening, cleaning—even though each, alone, cannot. Other patients require some help, usually from a nurse or social worker. This can be provided in a supervised hostel. Depending on the needs of the residents, there may be provision for meals, the cleaning of rooms, supervision of medication, physical nursing, counselling, or group psychotherapy. Some hostels are intended as a temporary home for patients who will soon be able to lead more independent lives. Others provide long-term care, for example for the mentally handicapped.

Conclusion. Although much of this article has been concerned with the ways in which psychiatric disorders and psychiatric treatment differ from the disorders and the treatment in other branches of medicine, it is important to end by emphasizing the close links between psychiatry and the rest of medicine. These are most apparent—and most important—in the area of professional standards, education, and training. They are also increasingly evident in the use of common methods of research (e.g. biochemical methods). Finally, methods of treatment are also moving closer together as psychiatrists develop new and effective drugs, and physicians pay increasing attention to the psychological and social aspects of care which are a central concern of psychiatrists.

See also PSYCHOLOGY.   M. G. GELDER

Further reading
Ackerknecht, E. H. (1968). *A Short History of Psychiatry*, trans. S. Wolff. New York.
Bloch, S. (1982). *What is Psychotherapy?* Oxford.
Clare, A. (1980). *Psychiatry in Dissent.* 2nd edn., London.
Farrell, B. A. (1981). *The Standing of Psychoanalysis.* Oxford.
Gelder, M., Gath, D. M. and Mayou, R. (1983). *Oxford Textbook of Psychiatry.* Oxford.
Lader, M. (ed.) (1980). *Priorities in Psychiatric Research.* Chichester, Sussex.
Shepherd, M. (ed.) (1982). *Psychiatrists on Psychiatry.* Cambridge.

PSYCHIC SURGERY, not to be confused with *psychosurgery, is the alleged performance of surgical procedures (e.g. removal of supposed *tumours) by paranormal methods which do not involve physical intervention. It has been reported particularly from the Philippines.

PSYCHOANALYSIS is a system of psychiatric theory and practice based on the ideas of Sigmund *Freud. The basic tool of psychoanalysis is the technique of free association, in which the patient is encouraged to express his thoughts, ideas, emotions, and memories with the minimum of intervention by the psychoanalyst, who listens, records, and eventually interprets. The final interpretation, when communicated to the patient, provides him with the insight into his motivation and behaviour necessary for him to solve his life problems. G. K. Chesterton defined psychoanalysis as 'confession without absolution'.

PSYCHOANALYST. A psychiatrist trained in the technique of *psychoanalysis. See PSYCHIATRY.

PSYCHOGALVANOMETER. A version of the *polygraph, for recording physiological changes associated with mental and emotional reactions.

PSYCHOLINGUISTICS is the branch of *linguistics dealing with the interrelation between the acquisition, use, and comprehension of language, and the processes of the mind. See LANGUAGE, COGNITION, AND HIGHER CEREBRAL FUNCTION.

PSYCHOLOGY IN RELATION TO MEDICINE

Introduction. Modern psychology may be defined as 'the study of behaviour and experience' and as such may be regarded as an extension of the biological study of structure and function. Psychologists' interest in behaviour is shared with ethologists, especially since the latter have taken to the study of human interactions, particularly those between mother and child. The study of human experience, conscious thought, and feeling has its roots in philosophy but now draws on many fields including those of communication and computer science. Sociology and anthropology are also highly relevant to psychology: all behaviour has a biological basis but is greatly influenced by the personal and social context in which it occurs.

Psychology has clear relevance to the practice of medicine as that practice involves a special form of relationship between doctor and patient in which the behaviour and experience of each and their mutual understanding is of prime importance. In fact, psychologists have contributed in a practical and useful way to the study of efficient doctor–patient *communication and the closely related and important matter of *compliance with medical advice (Ley, 1982). A physician or surgeon may not require specific training in psychology for the technical aspects of his practice in the same way as he requires knowledge of anatomy and physiology but it is important that he practises with insight into

and awareness of the personal and social influences bearing not only on his relationship with his patient but also on the form of manifestation or even the nature of his disease. All medical schools now include in their curriculum some general behavioural and social science as well as more specialized applications to clinical fields like *psychiatry. This does not imply that the traffic between psychology and medicine is one way. If one strikes a historical balance, psychology is found to owe more to medicine than the reverse.

Philosophical beginnings: medical influences. During the earliest historical period, *Aesculapian medical treatment was largely based on mysticism and superstition but later physicians were of a more speculative philosophical bent. This, allied to close observation of human beings in health and disease, inspired theorizing of a more scientific nature. Thus, by the 5th c. BC, *Hippocrates had conceived his elaborate biology in terms of the elements —earth, air, fire, and water—and the associated body humours—phlegm, yellow bile, blood, and black bile. *Galen, in the 2nd c. AD, added a psychological dimension by his doctrine of four temperaments—phlegmatic, choleric, sanguine, and melancholic—each associated with an excess of one humour over the others. These terms have survived in everyday language and the scientific concept of a relationship between physiological, temperamental, and psychological characteristics has also survived, sometimes in a form showing a clear line of descent from Galen (Eysenck, 1967).

The emergence of scientific psychology in the nineteenth century. Medical men also played an important part in the ultimate emergence of psychology from philosophy as a discipline in its own right. The Scottish surgeon Charles *Bell established the distinction between sensory and motor nerves and formulated the doctrine of the specific energies of nerves, later extended by the German physiologist Johannes *Müller, who argued that *consciousness consists of complexes of elementary *sensations. The task for psychology therefore seemed to be the analysis of consciousness into its elements, a sort of mental chemistry. Fechner, following up the work of his Leipzig colleague, Weber, established the methodology of 'psychophysics' to achieve, he hoped, an objective scale to measure subjective sensations. What is known as the Weber–Fechner Law is expressed by the equation $S = K \log I$, in which S represents sensation magnitude, K is a constant, and I the stimulus intensity in physical terms. Hermann von *Helmholtz, like Fechner a physician turned physicist, made important contributions to the study of perception and was the first to measure the speed of nervous impulses, thus opening the way to psychological reaction-time experiments to explore the processes intervening between stimulus and response.

It was in direct line with this tradition that Wilhelm Wundt, also medically qualified but appointed to the chair of philosophy at Leipzig, established in 1879 what is generally recognized as the first psychological laboratory. His department rapidly attracted many of those who founded the early departments of psychology in German, American, and British universities. By applying the experimental methods of his physiological precursors, Wundt set out to analyse consciousness into its sensory elements, to examine the manner in which these combine to produce the complex states of direct experience and to explain how these complexes acquire the non-sensory attributes of 'feeling' and 'emotion' which lead to appropriate action.

Apart from physiology, the other great biological influence on psychology was Darwinism which, though having less direct medical antecedents, had consequent medical relevance. In support of his arguments in *The Descent of Man* *Darwin carried out descriptive studies of the similarities in emotional expression between animals and man, leading to the publication of an important essentially psychological work (1872). His material included his own observations of the emotional expressions of children and mental hospital patients and he concluded that the various motor manifestations of *emotion are innate, but modifiable, vestigial remnants of earlier adaptive reactions. Thus, in contrast to mental chemistry based on introspection, Darwin studied overt behaviour in relation to environmental events and attempted to trace both the phylogenetic and ontogenetic history of these interactions. This set a tradition which is still followed, especially in child and abnormal psychology and related medical disciplines.

Variation within a species is a crucial aspect of Darwinian theory but the most significant contributions to the study of human individual differences came from Darwin's polymath cousin, Francis *Galton. Galton laid the foundations of psychometrics, the statistical methodology appropriate to the measurement of human abilities and other differential attributes. He also established the concept of correlation and its measurement by the calculation of a 'correlation coefficient'. Galton's pupils and assistants, many of them with medical qualifications, became the pioneers of mental testing in the UK and the USA. Galton was also an important influence on Alfred *Binet, director of the psychological laboratory at the Sorbonne, who in 1904 was appointed by the French Minister of Public Instruction to devise an objective means of detecting mentally defective children for placement in special schools. This appointment resulted in the creation in 1905 of the first version of the Binet–Simon Scale which has undergone numerous revisions and re-standardizations by various authorities to survive to the present time. Binet himself introduced the concept of 'mental age' (MA) in 1908, and in 1912 a German psychologist, Stern, proposed that an individual's mental age be related to his chronological age (CA) to indicate his '*intelligence quotient' (IQ) by the formula: $IQ = MA/CA \times 100$.

Galton's astonishing output also included contributions to criminology, particularly his discovery of identification by fingerprints, as well as studies of mental imagery and free association relevant to Freudian concepts of the unconscious and his championing of *eugenic concepts.

1870–1914: early American and British psychology. Darwinism was a strong influence on the directions taken by psychology in the USA where William *James, a qualified physician who never practised and a distinguished philosopher as well as psychologist, was an outstanding early figure. He adopted a biological stance in which he saw value in introspection but introspection directed at the dynamic 'stream of consciousness'. His analysis of the 'self image' is still reflected in current views of personality and psychopathology. Equally important was the vital role he assigned to 'habit', both in behaviour and in its neurological basis. He conceived of habits, acquired during the life history of an individual, as serving similar adaptive functions to instincts acquired during the evolutionary history of the species. This line of thinking led to a systematic view of psychology to be known as 'functionalism' which flourished particularly in Chicago.

The other main trend of contemporary importance in early American psychology was that towards '*behaviourism'. J. B. Watson is generally regarded as the founder of this doctrine but his was a very crude and extreme behaviourism. Greatly impressed with reports of the work of the Russian physiologist *Pavlov on conditioned reflexes, he rejected all forms of introspection and maintained that the only valid object of study for psychology is overt observable behaviour, analysed in stimulus–response terms at the molecular level of muscle twitches, glandular secretions, and the like. Thought was to be treated as internal speech, potentially recordable as minute movements of the speech apparatus.

Departments of psychology were set up in all the major American universities before the First World War but progress in the UK was much slower and owed much to those whose primary qualifications were in medicine. One such was W. H. R. Rivers who had worked in *neurology under Henry *Head and had trained in experimental psychology in Germany. He taught a course in psychology, and researched into visual perception and the effects of drugs on fatigue, in the physiology department at Cambridge. His interests became transformed when, with two other medically qualified pioneers of British psychology, William McDougall and C. S. Myers, he joined A. C. Haddon's famous 1898 expedition to the Torres Straits. This wedded him to anthropology and, in 1909, he handed over his lectureship to Myers who taught the first generation of Cambridge psychology graduates. These same Cambridge psychologists helped, as visiting lecturers, to establish psychology at University College, London. There, Charles Spearman was appointed reader and later professor but his chair remained that of philosophy until 1928. He remained close to the Galton tradition and argued that all intellectual tasks involved a general factor 'g' and another factor specific to the task. This was in direct contrast to the interpretation of similar data by E. L. Thorndike and other American psychologists who denied the existence of a general intellectual ability but argued for a number of distinct 'primary mental abilities'. This divergence led to very animated controversy for many years. At an earlier stage in his career, when experimenting with animals, Thorndike had formulated the 'Law of Effect' which, in one form or another, is basic to contemporary behaviourism. In essence, this 'law' implies that actions (responses) which are 'reinforced' by an event which satisfies a current need, for example by providing food or allowing escape from restraint, become associated with the context in which the action occurs (stimulus) and are repeated in similar contexts. Conversely, actions not so rewarded or punished drop out of the learner's repertoire in that context.

Psychopathology. Thus, by 1914, psychology had become clearly established as an independent academic discipline. However, despite the early heavy involvement of those trained in medicine, academic psychology at this time focused on the cognitive and rational and had little relevance to the irrationalities and emotional disorders associated with *psychopathology. Psychometrics had been applied to *mental deficiency and, to a lesser extent, to the insane. Neurology, from the more rational side of medicine, was better served. For example, E. W. Scripture, an American psychologist at Yale, later sought medical qualification, and in 1912 founded a speech laboratory at the West End Hospital for Nervous Diseases in London. There, his researches reflected both his medical and his psychological training. However, as mental disorder came to be regarded as a form of illness, not as evidence of demonic possession, practitioners, finding little in the existing psychology to aid them, developed their own practices and theories.

Hypnosis and French psychology. Hypnosis had an important role in this transition. The history of *hypnosis, like that of many psychological phenomena, passed through stages of mysticism and superstition, via serious medical application and speculation, to scientific experimental analysis. Much of the latter has been carried out by experimental psychologists but, during the period under discussion, hypnosis was closely associated with the treatment of neurotic disorders and with France. *Mesmer came to Paris from Vienna in 1777 with his theories of 'animal magnetism' and flamboyant group techniques. He had dramatic therapeutic successes but scientific investigation demonstrated that magnetism played no part in

these. Nevertheless, less showman-like forms of *mesmerism were used to achieve *analgesia in general and dental surgery despite antagonistic attitudes of the medical establishment. An 1838 formal resolution of the Council of *University College Hospital, London, forbade the practice of mesmerism in order to end its usage by one of the founder surgeons, John *Elliotson. It was James Braid, a Manchester physician, who coined the term 'hypnosis' and, by firmly rejecting all notions of magnetism, brought respectability to the practice in the 1840s. He explained the trance phenomenon in neurological terms but, mistakenly, likened it to sleep. Liébault and Bernheim, whose work at Nancy in France was influential in bringing the milder neurotic disorders within the range of psychiatry, disagreed and saw hypnosis as a psychological phenomenon depending on suggestion.

The work of J. M. *Charcot, neurologist at the *Salpêtrière Hospital in Paris, was of even greater seminal importance. He postulated a close relationship between hypnosis and '*hysteria', a condition in which physical symptoms are manifested without observable organic cause. For him, the hypnotic trance was itself an hysterical phenomenon to be employed more as a diagnostic than a therapeutic tool. Pierre *Janet, also at the Salpêtrière, extended this view. He considered that neurotics lack sufficient 'mental energy' to maintain the integration of the mind. In hysteria this results in 'dissociation', the independent action of different parts of the mind. In particular, unpleasant memories may be removed from conscious awareness. Janet argued that hypnosis was a similar dissociated state and discovered that, under hypnosis, hysterics could achieve vivid recall of forgotten events, often in a very emotional way. This he termed '*catharsis' and he employed the technique, now known as '*abreaction', to achieve some therapeutic success. Thus Janet developed some concepts of lasting value and moved along lines which Freud was to take much further.

Freud and psychoanalysis. Sigmund *Freud was born at Freiburg in Moravia but moved with his family to Vienna where he graduated in medicine and acquired postgraduate clinical and academic experience in neurology and neuropathology. These interests continued well into his psychological period, as shown by the publication of his well-regarded book on *aphasia in 1891 and his later abortive attempts at a reductionist analysis of his psychological theory into neurological terms. He established a relationship with Josef *Breuer (1842–1925), a practitioner and neurophysiologist of considerable distinction, who subscribed to a theory similar to Janet's of a limited pool of nervous energy, and treated hysterics by hypnotic catharsis, a term he coined independently of Janet. Freud was much impressed and, in 1885, visited Paris to study under Charcot and, four years later, visited Bernheim at Nancy.

Freud collaborated closely with Breuer who came to accept Freud's view that the lost memories of hysterical patients were not merely dissociated from the field of consciousness but were actively 'repressed' into unconsciousness by a mechanism, the function of which was to defend the self or '*ego' from the threat, not only of specific memories, but also of frightening impulses and emotions. This repressed material was thought to gain symbolic manifestation through the neurotic symptoms. In 1895 Freud and Breuer jointly published their *Studies on Hysteria,* but Breuer was already beginning to withdraw from the association. This was because he found the recurring sexual content of the repressed material embarrassing, as was the evident erotic response to him by some patients. He became unwilling to lay the same stress on these sexual aspects of neurosis as Freud, who proposed that the energy reservoir of their theory was of sexual energy or '*libido' and also claimed that it was conflict between sexual impulses and moral considerations which led to repression of the former.

Freud was not a particularly successful hypnotist and sought an alternative means of eliciting repressed material by extending Galton's techniques of free association. This brought the couch into what Freud christened '*psychoanalysis'. Patients also reported on their dreams which Freud regarded as disguised manifestations of repressed conflicts released during the relaxed vigilance of *sleep. His interpretations were based on his self-analysis which led to considerable modification and elaboration of his theory. He believed that psychopathology and the adult character originate in the course of the sexual development of childhood. He proposed several stages in this development during which 'libido' is directed to different '*erogenous zones' of the body and their related functions. Psychological development could become 'fixated' at one or other of these stages and, under stress, adult behaviour is likely to 'regress' to a style characteristic of the fixation. Of these stages—oral, anal, phallic, latent, and genital—the phallic is the one associated with the famous '*oedipal conflict' in which a boy becomes sexually attracted to his mother and aggressively jealous of his father from whom he fears retribution. Unsuccessful dealing with this conflict was considered to lead to *neurosis or sexual deviation. Freud's theory as it developed up to the First World War is described in his *Introductory Lectures on Psychoanalysis* which, even in translation (Freud, 1974), provide an excellent means of savouring the flavour and style of his thinking and argument. The essence was complete by that time but Freud continued to refine and elaborate his theories right up to his painful death in London at the age of 83. The later additions to his metapsychology include the incorporation of a death instinct, called 'thanatos', and his structural division of mind into 'id', the uncoordinated instinctual urges, the organized and reality-orientated

'ego', and the critical moralizing 'superego'. In psychoanalytic practice, the emphasis moved from the patient's gaining of insight to resolution of his 'transference', the shifting on to the analyst of intense feelings earlier experienced in relation to a parent or other important figure in the patient's life.

Even during the earlier period, psychoanalysis extended well beyond psychopathology to become a metapsychology applicable to all human activities. One of Freud's early works, *The Psychopathology of Everyday Life,* deals with slips of the tongue and similar 'parapraxes' and he opens his *Introductory Lectures* on this theme to demonstrate how trivial apparently accidental actions may be psychologically determined. Ultimately, he applied psychoanalytic concepts to such wide-ranging topics as art, occultism, religion, and anthropology. Few would deny that Freud was a genius and his ideas have penetrated the language and thinking of the West. But is it justified to place him, as is often claimed, alongside Copernicus, Newton, Darwin, and Einstein? One cannot blame him for his adoption of a mistaken contemporary neurophysiology, based on hydraulic-like enclosed systems of mental energies, but, despite the incorporation into general psychology of many of his concepts, several of these imply the identity of opposites in a way which makes them difficult to validate scientifically. The therapeutic efficacy of psychoanalysis is now dubious and its esoteric and allegorical language is more suited to artistic than scientific discourse. Its influence is, in fact, declining in science and medicine but continues to flourish in the world of literature and art.

Apart from Breuer, many orthodox psychiatrists rejected the sexual emphasis in Freud's early work, a reception similar to that awarded to Havelock *Ellis, the London non-practising physician, for his work on the psychology of sex. Freud greatly resented this reaction which he interpreted as psychodynamically determined. But his early books were well-received by others and, quite early, a Vienna Psychoanalytic Society was established and was in communication with psychiatrists elsewhere. In 1909 Freud was invited to America to receive a doctorate at Clark University, to lecture, and to meet many distinguished psychologists and psychiatrists. However, the Vienna Society soon exhibited a tendency to dissension and schism. In 1911 the famous psychiatrist *Bleuler resigned as did Alfred *Adler to form his own Viennese group. Later, the Swiss psychiatrist *Jung also disassociated himself.

The purposeful psychology of William McDougall. Meanwhile, a more consciousness-orientated dynamic psychology on a broader instinctual basis was developed in the UK by William McDougall, who was qualified in medicine, anthropology, and experimental psychology. After a period as a psychology demonstrator at University College, London, he became the Wilde reader in mental philosophy at Oxford where he remained until the First World War, after which he took up a chair at Harvard. The Wilde readership was not intended for empirical research but McDougall managed to obtain facilities at the physiology laboratory where he carried out high-quality experimental work on perception, psychophysics, and psychopharmacology. He wrote an early influential book on physiological psychology but his main theoretical impact came from his *Introduction to Social Psychology* (1908). In this he developed a concept of man as purposeful and goal-seeking, guided by prediction of the future on the basis of past experience, and activated by a large set of inherited 'instincts'. Each of these was characterized by a 'propensity' or 'disposition' to perceive a certain class of objects, to experience a particular emotional excitement when a relevant object is perceived, and to act in relation to it in a particular way. For example, the instinct of flight and the emotion of fear were considered to be innate, but fear of particular objects or situations might be learned, as might specific modes of escape. 'Sentiments', such as love or hate, were considered to be complexes of emotions related to specific persons or objects including the 'self'. McDougall's theories provided a reasonable basis for a psychology of motivation and personality but were marred by excursions into metaphysical animism and the extension of his list of instincts from those with a clear biological basis, such as hunger or sex, through such tendencies as gregariousness and pugnacity to broad social behaviour patterns like the acquisition of wealth, which was accounted for in terms of an acquisitive instinct. McDougall, like his fellow medically qualified academic psychologists, was more open to Freudian views than orthodox practitioners in the UK. He accepted the concepts of repression, dissociation, and the unconscious, but was critical of others which he described as 'ill-founded and somewhat fantastic'. In particular, he regretted Freud's 'almost ostentatious neglect of academic psychology' to extend a breach which was already wide. Therefore, McDougall adopted as a major aim 'to single out what is sound and true in these doctrines and to bring them into harmony with the main body of science'.

The First World War provided an exceptional opportunity for the pursuance of this aim. Pure research was halted but psychology's reputation for the usefulness of its practical application was greatly enhanced. Intelligence and aptitude testing made great strides and psychologists' contributions to the training of operators and their adaptation to new machines laid the foundation for post-war developments in industrial psychology. But consequences for psychological medicine were even more profound. Several British academic psychologists, such as McDougall, Rivers, and Myers, had qualified in medicine more to acquire academic respectability than to practise, and several of their early students, such as William Brown, went on to read medicine to avoid the strong prejudice against the encroachment on to clinical territory of the medically unqualified. However, when the war came they joined the RAMC and became involved with the *stress reactions of soldiers. Myers, in particular, did much to demonstrate the functional nature of '*shell-shock', a reaction which was claimed to result from minute brain haemorrhages caused by pressure waves from exploding shells. The publication of his war diary as a book, *Shell-shock in France, 1914–18* (1940), was long delayed but an earlier account of similar material was provided by Elliot-Smith and Pear, a non-medical psychologist (1917). It was demonstrated that sufferers were not cowards or moral weaklings but might even have excellent combat records. Most importantly, it was demonstrated that these reactions could often be treated effectively and quickly by eclectic psychological techniques involving both psychodynamic elements and retraining methods adumbrating later behavioural approaches to treatment. These experiences were reflected in the post-war establishment, on a voluntary basis, of the Tavistock Clinic in London for training, research, and the free out-patient treatment of neurotic conditions, and the foundation by Myers, then president, and Rivers of a section devoted to medical psychology and an associated journal within the British Psychological Society.

Between the wars. Within psychology generally, the period between the two wars was one of competing theoretical 'schools'. Of these, two had greatest relevance for medical psychology—behaviourism and psychoanalysis.

Behaviourism. Although Watson abandoned academic work for a career in advertising in 1920, Russian reflexology continued to influence American psychologists in their development of a systematic S–R psychology. Both stimulus(S) and response(R) may be described in molar or molecular terms. For example, one may distinguish between movements and acts, an act being a functional response, such as operating a lever or opening a door, which can be effected by a variety of movement patterns. Some theorists continued to insist, as had Watson, on molecular analysis but others, notably B. F. Skinner, who remains the dominant contemporary influence on behaviourists, stressed the effects on the environment of response acts which Skinner referred to as 'operants'. In 'operant conditioning', unlike Pavlovian or 'classical conditioning', acts carried out in a particular stimulus situation acquire an increased probability of recurring in that situation if 'reinforced'. Thus, in the famous 'Skinner Box', a rat may learn to press a lever to obtain a food pellet. Initially, the lever is depressed by accidental or exploratory movements but its reinforcement by food gradually increases the frequency and precision of the operant response. More complex operants which could not occur accidentally, not being in the animal's initial repertoire, may be 'shaped' by reinforcing a simple related response and then reinforcing successive approximations to the required operant. A vast amount of meticulous experimentation by Skinner and his followers has established an impressive set of lawful relationships between the various parameters of operant learning and, despite objections to some of their theoretical views, the practical power of operant principles has been demonstrated impressively with complex human as well as animal learning.

Skinner, while not denying the reality of subjective conscious experience, considers that it would not be fruitful to involve internal events in his system, which he believes to be an adequate account of all aspects of external, observable behaviour and sufficient for the control of that behaviour. Other behaviourists have had more regard for internal events or 'intervening variables' between stimuli and responses. E. C. Tolman went so far in this direction with his 'purposive behaviourism' that he included 'demands', 'expectancies', 'cognitive maps', 'signs', and 'significates'. For him, reinforcement only makes manifest learning which has already been acquired in a more cognitive manner and remained latent. Clark L. Hull included intervening variables in a formal theory in the style of physical science and even hoped that the relevant variables could ultimately be precisely quantified. He claimed that his intervening variables were abstract constructs definable only in terms of measurable stimuli and responses but the terms given them, for example 'habit strength', 'drive strength', 'inhibitory potential', seem to refer to physiological entities, potentially susceptible to direct measurement. Hull's ambitious hope for a rigorous quantitative analysis of behaviour was doomed to failure but others, still very active, make more limited but also more fruitful use of related hypothetical constructs.

Psychoanalysis. Jung and Adler, after their withdrawal from Freud's circle, developed their own psychodynamic theories and practices for which they coined the terms 'analytic psychology' and 'individual psychology' respectively. Jung, apart from being a successful psychiatrist, was a man of great breadth of scholarship with interests in anthropology, philosophy, religion, mythology, and mysticism. He was convinced of the importance of unconscious processes in psychopathology and used his own association tests and the analysis of dream symbolism to gain access to those processes. However, unlike Freud, he considered aspects of the unconscious as positive and creative in nature and helpful to the development of a mature personality. He elaborated the concept of a 'complex' as a set of emotionally toned unconscious ideas and attitudes which cluster around some conscious theme. Apart from a personal unconscious deriving from an individual's life history, Jung postulated a collective unconscious derived from mankind's racial history and containing 'archetypal' material concerning fundamental human needs and experiences such as birth, death, physical danger, food, and the cycles of the sun and moon. These 'archetypes' were said to be represented in dream images and other symbolic ways and also in the common elements of myth and folklore.

Jung also studied individual personality differences and stressed the distinction between extraverted and introverted attitudes. The extravert is an outgoing, sociable, practically orientated person while the introvert is inward-looking, unsociable, shy, and tends more to thought than action. He also claimed that individuals differ by their bias towards one or other of four psychological functions—perception, feeling, thinking, and intuition. These biases were seen as emerging during development to become a person's strategy of adaptation, the opposing tendencies becoming repressed to have an unconscious role. The 'self' has the task, seldom achieved, of integrating these various conscious and unconscious tendencies and Jung's therapy was largely aimed at aiding this integration. His approach was thus more positive and optimistic than Freud's and had features in common with contemporary 'humanistic' psychology.

Adler's 'individual psychology' is much closer to common sense than the doctrines of either Freud or Jung. He laid less stress on the unconscious but a great deal on social development. This directed his interest to child psychiatry and he founded several child guidance clinics. He emphasized striving for mastery of oneself and the social environment and distinguished between normality and neurosis in terms of realistic and unrealistic social goals. Aggression is more prominent in his teaching than the sex drive. He saw the inevitable weakness of childhood as leading to a sense of inferiority. In neurotics this is exaggerated, and false beliefs of personal imperfections generate a life-style characterized by maladaptive over-compensation. This pattern is laid down in childhood interactions with parents and siblings: he considered birth order among siblings an important factor. Nevertheless, the adult personality is open to a modification of life-style and reorganization of goals. A healthy adult compensates by submerging his egocentric striving in the pursuit of co-operative social goals and trusting relationships.

The influence of social factors was also recognized by others who, though deviating greatly from Freud's views, remained under the banner of psychoanalysis. Two German analysts who later moved to the USA, Karen Horney and Erich Fromm, are notable examples. Horney, a Berlin medical graduate, was clearly influenced by Adler and saw childhood's helplessness as creating a 'basic anxiety' which becomes exaggerated if parents do not display unconditional love. Conflicts arising in the social context of adulthood may also be important and need resolution during analysis. It is not surprising that Horney, a woman, was highly critical of Freud's chauvinistic account of female psychosexual development.

Erich Fromm was a social psychologist prior to his psychoanalytical training and was particularly interested in the relationship between the individual and society, which he interpreted in Marxian as well as Freudian terms. He saw human nature at any one time and in any one place as owing as much to culture as to biology. In a rigid culture a person's place is immutably defined and, therefore, raises no problem of adjustment, but in a free society, individuals have the difficult task of creating their individuality. The inevitable conflicts and stresses may produce neurotic reactions. Fromm even saw the emergence of totalitarian societies such as Nazi Germany as a reaction to the 'fear of freedom', the title of the English version of his most influential book.

Psychoanalysis in the UK, as might be expected, remained closer to the biological emphasis of Freud even when deviating from his views. Of particular note is the work of Melanie Klein with children. Freud's daughter, Anna, worked in Europe with children of three and upwards along orthodox psychoanalytic lines and made valuable observations on the 'ego defence mechanisms'. Two of these, 'projection' and 'introjection', are basic to Klein's theorizing which extended backwards to the early months of infancy. By projection someone attributes his own unacceptable impulses to another. Introjection implies the reverse, external influences becoming incorporated into the self. Freud saw the superego as formed by the introjection of parental demands and prohibitions as a resolution of oedipal conflicts around the age of four. Klein put superego development much earlier and her doctrines became dominant in the UK. Later, the Second World War brought Anna Freud to the UK with her father and, under her direction, the rival 'continental school' of child analysis flourished at the Hampstead Clinic.

General and applied psychology. Within general psychology, many rejected much of psychoanalysis but were interested in the study of personality. For them the main question was whether their approach should be 'idiographic', treating individual personality as an indivisible and unique whole, or 'nomothetic', describing individuals analytically in terms of their placement along various trait dimensions. According to this view, a person's undeniable uniqueness lies in the unique combination of traits he or she displays. During the inter-war period the idiographic approach dominated. For example, an influential American psychologist, G. W. Allport, defined personality as the 'dynamic organization within the individual of those psychophysical systems that determine his unique adjustment to his environment'. Allport employed a variety of empirical techniques but the most popular idiographic assessment technique, particularly in clinical setting, has been the ink-blot

association test originated by the continental psychiatrist *Rorschach. This type of test is described as a 'projective technique' as the subject is claimed to 'project' his style of viewing the world and his motives in his responses. The other main projective technique, the Thematic Apperception Test (TAT), involves the telling of stories based on human scenes presented on a series of cards. This was devised by another American psychologist, H. A. Murray, who proposed that personality should be described in terms of 'needs' within the individual and the 'presses' which the environment imposes on him. He analysed TAT stories into press/need interactions or 'themata', especially those involving the hero of the story with whom the storyteller was thought to identify.

The period between the World Wars saw the slow beginnings of clinical psychology as an applied field, although not yet a profession. A number of psychological clinics for the treatment of neurotic conditions were set up in the USA but without formal training courses or official recognition. In the UK there was great resistance to the intrusion of non-medical graduates into psychiatric territory. A few gained limited access for research, usually of a psychometric nature, and the assistance of these was sometimes sought for the assessment of *dementia. But it was in the more open realm of child guidance that psychologists with clinical interests gained most ground. Training became available at the Tavistock Clinic and the London Day Training College, the precursor of the University of London Institute of Education. In 1929 Lucy Fildes, a psychologist with research experience in mental deficiency and neurology and of practical child guidance in the USA, was appointed chief psychologist to a new multidisciplinary London Child Guidance Clinic which offered both treatment and training.

Meanwhile, British universities, unlike those in the USA, were reluctant to establish departments of psychology. Where they existed, interest tended to turn from instinct and emotion to cognitive and other skills, either by experimental analysis as at Cambridge or by psychometric studies as at London. Research fundamental to physiological psychology and relevant to neurology made important advances but with few contributions from psychologists. An exception was the work of K. S. Lashley of Harvard who tested the effects of extirpation of various parts of the rat brain on subsequent behaviour. Without denying the specific localization of certain sensory and motor functions, his findings indicated that, for complex functions such as learning, it is the amount of cortex rather than the site of removal which determines the degree of loss. The loss was also incomplete and relearning was possible. Lashley argued that these 'higher functions' have no corresponding neural centre but depend on the integrated functioning of the brain as a whole. He also found that removal of some specialized areas did not necessarily result in loss of the relevant function. He assumed that other parts of the brain took over, a capability for which he coined the term 'equipotentiality'. During the same period, physiologists such as Cannon, Bard, and Papez unravelled much of the physical basis of emotion in the *autonomic nervous system, *hypothalamus, and *limbic system to provide a foundation for much later research and speculation by psychologists.

The Second World War and after. The Second World War, like the First, provided an opportunity for psychology to prove its usefulness. Psychologists were recruited to a variety of roles, including the new field of 'human engineering' or '*ergonomics', the tailoring of the job or the machine to the man. For the related task of selecting the man for the job, psychometric techniques were greatly improved and new training techniques were developed. Brief forms of psychotherapy were developed to deal with psychiatric casualties, who also provided subjects in sufficiently large numbers for large-scale research into their condition requiring statistical analysis. Another innovatory type of study which has since flourished is that of 'group dynamics', the largely covert interpersonal interactions within small groups.

Experimental approaches to neuropsychology, neurosis, and personality. The war was followed by an explosive growth of psychology in all the major countries. This growth was not confined to practical applications but was also reflected in research output and in the range of theoretical speculation. A substantial proportion of the research has been relevant to medicine and much of this has emerged from multidisciplinary contexts in which psychologists collaborate with clinicians and biological scientists. The reciprocal relationships between behavioural, clinical, and biological observations in experimental and clinical contexts have greatly extended knowledge of brain functioning. *Neuropsychology, *psychopharmacology, and *psycholinguistics are related new specialisms within psychology. Interpretation of the data in these areas is never easy because of the richness of interconnections within the brain, the complex interactions of excitatory and inhibitory systems, and the fact that apparent equipotentialities, as postulated by Lashley, may represent the replacement of one control system by another which involves quite different mechanisms.

Of particular interest to psychologists has been the recent light thrown on cerebral asymmetry, the differential functioning of the two sides of the brain. It appears that the cerebral hemisphere non-dominant for language, usually the right, not only has a major role in the processing of spatial information but is also important in emotional reactions. Equally interesting was the demonstration by two psychologists, J. Olds and P. Milner, that a rat with an electrode implanted in a certain region of the brain quickly learned to press a lever to achieve electrical self-stimulation. Moreover, this stimulation proved to be more reinforcing than food. Later, evidence emerged of the existence of more diffuse 'pain' systems opposed to these 'reward' systems. Other important advances concern the role of chemical *neurotransmitters within the brain. Neurotransmitter dysfunctions are thought to underlie the more severe psychiatric disorders such as *schizophrenia and the recent discovery of morphine-like brain chemicals (*endorphins, the body's own endogenous analgesics) may throw fresh light on the nature of *addiction.

A great deal of the more behavioural research with both human and animal subjects has been concerned with the mechanisms and reactions underlying neurotic disorders. An experimental analysis of conflict between opposing motives was carried out by a prolific American psychologist, N. E. Miller, who also studied escape and avoidance as well as aggressive reactions to frustration. With J. Dollard (1950) he wrote an influential book which, while accepting the fundamentals of Freudian theory and practice, analysed them in terms of the psychology of learning and thinking, and the cultural context. Later, learning theorists such as H. J. Eysenck (1957) in the UK and A. Bandura (1961) in the USA rejected psychoanalysis and accounted for neurotic reactions as resulting from the faulty learning of maladaptive habits.

Behavioural models of neurosis are as much opposed to medical as to psychoanalytic models in so far as the former imply physical disease of the nervous system. *Anxiety is basic to most neurotic disorders and behaviourists regard anxiety as a form of conditioned fear. *Depression, similarly, has been analysed behaviouristically. For example, M. E. P. Seligman has argued from empirical data that some types of depression result from a learned form of helplessness. Animal experiments have demonstrated that psychological stress can produce physical symptoms such as gastric ulceration. Other more complex experiments with primates show how infant experience can affect adult social behaviour.

In the study of personality the nomothetic approach has mainly prevailed although there has been recent advocacy of what is described as humanistic psychology, focused on the individual person and his or her self-actualization. This is defined by A. H. Maslow as 'ongoing actualization of potentials, capacities and talents, fulfilment of mission, fuller knowledge and acceptance of one's intrinsic nature and a trend towards unity and integration'. It will be seen that this is a very value-loaded, and Western value-loaded, concept but such 'self-actualization' is the goal of a type of psychotherapy. One practitioner of what he calls 'client-centred therapy', C. R. Rogers, has also contributed research findings relevant to all forms of psychotherapy. Unfortunately, at the other end of the broad spectrum embraced by the term humanistic may be found bizarre forms of what are called 'encounter groups'.

Within the nomothetic approach to personality assessment the main technique is the self-completion questionnaire or inventory, usually with a large number of items contributing scores to a more limited set of scales relating to traits. In most of these questionnaires the traits measured are relevant to psychopathological as well as normal characteristics. Many inventories yield many trait scores: for example, a popular American questionnaire by R. B. Cattell is scored for 16 factors. But H. J. Eysenck, who is most active in this field in the UK, points out that these scores are not independent but inter-correlate to varying degrees. Therefore, his own scale is scored for a small number of higher-order factors to which several traits may contribute. For example, one of his main measures, that of extraversion/introversion, may be broken down into traits of sociability, impulsivity, and dominance. Similarly, several lesser traits play a part in his other major factor, emotional stability/neuroticism.

Developmental psychology is also relevant to aspects of medicine. Recent research has demonstrated that the world of the newborn infant is in no way the booming buzzing confusion it was thought to be by William James. Improved methods of investigation have demonstrated remarkable capabilities active almost from birth. For example, when appropriately supported, newborn infants will make purposeful reaching movements towards objects. Similarly, it is now evident that the infant is a social being from the beginning. Quite early, gaze is skilfully directed and maintained at the face of another person, which is important for the infant's control of its mother. At later ages, much has been learned about the processes and stages involved in cognitive and language development.

Darwin's continuing influence, particularly from his work on emotional expression, is very evident in the rise of *ethology, a term which has been given new meaning as the comparative study of behaviour with particular reference to *instinct-based behaviour. The 1973 Nobel prize in medicine was awarded to von Frisch, Lorenz, and Tinbergen for their outstanding pioneer contributions to this field. Complex sequences of adaptive behaviour which follow a regular pattern common to all members of a species, even when there is no opportunity for individual learning, are the mark of instinct and imply a genetic basis. But primarily inherited patterns of this nature can be open to varying degrees of modification from individual experience. Lorenz, who was the main integrator of ethological concepts, considered, however, that truly instinctive behaviour does always involve a core fixed action pattern occurring often at the consummatory end-point of the behavioural sequence. Another important concept is that of imprinting, a type of learning which occurs during a specific sensitive period in early life but also affects adult sexual and other social behaviour. Important, too, is a particular class of stimuli which have been shown to act as specific releasers of certain action patterns.

Recently, ethological studies have tended to move from the more rigid genetic patterns of insects, fishes, and birds to the more flexible behaviour of mammals, including primates. There is also considerable evidence that ethological concepts are relevant to human development, for example in relation to the evocation of and response to an infant's smile, the establishment of mother–child affectional bonds, and children's play. Early attempts to apply evolutionary and ethological principles to human culture and social life more generally were resisted by psychologists and anthropologists partly because of a naïve over-emphasis on 'survival of the fittest' which allowed some authors to argue for objectionable political implications. More recently, however, primate field studies, the linking of ethological with ecological analyses, and a change of emphasis from individual to group selection in evolutionary theory have increased relevance to human affairs. For example, altruistic behaviour becomes explicable when it is recognized that the important units in evolution are the genes within the individual rather than the individuals themselves (Dawkins, 1976). Evolutionary fitness comes not only from selfish behaviour but also from assisting others with related genes. The evolution of man has been directed towards flexibility of behaviour but this is within a biological inheritance of certain behavioural strategies relating to reproductive effectiveness which are recognizable across cultures (Crook, 1980).

Clinical psychology, the profession, its methods, and current trends. The post-war era is also notable for the steady growth of a profession of clinical psychology. In the USA the *Veterans Administration established training criteria at a Ph.D. level as early as 1946. The US Public Health Service soon followed suit and various university courses were established. By 1950 there were some 500 new recruits to the profession each year and growth has continued to make clinical psychology a major division of the American Psychological Association. Owing to the American health care system, many clinical psychologists practise privately within a system of state registration and this has sometimes led to competitive conflict with psychiatrists.

In the UK, although a small number of non-medical psychotherapists, trained in one or other of the psychodynamic schools, have treated patients referred via their training institutions privately, private practice is only now beginning to penetrate the main stream of clinical psychology. This is because the profession has grown up in the context of the *National Health Service which remains the main employer. As in the USA, the clinical division has become an important and flourishing component of the British Psychological Society. Following the British tradition in which the Ph.D. is strictly a research degree, the professional postgraduate qualifications are various types of Master's degrees or diplomas. Thus, although individual clinical psychologists may take doctorates, all have a good honours first degree in psychology followed by a 2-year university Master's course, which includes a research component, or an equivalent 3-year in-service training within the Health Service, culminating in an examination for a diploma awarded by the Psychological Society. These are the requirements for a basic grade post in the Health Service which then provides a career structure through senior, principal, and top grades. As yet, there is no statutory professional registration but a proposed Act will probably embrace the whole range of psychological activities.

Clinical psychology is very much an evolving profession and it may be illuminating to trace some of that evolution, concentrating on the British scene which is most familiar to the author. The University of London Institute of Psychiatry and the associated *Bethlem Royal and Maudsley Hospital played an important part, as they did in the advancement of British psychiatry. When the Maudsley Hospital reopened after the Second World War, its staff included Eysenck, later to become reader and, later still, professor of psychology at the Institute. His wartime research had applied psychometric techniques to the taxonomic problems of psychiatry and he set out to establish a postgraduate course in clinical psychology under the direction of Shapiro, who subscribed to his own experimental objective nomothetic approach. This was in marked contrast to the approach of the Tavistock Clinic, the other main London influence. There the orientation was psychoanalytic and psychological assessment was mainly based on projective techniques. These differences were strongly reflected in the training provided for clinical psychologists in each place. Other influential early training courses, such as that at the Crichton Royal Hospital in Scotland, took an intermediate position. The Tavistock approach has maintained a place in British clinical psychology but the Maudsley influence proved dominant. There the early stress was on assessment, regarding each single case as a miniature scientific investigation which need not be restricted to standard psychometric tests and might involve experimental methods. Although, if successful, these investigations yielded findings with implications for treatment, the psychologist rarely played any part in that treatment unless it was a form of remedial education: the treatment of emotional disorders was strictly a medical preserve.

Meanwhile, the research and theoretical interests of the department were directed at exploration of the relationships between psychiatric conditions and biologically based personality differences, and a behaviouristic explanation of those relationships and the aetiology of neurosis based on the learning theories of Pavlov and Hull. It was from the combined influence of these theoretical concepts and the experimental single-case approach that, during the 1950s, the form of treatment that came to be known as 'behaviour therapy' emerged within the psychology department of the Maudsley Hospital. Oddly enough, a quite independent parallel development took place in South Africa through the work of the psychiatrist J. Wolpe (1958) who later became influential in the USA. There, clinical psychologists remained wedded for some time to psychodynamic and psychometric approaches but a group of experimental psychologists in the radical behavourist Skinnerian tradition applied operant conditioning procedures in what was described as the 'behaviour modification' of institutionalized chronic psychotics, subnormals, and delinquents. Both behaviour therapy and behaviour modification, often in combination, have flourished greatly across the world as reflected in a vast literature.

The early conceptual basis of behaviour therapy, in contrast to behaviour modification, allowed for internal intervening variables and, as in psychodynamic theory, stressed the role of anxiety in the development and persistence of neurotic symptoms. Anxiety was regarded as a learned fear response to stressful environmental events. As a distressing emotional state it motivates the sufferer to engage in such anxiety-reducing strategies as phobic avoidance or obsessional rituals. More directly, through its somatic manifestations, anxiety may give rise to various *psychosomatic symptoms. The treatment, which was intentionally symptomatic, drew on a wide range of the findings of experimental psychology but with strong emphasis on principles of learning, relearning, and unlearning. Several of the early case studies, for example, involved procedures aimed at the 'voluntary control' of 'involuntary' physiological systems by the feedback of information from those systems (e.g. Jones, 1960), thus anticipating the now popular techniques of *biofeedback for the treatment of somatic disorders.

Whereas behaviour modifiers, while vastly increasing their range, have maintained a strict behaviourist stance, many behaviour therapists have not only paid great attention to the social context in which the disorder arises but also emphasize cognitive factors. Behavioural change is often accompanied and sometimes preceded by cognitive change: a change in attitude to or interpretation of his problems by the patient. Sometimes such a cognitive reorientation becomes the target of treatment, hence the emergence of terms such as cognitive behaviour therapy and behavioural psychotherapy. While overt behaviour continues to have an important role in behaviour therapy, there is now particular emphasis on the achievement of the self-management of that behaviour by the patient.

Apart from the assessment and treatment of patients, clinical psychologists are often active researchers. The validation of assessment techniques and the evaluation of treatment effects is a necessary clinical function but the clinic also provides real-life situations in which abnormal behaviour can be experimentally manipulated in an ethical manner. Also, representing as they do, an academic discipline highly relevant to medicine, clinical psychologists are inevitably involved in the training of other professional groups. Apart from nursing, occupational therapy, and other health-related professions, psychiatric examinations include papers in psychology and recent curriculum reforms have brought behavioural science into far greater prominence in undergraduate medical education.

During the early post-war years, apart from a minority who worked in neurological contexts, almost all clinical psychologists worked in close association with psychiatrists within mental illness or, less often, mental subnormality hospitals. In recent years, however, there has been a strong trend towards more independent operation from a variety of bases, the formation of new allegiances, and the tackling of new problems. This trend has been most evident in countries where, as in the USA, economic factors and traditional roles have been less limiting. The most striking move has been the one from the hospital into the community. Clinical and other psychologists now work within social service departments and others have direct relationships with general practitioners. Over 10 per cent of general practice patients exhibit some degree of mental disorder and there is also scope for preventive work. Behaviour therapy with children, for example, often involves training parents to apply its principles themselves in the home. Still close to the psychiatric sphere, psychologists are active, both in research and treatment, in fields such as addiction, sexual and marital disorders, and bereavement and the care of the dying (see DEATH, DYING AND THE HOSPICE MOVEMENT).

In the field of neuropsychology, clinical psychologists have remained within specialist neurological settings where they contribute to both the assessment and rehabilitation of patients. Psychometric tests are administered to those with suspected dementia and to assess the more general effects of brain damage. A combination of psychometric and experimental techniques based on research findings is applied to the unravelling of the more specific cognitive and executive defects resulting from localized lesions affecting speech and other higher cerebral functions. Functional analyses of this nature are closely akin to the experimental single-case investigations described earlier and lead naturally into rehabilitative procedures aimed at enhancing natural recovery processes by providing training in the impaired functions and/or developing compensatory use of unaffected capacities. For this purpose, and for monitoring improvement following medical or surgical treatment, attention is focused on disabilities which impair normal living. There are subtle disorders, as in some forms of constructional *apraxia, which, although disclosed in psychological investigations and possibly important for diagnosis, have little if any effect on the patient's everyday activities.

Excursions into clinical fields other than psychiatry and neurology have become so frequent as to gain the general title of 'behavioural medicine'. Much interest has centred on cardiovascular disorders such as *hypertension and *coronary heart disease. There is evidence of the potential modifiability of the aggressive striving behaviour relevant to the latter, and relaxation and biofeedback techniques have been shown to reduce the former. Attempts have been made to apply psychological techniques to the management of chronic pain, with inconclusive results but promising leads. Rehabilitation of the physically handicapped presents many problems open to psychological solutions and, when states may be beyond rehabilitation as in some *geriatric disorders, much may be done to improve the patients' quality of life by applying psychological principles to the design of prosthetic appliances. Other areas into which psychologists are venturing include psychological preparation for surgery, problems associated with *renal dialysis and *transplants, *obesity control, *headaches, *tinnitus, and even aspects of the treatment of *cancer. Health education is another related interest.

It is clear that psychology, which received much of its early sustenance from medicine, is now beginning to repay that debt in what promises to be a fruitful symbiotic relationship.

See also PSYCHIATRY.

H. GWYNNE JONES

References

Bandura, A. (1961). Psychotherapy as a learning process. *Psychological Bulletin*, **58,** 143–59.

Crook, J. H. (1980). *The Evolution of Human Consciousness*. Oxford.

Darwin, C. (1872). *The Expression of the Emotions in Man and Animals*. London. (Available in Thinker's Library edn, 1948.)

Dawkins, R. (1976). *The Selfish Gene*. Oxford.

Dollard, J. and Miller, N. E. (1950). *Personality and Psychotherapy*. New York.

Elliot-Smith, G. and Pear T. H. (1917). *Shell Shock and its Lessons*. London.

Eysenck, H. J. (1957). *The Dynamics of Anxiety and Hysteria*. London.

Eysenck, H. J. (1967). *The Biological Basis of Personality*. Springfield, Illinois.

Freud, S. (1974). *Introductory Lectures on Psychoanalysis*. Pelican edn, Harmondsworth.

Jones, H. G. (1960). The application of conditioning and learning techniques to the treatment of a psychiatric patient. *The Journal of Abnormal and Social Psychology*, **52,** 414–19.

Ley, P. (1982). Giving information to patients. In Eiser, J. R. (ed.), *Social Psychology and Behavioural Medicine*. New York.

McDougall, W. (1908). *An Introduction to Social Psychology*. (26th edn, 1945.) London.

Myers, C. S. (1940). *Shell Shock in France 1914–18*. Cambridge.

Wolpe, J. (1958). *Psychotherapy by Reciprocal Inhibition*. Stanford, California.

Further reading

Atkinson, R. L. and Atkinson, R. C. (eds) (1980). *Mind and Behavior: Readings from Scientific American*. San Francisco.

Beech, H. R. (1969). *Changing Man's Behaviour*. Harmondsworth, Middlesex.

Bower, T. G. R. (1974). *Development in Infancy*. San Francisco.

Broadhurst, P. L. (1963). *The Science of Animal Behaviour*. Harmondsworth, Middlesex.

Brown, J. A. C. (1961). *Freud and the Post-Freudians*. Harmondsworth, Middlesex.

Gibson, H. B. (1977). *Hypnosis*. London.

Hinde, R. A. (1970). *Animal Behaviour: a Synthesis of Ethology and Comparative Psychology*. 2nd edn, New York and London.

Kazdin, A. E. (1978). *Hypnosis*. London.

Kazdin, A. E. (1978). *History of Behaviour Modification*. Baltimore.

Mathews, A. and Steptoe, A. (1982). Behavioural medicine. Special issue of *British Journal of Clinical Psychology*, **21**, (4), 239–358.

Peck, D. and Whitlow, D. (1975). *Approaches to Personality Theory*. London.

Thomson, R. (1968). *The Pelican History of Psychology*. Harmondsworth, Middlesex.

Ullmann, L. P. and Krasner, L. (1975). *A Psychological Approach to Abnormal Behavior*. 2nd edn, Englewood Cliffs, New Jersey.

Walsh, K. W. (1978). *Neuropsychology: a Clinical Approach*. Edinburgh, London, and New York.

Yates, A. J. (1970). *Behaviour Therapy*. New York and London.

PSYCHOMOTOR. Descriptive of the motor expression of mental activity.

PSYCHONEUROSIS is synonymous with *neurosis.

PSYCHOPATHOLOGY is the study of the nature and causes of mental disorder.

PSYCHOPATHY is a personality disorder independent of *intelligence characterized by impulsive, egocentric, irresponsible, and antisocial behaviour; there is difficulty in forming normal relationships, and a manner which is either aggressive or charming or which alternates between the two.

PSYCHOPHARMACOLOGY is the branch of pharmacology concerned with the effects of drugs on mental processes and behaviour. See PHARMACOLOGY.

PSYCHOSEXUAL means pertaining to the mental and emotional aspects of sexual behaviour.

PSYCHOSIS is a term for any of the more serious mental disorders recognized by the lay public as constituting insanity, the defining features of which are loss of contact with reality and derangement of the personality. They include those attributable to organic lesions and states, though these are a small minority. Thought disorganization, profound *mood alterations, *hallucinations, and *delusions are characteristic manifestations. *Schizophrenia and *manic-depressive psychosis are examples.

PSYCHOSOMATIC DISEASE. Disease in which both mind (*psyche*) and body (*soma*) are involved. The term is usually employed with reference to disorders which, although of an unquestioned organic physical nature, are also strongly influenced by emotional and psychosocial factors. Examples include bronchial *asthma, *peptic ulcer, *migraine, *hypertension, *colitis, menstrual disorders, sexual dysfunction, skin diseases such as *eczema and *psoriasis, and very many more.

PSYCHOSURGERY. Brain surgery, of which *leucotomy is an example, undertaken with the object of altering behaviour in patients with severe chronic mental disorders refractory to other forms of treatment. See NEUROSURGERY; PSYCHIATRY.

PSYCHOTHERAPY is the treatment of psychiatric disorders by psychological methods, without the use of drugs or other physical interventions such as *psychosurgery or *electroconvulsive therapy. Psychotherapy consists essentially in listening and talking to the patient. *Psychoanalysis is an example, but most psychotherapy consists of much simpler techniques such as encouragement or reassurance.

PSYCHOTROPIC DRUGS. Drugs that have an effect on the mind, altering the mental or emotional state, for example *tranquillizers, *antidepressants, *hypnotics, etc.

PTOMAINE is a general term formerly applied to nitrogenous products of putrefied flesh (*ptoma* = corpse) considered to be poisonous.

PTOSIS is the drooping of one or both upper eyelids; it is sometimes also applied to downwards displacement of other organs or parts.

PUBERTY is the onset of the reproductive period of life, marked in girls by the *menarche and in both sexes by the development of the *secondary sexual characteristics.

PUBLIC HEALTH. 'Public health is the science and art of preventing disease, prolonging life and promoting mental and physical health and efficiency through organized community efforts for the sanitation of the environment, the control of communicable infections, the education of the individual in personal hygiene, the organization of medical and nursing services for the early diagnosis and preventive treatment of disease, and the development of social machinery to ensure to every individual a standard of living adequate for the maintenance of health, so organizing these benefits as to enable every citizen to realize his birthright of health and longevity' (C.-E. A.

Winslow (1923), *The Evolution and Significance of the Modern Public Health Campaign,* New Haven).

PUBLIC HEALTH ACT 1848. A major piece of British public health legislation, sometimes referred to as 'the Chadwick Act' after Sir Edwin *Chadwick, the civil servant who was largely responsible for framing its provisions (see COMMUNITY MEDICINE). These provisions invested local authorities with a number of important responsibilities, including the paving of streets, the construction of drains and sewers, the collection of refuse, and the procurement of water supply both for domestic use and for other purposes such as street cleaning and fire-fighting. The Act also instituted the *General Board of Health.

PUBLIC HEALTH ACTS 1875, 1936, 1961. Three major and comprehensive enactments concerning public health in England and Wales (the first is known as 'The Great Public Health Act'). They encompassed a huge variety of provisions. Among them were: sewerage and sewage disposal, including private sewers and cesspits; the sanitation of buildings; refuse; scavenging; the keeping of animals; public conveniences; verminous premises and persons; nuisances and offensive trades; water supply; preventing and notification of disease; registration and inspection of nursing homes; notification of births; maternity and child welfare; child life protection; baths, wash-houses and bathing places; common lodging houses; canal boats; water courses, ditches, and ponds; tents, vans, and sheds; hop-pickers; trade effluents; cleaning and paving of highways; inspection of markets and slaughterhouses; and other matters, including the administration of all the foregoing.

PUBLIC HEALTH IN THE USA. In the mid 19th c. there was great confusion in the USA and elsewhere as to the causes of disease. Although *Jenner's cowpox vaccine was known to provide protection against *smallpox, there were doctors as well as laymen who believed that *epidemics originated from noxious substances (*miasmas) exhaled into the atmosphere from putrefying animal or vegetable matter. A few individuals were groping to establish a public health movement but they concerned themselves primarily with defensive measures instituted locally to ward off epidemics or to correct environmental conditions that had become intolerable. Responsibility for action was a matter that had barely begun to be discussed. The times were ripe for the new concepts and policies that soon came in rapid succession—with consequences that inspired the president of an American university to reflect, in the mid 20th c. on the importance of public health:

. . . A historian a thousand years hence examining the records of our culture will conclude perhaps that the goal of physical well-being was one of the unifying forces of the twentieth century. . . . A widespread concern with allevi-

ating or eliminating suffering and a firm belief that suffering can be reduced by human efforts are certainly characteristic of America today.

. . . it is clear that if we are to attain the social objectives of making the new knowledge equally effective in the lives of all the people of a nation—let alone of the entire world—improving our methods of curing disease is not enough. The problem today is keeping people well . . .

. . . as the profession of public health advances . . . the entire people of a free and prosperous society will enjoy a state of health undreamed of even by the kings and nobles and the privileged classes of a few centuries ago. (Conant, 1949.)

Today one can easily see that public health in the USA has its foundations not only in the domain of biological and natural sciences, but also in the realm of social and political affairs. This article begins with a very brief indication of the kinds of scientific advances that gave rise to the first great successes of public health.

Origins of basic concepts. Although there are examples in which a disease has been prevented by actions taken without any knowledge of its cause—actions based solely on careful observation of the circumstances of its occurrence—such examples are exceptions. Successful preventive measures most often depend on accurate information about the cause and the factors influencing the course of a disease. This precept is vividly illustrated by the dramatic consequences of applying five sorts of new information about communicable diseases: the proof that *micro-organisms and *parasites can cause disease in man and animals; the recognition of the role of *carriers in certain diseases; the discovery of the wide variety of animal reservoirs of human diseases; the proof that certain *arthropods can transmit disease agents and sometimes serve as intermediate *hosts; and the demonstration on a wide scale that control measures appropriately designed and adapted to the habits and life cycle of an arthropod *vector can sharply reduce the *incidence of the disease in question.

Equally dramatic results accompanied the application of advances in the new science of *immunology. The initial work demonstrating the principles of active and passive immunity was that of European scientists. The subsequent advances have been prodigious. A glance at the list of vaccines currently recommended for public use indicates the firm place attained by active *immunization. American scientists had central roles in the development of several of the vaccines on the list, notably those against *yellow fever, *poliomyelitis, *louse-borne *typhus fever, *influenza, *measles, and *rubella (Snyder, 1976). In addition to the basic knowledge permitting the development of vaccines, immunological research provided many diagnostic procedures that are now indispensable in public health as well as clinical medicine.

By the mid-point of the 20th c. the application of the findings of *microbiology and immunology enabled public health to lift a great burden of communicable diseases from large segments of society. Meanwhile, the ideas and recommendations put forward in 1850 by Lemuel Shattuck, in his monumental report, gradually won acceptance in the USA (see below on 'Pioneers'). Scores of individuals over more than half a century, both doctors and laymen, participated in the process of working out an acceptable, and effective *modus operandi* for the practice of public health. The basic principles in the USA today are that:

1. The health of people generally can best be protected and improved by *organized community actions;*

2. Such actions must draw not only upon doctors, dentists and nurses, but also upon experts from such diverse fields as chemistry, education and communications, engineering, entomology, laboratory sciences, law, nutrition, pharmacy, public affairs, social work, veterinary medicine, and more recently, management sciences; in brief, *public health consists of a mosaic of professions;*

3. The most effective way to deal with complex health problems whether local, state, or national is to *mobilize the relevant experts for collaboration with community leaders* in analysing the particular problems and developing appropriate measures.

These principles have been put to use in hundreds of ways in the USA, ways that include programmes of governmental agencies, voluntary organizations, industries, even international groups. One might infer that public health now has all the administrative inventions it needs to deal with any problems that arise. Such may not be the case, however, because there are three new exceedingly complex issues demanding the attention of society in general, not just the health professions.

The first issue is 'comprehensive health care' and how it is to be provided. While the principal causes of death and disability in the USA were shifting from communicable diseases to chronic degenerative and neoplastic disorders, the nature of medical practice also changed. Doctors spent more of their time attempting to arrest the progression of chronic disease. Then came new methods of paying for medical care, methods that have had great impact on people's behaviour. Soon they began to expect personal health care to include both preventive and curative services; further, they wanted them to be provided in a single setting. A considerable proportion of doctors and patients alike now think that prevention should pervade all of the medical specialties. In other words, they want comprehensive health care.

The goal of comprehensive health care is utopian. One of the chief obstacles to its attainment is the fact that medical students and their teachers are traditionally attracted much more strongly by the very tangible satisfactions of direct patient care than they are by the abstract satisfaction of knowing that one's efforts have helped to keep large numbers of people from getting sick, a situation lacking personal contact with patients. One cannot realistically expect a sudden change in attitude of physicians such that they will devote adequate attention to preventive measures in all facets of medical practice. Thus, the comprehensive health care of tomorrow will be of better quality in its therapy than in its prevention. Consequently there will continue to be a need for those who do derive satisfaction from keeping people well, and who make it their careers whether as teachers, researchers, or practitioners. Later in this article there are comments on the growth of the medical–industrial complex and its future role in delivery of comprehensive health care.

A similar issue confronting society and especially its political elements is the question whether health is a universal human right. This idea took form slowly, through times of prosperity and depression, wars and their consequences, struggles over civil rights, and women's liberation. It gained support from the campaigns to reduce infant mortality, to educate the public in matters of personal hygiene, to establish nursing services for the poor, to provide care for the elderly, the handicapped, and the unemployed. As each such programme was sponsored by a voluntary organization or undertaken by an official agency serving community health needs, the idea of the individual's right to health grew in its appeal. By 1946 it had such a degree of public approval that it appeared as the basic tenet in the Preamble to the Constitution of the newly created *World Health Organization (WHO). The USA formally endorsed the concept along with the majority of the nations of the world. The language in the preamble is simple, direct, and clear, yet revolutionary to a degree not appreciated by all the governments when they signed the document, nor even now, decades later:

The States Parties to this Constitution declare, in conformity with the Charter of the United Nations, that the following principles are basic to the happiness, harmonious relations and security of all peoples:
Health is a state of complete physical, mental and social well-being and not merely the absence of disease or infirmity. The enjoyment of the highest attainable standard of health is one of the fundamental rights of every human being without distinction of race, religion, political belief, economic or social condition. . . .
Governments have a responsibility for the health of their peoples which can be fulfilled only by the provision of adequate health and social measures. (Preamble to the Constitution, *World Health Organization Basic Documents*, Geneva, 1963: 1–2.)

What was the effect in the USA of endorsement of this concept in the charter of the WHO? To what extent have the federal, state, and local governments provided people of all economic levels, religions, and races with access to health services? One must say, not enough, and point to the perplexing paradoxes of the health care situation in the nation (Somers, 1971). (See also GOVERNMENT AND MEDICINE IN THE USA).

The third new issue, rapid population growth, rivals nuclear warfare in its implications for the world. It affects public health directly and indirectly, in the USA as well as in every other nation, now and far into the future. It affects environmental resources, agricultural practices, nutrition, hunger, the quality of life, and even the stability of governments. Gradually over the past few decades the health professions have become involved in several aspects of the control of human fertility. (For further comments on population issues, see below on 'Contributions to public health activities world-wide'.)

Pioneers in the USA. Who were the prime movers in bringing the profession of public health in America to its present state? This question will not be settled until historians centuries from now have had their say. From today's perspective there are more than a score who merit recognition for the high quality and significance of their ideas, their insights, their contributions to knowledge, or their administrative inventions. Since there is space in this chapter to cite only nine Americans who started new undertakings or explored new areas of importance to the health of the public, the selection must be highly arbitrary; apologies are due to the many perceptive and creative people who are not mentioned here.

Lemuel Shattuck (1793–1859) was the principal author of the *Report of the Sanitary Commission of Massachusetts, 1850.* Shattuck's contribution was described by an astute student of public health a century later as ' . . . one of the most remarkable documents—perhaps the most significant document—in the history of public health' (Winslow, 1948). The 50 detailed recommendations of the report deserve to be read in full because of their clarity, completeness, and vision of future developments. The subjects included the formation of State Boards of Health; periodic census enumerations; uniform nomenclature for recording diseases; periodic local surveys and analyses of causes of sickness in various localities among persons of different occupations; control of the sale and use of unwholesome, spurious, and adulterated articles intended for food, drink, or medicine; vaccination against smallpox; promotion of health in infancy and childhood so that a good foundation will be laid for a vigorous adulthood; protection of health of school children; measures to reduce the evils arising from the use of intoxicating drinks; town planning, control of overcrowded tenements, new housing for the poor; institutions to educate and qualify females for nursing; training of physicians to be preventive advisers and the establishment of sanitary professorships in all colleges and medical schools; the importance of mobilizing support among the public for health measures; the extension of health awareness into every home. Although the report was largely neglected for two decades, eventually nearly all of its detailed recommendations have been absorbed into the public health movements in the various states.

William Thompson *Sedgwick (1855–1921). The Massachusetts Board of Health in 1886 established the Lawrence Experiment Station and appointed Sedgwick as its director of research. Under his aegis this quickly became America's pioneer institution in environmental *sanitation, producing new knowledge and educating engineers, chemists, and biologists who were the early leaders in environmental sciences for the entire nation. Sedgwick developed a new course of instruction in sanitation and public health, based on his book, *Principles of Sanitary Science and the Public Health* (1902); the course inspired his students and brought general acceptance of the concept that careers in the environmental sciences are basic to public health. Sedgwick became professor of biology at the Massachusetts Institute of Technology, where he conducted an informal school of public health as a solo performance. Tributes to Sedgwick came in profusion from his colleagues and students. The American Public Health Association established the Sedgwick Medal as its most prestigious award (Jordan *et al.*, 1924).

Alice *Hamilton (1869–1970) was the first woman to be appointed by Harvard University to any of its faculties. Through her work on *lead poisoning, published in 1910, she established her ability as a scientist in the field of industrial medical problems. A long association with Jane Addams at Hull House in Chicago gave her a keen appreciation of the problems of the worker and the motivation to ferret out the hazards due to toxic substances in the worker's environment. In her teaching career over a 16-year period at the Harvard School of Public Health, Alice Hamilton inspired students, instructed her colleagues, and influenced industrial practices in many plants. Her books *Industrial Poisons in the United States* and *Industrial Toxicology (1934)* are classics. One of the founders of the *Journal of Industrial Hygiene,* she helped to guide its affairs and shape its influence on the development of the discipline for many years.

Charles Value Chapin (1856–1941) was a physician, epidemiologist, professor at Brown University, registrar and superintendent of health in Providence, Rhode Island, and president of the American Public Health Association. Chapin's notable, and at that time controversial, concepts of epidemiology were presented in his book *The Sources and Modes of Infection* (1910). His additions to epidemiological knowledge were matched by his innovations in the administration of public health and the control of communicable diseases. He practised what he preached by abandoning the traditional, but useless, routine terminal disinfection in the Providence Hospital. Chapin stressed the need for the critical evaluation of health department procedures, saying, for example: 'We are crowding our hospitals with scarlet fever cases and crying for more buildings, but who has figured the amount of case prevention and the cost per case, and has compared this cost with that of district-nursing of home-treated cases?' (Winslow, 1967).

A study of Chapin conducted for the Council on Health and Public Instruction of the *American Medical Association was the first comparative analysis of health department procedures anywhere in the world. From it evolved the widely used programme of the Committee on Administrative Practice of the American Public Health Association. A colleague summarized Chapin's achievements thus:

Dr. Chapin saw the change of emphasis from law enforcement to community education as the primary concern of public health administration; from isolation and quarantine as the methods of communicable disease control to a fundamental attack on causative agents when sources and modes of transmission and infection became known; and from care of children only when ill and convalescing to a whole scheme of prenatal and child hygiene as the foundation of sound health in adult life. (Winslow, 1967.)

Lillian D. Wald (1867–1940) graduated from the New York Hospital Training School for Nurses, and then enrolled in the Women's Medical College. During her medical student days she was asked to organize a home nursing service for immigrants on the Lower East Side of New York, and she found this so absorbing that she left medical school to make public health nursing her life work. She conceived the idea of a 'Nurses Settlement' which she proceeded to establish in 1895. By 1913 she had assembled 91 nurses who made 200 000 home visits to the poor that year. The movement spread over the USA. It extended into public schools, and soon was adopted by insurance companies for their policy holders. Meanwhile she broadened the Settlement into a neighbourhood centre with civic, educational, social, and vocational activities.

When the National Organization for Public Health Nursing was formed in 1912, Lillian Wald was chosen as the first president. She was the prime mover in getting Columbia University to set up a department of nursing and health. Among her other activities was the campaign to improve housing as a measure against tuberculosis. It was she who in 1905 first suggested the creation of a federal children's bureau to President Theodore Roosevelt (Smillie, 1955; James, 1971).

Wickcliffe Rose (1862–1931). As an agent and trustee of philanthropic funds, Rose became involved in advancing education in rural areas of the southern states where *hookworm disease was the great obstacle to education. He guided the Rockefeller Sanitary Commission's campaign against hookworm with great skill, enlisting the co-operation of officials in 11 states, educating the public as well as the medical profession, and obtaining the participation of the federal government. This success resulted in the appointment of Rose as the Director of the International Health Commission of the Rockefeller Foundation at the time of its establishment in 1913. After reconnais-

sance trips, Rose launched a mass attack on hookworm infection around the world—in 52 countries and 29 islands. The colleagues he assembled for the campaign examined and treated millions of people. 'The agency and the man were unique in the annals of preventive medicine, and in light of . . . the results achieved they were of epochal significance in the history of . . . public health . . . ' (Welch, 1932).

Thomas Parran (1892–1968) was the 'leading architect of the structure of American and international public health in the twentieth century'. Parran joined the United States Public Health Service in 1917 and acquired his early experience in Alabama, Missouri, and Illinois, learning the problems of county health departments. From those assignments he went to the venereal disease division of the Public Health Service. There he developed a plan for a national programme against *syphilis and *gonorrhoea, in the promotion of which he won an important battle against attempted censorship. In 1930 New York State put him in charge of its Department of Health. After six years he went to Washington as surgeon-general of the Public Health Service.

During his tenure as surgeon-general, Parran was responsible for the federal stimulus to medical research and for the growth pattern of the *National Institutes of Health. The Communicable Disease Center in Atlanta was founded under his aegis. Toward the end of his term he participated very actively in the design and creation of the WHO. On retiring from the Public Health Service in 1948 Parran began a new career. He established a school of public health in Pittsburgh, assembled an able faculty, and served as its leader for 10 years (*American Journal of Public Health*, 1968).

Margaret Higgins *Sanger (1879–1966) was one of the very few individuals early in the 20th c. who devoted their lives to the cause of birth control. A rebel against restraints of women's freedom, a campaigner against laws she believed unjust, a leader, and fighter, she lived to witness the accomplishment of many of the changes for which she had striven. While she was sometimes ungenerous in failing to recognize the contributions others were making to 'her' cause, even her critics acknowledged her extraordinary achievements. From a poor home in a small town in New York State, Margaret Sanger became a nurse, and despite frequent recurrences of tuberculosis she became a vigorous advocate of sweeping social reform. The term 'birth control' first appeared in her publication *Woman Rebel*. She deliberately defied the Comstock Law against dissemination of information about *contraceptives. Taken to jail eight times, she stirred public opinion and won decisions in the courts that were *de facto* repeals of restrictions.

Her clinical research bureau and its collection of case histories favourably influenced the previously hostile medical profession. She described the bureau 'not as an isolated social agency, but functioning as an integral factor of public and racial health, forming an integral part of all prenatal and postnatal agencies for maternal and child welfare' (Lader, 1955). Through her travels to Europe, the Soviet Union, China, Japan, and India, Margaret Sanger aroused interest in her cause and obtained wide participation in international meetings on population and birth control. Following the 1930 international conference of doctors and scientists in Zurich, which she organized, she helped to catalyse biochemical research by channelling funds into promising studies (Kennedy, 1970). Her leadership was responsible in large part for the formation of the International Planned Parenthood Federation with its 50 member nations and its programmes in more than 100 countries.

Alexander Duncan Langmuir (b. 1910) invented the administrative arrangements that were necessary to establish the Epidemic Intelligence Service (EIS), of the United States Public Health Service and to assure it of sufficient independence to permit its success. His skill and wisdom as director of the EIS made it a powerful organization, highly respected not only for the quality of its officers and staff but also for its rapid, effective responses to requests for assistance, its accuracy in analysis of outbreaks of illness wherever they might occur, and its benefits to health generally. Under Langmuir's tutelage hundreds of young physicians and other health professionals learned the value of the rigorous epidemiological discipline inculcated at the EIS when they became immersed in difficult health problems on assignments to localities in the USA or, in some instances, in other countries. One of the noteworthy consequences of Langmuir's stewardship of the EIS was its major contribution to the success of the global eradication campaign against smallpox (Foege *et al.*, 1975; Breman and Arita, 1980).

Contributions to public health activities worldwide.

The USA first became directly involved in international health activities as a consequence of its success in the control of yellow fever in Havana and in Panama during the construction of the canal. That involvement led in 1902 to participation in forming the International Sanitary Bureau (later the Pan-American Health Organization). In addition the USA supported the Office International d'Hygiène Publique from its origin in 1907 until it was absorbed into the WHO. Several Americans worked vigorously during the formative stages of the WHO to assure its establishment as an effective instrument for the achievement of common objectives for human health. Thomas Parran, while he was surgeon-general of the United States Public Health Service, was particularly effective in the negotiations that preceded the adoption of the charter of WHO.

The extent of commitment of the USA to the success of the WHO can be measured in part by the fact that from 1946 until the present approximately 30 per cent of its regular annual budget came from

the USA, a larger proportion than the total provided by the four next largest contributions, the Soviet Union, West Germany, the UK, and France (Goodman, 1971).

Over and above its annual contributions to WHO the United States government during the past two decades expended several billion dollars to support programmes in other countries for health and nutrition through the State Department (primarily by the International Cooperation Administration and the Agency for International Development); the Department of Health, Education, and Welfare (chiefly by the Public Health Service's Center for Disease Control); and nearly a score of other federal agencies. Private organizations likewise spent very substantial sums in this same period to promote the health and nutrition of other nations. The contribution of one private foundation is illustrated in the following paragraphs.

Malaria. In the 1930s the Rockefeller Foundation became involved in work that proved to be a landmark for international health. The *malaria-transmitting mosquito, *Anopheles gambiae,* while indigenous to Africa, had not been observed in the western hemisphere until it appeared in Brazil in 1930. Within a few years this species established itself in north-east Brazil, where it was responsible for a disastrous outbreak of malaria in 1938. A veteran malariologist described the situation in these terms:

There is no doubt that this invasion of *gambiae* threatens the Americas with a catastrophe in comparison with which ordinary pestilence, conflagration, or even war are but small and temporary calamities. *Gambiae* literally enters into the very veins of a country and may remain to plague it for centuries. (Barber, 1940.)

The International Health Division of the Rockefeller Foundation launched a campaign against *A. gambiae* in Brazil in 1939 under the direction of Fred L. Soper. Before the end of 1940, *A. gambiae* had been eliminated. This feat had repercussions extending far beyond Brazil: the results showed that a task presumed to be hopelessly difficult could in fact be done, given skilful leadership with adequate financial support. Advocates of global campaigns to eradicate malaria and smallpox cited this success in Brazil as a forceful argument in favour of their proposals. The argument was further strengthened when another incursion by *A. gambiae,* this time into Egypt from Sudan, was repulsed in the early 1940s, again under Soper's direction (Kerr, 1970).

In 1946 the Rockefeller Foundation and the government of Italy began an intensive campaign against malaria on the island of Sardinia, using residual spraying of the walls of all human dwellings. The insecticide was *dichlorodiphenyltrichloroethane (DDT). Before 1946 Sardinia was rated as one of the three most malarious areas in the world; the termination of malaria transmission on the island in 1949 was therefore a spectacular accomplishment (Goodman, 1971).

Although the extensive use of DDT in the early 1950s reduced the incidence of malaria in many regions, the disease continued to be a serious problem. In 1955 the World Health Assembly decided to implement a programme having world-wide eradication as its goal. By 1968 data collected by WHO indicated that of 1700 million people living in malarious areas 1350 million had been protected by the campaign and were living in improved economic conditions as a consequence (Johnson, 1969). The appearance of DDT-resistant anopheline mosquitoes and the emergence of strains of malaria resistant to therapy with the 4-aminoquinolines were setbacks to the progress of the campaign, as were the administrative and financial problems encountered in individual countries. Unfortunately, the present malaria picture suggests that global eradication is still a very distant goal.

Smallpox. The USA contributed both funds and experts to the world-wide campaign against small-pox. This disease had been eliminated from several countries in the 1950s but the national smallpox efforts had varied so greatly in effectiveness that eradication seemed only a dream. Nevertheless, WHO launched its campaign in 1958 and intensified the work a few years later by establishing regional reference centres, one of which was the Center for Disease Control (CDC) in Atlanta. Several members of the CDC staff were soon deeply involved in the eradication activities in West and Central Africa. By May 1970, after three and a half years of intensive field work in 20 African countries, they were able to show that smallpox was no longer occurring in this formerly endemic region, equal in size to the continental USA. Furthermore, they found that epidemiologically directed surveillance and containment activities were more effective than mass vaccination, an observation of great value to the eradication programmes in other regions. With the use of the surveillance and containment technique, progress became more rapid (Foege *et al.*, 1975). The goal of zero cases was reached in 1979—a triumph of international co-operation in which the USA played a very significant part. This is one instance of species eradication mourned by no one.

Malaria and smallpox are by no means the only examples of far-reaching contributions to international health by the USA, its official and voluntary organizations, its scientists and administrators. Accomplishments in the prevention of yellow fever, poliomyelitis, epidemic typhus, or measles could readily be cited to illustrate the point. Similarly, the many advances in nutrition and reduction of deficiency diseases are worthy of close attention, but the reader is referred to other articles in this volume for discussion of these matters.

There is one more subject, however, that must be presented in this section: the participation of the USA in efforts to reduce the burdens of rapid population growth that press upon most of the developing nations of the world. The magnitude of the problem is awesome both as to sheer numbers and complexity. 'At present and projected growth rates, the world's population would reach 10 billion by 2030 and would approach 30 billion by the end of the twenty-first century.' (Barnes, 1980). Figure 1 shows the changes in the size and distribution of the world's population since 1830 and a projection to the year 2000.

The official representatives of 135 nations meeting at the World Population Conference in Bucharest in 1974 endorsed without opposition the principle that all people have the basic human right to decide freely and responsibly the number and spacing of their children and to have the information, education, and means to do so (Piotrow, 1974). Acceptance of this principle means that members of the health professions, as public servants, have the obligation to assist in providing the necessary information and services for fertility control. A start has been made in this direction and, all things considered, it is an impressive one. American scientists have been intimately involved in the development of the contraceptives and *intrauterine devices that so many millions of healthy women are using in the USA and in scores of other countries. The director of the Office of Population of the Agency for International Development reported that the recent reductions in fertility in many countries had clearly been assisted by programmes providing contraceptive information and services (Ravenholt and Chao, 1974). In 1980, the United States Government donated approximately 187 million dollars for support of population and family planning assistance in other countries; contributions by two major

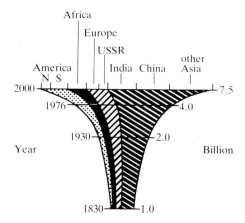

Fig. 1. Actual and predicted population growth, showing regional differences, 1830–2000. (Adapted from Rudel, W., Kinel, F. A. and Henzl, M. R. (1973). *Birth Control: Contraception and Abortion.* New York, and from *The New York Times*, 20 April 1970)

foundations in the USA raised the figure to 200 million dollars, about half of the total funds donated by the industrialized nations for population assistance (Lewison, 1983). An enormous amount is still to be done: at least 50 million women not using oral contraceptives in less-developed countries would do so if they became readily obtainable; equally large numbers of people would accept sterilization, terminate their pregnancies, or use one of the other effective methods of birth control if such were generally and appropriately available.

Some observers believe that voluntary programmes of family planning will not succeed in bringing population growth to a halt. Garrett Hardin (1972) concluded that mankind must adopt 'mutual coercion, mutually agreed upon' as the solution. Mark Twain lamented the advent of improvements in medical practice because, he said, doctors had done so much in former times to keep population growth in check (De Voto, 1962). Both Hardin and Mark Twain, however, surely would agree that the health professions in concert with national leaders should strive to stabilize the total world population at a level low enough to permit people everywhere to enjoy a life of peace, civility, dignity, and meaning.

Status of public health in the USA. Widely voiced concern about the rising costs of medical care might lead one to infer that the health of people in the USA is worsening.

Table 1 shows some of the items that are frequently considered in assessing health status and compares the data for 1980 with those of 1870. The differences are striking, to say the least. The nation grew in total population nearly sixfold. Live births per 1000 women aged 15–44 dropped to less than half the figure in 1870, as did the crude death rate. The greatest change occurred in the number of infant deaths: in 1980 the figure was one-fifteenth of that of a century before. As an accompaniment to those developments, life expectancy at birth nearly doubled, the proportions of the population across the age range became more evenly distributed, and the median age increased by 10 years. These comparisons assume that when figures for 1870 are not available for the entire country, the data recorded for Massachusetts may be taken as approximating the situation in other states.

Table 2 compares the principal causes of death, now and a century ago. The five communicable diseases that accounted for such a large proportion of deaths in 1870 do not appear in the list for 1980.

Changes in causes of mortality of this magnitude, affecting millions of people in such a short time, were unknown in previous eras. It is probable, moreover, that changes also occurred in the duration of disability from preventable disorders, especially in childhood and early adulthood. Although there are no records for the 1870s with respect to the number of days per year that the

Table 1. Health statistics for the USA (figures rounded to the nearest whole integer)

	1870	1980
Total population	39 819 000	226 500 000
Births per 1000 women		
aged 15–44	167	70
Life expectancy at birth		
(years)	43[a]	74
Percentage of population		
under age 5	14	7
5–20	33	25
21–64	51	56
65+	3	11
Median age of population	20	30
Death rate per 1000	19[a]	9
Deaths under 1 year per		
1000 live births	188[a]	13

[a] Data available only for Massachusetts

Table 2. Principal causes of death in the USA (approximate rates per 100 000 population)

1870[a]		1980	
Pulmonary		Heart disease	343
tuberculosis	343	Malignant	
Typhoid fevers	92	neoplasm	186
Diphtheria	46	Cerebrovascular	
Measles	19	diseases	77
Smallpox	9	Accidents	48
		Chronic obstructive pulmonary	
		diseases	25

[a] Data available only for Massachusetts

Sources for Tables 1 and 2: Adapted from the US Bureau of the Census, *Historical Statistics of the United States, Colonial Times to 1957*; and from the *Statistical Abstract of the United States, 1980*. Washington, DC.

average person was sufficiently disabled to require confinement to bed, one can infer from accounts of life in those times that the figure must have been far greater than the average period of six days estimated for the 1970s.

Statistics such as these tempt one to think that the present status of human happiness and the quality of life now are better than they were 100 years ago. It would be unwise, however, to make assertions because there are not as yet any generally accepted definitions or quantitative criteria for measurement. Indeed, questions raised by the Secretary of Health, Education, and Welfare in 1972 concerning the impact of federal programmes resulted in an 18-page paper by his staff. Their report stressed the imperfections of current data, outlined the disagreements over criteria for evaluation of the quality of life, and predicted the futility of any federal attempt in the near future to establish indices for measuring the impact of governmental programmes on health and welfare (Francis, 1973).

The lack of criteria has not deterred discussion of the issues. Health is widely assumed to consist of far more than the absence of disease or physical disability. Just as the physical health of people is clearly affected by housing conditions, environmental defects, automobiles, and conditions of employment, so too are mental health and well-being affected by the social changes accompanying rapid urbanization and technological developments (see SOCIOLOGY). On these matters the reader is urged to consult the special issue of *Daedalus* in 1977 that presents 18 essays on various aspects of health in the USA, ranging from the perceptions and expectations of people regarding health and medical care to the impact of technological advances on the economics and growth of the health care industry (Knowles *et al.*, 1977).

That health care *has* become an industry is now beyond question: its 4.5 million employees make health the largest industry in the USA in terms of workers and the third largest in terms of income produced. Total expenditures for health care in 1980 amounted roughly to 9.4 per cent of the gross national product of the USA. But the benefits of the industry are not equally distributed among the population. By what means can access be provided to all the people regardless of their status? What methods of financing should be used? One proposal from academe favours a new organization in the federal government and a system of regional health boards (Rutstein, 1974); another prefers 'income-graded' catastrophic health insurance (Wildawsky, 1977).

Within the past three decades relations have changed profoundly between the increasingly consumer-orientated public, the federal government, and the health professions, particularly organized medicine. Industry has entered the field of providing medical services to such a degree that its activities are sometimes labelled ominously as 'the medical–industrial complex'. Starr's book, *The Social Transformation of American Medicine* (1982), describes the evolution of the health care system and the intensifying conflicts within it. From the perspective of the sociologist, Starr considers the implications of current trends as well as the ways in which medical corporations probably will become the dominant force in delivering health care in future decades.

Issues in allocation of public funds for health. Both the public and the members of the health professions face difficult decisions. How much of the nation's resources should be expended for health? How much of the financial and intellectual resources should be allocated to programmes for reducing the effects of common causes of disability and death and how much to the pursuit of highly expensive procedures that are restricted in application to a very small fraction of the population at large? For example, is it right to spend public funds for the costly programmes of renal dialysis and black lung disease, or for organ transplants, if this means curtailing the immunization of the public against a disease such as poliomyelitis that can cause widespread misery and disability? The realization is spreading that the nation is reluctant to pay for the universal application of every advance in technology (Handler, 1976). (See also HEALTH CARE ECONOMICS.)

No matter how painful the effort, the process of ordering national priorities for the expenditure of public funds for health must begin soon. To succeed in this process, ways must be found to escape from the political tyranny of single-issue minorities with their militant intolerance and their unwillingness even to let other viewpoints be heard (Staub, 1980). Ways must also be found to deal with the new phenomenon in our society—the increasing public preoccupation with disease, the widespread notion that the human

body is fundamentally flawed, subject to disintegration at any moment, always on the verge of mortal disease, always in need of continual monitoring and support by health-care professionals. . . . [Somehow it must become part of the public perception that] . . . human beings are fundamentally tough, resilient animals, marvellously made, most of the time capable of getting along quite well on their own. The health care system should be designed for use when it is really needed and when it has something of genuine value to offer. If designed, or redesigned, in this way the system would function far more effectively, and would probably cost very much less. (Thomas, 1977).

Even more important, in the next few decades at least, than redesigning the health care system will be to advance the art and the science of educating the public in matters of health. The accomplishments of the health sciences are of no benefit until they are incorporated into the practices of considerable segments of the population. The key elements in effecting changes in the perceptions of people and their behaviour are accurate information, skilful communication thereof, and finally motivation of those individuals in a community who will use the information for their own benefit, thereby influencing the behaviour of those around them.

Success in this enterprise would go far toward improving the health of the public at large. It would also reduce the enormous expense of operating the health care system itself, a matter that surely will be of concern to the taxpayer of tomorrow.

J. C. SNYDER

References

American Journal of Public Health (1968). Editorial. Dr. Thomas Parran 1892–1968. *American Journal of Public Health*, **58**, 615–8.

Barber, M. A. (1940). The present status of *Anopheles gambiae* in Brazil. *American Journal of Tropical Medicine*, **20**, 264.

Barnes, G. O. (ed.) (1980). *The Global 2000 Report to the President of the United States Entering the 21st Century* (Report prepared for the Council on Environmental Quality and the Department of State), Vol. 1. New York.

Breman, J. G. and Arita, I. (1980). The confirmation and maintenance of smallpox eradication. *New England Journal of Medicine*, **303**, 1263–73.

Chapin, C. V. (1910). *The Sources and Modes of Infection*. New York.

Conant, J. B. (1949). Foreword. In Simmons, J. S. (ed.), *Public Health in the World Today*. Cambridge, Massachusetts.

De Voto, B. (ed.) (1962). *Mark Twain Letters from the Earth*, pp. 90–2. New York.

Foege, W. H., Millar, J. D. and Henderson, D. A. (1975). Smallpox eradication in West and Central Africa. *Bulletin of the World Health Organization*, **52**, 209–22.

Francis, W. J. (1973). *A Report on Measurement and the Quality of Life*. Washington, DC.

Goodman, N. M. (1971). *International Health Organizations and Their Work*. 2nd edn, Edinburgh and London.

Hamilton, A. (1934). *Industrial Toxicology*. 2nd edn., New York and London.

Handler, P. (1976). *Quo Vadis, U.S. Medicine? Epilogue: Essays at the Bicentennial of Medicine in the United States*. In DHEW Publication No. (NIH) 77–1176. Washington, DC.

Hardin, G. (1972). *Exploring New Ethics for Survival. The Voyage of the Spaceship Beagle*. New York.

James, E. T. (1971). *Notable American Women*. Cambridge, Massachusetts.

Johnson, D. R. (1969). Malaria eradication: what it has achieved. *Mosquito News*, **29**, 523–32.

Jordan, E. O., Whipple, G. C. and Winslow, C.-E. A. (1924). *A Pioneer of Public Health: William Thompson Sedgwick*, p. 85. New Haven.

Kennedy, D. M. (1970). *Birth Control in America. The Career of Margaret Sanger*. New Haven.

Kerr, J. A. (1970). *Building the Health Bridge. Selections from the Works of Fred L. Soper, M.D.* Bloomington, Indiana.

Knowles, J. (guest ed.) (1977). Doing better and feeling worse: health in the United States. *Daedalus: Journal of the American Academy of Arts and Sciences*, **106**, No. 1, 1–278.

Lader, L. (1955). *The Margaret Sanger Story and the Fight for Birth Control*. New York.

Lewison, D. (1983). Sources of population and family planning assistance. *Population Report*, Series J, No. 26, Baltimore.

Piotrow, P. T. (1974). World plan of action and health strategy approved at population conferences. *Population Report*, Series E, No. 2, Washington, DC.

Ravenholt, R. T. and Chao, J. (1974). World fertility trends, 1974. *Population Report*, Series J, No. 2, Washington, DC.

Rutstein, D. D. (1974). *Blueprint for Medical Care*. Cambridge, Massachusetts.

Sedgwick, W. T. (1902). *Principles of Sanitary Science and the Public Health*. New York.

Shattuck, L., Banks, N. P. Jr and Abbott, J. (1948). *Report of the Sanitary Commission of Massachusetts 1850* (reprinted). Cambridge, Massachusetts.

Smillie, W. G. (1955). *Public Health, Its Promise for the Future: A Chronicle of the Development of Public Health in the United States, 1607–1914*. New York.

Snyder, J. C. (1976). Public health and preventive medicine. In Bowers, J. Z. and Purcell, E. F. (eds), *Advances in American Medicine: Essays at the Bicentennial*, vol. 1, pp. 384–457. New York.

Somers, A. R. (1971). *Health Care in Transition: Directions for the Future*. Chicago.

Starr, P. (1982) *The Social Transformation of American Medicine*. New York.

Staub, H. O. (1980). The tyranny of minorities. *Daedalus: Journal of the American Academy of Arts and Sciences*, **109**, 159–68.

Thomas, L. (1977). On the science and technology of medicine. *Daedalus: Journal of the American Academy of Arts and Sciences*, **106**, 35–46.

Welch, W. H. (1932). *Wickliffe Rose 1862–1931*. Memorial Address, Rockefeller Institute for Medical Research. New York.

Wildawsky, A. (1977). The political pathology of health policy. *Daedalus: Journal of the American Academy of Arts and Sciences*, **106**, 105–24.

Winslow, C.-E. A. (1948). Foreword. In Shattuck, L. *et al.* (eds). *Report of the Sanitary Commission of Massachusetts 1850* (reprinted). Cambridge, Massachusetts.

Winslow, C.-E. A. (1967). *The Conquest of Epidemic Disease, A Chapter in the History of Ideas* (reprinted). New York.

World Health Organization (1963). *World Health Organization Basic Documents*. Geneva.

PUBLIC HEALTH LABORATORY SERVICE (PHLS). A government-funded agency responsible in the UK for the surveillance of communicable diseases and for the provision of a microbiological laboratory service for the diagnosis, control, and prevention of such diseases. In addition to its Centre for Applied Microbiology and Research (CAMR) and the Communicable Disease Surveillance Centre (CDSC), the PHLS operates 52 regional and area laboratories and 24 reference and special laboratories throughout the UK. The information collected by the CDSC is disseminated in the weekly publication *Communicable Disease Report*.

PUBLIC VACCINATOR. The office of public vaccinator was created in 1871, when England and Wales were divided into districts each under the charge of a public vaccinator, a general practitioner under contract to vaccinate without a fee.

PUDENDA. The external *genitalia, particularly of females.

PUERPERAL FEVER is fever following childbirth, due to *streptococcal infection of the birth canal and surrounding tissues leading to *septicaemia—the once deadly 'childbed fever'. Both the incidence and the danger of this complication have been drastically reduced by *aseptic methods and *antibiotics respectively, though in the UK puerperal fever is still a *notifiable disease. See also OBSTETRICS.

PUERPERIUM. The period following *childbirth, which lasts until the maternal pelvic organs and tissues have returned to their normal condition.

PULEX IRRITANS, the human *flea, is parasitic on the skin of man. Individual sensitivity varies, but pulicine bites can be very irritant, causing the condition sometimes known as flea-bite *dermatitis. Unlike some other species, notably the rat flea *Xenopsylla* which transmits *plague, *Pulex irritans* is not normally a vector of infectious disease.

PULHEEMS is the acronymic classification of medical fitness used by the British army, the letters representing: physical capacity (P); upper limbs (U); lower limbs (L); hearing (H); visual acuity (EE); mental capacity (M); and emotional stability (S). A numerical grade is assigned to each letter.

PULMONARY ARTERY. The blood vessel which conducts deoxygenated blood from the right *ventricle of the *heart to the lungs. It consists of a main trunk and right and left pulmonary arteries going to the right and left lungs respectively.

PULMONARY DISEASE. See CHEST MEDICINE.

PULMONARY FUNCTION. See RESPIRATORY PHYSIOLOGY.

PULMONARY OSTEOARTHROPATHY is *clubbing of the fingers, painful swelling of the distal joints of the extremities with associated soft tissue swelling, and radiological evidence of sub-periosteal new bone formation in the shafts of the long bones: a syndrome also known as hypertrophic pulmonary osteoarthropathy. It almost invariably signifies serious disease of the lungs or heart, particularly *bronchogenic carcinoma, of which it may be the first overt manifestation, or chronic lung sepsis (*abscess, *empyema, *bronchiectasis). Finger clubbing alone, without obvious new bone formation, occurs in *infective endocarditis, cyanotic *congenital heart disease, pulmonary arteriovenous malformations, and certain diseases of the intestine and liver (e.g. *Crohn's disease, *ulcerative colitis, and some types of *cirrhosis of the liver). It may also be congenital and of no pathological significance.

PULSE. A pressure wave in a blood vessel, corresponding to the heart beat, which can be seen or felt or both. The arterial pulse is easily felt at a number of sites and its rate is commonly used as an index of heart rate; careful and skilled examination of the arterial pulse can provide other valuable information about the state of the heart, circulation, and arteries. The central venous pulse can usually be seen (but not felt) just above the medial third of the clavicle and similarly repays detailed study.

PULSUS ALTERNANS is an arterial *pulse in which the beats are of alternating strength, due to a corresponding alternation in left ventricular (and therefore arterial) systolic pressure. The phenomenon may be detected on routine palpation of the radial pulse, or may be first noticed when taking the blood pressure: as the *sphygmomanometer cuff is deflated, the brachial arterial sounds abruptly double in rate as the systolic pressure achieved by the weaker beats is reached. Pulsus alternans occurs in left ventricular failure, and though the precise mechanism is not understood, is generally recognized to be of poor prognostic significance.

PULSUS PARADOXUS. A marked decrease in amplitude of the arterial pulse during inspiration constitutes a paradoxical pulse. This physical sign, which is particularly characteristic of *pericardial effusion and constrictive *pericarditis, is badly named, since it represents an exaggeration of a normal phenomenon. Normally, the inspiratory fall in intrathoracic pressure sucks in a greater volume of blood to the right side of the heart, augmenting its output and partially compensating for the simultaneous increase in pulmonary vascular capacity; the output from the left heart either falls a little, or not at all. Pulsus paradoxus indicates that the right heart is unable to achieve this compensatory increase in output, usually because its expansion is limited by a tense or rigid pericardium but sometimes because the myocardium itself is rigid ('constrictive' *cardiomyopathy, or extreme right ventricular dilatation). The sign may also occur when the respiratory swing in intrathoracic pressure is exaggerated, as for instance in obstructed or stertorous breathing.

PUNCH-DRUNK SYNDROME. The syndrome exhibited by certain professional boxers resulting from repeated *trauma to the head. The manifestations are those of chronic *encephalopathy, with muscular incoordination, hesitancy of speech, slowness of thought, and memory loss.

PUNCTURE BIOPSY involves the removal of a sample of tissue from a patient for histological examination by means of needle puncture and aspiration (also known as needle or aspiration *biopsy).

PUPIL. The circular opening enclosed by the *iris that admits light into the eye.

PURGATION is the administration of a purgative or *laxative in order to induce defaecation.

PURGATIVE is a synonym for *laxative.

PURINES are substituted derivatives of purine, a bicyclic organic base with the formula $C_5H_4N_4$ related to uric acid. The biological importance of purines is due to their presence in *adenosine triphosphate (ATP) and *nucleic acids. Adenine and guanine, two of the nucleotide bases of *deoxyribonucleic acid (DNA) and *ribonucleic acid (RNA) are examples of purines.

PURKINJE (PURKYNE), JAN EVANGELISTA (1787–1869). Czech physiologist, MD Prague (1819). Purkinje took holy orders at an early age, but renounced them in 1807. He was appointed professor of pathology and physiology in Breslau in 1823, and moved to the chair of physiology in Prague in 1850. A histologist of distinction, he was the first to use a *microtome and *Canada balsam. He described the cells in the *cerebellum (1837) and the fibres in the *myocardium (1839), both of which bear his name. He noted *ciliary action in 1835. His physiological research was centred on sensory phenomena, especially vision, and the maintenance of equilibrium and posture. He invented the term '*protoplasm' (1846). In 1823 he analysed and classified fingerprints.

PURKINJE CELL, FIBRES, VESICLE, ETC. Among the various structures and physiological phenomena to which the name of *Purkinje is attached, the most frequently encountered are: Purkinje cells (also Purkinje corpuscles, Purkinje layer), which are large branching neurones in the cortex of the *cerebellum; Purkinje fibres (also Purkinje network), which are specialized subendocardial myocardial fibres responsible for conducting the exciting impulse to the ventricular muscle of the *heart; and Purkinje vesicle, which is the nucleus of an *oocyte.

PUROMYCIN is an *antibiotic produced by the fungus *Streptomyces alboniger* with antineoplastic and antiprotozoal activity. It has been used in the treatment of *tumours, *trypanosomiasis, and *amoebiasis.

PURPURA is a condition marked by multiple spontaneous capillary haemorrhages chiefly in the skin and mucous membranes. Purpura is distinguished morphologically from the smaller pin-point or punctate haemorrhages known as *petechiae and from the larger black-and-blue haemorrhages of bruising known as *ecchymoses. There are numerous causes of purpura, which are usually classified into two main groups, namely, those associated with a low circulating level of blood *platelets, the thrombocytopenic purpuras, and those not so associated, the vascular purpuras.

PURULENT means associated with the presence or the formation of *pus.

PUS is a yellowish fluid of varying consistency formed as a product of *inflammation, notably with particular species of bacteria known on that account as pyogenic. The main constituents of pus are white blood cells, bacteria, necrotic tissue, the debris of all these, and tissue fluid.

PUSTULE. A pimple containing visible *pus.

PUTREFACTION is enzymatic and bacterial decomposition of organic material.

PYAEMIA is the presence of pus-forming (pyogenic) micro-organisms in the blood circulation, which may be associated with the formation of *abscesses remote from the site of original infection: a form of *septicaemia.

PYELITIS is inflammation of the renal pelvis, a frequent result of bacterial infection. Since the

kidney substance is inevitably also involved to some extent, the term pyelonephritis is virtually synonymous. See NEPHROLOGY.

PYELOGRAPHY is the *radiographic visualization of the pelvis of the kidney after it has been filled with a radio-opaque dye. There are two main methods. The first is known as intravenous pyelography (or excretory urography). An iodinated contrast medium which is both excreted and concentrated by the kidney is injected intravenously, after which a number of X-ray films are taken at appropriate intervals; initially, the kidneys are seen in outline and then the dye is concentrated in the renal pelves and *ureter, revealing any anatomical abnormality. Impairment of renal function may be suggested by delayed or deficient excretion by one or both kidneys. The other method, known as retrograde pyelography, is independent of the state of renal function. Here a *cystoscopy is performed and a catheter inserted under direct vision into one or other ureteric orifice, allowing contrast medium to be injected directly into it; the medium spreads in a retrograde fashion to fill the rest of the collecting system of the kidney.

PYELONEPHRITIS. See PYELITIS.

PYKNIC. One of the constitutional types described by Kretschmer, the pyknic habitus is a short stocky build associated with a cheerful extraverted social temperament and swings of mood. When those of pyknic constitution suffer a mental breakdown, the resultant illness is likely to be of the *manic-depressive variety. Kretschmer's 'pyknic' is approximately equivalent to Sheldon's '*endomorph'.

PYKNOLEPSY is a name sometimes given to *petit mal epilepsy when attacks are very frequent, of the order of 100 or more a day.

PYKNOSIS is cell degeneration, marked by contraction of the cell nucleus into a dense featureless mass.

PYLORIC STENOSIS is an outflow obstruction from the *stomach due to contraction of the pyloric orifice. In adults this may result from scarring due to *peptic ulceration or from the presence of a *tumour in the pyloric region. Congenital pyloric stenosis of genetic origin occurs in newborn infants.

PYLOROPLASTY is the surgical re-formation of the pylorus, the narrow muscular tube connecting the *stomach to the *duodenum.

PYLOROSPASM is spasm of the pyloric muscle.

PYODERMA is any skin disease associated with *pus formation.

PYOGENIC. *Pus-forming.

PYOMYOSITIS is *myositis with *pus and *abscess formation, usually due to *staphylococci and occurring more commonly in the tropics.

PYONEPHROSIS is suppurative infection of the kidney, in which the renal parenchyma is partly or completely destroyed by a collection of *pus.

PYOPNEUMOTHORAX is the simultaneous presence of air and *pus in the *pleural cavity.

PYORRHOEA is any flow of *pus; when otherwise unqualified, it usually means pyorrhoea alveolaris, purulent *periodontitis.

PYRAZINAMIDE is an antibacterial drug used in the treatment of *tuberculosis, normally in combination with other drugs. Its value is limited by the development of drug resistance and by its side-effects, notably liver damage.

PYREXIA is a synonym for *fever.

PYRIMIDINES are substituted derivatives of pyrimidine, an organic base with a heterocyclic 6-membered ring structure (formula $C_4H_4N_2$). Cytosine, thymidine, and uracil, nucleotide bases found in *nucleic acids, are pyrimidines.

PYROGEN. An agent which produces *fever.

PYROSIS is a synonym for *heartburn.

PYURIA is the presence of *pus in the *urine.

Q

Q FEVER is a severe but self-limiting influenza-like illness due to the micro-organism *Coxiella burnetii*. *C. burnetii* is a species of the **Rickettsia* group, but Q fever differs in two respects from other rickettsial infections like *typhus: firstly in being transmitted to man by inhalation and secondly in not being marked by a skin rash. The organism, moreover, is remarkably resistant to drying and to exposure in soil and dust. A reservoir exists in wild animals, maintained through transmission by *arthropod vectors; man becomes liable to infection when this spreads to domestic animals, particularly cattle, sheep, and goats. Clinically, the pattern is one of high fever, with malaise, muscle pains, headache, and other febrile manifestations; a mild pneumonia is not uncommon. The overall mortality rate is less than 1 per cent, and the response to antibiotics is favourable. The only serious complication is *endocarditis, and this is rare. Q stands for query.

QUACKS. Medical impostors or charlatans. See FRINGE MEDICINE, CULTS, AND QUACKERY.

QUADRIPLEGIA is paralysis of all four limbs.

QUADRUPLETS. Four offspring from a single gestation. See MULTIPLE BIRTH.

QUAIN, RICHARD (1800–87). Anglo-Irish surgeon, MRCS (1828), FRS (1844). Quain was the first assistant surgeon appointed to *University College Hospital, London, in 1834, later becoming surgeon and professor. He was one of the foundation fellows of the Royal College of Surgeons of England in 1843 and became president in 1868, as well as surgeon-extraordinary to the Queen. A cousin of Sir Richard *Quain, he was a cautious surgeon, jealous and ready to impute improper motives to his colleagues.

QUAIN, SIR RICHARD, BT (1816–98). Anglo-Irish physician, MD London (1842), FRCP (1851), FRS (1871). Quain was elected a fellow of *University College, London, in 1843; he became assistant physician to the Brompton Hospital for Chest Diseases in 1848 and physician in 1855. He was appointed physician-extraordinary to the Queen in 1890 and raised to the baronetcy in 1891. He was president of the *General Medical Council from 1891 to 1896.

QUARANTINE is a period, originally (for a ship) of 40 days (derived from the French *quarante*), of compulsory isolation or detection in order to prevent contagion or infection. The term is now used extensively in other contexts, as for example in relation to the period of six months for which an imported dog must be kept 'in quarantine' in the UK in order to prevent the importation of *rabies.

QUARANTINE LAWS. Improvements in knowledge, sanitation, therapy, and prophylactic *immunization during the present century have led to increasing relaxation of various quarantine regulations in respect of infectious diseases. In order to replace these, and in the light of increasing international air travel, the *World Health Organization (WHO) in 1969 issued International Sanitary Regulations to set standards for reporting of diseases and quarantine measures, including maximum quarantine requirements that could be imposed on international traffic. These regulations were concerned with six designated 'quarantinable diseases', namely *cholera, *plague, *yellow fever, *smallpox, louse-borne *relapsing fever, and louse-borne *typhus. Subsequently, WHO International Health Regulations revised the standards applicable to the first four of these diseases, and downgraded the two last to 'diseases under surveillance' (along with *malaria, *influenza, and *poliomyelitis).

A quarantine law which remains strictly in force is that governing the importation of live animals into the UK, which has been free of endemic *rabies for some 70 years. Under the Rabies (Importation of Dogs, Cats and Other Animals) Order 1974 it is an offence to import into the UK most mammals except with an advance licence, which requires the animal to be retained in approved quarantine premises for six months. This applies to any animal that has been in a foreign port regardless of whether or not it actually landed and whether or not it has been vaccinated against rabies. Contravention can result in a prison sentence and destruction of the animal.

QUARANTINE PERIOD. A period of isolation or detention imposed on those who have or may have been in contact with an infectious disease in order to prevent further transmission, the period being normally equal to the maximum *incubation period of the particular infection. With the common infections, quarantine periods are now rarely strictly observed, ordinary medical surveillance of contacts being regarded as adequate; however it may be advisable in some instances to keep contacts away from, for example, schools and places of public entertainment.

QUARTAN FEVER is a fever recurring at 72-hour (not 96-hour) intervals, as in the type of *malaria due to *Plasmodium malariae,* a parasite which has an asexual life cycle of 72 hours.

QUECKENSTEDT, HANS HEINRICH GEORG (1876–1918). Queckenstedt was Chief of Medical Services in Hamburg, Germany. In 1916 he devised a test to show if the *spinal canal is blocked (see QUECKENSTEDT'S TEST). Queckenstedt was killed by an army wagon on the last day of the First World War.

QUECKENSTEDT'S TEST. A hollow needle with a pressure-measuring device is introduced into the *cerebrospinal fluid in the lumbar region by *lumbar puncture. The jugular veins in the neck are then compressed. This dams back blood in the cranial cavity. Cerebrospinal fluid is therefore compressed and the rise in pressure is transmitted to the spinal canal. If there is a block, the pressure does not rise. If there is a partial block, the pressure rises more slowly than normal and falls back more slowly too.

QUERVAIN, FRITZ DE (1868–1940). Swiss surgeon, MD Berne (1892). De Quervain was a pupil of *Kocher; he was granted the title of professor of surgery in Berne in 1907, becoming *ordinarius* in 1909 and moving to Basle in 1918. He described a non-suppurative form of thyroiditis (de Quervain's thyroiditis, 1904) and chronic stenosing vaginitis of the thumb (de Quervain's disease, 1895).

DE QUERVAIN'S DISEASE is painful *stenosing vaginitis of the thumb.

DE QUERVAIN'S THYROIDITIS is an inflammatory condition of the *thyroid gland, also known as subacute granulomatous thyroiditis, which usually follows a virus infection and which is characterized by painful swelling of the gland. Disturbance of thyroid function, if it occurs, is transient and the disease is self-limited.

QUETELET, LAMBERT ADOLPHE JACQUES (1796–1874). Belgian statistician and astronomer. Quetelet became professor of mathematics at the Collège de Ghent in 1815 and astronomer at the Brussels Royal Observatory in 1833. The founder of *vital statistics and the first to conceive of the 'average man', he devised a technique for the application of statistics to the data of biology and the social sciences.

QUICKENING. The first perception by the mother of fetal movement, usually early in the fifth month of pregnancy.

QUINCKE, HEINRICH IRENAEUS (1842–1922). German physician, MD Berlin (1863). After working in physiology under Brücke in Vienna Quincke was made an assistant to *Frerichs in Berlin in 1867. He became professor of medicine in Berne in 1873, moving to Kiel in 1878, and to Frankfurt in 1908. A general physician of great ability, he described the capillary *pulse (1868) and *angioneurotic oedema (Quincke's disease, 1822). He was the first to use *lumbar puncture for therapeutic and diagnostic purposes (1895).

QUINIDINE is one of the *cinchona alkaloids, used mainly for its anti-arrhythmic and myocardial depressant effects.

QUININE was the first, and is still one of the medicinally important *alkaloids of cinchona bark, obtained from a genus of South American trees (quinoline alkaloids). Though for most antimalarial purposes quinine has been superseded by synthetic compounds, it remains a valuable agent for the treatment of malignant tertian (falciparum) *malaria resistant to *chloroquine. Its wide variety of pharmacological actions finds other therapeutic applications, for example in controlling the familiar affliction of night *cramps.

QUINOLINE is a *quinine derivative with *antiseptic and *antipyretic properties.

QUINSY is an *abscess in the peritonsillar region and is an occasional complication of pharyngeal infections.

QUINTUPLETS. Five offspring from a single gestation. See MULTIPLE BIRTH.

R

RABELAIS, FRANÇOIS (?1494–?1553). French physician and writer, MD Montpellier (1537). Rabelais was tonsured as a Franciscan at an early age, but changed to the Benedictine order about 1525. He matriculated at *Montpellier in 1530 and proceeded MB within the year. In 1532 he was appointed physician to the Hôtel-Dieu in Lyon, where he lectured on anatomy. Here he wrote the works which have made his memory imperishable, *Pantagruel* (1533) and *Gargantua* (1535). The first was condemned by the Sorbonne in 1533. He left Lyons to travel with his patron. In 1546 he was town physician in Metz, but he encountered many vicissitudes in his later years.

RABIES is an almost uniformly fatal virus infection transmitted to man by the bite of an infected animal, usually a dog. In many countries, the virus (a large bullet-shaped ribonucleic acid (RNA) virus belonging to the *rhabdovirus group) is enzootic in wild warm-blooded animals; though the chief danger to man occurs in communities where rabies in domestic animals (dogs and cats) is inadequately controlled. Some countries (e.g. the UK and Japan), which have been able to eliminate the disease, maintain this situation by stringent control of the importation and *quarantine of animals. Once signs of infection appear (the incubation period varies from a week or two to several years), treatment has little or no influence on the ultimate outcome. It is, however, possible to reduce the likelihood of infection after the bite of a rabid animal by a combination of active and passive *immunization.

RACE, ROBERT RUSSELL (1907–83) British haematologist, MRCS England, LRCP London (1933), FRCP (1959), FRS (1952). Race made a memorable contribution, with *Fisher, to the genetics of blood group inheritance, particularly with the *rhesus factors. He introduced the CDE/cde system, which has helped illuminate many areas of *haematology.

RACHISCHISIS is the absence of the vertebral arches of the spine in the lumbar region, a severe form of *spina bifida.

RACIAL FACTORS IN DISEASE. Like other genetically determined characteristics, such as skin colour, facial appearance, height, etc., disease of genetic origin or having a contributory genetic component, may vary in incidence between different racial groups. For instance, *sickle cell anaemia does not occur among Caucasians and *cystic fibrosis is rare in those of Negro origin; *gout is common among Maoris; *phenylketonuria is rare in Jews but *Tay–Sachs disease is relatively common: *thalassaemia occurs chiefly in people originating from South-East Asia and the Mediterranean littoral; and there are many other examples. See also GENETICS.

RAD. The unit of absorbed dose of ionizing *radiation. One rad is equal to an energy absorption of 0.01 joule per kilogram of irradiated material.

RADCLIFFE, JOHN (1650–1714). British physician, DM Oxford (1682), FRCP (1687). Radcliffe was elected a fellow of Lincoln College, Oxford, in 1669 and practised in Oxford until 1684 when he moved to London. Although notably lacking in the social graces he became the leading physician in London and was appointed to Princess Anne in 1686. About 1695 she dismissed him for his unacceptable candour as did William III later. He is said to have refused to see Queen Anne when she was dying. From 1690 to 1695 he was Member of Parliament for Bramber and from 1713 to 1714 for Buckingham. Radcliffe was the original owner of the gold-headed cane and left a large fortune to Oxford University from which were built the Radcliffe Camera, the *Radcliffe Infirmary, and the Radcliffe Observatory.

RADCLIFFE INFIRMARY, Oxford, England, is named after the physician John *Radcliffe who graduated from Oxford and practised in London. In 1724 he left a benefaction to Oxford University, especially to pay for the building of a library and the salary of a librarian. The edifice is the renowned Radcliffe Camera. The Infirmary was opened in 1770 and named after him; although he did not specifically make any mention of such an institution in his will, his trustees used part of the residue of his estate for the erection of a building to become the Infirmary, on land donated by Thomas Rowney. It went through many vicissitudes over two centuries, such as beset all hospitals, especially in association with ancient universities. Clinical instruction for undergraduates occurred sporadically, occasionally disappearing. Henry Acland in the 19th c. seemed to feel that a medical education should consist of basic sciences in the University, followed by clinical education elsewhere, a pattern which was adopted against some opposition. William *Osler came from the USA as regius professor of medicine and an illustrious period began at the

Radcliffe and in Oxford leading ultimately to the opening of an Oxford clinical school. In 1918 an orthopaedic department began and later flourished under Girdlestone and H. J. Seddon. Farquhar Buzzard was made regius professor in 1928. Lord Nuffield (see MORRIS) made enormous benefactions in the 1930s and clinical chairs in surgery, medicine, obstetrics, and anaesthesia were founded and filled by the distinguished Hugh *Cairns, L. J. Witts, Chassar Moir, and R. R. Macintosh. Pomfret Kilner, one of the founders of modern plastic surgery in the UK was also ultimately made a professor in that subject. Further renowned names associated with the Infirmary were J. Trueta in traumatic surgery (from experience in the Spanish Civil War) and John *Ryle, who held the first chair of social medicine in the UK, coming from a lucrative London practice as a physician, as well as Ritchie Russell in neurology and Sir George *Pickering. A clinical medical school is now firmly established in Oxford using the new John Radcliffe Hospital and the Radcliffe Infirmary, amongst others, for teaching. These form a central pillar of the medical services of the Oxford Region of the *National Health Service.

RADIATION is the emission of any rays, wave motion, or particles (e.g. *alpha particles, *beta particles, *neutrons) from a source.

RADIATION, IONIZING: ITS BIOLOGICAL EFFECTS

Introduction. The biological effects of ionizing radiation have been investigated for more than 80 years. From the wealth of information about such effects that is now available, it may be inferred that they are better known than those of any other physical or chemical agent. The evolution of our knowledge of radiation injury—and, in turn, the development of principles and procedures for radiological protection—have thus provided lessons of strategic importance in addressing the health hazards of other environmental agents.

Historical background. Within months after its discovery by *Roentgen, in 1894, the *X-ray was introduced widely into the diagnosis and treatment of disease. At the same time, harmful effects of radiation were encountered almost immediately. The first such effects to be recognized typically appeared within hours or days after exposure and rapidly subsided.

It was not until 1902 that *cancer, arising on the hand of a radiologist at the site of long-standing radiation-induced skin damage, was recognized as a potential late-occurring complication of radiation injury. In the ensuing decades, before safety measures were improved, similar growths occurred in scores of pioneer radiation workers.

Because such cancers were characteristically preceded by long-standing and progressive skin damage, it was generally assumed that such damage was a prerequisite for cancer formation

and that carcinogenic effects of radiation would not occur in the absence of gross tissue injury. By the middle of the century, however, the frequency of *leukaemia in A-bomb survivors, radiologists, and certain groups of medically irradiated patients suggested that the incidence of this *malignant disease might increase in proportion to the dose, without any threshold.

The implication that any dose of radiation, however small, might involve some risks of serious injury aroused concerns which have persisted to the present. As a result, radiation protection standards no longer assume the existence of a level of exposure that is totally 'safe'.

Nature of ionizing radiation. Ionizing radiation, in contrast to other forms of radiant energy, imparts enough localized energy to a material in which it is absorbed to cause *ionization, as well as excitation, of the atoms and molecules with which it interacts. Ionizing radiations are of both electromagnetic and particulate types. The former type includes *electrons, *protons, *neutrons, *alpha particles, and other atomic particles of varying mass and charge.

Ionizing radiation is measured in several units. The oldest unit, the Roentgen (R), is a measure of the quantity of ionization induced in air. The principal units used for expressing the dose absorbed in tissue are the *rad* (1 rad = 0.01 joules per kilogram, or 100 ergs per gram of tissue) and the *gray* (1 Gy = 1 joule per kilogram of tissue = 100 rad). The *rem* and the *sievert* have also been introduced to enable doses of different types of radiation to be normalized in terms of biological effectiveness, since particulate radiations generally cause greater injury for a given dose in rads or grays than do X-rays or gamma rays. One *rem*, defined loosely, is the amount of any radiation which produces a biological effect equivalent to that produced by one *rad* of gamma rays; and one *sievert* (Sv) is the amount of any radiation which produces a biological effect equivalent to that produced by 1 *gray* of gamma rays (1 Sv = 100 rem). For expressing the collective dose to a population, the *person-rem* and *person-Sv* are used, each unit representing the product of the average dose per person times the number of people exposed (e.g. 1 rem to each of 100 people = 100 person-rem = 1 person-Sv). For measuring the amount of radioactivity contained in a given sample of matter, the *curie* (Ci) and the *becquerel* (Bq) are the customary units; one Ci is that quantity of a radioactive element in which there are 3.7×10^{10} atomic disintegrations per second, and 1 *becquerel* is that quantity of a radioactive element in which there is one atomic disintegration per second (1 Bq = 2.7×10^{-11} Ci).

Sources and levels of radiation in the environment. Life has evolved since its inception in the presence of natural background radiation. This radiation comes from three main sources: (i) cosmic rays, which come from outer space; (ii) terrestrial radiations, which are emitted by radium, thorium, uranium, and other radioactive elements in the earth's crust; and (iii) internal radiations, which emanate from potassium-40, carbon-14, and other radionuclides present in living cells themselves. The average total dose received annually from these three sources by a person at sea-level is about 0.80 mSv, or 80 mrem; however, a dose twice this size may be received at higher elevations, where cosmic rays are more intense, or in regions where the soil's radium content is increased (Table 1).

Table 1. Estimates of annual doses of whole-body radiation to the US population

Source of radiation	Average dose rates (mSv/year)
Natural	
Environmental	
Cosmic radiation	0.28 (0.28–1.30)[a]
Terrestrial radiation	0.26 (0.30–1.15)[b]
Internal radioactive isotopes	0.26
Subtotal	0.80
Man-made	
Environmental	
Technological enhanced	0.04
Global fallout	0.04
Nuclear power	0.002
Medical	
Diagnostic	0.78
Radiopharmaceuticals	0.14
Occupational	0.01
Miscellaneous	0.05
Subtotal	1.06
Total	1.86

[a]Values in parentheses indicate range over which average levels for different states vary with elevation.
[b]Range of variation (shown in parentheses) attributable largely to geographic differences in the content of potassium-40, radium, thorium, and uranium in the earth's crust.
Source: From National Academy of Sciences Advisory Committee on the Biological Effects of Ionizing Radiation (BEIR) (1972, 1980). *The Effects on Populations of Exposure to Low Levels of Ionizing Radiation.* Washington, DC.

In addition to natural background radiation, man is now exposed to radiation from artificial sources, the largest of which is medical radiography. Although the doses from different types of medical and dental examinations vary widely, the annual dose to the population from medical irradiation in developed countries is estimated to approach that received from natural background (Table 1). Other sources of man-made radiation include radioactive minerals in crushed rock, building materials, and phosphate fertilizers; radiation-emitting components of TV sets, smoke detectors, and other consumer products; radioactive fall-out from atomic weapons; and nuclear power (Table 1).

Interaction of radiation with matter. As radi-

ation penetrates matter, it gives up its energy through random interactions with atoms and molecules in its path. These interactions result in the formation of ions and reactive radicals which, in turn, can break chemical bonds and cause other forms of molecular damage.

The distribution of ionization events along the path of an impinging radiation depends on the energy, mass, and charge of the radiation and, to a lesser extent, on the density of the absorbing tissue. In general, X-rays and gamma rays produce ions sparsely along their tracks and hence are characterized by a low rate of linear energy transfer (LET). As a result, they tend to penetrate deeply into or through the body. Charged particles, on the other hand, are characterized by higher LET and shallower penetration; for example, alpha particles characteristically travel only a few micrometres in tissue.

The anatomical distribution of the dose from an internally deposited radioelement, whatever the nature of its emitted radiations, is determined by the uptake, tissue distribution, retention, and metabolism of the radioelement. These properties tend to be highly specific for each radioelement. For example, the pattern of uptake and retention of radioactive iodine by the normal *thyroid gland is so predictable that this radionuclide is used clinically in assaying thyroid function, whereas with radium the skeleton is the principal site of deposition.

Since the production of biological injury is correlated with molecular damage and, in turn, with the density of energy deposition, radiations of high LET (e.g. protons and alpha particles) generally are of higher relative biological effectiveness (RBE) for damaging the cells they traverse than are radiations of low LET (e.g. X-rays and gamma rays).

Major types of radiation injury. Although any living organism can be killed by radiation if it is exposed to a large enough dose, the effects of irradiation in a given situation depend on the dose and the conditions of exposure (Table 2). For

Table 2. Some effects of the acute whole-body irradiation in relation to dose

Tissue dose (Sv)[a]	Biological effect
0.1	Immediate increase in frequency of chromosome aberrations in circulating lymphocytes
0.5	Increase in lifetime risk of cancer [b]
1	Transitory nausea and vomiting
10	Death within 4–6 weeks from injury to marrow
20	Death within 7–14 days from injury to intestine
50	Death within 24–72 hours from injury to brain

[a]Dose received in a single, brief exposure.
[b]See Table 3.

example, exposure of germ cells (i.e. those involved in reproduction) to radiation can cause *genetic effects which are expressed only in the descendants of an exposed individual; whereas exposure of other cells of the body can affect the exposed individual himself. Effects of the latter type (i.e. somatic effects) include both early reactions which appear almost immediately after irradiation, and late reactions, which may be delayed for decades (e.g. certain radiation-induced cancers).

Radiation injuries are classified for purposes of radiological protection into two categories: (i) *stochastic* effects, which vary in frequency, but not severity, with dose; and (ii) *non-stochastic* effects, which vary in both frequency and severity with dose. The latter require injury to many cells, with the result that such effects do not occur below a certain threshold dose. In contrast, each stochastic effect is attributed to injury of a single cell, damaged individually, with the result that no threshold for the effects is presumed to exist. Included in this category are *mutagenic and *carcinogenic effects.

Effects of radiation on cells. At the cellular level, radiation injury may take various forms, including inhibition of cell division, damage to *chromosomes, *gene mutation, *neoplastic transformation, and various other changes. All such effects are thought to be end-results of molecular lesions caused by radiation-induced ions and free radicals.

Radiation can alter essentially any molecule within the cell, but alterations in *deoxyribunucleic acid (DNA) are the most critical, since damage to a single gene can profoundly affect the cell in question. A dose of X-radiation sufficient to kill a cell (e.g. 1–2 Sv) produces dozens of strand breaks and other changes in its DNA. Although many of the changes are reparable, the type of DNA lesion caused by a given dose of high-LET radiation is likely to be less reparable than that resulting from the same dose of low-LET radiation. The lesion that ultimately results, and whether it is permanent, may depend as much on the action of DNA repair processes as on the nature of the initial alteration itself.

Radiation may also damage membranes and other cellular structures, but it is not certain whether such damage leads to significant biological effects on the cell, except possibly at extremely high doses. The molecular basis for most types of cellular injury remains as yet poorly understood.

Damage to chromosomes. The production of chromosomal abnormalities is one of the most thoroughly studied effects of radiation. These abnormalities, which include changes in chromosome number and structure, result from the breakage and rearrangement of chromosomes and from interference with the normal segregation of chromosomes to daughter cells at the time of cell division. The majority of the aberrations are 'unstable', in that they interfere with *mitosis and

thus cause the affected cells to die when they attempt to divide.

The frequency of chromosomal aberrations increases as a linear non-threshold function of the radiation dose in the low-to-intermediate dose range. The increase for a given dose is lárger with high-LET radiation than with low-LET radiation. In human blood lymphocytes irradiated in culture, the frequency of such aberrations approximates to 0.1 per cell per Sv.

Although a small percentage of chromosome aberrations is attributable to natural background radiation, they can also be caused by certain viruses, chemicals, and drugs. Their ultimate implications for the health of an affected individual are not known.

Damage to genes. Since *Muller's pioneer studies with the fruit fly, *Drosophila*, in 1927, mutagenic effects of radiation have been investigated extensively in many types of organism. Although heritable effects of radiation on human germ cells remain to be documented, the wealth of information that is available from other species, especially the mouse, provides a basis for predicting genetic effects of irradiation in man.

In mouse spermatogonia and oocytes, the frequency of mutations per locus is increased by about 10^{-5} (or by about 100 per cent) per Sv, depending on the conditions of irradiation. The fact that no increase in genetic abnormalities has been detectable in the children of atomic bomb survivors is thus not unexpected, given the relatively small number of such children (78 000) who have been available for examination and the small size of the average gonadal dose (0.5 Sv) received by their parents. On the basis of the available data, it has been estimated that the dose required to double the frequency of mutations in the human species probably lies between 0.2 and 2.5 Sv, and hence that only a small percentage (0.1–2.0 per cent) of genetically related disease in the general population is attributable to natural background irradiation.

Effects on cell survival. Dividing cells, as a class, are comparatively radiosensitive. Hence the susceptibility of cells to killing by irradiation generally increases with their rate of proliferation. As measured by ability to multiply, the survival of cells tends to decrease exponentially with increasing dose (Fig. 1). The dose required to reduce the number of surviving cells by 50 per cent approximates to 1–2 Sv for most rapidly proliferating mammalian cells, including cancer cells.

At lower doses, survival may decrease less steeply, giving rise to a shoulder on the dose–survival curve, which is LET-dependent. When a dose is fractionated into two or more exposures, such a shoulder tends to reappear between exposures, owing to repair of sublethal damage during the interim. As a result, a dose of low-LET radiation that is delivered in many small increments over an extended period tends to kill

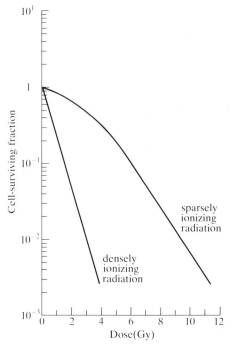

Fig. 1. Characteristic survival curves for clonogenic mammalian cells exposed to ionizing radiation, as scored by ability to proliferate and form macroscopic colonies. (Modified from Hall, E. J. (1978). *Radiobiology for the Radiologist*. 2nd edn, New York.)

fewer cells than the same dose delivered in a single brief exposure.

Effects on tissues. The effects of radiation on multicellular tissues involve indirect reactions, some of which evolve slowly, as well as direct injury to cells. For example, although mitotic inhibition and cytological abnormalities are often detectable immediately after irradiation, *fibrosis and other degenerative changes may not appear until months or years later. Tissues in which cells proliferate rapidly generally exhibit injury sooner than others; however, susceptibility to long-term damage is not always correlated with mitotic rate.

In proliferating tissues, depletion of cells by irradiation elicits compensatory proliferation of uninjured cells, so that the net effect is generally smaller when a dose is spread out in time than when it is received in a single brief exposure. By the same token, the effects of a given dose are generally more severe when a whole organ or the whole body is irradiated than when only a part of an organ or a part of the body is exposed.

Since the effects of irradiation can vary appreciably, depending on the tissue irradiated and the conditions of exposure, no attempt is made here to review such reactions comprehensively. Certain tissue reactions, however, which are particularly relevant to occupational or accidental irradiation, are characterized briefly below.

Skin. Because of the superficial location of the skin, its response to radiation has been studied more extensively than that of any other organ. The effects of radiation on the skin include various reactions, the frequency, severity, and timing of which depend on the conditions of exposure.

The earliest outward reaction is transitory reddening, or erythema, which may become evident within hours after a dose of 6 Gy or more. This reaction results from dilatation of capillaries by *histamine-like substances released from injured *epithelial cells. The initial erythematous reaction, which typically lasts only a few hours, is followed 2–4 weeks later by one or more waves of deeper and more prolonged erythema. With a larger dose, dry desquamation (scaling), moist desquamation (blistering), and necrosis (breakdown) of the epidermis may ensue, followed by epilation (shedding of hair) and pigmentation. Long-term sequelae, developing months or years later, may include atrophy of the epidermis, sweat glands, sebaceous glands, and hair follicles, and fibrosis of the dermis. (See SKIN.)

The early effects (erythema, dry desquamation, moist desquamation, and necrosis) are attributed primarily to injury of proliferating germinative cells in the basal layer of the epidermis, and to the resulting interference with renewal of epidermal cells. The late changes, on the other hand, are thought to result from injury of blood vessels in the dermis as well as of epithelial cells in the epidermis.

The severity of reaction increases with the area as well as the depth of skin that is irradiated. It also depends on the anatomical location, vascularity, and oxygenation of the skin, as well as other factors. The threshold dose for erythema over a 10 cm² field varies, from 6 to 8 Gy delivered in a single brief exposure to more than 30 Gy fractionated over a period of several weeks.

For dry desquamation, moist desquamation, and necrosis, the thresholds are considerably higher than for erythema. For damage to hair follicles, on the other hand, the threshold is lower than for erythema; that is, a dose of 3–5 Gy delivered in a single brief exposure can cause temporary epilation, while 7 Gy in a single exposure, or 50–60 Gy fractionated over several weeks, can cause permanent epilation.

Bone marrow and blood-forming tissues. Blood-forming, or haemopoietic, cells are among the most radiosensitive cells in the body. Many such cells show cytological changes within minutes after a dose in excess of 1 Sv, and subsequently die as they attempt to divide. The killing of such cells can impair the normal replacement of ageing blood cells, causing the blood count to fall. Since mature blood cells are generally radioresistant, however, their numbers decline gradually; maximum depletion of *leucocytes and *platelets is not reached until 3–5 weeks after intensive whole-body irradiation.

While less than 0.5–1.0 Sv of whole-body irradiation produces too little depletion of haemopoietic cells to cause death, a dose above 10 Sv is invariably lethal if absorbed within minutes or days, as in a radiation accident or nuclear explosion. Infection and haemorrhage, resulting from damage to haemopoietic cells, are the principal causes of death under such circumstances. Larger doses can be tolerated if accumulated gradually over weeks or months. Few systemic effects are observed even after a dose of 20 Sv if only a small volume of *bone marrow is irradiated.

*Lymphocytes, like haemopoietic cells, are highly radiosensitive, undergoing degeneration almost immediately after irradiation. Severe damage to lymphoid tissues, if generalized, may result in profound depression of the immune response. (See IMMUNOLOGY.)

Gastro-intestinal tract. The reaction of the gastrointestinal tract to radiation is comparable in some respects to that of the skin. Germinative cells in the mucosal epithelium are highly radiosensitive, and their killing by radiation may interfere with the normal replacement of cells lining the gastrointestinal tract. If the depletion of such cells is severe, *ulceration and, ultimately, denudation of affected parts of the *mucosa may result. This effect can cause a fatal *dysentery-like syndrome if a large part of the small intestine is exposed acutely to a dose in excess of 10 Gy, as may occur in a radiation accident. Under such conditions, death occurs within several days.

Long-term complications which may develop months or years after intensive localized exposure of the gastrointestinal tract, include perforation, *fistula formation, and *stricture.

The *mucous membranes lining the oral cavity, pharynx, oesophagus, and rectum are less radiosensitive than those lining the stomach and intestine. By comparison, the liver and other parenchymatous organs of the digestive system are relatively radioresistant.

Gonads. The *testis is among the most radiosensitive organs of the body because of the high radiosensitivity of spermatogonia and other immature sperm-forming cells. Acute exposure of the testes to a dose as low as 0.15 Sv can depress the *sperm count temporarily, and a dose of 2 Sv or more can cause permanent sterility in some exposed men.

Oocytes are also highly radiosensitive. A dose of 1.5–2.0 Sv to the *ovaries causes temporary sterility, and a dose of 2.0–3.0 Sv permanent sterility, in some exposed women.

Lens of the eye. Irradiation of the lens can cause opacities or *cataracts, the frequency and severity of which increase with the dose. Although microscopic opacities have been observed after a dose of 1–2 Sv received in a single brief exposure, the threshold for a vision-impairing opacity is estimated to vary from about 2–3 Sv received in a single exposure to 5.5–14 Sv received over a period of months. Such opacities may not become evident until months or years after irradiation.

Some of the pioneer *cyclotron physicists developed cataracts as a result of occupational exposure to neutrons in the 1940s, indicating for the first time the high relative biological effectiveness of neutron radiation for lens damage.

Radiation sickness. As mentioned above, intensive irradiation of a major part of the haemopoietic system or of the gastrointestinal tract may kill sufficient numbers of cells in these tissues to cause radiation sickness, or the 'acute radiation syndrome'. In both the haemopoietic and intestinal forms of the syndrome, *anorexia, nausea, and vomiting typically occur within a few hours after irradiation. These prodomal symptoms characteristically subside within 24 hours, to be followed by a symptom-free interval until the main phase of the illness.

The main phase of the intestinal forms of the syndrome typically begins 2–3 days after irradiation, with abdominal pain, fever, and increasingly severe diarrhoea, dehydration, debilitation, disturbance of salt (electrolyte) and fluid balance, toxaemia, and shock. The disorder characteristically ends in death within 7–14 days.

The main phase of the haemopoietic form of the syndrome typically begins 2–3 weeks after irradiation, with reduction in the number of granular white blood cells, or leucocytes, (granulocytopenia) and platelets (thrombocytopenia) and other complications of radiation-induced aplasia of the bone marrow. If damage to the marrow is sufficiently severe, death may ensue 4–6 weeks after irradiation, from *septicaemia, exsanguination, or other complications.

A third form of the acute radiation syndrome, the cerebral form, may result from acute exposure of the brain to a dose in excess of 50 Gy. In this syndrome, the same prodromal symptoms as above—anorexia, nausea, and vomiting—occur almost immediately after irradiation, and are followed within minutes or hours by increasing drowsiness, *ataxia, confusion, convulsions, loss of consciousness, and death. Although the brain is relatively resistant to radiation injury, a large enough dose can cause prompt destruction of *neurones, with cerebral inflammation, *oedema, and death.

Effects on growth and development of the embryo (teratogenesis). Embryonal, fetal, and juvenile tissues are highly radiosensitive, in keeping with their highly proliferative character. Acute exposure to 0.25 Sv during a critical stage in organogenesis has been observed to disturb prenatal development in experimental animals. Comparable effects have been observed at higher doses in prenatally irradiated children. In atomic-bomb survivors who were irradiated early in prenatal development, for example, the incidence of mental retardation is increased as a function of the dose.

Because radiation-induced *malformations result, in general, from the killing of cells at critical and sharply circumscribed stages in embryonal organogenesis, their frequency in experimental animals decreases markedly as a dose is spread out in time.

Effects on cancer incidence. Observations on atomic-bomb survivors, patients exposed to radiation for medical purposes, and various occupationally exposed groups indicate that most, but not all, types of cancer are increased in frequency by irradiation, depending on the conditions of exposure. A cancer induced by radiation, however, has no distinguishing features by which it can be recognized as such, and it may not appear until years or decades after irradiation. Hence, the possible link between the occurrence of a cancer and previous irradiation can be inferred only statistically, on the basis of appropriate *epidemiological evidence.

The epidemiological data come predominantly from observations at relatively high doses (0.5–2.0 Sv) and in no instance cover a wide enough range of doses and dose rates to define the precise shape of the dose–incidence curve. Thus, the carcinogenic risks of low-level irradiation can be estimated only by extrapolation from observations at higher doses and dose rates, based on unproven assumptions about the dose–incidence relationship. The most extensive information about the dose–incidence relationship pertains to leukaemia and cancer of the female breast.

For leukaemias other than that of the chronic lymphatic type, the incidence is increased during the first 25 years after irradiation. The overall excess of all such leukaemias combined amounts to approximately 1–2 cases per year per 10 000 persons at risk per Sv to the bone marrow. The relationship between the cumulative incidence and the dose can be represented by a linear non-threshold function, but various other dose–incidence functions which are more consistent with observations in experimental animals (e.g. a linear-quadratic function) fit the data equally well. Interpretation of the dose–incidence relationship is complicated by unexplained variations among different types of leukaemia in the magnitude of the radiation-induced increase for a given dose, age at irradiation, and time after exposure.

For cancer of the female breast, the relation between incidence and dose appears consistent from one population to another, whether the population was irradiated instantaneously (as in the case of the atomic-bomb survivors) or irradiated over many months (as in the case of women who received multiple fluoroscopic examinations of the chest during treatment for pulmonary *tuberculosis). This consistency of the dose–incidence relationship suggests that successive small widely spaced exposures are fully additive in their cumulative carcinogenic effects on the breast. Such a relationship implies that the incidence

increases as a linear non-threshold function of the dose.

Other evidence that carcinogenic effects may occur at low doses is the increased incidence of thyroid *tumours in persons who have received doses as low as 0.06–0.20 Sv to the thyroid gland in childhood, and the association between prenatal irradiation and cancer in childhood. The latter, although not proved to be a cause–effect association, implies that prenatal diagnostic X-irradiation may increase a child's risk of juvenile cancer by as much as 40–50 per cent.

Table 3. Estimated lifetime cancer risks of low-level radiation

Site	Risk per 10 000 person-Sv	
	Fatal cancers	Incident cancers
Bone marrow (leukaemia)	15–40	15–50
Thyroid	1–10	25–120
Breast (women only)	30–100	40–200
Lung	25–130	25–140
Stomach Liver Colon	3–50 (each)	5–60
Bone Oesophagus Urinary Bladder Pancreas Lymphatic tissue	2–15 (each)	5–30
Skin	—	1–2
Total (both sexes)	70–500	140–1000

Sources: Jablon, S. and Bailar, J. (1980). The contribution of ionizing radiation to cancer mortality in the United States. *Preventive Medicine*, **8**, 219–26; National Academy of Sciences Advisory Committee on the Biological Effects of Ionizing Radiation (BEIR) (1980). *The Effects on Populations of Exposure to Low Levels of Ionizing Radiation*. Washington, DC; United Nations Scientific Committee on the Affects of Atomic Radiation (1977). *Sources and Effects of Ionizing Radiation*. Report to the General Assembly, with annexes. New York.

Many other types of cancer are also increased in frequency in irradiated populations (Table 3). Although the relevant data are not adequate to characterize the shapes of the dose–incidence curves in most instances, they suffice to indicate that the excess is dose-dependent and that it is generally larger with high-LET radiation than with low-LET radiation. The data also indicate that the excess for a given dose varies appreciably among cancers of different organs.

Following exposure to whole-body irradiation, the total excess of all cancers combined approximates to 0.6–1.8 cases per 1000 persons at risk per Sv per year, beginning 2–10 years after irradiation and continuing indefinitely thereafter. This corresponds to a cumulative lifetime excess of approximately 20–100 additional cancers per 1000 persons at risk per Sv, or an increase of 10–60 per cent per Sv in the relative risk of cancer.

Although these estimates are uncertain, efforts to refine them cannot rely solely on epidemiological studies, since the number of cancers attributable to low-level radiation is so small that any epidemiological study undertaken to measure risks at doses of 1–50 mSv would require a prohibitively large population (i.e. hundreds of thousands of persons). Further efforts aimed at risk assessment must, therefore, include research into the mechanisms of the effects in question, through experiments in laboratory animals and other model systems, in order to refine our understanding of dose–effect relationships.

Comparative magnitude and acceptability of radiation risks. From the above risk estimates, it appears that only a small percentage (1–3 per cent) of all cancers in the general population is attributable to natural background radiation, although up to 20 per cent of lung cancers in non-smokers may result from inhalation of *radon and other naturally occurring radionuclides present in air. The number of cancers attributable to occupational irradiation may, similarly, be inferred to represent less than 1 per cent of the natural incidence of cancer in radiation workers. Hence the average risks to such workers, reckoned in loss of life expectancy, appear to be no greater than those in other 'safe' occupations.

Since no amount of radiation is assumed to be entirely without risk, some level of risk must be assumed to accompany any activity involving radiation exposure, no matter how small the dose. Although some such risks may be negligibly small in comparison with other risks encountered in daily life, no risk is in principle acceptable if it is readily avoidable or if its acceptance fails to provide a commensurate benefit.

A decision about the acceptability of a risk also depends on the perceived, as well as the real magnitude of the risk. A risk tends to be less acceptable to the extent that it is involuntary. The weighing of risk and benefit thus involves value judgements, which can vary widely among individuals and groups. A decision on the social acceptability of a risk cannot, therefore, be relegated to scientists alone. It constitutes a public matter, in which society as a whole must be represented. (See RELIGION, PHILOSOPHY AND ETHICS IN RELATION TO MEDICINE.)

While the risks associated with low-level irradiation from many man-made sources, such as nuclear power plants, ordinarily appear so small as to be readily acceptable, the consequences of a serious radiation accident could be catastrophic. Pessimistically, for example, it has been estimated that an extremely serious nuclear power plant accident could cause hundreds of prompt deaths from radiation sickness in the local population, and thousands of cancer deaths during subsequent decades in persons residing down-wind from the reactor. Similarly, a large-scale nuclear war would almost certainly assume the proportions of a holocaust, resulting in hundreds of millions of deaths from early and late effects. These worst-case possibilities, with their psychosocial and political ramifications, influence public perceptions of the risks associated with nuclear power and, to a lesser extent, radiation devices in general. Such considerations cannot be neglected in the development of public policies to deal with radiation hazards. A. C. UPTON

Further reading
Hall, E. J. (1978). *Radiobiology for the Radiologist*. 2nd edn, New York.
Jablon, S. and Bailar, J. (1980). The contribution of ionizing radiation to cancer mortality in the United States. *Preventive Medicine*, **8**, 219–26.
National Academy of Sciences Advisory Committee on the Biological Effects of Ionizing Radiation (BEIR) (1980). *The Effects on Populations of Exposure to Low Levels of Ionizing Radiation*. Washington, DC.
United Nations Scientific Committee on the Effects of Atomic Radiation (1977). *Sources and Effects of Ionizing Radiation*. Report to the General Assembly, with annexes. New York.

RADICAL. A group of atoms, usually incapable of independent existence, forming part of a molecule and maintaining its identity during chemical changes affecting the rest of the molecule (e.g. NH_4^+, the ammonium radical).

RADICLE, meaning a small root, is a term applied anatomically to the smallest subdivisions of a branching structure.

RADICULITIS is inflammation of a root of a spinal nerve.

RADIOACTIVE SUBSTANCES ACT 1960. This UK Act regulated the keeping and use of radioactive substances and radiation equipment and made provision as to the accumulation and disposal of radioactive waste.

RADIOACTIVITY is the property of spontaneous disintegration possessed by certain unstable atomic nuclei, the disintegration being accompanied by the emission of either *alpha or *beta particles and/or *gamma rays.

RADIOBIOLOGY is the branch of biology concerned with the effects of *radiation on living organisms and the behaviour of radioactive substances in biological systems.

RADIO-COBALT UNIT. Megavoltage apparatus for the *radiotherapy of cancer which uses as the radiation source an isotope of cobalt, ^{60}Co; this isotope, which is easy to produce in a reactor, emits penetrating *gamma rays with a penetration equivalent to *X-rays from a three million volt X-ray machine but can be contained in a much more compact unit (also known as a cobalt teletherapy or cobalt bomb unit). ^{60}Co decays at a rate of about 1 per cent a month (half-life 5.3 years); the source therefore requires replacement after 5–10 years. The radio-cobalt unit was developed in Canada in 1951 and is now one of the two major types of megavoltage equipment in general use (the other being the *linear accelerator).

RADIOGRAPHY is the formation of images on photographic material or fluorescent screens by short wavelength radiation such as *X-rays or *gamma rays. See RADIOLOGY.

RADIOIMMUNOASSAY is a technique for measuring minute quantities of any substance to which an *antibody can be produced. A preparation of the antibody is first saturated with a known quantity of the substance which has been tagged with *radioactivity. The extent of displacement of the radioactive label by the test material when this is added is a measure of how much of the non-radioactive substance it contains.

RADIOISOTOPE. An *isotope possessing *radioactivity, which can therefore be used in physiological and diagnostic studies or to bring therapeutic radiation to bear on tissues in which it is concentrated.

RADIOLOGICAL PROTECTION ACT 1970. This Act created a National Radiological Protection Board for the UK, with the functions of undertaking research and providing advice and services in connection with protection from *radiation hazards. It provided that the new Board would take over the Radiological Protection Service, which was formerly administered by the *Medical Research Council, and the Radiological Protection Division of the UK Atomic Energy Authority's Health and Safety Branch; the Board also took over the functions of the Radioactive Substances Advisory Committee appointed under the Radioactive Substances Act 1948, which was thereby repealed. The Board is subject to the directions of the Health Ministers of England, Scotland, Wales, and Northern Ireland.

RADIOLOGIST. A specialist in the use of electromagnetic radiation for diagnostic imaging. See RADIOLOGY.

RADIOLOGY

Window on the world of disease. Radiology is the field of medicine in which electromagnetic waves are utilized to produce images of normal and abnormal organs in order to permit the accurate diagnosis of disease. In roentgenography, *X-rays generated in an X-ray tube penetrate a selected region of the body, are absorbed in different degrees by different tissues (depending on their specific density), and finally, as remnant unabsor-

bed radiation, blacken a film to produce an image. The chest X-ray is a familiar example. Fluoroscopy (or *radioscopy) utilizes a tube and a fluorescent screen (as a substitute for film) so that moving organs can be viewed in real time. The sonic beam directed at organs by *ultrasound produces an image of reflected waves that depends largely on structural characteristics and tissue interfaces to define 'density' differences. Computed tomography (more often called *computerized axial tomography or CAT scanning in the UK) uses a moving external beam to produce a large series of transmitted and attenuated X-rays that register on multiple detectors, are then digitized by a computer, and are finally reconstructed to afford a cross-sectional view. In *nuclear medicine, an internal source of *radiation—a radioactive isotope—is injected into the body and then registers on external detectors (such as a *gamma camera), producing an image that depicts the distribution of the isotope in tissue.

There are many other specialized branches of radiology, including *arteriography, cardioangiography (or *angiocardiography), *venography, *mammography, and interventional radiology, all of major clinical importance.

How and where did it all begin?

The past. On 8 November 1895, Wilhelm Conrad *Roentgen, during an experiment with the Hittorf–Crookes tube, observed a bright fluorescence of barium platino-cyanide crystals. He assumed initially that the fluorescence might be caused by cathode (beta) rays. Using a fluorescent screen, he removed it beyond the range of cathode rays; when the fluorescence persisted, he realized that the effect was produced by a new kind of rays. Not long afterward, he replaced the screen by a recording photographic plate. One of the dramatic results of this experiment was a picture of his wife's hand. On 28 December 1895, after eight weeks of intensive investigation, Roentgen delivered the manuscript reporting his discovery of X-rays to the Physical Medical Society of Wurzburg. Printed as a preliminary communication in the annals of the society, it was a remarkably succinct and careful description of the behaviour of X-rays (Roentgen, 1895). Two classic papers of March 1896 and May 1897 completed Roentgen's early account, and little was added to these fundamental observations for many years.

By early January 1896, word of Roentgen's discovery and its import had spread around the world. Almost immediately the possibilities of applying the new 'photography' to traumatic lesions of bone fired the imagination and, within a month, X-rays of *fractures had been obtained and published. Early in the year, Edison and many others began intensive work on the fluoroscope. By the end of March 1896, Becher had outlined the stomach and intestines of a dead guinea-pig with lead subacetate and had mentioned the idea of delineating *fistulae in this way (Becher, 1896). In 1896, Walter B.

*Cannon, then a medical student, later to become a great Harvard physiologist, undertook a study, suggested to him by H. P. *Bowditch of Boston, of the feline gastrointestinal tract. Mixing bismuth subnitrate with the food, he observed the movements of the opaque mass in the stomach and subsequently described in detail the nature and site of *peristaltic activity as he saw it on the fluoroscopic screen (Cannon, 1898). He noted in particular the 'extreme sensitiveness' of the cat stomach to anxiety or rage and the marked inhibition of peristalsis that resulted. The usefulness of contrast agents was already becoming apparent. Before the year ended, the first textbook on the subject of X-rays had been published.

Visualization of the blood vessels in a human pathological specimen was achieved several months earlier. In January 1896, soon after the announcement of Roentgen's discovery, Haschek and Lindenthal injected an opaque mixture into the blood vessels of an amputated hand. A published photograph of their original X-ray showed clearly the potential of the method for visualizing the vascular bed. Also of interest that year was the appearance of a volume entitled *The X-ray, or, Photography of the Invisible and its Value in Surgery* (Morton and Hammer, 1896). This collaborative effort by an electrical engineer and a 'professor of the diseases of the mind and nervous system' at the New York Postgraduate Medical School, reflected a growing interest in the new field of roentgenology. In the text were not only chapters on normal anatomy, fractures and dislocations, stiff joints, and foreign objects in the body, but also a section on medicolegal applications of X-rays.

By 1900 a volume entitled *The Use of the Roentgen Ray by the Medical Department of the U.S. Army in the War with Spain* had been published (Borden, 1900). Gunshot fragments in the soft tissues and traumatic lesions of bone were illustrated in large plates in this volume.

By the time that Voelcker and Lichtenberg (1906) introduced retrograde *pyelography to the field of *urographic diagnosis, a number of medical schools had organized departments of roentgenology. In Kassabian's voluminous textbook of 1907, *Roentgen Rays and Electrotherapeutics*, the chapters on diseases of the thorax and diseases of the abdominal organs warranted 60 pages for adequate description. Cannon's research interests in gastrointestinal physiology bore remarkable fruit within a decade after the discovery of X-rays, as clinical radiology of the gastrointestinal tract became a reality. By 1908, the radiographic appearance of *gastric ulcer and gastric *carcinoma had been fully described. Imaging studies of peristaltic activity in the gastrointestinal tract of man rapidly became as important as bone and joint radiology.

Important technical improvements early in the century made radiography safer and more effective and new areas became more accessible. In 1918,

*Dandy of *Johns Hopkins performed the first air *ventriculogram, visualizing enlarged *ventricles in children with *hydrocephalus. Soon afterwards, the discovery that intravenous sodium iodide was not only excreted by the kidneys but opacified the urine, led to the description of clinical urography in 1923. About the same time that intravenous contrast agents were first injected in the arteries and veins of living subjects (Abrams, 1981a), Graham and Cole used their knowledge of physiology and chemistry to develop *cholecystography by utilizing brominated phenolphthalein, excreted into the biliary tract (see BILE DUCT) (Graham, Cole, and Copher, 1924). A year later, Merrill Sosman of the Peter Bent Brigham Hospital observed cyclic reopacification of the *gall bladder three days after the 'Graham–Cole' test. Realizing that the opaque salt must have been reabsorbed from the gastrointestinal tract, he pointed out the possibility of using an oral agent to render the gall bladder opaque. Oral cholecystography was first applied to man during the same year.

Bronchography (visualization of the *bronchi) in 1922, *carotid arteriography (demonstration of the blood vessels to the brain) in 1928, laminography (focused sectional imaging of visceral and bony structures) in 1929, and angiocardiography (contrast visualization of the cardiac chambers and great vessels) in 1931 were all important milestones in the development of radiology. Image-amplified fluoroscopy, developed during the 1940s and 1950s, constituted the most important technical advance. This removed fluoroscopy from a dark room and a relatively poor image at high X-ray dose, to a setting in which both the accuracy and the versatility of the method were remarkably increased (Chamberlain, 1942).

The present. Radiology in the 1980s, besides shedding important light on disordered physiology, represents the most important approach to delineating gross pathological anatomy in living man. It is literally the foundation of every creative new surgical therapeutic approach of the 20th c. Without sophisticated radiology, there could be no advanced surgery of the central nervous system, of the lungs, of the stomach, duodenum, and large bowel, of the kidneys, and certainly not of the heart or vascular bed. The method depicts the relationship of gross pathology to clinical signs and symptoms with a special kind of elegance. If there is dullness to percussion together with increased breath sounds, the chest film will show the consolidative process characteristic of *pneumonia; if the dullness is accompanied by diminished breath sounds *pleural effusion will be evident. Radiology reflects functional anatomy with clarity and an unimpaired fidelity to fact (the structure of bones and joints; the position of calcified *valves in the cardiac mass; the relationship of the pons to the fourth ventricle and the sella turcica; pathology (the difference between *tuberculosis and carcinoma in the lung; ulcer and *neoplasm of the stomach; papillary necrosis and medullary sponge kidney; physiology (the mode of *oesophageal and gastric peristalsis; *urinary bladder emptying in health and disease; the mechanics of *myocardial contraction or valve motion); pharmacology (the effect of a fatty meal on the gall bladder; of epinephrine (*adrenaline) on normal and neoplastic vessels in the kidney); and the whole gamut of diagnostic medicine visualized differentially (*haematemesis caused by ulcer, carcinoma, varices, or acute gastritis).

The radiologist as a consultant and a teacher may work with medical students and residents. But throughout his professional life, his teaching is also levelled at the internist, the paediatrician, the surgeon, and indeed all of the specialists in medicine, with the possible exception of the psychiatrist. He spends relatively less time with patients and a great deal more with physicians than most of his colleagues, and he must speak their language with lucidity and sophistication. His opinions are almost invariably subject to verification by the clinical course of the patient, the surgeon's knife, or the pathologist's microscope. Because he deals in gross disorders of visceral anatomy and physiology with a high degree of specificity, he and his colleagues may together learn in a continuum not only about the accuracy of diagnostic indices but equally about the chronology and biology of disease. In no other way can the sequence of visceral and peripheral changes be mirrored with such precision over a period of many years, with the original data intact for all to see and the professional commitment available for all to analyse.

Research in radiology. Research in radiology until the last 15–20 years was largely technical and/or reportorial. For good reasons, clinical observation and analysis formed an important element in the scholarly activity of the radiologist: after all, the first gastrointestinal study is only 65 years old; that of cerebral arteriography is 50 years old; that of angiocardiography is 40 years old; and cinefluorography has been applied to man at acceptable dose levels for barely two and a half decades. It is hardly unexpected, therefore, that a wealth of interpretive correlations have amplified and deepened the whole framework of medical diagnosis in the years since Roentgen.

Techniques developed in the sixties and seventies were concentrated on the vascular bed: arterial, venous, and lymphatic (Abrams, 1981b). These methods added broad dimensions to our capacity to diagnose disease, as well as to analyse the spread of neoplasms in the lymphatics and to undertake fundamental cardiovascular investigations. In the modern era, research in diagnostic radiology finds its natural application in the study of function, normal and abnormal, and the Roentgen approach is uniquely capable of recording information of value and significance when correlated with other physiological parameters. As a

clinical investigator, the radiologist has continuing opportunities to study blood flow and circulatory dynamics as a part of his examination. With the gastroenterologist he may concentrate on the problems of intestinal motility in man; with the urologist on bladder and kidney function; with the neurologist on cerebral blood flow. In the laboratory he may work in the areas of physiology, pharmacology, neuroanatomy, microradiography, biochemistry, and others.

It is important to emphasize that the field of radiology goes far beyond the application of external radiation to the diagnosis and characterization of human disease. Nuclear medicine, with its internal sources of radiant energy, has become an important segment of the field, because of its imaging yield and also because of its capacity for dynamic retrieval of physiological data. Radioactive isotopes have been applied to the study of virtually every viscus in man, and multiple relatively non-invasive techniques of studying normal and abnormal physiology have been devised.

Another important growth sector within the discipline is diagnostic *ultrasound, which has suddenly become the centre of an explosion in technology. The data derived from B-scanning, dynamic real-time scanning, and *echocardiography have given a remarkable impetus to obtaining sharper and more dynamic images. An important advantage of ultrasound is its non-invasive character and the fact that it has no demonstrated injurious effects, in contrast to X-rays and gamma rays. In *obstetrics, the logarithmic growth rate of this technique is based not only on its ability to locate the placenta and characterize fetal growth and development, but also on the fact that it does not expose patients to ionizing radiation.

Radiological methods have become so integral an element in our approach to visceral disease in man that it seems highly likely that many of the conventional radiological examinations now in use will continue to be applied for a long period. The special procedures are equally important in their yield of diagnostic and physiological information. Although some may be modified or replaced within the coming years, this will occur only when major improvements in information gathering techniques have become available.

Within the past 15 years, the field of so-called 'interventional' radiology has become an important aspect of patient care. The intravascular *catheter is used today not only to inject contrast agents in order to define the site of gastrointestinal or intracranial bleeding, for example, but also in some circumstances to infuse pharmacological agents that constrict the vascular bed and stop the bleeding. A whole new field of pharmacoangiography has thus developed. Similarly, the radiologist has become concerned with the technology of balloon catheters, as a means of obstructing flow in circulatory beds in which uncontrolled haemorrhage is a threat to life. There has been increased interest in the character of intravascular *embolic materials, and the delivery of these materials to control local bleeding without rendering other segments *ischaemic has become both an art and a science.

Using ultrasound or computerized axial tomography (CAT) the radiologist has become involved in *biopsy of the liver, pancreas, lymph nodes, retroperitoneum, and kidney. He can drain abdominal and pelvic *abscesses non-operatively, and leaves catheters *in situ* for longer-term evacuation of *pus. He removes *gallstones and actively intervenes in the face of *intussusception and *volvulus of the colon. He infuses chemotherapeutic agents and/or embolic materials into neoplastic beds. Percutaneous lung biopsy performed with the image-amplified fluoroscope is now a standardized procedure (Herman and Hessel, 1977). Venous sampling is an everyday occurrence in the radiology department: used for *parathyroid and *adrenal tumours and for renovascular *hypertension, it requires specific skills to place the sampling catheter precisely in the venous drainage sites necessary for specific sampling (Paster, Adams, and Abrams, 1974). In the patient threatened with pulmonary embolism from peripheral venous *thrombosis, the radiologist may now place a filter in the inferior vena cava to stop the progress of a clot towards the lung. When the intestine is deprived of adequate blood supply because of vasoconstriction of its vascular bed, he may find it necessary to infuse *vasodilator drugs. As a therapist, the diagnostic radiologist has even become involved in adrenal ablation and in the distribution of radioactive microspheres to pancreatic carcinoma via the selective arterial catheter.

Most of these techniques have been developed in the experimental laboratory, originating in the clinical setting and ultimately returning there. Problems which cannot be solved in clinical investigation, unanswered questions about the diagnosis or treatment of disease in man—these are the stimuli that prompt the establishment of animal models in the radiology laboratories. The radiologist, involved in the use of *vasopressin in the mesenteric circulation to control bleeding, has taken a new look at the systemic effects of the drug on other vascular beds in animal models. Because he deals with renal ischaemia commonly, and because the collateral circulation of virtually all visceral systems is very much a part of his angiographic studies, the stimulus for this circulation has become a focus of concern (Cowan *et al.*, 1978). Because he applies pharmacodynamic responses to enhance perfusion of tumours, it is natural that he would be interested in the nature of the tumour vascular bed and in its differences from the norm (Abrams, 1964; Young, Hollenberg, and Abrams, 1979). The *oliguric or *anuric patient has been studied so frequently by radiological methods that it seems quite natural for models of unilateral renal failure to be explored intensively in the radiological animal laboratory, with a view to reversing the pre-glomerular vasoconstriction that exists in this setting (Knapp *et al.*, 1972). The angio-architecture of the lymph node during the immune response (Herman, Yamamoto, and Mellins, 1972); the renal vascular changes that accompany hypertension (Abrams, 1983); the development of new tissue-specific and tumour-specific radiopharmaceuticals for diagnosis and treatment (Kaplan and Adelstein, 1976); the assessment of varying tissue response to ultrasound, and the capacity to distinguish between normal and neoplastic tissue—all of these represent but a few of the explorations in which radiology is now involved.

An important area of research in radiology is concentrated on decreasing the radiation dose and increasing the information yield. This is a critical focus because medical radiation is the most important single man-made source of the radiation burden borne by the population of the world. Because radiology is so important to diagnosis, over 140 million X-ray examinations are performed in the USA each year. This means that every man, woman, and child, on average, has a radiographic examination annually or bi-annually. The matter of decreasing dose or improving the quality of data retrieval is obviously the subject of a large and important sector of radiological research; namely, equipment development, technology assessment, and diagnostic decision-making (Abrams, 1979). Concern for the impact of radiological examinations on clinical management and health outcome has brought the radiologist directly into the field of utilization and cost-effectiveness studies (Abrams and McNeil, 1978a, b).

The future. The last decade has seen the most important development in the imaging field since image-intensified fluoroscopy became a reality. The principle behind computerized axial tomography (CAT scanning) has been known for a long time: namely, that different tissues attenuate monochromatic or polychromatic X-ray beams to a different degree so that the 'attenuation' or 'absorption' coefficient varies significantly. Except when these tissue differences were very great, however, they could not be depicted by conventional radiography. It was Hounsfield, an English physicist, who devised an instrument to detect the relatively fine differences and then put the computer to work depicting them as a reconstructed transaxial image (Hounsfield, 1973).

Because the scanning time was relatively long and demanded immobilization, the process was highly sensitive to motion blurring. Consequently the initial application of CAT was to the brain, because patients could lie with the skull immobilized for relatively long periods. It soon became clear that CAT could detect intracranial tumours, cerebral *subdural haematoma, brain *infarctions, and other abnormalities which previously had been definable only by relatively invasive approaches. Once cranial CAT had been proved useful, it was only a matter of time before the method was applied to body scanning. Because attenuation coefficients differ among various organs, it is possible to identify specific masses or viscera within the abdomen and thorax on these scans. For example, radiolucent gallstones may be apparent within the lumen of the gall bladder, which in turn is different in density from the surrounding liver. Dilated biliary radicles are also detectable. None of these structures can, of course, be visualized on standard X-rays without special studies. Since the scanner is exquisitely sensitive to small amounts of iodine (in the contrast medium), the biliary tree, including the common duct, may be visualized in the *jaundiced patient—something not possible previously without direct puncture of the liver.

Another important advantage of CAT is its ability to detect *metastatic foci of disease at a relatively early stage. In the liver, for example, such lesions are apparent on routine scans if they are above a certain size; otherwise, they readily become visible following pharmacological enhancement. Indeed, an entire new field of radiopharmacology has developed in order to augment the capabilities of CAT.

CAT has proved to be highly accurate in detecting diseases in the *pancreas, which is ordinarily very difficult to evaluate. Visualization of small pancreatic lesions after pharmacological enhancement, followed by ultrasonically guided, fine-needle aspiration biopsy, allows diagnosis that would otherwise be possible only after far more complex procedures. CAT has similar advantages for evaluation of the *adrenal gland, the bladder, the *prostate, the *uterus, the *ovary, the retroperitoneum, the *spleen, and the kidneys.

In the thorax the vascular structures of the lungs may be seen; perhaps more importantly, the *mediastinum may be dissected atraumatically, and the oesophagus, tracheobronchial tree, and vascular structures are all readily separated.

CAT is highly effective in planning radiotherapeutic treatment. It represents an ideal tool for imaging both the tumour mass itself and its relationship to surrounding organs. The image can be digitized and, with the aid of the computer, superimposed isodose curves permit calculation of dosages to the tumour and surrounding tissues. This is also an accurate method of monitoring the results of tumour therapy.

With the new developments in CAT and ultrasound, and with the investigation of new radionuclides that are tumour-specific or tissue-specific and therefore serve to advance either imaging or therapy, radiology has entered a period of remarkable growth and change. Emission tomography (using internal sources of energy or radioisotopes, e.g. *positron emission tomography) is now being applied to the study of intracranial and cardiac disease, with promising results. Digital radiography is designed for instantaneous storage of the image in digital form in the computer, reconstruction of the image after processing, and image storage on a tape or disk. In vascular radiology, digital subtraction allows the elimination of some of the more invasive intravascular catheter procedures. *Nuclear magnetic resonance (NMR), a method used in biochemistry until recently, is now being adapted for imaging, and holds great promise both for diagnosis and for the study of disease. As used for imaging, NMR depicts tissue proton distribution and concentration, measuring 'relaxation' times and spin density to produce an image that is reconstructed in cross-section. NMR can detect plaques in *multiple sclerosis, brain tumours, and areas of decreased blood flow in the brain or heart.

Thus, radiology, the field of diagnostic imaging, employs multiple modalities in order to define both the character and extent of disease. In less than a century, it has become a critically important tool in the exploration and management of disease in living man.   H. L. ABRAMS

References

Abrams, H. L. (1964). Altered drug response to tumour vessels in man. *Nature*, **201**, 167.

Abrams, H. L. (1979). The 'overutilization' of X-rays. *New England Journal of Medicine*, **300**, 1213.

Abrams, H. L. (1981a). The development of angiocardiography. In Snellen, H. A., Dunning, A. J. and Arntzenius, A. C. (eds), *History and Perspectives of Cardiology: Catheterization, Angiography, Surgery, and Concepts of Circular Control*. The Hague.

Abrams, H. L. (1981b). Research in diagnostic radiology: a holistic perspective. *Clinical Radiology*, **32**, 121.

Abrams, H. L. (1983). Renal arteriography in hypertension. In Abrams, H. L. (ed.). *Abrams' Angiography: Vascular and Interventional Radiology*. Boston.

Abrams, H. L. and McNeil, B. J. (1978a). Medical implications of computed tomography ('CAT scanning'). Part I. *New England Journal of Medicine*, **298**, 255.

Abrams, H. L. and McNeil, B. J. (1978b). Medical implications of computed tomography ('CAT scanning'). Part II. *New England Journal of Medicine*, **298**, 310.

Becher, W. (1896). Zur Anwendung des roentgenischen Verfahrens in der Medizin. *Deutsche Medizinische Wochenschrift*, **22**, 202.

Borden, W. C. (1900). *The Use of the Roentgen Ray by the Medical Department of the U.S. Army in the War with Spain*. Washington, DC.

Cannon, W. B. (1898). The movements of the stomach studied by means of the roentgen ray. *American Journal of Physiology*, **1**, 359.

Chamberlain, W. E. (1942). Fluoroscopes and fluoroscopy. *Radiology*, **51**, 359.

Cowan, D. F., Hollenberg, N. K., Connelly, C. M., Williams, D. H. and Abrams, H. L. (1978). Increased collateral arterial and venous endothelial cell turnover after renal artery stenosis in the dog. *Investigative Radiology*, **13**, 143.

Graham, E. A., Cole, W. H. and Copher, G. A. (1924). Visualization of the gallbladder by the sodium salt of tetrabromphenolphthalein. *Journal of the American Medical Association*, **82**, 1777.

Haschek, E. and Lindenthal, O. T. (1896). A contribution to the practical use of the photography according to Roentgen. *Wien Klinische Wochenschrift*, **9**, 63.

Herman, P. G. and Hessel, S. J. (1977). The diagnostic accuracy and complications of closed lung biopsies. *Radiology*, **125**, 11.

Herman, P. G., Yamamoto, I. and Mellins, H. Z. (1972). Blood microcirculation in the lymph node during the primary immune response. *Journal of Experimental Medicine*, **136**, 697.

Hounsfield, G. N. (1973). Computerized transverse axial scanning (tomography description system). *British Journal of Radiology*, **46**, 1016.

Kaplan, W. D. and Adelstein, S. J. (1976). The radionuclide identification of tumors. *Cancer*, **37**, 487.

Kassabian, M. K. (1907). *Rontgen Rays and Electrotherapeutics with Chapters on Radium and Phototherapy*. Philadelphia.

Knapp, R., Hollenberg, N. K., Busch, G. J. and Abrams, H. L. (1972). Prolonged unilateral renal failure induced by intra-arterial norepinephrine infusion in the dog. *Investigative Radiology*, **7**, 164.

Morton, W. G. and Hammer, E. W. (1896). *The X-ray, or, Photography of the Invisible and its Value in Surgery*. New York.

Paster, S. B., Adams, D. F. and Abrams, H. L. (1974). Errors in renal vein renin collections. *American Journal of Roentgenology*, **122**, 804.

Roentgen, W. C. (1895). On a new kind of rays. *Erste Mitt Sitzber Phys-Med. Ges. (Wurzburg)*, 137.

Voelcker, F. and Lichtenberg, A. (1906). Pyelographie (Rontgenographie des Nieurenbeckens nach Kollargolfullung). *Münchener Medizinische Wochenschrift*, **53**, 105.

Young, S. W., Hollenberg, N. K. and Abrams, H. L. (1979). The influence of implantation site on tumor blood flow and growth. *European Journal of Cancer*, **15**, 771.

RADIO-OPAQUE SUBSTANCES are impervious to *X-rays and therefore employed as contrast media to outline hollow structures in various radiographic techniques. See RADIOLOGY.

RADIOSCOPY is the examination of structures and their movement from *X-ray images projected on to a fluorescent screen (also known as fluoroscopy).

RADIOTHERAPIST. A specialist in the application of ionizing radiation to the treatment of disease. See RADIOTHERAPY.

RADIOTHERAPY (also known as radiation therapy or radiation oncology) is the branch of clinical medicine concerned with applications of *ionizing radiation in the treatment of disease, and is now devoted almost entirely to the treatment of *cancer. Its success in the cure of a malignant tumour depends on the greater ability of normal tissue to recover under suitable conditions from a given dose of radiation, compared with that of the tumour. The agents employed—either electromagnetic radiations (photons) such as *X-rays and *gamma rays, or corpuscular radiations (particles) such as *electrons, *neutrons, *protons, and *pions—have in common the ability to produce ionization in living matter, and the biological effects depend on the intensity and distribution of this ionization. The method of radiotherapy used depends on the type of tumour, on its size and anatomical position, and on the extent of spread. It may be applied by directing external beams of high-energy radiation to a defined volume of the body, or by inserting radioactive sources in or around the tumour, or less commonly by administering radioactive isotopes systemically. Radiotherapy may be prescribed with a view to possible cure of the tumour, or when because of spread this is not feasible, as a palliative measure to control local tumour deposits and relieve symptoms.

When a beam of X-rays impinges on matter the penetration depends on the energy and this in turn depends on the generating voltage. For instance X-ray beams used for treating skin cancer have energies of 50 000–140 000 electron-volts, while megavoltage beams used for treating deeply placed tumours have energies of over 1 million electron-volts (1 MeV). *Linear accelerators for clinical use produce X-rays of 4–35 MeV compared with the 1.25 MeV of the gamma radiation from a *radio-cobalt unit. The energy of an X-ray beam is mainly absorbed by ejecting electrons from the atoms through which it passes, independent of the manner in which these are combined into molecules. The ions produced are concentrated along the track of the ejected electron (Fig. 1) and the biological effects are due directly to this energy deposition. The ionization effect being fundamental, this is used in the measurement of the quantity of radiation: the modern (SI) unit of absorbed dose is the gray, one centigray (cGy) being equivalent to an energy absorption of 100 ergs per gram (0.01 joules per kilogram) and corresponding to the previous dosage unit of the rad.

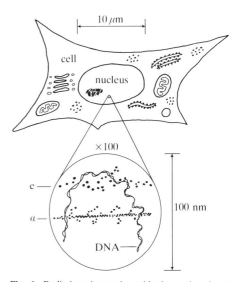

Fig. 1. Radiations interacting with tissue give rise to concentrated columns of ionization along their tracks, less intense for photons and electrons (e) than for heavy particles (α). The sensitive biological targets within a cell are very small. (Reproduced by courtesy of Professor J. Fowler and Messrs Hilger Ltd)

The biological effects of radiations are complex because many different parts of the intricate cellular mechanism are affected. The energy of the radiation dissipated by ionization is immediately used in chemical reactions in an extremely short time, perhaps a millionth of a second. Several hundreds of these primary reactions may occur inside a single cell submitted to as little as 1 cGy of radiation, but not all may result in biological effects. Visible cellular damage, appearing after an interval of hours or weeks, affects both nucleus and cytoplasm; chromosomes may be broken and may reconstitute abnormally, abnormal vacuoles may form, and the mitochondria on which respiratory enzymes are organized may appear abnormal (see CELL). Cells are rarely killed immediately but die after one or several divisions. The inhibition of *mitosis is usually related to interference with *deoxyribonucleic acid (DNA) synthesis, the important lesion being double strand breakage. Cells are more sensitive in certain phases of the cell cycle, particularly in early DNA synthesis (S) phase and in the mitotic (M) phase. The reproductive integrity, or the capacity of a cell for indefinite proliferation in a suitable environment, is fairly easily destroyed by irradiation, and physical factors of radiation dose and its distribution in time and space are important in determining the observed effect. While the higher the dose the greater the proportion of cells sterilized, the milieu of the cell at the time of irradiation is also significant, and especially the *oxygen supply: cells that are fully oxygenated are sterilized experimentally by about one-third of the dose necessary to produce the same degree of damage if the cells were completely devoid of oxygen (anoxic). The technique of *clonal cultivation of mammalian cells *in vitro* has permitted the quantitative analysis of radiation-dose/cell-survival relationships, and the resulting survival curves (Fig. 2) prove to be exponential, after an initial 'shoulder' region shown to be due to recovery from sublethal damage. With multiple exposures, new variables are introduced into the response, with recovery in varying degrees occurring in the intervals between subsequent doses.

The effects of irradiation on normal tissue have been studied in great detail both clinically and experimentally for, in essence, they are the limiting factor in the local cure of cancer by this means. The expression of cellular radiation-induced changes in tissues depends particularly on their normal replacement rate or 'cellular turnover', rapidly replicating tissues showing their responses early. Skin reaction, shown by redness (erythema) confined to the irradiated area, appears after 8–14 days and gradually subsides with scaling and perhaps residual pigmentation. Similarly, when the mouth or upper respiratory tract are irradiated a *mucosal surface reaction occurs; and during abdominal or pelvic irradiation, diarrhoea may occur from the effect on the intestinal mucosa. When large volumes of tissues are irradiated, depression of the

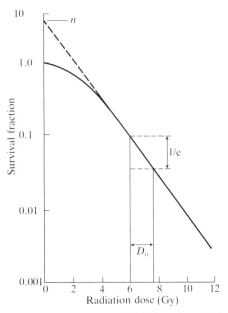

Fig. 2. A dose-response curve for the loss of reproductive capacity of mammalian cells from irradiation consists typically of an exponential straight portion, preceded by a 'shoulder' due to recovery from sublethal damage. Curves from different cell lines, both normal and malignant, can be compared by their mathematical characteristics of D_0, the dose necessary to reduce survival to $1/e$ (or 37 per cent), and the 'extrapolation number' n which is a measure of the initial shoulder. Some of the more radioresistant tumours have high extrapolation numbers

blood-forming *bone marrow is often the limiting factor, the circulating *lymphocytes being rapidly affected, then the *platelets, and a little later the granular cells (*granulocytes). All these effects are dose-dependent: a large body of information has been acquired over the years on the radiation tolerance of normal tissues under various conditions, so that in clinical practice the dose schedule can be chosen to enable these tissues to recover. Whatever the tissue or anatomical region, radiation tolerance varies inversely with the volume irradiated, so that the larger the volume which has to be included in the field, the lower the dose permissible.

While the acute and subacute effects on rapidly responding tissues are responsible for the symptoms which occur during and immediately after a course of radiotherapy, the truly dose-limiting effects in local cure of cancer are late tissue reactions in which a common factor is an effect on the vascular and *connective tissue present in all organs. Small *arterioles and *capillaries are particularly vulnerable, and subsequent impairment of blood supply aggravates the direct effect on connective tissue cells, resulting in late *fibrosis and *atrophy. Depending on the organ affected the latent period for vasculoconnective tissue damage varies from a few months to several years. The tumour itself receives its blood supply from the host tissue, and the stroma of the 'tumour bed' necessarily receives the full dose and cannot be spared the brunt of irradiation. Certain 'critical organs' are, however, particularly sensitive—importantly the eyes, the lungs, spinal cord, and kidneys—and appropriate measures are taken to shield them during routine radiotherapy. The *gonads are also highly radiosensitive and for both somatic and genetic reasons particular care is taken to avoid their being irradiated. Clinical experience over half a century has shown that fractionation, the spreading of dose over a period of time, is more effective than is a single dose in eradicating tumours with a minimum of normal tissue damage. For curative treatment the radiation dose is thus commonly divided into a number of fractions given daily or thrice weekly over a period of 3–6 weeks, depending on the type of tumour, its site, and the volume to be irradiated.

Tumours (see ONCOLOGY) vary greatly in their clinical response to irradiation and in general the more cellular the tumour and the more primitive the cell type the greater the likelihood of radiosensitivity. Tumour growth is the result of a complex balance between cell production and cell loss. The average time for a human tumour to double in size varies widely, but is often about 3 months (in contrast to 1 week for experimental tumours in mice); however, it may be as short as 1 week in embryonal tumours or as long as several years for *adenocarcinoma. The 'growth fraction', the proportion of actively proliferating cells, may also vary from 100 per cent in embryonal tumours to 5 per cent in breast cancer; in the former most new cells contribute to the net growth of the tumour. Again the 'cell loss factor', due to cell death and exfoliation, varies greatly but is often of the order of 75 per cent. The kinetics of tumour cells is also influenced by the proliferation rate and pattern of branching of the vascular capillary network supplying the tumour which is again vulnerable to irradiation. The effect of radiotherapy depends on the relative kinetics and sensitivities of tumour and normal tissues within the beam: after radiation dosage capable of sterilizing a high proportion of malignant cells an embryonal tumour (with a high growth fraction and cell-loss factor) may rapidly regress even within days, while a well-differentiated adenocarcinoma with low growth parameters may take months to regress. Large tumours are more difficult to control locally than are small ones, partly because of the number of cells to be sterilized but also, from outstripping the blood supply and spontaneous cell death, they have regions which are practically anoxic and in which the cells can survive the largest dose of radiation tolerable by normal tissues. For practical purposes three grades of responsiveness are recognized, tumours being subdivided into those of high, moderate, and low radiosensitivity. The most sensitive are mainly those of embryonal or lymphoid

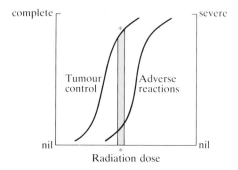

Fig. 3. The degree of tumour control and the adverse responses of normal tissues appear as sigmoidal curves when plotted against radiation dose. The skill of the radiation oncologist is to choose a dose regimen (such as *) giving the best differentiation between good and adverse responses

origin: they respond to dosage which may be tolerated by a large volume of tissue, and can be treated even when extensive; examples are the primitive tumours of childhood and the *lymphomas (including *Hodgkin's disease). Tumours of moderate radiosensitivity arise mainly in surface *epithelium or *glands, for example carcinomas of skin, upper respiratory tract, breast, and uterus, and they can be sterilized by high radiation dosage if confined to a reasonable compass. Those of low radiosensitivity are a heterogeneous group including bone *sarcoma, malignant *melanoma, and gastro-intestinal cancer but, applying recent research, radiotherapy may have an adjunctive role in controlling such tumours after surgery.

Bearing in mind these fundamental considerations the skill of the radiotherapist is to select in the circumstances of the individual patient an effective radiation dose and technique which will give clear differentiation between good and adverse responses (Fig. 3). The current scope and application of radiotherapy will be considered presently.

The development of radiotherapy. Very soon after the discovery of X-rays by *Roentgen in 1895 and of radioactivity by Becquerel in 1896 it became evident that the radiations produced or emitted had remarkable biological effects. The observation of reddening of the skin and loss of hair noticed in the operators after a few weeks led quite quickly to attempts to use these effects in treatment. Leopold Freund of Vienna may be regarded as the 'father of radiotherapy' by producing epilation in a hairy mole in November 1896. The responses of normal and pathological tissues were gradually documented and indicated a selective biological effect: some tissues would be completely destroyed and the growth of some forms of cancer arrested, leaving other tissues apparently healed and intact. The first cancer cure by X-rays—that of a basal cell carcinoma (*rodent ulcer) of the nose—was recorded by Thor Stenbeck from Sweden in 1899. A few medical pioneers in both Europe and America over the next two decades laid the foundations of therapeutic radiology, although their methods could only be those of trial and error, their apparatus unreliable in both quantity and quality of its output, and methods of dose determination imprecise. They soon observed that in addition to beneficial effects such as tumour regression there were many instances of severe damage caused by exposure to radiation. Persistent *ulceration followed high dosage in the treatment of some patients; chronic *dermatitis and subsequent carcinogenesis occurred on the hands of pioneer radiologists from the cumulative effect of multiple small doses, each of which had produced no appreciable clinical effect. There were also a number of premature deaths from unexplained *anaemia among radiation workers. Thus attention became increasingly directed to the study of protection methods and ultimately to the setting of international standards. (See also RADIATION, IONIZING.)

While radiotherapy was first applied in a variety of proliferative diseases, because of undesirable latent effects it became used predominantly in the treatment of cancer, first of superficial forms until with technological development it was possible to irradiate deep tumours. Despite significant advances the clinical studies were for many years at a disadvantage in that treatment with X-rays was carried out by general radiologists who, at the same time, were developing the specialty of X-ray diagnosis, while the development of treatment with *radium was mainly in the hands of some surgeons, gynaecologists, and dermatologists who had a particular interest in cancer. The essential similarity of both forms of radiation was inadequately recognized, with a tendency towards the development of two distinct forms of treatment which persisted in many countries for half a century. Those who devoted their energies to the total clinical investigation of therapeutic radiology and cancer were quite a small band, notably in Sweden, France, the UK, and the USA in the period between 1925 and 1950, and their clinical enterprise enabled radiotherapy to develop to the present time, when it is recognized as one of the most important methods of treating cancer. Their efforts were, however, very much dependent on scientific progress in physical and biological disciplines, and the development of radiotherapy has been characterized by the closest collaboration between doctors and scientists—starting earlier than in any other branch of medicine—and continuing actively at the present time.

Radiation sources. The early development of X-ray therapy was inhibited by the erratic behaviour of the apparatus and the low penetration of the radiations. With the introduction of the hot-cathode high-vacuum tube by Coolidge in the USA in 1914 it became possible to have stable penetrating beams, ultimately of over 250 kV and capable of 'cross-firing' a deep tumour, and this heralded

the era of 'deep X-ray therapy' which began in the 1920s. Notable responses were obtained in a number of previously untreatable tumours, but the limiting factor was still the inevitable skin reaction at the portals of beam entry. The penetrating power depending essentially on beam energy, physicians strongly supported the engineers in their search for new methods of high voltage generation. At the instigation of Rutherford, Cockcroft and Walton in 1931 developed a voltage multiplier, used the following year at Cambridge to accelerate protons and to cause the first artificial atomic transmutation. By combining this circuit with a continuously evacuated tube Allibone achieved the goal of 1 000 000 volts, and the first clinical equipment so designed was installed at *St Bartholomew's Hospital in London in 1936. In addition to the planned advantage of higher depth dose, were found further benefits of reduced skin reaction, stricter beam collimation to avoid vital structures, uniform energy absorption in different tissues, and a high radiation output. Such diseases as inoperable rectal carcinoma became controllable for the first time, and this was the portent of the new era of 'megavoltage' X-ray therapy which continues to the present time.

The search for methods of providing reliable and versatile high energy beams continued in the next decade as a by-product of physical research, particularly in the USA. R. van de Graaff had conceived an ingenious electrostatic generator with very high voltage achieved by conveying charged particles from ground potential to the output terminal by a rapidly moving insulated belt. In the energy range of 2–4 million volts these generators were surprisingly compact and gave many years of use in therapy until replaced by the most modern types of equipment. The attainment of really high energies required a different approach, that of accelerating a particle many times through a relatively small potential difference. The *cyclotron constructed by E. O. Lawrence and M. S. Livingston in 1932 used the principle of magnetic resonance to maintain particles in circular orbit, and although electrons cannot be so accelerated to produce X-rays, very high energy (up to 200 MeV) can be achieved for protons and deuterons. When the high-speed alpha particles from the cyclotron impinge on a beryllium target, intense beams of neutrons are produced and may be used in cancer therapy. Another important milestone was the *betatron, a device for accelerating electrons developed by D. W. Kerst at the University of Illinois in 1943. Electrons are accelerated in a circular orbit by a changing and increasing magnetic field, and the resulting beams of 15–40 MeV electrons and X-rays had a valuable place in therapy.

The two major types of megavoltage equipment now in common use, the *radio-cobalt unit and the *linear accelerator, depended on developments in nuclear physics and in electronics which occurred during the Second World War. While teletherapy machines containing a radium source of 4–10 g had been developed in the 1930s, their use was limited by the very high cost of the radium and by difficulties of shielding. All this was changed in 1951 when strong sources of cobalt-60 were made available in Canada from the heavy water pile at Chalk River. H. E. Johns realized that it was now feasible to place a small source at a relatively large distance from the patient and emulate a high-energy X-ray machine. Thus was developed at Saskatoon the radio-cobalt unit which has proved to be one of the major steps in progress in the history of radiotherapy. From 1951 the production of cobalt sources and units expanded to an extent that 25 years later more radiotherapy was carried out with these units throughout the world than with all other types of radiation.

As a direct result of war-time radar research, D. W. Fry and his colleagues at Malvern, England, succeeded in 1946 in accelerating electrons by radiofrequency waves to produce the first 'linear accelerator'. The electrons injected when the wave velocity is least are carried forward with increasing velocity on the crest of the wave, much as a surfboard rider is carried on the crest of an ocean wave, and with powerful radiofrequency (RF) generators (klystrons) electrons could be accelerated to energies in the megavoltage range. The possibilities of medical application were immediately seized upon and linear accelerators producing X-rays or electrons in the 4–36 MeV range have been developed since 1950. They have the particular advantage of producing a high output of closely collimated high energy X-ray beams which in highly developed countries are becoming the mainstay of external beam radiotherapy (Fig. 4). Both radio-cobalt units and linear accelerators are now 'isocentrically mounted', that is the source can be made to move in an arc of constant radius about the centre of the tumour volume, a further adjunct to precision of treatment.

Within three years of its discovery radium was applied in the treatment of cancer and for 70 years it remained the most useful method of radiotherapy for small tumours which were accessible near the surface or in body cavities. During this period there was steady progress in the technique of applying the sources, particularly for gynaecological purposes, which became a highly skilled procedure. With the advent of artificially produced radioisotopes from the nuclear pile more convenient sources of localized gamma-radiation have been produced—such as caesium-137, cobalt-60, and iridium-192—and, with advantages of better radiation distribution and ease of protecting personnel, these have almost entirely superseded the use of radium in developed countries. Nevertheless the achievements of the radium era were real; they provided the basis of scientific radiotherapy and the technical methods developed are still current in the applications of the newer sealed sources.

With the wide range of artificial radioactive isotopes which became available in the 1950s, many were applied in medical science and gave rise to the new specialty of *nuclear medicine. As agents for systemic therapy their effects are limited mainly by their metabolic pathways, and only radioiodine (^{131}I) for *hyperthyroidism and certain cases of *thyroid carcinoma, and radioactive phosphorus (^{32}P) for *polycythaemia have proved their value.

Measurement of radiations. Early workers with both X-rays and radioactive substances used the deflections of a gold-leaf electroscope as an indicator of activity, and as the ionization effect was fundamental this has been the basis of most methods of quantitation throughout this century. Early radiation units based on fluorescence, blackening of silver bromide film, colour changes of platinobarium cyanide capsules, and skin erythema gradually gave place to those based on ionization, culminating in the international recognition of the '*roentgen' (R) as the unit for X-rays in 1928. There were still substantial difficulties in obtaining precise comparison at all X-ray energies, and particularly with radium, but by 1937 it was possible to extend the roentgen to be the unit of quantity of either X- or gamma-radiation. Whereas the roentgen (measured as ionization in air) gives an exact description of radiation *exposure*, the quantity of importance for radiotherapy is the *absorbed dose* in tissue which depends also on the 'quality' (spectral distribution) of the radiation and on the nature of the tissue irradiated (whether fat, muscle, or bone). A new unit, the rad was therefore defined in 1953 as the energy imparted by ionizing radiation to matter in a volume element, that is, 1 rad = 100 erg per gram. With the extension in 1980 of the SI system to radiological units the SI unit of absorbed dose is the gray (Gy), named after the English physicist and radiobiolog-

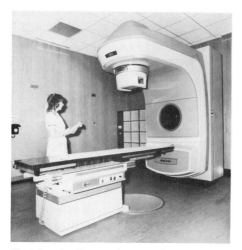

Fig. 4. A modern linear accelerator producing beams of X-rays or electrons at energies of from 4 to 24 MeV for megavoltage radiotherapy

ist L. H. Gray (1905–65), and equal to 1 joule per kilogram; thus 1Gy = 100 rad (or 1 rad = 1 centigray).

The curie (Ci) was first suggested as a unit of radioactivity in 1910, but defined only for use with *radon as the quantity in radioactive equilibrium with one gram of radium. With the advent of radioactive isotopes, it was extended to cover these, and defined as the unit of activity which gives 3.7×10^{10} disintegrations per second. As an idea of magnitude it may be mentioned that a dose of radioiodine for tracer studies may be 50 *micro*curies, that of radioiodine given systemically for thyroid cancer 150 *milli*curies, while the activity of radio-cobalt in a teletherapy machine may be 5000 *curies*. The new SI unit of radioactivity is the *becquerel* (Bq) which equals one disintegration per second (i.e. 1 Bq = 3.7×10^{-11} Ci).

Throughout the development of radiotherapy there has been a great deal of detailed exploration by physicists of the distribution of radiations in the body and of the best means of achieving uniform irradiation of the tumour while sparing normal tissues. In the second decade of the century it became known that one of the most important factors was scattered radiation created by the primary beam at a depth, and that this depended on its 'quality' (energy and filtration). In 1918–21 Friedrich and Dessauer in Germany charted the absorption under various technical conditions in media which simulated tissue and opened the way to much technical progress. The pictorial representation of percentage depth doses as 'isodose curves' was due to Otto Glasser in 1920, and now the clinician had a graphic representation of the radiation as well as methods for measuring and expressing its quantity and quality. Thanks to the work of a generation of hospital physicists, and particularly of Mayneord in London in the 1930s, the combination of isodose curves into two- or three-dimensional radiation distribution for an individual patient has become part of standard radiotherapeutic practice (Fig. 5). For radium and other interstitial gamma-ray sources the problems of obtaining uniformity of radiation distribution were more complex. The distributions around radium sources of various geometric shapes and combinations were examined *inter alia* by Sievert in Stockholm between 1920 and 1932, but of the several dosage systems devised the most practicable was that of Paterson and Parker (1934 and 1938), and the general adoption world-wide of this 'Manchester System' was an important milestone in the radiotherapy of accessible cancer.

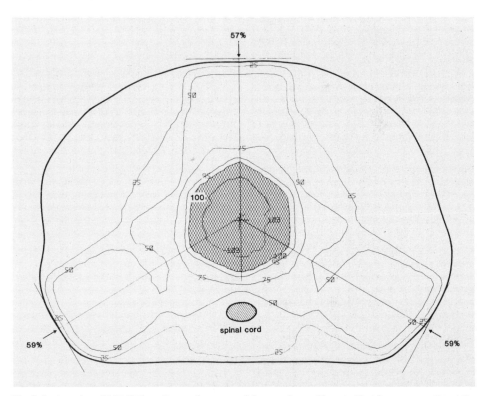

Fig. 5. Isodose plan of 8 MeV X-ray therapy for cancer of the oesophagus. Three incident beams summating at the tumour (cross-hatched area) are so arranged as to minimize dosage to the lungs and spinal cord which are particularly vulnerable to irradiation

Radiation protection. The adverse effects which could follow radiation exposure both in patients and in radiation workers became increasingly apparent in the early years of this century, particularly those involving the skin, the eyes, and the blood-forming bone marrow, but full appreciation of their incidence was delayed by the long latent periods which often elapsed before their significance became apparent. While protection of X-ray tubes became increasingly efficient there was for many years undue exposure from X-ray fluoroscopy and from handling of radium and its products, to the extent that many of the early workers eventually succumbed to skin malignancies or *aplastic anaemia. A monument was erected in Hamburg in 1936 by the German Roentgen Society to X-ray and radium martyrs who eventually numbered several hundreds. A British X-ray and Radium Protection Committee formed in 1921 to recommend measures of radiation protection had a salutary effect and led to the formation in 1928 of the body which became the International Commission on Radiological Protection (ICRP). From their initial deliberations a 'maximum tolerance dose of X-rays' was derived, based on the working conditions of a number of experienced radiologists who had escaped injury and still enjoyed normal health: by 1937 this was regarded as 1 roentgen (R) per week. These recommendations were adopted world-wide and resulted in overt radiation damage to those occupationally employed in medicine becoming a thing of the past.

With the advent of atomic fission, artificial radio-isotopes, and nuclear energy, concern for radiation protection has greatly increased and has led to a vast amount of biological and physical research which has been applied to the diverse uses of ionizing radiations in medicine. The long-term effects of radiation may be classified as 'somatic', affecting that individual, or 'genetic', affecting subsequent offspring. 'Stochastic' effects are those for which the probability of an effect occurring rather than its severity is regarded as a function of dose, without any threshold. 'Non-stochastic' effects are those for which the severity of the effect varies with the dose, and for which a threshold may therefore occur. *Hereditary effects and carcinogenesis are regarded as being stochastic, and at the low doses now encountered by radiation workers are the main consideration. In the past the emphasis in radiation protection science was on keeping exposure below a maximum permissible dose level, without identifying the order of risk, other than that it was small, but since 1977 the emphasis of the ICRP recommendations has been on quantifying the probability of deleterious effects in the irradiated person. These are framed in terms not simply of exposure dose, but of 'dose equivalent' which takes into account the absorbed dose in rad, the quality and the relative biological effectiveness of the radiation, and the relative risk of irradiating a specified organ compared with that of irradiating the whole body. This 'dose equivalent' is stated in sievert (Sv) (1 Sv = 100 rem), and the annual dose equivalent limit for occupationally exposed workers is at present 50 mSv (5 rem). (See also RADIATION, IONIZING.)

A patient undergoing modern X-ray therapy is protected by the beam being limited to a definite geometric size by collimators, and by an intricate system of 'fail-safe' dosimetric devices which ensure that the dose prescribed is accurately given. The whole-body dose from 'scatter' is still beyond the limit tolerable for continuous exposure in a radiation worker, who must therefore control the apparatus from outside the room. The treatment room walls are protected by considerable thicknesses of concrete. Radiation workers wear sensitive film badges which are measured regularly to ensure that no undue exposure has occurred. Provided that the stringent rules are at all times followed, the environment of a radiotherapy department now carries no significant risk for those employed. In most countries a considerable amount of local legislation now controls the use of radiations, and in the EEC a general directive came into force in 1980 from which member countries prepared their own legislation. In the UK this is controlled by the Health and Safety Executive (HSE), mainly under the *Health and Safety at Work Act (1974). (See also RADIOACTIVE SUBSTANCES ACT 1960; RADIOLOGICAL PROTECTION ACT 1980.)

Radiobiology. The first biological response to be quantitatively studied was the reddening (erythema) produced in human skin, and since skin tolerance was a limiting factor in many procedures throughout the first half of this century it was subjected to extensive physical and biological investigation. A biological unit, the 'skin erythema dose' (SED) was widely used until superseded in 1928 by the 'roentgen'. At the tissue and cellular levels a wide range of indicators of radiation response was used from the earliest days. Already in 1903 Perthes had noticed abnormal mitosis in the ova of *Ascaris* and soon confirmed the finding in mammalian tissue, both normal and neoplastic. In 1906 two French observers, Bergonié and Tribondeau, summarized their work on the germinative tissues of the male rat in a general statement: 'the sensitivity of cells to irradiation is in direct proportion to their reproductive activity and inversely proportional to their degree of differentiation'. This 'law' was to be quoted in and out of context (for it was derived from a specific tissue having an orderly progression of cell division and differentiation) and was to have an important influence on radiobiological thought for generations. But most tissues including tumours are heterogeneous, and their radiation responses are extremely complex: so the advances and techniques of cytology and histology of each decade were used to explore and explain the effects. In addition to direct action on tumour cells radiation was seen to damage selectively small blood vessels and thus indirectly to affect normal and neoplastic tissues: the investigation of this latter effect on vasculoconnective tissue was subsequently to become increasingly important.

A major discovery by Regaud in 1919 was the culmination of a long period of work on the mechanism of radiation sterilization of ram testis. He showed conclusively that 'fractionation' of radiation dosage, splitting it into a number of exposures over a period of time, could permanently eradicate spermatogenesis whereas no single dose could then do so without inflicting serious damage to the normal skin. Very imaginatively he likened this phenomenon to the eradication of a tumour, and suggested that fractionated radiotherapy might be clinically advantageous. In Paris he and his colleague Coutard applied these principles of fractionated daily radiotherapy in the treatment of patients with a variety of accessible cancers, and in the 1920s produced tumour regressions and five-year survivals which were absolutely revolutionary for that era. Permanent cures of a very significant fraction of patients with cancers of the head and neck were achieved for the first time in history. It has since been established that the overall protraction of treatment, and the number, size, and distribution of the individual doses, are of critical importance to the protection of the host's vasculoconnective tissue and to the prevention of late radiation damage such as *necrosis. The significance of introducing fractionation into radiotherapy has in fact been compared with that of introducing *asepsis into surgery: it has been one of the most important factors in the development of radiotherapy as a medical specialty.

Cells in process of division had long been known to be more sensitive to irradiation, and the advent of in vitro *tissue culture enabled Strangeways in 1920 to eliminate variables such as the blood supply. He and Hopwood showed that the most sensitive phase of cell division was prophase, and their work with Canti heralded a more quantitative approach. In the next two decades there was great interest in the physical and chemical processes of radiation absorption, in the recognition of single- and multi-hit types of action in vulnerable macromolecular targets of cell nuclei, in the production of chromosomal damage, and in the mechanisms of cell death. In the burst of biological interest and research which accompanied the development of the atomic bomb and nuclear energy around 1945, the topics were pursued by classical methods of cytology and histology since the important developments of quantitative radiobiology were yet to come. Fundamental were the effects on mitosis, and the technique of *autoradiography (introduced by Howard and Pelc in 1953 and which revolutionized the study of cell biology), allowed detailed investigation of effects on DNA synthesis. This ability to identify two discrete phases in the cell cycle (S-phase by radioactive tracers and mitosis by microscopy) made it possible to measure the duration of the cell cycle in many tumours and normal tissues, and led later to the high technology of fluorescence-activated cell sorters capable of identifying the DNA content of single cells and of identifying resistant and sensitive subpopulations.

The seminal development in modern radiation biology was the discovery by Puck and Marcus in 1955 of the technique of clonal cultivation of mammalian cells in vitro which permitted quantitative analysis of radiation-dose/cell-survival relationships: it heralded an unprecedented quarter-century of activity in cellular radiation biology. Such survival curves (Fig. 2) proved to be exponential in shape, after an initial 'shoulder' region which the later work of Elkind and Sutton showed to be due to cellular recovery from 'sublethal' damage. These discoveries, which extended the horizons of radiobiology, became relevant to radiotherapy once it was appreciated that what was being measured—the capacity of proliferating cells for indefinite replication and growth in a suitable environment—is in most tissues subject to a variety of *homeostatic and reparative influences. Taken in context, cell survival curves have proved a versatile tool in elucidating basic mechanisms for radiotherapy, and now there are numerous techniques for measuring the lethal effects of radiations on cells, be they established cell lines, fresh explants from tumours, or normal tissues. Proceeding from a single radiation exposure to multiple fractionated exposures, a number of new variables are introduced into the response and the single-dose survival curve is no longer applicable. Several important parameters which come into play have been recognized: they include cell recovery, repair, repopulation, redistribution in the cell cycle, and particularly reoxygenation.

A host of chemical and pharmacological agents have been found to modify the biological effects of radiation, but none is simpler than *oxygen and none produces such a dramatic response. As early as 1921 it had been noted by Holthusen in Hamburg that Ascaris ova were relatively radio-resistant in the absence of oxygen. The effect was explored in England by Mottram in the 1940s, culminating in its quantitative measurement by his colleagues Gray and Read using growth inhibition of broad bean root as the test system. In a classic study of 1953 Gray (already mentioned for his fundamental work on dosimetry) showed that cells with normal oxygenation are sterilized by about one-third of the dose of radiation that would be necessary if they were completely lacking in oxygen (anoxic). Because of the tenuous blood supply and spontaneous cell death, many experimental tumours were shown by Gray and his colleagues to have regions, or at least groups of cells, which are practically anoxic and these may survive the largest dose of radiation which normal tissues can tolerate—and consequently lead to a recurrence of growth. Appreciation of the oxygen effect and suggestions for overcoming it have had a profound effect on radiobiological and therapeutic thought in the subsequent three decades.

Quantitative cellular radiation biology has already in its 25 years contributed greatly to the advance of radiotherapy especially by providing concepts and understanding of basic mechanisms. The present understanding of cell, tissue, and tumour kinetics, dose-response and dose-time effects, chemical and pharmacological modifiers of radiation response, and particularly of the oxygen effect are all due to sophisticated applications of cell-survival curves. These advances are likely to continue in relation to radiation effects on organized tissues, the use of new radiation modalities, and combined therapy with cytotoxic drugs (antineoplastic chemotherapy).

Present scope and application of radiotherapy. Once a definite pathological diagnosis of cancer has been made it is necessary by clinical examination and special investigations to determine as accurately as possible its extent as regards both local spread and possible remote deposits—the 'stage' of the disease—as a factor in selecting the best treatment. Depending on the type of tumour the staging procedures may include various forms of *endoscopy, routine radiological investigations, biochemical and haematological tests, and special imaging procedures such as scans by *computerized axial tomography, *ultrasound, or radio-isotopes. The general condition of the patient is at the same time assessed, particularly with regard to related or coincidental medical conditions. The choice of treatment, whether by surgery, radiotherapy, or chemotherapy, depends essentially on the type of tumour, its pathological degree of malignancy, and on the extent of spread. In general, surgery is most successful for discrete well-differentiated tumours, particularly those manifest by their 'space-occupying' or 'mass' effects, while irradiation can succeed with more diffuse and anaplastic processes. In the long term well-differentiated tumours can be controlled, but the most rapid radiation responses occur in the more primitive types. On the other hand, tumours consisting of cells with a high rate of turnover (such as lymphoma or leukaemia) have also a high propensity for *metastasis. They may respond to chemotherapy, which although having at present limited effect on the common solid tumours (squamous or adenocarcinoma), may be active for widely disseminated tumour cells provided that these are sensitive to the drugs and the 'tumour burden' of the body is low. The decisions which have to be made at this stage are therefore: whether treatment can be potentially curative for regionally localized disease, or merely palliative for relief of symptoms; which shall be the main line of treatment; and how one method may be phased with others. These decisions are based on accumulated clinical experience and on the results of clinical trials which are constantly being updated.

Whichever method of radiotherapy is used to achieve the physical requirements of adequate and uniform irradiation of the tumour-bearing volume, with sparing of normal tissues, the treatment plan is the end-result of a detailed process of assessment which takes into account both the biological nature of the tumour and its spatial distribution within the body as seen in various cross-sections. This 'treatment planning' is carried out by the radiation therapist in collaboration with a physicist (radiation dosimetrist). Use is often made of a 'treatment simulator', a special diagnostic X-ray machine which can relate the tumour-imaging data to exact landmarks and also check on the accuracy of the radiation beams ultimately selected. CAT scanning is often a particularly valuable aid, for it not only provides an exact contour of a body section and representation of the outlines of organs with evidence of tumour involvement, but it can quantitate the 'density' of anatomical structures in the section and develop isodose curves with homogeneity corrections (Fig. 6). The tumour-bearing area having been delineated on the body section, together with the position of 'critical organs' such as the spinal cord or kidneys which need to be avoided, from the data supplied by the planning computer an appropriate technique is selected. The prescribed radiation dose and its fractionation depend on many factors including the type of neoplasm and the size of the target volume. Commonly the total dose is in the range of 3500 to 6500 centigrays and the treatment is given daily, or 3 times a week, for 3–6 weeks.

For small accessible tumours the most suitable method of irradiation may be by brachytherapy, the application of radioactive sources within or close to the tumour. The interstitial implantation of tumours such as those of the mouth or breast has been practised successfully for many years, with radium needles now being superseded by iridium-192 wires, or caesium-137 needles for greater geometric accuracy and for ease of personnel protection. In intracavitary therapy for gynaecological tumours such as carcinoma of the uterus, radioactive sources are placed within the natural body cavities. Again, originally carried out with radium,

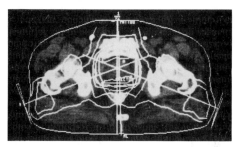

Fig. 6. CT scan of pelvis with computer-generated radiation plan for 8 MeV X-ray therapy of prostatic cancer. (Reproduced by courtesy of Dr J. Dobbs, Institute of Cancer Research, London)

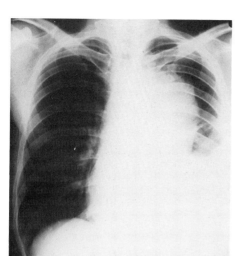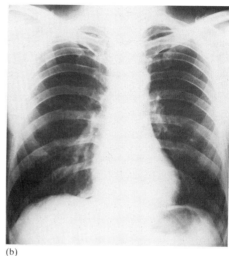

(a)   (b)

Fig. 7. Response of lymphoma of mediastinum to X-irradiation. (a) Large mediastinal mass and left pleural effusion at presentation. (b) Normal chest radiograph six months after treatment. The patient was well 15 years later

this treatment is now delivered by radiocaesium or by the Cathetron technique which uses high-activity cobalt-60 sources.

The results of radiotherapy for localized cancer can be highly satisfactory. For instance, in carcinoma of the *larynx 80 per cent of irradiated patients are cured and retain a normal voice. Similarly, for early carcinoma of the uterine *cervix 80 per cent of patients can expect to be cured following radioactive caesium treatment. The wide variety of tumours which may be controlled by irradiation range from those of common occurrence such as breast carcinoma to such rarities as those of the *pineal gland. Technical innovation, especially the use of megavoltage methods, has brought increased cure rates in many tumours, from those of the head and neck to advanced *prostatic cancer. The great versatility of megavoltage equipment opened the way to entirely new treatment approaches for Hodgkin's disease: its radiosensitivity allows wide fields to be irradiated and early disease to be eliminated before it is clinically identifiable; cure rates of over 90 per cent are now regularly reported for the early stages, and even when the disease has spread widely in the *lymphatic system, long-term control is possible in over 60 per cent. Postoperative irradiation of the abdominal *lymph nodes for *seminoma of the testis has improved the survival rates from 50 per cent to over 80 per cent. While some deeply placed tumours such as those of the *bladder frequently respond well, others such as those of the *oesophagus are difficult to control. In others such as *bronchogenic carcinoma a satisfactory local response is often vitiated by the appearance of remote metastases. But even when actual cure has not been attained there may be valuable long-term relief of symptoms (Fig. 7) and, especially in head

and neck tumours, the best palliation may come from a frustrated attempt at cure.

Unfortunately, about half of the patients presenting at radiotherapy departments have no prospect of cure because of the advanced stage of the disease from local spread or from secondary deposits at the outset. Beneficial palliation of symptoms may nevertheless be achieved: examples are the healing of ulceration, the control of profuse haemoptysis (spitting blood) from bronchial carcinoma and of *dysphagia in *pharyngeal carcinoma, the rapid relief of pain from bone metastases (Fig. 8), the avoidance of paralysis from spinal deposits, and the relief of cerebral symptoms from those in the brain. At the present time radiotherapy is certainly the most versatile method in the palliative treat-

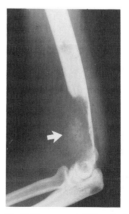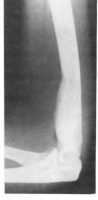

Fig. 8. Response to X-irradiation of secondary deposit of breast cancer in the humerus showing recalcification. Relief of pain and prevention of fracture were important clinical benefits

ment of cancer, and when applicable certainly the most effective. Such treatment should not, of course, be considered in isolation for it is but part of the general care of the patient.

Multimodality treatment. While radiotherapy alone may in certain instances be the treatment of choice (e.g. in early laryngeal cancer) it is now frequently administered in combination with surgery or with the use of *cytotoxic drugs. When combined with surgery it may be given preoperatively to reduce tumour mass, or postoperatively to sterilize any residual tumour seedlings. Chemotherapeutic agents may also be used in combination with radiotherapy in an attempt at increasing the local effect either by additional 'cell killing' or by potentiating the radiation effect itself. With a quite different aim, cytotoxic drugs or *hormones may also be combined with surgery or with radiotherapy, to try to control 'silent' remote deposits (micro-metastases) before they become apparent. Multimodality treatment is exemplified in the modern management of breast carcinoma, which involves both the treatment of the tumour to prevent local recurrence and the control of possible blood-borne micro-metastases. By depending on the efficacy of modern megavoltage X-ray therapy the initial surgical excision can be less radical and mutilating, and it is often possible to conserve the breast. On the other hand, in cases deemed from the pathological data to be at high risk of developing metastases, 'adjuvant' chemotherapy may then be administered using a combination of such cytotoxic agents as cloxorubicim (Adriamycin®) and *cyclophosphamide or by a hormonal agent such as *tamoxifen.

The treatment of malignant disease by combinations of radiation and drug therapy is becoming increasingly popular, spurred by the notable successes of this approach in the highly malignant tumours of childhood. Because of the possible interactions of radiation and drug effects the closest collaboration is needed between the various specialists involved, and this has at the same time resulted in much greater understanding of the problems.

Prospect. The remarkable development of radiotherapy in the middle decades of this century came from the effective application in a fully clinical context of physical technology and radiobiology; notably the enhancement of the 'therapeutic ratio' of effects on tumour/host by dose-fractionation and using megavoltage radiations. Coupled with this was the adequate formal training of the specialists concerned in radiotherapy and oncology. At the outset, radiation provided the only alternative to surgery in the treatment of cancer, but in the last two decades chemotherapy has come to occupy an increasingly important place. When metastatic spread is so often the lethal factor in the common forms of malignant disease it may therefore be asked whether radiotherapy, a mainly local method of treatment, is likely to

maintain its position and what further progress is feasible. In practice the situation is quite otherwise. While chemotherapy is increasingly capable of dealing with small foci of tumour cells, however disseminated, it has so far proved of limited value in achieving regression and sterilization of the primary mass in the common tumours, so that increasing numbers of patients, rescued from the development of metastasis in vital organs, may survive with the disease at the primary site uncontrolled and requiring treatment. For this, and such reasons as the changing age distribution of the population, the advent of new radiation techniques, the use of multimodality regimes, and the requirements of palliation, the total demand for effective radiotherapy is likely to increase in the foreseeable future.

Clearly there is obvious benefit to be gained from making local treatment more effective. Bearing in mind the basic problem of delivering a lethal dose of radiation selectively to the tumour, the causes of failure are numerous and interrelated and can affect either side of the equation for the 'therapeutic ratio'. Uncertainty as to the precise size and situation of a tumour is diminishing with the use of sophisticated imaging techniques, especially data from CAT scanning; there may be similar benefits from *nuclear magnetic resonance (NMR) imaging. Modern linear accelerators can deliver a requisite dose at any prescribed depth, and the highest dose increment can be further localized precisely by photon or electron beams or by interstitial implantation of sealed sources such as iridium-192 or iodine-125. But apart from work on high-energy particle acceleration, advances in radiotherapy physics are more likely to be in applying treatment precisely in the individual patient than in fundamental research. From the radiobiological point of view human tumours have been shown by their radiation dose–response relationships to be heterogeneous both in the proportion of clonogenic cells and in other factors causing radioresistance, so that clinically a treatment strategy aimed at modifying one major factor may give less impressive results than those obtained with homogeneous animal tumours. The *clinical* problem of tumour radio-resistance can be seen as the inability to identify predictively its cause in the individual patient: however, radiobiological research does provide important pointers. The radio-protective effect of oxygen lack on tumour cells has been investigated for 25 years, for it is well recognized experimentally as a potential cause of radioresistance. Several means have been tried to overcome this hypoxic protection of clonogenic cells. The patient may be irradiated in a *hyperbaric oxygen chamber whereby the increased concentration of dissolved oxygen diffuses into the tumour centre. So far only marginal benefit has been recorded in a few situations—some 10 per cent improvement in head and neck cancer and in carcinoma of the uterine cervix—and the technical difficulties have limited the widespread use of this method. More promising are the possibilities of chemical radiosensitization of hypoxic cells. The proposal in 1963 by Adams and Dewey that the ability of a few chemical compounds to sensitize hypoxic bacterial cells was related to their electron-affinity, led to the production of a group of 'oxygen-mimics', notably the nitroimidazoles (such as misonidazole), and new drugs are being developed with greater sensitizing efficiency and reduced toxicity which may provide the hoped-for gain. In experimental animals hypoxic regions, from cells overgrowing their supportive vasculature, occur in nearly all solid tumours but it is not fully established that the protective action of hypoxia against photon irradiation commonly impedes local tumour control in man. For while a significant proportion of tumour cells may initially be hypoxic, the first few doses of a fractionated course of radiotherapy may kill off well-oxygenated cells and lead to reoxygenation of residual hypoxic cells. This has led to further attempts to optimize fractionation beyond the customary pattern of daily treatment: hyper-frac-tionation, with two or three fractions of radiation each day, also has the potential advantage of greater inhibition of 'repair of sublethal damage' in the hypoxic than in the fully oxygenated cells.

While high-energy electrons have biological properties very similar to those of X-rays, heavy particles such as neutrons and protons produce very dense ionization along their tracks—they are the so-called high-LET (linear energy transfer) radiations (see Fig. 1)—and they show three major radiobiological differences from photons: they are more effective against hypoxic cells, there is less repair of sublethal damage and there is less dif-ference in radiosensitivity at different phases of the cell cycle. Clinical studies of neutron therapy have been promising, with increased local control of certain tumours, but the effect on the 'therapeutic ratio' is as yet undecided, and new very high energy cyclotrons are being installed in both the UK and the USA to try to elucidate this in controlled trials. The other high energy particles of interest—pro-tons, helium ions, or negative pi-mesons—have similar potential advantages to neutrons, but better isodose distribution (in fact, that for pions is almost ideal for deep-seated tumours). Large and vastly expensive machines are, however, required to produce these particle beams, and they will consequently be of limited availability. A few are already in use for clinical research—at Los Alamos (New Mexico), at Vancouver, and at the SINR facility near Zurich.

On the opposite side of the coin the selective biochemical protection of normal tissues has experimentally become a possibility. When ion pairs are produced by photons depositing energy in DNA, they are associated with the formation of hydroxyl- and hydrogen-free radicals and hydrated electrons. The cell damage from this radox process may be 'fixed' by oxidation, but it may equally be 'repaired' by reduction. The use of sulphydryl compounds to repair free-radical lesions in the DNA of oxygenated normal tissue is possible, moreover with decreased protection of hypoxic tumour cells.

In a quite different field, heating of cancer cells (hyperthermia) makes them more sensitive to radi-ation; the thermal enhancement for tumour is greater than that for normal tissue, and hypoxic cells are less protected than are the well-oxygenated. Combined hyperthermia and radi-ation may therefore offer advantages when the technical difficulties of thermal gradients and quantitation in tissue have been overcome.

The magnitude of benefit from such advances can only be guessed, but it is more likely to come from the summation of a number of improvements, each small in itself, rather than from any single breakthrough.

Whatever the improvements in radiotherapy of local disease, it is certain that the future advances in the care of patients with cancer will come from multimodality therapy in which the individual agents of surgery, radiation, and cytotoxic drugs will be used to their best advantage in a planned schedule—selected not only from knowledge of their effects on groups, but also with reference to the clinical and biological features of the tumour in the individual patient. Whether the chemical agents are used for their additive effects before, during, or after radiotherapy, or whether as adjuvant therapy for micro-metastases, the poss-ible interactions are such as to require the closest collaboration of the various specialties.

Such collaboration between surgical, medical, and radiation oncologists is ideally pursued in a department of clinical oncology in which each specialty contributes its own expertise. Early in the development of radiotherapy, experience in Stock-holm, Paris, London, Manchester, and New York showed the advantages of having well-equipped departments devoted to the care and investigation of patients with cancer, in which a wide variety of tumours could be studied in adequate number, with detailed documentation and analysis. The high cost of modern linear accelerators and other equipment means that such facilities have to be centralized in a limited number of hospitals to which patients are referred, often on a regional basis. Peripheral clinics at district hospitals provide an integrated service both for reference and follow-up, so that the collaboration between specialists at the centre is reflected in continued contact with referring physicians. While the high cost of radio-therapeutic equipment was the original *raison d'être* for such centres, it should in future be the opportunity for collaboration between the various specialties in clinical oncology. A. JONES

Further reading
Denekamp, J. (1982). *Cell Kinetics and Cancer Therapy.* Springfield, Illinois.
Fletcher, G. H. (1980). *Textbook of Radiotherapy.* 3rd edn, Philadelphia.

Fowler, J. F. (1981). *Nuclear Particles in Cancer Treatment*. Bristol.

Freund, L. (1904). *Elements of General Radiotherapy*. New York and London.

Glasser, O. (ed.) (1933). *The Science of Radiology*. London.

Halnan, K. (ed.) (1982). *The Treatment of Cancer*. London.

Regato, J. A. del (1976). Claudius Regaud. *International Journal of Radiation Oncology, Biology and Physics*, **1**, 993.

RADIUM is a naturally occurring radioactive element (symbol Ra; atomic number 88 and, for the most stable isotope, with a half-life of 1620 years, relative atomic mass 226). It is a rare metal, which chemically resembles *barium. Radium is used as a source of *beta particles and *gamma rays in *radiotherapy.

RADON is a short-lived radioactive gaseous element (symbol Rn; atomic number 86 and, for the most stable isotope, with a half-life of 3.825 days, relative atomic mass 222). Radon, which is the immediate decay product of *radium, belongs chemically to the inert (noble) gases.

RAGWORT is the name for various flowering plants of the genus *Senecio* (family Compositae), the commonest species being *S. vulgaris*. Ragwort (or ragweed) pollen is highly allergenic and a common cause of allergic rhinitis (see ALLERGY). The common ragwort has yellow daisy-like flowers and is widely distributed in dry grassland; it is closely related to the groundsels.

RALES are moist bubbling sounds heard on *auscultation of the lungs, coarser than *crepitations, indicating the presence of fluid in the air-passages.

RAMAZZINI, BERNARDINO (1633–1714). Italian physician, MD Parma (1659). Ramazzini was appointed professor of theoretical medicine in Modena in 1682; he moved to the chair of practical medicine in *Padua in 1700. Ramazzini was the first physician to be interested in *occupational disease. In *De morbis artificum diatriba* (1700), he described some 40 industrial diseases. He was also a pioneer of *epidemiology.

RAMON Y CAJAL, SANTIAGO (1852–1934). Spanish neuroanatomist, MD Saragossa (1876). After graduation Ramon was sent to Cuba with the army, but was invalided with malaria. He occupied the chair of anatomy in Valencia (1883), of histology in Barcelona (1887), and of histology and pathological anatomy in Madrid (1892). He improved *Golgi's staining methods and studied systematically the microscopic structure of the central nervous system, confirming the *neurone doctrine. His researches were published in Spanish and were not generally available, but they were embodied in his work *Textura del sistema nervioso*

del hombre y de los vertebrados (1904). He received the Nobel prize with Golgi in 1906.

RAMUS is the anatomical term for a branch.

RANITIDINE is, like *cimetidine, an *H₂ receptor antagonist used in the treatment of *peptic ulcer and other conditions where reduction of gastric acidity is likely to be of benefit, such as *reflux oesophagitis and the *Zollinger–Ellison syndrome. It is more potent than cimetidine, and has fewer side-effects; in particular, it does not cause anti-androgen effects such as *gyaecomastia and *impotence.

RANSON, STEPHEN WALTER (1880–1942). American neuroanatomist, MD Rush Medical College (1907). Ranson's professional career was spent mainly at Northwestern University. His writings and textbooks served as major sources of *neuroanatomical information for many years. He and colleagues demonstrated neural connections between the *hypothalamus and the *pituitary gland.

RANVIER, LOUIS ANTOINE (1835–1922). French anatomist, MD Paris (1865). Ranvier worked with Claude *Bernard at the Collège de France where he became professor of general anatomy. He wrote a successful textbook of pathology (1869–76), described the constrictions on medullated *nerve fibres (nodes of Ranvier, 1878), and suggested the concept of the *reticuloendothelial system (1900), and the name 'clasmatocyte' for what is now called the *macrophage.

RAPE is sexual intercourse with a woman without her consent. See SEXUAL OFFENCES ACTS.

RASH. Any temporary skin eruption.

RAT-BITE FEVER is an uncommon condition occurring under poor sanitary conditions where *rats flourish, due to either of two distinct microorganisms *Streptobacillus moniliformis* and *Spirillum minus*. The mortality is low, and the infection responds well to antibiotic treatment.

RATHKE, MARTIN HEINRICH (1763–1860). German embryologist, MD Berlin (1818). Rathke was chief physician to the Danzig Hospital; in 1829 he became professor of physiology at Dorpat. An early embryologist, he is known for Rathke's pouch, a depression in the roof of the embryonic mouth, from the walls of which the anterior hypophysis (*pituitary) is developed.

RATIONALISTS are those who regard reason as the chief source and test of knowledge.

RATIONALIZATION is the mental defence mechanism whereby actions or attitudes are justified after the event by the finding of reasons for them.

RATS are small rodents of the genus *Rattus*, of which the best known are the black rat (*Rattus rattus*) and the brown rat (*Rattus norvegicus*). They live in close relationship to man and are the vectors of a number of communicable diseases, including *leptospirosis, *plague, *typhus, *relapsing fever, *rat-bite fever, and several forms of *helminthiasis, as well as *food poisoning. Various in-bred strains are used as laboratory animals.

RAY. The rectilinear path along which directional energy (e.g. electromagnetic, particulate) travels from its source.

RAYNAUD, MAURICE (1834–81). French physician, MD Paris (1862). Raynaud worked at the Hôpital Lariboisière and la Charité. In his thesis he described intermittent cyanosis and/or pallor of the extremities very occasionally progressing to gangrene (*Raynaud's disease or phenomenon, 1862).

RAYNAUD'S DISEASE OR PHENOMENON. Raynaud's phenomenon is the familiar syndrome characterized by intermittent restriction of blood supply to the fingers and toes (and sometimes the ears and nose), most often in response to cold. There is numbness, tingling, pain, and obvious pallor of the affected extremities, occasionally with blueness. Warmth relieves the symptom after some minutes or hours as the blood vessels dilate again, and this phase may itself be quite painful. The phenomenon is a nuisance, but rarely harmful; occasionally it is progressive, and causes atrophic changes or rarely even *gangrene in the terminal extremities. Raynaud's phenomenon may be a symptom of more serious underlying vascular, neurological, or collagen disorder; it may be occupational, classically in those who operate pneumatic drills; or it may be due to the action of certain drugs or chemicals. More often, it is 'idiopathic', that is no cause is found, when it is termed 'Raynaud's disease'.

REACTION, in *psychology, is any mental, emotional, or *psychomotor response to the stimulus of an event or situation; in chemistry, it is any process involving chemical change.

READ, SIR WILLIAM (d. 1715). British mountebank and itinerant oculist. Read became oculist to Queen Anne who knighted him in 1705 for curing seamen of blindness without fee.

RÉAUMUR, RENÉ-ANTOINE FERCHAULT DE (1683–1757). French scientist, naturalist, entomologist, and physician, Réaumur wrote a monumental work on insects, the six-volume *Mémoires pour servir à l'histoire des insectes* (1734–42), and discovered regeneration of lost limbs in Crustacea. He made technical improvements in the iron and steel industries. He is mainly remembered for his thermometric scale, now obsolete, which took the freezing point of water as zero but the boiling point as 80°. The *Celsius scale takes the boiling point as 100°.

RECEPTORS. The term 'receptor' is used in two different senses in medicine: firstly, to describe a specialized nerve ending which detects and responds to a particular stimulus such as touch, light, heat, pain, etc.; secondly, to describe a chemical component of a molecule or cell which has an affinity for a particular substance (e.g. hormone, toxin, antigen, neurotransmitter, etc.) and therefore binds with it, with consequent chemical, immunological, or cellular effects.

RECERTIFICATION. Periodic relicensing of medical practitioners, as required by some states in the USA. See MEDICAL EDUCATION IN THE USA AND CANADA.

RECESSIVE describes a genetically determined characteristic which is manifest only in *homozygotes, that is individuals who inherit the responsible *gene from both parents. It is not detectable, except sometimes by special tests, in *heterozygotes, who possess only one such gene. See GENETICS.

RECIDIVIST. A habitual criminal, who persistently relapses into crime despite punishment or attempts at reform.

RECKLINGHAUSEN, FRIEDRICH DANIEL VON (1833–1910). German pathologist, MD Berlin (1855). After studying under *Virchow Recklinghausen was made professor of pathological anatomy at Königsberg in 1865, later at Würzburg, and in 1872 at Strasbourg. Much of his research was on diseases of bone and tumours. He described multiple *neurofibromatosis (1882), adenomyosis of the uterus (1896), and *osteitis fibrosa cystica (1891).

VON RECKLINGHAUSEN'S DISEASE, when otherwise unqualified, is synonymous with multiple *neurofibromatosis; 'von Recklinghausen's disease of bone' is another name for osteitis fibrosa cystica, the bone condition which results from *hyperparathyroidism.

RECOMBINANT DNA TECHNOLOGY. See GENETIC ENGINEERING.

RECORD LINKAGE is the process of combining terms of information or sets of data relating to the same subject but obtained from different sources. The essential requirement of record linkage, which has received much emphasis in recent years as a technique of medical epidemiology, is that the individual subject or patient must be uniquely identifiable either by means of name and other personal data or by a code of some sort. Medical record linkage has been defined as '. . . . . . the process of bringing together selected data of biological interest for a population commencing with the conception and ending in death, into a series of personal cumulative files, the files being so organized that they can also be assembled in family groups' (Acheson, E. D. (1967), *Medical Record Linkage*, London.)

RECTUM. The terminal portion of the large intestine, connecting the pelvic *colon to the *anus.

RECURRENT LARYNGEAL NERVE. This nerve is an important branch of the *vagus (Xth cranial) nerve; it supplies motor fibres to the intrinsic muscles of the *larynx (except the cricothyroid). Lesions of the nerve cause *dysphonia, and are not uncommon; because of its anatomical course (it leaves the vagus in the thorax and runs upwards into the neck, behind the *thyroid gland), it is vulnerable to damage by neck tumours, bronchogenic carcinoma, and operations on the thyroid. The nerve on the left side may be damaged by an *aneurysm of the *aortic arch.

RED BLOOD CELL. See ERYTHROCYTE.

RED CRESCENT. In Muslim countries, a red crescent replaces a red cross as the symbol of the International Red Cross, the humanitarian agency dating from 1864 which arose out of the work of Jean-Henri *Dunant, the Swiss philanthropist. See also RED CROSS.

RED CROSS, INTERNATIONAL, AND THE BRITISH RED CROSS SOCIETY

The International Red Cross. On the evening of 24 June 1859 Jean-Henri *Dunant, a young Swiss, found himself by chance in the Lombardy village of Castiglione, during the Italian Campaign to free Italy from Austrian occupation. Throughout the day some 300 000 soldiers, with accompanying horses and artillery, had been engaged nearby in battle. Fought in a confined space surrounded by hills, the main thrust had centred in and around the village and heights of Solferino which was to give the battle its name. When the fighting ceased abruptly in the late afternoon some 40 000 men were dead, wounded, or missing.

Although the medical services of the victorious French were well organized by the standards of the day, the scale of the casualties was beyond their ability to cope. The addition of enemy wounded abandoned by fleeing comrades completely overwhelmed them. To speed their retreat, the Austrians had commandeered most of the carts in the district, thus adding to the difficulties. Those wounded who could neither walk nor crawl had to depend on the few ambulance wagons the French had in the field. Hundreds did not survive the wait.

Castiglione became a huge casualty clearing station with the wounded packed tightly wherever there was space for a man to lie. Of those lying in the streets or gardens, many were without shelter from the burning sun. There was a shortage of food, medical supplies, water—everything. Above all, there was a shortage of people to look after the casualties.

Aghast at the conditions, Dunant was tireless in tending the wounded and persuading others to help. At first the villagers were reluctant, afraid of reprisals should the occupying power regain control and find they had helped the enemy. 'Tutti fratelli' Dunant repeated again and again, explaining that we are all brothers and that, once wounded, a man became a victim deserving of help regardless of the side he had been on.

Afterwards Dunant could not forget the suffering he had witnessed and to exorcize his ghosts wrote a book called *A Memory of Solferino*. In it he pleaded for neutral status for the wounded, those tending them, and whatever was used to transport and house them. Mindful, too, that the resources of military medical services are seldom unlimited, he also suggested that each country should train volunteers in peacetime to supplement the medical services of armies in time of war. The book captured the imagination of the rich and influential of mid 19th c. Europe. On 26 October 1863 a small Committee, of which he was secretary, hosted an international congress in Geneva at which Dunant's proposals were accepted. Before the year was out the first National Relief (to become Red Cross or Red Crescent) Societies had been formed. Recognizing that more than pious hopes would be required to make sure that the neutral status of the wounded would be respected at all times, the Committee persuaded the Swiss government to convene a Diplomatic Conference in Geneva the following year. It was attended by representatives of many European countries, among them Great Britain. Two weeks later, on 22 August 1864, an international treaty, the Geneva Convention for the Amelioration of the Condition of the Wounded of Armies in the Field, was signed.

In the course of its deliberations it had become apparent to the Conference that something would be needed to differentiate members of the medical services—and their volunteer helpers—from combatant troops, keeping them safe from attack; an immunity they had not enjoyed hitherto. A similar immunity was required for hospitals, permanent and temporary, and ambulance wagons. The emblem chosen, and incorporated into the 1864 Convention, was a red cross on a white field—the Swiss flag in reverse. Although it had no religious significance and was not intended to have any, a crescent was substituted in certain Muslim countries where the red cross was seen as a symbol of Christianity. With a third emblem, no longer in use, the crescent was legalized and officially adopted in 1929 at a diplomatic conference. At the same time, the signatory governments stipulated that no further emblems would be considered as a visible sign of protection accorded by the Geneva Conventions.

In 1919 the International Red Cross extended its activities to include help for the victims of natural disasters. A League of Red Cross Societies was set up to co-ordinate this work and to help new societies to develop.

By its 120th anniversary, in 1983, the Red Cross movement had over 200 million members: practically every independent state in the world was a signatory to the Geneva Conventions—which by that time numbered four—and most signatory countries had a national Red Cross or Red Crescent Society.

Although National Societies are autonomous they are bound by the principles and statutes of the Red Cross, which oblige them to support each other, and by the Red Cross objectives for war and peace which are common to all societies. Individual societies engage in peacetime programmes appropriate to their national needs. *Primary health care has an important role in developing countries, for instance. Disaster-preparedness programmes have a vital part in countries which lie in natural disaster belts. In some countries the blood donor service is one of the principal activities, while in others welfare services predominate.

In 1901, Henry Dunant was joint recipient of the first Nobel peace prize. Subsequently it was awarded to the International Red Cross in 1917, 1944, and 1963.

The British Red Cross, founded in 1870, was known in its early days as the National Society for Aid to the Sick and Wounded in War. Its first essay in the field of relief was to raise money to give aid impartially to both sides in the Franco-Prussian War. Thereafter, following the pattern of need so clearly established in the aftermath of Solferino, it proceeded to develop its help for war victims in three areas; first aid/nursing; transportation for the wounded (casualty evacuation); and welfare—the supply of medical stores and equipment, clothing, food, and comforts. In 1880 the first small group of eight nurses went to the military hospital in Netley to be trained for wartime nursing duties. Two years later, in 1882, the War Office made its first request for Red Cross nurses to go to Egypt. They were to be the forerunners of many thousands whose services were to be called upon in years to come.

Initially the relationship of the Society (which became the British Red Cross in 1905) with the military medical services was informal. It was given official status in 1907 when the Territorial and Reserve Forces Act of Parliament defined its wartime role as that of 'providing supplementary aid to the Territorial Medical Services to meet the needs of war'. The Society was granted a Royal Charter of Incorporation in 1908 'for the primary object of furnishing aid to the sick and wounded in time of war'.

In 1909, consequent upon the change in status, the Society's County Branches were called upon to appoint Directors 'who would raise as many Voluntary Aid Detachments as possible'. Female members of Voluntary Aid Detachments (soon to become known as VADs) were required to have a First Aid and Nursing Certificate and were trained to carry out nursing duties on military lines of communication. Male members with First Aid Certificates were trained in casualty collection.

The military casualties of the First World War exceeded in number anything previously experienced in modern warfare and the strain on the medical resources of the military was enormous. As a result, VADs served in military hospitals and in convalescent homes both at home and overseas, the distinctive red cross on the veils and aprons of the female members becoming a familiar and comforting sight. Transportation for the huge numbers of wounded was another major Red Cross undertaking. Ambulance trains and motor launches designed to carry the wounded were provided by the Society for use in many parts of the world but its biggest contribution was the provision of innovatory motor ambulances and drivers. Fleets of vans (with crews) converted to a variety of uses from mobile soup kitchens and workshops to travelling dental surgeries, bacteriological laboratories, and X-ray units were another gift.

While there was still a requirement for VADs in the Second World War of 1939–45—they were attached to medical units of all three services as well as to civilian hospitals—and for Red Cross ambulances and drivers, a significant part of the Society's effort was concentrated on welfare services. Many of these were provided for the wounded and the convalescent but a gigantic operation was mounted on behalf of prisoners-of-war. The third (1929) Geneva Convention which was signed by most of the countries signatory to the earlier Conventions, including the UK and Germany (but not Japan and Russia who did not sign that particular treaty until 1949), allowed much more to be done for prisoners of war than had been possible previously. The all-Swiss International Committee of the Red Cross in its role as neutral intermediary was able to visit camps to make sure that prisoners were being treated properly and accorded their rights. The Red Cross was permitted, too, to establish a message service enabling prisoners to write to their relatives and to receive messages in return. Red Cross parcels could be sent to prisoners-of-war. Between 1939 and 1945 the British Society packed and dispatched, via the International Committee in Geneva, over four million standard food parcels alone. Other parcels contained clothing, mending materials, games, books, and a variety of other much-needed and appreciated items. Even an educational service was provided so that people in POW camps could study and take examinations while waiting for the end of the war and their release.

In peacetime the British Society continues to have an obligation to maintain a trained membership ready to act in support of the public authority in local emergencies and to provide teams to augment the health services, military and civilian, in time of national emergency.

The absence of a global war since 1945 has enabled the Society to pay more attention to the peacetime objects namely: 'the improvement of health, the prevention of disease and the mitigation of suffering throughout the world'. First-aid duties at public and sporting events play a major part in the Society's peacetime life. Nursing, too, continues to have a role, although less help is required in hospitals than previously. Transportation is an important service for the sick, the disabled, and the frail elderly. Medical equipment, such as wheelchairs, bed blocks, bed pans, and bed cradles, is available on short-term loan from Red Cross Medical Loan Depots in most parts of the country.

Courses in first aid, home nursing, and other associated subjects are available to the public as well as to members. A major development in the Society's training programmes since the *Health and Safety at Work etc. Act 1974 has been the introduction of, and steady increase in, First Aid at Work courses which are held all over the country.

Welfare activities are many and varied. The Beauty Care Service, for example, is designed to boost the morale of long-stay patients in hospitals and in homes for the elderly. Another example is the tracing service. One of the distressing aspects of war—or natural disaster—is to be without news of missing relatives. The Red Cross Tracing Service was started in Switzerland in 1870, by the International Committee, to provide relatives with information on war casualties. Today it is actively supported by many national societies, among them the British. Recent conflicts in Indo-China, Cyprus, the Middle East to name a few, have provided their quota of missing people. A surprising number, too, of those missing since the Second World War are still being found and reunited with relatives who long believed them dead.

The British Red Cross makes contributions in cash, kind, and personnel to the relief work of the International Red Cross. Doctors, nurses, nutritionists, physiotherapists, pharmacists, sanitary and water engineers, motor mechanics, and logistics specialists are recruited on short-term contracts for service in conflict or disaster areas in different parts of the world, as occasion demands.

The Youth Section was started in 1924. Young members study a wide variety of subjects from first aid and nursing to accident prevention and international understanding. Training is put to full use on the holidays for handicapped children which county branches run every summer. Guests are paired with young members who look after them, help them with their toilet, to dress, eat, and so on.

The Society operates through local offices in England, Wales, Scotland, Northern Ireland, the Channel Islands, the Isle of Man, and the UK's remaining colonies and dependencies. The Society's governing body is the Council which is responsible for its policies, for the formation of branches and for presenting the conditions of membership. The Trustees who manage the Society's affairs, at national and local level, discharge all the responsibilities laid by law on Charity Trustees (see CHARITIES ACT, 1960). To train its members and maintain its services it relies on donations from the public.   ANN CLAYTON

Further reading

Many publications on different aspects of the Red Cross are published by the International Red Cross in Geneva and are obtainable from The Henry Dunant Institute, 114 Rue de Lausanne, 1202 Geneva, Switzerland. Many others about the International Red Cross and the British Red Cross Society are obtainable from the Supply Department, British Red Cross, 4 Grosvenor Crescent, London SW1X 7EQ, and include:

Boissier, P. (1947). *Henry Dunant*. Geneva.
Dunant, H. (1862). *A Memory of Solferino*. Geneva.
Junot, M. (1951). *Warrior Without Weapons*. London.
Oliver, B. (1966). *The British Red Cross in Action*. London.

REDI, FRANCESCO (1626–97/8). Italian physician, MD Pisa (1647). Redi was chief physician to the court of the Medicis and a pioneer parasitologist. In 1668 he disproved the widely held belief in the spontaneous generation of insects, showing that maggots developed from eggs laid by flies. He made valuable studies of *toxicology and *snake venoms.

RED TIDE is a red discoloration of sea-water due to the presence of enormous numbers of dinoflagellates, *protozoal organisms of the order Dinoflagellata, class Phytomastigophora. Red tides may be very destructive of fish and invertebrate life; species of the genus *Gonyaulax* are neurotoxic, and their ingestion by bivalve molluscs leads to 'paralytic shellfish poisoning' in man, a severe form of food poisoning which may be fatal. The neurotoxic alkaloid involved is saxitoxin.

REED, WALTER (1851–1902). American military medical officer, MD University of Virginia (1869). Following some years of conventional military medical service, Reed became professor of bacteriology at the Army Medical School in Washington, DC. In 1898 he was appointed head of a medical commission to Cuba, charged with study of the cause and mode of transmission of *yellow fever, which was causing serious morbidity and mortality among American troops there. By 1900, using human volunteers (members of the commission and soldiers), Reed's group had established that the disease is contracted by bite of an infected mosquito. This led directly to control of the disease in Cuba, and, shortly thereafter, in Panama, by eliminating mosquito breeding places. It is believed that the Panama Canal could not have been built without control of yellow fever. (See also TROPICAL MEDICINE.)

REFLEX. Any involuntary or automatic response to a stimulus. The nervous pathway mediating a reflex is termed a reflex arc and represents a circuit by which the *receptor which has been stimulated is connected to the effector organ which responds.

REFLEX ARC. See REFLEX.

REFLUX. Retrograde flow.

REFLUX OESOPHAGITIS is inflammation of the lower part of the *oesophagus caused by regurgitation of gastric contents containing acid and *pepsin. See also HIATUS HERNIA; HEARTBURN.

REFRACTION is the deflection of light waves as they pass from one medium to another of different optical density, the deflection occurring at the boundary between the two.

REFRACTIVE ERROR is any impairment of the lens function of the eyes, such as *myopia, *hypermetropia, *presbyopia, etc. See OPHTHALMOLOGY.

REFSUM'S DISEASE is a rare *recessive disorder associated with an inability to metabolize a particular *fatty acid (phytanic acid). The chief manifestations are motor and sensory *neuropathy, *deafness, *ataxia, *retinal degeneration, *cardiomyopathy, and *ichthyosis.

REFUSE DISPOSAL. In the UK responsibility for refuse is distributed as follows: in England, district and London borough councils must collect the refuse, county councils and the Greater London Council must dispose of it; in Scotland and Wales, district councils must both collect and dispose of it. An exception concerns remote dwelling-places, where councils are not obliged to provide a service unless the Secretary of State for the Environment requires them to do so. Services which the majority of councils provide, though they are not obliged to do so, include the provision of bottle-banks, the removal of abandoned cars, the disposal of rubble, and the collection of unwanted large household items like cookers and refrigerators.

REGENERATION is the replacement or regrowth of a substance or structure in its original form and by natural processes.

REGIMEN. A course of diet, exercise, or mode of living prescribed for health reasons.

REGIMEN SANITATIS SALERNITANUM. The *Salernitan Guide to Health,* a famous and popular work of the 12th c. *Salerno school of medicine, probably by a number of authors. Written in verse, the *Guide* appeared in many versions, editions, and translations, one of which includes the well-known couplet:

Use three physicians still, first Doctor Quiet,
Next Doctor Merryman and Doctor Diet.

The *Guide* was essentially a handbook of home medicine. It is said to have been written for the crusader, Robert, Duke of Normandy, when he visited Salerno.

REGIONAL ANAESTHESIA. See LOCAL ANAESTHESIA.

REGIONAL ILEITIS. See CROHN'S DISEASE.

REGISTRAR. One whose responsibility it is to maintain records. In many organizations in the UK, such as universities and the *General Medical Council, for example, the Registrar is the chief administrative officer. In the context of hospital medicine in the UK, a registrar is a doctor undergoing further training with a view eventually to attaining consultant status, that is to becoming a recognized specialist in one of the branches of medicine. 'Registrar' when otherwise unqualified denotes a person usually in the third or fourth year following graduation in medicine (second or third year following full registration), whereas a 'senior registrar' is already likely to have served as a registrar for two years and to be undertaking a final period of training and preparation while awaiting a *consultant post. The former grade of 'junior registrar' is now rarely used, having been replaced by 'senior house officer'. The fact that many present-day registrars have the task of completing and ensuring the accuracy of case-records among their duties recalls the origin of the term. See POSTGRADUATE AND CONTINUING MEDICAL EDUCATION.

REGISTRAR GENERAL. An officer having the superintendence of the registration of all births, deaths, and marriages in England and Wales. He is appointed by the Queen under the terms of the Registration Service Act 1953, which obliges him to supply registrars of births and deaths with durable register books, strong fire-resisting storage boxes, and forms for certified copies. The Registrar General is also responsible for making arrangements for taking a population census when an Order in Council made by the Queen so directs. See also OFFICE OF POPULATION, CENSUSES, AND SURVEYS.

REGISTRARS OF BIRTHS AND DEATHS. Under the UK Registration Service Act 1953, each county council, county borough council, and London borough council is obliged to make a scheme, known as 'the local scheme', for the organization of the registration service in its area and to have the scheme approved. The area of each council is divided into districts and subdistricts. For each district, a superintendent registrar of births, deaths, and marriages is appointed, and for each subdistrict a registrar of births and deaths, who may also have conferred on him by the local scheme the function of a registrar of marriages for the purposes of the Marriage Act 1949. A registrar of births and deaths in England and Wales must register the birth of every child within his subdistrict within six weeks of its occurrence. The death of each person must be registered within a similar period.

REGISTRATION in UK medicine is one of the responsibilities of the *General Medical Council (GMC), the statutory professional body for governing the professional standards and conduct of doctors. Registration involves the keeping of the *Medical Register* which is the official reference of enquiry as to whether a person is qualified in medicine or not. Unless a doctor's name is on the *Register*, he is precluded from filling a public office, from using dangerous drugs, from signing death certificates, and from performing certain other duties such as the issue of statutory certificates. Registration requires satisfactory completion of a course of study approved by the GMC. After the final examination, provisional registration is granted. Before the student proceeds to full registration, he must work as a house officer for one year in a recognized hospital, six months in surgery and six months in medicine (with certain alternatives). Registration of Commonwealth and foreign medical graduates wishing to work in the UK is also the responsibility of the GMC.

In other countries, registration of medical graduates is sometimes carried out by a similar national body, sometimes by Ministries or Departments of Health, sometimes by registration authorities of individual states (as in the USA, Canada, and Australia), and sometimes by local medical associations.

REGISTRATION ACT 1836. The Births and Deaths Registration Act 1836 was an enactment which provided for the registration of births, deaths, and marriages in England. It has been superseded by subsequent Acts, the latest being the Births and Deaths Registration Act 1953. Intervening legislation was enacted in 1837, 1858, 1874, and 1926.

REGURGITATION is retrograde flow, particularly with reference to the return of swallowed food and drink into the mouth and to the backwards leakage of blood across an incompetent cardiac valve (e.g. mitral regurgitation, aortic regurgitation, etc).

REHABILITATION

Definitions of rehabilitation abound. Indeed, rehabilitation is a general term applied with equal correctness to restoring old houses, to helping alcoholics, and to many others aspects of care of both mental and physical illness. While the importance of rehabilitating those with mental illness is well recognized (see PSYCHIATRY) this article will deal solely with problems consequent upon *physical* disease.

The Mair Report (Mair, 1972) on the organization of rehabilitation services for Scotland stated 'rehabilitation implies the restoration of patients to their fullest physical, mental and social capacity'. This definition is important in implying that it is not invariably necessary to do things to the patient.

The *World Health Organization (WHO) definition is longer and more generally accepted: 'As applied to disability, rehabilitation is the combined and co-ordinated use of medical, social, educational and vocational measures for training and retraining the individual to the highest possible level of functional ability'. This definition recognizes that the best results come from a co-ordinated and direct approach. There are, however, cynics who consider that the process of rehabilitation constitutes treatment of the patients so that planned withdrawal of services may convert a consumer of health and welfare services into a contributor to them (in the form of taxes paid). Many severely disabled people in industrial societies would welcome the opportunity to work and thus to contribute to society: indeed, many do, but some cannot. Nevertheless, most of those in developing countries have little chance to do so, where unemployment rates (if known) may be as high as 25 per cent or even 40 per cent.

The objectives of rehabilitation thus are clear: to restore the subject to his maximum function and to maintain him there.

Causes of disability. Adults in the Western world can usually expect some five decades free of disability. Subsequently they may be subject to *degenerative diseases such as *osteoarthritis and *atherosclerosis (causing strokes, *heart attacks, and peripheral vascular disease).

Younger people often need rehabilitation services to enable them to overcome—at least to some extent—the effects of *congenital disorders, principally *cerebral palsy and *spina bifida and, rarely, such diseases as inflammatory arthritis. In such cases, we more properly talk of 'habilitation'. However, in other young people, perhaps with head or spinal injury or other multiple injuries often attributable to road accidents, where the individual was previously physically normal, it is again correct to speak of rehabilitation.

We are thus faced with many different diseases and situations: the condition may have been due to a single incident such as a road traffic accident resulting in paralysis of the legs (paraplegia); the patient must learn to come to terms with his new situation which, though irreversible, is (almost) static. Some diseases, however, such as *muscular dystrophy, progress steadily and inexorably: *motor neurone disease, another example, is often fatal in under five years and is distressing to watch or experience. Many people find it difficult to adjust to chronic disease, particularly when its course is fluctuating, as is often true of *multiple sclerosis, and the principal need of such sufferers may be repeated access to rehabilitation services.

In the Third World, major causes of disability are different and often preventable by simple measures—clean water, and *immunization against *poliomyelitis and other diseases. Much of the discussion in this article must be understood in the light of the limited resources and different priorities available in such countries, often with a total absence of paramedical (rehabilitation) staff; this makes much of current practice in industrialized nations inappropriate to less developed countries, even though the same principles apply.

Much disability is of traumatic origin and it is regrettable that advances in rehabilitation techniques have often been related to war. Sir Robert *Jones, in the First World War, set up his famous workshops to provide work for disabled war veterans: in the basement of Shepherd's Bush Hospital a workshop was fitted with lathes and carpentry tools and men were paid for their work, which also produced an increase in muscle strength and range of joint movement. Second World War pilots were few and often returned rapidly to fighting in the Battle of Britain with the help of intensive rehabilitation, which was of proved effectiveness. Veterans of the Vietnam war in the USA enjoy services which are much better co-ordinated than those available to civilians; advances in equipment design have also resulted.

Terminology. There is much confusion of terminology, partly arising from the need to remove from common parlance words that had become pejorative: the 'cripple' is now a 'disabled' or 'handicapped person'. But not everyone with a disability is handicapped: some people lacking all or part of an arm or leg lead a normal life. The dustman who has a disease leaving him without useful speech may still be able to pursue his normal work, unlike the barrister; it is the interaction of disorder and circumstance that determines outcome. The WHO classification developed by Wood (1980) overcomes many of these difficulties and allows precise definition: thus, it speaks of impairment, disability, and handicap. Impairment has been defined as 'lacking part or all of a limb, or having a defective limb, organ or mechanism of the body'. Disablement is 'the loss or reduction of functional ability'. Handicap is 'the disadvantage or restriction of activity caused by disability'.

However, in many situations the simpler classification of Agerholm (1975), a pioneer in rehabilitation, particularly of young people, is preferred. The separation of intrinsic versus extrinsic handicaps and functional assessments, such as that of Steinbocker et al. (1949), used for many years in rheumatology, also have their uses. Self-assessment has been proved to be valid and the Health Assessment Questionnaire developed at Stanford (Fries et al., 1980), may well replace that of Steinbocker. In the important national survey of the disabled completed in the UK by Amelia Harris in 1971, self-assessment was shown to be acceptable. Here, for the first time, the extent of disability within a population was shown: some 3.5 million adults were identified, of whom approximately one-third were severely handicapped; there were only minor regional variations. Few other countries, even in the developed world, have comparable reliable figures. Overall, 450 million people are thought to be disabled in the world. One-third of all people are impaired, and probably some 3 per cent of the population is severely disabled.

Resources available to the disabled. In general these can be divided into restorative (largely medical) and supportive services. Thus a disease process can be modified to prevent disability (e.g. good control of *diabetes may prevent blindness; control of *hypertension may prevent strokes, or further strokes where a first has been suffered). Or one can draw on all the patient's resources (with treatment such as *physiotherapy and *occupational therapy, for instance, to maintain walking for as long as possible in a progressive neurological disorder); or to contain disability one can alter the environment (e.g. make the kitchen accessible to someone wishing to use it from a wheelchair). Finally, one can accept the disability and put in support services (the nurse or bath attendant to help the frail subject bath in safety; the provision of *meals on wheels). These supportive benefits are usually most widely available in societies where there is some form of socialized medicine. Otherwise the family must provide and voluntary societies help as best as they can. Such voluntary help is patchy and one of its functions may be to innovate, to pilot good practice, and to support new developments and research.

Organization of services. The principles of rehabilitation remain unchanged across the globe but the organization of the services required is vastly different, even from one developed country to another. This is inevitable, given the social content of the specialty and the variety of social systems within which it operates. Here the UK situation will be described in detail, as one example.

Medical services. The *general practitioner is the first point of referral for a patient and, in his team, the *district nurse provides nursing at home and is a valued source of information on matters such as how and where to obtain equipment (e.g. incontinence appliances). Referrals are made from the primary care team to the hospital services for medical and surgical help, and to the local authority (social services department) for aids to daily living, for ramps and rails, home helps, meals on wheels, day care facilities, etc., and to the Artificial Limb and Appliance Centre for wheelchairs (Fig. 1) and prostheses. The general practitioner has also direct access to the Disablement

Fig. 1. A self-propelled electric wheelchair for outdoor use. (Reproduced by courtesy of Vessa Ltd)

Resettlement Officer employed by the Manpower Services Commission and located at Job Centres.

Community services are organized by the District Health Authority and their availability differs widely (see also COMMUNITY MEDICINE). Community physiotherapists are becoming more widely available to instruct disabled people and their relatives in their home in the best way of managing (e.g.) their mobility problems. Often this involves teaching the safest and most practical method of transferring from bed to chair (or commode or wheelchair) or of standing. Community occupational therapists are usually employed either by the social services or by the health authority and are available to patients at home and in local authority institutions, their work being an extension of that of their colleagues in hospital. There is increasing emphasis on the disabled person having a part in the decisions which most affect him, particularly including where he will live, be it an institution or, preferably, at home. To remain at home may require many home adaptations. A recent code of practice published by the Royal Association for Disability and Rehabilitation (RADAR) (1983) makes it clear that the disabled person is best served in this respect by an occupational therapist whose expertise on his behalf is accessible to social services and other bodies such as the Housing Department and the Department of the Environment (who may give grants for home adaptations). (See also SOCIAL WORK.)

Hospital services; rehabilitation units. Departments of rehabilitation exist in most district general hospitals and consist of the departments of physiotherapy, occupational therapy, and speech therapy, available to in-patients and out-patients. Many patients (e.g. those recovering from a meniscectomy (removal of a cartilage from the knee joint)) require treatment from only one department. Those with more complex disabilities (e.g. head injury) require co-ordinated and progressive care from several departments and may be treated in specialist units. Thus there are nine spinal injuries units spaced over the country; several neurosurgical units have access to head injury workshops and some patients with stroke are fortunate enough to be treated in stroke units. The value of these units remains to be proved but much evidence on the value of rehabilitation units in general has been obtained by Evans (1981) working at the United Services Medical Rehabilitation Unit at Chessington, Surrey.

Rehabilitation units usually treat a wide range of new disabilities; some may specialize, as, for example, in neurological disease. Some are small in-patient units concentrating on severe and often multiple disabilities (Leeds); some have arisen from provision for one group of workers such as coal-miners, as in Durham, where their worth has been proved; they are geared to a more active later phase of treatment. Mary Marlborough Lodge at Oxford under Philip Nichols was a pioneer unit in the assessment of and research into severe disability. Specialist units for children (usually with cerebral palsy) also exist (Cheyne Walk, Chelsea, London), some attached to special schools and pioneering new developments (Chailey Heritage). One, Garston Manor Rehabilitation Centre is unique in having an Employment Rehabilitation Centre alongside it. In the 1970s the then Minister of Health, Sir Keith Joseph, designated certain centres of excellence as National Demonstration Centres, demonstrating and teaching good practice in the specialty.

Staffing of rehabilitation units. These units are usually under the direction of a physician or surgeon. The nursing officer of the ward remains the key figure, co-ordinating the management of the individual patient, ensuring that what was learnt in occupational therapy or physiotherapy departments is practised in normal daily activities such as eating, washing, dressing, and use of the toilet. It may take many weeks and months to regain these simple skills after an accident or an event such as a stroke, and to learn to use arms and legs again.

The occupational therapist (ergotherapist, OT) and her aides are available to assess the patient's ability in self-care. Toileting is an area of particular importance where inadequate performance/arrangements preclude a return to normal activity (Fig. 2). She may assess the patient's potential and ability in other areas, such as food preparation, budgeting, and handling, mobility inside and outside the home, and vocational skills. She will help retrain in these and often has to help the patient adjust to such impairments as a poor short-term memory or partial field of vision. She may aim to increase the attention span and she may use a variety of normal teaching methods and liaise with

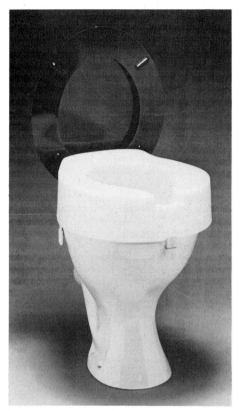

Fig. 2. A raised toilet seat especially designed for a patient with arthritis in the hips and knees. (Reproduced by courtesy of Nottingham Medical Aids Ltd)

the rehabilitation team. Their function of analysing speech problems (a field which is developing increasingly a scientific base; see LANGUAGE, COGNITION, AND HIGHER CEREBRAL FUNCTION) and of giving treatment, brings them close to a patient as they help to improve his communication (whether verbal or non-verbal, by voice or by electronic communicator, often called a communication aid).

Other members of the team vary according to need and include:

Clinical psychologist. He or she is especially useful in those with head injuries and with discrete neurological deficits. A variety of techniques are used for assessment and treatment including behaviour modification (see PSYCHOLOGY).

Social worker. His or her function is not only to assist the patient to obtain benefits, funds, and suitable housing, but also to counsel the patient and relatives so that their grief and depression (and often anger and guilt) in the face of a changed personality, changed abilities, or reversed roles may be worked through to the family's eventual benefit (see SOCIAL WORK).

*Health visitor. This appointment is peculiar to the UK; the value of this (rare) member of the rehabilitation team has been pioneered in the

teaching staff. She performs job evaluations which are useful to industrial rehabilitation units and to potential employers. She may be responsible for making individual splints. She is particularly responsible for modifying home and workplace to increase the patient's independence (Fig. 3).

Physiotherapists are also invaluable and in rehabilitation have a great part to play in teaching patients to relearn not only individual muscle movements but also patterns of movement and normal activities. The physiotherapist gives both individual and group therapy, and (it is to be hoped) has access to hydrotherapy (exercises in warm water). In rehabilitation units in more developed areas her function is less that of using individual physical treatment techniques (heat, ice, *ultrasound, etc.) and more that of improving physical function, mobility, and endurance, and maximizing muscle power. She also seeks to preserve and increase joint range and to prevent *contractures that may arise with prolonged unconsciousness. Remedial gymnasts performing similar functions are available in some places.

*Speech therapists are also valuable members of

Fig. 3. A trolley which enables a patient with arthritis to move objects around the home

rehabilitation unit in Leeds. She is a practical nursing adviser available to patients at home and is often also part of the primary care team.

In many units one finds other specialists such as *disablement resettlement officer, rehabilitation officer, bioengineer, appliance officer,* according to the main interests of the unit and often also there are associated research teams (see also PROFESSIONS SUPPLEMENTARY, ETC. IN THE UK).

Younger disabled units (YDU) have been established in many parts of the country to provide residential accommodation for those most severely disabled adults who do not have resources to manage at home; they avoid the placement of such individuals in geriatric units. These units function in many ways, varying from the simple one of providing permanent care to the more dynamic approach of providing intermittent and holiday relief, treatment, and a wide range of activities and support. Such units have more therapists available and aim to allow the residents much freedom and responsibility. Most purpose-built YDUs provide accommodation for 20–25 persons at ground level and many are in hospital grounds. Many similar residential units have been established and funded through voluntary effort. Among the most notable in the UK are the Cheshire and Sue Ryder homes, initiated by Group Captain Leonard Cheshire, VC, OM and his wife, Baroness Ryder, and the many homes and schools for disabled children, such as those of the Shaftesbury Society. It is hoped that more developments of the type pioneered by Habinteg (an organization building specialized housing for the disabled; 6 Duke Mews, London W1M 5RB) will arise, with severely disabled people living in adapted housing in the community but provided with a high level of support services (including nursing and care assistants). They are a potentially valuable resource of expertise for the surrounding community.

Aids centres. At the beginning of the 1970s it was realized that simple technical aids could contribute much to independence. For instance, the conventional water tap (faucet) cannot be manipulated by someone with a poor, painful grip; a tap-turner with a long handle compensates. The Disabled Living Foundation in London was founded by Lady Hamilton and now some 15 independent centres in the UK provide professional (usually OT) help and an extensive display of equipment, together with information. Similar aids centres are now found in many industrialized countries. Communication aids centres are also being developed in the UK to provide similar expertise and advice about equipment (often computer-based), designed to increase communication between speech-disabled persons and others.

Environmental and speech aids. Most aids to independence have been produced using only simple engineering principles. The situation is now changing rapidly and the field of environmental aids, teaching aids, and communication aids is expanding fast. Many new aids are based on the microchip. Developments in the field are well exemplified by alarm systems and environmental controls. Domestic alarm systems are useful for disabled people living alone. They often consist of a bell, buzzer, or flashing light situated in a prominent position. Like many communication devices they can be activated in several ways such as by a pull cord, push-button, or suck/blow controls. They are cheap, simple, and reasonably reliable. However, in an emergency they may not be reached by the person at risk: thus, body-worn devices have been developed. Others can be attached to clothing or a walking stick and are activated by greater-than-normal angles. Some patients are better served by an alarm system consisting of both a body-worn transmitter and a central receiver. The 'phone alerts' and similar systems are versatile and reliable but are limited by the range of the transmitter. The citizens' band wavelength can function as an emergency call system as well as offering an interactive leisure pursuit.

Environmental controls. The longest established of these is the 'Possum' (i.e. patient-operated selector mechanism) range (Fig. 4). The Possum PSU3 system comprises an indicator panel showing up to 11 electrical appliances (such as telephone, television, front door lock) which can be turned on or off. The Hugh Steeper Environmental Control is similar. For the most severely disabled there is a whistler aid, in which up to six devices can be activated by the whistling of certain tunes. Where there is any remaining residual movement, this can be utilized to control the required devices through a variety of interfaces such as microswitches, pressure pads, or joy sticks operated (e.g.) by the mouth, chin, or limb. Voice input modules can be attached to computers which thus respond to spoken commands by activating environmental controls.

Domestic equipment can be operated by remote control using infra-red beams. Radar beams and sonic beams are also in use.

Disabled people can have access to printed and

Fig. 4. One example of Possum equipment (see text). (Reproduced by courtesy of Possum Controls Ltd)

spoken outputs. Thus the Possum Text Processor allows the subject to compose text on a visual display unit and edit and correct it before the typewriter produces a written copy. Such copy can be stored in the memory of the equipment to be used at a later date.

Communication aids are now produced in a great variety. Some have only a very simple format—often of pictures—readily understood by those whose language processes are severely disrupted. Others (such as the Canon Communicator) look like a calculator, are as portable, and produce a length of printed tape. Some can produce a written output in another language, assisting the disabled traveller. Others use a voice synthesizer to produce a spoken output which gives to the non-vocal the immediacy of the spoken word. Much research is in progress to determine the best form of speech synthesis in terms of unlimited vocabulary and voice quality.

Rehabilitation outside the hospital. Rehabilitation is said to begin in the ambulance bringing the patient to hospital: it certainly does not end at the hospital gates as the patient leaves; indeed, the process of returning to useful life is only just then beginning. Handicapped adolescents are often immature and have lost much schooling. Although some benefit from residential facilities to give independence or mobility training (e.g. Banstead Place, part of the Queen Elizabeth Foundation for the Disabled), more will benefit from local authority further education training near home. Courses for handicapped school-leavers can open the way to the young person's attendance at other further education facilities, access permitting.

Employment rehabilitation (Manpower Services Commission). The history of employment rehabilitation is entwined with that of medical rehabilitation and ideally still remains closely linked. The Vauxhall (GM) Motor Works (Luton, Bedford) provided an excellent early example of good practice which, sadly, has not been followed. Workers unable, or not yet ready, to return to their full-time employment came to work daily in the rehabilitation centre and underwent a graduated programme which fitted them to return to the shop floor relatively soon afterwards. Employment Rehabilitation Centres are spread over the country, mainly in industrialized areas; all except one are non-residential, providing a variety of assessment courses for disabled and non-disabled workers in which the worker has the opportunity of trying lighter or heavier work (e.g. wood and metal work, packing and assembly, clerical work, etc.). After several weeks' attendance, a report is prepared and the subject is recommended for (say) sheltered work (e.g. in a Remploy factory), for work in 'open' industry, or for retraining. A (voluntary) register of disabled people is kept at Job Centres; and employers with over 20 employees must by law employ 3 per cent of registered disabled persons. However, in times of high unemployment many disabled people remain unemployed for long periods. Those with higher qualifications may seek employment using the Professional and Executive Register; most people seek the services of the disablement resettlement officer at the local Job Centre. Aids and adaptations to work, grants, and help with fares are all available through the Manpower Services Commission. In the USA one finds sophisticated job evaluation schemes (including work sampling). Their usefulness for the disabled worker in the UK is undergoing preliminary examination.

Voluntary and self-help groups. Expectations and disabilities constantly change and voluntary organizations remain necessary even in countries with well-developed health and welfare services. They are helpful in three areas:

1. Self-help, mutual support, and education;
2. As pressure groups seeking improvements in facilities; and
3. In promoting new developments and research.

These groups include general organizations such as the Royal Association for Disability and Rehabilitation (RADAR) and ones specific to a medical condition (such as Arthritis Care in the UK, and the Rheumatism and Arthritis Association of Victoria, in Victoria, Australia). In the USA, patient organizations also achieve a great deal and ensure that the Rehabilitation Act of 1973 (quoted in Hale, 1979) is enacted (e.g. the Independent Living Foundation in Berkeley, California). Information on disability groups, rights, and benefits is becoming easier to obtain and many valuable publications are available (see Appendix to this entry).

Services for the blind have been long-established, are well developed, and are not medically based, being provided in the UK by the Royal National Institute for the Blind.

Services for the deaf are provided by the National Health Service and by the Royal National Institute for the Deaf.

Legislation is crucial to the development of minority rights. Although one in 10 adults in the UK will be disabled at some time, little specific legislation has been enacted until the last few decades.

In 1601 the *Poor Law was enacted, care of the sick, poor, and homeless passing to the local authority, where it still resides. In 1944 the *Disabled Persons (Employment) Act was passed following the *Tomlinson Report* (this recommending the disabled persons' register or quota, and industrial rehabilitation). The *National Health Service Act, the *National Insurance Act, and *National Insurance (Industrial Injuries) Act in 1946 laid the foundation of the Welfare State. Three rehabilitation reports, of Piercey in 1956, Tunbridge in 1972, and Mair (Scotland) in 1972 have highlighted current deficiencies and made recommendations. But perhaps the most significant Act—with its recent amendments—has been the Chronically Sick and Disabled Persons Act 1970. In essence this is an enabling act which states:

I:

1. It shall be the duty of every local authority having functions under section 29 of the National Assistance Act 1948 to inform themselves of the number of persons to whom that section applies within their area and of the need for the making by the authority of arrangements under that section for such persons.

2. Every such local authority:

(a) shall cause to be published from time to time at such times and in such manner as they consider appropriate general information as to the services provided under arrangements made by the authority under the said section 29 which are for the time being available in their area; and

(b) shall ensure that any such person as aforesaid who uses any of those services is informed of any other of those services which in the opinion of the authority is relevant to his needs.

3. This section shall come into operation on such date as the Secretary of State may by order make by statutory instrument.

II:

1. Where a local authority having functions under section 29 of the National Assistance Act 1948 are satisfied in the case of any person to whom that section applies who is ordinarily resident in their area that it is necessary in order to meet the needs of that person for that authority to make arrangements for all or any of the following matters, namely:

(a) the provision of practical assistance for that person in his home;

(b) the provision for that person of, or assistance to that person in obtaining, wireless, television, library or similar recreational facilities;

(c) the provision for that person of lectures, games, outings or other recreational facilities outside his home or assistance to that person in taking advantage of educational facilities available to him;

(d) the provision for that person of facilities for, or assistance in, travelling to and from his home for the purpose of participating in any services provided under arrangements made by the authority under the said section 29 or, with the approval of the authority, in any services provided otherwise than as aforesaid which are similar to services which could be provided under such arrangements;

(e) the provision of assistance for that person in arranging for the carrying out of any works of adaptation in his home or the provision of any additional facilities designed to secure his greater safety, comfort or convenience;

(f) facilitating the taking of holidays by that person, whether at holiday homes or otherwise and whether provided under arrangements made by the authority or otherwise;

(g) the provision of meals for that person whether in his home or elsewhere;

(h) the provision for that person of, or assistance to that person in obtaining, a telephone and any special equipment necessary to enable him to use a telephone.

In the USA the Rehabilitation Act 1973, Title 5, in particular Section 504, was crucial in forbidding bodies receiving Federal funds from discriminating against people in areas such as access, employment, health, social services, and transport. It was followed by a mass of regulations from various departments of Federal government amplifying the legislation. In Scandinavia the disabled have formed an effective pressure group for at least three decades and a significant part of the national budget has been devoted to their well-being. In Holland, provision is also well advanced, both in social areas and in hospital rehabilitation departments.

Learned societies include:

International. International Rehabilitation Medicine Association (IRMA); International Federation of Physical Medicine and Rehabilitation; Rehabilitation International (US-based).

UK. Group for the Management of Disability; British Paediatric Association—all children's disorders; British Society of Rheumatology (the result of a merger between the Heberden Society and the British Association of Rheumatology and Rehabilitation); British Geriatric Association; Society for Research in Rehabilitation—multidisciplinary.

Examples of medical (as opposed to social) rehabilitation. *Amputation and provision of prostheses.* Perhaps the simplest example of rehabilitation of physical disease is the replacement of part of a lower limb by a *prosthesis. Where the *amputation takes place in a young person, distally, say at the ankle, rehabilitation consists of the provision of a replacement prosthesis which can be inserted in a shoe and which is easily disguised. Normal walking is quickly resumed with little or no physiotherapeutic training.

A below-knee prosthesis is virtually undetectable in normal use (Fig. 5), but, as amputation takes place at higher levels or is bilateral, so training the patient becomes harder; energy expenditure in walking becomes greater and the elderly patient has much difficulty in gaining new skills. Best results are achieved with early training (even before amputation, if possible) with early mobilization, and with intensive exercise in a unit well-versed in the techniques. Meticulous surgery is required with close attention to the provision of a well-modelled, well-nourished stump and the prevention of undesirable contractures. The muscles to be used to control the prosthesis have to be strengthened and where amputation is high, much of the body's weight will initially be taken by the muscles of the shoulder girdle, which should be strengthened. As with all rehabilitation, the patient is better able to respond to training if he is otherwise fit and well, alert, co-operative, and motivated to return to his former life-style, and not obese. Very elderly patients may be too ill generally, too tired, and lacking in resources to cope with walking again after high amputation and may have to be trained in leading life from a wheelchair. Many patients using above-knee prostheses will be given pylons during retraining, while their individually made prosthesis is produ-

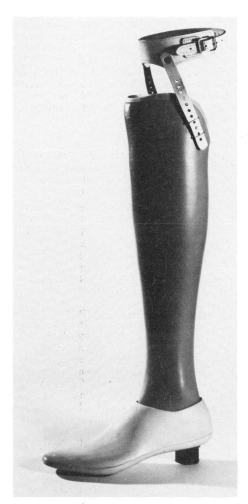

Fig. 5. An artificial leg provided for a below-knee amputation, using a patella tendon bearing with a plastic socket, cuff suspension, an articulated ankle, and a moulded foot. A cast of the patient's stump must be made and appropriate measurements taken before making and supplying such a prosthesis. (Reproduced by courtesy of the Artificial Limb and Appliance Centre, Department of Health and Social Security; Crown copyright)

Fig. 6. A myoelectric (electrically powered) prosthetic hand. (Reproduced by courtesy of Hugh Steeper Ltd)

ced by suppliers working to the specifications produced by the Artificial Limb and Appliance Centres (ALAC) in the UK. Mechanisms for provision of such aids, of wheelchairs, of bicycles, and other equipment differ widely from country to country. Modular prostheses are becoming more readily available, and can be obtained and altered so speedily that pylons may be unnecessary. The Pneumatic Post-Amputation Mobility Aid (PAM) is used to speed return to walking, being used for a short time after the operation until the temporary prosthesis is available. The necessity for meticulous stump bandaging is thus declining.

Upper limb prostheses. Captain Hook in *Peter Pan* had a split hook instead of a hand. Many today still rely on such a simple device for it is reliable, sturdy, and effective. However, there is no sensory feedback from such apparatus to the brain, so that the child may reject the prosthesis, and all potential users have to be convinced of its functional worth. This applies especially to complex disabilities in which powered prostheses (Fig. 6), such as those pioneered by Lawson of Canada and Simpson of Edinburgh, are tried. Congenital deformities and absence of a limb were frequent in the babies which followed the prescription of *thalidomide for pregnant women. A Swedish powered (myoelectric) hand is still being evaluated in young children and its early success suggests that it will be offered to older children.

Rehabilitation of the hand. There is now much interest in the total pre- and postoperative care of the hand, particularly following the development of prostheses for the proximal interphalangeal and metacarpal joints. Developments in the surgery of the hand owe much to Flatt (1978, 1979) and Swanson. Interest in total care was first stressed by Wynn Parry with the publication of his book *Rehabilitation of the Hand* in 1958. Much scientific work and research is reported at the international congresses organized by the International Federation of Societies for the Surgery of the Hand.

Spinal injuries. Injuries to the spine can occur along its length. When they damage the *spinal cord within it, they lead to either a *paraplegia (in which the legs are affected), or a *quadriplegia (or tetraplegia), in which all four limbs and trunk are paralysed, due to damage to the cervical portion of the cord. Damage is often irreversible. Less commonly other non-accidental causes may lead to progressive disability. Not only is there loss of ability to move the limb but the limb muscles may be released from higher control (*spasticity) and may take up abnormal postures and movements. Uncorrected, these lead to contractures. Inability to move the body leads to the development of skin *necrosis due to high local pressures and shearing stresses on the skin. *Anaesthesia of the affected area and *incontinence compound the problem. Pressure sores develop. Reflex activity of the bowel and bladder is abolished in most spinal cord injuries; urinary tract infections are common, leading to renal and bladder stones and eventual renal failure.

Quadriplegia is associated with paralysis of respiratory muscles. Indeed an injury above the fourth cervical segment is incompatible with life. Sensory loss has been mentioned; in addition the *autonomic nervous system regulating bodily functions is damaged too, resulting in sudden changes, for example, in *blood pressure, in *temperature control, and in *sweating.

The survival of such patients receiving full support now approaches the normal but such patients rarely survive long in developing countries. Survival is also closely geared to the development of specialist units and to the speed with which patients reach them. Continuing survival is related to the extent of the lesion, the ability of the patient and family to deal with the disability, and the provisions that are made for such subjects, particularly for follow-up care.

A specialist centre was set up in the UK after the Second World War at *Stoke Mandeville (1944), with the pioneering work of Sir Ludwig *Guttmann (1976). The continued interest of such patients in life—and their ability often to live a remarkably full life—also owes much to his development of the use of games in therapy. The International Paraplegic Olympics held at Stoke Mandeville and subsequently at Olympic sites following the pattern of the Olympic Games are now famous. (See SPORT AND MEDICINE.)

The Spinal Injuries Association provides patients with their own organization. International meetings are organized by the International Rehabilitation Medicine Association (IRMA), Admin. Secretariat, Oberwilerstrasse 23, CH-4012, Basle, Switzerland; and also by Rehabilitation International, 432 Park Avenue South, New York, NY 10016. UK meetings are organized by the Society for Research in Rehabilitation (SRR), Department of Speech Therapy, Frenchay Hospital, Bristol. *Paraplegia* is the specialist journal.

Hemiplegia is paralysis of half the body, that is a hand, arm, and ipsilateral leg, often with loss of sensation, balance, and visual field, with associated speech problems in right hemiplegia or of visuospatial competence in left hemiplegia (see NEUROLOGY). In spite of the fact that the single largest cause of chronic disability in the Western world arises from stroke, there had been little interest in the management of adult hemiplegia

until the work of the Bobaths became more widely known with the publication of the book, *Adult Hemiplegia*, in 1978. Several techniques of physiotherapy treatment now exist and almost all stress the importance of adopting a bilateral approach. They seek to prevent the patient's rejection of his hemiplegic side and to re-establish the paralysed side as an active part of his body. Considerable success has followed the adoption of such techniques, even when hand function has not been restored, by the use of such therapy (based on the developmental sequence of walking and on the modification of dynamic spastic patterns and their decrease by alteration in body positions out of the spastic posture). Many patients are able to stand and walk, and gain some independence. To be successful, as with other rehabilitation, the approach has to be holistic and the various therapists work closely together (in all neurological disabilities the whole range of rehabilitation staff will often be required).

Rheumatology. Chronic rheumatic disorders are extremely common: rheumatoid arthritis itself occurs in over 1 per cent of the population; chronic rheumatic disorders account for some 20 per cent of chronic disability in the adult population. Much of the expertise developed in rehabilitation in the UK is closely linked with the growth of the specialty of physical medicine and rheumatology, under the umbrella of the British Medical Disability Society and the British Society for Rheumatology, in contradistinction to the situation in North America. Rehabilitation of rheumatic patients is seen as part of the total management of the patient: that is, drug therapy to control or modify the disease is seen as part of a spectrum of help comprising physiotherapy in which joint range and muscle power are conserved; occupational therapy (the provision of aids and splints and instruction in joint protection; the maintenance of self care and domestic and vocational functions; education, self-help groups, and involvement of the services of the Manpower Services Commission) supplements medical help. Rheumatology and rehabilitation itself may take place in specialist units or (as in East Germany) in rheumatological rehabilitation centres or in spas (as in Switzerland). (See also RHEUMATOLOGY.)

History. Since rehabilitation is relatively young, indeed unrecognized in some countries which have no relevant training structure for their doctors, it is difficult to give a cohesive history. A few landmarks will be mentioned.

Much of the early work in the UK arose from war experiences. During the First World War Sir Robert Jones provided remedial work for disabled servicemen. The Ministry of Pensions established government instructional factories to retrain disabled servicemen. These became Government Training Centres, now Skill Centres.

Interest lapsed until the Second World War, when the Royal Air Force developed excellent residential rehabilitation centres under Sir Reginald Watson-Jones, Sir Henry Osmond-Clark, and Group Captain C. J. S. O'Malley. In 1944, Sir Ludwig Guttmann started the first spinal injuries unit at Stoke Mandeville and thereafter others opened in many countries including the USA, Canada, France, Scandinavia, Switzerland, and Australia. The accent now is on a more aggressive approach with early stabilizing surgery plus more interest in reconstructive upper limb surgery, particularly stimulated by the work of Zancolli in Argentina.

At the end of the war, many of the service doctors with such expertise returned to civilian life. Cooksey set up a rehabilitation unit at *King's College Hospital, in which the emphasis was more on domestic resettlement. Philip Nichols established a unique enterprise in Oxford at the Mary Marlborough Lodge, where comprehensive assessments of disabled patients' needs were undertaken. Gardening for the disabled was developed here, too. Some of the medical officers who had been in charge of the service rehabilitation units organized similar units in civil life—notably, Clacton, Durham, Garston Manor, and Camden Road Day Centre. Peter London developed rehabilitation workshops for the severely head-injured patient (The Lame Brain) as an annexe of the Birmingham Accident Hospital. Many other physicians returned to major teaching hospitals to run physical medicine departments which were closely linked with developing rheumatology services. Although this link continues in practice in the UK, the advisory bodies to the Royal Colleges of Physicians on both subjects (i.e. rehabilitation and rheumatology) are now separate. The decision has been made that each medical specialty should be responsible for the long-term care of its own patients. It is recognized, nevertheless, that regional services will be needed to deal with less common problems (such as spinal injuries) requiring highly specialized care.

In the North American subcontinent developments of the two specialties have always been separate. The US Military Services followed the lead of the Royal Air Force and opened service rehabilitation units under the inspiration of Howard A. Rusk. In peacetime, the *Veterans Administration Hospitals became active rehabilitation units and a similar pattern was followed in Canada and Australia. Rehabilitation as a medical discipline was originally linked with physical medicine (or physiatry in the USA) and in many countries that link still exists. A major concern has been in the field of physical treatments using such modalities as heat, ultrasound, ultraviolet light and electrical stimulation. Pioneer workers included Bauwens (UK), Lehmann, Krusen, and Licht (USA), Bourgignon (France), and Cumberbatch (Germany).

Many nations founded academies of physical medicine and rehabilitation with examinations to be passed before practice was allowed. In most European countries, physical medicine specialists are responsible for most rehabilitation, at least for locomotor and neurological disorders, and rheumatology is a quite separate specialty with no commitment to rehabilitation.

Scandinavia (Olle Hook, Nachemson, and others) has established a reputation for work on the scientific analysis of effects of exercise on human physiology and the *Scandinavian Journal of Rehabilitation Medicine* was the first journal to deal specifically with rehabilitation. The *International Journal of Rehabilitation Medicine* followed soon after and now attracts articles on all aspects of rehabilitation from many disciplines from all parts of the world.

Recently academies of rehabilitation medicine have been started in Singapore and Australia with special qualifying examinations.

There is a growing awareness of the needs of patients with problems of the special senses—Bach y Rita (California) has developed sensory substitute mechanisms for the blind. There are exciting advances in problems of the partially sighted and in implants for the deaf.

Severe head injuries present a particularly difficult problem with intellectual, behavioural, and physical disabilities. Special centres with a multidisciplinary approach are required (as found at Chessington (RAF), St Andrews, Northampton, and Tel Aviv, Israel).

Alongside the development of comprehensive rehabilitation services in the last 40 years has been the appreciation of the importance of return to work. Vocational counselling and retraining centres were pioneered in the UK and the USA and are now a feature of all rehabilitation projects throughout the world. Much attention has been paid to the design of aids to daily living and the solution of problems of disability in the home by modifying the working environment in the kitchen and easing the difficulties of bathing, toilet, dressing, feeding, and transfer from bed to chair. These are the particular responsibility of the occupational therapist. Paul Brand (Vellore, India) especially in his work on leprosy showed how simple apparatus and basic principles can transform the life of the disabled with minimal financial outlay. Educating society to accept disabled people is probably the last great barrier to rehabilitation.

Appendix. *Organizations, journals, etc. referred to in the text.*

Artificial Limb and Appliance Centre, Roehampton Lane, London SW15 5TR, UK

UK Manpower Services Commission, Selkirk House, 166 High Holborn, London WC1V 6PS, UK

Chartered Society of Physiotherapists, 14 Bedford Row, London WC1R 4ED, UK

College of Occupational Therapists, 20 Rede Place, Bayswater, London W2 4TU, UK

Royal Association for Disability and Rehabilitation (RADAR), 25 Mortimer Street, London W1N 8AB, UK

College of Speech Therapists, Harold Poster House, 6 Lechmere Road, London NW2 5BU, UK

Joint Aids Centres Committee (JACC), Leicester Aids Centre, 76 Clarendon Park Road, Leicester LE2 3AD, UK

Disabled Living Foundation, 346 Kensington High Street, London W14 8NS, UK

Queen Elizabeth Foundation for the Disabled, Leatherhead, Surrey KT22 0BN, UK

Royal National Institute for the Blind, 224 Great Portland St, London W1N 6AA, UK

Royal National Institute for the Deaf, 105 Gower St, London WC1E 6AH, UK

International Rehabilitation Medicine Association (IRMA), Hon. Sec. Dr. M. Grabois, Dept. Physical Medicine, Baylor College of Medicine, 1333 Moursund Ave., Houston, Texas 77030, USA. Journal address: ARC Epidemiology Research Unit, Stopford Building, Oxford Road, Manchester M13 9PT, UK

Self-help groups

Arthritis Care, 6 Grosvenor Crescent, London SW1X 7ER, UK

Rheumatism and Arthritis Association of Victoria, Victoria, Australia

Independent Living Foundation, Berkeley, California, USA

Sexual Problems of the Disabled (SPOD), 49 Victoria Street, London SW1H 0EU, UK

Spinal Injuries Association, 5 Crowndale Road, London NW1 1TU, UK

DIAL(UK), 117 High Street, Clay Cross, Chesterfield, Derbyshire, S15 9DZ, UK

Possible source books for relatives

Allbeson, J. and Douglas, J. (1983). *National Welfare Benefits Handbook.* London.

Chartered Society of Physiotherapists (1980). *Handling the Handicapped.* Cambridge.

Cochrane, G. and Wilshire, E. R. (1979–81). *Equipment for the Disabled.* Vols on *Leisure and Gardening* (1979); *Hoists and Walking Aids* (1980); *Disabled Child* (1980); *Home Management* (1981); *Clothing and Dressing, etc.* (1981). Oxford.

Darnborough, A. and Kinrade, D. (1981). *Directory for the Disabled.* 3rd edn, Cambridge.

Darnborough, A. and Kinrade, D. (1981). *Motoring and Mobility for Disabled People.* London.

Fallon, B. (1978). *So You're Paralysed.* London.

Goldsmith, S. (1976). *Designing for the Disabled.* 3rd edn, London.

Hall, G. (ed.) (1979). *Source Book for the Disabled.* London.

Harpin, P. (1984). *With a Little Help.* London.

Lane, M. and Mara, J. (1976). *Kitchen Sense for Disabled or Elderly People.* London.

Lifchez, R. and Winslow, B. (1979). *Design for Independent Living: The Environment and Physically Disabled People.* London.

Mandelstan, D. (1978). *Incontinence.* London.

Nichols, P. (1980). *Rehabilitation Medicine: the Management of Physical Disabilities.* 2nd edn, London.

Russell, P. (1978). *The Wheelchair Child.* London.

Stone, J. and Taylor, F. (1977). *A Handbook for Patients with a Handicapped Child.* London.

M. ANNE CHAMBERLAIN

References

Agerholm, M. (1975). Handicaps and the handicapped: nomenclature and classification of intrinsic handicaps. *Journal of the Royal Society of Health,* **95,** 3–8.

Bobath, B. (1978). *Adult Hemiplegia: Evaluation and Treatment.* London.

Evans, C. (1981). *Rehabilitation of Head Injuries.* London.

Flatt, A. E. (1978). *Care of Congenital Hand Anomalies.* London.

Flatt, A. E. (1979). *Care of Minor Hand Injuries.* 4th edn, London.

Fries, J. F. *et al.* (1980). Stanford Health Assessment: measurement of patient outcome in arthritis. *Arthritis and Rheumatism,* **23,** 137–45.

Guttmann, L. (1976). *Spinal Cord Injuries—Comprehensive Management and Research.* 2nd edn, Oxford.

Hale, G. (1979). Rehabilitation Act of 1973, USA; UDS Federal Act of 1972. *Source Book for the Disabled,* 47–53. London.

Harris, Amelia (1971). *Handicapped and Impaired in Great Britain,* Part I. London.

Mair, A. (1972). *Report of Standing Medical Advisory Committee of the Scottish Health Services Council* (The Mair Report). London.

Ministry of Labour and National Service (1956). *The Rehabilitation, Training and Resettlement of Disabled Persons* (Piercy Committee Report). Cmd. 9883. London.

Periquet, A. O. (1984). *Community-based Rehabilitation Services: the Experience of Bacolod, Philippines and the Asia/Pacific Region.* New York.

Royal Association for Disability and Rehabilitation (1983). *A Code of Practice on the Provision of Services by Social Service Departments under Section 2 of the Chronically Sick and Disabled Persons Act 1972.* London.

Steinbocker, O., Traeger, C. H. and Batterman, E. C. (1949). Therapeutic criteria in rheumatoid arthritis. *Journal of the American Medical Association,* **140,** 659–62.

Tunbridge, R. (1972). *Report of Subcommittee of the Standing Medical Advisory Committee of the Central Health Services Council.* London.

Wood, P. H. N. (1980). The language of disablement: a glossary relating to disease and its consequences. *International Journal of Rehabilitation Medicine,* **2,** 86–92.

Wynn Parry, C. B. (1966). *Rehabilitation of the Hand.* London.

REICHERT, KARL BOGISLAUS (1811–83). German anatomist, MD Berlin (1836). Reichert was successively professor of anatomy in Dorpat (1843), physiology in Breslau (1853), and anatomy in Berlin (1858). He introduced the cell theory into *embryology and made valuable studies of the germ layers.

REIL, JOHANN CHRISTIAN (1759–1813). German physician, MD Halle (1780). Associated with the University of Halle, Reil became professor of medicine when it reopened after the Napoleonic war. He described the *insula (island of Reil) in the brain, and was a leading medical educator, but later immersed himself in nature-philosophy and metaphysical speculation. He died of *typhus acquired while in charge of a military *lazarette.

REINFORCEMENT. The strengthening of a response to a stimulus by some means.

REINNERVATION. The attachment or growth of a living nerve into a denervated and paralysed muscle with the object of restoring its function.

REITER, HANS (1881–1969). German physician, MD Leipzig (1906). Reiter described the sexually transmitted disease now named after him (see REITER'S SYNDROME; VENEREOLOGY). He probably did not recognize its essentially venereal nature.

REITER'S SYNDROME is the association of *non-specific urethritis, *conjunctivitis, and *polyarthritis, occurring most commonly in young males and thought to be usually of venereal origin with a similar aetiological pattern to that of non-specific urethritis itself. The causal agent appears to be a *mycoplasma.

REJECTION is the process by which the body destroys tissue which has been transplanted into it, unless the donated tissue is genetically identical (syngeneic) with that of the host, or unless the host's *immune system is depressed. Rejection serves as a defence against invasion by pathogenic micro-organisms but is a major obstacle to successful organ *transplantation. Except in the case of incompatible *blood transfusion, where immediate rejection results due to pre-existing host *antibody to *antigens on the transfused cells (ABO antigens), rejection is caused by host reaction to the major histocompatibility (MHC) antigens on the surface of the transplanted cells (see HLA). The host lymphocytes (T and/or B cells, with their non-specific adjuncts such as complement and macrophages) attack the graft: antibody generated by B cells destroys free cells and vascular endothelium, initiating inflammation, while T cells attack solid tissue directly or via macrophages.

The enormous experience accumulated with kidney grafting has shown that rejection can be classified as: immediate, due to ABO incompatibility or MHC presensitization; acute (weeks or months), due to B-cell (antibody) or T-cell response to MHC antigens; or chronic (months to years), usually due to immune complex deposition. Immunosuppressive drugs nevertheless now enable the successful survival of many transplants other than those from identical twins. Tissues like cornea and cartilage which do not naturally contain blood vessels are not normally rejected after transplantation. See GENETICS; IMMUNOLOGY; TRANSPLANTATION.

REJUVENATION is the restoration of youthfulness, or of some of the mental or physical characteristics of youth: the aim and claim of innumerable popular remedies.

RELAPSE. The recurrence of illness after partial or complete remission.

RELAPSING FEVER is an infection marked by recurrent fever, in which haemorrhage and jaundice are frequent features, due to *spirochaetal organisms of the genus *Borrelia*. There are two forms, with different *arthropod vectors: epidemic or louse-borne relapsing fever, due to *B. recurrentis* and transmitted from person to person (there is no animal reservoir) by the *body louse *Pediculus humanus humanus*; and endemic or tick-borne relapsing fever due to various *Borrelia* species, notably *B. duttoni*, which is primarily a *zoonosis and is transmitted to man by various *tick species of the genus *Ornithodorus*. The former infection is world-wide, whereas the distribution of the latter is determined by that of the tick vectors and is restricted to certain endemic regions, mostly tropical and subtropical. Louse-borne relapsing fever is internationally *notifiable to the *World Health Organization.

RELAXATION is a lessening of muscular tension or tone, which occurs when muscular contraction has ceased. Total relaxation can be achieved by preventing excitatory nervous stimuli from reaching the muscles. Drugs such as *curare have this effect, and are often used in conjunction with general anaesthesia to facilitate surgical operations; since spontaneous breathing is then no longer possible, pulmonary ventilation must be assured by artificial means. The severe and life-threatening muscular contractions of *tetanus may need to be similarly controlled. The word 'relaxation' is also though less precisely used to mean lessening of mental and emotional 'tension'. Here the group of drugs known as '*tranquillizers' may be of value.

RELIGIO MEDICI was the first published work (1642) of Sir Thomas *Browne, believed to have been written during the four years he was engaged in medical practice in Oxford (1634–7) before he settled at Norwich in 1637. *Religio medici* is essentially an examination and an affirmation of Browne's religious faith, a private document written, it is said, without any thought of publication, this being forced by the appearance of a pirated version.

RELIGION, PHILOSOPHY, AND ETHICS IN RELATION TO MEDICINE. From time immemorial the practice of medicine has been bound up with religion and philosophy. Sometimes practitioners have promoted that association as beneficial to the art and to patients; as often, they have repudiated it as detrimental to both. When religion shades off into magic and philosophy into sophistry, a rational scepticism affords the easiest refuge. Ethics, the compound of what religion approves, what is believed to be good, and what is found to work, varies with the varying strengths of each ingredient. And since Western religion, philosophy, and science all derive from those civilizations cradled between the eastern Mediterranean and the Persian Gulf we should expect both continuity and variety as the credal, the reflective, and the empirical elements in turn dominate and recede.

Ancient Egypt had its physicians, exorcists, sorcerers, and priests. The practice of medicine was divided between them, in ways not always distinct. Confession, prayer, invocation, or incantation would accompany empirical remedies, and all under the eye of the tutelary gods. The rituals of the one might or might not hinder the scientific development of the other. The Sumerian texts of Mesopotamia yield early evidence of a similar compound. Religion dominated medicine like everything else. Health was a blessing, disease a curse, even a punishment for sin personal or corporate. Rites of purification and reconciliation were therefore as much part of therapy as was physical medicine, with exorcism, incantation, divination, and hepatoscopy, astrology, and the horoscope for added measure in some traditions—all designed to remove the cause of illness and to adjust the patient to his environment, natural and divine. Physicians ranked with priests and magicians as the educated classes in society. Within this context medicine as an empirical science grew fitfully, an ethic evolved, and laws were enacted to protect the patient as well as to reward the practitioner for success and to punish him for failure (Sigerist, 1951).

From this matrix emerged two traditions formative of Western medicine and its ethics: the Hebrew, bifurcating into the Jewish and Christian religions; and the Greek, in which medicine, striving with its twin, philosophy, created the Hippocratic corpus and ideal.

The Hippocratic corpus: Greek medicine and philosophy. The stature of *Hippocrates as man and physician is not diminished by the inability of scholars to determine either which of the writings in the corpus are his or which of the recensions of the *Hippocratic Oath came closest to the original (Jones, 1923; Nutton, 1981). Despite the invocation of the gods with which the Oath begins, it was adopted and transmitted, with minor changes, by Christians, Jews, and Muslims alike; and, beginning with Arab civil powers and continuing in some Scottish and continental medical schools into the 20th c., its administration was widely required upon entry into medical practice. Whatever its origin, therefore, whether for a circle of adepts or for wider use, its intrinsic worth gave it universal appeal—an appeal to what came to be called *recta ratio,* natural fitness as perceived by the educated conscience, by moral reasoning. If one of Hippocrates' tasks was to free medicine from bondage to philosophy and religion, his work was in the course of time validated by the one and baptized by the other. Hippocrates did indeed ridicule the metaphysicians and sophists of his day, as *Galen did after him. He did indeed strike at religion, and the whole theory of possession, when he asserted that there must be a natural cause for *epilepsy, which his contemporaries called 'The Sacred Disease'. In their place he asserted an ethical obligation to observe: good practice (which he called the art, or the handicraft) rests on good knowledge, gained by observation. Good theory is grounded in perceived fact, 'a composite memory of things apprehended by sense perception', not in speculation.

The empirical features were those surrounding the patient, as well as his own constitution, manner of life, physical characteristics, and the symptoms of his disease: his habitat, the seasons, climate and weather, the location of his city, the social habits of its citizens. The signs to be looked for were those of a capacity to recover: 'one who has knowledge of these matters can know whom he ought to treat, as well as the time and method of treatment'. Doctors are more to be praised than blamed for refusing to take on cases for which they have no acceptable remedy. 'Medicine . . . is to do with the sufferings of the sick, to lessen the violence of their diseases, and to refuse to treat those who are over-mastered by their diseases, realizing that in such cases medicine is powerless.' (The same precept is firm in Egyptian, Hittite, and Babylonian writings also.)

The grounding of medicine in good science stands on this first obligation, to observe. The art of medicine, in the Hippocratic tradition, stands on two more: of self-respect in the physician, and of respect for the patient. One of the precepts enjoins care of the sick to make them well, care for the healthy to keep them well, and 'care for onself, so as to observe what is seemly'. Quackery lowers medicine in popular esteem. 'Many are physicians by repute, very few are such in reality.' The dishonourable are the least troubled by loss of honour. To become a good physician a man requires, first, natural ability; then, teaching from childhood up in some suitable place of learning; then, long diligence to make that learning second nature. Only excellence will suffice, in 'quickness, neatness, painlessness, where each is called for'. Appearance, dress, social conduct, must be fitting. The physician must keep watch over himself, 'and neither expose much of his person nor gossip to laymen, but only what is absolutely necessary, for . . . gossip may cause criticism of his treatment'. 'The intimacy between physician and patient is close. Patients in fact put themselves into the hands of their physician, and at every moment he meets women, maidens, and possessions very precious indeed. So towards all those self-control must be used. Such then should the physician be, both in body and in soul.' Fees should be charged according to the patient's means. Do not worry a patient about fees; treat him: 'it is better to reproach a patient you have saved than to extort money from those who are at death's door'. Sometimes attendance should be given for nothing, 'for where there is love of man (*philanthropie*) there is also love of the art (*philotechnie*).

'The art has three factors, the disease, the patient, the physician. The physician is the servant of the art. The patient must co-operate with the physician in combating the disease.' The relation of doctor to patient was what we should now call paternalistic or authoritarian; but that was held to be in the patient's interest, which it was the physician's first duty to serve. He was thought to know best. 'Some patients ask for what is out of the way and doubtful, through prejudice, deserving indeed to be discouraged, but not to be punished. Wherefore you must reasonably oppose them. Ground your treatment only on examination.' 'If he be under orders the patient will not go far astray.' The physician is to visit frequently, checking patients' veracity about taking their medicines: 'What they have done never results in a confession, but the blame is thrown upon the physician.' 'Perform all things calmly and adroitly, concealing most things from the patient while you are attending to him. Give necessary orders with cheerfulness and serenity, turning his attention away from what is being done to him; sometimes reprove sharply and emphatically, and sometimes comfort with solicitude and attention, revealing nothing of the patient's future or present condition. For many patients have for this cause taken a turn for the worse.' Leave a pupil, an initiate, to see that treatment is followed between visits; 'never put a layman in charge of anything; otherwise, if a mischance occurs, the blame will fall on you'.

Yet the patient is no cipher. 'Life is short, the Art long, opportunity fleeting, experience treacherous, judgement difficult. The physician must be ready, not only to do his duty himself, but also to secure the co-operation of the patient . . .' 'Do not hesitate to enquire of laymen if thereby there is likely to result improvement of treatment.' In treating joints and fractures, 'ask the patient' about the comfort or press of a bandage. Of someone who put up an arm in an unnatural position he wrote 'and perhaps our theorizer would not have committed this error if he had let the patient himself present the arm'. 'It is disgraceful in any art, and especially in medicine, to make parade of much trouble, display and talk, and then do no good.'

Of the necessity for 'informed consent', now almost a fetish in medical ethics, there is no trace in the Hippocratic corpus or in the tradition for a long time after (Polani, 1983). Two other principles of ethics, cherished today, however, are firm and clear in the text of the Oath itself: the principles of professional conduct and of *professional confidence. 'In every house where I shall come I will enter only for the good of my patients, keeping myself from all intentional ill-doing and all seduction, and especially from the pleasures of love with women or with men, be they free or slaves. All that may come to my knowledge in the exercise of my profession or outside of my profession or in daily commerce with men, which ought not to be spread abroad, I will keep secret and will never reveal.' The qualification on the rule of silence is important: it forbids disclosure only of what ought not to be disclosed; some disclosure is sometimes a professional duty.

Galen, Avicenna, and Averroes and transmission of the Hippocratic tradition. The Hippocratic ethics survived the cities which gave it birth,

though with inevitable adaptation. *Galen in the 2nd c. AD maintained the opposition to philosophers who tried to schematize medicine or to moralize it, and so to restrict it as an empirical science. 'Iatrosophists' and 'iatrophilosophers' were even more contentious in Rome, when Galen worked there, than they had been in the Greek islands and cities. As against the dogmatists who would impose an order on visible things on the basis of an invisible 'nature' of things, Galen asserted that 'empiricism suffices to discover everything used in healing'. He sought a method of organizing experience or empirical observations in the service of the art, even taking account of random possibilities, 'so that there is no assurance of uniformity however many you observe'. 'On the whole, the conclusion known as *epilogismos* prescribes the doing of what should be done on the basis of the good or evil which is inherent in the thing and accompanies it, whereas the conclusion known as *analogismos* prescribes action on the basis of the nature of things.' The empirical features do not themselves dictate the course of action; they are the most trustworthy material upon which reason can work. 'The art of healing was originally invented and discovered by the logos in conjunction with experience. And today also it can only be practised excellently and done well by one who employs both of these methods.' So, 'the best physician is also a philosopher'. The efficient healer must be trained in logic, the science of how to think; in physics, the science of what is; and in ethics, the science of what to do (Brock, 1916; Walzer, 1944; Stannard, 1981).

Belief in medicine as an art with its ethics grounded in philosophy and science passed from Greece and Rome into the three main currents of mediaeval civilization, the Arab (including the Islamic and the Persian), the Christian, and the Jewish. Hippocrates and Galen circulated in Arabic translation. *Avicenna, in his *Canon of Medicine,* created a synthesis of Greek and Arab medicine and personal clinical observation, based on a philosophy compounded of *Aristotle, Plato, Neo-Platonists, and Stoics. In *Averroes, Greek philosophy and Hippocratic and Galenic medicine reached the height of its influence in the Arab world before it became overlaid by Islamic theology. Both Avicenna and Averroes had a profound influence on European thought because they transmitted the Greek tradition through centuries when, in the Latin West, Greek influence was low (Marmura, 1967; MacClintock, 1967; Iskandar, 1981).

Monastic writings. Yet the Hippocratic influence did survive in Europe throughout the darkest period, *c.* AD 400–1100. *St Cosmos and St Damian, twin physicians known as 'silverless' (*anarguroi*) because they practised without reward, and honoured as martyrs by the 5th c., became patron saints of medicine. The literary evidences are in monastic treatises written for monks charged with the care of the sick. There are more borrowings from Hippocrates, chiefly *Decorum* and *Precepts*, than from biblical or clerical sources; though there was fusion between the concepts of classical antiquity and Christianity. In ethics they found no conflict of ideals; in etiquette they used Hippocratic standards of character and deportment to teach their own practical wisdom. St Jerome, in one of his letters, writes of the clergyman's duty of visiting, and warns of its perils: 'Hippocrates, before he will instruct his pupils, makes them take an oath and compels them to swear obedience to him. That oath exacts from them silence, and prescribes for them their language, gait, dress and manners. How much greater an obligation is laid on us who have been entrusted with the healing of souls' (Jerome, St, 394). Later evidence came from Visigothic Spain, in the 5th c., Ostrogothic Italy in the 6th c., and from Northern Europe—traditions predating the Salernitan revival. So Europe in the 10th c. knew precepts with a Hippocratic ring: 'The physician ought to know the past, to perceive the present, to recognize the future.' 'He should endure peacefully the insults of the patient, since those suffering from melancholic or frenetic ailments are likely to hurl evil words at the physician; these should be ignored, for they are not deliberate but rather the result of the harsh annoyance suffered by the patient' (MacKinney, 1952).

Maimonides. In the Jewish tradition, the crowning embodiment of Greek philosophy and medicine was *Maimonides. Expelled in youth from Moorish Spain he settled in Egypt as medical author, court physician, and servant to the Jewish community. Though a severe critic of Galen—for contradictions in medicine and ignorance in philosophy and theology—he could argue that it is not necessary to repudiate Greek science and philosophy to preserve religious faith and obedience. They are compatible, given the necessary intelligence; only when vulgarized could philosophy threaten society and disturb faith (Penes, 1967).

The Renaissance ideal of the philosopher-physician. The ideal of the philosopher-physician flourished during the Renaissance in the universities of northern Italy, particularly in *Padua—the resort of the keenest aspiring physicians from all over Europe, including William *Harvey. In Padua a doctorate in arts, that is in natural philosophy, was taken as a stepping-stone to a career in medicine; the route to a medical chair was through a teaching post in logic or philosophy. Among the teaching texts were the *Aphorisms* of Hippocrates, Galen's *Ars medica,* and Avicenna's *Canon. Philosophus et medicus* became a title of distinction (Byleby, 1979). In 16th c. England the Oath was the most frequently printed of all the Hippocratic writings. Four distinct English translations were in circulation, with commentaries, omissions, and additions. The Hippocratic ideal was displayed as the model for the physician and as the ground for

extensive reform in medical practice (Larkey, 1936).

How the tradition was received and transmitted is illustrated in the writing of Thomas *Vicary. He was five times master of the *Barber-Surgeons' Company, resident surgical-governor of *St Bartholomew's Hospital, and chief surgeon to Henry VIII, Edward VI, Mary, and Elizabeth I. In 1548 he published *The Anatomie of the Body of Man.* Though pre-Vesalian in its anatomy, his book was reprinted by four surgeons from his own hospital in 1577; and, with frequent supplements, it held the field for 150 years. Galen is echoed in the Epistle Dedicatory of the surgeon-editors when they commend their practice as 'onely grounded upon reason and experience, which are the principle rootes of Phisicke and Surgerie'. Galen is commended by Vicary to 'the younger brethren of the Fellowship practising surgerie' as 'the Lanterne of all Chirurgions' and as 'the prince of Philosophers'. His first chapter is in effect an essay in medical ethics, in which Avicenna, Galen, and Aristotle are freely quoted.

He writes of what is to be looked for in choosing a surgeon. He must know the anatomy, and be learned, not only in 'Chirurgery and Phisicke' but also 'in Natural Philosophie, and in Grammar, that he speake congruitie, in Logike, that teacheth him to proue his propositions with good reason, (and) in Rethorike, that teacheth him to knowe things natural and not natural, and thynges agaynst nature'. Moral virtue is also required—'he must be wel manered'. Among the precepts offered are these, straight from the Hippocratic tradition:

likewise they shal geue no counesayle except they be asked, and then say their aduise by good deliberation . . .

likewise they must be as priue and as secrete as any Confessour, of al thinges that they shal heare or see in the house of their Pacient.

they shal not take into their cure any maner of person, except he wyl be obedient unto their precepts . . .

also that they do their diligence aswel to the poore as to the riche.

They shal neuer discomfort their pacient, and comaunde all that be about him that they doo the same; but to his freendes speake truth, as the case standeth.

They must also be bold in those thinges whereof they may be certayne, and as dreadfull in al perilles.

They may not chide with the sicke, but be alwayes pleasaunt and mery.

They must not couet any woman by waye of vylanie, and especially in the house of their pacient.

They shal not, for couetousnes of money, take in hande those cures that be vncurable, nor neuer set any certaine day of the sicke-man's health, for it lyeth not in their power.

They must also be gracious and good to the poore, and of the riche take liberally for bothe.

There is no need for a man to praise himself, 'for his works wyll euer get credit ynough'. Neither should he despise other surgeons, 'for it is meet that one Chirurgion should loue another, as Christe loueth us all'.

Vicary lived as he taught. Though he was well rewarded in the royal service, he was a faithful servant of the poor at St Bartholomew's Hospital (Vicary, 1548).

The ethics which Vicary transmitted was not, then, an abstract set of philosophical principles; it was an ethics of practice, set out at the beginning of a medical textbook, well-used for something approaching two centuries. It is not to disparage Thomas *Percival, therefore, to question whether he was quite as much the innovator as his modern admirers suggest. The Judicial Council of the *American Medical Association, for instance, in its annual publication of *Current Opinions and Principles of Medical Ethics,* writes that 'The most significant contribution to ethical history subsequent to Hippocrates was made by Thomas Percival, an English physician, philosopher and writer' (AMA, 1982).

Percival's code of professional conduct.
Percival's *Medical Ethics* was indeed a monument—systematic, comprehensive, written with a grave moral calm. Yet it presupposes an existing community—'the gentlemen of the Faculty'— divided on an ethical issue, and therefore not unaware of the claims of professional conduct. An outbreak of *typhoid, or of *typhus, in Manchester in 1791 overtaxed the staff of the infirmary. When the governor augmented it, there was friction between the old staff and the new, and some resigned. Percival was asked to frame 'a scheme of professional conduct relative to hospitals and medical charities'. His text was printed for circulation among friends, for criticism, and published in 1803. It was subtitled: *A Code of Institutes and Precepts adapted to the Professional Conduct of Physicians and Surgeons: I In Hospital Practice; II In private, or general Practice; III In relation to Apothecaries; IV In cases which may require a knowledge of Law.* Among the few authorities whom he quotes is Hippocrates, 'the father of physic', 'in the oath enjoined on pupils, which some universities now impose upon the candidates for medical degrees'.

The patients in the hospitals and charitable institutions for whose doctors the first section was written were the poor. More significant, therefore, is his consideration for their sensitivity. 'The *feelings* and *emotions* of the patients, under critical circumstances, require to be known and attended to, no less than symptoms of their diseases.' Timidity may contraindicate venesection; even prejudices are to be respected. Patients should be interrogated in a voice that cannot be overheard; secrecy should be strictly observed; females should be treated with scrupulous delicacy. 'The character of a physician is usually remote either from superstition or enthusiasm'; but patients are not, always; therefore, let the chaplain perform his office in restraint of both.

The gentlemen of the faculty are responsible for the goodness and honour of each other. Therefore let there be the utmost confidence between them, especially physicians and surgeons, and in the pursuit of new methods and in the better recording of cases. In consultations the junior should present his opinion first; then progressively up the scale of seniority. It is for the good of patients, especially of the poor, 'that new remedies and new methods of chirurgical treatment should be devised. But in the accomplishment of this salutary purpose, the gentlemen of the faculty should be scrupulously and conscientiously governed by sound reason, just analogy, or well authenticated facts. And no such trial should be instituted without a previous consultation of the physicians or surgeons according to the nature of the case.' During operations there must be no unauthorized spectator; and silence is to be kept, except that one may speak occasionally to comfort the patient, 'and to give him assurance, if consistent with truth, that the operation goes on well, and promises a speedy and successful termination'. There is no mention anywhere of obtaining the patient's consent.

His injunctions for the general practitioner cover both ethics and etiquette. Secrecy and delicacy are enjoined. So is sobriety, so that in an emergency 'for which no professional man should be unprepared, a steady hand, an acute eye, and an unclouded head, may be essential to the well-being, and even to the life, of a fellow-creature'. A bad prognosis must be given, on proper occasions; but preferably not by the physician himself. Precedence is established by seniority of residence in the town. The academically educated should not exclude from their fellowship those qualified without such advantages. Visits should not be so frequent as 'to give rise to such occasional indulgences as are subversive of all medical regimen'. Fees ('pecuniary acknowledgments') are delicately treated. Members of the profession, including *apothecaries, and their wives and children, are to be treated gratuitously—though the opulent may bestow a fee if they wish to. 'Clergymen, who experience the *res angusta domi*, should be visited gratuitously by the faculty. And this exemption should be an acknowledged general rule, that feeling of individual obligation may be rendered less oppressive.' Yet they too may pay if they have means. Military and naval subaltern officers, in narrow circumstances, are also proper objects of professional liberality.

At the close of every interesting and important case, especially fatal cases, there is a duty calmly to review and reflect on the management of it, without self-deception. 'Regrets may follow, but criminality will be thus obviated. For good intentions and the imperfections of human skill which cannot anticipate the knowledge that events alone disclose, will sufficiently justify what is past, provided the failure be made conscientiously subservient to future wisdom and rectitude in professional conduct.' The doctor should observe the Sabbath, to fit in his visits between the hours of divine service, not least so that those in the patient's household will not stay at home in case he should call!

The apothecary is to be trusted and respected for his knowledge, for his proximity to the patient, and for his professional integrity. 'He is the physician of the poor in all cases and of the rich when distress or danger is not very great.'

One subject ventilated interminably in recent years, and which moralists unravel in terms of the principle of double effect, has summary treatment in Percival: 'When medicines which are administered to a sick patient with an honest design to produce the alleviation of pain, or cure of his disease, occasion death, that is misadventure, in the view of the law, and the physician or surgeon, who directed them, is not liable criminally, though a civil action might formally lie for neglect or ignorance.' Despite this, physicians must use the healing art with knowledge, tenderness, and discretion. Rash experiments, or mistakes due to rash inattention or ignorance, are, 'in the eye of conscience, a crime both against God and man' (Percival, 1803).

Contemporary interest in medical ethics in the UK and USA. Today, although it is difficult to find a working doctor who has ever read a word of Hippocrates (except perhaps the Oath), Vicary, or Percival, 'medical ethics' is a growing academic subject and, in terms of publishing, a growth industry. At its best the pursuit is where the Hippocratics strove to locate it, in philosophical reflection rooted in the practice of medicine. At its worst it becomes a television feature in which viewers are deluded, by a slanted presentation of the 'facts', into mistaking a gut reaction for a moral judgement. In between it becomes an exercise for philosophers having no organic relation to medical practice but using medical issues as the material for mere argument; or for lawyers exploiting the opportunities of a consumerist and insurance-bound society, for whom 'ethical' comes to mean that which will give a 'health care professional' a successful defence in a malpractice suit, and 'unethical' that which will cost him or his insurers damages in a court of law

In a typical British symposium on medical ethics today the leading contributors would be medical scientists or practitioners, chosen from the relevant specialty. There might also be a philosopher, a moral theologian, a lawyer, a social worker or some other lay representative of the social or public interest, or possibly a sociologist. The medical members would set out the empirical features of the matter to be discussed, so exposing the points of moral claim or of ethical doubt. These the non-medicals would identify and examine from their respective disciplines. The purpose of the exercise would be practical: to provoke medical students to reflection; to articulate ethical difficulties faced by medical or nursing staffs in hospitals, or by doctors in general practice; to draw guidelines for innovative or controversial procedures for members of a Royal College; to approve research proposals in hospitals or academic clinical or research institu-tions; to help to inform public opinion, or to contribute to a possible legislative process, when controversy surrounds some new medical advance, as in transplant surgery or assistance in human reproduction.

Such are the activities of the London Medical Group and of the other Medical Groups in teaching hospitals all over the UK, loosely associated in the Institute of Medical Ethics (IME); of the Linacre Centre, established under Roman Catholic auspices for the study of the ethics of health care; of the *Ciba Foundation in some of its symposia (Wolstenholme and O'Connor, 1966; Ramsey and Porter, 1971; Wolstenholme and FitzSimons, 1973); of the Centre of Law, Medicine and Ethics at King's College London; of the Open Section of the *Royal Society of Medicine; of working parties set up by the Council for Science and Society; of formal Research Ethical Committees attached to teaching hospitals and District Health Authorities. The Royal College of Obstetricians and Gynae-cologists appointed such a mixed Ethics Commit-tee to formulate the College's evidence to a Government Inter-Departmental Committee on *fertilization in vitro (RCOG, 1983). The Royal College of General Practitioners has another to validate the ethics of *clinical trials of new medi-cines in general practice. The method of interdis-ciplinary study in medical matters was pioneered by the Church of England in a series of reports, from about 1958 to 1975, each of which made a notable contribution to subjects then in public debate (Church of England, 1958, 1959, 1960, 1962, 1965a, 1965b, 1975). The method produces a continuing literature: for instance, the Journal of Medical Ethics, published quarterly since 1975 by IME; and a Dictionary of Medical Ethics, first published in 1977 and revised and amplified for a second edition in 1981 (Duncan et al., 1981).

The teaching of medical ethics in British *medi-cal education is more a by-product of these wide-spread associations than taught in formal academic courses. The ethics of practice are, no doubt, transmitted by *consultants to their juniors and students in normal clinical training. But the discur-sive element, with its philosophical and social ingredients, is commonly explored in the voluntary Medical Groups in the teaching hospitals. The University of London conferred the personal title of professor of medical law and ethics on a law teacher at King's College in 1983; there is still no established chair in the subject in the UK. This contrasts with widespread academic recognition in the USA; but it does not represent a lower standard of activity.

In the USA there are two distinguished and well-endowed institutions for multidisciplined ethical study in the Hastings Center and the Kennedy Center, both of which publish extensively. By and large, however, the discussion of medical ethics is more heavily overshadowed by philosophy and by law than it is in the UK. Proceedings of an annual Transdisciplinary Symposium on Philosophy and

Medicine appear, with other titles, in a series under that heading published by D. Reidal Publishing Company. It is clear that such co-operation brings the best out of both disciplines, if aptness to an ethics of practice be the criterion, with the philosophically minded physician coming nearer to the mark than the non-medical philosopher (Pellegrino and Thomasma, 1981). Articles in the philosophical journals, however, by philosophers working without close involvement with physicians, sometimes exhibit a distance from clinical realities which evoke sympathy for Hippocrates and Galen in their striving, if not for the autonomy of medicine, at least for the primacy of empirical experience. The place of law in medical ethics in the USA is largely a product of the nation's awareness of the monetary advantages to be gained by a successful action for malpractice or negligence, or even for accident or honest mistake. There are departments of legal medicine in many universities; and medical schools have associate or assistant professors in such medical specialties as paediatrics, obstetrics, or psychiatry, with the qualifier '(Law)' inserted in the title. Inflated risks of litigation, encouraged by the contingency fee system in legal practice, and of crippling awards of damages, have promoted 'defensive medicine'—playing safe, when a normal initiative might be in the better interest of the patient and of the art—and have added high insurance premiums to the already heavy costs of medical care.

Origins of existing codes: professional awareness, organization, and discipline. The origins of the present concentration on medical ethics are complex. They stem in part from the extended notion of professional obligation in the 19th c. Medicine was numbered among the 'professions'—associations characterized by their possessing a tradition of learning or skill, with an obligation to enhance it and to induct pupils into it, and to offer a service to a public requiring it under ethical regulation; with social status and financial reward in return. A Hippocratic saying captured these elements: 'to heal the patient, and not to overlook the reward, to say nothing of the desire that makes a man ready to learn'. Medical education and the drawing of limits between acceptable and unacceptable practice, and the discipline of the profession, became a national responsibility. The first meeting of the *American Medical Association in Philadelphia in 1847 made this its aim; and the code of ethics which it then established was based on Percival's *Medical Ethics* (AMA, 1982). In England the *General Medical Council was established by statute in 1858, with statutory responsibility for the qualification and registration of all medical practitioners. Only then was there achieved what the physicians of England had asked for in a petition to Henry V in Parliament in 1421:

Hey and most mythty Prince, noble and worthy Lordes Spirituelx and Temporelx, and worshipfull Commones, for so moche as a man hath thre things to governe, that is

to say, Soule, Body, and wordly Goudes, the whiche ought and shulde ben principaly reweled by thre Sciences, that ben Divinitie, Fisyk, and Lawe, the Soule by Divinite, the Body by Fisyk, wordly Goudes by Lawe, and these conynges sholde be used and practised principaly by the most connyng men in the same Sciences, and most approved in cases necessaries to encres of Vertue, long Lyf, and Goudes of fortune, to the worship of God, and comyn profyt. But, worthy Soveraines, as hit is knowen to your hey discrecion, many unconnyng an unapproved in the forsayd Science practiseth, and specialy in Fysyk, so that in this Roialme is every man, be he never so lewed, takying upon hym practyse, y suffred to use hit, to grete harme and slaughtre of many men: Where if no man practised thereyn but al only connynge men and approved sufficeantly y lerned in art, filosofye, and fisyk, as hit is kept in other londes and roialmes, ther shulde many men that dyeth, for defaute of help, lyve, and no man perysh by unconnyng. Wherefore pleseth to youre excellent Wysdomes, that ought after youre soule have mo entendance to your body, for the cause above sayd, to ordeine and make a Statuit, perpetually to be straytly y used and kept, that no man of no maner estate, degre, or condicion, practise in Fisyk, from this time forward, but he have long tyme used the Scoles of Fisyk withynne som Universitee, and be graduated in the same; that is to say, but he be Bachelor or Doctour of Fisyk, having Lettres testimonyalx sufficeantz of on of these degrees of the Universite in the whiche he toke his degree yn; under peyne of long emprisonement, and paying XL li. to the Kyng; and that no woman use the practyse of Fisyk undre the same payne, And that the Sherrefe of the Shire make inquisicion in thaire tornes, if ther be eny that forfaiteth ayens this Statuit, under a payne resonable, and theme that has putte this Statuit in execucion without any favour, under the same peyne. Also, lest that they the whiche ben able to practyse in Fisyk ben excluded fro practysing, the whiche be nought graduated, plesith to your hey prudence, to send Warrant to all the Sherrefs of Engelond, that every practysour in Fisyk nought gradeuated in the same science that wile practyse forth be withynne on of the Universitees of this lond by a certeine day, that they that ben able and approved, after trewe and streyte examinacion, be receyved to theyr degree, and they that be nought able, to cese fro the practyse into the tyme that they be able and approved, or never more entremete thereof; and that therto also be iset a peyne convenient.

Parliament, in reply, empowered and authorized the Lords of the King's Council to make such an ordinance as would assure that only those should practise Physic who had studied the same in the Universities, and Surgery, only those who had learned it from masters of that art (*Rotuli Parliamentorum*, IV, pp. 130, 158).

The corporate identity and discipline of physicians, surgeons, and apothecaries was kept alive, fitfully no doubt, from the Lancastrian to the Victorian era by their respective Royal Colleges and Companies, in London and Edinburgh, and by local medical societies in provincial cities and towns. But it was the 19th c. which gave to medicine its present professional identity, and the 20th c. which brought it into a *National Health Service (NHS) with further statutory requirements and controls.

The second provocation to ethical awareness was the development of a new scientific base for medicine, with new techniques and a new technology which enabled doctors to attempt tasks never undertaken before and, in many of them, to succeed. This also began in the 19th c. and it went further, and more rapidly, in the 20th c. The advances in technique and *antisepsis which made the termination of pregnancy possible by direct means, instead of indirect, caused a sharp rise in the *abortion rate and so provoked the Papacy into the novel and extreme reaction of a total prohibition, signalized by Pius IX's bull *Apostolicae Sedis* of 1869. As with *anaesthesia, *analgesia in *childbirth, and *contraception, so with transplant surgery, *neurosurgery, *psychopharmacology, *artificial insemination, *in vitro* fertilization, and *embryo replacement, each new advance has met with moral questioning and downright opposition; each one heightened public anxiety that there were rights and wrongs in medicine not always observed.

Examples of unethical human experiments. The final provocation came with the exposure of the scientific and medical experiments forced upon Jews and other disadvantaged persons in Nazi Germany before and during the Second World War. The Nazis were not the first to experiment on human subjects in ways which are now judged unethical: in 18th c. England *inoculation of *smallpox was tested on criminals and orphans before it was administered to children of the blood royal. Neither were they the last: some innovative procedures in several medical specialties in the UK in the 1960s called out the protest of Pappworth in his much controverted *Human Guinea Pigs* (1967); and the Willowbrook study of children in the USA infected with *hepatitis drove Paul Ramsey to the best of his argumentative ethical reasoning in *The Patient as Person* (1970). Continued abuses of *psychiatry in the USSR occasioned the protest of the World Psychiatric Association in 1977 and the subsequent withdrawal of the Soviet Union from the Association.

The Nuremberg Code and subsequent codes of practice. Yet the Nazi atrocities, in their extent, their ruthlessness, and their futility, came as such a shock to Western consciousness as to give the final thrust to the tide of ethical assertion. Since protest alone is ineffective as a remedy, codes and declarations have been drawn and promulgated by authoritative bodies; and these now have a recognized moral status throughout the world. The first was the Nuremberg Code, laying down, in the judgment of the tribunal which pronounced sentence on 23 German defendants, 10 standards to which physicians must conform when carrying out experiments on human subjects. These were amplified in the Declaration of Helsinki (1964, revised 1975), the work of the *World Medical Association (WMA). The WMA published also the Declarations of Geneva (1948, revised 1968)— a modernized version of the Hippocratic Oath; of Sydney (1968), on the determination of death; of Oslo (1970), on therapeutic abortion; of Tokyo (1975), regulating the conduct of doctors in rela-

tion to torture and other cruel, inhuman, or degrading treatment or punishment; and of Lisbon (1981), on the rights of patients. The Declaration of Hawaii (1977) on the uses and misuses of psychiatry was the work of the World Psychiatric Association (Duncan *et al.*, 1981). The WMA revised all its Declarations at a meeting in Vienna in October 1983.

Yet another document is in prospect, the *Proposed International Guidelines for Biomedical Research,* a joint project of the *World Health Organization and the Council for International Organization of Medical Sciences (WHO, 1982). The draft takes note of special considerations for research in developing countries; and it reflects recent study in the USA of means of compensating subjects injured in research procedures (President's Commission, 1982).

In addition to these international declarations, national bodies also produce codes of ethical conduct, or of criteria by which procedures in research or in clinical care are to be judged. In 1962 the British *Medical Research Council issued a Statement on Responsibility in Investigations on Human Subjects (MRC, 1962–3). This was more strict in some respects than the Helsinki Declaration was to be; it allowed no proxy consent for research procedures not designed to be of direct benefit to individuals incompetent to consent for themselves, which Helsinki, even in its revised form, appeared to tolerate. The Royal College of Physicians of London issued a statement in 1973 on Supervision of the Ethics of Clinical Research Investigations—from which stemmed the institution of Research Ethical Committees. The Royal Colleges together (Physicians, Surgeons, Obstetricians and Gynaecologists, Radiologists, Psychiatrists, and General Practitioners), acting either through their presidents or through joint working parties, have pronounced on particular ethical issues commanding public attention. One was to discourage medical participation in strikes threatened in the conduct of a dispute over hospitals in the NHS. Another statement, issued jointly with the British Medical Association (BMA) in 1977, discussed the ethical responsibilities of doctors practising in the NHS. Two others gave authoritative guidance on the diagnosis of *brain death and of death respectively (Royal Colleges, 1975, 1976, 1977, 1979). The British Paediatric Association (BPA) issued guidelines on research involving children (BPA, 1980). The Association of the British Pharmaceutical Industry (ABPI) issued in 1983 a Code of Practice for the Clinical Assessment of Licensed Medicinal Products in General Practice, agreed between the APBI, the Royal College of General Practitioners, and the BMA and after consultation with the Department of Health and Social Security (ABPI, 1983).

It is evident that medical ethics is now a matter of public interest and public debate, no longer a set of private conventions for the regulation of a corporate self-interest within the profession. Responding to this change, the BMA, which formerly issued its little book of medical ethics to members only, now publishes its *Handbook of Medical Ethics* (1984) for general circulation. About one-half of it discusses the relationships of doctors with individuals and with groups, and (in so summary a fashion as to explore none of them with thoroughness) some ethical dilemmas now uppermost in the public mind. The other half deals with etiquette, professional discipline, the law, and the ethical codes, including resolutions of the BMA Annual Representative Meetings. The American Medical Association publishes similarly every year the Current Opinions of its Judicial Council. In this about one-quarter deals with ethical issues in the broader sense—though the AMA book differs from the BMA one in that it treats these specifically in terms of what doctors ought or ought not to do, rather than discussing them in general; and the rest concerns the profession's self-regulation, very much preoccupied with self-protection against commercial and monetary pressures.

What, in general, may be said about these declarations and codes? They are not peculiar to medicine and medical research: many circulate in the business world, though they attract less public notice. They carry considerable authority in so far as they are drawn up carefully by specialists in the respective disciplines and are published by respected authorities. They put on record not only goals to which practitioners should aspire but also criteria by which their work can be judged, ethical or unethical as the case may be. The MRC Statement and the Helsinki Declaration on medical research are widely used by funding bodies when deciding whether to finance a research project, and by Research Ethical Committees when deciding whether the research may be undertaken. The codes have no legal force. Yet in legal proceedings conformity with or departure from their requirements would weigh presumptively for or against a defendant.

No code can relieve the practitioner of moral judgement or responsibility. He has to determine his own duty to each patient or research subject in the light of each one's circumstances as well as in the light of the code and of the state of the law. Interpretation is not always easy. Such are the contradictions in the guidelines issued for paediatric research that a group appointed by the Institute of Medical Ethics spent three years in trying to derive a consistent ethic from them (Nicholson, 1985). Further refinement might make the distinction between 'therapeutic' and 'non-therapeutic' research as clear as it is popularly assumed to be; yet still there will remain the question, which procedures in any given regimen fall into which category, and what are the ethical consequences of the allocation?

Some contemporary ethical issues. Any sketch of the issues in medical ethics most prominent in

present discussion must be selective. Two works of reference are readily available. One is the *Dictionary of Medical Ethics* (Duncan *et al.*, 1981) produced in the UK—compact and practical. The other is the *Encyclopaedia of Bioethics* (Reich, 1978), an American production in four volumes, lavishly printed, handsomely bound. Discussion is generated and continued in the journals, medical, philosophical, and specifically ethical, of which the *Journal of Medical Ethics* is the leading UK example, matched by the *Journal of Philosophy and Medicine* edited in the USA.

Medicine has an ethical dimension because of the nature of man and the nature of the medical profession. Man is vulnerable and mutually dependent. He is intellectually aware of the concepts of health, well-being, and happiness, and he pursues them. He is sentient, aware of pain and distress, and he seeks to prevent them, for others as well as for himself. He is both self-regarding and altruistic; self-loving but also social and benevolent. He knows the good, and values it the more when he can choose it or will freely for himself. Man is a moral being because he is a choosing being (Oppenheimer, 1975). He needs the profession of medicine for his health and comfort. The profession wields power, the power inherent in knowledge and skill, to match the patient's vulnerability. Ethics imposes a moral control over the exercise of power. It regulates the degree to which self-interest may be satisfied, in terms of status and financial reward, by the use of power. It regulates the relation between doctor and patient in ways designed to protect both from embarrassment. (The ethics of the patient are the least attended to in present discussions; his reciprocal duties have yet to be explored.) More and more in recent tendency ethics exalts the element of choice, of willing the good, in the patient—what is called his autonomy—and restricts the action of the physician in ways which are called authoritarian or paternalistic. Central to discussion in medical ethics is the question of consent.

Consent to treatment. It is easy to ring the changes on such terms as 'free and informed consent', in order to emphasize the elements of freedom to decide and essential knowledge on which to decide. Behind lie two deeper questions, the one dogmatic, the other practical. What is believed to be the true nature of man? And when does a social obsession with consent begin to inhibit good medicine?

The reality of the first question is brought out when Jewish, Christian, and humanist presuppositions are compared. The Christian tradition has so assimilated the philosophical notion of human autonomy as to distinguish between 'ordinary' or established treatment, which the physician is obliged to offer and the patient to accept, and 'extraordinary' treatment, involving undue hardship, distress, or risk, which the patient is free to refuse even though refusal might shorten his life; and this the physician is forbidden to impose on him against his will. In this tradition the forcible feeding of hunger-strikers is forbidden: the prisoner or patient is free, should he so choose, to die. In the Jewish tradition every moment of life is infinitely precious; and since the doctor is the servant of life, his duty is to preserve his patient's life by all means within his power up to the time when the death process has visibly begun—taking care, meanwhile, to relieve all relievable suffering. He does not require the patient's consent; he may overrule his refusal. Difference in practice between these two beliefs will reflect the personalities and skills of the respective practitioners; but the traditions are firm, and their implications for consent are clear (Dunstan and Seller, 1983). Our preoccupation with consent is novel. Legal redress for a patient against a doctor traditionally rested on the tort of assault or battery. It was not until the 1940s and 1950s that courts in England and America turned from that blunt instrument to bring failure to gain informed consent under the tort of negligence (Kennedy, 1983). Consent as an ethical requirement is not to be found in the Hippocratic tradition; yet it does lie in the theological. St Thomas Aquinas has it in his treatment of mutilation:

If a corrupt member threatens the whole body with corruption it is licit, if the owner so wills (de voluntate ejus cujus est membrum putridum) to cut it away for the sake of the health of the whole body, since every man has a duty of care for his own health. And the same reasoning applies when willingness is expressed by one whose duty it is to look after the health of him who has the corrupt member. Otherwise it is altogether wrong to mutilate anyone.' (Summa Theologiae, 2a2ae. 65, 1)

Here the principles of consent and proxy consent are stated.

The requirement of consent is rigorously asserted today, especially in the USA, in terms of the rights of patients. The question, inflamed by undoubted errors and abuses of human liberty, has become ideologically and politically divisive, particularly in the care of the mentally ill. Granted their incapacity, because of their impairment, to give informed consent, how far may they be treated, how long may they be detained, without consent or against their stated will? (Sherlock et al., 1983). The question engaged doctors and philosophers in the eighth Transdisciplinary Symposium on Philosophy and Medicine in Connecticut in 1978. The conclusion that emerged is firm: not to treat patients incapable of giving informed consent was unconscionable (Spicker et al., 1981). It is not easy for legislators to reconcile that judgement with the demands of civil libertarians determined to champion the perhaps unwittingly aggrieved.

Surgeons are sometimes inhibited in their management of *Jehovah's Witnesses who will not consent to the *transfusion of donated blood— some, indeed, refusing to allow their own blood to be taken and stored against their possible need of it. In the last resort an adult may be presumed to accept the consequences of his own refusal. When parental consent is refused for the transfusion of a child the doctor's decision is more difficult. Should he override the parental veto he might incur the risk of civil action; though in an English court the concept of necessity might afford him a good defence. He might have the child taken into the care of the Local Authority, or declared a ward of court, and so secure proxy consent. Should he transfuse the child and the fact become known the parents may reject the child. Concealment would require the strict privacy of the case notes and the loyal silence of attendant staff. Both are now under threat: the one from the campaign to open case notes to patients' inspection; the other from investigative journalism and from vigilante groups in defence of 'life'.

Consent is an issue also in research procedures, especially when the subjects are children. The age at which children may consent to medical procedures of all sorts is itself disputed. In practice an assessment of capacity to judge replaces reliance on an (uncertain) legally defined age. It is often stated, as if disposing of the problem, that proxy consent for a child subject was permissible only if the research were 'therapeutic', that is, intended to be potentially of benefit to the child; but not if it were 'non-therapeutic', that is, designed to formulate knowledge potentially of benefit to children as a class, but not necessarily to this child. The distinction is too simple. Rigidly pressed, it would prohibit all studies designed to measure normal ranges or reactions—a necessary preliminary to recognizing the abnormal. Some investigations are by observation only; they are non-invasive and could do no harm. Others do not fall neatly within the categories stated. In the course of a regimen designed for the child's good ('therapeutic') there may conveniently, and without detriment to the child, be intruded a measurement or observation not so intended ('non-therapeutic'). Is parental consent to be required for this also? May it in fact be given? Parents are not always present at the opportune moment. Must the opportunity be lost? The ethics of the matter are vigorously debated.

Proxy consent for a procedure beneficial to the patient stands on the presumption that he would and should have consented, had he been competent, because (as Aquinas said) we ought to will our own physical well-being. McCormick (1974) would allow a proxy consent also to non-beneficial procedures involving minimal risk, on the ground that we ought to will also the good of others and therefore the means to that good. The child, by nature altruistic, would and should so will if he were capable. Ramsey (1976) rejects this argument, precisely because of the moral assumption built into that word 'should'. Janofsky and Starfield (1981), commenting on proposed federal regulations for institutional review boards, concentrate, not on the dichotomy of 'therapeutic' and 'non-therapeutic', but on the degree of risk entailed; only after this has been assessed as more than minimal need the questions of benefit, the child's capacity to assent, and parental permission be considered. Vandeveer (1981) rejects the notion of proxy 'consent' as a fiction anyway; what matters is that the child's rights and interests be respected; an infringement of these (but not every infringement) could be justified if there were high probability that the child would be no worse off. But the judgement in particular cases would be difficult.

Issues of consent arise in transplant surgery, as when it is desired to take *bone marrow from a child or a paired organ from an identical twin. Is the emotional pressure to donate so strong as to lessen freedom in consent? The consequences are not always without psychological strain. What should be the basis for a law governing cadaver transplants? If it were a 'contracting out' basis, a law, that is, which permits the removal of organs after death unless the deceased had in life expressly forbidden it, more organs would be available than on a 'contracting in' basis, which licenses the removal of organs only if permission has been given, either by the deceased or by his next of kin after death. 'Contracting out' is opposed on the ground that it would license one more exaction by the state against the individual, one more inroad upon consent. 'Contracting in' is opposed because it loses precious time, and useful organs as well.

Consent is in issue in the new interventions in human reproduction. Should a woman's consent be required to determine the destiny of an oocyte (egg or *ovum) taken from her at *laparoscopy or during *sterilization—whether it is to be *fertilized and given to another woman, or fertilized and frozen for research? Who may consent to the destruction of *semen or of embryos in cryostorage? Should they be compulsorily destroyed on the death of the donor?

Artificial insemination (donor), in vitro *fertilization, embryo transfer*. The social, legal, and ethical implications of the new medical interventions in begetting, much controverted, have been investigated by a Departmental Committee chaired by Dame (now Baroness) Mary Warnock. Its report was published in 1984 (HMSO, 1984). The practice of *artificial insemination from donated semen (AID) has spread for 40 years while the ethical issues, though discussed, have remained unsolved. The intrinsic ethics are still masked, in the UK, by laws unrevised to cover new possibilities, especially those which leave parents no option other than to falsify the register by entering the husband's name as the father of the child, or to leave the column blank with the imputation of bastardy for the child. They were also masked until recently by the secrecy of the practice, which protected it from the normal scrutiny of published reports. The second impediment is being removed by the opening of centres in teaching and general hospitals and by agreed protocols for recording. The ethics then call to be weighed in relation to the agents involved—the donor, the recipient couple, the practitioner—and in relation to kindred and the wider society. The donor has a duty of full disclosure of any family or personal history which might adversely affect a child born of his semen. This duty he might be tempted to overlook if his primary motive is to collect payment for his donation— a temptation avoided in the CECOS system in France which forbids payment and takes donations only from married men with children of their own, and only with the consent of their wives. He has an interest in secrecy, particularly while the law attaches responsibilities to his paternity if it were known. Yet the pledge of anonymity to him deprives the child of ever knowing his father's identify, a disadvantage which the law has gone some way to removing for adopted children by opening the register of adoptions to them at majority.

The recipient couple have to assure themselves that their receiving semen *ab extra* is compatible with their belief about the nexus of marriage and begetting: is the semen accepted as no more than an impersonal fertilizing agent, or does it in some sense adulterate their marriage? They have to decide whether to conceal the contrived conception from the child—with the risk of accidental disclosure with traumatic effect—and from their own kindred, who may have material interests at stake as well as familial feelings. The practitioner is under duty to assure himself, so far as he can, of the veracity and personality of the donor and to apply whatever tests may be available to exclude genetic or viral taint in his donation. Similarly, in the interest of the child to be born, he must assess the personality of the applicant couple and the stability of their union. To compile accurate but confidential records also is now becoming a professional duty, employing codes to protect anonymity while creating archives adequate for research (Brudenell et al., 1977; Dunstan, 1983; Snowden, 1983; Snowden and Mitchell, 1981).

Artificial insemination by donor has been overtaken by, and then taken up into, *in vitro* fertilization (IVF); this can be followed by embryo replacement, in the *uterus of the donor of the oocyte, or embryo transfer, into another woman, or by observation and experimental research on the unimplanted cleaving embryo (Edwards and Purdy, 1982). Any discussion of the ethics must be tentative because practice is developing so rapidly, both in the fundamental science and in its applications. LeRoy Walters, in a Hastings Center Report (1979), surveyed the (largely theoretical) discussion in the literature up to that time. R. G. Edwards, who with P. C. Steptoe and Jean Purdy pioneered the scientific and clinical work and produced the first IVF baby, Louise Brown, in 1978, outlined, at the First Bourn Hall Meeting of IVF practitioners, a programme of observation, research, and application in terms which required ethical answers to his questions: this is what it would be very useful for us to do; may we do it

(Edwards and Purdy, 1982)? The ethics of the clinical gynaecology involved have been tested step by step. They involve risk to the mother at laparoscopy, at implantation, and in pregnancy, and risks of damage to the embryo during fertilization, cleavage, and replacement. The new questions concern the embryo at its preimplantation stage, now that it can be preserved in that state for a period not yet determined. If more oocytes are taken and fertilized than are required for the intended pregnancy (including those frozen for implanting at the next cycle if the first did not succeed), is it licit to kill the survivors? Or may they be used for study up to the early stages of organogenesis? Or for the extraction of genetic material for the attempted repair of other embryos genetically defective? Is artificial twinning licit with a view to chromosomal analysis of the one as a guarantee of the genetic adequacy of the other?

More questions surround the recipient of the embryo. For those who would accept IVF as such, the return of the embryo to the donor of the ovum presents no problem: she is being helped to achieve her own pregnancy. But what of surrogate motherhood, in which a woman receives the product of another couple's joint donation under contract to return the child at birth to its genetic parents? Or of embryo transfer, in which a fertilized ovum is recovered by lavage from the uterus of a donor woman and transferred (in a synchronized cycle) to the uterus of an infertile woman, to become her 'own' child?

To these questions conflicting answers are given. The whole IVF process is opposed by some as an interference with nature beyond necessity. Others would accept the clinical application to the donor couple but reject, for a mixture of social and ethical reasons, its extension to third parties. Others, accepting it as a remedy for infertility, reject all experimental observation or interference with the embryo on the ground that, without capacity for consent, it should enjoy the full protection due to a human being. (These overlook the number of embryos used and discarded in the years of trial and the failures necessary to achieve the first successful pregnancy.) Yet others would accept observation and experiment on unimplanted embryos up to a stated term: the Ethics Advisory Board of the US Department of Health, Education and Welfare and the British Medical Research Council, both in 1982, set this term at the time when implantation would normally have been complete. This would allow about 14 days. The Warnock committee adopted 14 days, up to the emergence of the 'primitive streak', on the grounds that individuation was by then established.

The issue turns on the moral status attributed to the human embryo. There is an absolutist view which, arguing from the composition of the blastocyst from two human *gametes and its being therefore genetically human, would attribute to it the full status of a human being from the moment of

fertilization, and so give it the full corresponding ethical and legal protection. On this view even postcoital contraception, whether hormonal or mechanical, is an unethical and criminal assault. Others (RCOG, 1983; Dunstan, 1983; Council for Science and Society, 1984) reject this view. It ignores, they argue, products of conception like the *hydatidiform mole which, though of human genetic stock, cannot be called human. It takes no account of the high rate of loss, in the natural process, of embryos which never implant. It ignores centuries of moral tradition, accepted almost without challenge even in the Roman Catholic Church until the later 19th c., which, while in no way trivializing unborn human life at any stage, matched its protection with its growth towards maturity. It was not, in this tradition, recognized as a human being until it was *animatus, formatus*, or *effigiatus*, that is, visibly human in form; and this was from something like 40 days from conception. The tradition continued in terms given to it by Aristotle, matching the philosophical theory of animation (the theory relating the characteristic form of a substance to the *psyche* or *anima* informing it) to what the eye could see in early embryonic growth. The matching of protection to growth was older. It formed part of the Hittite penal code. And in the translation of the Hebrew Old Testament into Greek (the *Septuagint*) this principle replaced a Babylonian one in the law of Exodus 21: 22 (Chollet, 1923; Delmaille, 1935; Sigerist, 1951; Driver and Miles, 1955; Dunstan, 1984). Modern embryologists, seeking to relate the duty of protection to fetal growth, tend to link it with the presumed emergence of a nervous capacity for 'awareness'; experiment should cease before the fetus could in any sense be aware of its environment or of any interference with it (Grobstein, 1979). Mahoney (1984) has attempted to restate Roman Catholic teaching in terms which take account both of the older moral tradition of delayed animation and of the established knowledge of embryonic development.

Professional confidence. The principle that a patient's confidences are safe in his doctor's keeping is, like the principle of consent, one to which present feeling is sensitive. It is firm in the Hippocratic tradition. It has a simple purpose, to safeguard a patient's interest in health: he must feel free to tell his doctor all that he may need to know without fear that his confidence will be betrayed. (The seal of the priest's confessional stands on a similar footing, to safeguard the penitent's ultimate interest, his soul's health or salvation.) Confidence in particular relationships extends to the general: the public as a whole must be able to trust the profession as a whole to keep its secrets.

New technology in health care and its administration is said to put this confidence at risk. Record keeping is not only the doctor's personal responsibility; it is shared by secretaries in general practice and by clerks and technicians in hospitals, especially when records are kept on computers. It is often said, without convincing evidence, that the computer is less secure than the filing cabinet; and public anxiety is thereby increased. Temptations to improper disclosure are strong when there is journalistic interest in a particular case, with money available, and when even responsible newspapers have sometimes published 'leaked' material without scruple (see MEDIA, THE). The rule of secrecy must be a corporate possession if it is to be maintained.

A narrow keeping of the rule may, however, prove adverse to a patient's interest. Cases have occurred in which children are known to more than one person to be at risk from assault, 'non-accidental injury'—general practitioner, hospital casualty officer, social worker, health visitor, probation officer, police officer, school teacher. Reluctance to communicate with other professional people has led, it is alleged, to further injury, sometimes to death. In reaction comes the proliferation of case conferences, and a general mounting of anxiety and suspicion. Registers of children at risk, a means of more ready identification, are held to impute stigma, putting parents under perhaps unjustified suspicion. There is a positive need to develop a corporate ethic of confidence in which knowledge can be shared between responsible professional people, in the assurance that it will not be misused or spread further.

The rule of confidence is not absolute, because the interest of the patient is not absolute. Occasions arise when it may be overridden in the interest of society. Doctors are under obligation to notify listed infections and contagious diseases; a doctor in industrial medicine may be obliged to notify employers of a relevant disability in an employee. A court of law may require a doctor to disclose information in the interest of justice in a serious case. The principle creates a very strong presumption in favour of secrecy; the presumption may be rebutted only for grave cause when either the patient's interest or a serious interest of society requires it, the first judged by the corporate mind or convention of the profession, the second by statutory or judicial authority.

The doctor is professionally the servant of life. Is he then bound to prolong life by all possible means, regardless of its quality? The question is faced, first in the care of severely handicapped newly born children, secondly in the care of the dying.

Severely handicapped infants. Advances in the detection of *spina bifida by assay of *alpha-fetoprotein, and possibly in its prevention by *vitamin supplement in pregnancy, may lessen the incidence of children born with this handicap. Meanwhile decisions are called for because of possibilities unavailable to earlier generations. The invention of a *shunt for the relief of *hydrocephalus and the successful treatment of infections with *antibiotics enabled severely handicapped children to survive who formerly would have died early in infancy. Surgical operations very early in life increased their chance of survival, but, in many cases, only at the cost of more surgery of increasing severity extending into adolescence and early adult life; and all of it palliative, none curative. In a 10-year study in the Sheffield Children's Hospital the effects of a policy of active intervention in every patient seen became the basis of a new policy. Experience made it possible to predict, in the first day or two of life, those children with neural tube disorders who, given minor surgery, could expect a life without gross or severe handicap; those who, given surgery, would face a life of known *minimum* suffering, dependent upon increasingly severe palliative intervention; and those for whom there could be only an early death. An ethic of practice developed accordingly. To the first group appropriate surgery would be given. For the third group there would be no intervention, only normal nursing care, including feeding and analgesia necessary to relieve distress. For the intermediate group clinical judgement, varying from surgeon to surgeon, would determine what intervention was appropriate, if any.

In the event, clinical decision became complicated by other factors. An increasingly publicized notion of parental 'rights' raised the question, how far may the paediatrician become the agent of the parents in his management of the child? Is the final decision on whether or how to treat his or theirs? Indecision on that question brought a paediatrician into court on a charge of murdering a child born with *Down's syndrome. The paediatrician marked the case-notes, 'Parents do not wish it to survive. Nursing care only.' He also prescribed dihydrocodeine (DF 118) orally in 5 mg doses to alleviate distress as and when it arose, not more than every four hours. The child died 60 hours after birth. The prosecution was brought, at the instance of an organization called Life, on the grounds that the purpose of the DF 118 was to accomplish the death of the baby, in that it stopped the child sucking and suppressed the part of the brain which enabled it to breathe and control its lungs. The prosecution was obliged, in view of evidence for the defence, to reduce the charge to attempted murder. The baby weighed as much at death as it had at birth—not at all unusual. The jury were not convinced that the facts alleged established a guilty intent; the paediatrician was acquitted (*British Medical Journal,* and *Lancet,* 14 November 1981). The judge does not seem to have adverted to the question of parental rejection.

In a civil case three months earlier, however, the question was ventilated. A Down's syndrome baby was born with an intestinal *atresia on which the paediatric surgeon was confident he could operate with success. The parents refused consent to the operation. The Local Authority, expecting to be able to place the child for adoption, had the child made a ward of court. The judge at first gave consent for the operation, and then withdrew it. The Court of Appeal reversed his refusal, adjudging that he had erred because he was influenced by the views of the parents instead of deciding what was in the best interests of the child. 'While great weight should be given to the views of the parents, those views did not necessarily prevail.' The Court *authorized* the operation—it did not order it: clinical discretion was left unimpaired either by parental pressure or by the authority of the Court (*The Times* Law Report, 8 August 1981).

It is pertinent to observe what complications follow when duties are confused with rights. Parents have a duty to their children, to secure their interest in health, as in education. That duty they discharge, when necessary, through the agency of the doctor for health, as of the teacher for education. The nearest they come to a right in either matter is a claim on the protection of law to enable them to fulfil those duties. They have no 'right' to deny a child that which his essential interest—life—requires. Their opinion or wish is circumstantial only: one of the factors to be considered by the doctor in making his clinical decisions, what is the best for his patient, the child.

Terminal care and euthanasia. Similar issues arise in terminal care. It is for the physician to decide when he can no longer serve his patient's interest in living, and turn to serve his interest in dying, in dying well. As with the care of severely handicapped children, professional judgement must weigh two possibilities. To give up attempts to cure too early, or to innovate too seldom, would weaken the drive towards more effective medicine on which progress has grown. To attempt to cure too long, or to innovate too readily, would subject the patient to unjustified distress. Recent tendency has been to protect the patient from over-aggressive intervention.

Advocates of what is called '*euthanasia' would impose upon the doctor at least a liberty and at most a duty to kill the patient, at his own instance and by painless means, if he thought he would spare him thereby prolonged suffering or protracted and 'useless' dependence on others. In fact, neither in ethics nor in law is the doctor authorized to kill—as is the soldier in war, or the policeman in defined circumstances, or the public executioner in societies which retain capital punishment. Neither has he need to kill, for he has better remedies. Thanks to advances in pharmacology and clinical skill the pains and distresses of death can be controlled, and without suppression of sense or distortion of personality, where the resources are available. Thanks to a widened understanding of the scope of nursing care, the patient can be helped to accept dependence and rise to the spiritual and social opportunities attending his dying. The hospice movement exists to extend both skills, the medical and the nursing, in the care of dying patients, whether at home or in hospitals of whatever sort (Saunders, 1981, 1984; Twycross and Ventafridda, 1980) (see DEATH, DYING, AND THE HOSPICE MOVEMENT). Euthanasia will continue to appeal, while these skills extend, only as it can appeal to fear.

The care of the dying is not without its ethical options. A *pneumonia supervening upon a terminal illness with a prognosis of increasing distress for which only palliative management is available, could in theory be treated with an antibiotic specific to it. That treatment would be normal or 'ordinary' for a young patient without complications. But for a patient whose interest is now not in a prolonged life but in a good death, it would be 'extraordinary', a remedy which the physician is not bound to offer nor the patient to accept. Pain and distress can be relieved by appropriate medicines. These, by relieving strain, may prolong life. They may, on the other hand, hasten death a little by provoking conditions in which a fatal pneumonia supervenes. The principle of double effect is invoked to distinguish the morality and legality of this action from that of administering deliberately to kill. The analgesic is given with the direct intent of relieving pain, an intent within the physician's duty; and it achieves that effect. It may result in a second effect, foreseeable as a possibility but not intended—the fatal pneumonia. The doctor is not guilty (as Thomas Percival saw), morally or in law, of unlawfully occasioning that death. (A parallel case would be that of the ship's captain who, in an emergency, orders the closing of watertight doors in order to save as many of the ship's company as he can. If, despite precautions, some are trapped and perish in the flooded holds, the captain is not guilty of their death.) Philosophers can point to logical difficulties and practical evasions in the interplay of intention, act, and omission in the causation of death (Glover, 1977), but the distinctions are defensible in ethics and law, and of proven value in the art of medicine. While they are used with integrity, doctors will be trusted to use them and their patients will benefit. They require in the physician the ancient compound of clinical competence, a capacity for insight and moral reasoning, and a good conscience. Medical ethics are the ethics of trust.

Trust between patient, doctor, and nurse enables truth to be faced. A patient may need to know if soon he is likely to die: a will to be made, relationships to be fulfilled or repaired, forgiveness to be sought or offered, God to be met. He may fear that knowledge, or be anxious about dying. If he does not know, he may be bruised by too insensitive a telling. If he does know, he may not be helped by a conspiracy of silence. The question, therefore, whether or not he should be told is the wrong question. The right question is, what quality of relation between him and his doctor and nurses will enable him to articulate his need and to face the truth—whether known or yet to be learned? The relation must plainly be one of mutual trust (see also COMMUNICATION BETWEEN DOCTORS AND PATIENTS).

Religion, philosophy, and medicine. So far, the empirical and the reflective elements in medical ethics have been sketched. What now of the credal, of religion?

Primitive belief and practice. Religion has been and is a factor in healing for various reasons and in a variety of ways. At a primitive level it is the substitute for an empirically grounded theory of causation in malfunction or disease. Illness is brought about by powers external to man or the world: by the gods, the stars, spirits of evil or of the dead. It is the function of religion to manipulate or to neutralize these powers—the task of priests, diviners, astrologers, soothsayers, exorcists, witch-doctors. Not all gods are indifferent or malign; some are beneficent, the healer gods: Gula, Kur-rak, Thoth, *Imhotep, *Asclepius, Hygieia. Religion could invoke these and prepare the patient in mind and body to receive divine aid. Healing would come from some adjustment between the patient and his environment, diverting hostile forces, invoking the benign; strengthening the patient against the one, making him receptive of the other. Some physicians went along with this: it was convenient for heavenly agents at the shrines to incur the odium of painful manipulations. Some were sceptical. Others saw plain quackery and resented it, as inimical to the search for knowledge of cause and outcome.

Hebrew ethical monotheism. Such in general was the picture—overlooking significant variations—of religion and medicine in Egypt and Mesopotamia, among the Hittites, Assyrians, and Babylonians, and of ancient Greece. The ethical monotheism of the Hebrews gave men a new creed, a new theory of causation, and a new ethic. None of these emerged fully grown; the revelation or perception grew over time. In its fullness, as found in the Psalms and the major prophets, the Lord alone was God, the creator of heaven and earth. He therefore was supremely responsible for all that is, all that occurs, in the world, whether by permission or by the direct hand. But since His nature was righteousness and steadfast love, all events, all His acts, had moral significance. The nation's sufferings were occasioned by the nation's sins; and so personal suffering was occasioned also by personal sin. Job contested this doctrine, protesting his innocence the more as his comforters loaded him with guilt. But the doctrine persisted. Despite theological change, it persists in popular emotion to this day. 'Why should it happen to me? What have I done to deserve this?' Repentance would bring forgiveness and restoration both to divine favour and to health. The doctrine was promulgated regularly by bishops in the later Middle Ages, calling for repentance and works of devotion in face of natural calamities—pestilence, foul harvest weather, war. The language of their mandates was translated into the English of the *Book of Common Prayer* in the exhortation to be read (but now never read) to the sick man upon his bed (Dunstan, 1974).

The doctrine, behind all its limitations and distortions, had three merits. First it assumed that the natural universe was ordered, not capricious, and could therefore be studied; science in such a world was possible. Secondly it assumed the priority of good, of health and well-being; evil and suffering were departures from the primary good and were not absolute; suffering could indeed effect redemption from evil. Thirdly it is in part compatible with the understanding of *psychosomatic disorder and of the therapies which go beyond physical treatment: some maladies—not all—are the product of guilt, as some guilt is the product of religious indoctrination; and release from guilt can contribute to the cure. Jesus lived and worked with this faith. Like Job, he denied the universal and inevitable connection between calamity and sin (Luke 13: 1–5; John 9: 2–3); but he associated some of his healings with forgiveness of sin; and in some he employed methods used by healers of his day—touch, anointing, exorcism. His earliest apostles did the same.

The compound of Hebrew theology, Greek philosophy, and Hippocratic medicine in Christian tradition. The regular practice of medicine, orthodox with the orthodoxies of each age, continued within this pattern of belief. In Ecclesiasticus, one of the books of the Old Testament written in Greek and not in Hebrew (and therefore relegated by some Churches of the Reformation to the Apocrypha) the son of Sirach wrote the celebrated paean of praise for the physician, with the theological overtones clear:

Honour a physician according to thy need of him with the
   honours due unto him;
For verily the Lord hath created him.
For from the Most High cometh healing;
And from the king he shall receive a gift.
The skill of the physician shall lift up his head;
And in the sight of great men he shall be admired.
The Lord created medicines out of the earth;
And a prudent man will have no disgust of them.
Was not water made sweet with wood,
That the virtue thereof might be known?
And he gave men skill,
That they might be glorified in his marvellous works.
With them doth he heal a man,
And taketh away his pain.
With these will the apothecary make a confection;
And his works shall not be brought to an end;
And from him is peace upon the face of the earth.

My son, in thy sickness, be not negligent;
But pray unto the Lord, and he shall heal thee.
Put away wrong doing, and order thine hands aright.
And cleanse thy heart from all manner of sin.
Give a sweet savour, and a memorial of fine flour;
And make fat thine offering, as one that is not.
Then give place to the physician, for verily the Lord hath
   created him;
And let him not go from thee, for thou hast need of him.
There is a time when in their very hands is the issue for
   good.
For they also shall beseech the Lord,

That he may prosper them in giving relief and in healing
for the maintenance of life.
He that sinneth before his Maker,
Let him fall into the hands of the physician.
(Ecclesiasticus 38: 1–15)

In the New Testament we have the Gospel
according to St Luke, 'the beloved physician' (Col-
ossians 4:14), St Paul's companion on his journeys,
which he narrated in the Acts of the Apostles.
Christianity, therefore, launched into the Hellenistic world by St Paul (who himself, in the first two
chapters of Romans validated for Christian
theology the Gentile conscience, Gentile reasoning), was well equipped to take Hippocratic medicine into its system. This it did, accepting the
empirical and philosophical base, excising the
appeal to pagan divinities, and strengthening the
ethical impulse with motives derived from its own
faith. The Church became one carrier of Greek
medicine into the modern world. It was a conservative carrier, more of a mind to care than to cure,
and dissuading from rather than promoting radical
advance in the science or the art. These had to wait
for the new men of the Renaissance—for the curiosity and matchless eye and hand of *Leonardo da
Vinci in dissection, the challenge of *Vesalius to
Galen, the wild essays of *Paracelsus into
*chemotherapy.

Present-day Christian practice. In Christianity
today the elements in its tradition remain with
varying emphases in different Churches. Orthodox
medicine is commonly accepted, though fringe
groups, who would call themselves Christian, like
Jehovah's Witnesses and Christian Scientists,
reject parts of it. Prayer for the sick, and for
doctors, nurses, and hospitals, and thanksgiving
after recovery, are universal. Unction, the anointing of the sick, raised to the status of a sacrament in
the late medieval Church, is administered routinely
in the Roman Catholic Church and selectively in
the Anglican and Episcopalian. For some centuries
it became Extreme Unction administered as part of
the last rites in immediate preparation for death.
Now it is regarded as a sacramental ministry to the
soul in sickness, contributing either to recovery, or
to a creative patience in chronic disease, or to
preparation for death. Confession of sin, and
absolution, would normally accompany it
(McClain, 1967).

The Roman Catholic Church associates healing
cults with particular shrines. These were many in
the Middle Ages, originating in the veneration of
the outstanding sanctity of a local man or woman.
The tomb of Edmund Lacy, for instance, the 15th
c. bishop of Exeter, was the centre of a therapeutic
cult until it was desecrated at the Reformation
(Radford, 1949). In his lifetime Lacy had compiled
a liturgical office of St Raphael, the angel of healing in the Book of Tobit, and promoted his cult,
with papal approval (Dunstan, 1972). Modern
shrines are associated with visions, as of the Bles-
sed Virgin Mary, vouchsafed these. Of these the

most notable in Western Europe is at *Lourdes,
visited by pilgrims in thousands, some sick, some to
pray for the sick; cures and remissions are
reported. These cults are controlled liturgically
and by canon law, and tests for 'miracles' are
increasingly stringent (Casey, 1967). A more
cautious theology, recognizing that in the New
Testament the healings performed by Jesus and the
Apostles were written of as 'signs' of the coming of
God's kingdom, does not look for them as direct
divine interventions in the same way now (Habgood, 1981).

The laying on of hands has, in some congregations, passed from the private ministration of the
priest or minister into the open as a congregational
event, accompanied by corporate expressions in
sound and action called 'charismatic' and evoca-
tive of what adherents believe to be the practice of
early Christian congregations. Exorcism, reduced
to a harmless ritual in Catholic wisdom, erupts
occasionally in other churches in its more intense
forms, sometimes with terrifying and even fatal
results. After notorious outbreaks in the recent
past, Anglican bishops, halting between a waver-
ing conviction as to the objective validity of the
process and pressure on prudential grounds to
forbid it, contented themselves with the pious
language of 'regulation'.

The corporate activity of the Church, however,
engaging lay strength, initiative, and enthusiasm,
issues in the founding and support of Christian
communities and institutions in which orthodox
medicine can find its place in the care of the whole
person, his spiritual as well as his physical and
mental reality. When the municipal hospitals of the
Roman Empire decayed, the Church was ready to
replace them: hospitals for the sick, for lepers, and
for the aged poor were founded and sustained
throughout the Middle Ages, and were supplemented by lay or liberal philanthropy in the
centuries before a state health service was conceived to be a national responsibility. Hospitals
and medical care were, with education, the spearhead of missions overseas; in the confident expansion of the 19th c. they were the main carriers of
Western medicine abroad. The impulse which sent
Albert *Schweitzer to French Equatorial Africa
today sends Mother Theresa to Calcutta and Dame
Cicely Saunders to establish the Hospice movement—the one to care for destitute children, the
other to enhance effective analgesic and general
medical care for the terminally ill, and a positive
concept of the value of dying (Saunders, 1981,
1984).

Orthodox Christianity claims no prerogative in
healing or in medical care. It contributes to the care
of the sick in offering communities in which
orthodox medicine can be practised at the highest
level locally attainable. It contributes to the forming of character and motive in doctors and nurses—
a factor felt so strongly by some as to impel them
into specific Christian associations, like the
Christian Medical Fellowship (Edmunds and

Scorer, 1958, 1967), guilds of Catholic doctors, or the Guild of St Barnabas for nurses. It contributes to the philosophy and ethics of medicine from its own theology. These insights and emphases have been summarized by the present Archbishop of York in an available essay (Habgood, 1981): belief in God as creator and in man as his creature on the one hand sets limits to man's assumption to himself of godlike powers and on the other gives man a stewardship in the natural order, in which his responsibility advances with his power. Belief in the incarnation of the Son of God, and a doctrine of salvation, give man new dignity, imprinting on him the capacity to bear the image of God; while the doctrine of original sin warns him of a bias towards evil and frustration in all human activities, when even good can be exploited for evil. The Christian is both committed to and sceptical of all effort for human betterment.

Rabbinic Judaism. Jewish medical ethics stands in a tradition of centuries in which rabbinic guidance is given on the interpretation of the Jewish law with regard to birth, death, and, above all, the preservation of life by permissible medical treatment. The Rabbis, like the Christians, took Hippocratic and Galenic medicine into their system, but they maintained a strict independence of judgement. The method is the application to particular cases of the Law, as contained in the Pentateuch and interpreted by the Targums (the early Aramaic translations and paraphrases), the Talmud (the binding precepts of the elders, with commentaries), and the Responsa of other Rabbis. The moral tradition is developed, as new demands and cases require, but always under the control of principles. The strongest of these is the overriding duty to save life, derived from the theological belief that every human life is infinitely precious to God. The work of the present Chief Rabbi of the British Commonwealth, Sir Immanuel Jakobovits (1975, 1983, 1984) demonstrates the method and its application to some contemporary questions concerning the beginning and ending of life, the control of pain, euthanasia, abortion, sterilization, and contraception.

Islam, the third great religion of the West, first received its medicine from Greece, having the Hippocratic and Galenic texts, especially the Oath and commentaries on it, translated into Arabic. There was close rapport also with Jewish practitioners; and a major work of practical medical ethics, *Adab at-tabib,* was written by a Jewish author in the 10th c. AD. This tradition was then overlaid—as it has been again locally in recent years—by an interposed Koranic or 'prophetic' orthodoxy, varying in intensity from place to place. This would permit, for instance, medical participation in the castration of eunuchs and in penal mutilation. Where Western medicine has penetrated however, Western attitudes, both strict and lax, tend to accompany it (Bürgel, 1981).

Hinduism. The basic texts of *Ayurveda,* Hindu

medical lore, date from before AD 700. They describe an ethic of mutual obligation between physician and patient, though the physician was not obliged to treat the incurable, the king's enemies, or certain disqualified classes of people. The ethics were highly protective of the physician; but he was liable to fine if guilty of incompetence, negligence, or malice. The taint of impurity or of unpropitiated sin infected his fee: he could not use it for charitable purposes. In the tradition, only when used to save the mother's life was abortion without sin. Experiments on animals or men were unknown. *Ayurvedic and Unani medicine and *homoeopathy are still taught and widely practiced; they coexist with Western practice, and only practitioners qualified in the latter may operate under the Medical Termination of Pregnancy Act 1971 (Derrett, 1981). Indian doctors today are deeply involved in campaigns for sterilization promoted by central and state governments; even in the short-lived imposition of compulsory abortion and sterilization for parents of more than an allowed number of children in the state of Maharashtra in 1976 (IPPF, 1976).

Buddhism. The Buddhist Path of Life enjoins the purification of the mind and compassion for all creatures. The Buddha is believed to have been a healer. Hospitals were set up as early as the 3rd c. BC. By the curing or relieving of their physical ills men are freed to cultivate their minds. But the mind itself, calm and trusting, is also an instrument of healing and of health. Strict adherents to the tradition of reverence for life find abortion and contraception unacceptable (Rivers, 1981).

Chinese medical ethics. The organization of medical care in the People's Republic of China, and the therapeutics of *acupuncture and the Chinese *materia medica,* are beyond the scope of this essay. Official policy in both the Nationalist and the Communist revolutions was to deliver medicine from its traditional attachments: first to the cult of the ancestors; then, since the last five centuries BC, to the conflict of demons; then to the Confucian doctrine of correspondence, the balancing of influences internal and external as the way to health; and lastly to the Tao which ambiguously both disdained medicine and cultivated it in the utmost prolongation of life. In practice the aim is to combine the best of Western medicine with the best of traditional practice, taking acupuncture, for instance, into the arts of anaesthesia. Convulsive changes of political and social ideology in recent years make the recognition of a characteristic medical ethic difficult. Whereas at one period all Western philosophy of medical science and practice was denounced as bourgeois, now Western philosophy of medical science and technology are under invitation to expand. The stern battle with population growth has entailed the sacrifice of some human liberties, including the free choice of family size. It remains to be seen whether the male contraceptive produced from cotton oil seed will prove both medically and personally acceptable (Unschuld, 1981).

Shinto in Japan is like Buddhism in that it offers more the ethics of a community life than of a professional practice, and in that it extends the mercy of the god to all creatures, animal as well as man. It has hygienic value, in its enjoining cleanliness of body and soul, to be attained by bathing and by rituals of the cult. A conscious search for a pure Japanese medicine (Wano-igaku) and its attendant ethics began at the beginning of the 19th c. with the rejection of prevailing medical knowledge, partly Chinese, partly European. Atsutane Hirata (1776–1843), in his book *Shizu-no-iwaya* (1811), required a high standard of ethical conduct from so solemn an undertaking as the practice of medicine (Higuchi and Ogawa, 1981). Today Western practice and concepts of medicine are fully integrated in Japanese medical practice, and Japanese students of medical law and ethics are fully conversant with developments in Europe and the USA (Bai, 1983).

Conclusion. 'From time immemorial the practice of medicine has been bound up with religion and philosophy': so this essay began. Does 'time' include the present with the past? is the statement still true? In one sense it is no longer true. Medicine has freed itself from the cultic prescriptions of religion; and most of the religions which claimed to possess therapeutic powers have died with the nations that practised them. In another sense the present is continuous with the past. The religions which still claim men's intellectual, moral, and spiritual allegiance, notably Christianity and Judaism in the West, Hinduism and Buddhism in the East, show a capacity, while cleaving to their fundamental theology and derived principles of behaviour, to accommodate new knowledge and formulate a new ethic for conditions and possibilities unknown before. For this reason, more than surviving, they flourish: commitment to medical science and practice is compatible with the practice of religion; indeed, the one may be deepened by the other. Contemporary Islam is divided. Part continues to accommodate Western medicine as once it took in the Hippocratic. Part imposes a new Islamic orthodoxy hostile to that liberality which the West regards as humane. Islam is old enough to change yet again.

Philosophy is a perennial discipline. It is an exercise of the mind, skilled to form consistent patterns of thought and ideas, as natural science seeks to form hypotheses to interpret the facts. Religion and medicine are both proper subjects for philosophical analysis. The three disciplines are still interlocked.   G. R. DUNSTAN

References

American Medical Association (1982). *Current Opinions of the Judicial Council of the American Medical Association.* Chicago.

Association of the British Pharmaceutical Industry (1983). *Code of Practice for the Clinical Assessment of Licensed Medical Products in General Practice.* London.

Bai, K. (1983). Personal communication. In Dunstan and Seller (1983).

British Medical Association (1984). *Handbook of Medical Ethics.* London.

British Paediatric Association (1980). Guidelines to aid ethical committees considering research involving children. *Archives of Diseases in Childhood,* **55,** 75–7.

Brock, A. J. (ed.) (1916). *Galen on the Natural Faculties.* Loeb Classics. New York.

Brudenell, J. M., McClaren, A., Short, R. V. and Symonds, E. M. (1977). *Artificial Insemination.* London.

Bürgel, J. C. (1981). Islam. In Duncan *et al.* (1981).

Byleby, J. J. (1979). Padua and humanistic medicine. In Webster, C. (ed.), *Health, Medicine and Morality in the Sixteenth Century,* Cambridge.

Casey, T. F. (1967). Lourdes. *New Catholic Encyclopaedia.* New York.

Chollet, A. (1923). Animation. In Naz, R. (ed.), *Dictionnaire de Théologie Catholique.* Paris.

Church of England (1958). *The Family in Contemporary Society.* London.

—— (1959). *Ought Suicide to be a Crime?* London.

—— (1960). *Artificial Insemination by Donor: Two Contributions to a Christian Judgment.* London.

—— (1962). *Sterilization.* London.

—— (1965a). *Abortion: An Ethical Discussion.* London.

—— (1965b). *Decisions about Life and Death.* London.

—— (1975). *On Dying Well.* London.

Council for Science and Society (1984). *Human Procreation: Ethical Aspects of the New Techniques.* Oxford.

Delmaille, J. (1935). Avortement. In Naz, R. (ed.), *Dictionnaire de Droit Canonique.* Paris.

Derrett, J. D. M. (1981). Hindu Medicine. In Duncan *et al.* (1981).

Driver, G. R. and Miles, J. C. M. (1955). *The Babylonian Laws.* Oxford.

Duncan, A. S., Dunstan, G. R. and Welbourn, R. B. (1981). *Dictionary of Medical Ethics.* 2nd edn, London and New York.

Dunstan, G. R. (1972). *The Register of Edmund Lacy Bishop of Exeter 1420–1455,* V, p. 249 (index). London.

Dunstan, G. R. (1974). Some late medieval ingredients in the Reformed English Church. In Simon, M. (ed.), *Aspects de L'Anglicanisme.* Paris.

Dunstan, G. R. (1983). Social and ethical aspects. In Carter, C. E. (ed.), *Developments in Human Reproduction and their Eugenic and Ethical Implications.* London and New York.

Dunstan, G, R. (1984). The moral status of the human embryo: a tradition recalled. *Journal of Medical Ethics,* **10** (1), 38–44.

Dunstan, G. R. and Seller, M. J. (1983). *Consent in Medicine: Convergence and Divergence in Tradition.* London.

Edmunds, V. and Scorer, C. G. (1958). *Medical Ethics: A Christian View.* (2nd edn, 1966). London.

Edmunds, V. and Scorer, C. G. (1967). *Ethical Responsibility in Medicine.* Edinburgh and London.

Edwards, R. G. and Purdy, J. M. (1982). *Human Conception in Vitro: Proceedings of the First Bourn Hall Meeting.* London and New York.

Glover, J. (1977). *Causing Death and Saving Lives.* Harmondsworth, Middlesex.

Grobstein, C. (1979). External human fertilization. *Scientific American,* **240,** 33–43.

Habgood, J. S. (1981). Christianity. In Duncan *et al.,* (1981).

HMSO (1984). *Report of the Committee of Enquiry into Human Fertilization and Embryology.* Cmnd. 9314 London.

Higuchi, S. and Agawa, T. (1981). Shinto. In Duncan *et al.* (1981).

International Planned Parenthood Federation (IPPF) (1976). The Maharashtra Scheme. *People,* **3,** 4. London.

Iskandar, A. I. (1981). Averroes. In Gillespie, C. C. (ed.) *Dictionary of Scientific Biography.* New York.

Jakobovits, I. (1975). *Jewish Medical Ethics.* New York.

Jakobovits, I. (1983). The doctor's duty to heal and the patient's consent in the Jewish tradition. In Dunstan and Seller (1983).

Jakobovits, I. (1984). *In vitro* fertilization and Jewish law. *L'Eyah,* **2** (6), 1–5.

Janofsky, J. and Starfield, B. (1981). Assessment of risk in research on children. *Journal of Paediatrics,* **98,** (5), 842–6.

Jerome, St (394). Ep. LII, *Ad Nepotianum.* In Wright, F. A. (ed.) (1954). *Select Letters of St Jerome.* Loeb Classics. New York.

Jones, W. H. S. (1923). *The Hippocratic Writings,* 4 vols. Loeb Classics. New York.

Kennedy, I. (1983). Consent in law. In Dunstan and Seller (1983).

Larkey, S. V. (1936) The Hippocratic Oath in Elizabethan England. *Bulletin of the History of Medicine,* **4** (3), 201–19.

McClain, J. P. (1967). Anointing of the sick. *New Catholic Encyclopaedia.* New York.

MacClintock, S. (1967). Averroes. In Edwards, P. (ed.), *Encyclopaedia of Philosophy.* New York and London.

McCormick, R. A. (1974). Sharing in Sociality: Children and Experimentation. Reprinted (1981) in *How Brave a New World?* London.

MacKinney, L. C. (1952). Medical ethics and etiquette in the early Middle Ages: the persistence of Hippocratic Ideals. *Bulletin of the History of Medicine,* **23** (1), 1–31.

Mahoney, J. and S. J. (1984). *Bio-ethics and Belief.* London.

Marmura, M. E. (1967). Avicenna. In Edwards, P. (ed.), *Encyclopaedia of Philosophy.* New York and London.

Medical Research Council (1962–3). Report of the Medical Research Council for 1962–3. Cmnd. 2382. London.

Nicholson, R. H. (1985). *Medical Research with Children: Ethics, Law and Practice.* London.

Nutton, V. (1981). Hippocratic Tradition. In Duncan *et al.,* (1981).

Oppenheimer, H. (1975). Ought and Is. In Dunstan, G. R. (ed.), *Duty and Discernment.* London.

Pappworth, M. H. (1967). *Human Guinea Pigs.* London.

Pellegrino, E. D. E. and Thomasma, D. C. (1981). *Philosophical Basis of Medical Practice.* New York and Oxford.

Penes, S. (1967). Maimonides. In Edwards, D. (ed.), *Encyclopaedia of Philosophy.* New York and London.

Percival, T. (1803). *Medical Ethics.* (ed. Leake, C. D. (1927). Baltimore).

Polani, P. (1983). The development of the concepts and practice of patient consent. In Dunstan and Seller (1983).

President's Commission for the Study of Ethics in Medicine and Biomedical and Behavioral Research (1982). *Compensating for Research Injuries.* Vol. I: Report. Washington, DC.

Radford, U. M. (1949). The wax images found in Exeter Cathedral. *Antiquaries Journal,* **29,** 164.

Ramsey, I. T. and Porter, R. (eds.) (1971). *Personality and Science: An Interdisciplinary Discussion.* Edinburgh and London.

Ramsey, P. (1970). *The Patient as Person.* New Haven and London.

Ramsey, P. (1976). *The Enforcement of Morals: Non-*

Therapeutic Research on Children. Hastings Center Report. New York.

Reich, W. T. (ed.) (1978). *Encyclopedia of Bioethics,* 4 vols. New York.

Rivers, J. (1981). Buddhism. In Duncan *et al.* (1981).

Royal College of Obstetricians and Gynaecologists (1983). *Report of the RCOG Ethics Committee on In Vitro Fertilization and Embryo Replacement.* London.

Royal Colleges (1975). *British Medical Journal,* **iv,** 401–2.

(1976). *Lancet,* **ii,** 1069–70.

(1977). *British Medical Journal,* **i,** 157–9.

(1979). *Lancet,* **ii,** 261–2.

Saunders, C. M. (1981). Hospices. In Duncan *et al.* (1981).

Saunders, C. M. (1984). *The Management of Terminal Malignant Disease.* 2nd edn, London.

Sherlock, R., Leaser, H. and Taylor, P. J. (1983). Consent, competency and ECT. I, II, III. *Journal of Medical Ethics,* **9,** 141–51.

Sigerist, H. E. (1951). *A History of Medicine,* I. New York.

Snowden, E. M. (1983). *Artificial Reproduction: A Social Investigation.* London.

Snowden, R. and Mitchell, G. D. (1981). *The Artificial Family.* London.

Spicker, S. F., Healey, J. M. Jr. and Engelhardt, H. T. Jr (1981), *The Law–Medicine Relation: A Philosophical Exploration.* Dordrecht.

Stannard, J. (1981). Galen. In Gillespie, C. C. (ed.), *Dictionary of Scientific Biography.* New York.

Twycross, R. G. and Ventafridda, V. (1980). *The Continuing Care of Cancer Patients.* Oxford.

Unschuld, P. U. (1981). Chinese medicine. In Duncan *et al.* (1981).

Vandeveer, D. (1981). Experimentation on children and proxy consent. *Journal of Medicine and Philosophy,* **6,** 281–93.

Vicary, T. (1548). *The Anatomie of the Bodie of Man.* (The text of 1577, edited by F. J. and P. Furnivall, (1888). Oxford.)

Walters, LeRoy (1979). *Human In Vitro Fertilization. A Review of the Ethical Literature.* Hastings Center Bulletin. New York.

Walzer, R. (ed.) (1944). *Galen On Medical Experience* (1st edn of the Arabic text, with English translation and notes). Oxford.

Wolstenholme, G. E. W. and FitzSimons, D. W. (1973). *Law and Ethics of A.I.D. and Embryo Transfer.* Amsterdam, London, and New York.

Wolstenholme, G. E. W. and O'Connor, M. (1966). *Ethics in Medical Progress* (paperback entitled *Law and Ethics of Transplant Surgery*). London.

World Health Organization (1982). *Proposed Institutional Guidelines for Biomedical Research Involving Human Subjects.* Geneva.

REM (roentgen equivalent man) is the unit dose of ionizing radiation that gives the same biological effect as that due to one roentgen of *X-rays. In the case of beta particles, and gamma- and X-radiations, the rem is equivalent to the rad, which is equivalent to an energy absorption by irradiated tissue of 0.01 joule per kilogram. The rad has now been supplanted by the gray (Gy): 1 Gy = 100 rad. See RADIATION, IONIZING; RADIOTHERAPY.

REMEDY. Any means of counteracting a disease process.

REMISSION. Temporary abatement of the manifestations of a disease.

REM (RAPID EYE MOVEMENTS) SLEEP is a phase of normal sleep, also known as 'paradoxical sleep'. During this period, rapid eye movements, *hypotonia, muscle twitching, and dreaming occur; it is an essential component of human sleep, thought to be necessary for brain repair. REM sleep is cyclical, and normally accounts for about 25 per cent of the normal night, though this proportion may be varied by the administration of hypnotic and stimulant drugs. It is the phase during which a subject is most difficult to arouse. See SLEEP.

RENAL COLIC is severe *colic, due usually to impaction of a *stone in the urinary tract.

RENAL DIALYSIS: TECHNIQUES AND CLINICAL APPLICATIONS. When the kidneys fail from acute or chronic disease, their functions are altered to different degrees (Table 1). Some *erythropoietin is produced outside the kidney and for this and other reasons the *anaemia of renal failure, although troublesome, is tolerable. The active forms of *vitamin D are now available as drugs which can be given by mouth. High *blood pressure can be combated with a wide range of drugs, which now include specific antagonists of *renin, provided that the excess of salt and water retained in kidney failure is removed. Only the loss of excretory function is immediately life-threatening.

The *gut absorbs water and many solutes indiscriminately, regardless of the body's need, a fact familiar to anyone who has been on a celebratory night-out. The chemical composition of our body fluids, which Claude *Bernard called the '*milieu

interieur', is precisely regulated (see HOMEOSTASIS) in spite of great variations of intake and output which we inflict on ourselves; the kidneys have a key role in this regulation. Such excretory and regulatory function can be permanently restored by renal *transplantation, which is applicable only to irreversible disease and which will not be considered here. Temporary replacement can be achieved by haemodialysis or peritoneal dialysis, although 'temporary' is an elastic term; for one of my medical colleagues it means '23 years so far'.

Haemodialysis (Fig. 1). Blood is taken from a suitable vessel and pumped through a tube of semipermeable membrane which allows the passage of the small molecules which accumulate in renal failure, but retains the *proteins and blood cells. As it passes down the tube it is 'washed' by a stream of fluid on the outside of the membrane that carries away the waste products. This dialysis fluid (erroneously called 'dialysate' in the medical literature) contains solutes like *sodium and *dextrose in the same concentrations as normal blood, so that these vital substances are not lost from the body unless they are present in excess. There are practical limits to what can be included in dialysis fluid so some important substances like *amino acids and *vitamins are omitted. These are lost from the body and must be replaced by eating an adequate diet or consuming dietary supplements like vitamin pills.

The principles of haemodialysis were described in 1913 by three Americans who built the first artificial kidney, or haemodialyser, from strips of celloidin tubing (*Abel *et al.*, 1913). They passed animal blood through it and prevented clotting with the *anticoagulant hirudin which is injected by leeches (*Hirudo medicinalis*) when they suck blood. A large-scale model was built by Haas in Germany at the end of the First World War and

Table 1. Functions of the kidney and their alteration in acute and chronic renal failure

Function	Change in severe (oliguric) acute renal failure	Change in chronic renal failure (CRF)
Excretion of water	Virtually abolished	Well-preserved in early CRF; progressively reduced in late CRF
Excretion of water-soluble compounds	Virtually abolished	Varies with the compound; in general, progressively reduced as CRF progresses
Production of erythropoietin (stimulates red blood cell formation)	Greatly reduced —progressive anaemia	Progressively reduced but not usually to zero; moderate to severe anaemia
Production of 1,25- and 24,25-hydroxycholecalciferol, the active forms of vitamin D	Reduced—low blood calcium is usual	Reduced in moderate to severe CRF—reduced blood calcium and tendency to bone disease
Production of renin—hormone which helps to maintain blood pressure and conserve sodium	Variable. Since the kidney is not excreting much sodium, effect minimized	Often increased—contributes to high blood pressure of chronic kidney disease; removal of both kidneys (to cure this) may cause low blood pressure
Production of prostaglandins and intrarenal hormones	Uncertain what part changes in secretion of such hormones plays in producing the symptoms of acute and chronic renal failure	

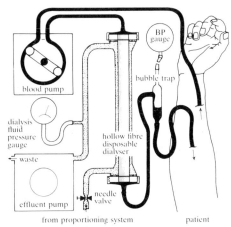

Fig. 1. A modern haemodialysis circuit (simplified). Blood is taken from the arterial tube and pumped through the hollow-fibre disposable dialyser before returning through an air trap to the patient. Dialysis fluid flows in the opposite direction from a proportionating system, which makes it from water and concentrate. A number of safety devices (not shown) monitor the temperature, flow, and pressure of the dialysis fluid and the presence of air bubbles in the blood stream

was used on a patient with renal failure but for a period which we now know to be quite inadequate and therefore with no benefit (see Haas, 1935). Haas tried again in 1928 when *heparin became available as an anticoagulant but again failed to produce any clinical improvement (Haas, 1928).

After the introduction of cellulose tubing (Cellophane) as sausage skin, Kolff in Holland designed an ingenious artificial kidney which he tried out on animals in the University of Groningen in 1938. When the Second World War interrupted his studies and he was banished to the small provincial town of Kampen he continued his work illegally and made six working artificial kidneys. One of these was used to save the life of the first patient to survive prolonged acute renal failure and some patients with chronic renal failure experienced gratifying, although only temporary, improvement (Kolff, 1965).

After the war, Kolff's machines were distributed to several countries, including the UK, but the technical problems of running them discouraged many workers. Alwall (1947) in Sweden and Murray *et al.* (1948) in Canada, working independently in the later years of the Second World War also produced artificial kidneys which were used successfully but it was Kolff, whose enthusiasm overcame the later technical difficulties, who is rightly hailed as the father of haemodialysis.

For the next 14 years the artificial kidney was used only to treat acute renal failure or to tide patients with chronic renal failure over temporary illness. Then in 1960, Quinton and his colleagues (1960) found a way to connect patients with chronic renal failure repeatedly to an artificial kidney.

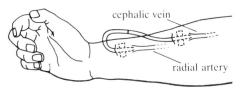

Fig. 2. The original Quinton–Scribner shunt for haemodialysis. Silicone tubes with stabilizing wings and Teflon tips have been inserted in the radial artery and cephalic vein and connected end to end. They are disconnected and attached to the machine during the procedure

They implanted a Teflon tube, into an artery and vein by the forearm or ankle and connected the vessels end-to-end between treatments (Fig 2). This system prolonged many lives but clotting in the tubes was a common problem which led to many revisions of the *shunt and made life a misery to some patients. In 1966 Brescia and his colleagues found a more permanent solution. They connected an artery to a vein in the forearm, causing a fast flow of arterial blood to course up the superficial vein, from which it could be withdrawn by inserting a wide-bore needle (Fig. 3).

When Scribner first described the prolonged survival of patients with chronic renal failure, treated by repeated haemodialysis, he was greeted with incredulity. It seemed too good to be true that so crude a system could happen to remove all the life-threatening impurities in the blood without depleting the patient of some vital substances. The general view was that Scribner's patients would suffer the fate of Lot's wife and turn into pillars of unremoved solute. Although Scribner's faith was rewarded, the patient who survives for many years on an artificial kidney does suffer from many complications which have turned this form of treatment into a whole new field of medicine (Table 2). The loss of vital solutes has proved a surprisingly unimportant problem. Loss of the *hormones which cause *vasoconstriction when blood volume decreases contributes to the syndrome of 'dialysis *hypotension' which limits the rate at which fluid can be removed, and therefore the amount that can be drunk between treatments. Most other lost solutes are readily replaced by the diet or by the body overproducing to compensate. Accumulation of unwanted solutes has proved a much more formidable problem. Several of these have been

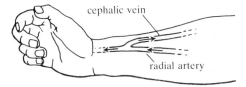

Fig. 3. Cimino–Brescia fistula. Arterial blood flows through the surgically created fistula into a superficial vein into which needles are inserted in the approximate direction of the arrow, identifying the cephalic vein

Table 2. Some complications of haemodialysis ('treatment with an artificial kidney')

Generic cause	Complication	Prevention or treatment
Technique failure	Air embolism Electrocution Blood loss from circuit Incorrect composition of dialysis fluid	All preventable by equipment design and training, but the high standards required greatly increase the cost of treatment
Loss of vital solutes	Low blood pressure (fainting) during procedure	Fluid restriction between dialyses; slow removal of fluid (prolongs procedure); more expensive alternatives like haemofiltration
	Vitamin deficiencies e.g. scurvy	Avoid by diet and supplements

Accumulation of dietary solutes—
  sodium, potassium, phosphates, etc.
	Fluid overload and
	  high blood pressure
	Life threatening high
	  blood potassium
	Bone disease due to
	  phosphate retention, etc.
		Dietary restriction
		Use of drugs which block gut
		  absorption of solutes
		More prolonged dialysis

Accumulation of toxins such as trace
metals, chloramines, etc. from the
water supply
	Bone disease and brain
	  disease (aluminium)
	Haemolytic anaemia (copper,
	  zinc, chloramines) etc.
		Purification of water supply; use
		of only high-grade approved
		materials in artificial kidneys and
		all ancillary equipment

Persistence of the primary disease and its complications such as high blood pressure and arterial disease	Heart attacks, strokes etc.	Best prevented by early treatment of these complications, early in the course of renal disease

derived from tap water used to make the dialysis fluid; initially, total purification of water for this purpose was deemed too expensive, since up to 100 gallons can be used in a single treatment, but fortunately water purification technology has advanced as the problem has emerged and it is now almost mandatory to treat tap water by an appropriate combination of reverse *osmosis and deionization before making the fluid.

Peritoneal dialysis (Fig. 4). The *peritoneum is a natural membrane through which solute exchange can take place between the blood in subperitoneal *capillaries and a dialysis fluid introduced into the peritoneal cavity. The technique was first used by Ganter in 1923 but it was rarely employed until Maxwell and his colleagues (1959) persuaded manufacturers to produce dialysis fluid, administration sets, and disposable *catheters containing a stylet commercially. Peritoneal dialysis was rapidly accepted as a treatment for acute renal failure and our understanding of the peritoneum was advanced by the careful studies of Boen (1964). However, repeated attacks of *peritonitis, partly caused by bowel trauma by the disposable catheter, limited its use in chronic renal failure until Tenckhoff et al. (1972) introduced a disposable silicone rubber catheter which could be implanted permanently through the abdominal wall and allowed repeated access to the peritoneal cavity, as the Quinton–Scribner shunt had done for the blood stream.

However, peritoneal dialysis remained a junior partner to haemodialysis until 1976 when Popovich et al. (1978) hit on the idea of leaving fluid in the peritoneal cavity throughout the 24 hours. This

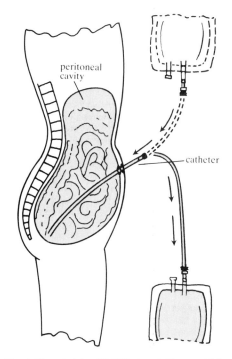

peritoneal
cavity

catheter

Fig. 4. The principle of CAPD. A sealed bag containing 2 litres of dialysis fluid is first emptied into the peritoneal cavity, then wrapped up and stowed in a pouch while the patient walks around, and finally hung below the abdomen to drain out the used fluid. The old bag is then changed for a full new one

Table 3. Some complications of peritoneal dialysis

Generic cause	Complication	Prevention or treatment
Introduction of bacteria into the peritoneum	Peritonitis	Prevent by design of equipment (easy and safe connections) and training; treat with antibiotics (usually successful)
Loss of function of the peritoneum	Loss of capacity to withdraw fluid; occurs for ill-understood reasons	Transfer to haemodialysis at least temporarily
	Loss of diffusion capacity due to adhesions after peritonitis	Transfer to haemodialysis permanently
Overdistension of abdomen	Hernias	Treat surgically; Temporary rest from CAPD (haemodialysis)
	Liability to chest infection	Treat with physiotherapy and antibiotics
Excess absorption of dextrose from PD fluid (added to abstract water from patient)	Weight gain High blood fat (?risk of heart attacks)	An alternative to dextrose is being sought; meantime the only remedy is self-discipline in fluid intake
Loss of protein and amino acids in PD fluid	Low blood proteins	Adequate diet (not always easy when fluid restricted)
Persistence of primary disease and its complications	As for haemodialysis	

greatly increased its efficiency in removing solutes of intermediate molecular weight and permitted patients to treat themselves at home after a short training period in hospital. This method of continuous ambulatory peritoneal dialysis (CAPD) has increased faster than any other treatment for renal failure over the last few years, although it still accounts for only about 20 per cent of all such treatment in the UK.

Figure 4 illustrates CAPD. Four times a day the patient empties his peritoneal cavity by draining the fluid into a disposable plastic bag. Using sterile precautions, he removes the used bag and replaces it with a new container of sterile fluid which he then pours into his peritoneum through the giving set. The whole exchange procedure takes about 40–60 minutes but much of the time can be usefully or pleasantly employed reading, watching television, etc. Some of the complications of peritoneal dialysis are listed in Table 3. Much the most important is peritonitis and the future of this technique hinges on whether better equipment and training can reduce the incidence of peritonitis to a more acceptable level.

Choice of treatment. Haemodialysis is the longer-established treatment for chronic renal failure and the better bet for young adults who must continue treatment for many years. Average survival in Europe is about 10 years and is improving steadily. Younger adults and older children can usually treat themselves at home after careful training for two months or so. The skills required are about comparable to those involved in learning to drive a car; like the latter, they are more easily acquired under 50 than at older ages, though there are notable exceptions. Treatment is required for about four hours three times a week.

CAPD is used for older patients, who find it easier to master the skills for this method, and for those with common tissue types who can, therefore, expect a kidney transplant after a short wait. Patient survival has not yet been charted for more than about 3–4 years but over that time span it is comparable to that for haemodialysis when similar patients are compared. However, a much higher proportion of patients have to abandon the method because of complications: its use therefore should be confined to centres which have the alternative of haemodialysis to offer the 'drop-outs'.

D. N. S. KERR

References

Abel, J. J., Rownstree, L. G. and Turner, B. B. (1913). On the removal of diffusible substances from the circulating blood by means of dialysis. *Transactions of the Association of American Physicians,* **28,** 51.

Alwall, N. (1947). On the artificial kidney I. Apparatus for dialysis of blood *in vivo. Acta Medica Scandinavica.,* **128,** 317.

Boen, S. T. (1964). *Peritoneal Dialysis in Clinical Medicine.* Springfield, Illinois.

Brescia, M. J., Cimino, J. E., Appel, K. and Hurwich, B. J. (1966). Chronic hemodialysis using venepuncture and a surgically created arteriovenous fistula. *New England Journal of Medicine,* **275,** 1089.

Ganter, G. (1923). Uber die Beseitigung giftiger Stoffe aus dem Blute durch dialyse. *München Medizinische Wochenschrift,* **50,** 1478.

Haas, G. (1928). Die Methoden der Blutawswaschung. *Klinische Wochenschrift,* **7,** 1356.

Haas, G. (1935). Die Methoden der Blutawswaschung. *Aberhalden's Handbuch. Biologischen Arbeitsmethoden,* V, 8, 717.

Kolff, W. J. (1965). First clinical experience with the artificial kidney. *Annals of Internal Medicine,* **62,** 608.

Maxwell, M. H., Rockney, R. E., Kleeman, C. R. and Twill, R. L. (1959). Peritoneal dialysis 1. Technique and applications. *Journal of the American Medical Association,* **170,** 917.

Murray, G., Delorme, E. and Thomas, N. (1948). Artificial kidney. *Journal of the American Medical Association*, **137**, 1596.

Popovich, R. P., Moncrieff, J. W., Nolph, K. D., Ghods, A. J., Twardowski, Z. J. and Pyle, W. K. (1978). Continuous ambulatory peritoneal dialysis. *Annals of Internal Medicine*, **88**, 449.

Quinton, W., Dillard, D. and Scribner, B. H. (1960). Cannulation of blood vessels for prolonged hemodialysis. *Transactions of the American Society of Artificial Internal Organs*, **6**, 104.

Tenckhoff, H., Meston, B. and Shilipetar, G. (1972). A simplified automatic peritoneal dialysis system. *Transactions of the American Society of Artificial Internal Organs*, **18**, 436.

RENAL DISEASE. Disease of the kidney. See NEPHROLOGY.

RENAL FAILURE describes the situation in which the *kidneys, because of disease or destruction, are no longer able to mantain physiological *homeostasis in respect of their several functions, in particular the excretion of nitrogenous and other waste products and the regulation of water, electrolyte, and acid–base equilibrium. The terms *azotaemia and uraemia (or uraemic syndrome) are virtually synonymous with renal failure. See RENAL DIALYSIS; RENAL FUNCTION TESTS; NEPHROLOGY.

RENAL FUNCTION TESTS. A wide variety of tests is available to assist in the evaluation of kidney function and the determination of the presence, extent, and type of renal functional impairment. They include: examination of the urine (particularly for the presence of *albumin and blood cells); assessment of concentrating and diluting capacity in response to varying water loads; measurement of urinary *electrolyte concentrations; assessment of acidifying capacity in response to administered ammonium chloride; blood biochemistry (particularly with respect to *acid–base balance, electrolyte concentrations, and concentrations of urea, creatinine, and serum proteins); *clearance tests; radiographic visualization of the urinary tract; other imaging techniques; and histological study of renal tissue removed by percutaneous needle *biopsy.

RENAL TUBULE. The basic functional unit of the kidney, also known as the nephron, of which there are about a million in each kidney. Each tubule, which consists of a *basement membrane lined with *epithelium, begins in the cortex (outer layer) as an expansion (*Bowman's capsule) surrounding a *glomerulus, and ends in a collecting tubule in the medulla (inner layer) which merges with others to drain into one of the calyces of the renal pelvis. In between these points, the tubule is divided into the following anatomical portions from above downwards: proximal convoluted tubule, Henle's loop with descending and ascending limbs, distal convoluted tubule, arched collecting tubule, and straight collecting tubule. See also NEPHROLOGY.

RENIN is an *enzyme secreted by the juxtaglomerular cells of the kidney in response to lowering of renal arterial *blood pressure. It catalyses the formation of *angiotensin I from a fraction of *plasma *globulin.

REOVIRUS. A group of *ribonucleic acid (RNA) *viruses responsible for various enteric and respiratory infections, including the common *cold.

REPRESSION is a concept extensively employed in psychiatry, denoting an unconscious mechanism whereby thoughts, ideas, memories, and impulses that are unacceptable to the conscious mind are banished from it and prevented from re-entering. Repression is the means by which the true nature of an emotional conflict may be concealed from the individual.

RESEARCH. Investigation towards the acquisition of new medical knowledge is broadly divided into basic or fundamental research, which may involve almost any branch of science and the application of which is unlikely to be planned or even foreseen; and applied research, itself divided into clinical research and research into methods and systems of health care. Financial support comes from a wide variety of public and private sources, the main agencies through which government funds are provided being the *National Institutes of Health in the USA and the *Medical Research Council in the UK. See FOUNDATIONS, ETC. IN THE UK; RESEARCH INSTITUTES; EXPERIMENTAL METHOD.

RESEARCH INSTITUTES, MEDICAL

Introduction. The independent medical research institute may be defined as a legally separate institution with its own research facilities and staff, unaffiliated in any formal or practical way with a larger parent body, with its own independent source of income, devoted solely to research in the medical sciences with no regulatory functions and no responsibility for teaching, for patient care except in connection with its research programme, or for making or selling pharmaceuticals or other products. By this definition the prototype is—or was—the Rockefeller Institute for Medical Research. It may, indeed, be questioned whether any other institution has ever met so strict a definition. A number, however, have approached it; this article will explore their development, primarily in the USA. 'Institutes' which are integral parts of medical schools or universities, those for which research is incidental to regulatory, administrative, patient-care, or other service functions, and industrial laboratories have been excluded. Even so, the number and variety of medical research institutes are so great that only a small proportion will be described—some because of their size and importance, others as representative of types and trends.

Since the beginning of the scientific revolution in the 16th c., scientists and physicians, their patrons, and governments have sought various means to promote scientific and medical research. Academies, societies, universities, and hospitals have all been created with support from government funds, private wealth, and personal income. As early as 1763 Johann Christian Senckenberg founded the Senckenberg Institute in Frankfurt with an endowment and necessary facilities for the pursuit of medical research. Only with the development of the German universities in the 19th c. did research emerge on an extensive scale as an organized, consciously promoted, societal activity with a firm institutional base. Combining teaching and research in so-called institutes, the universities provided both means and incentive for sustained discovery and the training of new investigators. They brought Germany into a position of world scientific leadership during the second half of the 19th c.

Even the German system did not always provide for brilliant investigators. Robert *Koch was still a district physician in 1875 when he demonstrated the complete life cycle of the *anthrax bacillus. Impressed by this and other achievements, the Imperial Health Office created a special bacteriological research laboratory for Koch in Berlin in 1880. Because of its desire to support a man of genius for whom there was at the time no suitable university post, the government had fortuitously created the first modern non-university medical research institute. In 1885, however, Koch left the Health Office to become professor of hygiene in the University of Berlin, with his own university institute.

In France, meanwhile, during the course of a long and productive career in teaching, academic administration, and research, Louis *Pasteur had by 1885 made fundamental contributions to chemistry and *microbiology, had greatly benefited the French wine and silk industries, and had discovered the first preventive *vaccinations (for anthrax and chicken cholera) since Edward *Jenner introduced *smallpox vaccination in 1798. In July 1885 came the first *inoculation against *rabies. As soon as its success was announced, persons bitten by rabid dogs started flocking to Paris from as far as Russia and the USA. In March 1886 Pasteur reported to the Academy of Medicine on the inoculation of 350 patients with only one failure and advocated establishing an institution to provide the anti-rabies treatment. The Academy of Sciences opened an international subscription for an establishment to be known as the Institut Pasteur (Pasteur Institute) to serve not only as an anti-rabies dispensary, but also as a centre for research in infectious diseases. An extraordinary and totally unprecedented outburst of popular enthusiasm followed. By November 1888 over 2.5 million francs had been subscribed. In addition to living quarters for Pasteur, the Institute, an autonomous corporation, had its own laboratories and

other facilities for treating patients threatened with rabies, for producing *vaccines, and for engaging in a wide range of investigations in microbiology. Separate research services were led by Emile Duclaux, Emile *Roux, Charles Chamberland, and Elie *Metchnikoff. Among the Institute's first significant announcements was the discovery of *diphtheria *toxin by Roux and Alexandre *Yersin. Soon the quarters which had seemed so spacious in 1888 became cramped. When Roux announced his successful use of diphtheria *antitoxin in 1894, a Paris newspaper opened another subscription, enabling the Institute to enlarge its facilities for the production of *serum. Other substantial gifts followed, one of which made possible the 120-bed Pasteur Hospital opened in 1900 for clinical investigation. In subsequent years the Pasteur Institute continued to produce important research results such as the development of *BCG vaccine for *tuberculosis. Many were reported in its own *Annales de l'Institut Pasteur*, started in 1887. It also continued to treat persons bitten by rabid animals: 45,751 from 1888 to 1923, with only 150 deaths.

The Pasteur Institute was the first modern, independently endowed non-university medical research institute. Its facilities and staff were outstanding, its research wide-ranging; it rapidly acquired world-wide fame and provided an inspiration and model for other institutes around the globe. Thus the next important medical research institute, the Russian Institute for Experimental Medicine, established in St Petersburg in 1890 grew out of Prince Alexander Petrovich Oldenburg's desire to found a rabies dispensary there. The plan was quickly enlarged to include fully equipped laboratories for physiology, biochemistry, bacteriology, pathology, and veterinary medicine, a hospital, living quarters for the director, and its own scientific journal. A number of outstanding scientists joined the staff, of whom the best known is probably I. P. *Pavlov, first head of the department of physiology. After founding the institute, Oldenburg turned it over to the imperial government, which thereafter provided financial support. After the Revolution it became part of the All-Union Institute of Experimental Medicine.

In the UK, too, the idea of establishing a Pasteur Institute arose soon after the success of the rabies treatment was confirmed. A self-constituted committee, in typically English fashion, met to consider the matter in 1889, but decided instead that it would be more efficient to stamp out rabies in the British Isles by enforcing a muzzling law and *quarantine (as indeed it proved to be). After raising some £2000 to send as a gift to Pasteur, the committee disbanded, only to reconstitute itself after tea when one member urged the need for a medical research institute anyway. Though hampered and harassed by England's strident *antivivisectionists, the organizing committee, under the leadership of Joseph *Lister, finally secured a charter for the British Institute of

Preventive Medicine in July 1891, very possibly with behind-the-scenes assistance from the Prince of Wales. The Institute's chief aims were to investigate means of preventing and treating infectious diseases, postgraduate education in *preventive medicine, and the production of sera and vaccines. In 1893 it amalgamated with the faltering College of State Medicine, a private institution, thus securing laboratory facilities in a rented building in Bloomsbury and the all-important licence, held by the College, to engage in animal experiments. In 1894 the British Institute began its work by producing diphtheria antitoxin, giving courses, and making bacteriological tests for local health authorities.

Money came in slowly at first. By 1897, £70000 had been raised, approximately half of it for the construction of a new building in Chelsea. A further ray of hope appeared when another committee, also headed by Lister, early in 1897 opened a public subscription to memorialize Jenner on the centenary of his great discovery, intending to use the money to support the Institute. The campaign goal was £100000. After two years the committee had raised £5770: £5000 from the first Lord Iveagh, £600 from the Duke of Westminster, £100 from Lister, and £70 above expenses from, as the historian of the Institute has written, 'the normally warm-hearted British public'. (Meanwhile the dog-loving British public, or at least 183607 of them, petitioned the Home Secretary not to permit the transfer of the animal experimentation licence from the Bloomsbury address to Chelsea, fortunately without success.) Despite the poor showing in the campaign, the Institute was renamed in honour of Jenner. This later caused conflict with a small business that manufactured vaccine, so in 1903 it became the Lister Institute of Preventive Medicine. Meanwhile, in December 1898, Lord Iveagh, whose fortune derived from the Guinness breweries, came to the rescue with a munificent gift of £250000, thus setting the Institute on its financial feet.

In contrast to the Pasteur Institute, the British Institute had been founded without any specific director ready to provide leadership for a nucleus of investigators and carry forward an existing programme of research. The first director, Armand Ruffer, whom Pasteur had recommended, left in 1896. His successor, a young bacteriologist named Allen Macfadyen, proved unsatisfactory and was not reappointed. In 1903 a new director was named, Charles James Martin, professor of physiology at the University of Melbourne, who had already made a name for himself in research. Martin fortunately provided the Lister Institute with able leadership until his retirement in 1930. His work on the physiology of body heat and heat regulation, Arthur Harden's studies on alcoholic fermentation, for which he shared the Nobel prize for chemistry in 1929 with Hans von Euler, and E. A. Minchin's elucidation of the highly complicated life cycle of the protozoon *Trypanosoma lewisi* (see TRYPANOSOMIASIS) were among the accomplishments of the Institute staff.

Meanwhile the *Royal Colleges of Physicians and Surgeons in London, following the example set in 1887 by the Royal College of Physicians of Edinburgh, set up a laboratory in 1890 at their conjoint Examination Hall where approved investigators might carry on research, although without remuneration. Several workers, some of them later highly distinguished, took advantage of this opportunity, but by 1901 the modest expense of even this arrangement was becoming a burden the Colleges could not bear. Just at this time Thomas Rudd approached Henry Morris, a prominent fellow of the Royal College of Surgeons and a leader in cancer research at the *Middlesex Hospital, with a proposal to establish a cancer research and treatment facility. Rudd averred that he could easily raise £100000 if a proper scheme were devised, and perhaps he could have, for his brother had been a partner of Cecil Rhodes and both were wealthy and had important connections. Rudd died before the plan could be matured, but Morris and others carried it forward, the two Royal Colleges agreed to participate in overseeing it and they made their laboratory available, no doubt with relief at this solution to their problem. With a distinguished body of trustees headed for years by the Duke of Bedford and, from 1904, royal patronage, the *Imperial Cancer Research Fund, as it became, attracted sufficient charitable donations and bequests to support a gradually expanding laboratory research (but not a treatment) programme. Under the guidance of a board of governors representing the two London Colleges and other professional organizations, the Cancer Fund's full-time workers from the beginning made solid contributions, particularly through studies on the *transplantation of animal *tumours, the histopathology of tumours, and mouse *genetics in relation to cancer. In 1912 the Fund moved its laboratories to larger quarters at the Colleges' new Examination Hall in Queen Square, Bloomsbury, and in 1923 opened an additional laboratory at Mill Hill on land provided by the *Medical Research Council. All its research was consolidated there in new buildings in 1939. In the 1960s it opened additional laboratories at Lincoln's Inn Fields, London. The Imperial Cancer Research Fund was one of the earliest independent institutes created for work in a field other than bacteriology, and one of the few to rely successfully on continuing charitable appeals for its major support (see FOUNDATIONS, ETC. IN THE UK). It also was among the first to demonstrate the value of a 'dread disease' as a fund-raiser and the virtue of having, at least in England, impeccable patronage.

In Germany, meanwhile, Koch wished to be relieved of his teaching duties. The German government therefore established the Koch Institute for Infectious Diseases for him in 1891, purely for research, according to the great bacteriologist's own design. It included both a substantial laboratory building and a special 108-bed hospital.

Koch's institute quickly became a new mecca for investigators. Among those who came was Shibasaburo *Kitasato of Japan, co-discoverer with Emil von *Behring of the diphtheria and *tetanus antitoxins, who returned to his homeland in 1892 to establish his own small private Institute for Infectious Diseases with the aid of a Japanese philanthropist. Soon thereafter the Japanese government began supporting the institute and in 1899 it assumed control. Like the Koch Institute it included both a scientific department and a special hospital for clinical studies. Under Kitasato's direction it continued as the leading Japanese medical research centre until 1914, when it was placed under the University of Tokyo. Kitasato and his staff thereupon resigned, to form the independent Kitasato Institute for Infectious Diseases, with income from endowment and the sale of biologicals.

Another of Koch's colleagues at the Institute was Paul *Ehrlich, whose contribution to the production and standardization of the diphtheria antitoxin helped advance its practical application. When increasing demand for this and related products placed a growing burden on the Koch Institute, the government set up a new State Institute for the Investigation and Control of Sera under Ehrlich's direction in 1896. Ehrlich soon felt the need for hospital facilities to continue and expand his research. None were available in Berlin, so with local assistance the government created a new Institute for Experimental Therapy for him in Frankfurt in 1899. Like its immediate predecessor, the new Ehrlich institute tested all sera and vaccines controlled by the state. It also provided certain laboratory services for the local health authorities and physicians. A third division, under Ehrlich's immediate direction, was devoted purely to research, primarily on immunology. To the Institute were later added a division for cancer research and, from a private donation, the Georg Speyer House Institute for Research in Chemotherapy.

Thus by 1900 major non-university medical research institutes existed in France, Germany, Russia, England, and Japan. Those in France and England were essentially private; the others were government-controlled. All but the Koch Institute also provided more or less routine services to public health authorities, treated patients on a regular basis apart from the research programme, or engaged in the production of diphtheria antitoxin and other biologicals: none operated solely on the basis of an independent income from endowment. All were clearly established because of the great practical benefits that had resulted from discoveries in bacteriology and most were founded by or for a great investigator who for some reason did not fit into or was inadequately served by the existing pattern of research facilities. The chief exception, the Lister Institute, was still

floundering and had yet to establish a research tradition.

In addition, many other smaller institutes were established in countries around the world. Albert *Calmette established the first of the overseas Pasteur institutes at Saigon in 1890. While working there, Yersin discovered the *plague bacillus in 1893. Two years later Yersin founded the second Indochinese Pasteur Institute at Nhatrang. Others were set up in French African colonies in Tunis, Algeria, and Dakar, as well as in a number of cities in France. In India, the Haffkine Institute was established in 1896 for plague research and four years later the Malay government established the Kuala Lumpur Institute for Medical Research. Turkey, Brazil, Mexico, Italy, and other countries also established new specialized institutions for serum production and bacteriological research during the 1890s.

The USA in this respect still lagged behind. During the 19th c. science had gained increasing support in the federal and some state governments and in a limited number of universities, such as Yale, *Harvard, *Johns Hopkins, and Chicago, where the German ideal of combining research and teaching had proved attractive to professors and worthy of support by philanthropists. Supplementing these were a wide variety of local and national societies and academies, including a limited number of institutions devoted at least in part to research. Some, intended for investigations in basic biological sciences, made contributions that would ultimately benefit human health and medicine, such as the Woods Hole Marine Biological Laboratory (Massachusetts) founded in 1888, and the *Wistar Institute (Philadelphia), revitalized and chartered in 1892.

Medical schools were also beginning to share in this movement to a limited degree, starting with the laboratory of physiology set up at Harvard in 1871 under Henry P. *Bowditch, the first American medical school professor to take up a full-time career in teaching and research. The University of Michigan set up a *hygiene laboratory in 1889, Pennsylvania in 1892. Johns Hopkins, however, seized the educational leadership by establishing its major preclinical departments on a full-time university basis when it opened in 1893 and by bringing to its faculty the best men it could attract instead of relying, as other schools generally did, on the leading local practitioners. In addition, a few health departments, notably Massachusetts and New York City, created bacteriological laboratories for sanitary investigations, diagnosis, and the production of diphtheria antitoxin. Besides their routine administrative responsibilities, some were also able to make contributions to medical science.

Most medical schools, however, were still largely proprietary and either independent or affiliated but loosely to a parent university or college. They lacked endowments or other significant sources of income beyond the students' fees, and the professors devoted most of their time to private practice. Even where there was a will, few schools had the means to create research laboratories. To those few American physicians who had been inspired by a year or two of post-graduate study at a German university with a desire to emulate the careers of their teachers, the prospect appeared bleak indeed.

It was just at this time that a new phenomenon appeared on the American scene, the business magnate of immense fortune who felt a moral imperative to return to the public a large portion of his wealth and who was ready to apply to his philanthropic endeavours the same breadth of vision and managerial talent that had enabled him to build the fortune in the first place. Two men stand out above all others, Andrew *Carnegie and John D. *Rockefeller. By the turn of the century both already had a long record of donations to charitable and educational enterprises, but now they were turning in earnest to the consideration of what to do with their money.

Carnegie was the first to announce in 1901 a truly major donation for the advancement of scientific research, an endowment of $10 million for the Carnegie Institution of Washington, incorporated in 1902. Although a number of persons had attempted to persuade him to use the money for a national university, Carnegie's first priority was scientific research. The most influential of his advisers on the Board of Trustees, Robert S. Woodward, C. D. Walcott, and John Shaw *Billings, had all been educated outside the graduate schools and had spent the major portion of their careers in government service. It is not surprising that they did not see the combination of teaching and research as the only feasible route to scientific advance. They took as their model not the German university institute but the Royal Institution in the UK, where Humphry *Davy and Michael *Faraday had pursued their highly important investigations in the physical sciences but did not teach. After an initial period of supporting individuals through grants-in-aid, reminiscent of the short-lived programme initiated by Billings at the National Board of Health some 20 years earlier, the Carnegie Institution adopted a policy of supporting its own laboratories in a variety of locations around the country. Carnegie money went primarily to the physical sciences, but at least three of its laboratories engaged in basic biological research of potential interest to medicine: the Station for Experimental Evolution at Cold Spring Harbor, organized in 1904 under C. B. Davenport, which has worked primarily in areas of heredity and genetics; the Nutrition Laboratory established in Boston in 1907 under Francis G. *Benedict, which has engaged in studies of normal human basal metabolism, and, in co-operation with E. P. *Joslin of Harvard, metabolism in persons with *diabetes; and the Department of Embryology established at Baltimore in 1914 under F. P. *Mall, which has worked on both *morphological and physiological development of the *embryo from formation of the egg to birth, in close co-operation with the Johns Hopkins medical school. Except for subsidizing *Index Medicus briefly, the Carnegie Institution did not support medical research as such, perhaps because John D. Rockefeller had already announced his intention of supporting that field.

Thinking and planning for some form of support for medical research had begun in the Rockefeller entourage at least as early as the summer of 1897, when Frederick T. Gates, Rockefeller's chief adviser in matters of philanthropy, out of personal curiosity, had read William *Osler's Principles and Practice of Medicine. Struck by the number of diseases for which medicine had no cure, Gates perceived a great opportunity. He promptly urged upon Rockefeller the advantages of founding a medical research institute, citing among other things the examples already set by the Koch and Pasteur institutes. Gates's initial expectation was that the prospective institute would be affiliated with a university—presumably the University of Chicago, which Rockefeller had already supported very generously. However, President William Rainey Harper, an able but sometimes impetuous academic empire-builder, may have unwittingly destroyed the university's prospects. Harper had for some time hoped to establish a medical school at the university. There had been talk of affiliation with Rush Medical College in Chicago, a typical American school of the time with no particular commitment to research, but Rockefeller had made clear his opposition. In January 1898 he and Gates learned that the university and Rush had affiliated anyway. Thereafter all thought of attaching the institute to the University of Chicago was out of the question.

By the spring of 1901, after the death of his grandson John Rockefeller McCormick from *scarlet fever, Rockefeller was ready to move ahead. L. Emmett *Holt, Christian Herter, William H. *Welch, T. Mitchell Prudden, Hermann M. Biggs, Simon *Flexner, and Theobald *Smith were brought together as a Board of Scientific Directors. Welch and Prudden initially would also have preferred to establish the institute at a university, but this idea was soon dropped, probably by decision of Rockefeller himself, to free the researchers from competing pressures. Clearly teaching and other academic routines were among the pressures to be avoided, as well as an atmosphere, common in most medical schools, which basically was not friendly to research. Also, Herter had carried out his research in his own private laboratory, Holt in a hospital, and Smith in the laboratories of the US Department of Agriculture and the Massachusetts State Board of Health. Biggs's career had been with the New York City Health Department while Welch and Prudden had both battled hard with New York medical schools over space and equipment. Only Flexner had from the beginning found a career in university medical schools, namely Hopkins and Pennsylvania. Like the trustees of the Carnegie Institution, this group would not automatically assume that a university was the only natural and necessary home of medical research.

A final pressure to be avoided was that stemming from the still bitter rivalry between *homoeopathic physicians and 'regulars'. Any regular school was inevitably antihomoeopathic and Rockefeller's personal physician was a homoeopath. By placing the proposed Rockefeller Institute in an independent position where its work, as Gates phrased it, could be 'purely scientific', it could be seen to rise above what some considered a purely sectarian conflict and to avoid an overtly antihomoeopathic stance that might antagonize Rockefeller. (To Gates, who had read Samuel *Hahnemann as well as Osler and concluded that the founder of homoeopathy 'must have been, to speak charitably, little less than a lunatic', this was evidently a matter of tactics; the Institute never had any connections with homoeopathy, which was simply ignored.)

Finally, it may be assumed that the decision to set up an independent institute was reinforced by the obvious success of the Pasteur Institute, although Welch was certainly more familiar with and attuned to German models than to the French.

Incorporated in June 1901, the Rockefeller Institute for Medical Research began operations with a series of small grants. Those continued at a rate of about 20 a year until 1907 and at a lower level until 1917, when they were stopped altogether. The directors soon decided, however, to push ahead with the establishment of their own laboratories. Once Rockefeller had pledged an amount of $1 million, to be spread out over 10 years, the Board secured Simon Flexner as director, after Theobald Smith had declined. In the fall of 1904 the Institute opened its first laboratories in rented buildings while construction started on permanent quarters, which were ready in 1906. In 1907 the Institute introduced spinal *injection of cerebrospinal *meningitis serum as a substitute for ineffective subcutaneous administration, its first prominent success. This evidently helped Rockefeller decide to give the Institute over $2.6 million for a permanent endowment and to fund the construction of a hospital for clinical research. When the hospital opened in 1910, he announced a further gift of over $3.8 million. Later gifts brought the total up to about $65 million by 1928. Compared to Carnegie's initial gift of $10 million to his Institution, Rockefeller had started off in a small way; once he was satisfied with the direction of the Institute's management, his gifts increased, and the final endowment was munificent indeed.

Research at the Koch and Pasteur institutes, founded for two outstanding individual scientists, inevitably centred about their interests. The Rockefeller Institute from the beginning took a broader view. Flexner and his immediate co-workers concentrated on infectious diseases, notably *poliomyelitis, but other early work ranged as widely as Alexis *Carrel's on *vascular surgery and *tissue culture, Peyton *Rous's on the *virus of chicken *sarcoma, and Jacques *Loeb's on the physical chemistry of *cells. At the hospital, rather than having outside attending physicians care for the patients while laboratory men did the research as Herter had originally planned, Rufus *Cole introduced a true clinical research programme carried out on a full-time basis by salaried physicians who were also responsible for patient care. At the time it was a revolutionary approach. As one of the early residents later wrote after he became regius professor of medicine at Oxford, 'I have often thought what a remarkable act of faith it was that we should all have been there consciously attempting to fit ourselves for full-time posts in medicine when no such jobs existed anywhere.' Like the Pasteur Institute, the Rockefeller Institute also acquired its own journal by taking over the *Journal of Experimental Medicine*.

In presenting his arguments, Gates had suggested to Rockefeller that even if his institute discovered nothing of value, the fact that he had made such a donation would encourage others to use their money in a similar way to the inevitable benefit of medical science. Quite early it appeared that Gates's prediction was coming true. At the dedication address of the first laboratory building in 1906, Welch pointed to the establishment of a Memorial Institute for Infectious Diseases founded in memory of John Rockefeller McCormick in Chicago in 1902 by Harold F. and Edith Rockefeller McCormick and the Henry Phipps Institute for the Study, Treatment, and Prevention of Tuberculosis founded in Philadelphia in 1903 as well as to the support of biological research of fundamental importance to medicine by the Carnegie Institution of Washington.

The McCormick Institute had been established by the McCormicks at the urging of Frank Billings after their son—John D. Rockefeller's grandson—had died of scarlet fever. Its first director was Ludwig Hektoen, who was also professor of pathology at both the University of Chicago and Rush Medical College. The new institute began operations in the Rush laboratory building with a small staff and in 1904 began publishing the *Journal of Infectious Diseases*. After various difficulties, the Institute made an arrangement with the trustees of the Annie W. Durand bequest to build a small contagious diseases hospital, which opened in 1913. Next to this was built a laboratory and administration building for the McCormick Institute. By 1915 its total resources including the Durand Hospital and other real estate amounted to nearly $2 million. Prominent among those who were working there, besides Hektoen, who remained director through most of its history, were the team of George and Gladys Dick.

Unlike Flexner at the Rockefeller Institute, Hektoen continued to serve as professor of pathology at Rush and Chicago as well as consulting pathologist to a number of hospitals. Also, the Durand Hospital was used for teaching undergraduate medical students at Rush and for a number of years the McCormick Institute produced diphtheria antitoxin for sale. The Institute remained dependent in part on the continuing support of the McCormicks. When this failed after Edith McCormick's death in 1932, no other sources of help were forthcoming; the hospital closed in 1933, the Institute a few years later. What remained of its properties went to the University of Chicago. The building was sold in 1943 to the Cook County Hospital and was reopened the following year as the Hektoen Institute, an independent corporation but closely affiliated with the hospital as its research arm. Though the McCormick Institute was established as an independent institution, the staff was never entirely divorced from local medical schools and hospitals; ultimately it lacked the strength to survive the Depression.

The Phipps Institute, as an independent organization, had an even shorter life. It originated when Phipps, an associate of Carnegie's in the steel business, retired in 1901 and sought some appropriate philanthropy to which he could devote his energies. Introduced to Lawrence Flick, an ardent campaigner against tuberculosis, and his work at the White Haven Sanatorium, Phipps decided to back Flick in his desire to set up an institute in Philadelphia for tuberculosis research, where he could demonstrate his ideas for treating the disease and for preventing it through hospitalization, improved diet, and education. In January 1903 Flick announced Phipps's intention to establish the institute with an endowment of $1 million. In February the Phipps Institute opened a dispensary, in April a small hospital—all in temporary quarters—and in September it was incorporated. In fact Flick seems to have devoted most of his efforts to the charitable treatment of the patients and the education of both the public and the profession on the contagiousness of the disease and means to prevent its spread. Flick was an enthusiast and an organizer, adept at getting publicity, but also at arousing opposition among more conservative members of the profession, especially for his continuing efforts to require physicians to report cases of tuberculosis to the health department. The Institute undertook some statistical, clinical, and pathological work, but Flick was not a laboratory scientist.

Despite the newspaper announcement, it would appear that Phipps never did provide the million-dollar endowment, though he did support the Institute through annual subventions. He declined to erect the permanent building that Flick thought had been promised, and eventually Phipps concluded that a more permanent form of government was necessary. For reasons that are not entirely clear but probably on the advice of Osler and Welch, with whom Flick had already clashed, Phipps decided in 1909 to turn the Institute over to the University of Pennsylvania and Flick resigned

as director. Since 1910 the Phipps Institute has been a unit of the University.

Despite the prominence and success of the Rockefeller Institute, the independently endowed non-university research institute did not become the pattern for medical philanthropy in the USA. For example, Henry Phipps's other major medical donations went to the Johns Hopkins medical school for a tuberculosis clinic and a psychiatric institute. In 1906 industrialists H. M. Hanna and Oliver H. Payne endowed the Henry Kirke Cushing Laboratory of Experimental Medicine in Cleveland but attached it to Western Reserve University. Harriet C. Prevost of Philadelphia in 1909 founded a department of research medicine at the University of Pennsylvania in honour of John H. Musser, for whom it was later named. In 1907 Mrs Russell Sage endowed the Russell Sage Institute of Pathology at New York's City Hospital on Blackwell's Island to promote research. In fact it seems to have emphasized clinical pathology and service to the physicians until 1913 when it was moved to *Bellevue Hospital in association with the Cornell Medical Division; its director, Graham *Lusk, became professor of physiology at Cornell. Similarly, special research laboratories at other hospitals were taken over as the hospitals, under the impetus of the reform in medical education, became affiliated with medical schools.

The history of the Memorial Hospital for Treatment of Cancer in New York exemplifies this trend. In 1902 it attracted the first major endowment for cancer research, $100 000 from Mrs Collis P. Huntington. In 1912 James Douglas added another $100 000 to endow 20 beds for clinical research and a clinical laboratory. Douglas believed that a university affiliation was essential for the research function, so when the hospital affiliated with Cornell in 1914 he brought the gift up to $600 000 and in 1917 he provided additional funds for a research laboratory, which became the hospital's postgraduate training centre. Other gifts culminated in 1945 in $4 million from Alfred P. Sloan and $4 million from a public campaign, making possible the establishment of the Sloan–Kettering Institute, which was also established as a graduate division of Cornell.

Once the reform movement in medical education was under way, philanthropists saw more future for both research and the educational system that underlay it in financing and speeding the reform of the medical schools rather than in establishing independent institutes. At the same time the invention of the big grant-giving foundations by Carnegie and Rockefeller demonstrated a more flexible way of supporting research directly when this seemed advantageous. Even the Otho S. A. Sprague Memorial Institute, founded in Chicago in 1911 for medical research, operated in fact in the manner of a foundation by supporting investigators in existing institutions—mostly the University of Chicago—rather than by building its own facilities. The George Williams Hooper

Foundation for Medical Research established in San Francisco in 1913 was placed under the University of California although the donor had originally thought to make it independent. For financial reasons if no other this was fortunate, since income from the million-dollar endowment in timber lands turned out to be more prospective than actual for many years. In time the Hooper Foundation developed increasingly close ties with the University of California medical school in San Francisco as that school improved. Despite its financial difficulties the Hooper Foundation established an excellent reputation under the first director, George Hoyt *Whipple, who began there the work for which he was later awarded the Nobel prize.

In Europe, meanwhile, the trend was the other way, in part from the example of the Rockefeller and Carnegie institutions, especially in Germany. There the old universities were defending their privileged status and the virtues of 'pure' science with increasing difficulty in face of growing demands for the technical education needed by industry. A new approach was advocated in 1909 by Adolf von Harnack, a theological scholar and director of the Prussian National Library, who rejected the traditional view that teaching and research were optimally combined and argued instead for specialized research institutes where the scientists and scholars would be free of teaching duties. Harnack claimed that German science was falling behind; to maintain its strength, and the strength of the German state, he sought donations from German industrialists to do for the Fatherland what Carnegie and Rockefeller were doing for America. Out of his efforts came the Kaiser Wilhelm Society for the Promotion of Sciences in 1911. The protecting hand of the monarch was expected to preserve the scientists' academic freedom against both the bureaucracy and the capitalist donors. In time the Society, renamed after the Second World War in honour of Max Planck, came to support a large number of autonomous scientific research centres in many different disciplines, including, in 1977, 22 in biological and medical sciences. Thus the state began to foster pure research institutes throughout the country as a matter of national policy.

In the UK, meanwhile, the *National Health Insurance Act of 1911 directed the government to set up a *National Institute for Medical Research for scientific investigation of matters relating to health. The *Medical Research Committee (later Council) was created in 1913 to carry out this mandate. For a period it seemed likely that the Lister Institute would be turned over to the nation as the nucleus of the National Institute but this was prevented by opposition from within the body of members and the Medical Research Committee instead went ahead with the foundation of the National Institute for Medical Research at Hampstead. Through the Medical Research Council, the British government also came to support many small specialized units around the country, mostly at universities and colleges. Many of these units were established either to support the work of distinguished scientists who became their directors or for investigation in a specific scientific field. The Laboratory for Molecular Biology at Cambridge was one such notable example.

In France, the government established a Fund for Scientific Research in 1901, most of which went for biological sciences, but not until after the Second World War did the central government embark in a substantial way on the support of its own research centres and laboratories through the National Centre of Scientific Research and the National Institute of Health and Medical Research.

Although the Rockefeller Institute remained unique in the USA as a large endowed independent medical research institute, other forms of operating medical research foundations came into being, established by practising physicians themselves and in most cases supported primarily from the returns of clinical practice. Perhaps the first of this type was started by Edward L. *Trudeau. Like many physicians of his era, Trudeau had developed a strong interest in tuberculosis after contracting the disease. At Saranac Lake, New York, where he had first gone in 1873, Trudeau established the Adirondack Cottage Sanitarium in 1885 to treat tuberculous patients of modest means. After his death, the Trudeau Foundation was created to control both the renamed Trudeau Sanatorium and, as a separate research institution, the Saranac Laboratory for the Study of Tuberculosis. The Laboratory continued, however, to rely heavily on gifts from individuals, foundations, and other institutions; out of an income of $63 000 in 1940 only 10 per cent came from the Foundation and 90 per cent from outside.

The Adirondack Cottage Sanitarium was conceived from the beginning as a semi-charitable enterprise. The same cannot be said of the partnership in medical practice set up in Rochester, Minnesota, by the brothers William J. and Charles H. *Mayo a few years later. As their practice prospered and the staff increased, the group came to be known as the *Mayo Clinic. At first incidentally, but in time in an organized fashion, the Mayos began devoting a portion of the Clinic's resources to clinical and eventually experimental research and informal postgraduate education. By 1914 the Mayos were millionaires and ready to seek more lasting arrangements for turning their wealth to public benefit. After extensive negotiations with the University of Minnesota, the Mayos created the Mayo Foundation for Medical Education and Research in 1915 to carry on their educational programme in association with and under the academic supervision of the graduate school of the university, with an endowment of $2 million controlled by the university. In 1919 the Mayos donated all properties owned by the Mayo Clinic to the newly created Mayo Properties Association, along with some $5 million in securities as endowment. The partnership was changed into a voluntary association of physicians, all paid by salary. The Mayo Properties Association (later Mayo Association) leased the properties back to the Mayo Clinic associates, and received in return the net earnings of the clinic, to be devoted to education and research. Under this arrangement both the clinic and its research and educational programmes have continued to prosper and expand. That the affiliation with the university was not purely nominal may be inferred from the fact that the joint review board headed by the dean of the graduate school, a historian, rejected a substantial proportion of the theses presented by the Mayo students until the clinic began to understand what graduate education, as opposed to postgraduate professional training, demanded.

The Mayos had been pioneers in setting up an institutional arrangement whereby the profits of private group practice could be used for the creation and continuing support of an educational and research institute. While they affiliated their foundation with a university, other clinics have since followed their precedent of setting up independent non-profit operating research foundations in association with private group practice. Thus George *Crile and his associates, impressed by their experience in the First World War with the benefits of a well-organized hospital service, after studying the Mayos' arrangements, created the Cleveland Clinic Foundation, a non-profit corporation, in 1921. In this case the physicians were salaried employees of the corporation itself, at the time a most unusual arrangement. It was their intent from the beginning to devote a substantial portion of the Foundation's income to research. For a number of reasons, including a disastrous fire in May 1929 and the subsequent stock market crash, it would appear that the research programme through the 1930s was not outstanding.

Another potential source of support for independent research institutions was also tried in the 1920s; the popular appeal for funds. One such originated in efforts led by the president of Panama and officers of the US Army, Navy, and Public Health Service to create a suitable memorial for William C. *Gorgas, the distinguished army sanitarian and Surgeon-General, after he died in 1920. The Gorgas Memorial Institute of Tropical and Preventive Medicine was incorporated in October 1921 and the Republic of Panama donated a site for a laboratory. Setting a goal of $6 million, the Institute contracted with a fund-raiser to bring in the money. Neither the public nor the medical profession responded, however, and two years later the Institute ended up owing the fund-raiser money. Only after the Republic of Panama donated a building in 1928 and Congress voted an annual $50 000 subsidy was the Institute able to open its research arm, the Gorgas Memorial Laboratory. With its own small professional staff and a succession of visiting scientists from American universities, the Gorgas Laboratory carried

out a modest but creditable research programme, centred on *malaria and other tropical parasitic diseases.

Equally frustrating, for a number of years through the 1920s, were the efforts of Major General Leonard Wood, Governor General of the Philippine Islands and a physician, and H. W. Wade to raise money for the support of a research programme at the Philippine Leprosarium at Culion. Eventually, in 1928, the Leonard Wood Memorial for the Eradication of Leprosy—Wood having died in 1927—was incorporated in New York with sufficient backing to establish a research facility at Culion and to support other research and related activities both in the Philippines (until the Japanese invasion in 1941) and elsewhere. Apparently the public was still reluctant to support medical research, perhaps especially on diseases that affected primarily foreign lands.

With the advent of the Great Depression, the Roosevelt administration, and a more interventionist attitude in the federal government in the 1930s, the situation with respect to support for medical research began to change in the USA. The Public Health Service began a slow expansion of its research activities when the Hygienic Laboratory set up in Washington in 1891 was transformed in 1930 into the National Institute of Health (NIH). Both the authority to investigate disease and the funding of the Public Health Service were significantly increased by the Social Security Act in 1935. In 1937, after years of effort by a small group in Congress, the National Cancer Institute was created. By 1940 the NIH budget had reached about $700 000, less than one-third of which was for grants. At the same time foundations were giving some $4.7 million for medical research. With the outbreak of the Second World War, social legislation was largely set aside, but after witnessing the enormous accomplishments of governmentally organized scientific research and development in medicine as well as in weapons, the public and Congress were much more favourably inclined to support medical research than ever before. Moreover, long-standing American opposition to federal intervention in education and the conservative opposition of the American Medical Association and others to any form of national health insurance, while strong enough to delay action in those areas for decades, were not applied against medical research (see GOVERNMENT AND MEDICINE IN THE USA).

This underlying sentiment was brought to effective focus through the highly skilled and persistent advocacy of a small group of dedicated persons, prominent among them Mary Lasker. In 1944 the American Society for the Control of Cancer, an organization run by medical professionals, raised $780 000 from public solicitations. In 1945 Mrs Lasker offered to run a fund-raising campaign provided that one-quarter of the proceeds went to research and one-half of the board would be lay persons. Under her leadership the newly renamed

American Cancer Society raised $10 million in 1946. In part, at least, as a response to this success, other disease-orientated voluntary health agencies revamped their public appeals and began devoting increasing percentages of their funds to research grants.

The same advocates were also prodding Congress, which was not unresponsive to demonstrations of public concern, and Public Health Service officials. In 1946 the NIH budget was increased to approximately $3 million, in 1947 to almost $8 million. In 1948 Congress created the first of a new wave of categorical institutes, the National Heart Institute, and the budget of the renamed *National Institutes of Health jumped to $26 million. The era of big federal money, destined to be greatly enlarged over the next two decades, had definitely dawned. It brought with it the growth of the huge government research establishment with its own laboratories and clinical centre in Bethesda, Maryland (a suburb of Washington), and an even greater expansion of money available for grants-in-aid. Most of the grants went to medical schools, with resulting problems for the schools that cannot be considered here. Although appropriated to finance research rather than education, the money in fact resulted in the training of a greatly increased number of research professionals. Medical research became for many young men and women not an activity they might hope to fit in as time could be spared from teaching or practice, but rather a feasible choice for a full-time career. Some years later, following the NIH model of providing research laboratories in close relationship with clinical facilities for patient care, the Medical Research Council in the UK supplemented its National Institute for Medical Research by establishing in the 1960s a Clinical Research Centre in close association with a district general hospital at Northwick Park near Harrow.

Meanwhile in the USA the cost of the war had greatly accelerated the tendency, already visible in the 1930s, to increase personal income and estate taxes on the wealthy. One result was a proliferation of foundations which made it possible to accomplish some goal, whatever the other motives involved, with tax-free dollars and in some cases to retain family control of a corporation that would otherwise have had to go public. Of some 5000 'not-small' foundations existing in 1959, nearly 90 per cent had been created since 1940. For many of these foundations, medical research was a safe conservative field to support. Most foundations, not surprisingly, were prepared to channel their contributions only to non-profit organizations, and the same restriction applied to many government grants.

One final factor affecting the independent medical research institute during the post-war period was the general inflation of prices, decreasing return on endowments in terms of purchasing power, and the greatly increased costs, beyond the rate of inflation, of doing research. This last consideration affected primarily the older independent institutes. In France, the Pasteur Institute, while continuing to expand in the immediate post-war decade, came to rely increasingly on outside funds. In the UK, although the Imperial Cancer Research Fund successfully met the post-war challenges, the Lister Institute found itself beset with growing financial difficulties. Some help was received from foundations and government grants, but by 1970 annual deficits were making serious inroads on the Institute's capital. At the end of 1975 it was forced to close its main research laboratories in Chelsea. The Rockefeller Institute for Medical Research, which for years had operated independently on the income from its endowment, during the 1950s found it necessary to seek outside funds, both private and governmental. It also transformed itself into the Rockefeller University, adding formal graduate education to its responsibilities, giving up its status as the premier independent non-university medical research institute.

The new sources of funds—federal government grants and contracts, voluntary health agencies, and an increasing number of foundations—combined with general prosperity, a tax structure that encouraged gifts, widespread popular support for medical research, and a growing body of trained researchers looking for jobs, were leading to the transformation of some of the older non-university research establishments and the creation of a large number of new ones heavily dependent on continuing outside support, primarily for project research rather than endowment.

Elsewhere, clinic foundations became increasingly common after 1940, as clinics sought outside philanthropic or government support which was available to them only as non-profit institutions. Thus the Menninger Clinic, begun in 1919 as a private medical partnership in conjunction with the Menninger Sanitarium, founded in 1925, gradually developed into a research and training centre. To permit acceptance of philanthropic support, the Menninger Foundation was created in 1941. A few years later the partners of the Clinic and the shareholders of the Sanitarium corporation donated their properties to the Foundation, much as the Mayos had done years before. A similar method was used, in frank imitation of the Mayo Clinic model, in the creation of the Alton Ochsner Medical Foundation in 1944 with the assets of the Alton Ochsner Clinic in New Orleans, and of the Lovelace Foundation for Medical Education and Research in 1947 with the properties of the Lovelace Clinic in Albuquerque, New Mexico, to name but two of many that have been created since the Second World War. Both have been since expanded their research programmes substantially with the support of government and other outside funds.

New, relatively small medical research institutes were also appearing. In 1944 Hudson Hoagland and Gregory Pincus, who had been working at Clark University since the 1930s on the physiology of the nervous system and the physiology of reproduction respectively, concluded that the facilities at Clark were inadequate and decided to establish a non-profit research institute without university affiliation. With community support they purchased a property in Shrewsbury, Massachusetts, for their laboratories and incorporated the Worcester Foundation for Experimental Biology. Starting with a staff of 12, with no endowment, and with no significant earned income, the Worcester Foundation, relying on gifts and grants, had by 1965 a greatly enlarged plant, a staff of 354, and 118 research grants totalling $3.6 million. In 1982 the research programme was reported to total $6.5 million. It is now a member of the Worcester Consortium for Higher Education and runs a post-graduate education programme in co-operation with Clark University, but retains its essential independence as a medical research institute supported by gifts and grants.

A similar organization is the Salk Institute for Biological Studies in La Jolla, California, founded in 1960 by and for Jonas Salk after the introduction of the *Salk vaccine for poliomyelitis had made him famous, with the backing of one of the nation's most successful voluntary health organizations, the National Foundation (formerly the National Foundation for Infantile Paralysis) and its dynamic president Basil O'Connor. It, too, was intended to provide Salk and his colleagues with an opportunity to carry on fundamental biological research without the distractions attendant on a university position. By 1982, with support from the government, foundations, industry, and individuals, it had a reported scientific staff of some 120 doctorate-level investigators.

The Worcester Foundation and Salk Institute are only two examples—more successful than many, to be sure—of a type of medical research institute common in the USA by 1982, created in an era of burgeoning public support and depending on that support for their continuance, in competition with university medical centres, operating foundations, and the government's own installations. Medical research institutes had been founded originally after the rise of bacteriology had demonstrated the practical value of medical research, either because there was no place within the existing system for an unusual individual investigator or because the existing system did not make adequate institutional provision for research and farsighted individuals saw the need and had the means to do something about it. After the Second World War medical research became so well supported that research institutes were sometimes founded or expanded, so it would seem, because the money was there. By the late 1960s, however, it was evident that the rate of increase in funds for research was beginning to slow down. How stable research institutes built on this kind of support and with this kind of competition might be in the long run is yet to be determined.

This survey has been, perforce, incomplete. It has not considered or even listed many other important research institutes in the USA, Canada, and the UK, and European coverage has also been selective. In the UK, for example, other cancer research institutes such as the Beatson, Bland-Sutton, and Ludwig Institutes are not mentioned, nor are the Kennedy Institute for Rheumatology and the Strangeways Laboratory in Cambridge. The Walter and Eliza Hall Institute in Australia is another example of a research establishment of world-wide renown which could have been included. But the intention of this article has been simply to describe and illustrate in a selective manner the forces which led to the establishment of independent medical research institutes and a few of the many notable contributions to medical science which they have made.   J. B. BLAKE

Further reading

Blake, J. B. (1957). Scientific institutions since the Renaissance: their role in medical research. *Proceedings of the American Philosophical Society*, **101**, 31–62.

Chick, H., Hume, M. and Macfarlane, M. (1971). *War on Disease: a History of the Lister Institute*. London.

Corner, G. W. (1964). *A History of the Rockefeller Institute 1901–1953: Origins and Growth*. New York.

Delaunay, A. (1962). *L'Institut Pasteur, des Origines à aujourd'hui*. Paris.

Fox, R. and Weisz, G. (eds) (1980). *The Organization of Science and Technology in France, 1808–1914*. Cambridge.

Harvey, A. M. (1981). *Science at the Bedside: Clinical Research in American Medicine, 1905–1945*. Baltimore.

Lape, E. E. (1955). *Medical Research: a Midcentury Survey*. 2 vols, published for the American Foundation. New York.

Mider, G. B. (1976). The federal impact on biomedical research. In Bowers, J. Z. and Purcell, E. F. (eds), *Advances in American Medicine: Essays at the Bicentennial*. New York.

Nielsen, W. A. (1972). *The Big Foundations*. New York.

Reingold, N. (1979). National science policy in a private foundation: the Carnegie Institution of Washington. In Oleson, A. and Voss, J. (eds), *The Organization of Knowledge in Modern America, 1860–1920*. Baltimore.

Shannon, J. A. (ed.) (1973). *Science and the Evolution of Public Policy*. New York.

Shryock, R. H. (1947). *American Medical Research Past and Present*. New York.

Strickland, S. P. (1972). *Politics, Science, and Dread Disease: A Short History of United States Medical Research Policy*. Cambridge, Mass.

Thompson, A. L. (1973). *Half a Century of Medical Research. Volume One: Origins and Policy of the Medical Research Council (UK)*. London.

RESECTOSCOPE. A surgical instrument designed for transurethral resection of the *prostate gland, employing an electrically powered wire loop for cutting tissue. See UROLOGICAL SURGERY.

RESERVOIR. A store, or place used for storage. In the context of *infectious diseases, reservoir denotes the place or manner in which the causative agent is perpetuated between outbreaks of clinical infection. Such a reservoir of infection may be provided by symptomless human carriers of the disease, as is the case with *typhoid fever, or by animals acting as alternate or intermediate hosts to the particular micro-organism, as is the case with *rabies and many other infectious and parasitic diseases.

RESIDENT is a US term for a medical graduate who has completed an *internship and who is engaged in specialized hospital training under supervision. See MEDICAL EDUCATION IN THE USA AND CANADA.

RESIDENT HOSPITAL APPOINTMENTS are training posts for medical graduates that carry the requirement of full- or part-time residence in hospital.

RESIDENT HOUSE OFFICERS are junior doctors undergoing further training and normally responsible for the day-to-day care of patients. In both the UK and the USA, a period spent as a resident house officer is an essential prerequisite for admission to independent medical practice, that is in the UK for admission to the full, rather than provisional Medical Register (see REGISTRATION; GENERAL MEDICAL COUNCIL). House officers are often resident in their first year after graduation, but many are also resident (i.e. living in hospital) for up to two or three more years.

RESISTANCE, ANTIBIOTIC. *Antibiotic resistance refers to the property possessed by certain members of a bacterial species which enables them to resist the effect of a drug which kills or prevents the growth of most other members of that species. Thus some *staphylococci produce an enzyme, penicillinase, which destroys benzyl-penicillin. Since resistance is genetically determined, resistant strains may emerge by the process of *natural selection during the course of treatment of an infection with an antibiotic. Resistance may also be transferred from one organism to another by means of the independent units of genetic material known as *plasmids or resistance transfer factors (RTF).

RESOLUTION is discrimination between objects or values that are close together, usually applied to optical systems. Resolving power, that is the ability to distinguish between two points or objects, is limited by the wavelength of the light employed; however great the magnification of the system, objects which are closer together than about half the wavelength of the light cannot be distinguished from each other. Hence the magnification of *microscopes employing ordinary light cannot usefully be greater than about 1500 times. Finer detail can only be resolved by decreasing the wavelength of the illumination. Electrons have a very short wavelength, explaining the high resolution which can be achieved by electron microscopes.

The word 'resolution' is also used in medicine in respect of pathological states, for example *pneumonia, to mean subsidence, clearing, or disappearance of the abnormal features.

RESONANCE is the slightly ringing, hollow sound elicited by *percussion when no solid or dense structure or substance (such as the liver or fluid in the pleural cavity) underlies the body surface area on which the *pleximeter finger is placed; resonance is increased over an air-containing viscus or cavity. Vocal resonance refers to the quality of the voice sounds heard on *auscultation.

RESPIRATION is the exchange of gases which occurs as a result of oxidative metabolism, by which *oxygen is taken up and *carbon dioxide released. This gas exchange occurs with respect to the atmosphere and the blood circulation in the lungs as a result of pulmonary ventilation (sometimes called external respiration), and similarly between blood and tissue in the peripheral circulation (tissue or internal respiration). See RESPIRATORY PHYSIOLOGY.

RESPIRATOR is a term sometimes used, though less so than formerly, to describe apparatus for artificially ventilating the lungs (see INTENSIVE CARE). It also meant a device for filtering or otherwise modifying the composition of the air breathed; during the Second World War 'respirator' was the official term for gas-mask.

RESPIRATORY DISTRESS SYNDROME is an alternative designation for *hyaline membrane disease; a similar syndrome associated with pulmonary *atelectasis but without hyaline membrane formation is known as idiopathic respiratory distress of the newborn. Severe rapidly progressive respiratory failure in the adult is sometimes termed adult respiratory distress syndrome.

RESPIRATORY EXCHANGE RATIO. See RESPIRATORY QUOTIENT.

RESPIRATORY FAILURE occurs when the respiratory system is unable to maintain normal body *homeostasis, notably with respect to arterial gas tensions of oxygen and carbon dioxide, indicating extensive impairment of lung function. See RESPIRATORY PHYSIOLOGY.

RESPIRATORY INFECTION is a very wide term embracing all conditions resulting from invasion by micro-organisms of part of the respiratory tract, from nasal air passages to lung parenchyma. It includes many conditions that are trivial and self-limiting, and many that are life-threatening. See CHEST MEDICINE.

RESPIRATORY PHYSIOLOGY, CLINICAL. The application of physiological measurements to patients with diseased lungs has had a considerable impact on the practice of respiratory medicine over the past 30 years. This has been a major factor in the transition of the chest physician from a 'tuberculosis doctor' to the modern specialist whose interests and expertise in pulmonary diseases are much more broadly based. (See also CHEST MEDICINE.)

Lung and chest wall mechanics. The nature and function of *breathing have been, from the time of the ancient Greeks, a source of fascination to inquisitive investigators. Both *Erasistratus, the Greek philosopher of the 3rd c. BC, and *Galen in the 2nd c. AD were aware that the lungs expanded as a result of the action of the *thorax—but their views on the mechanical function of the lungs were far in advance of any knowledge of pulmonary gas exchange. *Leonardo da Vinci likened the lungs to a bellows (an analogy which retains its usefulness) and he demonstrated that animals could be kept alive by artificial *ventilation, but it was only with the work of *Lavoisier and others in the late 18th c. that the process of tissue *respiration and the role of the lungs in providing *oxygen became clear.

*Borelli in the 17th c. was probably the first to make ventilatory measurements and he recognized the presence of the residual volume, i.e. gas remaining in the lungs after a maximal expiration. John Hutchinson, between 1846 and 1852, established the first generally applicable test of the 'bellows function' of the lungs—the *vital capacity—and he described the type of water-filled *spirometer with which it is still often measured (Fig. 1). Hutchinson also measured maximum respiratory pressures on over 2000 normal subjects and some 360 'diseased cases' and therefore lays claim to be the founder of clinical pulmonary function testing. Unfortunately, his example does not seem to have been followed for nearly 100 years. The understanding of respiratory mechanics, however, continued to develop—notably with the work of the Swiss physiologist Rohrer, who analysed in detail the forces operating on the respiratory system. By the 1930s occasional measurements of vital capacity were being reported in patients and the frequent use of induced *pneumothoraces for treatment of pulmonary *tuberculosis allowed direct measurement of intrathoracic pressures. During the Second World War the problems of aviators breathing gas at reduced pressure gave further impetus to investigating the mechanical performance of the lungs and thorax and, shortly afterwards, simple tests based on a single forced expiratory manoeuvre were introduced by Tiffeneau in Europe and by Gaensler in the USA. Initially, the volume of air expired forcibly in a given time was used as an indirect guide to the longer-established maximum breathing capacity, but the forced expiratory volume in one second (FEV_1) was soon recognized as a useful measurement in its own right; the FEV_1 and vital capacity (VC) remain the simplest and most useful clinical measurements of pulmonary mechanics and are the criteria by which ventilatory defects in disease are classified, as arising primarily

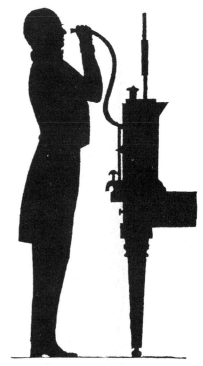

Fig. 1. Measurement of vital capacity of the lungs, showing the position of the body for filling the chest before breathing into the spirometer. (Reproduced from Hutchinson, J. (1846). On the capacity of the lungs, and on the respiratory functions, with a view to establishing a precise and easy method of detecting disease by the spirometer. *Medico-Chirugical Transactions*, **291**, 137–252.)

from volume reduction ('restrictive', with FEV_1 and VC reduced in proportion) or from *airway narrowing ('obstructive' with the ratio FEV_1/VC reduced). Although deceptively simple in practice, the forced expiratory manoeuvre has continued to excite physiologists with its complexity: despite detailed analyses by Mead and others, and most recently by application of wave speed theory, the exact events during forced expiration remain incompletely understood. An even simpler measurement made during the same manoeuvre is the peak expiratory flow (PEF): the development by Wright of simple inexpensive devices for its measurement has brought clinical respiratory physiology into the patient's own home or place of work. A further variant of the forced expiratory manoeuvre is the maximum flow volume curve, introduced by Hyatt, which in clinical investigation is of most value in distinguishing narrowing of the central airway from the more common diffuse airway obstruction associated with *asthma, *bronchitis, and *emphysema. The whole-body *plethysmograph offers an elegant technique for measurement of airways resistance and of absolute thoracic gas volumes and hence total lung capacity

(TLC). This was first described in the mid-1950s as a development of the tank respirator ('iron lung') in common use at that time for treatment of paralytic *poliomyelitis. The alternative technique for measurement of TLC by the dilution of an inert gas has a more venerable history, dating back to Lavoisier and Humphry *Davy, with helium now having replaced hydrogen as the tracer gas, the dilution of which by the resident gas in the lungs allows calculation of absolute lung volumes.

Pulmonary gas exchange and the control of respiration. The presence of both oxygen and carbon dioxide in blood became generally recognized by the mid-19th c., and carriage of the gases by *haemoglobin was established shortly thereafter. The first oxygen dissociation curve was probably that constructed by Paul *Bert in 1872 and he also demonstrated the importance of the oxygen tension in inspired air rather than the total barometric pressure at simulated *altitude. The acid–base status of the blood was soundly established by *Henderson in the early 20th c., when he applied the Law of Mass Action to the CO_2–bicarbonate equilibrium in blood; the *pH notation was subsequently substituted for *hydrogen ion concentration and Henderson's equation became the Henderson–Hasselbalch equation to the subsequent confusion of several generations of medical students! At about the same time a notable controversy surrounded the mechanism of gas exchange in the lungs, centring on the way in which oxygen crosses the alveolar–capillary membrane. One school, led by Christian *Bohr and J. S. *Haldane, maintained that simple diffusion was not sufficient in all circumstances to account for the uptake of oxygen and that the *alveolar epithelium must be able actively to secrete oxygen into the blood. The opponents of this theory, led by August and Marie *Krogh and Joseph *Barcroft, argued that passive diffusion along a partial pressure gradient was the only mechanism operative. The controversy led to several expeditions to perform studies under hypoxic conditions at altitude (notably to *Pike's Peak in Colorado and Cerro de Pasco in Peru) and led indirectly to the development of a simple test of respiratory function which remains in use today. Marie Krogh introduced measurement of the diffusing capacity of the lung for *carbon monoxide, initially as an indirect means of assessing oxygen diffusion across the alveolar–capillary membrane. Like the FEV_1, the test (now sometimes known as the CO transfer factor) has superseded the measurement it was originally used to estimate: although it was not generally used in clinical testing until 40 years after its description in 1914, it is now regularly in use in most clinical lung function laboratories. It gives a simple overall assessment of the integrity of the gas-exchanging surface of the lungs: its disadvantage is a lack of specificity as it is impaired by conditions as diverse as emphysema, diffuse interstitial pulmonary fibrosis, and pulmonary vascular

obstruction—but, when combined with measurements of dynamic and static lung volumes, characteristic patterns of pulmonary dysfunction which relate to different types of pathological change can be identified.

Although Haldane's views on oxygen secretion proved incorrect, he made several other enduring contributions to the subject—notably his tables for the guidance of divers to avoid the problem of the '*bends' by staged ascent from depth (see ENVIRONMENT AND DISEASE), and his work on control of breathing and on analysis of alveolar air. The important role of the *central nervous system in breathing had been recognized by Galen, initially by observation that certain gladiators with neck injuries failed to breathe spontaneously, whereas in others, breathing movements continued (because innervation of the diaphragm was spared). By the 19th c. the neural control of respiration was well worked out in experimental animals and the importance of carbon dioxide began to be recognized, but it was Haldane who was responsible for establishing the quantitative role of CO_2 in ventilatory control in human subjects. This was aided by his technique of sampling alveolar gas and by his development of the gas analysis apparatus which bears his name and which became a mainstay of physiology laboratories (and the *bête noire* of numerous medical students) until the recent era of electronic gas analysers. Haldane also clearly understood the implications of imperfect matching of ventilation to *perfusion in different parts of the lung, long before techniques were available for their demonstration. It is self-evident that for optimal gas exchange the supply of fresh inspired air and of desaturated pulmonary arterial blood need to be reasonably matched in all the alveolar–capillary 'units' in the lung. Gravity produces regional differences of both ventilation and perfusion, so that, even in normal subjects, some 'mismatching' occurs. More importantly in diseased lungs, microscopic damage to small airways or alveoli affects local ventilation and, similarly, disease of small blood vessels impairs local perfusion, so that ventilation/perfusion (V/Q) mismatching within lung regions may be quite severe with the net result of reduction in arterial pO_2 and a rise in pCO_2. A major problem in diseased (and to a lesser extent in normal) lungs has been access to a representative sample of alveolar gas, the composition of which, because of V/Q mismatching, varies from place to place in the lungs and also varies from time to time during the breathing cycle. An ingenious way round this problem was suggested by Riley in the 1940s: he proposed a lung model containing three compartments—a 'physiological' dead space (i.e. no blood flow), a 'physiological' shunt (i.e. no ventilation), and a third 'ideal' alveolar compartment. The gas tensions in this 'ideal' compartment are easily obtained from those of arterial blood and this model analysis has been very profitably applied to conditions such as *respiratory failure, notably by

Campbell. Use of this type of analysis was greatly aided by the development in the 1950s of reliable and accurate *electrodes for the measurement of arterial blood gas tensions to replace the earlier tedious volumetric and equilibration techniques. Subsequently, regional lung function has been extensively studied by means of *radioisotopes, and recently West and his colleagues, using elegant techniques involving several inert gases, have been able to produce detailed descriptions of the distribution of ventilation and perfusion in diseased lungs.

The modern lung function laboratory. In the modern lung function laboratory a multiplicity of tests is available, often using highly sophisticated and automated equipment. Tests of respiratory function have proved to be of great value in the clinical assessment of patients with respiratory disease, in following the effects of therapy, in the recognition and control of industrial hazards, in epidemiological studies to identify latent disease in the community, and in clinical research. Generally speaking, the simpler tests such as spirometry, peak flow measurement, CO diffusing capacity, and the estimation of blood gases are the most useful and instructive in clinical practice, so that the peak flow or FEV_1 is now to asthma what the *blood sugar level is to *diabetes. These tests essentially assess the function of the 'whole organ': other techniques relating to lung biochemistry, immunology, or molecular biology have recently become important research tools and doubtless will be increasingly applied to clinical problems. Nevertheless, research in the more traditional areas of clinical physiology continues to reap rewards. Areas of active growth include the study of respiration during *sleep (where the grossly disordered breathing now recognized in many conditions was quite unsuspected 10 years ago), and a resurgence of interest in function of the respiratory muscles, which has led to the intriguing suggestion that *fatigue of the muscles in some diseases might lead to failure of the bellows function of the respiratory system, perhaps akin to the more familiar failure of the muscle of the heart.

G. J. GIBSON

Further reading
Gibson, G. J. (1984). *Clinical Tests of Respiratory Function*. London.
Perkins, J. F. (1965). Historical development of respiratory physiology. In Fenn, W. O., and Rahn, H. (eds), *Handbook of Physiology, Section 3: Respiration*, vol. 1, ch. 1. Washington, DC.
West, J. B. (1977). *Pulmonary Pathophysiology: the essentials*. Baltimore.

RESPIRATORY QUOTIENT is the volume of *carbon dioxide excreted by the lungs divided by the volume of *oxygen taken up, usually abbreviated to RQ. The RQ is alternatively termed the respiratory exchange ratio (RER).

REST. Physical rest has long been an established principle of therapy, and remains so. There are many instances, of which cardiac decompensation can be a striking example, where rest alone can visibly reverse the course of an illness. In others, the nature of the condition itself, whether influenza, a sprained ankle, or a slipped disc, dictates that rest be part of the treatment. However it is also true that appropriate and graduated activity is an important stimulus to the processes of repair and growth after injury; and the deleterious physical and mental consequences of prolonged immobility are well-known. Complete rest should therefore only be ordered when judged strictly necessary, and should not be of unduly long duration. Modern surgical and obstetric practice accords with these principles.

Similar considerations apply to mental and emotional rest, as when, for example, induced by tranquillizing agents.

REST HOMES are establishments for the residence of those in need of special care and attention, such as invalids and old people.

RESURRECTIONISTS were professional criminals, also known as 'resurrection men' or 'bodysnatchers', whose trade was the clandestine exhumation of recently buried corpses and their profitable sale to teachers of anatomy before the *Anatomy Act 1832 provided medical schools with a legitimate source of bodies for dissection. See BODY-SNATCHERS; ANATOMY.

RESUSCITATION is the restoration by artificial means of pulmonary ventilation and effective circulation when these vital functions have ceased (cardiopulmonary arrest). The immediate or first-aid steps are: establishment of an airway; artificial ventilation by means of the operator's expired air (mouth-to-mouth or mouth-to-nose); and maintenance of circulation by means of external cardiac compression. Where necessary, more sophisticated life-support techniques can take over subsequently.

RETARDATION, when otherwise unqualified, usually means 'mental retardation', a term equivalent to *mental subnormality. 'Psychomotor retardation' refers to the abnormal slowness of thought and movement characteristic of patients with depressive disorders (see DEPRESSION).

RETE. Anatomically, a network or *plexus.

RETENTION OF URINE is the accumulation of urine within the *bladder as a result of failure to urinate. The bladder becomes distended, so that it can be detected above the pubis by palpation and percussion through the abdominal wall. The cause may be mechanical obstruction, for example urethral compression by an enlarged *prostate gland, or it may be neurogenic dysfunction of the bladder. In the latter case, urinary retention may be accompanied by *incontinence ('retention with overflow').

RETICULOCYTE. An immature *erythrocyte, distinguished by the presence of a fine network (reticulum) on basophilic staining. The appearance of large numbers in the circulation (reticulocytosis) is an indication of active *erythropoiesis, such as that which follows blood loss from *haemorrhage or *haemolysis.

RETICULOENDOTHELIAL SYSTEM (RES) is the term for the body-wide system of *phagocytic cells of which the *macrophage is the essential unit, together with other cells of similar type and function also derived from the *bone marrow via the blood *monocyte (*histiocytes, *Kupffer cells, microglial cells, and others). Reticular cells (the supporting cells of lymphoid organs) and endothelial cells (lining blood vessels), though not so derived, are also phagocytic and are considered part of the RES. The essential function of the RES is the scavenging of foreign particulate matter, bacterial debris, degenerate cells, etc.

RETICULOENDOTHELIOSES are proliferative disorders of the *reticuloendothelial system.

RETICULOSIS is any proliferative disorder of the *reticuloendothelial system (a system of cells and tissues with marked *phagocytic properties which forms part of the immune defence mechanism).

RETINA. The retina is the light-sensitive structure of the eye, which is in the form of a membrane lining the interior; it has an outer pigmented layer and an inner transparent nervous layer next to the vitreous body. The nervous layer contains the sensitive nerve-endings which are of two kinds, the rods and the cones. The latter, being themselves of three types, are sensitive to colour and function only in strong light; the rods function in poor light, and are sensitive only to blue and green. They are continuous with the *optic nerve, which carries impulses back to the visual cortex of the brain.

The retina is embryologically part of the brain. It develops as a hollow outpouch of the brain wall, the end of which is invaginated to form a two-layered cup which becomes the two layers of the retina, the stalk forming the optic nerve. See OPHTHALMOLOGY.

RETINACULUM is an anatomical term for a band or sheet of *connective tissue which retains a structure in place.

RETINITIS PIGMENTOSA is a genetically transmitted degeneration of the *retina characterized by atrophy, attenuation of blood vessels, clumping of pigment, and contraction of vision. The pattern of *genetic transmission varies.

RETINOL. See VITAMIN A.

RETINOPATHY is any pathological condition of the *retina.

RETINOSCOPY is measurement of the refractive power of the eye by observation of the movement of a beam of light reflected from the retinal surface.

RETRACTOR. A surgical instrument, of which there are many designs, for restraining and separating the edges of an incised wound and the structures underlying it.

RETROCOLLIS is a form of *torticollis or wryneck in which muscular spasm displaces the head and neck backwards.

RETROLENTAL FIBROPLASIA is a condition, now known to be due to the administration of excessive concentrations of *oxygen to newborn infants, in which intense spasm of the retinal vessels leads to necrosis and fibrosis of the retinal tissue; a fibrous mass develops at the back of the eye. Since the aetiology of retrolental fibroplasia was elucidated in the 1940s, oxygen has been administered to premature infants with extreme caution, intermittently, and in dilute concentrations.

RETROPULSION is a physical sign sometimes demonstrated by patients suffering from *parkinsonism: if the standing patient is suddenly pulled backwards, he is unable to prevent himself taking a few more steps in a backwards direction.

RETROVERSION is backwards displacement or rotation of an organ, and is usually used with reference to the upper part of the *uterus.

RETROVIRUS. A member of a group of RNA viruses, the RNA of which is copied during viral replication into DNA by reverse transcriptase. The viral DNA is then able to be integrated into the host chromosomal DNA. Retroviruses are thus potentially *oncogenic. There is strong evidence that the *aquired immune deficiency syndrome (AIDS) is due to a retrovirus of the HTLV (human T-cell lymphoma virus) group.

RETZIUS, ANDERS ADOLF (1796–1860). Swedish anatomist, MD Lund (1819). Retzius studied in Copenhagen and Stockholm, and became professor of comparative anatomy in the veterinary school in the Swedish capital, and later held the chair of anatomy and physiology at the Carolinian Institute. He described the space in front of the *urinary bladder which allows it to expand and contract freely, and this space is now known as the cave of Retzius. He made many new observations in animals; certain *gyri in the brain were named after him, as has been a *ligament of the ankle joint; he discovered the canals in the *cornea of the eye, which were later named after Schlemm. He was an anthropologist who measured physical features of the body and he introduced craniometry, the measurement of skulls, on which skull indices could be based and which distinguishes brachycephalic, mesocephalic, and dolichocephalic human types.

REVERSION is used in respect of the *tuberculin test to denote a return to a negative reaction in an individual who was previously positive ('Mantoux reversion', the opposite of 'conversion').

RHABDOMYOMA. A non-malignant *tumour of skeletal muscle.

RHABDOVIRUS. A group of rod- or bullet-shaped ribonucleic acid (RNA) *viruses which includes the causative agent of *rabies.

RHAZES (ABU BAKR MUHAMMAD IBN ZAKARIYYA) (c. 864–925/35). Persian physician. Details of Rhazes' life are scanty. He directed a hospital in his native town of Rayy and later in Baghdad. He distinguished *smallpox from *measles, giving excellent accounts of each. He described the *guinea worm (*Dracunculus medinensis*), the *recurrent laryngeal nerve, and *spina ventosa. He is best known for his immense Graeco-Arabic encyclopaedia of medicine, *Kitab al-hawi*, translated into Latin as *Liber continens* in 1279. It was antireligious and critical of *Galen in tone. The ninth book was the main source of therapeutic knowledge for three centuries.

RHEOLOGY is the science of the deformation and flow of matter; it is often used in medicine in respect of the study of blood flow in the *circulatory system.

RHESUS FACTOR is a complex of blood group *antigens of particular importance because of the association of one of them (possessed by 85 per cent of the population, termed 'rhesus-positive', the remainder being 'rhesus-negative') with *haemolytic disease of the newborn. A rhesus-positive baby may be born with the condition if its mother is rhesus-negative and has developed antibodies as a result of a previous rhesus-incompatible pregnancy or blood transfusion. See also BLOOD TRANSFUSION; GENETICS.

RHEUMATIC FEVER is an acute febrile illness with a marked tendency to recur, associated in some indirect way with haemolytic (group A) *streptococcal infection and occurring predominantly in childhood and early adult life. The chief manifestations are in the joints (migratory *polyarthritis), the skin and subcutaneous tissues (*erythema and palpable *nodules), the heart (*endocarditis), and the central nervous system (*chorea). The importance of rheumatic fever lies in its frequent legacy of permanent damage to the heart valves; it is the major cause of acquired *valvular heart disease. The risk is greater the

younger the age at the first attack, and when attacks are recurrent; and antibacterial prophylaxis against further streptococcal infections in susceptible patients is an essential part of management. The likelihood of adult heart disease is little correlated with the severity of the acute rheumatic episodes, which may pass unnoticed altogether or be dismissed as 'growing pains'. See also RHEUMATOLOGY, RHEUMATISM, AND OTHER CONNECTIVE TISSUE DISORDERS.

RHEUMATISM is a generic term for a number of disparate conditions, the common denominator of which is the occurrence of pain with or without signs of inflammation in joints, muscles, tendons, and connective tissues. It embraces, for example, *rheumatic fever, *rheumatoid arthritis, other forms of *arthritis, and conditions with such imprecise labels as *fibrositis. See RHEUMATOLOGY, RHEUMATISM, AND OTHER CONNECTIVE TISSUE DISORDERS.

RHEUMATOID ARTHRITIS is a chronic and often progressive *polyarthropathy of unknown aetiology, affecting primarily joint *synovial membranes, though other tissues and organs may also be involved. There may be extensive deformities and corresponding disability in advanced cases. There is evidence that a disordered *immune system plays a part in pathogenesis. See RHEUMATOLOGY, RHEUMATISM, AND OTHER CONNECTIVE TISSUE DISORDERS.

RHEUMATOLOGIST. A specialist in the rheumatic disorders. See RHEUMATOLOGY, RHEUMATISM, AND OTHER CONNECTIVE TISSUE DISORDERS.

RHEUMATOLOGY, RHEUMATISM, AND OTHER CONNECTIVE TISSUE DISORDERS

Introduction. 'Rheumatism' is a lay term meaning little except pain and stiffness on movement and derived from the Greek for 'flow', applied to a watery humour—'a defluxion of Rheum' (*OED*). It has no real medical meaning and yet still contributes to the folklore of disease through its riparian connections with wetness, damp, moisture, colds, and mucous secretions.

Listed in the last edition of *Joint Disease* by Huskisson and Hart (1978) were 208 morbid conditions derived from the whole range of human disease and covering illnesses affecting joints, muscle, bone, and connective tissue, or symptoms relating thereto. More such conditions appear anew each year. Thus it may be seen that those doctors who deal with 'rheumatism' (rheumatologists) have to cover a very wide (if ill-defined and still burgeoning) field, despite their recently acquired specialism: the patients that are referred to them from general practice or from their hospital colleagues suffer from diseases formerly (and indeed sometimes still) treated by cardiologists, dermatologists, endocrinologists, chest physicians, nephrologists, gastroenterologists, neurologists, and orthopaedic surgeons, as well as paediatricians and geriatricians. A competent rheumatologist must therefore not only be cognizant and effective over such a wide field, but must be able also to co-operate agreeably and to good purpose (for the patient) with his colleagues in the hospital, in the laboratory, and in general practice, together with the growing army of professional health workers that he is now largely dependent upon for the implementation of his plans for the individual patient.

A modern quasi-official definition of rheumatology is given by the Careers Service information sheet of the British Medical Association (January 1974). It is 'a specialty within internal medicine dealing primarily with disorders of the locomotor system' demanding 'as good a knowledge of general medicine as any other specialty and better than most'. The rheumatologist caters for patients with inflammatory *arthritis, *osteoarthritis, *connective tissue disorders, soft tissue *rheumatism, and other inherited and acquired disorders of the locomotor system. But it was not always thus.

Rheumatic disease before the 20th c. Mankind and indeed other animals have always suffered from diseases of various kinds affecting or ascribed to the locomotor system but there is no known living animal model of *ankylosing spondylitis or of *rheumatoid arthritis, despite the description of similar lesions in monkeys by Sokoloff et al. (1968), and by Bywaters (1981). Studies of neolithic skeletons and Egyptian mummies have posed interesting questions: they have shown the effects of trauma, of osteoarthritis, and rarely of ankylosing hyperostosis, but so far studies of material available before 1693 has revealed no indubitable evidence of those two most severe and painful inflammatory diseases affecting the skeleton, rheumatoid arthritis and ankylosing spondylitis, despite earlier claims to the contrary. This has led some to enquire whether these are 'diseases of civilization' and indeed a case could be made out for suggesting that socially conditioned disease (e.g. *cancer) arises in the end stages of *evolution, affecting the elderly and helping to maintain a fully contributory tribe. Prolonged life such as we have today is not predicated by the *genes we are born with, developed for a shortened reproductive span. The fact remains that no rheumatoid skeletons have been found; this may have been due to early decay of eroded bone, to recent inception of the disease, or to the fact that few then lived long enough to develop it. Today many of us in this privileged Western world live to more than the Psalmist's three-score years and ten, but whatever intellectual contribution the elders of the tribe may make, the new diseases associated with prolongation of life have made a dramatic social impact on the developed cultural scene. Rheumatology was one of the first specialties to be involved but is also involved in earlier life; the conquest of *infectious diseases through *vaccination and *antibiotics has meant the prolonged but fraught survival of young patients with juvenile chronic arthritis, *lupus erythematosus, and *dermatomyositis who used to die largely of *sepsis. This has entailed a large continuing outlay on social services throughout the country—but worthwhile on all counts, despite our present inability to cure these diseases (see HEALTH CARE ECONOMICS). It has been difficult for our health planners to adapt to this changing aspect of disease; but the massive voluntary financial support from the public, both in the UK and USA, for cancer, heart disease, and arthritis research assures at least that we are able to recognize and develop our opportunities in this field of *chronic and *degenerative diseases. Opportunity is open wide but options are straight and narrow, as medicine becomes exponentially more expensive in terms of global demand, productivity, and technological complexity.

The historical development of rheumatology. 'Rheumatology' designates both the science (the knowledge of the rheumatic diseases) and the art (the practising specialty as a guild). It is impossible to separate these two aspects because developments in the art and organization depend on social need and to a considerable extent also on the science and its technical advances. The increased social need and demand, as exemplified, for instance, in our own ageing society, has largely determined the development of the specialty. This review must of necessity refer to major scientific advances, but we should remember that social developments often, and indeed, usually, preempt those of science. No country can achieve progressive health betterment (and there are today good indices of this (Rutstein, 1974)) without social change. Indeed, in most developed countries, *rheumatic fever and rheumatic heart disease have diminished, not because of *antibiotics but because of better social conditions, better temperature regulation, more space and hence less overcrowding and contact and less *passage of the Group A, β-haemolytic *streptococcus, with a resultant decrease in its antigenicity and *virulence (Bywaters, 1984). In less well-developed or developing countries, rheumatic fever and rheumatic heart disease still pose major problems, even in competition with *parasitic diseases—crowding due to heat and poverty perpetuating the infection and the still ill-understood mechanism of its action. Although regular antibiotics may prevent recurrences and hence ultimately diminish to some extent cardiac disease, only social betterment (a receding dream globally despite the slogans of the *World Health Organization), will diminish this streptococcal disease.

Social changes however, determine the pattern of disease even in fully developed countries: people survive to a greater age and thus develop cancer and degenerative disease such as osteoarthritis. Many who now develop rheumatoid arthritis have survived for a much longer period than in earlier pre-war years because of antibiotics. In the old days, infection was the killer: now it is *infarcts and cancer which finally carry off doctor and patient alike. Altered sexual mores have seen a recrudescence of *venereal diseases and of the (virus-mediated) novel and still ill-understood *acquired immune deficiency syndrome (AIDS). Thus, in this account of the development of the specialty we should try to determine the social factors responsible for our present and future response patterns, whether or not society will do anything about them.

The specialty of rheumatology. Specialism, which dominates today's medicine, depended originally on the development of new techniques (e.g. surgery, radiology, pathology) and is still based on this now, although the term 'technique' must now be widened to include social or communicative expertise, as in geriatrics or paediatrics. Even in family medicine, the typical group practice of today often includes doctors with special interest (such as obstetrics or psychiatry). In hospital medicine, despite a long-drawn-out rearguard action by the generalists in the 1920–1930s, specialism has come to stay—a pyrrhic victory in so far as rheumatology is concerned, since there is still need in the UK for physicians with a wide knowledge of medicine, even (with today's migration opportunities) of *tropical medicine (Peart, 1983).

Rheumatology, which today is a separate specialty within *internal medicine, was first associated with internal and external application of *spa water. The developing recognition of rheumatic diseases (see Copeman, 1964, for individual references), retrospectively identified in the aphorisms of *Hippocrates on *gout, in the works of the early Arab physicians, and in well-known mediaeval writings, began to assume modern shape with the famous descriptions of gout and rheumatic fever by Thomas *Sydenham, at last releasing us from the thrall of authoritarian Galenism, although still requiring and prescribing *galenicals. Indeed it was not until Maclagan in 1874 (Bywaters, 1963) introduced salicylin for rheumatism (on 'the Doctrine of Signatures') that synthetic drugs—the first of which was salicylic acid (Kolbe and Lautemann, 1860; Bywaters, 1963)—began to be used for the rheumatic diseases.

By the mid 19th c. Sir Alfred *Garrod had put gout and chronic arthritis on the clinical map and indeed proposed the term 'rheumatoid arthritis' still in current and universal use (although with varying geographical connotations). Not, however, until the turn of the century was the rheumatoid variety of chronic arthritis differentiated from osteoarthritis, largely as the result of earlier pathological enquiries by Robert *Adams (1857) and (from Boston) by Nichols and Richardson (1909), as well from the use of *X-rays, of which the first published rheumatoid hand was figured by Bannatyne (1896) followed by Barjon (1897). Confusion reigned until about the 1930s

because, firstly, osteoarthritis as defined radiologically could be secondary to previous traumatic or inflammatory damage to a joint; secondly, because many older people with osteoarthritis could later develop primary rheumatoid arthritis, and thirdly, because of poor academic representation in the specialty, inadequate teaching, and lack of interest. This particular problem, fortunately, seems now to be solved, although a small and vocal group continue to claim that osteoarthritis is an inflammatory disease due to crystals, trauma, etc.

Although, therefore, the scientific basis for the specialty had already expanded with *nosological differentiation, clinical practice continued on much the same lines as in the preceding century until after the Second World War (see below) with one major (and aberrant) deviation—the *focal sepsis and vaccine 'industry'.

Microbial theories, focal sepsis, and vaccine therapy. *Pasteur inaugurated (and like most initiators whose names have survived, got it right) a new epoch in medicine with consequential social change—a new and younger, and at the same time an older, society: the new concept of infection, proved and fully accepted, became the 'ignis fatuus' of chronic rheumatism, as of many other chronic and resistant diseases. Innumerable *bacteria were identified as direct causal agents, and then disproved (as in cancer also). Indeed this approach continues and with the discovery of new organisms such as *Legionella* (see LEGIONNAIRES' DISEASE) and the *tick-borne *spirochaete of Lyme disease (Steere et al., 1977) is still a possible explanation of some diseases. In the absence of such directly responsible agents, a new movement was born—the crusade to identify and eradicate *focal sepsis* as a source of bacterial toxins acting at a distance. William Hunter (1901) in the UK (perhaps preceded by Benjamin *Rush of Philadelphia in 1819) and later Frank Billings of Chicago, from 1909 (see Billings, 1916) initiated what was to become a universal method of treating, not only chronic arthritis, but also *gastritis, *neuritis, *backache, etc. For dentists and surgeons, this was a bonanza: teeth, *tonsils, and *adenoids were vigorously removed, as were *appendices, *prostates, and *gall bladders. *Sinuses were cleansed and drained and the *colon itself, that mighty repository of bacterial life (and death) was removed sometimes, washed out often, and 'disinfected' regularly, over a period of nearly half a century. The patient was often left with his arthritis, but it 'might have been worse'. Very occasionally, following such treatment the arthritis got better—to everyone's delight. If it did not, vaccines were made of autogenous or more usually exogenous bacteria of various kinds and injected regularly—perhaps as a penance for removing so many bacterial nests previously! Vaccines and the removal of septic foci remained the mainstay of the treatment of chronic arthritis, *fibrositis, and unspecified rheumatism—lauded in major textbooks of orthodox medicine and a major industry for bacteriologists as well as for surgeons. A few sceptical voices were raised in the late 1930s, from Edinburgh (Davidson *et al.*, 1949), Boston, etc.; nevertheless, vaccine treatment survived in England and elsewhere until the 1980s when the (private) Charterhouse Rheumatism Clinic in London closed (Crowe, 1930). In retrospect, the sole value of vaccine therapy was as a harmless *placebo, inspiring hope in both patient and doctor and bringing both together at regular intervals for mutual encouragement. Much less can be said for a lot of pill treatment today and perhaps less still for the *injections and *suppositories so popular in other parts of Europe.

Diathesis. An even earlier concept had been evoked to account for the apparently random attack of environmentally produced disease. Everyone affected had sat or lain down on damp grass, or had been exposed to mists, but only a few got rheumatism. *Diathesis—a congenital disposition—was the answer. In the 19th c., beside the well known 'gouty diathesis', there were diatheses—mostly in French, such as 'herpetisme', 'scrophulisme', and 'dartisme', to name but three. Today we recognize not only the *hereditary basis of structural and many *metabolic diseases, such as the *haemoglobinopathies, but also that of a few apparently 'endocrine' and 'inflammatory' diseases, with the discovery of tissue or histocompatibility antigens (*HLA). We have not finally solved this problem of seed and soil (nature and nurture) despite most valuable studies of *identical twins reared apart. Indeed, epidemiological studies—even of twins, families, and cohorts with tissue typing and a continuing study of any intermittent infections—would be most difficult to do. The alternative approach of sequencing *deoxyribonucleic acid (DNA) from selected *lymphocytes of known histocompatibility lymphocyte-A antigen (HLA) constitution and disease origin may be a shorter but more operationally viable route to this central problem of 'diathesis'—the predisposition.

Hydrotherapy and the spas. Thus, rheumatology during the first third of the 20th c. was still only distantly related to the slow progress of general internal medicine with its early discoveries of *insulin by *Banting, *Best, and McLeod in 1922 and Castle and *Minot's liver factor, even up to 'red *Prontosil®' in the 1930s. It was on its own and did not register as a specialty, despite the efforts of Fortescue Fox in the UK and van Breemen in Amsterdam to force social and medical recognition. It continued in the tradition of balneology (see BALNEOTHERAPY) and climatology (see CLIMATOTHERAPY) and later physical medicine, catering especially for the well-to-do, and sustaining the fashionable spas in Europe and in the UK, which, besides Bath in the forefront, boasted numerous other watering places, derived in large part from the holy or healing wells of the long-

distant past. As late as 1964, the British Spas Association listed eight such centres in England and Wales offering therapeutic facilities. More recently—although we have recognized the spa as a recreational and leisure resort, as well as the value of *hydrotherapy in *rehabilitation and of assisted exercise for weak limbs—ordinary tap-water pools with enthusiastic attendant *physiotherapists have been found to do just as well. Recently, despite the vested interests of physical medicine apparatus suppliers, these gentle naiads do seem now to be concentrating sensibly on simple encouraged exercise, leaving the diathermy, galvanotherapy, faradotherapy, and infrared with which they were previously concerned (as well as massage, effleurage, petrissage, foulage, pincement, hacking, kneading, swooping, and traction) to recede into limbo (or perhaps Soho!) even without benefit of controlled trials. Rehabilitation has finally emerged as a specialty respected by its peers.

The departments have changed names, as have learned societies, the specialist journals, and the abstract headings. The Royal College of Physicians of London has at last allowed that 'every specialty in Medicine must be responsible for its own rehabilitation practice', apart from highly complex problems such as those of *stroke, *paraplegia, and other post-traumatic lesions which demand full specialty-status attention. It is a far cry from the Cranach vision of revivification in the 'Fountain of Youth' (1546), but the waters still remain centres of health and enjoyment and (in its broader sense) 'healing' (Kersley, 1981).

Post-war rheumatology: the *annus mirabilis* of 1948. After the austerities and single-mindedness of the Second World War and its aftermath, lasting in the UK at least through 1947, 1948 proved (and not only for rheumatology) an *annus mirabilis*, in which the specialty came of age and was globally recognized. Most of these developments were celebrated in the first post-war International Congress of Rheumatology in New York (1949), with renewal of scientific communication and of old friendships. These advances paved the way for the new 10-lane highway which rheumatology was now to become. 1948 saw the recognition of the LE cell (often diagnostic of *systemic lupus erythematosus) by Hargreaves, the rediscovery of the Rose–Waaler blood test for rheumatoid arthritis (which retrospectively vindicated the streptococcal agglutination test of Russell Cecil), the recognition by Wolfson of the uricosuric effect of carinamide (later probenecid, Talbott *et al.*, 1951) for the treatment of gout, serendipitously discovered in its trial as an agent for blocking the excretion of *penicillin which was then very costly. In the same year, studies on *adrenocorticotrophic hormone (ACTH) by Thorn, and on *cortisone were conducted by *Kendall and *Hench, resulting in their Nobel prize award. Although *glucocorticoids have not proved to be the panacea that many hoped for at the time, they have proved, within limits, to be most useful therapeutic agents in the field of rheumatology, although often grossly abused. But perhaps the most important scientific development of 1948 was that of the fully controlled double-blind and often multicentre clinico-therapeutic trial (see CLINICAL TRIALS); in the few years that followed the original *tuberculosis trials, rheumatology began to spearhead this sophisticated attack on problems which had been hitherto almost anecdotally approached. This was none too soon, because soon after, Irgapyrine® and the recognition of phenylbutazone (Butazolidine®) as its active constituent heralded the phenomenal rise of the synthetic drug industry, especially in the rheumatic field and also the beginning of so many of our present ethical, pharmaceutical, and legal problems. It is of considerable interest that in 1983 the USSR published an 'unprecedented' double-blind therapeutic trial, 20 years after the British Council sent Witts, Scadding, and myself to explain the principles in that country.

Over and above this explosion of scientific rheumatology, the advent of the *National Health Service (NHS) in the UK in that same year meant that we were able to implement many such advances for the benefit of all. Since 1912, when the Liberal leader, David Lloyd-George, brought in *National Health Insurance for workers and their families, there had been a tradition of medical care given freely as needed, side-by-side with private medicine and charitable hospital services. Medicines were cheap—chalk, *aspirin, *valerian, etc. But complexity increased and by 1938 the hospitals were bankrupt and their take-over in 1939 by the government for national defence needs made the NHS inevitable by 1948. In no field has it proved more successful than in that of rheumatism and other chronic diseases of the more elderly. In countries without prepaid insurance cover, the plight of patients with chronic rheumatic disease is desperate. Today, even in the UK, cost–benefit problems are looming, as, for instance, with *hip replacement which could improve the quality of life for so many more than is at present possible with current resources.

The commoner 'rheumatic' diseases. *Backache.* Almost everyone has backache sooner or later. Fortunately in most people it is short-lasting. A few go on to develop intractable symptoms which limit their activities, but this is a very small portion of the total, and therefore backache is usually treated in the acute stages with bed rest, later with graded exercise in a corset or back restraint apparatus, and only finally, if it lasts for an undue length of time, do we have to consider the possibility of surgical relief. Surgical relief can help most those patients who have had a *prolapse or *hernia of the cartilaginous disc between the bony bodies of the *vertebrae which presses on the nerves of the *spinal cord, and even then it is not entirely satisfactory and the pain may well recur. Surgery (*spinal fusion) may also be necessary for spondylolisthesis (when one vertebral body slips forward over the one beneath it).

Soft tissue rheumatism. Under this heading are included all the other connective tissue conditions often due to minor traumata, such as *sprains, *bursitis, *tennis elbow, *frozen shoulder (pericapsulitis of the shoulder joint), affecting the locomotor system exclusive of serious lesions of the actual joints, bones, and muscles. They usually 'mend' on their own, provided that no further strain or stress is encountered. In more severe cases, injection of *corticosteroid may provide the stimulus for recovery.

'Osteoarthritis' or degenerative joint disease. The term osteoarthrosis is now generally preferred to osteoarthritis as the condition is degenerative and not inflammatory. It implies wearing out of the cartilage covering the bony ends forming the joint, occurring with increasing age, faulty use, or malalignment. The hip is involved particularly often because it bears in walking the main weight of the body, but fortunately this joint can now be replaced with metal and plastic by the surgeon. Otherwise, osteoarthrosis affects mainly the knees, the basal thumb joints, and the terminal joints of the fingers where it is more of a nuisance than a real disability (except for pianists, etc. for whom stabilizing operations may be necessary).

Gout and pseudogout. These are both due to the irritation by crystal formation in the tissues (respectively due to sodium urate and calcium pyrophosphate). Gout can now be cured or at least controlled by drugs such as *allopurinol which gradually dissipate the abnormally accumulated urate in the body fluid and in the solid crystal masses.

Rheumatoid arthritis. This is a chronic and often progressive inflammation of many joints—cause unknown. It affects all ages, particularly middle-aged women. It is important to maintain movement and strength through exercises, aided by analgesic drugs like aspirin, and the *non-steroidal anti-inflammatory drugs (NSAID) of which there are now many varieties. The patient must find one which suits him best and which has least (for him) side-effects. More progressive and severe cases should be treated with stronger drugs such as *penicillamine or *gold. Occasionally surgery and rarely *immunosuppressive drugs may be needed.

Ankylosing spondylitis. This occurs in some genetically predisposed (see HLA) young men and boys, with joint swelling, stiffness of the spine, and sometimes eye involvement. A precipitating agent may be microbial but is not yet identified. Postural exercises and *analgesic drugs usually procure a satisfactory life style.

The connective tissue diseases. These include systemic lupus erythematosus, poly- and *dermatomyositis, *systemic sclerosis, and peri- or *polyarteritis or *vasculitis. These various diseases affect tissue widely in the body and particular organs within the body. They appear to be due to an as yet unidentified aberration of the immunological system, which was established to protect the organism from environmental (e.g. bacterial) assaults.

Systemic lupus erythematosus affects young women particularly and is characterized by fever, rash, arthritis, and sometimes by cerebral or lung dysfunction. It is treated by steroids and immunosuppression, as indeed are the other types of connective tissue diseases listed above.

More recent developments in rheumatology. The years since 1948 have seen the loss of Empire (colonial markets, raw materials, and cheap labour), leading, in medicine as in other fields, to a much more sophisticated economy with an even greater dependence on technology. Five such fields greatly affecting the practice of rheumatology might be briefly mentioned here: immunology, biochemistry, pharmacology and therapeutics, orthopaedics, and communication.

Immunology. Perhaps most important of these five for our understanding of the rheumatic diseases is immunology. From earlier and humble beginnings in vaccination and serology and, starting perhaps in 1948, the systemic and inflammatory rheumatic and connective tissue diseases have become complicated jigsaw puzzles involving the concepts of *autoimmunity and *graft-versus-host reactions, of immune-complex technology, complementology, and more recently studies of lymphocyte subsets, identified by the latest of new probes—*monoclonal antibodies. This and other results of cell hybridization promise much greater advances for the rheumatic diseases than the wrangles of yesteryear about immunosuppressive drug development and usage. Most of this major progress was made possible in the first place by the separative techniques introduced in the 1950s, secondly by our new knowledge of DNA and its reproduction, more recently by our knowledge of cell surface *receptors and by our realization of the links between genetic make-up and immunological defects.

Biochemistry. General developments in auto-analysis and radiobiochemistry have affected all fields. The many metabolic diseases of bone and joints have thus become much more easily studied at the local hospital level, making referrals to major academic centres less burdensome, except perhaps for the rarer genetic diseases involving such tissues, due to *enzyme deficiency, now susceptible to *transplantation.

Pharmacology and therapeutics. The unprecedented development of made-to-measure drugs following the first breakthrough on sulphanilamide as a substrate analogue inhibitor in the 1930s, has also brought problems as well as very considerable patient relief. Gout is now not only preventable but curable, even in patients with kidney disease. The benefits of the non-steroidal anti-inflammatory agents are undoubted although they have perhaps been over-advertised.

Orthopaedics. A major advance in remedial rheumatology was development of the artificial *prosthesis, pioneered by orthopaedic surgeons all over the world and perfected for the hip by the late Sir John *Charnley. This development will no doubt lead before long to continuing advance in replacement of other irremediably damaged joints, but in the meantime it has resulted in a much closer relationship between the rheumatology and orthopaedic departments. There can be few good hospitals or academic centres in either the UK or the USA that do not have combined weekly outpatient duties and ward rounds with occasional combined research sessions: this has led to considerable improvement in diagnosis and care for the average patient, quite apart from the provision of prostheses.

Rheumatism in children. In Eastern Europe, rheumatic fever and consequential heart disease are still dealt with by physicians working in institutes of rheumatology, although in most textbooks of medicine, the subject was long ago transferred to the section on heart disease. In most developed countries, rheumatic fever, primarily a disease of children, has almost disappeared. Although a centre at Taplow was set up by the Royal College of Physicians and the UK Ministry of Health in 1947 for research into the care of rheumatism in children and played a major part in educating the medical profession about the value of *prophylaxis, first used by Thomas and France in 1939, it had no sooner completed its major studies of rheumatic fever, clinical and laboratory, including participation in the first multicentre USA–UK controlled trial of *aspirin and *cortisone, than acute rheumatic fever decreased and its recurrences also. Since the late 1950s very little of this disease has been seen, thus enabling the hospital at Taplow to begin a long-term study of chronic rheumatism in children, of which we have now seen more than 2000 cases. Since the first series described by Sir Frederic *Still, published in 1898, this had been neglected, but with the control of infection and malnutrition it became relatively more prominent (a prevalence of 0.06 per cent of schoolchildren in six towns around Taplow). With 100 beds and with an enthusiastic staff, later including Dr Barbara Ansell, we put this neglected group of young patients into the limelight, ultimately forming an International Study Group, a Standing Committee of the European League against Rheumatism (EULAR) and a new subspecialty of paediatric rheumatology. This was later echoed in Scandinavia, the USA, and in other countries. Today in England, there are at least five regional groups who are able to undertake the multifarious responsibilities—therapeutic, orthopaedic, social, educational, and psychological, demanded by these young, underprivileged and often maltreated young people (sometimes they are under- and sometimes over-treated).

'Literature' and the information explosion. Every specialist gets the journals of his own specialty, but the rheumatologist, although well (perhaps too well) catered for, must seek for relevant information in a wide range of other specialty journals besides such stand-bys as the *British Medical Journal, Lancet, New England Journal of Medicine,* and the *Annals of Internal Medicine.* Pim Haas in his role of adviser to *Excerpta Medica (Rheumatology)* claims that only one in five articles of significant rheumatological interest appears in specifically 'rheumatological' journals. But in recent years, there has been a seemingly uncontrollable launching not only of straightforward rheumatology academic subscription journals such as *Journal of Rheumatology* and *Rheumatology International* but also periodic volumes such as *Seminars* and *Clinics in Rheumatic Disease.* Some of these have represented restyling of national journals such as *Clinical Rheumatology* (Belgium), but in addition there is a plethora of drug-house journals of all descriptions circulated freely, as well as, recently, abstract journals of various types dealing with rheumatology. All in all, there are now available almost twice as many journals, dealing with this specialty, as in the review by Morton and Bywaters in 1969.

Although many prefer to browse through journals, the tendency now is to develop on-line computer print-outs of 'relevant' papers from all over the world; however, the impression is that 30 per cent of those papers thus retrieved are, in fact, irrelevant and of the remainder, more than half are not useful. This is counter-productive, at least for people with broad interests. If one is interested only in *C-reactive protein, the above strictures perhaps do not apply. Nevertheless nothing is as rewarding as a regular periodical thumb-through of journals in a familiar top-class library—perhaps aided from time to time by specific literature searches. Even dependence on *Index Medicus* may not be very wise (Thorpe, 1972).

The present organization of the specialty in the UK and its relationship to the International League Against Rheumatism. We have already traced the development of the specialty from balneology, climatology, physical medicine, and rehabilitation to its present status as an integral part of general internal medicine. Today in the UK, rheumatologists belong to the British Society of Rheumatology (BSR), formed with some anguish in 1983 and uniting the two previously independent professional associations, the Heberden Society (founded in 1936 primarily as a learned society and originally limited to 100 members) and the British Association for Physical Medicine founded in 1943, later called the British Association for Rheumatology and Physical Medicine, which finally became the British Association for Rheumatology and Rehabilitation. This was a

more clinically orientated body which also negotiated politically with the Department of Health with regard to the professional status, responsibilities, and duties of its members. Since 1983, when these two almost identical lists of specialists were merged, the Heberden Society has been remembered in the Heberden Library in the Royal College of Physicians in London (a historical collection of books on rheumatism and gout) and in the Heberden Round and Oration. Both branches of this new society retain their own journals (for various economic reasons), but at least the much-valued secretariat, the regular meetings, and the list of members are now united, as is their membership of the British League against Rheumatism (BLAR), one of the 33 national leagues forming the European League against Rheumatism (EULAR) (two European nations are not represented in the League).

Together with this body, in BLAR are represented various other scientific societies and associations such as the British Orthopaedic Association, the Back Pain Research Society, as well as bodies more socially and therapeutically orientated in the fight against rheumatism, such as the British Rheumatism Association, the Horder Homes, and the paramedical professions such as the Social Services and the Chartered Society of Physiotherapists. Both the scientific and the social sides are entitled to send one delegate and a deputy to EULAR which meets every four years in a congress, and is one of three continental leagues comprising ILAR, the International League against Rheumatism (PANLAR (Pan-American), SEAPAL (Asian) and EULAR). Both EULAR and ILAR were democratized in the years following the European Congress of 1971 in Brighton, largely due to British efforts. The International League against Rheumatism was founded by van Breemen of Holland and Fortescue Fox in England in 1928. After six meetings in Europe, the war intervened and no meetings were held until 1947. That year saw the first specifically European Congress (in Copenhagen), and 1949 the Seventh International and first extra-European Congress in New York, a most prestigious occasion.

Today most countries in the world are represented and, with modern communication techniques and multichannel simultaneous translation, the original West European dream of a world-wide professional body of rheumatological knowledge and care has been realized (see INTERNATIONAL MEDICAL ASSOCIATIONS).

Besides the organization of periodic congresses, growing larger and more unwieldy each year, as did the brontosaurus, leaving behind a reminder of its passage as proceedings or excrementa (Bywaters, 1978), EULAR initiated the formation of standing committees on epidemiology, education, and international clinical studies including therapeutic trials, publications, international and national agencies, social and community agencies, surgery and paediatric rheumatology, plus subcommittees on pathology, radiology, and nomenclature.

Postgraduate training for specialty status in the UK. As with other specialties, the would-be consultant in rheumatology needs to have three years' general medical training following *registration, and after attaining membership of the Royal College of Physicians or the appropriate MD, should have four years in higher specialist training at senior *registrar level. Rheumatology has been a popular choice for the young resident, with its exciting immunological, general medical, and pharmacological opportunities, so much so that the openings for consultant status have not kept pace with the large numbers of well-trained senior registrars available. This is partly because the *Departments of Health, having agreed that each NHS area should have a rheumatology consultant, have not yet proceeded to fill all these vacancies, because of partly economic and partly local reasons. Thus 24 per cent of health district areas in the UK out of a total of 247 have no such specialist. The big cities and the southern part of England are well staffed but largely at the expense of the more northern areas (Wood and Badley, 1983). Posts in new and smaller subspecialties such as that of paediatric rheumatology are also sparsely distributed, although training opportunities have been greatly enhanced.

In 1936, when the *Royal Postgraduate Medical School of London was founded, most postgraduate students and residents came from the UK itself. However, during and after the war a much larger proportion came from abroad. This was balanced nationally after 1961 through the successful initiation, spearheaded by the *Nuffield Provincial Hospitals Trust, of postgraduate centres throughout the country, with tutors appointed by the Royal Colleges and continuing programmes of local postgraduate education for residents, general practitioners, and consultants alike. In the past, a great deal of specialist training in the UK (particularly at the Royal Postgraduate Medical School in London and also, in my own experience, at the *Medical Research Council Rheumatism Unit at Taplow) was taken up by graduates from overseas—Canada, Australia, New Zealand, India, and more recently European countries. These provided few problems with ultimate placement because the trainees returned to their own countries, and many of the present rheumatologists in Canada, New Zealand, and Australia were trained in England, particularly at the Royal Postgraduate Medical School, at Taplow, and in Manchester. Now because of financial shortage and increased fees, such overseas graduates are becoming fewer, but the influence of British rheumatology, with its emphasis on the clinical approach, has now been established the world over.

Conclusions. Every historical account should end with a brief look at the future. I do not expect that the present trend in '*alternative medicine'

will be sustained, although it will always appeal, as does '*fringe medicine' to a proportion of people, particularly in the rheumatism and cancer fields where there are as yet no specific cures. On the other hand, as people become better educated both scientifically and socially, 'consumerism' will undoubtedly increase. It has already been welcomed in rheumatology, with the establishment of the Arthritis and Rheumatism Council (ARC) in 1936, now with 900 branches throughout the country. This raises today over £6 000 000 yearly for research. The 'consumer', represented by the ARC and other bodies such as the associations for patients and helpers devoted to lupus erythematosus or spondylitis, has official delegates with voting rights in the British League against Rheumatism. Fortunately, 'malpractice' litigation (which in the USA is common and has resulted in enormous insurance premiums, particularly for orthopaedics) has not yet increased significantly in the UK, although pharmaceutical companies are becoming, quite rightly, apprehensive. The Press has been relatively co-operative, although always exploiting so-called 'breakthroughs' (see MEDIA). Television reporting is also usually well informed, and from time to time raises key issues, such as the occasional heavily subsidized visits of rheumatologists to specific drug-related symposia in pleasant Mediterranean sites. In general, however, relations with the drug companies are good and are improving. The major drug companies themselves are far more conscious of their social obligations with much better medical advisers. The specialty is well aware of its ethical duties, of its obligations to maintain the best service to its patients that it possibly can under existing social circumstances, and of the exciting possibilities in this and related research fields. It has achieved during the last 30 years momentous scientific advances and has applied them within a satisfactory and satisfying social framework.

Despite recent financial cuts at university, Medical Research Council, and health service levels (only temporary, we hope) there is every indication that this progress will continue, and that the recent and greatly increased knowledge in rheumatology will bear fruit in the fields both of prevention and treatment.

Appendix. Detailed and up-dated reports on individual rheumatic diseases, on their social significance, and on treatment currently available, written to suit both the family medical practitioner and the well-orientated patient, and very useful indeed also for medical students and consultants, are provided both in the USA (*Bulletin on Rheumatic Diseases* and other publications listed by the American Rheumatism Foundation) and in the UK (listed below). References for general reading published by and available from the Arthritis and Rheumatism Council together with the British League against Rheumatism at 41 Eagle Street, Holborn, London WC1R 4AR include:

Wood, P. H. N. (ed.) (1977). *The Challenge of Arthritis and Rheumatism.*

Rheumatism, the Price We Pay (1977). The impact of the rheumatic diseases on the individual and the country.

Rheumatism, a Case of Neglect (1977). A report on the lack of welfare facilities available and social support given to rheumatism sufferers.

Rheumatism: Why the Long Wait? (1977). The facts about the delays in treatment for sufferers in different areas of the country.

People with Arthritis Need Help and Support (1981). A report on services available for the rheumatic sufferer.

Arthritis: A Walking Miracle (1977). A review of surgical advances.

A Plain Man's Guide to Rheumatic Diseases (1982). Intended for the general public.

Reports on the Rheumatic Diseases. A series of pamphlets intended for the undergraduate and for postgraduate doctors.

People with Arthritis Deserve Well-Trained Doctors (1979). Report on the workshop on undergraduate education in rheumatology.

Arthritis Research. The Way Ahead (1977). A report on research achievements and a challenge for the future.

For more detailed medical references see J. T. Scott (ed.) (1984), *Textbook of Rheumatic Diseases*, 6th edn, Edinburgh.

Small handbooks on rheumatic diseases intended for the patient and to be passed on to him by the general practitioner in general circumstances include the following titles (published by the Arthritis and Rheumatism Council, London).

Gout
Lumbar Disc Disorders
Osteoarthrosis
Rheumatoid Arthritis
Ankylosing Spondylitis
Pain in the Neck
Marriage, Sex and Arthritis.
Your Home and your Rheumatism
Where a Young Person has Arthritis; a Guide for Teachers
Your Garden and your Rheumatism

E. G. L. BYWATERS

References

Billings, F. (1916). *Focal Infection.* New York.

Bywaters, E. G. L. (1963). The history of salicylates. In Dixon, A. S. J., Martin, B. K., Smith, M. J. H. and Wood, P. H. N. (eds), *Salicylates: an International Symposium.* London.

Bywaters, E. G. L. (1978). Congressosaurus internationalis in danger of extinction. *EULAR Bulletin*, **7**, 53–4.

Bywaters, E. G. L. (1981). Observation on chronic polyarthritis in monkeys. *Journal of the Royal Society of Medicine*, **74**, 794–9.

Bywaters, E. G. L. (1984). Rheumatic fever. In Scott, J. T. (ed.), *Textbook of Rheumatic Diseases.* Edinburgh.

Copeman, W. S. C. (1964). *A Short History of the Gout and other Rheumatic Diseases.* Berkeley.

Crowe, H. Warren (1930). *Handbook of the Vaccine Treatment of Chronic Rheumatism Diseases.* Oxford.

Davidson, L. S. P., Duthie, F. F. R. and Suger, M. (1949). Focal infection in rheumatoid arthritis. *Annals of Rheumatic Diseases*, **8**, 205–8.

Hunter, W. (1901). *Oral Sepsis as a Cause of Disease*, London.

Huskisson, E. C. and Hart, F. D. (1978). *Joint Disease: all the Arthropathies*, Bristol.

Kelley, W. N., Harris, E. D., Ruddy, S. and Sledge, C. B. (eds) (1981). *Textbook of Rheumatology.* Philadelphia.

Kersley, G. D. (1981). *The 3 R's, Rheumatism, Rehabilitation, Research as Viewed from Bath.* Bath.

Morton, L. T. and Bywaters, E. G. L. (1969). The literature of rheumatism. *Annals of Rheumatic Diseases*, **28**, 669–73.

Peart, W. S. (1983). Rebirth of the professor of medicine. *Lancet*, **i**, 810–12.

Rush, B. (1798). *Medical Inquiries and Observations*, Vol. V. Philadelphia.

Rutstein, D. D. (1974). *Blueprint for Medical Care.* Cambridge, Massachusetts.

Sokoloff, L., Snell, K. C. and Stewart, H. L. (1968). Spinal ankylosis in old rhesus monkeys. *Clinical Orthopaedics*, **61**, 285–93.

Steere, A. C., Broderick, T. F. and Malawista, S. E. (1977). Erythema chronica migrans and Lyme arthritis. *Annals of Internal Medicine*, **86**, 685.

Talbott, J. H., Bishop, C., Norcross, B. M. and Lockie, L. M. (1951). The clinical and metabolic effects of Benemid in patients with gout. *Transactions of the American Association of Physicians*, **64**, 372–4.

Thomas, C. B. and France, C. R. (1939). A preliminary report of the use of sulphonamide in patients susceptible to rheumatic fever. *Bulletin of the Johns Hopkins Hospital*, **64**, 67–8.

Thorpe, P. (1972). An evaluation of the rheumatology coverage of *Index Medicus. Journal of the American Society for Information Science*, **23**, 406.

Wood, P. H. N. and Badley, E. M. (1983). *The Availability of Rheumatological Specialists.* Arthritis and Rheumatism Council. London.

RHINITIS is inflammation of the nasal mucous membrane, as in the common *cold.

RHINOLOGY is the specialty concerned with disorders of the nose. See OTOLARYNGOLOGY.

RHINOPHYMA is a disfiguring irregular enlargement of the nose due to sebaceous hyperplasia, occurring in *rosacea.

RHINOPLASTY is any *plastic surgical procedure on the nose.

RHINORRHOEA is any discharge from or through the nose.

RHINOSCLEROMA is a chronic granulomatous condition affecting the mucous membrane of the nose and upper respiratory tract occurring in South-East Europe and South America and thought to be due to a bacterium *Klebsiella rhinoscleromatis*.

RHINOVIRUS. A large and widely distributed group of small ribonucleic acid (RNA) *viruses causing respiratory infections in man, including about half of all common *colds.

RHODES SCHOLARS are recipients of scholarships awarded annually since 1902 (the year of Cecil John Rhodes's death) to students from the USA, the British Commonwealth, South Africa, and Germany for study at the University of Oxford.

RHODOPSIN is one of the visual pigments of the *retina, also known as visual purple, occurring in the cellular elements responsible for dim-light vision (rods). Rhodopsin consists of a *protein (opsin) in combination with a prosthetic group synthesized from *vitamin A.

RHONCHUS. An extra sound heard accompanying the breath sounds on *auscultation of the chest in patients with partial obstruction of the air-passages by bronchoconstriction or relatively dry exudate; rhonchi are of variable pitch and have a whistling or wheezing quality.

RHYTHM is the pattern displayed by recurrent events, for example that of the *pulse beats felt at the wrist, the heart sounds heard over the precordium, the galvanometric deflections seen in the *electroencephalogram, etc. A regular rhythm is one in which the same event or sequence of events is repeated at uniform intervals, for example the arterial pulse in most normal adults. A biological rhythm is one which arises from any recurrent biological phenomenon. *Circadian rhythm implies a frequency of about 24 hours. Other adjectives may be descriptive (gallop rhythm, triple rhythm), may indicate the origin of the events (cardiac rhythm, sinus rhythm, ventricular rhythm), may simply be an arbitrary classification (alpha, beta, gamma rhythm), or may give an indication of the cycle length (circadian, ultradian, infradian). See also ARRHYTHMIA.

RIBES, CAMILLE LOUIS ANTOINE CHAMPETIER DE (1848–1935). French obstetrician, MD Paris (1879). Champetier de Ribes studied medicine in Paris, where he became director of obstetric services at the *Hôtel-Dieu in 1897. He is remembered especially for devising a balloon which, in its collapsed state was introduced through the uterine *cervix, and then inflated by the injection of fluid along its attached tube. The idea was to help the lower segment of the uterus to distend and after the bag was expelled the birth canal would be open enough to allow the presenting part of the fetus to follow. It was a method for the induction of labour and with a small weight or gentle traction on its protruding tube it could be made to bring pressure on to a bleeding *placenta praevia and so cut down the amount of bleeding. The method is no longer used though it was valuable in its time when operative intervention in pregnancy and labour was so dangerous to mother and child (see OBSTETRICS).

RIBOFLAVIN. See VITAMIN B.

RIBONUCLEIC ACID (RNA), a vital component of all living *cells, consists of a large number of nucleotides attached together in single file to form a long strand. Each nucleotide contains the sugar ribose and one of four different bases, namely adenine, guanine, cytosine, and uracil (the same as occur in *deoxyribonucleic acid (DNA) except that uracil replaces thymine). RNA is concerned in translating the structure of the inherited substance DNA into the structure of protein molecules. In some viruses RNA is the inherited material itself but it undergoes translation into DNA before replication in the host cell.

RIBOSOMES are granules of *protein and *ribonucleic acid (RNA) present in the cytoplasm of all living organisms, often attached to *endoplasmic reticulum. They are the site of protein synthesis. See CELL.

RICH, ARNOLD RICE (1893–1968). American pathologist, MD Johns Hopkins (1919). Rich joined the department of pathology at *Johns Hopkins, and eventually succeeded *MacCallum as its head. His principal interest was in the inflammatory reaction, especially as it pertained to the advantage or disadvantage to the host of *hypersensitivity to agents such as the tubercle bacillus. His textbook on the pathogenesis of *tuberculosis was for years a standard reference. He also showed that lesions morphologically identical with those of *polyarteritis nodosa could be induced in experimental animals by administration of drugs or foreign proteins.

RICHARDS, ALFRED NEWTON (1876–1966). American pharmacologist, Ph.D. Columbia (1901). Richards held academic appointments at Columbia and Northwestern University, then moved permanently to the University of Pennsylvania as head of the department of pharmacology. He exerted great influence in the growth and academic eminence of that university. During, and after the Second World War he played a powerful role in national scientific affairs, working through such organizations as the *National Academy of Sciences. His best-remembered scientific contribution was in the study of renal function, where he and colleagues developed the technique of micropuncture of *renal tubules.

RICHARDS, DICKINSON WOODRUFF (1895–1973). American physician, MD Columbia (1923). Richards continued his affiliation with Columbia, eventually becoming professor of medicine, in Columbia's division of *Bellevue Hospital. His special interest was cardiopulmonary physiology and disease, and the interrelationships between pulmonary and cardiac function. With Cournand he developed the technique of right heart catheterization, which enabled precise measurements of *cardiac output in various disease states. For this work Richards, Cournand, and *Forssman (of Germany, who had first succeeded in inserting a *catheter into his own right heart, via peripheral veins) were awarded the Nobel prize in 1956.

RICHET, CHARLES ROBERT (1850–1935). French physiologist, MD Paris (1875). Richet was attached to the Faculté de Médecine in Paris and was appointed professor of physiology in 1887. His earlier researches were on gastric secretion (1878), muscular contraction (1884–9), and the nervous control of the body temperature. His late interests were in *blood transfusion after immunization of the donor against the recipient's infection (1888) and in sensitization against foreign proteins (1895). He invented the term '*anaphylaxis'. For this work he was awarded the Nobel prize in 1913.

RICKETS is the defective development and growth of bones due to inadequate absorption and utilization of *calcium. The usual cause of rickets is *vitamin D deficiency in childhood. Vitamin D promotes calcium absorption from the intestine and its incorporation into bone structure; many diets contain only a small amount, but it is also formed within the body by the action of ultraviolet light on 7-dehydrocholesterol in the basal layers of the skin. Rickets results from the combination of inadequate light exposure and insufficient vitamin D intake; it is thus rare in Western urban communities except in certain special groups such as coloured immigrant children. It may also be caused by certain *inborn (inherited) errors of metabolism. The clinical features of rickets are soft and fragile bones, inadequate growth, deformities of the limbs, thoracic cage, pelvis, and skull, and characteristic X-ray changes. *Hypocalcaemia and *tetany may occur.

RICKETTS, HOWARD TAYLOR (1871–1910). American microbiologist and epidemiologist, MD Northwestern University (1897). Ricketts joined the department of pathology at University of Chicago, and developed a special interest in *infectious diseases. He carried out important field studies of *Rocky Mountain spotted fever, succeeding in transmitting the disease from man to laboratory animals, and demonstrating the causative organism, which was subsequently named for him: *Rickettsia*. He showed that this organism is carried in nature by *ticks, and transmitted to man by the bite of a tick. In Mexico in 1910, while studying *typhus fever, another rickettsial infection, he succumbed to it himself.

RICKETTSIA. A genus of very small intracellular *bacteria (at one time considered intermediate between bacteria and *viruses) transmitted by *arthropod vectors and responsible for *typhus fever and related diseases.

RICORD, PHILLIPE (1799–1889). French venereologist, MD Paris (1826). Born of French parents in Baltimore, Ricord moved to Paris in 1820 and rose to become chief surgeon to the Hôpital du Midi for *syphilis. Ricord was the leading venereologist of the century (see VENEREOLOGY). He finally proved that syphilis and *gonorrhoea were different diseases by innumerable inoculation experiments. He described the three stages of syphilis and published a standard book on venereal diseases (1838). He was appointed physician to Prince Napoleon in 1852 and to the Emperor in 1869.

RIEDEL, BERNHARD MORITZ KARL LUDWIG (1846–1916). German surgeon, MD Rostock (1870). After working in Göttingen Riedel became professor of surgery in Jena. He described ligneous or woody thyroiditis (*Riedel's thyroiditis, 1896) and *Riedel's lobe of the liver.

RIEDEL'S LOBE is an anatomically anomalous tongue of tissue protruding from the lower edge of the right lobe of the liver which may be palpable on examination of the abdomen and which, if not recognized as a normal variant, may cause diagnostic confusion.

RIEDEL'S THYROIDITIS is a rare condition of unknown aetiology in which the *thyroid gland and surrounding structures are invaded by a mass of hard sclerotic tissue, giving rise to a strikingly firm neck enlargement (and sometimes tracheal obstruction) which may be mistaken for thyroid *carcinoma.

RIFAMPICIN is a powerful antibiotic effective against a wide spectrum of bacteria including *mycobacteria. Its use is largely confined to the treatment of *tuberculosis and *leprosy.

RIFAMYCIN is a generic name for a group of *antibiotics, including *rifampicin, originally obtained from the mould *Streptomyces mediterranei*.

RIFT VALLEY FEVER is an *influenza-like illness of farm animals and man endemic in certain areas of Africa, originally described from the Rift Valley of Kenya. It is due to an *arbovirus.

RIGIDITY is inflexibility of the body or limbs due to increased muscular tone. It is characteristic of extrapyramidal neurological disorders such as *parkinsonism.

RIGOR is the sensation of shivering experienced when the body temperature rises sharply.

RIGOR MORTIS is the term for the increasing stiffness of muscles which develops after death.

RINDERPEST. Cattle plague, which caused a disastrous epidemic in the UK in 1865–6. See VETERINARY MEDICINE.

RINGER, SYDNEY (1835–1910). British physician and physiologist, MD London (1863), FRCP (1870), FRS (1885). Ringer was appointed to the staff of *University College Hospital in 1867, and became professor of medicine in 1887. He showed that isolated organs survived longer when calcium and potassium were added to the saline perfusate (Ringer's solution).

RINGER'S SOLUTION is a physiological *saline solution with potassium and calcium chlorides added.

RINGWORM is a common term for various *tinea infections in which centrifugal spread of the fungus in the skin accompanied by central healing of the lesion leads to a circular rash (tinea circinata).

RINNE'S TEST was first described by the German otologist Heinrich Adolf Rinne (1819–63). It determines whether *deafness is due to disease of the middle ear (conductive deafness). A tuning fork is set into vibration and alternately held half an inch from the external auditory meatus to assess air conduction and placed on the mastoid process behind the ear to assess bone conduction. Normally (and in sensorineural deafness such as that due to a lesion of the auditory nerve) the sound is heard louder and longer through the air. Should the reverse be the case, conductive deafness is indicated.

RIO-HORTEGA, PIO DEL (1882–1945). Spanish neurohistologist, MD Valladolid (1905). In 1918 Rio-Hortega developed a silver impregnation stain which allowed him to identify two new glial elements: the microglia and the oligodendroglia (see NEUROGLIA). Working at the National Institute for Cancer in Madrid he reclassified the *gliomata (1919). He left Spain during the Civil War and after a short period in England settled in Argentina.

RIOLAN, JEAN (1580–1637). French physician, MD Paris (1604). Riolan was professor of medicine at the Collège Royal and of anatomy and botany in the University of Paris; in 1633 he was appointed principal physician to Marie de Medici, the Queen Mother. His slavish veneration for *Galen led him to oppose any new current in medical thought. He recorded his disapproval of *Harvey's views in *Encheiridium* (1648) to which Harvey replied in 1649.

RIPPLE BED. A bed with a mattress consisting of a number of compartments which can be separately inflated and deflated, so varying the points at which pressure bears on the patient's body.

RIVA-ROCCI, SCIPIONE (1863–1937). Italian physician, MD Turin (1888). In 1896 Riva-Rocci devised the type of mercury *sphygmomanometer still in general use today.

RIVERS, THOMAS MILTON (1888–1962). American microbiologist, MD Johns Hopkins (1915). After military service in the First World War, Rivers joined the department of bacteriology at *Johns Hopkins, where his principal achievement was in determining the special growth requirements of *Haemophilus influenzae. In 1922 he joined the staff of the Rockefeller Institute, and began a lifelong investigation of viral diseases of man. In this he played an important part in establishing virology as a discipline separate from bacteriology. He studied *measles, *varicella, lymphocytic choriomeningitis, *psittacosis, and *smallpox. His books on animal viruses were standard references for many years.

RNA. See RIBONUCLEIC ACID.

ROAD ACCIDENTS. See SURGERY OF TRAUMA.

ROCKEFELLER, JOHN DAVISON (1839–1937). American industrialist and philanthropist. Soon after the first US oil well was drilled in Pennsylvania he began to invest in oil production enterprises, building refineries, and distributing the products. He founded the Standard Oil Company of Ohio in 1870. This expanded over the nation, and included other manufacturing and transportation interests, which yielded immense wealth to him. About the end of the century he turned his attention to philanthropy, and began to give large sums of money to religious and educational institutions. On the advice of his friend and clergyman, Frederick T. Gates, he founded the Rockefeller Institute for Medical Research in New York City in 1904. Later he established the General Education Board and the *Rockefeller Foundation, agencies which contributed to biomedical research, medical education, and control of world health problems, such as *malaria, *yellow fever, and *malnutrition.

ROCKEFELLER FOUNDATION. The Rockefeller Foundation was endowed by John D. *Rockefeller in 1913 'to promote the well-being of mankind throughout the world'. In its early years the main thrust of the Foundation was in public health and medical education. Now its work has expanded to include agriculture, natural and social sciences, and the arts and humanities. It has a board of trustees and officers concerned with the main activities, with headquarters in New York. Its work is carried out by making grants, supporting fellowships, and by field operations in which expert teams help developing countries until they are capable of managing their problems out of their own resources. In 1983 there were programmes in agricultural improvements; in supporting artists; in researching issues of importance to the arts and in American society; in assisting the development of equal opportunities for minorities; and in the field of international relations. In the field of medicine it has concern with reproductive biology, contraceptive technology, and social factors of significance in population control. Also the Foundation supports research into neglected diseases afflicting mainly the developing world, into epidemiology and other quantitative approaches to disease control and their incorporation into medical education, and the efficient use of biomedical information, which is accumulating so rapidly. It maintains a useful Conference Centre at Bellagio on Lake Como in Italy where experts are brought together to discuss and define problems of interest to the Foundation.

ROCKEFELLER INSTITUTE AND UNIVERSITY. See FOUNDATIONS IN THE USA; RESEARCH INSTITUTES.

ROCKY MOUNTAIN SPOTTED FEVER. Tickborne *typhus, due to *Rickettsia rickettsii.*

RODDICK, SIR THOMAS GEORGE (1846–1923). Canadian surgeon, MD McGill University (1869). Roddick was born in Harbor Grace, Newfoundland. He attended the Normal School in Truro, Nova Scotia, at the age of 14. Thereafter he served as an apprentice to surgeons in Truro and in St John's, and entered *McGill University as a medical student at the age of 18. Upon graduation at the top of his class, he became a house surgeon at the *Montreal General Hospital where *Osler was a student. Later Roddick brought back 'Listerism' from Edinburgh in 1872. By the age of 29 Roddick was already clinical professor of surgery, and when the *Royal Victoria Hospital was opened in 1893 he was named its surgeon-in-chief. He was dean at the time of the destruction of the medical faculty's building and worked tirelessly to have it replaced by a magnificent structure in 1912. Roddick's greatest work was, however, in forming the Medical Council of Canada, after 18 years of frustrating work through professional organizations (he was president of the Canadian and British Medical Associations in turn). As a result a medical graduate is able to write a single set of examinations permitting him to practise anywhere in Canada. He served for many years in the Canadian House of Commons.

RODENT ULCER. Basal cell *carcinoma of the skin, almost always situated on the sun-exposed parts of the face. It begins as a small nodule, which then breaks down in the centre to form an ulcer with firm raised edges. Although locally malignant, it rarely metastasizes, and is eminently curable.

RODS are the specialized retinal structures containing the visual pigment *rhodopsin which are the sensory receptors for vision at low levels of light intensity, sensitive to blue and green light only. See also RETINA.

ROENTGEN. The amount of *gamma- or *X-radiation that will produce ions carrying 2.58 × 10^{-4} coulomb of electric charge per kilogram of dry air.

ROENTGEN, WILHELM CONRAD (1845–1923). German physicist, Ph.D. Zurich (1869). Roentgen occupied the chair of physics successively at Strasbourg (1876), Giessen (1879),

Würzburg (1888), and Berlin (1899). It was at Würzburg that he discovered *X-rays. On 8 November 1895 while experimenting with a highly evacuated vacuum tube on the conduction of electricity through gases, he noted fluorescence of a barium platinocyanide screen lying nearby. Further investigation of this radiation showed that it could pass through some substances impervious to light. In view of its unusual features he suggested the name X-rays. For this discovery he was awarded the Nobel prize in physics in 1901.

ROGER OF PALERMO (Ruggiero Frugardi) (*fl.* 12th c.). Roger was the most distinguished of the surgeons of the school of *Salerno. Details of his life are lacking, but he published *Practica chirurgiae* (*c.* 1170) which became the standard textbook at Salerno. He was clearly experienced and skilled. He used seaweed or burned sponge for treating *goitre and believed *suppuration was essential for wound healing.

ROGERS, SIR LEONARD (1868–1962). British physician and pathologist, MD London (1897), FRCS (1892), FRCP (1905), FRS (1916). Rogers was commissioned in the Indian Medical Service in 1893, became professor of pathology in Calcutta in 1900, and was knighted in 1914. He returned to England in 1920 and was appointed physician to the Hospital for Tropical Diseases in London. One of the pioneers of *tropical medicine, Rogers identified *Entamoeba histolytica* as the cause of *amoebiasis and introduced *emetine in its treatment; he was the first to use *antimony in treating *kala-azar and hypertonic intravenous saline in *cholera.

ROGET, PETER MARK (1779–1869). Anglo-Swiss physician and savant, MD Edinburgh (1798), FRCP (1831), FRS (1815). After serving as physician to Manchester Infirmary from 1805 to 1808, Roget moved to London and became a lecturer at the *Great Windmill Street School in 1809. He was physician to the Northern Dispensary and the Millbank penitentiary. Roget was one of the founders of London University and secretary of the Royal Society from 1827 to 1848. He made many contributions to the *Encyclopaedia Britannica,* but his main claim to fame is his *Thesaurus of English Words and Phrases* (1852), of which there had been 76 impressions by 1983.

ROKITANSKY, KARL FREIHERR VON (1804–74). Austrian pathologist, MD Vienna (1828). Professor extraordinary of pathological anatomy in 1834, and *ordinarius* in 1844, Rokitansky was the leading teacher of his subject in Europe and a founder of the New Vienna School. His *Handbuch der pathologischen Anatomie* (1842–6), enjoyed a large circulation although neglecting morbid histology. The doctrine of 'crases' and 'stases' it contained was demolished by *Virchow. When he retired he had carried out more than 30 000 autopsies. He was the first to describe *acute yellow atrophy of the liver (1843) and acute dilatation of the stomach (1842).

ROLANDO OF PARMA (Rolando Capelluti) (*fl.* 13th c.). Italian surgeon. Rolando revised and re-edited *Roger of Palermo's *Practica chirurgiae* about 1230–40. A sound practical surgeon of his time, he was independent of Arabic sources and held that *suppuration was undesirable.

ROLANDO, LUIGI (1773–1831). Italian physician and anatomist, MD Turin (1801). Appointed professor of practical medicine in Sassari, Sardinia, in 1804, Rolando returned to Turin and the chair of anatomy in 1814. He described the *fissure of Rolando (the Rolandic fissure). After excising the *cerebrum and *cerebellum in animals he concluded that the first presided over voluntary and the second over involuntary movements.

ROLLESTON, SIR HUMPHRY DAVY, BT (1862–1944). British physician, MD Cambridge (1891), FRCP (1894). Rolleston was elected fellow of St John's College, Cambridge, in 1889, and physician in 1898. During the South African war he served as consulting physician to the Imperial Yeomanry Hospital and in the Second World War to the Royal Navy in the rank of surgeon rear-admiral. In 1925 he was appointed regius professor of physic at Cambridge. He was physician to Prince Albert (later George VI) in 1916, physician-in-ordinary to the King in 1923 and extraordinary from 1932 to 1936. He was made a baronet in 1924. Rolleston was a scholarly and widely read physician and medical historian and the co-editor with Sir Clifford *Allbutt of *A System of Medicine* (1905–11, 9 vols).

ROMANOWSKY, DIMITRI LEONIDOVITCH (1861–1921). Russian physician, remembered chiefly in connection with the eosin–methylene blue stain he developed (Romanowsky's stain) which was the forerunner of various other similarly based stains used for blood smears and malarial parasites (e.g. *Leishman's stain).

ROMANOWSKY'S STAIN. A microscopic stain for blood films made up of eosin and methylene blue.

ROMBERG, MORITZ HEINRICH (1795–1873). German physician and neurologist, MD Berlin (1817). After working as an *armenarzt* amongst the poor of Berlin (1820) Romberg became professor in the University in 1838. His main interest was in neurology and he published the first formal textbook of this subject, *Lehrbuch der Nervenkrankheiten* (1840–6). He was first to describe *achondroplasia (1817). He is now chiefly remembered for *Romberg's sign of spinal ataxia, unsteadiness when standing with the eyes closed and the feet together.

ROMBERG'S SIGN. Swaying or falling on closing the eyes while in a standing position with the feet together. It indicates sensory *ataxia, that is ataxia due to impaired *proprioception (lack of position and joint sense) in the lower limbs which is compensated by vision and therefore ataxia is aggravated by closing the eyes.

ROONHUYZE, HENDRICK VAN (b. ?–1625). Dutch surgeon. Roonhuyze practised in Amsterdam being the first to concern himself with orthopaedics. He was noted also for his operations on *hare-lip, for his obstetric skills, and for championing *Caesarean section. His son, Rogier, also an obstetrician, is said to have bought the secret of the *obstetrical forceps from Hugh *Chamberlen the elder.

RORSCHACH TEST. This psychodiagnostic method, also known as the 'inkblot test', was devised by the Swiss psychiatrist Hermann Rorschach (1884–1922). The subject is shown a series of 10 cards, each of which bears a bilaterally symmetrical inkblot, 5 of which are in black and white, 3 in black and red, and 2 multicoloured. He is invited to interpret what he sees on each card, and his responses are recorded. Scoring and analysis are complicated, but the test is said to be of value in the assessment of personality, intellect, and emotion, and to assist the differential diagnosis of psychiatric disorders. Objective validation of these claims has been disappointing.

ROSACEA is a chronic disorder of the skin of the nose, cheeks, and forehead—the 'blush area'—marked by persistent capillary dilatation, papule, and pustule formation, and in some longstanding cases, *rhinophyma.

ROSE, WICKLIFFE (1862–1931). See PUBLIC HEALTH IN THE USA.

ROSEOLA is an infection of infancy (also known as exanthema subitum or roseola infantum) presumed to be due to an as yet unidentified *virus. It is marked by fever for 3–4 days followed by the appearance of a rose-coloured macular rash. Recovery is uneventful.

ROSICRUCIAN. A member of a secret society or order said to have been founded in 1484 by a Christian Rosenkreuz. Its adherents claimed various forms of magical power and knowledge, such as the transmutation of metals and the prolongation of life. Some present-day societies purport to continue the Rosicrucian tradition.

ROSS, SIR RONALD (1857–1932). British malariologist, MRCS (1879), LSA (1881), FRS (1901). Ross studied at *St Bartholomew's Hospital, London and worked as a ship's surgeon before being commissioned in the *Indian Medical Service in 1881. He undertook research into *malaria with Sir Patrick *Manson, observing the parasite in the stomach of the anopheline *mosquito in 1897. He returned to England and became lecturer in the Liverpool School of Tropical Medicine in 1899 and professor from 1902 to 1912. He was awarded the Nobel prize in medicine 1902 for his work on malaria. In 1912 he came to London as physician for tropical diseases at *King's College Hospital.

ROTAVIRUS. A group of double-stranded *ribonucleic acid (RNA) *viruses associated with acute non-bacterial *gastroenteritis.

ROTHSCHILD REPORT. A report made in 1971 to the UK Government by the then head of its Central Policy Review Staff, Lord Rothschild, under the title 'The Organization of Government R. & D.' and published as part of a consultative document (Green Paper) *A Framework for Government Research and Development*. The main thesis of the Rothschild Report, which was the application of the so-called customer–contractor principle to the organization and funding of civil science, was subsequently accepted by the government, whose decisions were published the following year in a White Paper of the same title (Cmnd. 5046). In the case of medical research, the new arrangements required transfer of one-quarter of the annual financial allocation of the *Medical Research Council (the 'contractor') to the budget of the *Health Departments (the 'customers'), who were then expected to employ the money in commissioning research from the Council in areas of specific interest to them. The change was intended to move the balance of research expenditure in the direction of social need as reflected in the utilization of National Health Service resources; but it was much criticized by the medical and scientific community at the time as being simplistic and naïve, and ignoring the internally logical nature of advances in medical science. The fears proved well founded; no significant alteration in the rate of progress or pattern of research was discernible during the following years, while cumbersome paperwork procedures for 'accounting' for the transferred funds placed a bureaucratic burden on customer and contractor alike. On the advice of the Public Accounts Committee, the Rothschild arrangements were formally abandoned on 1 April 1981, when the transferred funds were returned from the Health Departments to the Council.

ROUNDWORM. Any *nematode worm parasitic in man or animals. Roundworms, when long and slender such as *Oxyuris*, may also be referred to as *threadworms.

ROUS, FRANCIS PEYTON (1879–1970). American experimental pathologist, MD Johns Hopkins (1905). After training in pathology at the University of Michigan, Rous joined the staff of the Rockefeller Institute in 1909, where he remained throughout a long professional career. In 1911 he demonstrated that a *sarcoma of chickens could be transmitted by an agent in cell-free sterile filtrates of the tumours, that is, a *virus. For this work he received the Nobel prize 55 years later. In addition he made significant discoveries with respect to other animal tumours caused by viruses, as well as those induced by irritation, for example tar cancers of the skin. During the First World War he conducted studies on the preservation of blood, and showed that by bleeding into a solution of citrate and sugar, blood could be maintained in fluid state, with cells relatively undamaged, for weeks. The reagent he helped to devise was called the Rous–Turner solution. This finding enabled the later practical development of *blood banks.

ROUS SARCOMA is a type of virus-induced *sarcoma occurring in fowls, described in 1911 by Francis Peyton *Rous.

ROUX, PIERRE PAUL ÉMILE (1853–1933). French bacteriologist, MD Paris (1878). Roux worked with *Pasteur at his institute, becoming director in 1904. His chief studies were on *rabies, *anthrax, and the preparation of *vaccines. With von *Behring he demonstrated the value of treatment with *diphtheria antitoxin and of immunization with toxin.

ROYAL APOTHECARIES. There are, by tradition, five general medical attendants in the *Royal Medical Household in the UK. They are: the apothecary to the Queen and to Household; the apothecary to Household at Windsor; the apothecary to Household at Sandringham; the apothecary to Household at Balmoral; and the apothecary to Household at the Palace of Holyrood.

ROYAL COLLEGE OF GENERAL PRACTITIONERS. See MEDICAL COLLEGES, ETC. OF THE UK.

ROYAL COLLEGE OF NURSING. See NURSING IN THE UK; MEDICAL COLLEGES, ETC. OF THE UK.

ROYAL COLLEGE OF PATHOLOGISTS. See MEDICAL COLLEGES, ETC. OF THE UK.

ROYAL COLLEGE OF PHYSICIANS AND SURGEONS OF CANADA began in 1929 after the usual stimuli, negotiations, arguments, and counter-arguments inseparable from the founding of such professional corporations. The general model adopted was that of the Royal Colleges of the UK (see MEDICAL COLLEGES, OF THE UK). The Act which went through Parliament made it clear that the new College was intended to stimulate postgraduate education and it was 'to act as an incentive to medical men, both physicians and surgeons, to aspire to higher qualifications and therefore higher standards of service to the public'. It does this still, as similar predominantly educational bodies do, by setting standards of experience required for admission to the stiff examinations for the fellowship. These are conducted in both English and French for a large variety of specialties. There is now a series of committees for the specialties and regional committees across the country all accountable to the Council which is the Governing Body. Naturally there are relationships established with many other bodies concerned with medicine nationally and internationally.

ROYAL COLLEGE OF PHYSICIANS AND SURGEONS OF GLASGOW. See MEDICAL COLLEGES, ETC. OF THE UK.

ROYAL COLLEGE OF PSYCHIATRISTS. See MEDICAL COLLEGES, ETC. OF THE UK.

ROYAL COLLEGE OF RADIOLOGISTS. See MEDICAL COLLEGES, ETC. OF THE UK.

ROYAL COLLEGES OF PHYSICIANS. See MEDICAL COLLEGES, ETC. OF THE UK.

ROYAL COLLEGES OF SURGEONS. See MEDICAL COLLEGES, ETC. OF THE UK.

ROYAL FREE HOSPITAL. The Royal Free Hospital, London, will ever be remembered for its prime place in the history of medical education for women. Prior to the middle of the 19th c. there was no medical education available to females in the UK, but in the first *Medical Register*, published as a result of the *Medical Act of 1858, there appeared the name of one woman, Elizabeth *Blackwell, who had obtained a medical degree in the USA. Mrs Elizabeth Garrett *Anderson in 1865 had complied with all the requirements for qualification of the Society of Apothecaries. Almost immediately after, the Society changed its rules to exclude women from its examinations. Sophia *Jex-Blake and others had persuaded Edinburgh University to educate them medically, but by technicalities they too were excluded from the practice of medicine. This aroused concern in London, where a medical school for women was set up in 1874, and among the governors were the Earl of Shaftesbury, Charles *Darwin, and Thomas Henry *Huxley. However, there was still no clinical instruction. Then in 1877 the Royal Free Hospital agreed to admit students of the school to its wards. The bridgehead was established, and was held because under an Act of 1876 Examining Boards were empowered to open their examinations to women. The Royal College of Physicians of Ireland did this in 1887, and in the same year the University of London admitted women to its degrees. In 1900 the University recognized the Royal Free Hospital School of Medicine as one of its schools. By the later 1940s men were first admitted to the school, just as women had to be admitted to the previously all-male schools in London. Now, as in other medical schools and

faculties the entry of men and women is approximately equal, so that the battle is won.

The hospital moved in 1982 from its more central site to one in Hampstead, a northern suburb of London. For the first time in its history this brought together the whole school in its preclinical and clinical parts, allowing for better integration of the curriculum.

ROYAL HOSPITAL, CHELSEA, by the Thames in London, is not a medical hospital but a home for old soldiers. It was founded in 1682 by King Charles II, and the original building, still standing, was designed by Sir Christopher Wren. The foundation was modelled on the Hôtel des Invalides in Paris, which was started by Louis XIV in 1670 for similar purposes. The Royal Hospital is run by a Board of Commissioners appointed by the Crown and supported by parliamentary grant since 1847. There are about 450 pensioners, almost all over the age of 65. They are familiar about London in their long scarlet coats with small black military caps, a uniform modernized from that of the first Duke of Marlborough's time. On ceremonial occasions the headgear is a tricorn. There is a small infirmary of about 80 beds for the weak and ill.

ROYAL MEDICAL HOUSEHOLD. The doctors serving the Queen in the UK are appointed by the Lord Chamberlain, who has overall responsibility for the Royal Medical Household. In 1983, this consisted of the head of the Medical Household, who was also physician, and two other physicians; the serjeant-surgeon; the surgeon; the surgeon-oculist; the surgeon-gynaecologist; the surgeon-dentist; the apothecary to the Queen and to Household; the physician to Household; the surgeon to Household; the surgeon-oculist to Household; the apothecary to Household at Windsor; the apothecary to Household at Sandringham; and coroner to the Queen's Household. In addition, the Medical Household in Scotland numbered three physicians, two surgeons, two extra-surgeons, the apothecary to Household at Balmoral, and the apothecary to Household at the Palace of Holyrood. (For comparison, the Royal Ecclesiastical Household numbers 36 chaplains.)

ROYAL NATIONAL INSTITUTE FOR THE BLIND (RNIB) began in 1868 when Thomas Rhodes Armitage of London lost his sight and then determined to help the blind to read. The British and Foreign Society for Improving the Embossed Literature of the Blind was formed. It soon became the British and Foreign Blind Association. In 1914 it became the National Institute for the Blind and took over the Moon works, which produced a form of embossed type that can be printed individually but not written by hand. It is easier to read than braille, but it is this latter system which has prevailed, with help from the RNIB, since it can be printed and written, which is a great advantage for communication. In 1915 the Institute founded St

Dunstan's Hostel for Blinded Soldiers and Sailors and this became independent in 1922. In the following few years the RNIB took over education in massage for the blind and this has developed into a School of Physiotherapy; it started after-care and home industries; published a journal; started the Sunshine Homes for Blind Babies; and opened the Chorleywood College for Girls—all an amazing record of achievement. This continues, for the Talking Book Service came in 1935, mainly for the elderly blind (a large group) who find learning braille particularly difficult. Now there are homes of recovery for those recently blinded, training centres for telephonists, typists, braille shorthand writers, and computer operators, homes for those with multiple handicaps, and a British Foundation for Research into Prevention of Blindness. Braille books are produced for undergraduates, the first braille book being translated by computer in 1968, and from 1982 the advanced autobraille printing press has been in use. A Royal Charter was granted in 1949 and in 1953 the present name was allowed. Books, tapes, and other facilities are available to the blind at subsidized prices. The RNIB spends over £1 million on braille productions, runs 40 establishments, employs 1300 people, and has a turnover of £11 million (in 1982), money coming mainly from donations and legacies. See also OPHTHALMOLOGY.

ROYAL NATIONAL ORTHOPAEDIC HOS-PITAL, London, was formed in 1905 out of the amalgamation of three small metropolitan hospitals, under some pressure from the King's Metropolitan Hospital Fund, which contributed moneys to all of them. The Fund wished for a new hospital to be built in central London, and another one in the country, in that order. The First World War interfered with this plan, but traumatic surgery and its aftermath gave a fillip after the war to the development of the hospital. The town branch was in operation in Great Portland Street, and a convalescent home became vacant at Stanmore, in the northern suburbs, and was acquired for the country branch, which was opened in 1922. The two parts of the hospital have developed in accordance with the changes occurring over the decades in orthopaedic practice and concern. There are workshops, interests in bio-engineering, limb fitting, *scoliosis, and crippled children's centres. A chair of orthopaedics was founded, with a benefaction from the National Fund for Research into Poliomyelitis and other Crippling Diseases, in the University of London, during 1965. Prior to this the University had started an Institute of Orthopaedics at the hospital in 1948. Its concerns were postgraduate teaching and research, overseen by a Director until the professor was appointed. At present the need for specialized hospitals in London, including those for orthopaedics, is being questioned. Because the lease of the Great Portland Street branch terminated during 1984, it was decided not to continue

with it, but to transfer some clinical facilities and the work of the Institute to the nearby Middlesex Hospital, with which there have always been close associations. The branch at Stanmore is to continue and a Spinal Injuries Unit is being built there. The record of service, teaching, and research of the Hospital and Institute is distinguished and has contributed to the great advances in orthopaedics that have been a feature of the 20th c.

ROYAL POSTGRADUATE MEDICAL SCHOOL. The Royal Postgraduate Medical School is associated with the Hammersmith Hospital in west London. The establishment of such a school was recommended by a committee under the chairmanship of the Earl of Athlone. In 1930 another committee recommended the siting of the school at Hammersmith, where it was opened in 1935, and it was granted a Royal Charter in 1966. At first it was part of the London University's British Postgraduate Medical Federation but seceded from it in 1974 to become a School of the University of London. It is the only postgraduate medical school in the UK. The hospital is almost entirely staffed by academics, except for juniors, who are provided by the *National Health Service. The school conducts advanced research in all major areas of medicine and has extensive teaching commitments to postgraduate students from all over the world. The hospital provides a major service to the population in its immediate vicinity, just as do other hospitals in the National Health Service, and because of the advanced nature of its work, it provides a consultative service for anyone referred to it. As might be expected it has a very distinguished research record covering many fields of medical practice.

ROYAL SOCIETY. The national academy of science for the UK and one of the oldest scientific societies of Europe. Its origins date back to the middle of the seventeenth century when a group of scholars began a series of meetings in London from about 1645. The Civil War and the Protectorate divided the group, some going to Oxford, where meetings continued in Wadham College, others remaining in London. After the Restoration, the group came together again in London and resumed their meetings. The foundation of the Society is regarded as having occurred in November 1660, at a meeting at which '. . . Something was offered about a designe of founding a Colledge for the Promoting of Physico-Mathematicall, Experimentall Learning'; this was the first meeting to be recorded in the Society's journal book. The Society's first Charter was granted by Charles II on 15 July 1662, and a second Charter granted less than a year later extended the Society's privileges; in the latter the Society is referred to by its full title as 'The Royal Society of London for Improving Natural Knowledge'. Medical men were among the founding fellows, and have continued to play an important role in the Society's affairs to the present day. The Society, which engages in a wide range of national and international scientific activities, is partly financed by an annual Parliamentary grant-in-aid, administered as part of the UK government budget for civil science through the Department of Education and Science.

ROYAL SOCIETY OF MEDICINE was founded in 1805 and received a Royal Charter in 1834, and a supplementary one in 1907. Its purpose was and is 'for the promotion of physic and surgery and of the branches of science connected with them'. It has an international membership and includes scientists and interested lay people. It carries out its work through 33 sections, each devoted to a wide area of medical and surgical practice. Each holds regular meetings on topics within its interest. Its headquarters in London incorporates a club with some residential accommodation and catering facilities. It maintains one of the best and most comprehensive medical libraries in the UK. Its purposes are essentially educational in the organization of meetings and symposia, in publishing a journal of proceedings, and in the production of audio-visual materials for teaching and learning. It is non-political, and continues to flourish as an independent educational body.

ROYAL TOUCH. See KING'S EVIL.

ROYAL VICTORIA HOSPITAL, Belfast, Northern Ireland, arose out of the Fever Hospital started in 1797. It became the Belfast General Hospital in 1848 after the opening of the Union Fever Hospital in 1845. A first charter changed the name to Belfast Royal Hospital in 1875 and a further charter in 1899 brought the present title. Because of the workload a new hospital was built in Grosvenor Road and was opened in 1903 by King Edward VII. Its in-patient work has increased 14-fold since that time. It is now a major regional centre for the whole of Northern Ireland for patients with complicated disorders, and for such specialties as radiotherapy, neurosurgery, and cardiology. It includes all the specialties of medicine and is the teaching hospital of the Queen's University of Belfast. The civil strife in Northern Ireland, especially since 1970 and often in Belfast, has given the hospital staff unrivalled experience in *surgery of trauma caused by many forms of weaponry and fire.

ROYAL VICTORIA HOSPITAL, Montreal, Canada, was founded in 1887, Queen Victoria's jubilee, by Sir George Stephen and Sir Donald Smith, who gave a million dollars for a hospital for the sick poor, without distinction of race or creed. There were also to be facilities for medical and nursing education. By 1894 seven beds were in use and soon the full complement of 260 beds was open. A nurses' home was provided in 1907 and a private wing in 1916. In 1926 a maternity hospital began and is now known as the Women's Pavilion. Later came the Psychiatric (Allan Memorial) Insti-

tute in 1944, a large surgical wing in 1956, and a medical one in 1959. Now (1984) there are 873 beds to which about 25 000 patients are admitted annually and there are 425 000 out-patient visits. All specialties are represented, with special interests in high-risk obstetrics, reconstructive surgery, emergency medicine, endocrinology, and geriatrics. Much research is carried out in all departments. It is a major centre (along with Montreal General Hospital) for the teaching of medical students of *McGill University, which has an innovative educational programme that has attracted interest world-wide. There is teaching for all other health care professions. Expansion of many of the hospital's activities is planned in the immediate future.

ROYAL VICTORIA INFIRMARY (RVI), Newcastle upon Tyne, England, began in 1751 because of the concern of local dignitaries and doctors for the sick poor. A house in Gallowgate was opened with space for 23 in-patients. Rooms close by were then rented and a foundation stone for a purpose-built hospital was laid in the same year. Patients came from Newcastle upon Tyne, Northumberland, and Durham, and the House Committee had representatives from all three. The new hospital was opened to patients in 1753 on a site close to the river, near a poor part of the city. By 1788 John Clark was appointed to the staff and pressed for extensions to the hospital, with a fever ward of 12 beds separated from the main building by a wall; despite dissension this was completed in 1803. A College of Medicine made a stuttering start in 1832 but became established in 1834, and the clinical facilities of the RVI were used for teaching students. Later the Medical School (at first part of the University of Durham, but from 1962 of the University of Newcastle upon Tyne) became nationally and internationally renowned. In 1874 Beatson was appointed as house surgeon, having trained with Joseph *Lister, and the *sepsis rates began to fall. Further wards were added in 1885, but plainly a new hospital was needed, away from a site now cramped by the encroachments of the railway and other buildings. In 1896 Queen Victoria's diamond jubilee was approaching and another public appeal was launched. The foundation stone of the new hospital, on its present site (Leazes), was laid in 1900 by the Prince of Wales, Albert Edward, and the Royal Victoria Infirmary was named, being opened in 1906. From the 1940s onwards there was rising specialization and chairs in various clinical subjects were founded, and the RVI increasingly co-operated with other specialist hospitals in the city, including those for maternity, children, eye and ear, nose, and throat diseases. Now it is but one part of a wide hospital teaching complex serving the Medical School. In the hospital George Murray first treated *myxoedema with thyroid extract and famous surgeons of the first half of the 20th c. included James Rutherford Morison and George Grey Turner.

RUBBER GLOVES. Latex rubber gloves are worn to prevent transmission of micro-organisms from and to the wearer's hands. The introduction of rubber gloves as part of *aseptic technique in surgical practice is credited to the surgeons of *Johns Hopkins Hospital, Baltimore, USA.

RUBEFACIENT is descriptive of agents causing *erythema.

RUBELLA is a common and mild virus infection, also known as German measles, affecting principally children and young adults. One attack usually confers lifelong immunity. The main features are slight fever, inflammation of *lymph nodes particularly behind the ears and below the occiput, and a transient pink *macular rash on face, trunk, and extremities in that order. Rapid recovery without complications is the rule. The incubation period varies between 14 and 21 days. The fleeting nature of the rash (which may not be detectable at all) and the mildness of the illness mean that the clinical diagnosis is rarely certain without recourse to laboratory investigations.

The major importance of rubella lies in the tragic consequences it produces in the fetus when a mother becomes infected during the first three or four months of pregnancy. Transplacental infection occurs, and the infant has a high probability (more than 50 per cent if infection is within four weeks of conception) of being born with *congenital heart disease, *mental handicap, eye *cataracts, *deafness, or a combination of these.

Active *immunization with live attenuated virus is effective. Girls who have not acquired natural immunity (ascertainable by serology) should be immunized before the reproductive period (unless there is any possibility of pregnancy already existing). Rubella during the first four months of pregnancy is an indication for therapeutic *abortion.

RUBNER, MAX (1854–1932). German physiologist, MD Munich (1878). Rubner was a pupil of *Ludwig and *Voit. He became assistant professor of hygiene in Marburg in 1885, before following *Koch in the Berlin chair in 1891. His main interest was in metabolism, but he made valuable practical contributions in the field of hygiene. He first described the specific dynamic action of foodstuffs.

RUDOLPH II (1552–1612). Rudolph was King of Hungary in 1572 and of Bohemia in 1575 before becoming Holy Roman Emperor in 1576. He was subject to severe *depression which led to loss of control in his rule, leading to dissension between Roman Catholic and Protestant factions, the ultimate result being the Thirty Years' War (1618–48).

RUELLE, JEAN DE LA (du Ruel; Ruellius) (1474–1537). French physician. Ruelle was physician to François I in 1509. He wrote much on botany, popularizing its study. He translated *Dioscorides in 1516 and in *De natura stirpium* (1536) gives a full description of a large number of plants, including many new species.

RUFFER, SIR MARC ARMAND (1859–1917). Anglo-French palaeopathologist, MB London (1887). Going to Cairo to convalesce Ruffer was appointed professor of bacteriology in the medical school and became the pioneer *palaeopathologist. He described *tuberculosis of the spine, *arteriosclerosis, *gall stones, and *schistosomiasis in mummies of 3000 BC. He was knighted in 1916.

RUPTURE is the usual lay term for *hernia.

RUSH, BENJAMIN (1746–1813). American physician and political figure, MD Edinburgh (1768). Rush studied medicine as an apprentice in Philadelphia and later obtained a medical degree at Edinburgh. He began practice of medicine in Philadelphia in 1769, and taught clinical medicine in the College of Philadelphia. He took an active interest in matters of public policy, including abolition of slavery and the temperance movement. He was a member of the Continental Congress, and a signatory of the Declaration of Independence. After the War of Independence he became a professor of medicine at the University of Pennsylvania. During the terrible *yellow fever epidemic of 1793 in Philadelphia he bravely remained in the city, caring for hundreds of victims. He became convinced of the value of drastic purgation, and engaged in a violent controversy with medical colleagues about the benefit of this treatment in patients with yellow fever.

RUTHERFORD, WILLIAM (1839–99). British physiologist, MD Edinburgh (1862). Rutherford was a Scotsman, known for his theory of hearing, as well as other physiological researches. The resonance theory of *Helmholtz noted the varying fibre lengths of the cochlear membrane, so that notes of varying pitch were assumed to cause vibration of only selected fibres. This accounted for only some of the observed phenomena. Rutherford proposed a telephone theory in which the whole membrane was thought to vibrate in response to sound, as in the diaphragm of a telephone microphone, which then generates electrical impulses in bursts. It seems likely that hearing is dependent both on peripheral and central analysis in the ear and brain to interpret sounds. Rutherford qualified in medicine in Edinburgh, studied in Berlin with *Dubois-Reymond and in several other continental cities. In 1869 he was appointed professor of physiology at *King's College, London, and he returned to Edinburgh as professor in 1874. He was noted as a fine musician with a good baritone voice.

RUXTON, BUCK (*fl.* 1935). British medical practitioner and murderer. Ruxton killed his wife and nursemaid, then dismembered their bodies in a bath, extracted some of their teeth, cut off ears and parts of the face, as well as finger tips, all to make recognition difficult. The parts of the two bodies were distributed widely on the moors near Edinburgh. More than 70 pieces were ultimately discovered. The forensic investigation was brilliant in reconstructing the two bodies as the parts turned up. Estimates of height and weight were made from fragments of the limb bones and these turned out to be remarkably accurate. The skulls were X-rayed and the images carefully superimposed on photographs of the dead women showing congruence of the bones with the features. The mode of dismemberment showed that the person responsible must have had medical and anatomical knowledge since joints were neatly disarticulated and features were removed to make identification difficult. After the remains were found on 29 September 1935 and the forensic work was done, it was discovered that two women had disappeared from Ruxton's household on 15 September of the same year. Search of the house revealed hair and blood-stains in the bathroom and on various parts of the stairs, and human remains in the drainage system. Ruxton was found guilty of murder and was hanged.

RUYSCH, FREDERIK (1638–1731). Dutch anat-omist. After apprenticeship he opened his own apothecary's shop in 1661, but when he graduated he began practice in The Hague. He was praelector in anatomy to the Guild of Surgeons in Amsterdam from 1666 until 1731; he was appointed doctor to the Courts of Justice in 1679, and professor of botany in 1685 as well as practising as an obstetrician. Ruysch was the first to demonstrate the valves in the *lymphatics (1665) and developed a method of displaying blood vessels by injecting them post-mortem with a material which solidified. He suggested that the *thyroid secreted some substance into the blood stream. He made an immense collection of anatomical and pathological specimens; this was sold after his death for a large sum.

RYLE, JOHN ALFRED (1889–1950). British physician, MD London (1919), FRCP (1924). Ryle was elected assistant physician to *Guy's Hospital, London, in 1924 and physician in 1930. In 1935 he was appointed to the chair of physic in Cambridge, but returned to work in London during the war until he was made professor of social medicine at Oxford in 1943. He became physician to the Royal Household in 1932 and physician-extraordinary to the King in 1936. Ryle renounced one of the largest consulting practices in London to become a pioneer of social and *preventive medicine.

S

SABIN, FLORENCE RENA (1871–1953). American biologist, MD Johns Hopkins (1900). Florence Sabin taught anatomy and histology at *Johns Hopkins until 1925, and then became a member of the *Rockefeller Institute, New York City. Early in her career she engaged in studies of neuroanatomy, but for the remainder of the time her focus was on the lymphoid and haematopoietic systems. She helped to elucidate the path of lymph flow through lymph nodes, and developed techniques for staining and observing living blood cells.

SABOURAUD, RAYMOND JACQUES ADRIEN (1864–1938). French dermatologist, MD Paris (1894). Sabouraud became director of the laboratories at l'Hôpital S. Louis in 1897 and later took charge of the municipal laboratory. He had no chair but was a popular teacher. Essentially a skin microbiologist, his studies of mycotic infections were of great value and he devised a culture medium for pathogenic fungi (Sabouraud's medium).

SACCHARIN is a non-nutritive sweetening agent manufactured from toluene. When pure, saccharin has about 550 times the sweetening power of ordinary sugar.

SACHER-MASOCH, LEOPOLD VON (1836–95). Austrian novelist. Sacher-Masoch described the sexual pleasure derived from being treated cruelly, now known as masochism. This is to be contrasted with sadism—sexual pleasure from causing pain in others. These are the extremes of the pleasure–pain principle, and in slight degree may be part of the make-up of many.

SACRED DISEASE was a name for *epilepsy, though to *Hippocrates it was 'nowise more divine nor more sacred than other diseases'.

SACROILIAC JOINTS. The two relatively rigid articulations between the sacrum (the bone formed by the five fused sacral vertebrae of the *spine) and the right and left iliac bones, through which the weight of the body is transmitted to the legs. Little movement occurs at the sacroiliac joints, which is supported almost entirely by ligaments, but some relaxation, allowing expansion of the pelvis, takes place during the later stages of pregnancy; aching of the lower back at this time may be due to tension of the ligaments supporting the joints. Inflammation of the sacroiliac joints produces important early radiological changes in patients with *ankylosing spondylitis.

SADE, COUNT DONATIEN ALPHONSE FRANÇOIS (1740–1814). French writer commonly known as le Marquis de Sade, he served in the army from the age of 14 years. Becoming notorious for his depravity and his vicious practices, he was condemned to death in 1772, but fled to Italy. Re-arrested in 1778 he was committed to the Bastille and transferred to Charenton asylum in 1789. Released and re-admitted he died demented. The term 'sadism', a sexual perversion marked by love of cruelty, is derived from his name.

SADISM is the derivation of sexual pleasure from the infliction of pain or humiliation on another.

SAFE PERIOD. The 'safe period' is that period of the menstrual cycle during which conception is least likely to occur, usually taken as the 10 days preceding *menstruation and the seven days following. In other words, sexual intercourse is avoided during the periovulatory period of the cycle. Since menstruation may itself not be strictly regular, the safe period is best related to the actual time of *ovulation; women who are not aware of its occurrence, for example by experiencing *mittelschmerz, may detect the accompanying slight pyrexia by taking daily measurements of body temperature. Restricting intercourse to the safe period is the so-called 'rhythm method' of contraception. It is unreliable, and can result in up to 20 pregnancies per 100 woman-years.

SAFETY OF DRUGS. See MEDICINES ACT 1968; MEDICINES COMMISSION; DUNLOP COMMITTEE; FOOD AND DRUG ADMINISTRATION; PHARMACOLOGY; PHARMACEUTICAL INDUSTRY.

ST ANTHONY'S FIRE is *erysipelas, to the nursing of which disease an entire monastic order (the Antonines, or Hospital Brothers of St Anthony) was exclusively devoted. The order was founded in 1095 by a Gaston de Dauphine, who believed he owed his recovery from erysipelas to the intervention of the saint, and over the next few centuries erysipelas hospitals were built by the Order throughout Europe. They disappeared from England and France when religious orders were suppressed in those countries. St Anthony's fire has also been taken to refer to *ergotism.

ST BARTHOLOMEW'S HOSPITAL, London,

was founded with the Priory of the same name in 1123, by Rahere, an Augustinian canon. It remains on its original site, from where it has ministered to the sick of the City of London for 860 years—an astonishing record of service. The first carers were monks and nuns. Some of their patients came from the nearby notorious Newgate Prison. In 1539 the Priory was closed at the Dissolution of the Monasteries by Henry VIII. He confiscated the property of the hospital, but allowed it to remain open. Under pressure from the City and his own surgeon Thomas *Vicary, Henry re-established the Royal Hospitals of St Bartholomew's, *St Thomas's, *Bethlem, and Bridewell. This same Vicary persuaded the king to grant a charter to the Royal College of Physicians (see MEDICAL COLLEGES, ETC. OF THE UK). The new establishment was managed by a Board of Governors under the City of London, and a matron and 12 sisters were appointed to care for the 100 patients. Three surgeons visited, but no physician was appointed until 1560. Nothing remains of the mediaeval hospital. James Gibbs designed the new hospital in the 18th c. There is a magnificent Great Hall in the North Wing. The staircase leading to it is decorated with murals by William Hogarth, who was a governor. In 1609 William *Harvey was appointed to the staff. Percivall *Pott was on the staff in the 18th c. There is a portrait of him by Joshua Reynolds in the hospital. John *Abernethy founded the Medical College in 1822, and James *Paget was the first warden. He became surgeon to Queen Victoria and admitted Elizabeth *Blackwell to studies in 1850. She was the first woman medical graduate of the USA. In 1877 a school of nursing was started. The Medical College is now part of the University of London. Since 1948 the hospital has been part of the *National Health Service, and combines with others in all its activities. It now has 711 beds and more than 80 departments, covering the whole range of hospital medicine. In 1980 the hospital treated 23 000 in-patients and 250 000 out-patients.

ST COSMAS AND ST DAMIEN were twin brothers, early Christian martyrs of Cyrrhus in Syria, who practised medicine without fees and who came to be regarded as patron saints of doctors. There are several versions of the saints' lives, and even the fact of martyrdom is uncertain; but there is little doubt that their cult adapted the ancient Greek practice of incubation (see TEMPLE MEDICINE) to the Christian faith, their patients sleeping overnight in their churches in order to dream of a cure.

ST FIACRE is the patron saint of *haemorrhoids. St Fiacre was the son of an Irish king; he emigrated to France and lived there as a hermit for many years.

ST GEORGE'S HOSPITAL was founded in 1733 at Hyde Park Corner in the West End of London, on which site its buildings have been a London land-mark for more than two and a half centuries. It has a distinguished record of service to medical education and medical research; Edward *Jenner was trained there, and among the many illustrious members of staff were John *Hunter, Matthew *Baillie, Thomas *Young, Benjamin *Brodie, and Stewart *Duke-Elder. St George's Hospital and its associated medical school have now been re-located in new buildings in Tooting, a southern suburb of London, a move which took place in phases during the 1960s and 1970s. The facilities at Hyde Park Corner were finally closed in 1980.

ST JOHN, ORDER OF; KNIGHTS HOSPITALLER; ST JOHN AMBULANCE

Historical background: the Knights Hospitaller. When the warriors of the First Crusade captured Jerusalem in 1099, they found there a hospice which cared for the sick and weary pilgrims to the Holy Land. It was run by a group of monastic brothers under the rule of St Benedict. The Crusaders gave this hospice money, land, and estates in the Holy Land and back in Europe, and in 1113 the Hospitallers became an independent religious order, recognized by the Pope, called the Order of the Hospital of St John of Jerusalem. The precincts and hospital of the Order were close by the Church of the Holy Sepulchre, in the Muristan. In their vows of poverty, chastity, and obedience, the brothers followed a monastic rule, and made another vow which no other Order made, 'to honour Our Lords the Sick', although Hospitaller nuns did not usually undertake nursing duties.

Late 12th c. rules of the Order show that they employed 'four wise doctors, who are qualified to examine *urine and to diagnose different diseases and are able to administer appropriate medicines', and they also employed surgeons. The Knights laid great stress on the importance of hygiene, good nursing, diet and a good knowledge of herbs and drugs.

By the mid 12th c., the Hospitallers had developed a military role, protecting travellers and pilgrims, and defending the states set up by the Crusaders from the attacks of the Saracens. The Knights garrisoned huge crusader castles, like Krak des Chevaliers and Margat (in Syria) and employed mercenaries. The other contemporary military religious order, the Knights Templar, also had these duties and took monastic vows, but did not have the Order of St John's additional commitment to care for the sick, although the Teutonic Knights were modelled on the Hospitallers.

The Latin states in the Holy Land fell successively to the Saracens, starting with Jerusalem in 1187. The Order moved its headquarters to Acre, and when that stronghold fell in 1291, the Knights moved to their estates in Cyprus. Shortly afterwards they captured for themselves the island of Rhodes and its neighbouring islands, and even established outposts on the mainland. Securing a headquarters outside Europe from which to pursue the crusading ideal saved them from the fate of the Templars, who were dissolved in 1312, their estates going to the Knights of St John. The Knights fortified Rhodes and developed a seafaring role, harrying Turkish shipping in the Eastern Mediterranean and employing privateers. Rhodes was a busy trading harbour and a noted port-of-call for pilgrims *en route* to the Holy Land, and other travellers. The hospital was renowned for the quality of its care, and the 15th c. building, now the National Museum in Rhodes, had separate wards for infectious diseases. An obstetric ward existed, and cots were provided for children born to pilgrims, as there had been in Jerusalem. Every Knight, including the Master of the Order, worked in the wards at some point in his career, although orderlies were employed, as well as the specialist physicians, surgeons, and pharmacists.

During the Rhodian period the organization of the Order became more structured as its international affairs became more complex, and they also had to rule a small country efficiently. At the conventual headquarters on Rhodes, the Knights were organized into Tongues, divisions according to language spoken. These were France, Auvergne, Provence, Germany, Italy, England, Aragon, and Castile. The representatives of each Tongue conducted its business in Rhodes and provided the great officers of the Order, like the Hospitaller, who was usually French, and the Turcopilier, responsible for coastal defences and the employment of mercenary troops, who was usually English. The head of the Order was called the Grand Master from the 15th c. onwards. He was elected for life and was advised by a council. Representatives of the whole Order met in General Chapter about once every five years.

The Order owned a great deal of property throughout Europe. This was organized into Priories, each with a Prior or Grand Prior at its head. Estates administered by the Priories were subdivided into commanderies, also called preceptories, each a unit of estate management. The commanders were responsible for the administration of land and resources in their own commanderies. From these came the men, money, and supplies to maintain the conventual headquarters and the Knights' hospitaller, military and religious roles. A letter from a 15th c. English commander, Hugh Middleton, writing from Rhodes to his agent in England who managed his commanderies, is mostly concerned with land and financial affairs, but also contains this request for medical information:

Item, to enquire diligently who helped to recure my Lord Cardinal [Beaufort, who died in 1447] that dead is—God have his soul—of the sickness that men call the palsy, and what leeches [doctors] had most fame in that cure, and labour over to them that I might have the receipts [recipes, prescriptions] sent over to me, or else if the medicines might be carried, that they be sent to me.

Few commanderies of the great system

throughout Europe had particular hospitaller duties, like running hospitals, but all had the monastic duty of hospitality and care of strangers and guests.

After several attempts by the Muslim powers to take Rhodes, notably in 1444 by the Egyptians and in 1480 by the Turks, the island and the surrounding fortresses fell to the Turks after a prolonged siege in 1522. The Knights and some of the Greek population were allowed to leave with all the honours of war. For some years they were without a central base, until the island of Malta was given to them by Charles V, King of Spain and Holy Roman Emperor. The Knights were soon called upon to defend their new headquarters. In 1565, under their Grand Master Jean de la Valette, they withstood a massive Turkish siege of the island. Soon afterwards, a new capital city was built—Valletta. Like the town of Rhodes, it had strong fortifications, a conventual church, auberges or inns to house the Knights of the different Tongues, a Grand Master's Palace, and a major hospital, the Holy Infirmary. Wounded and sick Knights, Maltese, slaves, and travellers were all cared for in the Order's several hospitals on Malta. In the 18th c. Grand Master Vilhena introduced a *quarantine hospital to counteract the spread of *plague and other infectious diseases. Travellers often deplored the inconvenience, but the penalties for disobeying the quarantine regulations were severe.

In 1676 a school of anatomy and surgery was founded by the Grand Master, which produced a number of qualified Maltese practitioners, including such pioneers as Michel'Angelo Grima (intestinal sutures), who became apprenticed when he was 12. Training particularly emphasized *wound surgery, as those injured in the Order's ships were returned to Malta for treatment, although each ship had its own surgeon. There was no shortage of corpses for *dissection, as it was directed that the bodies of Knights and patients from the Holy Infirmary should automatically be sent to be dissected as directed by the physicians and surgeons.

In England, the Order had its first grant of land early in the 12th c., and established its headquarters at Clerkenwell, just outside the city walls of London. English Knights of St John were not of the highest nobility, as they mostly were in other European countries, and were never very numerous. They were often holders of high office under the Crown, and in England served as Admirals of the Fleet, Treasurers of the Realm, and advisers to the Sovereign. All would have undertaken their military and hospitaller training at the headquarters of the Order, a supra-national organization, which none the less did not preclude service to a Knight's own nation. St John's Gate, the entrance to the Priory of Clerkenwell, still stands, as does the 12th c. crypt and part of the church. It now houses the headquarters of the Most Venerable Order of St John and its library and museum. Henry VIII dissolved the Order of St

John in England in 1540, as part of his dissolution of the religious orders and his reformation of the Church. Mary Tudor restored the Order briefly in the last year of her reign, but it fell into abeyance again under Elizabeth as the commanderies were again confiscated by the Crown, although there was never a formal act of dissolution. The Knights of Malta still continued to appoint titular Priors of England.

Throughout the 17th and 18th c. the crusading ideal and religious zeal of the Order gradually waned as times changed, although their hospitaller commitment hardly faltered. The French Revolution undermined the Order's failing finances, confiscating the large French estates, and in 1798 Malta itself fell to Napoleon's troops, with scarcely a shot fired. Some Knights went to Russia under the self-styled 'protection' of the Tsar, Paul I. The Order entered a period of decline and disarray. Eventually a new headquarters of the Order was established in Rome.

The Sovereign Military Order of St John of Jerusalem, called of Rhodes, called of Malta. Today, the members of the Sovereign Military Order of Malta, as it is commonly known, still have their headquarters in the Via Condotti in Rome. Although it is still a religious Order, the Grand Master is the head of a Sovereign Order that sends ambassadors to many countries and whose members are of aristocratic origin. Its members in the highest grade take monastic vows. Its role is entirely humanitarian and it is involved in hospitaller work all over the world. The care of pilgrims, to *Lourdes and to Rome, aid to Vietnamese refugees, and the care of *lepers are examples of the Order's world-wide charitable concerns. It has National Associations in most countries, including the UK.

The Johanniterorden. The Knightly Order of St John of Jerusalem (Bailiwick of Brandenburg) is based on a former province of the Hospitallers which adopted the Reformed Faith and continued in being. It was constituted as a separate Order by King William IV of Prussia in 1852. It now operates throughout West Germany and has commanderies in France, Switzerland, Finland, and Hungary. It runs hospitals, a first-aid service—the Johanniter-Unfall-Hilfe—and a nursing service.

The Order of St John in Sweden. This was formerly an association of the Johanniterorden, but was declared a separate Order in 1920 under the High Patronage of the Crown of Sweden. It runs various charitable projects.

The Order of St John in the Netherlands. Also formerly an association of the Johanniterorden, it declared itself a separate Order in 1945, under the Dutch monarchy. It undertakes various types of hospitaller and welfare work.

The Most Venerable Order of the Hospital of St John of Jerusalem. In the 19th c. there was a move to restore the Priory of England. The resultant organization founded in 1831 had a new lease of life in the 1870s, under the leadership of Sir John Furley, Sir Edmund Lechmere, and Major Francis Duncan. In 1888 Queen Victoria granted this organization a Royal Charter, making the British Order of St John a Royal Order of Chivalry with the Sovereign as its head. Since then a member of the Royal family has held the position of Grand Prior—at present held by HRH the Duke of Gloucester. The British Order of St John has Priories and Commanderies in many, mainly Commonwealth, countries, like Australia, Canada, and New Zealand.

The Royal Charter was granted in recognition of the valuable work done by the British Order of St John. In its early life, it had initiated several welfare projects. In 1870 John Furley had attended the first International Congress of the *Red Cross on behalf of the Order of St John. He had been struck with the realization that there was no provision for treatment and transport of the civilian population injured accidentally in peacetime.

In 1877, after much international correspondence and consultation with the foremost authorities of the day, the St John Ambulance Association was founded. Its aim was to train the public in 'aid to the injured', later called first aid. The first Association classes took place in the Woolwich dockyards, and Association Centres were set up all over the country, particularly along the industrial backbone of England, the Midlands, Yorkshire, and Lancashire, in the collieries, the main railway centres, and the manufacturing centres.

Today, the St John Ambulance Association still has the major responsibility for training industry, the police, the fire brigade, and the public in first aid. The training is intended to save life, to the point where superior medical knowledge and training may take over. Other courses run by the Association include Emergency Aid, Nursing, Home Nursing, and Hygiene, and a new First Aid at Work scheme to comply with the *Health and Safety at Work Acts. A major responsibility is the provision of textbooks. These are compiled jointly with the British Red Cross Society and the St Andrew's Ambulance Association (which provides similar services to Scotland). A Standing Committee of the Chief Medical Officers of these bodies prepares the text of the manuals and keeps them under constant review. Training for the Association and for the St John Ambulance Brigade is given by trained medical staff, who give their services voluntarily. Each registered First Aider must know the basic methods for saving and prolonging life and the procedures to be followed at an accident.

St John Ambulance Brigade. Following the success of the St John Ambulance Association and the obvious need for such an organization, the St John Ambulance Brigade was formed in 1887. This is a uniformed body of trained volunteers proficient in

First Aid who are present at public events to provide instant cover for accident and injury. They also provide a valuable supporting service to the statutory ambulance services in times of emergency, for example, a major industrial accident. St John Ambulance is organized on a county structure with local ambulance, nursing, cadet, and combined divisions and centres. Its headquarters are in Grosvenor Crescent, London, alongside those of the Joint Committee of St John and the Red Cross, and the Red Cross.

Early in its history the Brigade was required to support the *Army Medical Services, by providing hospital orderlies for the Boer War in 1899. During the First World War a Joint Committee of St John and the Red Cross was formed. This provided the Voluntary Aid Detachments (VADs), who acted in support of the Royal Army Medical Corps, the Military Home Hospitals Reserve, and the Royal Naval Sick Berth Reserve. The Brigade also ran its own hospital in the First World War, at Étaples, bombed in 1917, re-established at Trouville, and demobilized in 1919.

The St John role in Civil Defence was clearly established. In the inter-war years the first school for Air Raid Precautions for Brigade personnel was opened in 1935. By the end of 1939 more than 10 000 Brigade instructors had given lessons in anti-gas measures to Brigade members and the general public. The Joint Committee still exists, providing hospital welfare services (such as Hospital Library Services) and care of war disabled, amongst other things.

Other better-known St John activities include providing First Aid cover wherever crowds gather—theatres, football matches, etc. They provide cliff rescue services and river patrols as well as hospital nursing auxiliaries. Emergency aid services in co-operation with the police, ambulance, and fire services mean that St John members have given aid at such public tragedies as the Moorgate tube (subway) disaster and the Hither Green rail crash. Their voluntary work fills a gap for which society has made no other provision.

The St John Cadets, founded in 1922 as a youth movement to train and interest young people in the medical, nursing, and ancillary professions, also participate in welfare work, such as visiting the elderly, and the supplying of medical comforts. The St John Ambulance Overseas Relations Department is headed by a director in charge of a secretariat that co-ordinates and channels information to and from the many countries world-wide in which St John Ambulance operates, on a local basis, under a local St John Council, or under the Priories or Commanderies. In Australia, for instance, St John provides many of the state ambulance services. The flag of St John can be seen in over 50 countries.

The St John Ambulance Association and Brigade were amalgamated in 1968 to form St John Ambulance. More recent developments include the St John Aero-Medical Service, which had its origins in the first St John air attendant service in 1922. Its members accompany patients in transit from all over the world. The St John Air Wing has voluntary pilots who carry medical supplies or organs for transplant to wherever they are needed.

St John Ophthalmic Hospital. In 1882 the British Order of St John founded an eye hospital in Jerusalem, on the Old Bethlehem Road. Despite the historical vagaries of the area, the hospital, which is in the Sheik Jarrah district of Jerusalem, still continues its work of aiding those with eye disease, regardless of race, colour, or creed. Its work is supported by the other Orders of St John, especially the American Society of the Most Venerable Order, and other necessary external funding. Poor Arabs make up the majority of the patients, and the hospital provides training facilities for Arab nurses and orderlies. Doctors and surgeons are usually British or American, on short-term contracts. The hospital is run by the Warden and Matron under the direction of the Hospitaller. In conjunction with the Institute of Ophthalmology, London, the hospital is playing an important part in finding a cure for *trachoma. It also has an 'outreach' programme to tackle eye problems in outlying areas, and a 'sight' project that advises on and distributes preventive medicine packs and finds those in need of treatment.

The long tradition of caring for the sick established by the Knights Hospitaller continues today in the work of the Orders of St John.

PAMELA WILLIS

Further reading
Cassar, P. (1964). *A Medical History of Malta.* London.
Hume, E. (1940). *Medical Work of the Knights Hospitallers of St. John of Jerusalem.* Baltimore.
King, Sir E., and Luke, Sir H. (1967). *The Knights of St. John in the British Realm.* London.
Riley-Smith, J. (1967). *The Knights of St. John in Jerusalem and Cyprus 1050–1310.* London.
Schermerhorn, E. (1929). *Malta of the Knights.* London.
Seward, D. (1972). *The Monks of War.* London.

ST MARY'S HOSPITAL, London, is in the Paddington district of the metropolis. After being mooted from 1841, the building began in 1846, and five years later the hospital was opened for 50 in-patients. Two years later came the medical school as part of the University of London. Like so many similar institutions there has been much expansion and development over the years in both hospital and school. There was originally a board of governors, but now the various hospitals of the group are administered under the *National Health Service. Now in the group are Paddington Green Children's Hospital, Princess Louise Hospital for Children, St Luke's Hospital, Bayswater (terminal care), The Samaritan Hospital for Women (gynaecology), and the Western Ophthalmic Hospital. The school and the hospitals have a distinguished record of service, teaching, and research. It was in the microbiological laboratory that Alexander *Fleming discovered *penicillin in 1928. The tradition of investigation of infections had long been established, mainly by Almroth *Wright, who was appointed in 1902, and who introduced *vaccine therapy for many diseases. A. D. *Waller of the physiology department played a major part in the development of *electrocardiography. Lord Moran (see WILSON, CHARLES MCMORAN), Winston Churchill's physician, was at one time dean of the medical school.

ST THOMAS'S HOSPITAL, London, has one of the longest records of service to the sick of any institution in the world. Its origin has been placed in the Priory of St Mary the Virgin in about AD 1106. This was on the south bank of the Thames near the only bridge over the river from the City. Sick wayfarers were cared for by monks and nuns on their travels to London or southwards to Canterbury, where Thomas à Becket was murdered in the Cathedral and was canonized in 1173. His shrine became a place of pilgrimage and the hospital was named after him, remaining in close association with and part of the Priory. Richard (Dick) Whittington, Mayor of London, established a ward for unmarried mothers there (provided they would mend their ways!). Miles Coverdale printed the first full English translation of the Bible in the hospital precincts. The hospital fell on evil times and the monastic order was lax, and at the Dissolution of the Monasteries by Henry VIII it was virtually closed, but was restored by Edward VI in 1553. Since then its doors have never been closed.

Richard *Mead was appointed physician in 1703 and was contemporary with William *Cheselden, the surgeon. Thomas *Guy, the bookseller, was a governor and he built a hospital in the grounds of St Thomas's to take incurable and mental cases, at the suggestion of Mead, in 1721. Teaching of students took place from very early in the foundation, and John *Keats, the poet, is variously claimed as having studied first at St Thomas's and then *Guy's. Sir Astley *Cooper had established a fine anatomy school early in the 19th c. and students of both the hospitals were taught there and they attended the surgical operations now performed in each. But tensions were rising between them both, and when Guy's students were prevented from witnessing operations at St Thomas's unless they produced tickets, there was a riot which produced a total rift between the two hospitals. In 1847, during the Railway Age, schemes were afoot which meant that an extension of a railway would run through the site of St Thomas's, so it was compulsorily bought for £296 000 by the Charing Cross Railway, and a new position for the hospital had to be found. (The present London Bridge railway station is approximately where the old hospital used to be.) Temporary premises were found in Kennington's Surrey Gardens which had been a zoo, while the present site, opposite the Houses of Parliament, was being built on for the new hospital. This prime position was obtained for £100 000 through the

good offices of Sidney *Herbert, a member of the government of the day, under pressure from Florence *Nightingale, who wanted a place for her proposed school of nursing, which she thought was essential after her experiences in the Crimean War. The school was founded, revolutionizing concepts of nursing, ultimately throughout the world as a result of its pupils being in demand and disseminating the tradition everywhere.

During the Second World War the hospital suffered severe damage from enemy bombing, and though a few members of staff were killed no patients were. For much of the war many in-patient wards were evacuated to the country, though out-patient work continued in London, and there were emergency operations for casualties. In 1948 the *National Health Service took over the hospital. By the 1970s several local hospitals had become incorporated into St Thomas's and it was rebuilt on its site near Westminster Bridge. An interesting reversion of history is that the medical schools of Guy's and St Thomas's have combined once more to face the 1980s and beyond.

ST VITUS'S DANCE is Sydenham's *chorea (rheumatic encephalopathy), from the reputed power of St Vitus over nervous and hysterical afflictions.

SALBUTAMOL, known in the US as albuterol, is a selective beta$_2$–adrenergic stimulant of value as a *bronchodilator in bronchial *asthma and states of reversible airways obstruction. It is preferably administered by inhalation (of an *aerosol solution or in powder form) but is also effective by oral and parenteral routes.

SALERNO, on the west coast of Italy, just south of Naples, is famous in medical history for housing the first medical school of real pretensions in Europe, flourishing in the 11th and 12th c. It would be pleasing to think that it was here that Arabic medicine met the Christian medicine of the Benedictines of nearby Monte Cassino, but there is no firm evidence on this point. But it is certain that southern Italy and especially Sicily were much influenced both by Greek and Islamic cultures, as they moved along the Mediterranean. Several medical books were published from Salerno, and of especial interest is that there were female physicians and students. The practice of medicine came under the jurisdiction of the Emperor Frederick II, who in 1221 decreed that doctors would have to pass examinations set by the masters in Salerno. Moreover, no one was allowed to start an education in medicine until the age of 21, the prior three years being spent in the study of logic, and what is more the medical course lasted five years. This sort of pattern has therefore persisted for about 800 years.

There is a famous poem, *Regimen Sanitatis Salernitanum,* with editions varying from several hundred to a few thousand verses. It is literally a regimen of health and has references to healthy living, diet, liquor, sleep, and remedies of many kinds, including surgical. Castiglioni (a medical historian) thought it 'the backbone of all practical medical literature up to the time of the Renaissance'.

SALICETTI, GUILIELMO (Guilelimus di Saliceto) (*c.* 1210–77). Italian surgeon. Salicetti was professor of surgery in *Bologna (*c.* 1268); he moved to Verona in 1276. He was the leading Italian surgeon of the 13th c. and his *Cyrurgia*, which he completed in 1275 (first printed 1476), was a widely consulted textbook for many years. He reintroduced the knife in place of the *cautery favoured by the Arabs and regarded suppuration, inevitable after use of the cautery, as undesirable. He recorded *crepitus as a sign of fracture, distinguished between arterial and venous bleeding, noted contralateral paralysis in skull wounds, and appreciated the venereal origin of *chancres and *bubos.

SALICYLATE. Any salt of salicylic acid: the many preparations of aspirin (*acetylsalicylic acid) are examples.

SALINE. A solution of salt (sodium chloride: NaCl). Saline containing 0.9 g NaCl per 100 ml has the same *electrolyte strength as blood and is referred to as normal, physiological, or isotonic saline.

SALIVA is the fluid secreted by the parotid, submaxillary, and sublingual salivary glands. As well as assisting mastication by moistening the mouth, saliva contains an *enzyme, ptyalin, which initiates the process of *digestion by hydrolysing starch to maltose.

SALIVARY GLANDS. The three main pairs of glands which, together with a number of small accessory glands, are responsible for the secretion of *saliva; they are the *parotid, sublingual, and submandibular glands.

SALK VACCINE is inactivated *poliomyelitis vaccine, administered by injection.

SALMON, DANIEL ELMER (1850–1914). American veterinary pathologist, DVS Cornell University (1872), DVM (1876). Born in Mount Olive, New Jersey, for most of his career he lived in Washington, DC, and worked for the US Department of Agriculture, first (1879–84) as investigator, later (1884–1906) as chief of the Bureau of Animal Industry. He then became director of the National Veterinary School in Montevideo, where he remained for six years (1906–12). He died two years later, at the age of 64. Salmon is chiefly remembered because of the bacteria (*Salmonella*) which bear his name, but among his other scientific contributions was the discovery (in 1886 with Theobald *Smith) that bacteria could produce protective *immunity despite having been killed by heat.

SALMONELLA is a genus of *bacteria comprising many different species responsible for a variety of diseases in man and animals, including *typhoid and *paratyphoid fever and certain types of food poisoning. *Salmonella* (named after the American pathologist Daniel Elmer *Salmon) are rod-shaped, gram-negative bacilli which are distinguished from other enteric bacilli by their inability to ferment lactose.

SALPÊTRIÈRE (Hospice de la Vieillesse (femmes)) was founded in Paris by royal decree in 1656. The king gave the grounds and some buildings where there had been a small arsenal, and where saltpetre had been made. Cardinal Mazarin was also involved with the early years. The intention was to lodge women and children in need, and at first there were 628 women and 192 children aged from two to five years supervised by 27 male and female officers. By 1684 a special quarter for debauched women and prostitutes was established. They had to be kept separate for fear of corrupting other inmates. The rule for them and for women put there by parents and husbands was harsh, with a sparse diet, rough clothing, and rough sleeping in the cold. Women criminals were also sent there, and at their trials they paled when the populace shouted that they should go 'à l'hôpital'. In 1780 letters patent were issued which forbade the inmates of Salpêtrière being taken, when ill, into the Hôtel-Dieu, so an infirmary was built in the grounds. Eight years later, however, things had not improved. The institution had 8000 women inside and they slept four or five to a bed, and one observer felt that it would be better to let them perish than to keep them alive in such deprivation and squalor. Some of those who were mad were chained.

Matters improved when the Salpêtrière came under the control of a council for the hospitals of Paris; 4000 of the prostitutes, criminals, and children were discharged elsewhere, and the mortality dropped to one-quarter of its previous figure. The treatment of the mentally ill became renowned throughout Europe and attracted many students. Jean-Martin *Charcot was physician there from 1862. The original humanitarian purpose of caring for ageing indigent women also continued. Further evolution has made the place one of the most famous hospitals of Paris, and indeed in the world. Today the Salpêtrière functions as a major teaching hospital in which all major specialties are represented and many new buildings function alongside the old.

SALPINGITIS is inflammation of the *Fallopian (uterine) tube.

SALT is a compound formed when the hydrogen of

an acid is replaced by a metal. A salt is produced by the reaction of an acid with a base, water being formed at the same time. In common use the word salt refers to the compound sodium chloride (NaCl).

SALT DEPRIVATION. A condition of salt deprivation arises when too much salt (sodium chloride) is lost from the body, as in heavy sweating and in certain pathological conditions. Salt deprivation is common after exertion in a hot environment, causing weariness, prostration, and painful muscular cramps ('stoker's cramp'). It may be prevented by the use of salt tablets.

SALVARSAN is an *arsenic-containing organic compound, also known as arsphenamine, formerly used in the treatment of *syphilis.

SAL VOLATILE is ammonium carbonate or smelling salts, a traditional remedy for faintness.

SANATORIUM. An establishment for the reception and treatment of invalids, particularly those suffering from *tuberculosis. Since the advent of antituberculous chemotherapy obviated the need for special hospitals in which to treat tuberculosis, the word has largely fallen into disuse. It is still occasionally used in respect of convalescent homes and private hospitals for the treatment of, for example, *alcoholism.

SANDFLY is the name commonly applied to various species of the genus *Phlebotomus,* small biting dipterous flies common in tropical and subtropical countries. Female sandflies are responsible for the transmission of *kala-azar and other forms of *leishmaniasis, a South American bacterial infection called *Oroya fever (bartonellosis), and sandfly fever.

Sandfly (or pappataci) fever is an acute self-limiting febrile illness without any obvious diagnostic features and is difficult initially to distinguish from other causes of fever such as influenza, malaria, etc. It lasts, however, only 3–4 days, and requires no more than symptomatic treatment. It is caused by a group of viruses transmitted by the female *Phlebotomus papatasii.* The sandfly becomes infected by biting a patient with the acute illness, and remains infective for the rest of its life. There is no animal reservoir and maintenance of the virus is thought to be due to transovarial transmission within the sandfly population.

SANDFLY FEVER. See SANDFLY.

SANGER, MARGARET (1883–1966). American feminist leader, and world figure in the *birth control movement. As a nurse in a poor district of New York City Margaret Sanger became concerned about the problems of uncontrolled fertility in conditions of poverty. She became a leader in feminist causes, especially in education about methods of birth control. She established birth control clinics in the New York area, and was prosecuted for violations of the law and spent one 30-day term in gaol. Nevertheless she persisted, and founded the American Birth Control League in 1921; this later became part of a larger organization, the Planned Parenthood Federation of America. She wrote and published several books on birth control.

SANITARY INSPECTOR. A professional officer concerned with environmental sanitation and responsible for sanitary inspection. The designation of this officer varies widely from country to country, for example health inspector, public health officer, environmental health officer, etc. The term 'sanitarian' is sometimes used to cover all types of sanitary inspection personnel.

SANITATION. The establishment and maintenance of conditions favourable to health, particularly with respect to the provision of toilet facilities, drainage, and the disposal of sewage.

SANTORINI, GIOVANNI DOMENICO (1681–1737). Italian anatomist and physician, MD Pisa (1701). Santorini practised and demonstrated anatomy in Venice, where he was physician to the Spedaletto from 1706 to 1728. One of the outstanding anatomists of his time, his name is attached to some ten anatomical structures. He published *Observationes anatomicae* (1724).

SANTORIO, SANTORIO (Sanctorius) (1561–1636). Italian physician and physiologist, MD Padua (1582). After 14 years' practice in Poland, Santorio moved to Venice in 1599 and 12 years later to Padua. Sanctorius was one of the architects of the iatrophysical school of medicine. His main interest was in *mensuration and he tried to make it a support for humoral pathology. He devised an 'air thermometer', a hygroscope, and a device which he called the 'pulsilogium' for indicating the pulse rate. He invented instruments for extracting *stones from the bladder and a *trocar and *cannula. However, he is best known for his observations, published in *De medica statica* (1614), on his own changes in weight due to 'insensible perspiration' resulting from such physiological activities as eating, sleeping, and digestion.

SAPPHISM. See LESBIANISM.

SARCOIDOSIS is a chronic disease of unknown cause marked by the development of granulomatous tissue in various parts of the *reticuloendothelial system. Pulmonary infiltration, enlargement of mediastinal *lymph nodes, and involvement of the skin and eye are the commonest presenting manifestations.

SARCOMA. A malignant *tumour arising from

bone, connective tissue, muscle (*sarco* denotes 'flesh'), and other tissues, the embryonic origin of which is the *mesoderm. Sarcomas are much less common than *carcinomas (which arise from epithelial tissue) but are often highly malignant. An appropriate prefix is attached to indicate the tissue of origin when this is known, for example osteosarcoma (bone), chondrosarcoma (cartilage), lymphosarcoma, fibrosarcoma, etc.

SARCOPLASM is the substance in which the fibrils making up a muscle fibre are embedded.

SATIRES, MEDICAL are common at all times. Some members of the medical profession can often be seen as pompous, over-inflated, wrong-headed, or even plain stupid, and may therefore be figures of fun and suitable for lampooning. Vignettes of doctors at their most crass abound in literature and drama from Chaucer onwards, and no doubt much before. Such satire may provide amusing entertainment, made even better if the establishment should rise to try to defend itself against the attack. But they may also show a general dissatisfaction with medical attitudes, at least among the educated, to which the profession may have to respond in the constant dialogue between medicine and the society and culture in which it is practised (see MEDIA). The response may be slow and uneven and almost unconscious in the whole body of the profession, yet satire is one of the ways in which attitudinal change and practice may be brought about, so making practitioners more adaptive to the needs and wishes of those whom the profession is meant to serve.

SATURNISM. *Lead poisoning.

SATYRIASIS is pathologically increased sexual activity in males, the equivalent of *nymphomania in women.

SAUCEROTTE, NICOLAS (1741–1814). French army surgeon. Saucerotte joined the army as a surgeon in 1760, becoming master-surgeon in 1762. In 1764 he served as surgeon to the army of the King of Poland and in 1794 became chief surgeon to the French Northern Army. He was a neurosurgeon of some skill and established experimentally the fact of contralateral innervation. He described *acromegaly in 1772.

SAUERBRUCH, ERNST FERDINAND (1875–1951). German surgeon, MD Leipzig. Sauerbruch was a pupil of von *Mikulicz, and afterwards he held chairs of surgery successively at Marburg (1908), Zurich (1911), Munich (1918), and Berlin (1927). The leading German surgeon of his time, he was a pioneer of thoracic surgery (see CARDIOTHORACIC SURGERY) and devised a positive pressure cabinet in which he operated. He greatly improved the technique of *thoracoplasty. Interested and concerned with the broader issues of medicine he constantly warned surgeons against becoming mere technicians.

SAVE THE CHILDREN FUND, THE, started in 1919 in the UK, and has a headquarters in London. Its aims are to secure the welfare of children, wherever that is threatened by natural disasters, hunger, poverty, and disease. It is entirely non-political, and charity is its only source of finance. Funds are raised by hundreds of branches and thousands of volunteers throughout the country. Now there are similar funds in many advanced countries of the world including the USA, Canada, Australia, Denmark, and Norway, and others exist in some parts of the developing world, all with similar aims. Expert teams of agronomists, engineers, educationists, doctors, nurses, and others work in the field in many places. Their tasks are to help directly but especially to educate local people to help themselves, with the hope that later the various enterprises can be handed over to local initiative. There are campaigns for maternal and child welfare, in nutrition, in education, and against poliomyelitis and other infectious diseases, particularly gastroenteritis. There are teams for emergency relief and for refugees. In the UK there are special centres for help with children and their problems in inner city areas where other services seem to be failing relatively, for instance in support of distressed families, in certain aspects of medical care, and with pre-school children.

SAXITOXIN is the neurotoxic *alkaloid secreted by dinoflagellates of the genus *Gonyaulax* and responsible for paralytic shellfish or gonyaulax poisoning. See RED TIDE.

SCABIES is infestation of the skin with the itch mite *Acarus scabiei*, also known as *Sarcoptes scabiei*. The condition, which causes intense itching, is contagious.

SCAN. The record produced by a *scanner, or the procedure of scanning.

SCANNERS are instruments which make pictorial records of particular events (such as radioactivity, X-rays, ultrasound, etc.) by measuring different areas in turn and producing an integrated picture of variations over a part of the body or an organ such as the liver or the thyroid gland. In common parlance, 'scanner' when otherwise unqualified is usually taken to mean 'CAT scanner', that is a machine for *computerized axial tomography, which reconstructs X-ray tomographic images. Thus 'head scanner' and 'body scanner'. See also RADIOLOGY; NUCLEAR MEDICINE.

SCAR. The new fibrous tissue that remains after an injury has healed.

SCARLATINA is a synonym for *scarlet fever.

SCARLET FEVER is a streptococcal infection, usually of the throat, with certain strains of group A haemolytic *streptococci which elaborate 'erythrogenic' toxins, with the result that the usual manifestations of acute *pharyngitis are accompanied by a generalized skin *rash. This consists of a diffuse *erythema with punctate papules of a darker colour, the skin around the mouth typically being spared (circumoral pallor). Also characteristic is the peeling or desquamation which follows fading of the rash.

SCARPA, ANTONIO (?1714–1832). Italian surgeon and anatomist, MD Padua (1770). Scarpa was a pupil of *Morgagni whose assistant he became in 1772. In 1783 he was appointed professor of anatomy at Modena moving to the chair at Pavia in 1787, which he occupied until 1815, teaching surgery as well as anatomy. He was a great descriptive anatomist and dissector, making full use of the microscope. Although best remembered for his description of the *femoral (Scarpa's) triangle, his work on the ear, the olfactory apparatus, and the cardiac nerves was more important. He was a brilliant anatomical draughtsman as shown by his *Tabulae neurologicae* (1794).

SCHAFER, SIR EDWARD ALBERT SHARPEY. See SHARPEY-SCHAFER, SIR EDWARD ALBERT.

SCHAUDINN, FRITZ RICHARD (1871–1906). German protozoologist. Schaudinn took his doctorate in zoology at Berlin in 1894 and most of his short life was spent in study of the *protozoa. He became director of the Kaiserliches Gesundheitsamt in 1904 and of the Institut für Schiffs- und Tropenhygiene in Hamburg in 1906. In 1902 he claimed to have seen a *malarial sporozoite entering a red blood cell. The following year he distinguished the pathogenic *Entamoeba histolytica* from the harmless *Escherichia coli* and in May 1905, together with Hoffmann, he discovered *Spirochaeta pallida,* now known as *Treponema pallidum,* the causative organism of *syphilis.

SCHIFF, MORITZ (1823–96). German physician and physiologist, MD Göttingen (1844). In 1845 he started practice in Frankfurt, engaging in physiological research in a laboratory in his house. In 1854 he became professor of comparative anatomy in Berne, moving to the chair of physiology in Florence in 1862. He was unable to obtain an appointment in Germany, possibly because he was Jewish, possibly because he had been a member of the medical revolutionary corps in 1848. In 1876 he was made professor of physiology in Geneva. Schiff's main investigations were into the nervous system and dealt with the pathways for sensations of pain and touch in the *spinal cord. In 1856 he showed that *thyroidectomy in dogs and guinea pigs was followed by death. He made unsuccessful attempts to graft *thyroid tissue.

SCHISMATIC MEDICAL COLLEGES. See NESTORIAN MEDICINE.

SCHISTOSOMIASIS is a synonym for *bilharziasis.

SCHIZOID is a term descriptive of a personality which is withdrawn and introspective, with marked dissociation between the emotions and the intellect; in other words, a personality resembling that of *schizophrenia, but within the bounds of normality.

SCHIZOPHRENIA is the commonest psychotic illness, accounting for some 80 per cent of patients under the age of 65 who have been in hospital for two years or more. The term 'schizophrenia' was introduced by *Bleuler in 1911, replacing an older name 'dementia praecox', in order to describe the apparent splitting of the mind which is characteristic of the condition, part remaining in touch with reality and part not. The manifestations are protean, the commonest being withdrawal, regression, infantilism, asocial or antisocial behaviour, aberrant ideas, delusions, and hallucinations. Several clinical types are recognized: simple, paranoid, catatonic, hebephrenic, and mixed. The onset is usually in adolescence or early adult life and the course is chronic, sometimes with remissions. Despite intensive research over many years, the aetiology and pathogenesis of schizophrenia are still not understood. It is certain, however, that there is a strong genetic component.

SCHLEIDEN, JACOB MATTHIAS (1804–86). German physician and botanist, MD Berlin (1834). Schleiden never practised medicine, but held the chairs of botany successively at Jena, Frankfurt, and Dorpat. He was a popularizer of science and his textbook *Grundzüge der wissenschaftlichen Botanik* (1842) had great influence. He showed that plant tissues were made of groups of cells and he realized the importance of the nucleus, although he thought that it gave rise to young cells. Discussions with Schleiden inspired his friend, Theodor *Schwann, to formulate the 'cell theory'.

SCHMIEDEBERG, OSWALD (1838–1921). German pharmacologist, MD Dorpat (1866). After a short spell at Dorpat in 1872, Schmiedeberg became professor of pharmacology at Strasbourg where he remained until retirement. One of the earliest and greatest of German pharmacologists, he had many distinguished pupils including J. J. *Abel and A. R. *Cushny. He showed the *vagus to contain accelerator fibres (1871); extracted *muscarine from *Amanita muscaria* (1869); carried out important studies on *digitalis (1883); and deduced the formula of *nucleic acid (1896).

SCHÖNLEIN, JOHANN LUCAS (1793–1864). German physician. MD Würzburg (1816). In 1817 Schönlein became *privat-docent* in pathological anatomy at Würzburg, advancing to professor of special pathology and director of the clinic in 1824. In 1833 he was appointed professor of medicine in Zurich and in 1840 to the chair in Berlin. Schönlein was the founder of the school that believed that medicine could be studied like botany or zoology and that diseases could be classified like plants and animals. He was an outstanding clinician, one of the first to make the use of *auscultation and *percussion a routine, and to exploit clinical pathology. He was the first to lecture in German (1840). He described *peliosis rheumatica (Schönlein's disease) in 1837 and discovered the causative organism of trichophytosis (*Achorion schönleinii*) in 1839.

SCHOOL DENTAL SERVICE. Part I, Section 5, of the *National Health Services Act 1977 lays upon the Secretary of State for Social Services the responsibility in England and Wales for providing at appropriate intervals for the dental inspection of pupils in attendance at schools maintained by local education authorities and for the dental treatment of such pupils. Under schedule I of the Act he may also do so for pupils at other educational establishments including those privately owned and maintained (in which case payment may be made for the services). Prior to the 1974 reorganization of the NHS, the school dental service (which had existed in some form since 1907) was the responsibility of local education authorities, a Principal School Dental Officer with a staff of school dental officers being responsible to the *Medical Officer of Health. These staff were transferred to health authorities under the *National Health Service (Reorganization) Act 1973.

SCHOOL MEDICAL SERVICE. Like the *school dental service, a school medical service existed in the UK from 1907. It is now the responsibility of the Secretary of State for Social Services, under the *National Health Service Act 1977, and delegated by him to local health authorities, who provide regular medical inspection and treatment of pupils in schools maintained by local education authorities. Prior to the 1974 NHS reorganization, this responsibility rested with local education authorities.

SCHWANN, THEODOR AMBROSE HUBERT (1810–82). German physiologist, MD Berlin (1834). Schwann was a pupil of Johannes *Müller and his early researches were into muscular activity and metabolism. He described *pepsin and the *neurilemma and gave some hint of the germ theory of disease. In 1837 he published his classic declaration of the *cell theory in a book of microscopical investigations into the similarities of the structure and growth of animals and plants. In this year he was appointed to the chair of anatomy in Louvain, moving to Liège in 1849. He abandoned rationalism to become a mystic and for 40 years made no worthwhile contribution to physiology.

SCHWANN CELLS are large nucleated cells responsible for the production of *myelin in peripheral nerve fibres.

SCHWEITZER, ALBERT (1875–1965). German-French philosopher, theologian, and physician, Ph.D. Strasbourg (1899), DD (1901), MD (1911). After appointment as principal of the theological faculty in Strasbourg, Schweitzer decided that his duty lay in the medical care of the sick poor in Africa and trained in medicine. He settled in Lambaréné, Gabon, French Equatorial Africa, in 1913, built a hospital with his own hands, and maintained it. He was interned briefly in 1914 as a German subject and he returned to Africa to work in his hospital in 1925. In 1952 he was awarded the *Nobel peace prize.

SCIATICA is pain in the distribution of the *sciatic nerve, that is radiating from the buttock down the back and outside of the thigh and lower leg. See PROLAPSED INTERVERTEBRAL DISC.

SCIATIC NERVE. The largest nerve in the body, derived via the sacral plexus from the 4th and 5th lumbar and the 1st, 2nd, and 3rd sacral segments of the *spinal cord. Through its two main divisions, the tibial and the common peroneal nerves, it supplies motor fibres to the posterior (flexor) thigh muscles and to all muscles below the knee; and sensory fibres to the posteriolateral aspects of the leg and all the foot except the medial border.

SCIENTOLOGY is a system of beliefs supposedly based on the study of knowledge, founded by L. R. Hubbard in 1951; the founder's own definition is 'an applied religious philosophy dealing with the study of knowledge, which, through the application of its technology can bring about desirable changes in the conditions of life'.

SCINTILLATION COUNTER. A device for measuring *ionizing radiation. The radiation energy is absorbed by a phosphor, a substance which is luminescent, that is after a brief storage period it releases the absorbed energy in the form of light; the flashes of light are then converted into electrical pulses by a photomultiplier, counted, and recorded.

SCLERA. The thick white outer coat which covers most of the eyeball, merging into the *cornea in front and the sheath of the *optic nerve behind.

SCLERITIS is inflammation of the *sclera.

SCLERODERMA. See SYSTEMIC SCLEROSIS, PROGRESSIVE.

SCLEROSIS. Literally hardening; it is applied to any pathological process of which hardening is a feature, for example *fibrosis. See also SYSTEMIC SCLEROSIS, PROGRESSIVE; MULTIPLE SCLEROSIS.

SCOLIOSIS is spinal deformity due to curvature in a lateral direction.

SCOPOLAMINE is the alternative name for *hyoscine.

SCORPIONS are venomous arachnids found in many tropical and subtropical parts of the world, envenomation by which can sometimes cause serious reactions and even occasionally death.

SCOTOMA is a blind spot in the visual field (see OPHTHALMOLOGY).

SCRAPIE is an *encephalopathy occurring in sheep and goats, one of the prototypes of 'slow' infection of the nervous system (the incubation or latent period is up to four years). It can be shown to be due to a transmissible agent, but a *virus has not been identified.

SCREEN. The device employed for visualizing *X-ray images in *radioscopy.

SCREENING is any procedure undertaken in order to detect presymptomatic disease in a population.

SCROFULA is *tuberculosis of the cervical *lymph nodes or skin (scrofuloderma).

SCROTUM. The pouch of skin, fascia, and smooth muscle which contains the *testes and their accessory structures, enabling them to be maintained at a slightly lower temperature than the core of the body.

SCURVY is the condition which results from a deficiency of vitamin C (*ascorbic acid) in the diet. It is now extremely rare except in groups at special risk, such as the isolated elderly and the mentally handicapped. The clinical manifestations of frank scurvy (as opposed to the non-specific symptoms ascribed to putative 'subclinical' states) include follicular *hyperkeratosis of the skin, perifollicular *petechial haemorrhages, ecchymoses (bruising), swollen gums which bleed easily, *subperiosteal haemorrhages (in children), *hypotension, and *anaemia. Ascorbic acid is widely available in most foods of vegetable origin.

SCUTARI (now Uskiidar) was the suburb of Constantinople (Istanbul) in which were situated the military hospitals serving the Crimean battlefields, and the scene of Florence *Nightingale's first and greatest achievement. The accommodation, for more than a thousand men, had not been secured until many months after the war had started and was in a parlous condition when Miss Nightingale, with 38 nurses, arrived on 4 November 1854. Of the main hospital, Lytton Strachey later wrote:

In these surroundings, those who had long been inured to scenes of human suffering—surgeons with a world-wide knowledge of agonies, soldiers familiar with scenes of carnage, missionaries with remembrances of famine and of plague—yet found a depth of horror which they had never known before. There were moments, there were places, in the Barrack Hospital at Scutari, where the strongest hand was struck with trembling, and the boldest eye would turn away its gaze. (*Eminent Victorians*, London, 1918).

The transformation brought about by Miss Nightingale during the following six months represents a landmark in British history, military, medical, social, and administrative.

SEAT-BELTS are restraining belts which buckle across the chest and/or waist of passengers in aircraft, motor vehicles, etc. and which are designed to prevent the body being propelled forward in the event of an impact. The wearing of seat-belts by those in the front seats of motor cars is required by law in the UK.

SEBACEOUS CYST. A swelling of the skin, often on the scalp, neck, or forehead, due to blockage of the *duct of a sebaceous gland and distension with sebaceous secretion. Sebaceous cysts, commonly called wens, are often unsightly, but are readily removed by minor surgery.

SEBACEOUS GLAND. Any of the small glands found in the dermis or true *skin in relation to hair follicles; they secrete *sebum, which lubricates the skin and keeps it supple.

SEBORRHOEA is excessive production of *sebum by the sebaceous glands of the dermis. See SKIN.

SEBORRHOEIC DERMATITIS is a skin disorder affecting particularly the scalp and the skin flexures occurring in individuals with a tendency to *seborrhoea. The lesions are red and irritable, and shed loose greasy scales.

SEBUM is the yellow, greasy, semi-solid secretion of the sebaceous glands which lie in the *dermis of the skin.

SECONDARY HEALTH CARE is health care at the level normally provided by the consultants and their departments of a general hospital, to which patients are referred when necessary by those responsible for *primary health care, that is general practitioners.

SECONDARY SEXUAL CHARACTERISTICS are the physical manifestations of sexual maturity which begin to appear at the age of *puberty. In the female the most obvious of these include: rounding of the body contours; development of the breasts (thelarche); and growth of axillary and pubic hair. In the male the most obvious signs are: lowering of the voice (due to laryngeal enlargement); growth of pubic and facial hair; enlargement of the external genitalia; and body growth spurt.

SECRETIN is a hormone secreted by glands in the wall of the *duodenum in response to an acid stimulus; secretin in turn stimulates the *pancreas to produce pancreatic juice which is high in volume and bicarbonate concentration.

SECTION means cutting, or cut segment; sometimes it is an abbreviation for *Caesarean section. Occasionally it is used in the UK as a slang abbreviation for the process of compulsory admission to hospital of a patient under a specific section of the *Mental Health Act.

SEDATIVE. Any agent which slows down mental and physical activity and has a calming, relaxing effect; not significantly different from the later designation *tranquillizer.

SEDGWICK, WILLIAM THOMPSON (1855–1921). American public health authority, Ph.B. Yale (1877), Ph.D. Johns Hopkins (1881). Sedgwick held faculty positions at the Massachusetts State Board of Health. He was one of the early advocates of pasteurization of milk, and of the addition of chlorine to drinking water. See also PUBLIC HEALTH IN THE USA.

SEIZURE. A seizure is any sudden attack of illness, such as a *fit or a *stroke.

SEMANTICS is the science of the relationship between language and meaning.

SEMEN is seed-fluid, the white viscous secretion of the male genital organs; it is composed chiefly of *spermatozoa produced by the *testes, with contributions from the accessory reproductive glands (prostate, seminal vesicles, etc.).

SEMICIRCULAR CANALS. The three looped bony canals of the *labyrinth of the ear which lie in different planes at right angles to each other, so that acceleration of the head in any direction must cause movement of the fluid in one or more of them, which can be detected by the fine sensory receptors they also contain; together with the otolith organ, they comprise the vestibular apparatus of the ear subserving the functions of posture and balance via the vestibular division of the VIIIth cranial (auditory) nerve. See also OTOLARYNGOLOGY.

SEMICOMA is *stupor, distinguished from *coma by the fact that the patient will respond to sufficiently vigorous stimuli.

SEMINAL VESICLE. The organ which stores sperm in the male. It is attached to the back of the *bladder and its duct joins the *vas deferens to form the ejaculatory duct.

SEMINOMA. A malignant *neoplasm of the *testis.

SEMIOLOGY is the study of symptoms and signs.

SEMMELWEISS, IGNAZ PHILIPP (1818–65). Hungarian obstetrician, MD Vienna (1844). In 1846 when working at the *Allgemeines Krankenhaus in Vienna, Semmelweiss noted that the maternal mortality in the ward attended by students was far higher than in that staffed by nurses. He suspected the difference was due to the students coming directly from the dissection room and infecting the parturient women they examined. When he enforced their thorough washing, the maternal mortality fell from 9.9 per cent to 1.3 per cent. His views were not acceptable to his superiors and he left Vienna for Budapest, where he became professor of obstetrics in 1855. In 1861 he set out his findings in *Die Aetiologie der Begriff, und die Prophylaxis des Kindbettfiebers*. It was badly received and in 1865 he suffered a mental breakdown and died, ironically from *septicaemia from a wound infection.

SEMON, SIR FELIX (1849–1921). Anglo-German laryngologist, MD Berlin (1873), FRCP (1885). After training in Germany, Semon came to London in 1874 and was appointed physician to the Throat Hospital in Golden Square in 1877. He became physician in charge of the throat department at *St Thomas's Hospital in 1882 and laryngologist to the *National Hospital for Nervous Diseases in 1888. He was naturalized in 1901 and became physician-extraordinary to Edward VII. He was knighted in 1897. Semon was a highly skilled operator and worked with *Horsley on the thyroid. He enunciated Semon's law: 'a destructive lesion of the motor nerve to the intrinsic laryngeal muscles causes abductor weakness before adductor weakness'. See also OTOLARYNGOLOGY.

SENILE DEMENTIA is an insidious and progressive *dementia occurring in old age and affecting some 10 per cent of persons over 80 years of age; the onset is usually some time in the early 70s. The first and almost invariable manifestation is loss of memory, particularly for recent events, names, and places. A decline in all mental faculties follows, with disintegration of personality and deterioration of habits. Paranoid and persecutory ideas are common, together with disorientation and confusion. Urinary and faecal *incontinence constitute an additional problem. Senile dementia is associated with demonstrable *cerebral atrophy and neuronal loss. The pathological process is not at present reversible; it is usually that of *Alzheimer's disease.

SENILITY. See AGEING; GERIATRIC MEDICINE; SENILE DEMENTIA.

SENIOR HOUSE OFFICER is the grade of UK hospital appointment normally filled when the first (pre-registration) year after medical qualification has been completed; it was formerly known as 'junior registrar'.

SENIOR REGISTRAR. See REGISTRAR.

SENIUM. The period of old age, marked by deteriorating mental and physical powers.

SENN, NICHOLAS (1844–1908). American surgeon, MD Chicago (1868). Born in Switzerland, Senn studied medicine at the Chicago Medical College (1864–8), and later studied at Munich. He took up the practice of surgery, first in Milwaukee, then in Chicago, where he held faculty positions in several medical schools. He wrote extensively on a wide range of general surgical topics, and was one of the first to employ *X-rays in assisting with surgical diagnosis.

SENSATION is the awareness of a physical experience, dependent upon stimulation of sense receptors and transmission of impulses to the sensorium of the brain. This definition excludes 'sensations' experienced in dreams and *hallucinatory states, which must be ascribed to cerebral activity occurring in the absence of the appropriate afferent impulses.

SENSE. Any of the faculties, or any combination of the faculties, by which perception takes place.

SENSITIVITY is the level of responsiveness to sensory or other stimuli.

SENSORIUM. The whole nervous system apparatus involved in sensation considered collectively; or that part of the brain concerned with sensation; or the brain itself.

SENSORY DEPRIVATION is the removal of the external stimuli to which the human organism is normally subjected.

SENSORY SYSTEM. That part of the *nervous system, peripheral and central, concerned with the reception and appreciation of sensory stimuli.

SEPSIS is the infection of blood or other tissues by pathogenic bacteria.

SEPTICAEMIA is the presence and multiplication of pathogenic micro-organisms in the bloodstream.

SEPTUM. An anatomical structure which serves as a dividing wall or partition.

SEPULCHRE. A tomb or burial place.

SERJEANT-SURGEON. The chief surgeon of the UK *Royal Medical Household.

SEROLOGY is the laboratory analysis and study of

*antibodies in the blood circulation, for which blood *serum is conveniently used as the sample.

SEROTONIN is a vasoactive amine and local *hormone also known as 5-hydroxytryptamine; it is widely distributed in the body, and is found in particularly high concentration in the intestinal mucosa, the *pineal gland, and the central nervous system. It seems to have several physiological roles: these include *haemostasis (it is released by platelets and acts as a powerful vasoconstrictor); inhibition of gastric secretion; and neurotransmission within the brain (either excitatory or inhibitory according to site). Serotonin is derived from the *amino acid tryptophan.

SERPENT. The use of a serpent as a medical emblem derives from *Aesculapius, who was classically depicted, cloaked but bare-breasted, holding a staff with a serpent coiled round it. This emblem is not to be confused with the two entwined serpents of the *caduceus, which have no particular medical relevance. The Aesculapian snake is a species of rat-snake, *Elaphe longissima,* native to south-east Europe and Asia Minor. The present isolated populations which exist in Germany and Switzerland are the descendants of specimens brought to health resorts in those countries by the Romans. In ancient Greece, the Aesculapian snake was venerated as a symbol of renewal and treated as sacred; specimens kept in temples were encouraged to lick the wounds of the injured and sick as a means of promoting healing.

SERTÜRNER, FRIEDRICH WILHELM ADAM (1783–1841). German pharmacologist. Sertürner isolated *morphine from opium in 1805 and published the fact in the *Journal of Pharmacology* of Leipzig, in 1806. The work was overlooked for a short period but in 1817 the chemist Gay-Lussac drew attention to it.

SERUM, when otherwise unqualified, is taken to mean blood serum, which is the clear slightly yellow fluid which separates from blood when it clots. In composition it resembles blood *plasma, but with the fibrinogen removed. Sera containing *antibodies and antitoxins against infections and toxins of various kinds (antisera) have been used extensively in the prevention or treatment of various diseases (such as *tetanus and *diphtheria).

SERUM SICKNESS is an immune reaction to injected foreign serum or serum protein characterized by fever, *urticaria, joint pains, oedema, and lymph node enlargement. See ALLERGY; ANAPHYLAXIS.

SERVETUS, MICHAEL (Miguel Serveto) (?1511–53). Spanish physician and theologian. Servetus studied medicine in Paris and although he is known to have practised in Charlieu and

Avignon, it is not certain that he graduated. He wrote many contentious theological works in which he opposed the doctrine of the Trinity. In one of them, *Restitutio christianismi* (1553), in order to explain the introduction of the divine spirit into the body, he suggested that blood passed through the lungs to the left ventricle and was then distributed to the arteries. He was denounced by Calvin to the authorities in Geneva and burned at the stake.

SESAMOID BONE. A bone embedded in a tendon or joint capsule; the *patella is an example.

SETON. A thread of silk or other material laid down in a wound in order to initiate a passage for drainage.

SEVENTH DAY ADVENTISTS are the adherents of the largest of the Adventist churches, who keep the seventh day of the week (Saturday) as the sabbath rather than the first. Like other adventists, they are messianists, that is they believe in a Second Coming and the fulfilment thereupon of millennial expectations derived from their interpretation of the Bible. Seventh Day Adventists eschew meat, alcohol, tobacco, and the non-medical use of drugs. The sect operates over 325 medical units throughout the world.

SEWAGE. Liquid domestic and industrial waste, including human and animal excreta.

SEWAGE DISPOSAL. Sewage is water with an organic and a small inorganic deposit. Its lethal effect on the plant and animal life of rivers is due to its very high biochemical oxygen demand. The aim of purification techniques is the elimination of this demand, that is the removal of oxidizable matter. In the middle of the last century, before purification methods were used, the River Thames was described as a main sewer, devoid of plant and animal life. Sewage may be discharged untreated over land and into the sea, though even here some form of purification is desirable. In England and Wales, the bulk of treated sewage is disposed of into rivers.

Public sewage is the responsibility of the regional water authorities, set up in the UK under the Water Act of 1973, who inherited the obligation from local authorities, that is district councils. The latter remain responsible for controlling drainage and private sewers from buildings and groups of buildings. Environmental health authorities are concerned with approving sanitary facilities and drainage of new buildings.

SEWAGE FARM. An establishment where sewage is treated by maximizing contact with air and so allowing oxidation to occur.

SEX. See SEXOLOGY, MEDICAL.

SEX CHANGE is a phrase used to denote the

simulation, usually by a combination of surgical and pharmacological methods, of the secondary and external sexual characteristics of the opposite sex in patients suffering from persistent paradoxical gender identification.

SEX LINKAGE. A characteristic is said to be sex-linked when the gene that produces it is carried on one of the two sex chromosomes. See GENETICS.

SEXOLOGIST. A specialist in the management of sexual disorders. See SEXOLOGY, MEDICAL.

SEXOLOGY, MEDICAL

In the beginning. What is regarded as science—or non-science—is often dictated by man's attitudes and beliefs. The best definition of science is knowledge acquired by study. In other words, a science implies trained skills. If we look for the roots of sexual knowledge they can be seen growing in the Near East, Egypt, and Europe, nourished by the soil of early civilization. The 4000 years that ended about AD 1000 were sexist times with men seeing themselves as superior in every way to women, who were regarded as mere chattels—born the property of their fathers and then given to their husbands. Although for a while in Greece women gained a sexual niche in their own right as educated and much sought-after prostitutes (the *hetairai*), when the Christian Church took a hand in erecting the basic foundations upon which the science of sexology was built, then ancient Hebrew custom was the only bricks and mortar. And so sex became, under the founding fathers, a synonym for sin and *homosexuality, an enemy of the state.

The facts show that, in Europe and the West generally, sexology evolved as the study of a largely suspect and disgraceful subject. The Romans towards the end of their influence referred to all diseases of the sexual parts as *morbus indecens*. Elsewhere in Asia and in the Arab world the only respectable aspect of sexology was concerned with active processes of promoting *fertility. In China and India, as among the Arabs, *polygamy was encouraged with this in mind. The idea of chivalrous love, and if not some sexual freedom at least a freedom from the idea of sexual sin, gradually evolved in the Middle Ages and slowly a basis of learning about sex became possible, as it was no longer a taboo subject, for the first time.

The expanding world that brought us into the 19th c. crystallized the concept of woman as the mother. The early fathers of sexology eventually persuaded scientists also to look upon her as a person rather than a pure, inviolate, virtuous, and sexless mother creature who would be only a shadow of true femininity. During the mid 19th c. when Queen Victoria was on the throne of the UK, an ambivalent and sexist public morality prevailed. It is difficult to be sure exactly how far private sexual behaviour was influenced by such public attitudes, but it was in this restricted climate that the science of medical sexology or sexual medicine evolved. At this time society still saw the whole of the sexual life as a struggle against temptation, and early sexologists concerned themselves with the effects of sexual worry, fear, and sexual exploitation. But slowly sex was seen as a suitable subject for scientific study and modern medical sexology was painfully born of confused and often rather neurotic parents.

Into the 20th century. It took until the beginning of the 20th c. for men of science to feel secure enough in a more enlightened environment to make a tentative start initiating and publishing the results of sex research. Understandably these early works very often reflected the background and psychology of the sexologists themselves. Havelock *Ellis, an Englishman, experienced a youth filled with sexual guilt and torment. Eventually after painfully gaining a medical degree he felt sure enough of himself to become launched into a monumental examination of sexual mores, activities and parapsychology that culminated in his *magnum opus*, *The Psychology of Sex*. Today Ellis's contribution to sexology appears anecdotal and repetitive and its advances bibliographical rather than clinical. As a doctor, Havelock Ellis was singularly unsuccessful. He never really practised medicine or indeed treated or saw any patients. His main contributions to sexology as a science were to give the first fairly accurate description of varieties of sexual activity and to take a step towards divorcing the instincts of sex from the forces of sin. He reported sex as human behaviour and his books are really sexual anthologies.

Not all early sexologists were as permissive as Ellis, however. Richard von *Krafft-Ebing is remembered mainly for his exhaustive research into the psychopathology of sexual deviance. He gave us much of the basic language of the scientific sexologist, giving us *sadism (after the infamous Marquis de *Sade) to describe sexual pleasure derived from inflicting pain on others. He also coined the word *masochism (after the poorly constructed novels of *Sacher-Masoch), a condition in which self-infliction of pain, either in fact or in fantasy, brings a form of sexual pleasure. Krafft-Ebing firmly condemned homosexuality as evil and *masturbation as abnormal, and believed it was productive of many serious sexual and medical problems. He expected his work to be viewed scientifically and to make sure that lay people could not understand many of his case histories he insisted that they were published in Latin in his famous book *Psychopathia sexualis*.

Elsewhere, his contemporaries gradually took a more humanistic approach towards the practice of the science of sexology. Magnus Hirschfeld was a good example of this welcome change. He was a genuinely sympathetic psychiatrist from Germany who became interested in the problems of sexuality and in the relationship between sexual taboos (and restriction) and the subsequent development of sexual problems. He founded the Institute of Sexual Science in Berlin, a body that was very active in sex research in the early years of the century. Hirschfeld displayed a humane attitude towards such currently 'outrageous' subjects as homosexuality and sexual deviance. More important, perhaps, he fostered an attitude which suggested that the medical management of sexual problems was a worthy cause for doctors to support. Thus he may be looked upon as the father of sexual medicine. Unfortunately the Institute of Sexual Science crumbled under the heel of Hitler's influence in Nazi Germany in the 1930s and his work is largely forgotten today.

If Magnus Hirschfeld was the father figure of medical sexology, Sigmund *Freud is remembered as its high priest. Of course he made the most momentous contributions to the *psychoanalytical study of sex and human sexuality. It is, perhaps, strange to remember that to subscribe to Freud's views as outlined in his classic booklet, the *Three Contributions to the Theory of Sex* was tantamount to being labelled a heretic at the time they were published and medical men were virtually boycotted who associated with this 'evil and wicked man with an obscene mind'. Ernest Jones, the English psychiatrist who admired and supported Freud in the UK, was actually forced to resign his hospital appointments for enquiring into the sexual lives of his patients.

Freud's theories and contributions to sexology as a science seem somewhat odd and almost irrelevant, however, in the light of modern knowledge. Freud, who argued his theories on human sexology from his observations of his small, middle-class, mainly female, Viennese clientele, believed that poor levels of sexual desire stemmed from inhibitions that were generated throughout the sexual maturation process. He believed that because women were subjected to greater repressive influences during their formative years they were more likely to suffer from sexual problems than men. Along with this line of thought, Freud postulated unresolved conflicts occurring in the developing personality that he described as oedipal (see OEDIPUS COMPLEX). Oedipus, it will be remembered, in classical mythology married his mother unwittingly, and when this was found out she hanged herself, although Oedipus continued to rule in Thebes. Freud believed that unacknowledged homosexual or incestuous desires subsequently brought about suppression of sexual energy (libido) and this led to an aversion to heterosexual sex. Although some psychiatrists still use Freudian theories in their management of sexual problems (psychoanalysis), the modern medical sexologist has moved further towards a scientific attitude to this type of problem-solving and usually enjoys a greater success than does psychoanalysis as a result.

The present day. Today's science of sexology

was founded on the work of many men and women whose attitudes were more closely influenced by facts and experimental scientific principles than by beliefs about what happens in the unconscious mind. One of the prime movers in this new type of scientific approach was Alfred Kinsey and his team (Pomeroy, Martin, and Gebhard) whose research was based on the case histories of over 12 000 men and women recruited from a wide range of social, religious, and ethnic groups. Kinsey, of course, was an American and his studies are only valid in their own context. He and his team were thorough, and involved their (volunteer) subjects in the answering of complicated and probing questionnaires, often lasting several hours. Critics have questioned the normality of his cohorts. Nevertheless Kinsey and his colleagues swept away a lot of the 'folklore' of sex. They were the first to reveal an extraordinary diversity of sexual experience within their study subjects and provided new yardsticks of 'normalcy' relative to many heterosexual and homosexual practices.

Many of the Kinsey group's studies evoked considerable outrage and criticism when they were published between the years 1948–53. The high rate of *orgasmic response reported by women through oral, manual, and self-stimulation challenged the popular belief that *coitus was the only natural form of sexual satisfaction and that all other practices were somewhat deviant. Kinsey also catalogued the true extent of extramarital sexual experience in his study group and his reports that 50 per cent of the men and 25 per cent of the women interviewed partook of such experience challenged, for many, the concept of monogamous marriage. Similarly, his data on the extent of masturbation and homosexual experience in both sexes helped 'legitimize' such sexual practices.

Perhaps the most serious criticism of the validity of Kinsey's work involves the selection of his study subjects (the views of those who do not wish to talk about their sexual lives cannot be collated). There is also a mechanistic, anthropological flavour to Kinsey's classifications and recording. He was by profession an entomologist and seemed more interested in collecting data than in understanding feelings. Perhaps this and his insistence on an overall rejection of any normal–abnormal dichotomy in the field of sex was his greatest weakness. Nevertheless, his trojan work encouraged the evolution of the professional sex therapist.

Such was the popularization of sex therapy, that the names of William Masters and Virginia Johnson became household words. William Masters had been interested in the physiology of sex as a medical student and after qualification and postgraduate work as a *gynaecologist became particularly involved in the evaluation of *hormone replacement therapy in ageing men and women. Before William Masters decided to devote a large proportion of his life to unravelling some of the tangles that made sexual physiology a problem to those who wanted to help patients in this field, he

must have pondered over the professional fate that had befallen other eminent men who had pioneered sex research. As it happened, sexual medicine and medical sexology had generally proved to be a cruel and dangerous discipline.

For example, Eugen Steinach, in the latter years of the 19th c., had begun to carve an enviable reputation for himself among the great medical and scientific personages who were establishing the basic truths of *bacteriology and medicine in continental Europe. He had confirmed and extended the original work carried out by John *Hunter in 1762 that proved the part that the *testes play relative to sexual behaviour. He also devised a fine series of experiments that demonstrated the effect that sexual isolation produced on animal behaviour, and was the first scientist to link olfactory sensation (smell) and sexual arousal. Eventually he became a research biochemist with the German company, Schering AG, where he laid the foundations for the development of reliable assays of the newly discovered sex hormones. Later Steinach moved more into the clinical field and was instrumental in introducing a surgical treatment for *impotence. For years his reputation rose on the crest of a heady wave of medical and paramedical enthusiasm until eventually it became increasingly obvious that Steinach's operation only succeeded through a *placebo effect. His scientific reputation never recovered from this blow.

If William Masters had turned the pages of medical history a little further back he would have found similar evidence of professional hara-kiri being enacted by a most distinguished neurophysiologist of his day and age, Charles Édouard *Brown-Séquard. Brown-Séquard was perhaps the first medical scientist to enjoy a truly international reputation. A neurologist, he had held important medical posts at *Harvard, the *National Hospital for Nervous Diseases, Queen Square, and the Collège de France. He was founder-editor of two of the most distinguished learned journals of his day and enjoyed a worldwide reputation. This, however, foundered on the rocks of medical sexology when Brown-Séquard announced that he had discovered a cure for impotence (his own impotence, as it happened). This cure proved to be a crude extract of guinea-pig testes. At first the press and public alike were wild with enthusiasm and Brown-Séquard's name was on everyone's lips. As might be expected, however, the bubble of enthusiasm soon burst when it became common knowledge that the exciting new treatment just did not work, and its proud and famous promoter lost his enviable reputation as a scientist overnight.

Just how much episodes of a similar nature that destroyed other scientific reputations contributed towards a sense of professional wariness and that disinclination to wander down sexological avenues which persists to this day, is a debatable point. Nevertheless, the facts do show that few medical scientists of repute are now drawn to a career in sexual medicine. As a predictable result the subject has been taken over to a large extent by the psychologist, the sex counsellor, and also, unfortunately, in parts of the world by that smart gentleman whose real speciality is the diagnosis of the size of his client's bank balance—the paramedical *quack. It is, therefore, easy to see why William Masters and his (non-medical) assistant moved very warily into the field of sexual medicine in the 1950s—and when they did start to publish their results they did it in a curiously coy and often almost incomprehensible way. Nevertheless, the behaviourist approach to the solution of sexual problems was born and its influence on the subject has been immense.

As the years have passed many modifications to the Masters and Johnson approach have been made. Clearly it can only function in its 'pure' form in the context of private medicine, and probably only with rather sophisticated and up-market social groups. Slowly, in the UK, the medical profession has interested itself in the subject and many *family planning clinics provide sex counselling services. Some general practitioners, psychiatrists, and genitourinary specialists also provide sexual problem-solving services as part of their everyday work, and a monthly journal, the *British Journal of Sexual Medicine*, caters for the very varied interests of all practitioners of medical sexology and enjoys a large local and overseas circulation. Very slowly, physicians, psychologists, and others are beginning to learn that an eclectic approach to the subject is important. Before striking a more practical note and examining the ways in which the exponent of sexual medicine makes his diagnosis and treats his patient, mention must be made of the Institute of Psychosexual Medicine and the man who did most towards improving standards in this field, Michael Balint.

Balint undoubtedly pioneered an individual and innovative type of seminar training for doctors, the object of which was to allow the physicians themselves to see and understand the doctor–patient relationship in an entirely new light. It concentrated the doctor's attention on his own, often unconscious, motives which could influence the ways in which he dealt with patients. It also allowed a new and helpful insight into the ways in which patients relate to, and sometimes manipulate, their doctors.

Eventually, a nucleus of doctors from the Family Planning Association and other physicians, many of whom had been Balint-trained, founded the Institute of Psychosexual Medicine. This body, in turn, started training counsellors in a specialized modification of the Balint seminars which concentrated upon solving the problems of, mainly, but not exclusively, female sexual dysfunctions. The method assumes possession of basic medical knowledge of sexual anatomy and physiology and the seminar group members work with material rather than abstract ideas. The group leaders observe how their trainees react to the problems discussed and use their expertise to suggest sensible methods of solving problems. Always, great stress is laid on the principle of identifying motives and fears that lie behind the presenting complaints of patients and an awareness of what is happening, psychologically, between the doctor and the patient. Due care is taken to try to pinpoint psychological 'blind spots', experienced by all clinicians, which can, unless effectively identified, lead to much time-wasting within the doctor–patient relationship. Trainee counsellors are helped to recognize the unconscious elements in patients' communications with the doctor they are encountering, and to become aware of the part that fantasy plays in sexual life. It is also emphasized that the treatment of *psychopathology and personality disorder are outside the aims of such counselling. Finally, this type of seminar training stresses the use of the physical examination of the patient as a therapeutic device.

Some principles of sexual medicine. *History-taking.* When tackling any problem, doctors always start by taking a careful history of the complaint. Indeed, Sir William *Osler's advice that the good doctor should listen to the patient because he or she is trying to tell him what the *diagnosis is, is very relevant in sexual medicine. Taking a sexual history is a particular skill that, to some extent, doctors must be taught as part of their training. Experienced practitioners soon learn how to put their patients at ease and present a non-judgemental attitude. Of course, the more a patient feels the doctor will 'accept' in the way of symptoms, then the franker he or she will be.

Before taking a sex history, most doctors find it best to define the goals of the treatment that will be carried out and so to draw up a simple 'contract' with the patient. It is explained that treatment will allow the sex partners to think and communicate in a way that they have not been used to before. This in turn will tend to bring about a definition of their attitudes, concepts, and ignorances as far as sexual behaviour is concerned. Usually this will oblige the partners to communicate with one another and it is usually pointed out that these objectives may be somewhat traumatic. Understandably, perhaps, some folk opt out of therapy at this point; this is often a good thing, for it saves everybody time.

All sexual history-taking must be conducted in an atmosphere in which it is accepted that explicit answers only are worth while. Sometimes a great deal of judgement is necessary to decide what sort of words to use. The experienced physician in this field realizes that sexual words are a bit like dynamite, and have to be handled very carefully if patients are to feel comfortable and at ease.

To give an idea of the rough format of one type of sexual history-taking, the format used by Masters and Johnson is fairly typical and usually involves exploring the following problems. Was the patient's childhood happy or not? The patient's parental relationships are then explored with particular reference to death, divorce, separation, house moving, school changes, etc. The religion of the family and its socioeconomic status are discussed and orthodoxy, if any, is assessed. The patient's parental feelings towards sexual subjects are explored and any memory of sex games, particularly those that ended traumatically, are noted. The history will also delve into the adolescent and teenage years. Was this a happy time or not? Questions designed to find out approximately when the patient first *menstruated and masturbated and had a sexually orientated attachment, are posed, and the existence of homosexual and heterosexual affairs are noted. Feelings about sex at this time are explored. The premarital adult life is examined and the pattern of sexual experience at this time is explored. For instance, were long or short involvements common and were contraceptives used? The extent to which behaviour was moulded by religious beliefs, or parental or other taboos is noted, and the female's reaction to menstrual difficulties and contraceptive techniques is ascertained. Finally the sexual pattern at marriage is looked into carefully and frankly.

The treatment of sexual problems. It is important to realize at the start that there is no really hard information on what 'normal', 'healthy', 'adequate', or 'inadequate' sexual behaviour is. Many physicians and therapists have adopted a patient-centred definition of sexual problems; thus a sexual problem exists when an individual expresses a complaint about one or more cognitive, affective, or behavioural elements (see PSYCHOLOGY) of his sexual functioning or sexual relationship. (In addition, behaviour that produces demonstrably harmful consequences for the perpetrator or for others would also be defined as a problem, even if the patient does not complain of it.) More recently, we have begun to recognize sexual problem areas that do *not* involve discernible impairment of physiological functioning but are primarily subjective states. *Psychosexual dysfunctions are perhaps best defined as '*psychosomatic disorders which make it impossible for the individual to have *or enjoy* sex'. And so these are the 'diseases' we may expect those who practise sexual medicine to treat.

Sexual dysfunctions are generally subdivided into primary, that is, conditions that have existed since the inception of sexual activity, and secondary, that is, conditions developing after a period of adequate sexual functioning. This distinction is important only because primary conditions appear to be initiated by events or factors in the individual's development, whereas secondary conditions appear to be initiated by more recent events.

Male sexual dysfunctions include premature *ejaculation (ejaculation occurring before intromission or earlier following intromission than is acceptable to the patient or his partner). Usually treatment is straightforward and effective although no standardized therapy has evolved.

It is less easy to cure erectile failure which is also called impotence (the inability to achieve or maintain an erection before or during intromission). It can be primary or secondary and a variety of possible physical and psychological aetiological factors exist. In most cases therapy is time-consuming with a problematical outcome.

Retarded ejaculation or complete absence of ejaculation is a rare condition that must be differentiated from reflux ejaculation in which the *semen enters the *bladder rather than leaving the *penis during *orgasm.

Female dysfunctions also include several important syndromes. Orgasmic dysfunction or an inability to achieve orgasm is subdivided into several categories in women. Primary orgasmic dysfunction generally refers to women who have seldom or never experienced orgasm through any form of stimulation. In secondary orgasmic dysfunction, women develop impairment of orgasm subsequent to a period of unimpaired functioning. But this term has also been applied to women who are able to experience orgasm through one form of stimulation (usually self-stimulation) but not through another (usually coitus). It is fashionable these days to describe 'pre-orgasmic' rather than 'non-orgasmic' groups of women, so confident are sex therapists that women will be able to become orgasmic through treatment. Thus the term pre-orgasmic dysfunction has gained wide currency in the USA and has recently been introduced into the UK.

Dyspareunia and vaginismus are common problems too. They may be psychologically based but in many cases the aetiology is wholly or partially organic. Dyspareunia is recurrent pain or discomfort during intercourse, rendering the act difficult or unpleasant for the woman. Vaginismus is defined as a spastic involuntary contraction of the muscles surrounding the introitus to the *vagina, sufficiently strong to inhibit intromission. It is generally regarded as a *conditioned avoidance reaction to intercourse.

Organic disease and its effect on sexual function needs at least a brief mention in both sexes, for today it is widely accepted that organic pathology is a major cause of sexual dysfunction. Unfortunately, the area of sexual impairment related to various disease states has received little intensive study; therefore, it is difficult to determine the sexual effects of any disease *per se* in individual cases. For example, a *diabetic may indeed develop *autonomic neuropathy causing organic impotence as a result of his or her disease; however, the diabetic patient may also be experiencing general debility and *depression. Furthermore, if someone has been told by medical authority or has learned from other patients that erectile failure is, for instance, a common sequel of their physical disease, such knowledge may further depress sexual function.

The sexual responses of all individuals who are otherwise healthy may of course be affected by transitory factors, such as fatigue, natural fluctuations in libido, or mood change related to the menstrual cycle. Alcohol or drugs, oral contraceptives and other contraceptive materials, and minor genitourinary afflictions and medications also affect the sexual response. The part that *iatrogenic factors play in the aetiology of sexual dysfunction in both sexes is clearly much more important than hitherto thought.

Treatment strategies. These are varied and include anxiety dispersal, the restructuring of behaviour, and an attempt to restructure people psychologically. (The latter, of course, can be quite a problem, both practically and ethically.) The first two tasks, however, cover most eventualities. Three assumptions commonly guide the more widely used strategies for treating individuals and couples with psychosomatic sexual dysfunctions: anxiety (usually sex performance anxiety) is reduced in order to disinhibit the sexual response; patients with sexual problems who are experiencing their current patterns of sexual attitudes and behaviour as unrewarding will usually benefit by a restructuring programme; and finally, when dysfunction is maintained by ineffectual interpersonal communication, this must be modified in order to reverse the dysfunction.

Various authorities have identified differing factors in sexually dysfunctional individuals, which they feel contribute in the most major way to dysfunction. Helen Kaplan, for instance, comments that a lack of agreement about the nature of the experiences affecting sexual functioning is very important and she suggests a model of treatment worked out around remote and immediate causes. Supporters of the method of Masters and Johnson view historico-psychological factors and recent or ongoing experience as major facilitators of sexual anxiety and believe that usually this anxiety is related to expectations of sexual performance.

A common strategy in treating couples, and the basis of all the Masters and Johnson methods, is to prescribe situations in which the 'demand' for sexual performance is reduced or eliminated. First of all, sensuous touching with no expectations that arousal will occur is prescribed, together with the forbidding of genital stimulation or coitus. In order to minimize anxiety, a hierarchical order of tasks is prescribed, beginning with one that is least likely to provoke anxiety and allowing patients to 'act easy' with such tasks before progressing towards those more likely to produce anxiety. Such therapists assume that the more frankly erotic exercises and those more closely approximating coitus are the most anxiety-provoking. In many instances this assumption may be valid, especially if coitus is viewed as a demand for performance or has been the point in sexual activity at which previous failures have occurred. However, the nature of the anxiety-provoking stimuli may vary greatly from one individual to another.

Patricia Gillan has pioneered an alternative type of treatment which concentrates on facilitating sexual arousal. An inability to masturbate may well show a degree of sexual inhibition and so the Gillan stimulation therapy is very much in line with that recommended by Lobitz and the Lo Piccolos in the USA, who train both men and women with orgasm problems to masturbate with the help of erotic material. Gillan also believes that an encouragement to masturbate is in itself therapeutic. Most men and women develop some sort of masturbatory pattern at some time during adolescence. But a few men, and rather more women, do not masturbate. The psychological reasons for this seem complex and some sex therapists believe that this is linked with general sexual dysfunctioning. This has led to a system of masturbation training being developed, a practice sometimes rather coyly referred to as self-focusing.

Teaching female masturbation to those who do not spontaneously partake of this form of sexual behaviour is often difficult and a high degree of confidence between the person (nearly always female) who is giving advice and the patient must be forged. Women who have never masturbated are often unfamiliar with their bodies and often have phobias about touching themselves or examining themselves. Often they insist on undressing in private, or in the dark, even with their sexual partner. It could be that the act of masturbation is not entirely necessary for success of the Gillan-type treatment. The women who improve on this therapy may do so simply because they become more happy about themselves as sexual beings.

Other methods have, of course, been used to treat psychosomatic sexual dysfunction. At the University of California's Human Sexuality Program in San Francisco a multidisciplinary approach is favoured. Couples are typically treated first by the assignment of graduated exercises in the manner of Masters and Johnson. At other points in their treatment, implosive or flooding techniques (which do not utilize graduated approaches) towards relearning sexual behaviours may be used. For example, couples may be involved in film viewings during which they are exposed simultaneously to several films, depicting themes presumably capable of eliciting high levels of either anxiety or sexual arousal. Few British physicians are happy with such practices.

Other therapists use anxiety-reduction methods based on extinction techniques rather than on the graduated counter-conditioning approaches. Reports have appeared suggesting that a reversal of orgasmic dysfunction in women through the use of implosion occurs. This technique involves flooding the client with anxiety-provoking stimuli in order to induce maximal levels of anxiety and thereby extinguish it. Implosion may involve symbolic or realistic themes. Other sex therapists have reported successful results in treating sexual dysfunctions by means of guided imagery, a technique in which anxiety is extinguished by having clients imagine a realistic anxiety-provoking scenario related to their problem.

To sum up this vast subject, the use of graduated sexual assignments in the manner of Masters and Johnson appears to be a comfortable type of sexual therapy in most patients. Even when such behavioural techniques are modified to fit into the setting of a National Health Service they are time-consuming. Other quicker methods of sex therapy are more potentially hazardous to the patient and therapist alike. The use of sexual surrogates involved in therapy is a case in point. In all probability there is no method that *always* provides for a cure in sexual medicine, although what might be read from time to time on the subject sometimes persuades patients to the contrary.

E. J. TRIMMER

Further reading

Annon, J. S. (1976). *Behavioural Treatment of Sexual Problems*. Honolulu.

Bancroft J. and Myerscough, P. (1983). *Human Sexuality and its Problems*. Edinburgh.

Brecher, E. M. (1969). *The Sex Researchers*. London.

Masters, W. H. and Johnson, V. E. (1979). *Homosexuality in Perspective*. Boston.

Money, J. (1980). *Love and Love Sickness*. Baltimore.

Seymour-Smith, M. (1975). *Sex and Society*. London.

Trimmer, E. (1978). *Basic Sexual Medicine*. London.

SEXUAL INTERCOURSE. Sexual union, involving penetration of the vagina by the penis and usually, but not necessarily, seminal emission.

SEXUAL OFFENCES ACTS 1956, 1967, 1976. The UK Sexual Offences Act 1956 was amended by the Sexual Offences Act (Amendment) 1976. Among the provisions of the statutes, the following may be noted. In rape or unlawful carnal knowledge, the offence is committed by penetration only without emission, even when penetration is slight; consent is no defence when intercourse is unlawful. Rape is defined as intercourse with a woman who does not at the time consent to it, by a man who knows she does not or who is reckless as to whether she does; a husband separated from his wife under a separation order or agreement may be guilty of rape if he has intercourse with her without her consent. In rape, the anonymity of the complainant is preserved and other restrictions are placed on evidence. Other sexual offences include: intercourse after facilitation by the administration of drugs; intercourse with a girl under 13, or between 13 and 16; intercourse with an idiot, imbecile, or defective (these terms are now defunct and would be covered by 'severe subnormality'); incest; and the general offence of indecent assault.

The Sexual Offences Act 1967 concerned *homosexual practices, removing the prohibition on these provided they take place in private and between consenting adults.

Prior to these several enactments, to which should be added the Indecency with Children Act 1960, the misdemeanours they concern were offences under the Common Law and under the Offences Against the Person Act of 1861. It should be noted that an assault with intent to commit rape is still often prosecuted under the 1861 Act.

SHARPEY-SCHAFER, SIR EDWARD ALBERT (1850–1935). British physiologist, MB London (1871), FRS (1878). Sharpey-Schafer was associated with William Sharpey whose name he added to his own in recognition of his indebtedness. In 1874 he became assistant professor of physiology at University College, London, and in 1888 Jodrell professor. In 1899 he was appointed to the chair in Edinburgh. He was knighted in 1913. Sharpey-Schafer was a man of powerful personality who carried out important work on *cerebral localization and devised a method of *artificial respiration (Schafer's prone pressure method).

SHATTUCK, LEMUEL (1793–1859). See PUBLIC HEALTH IN THE USA.

SHEATH is an anatomical term denoting an enveloping tubular structure; it is also commonly used as a synonym for *condom, to mean an occlusive latex rubber cover for the penis worn during sexual intercourse to prevent conception and incidentally to provide some protection against sexually transmitted diseases. High reliability and ready availability in many parts of the world are its chief merits as a *contraceptive.

SHELLFISH POISONING. Shellfish are particularly liable to be the agents of bacterial *food poisoning (e.g. *Salmonella, Shigella*), since their breeding grounds may be contaminated by sewage and they filter large quantities of water. Another type of shellfish poisoning, in which muscular paralysis may follow ingestion of neurotoxic material, is due to dinoflagellates (see RED TIDE). It should also be remembered that in certain individuals shellfish can cause a severe *allergic reaction.

SHELL-SHOCK was a term used during the First World War to describe psychiatric disturbances developed by some soldiers in reaction to battle conditions, a form of war *neurosis, or battle exhaustion.

SHERRINGTON, SIR CHARLES SCOTT (1857–1952). British neurophysiologist. MD Cambridge (1892), FRCP (1912), FRS (1893). Sherrington was elected to a fellowship of Caius College, Cambridge, in 1887 and in 1891 became professor-superintendent of the Brown Institution. In 1895 he was appointed Holt professor of physiology in Liverpool and in 1913 Wayneflete professor at Oxford. He was president of the Royal Society from 1920 to 1925 and president of the British Association in 1922. In 1932, jointly with Lord *Adrian, he was awarded the Nobel prize in physiology for his work on the nervous system, and received the Order of Merit in 1924. After a few years as a pathologist, Sherrington turned to physiology, particularly of the nervous system. His researches over a period of 50 years explained *reflex action and laid the foundation of our present knowledge of *neurophysiology. They were embodied in his book *The Integrative Action of the Nervous System* (1906).

SHIFTING DULLNESS. Impaired resonance on *percussion of the abdominal flanks, the line of demarcation of which shifts when the patient is rolled to one side. This physical sign indicates the presence of fluid in the peritoneal cavity (*ascites).

SHIGA, KIYOSHI (1870–1957). Japanese microbiologist, MD Tokyo (1896). After graduation Shiga became an assistant to *Kitasato. From 1901–3 he worked with *Ehrlich, returning to take charge of a department of the Kitasato Institute. In 1919 he was made professor at Keijo, Chosan. He carried out valuable work on *plague and *tetanus but his name was made by isolating the *dysentery bacillus now known as *Shigella*.

SHIGELLA is a genus of gram-negative *bacilli responsible for bacillary *dysentery.

SHINGLES. See HERPES ZOSTER.

SHIVERING is a physiological method of heat production by means of involuntary muscle contractions. See also RIGOR.

SHOCK. The medical connotation of 'shock' is acute circulatory failure from whatever cause (e.g. blood loss, fluid loss, trauma, sepsis, myocardial infarction, cardiac arrhythmias, pulmonary embolism, pericardial effusion, burns, anaphylaxis, etc.). The common denominator is a fall in arterial blood pressure to 90 mmHg or less. The rest of the clinical picture varies with the precipitating cause, but characteristically includes the signs of generalized peripheral vasoconstriction, with cold clammy skin, pallor, peripheral cyanosis, rapid thready pulse, oliguria, hyperventilation, and mental confusion. It is important to distinguish this meaning from the loose use of the term to mean any sudden mental or emotional disturbance.

SHOPE, RICHARD EDWIN (1901–66). American virologist, MD University of Iowa (1924). Shope began his career in research at the Princeton branch of the *Rockefeller Institute, moving to the New York branch in 1949. His chief field of study was viral diseases of animals. He showed that influenza of swine is a complex infection caused by a filterable *virus and the bacterium *Haemophilus influenzae*. That virus was later shown to be related to some strains of human influenza virus, and there was serological evidence that it was related to, perhaps even identical with, the virus responsible for the world pandemic of influenza in 1918–19. In

the early 1930s he discovered that certain natural *tumours of wild rabbits, a fibroma and a papilloma, were caused by filterable viruses; these were later shown to be related to the fatal disease of rabbits, *myxomatosis. This work was later pursued by Peyton *Rous, who used it to add substance to the growing body of evidence that some animal and human tumours have their origin in viral infections. During the Second World War Shope headed a team which developed an effective *vaccine against a highly contagious disease of cattle: *rinderpest.

SHORT-SIGHTEDNESS. See MYOPIA; OPHTHAL-MOLOGY.

SHUNT. A short-circuit or bypass, usually between blood vessels, whereby blood flows from that with the higher intravascular pressure to that with the lower. A shunt may be physiological or pathological (congenital, acquired, or surgically induced).

SIALOGRAM. An X-ray picture of the *salivary ducts produced by injection of radio-opaque material into them.

SIAMESE TWINS are a developmental anomaly of monozygotic *twins in which there is a varying degree of fusion of the two bodies; they are also known as conjoined twins.

SIBBALD, SIR ROBERT (1641–1722). British physician and antiquary, MD Leiden (1660), MD Angers (1662), FRCP (1686). Sibbald practised in Edinburgh, founding the Botanical Gardens at Holyrood in 1667. In 1680 he obtained a Royal Charter to found the Royal College of Physicians of Edinburgh of which he was president in 1684. He was the first professor of medicine in Edinburgh (1665). He was knighted in 1682 and became physician to Charles II and later to James II as well as Geographer of Scotland.

SIBILUS. A *rhonchus of whistling character.

SIBLING (or sib). Brother, sister, or litter-mate.

SICK-ABSENCE is absence from employment due to illness. In the UK, sickness benefit can be claimed for medically certificated sick-absence under the state national insurance scheme by Class 1 (employed) and Class 2 (self-employed) contributors. Sickness benefit is paid for up to 28 weeks only, after which it is replaced by invalidity benefit.

SICKLE CELL DISEASE is a lifelong disorder due to an inherited abnormality of the *haemoglobin molecule, characterized by chronic *haemolytic anaemia, a sickle-shaped deformity of red blood cells, and intermittent 'vaso-occlusive crises' due to aggregations of sickled *erythrocytes blocking vessels and causing *infarction in various tissues and organs of the body. The disease is fully expressed only in the *homozygous state, that is when the abnormal gene has been inherited from both parents. The very high gene frequency in certain parts of the world, notably across the middle third of Africa and in populations elsewhere deriving from that area, is explained by the fact that the *heterozygous state (one abnormal gene only) confers some protection against the effects of falciparum *malaria in early life. The term 'sickle cell trait' is used to distinguish the relatively asymptomatic heterozygous state from homozygous sickle cell disease.

SICKNESS. Illness.

SIDE-EFFECTS are the unwanted pharmacological consequences of drug administration, which may be minor (e.g. dryness of the mouth, slight constipation) and considered acceptable in the light of the therapeutic value of the drug, or which may because of discomfort or danger require the drug to be withdrawn.

SIDS. See SUDDEN INFANT DEATH SYNDROME.

SIGMOIDOSCOPY is inspection of the interior of the pelvic *colon by means of an *endoscope.

SIGN. A manifestation of disease perceptible to an observer, as opposed to symptom, which is a manifestation of disease perceived by the patient himself.

SILICOSIS is a serious form of *pneumoconiosis due to inhalation of particles of silica (crystalline silicon dioxide), characterized by extensive damage to lung tissue.

SIMON, SIR JOHN (1816–1904). British pathologist and sanitary reformer, MRCS (1838), FRCS (1844), FRS (1845). In 1840 Simon became assistant surgeon to *King's College Hospital, advancing to lecturer in pathology and later to surgeon to *St Thomas's Hospital. In 1848 he was appointed the first *Medical Officer of Health to the City of London, and was successively Medical Officer to the *General Board of Health (1855), to the *Privy Council (1858) and finally the first Chief Medical Officer to the *Local Government Board (1871). His reports on the state of sanitation, the water supply, *vaccination, and *cholera had an immense influence on the public health of the nation. He was created Companion and then Knight Commander of the Order of the Bath in 1876 and 1887 respectively. He was acting president of the Royal College of Surgeons of England in 1878–9.

SIMON, THÉODORE (1873–1961). French psychologist, MD Paris (1900). With Alfred *Binet he introduced graded tests for patients with mental retardation, relating mental age to growth and chronological age. See PSYCHOLOGY.

SIMPSON, SIR JAMES YOUNG, BT (1811–70). British obstetrician, MD Edinburgh (1832). Simpson was appointed professor of midwifery in Edinburgh in 1839 when only 28. He introduced *chloroform as an anaesthetic in 1847, inhaling it experimentally with his assistants Matthews *Duncan and George Keith. In the same year he was made physician to the Queen in Scotland. He received a baronetcy in 1866. Simpson was the leading obstetrician of his day and one of the founders of *gynaecology. He invented the *uterine sound. In his later years he became a keen archaeologist.

SIMS, JAMES MARION (1813–83). American gynaecologist, MD Jefferson Medical College (1835). Sims practised medicine in Alabama, gaining attention by surgical skill in treatment of *vesicovaginal fistula. He devised the duckbill vaginal *speculum, and demonstrated usefulness of the 'Sims position' for vaginal examinations: patient on left side, with right thigh drawn up.

SINGER'S NODES are small white nodules which develop on the *vocal cords of those who are required to use their voices excessively.

SINISTRAL means left-handed, or on the left side of the body.

SINOATRIAL NODE. The normal cardiac *pacemaker, also known as the sinus node. It is a collection of specialized myocardial cells situated high up in the wall of the right atrium, near the opening of the superior vena cava. The sinoatrial node has a higher inherent rhythmicity than any other part of the myocardium and it therefore initiates the wave of excitation which produces each contraction of the heart.

SINUS, in the anatomical sense, is a term which is applied to a variety of channels or cavities (e.g. the *paranasal sinuses); in the pathological sense, sinus denotes a blind channel opening (and usually discharging pus) on to the surface of the body.

SINUS ARRHYTHMIA is a physiological waxing and waning of heart rate due to respiratory variation in vagal (parasympathetic) tone: the pulse quickens with inspiration and slows with expiration. This influence of breathing on heart rate is quite normal, but tends to be more marked at the extremes of age.

SINUSITIS is inflammation of one or more of the *paranasal sinuses.

SINUS NODE. See SINOATRIAL NODE.

SINUS THROMBOSIS is *thrombosis of a venous

sinus, particularly of one of the large intracranial venous sinuses of the *dura mater. Any of the latter may be involved, but most notable are cavernous, lateral and superior sagittal sinus thromboses. Before *antibiotics, septic *thrombophlebitis was a relatively common cause but it is now less so than aseptic *phlebothrombosis associated with various states that cause hypercoagulability.

SISTERS OF CHARITY OF ST VINCENT DE PAUL. Pre-eminent among the religious orders founded after the Renaissance with the objective of tending the sick and needy and hence anticipating the modern profession of nursing, St Vincent de Paul's order, the Sisters of Charity, was established in Paris in 1634.

SITUS INVERSUS is the combination of *dextrocardia with the transposition of the abdominal viscera.

SI UNITS. The Système International d'Unités was adopted in 1960 as the internationally agreed coherent system of measurement for all scientific purposes. It replaces previous systems, such as the centimetre–gram–second (c.g.s.) system and the foot–pound–second (f.p.s.) system.

There are seven basic units as follows: metre (m), length; kilogram (kg), mass; second (s), time; ampere (A), electric current; kelvin (K), temperature (absolute); mole (mol), amount of substance; and candela (cd), luminous intensity. In addition, there are two supplementary units: radian (rad), plane angle; and steradian (sr), solid angle. There are also a number of derived units, that is which can be stated in terms of basic units. These include: newton (N), force; pascal (Pa), pressure; coulomb (C), electric charge; farad (F), capacitance; ohm (Ω), electric resistance; siemens (S), electric conductance; weber (Wb), magnetic flux; tesla (T), magnetic flux density; henry (H), inductance; hertz (Hz), frequency; degree Celsius (°C), temperature; lumen (lm), luminous flux; lux (lx), illuminance; becquerel (Bq), radioactivity; and gray (Gy), absorbed dose (of radioactivity).

Decimal multiples are given by metric prefixes, and where possible a prefix representing 10 raised to a power that is a multiple of three should be used, for example kilo- (10^3), mega- (10^6), giga- (10^9), etc. and milli- (10^{-3}), micro- (10^{-6}), nano- (10^{-9}), etc.

SJOGREN'S SYNDROME is a condition, almost certainly *autoimmune in nature, in which there is progressive destruction of *salivary and *lacrimal gland tissue. The major features are dryness of the mouth (xerostomia) and of the eyes (keratoconjunctivitis sicca), often with some enlargement of the *parotid glands. There is an association with *rheumatoid arthritis and *systemic lupus erythematosus, and the condition is overwhelmingly commoner in women.

SKELETON. The bony framework of the body; all the bones collectively.

SKIN, the external covering or integument of the body, consists of two distinct layers: the outer epidermis (derived from ectoderm) and the inner dermis or corium (derived from mesoderm). The epidermis, which is avascular, has a basal layer of growing cells which migrate outwards, becoming flattened and losing their nuclei to become the outermost horny layer or stratum corneum in about two weeks from their formation; after about another two weeks they are shed completely, so that the total turnover time of epidermal cells is approximately one month. During the process of migration and differentiation the cells form a fibrous protein known as *keratin, which constitutes an integral component of the protective epidermal layer. The cells are therefore called keratinocytes. Mingled with them are some melanocytes, which are responsible for pigmentation.

Beneath the epidermis, resting in turn on a cushion of fat tissue is the main mass of skin, the dermis (sometimes called the 'true skin', or corium). It largely consists of vascular connective tissue which contains, along with blood vessels, fibrous protein, mucopolysaccharide, elastic fibres, and collagen, all the other structures found in skin: lymph channels, nerves, sweat and sebaceous glands, hair follicles, and a few cells, largely fibroblasts, mast cells, and histiocytes. See also DERMATOLOGY.

SKIN TESTS determine an individual's immunological reactivity to a substance by bringing it into contact with the skin by local application or by intra- or sub-cutaneous injection. See, for example, TUBERCULIN TEST.

SKODA, JOSEPH (1805–81). Austrian physician, MD Vienna (1831). Skoda became professor of medicine in Vienna in 1846. One of the leaders of the New Vienna School, he worked with *Rokitansky and his chief contribution was to correlate physical signs with pathological lesions. His *Abhandlung über Perkussion und Auskultation* (1839) is a medical classic and one of the foundations of physical diagnosis. A popular teacher and a therapeutic nihilist, he was the first in Austria to teach in German. He described the hyperresonant *percussion note above a *pleural effusion (Skodaic resonance).

SKODAIC RESONANCE is increased resonance on *percussion of the chest wall above the level of a *pleural effusion.

SKULL. The bony casing enclosing the *brain, also known as the cranium. The skull consists of a number of individual bones rigidly articulated to each other, with mobile articulations with the vertebral spine and the lower jaw.

SLEEP

Introduction. We evolved upon a rotating Earth in which light and dark, warmth and cold, came and went about every 24 hours and, in common with all other animals, we have within our genetic design an inherent rhythmicity that combines in a sensible manner with the alternation of light and dark. Some creatures have specialized and are nocturnal in habit, but man is among the majority, and during the light he is active and during the dark he rests. His nervous system imposes rest, sleep being a positive state of inertia and unresponsiveness to the environment.

Biological rhythms of about a 24-hour periodicity (circadian rhythms) can be found in isolated tissues but are normally co-ordinated in the whole body by the brain. If we fly to the other side of the northern hemisphere, our biological rhythm continues to make us sleepy and inefficient at times when those around us are alert, and it makes us wakeful while they rest. Social pressures will gradually force upon us new times for getting up in the morning and, over a period of weeks, we adapt fully to the new schedule. Merely engaging in regular night-shift working does not usually lead to full adaptation, for social pressures mean that, on non-working days, conventional patterns of wakefulness and sleep are allowed to continue.

The mental life of sleep has always held a special fascination and in most cultures the soul has been thought to leave the body during sleep, to mingle with supernatural beings, so to receive guidance for the future. The interpretation of dreams for prophetic purposes is familiar in the story of the boy Joseph, who grew to interpret Pharoah's dream, and in the dream-books of 19th c. Europe. The departure of the soul during sleep provides, in legal terms, a state of *automatism, and a defence, for example, to a criminal charge levelled against a sleep-walker. Sigmund *Freud considered his greatest work to have been his book *The Interpretation of Dreams* (1899) in which he saw the dream as a guardian against disturbance of sleep, and as revealing not the future, but the hidden personality traits of the individual.

The Russian physiologist *Pavlov found that his dogs frequently fell asleep during studies of *conditioning and he wrote that experimental sleep could be induced with the same exactitude as the reaction of a hungry dog to a piece of meat. He identified sleep with his concept of internal *inhibition of the *cerebral cortex. Another Nobel laureate, W. R. *Hess wrote extensively about sleep, seeing it as a positive state that he could induce in cats by electrical stimulation of the *thalamus and as a time for cellular renewal to complement the profligate work of waking life.

In the 1950s sleep was often seen as a negative state, of mere absence of arousal. It was a decade in which the regulatory role of the *brainstem reticular formation came to be understood. Formerly, Pavlov, for example, had supposed that wakefulness was determined by the intensity of sensory information reaching the cerebral cortex. Now it came to be realized that this was not the case, and that there is a key part of the brain, situated in the central core of the brainstem, excitement of which would lead to ascending and descending impulses that would activate the forebrain and the *spinal cord, raising their responsiveness to wakeful levels. In the 1960s there followed a recognition that sleep was not a unitary condition and that dreaming was especially associated in time with the rapid eye movement (*REM) or paradoxical phase of sleep. A great rise of knowledge about sleep followed this last advance, with some help from advances in pharmacological research.

Characteristics of sleep. The most important determinant of falling asleep is to have arrived at that phase of the circadian cycle during which we have learned to fall asleep. Falling asleep is, however, also promoted by sheer lack of sleep, by immobility, monotony, warmth, or lack of immediate purpose. The heart slows, the blood pressure falls, the muscles relax, the electrical resistance of the skin rises as insensible sweating diminishes, the pupils become small, and the electrical brain waves (electroencephalogram or EEG) change in appearance (see NEUROPHYSIOLOGY, CLINICAL). We first flit to and fro between wakefulness and drowsiness, while imperceptibly the control of our thoughts escapes us. Environmental cues become missed and reactions delayed whenever, for a second or more, the EEG displays slower waves. The tired car driver may at such a point leave the road without any reason other than his inattention.

As sleep deepens, the EEG displays the characteristic sleep spindles or groups of waves at 12–14 cycles per second (Hz), while slower waves of 1–3 Hz become more and more prominent. The body's *oxygen consumption falls and reaches its lowest while the EEG's slowest waves prevail. During this same slow-wave sleep of the early night the brain's blood flow and *glucose consumption fall and *growth hormone is secreted in greatest amounts. Circulating *cortisol and *adrenaline have by this time fallen to their lowest levels of the 24 hours. Soon afterwards body temperature falls to its lowest and at the same time the hormone *prolactin rises to unexplained heights, until, near the end of the sleep period, cortisol begins to rise again in pursuit of its after-breakfast peak.

Within sleep there can readily also be seen an ultradian rhythm of about 100 minutes periodicity. It is a rhythm detectable during wakefulness through, for example, variations in spontaneous activity or in day-dreaming, but the rhythm manifests itself prominently in sleep by the recurring periods of paradoxical (REM) sleep. In this form of sleep there are EEG waves in appearance near to those of drowsiness, jerky eyeball movements, extreme muscular relaxation, penile erection, enhanced brain blood flow, and irregularity of heart, blood pressure, and respiration. Although, in statistical terms, mental life most often deserves to be described as dreaming just after the very moment of one of the rapid eye movements during paradoxical sleep, mental life at any other time of sleep can be indistinguishable, and unequivocal dreaming is common when first falling asleep at night. The amount of sleep spent as paradoxical sleep is very high in the newborn but is low in *senile dementia or among adults with mental handicap. Among normal adults it correlates in amount closely and mundanely with gross body weight.

We need sleep and if, by selectively timed disturbances of sleep, we are prevented from getting either paradoxical sleep or sleep with the slowest EEG waves, then, when allowed to sleep undisturbed, we appear to compensate by spending extra time in the stage of sleep we have lacked. Popular misconceptions about needing to spend time in dreaming (misidentified with paradoxical sleep) in order to stay sane have no scientific basis.

The function of sleep. There is a widespread intuitive belief that sleep renews and restores. The apparent renewal is most evident for the brain. If total wakefulness is deliberately imposed on volunteers for several days and nights, they become unable to sustain attention or coherent thought because of brief 'microsleeps' that would lead them directly into full sleep were it not for relays of vigilant watchers. Judgement becomes impaired, visual and other misperceptions intrude, irritability and *paranoid ideas erupt, volition diminishes, energy is conserved, body temperature and muscular strength fall, while *nitrogen excretion rises and the *immune system that fights infection functions less effectively. A couple of subsequent nights of unbroken sleep, during which long periods of slow-wave sleep have priority, restore normal function. We need to sleep.

Tissues such as skin or the epithelium of the gut are constantly worn away and renew themselves by cell division, whereas the brain renews its structural components not by making new cells but by replacement of *protein molecules ('turnover'). Most research into these renewal processes has been conducted in rodents in which, in all tissues, there has been found to be a higher rate of renewal by cell division or by protein synthesis during that time of the 24 hours when rodents sleep, and this is true of brain protein synthesis. Limited research on man confirms a higher rate during sleep of cell division for at least skin, buccal mucosa, and red blood cell (erythrocyte) production. The hormone pattern of wakefulness, with high levels of cortisol and adrenaline, favours tissue breakdown or *catabolism and it inhibits protein synthesis, whereas the hormone pattern of human sleep, when catabolic hormones are low but growth hormone, prolactin, and *testosterone are high, will facilitate protein synthesis. More fundamentally, the high rate of cellular work during wakefulness lowers cellular levels of *adenosine triphosphate

(ATP), whereas rest allows the levels to rise to their highest during sleep and only when these levels are highest can protein synthesis proceed optimally.

Poor sleep. The complaint of poor sleep is one of the commonest any doctor encounters. Dissatisfaction with sleep is more frequent among women, among persons of anxious temperament, and among older age groups. Although objective measures of sleep fail to show sex differences, they do confirm that sleep becomes more broken with age, while also demonstrating that subjective impressions of delayed and diminished sleep usually provide an exaggerated indication of impairment. Nevertheless, the restorative function of a complainer's sleep cannot be measured and, on average, those who complain of poor sleep do sleep a little less, and do have sleep that is somewhat more broken by awakenings than that of other persons of the same sex, age, and weight.

The preferred duration of sleep, like any other biological measure, differs among individuals. A few people are happy, healthy and non-complaining on 3 hours a night, while some will gladly take 10 hours or more. Most people prefer 7–8 hours. A six-year follow-up of over a million Americans illustrated that those who had been markedly different from the average, in that they believed they slept more or fewer hours than the majority, had subsequently experienced a higher mortality rate.

People who are slightly obese sleep longer than those who are thin for their height and frame-size. Being very underweight, as in *anorexia nervosa, is associated with greatly reduced sleep, and subsequent re-feeding leads to weight gain and longer sleep. On a day-to-day basis normal people sleep best when they have partaken of accustomed foods at usual times. A malted milk drink at bedtime helps best the sleep of those who take it regularly, and may actually impair the sleep of those for whom it is unusual.

A reduction of sleep duration below normal, with greater brokenness of sleep, is commonly a consequence of enhanced *anxiety arising out of problems in daytime life. As worries recede, sleep improves again. Sometimes sleep is reduced for weeks or months as a result of mental illness, extremely so in the disorder known as *mania, characterized as it is by excess energy and confidence. The obverse disorder, *depressive illness, is more common and, especially in middle or later life, unaccustomed and persisting *insomnia accompanied by a black cloud of gloomy worries unjustified by the circumstances of daily life should provide a proper reason for seeking medical advice.

Drugs. Drugs taken to promote sleep were formerly provided by *alcohol, the *poppy, and extracts from plants containing *hyoscine and related compounds, the *mandrake root being the most famous. Conversely, *caffeine and other xanthines in *coffee and *tea have been natural substances capable of delaying and disturbing sleep, especially for the middle-aged or older.

Chemical compounds of non-plant origin have come into use in the past two centuries as promoters of sleep: *paraldehyde, *chloral, *bromides, *barbiturates, and methaqualone are compounds now obsolete. Currently, the *benzodiazepine derivatives are widely used, and are very much safer. They have many names but all have the same actions: they relieve anxiety and promote sleep. Where they do differ is in their potency and in their persistence in the body. Thus, flurazepam is usually taken in 30 mg doses and a bedtime dose tonight leaves almost as much active compound in the tissues throughout tomorrow, whereas lormetazepam is taken in only a 1 mg dose and is half-destroyed by breakfast time.

The regular intake of any of the sleep-promoting, anxiety-relieving compounds (which are also compounds that diminish liability to *fits), leads to compensatory adjustments in the brain. If intake of the drug suddenly ceases, then, as a consequence of the prior use of the drug, there is unnatural insomnia, with restlessness, anxiety, and an enhanced liability to fits. If large daily doses have been taken, the withdrawal picture may even be of *delirium tremens, although the less extreme syndrome is much commoner after benzodiazepines. Several weeks are always then needed before the *withdrawal phenomena fade and for return to a natural level of anxiety and a natural duration of sleep.

Sleep disorders. Although complaints of insomnia are commoner among older adults, some 5 per cent of adolescents regard themselves as sleeping badly, with associated feelings of unhappiness and low self-esteem. Looking at even younger children, no less than 40 per cent of parents of children under four regard their child as having a sleep problem, with rapid improvement after that age. Apart from simply waking and feeling lonely, there are a number of defined disorders of sleep that affect children and some adults.

Nightmares are common at any age and the true nightmare is a phenomenon of paradoxical sleep, made up of a relatively prolonged and fearful sequence within a dream, coupled with inability to move, and generally arising in the later night. Neither nightmares nor *night terrors denote mental disorder, although they are commoner when daytime life is anxious and nightmares are frequent after recent withdrawal of sleep-promoting drugs. Night terrors are features of the early night: they arise from EEG slow-wave sleep and are coupled with unelaborated mental life, such as a brief experience of being entrapped, and may be accompanied by shrieking and lashing out. Night terrors run strongly in families, together with a liability to sleep-walking and nocturnal shouting. They often begin around *puberty and occasionally persist into adult life. The child himself

remembers almost nothing of the nocturnal experience and the most important need is for reassurance of the family, together with simple precautions against injury while sleep-walking. It should be remembered that any drug that acts upon the brain may provoke night terrors and sleep-walking in occasional individuals.

Rhythmic movements can occur in sleep without disturbing it, for example, scratching. Some children and adults grind their teeth rhythmically during sleep, again sometimes as a consequence of taking a drug. It is not uncommon for children from 18 months of age to engage in rhythmic head-banging when feeling lonely upon being put to bed. Sometimes rhythmic humming noises accompany the movements. In a few children the head-banging comes to be dramatic, and to occur actually during sleep, yet without disturbing sleep, again with no memory of the events in the morning. The parents should be reassured that nothing serious will befall, and that the movements will nearly always disappear before adult life is reached.

*Bed-wetting is normal in young children and there is a large variation among individuals in the age at which bed-wetting ceases. It is usually a feature of slow-wave sleep, often in the first part of the night, and is not to be thought of as something that arises from mischievousness, or that will be cured by punishment. The most effective treatment is the buzzer device that is operated by wetness of the sheets, for in time it helps the individual to awaken before actually wetting the sheets.

Daytime sleepiness. While many people complain of lack of sleep, there are a few who complain of falling asleep too readily. In some cases this must be attributed to a constitutional need for more than the average hours of sleep, or to getting up early for work and then trying to remain awake in the evening in company with other family members. Sometimes, however, the liability to fall asleep must be regarded as a disorder, usually of unknown origin. Often it is manageable only by attempts at losing weight, and by the judicious use of deliberate naps and of caffeine or *amphetamine derivatives. Two syndromes that the average doctor may expect to encounter can, however, be defined.

One is known as idiopathic *narcolepsy with *cataplexy. It can begin at any age and is usually first manifested by spells of irresistible sleep, each lasting for about 10 minutes, a couple of times a day. The same person may during the day suddenly find himself partly or totally paralysed for a brief moment in response to an emotion characteristic for him or her, be it laughter, triumph, or anger. These brief paralyses are known as cataplectic attacks. About one person in a thousand suffers from idiopathic narcolepsy and the disorder should be more widely recognized as one that causes embarrassment and a liability to road accidents. That narcolepsy may in part be genetically determined is suggested by the finding that most sufferers have the antigen *HLADrW$_2$. Another reason for excessive sleepiness, particularly among males, is obstructed breathing that develops only during sleep. Children with large and infected *tonsils and *adenoids may be affected and also a proportion of obese adults. The obstruction means that every 20 seconds or so the sleeper almost awakens while engaging in violent snorting efforts to breathe, thereby greatly disturbing sleep. Successful treatment of the obstruction to breathing immediately relieves the sleepiness by day, and also excessive strain on the heart during sleep, though in some adult cases relief can only be achieved by a *tracheostomy for nocturnal use.

There are many other people who fall asleep by day more easily than they would wish and who are said to suffer from hypersomnia. Reduction of obesity, and arrangements to take deliberate daytime naps, will help them and the narcoleptics too. Caffeine or methylphenidate are sometimes employed, while clomipramine is effective in preventing cataplectic attacks.

Hypnosis. The Greek god of sleep was Hypnos and because many people in the course of hypnotic trances look like sleep-walkers the term '*hypnosis' came into use. However, despite the conventional instructions, 'You are falling asleep, you are falling asleep', the trance that is induced by the *suggestions of the hypnotist is not a state of sleep, but one of wakefulness and enhanced suggestibility. It is, of course, possible to induce a feeling of peace and *relaxation in the hypnotized subject and allow him to sleep.

Hints for good sleep. It is advisable to keep regular hours for getting up and going to bed. We should minimize alcohol intake and smoking, avoid evening caffeine, take plenty of regular exercise, and avoid being under-weight or severely over-weight. We should take evening meals at regular times and let them be of easily digestible food. Above all, we should seek to be satisfied with ourselves as we are, accepting our failures and disabilities, and being forgiving of others. We should not worry about how many hours of sleep we get; the brain will look after its needs.

I. OSWALD

Further reading
Adam, K. (1980). Sleep as a restorative process and a theory to explain why. *Progress in Brain Research,* 53, 289–305.
Carskadon, M. A., Dement, W. C., Mitler, M. M., Guilleminault, C., Zarcone, V. P. and Spiegel, R. (1976). Self-reports versus sleep laboratory findings in 122 drug-free subjects with complaints of chronic insomnia. *American Journal of Psychiatry,* 133, 1382–8.
Foulkes, D. (1966). *The Psychology of Sleep.* New York.
Kripke, D. F., Simons, R. N., Garfinkel, L. and Hammond, E. C. (1979). Short and long sleep and sleeping pills: is increased mortality associated? *Archives of General Psychiatry,* 36, 103–16.
McGhie, A. and Russell, S. M. (1962). The subjective assessment of normal sleep patterns. *The Journal of Mental Science,* 108, 642–54.
MacKenzie, N. (1965). *Dreams and Dreaming.* London.

Oswald, I. (1980). *Sleep.* 4th edn, Harmondsworth.
Williams, H. L., Lubin, A. and Goodnow, J. (1959). Impaired performance with acute sleep loss. *Psychological Monographs,* 73, no. 14.

SLEEPING DRAUGHT. A dose of medicine taken in order to promote sleep. See SLEEP.

SLEEPING SICKNESS. See TRYPANOSOMIASIS.

SLEEP PARALYSIS is temporary loss of muscle power on arousal from *REM sleep.

SLEEP WALKING. See SLEEP.

SLIT LAMP. An instrument which enables minute inspection of the structures of the eye by projecting into it a flat light beam of high intensity.

SLOANE, SIR HANS, BT (1660–1753). British physician, MD Orange (1683), DM Oxford (1701), FRCP (1687), FRS (1685). Sloane trained in medicine in Paris and Montpellier. In 1684 he returned to London and lodged in the house of Thomas *Sydenham. In 1687 he was appointed physician to the Duke of Albemarle, Governor of the West Indies, where he made a large collection of plants and natural curiosities. On returning to London he was made physician to Christ's Hospital in 1694. He attended Queen Anne and in 1716 was the first member of the medical profession to receive a baronetcy. He became physician-general to the Army in 1722 and physician to George II in 1727. He was secretary to the Royal Society from 1693 to 1712 and president from 1727 to 1741; from 1719 to 1735 he also occupied the position of president of the Royal College of Physicians of London. In 1712 he bought the manor of Chelsea where several streets still bear his name. He published in two volumes an account of his voyage to the West Indies and of the natural history of Jamaica (1707, 1725). After his death his collection was brought by the nation for £20 000 and went to form the basis of the British Museum.

SLOP, DR, is the irascible, clumsy, and bigoted Catholic doctor in Laurence Sterne's novel *The Life and Opinions of Tristram Shandy* (1760–7). In his eagerness to demonstrate a new type of *obstetrical forceps, Slop, a 'little, squat, uncourtly figure', inflicts permanent deformity on the hero's nose.

SLOW VIRUS INFECTIONS are infections which can be shown to be due to a transmissible agent but which have a very long incubation period, possibly lasting many years, and are then gradually progressive. *Kuru and *scrapie are examples.

SLYE, MAUD (1879–1954). American pathologist, AB (1899), Sc.D. (1937). Maud Slye studied at Brown University and the University of Chicago, where she spent most of her professional career, studying the occurrence of *cancer in different strains of mice. She investigated this from the standpoints of heredity, localization, and age incidence.

SLYKE, DONALD DEXTER VAN (1883–1971). American biochemist, Ph.D. University of Michigan (1907). Van Slyke joined the staff of the Rockefeller Institute, and remained there for 40 years, spending the last few years of his professional life at the Brookhaven National Laboratory. He developed many gasometric methods for *biochemical analyses. His two-volume work, (with J. P. Peters) *Quantitative Clinical Chemistry* was a standard reference for many years. Van Slyke was especially interested in the subject of acid–base balance, and the equilibria between gases and electrolytes. He and associates made noteworthy contributions to measurement of urea clearance by the kidney, and in the identification of glutamine as the source of urinary ammonia. See CHEMISTRY, CLINICAL.

SMALLPOX (or variola), a devastating and pestilential scourge all over the world and at all known periods of history until the present, had been finally eradicated as a human disease by the time the *World Health Organization made its historic declaration in May of 1980. Since there is no animal reservoir of infection, the virus, one of the group of orthopoxviruses which includes *vaccinia and a number of related animal poxviruses, can be assumed to exist no longer except where it is maintained in laboratories under the strictest security precautions. The last endemic infection occurred in 1977, and the record since then has only been marred by an accidental laboratory outbreak a year later in Birmingham, England. Vaccination against smallpox is no longer justified except in a small number of laboratory workers handling poxviruses. The chances of smallpox recurring as a result of mutation from a related wild species are considered to be remote.

SMEGMA is a soapy, cheesy secretion derived mainly from *sebaceous glands, particularly that which occurs under the *prepuce.

SMELL is the faculty of detecting odours. Loss of the sense of smell is termed anosmia. It is sometimes the result of local disease of the nose and is a not uncommon sequel of head injury. There are a number of rare causes, for example *cerebral tumour, and occasionally the sense of smell is congenitally absent.

SMELLIE, WILLIAM (1679–1763). British obstetrician, MD Glasgow (1745). After apprenticeship in Lanarkshire, Smellie studied in Paris, coming to London in 1739 where he rapidly acquired a large obstetrical practice. He was a friend of William *Cullen and of Tobias *Smollett, and in 1741 William *Hunter came to lodge

in his house. Smellie was one of the pioneer '*man-midwives'; he described a manoeuvre for delivering the after-coming head (Mauriceau–Smellie–Veit method) and devised special craniotomy scissors. See OBSTETRICS.

SMELLING SALTS. See SAL VOLATILE.

SMILES, SAMUEL (1812–1904). British physician and writer. Smiles studied at Edinburgh, and served his apprenticeship and later practised in Haddington. In 1838 he became editor of the radical *Leeds Times* and from 1854 to 1866 was secretary to the South-Eastern Railway. Thereafter he was occupied in writing, chiefly biographies and tracts. His best known publication was *Self-Help* (1859) which sold 250 000 copies in 25 years.

SMITH, SIR GRAFTON ELLIOT (1871–1937). Anglo-Australian anatomist and anthropologist, MD Sydney (1893), FRCP (1915), FRS (1907), Elliot Smith was elected to a research fellowship at St John's College, Cambridge, in 1896 and subsequently became successively professor of anatomy in Cairo in 1900, Manchester in 1909, and University College, London, in 1919. He was knighted in 1934. Elliot Smith was an anatomist of distinction who was fired with an interest in anthropology by working in Egypt, during which time he supervised the anthropological survey of Nubia.

SMITH, NATHAN (1762–1829). American physician, MD Harvard (1790). Smith practised and taught clinical medicine in several New England states. He is best remembered for a classical clinical description of *typhoid fever (then called typhus fever).

SMITH, THEOBALD (1859–1934). American bacteriologist and immunologist, MD Albany Medical College (1883). Smith carried out research in the field of veterinary bacteriorology in three institutions: the US Bureau of Animal Industry, the Massachusetts Board of Health, and the Princeton branch of the Rockefeller Institute. His discoveries, in the field of veterinary medicine, were of seminal importance to the study and understanding of human diseases. A list of his accomplishments includes: demonstration that an infectious anaemia of cattle (Texas cattle fever) is conveyed by an insect *vector, introduction of the fermentation tube in bacteriology, differentiation between typhoid bacillus and coliforms on the basis of gas formation, use of lactose and sucrose fermentation to differentiate gram-negative bacteria, cultivation of *anaerobes, determination of thermal lability of tubercle bacilli, differentiation between human and bovine strains of tubercle bacilli, induction of immunity in hogs by injection of heat-killed bacilli, discovery of *Vibrio fetus* in contagious abortion of cattle, recognition of bacterial dissociation resulting from serial *passage *in vitro,* differentiation of the flagellar and somatic antigens, standardization of *toxin and *antitoxin of *diphtheria and *tetanus, and demonstration of presence of *antibody in *colostrum. See also MICROBIOLOGY.

SMOG is a combination of smoke and fog, a form of air pollution which occurs in industrial areas where motor vehicles are in heavy use, particularly when temperature inversions are frequent. A layer of warm air is trapped close to the ground, so preventing the escape or dilution of chemical pollutants.

SMOKING AS A CAUSE OF DISEASE. The smoking of tobacco, particularly in the form of cigarettes, is now established beyond doubt as a potent cause of disease, most notably of lung *cancer, other cancers, chronic respiratory disease, ischaemic heart disease, peripheral vascular disease, and fetal growth retardation. *Tobacco tar and *carbon monoxide have been identified as two of the dangerous components of tobacco smoke; whether *nicotine also plays a part is much less certain, and it would not seem reasonable in the present state of knowledge to oppose the use of nicotine-containing chewing gum or of *snuff as smoking substitutes.

SMOLLETT, TOBIAS GEORGE (1721–71). British physician and novelist, MD Aberdeen (1750). Smollett studied at Glasgow and served as a naval surgeon before starting practice in London and later in Bath. His rough contentious manner proved unacceptable, but his lively and original novels have enjoyed lasting popularity. His best known works are *Roderick Random* (1748), *The Adventures of Peregrine Pickle* (1751), and *The Expedition of Humphrey Clinker* (1771).

SNAILS AS VECTORS OF DISEASE. Certain freshwater snails are of considerable medical and public health importance as vectors of *helminthic diseases, most notably of schistosomiasis (*bilharziasis) but also of other trematode infestations such as *paragonimiasis, for which the snails are intermediate hosts. The most important genera are *Bulinus, Planorbarius, Biomphalaria, Australorbis,* and *Tropicorbis.*

SNAKES are reptiles of the suborder Ophidia. Five families contain species which can be poisonous to man; these are the Elapidae, the Viperidae, the Crotalidae, the Hydrophidae, and the Colubridae. Their venom can be *neurotoxic, *myotoxic, *vasculotoxic, *cytolytic, *coagulant, or *anticoagulant, or some combination of these. The only poisonous snake found naturally in the UK is the familiar adder (*Vipera berus*). It is a shy creature, and rarely bites unless disturbed, usually by incautious handling. Its bite is unpleasant but only rarely fatal.

SNEEZING is the abrupt audible expulsion of air from the nose, reflexly induced by irritation of the nasal mucosa.

SNELLEN, HERMAN (1834–1903). Dutch ophthalmologist, MD Utrecht (1858). Snellen followed *Donders as professor of ophthalmology in Utrecht in 1877 and is known today for his printed *test types for testing visual acuity, which are still in use.

SNOW, JOHN (1813–58). British anaesthetist and hygienist, MD London (1844). Snow introduced *ether to the UK and administered *chloroform to Queen Victoria for the births of Prince Leopold and Princess Beatrice in 1853 and 1857. From his observations of the *cholera epidemic in 1848 he deduced that the infection was spread by the water supply and recommended the removal of the handle of the Broad Street pump to control it. He published his views in *On the Mode of Communication of Cholera* (1849).

SNUFF is ground *tobacco leaf or stalk, perfumed with a variety of essential oils, taken by insertion into the nostrils; *nicotine absorption occurs through the nasal mucous membrane. The taking of snuff is possibly the safest form of tobacco use, since the tobacco is not burnt and neither tar nor carbon monoxide is produced.

SOCIAL MEDICINE. See COMMUNITY MEDICINE; SOCIOLOGY IN RELATION TO MEDICINE; SOCIAL WORK AND MEDICINE.

SOCIAL SECURITY ACTS 1973, 1975. The 1973 Act repealed nearly all existing English national insurance (other than industrial injuries) legislation and substituted a new system embodying the essential purpose of the original but with certain changes and improvements. Among these were: wholly earnings-related contributions for employed earners instead of the previous hybrid structure of flat-rate and graduated contributions; earnings-related contributions for self-employed earners with earnings above a certain level, in addition to weekly flat-rate contributions; voluntary contributions for people who would otherwise be unable to qualify for basic pension and some other benefits; winding up of the previous state graduated pension scheme; recognition of occupational pension schemes for purpose of exemption from the reserve pension scheme; preservation of occupational pension rights on change of employment; an independent Occupational Pensions Board to administer the new arrangements affecting occupational pension schemes; a reserve pension scheme managed by an independent Board to provide earnings-related pensions for employees not covered by recognized occupational schemes.

The 1975 Act consolidated for England, Wales, and Scotland as much of the 1973 Act as established a basic scheme of contributions and benefits, together with the National Insurance (Industrial Injuries) Acts 1965 to 1974 and other enactments relating to social security.

SOCIAL WORK AND MEDICINE are both activities which have existed for many centuries. In the context of our own times, medicine has developed more quickly in the sense that it has established a comprehensive knowledge base and an understanding among ordinary people of what is expected from a person who is medically trained. Social work has also developed, especially in those countries where the state plays a large part in the provision of welfare services. There is not, however, anything like the same degree of agreement about the nature of social work, its knowledge base, and the credibility of social workers among the public at large.

What is social work? What, then, is social work? A definition of social work which would be accepted by many people is that it aims to enhance the social functioning of individuals, families, groups, and communities. This way of looking at social work has the great advantage of stressing the interaction of the individual with the environment rather than looking at either component in isolation. How social workers go about achieving this aim does depend very much on a number of factors which are themselves closely interrelated. The first of these is the power and authority given to social workers by their host society. In some countries, of which the UK is, perhaps, the best example, very wide legislative powers have been given to social workers in respect of many people with social problems, particularly children and the mentally ill. In other countries there is very little formal power of this kind and social workers may be employed by charitable and other organizations, for example, religious orders, to work with all kinds of people but without the power to compel the person to co-operate.

Another important factor is the way in which the social care system is organized. Extensive legislative powers often go together with the growth of large bureaucratic organizations and it is the organization which employs the social worker. A characteristic of such bodies is that they are hierarchical: there may be many managerial tiers between the social worker who sees the patient and the person who has the power to make the final decision to allow or disallow a particular course of action. This can lead to difficulties between doctors and social workers. Doctors, once they are beyond the training grades, are able, in general, to make their own independent judgements about the patients' needs without any kind of formal supervision. Social workers, even when they have considerable training and experience, are rarely in this situation.

The way in which social workers are trained is another important factor in determining how they attempt to achieve their aim of improving social functioning. There is a considerable variation between countries both in regard to the type of training given, its length and content, and where it is given within the education system. In the USA, training for social work has for many years been established within the universities and this gives social workers a status not enjoyed in other countries, where training may take place in a variety of educational institutions outside the university sector. This has an important bearing on the whole nature of doctor–social worker relationships in that doctors are invariably trained in universities, and opportunities for joint training—difficult enough in the best conditions—are lost if the two professions do not share similar educational bases.

The knowledge base of social work is itself of importance in determining how social workers achieve their aims. It is largely drawn from the social and behavioural sciences and includes sociology, psychology, anthropology, philosophy, economics, and social and public administration. This is clearly a different kind of knowledge base from that which informs medical training, with the exception of social medicine and psychiatry. The outcome of this difference of perspectives from the standpoint of medical practice and social work is that the doctor is trained to diagnose the patient's condition and then to solve the problem in such a way that may or may not involve the active co-operation of the patient. The social worker will, in contrast, be trained to regard the problem presented as belonging to the client. Social workers use the term client rather than patient, and believe that the client is best helped by being assisted to resolve the difficulty himself. This difference in approach can give rise to difficulties when the professions work together. The doctor may wish the social worker to take a more active part in solving the patient's problems; the social worker may want the doctor to recognize that the best solution is one in which the client comes to his own understanding of the nature of the problem and how it can best be resolved.

Methods. Given that the global aim of social work is to enhance the social functioning of individuals, families, groups, and communities, then it will be readily understood that different methods are needed to achieve this purpose. Social work methods can be divided into three broad groups: social casework, social group work, and community work. Social casework is by far the most common method used in social work in medicine and so will be dealt with in greater depth than the other two methods.

Social group work is a method in which the group itself is used as the means of exploring and resolving problems. It is used in a variety of medical contexts but has been found particularly useful in *psychiatry where individual and social functioning are so closely related (*group therapy). Many people with problems can derive considerable benefit from discussing their problem with others in the same situation with the help and guidance of a skilled therapist. It may be that greater use could be made of social group work in relation to other fields of medical work; *rehabilitation would seem one such area.

Community work is a method in which the whole community is involved in the identification, exploration, and resolution of problems. There are many examples of such work, especially in relation to disadvantaged groups of people, where the aim has been to raise the morale of the community. The very many large impersonal housing estates of Western Europe and the USA have been the site of much community work. Such work does very often have a major bearing on health and disease in the people within the community but is rarely the main focus of the work. The exception to this is in the developing countries where much effort is put into training community workers whose specific role is to teach about medical matters and provide a medical service.

Social casework in which the individual, alone or with their family, is the focus for treatment, is the most common form of social work in developed countries and the social work method which doctors are most likely to encounter. The range of problems dealt with by the social caseworker is enormous but the essential nature of the work is that the problem presented by the client is the focus for action. This may, and often does, involve the social worker in working not only with the individual client and his family, but also with any other significant person who has a bearing on the problem. This very often means the doctor, but can involve many other professionals, for example lawyers, housing officials, and non-professionals, like the next-door neighbour. Within the broad category of social casework, the social worker has three main roles.

The first is that of *assessor*. Social workers are very much involved in the assessment of the nature of the problem presented to them by the patient or client. The problems to be assessed will range from relatively simple matters, such as the eligibility of a person entering or leaving hospital for a particular service, to the exceedingly complex issues which arise in assessing the social and psychological components in, for example, the rehabilitation of those people with traumatic injury caused by industrial accidents. In the vast majority of cases this assessment process can, and should, include the active involvement of the client.

A second role is that of *advocate*. Even within social work in a medical context the social worker will encounter many people in great social need who may have insufficient knowledge or may be lacking in those social skills which would enable them to obtain those resources necessary to alleviate their condition, whether it be poverty or poor housing. The social worker's training will help the client through the exceedingly complex rules and regulations found in so many social welfare systems. It is not at all uncommon for social workers employed by one part of the system to spend a great deal of time and effort acting as advocates for a client in relation to another part of the same welfare system. Doctors often find this aspect of social work both mystifying and irritating in that so much of it would be unnecessary if welfare systems were better designed and more efficient. In the real world, however, this is very often not the case and so the advocacy role of the social worker is often vital to the well-being of the patient and much medical skill may be wasted if some of these more basic social needs are not supplied.

A third role is that of *therapist*. Here the social worker is not mainly concerned with the material needs of the patient but rather with the ways in which the patient's methods of solving problems can be improved by discussion and guidance. Again the range of problems which may respond to such methods is great, some involving the discussion of complex and personal problems as in those cases where physical illness is complicated by, say, marital conflict. Some kinds of problems may require only that the therapist draw attention to the inadvisability of certain behaviour. An example would be if a client did not adequately inform a potential employer of a dangerous medical condition; this situation is quite common in those with disorders such as *haemophilia and *epilepsy where misunderstandings of the nature of the disorder can give rise to negative attitudes on the part of employers. It may be that the therapist role of the social worker will overlap with that of other therapists such as psychiatrists, psychologists, and psychotherapists. Conflict and confusion can be avoided if the clear objective of the social worker's therapy is the enhancement of social functioning.

All the roles of the social worker referred to above are of potential value to the doctor and his patient. They will be of even greater value if they can be practised within a multiprofessional team. The invocation to practise teamwork has been made so often that it is in danger of becoming mere ritual. This should not be allowed to happen in the fields of social work and medicine. Medical and social problems are interrelated in such complex ways that both professions need to have the closest understanding of each other's work if the patient and client are to receive the kinds of help appropriate to their problems.   W. MORGAN

Further reading
Butrym, Z. and Horder, J. (1983). *Health, Doctors and Social Workers*. London.
Downie, R. S. and Telfer, E. (1980). *Caring and Curing*. London.
Garrad, J. and Rosenheim, M. (1970). *Social Aspects of Clinical Medicine*. London.
Huws Jones, R. (1971). *The Doctor and the Social Services*. London.

SOCIETY OF APOTHECARIES. See APOTHE-CARIES; PHARMACY AND PHARMACISTS; MEDICAL COLLEGES, ETC. OF THE UK.

SOCIOLOGY IN RELATION TO MEDICINE

Definition. In everyday speech the sociology of medicine is concerned primarily with sociological concepts and theories applied to aspects of medicine as an institution, and the individual in health and illness. Mitchell (1979) has suggested that some of the main concerns of sociology should focus on studies of social structure; the study of social composition—that is, the nature, proportions, and diversities of various groups, categories, and classes in society; the construction of accurate descriptive inventories of the social life of society; the study of culture and life-style and the elaboration and testing of methods of research, both qualitative and statistical.

Using the above as a framework, the specific theoretical and practical relevance of the application of sociology in medicine should include studies of beliefs in health and illness; inventories of the factors which promote or inhibit the attainment of health or those which produce illness and disease; the manner in which medical institutions and organizations affect the behaviour of individuals; and the relationship between these institutions, health occupations, and the wider society.

Other studies would examine the distribution of health care resources and differential *mortality and *morbidity rates as measures of inequality, and formulate social policies to increase availability, accessibility, and accountability in the delivery of health care. Underpinning and linking these activities would be a rigorous examination of methodology, with an acceptance that the best procedure must vary with the problem in hand.

Origins and history. The middle decades of the 19th c. were the years of social enquiry concerned with the relationship between man, disease, and the environment (see also COMMUNITY MEDICINE). Reports on the health of the great towns documented the incidence of disease in various groups in society, allied with penetrating descriptive studies of social conditions, in particular, in the writings of *Farr and *Chadwick. But by the last decades of the 19th c. Western medicine became dominated by the notion that most diseases were the result of infection by micro-organisms. In the five-year period from 1879 to 1884 the causative organism was identified for leprosy, typhoid, malaria, diphtheria, cholera, and tetanus, and instead of the totality of the human body and man in his social environment, theory and practice seemed to have benefited from biomedical innovations. It has been argued that 19th c. man appears to have internalized first the authenticity and then the utility of science as a way of perceiving the external world, and in this climate, medicine's time had arrived. The discovery of the *sulphonamides in the 1930s and *penicillin in the 1940s, with their dramatic impact on the infections, only served to justify this act of faith in the glittering prizes of science and technology. Yet some would suggest that two decades later the dream had faded with the persistence of mortality from *cancer, *stroke, and accidents with their behavioural and environmental components. The pendulum had moved imperceptibly from a dominant biomedical model to a rediscovery of the relationship between man, disease, and the environment. It was in this climate of opinion that the Royal Commission on Medical Education (*The *Todd Report 1968) recommended that the sociology of medicine should be included in the medical curriculum. The objectives of the discipline were defined clearly:

To give the student a comprehensive understanding of man in health and sickness and an intimate acquaintance with his physical and social environment. . . . Deliberate and sustained efforts should be made to show students the relevance of social phenomena, whether related conceptually, comparatively or historically to the roles and functions in society of doctors and organisations for medical care.

In 1969 the first meeting of the Medical Sociology Group was arranged under the aegis of the British Sociological Association, and the dissemination of information on research and teaching became an important objective; the journal *Sociology of Health and Illness—a Journal of Medical Sociology* was published and in 1982 Field and others produced *Medical Sociology in Britain, a Register of Research and Teaching* (4th edn) covering such relevant topics as health beliefs, illness behaviour, the health professions, general practitioner studies, social epidemiology, mental illness, and pregnancy and childbirth.

By the end of the seventies most British universities had adopted the proposals of *The Todd Report* and the sociology of medicine was an integral part of the medical course. As Jeffreys has argued, it would be naïve to suggest that this innovation did not cause conflict and difficulties, in particular in the perceived value of the sociological contribution compared with the biomedical sciences; yet some of the biomedical sciences also found themselves demoted in their share of curriculum time as priorities in medical education changed. Many would argue that the challenge of a viable alternative perspective in medical education remained; that is the significance of the social, cultural, and institutional contexts for understanding patients' experiences, medical practice and practitioners, and health and illness as a social as well as a biological phenomenon. This challenge was taken up by the *General Medical Council's Education Committee in 1980 and the objectives of the sociology of medicine were restated:

Teaching in sociology should concentrate upon the influences of social structure and processes on the prevalence, recognition and management of disease, the behaviour of patients and their families and the approach used by doctors in tackling problems of diagnosis and treatment. Teaching should include consideration of group and cultural characteristics. It should also be planned that the student may learn to assess and consider together the biological and sociological bases of human behaviour.

The social contexts of health and illness. *The biomedical model.* Underlying the proposals for the teaching of sociology within the medical curriculum is a central theme: the importance of both the biological and sociological nature of human behaviour (see PSYCHOLOGY). The concept of disease as deviation from a biological norm tends to dominate medical thinking and practice (e.g. the growth of specialization) and is also a common assumption held by the public, for it is in this arena where many of the critical encounters between doctors and patients occur. The patient's quest for a convenient label for the illness, and for treatment and cure, and the doctor's for a *diagnosis, treatment, and *prognosis dovetail together neatly. Those who argue for a broader view of disease not only leave room for non-biological variables but require a description of the social and cultural contexts in which individuals live and function; the very search for normality assumes sociomedical investigation. Thomas McKeown (1979) has argued that the reduction in mortality rates from the mid 18th c. was due, in the main, to improvements in hygiene and nutrition linked to increased food supplies. He goes on to suggest that the medical advances in the 20th c., in particular *immunization, only accelerated the already declining death rates from the infections, and concentrating today on technological advances and cure without the inclusion of environmental and behavioural factors is doomed to failure. Other authors have found little empirical evidence to suggest that there were significant improvements in diet before 1840 and have suggested that declining death rates were due, in the main, to inoculation against *smallpox. It is fair to say that the whole discussion of the role of medicine in relation to mortality in the 19th c. is full of uncertainty and conflicting interpretations. Yet it would be true also to say that the sociology of medical knowledge, only recently a concern of sociologists, relies on the social history of 19th c. medicine as a backcloth to current theories and practice.

Illness and illness behaviour. What are the principal health beliefs, outlook values, and customs of individuals in contemporary society? How is the world of the ill and healthy perceived, and how do men and women cope with the disruption of symptoms, and in what manner do they organize and interpret their experiences? It is clear from many studies, in particular the work of Cartwright, that to perceive *symptoms, that is deviations from an individual's assessment of normality, and to self-treat are common experiences in everyday life; in a recent comparative study in America and Europe covering 48 000 people in 12 industrial areas, investigators discovered that 143 per 1000 individuals considered themselves to be 'healthy' (no perceived morbidity) and the number reporting only minor or temporary conditions within a period of two weeks was found to be 244 per 1000. Approximately six out of 10 individuals

reported a wide range of conditions, particularly respiratory disorders, joint problems, shortness of breath, and anxiety. In another study in two London boroughs in a random sample of 1000 persons almost all reported at least one symptom of illness over a two-week period; of these, 168 consulted their general practitioner, 28 attended an out-patient clinic, and 5 were admitted to hospital. Of the remainder 188 took no action and 562 took some other action not involving doctors (e.g. self-medication). In this context health and illness are social concepts dependent on a cluster of factors. Some authors have emphasized the age, sex, occupation, and family status of individuals, others have reviewed the socialization process in health behaviour, the disruptive and perceived severity of the symptoms, the 'cost' of illness as against other competing goals, the knowledge of the disease process, the role of advisers, and the importance of self-cure, self-reliance, and self-medication. It has also been found that the availability and accessibility of health care and perceptions of the doctor–patient relationship have an important part to play in the decision to seek medical care. Underlying these determinants of illness behaviour is the assertion that illness and illness behaviour are culturally learned responses, and sole reliance on the biomedical model denies the complex relationship involved in a multidimensional view of health. The definition of health requires three basic perspectives: the sociocultural, the psychological, and biological. Yet in some of the research in these areas discussion remains at an atheoretical level, a cluster of the social and medical characteristics of those who consult, with the underlying assumption that the end of this complex social process is entry into orthodox medical care, thus distracting the researcher from examining other valued help or health-seeking activities. It is also clear that the measurement of impairment, disability, and morbidity requires acceptable cross-cultural definitions.

Patients and doctors: relationships and interactions. The act of consultation with those in the caring professions is the end of a process of advice seeking, symptom redefinition, and a search for meaning; the processes of nature require explanation. It is to Talcott Parsons (1954), an American sociologist, that we must turn to examine sickness as an institutionalized role essential for the proper function of society. He argued that in advanced industrialized societies we expect and count on individuals to perform their social roles, and if these interdependent roles are not adequately performed in, for example, illness, the individual deviates from our expectations and some form of social control is required; sick people must be turned over to the appropriate medical agency in order to return to their normal social roles. There are four basic characteristics of the patient's role: the non-responsibility of the individual for his or her condition; the exemption of the individual from normal tasks and obligations; the recognition that being sick is undesirable; and the need to seek competent help. Parsons also included a conceptual framework for the role of the doctor in contemporary society which also contained four specific characteristics: the extensive training, competence, and symbolic portrayal of the practitioner as the representative of health; the necessity for the physician to exhibit sympathy, but not empathy with the patient to prevent interference with the objective nature of treatment; the obligation to treat all patients alike, regardless of the patient's rank or status; and finally the power stemming from the professional's status which must be restricted to medical matters. There have been many criticisms of the Parsonian sick role, in particular its failure to encompass chronic and mental illness and attitudes to disability; the stigma attached to certain conditions may deny the reintegration of the patient in society and the reality we perceive is often socially constructed rather than 'real' in the biological sense. Erving Goffman (1963) distinguished broad categories of discrediting attributes, for example, deformity of the body and imputed character defect, which are likely to involve exclusion from society and even 'abomination'. When these characteristics overlap, individuals may form minorities of the disabled and words like 'epileptic' or 'spastic', used in a derogatory manner, are the consequence. The provisions of the *Disabled Persons (Employment) Act and of similar legislation in other countries have not yet resulted in striking improvements in employment opportunities for disabled people. The term 'spoiled identity' coined by Goffman, provides a useful concept to explain the way in which individuals become excluded from customary reactions and expectations. Various sociological studies of infirmity have analysed both those who stigmatize (e.g. the process by which defeatist medical viewpoints are formed) and the identification of the stigmatizing process itself. Sociological typologies constructed independent of, and complementary to, the medical one illuminate disability and emphasize alternative perspectives. It is also important to emphasize that the stigma attached to certain conditions, mental illness in particular, affects the implementation of social policy recommendations aimed at the reintegration of the individual and his family into the fabric of social life.

It is clear from the preceding section that there are considerable variations in the way that individuals and families view illness: some studies have suggested that, contrary to the Parsonian view, families may not be 'victims' of illness and that stress and crisis may be managed. Indeed the individual may engage in a series of coping and adaptive measures. The traditional one-to-one relationship in medicine as envisaged by Parsons has also given way to the 'team' concept which includes the skills of many other professionals and lay people. The asymmetrical doctor–patient relationship based on the doctor's superior knowledge and skills has tended to become more equal because of two major forces for change; the women's movement, and consumer advocacy, which seek to transform the passive patient into an active participant in treatment and cure. The possibilities for conflict, especially if doctors hold dissimilar views of their role in the therapeutic relationship, must be kept in mind. It is also true that a shift in emphasis towards *preventive medicine relies more on persuasion than authority and leverage as the agent of social control. Government statements concerning the role of prevention rather than cure, in for example, *Prevention and Health: Everybody's Business* (1976) have led to interesting studies concerning lay beliefs as to the *aetiology of disease important in any *health education programme. These studies have attempted to answer some of the following questions: What diseases are mentioned by individuals? Are patients drug-dependent? How do they view *alternative therapies? What role does heredity, behaviour, or the environment have in disease cause? Were lay explanations different from those in medical science? How far do individuals feel responsible for diseases with a self-induced component? The answers to these questions have important implications for the success of social policy and the doctor–patient relationship, where the 'well-informed' citizen may question the content and authority of medical knowledge.

The profession of medicine and the division of labour. A major concern in the sociology of medicine is the analysis of the characteristics of the profession of medicine in relation to other professions and the paramedical professions. Some sociologists have concentrated on the essential traits of professions, for example, skill, knowledge, training, professional codes of conduct, and ideals of public service. Others, Freidson (1972) in particular, have defined a profession as one that has achieved autonomy—a position of legitimate control over its work granted and sanctioned by society. Once an occupation has been granted autonomy the test of its position is self-regulation, that is self-imposed quality control. He suggests that autonomy in medicine is of special concern in that we will all enter its domain, and external controls may be required to limit autonomy and self-regulation. As Stacey has argued, this is a perennial question relating to the accountability of the professions, and the mechanisms for clinical audit and complaints procedures. Freidson is also concerned with what is termed the 'medicalization' of society: disapproved behaviour is more and more given the meaning of illness rather than sin or crime. Some would argue that labelling deviant behaviour as illness is a humanitarian compassionate process, while others would claim that the profession of medicine is reluctant to extend its territory into spheres where the application of scientific knowledge is less effective, as in, for example, the treatment of *alcoholism (see also ADDICTION). Many would also put forward the view that while medicine defends its autonomy, the profession also upholds the confidentiality of the doctor–patient relationship; the privacy of the *consultation is sacrosanct.

Research into the relationship between doctors, nurses, and other health care workers has benefited from a historical and a comparative approach. The growth of specialism towards the end of the 19th c., in, for example, the development of *obstetrics, led to the downgrading of the skills and status of *midwives and comparative studies have illuminated the role of present-day Western medicine on traditional health careers and health practices. There is some evidence to suggest that such health programmes now recognize the importance of working with lay beliefs and the sociocultural aspects of health care. Other authors decry the expansion of medicine and identify the family, self-care, and community resources as contributing to people's health almost as counterforces in their own right to the iatrogenic medical care system. The two spheres often appear as a battleground and these 'mediating' structures are regarded as effective and economic alternatives to medical care. It is also argued that in times of scarce health care resources, to suggest cutting the support to families in their care of the old and the ill should be treated with caution.

Freidson's concepts of autonomy and what is termed 'the medical division of labour' are also useful explanatory tools in the struggle for territorial recognition between doctors, doctors and nurses, and other professional workers. In a similar context there have been interesting research studies examining the relationship between hospital and community health care, the general practitioners, and consultants. Others have reviewed the position of *women in medicine and concluded that career advancement has been affected by family responsibilities, and part-time work or employment in selected specialties are often the only avenues open to women doctors. The role of trade unions within the health service, the rise of district management teams in the reorganized *National Health Service, and the work of *Community Health Councils have implications for the financial structure of the service, the allocation of resources between specialties, and the role of the hospital and community services. The recommendations of the Royal Commission on the National Health Service (1979) are essential reading in any attempt to predict the relationship between consumers and providers of health care in the decades ahead:

The impressive contribution which acute medicine has made in relieving illness and suffering seems likely to continue. Diagnosis is continually being improved and refined by technological advances. Techniques such as tomography, ultrasound and radio-isotope scanning have been major advances. . . . At the same time the emphasis on acute and high technology medicine is being challenged

and more thought is being given to the care of the chronically sick and elderly. These developments are likely to continue.

Inequalities and measurement in health. The *World Health Organization defined health as 'a state of complete physical, mental and social well-being, and not merely the absence of disease or infirmity' and, however one may quibble about this definition, it is clear that health is dependent on policies both inside and outside medical care and co-operation across institutional and professional boundaries. Marked discrepancies in mortality profiles and social class have been noted in the UK ever since this particular form of analysis was introduced in 1911, but caution must be exercised in the use of both measures. The five social classes from professional to unskilled (i.e. from I to V) are based on occupation, each occupation allocated a class according to the rules contained in the *Registrar General's handbook. There have been repeated reclassifications over time and any changes noted may be due to these reassessments. Sociologically, social class is the most variable of terms, loosely used to denote all those individuals who possess relatively the same amounts of power, income, wealth, and opportunity, or some combination of those characteristics. The classification of cause of death is dependent on information on death certificates classified according to the rules in another handbook—the *International Classification of Disease*—which has also been revised over the years. Reservations about the usefulness of such statistics appear in the writings of Chalmers and Alberman but, despite these misgivings over both measures, considerable variations in mortality by social class are apparent even in the younger age groups; for example, in 1977 the *infant mortality rate for males in England in social class V was over twice that for social class I.

In 1980 the UK Department of Health and Social Security published *Inequalities in Health, Report of a Research Working Group (The Black Report)* which concluded that inequalities in health have complex, multicausal explanations and are partly explained by 'the vicious circle by which (through a variety of mechanisms) poor families are locked into material, educational, environmental and social disadvantage . . . but there remains much that is probably not explainable in any direct fashion and must be attributed to the pervasive effect of the class structure'.

Recommendations for future policy included a shift towards community care in antenatal, postnatal, and child health services, and the care of the elderly and the disabled. Particular emphasis was placed on policies for prevention rather than cure as a commitment by government departments. Measures taken outside the health services concentrated on an attack on child poverty (*child welfare) and greater co-operation in funding between health districts, local authorities, and government departments.

While there is general agreement among sociologists that the sociology of medicine denotes the scientific study of the social behaviour of human beings in health and illness, there continues to be a measure of disagreement concerning the nature of scientific method as applied to social phenomena. There can be no doubt that the natural sciences, such as chemistry and physics, are capable of achieving extremely high levels of verifiability made possible by exact measurement. Yet medicine, as an applied science, inhabits a less certain world; some physicians have suggested that they have accepted the tools of scientific research but have failed to apply scientific discipline to their assessments in clinical practice—they have taken the view that acceptability is dependent on clinical experience, not upon the results of randomized controlled *clinical trials with all their ethical and practical difficulties. Sociologists share these concerns, but view with excitement the continuing dialogue between both disciplines as to the importance of measurement, the role of quantification and participant observation in reconstructing the process of becoming ill, the medical encounter, and the structure of the health care system.

In conclusion, the themes which should unite both sociology and medicine are as follows: the accurate collection of data; the careful evaluation of new procedures and techniques; an imaginative use of methodology; an appreciation of the socio-cultural, behavioural, and biological nature of health and illness; and the special concerns of the sick and the old in their heightened awareness of possible disablement or death. The issues that may cause conflict usually stem from an inability to accept a multicausal view of health and illness and a reluctance to break the mould with radical initiatives, in teaching, research, and professional training. The challenges in the years ahead lie in increased consumer participation in decision-making in health, in developing primary care and strategies for the prevention of ill health, in improving the cost-effectiveness and quality of services, in reducing the effects of chronic and degenerative disease, environmental risks, and poverty, and in the promotion of health within the context of a caring community.   A. HOLOHAN

References

Freidson, E. (1972). *Profession of Medicine.* New York.
Goffman, E. (1963). *Stigma.* New York.
McKeown, T. (1979). *The Role of Medicine: Dream, Mirage, or Nemesis?* Oxford.
Mitchell, D. G. (1979). *A New Dictionary of Sociology.* London.
Parsons, T. (1954). *The Social System.* New York.
Prevention and Health: Everybody's Business (1976). HMSO, London.
Royal Commission on the National Health Service (1979). *Merrison Report.* London.

SODIUM is a soft, silvery, white, very reactive, metallic element which reacts violently with water forming *hydrogen gas and sodium hydroxide (symbol Na, atomic number 11, relative atomic mass 22.990). Its compounds are widely distributed in nature, the commonest being common salt or sodium chloride (NaCl). Sodium has a fundamental role in physiology as the main extracellular *cation (cf. *potassium); *depolarization of excitable tissue is accompanied by an influx of Na⁺ ions across the cell membranes.

SODIUM, SERUM. Normal range: 136–46 mmol/l of the blood serum. See also HYPERNATRAEMIA; HYPONATRAEMIA.

SODOMY is anal intercourse, particularly between males.

SOEMMERRING, SAMUEL THOMAS (1755–1830). German neuroanatomist, MD Göttingen (1778). Soemmerring was professor of anatomy at Kassel (1779) and later at Mainz (1784). He described the crossing of the fibres of the *optic nerves in 1786 and published a classification of the *cranial nerves. He was one of the inventors of the electric telegraph.

SOFTENING is degeneration, particularly of brain tissue (encephalomalacia).

SOFT SORE is a synonym for *chancroid.

SOLIDISM was an early doctrine which referred all diseases to the state of, or to morbid changes in, the solid parts of the body.

SOMATOSTATIN is a polypeptide hormone (with 14 amino acids), secreted by the delta cells of the *islets of Langerhans and by cells in the *hypothalamus, which has an inhibitory effect on the release of a number of other hormones. These include *growth hormone (GH), *adrenocorticotrophic hormone (ACTH), and *thyroid-stimulating hormone (TSH), from the anterior *pituitary; *gastrin; *secretin; *glucagon; *insulin; and *renin.

SORE. Any circumscribed area of skin or mucous membrane which is tender, injured, ulcerated, or in some other way diseased.

SOUND is a physiological sensation received by the ear, generated by a vibrating source with a frequency in the range 20–20000 Hz (cycles per second) and transmitted as a longitudinal pressure wave motion through a material medium (e.g. air).

SOUTHWOOD SMITH, THOMAS (1788–1861). English Unitarian minister. Southwood Smith came under the influence of Jeremy Bentham, and became an ardent health reformer, working alongside Edwin *Chadwick. He made a report to the *Poor Law Commissioners in 1838 on the physical causes of sickness and mortality among the poor. These he had observed during epidemic fevers in

Nottingham during 1837–8. He was one of the founders of the Epidemiological Society in 1850, previously having written a small treatise called *Philosophy of Health* in 1835, and had been a member of the Health of Towns Association in 1840. He was a member of the original *General Board of Health which evolved over the course of time into the *Ministry of Health in 1917. In its turn this has become the *Department of Health and Social Security.

SPA. A mineral-water resort or mineral spring (after Spa in Belgium). See MINERAL SPRINGS.

SPALLANZANI, LAZZARO (1729–99). Italian physiologist, Ph.D. Bologna (1753/4). Soon after graduation Spallanzani was ordained and is usually known as Abbate Spallanzani. He became professor of philosophy in Modena (1763) and of natural history in Pavia (1769). His wide-ranging achievements have been under-rated. He studied respiration and the circulation, distinguished between putrefaction and fermentation, disproved spontaneous generation, and established the digestive power of saliva and gastric juice. He undertook artificial insemination in dogs and proved that spermatozoa were essential for fertilization of the ovum.

SPANISH FLY. See CANTHARIDES.

SPASM. Sustained involuntary contraction of a muscle or group of muscles, or sustained constriction of a small vessel or other channel.

SPASTIC DIPLEGIA, or Little's disease, is the condition afflicting many of those patients loosely known as 'spastics' or as suffering from *cerebral palsy. It is impairment or paralysis of voluntary movement affecting both legs. The muscles involved exhibit increased resistance to passive movement (spasticity); and this heightening of muscle tone tends to keep the legs extended and the feet in plantar flexion (pointing downwards). The legs tend to become crossed when the body is supported, and during walking (the 'scissors' gait). There are no sensory changes, the arms are usually unaffected, and mental defect is less common than in other forms of cerebral palsy.

The condition is present from birth, or from soon afterwards, although the diagnosis may not become apparent for some time. There is a strong association with prematurity, and it is thought that lack of oxygen permanently damages a particular area of brain tissue. Spastic diplegia is becoming less common as a result of improvements in the management of premature babies.

SPASTICITY. Increased tone of skeletal muscle, with exaggeration of the *tendon jerks or reflexes.

SPECIALIST. See POSTGRADUATE AND CONTINUING MEDICAL EDUCATION; MEDICAL PRACTICE.

SPECIALIST PRACTICE. See MEDICAL PRACTICE.

SPECTACLES are frame-mounted lenses which correct *refractive errors of vision, or reduce the amount of light reaching the eye. See OPHTHALMOLOGY.

SPECTROPHOTOMETER. A *photometer for comparing at various wavelengths the light emission from two sources (or the light absorption of two substances).

SPECTROSCOPY is the observation and analysis of spectra.

SPECULUM. An instrument designed to assist the examination of body cavities and passages. Some specula include reflecting mirrors, often of polished metal.

SPEECH is the utterance of vocal sounds codified into meaningful language.

SPEECH DISORDERS may be due to disturbances of articulation (anarthria, *dysarthria); of phonation (aphonia, *dysphonia); of language function (*aphasia, dysphasia); or to psychiatric illness. See LANGUAGE, COGNITION AND HIGHER CEREBRAL FUNCTION.

SPEECH THERAPISTS are staff professionally trained in the application and use of special techniques aimed at improving language and speech disorders. See LANGUAGE, COGNITION, AND HIGHER CEREBRAL FUNCTION; PROFESSIONS SUPPLEMENTARY, ETC. TO MEDICINE IN THE UK.

SPENCE, SIR JAMES CALVERT (1892–1954). British paediatrician and pioneer of social paediatrics, MB Durham (1914), MD Durham (1921), MRCP (1921), FRCP (1931). Spence was born and educated in the north of England and, though many national and international honours came his way, remained there for almost all his life. His early medical education was at the Newcastle upon Tyne medical school (at that time part of Durham University), from which he graduated in 1914 with honours, a result which surprised his contemporaries who knew him as a 'gay, versatile and athletic student' whose most obvious attainments had been at mountaineering and football. Immediately joining the Army, he served with the Royal Army Medical Corps at Gallipoli, in Egypt, and in France; when demobilization came in 1918 he had been twice decorated (Military Cross and bar). The next three years he spent in London, first as house physician at the Hospital for Sick Children, *Great Ormond Street, and then as John and Temple Research Fellow at *St Thomas's Hospital. He returned to Newcastle in 1922 as registrar in chemical pathology and medicine at the *Royal Victoria Infirmary, holding this position for five years. A period at *Johns Hopkins Hospital,

Baltimore, followed, during tenure of a Rockefeller research fellowship, after which he came back to Newcastle as a general physician on the staff of the Infirmary. Over the following years, his interest and activity in the medicine and welfare of children increased, extending beyond the bounds of the teaching hospital itself to other hospitals in the city (including the famous Babies' Hospital which he himself established) and to the municipal child welfare organization. Spence's department of child health acquired a world-wide reputation as a major experiment in social medicine, and in 1942 he became the first Nuffield professor of child health in the University of Durham (the second chair in this subject in the UK). Spence's interests, which had earlier tended to the more scientific aspects of his discipline, such as *clinical trials (e.g. his report in 1933 to the *Medical Research Council on the effect of calciferol in *rickets) were by now turned towards the larger issues of child development, growth, nutrition, and health (the classical 1000-family survey began in 1947, following his 1939 analysis of the causes of infant mortality and a smaller but important investigation of the health and nutrition of children between the ages of one and five). Among his many other contributions was his well-known and now widely emulated innovation of admitting mothers along with their sick children into single hospital rooms, eliminating the then considerable hazard of cross-infection and providing a kinder and more efficient as well as a safer environment for hospital care. Nationally, his influence on medicine, medical education, and the evolving *National Health Service grew far beyond the field of *paediatrics, being manifest particularly through his membership of three important bodies: the Medical Research Council, the *University Grants Committee, and the Central Health Services Council. His wisdom and his philosophy, in which scientific medicine and a profound humanism were combined, were greatly valued and much heeded. Sadly, his premature death occurred in 1954, when his powers and his influence were at their height.

SPERM. *Semen; or *spermatozoon.

SPERMATOZOON. A male gamete or germ cell, the essential generative component of *semen.

SPHINCTER. A circular muscle guarding the orifice of an organ and controlling passage through it, e.g. the anal sphincter.

SPHINGOMYELIN is one of a group of phospholipids (see LIPIDS) found in membranes and in brain and nervous tissue.

SPHYGMOGRAPH. Any instrument for recording the arterial *pulse.

SPHYGMOGRAPHY is the recording of arterial *pulse waves.

SPHYGMOMANOMETRY is the measurement of arterial *blood pressure. See KOROTKOFF SOUNDS.

SPICA. A spiral, figure-of-eight bandage, so called because of its resemblance to an ear of barley, often applied to anatomical features of differing dimensions, such as the thumb and the hand. A hip spica is a complicated *plaster-of-paris cast used in immobilization for fractures near or dislocation of the *hip joint.

SPIDERS are arthropods of the class Arachnida, order Araneida, suborders Labidognatha (true spiders) and Orthognatha (tarantulas or bird spiders). Almost all spiders envenomate their prey, but only a very few are of medical importance in the sense of biting and envenomating man. Of these, the best known are members of the genus *Latrodectus* (including the *black widow spider) and the genus *Loxosceles* (brown spiders).

SPINA BIFIDA is a condition which results from defective development of the posterior wall of the spinal canal, that is the neural arches (see SPINE), and thus one or more vertebrae remain incomplete. The defect may be a minor and symptomless one, discovered only on X-ray (spina bifida occulta). In more serious cases there is herniation of the meninges through the opening (meningocele); the spinal cord itself may be involved, with varying degrees of neurological disorder including total paralysis of the lower part of the body and incontinence. Sometimes an associated anomaly prevents normal circulation of *cerebrospinal fluid causing the condition known as *hydrocephalus, which may add mental retardation to the already formidable medical and social problems facing these babies if they survive.

Spina bifida is a relatively common congenital abnormality (approximately one in 300 live births). Controversy exists about its causation, particularly with regard to the relative importance of genetic and environmental factors. Prenatal detection is possible in some cases by examination of the amniotic fluid (see ALPHAFETOPROTEIN; AMNIOCENTESIS; ANENCEPHALY).

SPINAL ANAESTHESIA is a variety of regional *anaesthesia in which a *local anaesthetic agent is injected into the *subarachnoid space round the *spinal cord.

SPINAL CARIES is tuberculous *osteitis of the vertebrae and intervertebral cartilages.

SPINAL CORD. That part of the *central nervous system contained within the spinal canal of the vertebral column (see SPINE). It is continuous above with the medulla oblongata of the brain, beginning at the level of the foramen magnum of the skull and extending down the canal as far as the first lumbar vertebra. It comprises a central core of grey matter (nerve cells) surrounded by an outer layer of white matter (myelinated nerve fibres). In this grey matter incoming sensory fibres (neurones) form connections (synapses) with the cell bodies of other neurones, some of which give rise to fibres which synapse in turn with anterior cells in the anterior horn of grey matter from which motor fibres (lower motor neurones) arise and pass into the anterior roots. Other fibres carry sensation upwards in the columns of white matter to the brain. The posterior columns are concerned with fibres carrying fine touch, tactile discrimination, and position and joint sense, while the spinothalamic tracts of the lateral columns contain ascending fibres which have crossed the midline of the cord close to the central canal (which is continuous above with the fourth ventricle of the brain) and which carry the sensations of pain and temperature. There are also several descending pathways in the lateral columns such as the corticospinal (pyramidal) tract which carries messages from the brain to the anterior horn cells in order to initiate movement. Thirty-one pairs of spinal nerves arise from the cord (8 cervical, 12 thoracic, 5 lumbar, 5 sacral, and 1 coccygeal). These spinal nerves are formed by the union of posterior roots which carry incoming sensory impulses from peripheral nerves into the spinal cord (via cell stations attached to these roots in each intervertebral foramen, called the posterior root ganglia) and anterior roots which carry impulses outwards from the cord that pass down the motor nerves to supply the voluntary muscles (see NEUROMUSCULAR DISEASE). The cord is surrounded by three protective membranes or *meninges, the innermost pia mater, the arachnoid, and the outermost dura mater.

SPINAL DYSRAPHISM is a *neural tube defect. See SPINA BIFIDA.

SPINAL FUSION is surgical *ankylosis of one or more vertebral joints of the *spine.

SPINAL TUMOUR. A variety of neoplasms may arise either within the spinal cord itself (the commonest being *astrocytoma and *ependymoma) or outside the cord but within the spinal canal (most commonly *neurofibroma and *meningioma). Tumours arising outside the canal, for example in the vertebral bodies, may invade or compress the cord and its roots; these are usually metastatic (from the breast, lung, prostate, kidney, etc.).

SPINA VENTOSA is *tuberculous dactylitis (inflammation of the digits) occurring in infants and young children affecting one or more of the fingers and toes. It causes a hard red spindle-shaped swelling of the entire digit, usually with *abscess formation. Permanent deformity may result.

SPINE. The spinal or vertebral column, or backbone, is the distinguishing characteristic of vertebrates. It may be described as a jointed hollow rod enclosing the *spinal cord. In man, the spine consists of 33 vertebrae (7 cervical, 12 thoracic, 5 lumbar, 5 sacral, and 4 coccygeal), the upper 24 of which form separate bones with flexible joints occupied by the intervertebral *discs. Each *vertebra consists of a main weight-bearing rounded body, from the back of which projects a neural arch forming part of the spinal canal containing the *spinal cord. The neural arch has three projections, right and left transverse processes and a posterior spinous process, which serve as points of attachment for muscles.

SPIRITS, in the medical context, usually implies a solution in *ethanol (ethyl alcohol): alternatively, it means any liquid obtained by distillation.

SPIROCHAETES are spiral *bacteria. Spirochaetales is one of the 10 orders of the class Schizomycetes (bacteria); it has two families (Spirochaetaceae and Treponemataceae), each of which is subdivided into three genera and numerous species. The term 'spirochaete' therefore applies to a vast number of different bacteria and most of these have no medical importance. Those which do include the agents of *syphilis, *yaws, *bejel (or non-venereal childhood syphilis), *pinta (a skin disease of tropical S. America), *relapsing fever, *rat-bite fever, and the various forms of *leptospirosis.

SPIROMETER. An instrument for measuring the volume of air taken in and out by the lungs during breathing.

SPLEEN. A large unpaired organ situated in the left upper part of the abdominal cavity between the stomach and the left kidney, behind the left lower ribs and underneath the left hemidiaphragm. It is purple and pliable, oblong in shape and about 125 mm along the long axis. It is rarely palpable in health, but readily becomes so in a number of pathological conditions leading to an increase in size (splenomegaly) and a firmer consistency. It has a fibrous structure occupied by blood and lymphoid tissue.

The spleen has a number of functions: in fetal life and in the newborn it is a site of new red blood cell formation, a function to which it can revert in later life under certain conditions; it acts as a reservoir of blood; it sequesters and destroys ageing or imperfect red blood cells; it is part of the immunological system, producing *antibodies, *plasma cells, and *lymphocytes; it is also part of the *reticulo-endothelial system. None of these functions, however, is vital or unique, and surgical removal of the spleen (occasionally necessary, e.g. after abdominal trauma) does not usually produce obvious ill-effects in adults. Removal is also needed in some blood diseases (see HAEMATOLOGY).

SPLENOMEGALY is enlargement of the *spleen.

SPLINT. Any device for immobilizing part of the body.

SPONDYLITIS is inflammation of the vertebrae. See also ANKYLOSING SPONDYLITIS.

SPONDYLOSIS is any non-inflammatory (e.g. degenerative) disorder of the spine.

SPONGIFORM ENCEPHALOPATHY is a term descriptive of the pathological appearance of the brain in certain putative *slow virus infections of the central nervous system, such as *kuru, *scrapie, and *Creutzfeldt–Jacob disease.

SPORE. A resting or dormant form assumed by certain bacteria (e.g. species of *Clostridium*) in which they are able to survive a wide variety of environmental changes.

SPOROTRICHOSIS. A mycosis due to the fungus *Sporothrix schenckii*, commonly found as a mould on vegetation and wood. The infection is a chronic *granulomatous process usually limited to the skin and regional *lymphatics but like other mycoses it may become disseminated under certain conditions, notably in *immunosuppression from any cause. A rare pulmonary form may follow inhalation of spores. Sporotrichosis occurs most frequently in Central and South America.

SPORT. An unusual variant appearing as a result of *genetic mutation.

SPORT AND MEDICINE

Historical. Sport is one of the oldest organized activities known to man, derived from training for the hunt and for battle. Many modern events in sport such as the javelin and discus in the track and field programme display this origin.

Whilst sport was originally an applied form of training it had nevertheless certain intrinsic attractions which enabled different events to develop as recreational activities in their own right. This civilizing influence became manifest in the ancient Olympic Games, some of the events being little different from those of today.

The relationship between sport and medicine has always been at best problematical. The benefits of *exercise have long been known while those of training for sport have been perhaps more dubious. Plato's concept of the athlete as a 'sickly thing' is certainly not in keeping with modern attitudes to sport.

The first physician recorded as interested in dealing with medical problems of sport was *Galen of Pergamum, 'team physician' to the gladiators, and later to become court physician to the Emperor Marcus Aurelius.

With the collapse of the Hellenistic civilizations the ideals of the Olympic Games collapsed too, to be replaced in Rome by the excesses of the circus and the development of gladiatorial combat (which really have no role in the direct evolution of true sport, though perhaps they are still reflected these days in bull-fighting and cock-fighting). Despite such aggressive activities in the arena the Romans developed a system of hygiene and exercise totally separate from sport as set out in such treatises on health through exercise as *De sanitate tuenda* by Hieronymus Mercurialis.

In the Middle Ages sport once again reverted to martial preparation—the Battle of Agincourt was won by English bowmen who had been forbidden to play football because it interfered with their archery practice!

The increasing leisure of the aristocracy in more settled Elizabethan times allowed sport to become more popular as a recreational activity, and royal or 'real' tennis, as distinct from lawn tennis, for example, achieved royal recognition when Henry VIII built his court at Hampton Court (though royal tennis is of older origin if Shakespeare's representation of the Dauphin's gift to Henry V is anything to go by). Elizabethan sport was thus descended from the courtly practices instilled in young esquires training for knighthood, many of whom had undergone their schoolboy training in monastic institutions which were forerunners of the English public schools. And it was later in the English public school system particularly that sports were nourished for their character-building potential. It is said that by contrast with Agincourt the Battle of Waterloo was won on the playing fields of Eton. Whether this was a result of the high ideals of leadership generated thereon or simply because Eton schoolboys had learnt the ability to survive in the organized thuggery that was football in those days is uncertain.

Sport, however, remained an occupation of the well-to-do higher social classes until the turn of the century when it was the enthusiasm of the Baron Pierre du Cubertin in founding the modern Olympic movement that gave impetus to sport as a universal activity in terms both of geographical spread and social distribution. At the same time gymnasiarchs such as Per Hendrick Ling developed the codes of health-giving gymnastics so that sport again achieved its object of being a health-giving activity.

In the latter part of the 20th c. commercial interests have given a further nudge to the development of sport, producing a number of disturbing problems in their train. Financial rewards are often now immense but bring in their train tremendous pressures on participants both physically (in the training needed for expert performance at the highest level) and psychologically (in the stresses imposed by the need to win). A further twist has been added by the overt nationalism expressed in the somewhat cynical Eastern European concept that sportsmen are the new soldiers who have to fight the ideological battles on the playing field rather than on the battlefield. Despite all these difficulties, sport remains in the main a universally enjoyable and rewarding experience which, particularly in civilized countries, plays a more and more important part in the social well-being of individuals and communities. And many doctors have excelled in sport—Sir Roger Bannister, when a medical student, ran the first four-minute mile (see also DOCTORS AS ATHLETES; DOCTORS IN OTHER WALKS OF LIFE).

Sports medicine. The idea that sports medicine is a particular specialty within medicine as a whole is relatively recent and somewhat suspect. It is better defined as the appropriate application of the whole range of medicine to sport and of sport to medicine, and can be conceived as demonstrating four main components: man as an athlete; the athlete as a person; the athlete as a patient; and the patient as an athlete.

Man as an athlete. Vigorous physical activity as characterized by sport makes specific physical and mental demands on the participant. Training is the process by which the capacity to meet these demands may be developed and it produces significant changes in the individual—it is virtually only in the sporting and perhaps in the military service contexts that high human physical performance is required. The ability of an individual to cope with a physically very demanding training programme depends on a multiplicity of factors and although attempts have been made to formulate the work demands of certain types of activity, for example sprinting, these remain essentially academic paradigms rather than directly applicable 'instructions'. The basic characteristics that determine physical performance, particularly those that are amenable to modification, are however relatively easy to define, the scientific fields covering them including applied physiology, psychology, anthropometry, biomechanics (the mechanics of movement in living creatures), kinesiology (the scientific study of human movement, relating mechanics and anatomy), and biochemistry. Research on the physiology of exercise has yielded considerable information of value in the investigation of diseases of skeletal muscle, to quote but one example.

The essential components of physical fitness can be considered under two headings; 'General' and 'Specific': the former includes components common to all activities including general physiological (e.g. cardiovascular) fitness and psychological health, whereas the specific components are speed, strength, local endurance, skill, and flexibility, all of which relate in a very specific way to the particular activity in question. As a general rule any form of physical training will tend to improve general physiological fitness, but the specific nature of the fitness developed (e.g. cardiovascular endurance) is a reflection of the actual activity carried out; this is even more true of the specific factors making up fitness and is the basis of the principle of specificity of training. For example, a man may be fit to run a marathon in 2 hours and 20 minutes and yet be quite unable to survive five minutes in a game of rugby football or squash rackets.

General cardiovascular fitness relates to the ability of the individual to supply energy to his working muscle groups, by means of oxygenated blood pumped by the heart through the blood vessels and to remove waste products therefrom. Certain physiological parameters have suggested themselves as indices of training potential but because of the multifactorial nature of fitness the validity of these parameters remains in doubt. As an example, the maximum voluntary oxygen uptake (VO_2max) is commonly regarded as an index of cardiorespiratory endurance potential, yet there are many individuals with relatively low uptakes and relatively limited respiratory turnovers who even in endurance events perform extremely well because of a high degree of efficiency elsewhere. By contrast other individuals with high endurance capacities are often unable to capitalize on their potential because of inadequacy of co-ordination and inability to develop sufficiently mechanically efficient patterns of movement.

Certain fitness components can be developed or realized apparently quite rapidly while others demand time (although there is considerable variation between individuals).

Skill is essentially a matter of developing patterns of movement to the level of *conditioned reflexes, so that they can be carried out with the maximum of efficiency and the minimum of effort, but these patterns nevertheless remain under higher control so that the reflex response can be modified for the particular needs of the occasion. An example from the English game of cricket of this type of skill development is seen in the opening batsman who has to develop his batting technique to reflex level to cope with the opening fast bowler and yet needs to be able to modify this technique minutely to account for changes in the swing, in the air, or in pace off the wicket caused by climatic variation—somewhat similar problems face the baseball batter facing a skilled pitcher. Even in the individual exhibiting a high degree of motor educability the development of skill takes time although some individuals appear particularly gifted and have a remarkable initial degree of co-ordination, such as the eye/hand co-ordination of fast ball players. By contrast, strength appears to be developed quite rapidly, though perhaps it is more true to say that it is the ability of the muscle to realize progressively higher tensions (which it already has the potential to develop) which is gained rapidly, while development of strength due to increase in muscle fibre bulk takes place more slowly.

In general the body's response to activity is two-stage. The immediate or primary physiological changes are directed towards returning the body to the *status quo ante* exercise and a series of fast responses are demonstrable, an example being the increase in pulse rate that follows exercise. As soon as the pre-exercise state has been regained the physiological responses to the exercise are switched off. When the stimulus of exercise is maintained and repeated regularly before the subject has fully recovered from the previous bout, a secondary process of adaptation occurs which alters the pre-exercise state so as to diminish the need for so great a primary response. Thus in the cardiovascular system, for example, continuous exercise promotes a secondary physiological cardiac enlargement which allows for the maintenance of the necessary increased cardiac output during exercise without the need for such a high pulse rate. This adaptation or 'training effect' is a specific response to continuing exercise in that it disappears once exercise is discontinued.

In addition to functional physiological changes there are associated changes in biochemistry. Among the most interesting of these noted recently have been the changes in the *fat content of the body, particularly in the *brown fat deposits in some individuals, and in the *mitochondria in skeletal muscle, associated with endurance as opposed to strength training. The study of these phenomena and their application in the sporting context is part of the first element of sports medicine, the understanding of *man as an athlete.*

Study of the physical constitution of the individual and the extent to which this may be modified by training and of the role of the mind in physical performance are other important components of this element. It is known, for example, that physical performance capacity far outstrips achievement level except under conditions of extreme motivation (as in emergency or survival situations). From the long-term point of view in sport, as indeed in any other physical performance areas, interest will lie in the mobilization of motivation to achieve that performance of which the individual has already been theoretically capable in purely physical terms.

The athlete as a person. The second element of sports medicine studies the trained athlete as a man or woman in relation to the environment. It takes into account the peculiar factors of age and gender which may influence athletic performance, and the clinical problems that derive therefrom.

Sport is typically an activity of the second and third decades and it is within these decades that most clinical problems arise; nevertheless, participants' ages range widely from the very young to the elderly. Children are now being taught to swim before they can run and the foundations of a competitive career in sport may be laid among six-to eight-year olds (as it often is in ballet and music). Development of relatively intense training programmes for the young imposes peculiar clinical problems which are not part of normal *paediatric medicine—a particular problem is that overload injury in adolescents tends to affect the skeletal system rather than soft tissues, damage sustained before skeletal maturity subsequently giving rise to permanent disability.

In middle age, athletic activity may prove incompatible with the early *degenerative changes which affect not only the locomotor system but also the cardiovascular system. The incidence of myocardial infarction and *coronary thrombosis in middle-aged sportsmen, particularly those who, when improperly trained, unwisely engaged in high-grade competitive activity, is cause for concern. This has been exemplified by comments on the risk of such illness in middle-aged squash rackets players which has attracted attention in recent years. Perhaps the major problem is less the risk of myocardial infarction than the fact that when such an infarction occurs, if it does so in an actively exercising heart the result is likely to be far more serious than in the heart which is sustaining a relatively low cardiac output.

The ambivalent relationship of physical activity to maturity manifested on the one hand by the apparent benefits of long-term exercise in the prevention of cardiac disease and on the other by the problems of the 'Peter Pan syndrome' is well known. (Peter Pan was the ever-young hero of J. M. Barrie's famous play—and the expression Peter Pan syndrome is applied to those athletes who appear unable to accept the inevitable reduction of physical prowess with increasing age.) Even in the elderly subject, sporting activity is becoming more popular, not only through such obvious games as bowls (which incidentally carries the highest mortality rate in terms of number of deaths occurring per *n* hours of play!—although in these cases death is not of course a direct consequence of the game itself) and golf, but also through more overtly energetic activity such as marathon running. The peculiar physiological problems associated with training in the different age groups and the variable spectrum of age-related clinical conditions in sport forms a major part of this element of sports medicine.

Differences in gender introduce important problems. The fundamental differences between male and female are hardly to be denied, yet peculiarly the definition of femininity does not rest absolutely on any single parameter. Thus it is possible to derive definitions of femininity on anatomical, physiological, psychological, biochemical, genetic, or chromosomal bases, the end-points of which do not necessarily coincide. This may provide problems in sex definition in those sporting activities where there are manifest differences in capability between men and women, necessitating the segregation of the sexes for competitive purposes. While it is certainly true to say that some female athletes and sportswomen may perform better than some males, on balance a masculine male is always capable of higher performance than any female, bearing in mind that sports have evolved from activities specifically designed to emphasize masculine characteristics.

In recent years the role of women in sport has undergone dramatic change, in part as a result of a sympathetic understanding and re-evaluation of woman's physical capacity. The argument of equal pay (and perhaps equal opportunity) for equal work is almost universally accepted but what many feminists will not admit is that in a sporting context many women are not capable of equality of work as compared with their male counterparts. There seems little justification for offering the same prize money for men and women in events such as lawn tennis when the performance of even the best of the women cannot match up to that of the best of the men. In those activities, however, where there is no inbuilt inequality, for example equestrianism, male and female can and do compete on level terms—indeed it might be argued that masculine characteristics such as bigness of frame and strength may be to the disadvantage of the male competitor in events of this type. The anatomical and physiological differences between the average male and the average female competitor significantly influence responses to training and the actual performance of certain sporting activities as well as the clinical problems that may derive therefrom. Femoral obliquity in females is a known predisposer to anterior knee pain syndromes of the *chondromalacia patellae type. The fact that it seems relatively less common in female athletes than in females generally may be a reflection of the fact that female athletic activity tends to appeal more to a population of women with masculine characteristics and less oblique femora. It is in this area of clinical anthropometry that much research in the comparison of male and female sporting performance has yet to be done.

Female athletes also face the additional problems of the effects on physical performance of their menstrual cycles, although in some athletes a degree of *amenorrhoea may develop with an apparent suppression of the cycle and of *ovulation. The majority, however, continue to experience *menstruation and although physical fitness and athleticism appear to have a beneficial effect on the facility with which a woman copes with menstruation, problems do occasionally arise. The availability of suitable hormone preparations for menstrual control has greatly facilitated the preparation by the female athlete for major competition and has in fact made fair competition between female athletes possible.

Apart from such obvious influences on athletic activity as age and gender, the specific environment in which the athlete finds himself is also highly significant. Modification of physiological response due to variation in climate is well recognized; factors such as temperature, humidity, and *altitude (with reduced oxygen tension in the inspired air) are all examples. These environmental factors may influence athletic activity either advantageously, or otherwise, and a proper understanding of these factors and of methods by which the disadvantages can be offset is an essential component of the scientific basis of training as is environmental engineering, an evolving art in the preparation of suitable locales for athletic activity.

And jet lag, resulting from long-distance travel, must be avoided or overcome.

In addition to the ambient environment there are other significant factors relating to the immediate environment, specifically clothing and footwear. The demands of the high performance athlete in terms of, for example, heat exchange and water loss, significantly influence the type of clothing most appropriate for various forms of athletic activity. The same considerations also apply to footwear. The average individual walking relatively slowly over relatively short distances is able to cope with a much less exact shoe fitting and much less carefully designed padding than the long-distance runner running over 100 miles per week. Similarly, unsuitable equipment for athletic activity such as the wrong-sized racket handle in tennis, inefficient rowing rig, inadequately adjusted asymmetric bars for the female gymnast, may cause real problems and precipitate injury in the trained performer.

In recent years much attention has been paid to the alteration of the internal environment in the athlete by drugs, a process commonly known as 'doping'. Various procedures have been used from time to time, including those designed to affect performance while being taken (involving the use of *sedatives to damp down nervous reaction in sporting competition—e.g. the use of *diazepam in shooting—or the use of *stimulants to offset the onset of fatigue—e.g. the use of *amphetamine in a variety of endurance events). In some instances drugs are taken to have a distant effect, that is significantly to influence the training process without necessarily being present in the body when competition is taking place. In the latter category are the *anabolic steroids.

The extent to which drugs may or may not work is, in fact, equivocal and there is little concrete scientific evidence available to justify their use in purely biological terms. However, if athletes believe that drugs will help them perform better, then they will use them, as has been evidenced by the large number of positive dope tests that have been found since the introduction of dope control in the late 1960s. So much is this the case that dope control has become a growth industry in support of sport from the Olympic Games downwards and many sophisticated tests have had to be evolved to trap the athlete who resorts to the use of drugs in attempts artificially to improve performance.

The athlete as a patient. The third great element of sports medicine covers the athlete as a patient, and embraces three major fields—sports traumatology, internal medicine, and sports psychiatry.

1. *How injuries occur.* Inevitably perhaps, most attention is paid to sports injuries; many of these are dramatic, frequently affecting well-known and important sports personalities. By often providing an immediate interruption of sporting activity with inevitable subsequent disability they create a

demand for instant action. Many of the injuries which occur in sport are not different from those that occur in other activities, since while the human body is able to differentiate between types of stress applied to it (i.e. the pathological response to a direct blow is different from that of a sudden stretch), it is not able to identify the particular activity in which an injury is sustained; thus in general there is little difference in the pathological response to a blow sustained on a football field and one sustained tripping over in the home or out in the street. However, the condition of the tissue involved at the time of injury will often significantly influence the effect of that injury. For example, extravasation of blood will generally be greater in fit and exercising muscle than in unfit and unexercised muscle when the same blow is applied to each. This peculiar vulnerability of exercising tissue to damage is particularly significant in athletic patients.

Most injuries in sport are instantaneous, that is to say, they occur as a result of the application of sudden immediate stress to the body to which it has no opportunity to adapt. These injuries (which occur in other activities as well) are most common in body contact sports where the forces applied are multiplied by the external agents involved as they are in vehicular and similar injuries.

A classification of *aetiology of injury in sport relating the causative mechanisms to the injury sustained has been evolved, and is useful since its application very often gives guidance as to the nature of the injury involved. In injury it is mechanism that matters rather than the activity in which the mechanism is found. It is thus meaningless to talk about 'football injuries' or 'tennis injuries' since no such sport-related as opposed to mechanism-related 'injuries' exist. Classification of injury by sport tends anyway to be unnecessarily exclusive and too often to obscure the need to approach analytically each injury as an individual incident. It is true that certain injuries tend to occur repeatedly in certain sports, essentially because the mechanism of injury is inherent in the way in which the particular sport is played or practised. Thus *meniscal injuries of the knee are common in Association football ('soccer') because the game involves the application of rotational stress to the flexed weight-bearing knee, whereas in American and Rugby football *ligament injuries are more common since the stresses applied tend to be linear rather than rotational. This concept of mechanism as the immediate cause is essential to an understanding of injury in sport (as indeed it is in understanding injuries generally).

Sport is peculiar in the extent to which self-inflicted or intrinsic injuries occur. These do not involve external forces or outside agents but are the result of the generation of excessive force within the body. For example, failure of muscular co-ordination causes muscle tears or strains. These may be precipitated by external factors such as the environment (when the ground underfoot is uncertain the foot tends to slip adding further stress to the player's inadequate co-ordination, so precipitating injury). Such injuries tend to be relatively minor since as a rule the forces generated within the body cannot be as great as those externally generated. Even so, the force of muscular contraction can be so powerful as to cause fractures of the shaft of the humerus (as in thrower's arm). Since these injuries tend to be due to faults in the sportsman's technique, an essential component of the treatment phase is the appropriate development of the required motor skill to prevent recurrence.

One other major group of injuries occurs in sport, and more commonly in sport than elsewhere (although they do occur amongst individuals in the fighting services, in people starting in new and unaccustomed jobs, and in the occasional do-it-yourself enthusiast): the over-use injuries. These are the result of failure of the body to recover sufficiently after one episode of exercise before another episode is superimposed. Excess stress in activity will through normal physiological processes induce a low-grade transient *inflammatory response. Given time, this inflammation will subside (usually rapidly) before the next bout of activity but when this is not the case repeated activity may produce a summation of inflammation or 'micro-trauma' leading to injury. Sometimes a single episode of prolonged activity may of itself be sufficiently severe to induce an immediate summation of inflammation and acute over-use injury. Thus while a stress fracture or *tenovaginitis (inflammation of the fibrous *tendon sheath) develops slowly as a result of repeated insults, acute *tenosynovitis or the simple skin blister may be the results of single episodes of over-activity.

The over-activity may occur either at a time when the individual is taking up exercise de novo or may occur as a result of a drastic change in the training programme which, while not over-loading the body as a whole, has the effect of over-loading one particular part or system thereof. At one time, when long-distance runners tended to train cross-country during the winter season, only running on the track with an altered leg and foot action during the summer months, *Achilles tendon problems were common during the transitional period in the spring. Such injuries are less commonly concentrated at this time of the year now as a result of the availability of all-weather tracks for training throughout the year.

Patterns of injury in sport are readily established and it has thus become possible to identify significant problems in sport, many of which can be tackled by appropriate preventive means. The management of injury in sport as elsewhere involves both prevention and treatment. Prevention demands an understanding of the relationship of the injury to the activities involved in the sports programme.

One of the practical problems derives from the fact that steps necessary to reduce inherent risk of injury may denature the sport itself. A classic example of this is to be found in boxing. There is no doubt that severe brain damage is a consequence of long-term repeated head injury, and even today the '*punch-drunk syndrome' may be observed in retired boxers who have relatively recently given up the sport, despite the introduction over the past two decades of improved methods of control and protection of boxers (the same problem, however, can be seen in participants in other sports, such as Rugby Union football and National Hunt horse racing). This presents a real moral dilemma in that it may well be necessary to consider abolishing sports which carry unnecessary risk—but where is the line to be drawn? The situation is further complicated by the fact that too often little is known of the mechanics of the sport itself and many methods designed to protect against injury may in fact have the opposite effect. For example, in boxing the increase in padding of the glove may render the boxer able to accept more punishment in terms of total energy absorbed by the head, while diminishing the effect of any single blow. The relative danger of a single sharp blow causing unconsciousness as opposed to repeated not-so-hard blows that do not render the victim unconscious but may have a cumulative effect, is uncertain.

The concept of prevention of injury by regulation of the manner in which a sport is conducted is readily accepted and the laws of many sports, particularly the most vigorous, contain specific regulations to limit and control violence and to prevent injury. However, changing patterns in the way in which games and sports are practised lead to changing patterns of injury, so that regular monitoring and appropriate action is called for. Sadly, this is not always forthcoming, and even when it is, the last result may be worse than the first unless there is a proper understanding of the likely consequences of changes in the game. For example, the increased incidence of cervical spinal injuries in Rugby Union football in recent years has come about because of changes in the way the game is played and unfortunately some of the revisions intended to reduce that incidence have been not only pointless but have possibly made injuries more common. By contrast, in American football the outlawing of 'spearing' has reduced the incidence of such neck injuries. Only a real understanding of the mechanism of an injury allows proper preventive measures to be adopted.

At the level of the game itself, injury prevention involves a series of different factors, the first of which is a proper adherence to the rules under the supervision of the referee or umpire who sees that they are correctly interpreted on the field of play not only in letter but also in spirit. But in the last analysis, even the best referee is unable completely to prevent injury if players themselves do not play their part in controlling themselves. Whatever the rules may be in relation to what is or is not permitted in, for example, a rugby scrum, if a player himself breaks the rules the referee can do nothing about it at the time and can only penalize the player *after* the rule is broken, by which time the damage is done!

Quite apart from the simple matter of obeying the rules of the game, prevention of injury is enhanced by proper preparation and fitness for the game. This means the development of adequate levels of skill, endurance, and general fitness on the one hand and the proper recovery and redevelopment of those skills after injury on the other. One sad consequence of the admission of substitutes to play in many sports today has been the tendency to allow people on to the field whose fitness is suspect, on the basis that if they break down they can always be replaced. This has been the inevitable consequence of encouraging people to play while they are still vulnerable and often exacerbates rather than diminishes the effects of injury.

Because players are more liable to injury when fatigued or suffering from the effects of a previous injury, technique becomes a most important component of fitness in the prevention of injury. This is seen in body-contact sports such as football or the grid-iron game in which major injury tends to be relatively rare and to occur in the early part of the game, whereas minor injury is relatively frequent and occurs in the latter part of the game. The same effect of fatigue is seen in other fields of sport, such as adventure sport (e.g. mountaineering and canoeing) and skiing where injury is much more likely in the last period of activity when the victim has become tired. The importance of being fit to do the sport cannot be overemphasized.

The third factor in the prevention of injury is the provision of adequate and safe clothing, footwear, and equipment. In many sports, protective clothing is essential to diminish the risk of injury. Such clothing must comply with a number of basic requirements if it is to do its task properly. It must provide complete or adequate protection to the appropriate part of the body under conditions of use, and should withstand any foreseeable impact. It must be made of a material such as to allow proper cleansing and it must also retain its properties for a reasonable and stated period of time. Protective clothing is not acceptable if it loses its capacity to protect. It must be designed and made so as to allow the wearer appropriate freedom of action without interfering with his activities in a possibly dangerous way, and it must also be constructed and worn so that it does not put other players at risk. Too often so-called protective clothing has the opposite effect—the development of the ski-boot is a classic example. As the boot was made higher and higher to protect the site of injury (just above the top of the boot) so the injuries were pushed higher still up the leg. It was only the development of proper safety bindings that really provided adequate prevention of the serious injuries that may occur in skiing.

The fourth and essential factor in injury prevention is the application of common sense. The latter is almost incapable of definition but it should reflect an understanding of the nature of sport as being essentially recreational and a vehicle for the expression of higher ideals, whatever the importance of any particular event. Thus all sportsmen and women from the very beginning of their careers must be brought to understand that sport is not a selfish activity but one to be shared, and that each participant has a responsibility not only to himself but to all the other players as well. This sense of responsibility is the key to the prevention of injury, and is too often thrown away when winning becomes all-important, whatever the cost.

2. *Treatment of injuries* in sport logically follows accurate diagnosis along clearly-defined and well-tried lines. Sportsmen as a whole, however, tend to differ from the population at large in so far as many are impatient of delay and require to return to sporting activity as early as possible. Loss of fitness occurs very rapidly following injury, particularly at the highest levels, so that even a relatively short period away from training evokes the need for substantially longer periods of reconditioning and rehabilitation before the pre-injury level of fitness is regained. Treatment of these injuries, therefore, involves selecting the method which offers the most rapid return to normal function without prejudice to the patient's long-term future. This is now becoming generally recognized, although there are still those who feel that unqualified rest is the right treatment for any injury, even minor soft-tissue injury. Unqualified advice to rest is, in the case of the average sports injury, too often an indication of the physician's ignorance or disinterest. Even when the injury manifestly precludes further immediate training, much can be done to preserve morale and general fitness by programmes of activity involving other parts of the body. Thus, by appropriately modified training, a footballer who breaks his wrist is able to remain in condition so that as soon as his plaster has been removed and his wrist mobilized he can return to the game (it is obvious that footballers cannot play while in plaster!).

The increased incidence of over-use injuries on the one hand and the demands of patients for early return to sport on the other (which might be regarded as mutually exclusive) have necessitated the evolution of methods of treatment, based on concepts of pathology which appear valid, which have been dramatically successful in returning patients safely and effectively to activity at an early stage. A useful spin-off has been the application of these techniques to other individuals requiring rapid return to activity (e.g. self-employed manual workers etc.). An aggressive approach to treatment in sports injury shows clearly the extent to which disability and *morbidity can be reduced by often quite simple means. This is particularly true of the case of decompressive surgery for relief of excessive tissue tension, and represents no more than the extension of well-tried methods (such as tendovaginotomy—longitudinal splitting of the tendon sheath—for chronic *tenovaginitis of the thumb (de Quervain's disease) to a whole range of soft-tissue disorders including compartment syndromes (such as the *anterior tibial syndrome) and various tendinopathies (lesions of tendons)).

It is often asked whether diversion of scarce resources to the management of sports injuries, in particular apparently minor soft-tissue injuries, is economically justified—the answer must be 'yes' in the context of the evolution of techniques applicable to patients as a whole, not merely to those injuries sustained during sporting activities.

3. *General medical problems* in sport are not uncommon and previously held views that many diseases were incompatible with sporting activity have had to be revised. The possession of high levels of physical fitness is not necessarily a protective influence—indeed it may be the opposite. It is, for example, well known that the onset of paralytic *poliomyelitis is often more severe in the physically active than in the sedentary. Equally, the effect of a *coronary thrombosis and myocardial infarct is often more severe in the active individual than in the inactive—and especially if occurring during exercise (e.g. while playing squash), while the heart is in a physiological high-output state.

Physical activity is possible, even at a very high level, provided that the nature of the disease is clearly understood and its effects properly offset. Where the disease process is of itself a limiting factor, the levels of performance to which the patient may aspire will clearly be restricted. The development of techniques for enabling people to remain physically active with a variety of generalized diseases has been most valuable. Studies in exercise-induced *asthma and of asthmatic sportsmen have facilitated the development of aerosol preparations enabling asthmatics generally to remain physically active.

4. *Psychological disorders*. Athletes and sportsmen, being human beings, are prone to the same type of psychological disturbances as less active members of the population. While it is true that supreme athletic prowess is unlikely except in the most psychologically well-balanced individual (in terms of *psychological traits, e.g. neuroticism/ stability and intraversion/extroversion, top-class athletes appear to be more normal than the norm!), a wide spectrum of *personality types is found across the whole field of sport, and personality disorder may manifest itself in problems relating to sporting activity. Thus, some athletes will present with bizarre locomotor disorders which are finally revealed after extensive investigation to be *hysterical in origin, or to relate consciously or subconsciously to attempts at secondary gain. *Psychopaths may find their outlet in sporting activity, often to the disadvantage of other players, and odd performances in sport may be a manifestation of *manic-depressive illness.

Sporting activity, more so at a high level where the lifestyle is artificial, induces intense physical and psychological stresses which often bring to the surface latent psychological as well as physical disorders. The young athlete in particular is vulnerable to severe pressures from parent and coach, and may often collapse, psychologically as much as physically, under too great a burden. Identification and management of cases of this type is an important and fascinating component in the third area of sports medicine.

The patient as an athlete. The final area where medicine and sport impinge embraces two fields: the use of sport as therapy and the role of sport for the disabled.

Sport may be extremely valuable as therapy in so far as it provides (controlled) exercise in what should be essentially a pleasant and mentally stimulating context. It offers the same advantages as *occupation (work) therapy in that the indirect approach encourages the patients to exercise the stiff painful part of the body or regain all-round mobility and general fitness.

As a rule, sports therapy should be prescribed only for individuals who are generally physically active and interested in physical recreation—the object of 'sports therapy' is self-defeating when applied to those individuals who have no interest whatever in physical recreation and, indeed, dislike it.

The evolution of sport as therapy was extended to the encouragement of sport (and, indeed, where appropriate the modification of certain sports) for participation by disabled people as a normal form of physical recreation. The chief architect of this movement was Sir Ludwig *Guttmann who devised the programme of sports for *paraplegics which led to the Stoke Mandeville Games and the World Sports Movement for the Disabled. It is essential in sport for the disabled that the interest should come from disabled patients themselves. Too often the emphasis has come from clinician, coach, family, or governing body and the patient has often found himself/herself pressurized into a sporting situation in which he/she subsequently becomes what amounts almost to a circus act. Sport for the disabled should be organized and run by the disabled—it is encouraging to see the extent to which disabled people are taking up the challenge of administration in these spheres.

The general principle underlying sport for the disabled is straightforward. It involves the selection of recreational physical activities within the capacity of the disabled individual which in their practice will not further prejudice or put at risk the health of the participant. Development of appropriate programmes demands imagination and a sympathetic approach, wherein the ideal is the integration of the disabled individual with the able-bodied in the same sporting environment. Quite apart from the immediate pleasure and satisfaction gained, this leads to the reintegration of the participant into society as a whole. In general (and this varies from country to country) disabled people find themselves isolated from the main stream of society. Sport has a marvellous reintegrating influence, provided that the disabled sportsman is able to participate *on level terms.* This is the case in such sports as archery and small-bore rifle shooting (prone lying). Where such integration is not possible, segregated sport is at least better than nothing in that it offers to disabled people opportunities for physical recreation which might otherwise not exist. However, segregation inevitably encourages a degree of isolation and this must be clearly understood. It is always disappointing to see disabled people participating amongst themselves alone in a sport where those same individuals might be able to participate with the able-bodied in other sports, given appropriate opportunity.

Sport is coming to play a progressively greater part in the social and economic life of the community. This is true not only in the highly developed nations of the West, but is reflected in a world-wide movement. Whatever personal attitudes to sport may be, it is here to stay as a significant influence in human life. Like all other human activities, it throws up its own problems which present a variety of interfaces with medicine. In the past these interfaces have often been neglected and it is only recently that they have attracted informed and responsible attention. Even today whole areas of these remain clouded, with a wide variety of problems—scientific, clinical, human, and organizational—yet to be solved. 'Sports medicine', the collective term given to the activities that occur at the interfaces between medicine and sport, is not a specialty. It is a *specialism* involving the application of skills, knowledge, and experience in different fields of clinical medicine and the related applied sciences to those peculiar problems thrown up by sporting activity. It is full of challenge and interest and offers opportunities on the one hand to push back the frontiers of knowledge in the study of the 'high performance' human ('*Homo sportans*'!) and on the other to improve the lot of people as a whole in evolving and applying means of rapid restoration of function and health.
                                                    J. G. P. WILLIAMS

Further reading

FIMS (1975). *Problems of Sports Medicine and Sports Training and Coaching* (1975) and *Basic Book of Sports Medicine* (1978). Published by Olympic Solidarity. Available through National Olympic Committees.

Muckle, D. S. (1982). *Injuries in Sport.* Bristol.

O'Donoghue, D. H. (1983). *Treatment of Injuries to Athletes.* 5th edn, Eastbourne, Sussex.

Ryan, A. J. and Allman, F. L. (1974). *Sports Medicine.* London.

Williams, J. G. P. (1980). *Atlas of Injury in Sports.* London.

Williams, J. G. P. and Sperryn, P. N. (1976). *Sports Medicine.* 2nd edn, London.

Journals of interest

American Journal of Sports Medicine. 105 Physicians Building, Columbus, Georgia 31901, USA.

British Journal of Sports Medicine. (39 Linkfield Road, Mountsorrel, Loughborough, Leicestershire, UK.)

Journal of Sports Medicine and Physical Fitness. (Corso Bramante 83–5, 10126 Torino, Italy.)

Medicine and Science in Sports. (1440 Monroe Street, Madison, Wisconsin 53706, USA.)

The Physician and Sportsmedicine. (4530 West 77th Street, Minneapolis 55435, USA.)

SPOT. See MACULA; TACHE.

SPRAIN. A joint injury which results in partial rupture of one or more of the supporting *ligaments.

SPRUE is adult *coeliac disease, or *gluten-sensitive enteropathy. A condition with similar features of intestinal malabsorption known as tropical sprue occurs in certain tropical regions; its cause is uncertain but it is not due to sensitivity to gluten and it responds to treatment with vitamin supplements and antibiotics.

SPUTUM is the matter ejected from the respiratory tract, the product of coughing or hawking. Expectoration of sputum indicates inflammation of the lungs, bronchi, or trachea. The material varies in colour, consistency, and volume according to the nature and state of the underlying infection, but is basically a mixture of *pus and *mucus. Microbiological and cytological studies can be helpful in diagnosis.

SQUINT. Faulty alignment of the visual axis of one eye, also known as strabismus. Squint is described as convergent, divergent, or vertical according to whether the squinting eye is deviated inwards, outwards, or either upwards or downwards. Most squints are congenital, and due to faulty insertion of the eye muscles; in this case, the visual axes move together and the squint is therefore called 'concomitant', the degree of squint remaining constant whatever the direction of gaze. But where squinting is due to damage to one of the nerves supplying the eye muscles, the squint varies with the position of the eyes and is termed 'non-concomitant' or paralytic; this variety of squint is usually accompanied by double vision (diplopia). See also OPHTHALMOLOGY.

STACPOOLE, HENRY DE VERE (1863–1951). Irish physician and novelist. Stacpoole trained in London, but only practised briefly before devoting himself to authorship. He wrote many novels of which the best-known is *The Blue Lagoon* (1908), which was reprinted 23 times in 12 years.

STAGING OF DISEASE refers to the classification of *malignant disease according to the anatomical extent of the primary *neoplasm, of involved regional *lymph nodes, and of *metastases. Accurate staging prior to the initiation of treatment is important for several reasons, as follows: it allows prognosis to be estimated; it determines the pro-

gramme of treatment most likely to be effective; it provides a reference point by which the efficacy of treatment can subsequently be measured; and it allows comparison of different treatment regimens and of the same regimen at different times and in different medical centres. Staging usually requires not only careful clinical examination but a whole range of ancillary investigations which may need to include *laparotomy or *laparoscopy. It is of obvious advantage if staging criteria can be internationally agreed; in the case of *Hodgkin's disease, for example, this was achieved at the Ann Arbor Conference of 1971.

STAHL, GEORG ERNST (1660–1743). German physician, MD Jena (1684). Stahl became professor at Halle in 1694, court physician in Weimar (1687), and later physician to Frederick William I (1715). A most successful practitioner, his views exerted great influence on medical thought, counteracting the growing mechanistic outlook. He denied that the body was governed by physicochemical laws, holding that the soul or 'anima' presided over all bodily activities and that when it departed death and putrefaction resulted. Interested in chemistry, he believed that something he called '*phlogiston' was given up when combustion took place. This hypothesis was widely accepted and delayed the advance of chemistry for half a century.

STAINS AND STAINING METHODS. See PATHOLOGY; MICROBIOLOGY.

STALLARD, HYLA BRISTOW (1901–73). English eye surgeon. Stallard had a very distinguished career as practitioner, writer, editor, and athlete. He represented England in athletics (1921–7), Great Britain in the Olympic Games of 1924, and the British Empire against the USA in 1924.

STAMMERING, in English usage, is synonymous with stuttering, a common speech disorder occurring in about 1 per cent of children of school age, much more often in males. It may be a temporary condition associated with a period of anxiety during early childhood but it sometimes persists in a chronic form into adult life. Stammering consists of either an explosive repetition of the initial letter of a word before the word is finally achieved or of a total blocking of speech followed by a rush of words; the two may occur together, and are often combined with a compulsion to finish a word once it has been embarked upon. There is no clear agreement about causation; it may be that psychological and physical factors can both be involved but in either case the psychological problems for the sufferer from established stammering can be severe.

STANDARDIZATION is the formulation and observance of standards in respect of quality, potency, ingredients, method of preparation, etc. of biological and pharmaceutical substances.

STANDARDIZED MORTALITY RATIO. The ratio of observed to expected deaths in a sub-population (e.g. cigarette smokers) multiplied by 100, the expected deaths being calculated as the sum of the expected deaths in each age group on the basis of the overall population mortality for that age group. Sometimes abbreviated to SMR. See also EPIDEMIOLOGY.

STAPEDECTOMY is the surgical excision of the *stapes, a method of treating deafness due to *otosclerosis. The stapes is replaced with a small plastic rod, restoring mobility to the system.

STAPES. The innermost of the chain of three tiny bones (auditory ossicles) which transmit sound vibrations from the *tympanic membrane across the *middle ear cavity to the inner ear.

STAPHYLOCOCCUS. Spherical gram-positive bacteria with a tendency to grow in clusters resembling bunches of grapes. Staphylococci are widely distributed in the environment and are frequently present on the skin and in the nasal cavity of healthy subjects. They vary in their capacity to produce infection, most of those that do so belonging to a species called *Staphylococcus aureus* (or *S. pyogenes*). Staphylococci are responsible for many types of superficial infection, particularly those in which *pus formation is a feature (*boils, *carbuncles, *impetigo, etc.). They also cause a variety of more serious deep infections, including *septicaemia, *osteomyelitis, *enteritis, *pneumonia, and *abcesses in almost any part of the body. Certain strains elaborate an *enterotoxin which produces *food poisoning. Many staphylococci have acquired resistance to particular antibiotics and are especially dangerous on that account; this is often the case in nosocomial (hospital-acquired) infections.

STAPHYLOCOCCUS AUREUS is an important *pathogen responsible for a large variety of *pyogenic infections. See STAPHYLOCOCCUS.

STARCH is the principal storage form of *carbohydrate in plants (cf. *glycogen in animals). Starch is an insoluble mixture of two *polysaccharides, amylose and amylopectin.

STARLING, ERNEST HENRY (1866–1927). British physiologist, MD London (1889), FRCP (1897), FRS (1899). Starling was appointed a demonstrator of physiology at *Guy's Hospital, London, in 1889, and he became professor at University College, London, in 1899. He worked in close association with Sir William *Bayliss on the discovery of *secretin (1902). He enunciated his 'law of the heart' which stated that the energy of contraction is a function of the length of the muscle

fibres. He was the author of the standard textbook *The Principles of Human Physiology* (1912). In 1917 he was created Companion of the Order of St Michael and St George.

STARVATION. In total starvation, the energy expenditure necessary for existence leads to progressive consumption of the body's energy reserves: when *carbohydrate and *fat are exhausted, then *protein must be consumed. The duration of survival in total food deprivation is variable, but averages about four weeks, at which time body weight has been about halved. See HUNGER STRIKE; KWASHIORKOR; MARASMUS; FAT; ENERGY REQUIREMENTS; NUTRITION.

STATISTICS gets its name from activities introduced several centuries ago, when nations (or states) began the 'political arithmetic' of counting their people, births, deaths, imports, and exports. The collectors and analysts of the data were called statists, and the descriptive information became statistics. About a century ago, because of the difficulty of examining and counting all the entities about which information was desired, techniques were developed to estimate the total results by using data found in smaller samples. The processes used to assemble samples from a larger population and to use the sample data for inferences about the population gave statistics a new component, based on mathematical principles of probability.

These descriptive and inferential components continue to occur in both the language and concepts of statistical activities today. The term *statistic* can refer to at least three different items: a single piece of data, such as a person's weight; a summary statistic, such as the mean weight of a group of people; and a test statistic, such as t or *chi-square*, that is used inferentially for making estimates from a single sample or for contrasting the differences found in two samples. Thus, a test statistic can help us decide whether the increment found in the mean weight of two groups is substantially different from what might have occurred by chance alone.

The discussion that follows is divided into two parts: the procedures involved in the first two types of descriptive statistics, and the inferential procedures used for the tests conducted in the third.

Descriptive statistics. It contains at least five major ingredients: the variables that are used for individual descriptions; the expressions that summarize the collection of data for a single variable; the rates and ratios that occur as quotients of frequency counts; the methods used to cite a contrast in two numbers; and the calculations of association for the relationship between two (or more) variables or groups.

Types of variables. The name *variable* is given to a class of data that is expressed in a scale of values for different categories. The scale of categories can be ranked or unranked.

If the intervals between each pair of adjacent categories in a ranked scale are measurably equal, the variable is called dimensional. Examples of dimensional variables are *number of children in a family*, expressed in a scale of 0, 1, 2, 3, . . . and *weight in kg*, expressed as . . ., 68, 69, 70, 71, . . . Dimensional variables are sometimes called interval or continuous. If the intervals between adjacent ranked categories are not measurably equal, the variable is ordinal. Examples of ordinal variables are: *student's rank in class*, expressed as . . ., 9, 10, 11, . . .; *severity of illness*, expressed as mild, moderate, or severe; and *briskness of reflexes*, expressed as 0, 1+, 2+, 3+, or 4+.

A nominal variable contains categories that are unranked. Examples of nominal variables are: *occupation*, expressed as merchant, labourer, politician, etc.; and *citizenship*, expressed as British, American, Canadian, etc. A binary variable is expressed dichotomously in two categories as yes or no (or present or absent). Examples of binary variables are: *presence of chest pain* and *existence of previous episode of myocardial infarction*.

A particular person can be described statistically as having the values of male in *gender*, 52 in *years of age*, engineer in *occupation*, moderate in *severity of illness*, and acute myocardial infarction in *diagnosis*.

Summaries of a univariate collection. A collection of univariate data can include values of the same individual variable, such as systolic blood pressure, for each member of a group of people, or repeated measurements of the same variable for a single person.

1. *Frequency counts.* The simplest way of summarizing a collection of univariate data is to count n, the total number of members in the group, and to enumerate the frequency with which each value of the variable has occurred in the group. These direct frequency counts are especially useful for nominal, binary, or ordinal variables that have a small number of categories. Thus, a group of 67 people can be cited as having 42 men and 25 women for the variable *gender*; 16 yes and 51 no for *diagnosis of previous myocardial infarction*; and 36—none, 17—mild, 12—moderate, and 2—extreme for *severity of *dyspnoea*. The many categories of a dimensional variable are sometimes consolidated into an ordinal array for citing frequencies. Thus, in the people just cited, we might count 2 persons with age ≤40; 6 with age 41 to 50; 11 with age 51 to 60; and so on.

2. *Relative frequencies.* To help standardize the results for groups of different size, the relative frequencies of each observed value are commonly cited as a proportion (or percentage) of the total. Thus, the 67 people mentioned in the previous section contain 0.37 (=25/67) as the proportion of women. Proportions are usually multiplied by 100 and expressed as percentages. The percentages in the cited group for the variable *severity of dyspnoea* would be 54 per cent, none; 25 per cent, mild; 18 per cent, moderate; and 3 per cent, extreme.

3. *Distribution curves.* The collection of data for a particular variable is often depicted in a table or graph that shows, at each value of the variable, the associated frequency count or proportionate relative frequency. In a graph, the values of the variable are placed on the abscissa (x-axis) and the associated frequency values are shown on the ordinate (y-axis).

When ordinal and dimensional variables are arrayed according to the rank of their values, the heights of the adjacent frequency columns can be shown in bars that form a histogram. Alternatively, the frequency values can be shown as points that are connected with lines to form a frequency polygon. Since the values of nominal variables cannot be arranged in rank order, the associated frequencies can be shown as proportions in a 'pie graph' or as a group of non-continuous vertical columns that form a 'bar graph'.

These tabular listings and graphic portraits indicate the distribution of the variable. When shown as a frequency polygon, the distribution appears as a curvilinear line whose shape helps illustrate the characteristics of the data. These characteristics are particularly important in certain types of inferential statistics, where a specific shape is assumed for the distribution of the parent population from which a sample is taken.

The most popular statistical distribution has a 'cocked-hat' or 'bell-shaped' form that is called a normal or Gaussian curve. It has a centripetal symmetry around a single apex, which occurs at the central value. If the apex of a distribution is displaced substantially to the right or left of the centre, the curve is skewed.

In statistical inference, the relative frequency found at each demarcated category along the abscissa of the curve can be regarded as the likelihood or probability of obtaining that value if any single member of the population were randomly selected from the distribution. The area that lies under the curve beyond the selected value will represent the probability (or P value) of obtaining a more extreme value if some other random choice were made. Since the sum of the relative frequencies is 1, the total area of probability that lies under the curve is also 1.

Central tendency. To summarize a collection of data, we would like to have a single value, acting as a centre or focal point, that provides a reasonable idea of the contents. This *index of central tendency* is chosen according to the type of variable and the purpose of the selection.

For nominal, binary, and ordinal variables, the values of individual data cannot be added. They can be summarized by citing the relative proportions for each category. The category that occurs most frequently is called the *mode*. Thus, for the group of people cited earlier, the modal value of *gender* is men, occurring in 63 per cent (=42/67).

Because ordinal values can be ranked, their central focus can be cited as the *median*, which is the value that occurs midway in the distribution of ranks. For the 67 people under consideration, the median occurs at the 34th rank. Since 36 people had none in *severity of dyspnoea*, the median value for *dyspnoea* would be none.

Dimensional variables can be summarized with modes and medians, but the data can also be added and averaged. The classical average is the arithmetical mean, usually expressed as $\bar{x} = (\Sigma x_i)/n$ where x_i denotes any single value in the data, Σ denotes the addition of all the values, n indicates the number of members in the group, and $\bar{x}$ is the mean. Thus, if 212, 237, 250, 251, and 283 represent a series of serum cholesterol values, their mean is 1233/5=246.6. Because the location of the mean can be greatly affected by large 'outlier' values at the extremes of the dimensional data, the median (in this instance, 250) is often preferred as a single index of central tendency. For example, suppose the survival times (in months) for 11 patients with advanced cancer are: 1, 1, 2, 2, 2, 3, 3, 3, 3, 4, and 8. The mean value for this group is 2.9 months. If the last-cited patient had survived 40 rather than 8 months, however, the mean value would become 5.8. Furthermore, if the last patient were still alive, the mean survival time could not be calculated. By contrast, the median value in this group would be 3 months, regardless of what happened to the last patient.

Dispersion. An additional salient characteristic of a group of data is its dispersion, or spread. For non-dimensional data, spread is indicated by the proportions cited at each category. For dimensional data, a simple index of dispersion is the *range*, which is the difference between the highest and lowest values of the data. Like the arithmetical mean, the range can be greatly affected by outlier values. Thus, in the foregoing group of 10 patients with cancer, the range for survival time can be 7 (=8−1) or 39 (=40−1), according to the fate of the last patient.

The most popular expression for the spread of dimensional data is the *standard deviation*. It is derived by calculating the *deviance*, S_{xx}, as the sum of squared deviations from the mean. Thus $S_{xx}=\Sigma(x-\bar{x})^2$, which, for calculational purposes is expressed as $\Sigma x^2-[(\Sigma x)^2/n]$. The deviance is divided by $n-1$ to form the *variance*. The square root of the variance is the standard deviation, $s=\sqrt{[S_{xx}/(n-1)]}$. For the five people whose cholesterol values were cited earlier: $S_{xx}=306703-[1\,520\,289/5]=2645.2$, and $s=\sqrt{(2645.2/4)}=25.72$.

The main advantage of the standard deviation is that 95 per cent of the data in a Gaussian distribution lie in a symmetrical zone that spans almost two standard deviations ($\bar{x}\pm1.96s$) around the mean. By doubling the value of s, the reader can get a quick idea of the spread of the distribution. The main disadvantage of the standard deviation is its distortion by outlier values. Thus, for the first

group of cancer survivors in the previous example, $s=1.92$, but for the second group, $s=11.4$. If we double the latter value and add and subtract it to get a 95 per cent range around the mean, the result is a span from −17.0 to 28.6, which has an impossible lower value.

To avoid this type of problem, the inner 95 per cent zone of a collection of data is increasingly cited with a *percentile* technique. When the array of values in a distribution is arranged in rank order from the lowest to highest, the particular value that occurs at each 100th of these ranks is a percentile. The 95 per cent inner range of the distribution is obtained from the values that correspond to the 2.5 and 97.5 percentile ranks. The percentile method, which has now become an accepted standard for citing the distribution of heights and weights of normal growing children, is not as mathematically easy to work with as a standard deviation, but offers the major advantage of being applicable to any form of dimensional data, regardless of distributional characterics.

Rates and ratios. Although proportions (such as the percentage of patients surviving 5 years) are often called rates, the term rate is most properly used for a quotient of frequency counts for two different variables. For example, in an annual mortality rate, the denominator consists of the census count of people in a defined geographical region during a particular year. The numerator consists of death certificate enumerations for people in that region who died during that year. The calculated quotient is often multiplied by 1000 or by 100 000 to yield a number cited as an annual mortality rate per 1000 or per 100 000.

In epidemiological data, a *prevalence rate refers to the frequency with which an event exists at a particular time in a particular group. An *incidence rate refers to the frequency with which new occurrences of an event are noted as the group is observed during a defined period. For example, in a group of 2000 schoolchildren examined today, if 50 have positive throat cultures for streptococcal infection, the prevalence rate is 25/1000. If the 2000 children are repeatedly examined during the next year and if 80 develop new infections, the incidence rate is 40/1000 for that year.

Two rates are sometimes divided to form a ratio. For example, if we know the attack rate of infectious hepatitis in people who eat raw clams and the corresponding attack rate in people who do not eat raw clams, we can divide the two rates to form a risk ratio for infectious hepatitis in raw-clam eaters.

Expressions of contrast. The distinction noted in a contrast of two numbers can be cited for substantive magnitude or 'quantitative significance' by examining an absolute increment, ratio, or proportionate increment. For example, if the rate of success is 50 per cent with new treatment A and 33 per cent with old treatment B, the absolute increment shows treatment A as 17 per cent higher than B; the ratio shows that success occurred 1.52 times (=50 per cent/33 per cent) more often with A than with B; the proportional increment shows that treatment A was 52 per cent [= (50–33)/(33)] relatively more successful than B. (If expressed for the effects of B relative to A, the corresponding three values would be −17, 0.67, and −34 per cent.)

Since all of these expressions can be used to describe a single comparison, decisions about quantitative significance can be tricky. A 'baseline' value, such as treatment B, must be chosen; both the increment and the ratio (or proportionate increment) must be examined concomitantly; and a judgement must be made about the magnitudes that are important. For example, one treatment may seem substantially better than another if the ratio of success is 3.5 times higher, but if the actual proportions of success for the two treatments are 7 per cent and 2 per cent, the increment of 5 per cent may make the ratio seem less impressive. Nevertheless, if 'success' is measured by survival rather than by improvement of headache, an increment as small as 5 per cent may seem impressive.

Associative statistics. An association can be determined for two (or more) variables or groups whenever their points of data can be linked via a particular person, time period, or a pair of measurements for the same entity. Thus, we can relate haematocrit and cholesterol values for each of a group of people; the sale of backgammon sets and the number of crimes committed during each of a group of years; the values of weight before and after a reduction diet; or the measurements of cholesterol determined for the same specimens in two different laboratories or on two tests in the same laboratory.

With the assumption that the two variables are *dependent*, that is, that the value of one is affected by the value of the other, we can mathematically determine the dependence of either haematocrit on cholesterol or cholesterol on haematocrit. (In biological reality, of course, neither one of these variables may be affected by the other.) Alternatively, the two variables can be regarded as *interdependent* and cited for correlations by noting whether the values of one variable tend to rise or fall as the other variable's values rise or fall. A correlation can be determined mathematically even if the variables are as unrelated as crime and backgammon sets.

The dependent or interdependent expressions of association depend on the *co-variance* calculated for the products of the individual deviations of the two variables. For a single variable, x, we previously saw that the variance depends on $S_{xx}=\Sigma(x-\bar{x})(x-\bar{x})$. For two variables x and y, the covariance S_{xy} depends on $\Sigma(x-\bar{x})(y-\bar{y})$.

The regression coefficient. The dependent relationship of y on x is commonly expressed as the equation for a straight line, $y=a+bx$, which represents the regression of y upon x. The a and b

values for the equation are usually calculated from the data by using the method of least squares to fit a straight line to a series of points. With this procedure, b, the slope of the line, is determined as $b=S_{xy}/S_{xx}$. It is often called the *regression coefficient*. The value of a, which is the y-intercept of the line when $x=0$, is calculated as $\bar{y}-b\bar{x}$. The line can be drawn by connecting the point $(0, \bar{y}-b\bar{x})$ to the point $(\bar{x}, \bar{y})$.

If y is believed to depend on only one variable, x, the foregoing relationships are called simple regression. If y depends on more than one independent variable, the dependency equation of *multiple linear regression* describes a linear 'surface' in multidimensional space. The expression is $y=b_0+b_1x_1+b_2x_2+b_3x_3+ \ldots$, where x_1, x_2, and x_3 represent three different variables.

The correlation coefficient. The interdependent relationship of two variables, x and y, is expressed with a correlation coefficient, r, which is calculated as $S_{xy}/\sqrt{[(S_{xx})(S_{yy})]}$. Its absolute value ranges between 0 and 1. When r is close to 1, the correlation is high. When r is near 0, the two variables have little or no correlation. When r is negative, the variables correlate inversely, so that one of the variables tends to rise as the other falls.

Precautions. Because regression and correlation coefficients are calculated with mathematical models that fit a straight line (or its multidimensional equivalent) to the data, the results may be misleading if the data do not actually have a linear relationship or if the relationship becomes non-linear beyond the points contained in the data. A separate problem, when multiple variables are used, is that the customary linear model regards each variable as making a separate additive contribution, ignoring the *synergistic effects (which statisticians call 'interactions') that can occur when certain features (such as old age and major co-morbidity) are present concomitantly. The problem can be avoided if the multiple regression equation has been expanded to include appropriately chosen 'interaction terms'.

Since correlation coefficients indicate association rather than agreement, they are not the best way to express results when quality control is tested for laboratory procedures or for observer variability. Since the closeness of fit in a correlation is expressed better with r^2 than with r, 'impressive' values of r, such as 0.5, have achieved a proportional reduction in variance of only 0.25. Finally, when a correlation coefficient is converted to a P value (as described later), the likelihood of obtaining 'statistical significance' depends mainly on the size of the sample. Thus, if the number of observations is sufficiently large, a correlation coefficient as unimpressive as 0.01 can become 'statistically significant' at $P < 0.05$.

The coefficients of regression and correlation are calculated as described if the data are dimensional. For calculating correlations in non-dimensional data, the available procedures include Spearman's rho, Kendall's tau, and such coefficients as phi and kappa. When the dependent variable is expressed in nominal, non-ranked categories, its relationship to the independent variables is determined with discriminant function analysis, rather than with the standard regression model.

Inferential statistics. Statistical inference is used in two major ways: to estimate the parameter of a parent population, using results found in a sample of that population; and to perform stochastic or probabilistic contrasts of 'statistical significance' for the numerical results in two (or more) groups.

Parametric estimations. The simplest illustration of parametric estimation is a political poll. If a properly performed survey of 200 voters show 53 per cent favouring party A, 43 per cent favouring party B, and 4 per cent undecided, we would estimate that the larger electorate will be similarly distributed, but the reliability of this estimate depends on the number of people sampled.

To determine reliability, we first calculate the *standard error* of the sample means or proportion as $s/\sqrt{n}$. For a proportion, p, the standard error is calculated as $\sqrt{[p(1-p)/n]}$. Thus, for the cited poll of 200 people, the standard error is $\sqrt{[(0.53)(0.47)/200]} = 0.035$, or 3.5 per cent. We next determine a confidence interval by multiplying the standard error by a factor derived from considerations of probability. For 95 per cent confidence intervals, this factor is 1.96. The product is then added and subtracted from the observed proportion or mean to form the confidence interval. Thus, for the cited value of 53 per cent, the confidence interval is $53\% \pm (1.96)(3.5\%) = 46.1\%$ to 59.9%, and we can be 95 per cent 'confident' that the true parameter lies in that interval. Since this sample shows that the true populational parameter may be below 50 per cent, party A cannot be fully assured of an election victory. On the other hand, if the proportion of 0.53 had been found in a poll of 1500 rather than 200 people, the standard error of the proportion would be 1.3 per cent and the 95 per cent confidence interval would run from 50.5 per cent to 55.5 per cent. With this result in the larger sample, party A could feel more 'confident' of victory.

For a confidence interval to be applied appropriately, the sample under study should have been obtained by a randomization procedure that gives every member of the parent population the same chance (or probability) of being selected. To avoid the errors that can occur when selections are made in a casual or haphazard manner, a formal randomization mechanism is commonly derived from tables of random numbers.

Although the therapeutic agents tested in *clinical trials are often assigned by randomization, the people studied in the trials are not randomly chosen. They consist of patients conveniently available to the investigator. Randomly chosen samples have seldom been used for any of the existing studies of aetiology or therapy that appear in contemporary medical literature. For this reason, a major problem of statistical inference in medical research is biased sampling. Whenever the person who selects a sample can make deliberate choices, rather than using a random mechanism, the opportunity exists for overt or subtle forms of bias to enter the selections. If the sampling mechanism allows distortion, an increasing size of the sample will simply increase the distortion, which may be difficult or impossible to remove unless the scientific source of the problem is suitably recognized.

Stochastic contrasts. After previously evaluating the increment and ratio for success rates of 50 per cent with new treatment A and 33 per cent with old treatment B, we may have decided that the distinction was 'quantitatively significant'. Our possible enthusiasm for treatment A might vanish, however, if we discovered that treatment A was given to only 2 patients and treatment B to 3, so that the compared data were actually 1/2 v. 1/3. With numbers this small, the distinction could easily arise as an act of chance. On the other hand, if the compared numbers were 150/300 v. 100/300, the success rates would still be 50 per cent and 33 per cent, but the results would be more persuasive.

The role of statistical 'tests of significance' is to establish the numerical magnitudes that allow a quantitatively impressive difference to be regarded as stochastically (or 'statistically') significant. The reasoning follows the same general pattern used to prove theorems in elementary geometry. We begin by making an assumption that is actually contrary to what we want to establish. If the consequences of the assumption lead to an obvious absurdity or impossibility, we reject the assumption. In the statistical use of this reasoning, the process is slightly modified. We reject the original assumption, not if it leads to an impossibility (which would have a probability of 0), but to a sufficiently remote possibility. The statistical procedure follows a distinctive sequence of steps:

1. We have observed a distinction, d_o, in the results of 2 groups, A and B.
2. As a null hypothesis, we assume that the causal or therapeutic agents given to groups A and B are not really different.
3. If these agents are essentially identical, we can determine the relative frequency with which various results could occur by chance in the observed groups.
4. Among these diverse results, we can note the relative frequency with which random chance would produce a distinction that is as large as d_o, or even larger. This relative frequency is called a P value.
5. The 'remote possibility' mentioned earlier is demarcated by a selected boundary level, called α or the rejection zone. If P is at or below α, the observed event will be regarded as too uncommon to be ascribed to random chance. Accordingly, the null hypothesis (that agents A and B are similar)

will be rejected; and the difference in groups A and B will be regarded as stochastically impressive or 'statistically significant' at the calculated level of P.

6. The value usually chosen for α is 0.05 (or 1 in 20). Since 95 per cent of the data of a Gaussian distribution are encompassed by an interval that extends 1.96 standard deviations on both sides of the mean, the 5 per cent of data that are not included in this interval are regarded as the uncommon, unusual, or extraordinary members of the distribution. With this standard, P values of 0.05 or below are proclaimed to be 'statistically significant'. (Because a stochastic contrast involves an appraisal of the null hypothesis, the procedure is often called hypothesis testing.)

The standards of these decisions are entirely arbitrary. For greater confidence, α may be decreased to levels of 0.025, 0.01, or 0.001, and in some circumstances, the decisive level of α may be set higher than 0.05. The nomenclature that juxtaposes the words 'statistically' and 'significant' is also arbitrary. The substantive significance of the observed statistics depends on the clinical importance of the events and on the relative magnitude of d_o, not on the calculation of P. Another noteworthy point is that rejection of the null hypothesis implies that the observed difference did not occur by random chance, but there still exists a P probability that chance alone was responsible. Finally, the statistical decision refers only to the numerical role of random chance. The decision provides no information about the non-random phenomena caused by distortions, bias, and other sources of error in the design of the research and collection of data.

Mathematical strategies. After the null hypothesis is involved in the second step of the statistical procedure, the third and fourth steps—which lead to a P value—can be performed using two different types of mathematical strategies: non-parametric and parametric.

In the non-parametric approach, the observed data would be permuted into all the possible arrangements of combinations that could occur for the observed sample sizes. For each arrangement, we would note the means (or proportionate results) in each group and then determine the incremental difference in the contrasted means (or proportions). The relative frequencies found in the distribution of these differences in the array of arrangements would provide direct probabilities for the likelihood (i.e. the P value) that chance alone could create a difference at least as large as the one actually observed in the data.

In the parametric approach, a particular test statistic, such as Z, t, or chi-square is calculated from the observed data. The test statistic found for the observed groups is regarded as a random sample from a theoretical distribution whose parameters are estimated from the observed data. Such names as Gauss, Poisson, and Bernoulli are used for these theoretical distributions. The cal-

culated value of the test statistic for each distribution will correspond to a P value listed in an appropriate table.

The parametric approach has been popular because of its mathematical elegance, because the test statistics are easy to calculate, and because the P values, especially when sample sizes are large, are similar to what is noted for the direct probabilities provided by the non-parametric tests. The growing popularity of non-parametric tests arises because they require no unproved assumptions about parameters and distributions, because they provide direct values of probability, and because—in an era of digital computers and programmable calculators—they have become relatively easy to calculate.

Types of tests. The choice of a 'test of significance' depends on many features including the type of data, sample sizes, number of groups, and relationship under study. Table 1 shows the tests that are commonly used for a contrast of two groups.

Table 1. Tests of significance of two groups

Type of data	Parametric test	Non-parametric test
Dimensional	t test (small sample) Z test (large sample)	Pitman–Welch permutation test
Ordinal	None, although t and Z tests are sometimes used	Mann–Whitney U test
Dichotomous or nominal	Chi-square test	Fisher–Irwin exact probability test

When the two groups have been 'matched', so that a single set of differences can be contemplated, the corresponding respective procedures are the paired t-test for dimensional data, the Wilcoxon signed ranks test for ordinal data, and the McNemar chi-square test for dichotomous data. When more than two groups are being contrasted simultaneously, the chi-square test is still applicable for dichotomous or nominal data, but the F test of the analysis of variance is used for dimensional data. For ordinal data, several non-parametric procedures can be used, including the Kruskal–Wallis and Friedman tests.

For an index of association, such as a regression or correlation coefficient, the populational parameter for the index is assumed to have a value of 0 under the null hypothesis. The observed value of the index is then contrasted against 0, using a t test or some other suitable procedure.

Examples of calculations. Four of the tests just mentioned can be illustrated with calculations performed for a set of data showing survival times for patients with advanced cancer treated in a randomized trial of agents V and W. For agent V, the survival times in months were: 1, 3, 3, 3, 7, 9,

11, 12, 12, 14, 17, 21, 29, 31, 33, and 37. For agent W, the survival times were: 2, 5, 6, 8, 14, 16, 19, 27, 28, 28, 38, 39, 41, 47, 50, 51, and 54.

For agent V the summaries show the following: sample size, $n_V = 16$; median $= 12$; the mean $\bar{x}_V = 15.19$; and standard deviation, $s_V = 11.73$. The corresponding summaries for agent W are $n_W = 17$; median $= 28$; $\bar{x}_W = 27.82$; and $s_W = 17.59$. The investigator, impressed by the quantitative increment in the means ($\bar{x}_W - \bar{x}_V = 12.63$) and by the ratio of survival averages, $\bar{x}_W/\bar{x}_V = 1.83$, now wants to determine the stochastic (i.e. 'statistical') significance of the results.

Appraisal of difference in means. Of the various procedures available for appraising the difference in means, the two most commonly used are the Z test and t test.

1. *The Z test.* A critical ratio, or 'test statistic' is formed as:

$$Z = (\bar{x}_W - \bar{x}_V)/\sqrt{(s_W^2/n_W + s_V^2/n_V)}.$$

In the cited example,

$$Z = (27.82 - 15.19)/\sqrt{[(11.73)^2/16 + (17.59)^2/17]}$$
$$= 12.63/5.18 = 2.44.$$

This value of Z is then interpreted with a table showing relationship of P values and Z values for a Gaussian distribution. The table shows that $P = 0.015$ when $Z = 2.44$. Since this P is below the demarcation value of 0.05, the difference would be proclaimed 'stochastically significant'.

2. *The t test.* The Z test uses a Gaussian distribution, which is not wholly appropriate when the sample size is relatively small. In this situation, the t distribution described by W. S. Gossett (writing under the pseudonym of 'Student') is more suitable. For the interpretation of the t distribution, the variance of the difference in the two means is preferably calculated by a 'pooled' formula, and the result is interpreted using the 'degrees of freedom' in the two samples. The latter is calculated as $n_W + n_V - 2$. The formula for t is:

$$t = (\bar{x}_W - \bar{x}_V)/s_p\sqrt{(1/n_W + 1/n_V)}, \text{ where}$$
$$s_p = \sqrt{\{[(n_W-1)s_W^2 + (n_V-1)s_V^2]/(n_W+n_V-2)\}}$$

In the cited example,

$$s_p = \sqrt{\{[(15)(11.73)^2 + (16)(17.59)^2]/16 + 17 - 2\}} = \sqrt{226.27} = 15.04 \text{ and}$$
$$t = (27.82 - 15.19)/[15.04\sqrt{(1/16 + 1/17)}] = 2.41.$$

This value of t, which is quite similar to the result obtained with the formula for Z, would be interpreted, at 31 degrees of freedom, in an appropriate table. The result would show that $P < 0.025$ and is also stochastically significant.

Appraisal of difference in proportions. The data for agents V and W can also be examined by comparing the survival proportions (which are usually called rates), rather than the survival times. For example, the two-year survival rates are 25 per cent ($=4/16$) for agent V and 59 per cent ($=10/17$) for agent W. This distinction seems 'quantitatively

significant' because the incremental difference is 34 per cent ($=59\%-25\%$) and the ratio is 2.4 ($=59/25$). To examine the stochastic significance of the difference, we can use the chi-square test or the Fisher–Irwin exact probability test.

1. *The chi-square (χ^2) test.* For this test, the data are arranged in a fourfold table (Table 2). [The letters shown in parentheses are later included in the formula for calculating χ^2.]

Table 2

	Alive at 2 years	Dead at 2 years	Total
Treatment V	4 (a)	12 (b)	16 (n_1)
Treatment W	10 (c)	7 (d)	17 (n_2)
Total	14 (f_1)	19 (f_2)	33 (N)

The calculational formula is

$$\chi^2 = [(ad - bc)^2 N]/f_1 f_2 n_1 n_2,$$

and for these results,

$$\chi^2 = \{[(4 \times 7) - (12 \times 10)]^2 \times 33\}/14 \times 19 \times 16 \times 17 = 279\,312/72\,352 = 3.86.$$

At one degree of freedom for this value of χ^2, the corresponding P falls below 0.05

An unresolved controversy exists about whether to use a 'correction' proposed by Yates in the calculation of χ^2, particularly when the table contains relatively small numbers, as in this instance. With the Yates correction, the numerator of the χ^2 formula is changed to $[|ad - bc| - (N/2)]^2 N$. For these results the numerator would be $[|28 - 120| - 16.5]^2 \times 33 = (75.5)^2 \times 33 = 188\,108$. When divided by the denominator of 72 352, this yields $\chi_c^2 = 2.60$, and the result is no longer 'significant'.

2. *The Fisher–Irwin exact probability test.* Perhaps the best way to test the foregoing table is to use the Fisher–Irwin exact probability test, which uses specially arranged random permutations of the observed numbers to determine the probabilities. If the two treatments are identical, the probability that the particular fourfold table arose by chance is $p = (f_1! f_2! n_1! n_2!)/(a! b! c! d! N!)$, which is calculated as $p = [(14!)(19!)(16!)(17!)]/[(4!)(12!)(10!)(7!)(33!)] = 0.04323$. This is the probability for the individual table $\begin{Bmatrix} 4 & 12 \\ 10 & 7 \end{Bmatrix}$. To complete the 'tail of probability', we would need analogously calculated individual p values for the more 'extreme' tables. These would be:

$$\begin{Bmatrix} 3 & 13 \\ 11 & 6 \end{Bmatrix}, \begin{Bmatrix} 2 & 14 \\ 12 & 5 \end{Bmatrix}, \begin{Bmatrix} 1 & 15 \\ 13 & 4 \end{Bmatrix}, \begin{Bmatrix} 0 & 16 \\ 14 & 3 \end{Bmatrix}.$$

The respective p values are 0.00846, 0.0009, 0.00005, and 0.0000008. The total probability for these five tables is 0.0526, which is the sum of their individual p values.

To get the tail of probability in the other direction, the tables to be examined would be:

$$\left\{\begin{matrix} 14 & 2 \\ 0 & 17 \end{matrix}\right\}, \left\{\begin{matrix} 13 & 3 \\ 1 & 16 \end{matrix}\right\}, \left\{\begin{matrix} 12 & 4 \\ 2 & 15 \end{matrix}\right\},$$

$$\left\{\begin{matrix} 11 & 5 \\ 3 & 14 \end{matrix}\right\}, \left\{\begin{matrix} 10 & 6 \\ 4 & 13 \end{matrix}\right\}.$$

The individual probabilities for these five tables are 0.0000001, 0.0000116, 0.000302, 0.00363, and 0.02328. Their sum, which represents the opposite tail of probability is 0.0272. The total probability for the two tails is thus $0.0526 + 0.0272 = 0.0798$. Since this value exceeds the usual 0.05 demarcation of significance, the result would not be regarded as 'significant'. In this instance, which will not always be the case, the corrected χ^2 value agrees more closely with the Fisher exact probability test than does the uncorrected χ^2.   A. R. FEINSTEIN

Further reading
Bulmer, M. G. (1967). *Principles of Statistics*. 2nd edn, Edinburgh.
Feinstein, A. R. (1977). *Clinical Biostatistics*. St Louis.
Feinstein, A. R. (1985). *Clinical Epidemiology*. Philadelphia.
Fleiss, J. L. (1981). *Statistical Methods for Rates and Proportions*. 2nd edn, New York.
Freeman, L. C. (1965). *Elementary Applied Statistics*. New York.
Hill, A. B. (1971). *Principles of Medical Statistics*. 9th edn, London.
Huff, D. (1954). *How to Lie With Statistics*. New York.
Langley, R. (1968). *Practical Statistics for Non-Mathematical People*. London.
Moroney, M. J. (1962). *Facts from Figures*. London.

STATUS EPILEPTICUS is a series of successive epileptic fits lasting for hours or even days, without return of consciousness between attacks.

STEATORRHOEA is the occurrence of pale bulky frothy *stools, indicating the presence of excessive quantities of fat in the faeces, characteristic of intestinal malabsorption syndromes (e.g. *coeliac disease and *sprue).

STENOSING TENOVAGINITIS. A painful localized form of *tenosynovitis involving the common sheath of the tendons of two thumb muscles (abductor pollicis longus and extensor pollicis brevis).

STENOSIS is abnormal narrowing of a passage or orifice.

STENSEN, NIELS (Nicolaus Steno) (1638–86). Danish anatomist, MD Leiden (1664). Stensen described the *parotid duct (Stensen's duct, 1661) in sheep and gave an account of his researches in *De musculis et glandulis* (1664). He was also a notable geologist. In 1667 he joined the Catholic church, was ordained in 1675, and renounced medicine to become Bishop of Titiopolis.

STEREOTAXIS is precise positioning in space; in stereotactic, or stereotaxic, surgery, a lesion is produced deep in the brain in a group of cells which has been localized in three dimensions.

STERILITY, in the microbiological context, is the state of being free from living micro-organisms. Otherwise, sterility means inability either of male or female to produce offspring.

STERILIZATION, in the microbiological context, means the total elimination of all living micro-organisms by physical or chemical methods. Otherwise it means the act of rendering an individual incapable of reproduction, usually by obliteration of the *vasa deferentia in the male or of the uterine (Fallopian) tubes in the female.

STERN, KARL (1906–75). German-Canadian psychiatrist and author, MD Frankfurt (1932). Born in Germany, Stern studied at Munich, Berlin, and Frankfurt; he also studied at the *National Hospital for Nervous Diseases, Queen Square, London, before going to Canada in 1939. With a strong background in neuropathology he was a research fellow of the Montreal Neurological Institute with his colleague from *Rio-Hortega's Madrid laboratory, Miguel Prados. Both moved to the Allan Memorial Institute of Psychiatry at *McGill when it opened. Stern was closely allied with the Verdun Protestant Mental Hospital for many years, later becoming professor of psychiatry at the University of Ottawa. Prior to his retirement he served as psychiatrist-in-chief of St Mary's Hospital, Montreal. His non-medical writing including such volumes as *The Pillar of Fire* (1951); *The Third Revolution* (1954).

STERNBERG, GEORGE MILLER (1838–1915). American military surgeon and bacteriologist, MD Columbia University (1860). Sternberg served in the US Army during the Civil War, the Indian campaigns in the American West, and the Spanish–American War, having by then become surgeon-general. His main scientific interest was in the field of bacteriology, and he was one of several workers who independently discovered the *pneumococcus. He developed the technique of *photomicrography, and published a manual which became the authoritative American work on the subject. As surgeon-general he organized and supported Walter *Reed's *yellow fever commission in Cuba, which established the role of the mosquito in transmitting the causative agent.

STERNBERG, KARL (1872–1935). Austrian pathologist, MD Vienna (1896). After working as assistant to Paltauf in Vienna, Sternberg was granted the title of professor in 1908, advancing to *ordinarius* in 1926. He described the characteristic giant cells of *Hodgkin's disease (Sternberg cells, 1898) and published an account of the disorder (sometimes called Paltauf–Sternberg disease), and of '*lymphosarcoma cell' leukaemia (Sternberg's leukosarcoma).

STERNUM. The breast bone, the central structure of the front of the bony thoracic cage, to which the cartilages of the upper ribs are attached.

STEROIDS are a group of chemically similar but biologically diverse derived *lipids, being saturated hydrocarbons with 17 carbon atoms arranged in four linked rings (three six-membered and one five-membered, with six atoms shared between rings). Steroids include sex hormones, adrenal hormones, bile acids, cardiac glycosides, sterols such as cholesterol, and other substances of biological importance. See also CORTICOSTEROIDS.

STETHOSCOPE. An instrument for coupling the examiner's ear to the patient's body surface for purposes of *auscultation. The stethoscope, which was invented in 1816 by *Laennec, enabled direct auscultation to be replaced by the more elegant, more hygienic, and more efficient technique of 'mediate' or indirect auscultation. Laennec employed a single rigid wooden tube for the purpose, and a not dissimilar monaural instrument is still employed in obstetrics for the auscultation of fetal heart sounds. The familiar modern stethoscope, however, is binaural and has two flexible tubes connecting the earpieces to a chestpiece which is either an open bell or a closed diaphragm or (best) a combination of the two. The bell, especially when loosely applied, is sensitive mainly to lower sound frequencies, the diaphragm to high frequencies. The overall efficiency of a stethoscope is related directly to the area in contact with the body surface (i.e. the area of the diaphragm, or of the opening of the bell) and inversely to the total volume of the system which should therefore be kept to a minimum (by, e.g. using tubing of small internal calibre and keeping it as short as possible).

STIGMA. Any identifying mark or 'fingerprint' which is characteristic of a particular condition. The plural form stigmata when otherwise unqualified refers to marks, usually haemorrhagic or purpuric, located in the sites of the wounds of the crucified Christ; such marks are alleged or recorded as having appeared on the bodies of numerous saints, mystics, and others over the last 2000 years, as for instance those which were impressed on St Francis of Assisi on 15 September 1224 by a seraph with six wings. The full set of stigmata includes marks corresponding to the crown of thorns and to the spear wound as well as to the wounds on the hands and feet.

STILBOESTROL is one of the synthetic *oestrogens, now used mainly in the treatment of neoplastic conditions such as postmenopausal breast cancer (though here it is being replaced by the oestrogen antagonist *tamoxifen) and cancer of the prostate. Toxic side-effects are common, including nausea, fluid retention, and arterial and venous thrombosis; in the male, it causes impotence and *gynaecomastia. The use of stilboestrol should be avoided in pregnancy, since in high dosage it has been shown to be associated with the development of vaginal carcinoma in female offspring.

STILL, SIR GEORGE FREDERIC (1868–1941). British paediatrician, MD Cambridge (1896), FRCP (1901). Still was appointed physician to the Hospital for Sick Children, *Great Ormond Street, London, in 1895 and in 1899 physician for diseases of children to *King's College Hospital, becoming professor in 1906. He was made physician-in-ordinary to the Duke and Duchess of York in 1936 and physician-extraordinary to the King in 1937 in which year he was made Knight Commander of the Royal Victorian Order. Still was the outstanding British paediatrician of his day; he described juvenile *rheumatoid arthritis ('Still's disease') in his thesis for the MD.

STILLBIRTH. Birth of a dead child. In the UK, the arbitrary division between spontaneous abortion and premature stillbirth is drawn at 28 weeks' *gestation.

STIMULANT. An agent which increases the activity of an organ, tissue, system, or function. The term when otherwise unqualified usually means '*central nervous system (CNS) stimulant'. The most widely used CNS stimulant is *caffeine, present in tea, coffee, and cola beverages. Other weak CNS stimulants include *pemoline, *fencamfamin, *meclofenoxate, and *prolintane; the last of these is sometimes contained in vitamin preparations but they are of doubtful therapeutic value. *Cocaine and the *amphetamine drugs are more powerful stimulants of the CNS but they are on that account dangerously *addictive; they have no place in the management of *depression.

STING, INSECT. The reaction which follows envenomation by stinging insects, notably species of Hymenoptera (e.g. bees, wasps, hornets); although unpleasant and often very painful, it is normally localized to the region of the sting. Systemic manifestations are usually an indication of *anaphylaxis but may also arise as a result of the direct action of the venom toxins in cases where multiple stings have been inflicted. It should be noted that severe stings may also be due to non-insect arthropods such as *scorpions. See also ALLERGY.

STITCH. A sharp pricking painful sensation in the side of the lower chest due to *cramp of the intercostal muscles.

STOCHASTIC. See STATISTICS.

STOKE MANDEVILLE HOSPITAL. A general hospital has been in existence at Stoke Mandeville near Aylesbury in Buckinghamshire, UK, since the Second World War, but the name 'Stoke

Mandeville' is generally associated with the world-famous spinal injuries centre established by Sir Ludwig *Guttmann in 1944. See also REHABILITATION; SPORT AND MEDICINE.

STOKES, WILLIAM (1804–78). Irish physician, MD Edinburgh (1825), MD Dublin (1839), FRS (1861). Stokes was appointed physician to the Meath Hospital in 1825 and from 1845 was regius professor of medicine in Dublin. He was made physician-in-ordinary to Queen Victoria in Ireland in 1861. With *Graves he reformed the clinical teaching in Dublin. He described *Cheyne–Stokes respiration (1846) and *Stokes–Adams syndrome (1846).

STOKES–ADAMS SYNDROME is characterized by attacks of unconsciousness due to cerebral *anoxia as a result of (usually) temporary cessation of cardiac ventricular contraction in patients with atrioventricular *heart block. The patient suddenly blanches and falls to the ground. After a few seconds, acute cerebral anoxia often causes convulsive movements. If cardiac ventricular standstill persists, life ceases. More often, probably as a result of anoxic stimulation of the myocardium, ventricular contraction resumes spontaneously. Return of circulation is accompanied by a characteristic flushing of the skin. Artificial 'pacing' of the heart in patients with atrioventricular heart block removes the risk of this very serious complication.

STOMACH. An important organ of *digestion, comprising an expansion of the upper gastrointestinal tract situated in the upper abdomen below the *diaphragm, connecting the lower end of the *oesophagus with the *duodenum, the beginning of the small intestine. It has a muscular wall which churns the mixture of food and digestive enzymes, and forwards it into the duodenum. The lining, or mucous layer, contains glands which are responsible for the secretion of *mucus itself, *hydrochloric acid, the digestive enzyme *pepsin, and a protein promoting *vitamin B_{12} absorption called '*intrinsic factor', together with various other substances. Nervous control of the stomach is entirely mediated by the *autonomic nervous system. Hormonal influences are also important. See GASTROENTEROLOGY.

STOMACH PUMP. A device for washing out the *stomach contents.

STOMATITIS is inflammation of the *mucous membrane of the mouth.

STOMATOLOGY is the study of the mouth and its diseases.

STONE. A stone, or calculus, is an abnormal concretion or hard mass developing in a duct or hollow organ. The commonest stones are those which occur within the renal and the biliary tracts, where they predispose to infection and may cause obstructive effects. Stones may also develop within the ducts of *exocrine glands, such as the pancreas, the salivary glands, and the breast. Stones vary in composition according to site and the factors which led to their formation, but usually involve the precipitation of *calcium salts.

STOOL. The *faeces resulting from a single bowel movement.

STOPES, MARIE CHARLOTTE CARMICHAEL (1880–1958). British pioneer of contraception, Ph.D. Munich (1903), D.Sc. London (1904). Marie Stopes was trained as a botanist and in 1911 she was married for the first time. The marriage was annulled in 1916 for non-consummation and in 1918 she married Arthur Verdon-Roe, who was also interested in *birth control. She founded the first contraceptive clinic in the UK in 1921. She wrote numerous books on sex and contraception; the first, *Married Love* (1918), was translated into 13 languages.

STORAGE DISORDER denotes any disease in which a metabolic defect results in the abnormal accumulation within the body of a substance or class of substance, for example the *lipidoses. Many such disorders are known, involving *fat, *carbohydrate, *protein, or other substances, such as *iron in *haemochromatosis. Storage disorders are usually associated with absent or defective *enzymes and genetically determined.

STOUT is a dark slightly sweet variety of strong ale (also known in Ireland as porter) sometimes claimed to be of medicinal value.

STRABISMUS. See SQUINT.

STRAIN. A group of organisms within a species sharing some defining characteristic.

STRANGULATION is killing by compression of the throat, interrupting arterial circulation to the head and/or ventilation of the lungs. It is also applied to circulatory obstruction of an organ or part due to compression of the blood vessels supplying it, as in 'strangulated *hernia'.

STRANGURY is slow, difficult, and painful discharge of urine.

STRAWBERRY MARK. A vascular *naevus, bright red in colour, which eventually shrinks and disappears spontaneously.

STREPTOCOCCUS is one of a large and heterogeneous group of gram-positive spherical bacteria named for their common tendency to grow in chains. They can be classified in a number of ways, one of which is their capacity to cause *haemolysis when grown on an appropriate blood *medium.

Alpha-haemolytic streptococci, which cause partial haemolysis, are particularly associated with *infective endocarditis and with *dental caries. Beta-haemolytic streptococci cause complete haemolysis and are further subdivided on the basis of a polysaccharide antigen into 18 groups labelled A to T; of these, group A organisms (also known as *Streptococcus pyogenes*) cause over 90 per cent of human infections, particularly of the upper respiratory tract (e.g. *tonsillitis, *scarlet fever, *otitis media), skin and subcutaneous tissues (e.g. *cellulitis, *erysipelas, *wound infections), and blood (*septicaemia), and are also responsible in some indirect way for *rheumatic fever and *glomerulonephritis. Gamma streptococci cause no haemolysis; they include most of those found in the gastrointestinal tract, and are not infrequently involved in urinary tract infections.

STREPTOMYCES is a genus of micro-organisms, many of which are free-living or saprophytic in soil and some of which have proved valuable as sources of *antibiotics such as *streptomycin and the *tetracyclines.

STREPTOMYCIN is an *antibiotic produced by the soil micro-organism *Streptomyces griseus*, discovered by *Waksman in the USA in 1944. It is active against a range of bacteria, including gram-negative and acid-fast organisms, its main use now being in the treatment of *tuberculosis. Streptomycin is pH-sensitive and is little absorbed from the alimentary tract, so that for systemic infections it must be administered by parenteral injection. The major side-effect is damage to the auditory nerve, which may be permanent; it should therefore be given with caution, particularly in elderly patients and those with impaired renal function.

STREPTOTHRIX was formerly the name of a genus of micro-organisms, the species of which have now been reclassified under different genera such as *Streptomyces, Nocardia, Actinomyces*, etc.

STRESS is the totality of the physiological reaction to an adverse or threatening stimulus, or the stimulus itself. Such stimuli include all forms of physical, mental, and emotional trauma, in fact any event which threatens to disturb the body's *homeostasis. The hormones of the *adrenal cortex play a particularly important role in the adaptation to stress. In the view of some, failure of the system to cope with stress leads to the development of the so-called 'stress diseases'.

STRETCHER. A frame consisting of two poles separated by cross-bars on which canvas or other material is stretched, for the carrying of sick or wounded persons.

STRIA. A linear streak on the surface of the body due to weakening of elastic tissue and suggesting past or present stretching of the skin and sub-cutaneous layers. Abdominal striae are common in women who have been pregnant (striae gravidarum) and can follow abdominal distension from any cause. Characteristically purplish striae occur in the flanks and on the thighs of patients suffering from *hyperadrenalism or who have been given *corticosteroids.

STRIATED MUSCLE. See MUSCLE.

STRICTURE. An abnormal constriction of a duct or other passage.

STROKE. A sudden impairment of brain function due to haemorrhage from or obstruction of one or more cerebral blood vessels. Also called apoplexy.

STROKE VOLUME is the volume of blood ejected by the heart at each beat, which may be calculated by dividing the *cardiac output (minute volume) by the *pulse rate.

STROMEYER, GEORG FRIEDRICK LOUIS (1804–76). German surgeon, MD Berlin (1826). The leading military surgeon of his day, Stromeyer was surgeon-general in the Schleswig-Holstein and Hanoverian armies (1854). He was professor of surgery successively at Erlangen (1834), Munich (1841), Freiburg (1842), and Kiel (1848). Stromeyer was one of the early *orthopaedic surgeons and popularized the subcutaneous *tenotomy devised by *Delpech.

STRONGYLOIDES is a genus of *nematode worms, species of which are intestinal parasites of man and animals; the human species is *Strongyloides stercoralis*, occurring mostly in tropical and subtropical regions. Infestation, which because of autoinfection may persist over many years, may be asymptomatic when mild; heavier infection causes abdominal symptoms and *malabsorption. A dangerous hyperinfection syndrome can occur in patients whose immune defences become depressed.

STRÜMPELL, ERNST ADOLF GUSTAV GOTTFRIED VON (1853–1925). German neurologist, MD Leipzig (1875). After being assistant to *Wunderlich, Strümpell followed *Erb in the chair at Leipzig (1883), moving thence to Erlangen (1886), Breslau (1903), Vienna (1909), and back to Leipzig in 1910. Although first interested in biochemistry, he turned to neurology and published many clinical papers. He described spondylitis deformans (Strümpell–Marie's disease, 1884), acute polioencephalitis (Strümpell–Leichtenstern disease, 1891), and 'pseudo-sclerosis' (Westphal–Strümpell disease, 1897).

STRYCHNINE is a highly poisonous *alkaloid obtained from the seeds of a tropical tree *Strychnos nux-vomica*, small doses of which have traditionally been used as an ingredient of 'tonic' medicines. In larger amounts, it produces a condition resembling *tetanus, with violent muscle contractions, *convulsions, and *opisthotonos leading to death by *asphyxia.

STUPOR is a state of depressed consciousness in which only vigorous or painful stimuli will cause the patient to demonstrate an observable response. Cf. COMA.

STURGE–WEBER SYNDROME is the combination of a congenital port-wine stain (capillary *haemangioma) on the face in the distribution of the *trigeminal nerve and a similar vascular malformation in a part of the *meninges and *cerebral cortex. The latter leads to *calcification (seen on X-ray), *epilepsy, and *cerebral atrophy on the affected side. Other congenital anomalies may be associated.

STYE. A purulent *staphylococcal infection of the *sebaceous glands of the eyelids.

SUBACUTE BACTERIAL ENDOCARDITIS. See INFECTIVE ENDOCARDITIS.

SUBACUTE COMBINED DEGENERATION. See PERNICIOUS ANAEMIA.

SUBACUTE MYELO-OPTIC NEUROPATHY (SMON) is a disorder characterized by numbness and weakness of the lower limbs with difficulty in walking and impairment of vision. The condition is progressive over a few weeks. The pathological changes seem mainly to be in the dorsal and lateral columns of the spinal cord, the peripheral nerves, and the optic nerves. A large number of cases were reported in recent years from Japan, with sporadic cases elsewhere but it is now rare. It is now evident that the cause was the chemical antibacterial agent *clioquinol (iodochlorhydroxyquinoline), known under the proprietary name Enterovioform®, used as an antidiarrhoeal agent. The marked decrease in incidence of SMON is presumed to be due to the withdrawal of this compound for other than topical use.

SUBACUTE SCLEROSING PANENCEPHALITIS is a rare progressive encephalitis affecting children and young adults, in which mental and neurological deterioration leads to death within months or a year or two. A viral aetiology is now established, usually involving an altered form of the *measles virus.

SUBARACHNOID HAEMORRHAGE. Haemorrhage into the *subarachnoid space is usually due to rupture of a small ('berry') aneurysm on one of the arteries on the surface of the brain or to bleeding from a congenital arteriovenous malformation. Subarachnoid haemorrhage is one of the causes of sudden death or unconsciousness; but when consciousness is retained, the characteristic manifestations are severe headache combined with those arising from meningeal and spinal root irritation. *Lumbar puncture reveals bloodstained *cerebrospinal fluid.

SUBARACHNOID SPACE. The space between the *arachnoid mater and the *pia mater, which is criss-crossed by a cobweb-like network of fine threads through which the *cerebrospinal fluid circulates. See also MENINGES.

SUBDURAL HAEMORRHAGE. Bleeding into the subdural space (i.e. between the *arachnoid and *dura mater) is usually a complication of *head injury. A chronic subdural *haematoma may follow relatively minor closed injury, especially in older patients; because cerebral dysfunction due to compression of the brain develops only gradually and may be delayed by an interval of several weeks, by which time the original injury has often been forgotten, this type of subdural haemorrhage notoriously presents diagnostic difficulty.

SUBLIMATION, in psychoanalytic *psychology, is the process of modifying instinctual impulses into a socially acceptable form of activity. Thus, for example, aggression is sublimated by playing rugby football.

SUBPERIOSTEAL HAEMORRHAGE is the extravasation of blood beneath the periosteum, the connective tissue sheath which envelops bone; subperiosteal haemorrhage is a common and painful consequence of *trauma.

SUBSULTUS TENDINUM is a convulsive twitching movement of the muscles and tendons seen in certain severe fevers.

SUCCUSSION SPLASH is a splashing sound produced when a patient is shaken or moves suddenly, indicative of fluid and air in a body cavity. The splash heard when gas and fluid (usually pus) are present in the pleural cavity is traditionally termed 'Hippocratic succussion'.

SUDDEN INFANT DEATH SYNDROME (SIDS or cot death). Babies not more than a few months old, and apparently healthy, may be found dead in their cots. The cause seems to be respiratory failure of acute onset, though why this should happen is still not known. Suggested possible causes have included acute virus infection, allergy to milk, or some failure of response of the respiratory centre in the brain to fluctuations in the gases normally being carried in the blood (oxygen and carbon dioxide). No fully satisfactory explanation has been found to cover all cases. There are usually no clues to be found at autopsy. Parents are shattered when this tragedy befalls them. They feel guilt and remorse particularly painfully, yet in reality they should neither be blamed nor blame themselves, though this last is a natural and usual reaction.

Their grief is great and often hidden. Subsequent babies are a source of continuous anxiety to them until the child is well into its second year. The major mortality is at 3 to 4 months of age and diminishes up to one year.

It is particularly unfortunate that at one time cot deaths were often assumed to be caused by parents smothering their children. This notion still lingers in some members of the public and sometimes in the police, who may be called in since this is a sudden death. They, and others, can make the parents unnecessarily and miserably unhappy, when their need is for comfort and understanding. An association of parents who have suffered such a loss has been formed in the UK in order to promote research and greater public understanding.

SUFFOCATION is the interruption of breathing by deprivation of air.

SUGAR is, in general, any sweet soluble monosaccharide or disaccharide. In particular, the word is applied to *sucrose, the sugar of cane-sugar, beet sugar, maple sugar, etc., a white sweet crystalline disaccharide of melting point 160–186 °C and formula $C_{12}H_{22}O_{11}$; sucrose, also known as saccharose, is found in many plants but not in animals (except in the alimentary tract after ingestion).

SUGGESTION is the process of influencing an individual so that he shows uncritical acceptance of an idea or belief. Suggestion plays a large part in *hypnosis and *faith healing.

SUICIDE has existed as a form of behaviour since the beginnings of recorded history. Psychiatric and anthropological studies clearly demonstrate that suicide is a universal phenomenon and that it occurs in primitive as well as developed societies. Attitudes in various societies have varied widely from approval and encouragement to the severest condemnation and punishment. Cultural changes have given rise to changes in social conditions, ideologies, and institutions which have been accompanied by changes in suicidal practices.

Suicide is a major social, psychological, and medical problem, and in most developed nations it is among the first 10 causes of death. Each year about 25 000 persons in the USA kill themselves. In 1970, Mintz reported a public health survey in Los Angeles in which the number of living Americans with histories of having attempted suicide (parasuicides) was estimated at 5 million persons. In England, Wales, and Scotland there are about 5000 suicides and 100 000 parasuicides every year. The ubiquity of suicidal thoughts is indicated by a study which showed that 80 per cent of young adults admitted that, at one time or another, they had thought about ending their lives.

The annual rate of 12 suicides per 100 000 population in the USA is midway between countries with an unusually high rate, such as Hungary with 29.8, Austria with 22.8, West Germany with 20.0, Denmark with 19.3, and Sweden with 18.9, and those with low rates, such as Greece with 3.2, Northern Ireland with 4.8, Italy with 5.4, and Norway with 7.7. Undoubtedly there is underreporting because of the legal and social repercussions on survivors and the equivocal nature of the death in many instances. Dublin (1963), a leading statistician on the subject, estimated that the number of suicides in the USA is from one-quarter to one-third higher than reported.

The suicide rate in men goes up with age, and in women the rate reaches a peak in their fifties and then gradually recedes. An alarming recent change in most Western nations since the Second World War is the increasing rate of suicide in young people in their teens and twenties.

The history of suicidal behaviour. The earliest writings stress the philosophical, religious, and social aspects of suicide and, where psychopathological evidence was available, the accounts were usually in the form of works of government, history, philosophy, culture, or literature rather than medical tracts. During the early history of Greece, suicide was in disfavour except under a few specific circumstances, such as incurable illness, old age, grief, or some other calamity. Suicide among the ancient Jews appears to have been rare, although not specifically prohibited or condemned. When suicide did occur, it was generally to escape the consequences of political or military defeat. In the Roman Republic, with its emphasis on civic duty, moral virtue, and individual sacrifice, recorded suicide was predominantly of the heroic type; however, it was also permissible as an alternative to shame or chronic incurable disease. Early Christians, such as St Augustine, considered that suicide was a mortal sin and a crime because it precluded the possibility of repentance and because it violated the Sixth Commandment against killing. Social condemnation of suicidal behaviour became embodied in legal and religious prohibitions.

Although suicide has been considered to be rare in the Middle Ages, reliable information is not available. Throughout the Middle Ages there was recognition that mental and emotional disorders might lead to suicide. Melancholy, the 'black' *humour, which was considered to be a vice leading to the sin of suicide, was held to be due to the influence of the devil.

Not until the social upheavals accompanying the Renaissance and the Reformation was there some softening of the harsh mediaeval attitude towards suicide. With the increased feeling that men were masters of their own destinies, philosophers such as More, Dunne, Montaigne, Rousseau, Erasmus, and Voltaire wrote defences of suicide.

Beginning in the mid 18th c., mental disorders began to be considered as causes of suicide. *Esquirol maintained that it was not a disease *per se*, but a symptom of *insanity. Early studies linked insanity, alcoholism, physical illness, family troubles, love problems, and poverty, with suicide. As medical studies enhanced understanding of the deep-seated psychological reactions that precede suicidal acts, cultural attitudes began to change. Gradually the laws against attempted and completed suicide have been repealed, until at present few nations or states retain legal restrictions against suicidal behaviour.

In the UK, under the Suicide Act 1961, it is no longer a crime to commit, or to attempt to commit, suicide, but it is a criminal offence, punishable by up to 14 years in prison, to 'aid, abet, counsel or procure' the suicide of another person. This, of course, raises the question of *euthanasia, still a fertile source of debate. An organization once called EXIT, now the Voluntary Euthanasia Society, has actively campaigned for a change in the law to allow an individual of sound mind, faced perhaps with an incurable disease, to terminate his or her life, if need be with the assistance of another person, possibly a member of the medical profession. Compulsory euthanasia (a decision by society that an individual's life should be terminated with or without his consent) is totally repugnant to the medical profession and doctors are also opposed to voluntary euthanasia if only because of potential abuses which might arise. But passive euthanasia (the withholding of treatment which might prolong the life and the suffering of a dying patient) is widely practised in many countries. Ethical dilemmas also arise when doctors are called in consultation in the case of patients who are on '*hunger strike'. Forced feeding has its advocates but a doctor has no moral obligation to intervene if a patient of sound mind is determined to end his life in this way. But in the case of other suicidal attempts (as by hanging, drug overdoses, the cutting of arteries or veins) which present as medical emergencies, the doctor has an obligation to act rapidly in an attempt to save life, irrespective of the wishes of the patient. (See also ETHICAL ISSUES IN MEDICAL PRACTICE; RELIGION, PHILOSOPHY, AND ETHICS.)

The twentieth century. The modern era of the study of suicide began at about the turn of the 20th c. with two main types of investigation, psychological and sociological, associated with the names of Sigmund *Freud and Emile Durkheim, respectively.

In his classic sociological study, Durkheim (1952) used statistical comparative studies of suicide rates among different groups to support his argument that suicide is the result of a society's strength or weakness of control over the individual. He postulated three basic types of suicide, each associated with an individual's relationship to his society. One type, the 'altruistic' or institutionalized suicide, is required by the customs of the society. In India, since time immemorial suttee has been practised, influenced by the religious belief that death was followed by living again

with the lost one. The suttee practice of burning with the dead on the funeral pyre was committed most often by wives, but sometimes by mothers, to avoid separation from the lost loved one. Although the altruistic type of suicide is rare today, it was more common in the past in both Western and Eastern societies.

Most suicides in Western developed countries are 'egoistic'—Durkheim's second category. Egoistic suicide is brought about by the individual's weak ties to or integration with the social group. The high rate among unmarried older men is accounted for in Durkheim's theory by their lack of ties to social groups. Catholic countries, he argued, have lower suicide rates than Protestant countries because of their greater social integration and cohesion (but this is also probably because the Roman Catholic Church still regards suicide as a mortal sin).

The last category, 'anomic' suicides, occur when there is a sudden and traumatic disruption of the accustomed relationship between an individual and his society. This results in weak social control and the resultant emergence of unrestrained self-destructive forces in the individual (e.g. the divorced or separated or those with loss of money or status).

Books by Cavan (1926) on suicide in Chicago, Schmid (1928, 1933) on suicide in Seattle and Minneapolis, Sainsbury (1955) on suicide in London, Dublin and Bunzel (1933) and Henry and Short (1954) on suicide in the USA have provided knowledge about the ecology of suicidal behaviour. Sociological and psychiatric studies in the USA and Europe show that completed and attempted suicide, as well as some other forms of social deviance, tend to occur more frequently in the central business districts and contiguous areas of large cities. Suicidal behaviour tends to be associated with urban districts that have low levels of social integration and high levels of social disorganization and social isolation.

Psychiatric and psychoanalytic contributions. Freud (1917) emphasized the importance of unconscious hostility and unresolved grief over lost loved ones (bereavement) in the psychogenesis of suicidal reactions. The loss or threatened loss of an ambivalently loved person often causes the individual unconsciously to turn his *aggression back upon the self in self-destructive ways.

Sullivan (1956) regarded suicide as an eventuality that might occur in a number of clinical syndromes, and its roots were of great complexity. He viewed anxiety that grew out of unfavourable interactions between people as the main factor leading to *psychopathology. Although he stressed the importance of experiences occurring early in life, he considered that reactions to stressful situations throughout life were of great significance in contributing to suicidal behaviours. Of especial importance, in his view, were circumstances that created a sense of worthlessness when the individual falls short of his own expectations and of others' expectations of him.

The psychoanalyst Rado (1951) considered that *depressive illness was a basic disturbance in hedonic control of the organism, and that the longer a depressive cycle lasted, the more gravely it violated the minimal pleasure requirements for existence. The shift in the balance between pleasure and pain results in a disastrous dominance of pain. Depression is instigated by a real or imagined loss of loved one, health, or financial security, and is accompanied by rage and guilty fear that is turned against the self and is expressed in self-reproach, self-contempt, and the need for expiation that can result in suicidal behaviour.

The numerous psychodynamic studies of depression and suicidal behaviour have contributed to our understanding but have not produced a theory which has broad acceptance as an explanation of the complexities of suicidal behaviour. The diversity of types and motivations does not lend itself to a psychological formulation which has universal application. The conscious and unconscious meanings of suicide vary with individuals, both in the same society and between different cultures. A Dutch psychoanalyst, Meerloo (1962), has described 54 different conscious and unconscious motivations for suicide. Some of the more important, predominantly unconscious, suicidal wishes have been summarized by Litman and Tabachnick (1968) as follows: (i) a desire for escape, sleep, surcease, or death; (ii) a guilt wish for punishment, atonement, sacrifice, or making restitution; (iii) a hostile wish for revenge, power, and control, or to punish and to commit murder; (iv) an erotic wish for masochistic surrender or for reunion with a dead loved one; and (v) a hope for rescue, rebirth, rehabilitation, or a new life.

In his book *Man Against Himself,* Menninger (1938) described three related hostile wishes, any one or more of which may contribute to the suicidal drive: (i) the wish to kill; (ii) the wish to be killed; and (iii) the wish to die. Menninger, and more recently Farberow (1980), have been leading investigators on the subject of indirect or partial suicide defined as behaviours in which the subject unconsciously acts out self-destructive drives in ways that are actually or potentially injurious or even fatal to himself. These behaviours include alcohol and drug *addiction, martyrdom, *masochism, antisocial behaviour, multiple surgical operations, purposive accidents, and some *psychosomatic diseases.

Difficulties in determining whether a suicide has taken place have given rise to devising better means of determining suicidal deaths. One method that supplements medical post-mortem findings and police investigations (see FORENSIC MEDICINE) is the psychological autopsy. Through interviewing the families, friends, and others acquainted with the deceased, an attempt is made to reconstruct the victim's life and the circumstances surrounding his life in order to define more accurately whether or not a suicide had occurred in deaths that are equivocal, and to understand the individual suicide by appraising the possible cause or causes.

Attempted and completed suicide compared. About ten times as many people make unsuccessful suicide attempts as commit suicide. Statistics on suicide in the 19th and 20th c. indicate that more men than women commit suicide (about 3 to 1) and that more women than men attempt suicide (again about 3 to 1). The average age of completed suicides (about 50) is considerably older than the mean age (roughly about 34) of those who attempt suicide. In general, completed suicides tend to use more lethal methods, such as firearms and hanging, than do the attempters, who often employ drugs.

Stengel (1964), on the basis of both clinical and statistical comparisons, suggested that in the main, persons who attempt suicide and those who commit suicide represent two different, albeit overlapping, populations: (i) a large group of those who attempt suicide, few of whom eventually actually commit it; and (ii) a smaller group of completed suicides, approximately one-third of whom have previously attempted suicide.

A basic difference between the attempted and completed suicide populations is the degree of suicidal intent. Persons in the attempted suicide category show a continuum of suicidal intent ranging from a suicide gesture group who show little or no suicidal intention, through a large group of ambivalent attempters, and finally a serious suicide attempt group who, like the completed suicides, have a high degree of intent to kill themselves. Those in the gesture group perform their self-destructive acts, such as nicking their wrists, in ways that make death unlikely. In the ambivalent class are individuals who are often confused and indecisive in their intention, but whose wish to die is strong enough for them to risk death. Most of the serious suicide attempters would die were it not for intensive medical efforts to save their lives.

Facts and fables about suicide. Shneidman (1976) wrote about the misconceptions of suicide—the popular myths of suicide. These eight fables are listed below, together with the authenticated facts demonstrated by those who have done research on suicide in the past 60 years.

1. *People who talk about suicide do not commit suicide.* Fact: eight out of ten individuals communicate their intention to kill themselves before they commit suicide. Usually, they express their intention explicitly and directly, although sometimes they may make indirect and non-verbal communications about their suicidal wishes and plans. It is dangerously negligent to disregard their suicidal ideation, threats, or gestures.

2. *Suicide occurs precipitously and without warning.* Fact: studies reveal that the suicidal person gives many clues, warnings, and threats concerning suicidal intentions. If they are heeded, death can be averted.

3. *Suicidal individuals are fully committed to*

dying. Fact: most suicidal persons are ambivalent and undecided about living or dying, and they 'gamble with death', leaving it to others to rescue them.

4. *Suicide is a problem of lifelong duration.* Fact: individuals who wish to kill themselves are suicidal only for a limited period of time.

5. *Improvement after a suicidal crisis means that the suicidal risk is over.* Fact: remobilization of suicidal morbidity can ensue after apparent improvement. The individual should be considered vulnerable for about three months following a suicidal crisis.

6. *The poor or the rich are most likely to kill themselves.* Fact: all socioeconomic strata are proportionately represented.

7. *The propensity to commit suicide is inherited.* Fact: there is no scientific evidence that a self-destructive potential is inherited.

8. *All suicidal persons are insane.* Fact: studies demonstrate that a minority of individuals who commit suicide are psychotic at the time of their death. Most suicidal persons are extremely unhappy and depressed. Beck (1974) has shown that an attitude of hopelessness correlates highly with severe suicide risk.

Suicide and psychiatric diagnosis. Systematic psychiatric studies by Robins *et al.* (1959), Dorpat and Ripley (1960), and Barraclough *et al.* (1974) demonstrate that at least 94 per cent, maybe more, of those who commit suicide have some kind of serious psychiatric illness. About half have a serious depressive illness, approximately one-quarter suffer from chronic alcoholism, and a smaller but significant number suffer from *schizophrenia. A variable but small number of cases of *psychopathy (antisocial behaviour pattern), drug addiction, and organic brain syndrome appear in some series.

Follow-up studies indicate that about 15 per cent of those persons diagnosed as having either a depressive illness or chronic alcoholism will die by suicide, as well as 10 per cent of schizophrenics and 10 per cent (or more) of *opiate users.

Psychiatric treatment. Patients posing a serious suicide risk are often referred to a psychiatrist and hospitalized in psychiatric hospitals or in psychiatric wards of general hospitals. The specific treatment measures used depend on the patient's needs and the clinical diagnosis. Individual, group, and family *psychotherapy, electric shock treatment (*electroconvulsive therapy), and the use of *psychotropic drugs are the main therapeutic approaches to the treatment of the suicidal. Electric shock treatment is usually reserved for those patients who are refractory to other kinds of treatment. Obviously there are no drugs that are antidotal to suicide. There are, however, drugs that have been used effectively to reduce the *anxiety and depression underlying self-destructive tendencies. *Tranquillizing medications, especially those in the *phenothiazine class, are valuable adjuncts in the treatment of schizophrenic disorders. There are two classes of *antidepressant drugs, the tricyclics and the *monoamine oxidase inhibitors (MAOIs), with confirmed efficacy in the treatment of depressive illnesses.

Suicide prevention. The pioneer suicide prevention service, the Samaritans, was founded by the Reverend Chad Varah in 1953 in London, and has more than 150 centres in the UK. In the USA, the crisis intervention work and the suicide prevention and research services of the Los Angeles Suicide Prevention Service, established in 1955, have been widely emulated. Today there are more than 300 suicide prevention centres in the USA. Typically they are 24-hour telephone answering centres that provide short-term crisis intervention services. They use both professional and lay volunteer staff. Suicide is not solely a medical problem, and many kinds of persons, including lay volunteers—provided that they are adequately screened, trained, and supervised—can and do serve as effective life-saving counsellors in the prevention of suicide.

The study of suicide as an interdisciplinary subspecialty has developed since 1950. Most of those involved are also mental health professionals, that is psychiatrists, psychoanalysts, psychologists, or social workers. Some are anthropologists, epidemiologists, sociologists, clergy, or other professionals, and they, together with the mental health professionals, are involved in suicide research, education, prevention, and intervention.

T. L. DORPAT

References

Barraclough, B. *et al.* (1974). A hundred cases of suicide: clinical aspects. *British Journal of Psychiatry*, **125**, 355–73.

Beck, A. (1974). Hopelessness and suicidal behavior. *Journal of the American Medical Association* **234**, 1146–9.

Cavan, R. (1926). *Suicide*. Chicago.

Dorpat, T. and Ripley, H. (1960). A study of suicide in the Seattle area. *Comprehensive Psychiatry*, **1**, 349–59.

Dublin, L. (1963). *Suicide: A Sociological and Statistical Study*. New York.

Dublin, L. and Bunzel, B. (1933). *To Be or Not to Be: A Study of Suicide*. New York.

Durkheim, E. (1952). *Suicide: A Study in Sociology*. London.

Farberow, N. (1980). *The Many Faces of Suicide—Indirect Self Destructive Behavior*. New York.

Freud, S. (1917). Mourning and melancholia. In *Standard Edition of the Complete Psychological Works of Sigmund Freud*, Vol. 14. London.

Henry, A. and Short, J. (1954). *Suicide and Homicide*. Glencoe, Illinois.

Litman, R. and Tabachnick, N. (1968). Psychoanalytic theories of suicide. In Resnick, H. (ed.), *Suicidal Behaviors*. Boston.

Meerloo, J. (1962). *Suicide and Mass Suicide*. New York.

Menninger, K. (1938). *Man Against Himself*. New York.

Mintz, R. (1970). Prevalence of persons in the city of Los Angeles who have attempted suicide. *Bulletin of Suicidology*, **7**, 9–16.

Rado, S. (1951). Psychodynamics of depression from the etiological point of view. *Psychosomatic Medicine*, **13**, 51–5.

Robins, E. *et al.* (1959). Some clinical considerations in the prevention of suicide based on a study of 134 successful suicides. *American Journal of Public Health*, **49**, 888–9.

Sainsbury, P. (1955). *Suicide in London*. London.

Schmid, C. (1928). *Suicide in Seattle, 1914 to 1925: An Ecological and Behavioristic Study*. Seattle.

Schmid, C. (1933). Suicide in Minneapolis, Minnesota: 1928–32. *American Journal of Sociology*, **39**, 30–48.

Shneidman, E. (ed.) (1976). *Suicidology: Contemporary Developments*. New York.

Stengel, E. (1964). *Suicide and Attempted Suicide*. Baltimore.

Sullivan, H. (1956). *Clinical Studies in Psychiatry*. New York.

SULPHONAMIDES, introduced into medicine by *Domagk in 1935, ushered in the modern era of *chemotherapy. They have been used since that time against a wide variety of bacterial and protozoal infections and still have an important role, though less so than formerly, since they have to a large extent been superseded by *antibiotics. Sulphonamides, which are derivatives of the original sulphanilimide and contain the sulphonamide group —SO_2NH_2, exert their antibacterial action by preventing bacterial uptake of para-aminobenzoic acid which is required for the synthesis of folic acid and which is hence essential for bacterial metabolism. They are effective by mouth. Sulphonamides are toxic and side-effects are unfortunately not uncommon, and are occasionally serious.

SULPHUR is a non-metallic element (relative atomic mass 32.064, atomic number 16, symbol S) occurring in nature in several allotropic forms. It is present in the *amino acids cysteine and methionine and hence in many *proteins. Sulphur atoms form cross-links between amino acids containing them, either in the same chain (as in *oxytocin and *vasopressin) or between two chains (as in *antibodies and *insulin). The amino acid resulting from a sulphur bond between two molecules of cysteine is called cystine. Inorganic sulphur preparations have found various applications in medicine, particularly in diseases of the skin; as have sulphur-containing compounds generally (e.g. the *sulphonamides).

SUMMERSKILL, EDITH CLARE (Baroness Summerskill of Kenwood, life peeress) (1901–80). British physician and politician, MRCS, LRCP (1924). In 1925 Edith Summerskill married Dr Jeffrey Samuel and practised in partnership with him throughout much of her active political life. From 1934 to 1941 she was a member of the Middlesex County Council and from 1938 to 1955 she sat as a Labour Member of Parliament, first for Fulham and later for Warrington. She was parliamentary secretary to the Ministry of Food from 1945 to 1950 and Minister of National Insurance in 1950 and 1951. In 1954 she was chairman of the Labour Party. Edith Summerskill was made a Privy Councillor in 1949, created a life peeress in 1961, and Companion of Honour in 1966; throughout her life she was a vigorous champion of feminist causes.

SUN YAT-SEN (1866–1925). Chinese statesman and physician. MB, BS Hong Kong (1892). A farmer's son, born in a small village in Hsiang Shan (Xiangshan) district in Kwantung (Guangdong) province, China, he was educated at school in Honolulu and at Queen's College, Hong Kong (1884–6), where he became a Christian. Later he qualified in medicine in Hong Kong. In 1894 he left China during the Sino-Japanese war but returned in 1895 to lead an unsuccessful armed rising. When this failed he fled to Japan, then the USA and Europe, living for part of the time in England (1896–7) before returning to Japan in 1897. Shortly after his arrival in London he was kidnapped by members of the Chinese Legation, being released only after he had smuggled a message to his former medical school principal, Dr James Cantlie. Later he was involved in organizing many Chinese uprisings of which that of October 1911 was successful. The Manchu dynasty was deposed and Sun became the first president of the Chinese Republic, resigning in 1912. He then founded the Nationalist party (the Kuomintang) and spent the remainder of his life trying to bring unity to China.

SUNBURN is the familiar syndrome provoked by excessive exposure to sunlight, of which the ultraviolet component is chiefly responsible. It is characterized by erythema, tenderness, and discomfort and in severe cases vesiculation, followed by desquamation and a variable degree of pigmentation. Individual susceptibility varies, and may be enhanced by drugs (e.g. *sulphonamides) and by disease (e.g. *lupus erythematosus, *porphyria). Repeated exposure to sun over long periods accelerates the ageing process in skin, and confers an increased liability to skin cancer. Sunburn is sometimes termed actinic dermatitis.

SUNSTROKE. See HEAT AS A CAUSE OF DISEASE.

SUPEREGO is a psychoanalytical term designating a hypothetical structure built up in the unconscious by early experience, mainly parental, which acts rather in the manner of a conscience, causing guilt and anxiety when primitive impulses are gratified.

SUPERIOR SAGITTAL SINUS. One of the major venous sinuses of the *dura mater, an unpaired channel which runs anterioposteriorly in the midline. See also SINUS THROMBOSIS.

SUPPORTIVE CARE is the provision of assistance and facilities to the elderly and infirm in respect of everyday living requirements.

SUPPOSITORY. A medicated plug of material, solid at room temperature but designed to melt at body temperature, for insertion into the rectum, vagina, or urethra; the purpose being either to introduce a drug into the systemic circulation by means of absorption from the mucous membrane or to exert a local action on the mucous membrane itself. The base of the suppository is cocoa butter, gelatin, or one of a number of other substances with suitable physical characteristics.

SUPPRESSION has various senses: in *immunology, it is the inhibition by suppressor T-cells of B- and T-cell responses, or the depression of immune responses generally by drugs or other immunosuppressive agents such as irradiation; in *genetics, it is the restoration of a character lost by *mutation by the occurrence of a secondary mutation; in *psychoanalysis, it is the deliberate dismissal from consciousness of unpleasant thoughts, memories, and ideas, as opposed to the unconscious mechanism of *repression.

SUPPURATION is the process of *pus formation. See also INFLAMMATION.

SUPRARENAL GLAND is synonymous with *adrenal gland.

SURFACTANT. A surface-active agent, a substance which when introduced into a liquid affects those properties which depend on surface tension, that is spreading, wetting, etc. Detergents are surfactants. Pulmonary surfactant refers to the phospholipid secretion of alveolar cells which acts in this way, reducing the surface tension of fluid within the lungs.

SURGEON. Literally, one who treats disease with his hands. See SURGERY, GENERAL.

SURGERY, GENERAL

Origins and traditions in prehistory. The origins of surgery in prehistory cannot be separated from speculation and fantasy. The facts which we possess are few, but with limited imagination and extrapolation from the practices of certain primitive tribes in recent times, we can build up a picture that serves as an introduction to the development of surgical practice which is reasonably well documented from 2000 BC onward.

Before there was any knowledge of the pathogenesis of disease it is difficult to be certain why skulls were subjected to *trepanning. However, there seems no reason to doubt the popular notion that it was to release some demon entrapped in the skull. It is one of the early operations of which we have definite proof, for skulls have been found dating back to 10 000 BC in which the growth of new bone around the site of trepanning suggests that some subjects lived following the operation. The practice had evidently spread widely and trepanned skulls have been found not only in Europe but also in Mexico and Peru. However, none has been found in India, China, or Egypt. In recent times there are accounts of trepanning by tribes in islands off New Guinea.

The instruments used would clearly have been the implements available at the time and not specifically designed. Initially, flints are likely to have been employed but eventually metal instruments were to become available. Flints would also have been suitable for scarification. *Cautery at the site of an *abscess or as a counter-irritant over a *dermatome related to a deeper internal pain (which is still common in the Middle East and the African continent) may also have been undertaken, but no proof remains.

Human sacrifice was unquestionably practised fairly widely at one time but eventually mutilating surgery took its place. A primitive, crude, and empirical medicine may have preceded magic and priestly medicine, but their paths probably became intertwined at an early stage and have never since been completely separated.

The primitive and ancient world. Speculation gives way to pictorial and written record about 2000 BC in Babylon, with the seal of the surgeon Urlugaledin and the stele of the great law-giver Hammurabi defining a code of medical practice with some quite specific instructions, which serve to illustrate the development of the art of surgery by that time, as the example below shows.

If a physician operates on a man for a severe wound (or makes a severe wound upon a man) with a bronze lancet and save a man's life, or if he opens an abscess (in the eye) of a man with a bronze lancet and saves that man's eye, he shall receive 10 shekels of silver (as his fee).

It was from this time that the rod and serpent Sachan, the signs of the god Ninazu and his Son Ningischzida, were used as symbols of healing. The existence of surgical implements from Nineveh fashioned in bronze with both smooth and serrated edges confirm the transition of medicine from something magical to a developing art determined by the experience of those engaged in its practice.

Accounts of Egyptian surgery are to be found in various papyri dating from about 2000 to 1500 BC. The *Edwin Smith papyrus, somewhat speculatively attributed to *Imhotep, physician to King Zoser, gives a good but limited account of the practice of medicine in the 2nd millennium and also suggests a link with Babylonian and Assyrian medicine. It is interesting in that it demonstrates that the art of examination and observation at this time were already regarded as important in the clinical assessment which, in the developing science of surgery, had to precede treatment. In the papyrus there are records of detailed examinations of 48 patients and from these we know that the *pulse was thought to be important in assessing patients with head injuries, and the probing of wounds in establishing their depth before treatment was undertaken. Following such an examination it became possible for the surgeon to give some prediction of the probability of cure. Methods of wound closure and *splinting are also given in some detail.

The *Ebers papyrus is a collection of medical texts. Some of the material belongs to an earlier period but the rest records the extensive practice at the time. It is of surgical interest because there is an account of *circumcision which was apparently carried out at the age of 14 and was practised amongst Egyptians, Ethiopians, and Copts. Whether the reason was for *hygiene or supposed increased *fertility is obscure.

The systematic arrangement of the papyrus suggests that it was used as a working textbook. This and the Kahun medical papyrus from the Faiyum, which is entirely devoted to *gynaecology, may mean that there was some specialization and instruction organized in schools or through apprentices, as was known to be the custom in surgical training in the Middle Ages. The historical origin of the *Barber-Surgeons in the Middle Ages may also be traced back to the Egyptian priesthood who regularly cut their hair or shaved their heads every third day, as well as undertaking ritual surgical circumcision. The detailed written account of circumcision in the Book of Genesis written about 800 BC confirms its wide practice and perpetuates the erroneous concept of ensuring fertility in addition to considerations of ritual and hygiene. Flint instruments used at this time are still in existence. From the 3rd millennium BC, knives were probably used for evisceration before burial, as well as circumcision and other simple operations. Any anatomical knowledge which accumulated was probably kept by the technicians and not disseminated. Formal anatomical records were not made until the Alexandrian School in the 3rd c. BC.

Between the third and first millennium BC there were significant migrations into the Mediterranean basin, bringing primitive civilization and culture which then spread to India. There was, therefore, a certain uniformity of medical practice spreading centrifugally from the Eastern Mediterranean.

The development of Indian surgery, however, seems to have been in advance of that of classical Greece in many respects. An operation for *fistula-in-ano and some plastic operations on ears, nose, and cheeks are described in sacred Indian texts such as *Susruta*. These included the most suitable incisions in different regions, indicating some knowledge of lines and stress and tension which anticipate the formal description of Langer's lines. The use of metals in India and China preceded that in Europe and the Mediterranean basin and the availability of instruments must, to some extent, have dictated the development of surgery.

There is a tradition that *acupuncture with metal needles was started in China by the Emperor Shen Nung in the 3rd millennium BC, as recorded in the *Nei Ching*, but a more widely held view is that this practice dates from the 3rd c. BC. *Castration was certainly practised at this time and was accomplished by a combination of *ligation and *amputation.

It is likely that ordinary domestic implements would initially have been used surgically. In this respect it is interesting to note in the Mediterranean basin a similarity of design of the spouts of jugs in the proto-palatial period (2000–1750 BC) at Knossos and modern vaginal and anal *specula and various *forceps and malleable spoons and knives from the neo-palatial period (1750–1400 BC) with those of the Middle Ages and even today.

Classical times. The speculation about medical practice in the 3rd millennium BC gives way to more detailed documentation in the Greek world about 500 BC. Initially, we learn from the Homeric writings such as the *Iliad* that, by this time, wounds were accurately described and that there was considerable knowledge about extracting foreign bodies and stopping *haemorrhage. Achilles binding Patroclus' wound is illustrated on the bowl of Sosia (5th c. BC) and is, incidentally an early example of the application of a *spica (figure-of-eight) bandage.

However, the cult of *Aesculapius, which came to dominate medical thinking in Greece and Asia Minor, being introduced in Athens in 429 BC, was to a large extent mystic with little relevance to the development of surgery. Such medicine as was practised was once more in the hands of the priests rather than the laity, as had been the case in the Homeric period.

From the many cult centres in the Aegean a form of cleansing and treatment developed, which was to herald the start of medicine and surgery as both an art and a science. Traditionally, the school at Cos with *Hippocrates was the most important although others, such as that of *Alcmaeon of Croton, who practised anatomical dissection, must surely have contributed to the growing knowledge.

The Hippocratic writings describe a number of surgical instruments—sounds, knives, curettes, trephines, forceps, and specula—which indicate an increasing range of surgical skills. Some of the procedures such as the reduction of *dislocated joints, operations for fistula-in-ano, *haemorrhoids, and *cataracts are also described in some detail. It was known that pure boiled water or wine benefited the healing of wounds, although there was no knowledge of *asepsis.

The empirical school at Alexandria, and particularly *Herophilus of Chalcedon, who about 300 BC practised both animal and human dissections, advanced anatomical knowledge. He differentiated between *nerves and *arteries much more clearly than Hippocrates and advanced the knowledge of *neuroanatomy. The period of greatest development in this school came when *Heracleides of Tarentum in the 2nd c. BC undertook operations for *hernia, vesical *calculi (bladder stones), and cataracts. With the development of the Roman Empire it was inevitable that medicine should reach a certain pre-eminence and the documentation of this we owe largely to Aulus Cornelius *Celsus, who died about AD 50. It is likely that he was merely an encyclopaedist rather than a practitioner but he gave the first and classical definition of *inflammation and in the sixth and seventh book of *De artibus* we find particularly detailed accounts of surgical procedures. The techniques he records, and of which there was not good evidence previously, are the resection of protruding fragments of bone in open *fractures and of the *omentum following penetrating injury of the abdomen. Operations for *phimosis, abdominal *paracentesis, gut *anastomosis, and certain plastic operations including one for *exophthalmos, are also described. In discussing breast *cancer, although he recommends excision for an early lesion, he records that surgery aggravates the problem when the *tumour is advanced.

Clearly, one must expect advances in the surgery of *trauma in an empire with an active military commitment such as that which the Romans had. However, advances in other branches of surgery always follow, as we repeatedly discover through history. There was no exception at this time and the developing technology can be seen in the many instruments preserved at Pompeii after the volcanic eruption in AD 79.

In 46 BC Julius Caesar had granted the treasured rights of Roman citizenship to all physicians. This was to increase the dignity and practice of medicine. One of those Greek surgeons who came to Rome and were destined to fill important positions looking after the gladiators was *Galen (AD 138–201). He had been born in *Pergamum, an ancient shrine of Aesculapius, and was destined to dominate medical thought for some centuries to come. Many of his views and writings were not original and, unfortunately, their derivative nature was to delay progress by failing to establish the value of first-hand observations. Errors were thus perpetuated. Of surgical interest, however, he records that an escape of air from the *thorax indicates that a penetrating injury has perforated the lung, and the new technique of resection of the ribs and sternum for *empyema and *tracheotomy are described. Undoubtedly, procedures of this complexity were being attempted in various centres within the Roman Empire and perhaps even in the Orient. The lack of development of *analgesia and *anaesthesia were among the factors which clearly were to limit the possibility of undertaking even major operations. It is likely that *Hua T'o (AD 115–205), accepted as the father of Chinese surgery, had a greater knowledge and access to *opiates, allowing him to perform relatively major procedures under the influence of *narcotics. He is known to have had a powder which effervesced in wine and produced a certain degree of anaesthesia.

As the organization and pre-eminence of the Roman Empire passed its zenith, the impetus was lost from many aspects of life including medicine. Other centres grew up, once more, further east in Asia Minor and most notably at Byzantium and Alexandria.

Writings from this period have some points of surgical value. *Antyllus from Pergamum gave a good account of arterial *aneurysms and details of exposure and ligation above and below. He also discussed indications for the plastic surgery of the eyelid, nose, and cheek.

Actinus of Amida, a Byzantine writer of the 6th c. who studied medicine in Alexandria, describes *tonsillectomy and ligation above an aneurysm of the brachial artery. The importance of Alexandria as a centre of medical learning continued into the 7th c. The last great Byzantine physician, *Paul of Aegina, who studied there in the mid 7th c., discussed in his *Epitome* cancer of the *uterus and breast, for which he recommended surgery. He gives detailed accounts of *lithotomy with the patient positioned in what was to become the classical lithotomy position, and also repair of *inguinal hernia by reducing the intestines with a sound and uniting the bulges on either side with *sutures.

Surgical writings of importance gradually dwindled. Medicine, which had thrown off empirical priestly and mystic associations, to flower in the period of Hellenic philosophy and science and to be consolidated during the great period of the Roman Empire, returned to the shadow of the Church. Once more doctrinaire stances and compassion dominated clinical science. Many of the ideas and traditions of Greek medicine, however, were to be kept alive in the Arab world. During this period surgery inevitably suffered a decline. With strict religious prevention of practical anatomical dissection, many techniques were lost and much had to be re-learned in the renaissance of medical science in mediaeval Europe.

Arab legacy. The schismatic dispute in AD 431 involving *Nestorius, the Patriarch of Constantinople, caused him to flee with followers to Mesopotamia and a medical school was eventually established there. This had far-reaching implications for surgery in that the Greek writings and thought were preserved. Even when the *Nestorians were subsequently expelled from Edessa, they took their libraries with them to Jundishapur, which was to become the important nucleus of the Muhammadan tradition of surgery. Some of the Greek documents were translated by Hunain ibn Isháq and when he was eventually appointed court physician to Al-Mamun, Caliph of Baghdad, the centre of learning was transferred there and it became an important centre with a large hospital. It was here that Ar-Razi (*Rhazes) came from Teheran in the late 9th c. to study and it was from Baghdad that he published his encyclopaedic medical work, *Hawi*, or *Continens*. This records bleeding by *cupping and the application of *leeches. It also suggests the use of animal gut for suturing abdominal wounds, which is therefore traditionally attributed to Rhazes.

Amongst the writings at this time is the *Canon* of *Avicenna. His *Canon* contains the suggestion that pig bristles should be used for sutures, and also the first main reference to *obstetric forceps for extracting a dead fetus. Despite the advances for which he was responsible, his acceptance that surgery was a separate branch of medicine to be practised by those in an inferior position, took centuries to eradicate and undoubtedly hindered surgical progress.

The Arab world embraced the Mediterranean basin not only in the East but also in the West with an important presence in Spain. Albucasis, born in Cordoba in AD 936, kept alive the idea of Paul of Aegina and they were disseminated in his *Altasrif* within the western Arab world. It became a valuable surgical source book with good accounts of the techniques of cautery, lithotomy, and amputation.

The ideas, traditions, and to some extent the skills of the classical world were preserved in the Arab world. Valuable additions were also made, as we know from writings of Rhazes, Avicenna, and Albucasis. The magnitude of this should not be underestimated, for surgical eclipse in Europe was almost complete during this time, partly through economic decline and partly through the dominance of the Church.

Mediaeval renaissance. The reawakening of surgical interest and practice which took place in Europe was, on the whole, in a climate of thought created by religious dogma that was certainly restrictive if not openly hostile. Although St Benedict of Nusia had in AD 529 founded a monastery at Monte Cassino whose work was to a large extent directed towards healing, the belief in the evils and uncleanliness of the body was firmly held. It was considered wrong even to cut for stone—especially as the site of the operation required the exposure of parts of the body not fit to be observed. A further blow was dealt in 1215 by Pope Innocent III who formulated the views of the Church in *ecclesia abhorret a sanguine*. The shedding of blood was thought to be so abhorrent that occupations which entailed bloodshed were rather selfishly relegated to the lowly strata of society. It was with this background of opinion that the surgical activities, even of monks committed to surgical work, had been restricted by the Council of Tours in 1163.

However, ripples of surgical enlightenment were beginning to appear on the surface. The Church was unable to stop the Arab influence coming back into European culture. Constantine the Moor, born in Carthage in AD 1010, eventually arrived in Monte Cassino in AD 1072 and translated the *Pantegni* of Heli ibn al Abbas, an Arabic version of an original Greek text, into Latin. The section which is devoted to surgery discusses suturing methods, the ligating of blood vessels, fractures, and inflammation. None of this was new but when reintroduced to Europe after a dormant period it was natural that it would be looked at objectively. One of the centres where this happened was *Salerno. Constantine himself had been there before going to Monte Cassino and the city was already a centre of healing and destined to become one of the first universities. From it was published *Regimen sanitatis Salernitanum*, by tradition compiled and edited by John of Milan. This and *Practica chirurgiae*, compiled in 1170 by Guido Aretino (a pupil of Roger Frugardi who was one of the most distinguished surgeons of this period in Salerno), bear witness to the pre-eminence of this university in the field of medicine and surgery. This remained so for some 150 years with the *Practica* or *Rogerina* being developed through several editions (e.g. *Glossulae quatuor magistrorum super chirurgium Rogerii et Rolandi*) as the most important working surgical treatise of the time with sections on wounds of the head, fractures of the skull, and diseases of the neck and limbs.

The mediaeval medical renaissance was disseminated throughout Europe and an example of this is well documented in the foundation of *St Bartholomew's Hospital in London. Rahere, a monk and Canon of St Paul's, fell ill when in Rome and thinking that he might die, swore that he would found a hospital if he recovered and returned to his native land. Following a vision of St Bartholomew he decided to dedicate the hospital to the Saint. In due course he received permission from the King and the ground was dedicated by the Bishop of London in 1123.

It was important that medicine should be practised and documented within religious foundations for, despite the restrictions, prejudice, and dogma, enquiring and trained minds inevitably came to consider the problems presented by disease, injury, and healing. Roger Frugardi still believed that *pus was laudable and inseparable from good healing. However, by 1266 this was being denied by Theodoric of Cervia, a chaplain of the Order of Teaching Friars. In 1266 he outlined principles of healing and advocated both cleanliness and debridement (removal of dead tissue). For such original scientific thinking to be fostered within the Church was an important and significant development which, happily, spread to the universities. In addition to the preoccupation of surgeons with wounds received in battle, they were now beginning to think about such matters as the merits of *incision as opposed to cautery in healing (Guglielmo *Salicetti in *Cyrurgia* 1210) and the differential diagnosis of benign breast lumps and cancer (Lanfranck, *Chirurgia magna*). An age of scientific observation linked with surgical endeavour was developing out of an inheritance of prejudice and mysticism.

European enlightenment. The French school was pre-eminent and started with Lanfranck. In addition to his technical achievements he clearly understood that a knowledge of medicine was also essential for the surgeon. The belief that he should not merely be a technician but a physician who practises surgery—and able to appreciate and be able to meet the whole needs of the patient and his family—is suggested by Lanfranck's contemporary Henri de *Mondeville. He wrote about the qualities of the ideal surgeon, including the need to counsel both the patient and relatives about prognosis.

Some small technical advances were made at this time. Lanfranck's pupil Jehan Yperman was appointed surgeon in Ypres in 1308 and described a metal shield for allowing cautery at relatively small and precise points. The great Guy de *Chauliac, surgeon to three Popes, wrote a comprehensive textbook of surgery (1363) in which he describes radical cure of hernia but he is perhaps popularly remembered now for the chain hoist still seen hanging over many surgical beds. His textbook of surgery was translated into English (the *Questyonary of Surgeans*), French, Provençal, Dutch, and Hebrew. It maintained its importance until the writings of Ambroise *Paré 200 years later.

Just as the needs of armies and wounds of battle have dictated much of surgical organization and practice over the centuries, the devastation of the *plague (Black Death) which gripped Europe in 1347 focused public attention to some extent on the need for organization of the medical services of the community. This in turn was destined to affect surgery and surgical practice.

Although it was realized that there were no medical and surgical means able to contain the disease, the existing Guilds of Barbers and Surgeons were recognized as important bodies which could be used in the detection of disease and organization of community care in the overwhelming crisis. Following this in England, the Guilds of Barbers and Surgeons (officially recognized in 1368) increased in importance and began to exercise jurisdiction over the practice and standards of the profession. A system of apprenticeship was established by the early Guilds but it was not until 1629 that this was eventually supplemented by a series of lectures.

Inevitably, certain jealousies and restrictive practices developed in England between groups. These were not totally lacking on the European Continent, where surgery was a despised profession. Although barber-surgeons performed *venesections and many operations in France, Ambroise Paré was at first refused admission to the College of St Come because he could not write Latin and was, therefore, considered unworthy of the honour. The court, Church, and universities had a somewhat greater influence on the structure of the developing profession in the rest of Europe than the Guilds and Colleges in England.

Some important English surgeons emerged at this time. John of *Gaddesden, physician to Edward II and probably the model of Chaucer's doctor of physic, and John of Mirfield (d. 1407) span the 14th c. From their writings *Rosa anglica* and *Breviarium Bartholomei* respectively, we get a good idea of clinical practice at this time. They are both probably a compilation of writings from several authors and describe injuries, hygiene, diet, and dressings. The development of surgical techniques clearly changed little during this time

but John of Mirfield is credited with observing that an injury on the right side of the head may lead to *paralysis on the left side of the body.

It was John of *Arderne who contributed most from England during the 14th c. His experience had largely been obtained on the battlefield but the writings for which he is justly remembered were on fistula-in-ano. Until his detailed account of treating it with a grooved probe, ligature, and scalpel, his contemporaries considered it as largely incurable. His manuscript *De arte phisicale et de chirurgia* (1412) remains as a good record of his practices which were representative of the best in England at this time.

Despite the importance of surgeons to the armies of Europe over many generations they remained socially and academically inferior to physicians. The development of specialized surgical techniques did nothing to remove this trend. John of Mirfield is quoted as having said:

Long ago, unless I mistake, physicians used to practise surgery, but nowadays there is a great distinction between surgery and medicine and this, I fear, arises from pride, because physicians disdain to work with their hands though, indeed, I myself have a suspicion that it is because they do not know how to perform particular operations; and this unfortunate usage has led the public to believe that a man cannot know both subjects, but the well informed are aware that he cannot be a good physician who neglects every part of surgery, and, on the other hand, a surgeon is good for nothing who is without knowledge of medicine.

It was not unnatural that surgeons and barbers, being denied university education, should protect their interests by the formation of Guilds. In France during the 13th c. the College of St Come was founded (or refounded, for Malgaigne states that it was originally established in 1033) and to some extent protected the interests of surgeons. The members were, however, oppressed by the physicians and beaten in competition by those whom they regarded as inferior—namely the barber-surgeons who performed venesections and many of the operations of surgery. The position was not dissimilar in England and a Company of Barbers and the Guild of Surgeons fulfilled a similar function between 1300 and 1540 when the two companies merged and were incorporated in the City of London as the Company of *Barber-Surgeons with Thomas *Vicary as first Master. It was not until 1745 that the definitive Company of Surgeons was founded and 1840 before it was dignified by having a Royal Charter. Progress towards academic and social acceptance had been somewhat faster on the Continent and, as early as 1672, Louis XIV of France had ordained that public demonstrations of surgery be given annually in the Royal Garden.

By the mid 16th c. the barber-surgeons, *phlebotomists, and the travelling *lithotomists were fused into a recognizable profession in Europe, with leaders emerging in each country. One of the greatest of these was Ambroise Paré.

He started life as a military surgeon and came to Paris in 1532, ignorant of Latin and Greek but with an intelligence and originality which was to dignify surgery and leave us with the important and immortal concept that, although the surgeon dressed wounds, God healed them. Compared with his personality and independent mind and the fact that he helped release surgery from dogma, his reintroduction of ligatures in amputation and belief that treating gunshot wounds with boiling oil was harmful to the tissues were comparatively modest advances. His contemporaries in England were William Clowes (b. 1540), who described ligating an omental mass and leaving long tails on the ligatures so that they could be extruded, and William *Chamberlen, a Huguenot, who designed *midwifery forceps. An ingenious technique was introduced about this time by Jean Tagout of Belgium who, in 1543, described the injection of alum and silver into a *sinus tract to find where a bullet had lodged. These were, however, minor advances and somewhat pedestrian when compared with the art of lithotomy or cutting for stones so skilfully practised by Jermain Colot, Pierre Franco, and Frère Jacques, who developed an approach lateral to the mid-line to avoid damaging central structures.

Anatomical awareness. The rising status of surgeons and interest in their profession inevitably led to an interest in *anatomy. It was Andreas *Vesalius and his contemporaries in the Italian school who founded the modern science of anatomy in the 16th c. This had been stifled by religious scruples between the 2nd and 16th c., except for the remarkable textbook of anatomy written in 1316 by Mondino de Luzzi (*Mundinus) of Bologna. Vesalius performed dissections in Bologna, Pisa, Basle, and Padua which formed the basis of his book *De humani corporis fabrica* published in Basle in 1543. Gabriel *Falloppio, a pupil of Vesalius, succeeded him as professor in Padua in 1551. He is chiefly remembered for his description of the human oviducts.

Although a human body had been dissected publicly in Venice in 1308, resistance remained largely from the Church and it was not until 1540 in England that the barber-surgeons were given permission to have four bodies each year to dissect, although it was known that clandestine dissection had been carried out frequently in the past. The legal practice of dissection was ultimately immortalized in 1752 in a particularly vivid way by Hogarth in his picture 'The Reward of Cruelty' depicting the dissection of Thomas Nero in Surgeons' Hall by John Freake.

The first proposal that the Company of Surgeons in England should build an anatomical theatre was by Michael Andrews in 1636 and it was opened two years later.

Surgeons were understandably preoccupied with the organization of their profession, for raising standards of surgical practice and improving the education of barber-surgeons' apprentices. Society was still served by quacks and pseudo-surgeons, including cutlers, cooks, tooth-drawers, sow gelders, and witches, who had little honesty and skill in surgery. However, out of the disorder significant figures emerged, whose surgical stature was to serve as a foundation for the great developments which were to come. John *Woodall is remembered surgically for abandoning the current method of amputating *gangrenous limbs by cutting through the dead tissue below the line of demarcation of viability; he recommended cutting through the healthy tissue above. He illustrated well that surgeons who are pre-eminent in their field usually have, in addition, a great understanding of medicine. Although he does not receive the credit for discovering the cause and cure of scurvy, in his *Surgeon's Mate* (1617) is to be found one of the best accounts of *scurvy ever written, showing a full knowledge of the value of lemon juice. This work was a comprehensive surgical handbook for ships' surgeons, their mates, and probably ships' captains who found themselves without a surgeon on board and might need information about instruments and their use in accident surgery, bowel obstruction, and other medical topics (see also NAVY, ROYAL). The range of operations was very limited and the art of surgery still comparatively primitive as a result of *sepsis and the lack of *anaesthesia.

Many leading surgeons, despite the knowledge in basic sciences developing in parallel, were both critical and scornful of attempts to investigate the causes of disease rather than concentrating on surgical technique. Operations without anaesthesia on a delicate organ such as the eye demanded great manual dexterity. It was understandable, therefore, that many should feel that surgery was not capable of further refinement or advance. Percivall *Pott, appointed assistant surgeon to St Bartholomew's Hospital in 1745, to his credit took a contrary view:

Many and great are the improvements which the chirurgical art has received in the last 50 years; and many thanks are due to those who contributed to them; but when we reflect how much still remains to be done it should rather excite our industry than inflame our vanity.

This reference to vanity reflected the mental attitude of many of the contemporaries who were not only individualists but had fixed ideas which prevented their accepting or seeking any innovations apart from minor modifications in technique. The dismal state of surgical practice in London at the beginning of the 18th c. is summed up adequately in an anonymous letter (published in 1703) to Charles Bernard, serjeant-surgeon to Queen Anne:

A cheat in physic or chirurgerie is so very facile and so difficult to discover. Chirurgerie has somewhat of a disadvantage, whereas, in physic very often an abuse is never detected.

Later in the same letter the anonymous writer

refers to a surgeon calling himself the 'unborn doctor' who specialized in the amputation of breasts for cancer. He claimed cures by referring new patients to those whose breasts had been removed and who had allegedly been cured. The number of breasts removed by this surgeon was 'scarce to be believed' and later in the letter he drew attention to Bernard's statement that he had never seen a cure of the disease and that rapid dissemination followed operation. Bernard was probably the first English surgeon to make this observation and many breasts were undoubtedly removed until this time, for innocent conditions mistaken for cancer. However, the march of clinical experience could not be arrested and it became recognized that prognosis was worse if there were 'knots' in the axilla and that operations would be unsuccessful if the growth was fixed to the chest wall.

Before this time, surgery largely entailed removal of any affected part—of a limb if the main artery was the site of an aneurysm or if there was an open fracture—because of the fear of infective complications. Percivall Pott himself would have lost a leg after a compound fracture of the tibia sustained when falling from his horse in Southwark in 1756 had not his old master Edward Nourse intervened to prevent it. It was, incidentally, during his convalescence from this accident that Pott wrote his important treatise *On Ruptures*. He described methods of reduction and added that when a hernia appeared to be irreducible, venesection should be performed with the object of obtaining complete muscular relaxation of the patient's wound from loss of blood—thus permitting reduction. Only in the presence of *strangulation was the operation to be undertaken, when the risks of *infection were preferable to the inevitable result of intestinal gangrene.

The lack of knowledge about the cause and treatment of infection prevented surgery from being used for anything but relatively minor conditions, as well as making operation on the body cavities extremely dangerous. Even the giants of the profession, such as Pott, were very conservative in both treatment and ideas.

Developments, however, took place during the 18th c. which mark a significant advance in the surgical approach to various serious clinical problems such as an aneurysm of the external iliac artery. David Tait writing in the *Edinburgh Medical and Surgical Journal* acknowledges the dramatic nature of the advance which *Abernethy made:

When, 30 years ago, Mr Abernethy formed the firm resolution of cutting open the walls of the belly and feeling the external iliac—he made a mighty step in advance—he formed an epoch in the history of his profession.

The true founder of scientific surgery in the 18th c. was undoubtedly John *Hunter. The method of his scientific argument with a clarity of inductive and deductive reasoning allowed him to approach and solve problems far ahead of his generation. This was seen not only in his ability to advance surgical technique but also in his enunciation of the general principles of inflammation and their application to various diseases. He always tried to link structure and function and to know not only the diseases but their causes. He was the founder of the science of experimental and surgical pathology and was able to convince his generation, and subsequent generations, that there were processes of disease which could be studied scientifically. High (Hunterian) ligation of a popliteal aneurysm remains as a comparatively humble but effective and logical method of treating aneurysms of the popliteal artery.

The scientific approach to pathology and the understanding of function is most strikingly displayed in John Hunter's (*Hunterian) Museum at the College of Surgeons in London. It has rightly been described as a treasury of experience and a storehouse of facts in a visible and palpable form, to which the young medical student may resort to increase, and the old one to refresh, his knowledge.

Hunter's legacy was left at a time when there was still religious prejudice which prevented official legislation from allowing the lawful supply of bodies for dissection in England and Europe. Thomas *Burke was hanged in 1828 for assisting the death of aged inmates of a hostel in Edinburgh in order to supply bodies for dissection. It took nearly three centuries in England, from 1540, when the barber-surgeons were allowed four corpses of criminals for public dissection, until the Anatomy Act of 1832 for the legal supply of bodies for medical students to be assured.

World growth. Within Europe there had been a tradition of travel between centres such as Salerno, Padua, Montpellier, Basle, and London. The time had now arrived for the European tradition to be carried to the New World. Philip Syng *Physick was an American pupil of John Hunter who, having qualified in Edinburgh, returned to Philadelphia in 1792. His inventive and unrestricted American mind brought many modifications in techniques and instrumentation. He became, with Alexander *Monro of Edinburgh, the first to wash out the stomach and was known to have undertaken *Caesarean section in 1824. He designed a wire snare for removing tonsils and also a flexible pewter cannula for insertion into the *ventricle of the brain through a trephine hole. He was the first full professor of surgery at the University of Pennsylvania—a position which he held for 13 years. It is interesting to speculate on the restrictive practices within the profession in England which delayed the establishment of the first chair of surgery within the University of London until 1919, when George Gask was appointed as professor at St Bartholomew's Hospital.

A great American tradition developed. Henry Jacob *Bigelow of Boston was an inventive genitourinary surgeon who favoured the crushing of bladder stones and bladder irrigation, designing his own instruments. A similarly ingenious surgeon, John B. *Murphy, developed a 'button' for end-to-end anastomosis of the intestine. Charles *McBurney is remembered in the annals of clinical surgery for his grid-iron abdominal incision for appendicectomy. The international pre-eminence of W. F. *Halsted and of Harvey *Cushing, the leading neurological surgeon, both of *Johns Hopkins Hospital, consolidated the position of American surgery. Halsted introduced his radical *mastectomy in 1882 and Cushing's classic monograph on *pituitary diseases and surgery was published in 1912.

Their distinction meant that young surgeons from Europe travelled to see their work—the science and technology of surgery had indeed become an international commodity. The USA had more to offer, however, and in this great continent they were able to plan and develop surgical services dictated by the needs of a fast-developing industrial nation with enormous distances and an almost pathological demand for the best and most up-to-date services. A prime example of this was the concept of W. J. *Mayo and C. H. Mayo who founded the *Mayo Clinic to provide medical services of unparalleled excellence and organization in Rochester, Minnesota.

International standardization of practice. In 1881, a year after von *Mikulicz had operated on a patient with a perforated *peptic ulcer, Theodore *Billroth performed the successful resection of a *carcinoma of the pylorus (distal aperture of the *stomach). This was a momentous step in surgery, acclaimed the world over. It was, however, the third hazardous operation he had introduced for in 1872 he resected the *oesphagus and in 1873 performed a laryngectomy. It was not until 1897 that total *gastrectomy was undertaken by Schlatter. Such developments attracted innumerable visitors from around the world. Travel was not easy and those who came were able to reproduce in their own country the sophisticated operations which they saw. They were now secure in the knowledge that the local conditions and expertise were sufficient to ensure that any developments in Europe or America could become universal practice. Apart from occasional specific exceptions, a remarkable uniformity of practice was possible. Results could be compared, techniques modified and an art and mystery became a biological science. Two big barriers remained which had yet to be overcome before the practice of surgery could expand—namely the limitations imposed by lack of anaesthesia, and sepsis.

Pain and anaesthesia. Many potions and concoctions have been used through the ages to relieve the pain and suffering of injury and surgery. *Opium prepared from poppy seeds and Indian hemp (*Cannabis indica) were known to the ancients as well as *mandrake (Atropa mandragora) and

*henbane (Hyoscyamus). In more recent times *alcohol was employed for its analgesic and paralytic qualities. Joseph *Priestley discovered *nitrous oxide in 1772 and Humphry *Davy experienced its ethereal qualities in 1799 and suggested that the gas might be used for the relief of pain. The discovery of *morphine and its soporific effects by Friedrich Wilhelm *Serturner in 1806 was an important milestone.

In January 1842 William Clarke, a medical student, used *ether while a tooth was extracted from a friend, and *Long of Athens, Georgia, gave ether later in 1842. However, it was William *Morton who used it in a public demonstration in Boston in 1846 and shortly after that the physician-poet, Oliver Wendell *Holmes, suggested the term *anaesthetic. By December 1846 news had travelled to London and William Squire at University College Hospital used it successfully on a patient of Robert *Liston, who insisted that 'this Yankee dodge beats mesmerism hollow'. In March 1847, M. J. P. *Flourens claimed that *chloroform had an effect similar to that of ether and although there is little doubt that chloroform was used from then on by Holmes Coote, it was popularized by James *Simpson of Edinburgh when, on 15 November 1847, he anaesthetized a four-year-old patient. Religious objections were raised once more, as they had been in the days of resistance to the dissection of bodies. Opponents quoted Genesis 3:16 'Unto the woman he said I will greatly multiply thy sorrow and thy conception; in sorrow thou shalt bring forth children.' However, Simpson cleverly retorted with Genesis 2:21 'And the Lord God called a deep sleep to fall upon Adam and he slept; and he took one of his ribs and closed up the flesh instead thereof.'

There was considerable resistance to these new agents initially, but after Queen Victoria had chloroform administered in 1853 for the birth of Prince Leopold, it became generally accepted. John *Snow, who had delivered the Prince, devoted the rest of his working life to the practice of anaesthesia. The earliest textbook Anaesthetics and their Administration was written in 1893 by Sir Frederick Hewitt. Although the first full-time anaesthetist in the USA was Griffith Davis, who was appointed in 1904, an academic chair of anaesthetics in the USA was not filled until 1936. This provides a contrast with the establishment of the first chair of surgery over a century earlier.

It is interesting that the *pharmacology of local anaesthetics reached an important milestone at the time when *inhalation anaesthesia was first used. *Cocaine was isolated from Erythroxylon coca by A. Niemann in 1858. It was used as a local anaesthetic by Karl Koller in 1884 and by Halsted in 1885 for an infiltration anaesthetic block. Numerous agents for general anaesthesia, *local anaesthesia, and *relaxation were to be introduced by the pharmacologists and assessed by the clinicians over the next few decades.

The benefits which followed the introduction of

general and local anaesthesia were quite inestimable. They were to release the patient from fear and pain and surgeons from the need to exercise excessive speed. Anatomical dissections were to become possible and injury to tissue less. The surgeon was allowed to seek a better anatomical and physiological solution to operative problems. Anaesthetists became indispensable allies in whose hands subsequently blood transfusion, fluid balance, and the most essential and complicated aspects of postoperative care were to become vested. This allowed great developments in general surgery and ultimately led to advances in thoracic and cardiac surgery and neurosurgery. Anaesthesia was to prove the catalyst of surgical development between 1850 and 1950, when John Gillies introduced *hypotensive anaesthesia to reduce the loss of blood during surgery. Since then the supportive role of anaesthetics has diversified even further with *resuscitation and *intensive care.

Infection. The tide of history has often been ruled by disease and plague. In surgery, infection remained, after anaesthesia, as the factor which prevented its advance. The key to a greater understanding of surgical infection had existed since Alexander Gordon of Aberdeen claimed in 1795 that infection and fever was carried from woman to woman by the *midwife. However, it was not until Ignez Philipp *Semmelweis in 1847 had formulated his doctrine of *puerperal fever that the message was clearly received. Mortality from postoperative infection at this time was still unacceptably high after most elective procedures, being 43 per cent at the *Edinburgh Infirmary in 1847 following amputation (Erichsen) and the incidence of gangrene following a compound fracture in which the bones had pierced the skin was as high as 90 per cent.

Joseph *Lister started his medical studies at *University College Hospital the year after Semmelweis published his views of puerperal fever. As a child he had developed an interest in *microscopy from his father who had been made a fellow of the Royal Society for work on microscopical lenses. By 1860 Joseph Lister was appointed regius professor of surgery at Glasgow. His contributions to general surgery were significant by any standards, devising an amputation of the thigh through the *condyles (1860), a new operation for excision of the wrist joint (1865), radical mastectomy planned on anatomical principles (1867), and various operations and instruments for *urethral surgery. However, as we read in the *Lancet* in 1855, the excision of the wrist joint led to six cases of gangrene and one of *pyaemia.

Fortunately, Lister was acquainted with the growing influence of the ideas of *Pasteur. This led him to speculate about how micro-organisms could be destroyed by some chemical agent. Lister himself had seen *carbolic acid used to disinfect sewage at Carlisle and as a result of this he tried carbolic acid in a case of compound fracture in 1865. Initially it was applied undiluted with lint.

This damaged the tissue and in 1866 he mixed the carbolic acid with linseed oil and common whitening. The cases of compound fracture on which he used this less damaging mixture were recorded in the *Lancet* in 1867. Nine of the 11 patients were alive with intact limbs at six months after surgery. With the confidence of this success he recommended that even silk ligatures should be carbolized to prevent secondary sepsis and haemorrhage at the site of ligated vessels.

The concept of airborne micro-organisms being important in infection was beginning to be more widely appreciated. John Tyndall produced evidence at a meeting of the Royal Society in 1875 which was subsequently incorporated into a collection of essays entitled *Floating Matter in the Air in relation to Putrefaction and Infection*. Lister, in an attempt to kill the micro-organisms in the air which might settle on wounds and lead to infection, attempted to create a bactericidal microcosm by operating within a sterile environment created and maintained by a small hand spray filled with dilute carbolic acid. Even though this was developed into a more powerful steam-projected spray, Lister abandoned this in 1887. The simple gauze dressings impregnated with carbolic acid, however, which he recommended were used widely until 1889 and thereafter were replaced by gauze impregnated with mercuric cyanide and zinc. His thinking was generally accepted and immediately led to developments such as that by Karl *Thiersch of Munich who in 1874 introduced a method of skin *grafting which would have otherwise been impossible.

Although this method did much to reduce sepsis, the latter still occurred and Lister's shrewd surgical judgement led him to advocate the adoption of india-rubber drains, first used by Chassaignac in 1859, to allow any pus which might form to drain away freely. Lister's great contribution to surgery resulted from his ability to relate advances in other fields to those of his own, and to solve problems which had eluded surgeons through generations. Perhaps this can be described as genius, or perhaps explained in the words of Pasteur, to whom he owed so much: 'In the field of experimentation, chance favours only the prepared mind.' Lister's mind was certainly prepared and, happily, it was not as inward-looking as those of his surgical contemporaries, and therein lay his greatness.

Modern times. Our surgical inheritance is long but that of classical times can be thought of as a period of gestation. The century from 1850 to 1950 was an essential period of learning and development for the great advances in specialization which inevitably were to take place once the barriers of pain, physiological homeostasis, and infection were removed. Two World Wars intervened and each brought significant advances in their time. The surgery of trauma and war has always been a sad and urgent necessity and has, through the ages, led to advances.

One notable development which became an important and life-saving advance resulting from the impetus of war was the science of *blood transfusion. This had been anticipated in the 16th c. when Hieronymus Cardanus and Magnus Pegelius suggested cross-transfusion. Between 1814 and 1836 James *Blundell at *Guy's Hospital in London demonstrated the value of cross-transfusion in resuscitating exsanguinated dogs. George *Crile of Cleveland in 1907 successfully performed transfusions in seven patients. Thereafter, work on *blood groups, *anticoagulation, and the preservation of blood enabled transfusion to become a realistic possibility and the collection and preservation of blood was an important by-product of the First World War.

The work of plastic surgeons, such as Harold *Gillies at this time and subsequently Archibald *McIndoe, in rehabilitating badly burned air-crew during the Second World War in England was a stimulus to plastic surgery which resulted from the conflict.

The miracle of *penicillin, discovered by Alexander *Fleming and later developed during the war with dedication and single-mindedness by Howard *Florey and E. B. *Chain, would not have been possible in a time of peace and security.

Apart from the impetus of two World Wars, steady progress in elective surgery was being made. Ingenious surgeons began to take liberties and make advances which established them as pioneers of the new science. This was justified once the pain and the *mortality and *morbidity of infection as well as *shock had been reduced to an acceptable level. Almost all organs now became amenable to elective surgery.

Sir Victor *Horsley in 1885 carried out physiological experiments on the function of various parts of the brain. He developed an antiseptic modelling wax from beeswax and almond oil to reduce the bleeding from the edges of the cranial bones. Although he did not fully appreciate the mechanism, he found that the application of living *muscle tissue to the bleeding surface of the brain reduced haemorrhage. In 1887 he successfully removed a tumour of the *spinal cord—the first operation of its kind.

Chest disease in the form of *tuberculosis was a widespread scourge. Various methods of draining tuberculous abscesses were devised, in conjunction with artificial *pneumothorax which temporarily rested the lungs. Occasionally chest diseases appeared to demand pulmonary resection. This reached a sufficiently advanced stage in 1931 for Rudolf Nissen to achieve complete resection of one lung.

Following the initial success with intestinal surgery in the second half of the 19th c., Vincenz Czerny resected the upper oesophagus in 1877 for cancer, and Franz Torek resected the thoracic oesophagus in 1913. Resection of the small and large bowel for tumours, *diverticular disease, vascular lesions, and regional *enteritis became

common practice. Success was dependent on great skill and also on a ritual of technique learned from those who were thought of as the old masters but who were, in effect, merely the great men of the previous generation; the field was moving fast.

Paediatric surgery did not lag behind, despite the rather specialized anaesthetic techniques required. Conrad Ramstedt in 1912 described two cases of pyloromyotomy for congenital hypertrophic *pyloric stenosis. The abundance of vascular injuries over the centuries produced an early interest in vascular surgery. Von Eck undertook the first portacaval anastomosis in 1877 and Berkeley *Moynihan in 1895 excised an aneurysm of the subclavian artery. It was not, however, until 1944 that John Alexander and F. X. Byron successfully resected a *coarctation of the aorta. The modern age of vascular surgery was ushered in when in 1964 DeBakey used synthetic Dacron vascular grafts.

Elective, or so-called 'cold' surgery (as distinct from emergency surgery), had, in the early days, understandably been preoccupied with solving mechanical problems. Stones had been removed from the bladder from early times and by 1905 Howard Lilienthal had reported 31 suprapubic transvesical *prostatectomies without death. This had been refined by Terence Millin, who in 1945 described retropubic prostatectomy. Intestinal obstruction from a variety of causes and perforated peptic ulcers posed little problem now for surgeons, and the mortality of Caesarean section even for *placenta praevia, first undertaken by A. C. Bernays in 1893, was now acceptably low. Delicacy of technique and perfection of sutures allowed the restoration of continuity of even small structures such as the *bile duct, which was accomplished by W. J. Mayo in 1905.

Classically, operations had primarily been directed towards solving mechanical problems, and clinical benefit resulted with restoration of function. Many interesting physiological observations were ultimately made on the alteration of function of organs before and after such surgery. *Renal failure and *diuresis, for example, were studied in patients after surgery for urinary obstruction. Astley *Cooper undertook experimental thyroidectomies in animals to elucidate the changes which were seen after the technical problems of thyroidectomy (for *goitre causing laryngeal obstruction) had been mastered by pioneers such as Theodor Kocher, who published a series of 13 thyroidectomies in 1872 with only two deaths. In studies of function following surgery physiologists and physicians worked closely with surgeons. It soon became evident that surgery was a tool by which normal function could be altered, and also through which physiological normality could be restored, after removal of an abnormally functioning organ.

An early example of normal function being altered by surgery was *castration, which had been practised from the earliest times—initially on those in charge of harems and subsequently to prevent the breaking of voices of ecclesiastical choristers. In 1881, tubal ligation for *sterilization was introduced by W. P. Langren and, in recent times, both *oophorectomy and *adrenalectomy have been used to alter the *hormone environment of certain tumours, such as breast cancer, in an attempt to reduce their dissemination.

Following a greater understanding of *thyroid function and its control of the *basal metabolic rate, Sir Patrick Watson in 1872 undertook a partial thyroidectomy for exophthalmic goitre. The first sub-total thyroidectomy for this condition was undertaken by Ludwig Rehn in 1884. The possibility of ablative endocrine surgery having far-reaching metabolic consequences led to a close association between physicians and surgeons, which was to herald a new co-operation between specialists who had differing but essentially complementary expertise.

A similar co-operation was to exist in the field of heart surgery. The preparation of patients for surgery at a time which was considered optimal was clearly within the discretion of the physician as well as that of the surgeon. It was such a co-operation which enabled Henry Souttar in 1925 to attempt digital fracture (i.e. breaking open with a finger) of a mitral valve stenosis (see CARDIOTHORACIC SURGERY) via the auricle. Subsequently, success with instrumental dilatation of the mitral valve was achieved by Dwight Harken of Boston in 1948. Two other successes in cardiac surgery took place, first when Robert Gross in 1939 successfully ligated a patent *ductus arteriosus in children and later when Alfred *Blalock in 1949 anastomosed the left subclavian and left pulmonary artery to reduce the effect of the congenital abnormality of *Fallot's tetralogy.

After the development and insertion of artificial, mechanical, and denatured animal valves into failing hearts, which had considerable clinical success, the ultimate goal in cardiovascular surgery appeared to be the *transplantation of a healthy heart from a donor who had suffered irreversible brain damage (see CARDIOTHORACIC SURGERY). Such a dramatic achievement was accomplished in man by Christiaan Barnard in 1967. This followed considerable pioneering work in many laboratories throughout the world which was possible only as a result of enormous advances in our understanding of *immunology. However, many scientific and ethical problems were posed by the achievement; techniques had, to some extent, advanced too rapidly.

The concept of organ transplantation had been a dream for generations and had become a reality in the mid-1950s when Hume performed nine kidney homotransplants in patients and Goodrich undertook the first successful liver transplant in man in 1956. However, despite the initial enthusiasm for spare-part transplantation surgery, the problems of immunological *rejection, availability of organs, finance, and ethics all dictated that what originally appeared to be the ultimate goal might

not be so. In 1982 the first artificial hydraulic heart was inserted into a patient.

The field of *orthopaedics illustrates what has, in many respects, been a happier revolution, raising less controversial ethical and financial problems. In addition, the surgical techniques have developed in parallel with related disciplines such as those of immunology. After the days of external fixation of fractures, the inevitable progress to internal fixation took place with plates and intra-medullary nails. By the mid 1960s, the development of biologically inert implantable material was such that very satisfactory artificial hip joints of varying design were being widely inserted following pioneering work in many centres. These demanded a high technical ability and a close liaison with mechanical engineers and chemists who developed biological cements.

Clearly, such a stage of sophistication and technical expertise has been reached in various branches of surgery that the classical concept of general surgery is somewhat outmoded. It will, however, always remain as the training ground of all super-specialists and within it there will always be areas of special expertise, demanding skills and experience equal to those of what we now regard as the specialized branches of surgery. These have previously been organ-specific, such as *ophthalmology, or system-specific, such as *gynaecology and *gastroenterology, but may now also need to be disease-related.

Although all general surgeons, for example, treat cancer, the multidisciplinary approach required now dictates that, at least in some specialized centres, there should be surgeons who have a greater commitment and knowledge in this field. At one time cancer surgery meant merely more radical surgery, as when *Wertheim in 1900 developed his radical *hysterectomy or when Ernest Miles of the Royal Marsden Hospital, London, undertook the first synchronous combined abdominoperineal excision of the *rectum. Now, however, cancer surgery is undertaken in close association with physicians who undertake *chemotherapy and *radiotherapy. A new area of specialization within general surgery has been born and is now called surgical *oncology.

Technical developments in *fibre-optics, microvascular anastomosis (*microsurgery) and *lasers are being introduced into general surgery which will further increase specialization. The contention of Percivall Pott that 'much still remains to be done' and that this should 'excite our industry' is as true today as it was in 1745. The words of Khalil Gibran should be our ideal: 'The timeless in you is aware of life's timelessness and knows that yesterday is but today's memory and tomorrow today's dream'.

See also NEUROSURGERY; PLASTIC AND MAXILLOFACIAL SURGERY; CARDIOTHORACIC SURGERY; ORTHOPAEDICS; SURGERY OF TRAUMA; UROLOGICAL SURGERY; VASCULAR SURGERY.

H. WHITE

Further reading

Bennion, E. (1979). *Antique Medical Instruments.* London.

Bishop, W. J. (1960). *The Early History of Surgery.* London.

Cartwright, F. F. (1967). *The Development of Modern Surgery.* London.

Castiglioni, A. (1936). *Storia Della Medicina.* Milan. (Translated by Krumbhaar E. B. (1941). *A History of Medicine,* New York.)

Cope, Z. (1959). *The History of the Royal College of Surgeons of England.* London.

Dennis, F. S. (1905). *The History and Development of Surgery During the Past Century.* (Reprinted from *American Medicine,* **9,** Nos. 4-7.)

Graham, H. (1939). *Surgeons All.* London.

Hurwitz, A. and Dagensheim, G. A. (1958). *Milestones in Modern Surgery.* London.

Meade, R. H. (1968). *Introduction to the History of Surgery.* Philadelphia.

Power, D'A. (1933). *Short History of Surgery.* London.

Richardson, R. G. (1968). *Surgery Old and New Frontiers.* New York.

Zimmerman, L. M. and Veith, J. (1961). *Great Ideas in the History of Surgery.* Baltimore.

SURGERY OF TRAUMA

Introduction. Man has been concerned with the management and treatment of injury since earliest times. One can be reasonably sure of this since the outer surface of the body is covered by the largest sense organ, namely the *skin, which is richly endowed with nerve endings that record the sensations of touch, pain, heat, and cold. Any injury will stimulate these nerve endings, thus rapidly drawing the lesion to the attention of the person injured. In addition, if the skin has been damaged there will also be exudation of blood and tissue fluids. It would then be reasonable to expect that the person involved would tend to the injuries either by self-help or by seeking the assistance of another person. It is interesting to consider the outcome of injuries which are simply left to nature and are not afforded any form of treatment. There is, in fact, a vast spectrum of injury ranging from a minor scratch or abrasion to the opposite extreme of gross physical mutilation. Even today, despite all the skills and benefits of modern medicine and surgery, there are many injuries which are simply incompatible with life. Examples include gross brain injury and wounds of the heart and great vessels, like those which occasionally result from the impact of an automobile steering wheel on to the chest wall, causing rupture of the heart. Between the two extremes, there are many injuries which would recover uneventfully even without treatment. However, some patients with severe injury might not succumb but would recover incompletely, being left with some permanent disability or deformity. Included in this group would be some persons sustaining fractures of bones. In fact, if one examines the healing, looking at the capacity of various tissues of the body, one finds that it is unusual for a person to die of fractures; of all the tissues, bone will often repair itself most

soundly, bridging a gap by forming new bone, whereas in other tissues any gap is bridged by *scar tissue.

Scar tissue differs considerably from its parent tissues. The scar of a deep cut in the skin is permanent. It is visibly different from the surrounding skin, its texture is different, and cutaneous scars are usually devoid of nerve endings and therefore insensitive, while *hair follicles and *sweat glands are also absent.

Bones, however, show remarkable powers of recovery even under adverse circumstances. For example, a patient who fell from a tree sustaining a fracture of one femur was taken to a dwelling in the jungle where he lay for five months with 90 degrees of angulation at the fracture site. This fracture healed soundly, still angled, but he was able to walk and was pain-free, albeit with a shortened and much deformed leg.

The body's defences against injury. Nature's defence mechanisms against physical injury are numerous and formidable. Provided that no vital structure has been damaged there is a good chance of recovery without external intervention. In the depths of an open wound the blood vessels retract and contract, slowing down blood flow. Any blood which has been spilt from damaged blood vessels will rapidly *clot, tending to seal the wound. If blood loss has been considerable there will be a fall in *blood pressure, again tending to reduce the amount ejected from the wound with each heart beat. After substantial blood loss there will often be a feeling of weakness and faintness, compelling the injured person to lie down. This state is known as *shock. The cold, clammy skin of the shocked patient is a true reflection of the physiological redistribution of the circulating blood, which is conserved and largely diverted from skin and muscle to organs such as the brain, heart, liver, and kidneys. Mediated by the *hormonal output of the *pituitary and *adrenal glands, urinary output and consequently that of the *electrolytes contained in *urine is reduced, thus conserving body fluids. During the recovery phase the injured person will then experience thirst and will increase his intake of fluid in an attempt to replenish the depleted blood volume. As recovery continues he begins to feel stronger and his intake of food increases in order to make up for loss of *protein and of other blood components. Should the wound become infected, the body can call upon numerous defence mechanisms (including white blood cells (*leucocytes) and *antibodies) in order to cope with the onslaught of the bacteria, provided that the infection was not overwhelming.

History. The earliest historical records of accident surgery are shrouded in mystery, as there were no written texts of those times. There are available however, fossilized remains which show that many centuries ago attempts were made to align fractures and that wounds were *sutured, perhaps with small bone needles. Primitive surgery included the fashioning of *trephine holes in the skull as a form of treatment. Fossilized remains often showed healing at the edge of the trephine holes, indicating that the patients or victims survived the operation.

The oldest written medical texts are the clay tablets, found in Abrahamstown in Mesopotamia, the cradle of civilization lying between the Tigris and Euphrates valleys, of the 4th millennium BC. In 1861 Edwin Smith, an American amateur Egyptologist, discovered papyri in Luxor, Egypt (see EDWIN SMITH PAPYRUS) and in 1875 George Ebers, a German Egyptologist unearthed others (see EBERS PAPYRUS). These seem to have been written about 1600 BC. The finding of the Rosetta Stone in 1799 had provided the key whereby the hieroglyphics could be deciphered. The Luxor papyri provided details of the treatment of accidental injury. The use of herbal medicines was described, as was the care of injuries, including the treatment of wounds by suture and plasters. Fracture treatment was mentioned using *splints made of hollowed-out ox bones supported by straps made of bandages soaked in resin. *Cauterization was recommended for the treatment of wounds. In addition to the ancient Egyptian papyri, Mesopotamian texts were found written on clay tablets. Ancient Chinese records were also found on bones or strips of bamboo. Texts from India of about 1500 BC were found written in Sanskrit, in the form of four holy books. Cauterization was mentioned there for wounds and snake bite and the use of a *catheter-like instrument was described for treating urinary retention. Surgical operations were recorded on the abdominal viscera, including removal of urinary *calculi by *lithotomy; *Caesarean section and ocular *cataract extraction from the eye, and the construction of artificial limbs were described. There was also mention of a form of cosmetic surgery, whereby the nose was reconstructed in wives who had had the organ cut off as punishment for adultery. This was undertaken by way of a pedunculated flap from the cheek, forehead, or upper arm (see PLASTIC SURGERY). In ancient India hospitals were established more than 100 years earlier than in the West. These hospitals were established by religious orders, as were others established later in Europe after the introduction of Christian orders. For several centuries the progress of medicine and surgery was impeded by the association of learned men with religious orders. This in turn led to the belief that ill health could only be cured by divine intervention via the intermediary of the priests. The treatment of injuries therefore fell into the hands of untrained practitioners, who were held in very low regard in the community. It was not until the Middle Ages that any scientific study of medicine and surgery began. Any anatomical knowledge was gleaned mostly from animal dissections.

Andreas *Vesalius was the founder of human anatomy. Following his teachings, Ambroise *Paré, a French *barber-surgeon, rose to fame at about the time of the invention of gunpowder, which produced a new type of wound. For many years he was a skilful wound surgeon with the French army, finally achieving the patronage of four successive kings of France. He invented many surgical instruments, some of which are still in use today. He revolutionized the treatment of fractures and gunshot wounds and abolished the treatment of wounds by cautery with boiling oil, preferring to use less painful and less irritant wound salves.

In the UK following the days of the barber-surgeons of the Middle Ages, surgery became more organized and respectable as a profession. As scientific knowledge accumulated it became obvious that any one man could not be thought competent to deal with every type of surgery. In the past 30 years there has been more and more specialization and although today there are still surgeons designated as general surgeons, their work is no longer of an all-embracing general nature. The advent of specialists in orthopaedics, plastic surgery, urology, neurosurgery, ophthalmology, and otolaryngology has undoubtedly advanced specialist knowledge and research. However, in the management of trauma, one is frequently faced with multisystem injuries, which do not fall precisely into the realm of any one specialty and to this end over the past 15 years much thought has been given to the staffing and training of consultants and doctors, whose career is concerned with the management of accidents and emergencies, including the treatment of trauma. Most hospitals in the UK have an area designated for the treatment of accidents and emergencies. From the inception of the *National Health Service there were misgivings about the provision of treatment of accidents and functioning of hospital casualty departments as they then were. With increasing demands on hospital casualty departments, a report from the British Orthopaedic Association in 1959 led to the setting up of the Accident Services Review Committee of Great Britain and Ireland; its first report was published in 1961. This suggested a comprehensive provision for all types of injury through a three-tier system, with peripheral casualty services provided for the treatment of minor injuries and the needs of local casual patients, staffed mainly by general practitioners. Secondly, an accident unit was recommended as part of a district general hospital under consultant supervision, together with accident beds at a rate of 25 per 100 000 population; and lastly there were to be a number of central accident units, usually at teaching hospitals where there would be the added facility of specialized units being able to deal with patients with complicated injuries. This latter type of unit would deal with a population of perhaps 1–2 million persons. In 1962 a medical advisory committee was set up by the *Ministry of Health. The aims of this committee were similar but provision for emergencies other than accidents was emphasized and the present concept of accident and emergency services and departments was developed. The committee did not support the three-tier system, on the basis that specialist services should not necessarily be concentrated in one hospital within a region. To cope with the added load of emergencies other than accidents, the suggestion was made that for every 100 000 of the population, 30–35 accident beds should be provided.

Between 1962 and 1972 there was a considerable increase in demands on accident and emergency departments. In Scotland there was a 61 per cent increase in the number of first attendances. A national inquiry in 1966 found 883 hospitals providing some sort of emergency treatment, but only 335 offering a 24-hour emergency service. Only 227 dealt with more than 10 000 new attendances per year. In a significant number of casualty departments, no more than one new patient per week was seen.

It has been suggested that the figure of 150 000 population justifies an accident and emergency department. It is felt that 25 000 to 30 000 new attendances per annum justify a fully equipped department with a consultant in charge. Apart from population and work-load, another factor to consider is geography. In an area where the population is widely dispersed, an accident and emergency department may be justified despite a smaller work-load. From a practical point of view, it would be reasonable to suggest that most major district general hospitals should have an accident and emergency department. This would mean about 250 in England and Wales.

Consultants in accident and emergency departments. In 1962 a survey of 228 casualty departments revealed that 174 were the responsibility of orthopaedic surgeons. In only 18 of these departments was there a full-time orthopaedic consultant in charge. In the others the supervision was carried out on a day-to-day basis by the orthopaedic consultant on duty. In some other departments, general surgeons provided the supervision. In a few, particularly in large cities and especially in London, a general physician was responsible for the overall supervision. The routine work was left to less experienced staff and opportunities for training were few. In some departments the responsibility was given to the most recently appointed surgeons or physicians, in addition to their normal clinical duties. Clearly, the system was unsatisfactory and inefficient.

In 1971 the Joint Consultants Committee considered the problem. It was agreed that 32 experimental consultant posts would be set up. At present the total number of departments supervised by consultants in trauma and orthopaedic surgery is 115. The total number of departments supervised by a consultant in accident and emergency is 126. To cope with the changing pattern and the evolution of the new type of consultant in accident and emergency, a number of senior registrar training appointments have been made. At present there are approximately 50 such posts in the UK. These training posts are at present filled by doctors who, in addition to their basic medical degree, have obtained a higher qualification. The most frequent higher qualification is a fellowship of one of the Royal Colleges of Surgeons, but higher qualifications in medicine or anaesthesia, or membership of the Royal College of General Practitioners, may each be acceptable qualifications for higher training in accident and emergency medicine. (See POSTGRADUATE AND CONTINUING MEDICAL EDUCATION.) The aim of the training programme is to ensure that the trainee will have had broad-based experience in the diagnosis and management of all types of conditions which may be seen in an accident and emergency department and in addition to give the opportunity for the trainee to develop any special skill or interests which he chooses to pursue. In this way it is anticipated that, when the time comes for him to take up a consultant appointment, in addition to fulfilling his task as administrator and co-ordinator of accident and emergency services, his special clinical expertise will be an asset to his hospital.

The role of the accident surgeon. *Organization of accident services.* During and since the last two World Wars considerable thought has been given to the organization required for the treatment of large numbers of injured persons. With the increased volume of road traffic, faster railway trains, and aircraft carrying hundreds of passengers, together with the ever-present threat of casualties resulting from terrorist acts, or of nuclear warfare, renewed impetus has been given to the evolution of schemes whereby mass casualties might be handled. A more detailed appraisal has been made of the old military term of '*triage' or casualty sorting into groups, depending upon the type of injury or prospects of survival and relating to the quality of survival. Apart from the actual numbers of casualties and their individual conditions, knowledge of the geographical location of the incident, together with the accessibility of available medical facilities and personnel, is essential. Because large numbers of injured will require transportation, information regarding the availability of ambulances, vehicles, aircraft, and possibly of ships must be to hand. It is known from experience that communication plays a large part in the handling of any disaster, but nowadays it is usually a fairly simple project to establish a reliable radio link, along the various parts of the evacuation chain. If one accepts that the medical and surgical facilities are adequate to deal with the flow of casualties, then triage can proceed in a logical manner. It can take place at any point along the line of transportation from the location where the injury occurred to the admissions or casualty department of the hospital where definitive treatment is available. Depending on circumstances, the sorting may have to be undertaken by persons other than medical personnel, for example ambulance men, nurses, or first aid workers. The task should be allotted to the best qualified person available and ideally should be carried out by a doctor who has had prior experience in the handling of casualties, so that a quick accurate assessment can be made of the clinical situation and decisions can be made as to whether the casualty requires immediate treatment or is fit to wait for delayed treatment, perhaps after a journey of a number of hours. In practice it is usual to allot the injured into various groups, as follows:

1. *Group A.* Persons with very slight injuries which can be managed by self-help. This group should be rapidly diverted to avoid impairing the flow of more seriously injured.

2. *Group B.* Persons with injuries which are slightly more serious but not life-threatening, which can be treated by simple measures such as splints, bandages, etc. After first-aid treatment, these casualties are then fit for transportation over considerable distances to remote hospitals where they can receive definitive treatment.

3. *Group C.* Persons who require *resuscitation and/or operation. This group is further subdivided, as follows:

(i) *Priority 1* are persons who require urgent treatment for life-threatening injury. Usually this type of patient is suffering from the effects of *haemorrhage or *asphyxia. Asphyxia may develop from faciomaxillary injuries, respiratory obstruction, open chest wounds, or tension *pneumothorax. Haemorrhage may result from injury to the heart or large blood vessels from multiple wounds, multiple major fractures, abdominal injury with visceral damage or evisceration. Included in this group are severe *burns involving over 20 per cent of the body surface. As shock will be a marked feature of most of these injuries, resuscitation will be required along with some form of operative treatment.

(ii) *Priority 2.* Many patients in this group will require early surgery, but perhaps with less urgency. The group will include cases of intestinal perforation, chest wounds without asphyxia, closed head injuries, and wounds of the genitourinary system.

(iii) *Priority 3.* Patients in this group require surgery, but some delay will not cause any immediate risk to life or limb. Included in this group are extensive soft tissue injuries, fractures and dislocations, face and eye injuries, and burns involving less than 20 per cent of the body surface. After primary treatment these patients will be fit to travel considerable distances.

4. *Group D.* This group includes casualties who have died or who have sustained injuries of such severity that there is no hope of survival.

In a situation where the number of casualties vastly overloads the medical facilities available, a different form of classification must be undertaken so that the medical care available can provide the greatest benefit for the largest number of persons. In addition to considering the gravity of the injuries, one must assess the likelihood of obtaining good-quality survival. The NATO Armed Services have implemented the following classification: T1—immediate treatment; T2—delayed treatment; T3—minimal treatment; T4—expectant treatment.

1. *T1—immediate treatment.* Casualties in this group require immediate surgical operation to save life or limb. The time spent on operation should be limited to about 20 minutes and should only be offered to patients in whom chances of reasonably good-quality survival can be anticipated. Such an operation might include the release of respiratory obstruction, the control of severe haemorrhage, or amputation of one or more limbs.

2. *T2—delayed treatment.* Assessment of these patients shows that complex and time-consuming operations will be necessary, but their chances of survival will not be impaired by some delay. Recovery might be improved by *antibiotics, intravenous fluids, *analgesics, nasogastric suction, and catheterization. Included in this group are major fractures, abdominal and thoracic injury, and burns of up to 30 per cent of the body surface.

3. *T3—minimal treatment.* This group will include patients with relatively minor injuries, which can be treated either by self-help or by untrained personnel; included are abrasions, lacerations, closed fractures, and burns involving up to 10 per cent of the body surface area.

4. *T4—expectant treatment.* This group includes patients who have injuries which are so severe that if they were treated under the best possible conditions the outlook would be poor. These patients should be made comfortable, perhaps with analgesics and simple supportive measures, but should not be put forward for evacuation. These patients would not be abandoned but might be subject to review at a later stage when the casualty flow had subsided.

Although it may appear simple to group casualty patients into neat categories, in reality the situation is much more difficult. It is impossible to visualize what the next disaster might involve. Additional factors such as weather, darkness, failure of electricity supply, or contamination by chemical or radioactive materials, may complicate the situation. In the UK disaster plans have been made, involving a broad national outline, subdivided into more practical regional disaster plans. Since the distribution of medical facilities is not uniform throughout the country, the arrival of a number of casualties at one hospital might pose no problem whatever, whereas at a smaller hospital the facilities might be overwhelmed. In view of this situation it has been necessary to draw up lines involving evacuation towards larger cities with greater medical and surgical capacity. Formulating the major disaster plans for a region is not an easy project. One is planning for an unpredictable situation which may happen at any time in the future (e.g. a major train or aircraft crash, or nuclear war) but at a time as yet unknown. Large numbers of personnel might be called upon to assist. In addition to medical and nursing care, assistance is required from police, ambulance services, the fire brigade, radioactivity experts, gas and electricity personnel, social security, and various local public organizations. Since one is making plans for an unknown event, it is impossible to designate officers by name. Although regular major disaster training exercises are undertaken, it is exceedingly difficult to simulate a realistic incident. To do this effectively would require the date and time of the exercise to be known only by one person. An effective exercise would mean bringing hospitals to a standstill, cancelling operation lists, evacuating wards of patients, and bringing all the traffic of a city to a halt by setting up road blocks to ensure the free flow of ambulance traffic from the site of the incident. Clearly at best any planning will be a compromise, because it is unrealistic to expect that any disaster will occur according to a predictable set of rules. Nevertheless, it is important that any country be kept in a state of readiness. Undoubtedly if simple basic rules are well known and understood, improvisation and ingenuity will lead to the best use of the available resources to deal with the situation in hand.   D. D. MILNE

Further reading

Brim, C. J. (1936). *Medicine in the Bible*. New York.
Bryan, C. P. (1930). *Papyrus Ebers*. London.
Camp, J. (1978). *The Healer's Art*. London.
Kirby, N. G. and Blackburn, G. (1983). *Field Surgery Pocket Book*. London.
Lewin, W. (1978). *Medical Staffing of Accident and Emergency Services*, Report to Joint Consultants Committee. London.
Venzmer, G. (tr. Koenig, M.) (1972). *5000 Years of Medicine*. London.

SURGERY, OPEN HEART. Operative surgery on the dry non-beating heart, cardiopulmonary function being temporarily taken over by a *heart–lung machine (extracorporeal oxygenator). See CARDIOTHORACIC SURGERY.

SUTHERLAND, EARL WILBUR (1915–74) American biochemist, MD Washington University, St Louis (1942). After internship and military medical service, Sutherland gave up clinical medicine for biochemical research, at Washington University, Case Western Reserve University, Vanderbilt University, and the University of Miami. His first investigations were on carbohydrate metabolism in muscle and liver tissue. In the course of this he discovered the presence, in almost all cells, of adenosine-3′,5′-phosphoric acid (cyclic adenosine monophosphate (*cyclic AMP)). Much subsequent work by Sutherland and colleagues showed that cyclic AMP mediates the

action of many extrinsic *hormones on the intrinsic processes of cells—the so-called 'second messenger' concept. For this work he was awarded a Nobel prize in 1971.

SUTTEE is the Indian custom of widow-suicide by self-immolation on the husband's funeral pyre (see SUICIDE).

SUTURE is the surgical insertion of a stitch or stitches, the stitch itself, or the material employed for stitching; the inflexible fibrous articulations between the component bones of the skull are also referred to as sutures.

SWAB. A wad of cotton wool or other absorbent material for mopping up blood or other fluids, cleaning a patient's mouth, applying antiseptics to the skin, taking bacteriological specimens, etc.

SWAMMERDAM, JAN (1637–80). Dutch biologist, MD Leiden (1667). Swammerdam never practised medicine, spending his brief life in physiological and biological research. He devised a muscle-nerve preparation and showed that there was no increase in muscle bulk with contraction. He made many observations on insects and their development and described the red blood cells in a frog's web (1658). His great work *Bijbel der Natuure* was published nearly 80 years after his death by *Boerhaave (1757–8).

SWEATING is the secretion of a weak saline solution by the sweat glands of the skin, the evaporation of which plays an important part in thermoregulation. In extreme climatic circumstances, fluid loss by this means may be as much as 10 litres a day.

SWELLING is enlargement of any part, region, or organ of the body.

SWIETEN, GERARD VAN (1700–72). Dutch physician, MD Leiden (1725). Van Swieten practised in Leiden, but, as a Catholic, was debarred from a university appointment in the Netherlands. In 1745 he accepted an invitation from Maria Theresa to become her court physician in Vienna. He completely reorganized the medical faculty establishing the great Vienna School and earning a reputation as a clinical teacher. He was much influenced by *Sydenham and *Boerhaave, publishing a commentary in five volumes on the aphorisms of the latter (1754–5).

SWIMMING. Surface swimming (i.e. excluding deep diving) in pools, rivers, and the sea is a valuable form of symmetrical whole-body exercise which presents few medical hazards. In Europe, fear of infection, probably well-justified at that time, led to a decline in popularity of bathing during the Middle Ages which only recovered in the 19th c.; now, only bathing in highly polluted rivers is likely to result in enteric or other infections. The dictum that patients with plastic ventilation tubes (grommets) inserted in their *tympanic membranes should not go swimming has recently been questioned; the chemical and microbiological dangers are said to be less than those of submerging the head in bath water to rinse off shampoo. The sea, given calm water and an absence of dangerous currents, presents chiefly the possibility of occasional envenomation by certain marine animals, notably coelenterates, molluscs, echinoderms, and venomous fishes; their stings can be unpleasant but, in temperate waters at least, only rarely dangerous. 'Swimmer's itch' is a skin reaction to invasion by cercariae of Schistosoma spp. (see BILHARZIASIS), non-human as well as human, which can result from bathing in infested lakes in certain parts of the world including North America. Conjunctival irritation is a well-known consequence of using highly chlorinated swimming-pools. Chlamydial *conjunctivitis can also occur rarely, the organisms being transferred from the genital tract of the swimmer or his or her companions ('swimming-pool conjunctivitis'). Lastly, the danger of diving into unexpectedly shallow water should be mentioned; severe spinal injury, including *haematomyelia, can result.

SYCOSIS is suppurative infection of the hair follicles, particularly in the beard area of the face (sycosis barbae).

SYDENHAM, THOMAS (1624–89). British physician, BM Oxford (1648), MD Cambridge (1676), LRCP (1663). Sydenham was born in Dorset and matriculated at Oxford in 1642, but left to serve with the Parliamentary forces as captain of horse. He was taken prisoner in 1643 and resigned his commission in 1646. He returned to Oxford and graduated BM by order of the Chancellor, the Earl of Pembroke, in 1648. Recalled to the colours, he was seriously wounded in 1651. Later he studied in Montpellier, returning to practise in Westminster about 1661. He left London during the Plague in 1665. Sydenham has often been called 'the English Hippocrates'. He established the value of clinical observation in the practice of medicine and based his treatment on practical experience rather than upon the theories of *Galen. He was a sufferer from *gout of which he left a classic description (1649). He published Methodus curandi febris (1666) and Observationes medicae (1676).

SYLVIUS, FRANCISCUS (Franz de la Boë) (1614–72). Dutch physician, MD Basle (1637). After practice in Amsterdam Sylvius became professor of medicine in Leiden in 1658, where he established clinical instruction and won a great reputation as a teacher. A renowned anatomist he described the Sylvian *aqueduct and the *middle cerebral (Sylvian) artery. A leader of the *iatrochemical school he studied salts and ascribed all vital activity to a balance between acid and alkali. He was the first to institute laboratory teaching.

SYMBIOSIS is the living together of two dissimilar organisms in close association, the relationship being mutually beneficial. Examples are the association between cellulose-digesting bacteria and the herbivorous animals in whose alimentary tract they reside, and that between nitrogen-fixing bacteria and leguminous plants.

SYMBOLISM, in psychiatry, is the unconscious mental mechanism whereby an object, person, or idea is substituted for another that is causing an emotional or mental problem. Symbolism is an important component of dreams. It is also a characteristic of *schizophrenic thought disorder.

SYME, JAMES (1799–1870). British surgeon, MRCS (1821), FRCS Edinburgh (1828). Syme was appointed professor of clinical surgery and surgeon to the *Edinburgh Royal Infirmary, in 1833, and professor of clinical surgery at University College, London, in 1847, but the terms proved unsatisfactory and he returned to Edinburgh after three months. He was made surgeon-in-ordinary to the Queen in Scotland in 1838. Syme was the acknowledged leader of surgery in Europe; he devised the operation for *amputation through the ankle joint (Syme's amputation). He was Lord *Lister's father-in-law.

SYMONDS, SIR CHARLES PUTNAM (1890–1978). British neurologist, DM (1919), FRCP (1924). Symonds was appointed to the staff of the *National Hospital for Nervous Disease, Queen Square and *Guy's Hospital in 1920. During the Second World War he served as consulting neuropsychiatrist to the Royal Air Force. He was the first to describe clearly the clinical picture of spontaneous *subarachnoid haemorrhage. He was the leading clinical neurologist in the UK. He was created Companion of the Order of the Bath in 1944 and Knight Commander of the Order of the British Empire in 1946.

SYMPATHECTOMY is the surgical interruption of part of the *sympathetic nervous system, cutting off sympathetic impulses to a part, organ, or region.

SYMPATHETIC NERVOUS SYSTEM. Part of the *autonomic nervous system, which regulates the involuntary automatic functions of the body. The sympathetic nerves are derived from the thoracolumbar regions of the spinal cord (cf. the *parasympathetic system, which comes from the craniosacral portions of the neuraxis) and run in the first instance to a series of cell junctions or ganglia situated in longitudinal chains on either side of the spine; from here the sympathetic nerves, running mostly in conjunction with arteries, spread out to supply the whole body. In general, sympathetic stimuli produce effects directly opposed to those of parasympathetic stimulation. They include: dilatation of the pupils; stimulation of sweat glands; dilatation of muscle arteries but constriction of those supplying the skin and digestive organs; stimulation of the heart; increased ventilation of the lungs; and inhibition of digestive function. Similar effects (hence 'sympathomimetic') are produced by the circulating *catecholamines adrenaline and noradrenaline liberated by the *adrenal medulla.

SYMPATHOMIMETIC. See SYMPATHETIC NERVOUS SYSTEM.

SYMPTOM. A disease manifestation of which the patient complains, as opposed to one observed by others (cf. *sign).

SYMPTOMATOLOGY is most often used in respect of the totality of symptoms, either of a particular disorder or manifested by a particular patient; it is also the study of symptoms generally.

SYNAPSE. The site of impulse transmission between one nerve cell (*neurone) and another, where a nerve fibre (axon) of the first neurone terminates in close apposition to the cell body or a branch (dendrite) of the second. When excited, the first or presynaptic neurone releases a chemical *neurotransmitter substance which diffuses across the synaptic cleft to bind with receptors on the postsynaptic cell membrane, initiating the process of *excitation (depolarization) in the postsynaptic cell.

SYNCOPE is a sudden temporary loss of consciousness due to transient cerebral *anoxia; it is synonymous with faint.

SYNDROME. A collection of symptoms and signs which tend to occur together and form a characteristic pattern but which may not necessarily be always due to the same pathological cause.

SYNERGISM is the combination of two agents to produce an effect greater than the sum of their separate individual actions.

SYNGRAFT. A transplant of organ or tissue between genetically identical individuals, which in man means between monozygotic (uniovular or identical) *twins (cf. *allograft, *autograft, and *xenograft).

SYNOVIAL MEMBRANE is the lining membrane of joints, bursae, and tendon sheaths; it secretes the alkaline viscid synovial fluid, which acts as a lubricant.

SYNOVITIS is inflammation of a *synovial membrane, the smooth moist membrane which lines the interior of joints.

SYPHILIS. The most serious and the most feared of the sexually transmitted diseases, syphilis is due to infection with the spiral bacterium (spirochaete) *Treponema pallidum.* Apart from *congenital syphilis, infection is only acquired by close contact, almost always venereal in nature. The primary manifestations of the disease (SEE CHANCRE) are relatively minor and usually pass off without incident even when untreated; they are sometimes unnoticed altogether. The second stage, weeks or months later, takes the form of a mild general illness with lymph node enlargement and various types of rash, often mucocutaneous (see CONDYLOMA). During these first two stages, the patient remains infectious and able to pass the disease on to others. There follows a latent period which may last for years, or even a lifetime. Late, or tertiary, syphilis then supervenes, bringing with it the tragic and destructive lesions for which the disease has justly acquired its evil reputation. Late syphilis can affect almost any system of the body (see GUMMA), but those of most importance involve the central nervous system (see NEUROSYPHILIS; GENERAL PARALYSIS OF THE INSANE; TABES DORSALIS) and the heart and great vessels (particularly aortitis, aortic aneurysm, and aortic valve incompetence). The advent of *penicillin, to which *T. pallidum* has remained sensitive, has revolutionized the former unsatisfactory treatment of syphilis with various metal preparations which began in the 16th c. with mercury and further developed (1910) with *Ehrlich's 'magic bullet' arsphenamine (*salvarsan). In theory, since no animal reservoir for the organism is known to exist outside man and one or two higher primates, syphilis should be completely eradicable. Though reduced in incidence, however, it remains a major public health problem. See also YAWS; PINTA; BEJEL; VENEREOLOGY.

SYRINGE. An instrument for the injecting or withdrawing of liquids or gases, usually by means of manually applied pressure. The common form is a cylinder, in which the internal pressure is varied by means of a piston; the outlet of the cylinder is connected to a tube or hollow needle.

SYRINGOMELIA is a neurological condition, often progressive, in which an abnormal cavity (or syrinx) develops in the centre of the *spinal cord, usually most marked in the cervical region. The resultant interference with motor and sensory tracts causes muscular weakness and wasting with loss of *tendon jerks or reflexes in the arms and a characteristic type of sensory impairment known as dissociated anaesthesia, in which pain and temperature appreciation are lost while touch and tactile discrimination are preserved. When the signs suggest that the defect extends upwards into the medulla oblongata, the term syringobulbia is used. See also HAEMATOMYELIA; NEUROSURGERY.

SYRINX. A tube or channel, particularly a *fistula.

SYSTEM. Any one of the major physiological subdivisions of the whole organism, each comprising a set of cells, tissues, and organs subserving a broad general function (e.g. cardiovascular system, nervous system, endocrine system, immune system, reproductive system, etc.).

SYSTÈME INTERNATIONAL. See SI UNITS.

SYSTEMIC LUPUS ERYTHEMATOSUS is a chronic generalized inflammatory disorder of unknown aetiology, which may or may not be associated with a skin rash resembling that of local *lupus erythematosus. It is usually classified with the collagen or connective tissue disorders (e.g. *rheumatoid arthritis, *dermatomyositis, *poly-arteritis nodosa, *systemic sclerosis, etc.); and *autoimmunity seems to be involved in the pathogenesis. The clinical manifestations are varied and may affect, apart from the skin, the joints, other serous membranes, the kidneys, the central nervous system and other organs and systems of the body. See RHEUMATOLOGY.

SYSTEMIC SCLEROSIS, PROGRESSIVE is a chronic and serious disease of unknown aetiology, also and less accurately known as scleroderma, which appears to be primarily a disorder of *collagen. There is gradual and progressive thickening, hardening, and contraction of skin, particularly of the hands and face (acrosclerosis); at the same time, a similar process invades other organs and structures and may cause important damage to the digestive tract, the kidneys, the lungs, and the heart. *Morphoea, or true scleroderma is a localized form in which the pathological process is limited to the skin.

SYSTOLE is the contraction period of the heart, corresponding to the time interval between the beginning of the first heart sound to the end of the second. During this period, the atrioventricular valves are closed and blood is ejected from the right and left ventricles through the open pulmonary and aortic valves into the pulmonary artery and the aorta respectively (cf. *diastole).

T

TABES DORSALIS is one of the classical expressions of *neurosyphilis, now uncommon, of which the major manifestations are due to degeneration of the posterior columns and nerve roots of the *spinal cord. It is a late complication, which may not develop until as long as 20 years after the primary infection. Symptoms and signs include: 'lightning' pains in various parts of the body; tabetic 'crises' with severe abdominal pain and vomiting which may be mistaken for a surgical emergency; sensory *ataxia causing unsteadiness in the dark and a positive *Romberg's sign; loss of pain sensation and joint position sense; painless enlargement and disorganization of joints (Charcot's joints); absent tendon reflexes; muscular hypotonia; and small irregular unequal pupils which react to accommodation but poorly or not at all to light (*Argyll Robertson pupils). Unless *general paralysis of the insane coexists (taboparesis), the plantar responses are flexor and the mental state is unaffected.

TABLET. The usual form in which a drug or drug combination is presented for oral administration, an accurately measured dose being combined with a suitable *excipient and compressed into a convenient and preferably identifiable shape. It may be designed either for chewing or swallowing.

TABOO is a word of Polynesian origin denoting something prohibited, or restricted to a particular class of person, or sacred.

TABOPARESIS is *neurosyphilis with features both of *tabes dorsalis and *general paralysis of the insane.

TAB VACCINE is a killed *vaccine for active immunization against the *Salmonella organisms responsible for *typhoid fever and *paratyphoid fevers A and B.

TACHE. A stain, spot, or *macula.

TACHYCARDIA is a rapid heart rate, whether a physiological or pathophysiological reaction (e.g. to emotion, exercise, fever) or due to an inherent cardiac *arrhythmia.

TACHYPHYLAXIS is the phenomenon whereby repeated doses of a drug result in progressively smaller effects, or progressive increases in dosage are required to produce the same effect.

TADDEO, ALDEROTTI (also known as Taddes of Florence or Thaddeus Florentinus) (1223–1303). Taddeo was one of the early medical teachers at *Bologna, and Dante may have been among his students. Taddeo introduced the system of case histories to include all the features of disease in particular patients as a teaching method. It remains in use in all medical schools.

TAENIA is a genus of large *tapeworms (or cestodes) parasitic in mammals including man. There are numerous species, of which the two of most medical importance are *Taenia saginata* (the beef tapeworm) and *T. solium* (the pork tapeworm); for both of these, man is the only natural definitive host (see PARASITOLOGY). Intestinal infection occurs from eating raw or insufficiently cooked beef or pork which is contaminated with the intermediate or larval stage of the parasite; since completion of the life-cycle depends on intimate contact between cattle or pigs and human faeces, indigenous infection is uncommon in the USA and Western Europe. Despite the sometimes massive size of the worms (up to 10 m for *T. saginata* and up to 4 m for *T. solium*), intestinal infections cause little disturbance except revulsion and are usually recognized by the discovery of the gravid mobile segments in the faeces.

In the case of *T. solium*, however, man may also become the intermediate host with much more serious consequences. This is sometimes the result of autoinfection from faecal contamination. The larvae migrate to all parts of the body, die, and become calcified, causing symptoms perhaps many years after infection. These depend on the site; if in the brain, for example, epilepsy may result. This condition is known as cysticercosis.

TAGLIACOZZI, GASPARE (1546–99). Italian surgeon, Ph.D. Bologna (1570). Tagliacozzi is accounted the 'father of *plastic surgery' and was famed for *rhinoplasty, an operation condemned by the church. He also recorded plastic repairs of the lips, ear, and tongue using the predecessor of the pedicle graft.

TAIT, ROBERT LAWSON (1845–99). British gynaecologist, FRCS Edinburgh (1870), FRCS (1871). In 1871 Tait was appointed surgeon to the Hospital for Diseases of Women, Birmingham, becoming professor of gynaecology, Queen's College, Birmingham, in 1887. He was a pioneer of operative *gynaecology and one of the first to operate for tubo-ovarian abscess (1872), *hysterectomy for *fibroids (1873), and *ectopic pregnancy (1883).

TAKAYASU'S DISEASE is a condition, also known as 'pulseless disease' and 'aortic arch syndrome', in which there is progressive obliteration of the major arteries arising from the *aortic arch. It is relatively common in Japan, and affects women more often than men.

TALIPES is any congenital deformity of the foot (club-foot).

TALIPES EQUINOVARUS is a common variety of *talipes in which the foot is plantar-flexed and adducted, with the medial border raised.

TALISMAN. An *amulet or charm.

TALKING BOOKS are voice recordings of written material, made for the blind. See OPHTHALMOLOGY.

TAMOXIFEN is an *oestrogen antagonist which blocks receptor sites in target organs. It has become the drug of choice in the palliative treatment of postmenopausal breast cancer. See PHARMACOLOGY.

TAMPON. A plug of cotton wool or other absorbent material for insertion into body orifices in order to control *haemorrhage or a flow of secretions.

TAMPONADE is compression of the heart by an accumulation of fluid in the *pericardial cavity sufficient to embarrass cardiac function; this is particularly likely to be the case when the fluid accumulates rapidly, as with bleeding into the pericardium (haemopericardium).

TAPEWORM. Any cestode worm, that is, a member of the subclass Cestoda of the class Cestoidea. True tapeworms have a head (or scolex) and a number of segments (or proglottides). The adult worms are parasitic in the alimentary tract of vertebrates; the larval stages occur in the organs and tissues of animals acting as intermediate hosts. The subclass has 11 orders, of which two, the Cyclophyllidea and the Pseudophyllidea, contain species which are of medical importance. The species are *Diphyllobothrium latum (the fish tapeworm), *Taenia saginata (the beef tapeworm), Taenia solium (the pork tapeworm), Hymenolepis nana (the dwarf tapeworm), and Echinococcus granulosus (the agent of *hydatid disease). Infestation of man by other species is rare.

TARANTISM was an epidemic form of dancing mania prevalent in parts of Italy from the 15th to the 17th c. It was popularly supposed either to be caused by or to cure the effects of a bite of a spider.

TARANTULA. See SPIDERS.

TARSORRHAPHY is the surgical suturing together of the upper and lower eyelids along all (total tarsorrhaphy) or part (partial tarsorrhaphy) of their length.

TASTE is the sensation produced by particular substances when they come into contact with specialized *receptors (taste-buds) scattered throughout the mucous membrane of the tongue and palate. Impulses from the taste-buds are carried to the brain by fibres running in the *facial and *glossopharyngeal nerves.

TATTOOING produces an indelible mark or design on the skin by introducing permanent dyes through a needle puncturing the *epidermis into the *dermis. Transmission of *hepatitis B is an obvious hazard when the instruments are inadequately sterilized. The word 'tattoo' is derived from the Tahitian tatu, which means a puncturing. In the UK, except for Northern Ireland, the tattooing of persons under the age of 18 years is forbidden by law under the *Tattooing of Minors Act 1969.

TATTOOING OF MINORS ACT 1969. This UK Act prohibited the tattooing of persons under the age of 18 years, except in Northern Ireland and except when undertaken for medical reasons by a duly qualified medical practitioner. Tattooing was defined for purposes of the Act as the insertion into the skin of any colouring material designed to leave a permanent mark.

TATUM, EDWARD LAWRIE (1909–75). American geneticist, Ph.D. University of Wisconsin (1934). Tatum held faculty posts at Stanford and Yale, before joining the staff of the Rockefeller University in 1957. He was awarded the Nobel prize (with G. W. Beadle and J. Lederberg) for work leading to the 'one gene–one enzyme' concept, that is, that biochemical processes are regulated by genes.

TAXIS is the locomotory movement of an organism or cell in response to a directional stimulus (as in phototaxis, chemotaxis, etc.); also, the reduction by manipulation of a fracture, dislocation, or displacement of a part or organ.

TAXONOMY is the science of the classification of organisms according to their resemblances and differences.

TAY, WARREN (1843–1927). English ophthalmologist, MRCS (1866), LSA (1869), FRCS (1869). Tay described cherry-red spots seen by ophthalmoscopy at the back of the eyes, now known as part of *Tay–Sachs disease. He was educated at the London Hospital, being appointed assistant surgeon and ophthalmologist in 1869, surgeon in 1876, and consulting surgeon in 1902. He was one of the last men in London to combine the practice of general surgery with that of ophthalmology. He was also an authority on diseases of the skin and of childhood.

TAYLOR, JOHN 'CHEVALIER' (1703–72). English surgeon and oculist. Taylor was born in Norwich, elder son of a surgeon and apothecary. He went to London as an apprentice apothecary and studied surgery under William *Cheselden of *St Thomas's Hospital. Taylor set up as surgeon and oculist in Norwich, but meeting much opposition, he set out through the British Isles as an itinerant oculist, and did the same on the Continent. He became MD of Basle, Liège, and Cologne. In 1736 he was appointed oculist to George II. Taylor was a bombast who advertised his skills with little propriety and prefaced his operations with prolonged harangues about his prowess, which was in fact operatively good. He was well known in his time and referred to by Dr Johnson as 'an instance of how far impudence will carry ignorance'. Taylor was the author of several treatises on the eye. His son John followed him and became oculist to George III.

TAY–SACHS DISEASE is an inherited metabolic disorder (formerly known as amaurotic family idiocy), the infantile form of cerebral sphingolipidosis. The features are progressive dementia, paralysis, blindness, and death, the usual age of onset being 4–6 months. A cherry-red spot on each retina is characteristic. The genetic pattern is that of an autosomal *recessive trait, and the condition occurs mainly among the *Ashkenazi (i.e. Jews of middle and northern Europe). Detection of *heterozygote carriers is possible by serum enzyme studies in high-risk populations, and the *homozygous state can be detected prenatally in the fetus by *amniocentesis.

TEA is an infusion made from the dried and prepared leaves of a small evergreen tree of the genus *Camellia* (particularly *C. sinensis*), widely used as a beverage. Tea, which was known in China at least as far back as 2373 BC, contains tannic acid and the pharmacologically active substances *caffeine and *theophylline. Other herbal infusions, for example, 'bush tea', may contain plant derivatives which are toxic (see POISONOUS PLANTS).

TEACHERS OF NURSING ACT 1967. This UK Act amended Section 17 of the *Nurses Act 1957, which concerned the power of the *General Nursing Council to prescribe the qualifications of teachers of nurses. The amendment gave the Council discretion to grant certificates to persons other than those who had completed a prescribed course of training in an approved institution, provided they appeared to the Council (and to the Minister of Health) to be otherwise qualified for the teaching of nursing.

TEALE, THOMAS PRIDGIN (1800–67). British surgeon. Teale practised mainly in Leeds, England. He published papers on *neuralgic diseases, *hernia, *plastic surgery, and *amputations.

TEARS are the aqueous saline secretion of the *lacrimal glands.

TECHNICIANS are those whose profession concerns the technical aspects of medical and scientific work, such as the operation and maintenance of equipment, the laboratory procedures involved in biochemical analyses, histological preparations, etc. Special technical qualifications are normally required, though an increasing number of technicians also possess university degrees in science and occasionally doctorates. North American usage equates 'technologist' with 'technician'. In UK hospitals staff formerly called technicians are now called medical laboratory scientific officers (MLSOs). See PROFESSIONS SUPPLEMENTARY, ETC. TO MEDICINE IN THE UK.

TEETH. The main constituent of teeth is *dentine, which is identical to ivory. A layer of hard inorganic material, enamel, covers the dentine of the exposed portion or crown of each tooth, a layer of softer cement the concealed or root portion. Dentine resembles bone except that it contains no cells and no blood vessels. The cavity of the tooth is filled with the pulp, soft connective tissue containing blood vessels and nerves.

In man, the deciduous or milk teeth begin to erupt at about six months of life; there are 20 deciduous teeth in all, 5 in each quadrant of the mouth (2 incisors, 1 canine, and 2 molars). They have all usually appeared by the age of two years. From the sixth year onwards, they begin to be replaced by the permanent teeth, the full set of which numbers 32, 8 in each quadrant (2 incisors, 1 canine, 2 premolars, and 3 molars). The first to appear are the first molars, and the last milk teeth (the canines) have normally been replaced by the twelfth year. The third molars, or wisdom teeth, do not appear for a few more years and may not erupt at all.

TELANGIECTASIA. Dilatation of small blood vessels.

TELEOLOGY is the doctrine of causes, or interpretation in terms of purpose.

TELEPATHY. Extrasensory thought transference. See EXTRASENSORY PERCEPTION; PARAPSYCHOLOGY.

TEMPERAMENT is a combination of the characteristic qualities of an individual's emotional nature, his constitutional tendency to react to his environment in a certain way, and the quality and lability of his mood. *Galen recognized four types of temperament reflecting a preponderance of one or other of the supposed four body '*humours', namely sanguine, choleric, melancholic, and phlegmatic. There have been other more recent attempts to categorize differences in temperament. One such proposes a dimension based on proneness to a particular type of mental disorder: at one extreme of this is the 'cyclothymic personality', often jovial, friendly, and outgoing but with swings of mood and prone in the event of breakdown to develop *manic-depressive psychosis; the associated bodily habitus is 'pyknic', that is short, thick, and stocky. At the other end of this spectrum is the 'schizothyme', who is intraverted, withdrawn, and shy, and liable to develop *schizophrenia; here the habitus is tall, thin, and 'leptosomatic'.

TEMPERATURE is the measure of hotness, which can be defined as a property determining the rate at which heat will be transferred to or from a body. Temperature is thus a measure of the kinetic energy of the molecules, atoms, or ions of which matter is composed. The basic physical quantity, the thermodynamic temperature, is expressed in kelvin. Other scales of temperature are the *Celsius (centigrade), *Fahrenheit, and *Réaumur scales.

The normal body temperature when measured orally averages 37 °C (98.6 °F). It fluctuates slightly, being lowest in the early morning and highest in the evening. It also varies with the menstrual cycle, being lowest during menstruation and highest at ovulation.

TEMPLE MEDICINE. The temple medicine of ancient Greece probably began some time in the 8th c. BC, when temples were first erected to *Aesculapius, the god of medicine; they were called *asclepieia* (singular *asclepieon*). The medicine practised took the strange form known as 'incubation'. The patient, after sacrifice and purification, lay down to sleep near the altar of the god, whereupon the remedy for his illness was revealed to him, either in a dream or by a priest dressed to represent Aesculapius. On recovery, thank-offerings were presented to the temple, including models of the affected part in gold, silver, and wax, and a tablet was erected describing the illness and treatment. Other persons than the patient could incubate on his behalf, and in some temples there were professional dreamers who could be hired for the purpose. More than 300 such temples were mentioned by classical writers, the most famous being at *Epidaurus, Cnidus, *Cos, and *Pergamum. *Hippocrates is said to have been indebted to the clinical material accumulated on the tablets at Cos, but the Hippocratic school, though partly contemporaneous with the temple movement, was independent of it.

TEMPLE OF HEALTH. The principal temple of *Aesculapius, the god of medicine, in *Epidaurus.

TEMPORAL BONE. The paired skull bone which forms the flat part of the side of the head (temple) above the cheek-bone or zygoma; it houses the structures of the *middle and *inner ear and the *Eustachian tube.

TENDON. A fibrous cord, largely composed of *collagen fibres, attaching a muscle to a bone; also known as a sinew.

TENDON JERK (or reflex) is a spinal reflex elicited by tapping a *tendon to stimulate its stretch receptors; the stimulus evokes an involuntary contraction of the associated muscle or group of muscles.

TENNIS ELBOW is characterized by pain over the outer aspect of the elbow, localized to the region of the attachment of the common extensor tendon to the lateral humeral epicondyle but sometimes also present over the neck of the radius. It is associated with repetitive pronation and supination of the forearm, and with sports and occupations that require this movement (cf. 'golfer's elbow', which is medial humeral epicondylitis).

TENON, JACQUES RENÉ (1724–1816). French surgeon and ophthalmologist. Tenon joined the army as a surgeon in 1744 and later acquired renown as an anatomist and an ophthalmologist, describing several structures in the eye, including the fascial sheath of the eyeball (Tenon's capsule). In 1788 Tenon published a series of memoirs on Paris hospitals revealing their overcrowding, their squalor, and the total disregard for sanitation. These led the authorities to undertake great improvements.

TENOSYNOVITIS is inflammation of a *tendon sheath.

TENOTOMY is the surgical incision or division of a *tendon.

TENOVAGINITIS is synonymous with *tenosynovitis.

TENSION has various senses: stretching, the degree of stretching, or the state of being stretched; the partial pressure of a gas in a liquid (e.g. the oxygen tension of blood); a mental state of suppressed emotion, or conflicting ideas.

TERATOGENIC. Producing abnormal embryos. See TERATOLOGY.

TERATOLOGY is the branch of science which deals with the production, development, and classification of abnormal *embryos and/or *fetuses. The word 'teratology' is derived from the Greek word 'teras', meaning monster, so that the subject matter of teratology is literally the 'study of monsters'.

Early history. In a broad sense, teratology can be

thought of as one of the oldest branches of science. Man, from his earliest stages of evolution, must have felt awe, wonderment, and quite probably, fear at the birth of an abnormal infant. One of the earliest records of a malformed individual is Mellart's discovery of a sculpture of a double-headed goddess at a neolithic site in southern Turkey. The marble statue has been dated at 6500 BC and probably is based upon observations of dicephalic human 'monsters'. Today it is estimated that 3–6 per cent of newborns exhibit congenital malformations.

Almost certainly from the first observations of congenitally malformed individuals, parents, relatives, and society at large queried the cause and the meaning of these malformed individuals. Ancient peoples proposed many explanations for the birth of malformed children: these included lunar and stellar influences, divine intervention, and the belief of ancient Hebrews and Romans that sexual intercourse during the *menstrual period could cause the birth of a monster. The latter view persisted among learned men in the 17th c. and succumbed only after the investigations of such men as William *Harvey and Renier de *Graaf shed light upon the role of female processes in human reproduction.

In addition to supernatural theories, there existed other explanations for malformations based upon purely physical considerations. *Aristotle, who properly should be considered the father of teratology, was the first to make observations of animal development and attempted to explain the origin of 'monstrous' animals and humans in his work *On the Generation of Animals*. Aristotle postulated that monstrosities were produced by perverted male and female elements in generation. This hypothesis was translated in the practical sense into the view that traumatism and pressure on the early embryo could cause maldevelopment and the birth of a monster. Given the scientific context in which Aristotle worked, these observations and hypotheses are remarkable. For the next 18 centuries, however, mankind's insights into the causes of monsters gained little headway.

Teratology, as well as other branches of science, languished from the death of Aristotle until the onset of the Renaissance and the rebirth of *embryology, beginning with Volcher Coiter (1534–76), first in line of the Renaissance embryologists. Although embryology came out of the dark ages during the Renaissance, new theories seeking to explain the generation of monsters still involved mystical forces. One of the more prominent mystical explanations of monsters is the theory of maternal impressions. This theory had its origin in antiquity, probably serving originally as an explanation of why offspring differ from their parents and later as an explanation for every kind of anomaly and malformation. Proponents of this theory suggested that any specific birth defect was the result of a specific maternal impression

(psychogenic factors) occurring during *pregnancy. In support of this theory, William Dabney (1890) tabulated 90 cases involving maternal impressions that he believed to be 'worthy of credence'. His tabulation includes: (i) the name of the reporter; (ii) the journal or work in which the report may be found; (iii) the period of pregnancy at which the impression was made; (iv) the cause or nature of the impression; and (v) the nature of the defect of the child. One reported instance of maternal impression involved a woman who at one month of gestation observed at a circus a hydrocephalic cat preserved in alcohol. Eight months later, she gave birth to an infant with *hydrocephalus. Other accounts involved a woman who at three months of pregnancy was frightened by a monkey and subsequently gave birth to a girl with face 'singularly like a monkey's' and one who saw a hare and had a baby with a *hare lip. The theory of maternal impressions gained wide acceptance in the 17th c., in large part because the scientific knowledge necessary to refute such a theory was not yet available. Although scientific knowledge grew rapidly from the 17th c. onward, the theory of maternal impressions was still prevalent in the first half of the 20th c. Consider the quote from Bradley Patten's *Human Embryology* (1947): 'It is astonishing how many people believe that a fright or an unpleasant sight during pregnancy will cause a child to be marked in a manner suggesting the incident.'

With the increase in scientific knowledge in the 17th c. more plausible explanations for the production of monsters were proffered. Many of these can be grouped under the heading of mechanical factors, such as narrowness of the *uterus, faulty posture of the pregnant woman, external violence, length of the *umbilical cord, and amniotic adhesions. At one time or another each of these alone or in combination was considered the source of all human malformations. The amniotic theory of teratogenesis was most widely expressed by Étienne Geoffrey Saint-Hilaire in the 1820s. The validity of this theory has waxed and waned since that time, but even in recent times it has been invoked to explain the aetiology of certain birth defects (Torpin, 1968; Miller *et al.*, 1981).

The modern view. Although a variety of theories of teratogenesis, each with its own array of supporting evidence, was advanced prior to the beginning of the 20th c., the usefulness of most of these theories was minimal. It has been the 20th c. that has seen the field of teratology flourish. One of the major contributing factors to the flowering of teratology was the rediscovery of *Mendel's laws and Mendel's work in 1900. The framework of Mendelian *genetics provided the key to many observations of the *familial nature of numerous congenital malformations. The rapidity with which 20th c. investigators recognized and applied the findings of Mendelian genetics can be seen by the fact that Archibald E. *Garrod, in 1902, hypothesized that alkaptonuria was determined by a single recessive Mendelian factor (see INBORN ERRORS OF METABOLISM). Moreover, in 1905 W. C. Farabee first demonstrated that one type of brachydactyly of the hand (short fingers) exhibited Mendelian inheritance in man. Extensive research during the 20th c. has revealed that many malformations in humans have a genetic cause, ranging from *recessive *mutations (e.g. congenital *adrenal hyperplasia), *dominant mutations (e.g. *achondroplasia), *sex-linked (X-linked) mutations (e.g. oral-facial-digital syndrome), and abnormal chromosomal constitution (e.g. *Down's syndrome or trisomy 21). In addition, many anomalies and syndromes in non-human animals have been described which are known to have a genetic basis, and often these serve as experimental models for the human situation. Recently James Wilson (1973) estimated that between 20 and 25 per cent of all human congenital malformations are caused by genetic defects. The prevalence of genetically related congenital defects, the ability to detect certain genetic and chromosomally caused defects, and the recent developments in *amniocentesis have spawned the new discipline of *genetic counselling, which combines the fields of genetics and teratology.

Teratogens. Although approximately a quarter of all congenital defects have a genetic origin, the majority of defects such as *anencephaly, *spina bifida, and most forms of *congenital heart disease, have no known cause. Even before the research of the 20th c., it was well known that a variety of 'environmental' agents could be teratogenic in lower animals, particularly birds and fish. The science of experimental teratology, which seeks to explain all aspects of the processes that produce abnormal individuals, seems to have had its birth in the 1820s under the direction of Étienne Geoffrey Saint-Hilaire. He used artificially incubated chicken eggs exposed to a variety of physical agents in order to produce a variety of anomalies. These studies, coupled with those of Charles Fere at the end of the 19th c., clearly demonstrated that a variety of anomalies could be produced in chickens by different physical and chemical agents. Fere also made the significant observation that teratogen-induced growth retardation plays an important part in the aetiology of malformations. This important observation was confirmed by Charles R. Stockard's remarkable experiments with the marine minnow, *Fundulus heteroclitus,* from which he concluded that *all* teratogens must exert their effect by slowing or stopping growth. Stockard (1920) also made the important observation that the stage of embryonic development at which a teratogen was administered played a pivotal role in the type of defect(s) produced. This idea, expanded during the latter half of the 20th c., has become one of the principles of teratology formulated by James Wilson (1977).

By the end of the first quarter of the 20th c., the concept that environmental agents could cause malformations in lower animals stood on solid footing. None the less, a general feeling existed at this time that mammalian, and specifically human, development was impervious to environmental insult, by virtue of the fact that the embryo or fetus was shielded by maternal tissues. The collapse of this idea began with the pioneering work of Fred Hale in 1933, in which he showed definitively that *vitamin A deficiency in sows resulted in a variety of malformations, including severely malformed eyes, cleft lip, and *cleft palate. Hale's limited studies were followed by a long series of experiments on rodents by Josef Warkany and his colleagues in the 1940s and 1950s demonstrating that *nutritional deficiencies, for example, riboflavin and vitamin A deficiencies, could produce malformations in rodents. These studies placed mammalian teratology on a firm experimental basis. Despite the well-documented evidence for environmentally induced teratogenesis in mammals, birds, and fish, and the findings of Norman Gregg in 1941 that a viral infection, *rubella, during the first trimester of pregnancy could cause congenital malformations in humans, the scientific community at large still did not fully accept the idea that human congenital malformations could be related to exposure of pregnant women to environmental teratogens. This belief radically changed in 1960 with the discovery that *thalidomide taken by pregnant women, primarily in Germany, the UK, Australia, and Japan, was a potent human teratogen. Thalidomide is a synthetic drug which was marketed under a variety of trade names (e.g. Contergan, Distaval, Softenon, Talimol, Kevadon) as a sedative. The drug was initially synthesized by Chemie Grunenthal and by 1957 was widely prescribed as a 'safe' sedative. It was considered safe because overdose caused sound sleep but never produced fatal poisoning. The use of thalidomide from 1957 to 1961 increased steadily in a number of countries. In November of 1961, W. Lenz in West Germany and William G. McBride in Australia reported in the scientific literature and to two companies producing thalidomide, their evidence that the drug caused congenital defects in infants whose mothers had taken it during pregnancy. The primary defect observed was *phocomelia, in which the long bones of the extremities were reduced or absent. In addition to phocomelia, a variety of other anomalies were observed, including duodenal stenosis, anal atresia, absence of the spleen, and cardiac malformations. Although the exact number of affected children may never be known, it has been estimated to be over 10 000 world-wide.

An interesting and important side note to the thalidomide episode involves the refusal of the US *Food and Drug Administration to permit the sale of thalidomide in the USA. Thanks to the efforts of Helen Taussig and Frances Oldham Kelsey, the drug company's application for FDA approval was delayed until the teratogenicity of thalidomide was unequivocal. Their actions were responsible for avoiding a tragedy of immense proportions in the USA.

Although the personal tragedy of the thalidomide episode was enormous, one positive aspect did emerge; the myth that the human embryo or fetus was immune to environmental perturbation was forever shattered. This realization was accompanied by a resurgence in experimental teratology as it became clear that avoiding another 'thalidomide tragedy' was going to require a wealth of knowledge about normal development and the mechanisms by which it is perturbed by teratogens.

Research in animals and man. Research from 1960 to the present has involved four major efforts. One is the use of various animal species to determine whether a particular agent is teratogenic. Such studies have revealed that a wide variety of agents can be teratogenic in animals if administered at the appropriate dose and at the appropriate developmental stage. The results of many of these tested agents have been compiled in the *Catalog of Teratogenic Agents* by Thomas H. Shepard, *Drugs as Teratogens* by James L. Schardein, and *Birth Defects and Drugs in Pregnancy* by Olli P. Heinonen, Dennis Slone, and Samuel Shapiro.

Early animal testing indicated that different species often react quite differently to the same teratogen. This point is most dramatically made with respect to thalidomide teratogenicity. Humans and non-human primates are sensitive to thalidomide, rabbits are far less sensitive, and rats and mice are essentially insensitive. The knowledge that species can react differently to the same teratogen has spawned a wide range of investigations into the basis of this differential sensitivity, and numerous maternal or embryonic factors have been considered. One recent advancement that has had an impact on the analysis of species specificity is the development of *in vitro* culture methods for mammalian embryos in the early phases of organogenesis. This procedure, pioneered by Dennis New, has allowed investigators to separate maternal and embryonic components in attempts to understand the problem of differential sensitivity.

A second major research effort of the last 5–10 years has been a search for an effective teratogen screening procedure similar to the mutagen-screening *Ames test which uses simple bacteria as indicators of chemical or drug-induced damage to *deoxyribonucleic acid (DNA). A variety of systems, primarily *in vitro*, have been proposed as teratogen screens. These include the use of coelenterates, flatworms, fruit flies, chickens, mice, and rats as test animals. In addition, various organ and cell culture systems have been proposed, such as limb buds, palatal shelves, and tumour cell binding to lectin-coated surfaces. Each system has its own

advantages, but none has yet proved to be an effective screen. The main drawback of any proposed teratogen screening system is the problem of false negative findings—that is, agents that are negative as teratogens in non-human screening tests, but turn out to be teratogenic in humans. If thalidomide had been thoroughly pretested in rodents—the most common test animals used in screening potential teratogens—it would have been approved for human use as a non-teratogen. Perhaps in the future two or more of these systems can be combined to provide the necessary sensitivity and accuracy required in teratogen risk assessment.

A third major research effort has involved the search for human teratogens, using the conventional methods of *epidemiology. Although epidemiologists have not identified any human teratogens comparable to thalidomide, their findings have shown that many suspected human teratogens are only weakly, if at all, teratogenic. As new drugs and chemicals are released into the environment in ever-increasing numbers, the need for prospective epidemiological studies will also increase.

The fourth major research effort in teratology since 1960 has been in the area of teratogenic mechanisms, that is, the study of the underlying means by which teratogens perturb the normal development sequences and thereby produce congenital malformations. Like the 'cure' for cancer, the 'cure' for birth defects will require a detailed knowledge of the normal situation, the teratogen-perturbed situation, and the relationships between the initial perturbed state and the ensuing processes that lead to a recognizable malformation. The quest to prevent birth defects will require collaboration between investigators from a variety of disciplines such as embryology, anatomy, genetics, and biochemistry, to name a few. It is hoped that the stunning breakthroughs and insights recently achieved in molecular genetics, specifically *recombinant DNA technology, can soon be used to probe the intricacies of normal and abnormal mammalian development and therein to discover the keys to the aetiologies of congenital malformations. This is the challenge for teratology in the last two decades of the 20th c. and beyond.

P. E. MIRKES

References

Dabney, W. C. (1889). Maternal impressions. In Keating J. M. (ed.), *Cyclopaedia of the Diseases of Children*, Vol. 1. Philadelphia.

Heinonen, O. P., Slone, D. and Shapiro, S. (1977). *Birth Defects and Drugs in Pregnancy*. Littleton, Maryland.

Hickey, M. F. (1953). Genes and mermaids: changing theories of the causation of congenital abnormalities. *Medical Journal of Australia*, **1**, 649–67.

Miller, M. E., Graham, J. M. Jr, Higginbottom, M. C. and Smith, D. W. (1981). Compression-related defects from early amnion rupture: evidence of mechanical teratogenesis. *Journal of Pediatrics*, **98**, 292–7.

Patten, B. M. (1947). *Human Embryology*. Philadelphia.

Schardein, J. L. (1976). *Drugs as Teratogens*. Cleveland.

Shepard, T. H. (1980). *Catalog of Teratogenic Agents*. 4th edn, Baltimore.

Taussig, H. B. (1962). Thalidomide and phocomelia. *Pediatrics*, **30**, 654–9.

Torpin, R. (1968). *Fetal Malformations Caused by Amnion Rupture During Gestation*. Springfield, Illinois.

Warkany, J. (1959). Congenital malformations in the past. *Journal of Chronic Diseases*, **10**, 84–95.

Wilson, J. G. (1973). *Environment and Birth Defects*. New York.

Wilson, J. G. (1977). Current status of teratology—general principles and mechanisms derived from animal studies. In Wilson, J. G. and Fraser, F. C. (eds), *Handbook of Teratology*, Vol. 1. New York.

TERATOMA. A *tumour arising from several different types of tissue, or from persistent embryonic remnants.

TERMINOLOGY. See CLASSIFICATION; INTERNATIONAL CLASSIFICATION OF DISEASE.

TERTIAN FEVER recurs at 48- (not 72-) hour intervals, particularly the type of malaria due to *Plasmodium vivax* (benign tertian *malaria).

TERTIARY HEALTH CARE. The third order of medical care, namely that provided by 'super'-specialist physicians and surgeons (e.g. neurosurgeons, paediatric cardiologists) and by departments, not found in all general hospitals, into which expensive resources and skilled staff are concentrated (e.g. oncology, renal dialysis, cardiac surgery); patient reference to this level of health care is from both the *primary and *secondary tiers, but chiefly the latter.

TEST. Any examination, trial, or biochemical analysis.

TESTAMENTARY CAPACITY is the capacity of an individual to make a will. Testamentary capacity depends on an individual's ability to be aware of his estate and to express his wishes concerning its disposal to family, friends, charities, etc. Mental illness does not necessarily impair testamentary capacity, which may need to be judged by expert psychiatric and legal opinion.

TESTICLE. Synonymous with *testis.

TESTIS. The male reproductive organ or gonad which produces *spermatozoa and (in vertebrates) sex hormones.

TEST MEAL. A meal given for the purpose of allowing subsequent biochemical analysis of *stomach contents as an aid to diagnosis. As a diagnostic method, the test meal procedure has been largely superseded.

TESTOSTERONE is the main male sex hormone (*androgen), secreted by the Leydig (or interstitial) cells which constitute the endocrine tissue of the *testis. Testosterone promotes the formation of *semen, the development of the accessory sexual organs (*epididymis, *vas deferens, *seminal vesicle, and *prostate) and the development of male *secondary sexual characteristics. Testosterone is secreted in response to stimulation by the *luteinizing hormone (LH) of the anterior *pituitary gland, and in turn exerts a negative feedback action on LH secretion.

TESTS OF PATERNITY. Blood group analysis is used in order to disprove putative paternity (it cannot prove paternity). See HAEMATOLOGY.

TEST-TUBE BABY. See FERTILIZATION IN VITRO.

TEST TYPES are letters of varying sizes printed on a card, used in the measurement of visual acuity. See also SNELLEN.

TETANUS, or 'lockjaw' is due to the anaerobic spore-bearing bacillus *Clostridium tetani*, which when allowed to multiply under conditions where little or no oxygen is available produces a powerful and dangerous *neurotoxin. The vegetative organism lives freely (and harmlessly) in the intestine of animals and man, accounting for the wide distribution, particularly in well-manured soil, of tetanus spores; the spores, which are resistant to destruction by heat and other agents, remain viable for many years. Conditions favourable to their germination occur in necrotic tissue and in deep puncture wounds; when this happens, though the bacteria themselves remain at the local site, the neurotoxin which they elaborate spreads along the line of peripheral nerves to reach the central nervous system. Here its effect is to cause uncontrolled bombardment by nervous impulses of the body muscles, resulting in sustained and spasmodic contractions. The result is similar to that of *strychnine poisoning. Without treatment, death may occur from respiratory difficulty or from metabolic exhaustion. Active *immunization with a preparation of modified toxin is an effective method of prevention; and *antitoxin is an important component of treatment.

TETANY is a condition characterized by abnormal neuromuscular irritability leading to cramps and muscular spasm. In latent case, the patient may complain of numbness and tingling in the extremities, especially around the lips; and the heightened neuromuscular excitability can be demonstrated by tapping over the *facial nerve to induce contraction of the facial muscles (Chvostek's sign) or compressing the upper arm to occlude the blood supply, which causes the hand to assume the *main d'accoucheur* position (flexion of the wrist and metacarpophalangeal joints with extension of the fingers and adduction of the thumb: Trousseau's sign). When tetany is fully developed, the hands go into this position spontaneously, and there is plantar flexion of the feet (carpopedal spasm), contraction of the facial muscles (causing the 'risus sardonicus'), contraction of the laryngeal muscles with hoarseness and stridor ('laryngismus stridulus'), and sometimes generalized convulsions.

The condition is almost always caused by a decrease in the circulating concentration of ionized *calcium. Possible causes include: low calcium intake, as in *vitamin D deficiency and *malabsorption syndromes; *hypoparathyroidism, either idiopathic or iatrogenic following *thyroidectomy; respiratory *alkalosis due to over-breathing; metabolic alkalosis due to prolonged vomiting or excessive intake of alkali; impairment of renal function in certain cases; and several other rarer situations such as hypomagnesaemia (reduced *magnesium in the blood).

TETRACYCLINES are a group of broad-spectrum natural (from *Streptomyces aureofaciens) and semi-synthetic antibiotics; they were originally effective against a wide variety of organisms, but increasing bacterial resistance has lessened their usefulness. They remain the first line of treatment for infections due to *Brucella, *Rickettsia, *Mycoplasma, and *Chlamydia and are also of value in chronic bronchitis because of their activity against *Haemophilus influenzae. Tetracyclines are deposited in growing bones and teeth (causing staining), and should not be given to children under the age of 12 years nor to pregnant women. They are also contraindicated in patients with kidney disease.

TETRAHYDROCANNABINOL. See CANNABIS.

TETRALOGY OF FALLOT. See FALLOT'S TETRALOGY.

TETRAPLEGIA. See QUADRIPLEGIA.

THACKRAH, CHARLES TURNER (1795–1833). British physician, MRCS (1816). Thackrah was one of the founders of the Leeds Medical School and the author of the first book in England on *occupational diseases (1832).

THALAMUS. A region of the *brain situated between the cerebral hemispheres at the upper end of the brainstem which acts both as a sensory relay station and as a centre for *pain perception.

THALASSAEMIA is the name for a group of inherited *anaemias in which the basic abnormality is defective synthesis of one or other of the globin chains of *haemoglobin. The name derives from the first recognition of thalassaemia in people of Mediterranean origin (*thalassa* is Greek for 'sea'), but forms have since been described in a number of other racial groups. The two main types are labelled according to which of the two adult chains is affected, that is alpha- and beta-thalassaemia. The *heterozygous, partially expressed, or carrier state

is sometimes referred to as thalassaemia minor (or thalassaemia trait), the fully expressed *homozygous disease as thalassaemia major. The molecular genetics of thalassaemia is a rapidly advancing field of knowledge.

THALIDOMIDE $(C_{13}H_{10}O_4)$ is a drug which gained favour as a sedative and hypnotic following its introduction in Germany in 1958 but was withdrawn from use three years later when it became apparent that it caused serious congenital abnormalities in children born of women who had taken it during pregnancy. Prominent among these abnormalities was the otherwise rare condition of *phocomelia, in which the arms and legs fail to develop. The use of thalidomide is now restricted to one particular condition, a complication of *leprosy known as erythema nodosum leprosum, in which it is very effective. Thalidomide was never licensed for use in the USA. See also TERATOLOGY.

THAYER, WILLIAM SYDNEY (1864–1932). American physician, MD Harvard (1889). Thayer served throughout his professional career at *Johns Hopkins Hospital, where he was first an assistant, later a colleague, of William *Osler. Thayer made contributions to clinical knowledge of *malaria, *endocarditis, and *typhoid fever. His particular interest was in heart disease; he described the third heart sound, and wrote about various cardiac *murmurs.

THECA. An enclosing sheath, particularly the *dura mater of the spinal cord. See MENINGES.

THEILER, MAX (1899–1972). South African/American virologist, LRCP Cape Town (1918). Theiler was born and educated in South Africa; he studied in London, receiving MRCS and DTM & H in 1922; he transferred to Harvard, where he was instructor in *tropical medicine until 1930 and then joined the *Rockefeller Foundation, with which he was associated for the remainder of his career. He conducted research on several viruses found in tropical regions. His greatest achievement was in attenuating a strain of *yellow fever virus, so that a live virus vaccine, suitable for large-scale immunization of human beings could be developed. For this work he was given the Nobel prize in 1951.

THEOPHAGY is the sacramental and symbolic eating of a god as part of a religious ritual, such as that which takes place during the mass or communion service in the Christian church.

THEOPHYLLINE is one of the xanthine *bronchodilator drugs, now mainly used in oral sustained-release preparations in the control of bronchial *asthma.

THEORY. A hypothesis; or the principles of a science as opposed to the practice.

THERAPEUTIC NIHILISM is an attitude of extreme scepticism on the part of a doctor as to the value of treatment, particularly with drugs. Therapeutic nihilism may sometimes conceal a lack of familiarity with modern *pharmacology and methods of treatment.

THERAPEUTICS. The science of the treatment of diseases. See PHARMACOLOGY.

THERAPEUTIC SUBSTANCES ACT 1956. This UK Act consolidated the Therapeutic Substances Act 1925 and the Therapeutic Substances (Prevention of Misuse) Acts 1947 to 1953. It had two Parts. Part 1 imposed restrictions on the manufacture and importation of certain therapeutic substances. These were: vaccines, sera, toxins, antitoxins, and antigens; arsphenamine and analogous substances used for the control of infective disease; insulin; and preparations of the posterior lobe of the pituitary gland. Part II controlled the sale, supply, dispensing, and administration of penicillin and certain other substances capable of causing danger to the health of the community if used without proper safeguards; the other substances were to be prescribed by regulations made by the Secretary of State for Social Services after consultation with the Medical Research Council. The Act was repealed by the *Medicines Act 1968.

THERAPIA STERILISANS MAGNA is the theory of treating disease by means of an agent which destroys infecting organisms without harming the host, proposed by *Ehrlich.

THERAPY is the treatment of disease.

THERIAC is a supposed *antidote to venomous bites.

THERMISTOR. A semiconductor, the electrical resistance of which decreases rapidly as the ambient temperature increases; it is used as a sensitive temperature-measuring device or as a means of compensating for temperature variations of other components in a circuit.

THERMOCOUPLE. A temperature-measuring device consisting of two wires of different metals joined at each end. A current flows in the circuit when the two junctions are at different temperatures.

THERMODYNAMICS is the study of the general laws governing heat changes and the conservation of energy.

THERMOGRAPHY is the pictorial representation of an area in terms of its temperature and temperature differences. The most commonly used method detects and records infra-red radiation from the body surface, but other techniques are possible. Thermography can be employed to study superficial vascularity and as a method of detecting underlying pathological processes, for example tumours of the breast.

THERMOMETER. An instrument for the measurement of *temperature. Any physical property of a substance that varies with temperature can be used, for example, volume, pressure, electrical resistance, electromotive force, and so on, instruments being designed with regard to the desired temperature range, accuracy, and convenience. The familiar clinical thermometer of today was introduced by Sir Clifford *Allbutt in 1867.

THIAMINE is vitamin B_1, an essential dietary component also known as aneurin, deficiency of which results in *beriberi. Thiamine is required for the synthesis of the *coenzyme thiamine pyrophosphate, necessary for one of the steps in energy metabolism, and the body's requirement is approximately related to energy (i.e. *carbohydrate) intake. It is widely distributed in the diet, and deficiency under Western conditions is virtually confined to chronic *alcoholics (who have a large energy intake in the form of alcohol but little or no normal food).

THIERSCH, KARL (1822–95). German surgeon, MD Munich (1846). Thiersch became professor of surgery in Erlangen in 1854, moving to the chair in Leipzig in 1867. He served as a surgeon in the Schleswig-Holstein war of 1864 and was consulting surgeon to 12 Corps in the war of 1870. Thiersch was a strong supporter of Listerian doctrine and reawakened interest in the subject by his method of skin grafting (*Thiersch graft) introduced in 1874. He wrote on cancer (1865) and he also described phosphorus necrosis of the jaw ('phossy jaw') in 1867.

THIERSCH GRAFT. A very thin skin (split-skin) graft which, unlike the thicker *flap, does not need to retain its own blood supply during the period following transfer to the new site. See PLASTIC AND MAXILLOFACIAL SURGERY.

THIOURACIL is a drug which inhibits the synthesis of thyroid hormone by the *thyroid gland and is hence of value in the treatment of *thyrotoxicosis.

THIRD ORDER OF ST FRANCIS. This entirely lay Order, also known as the Franciscan Tertiaries, has numbered many famous men and women among its members, including the physicians and polymaths Luigi *Galvani and Roger *Bacon.

THIRST is the sensation of wanting to drink, mediated through osmotic and volume receptors and a thirst centre which is situated in the anterior *hypothalamus of the brain. The stimulus is plasma hyperosmolality; a 2 per cent rise is sufficient to cause thirst.

THOMAS, HUGH OWEN (1834–91). Orthopaedic surgeon, MRCS (1857). Thomas was descended from a family of skilled bone-setters and after apprenticeship to a relative in Liverpool, Dr Owen Roberts, he studied at Edinburgh. In 1866 he began practice in Liverpool and converted his house into a private hospital with eight beds, employing a smith and a leather worker to make splints. He devised the universally known Thomas's *splint, advocated passive congestion before *Bier, and used silver wire for internal fixation of fractures (1873). His work was largely unrecognized until revealed by his pupil and nephew Sir Robert *Jones.

THOMPSON, MARY HARRIS (1829–95). See WOMEN IN MEDICINE II.

THORACIC DUCT. The major vessel of the *lymphatic system, which empties into the venous system at the junction of the left internal jugular and left subclavian veins.

THORACIC SURGERY. See CARDIOTHORACIC SURGERY.

THORACOPLASTY is a surgical operation in which several ribs are removed, allowing the underlying lung to collapse, once widely used in the treatment of pulmonary *tuberculosis.

THORACOSCOPY is inspection of the pleural cavity by means of an *endoscope.

THORAX. The region of the body enclosed by the rib cage, extending from the first rib at the root of the neck to the *diaphragm.

THREADWORM. Any slender thread-like *nematode (roundworm), but usually refers to the small parasite *Enterobius* (or *Oxyuris*) *vermicularis*, also known as the pinworm, which commonly infests the lower intestine, particularly of children. Infestation is usually asymptomatic, apart from *pruritus ani due to the nocturnal laying of eggs by the female in the perianal area. Transfer of the eggs to the fingers by scratching and subsequent ingestion is the mode both of person-to-person transmission and auto-reinfection. Diagnosis and treatment are normally straightforward.

THRILL. Vibrations at the body surface which can be felt on palpation. The hand is relatively poor at appreciating the high frequency vibrations of which most thrills consist, and ability to detect them varies somewhat between observers. Over the precordium, thrills are cardiac *murmurs which can be felt as well as heard, with this additional significance: whereas a systolic murmur may or may not be due to heart disease, a systolic thrill is always pathological. At the apex of the heart, it allows mitral incompetence to be deduced;

localized to the lower sternal area, either tricuspid incompetence or ventricular septal defect; at the base, either aortic or pulmonary stenosis. See VALVULAR HEART DISEASE.

THROMBIN is an enzyme, formed from the precursor substance *prothrombin, which catalyses the conversion of the soluble fibrinogen into *fibrin. See HAEMATOLOGY.

THROMBOANGIITIS is *inflammation with *thrombosis of blood vessels. Thromboangiitis obliterans is an obliterative vascular condition chiefly of the lower extremities, also known as Buerger's disease; it occurs more often in younger men, is aggravated by smoking and is particularly common in Ashkenazi Jews.

THROMBOEMBOLISM is *embolism due to a detached *thrombus.

THROMBOPHLEBITIS. See PHLEBITIS.

THROMBOSIS is intravascular blood coagulation during life. The resultant clot, known as a thrombus, consists of *fibrin and *platelets, together with other blood cells; it may completely occlude the vessel within which it has been formed, causing obstruction to blood flow. Thrombosis occurs when flow is sluggish or stagnant, when the integrity of the vascular endothelium has been damaged by trauma, inflammation, or some other pathological process, or when blood coagulability is abnormally increased; sometimes these factors operate in combination.

THROMBOXANE is an endogenously produced substance related to the *prostaglandins, derived from arachidonic acid in the *platelets. In its active form, known as thromboxane A_2, it is a potent stimulator of platelet aggregation and constrictor of arteries, including the cerebral and coronary arteries. It rapidly hydrolyses to an inactive form, thromboxane B_2. *Acetylsalicylic acid (aspirin) exerts its anti-platelet-aggregating effect by blocking the production of thromboxane A_2.

THROMBUS. The intravascular clot of blood formed during the process of *thrombosis.

THROW-AWAY JOURNALS are journals distributed free of charge to the medical profession, or selected members of it, that depend for their income on revenue from advertising, chiefly of 'ethical' products of the *pharmaceutical industry. The opprobrious designation is sometimes but not always justified. See also MEDICAL JOURNALS.

THRUSH is oral *candidiasis, characterized by creamy white patches accompanied by *erythema on the oropharyngeal mucosa.

THUDICHUM, LUDWIG JOHANN WILHELM

(1829–1901). Anglo-German physician and bio-chemist, MD Giessen (1851), FRCP (1878). Thudichum settled in London in 1853 and was appointed lecturer in chemistry at *St George's Hospital (1858), moving to be the first lecturer in pathological chemistry at *St Thomas's Hospital (1865). He carried out much government research under the aegis of Sir John *Simon. The subject of pathological chemistry was then in its infancy and his work did not meet with general acceptance.

THYMUS. A lymphoid organ of vertebrates usu-ally situated in the pharyngeal or neck region. In man, as in other mammals, it lies in the anterior superior *mediastinum, behind the upper *sternum. From birth to puberty it doubles in size to reach a maximum, and thereafter gradually undergoes involution. Since *Galen declared the thymus to be the site of the soul, its function has been the subject of much speculation. Though still not fully understood, it is now known to play an important part in the body's cell-mediated immunological processes. *Myasthenia gravis, a putative autoimmume disorder, is sometimes cured by surgical removal of the thymus. See IMMUNOLOGY.

THYROID. The important endocrine gland situ-ated in the front of the neck which controls the overall rate of the body's metabolism. It consists of right and left lobes lying on either side of the *trachea joined by a small isthmus crossing the midline; it is normally neither visible nor palpable except occasionally as a result of physiological enlargement (e.g. during adolescence or pregnancy). Acting under the stimulus of the *thyroid-stimulating hormone (TSH) of the anterior *pituitary gland, the thyroid gland secretes the iodine-containing hormones *thyrox-ine and *tri-iodothyronine. It also secretes *cal-citonin. See ENDOCRINOLOGY.

THYROIDECTOMY is the surgical removal of all or part of the *thyroid gland.

THYROIDITIS is inflammation of the *thyroid gland.

THYROID-STIMULATING HORMONE (TSH) is the *hormone of the anterior *pituitary gland which controls the function of the *thyroid gland. TSH is also known as thyrotropin.

THYROTOXICOSIS is overactivity of the *thyroid gland, also known as hyperthyroidism. The abnormally elevated *metabolic rate which results causes weight loss (despite an often large appetite), heat intolerance and sweating, emo-tional lability and nervousness, tremor, and tachy-cardia. In the majority of cases of thyrotoxicosis the aetiology is unknown, although both *autoim-munity and genetic factors are thought to play a part; this group of patients often suffer from oph-

thalmopathy, chiefly *exophthalmos, as well as thyroid overactivity, a syndrome known as *Graves' disease. In the remainder, thyrotox-icosis is the result of *thyroiditis or of various types of thyroid or pituitary tumour.

THYROXINE is one of the two main *thyroid hormones, also known as tetra-iodothyronine (or T4), the other being *tri-iodothyronine (or T3). T4 is at least partly converted into T3 by deiodinating enzymes in the tissues, and T3, which is about four times more active than T4, is probably responsible for most of the metabolic effects of *thyroid secretion.

TIC. A tic, sometimes also known as a habit spasm, is a repetitious spasmodic movement involving a particular group of muscles, particularly of the face, neck, and shoulders. It is compulsive and unintentional, but not strictly involuntary since it can often be suppressed for a period by an effort of will. It may be aggravated by adverse psychological factors such as anxiety, and diminished by the administration of *tranquillizing drugs. It is to this category that the habitual winking, grimacing, and shrugging sometimes observed in otherwise nor-mal individuals belongs. Vocal tics also occur. Although very similar repetitive movements may sometimes occur in *encephalitis, or in the rare *Gilles de la Tourette syndrome, tics are usually held to be nervous mannerisms which have become persistent. Childhood tics often disappear with maturity.

TIC DOULOUREUX, also known as trigeminal neuralgia, is a syndrome affecting mainly older adults characterized by intense one-sided facial pain in the distribution of one or more divisions of the *trigeminal nerve. The pain is spasmodic, dagger-like, and very severe; it is often pre-cipitated by local stimuli such as eating, speaking, touching of certain areas on the face known as 'trigger spots', and cold draughts. Attacks occur at varying intervals, and tend to become more frequent with increasing age. The causation is usually obscure; in a minority of patients there is a mechanical lesion of the trigeminal nerve or its ganglion (pressure from an aberrant artery) and *multiple sclerosis is an infrequent association which should nevertheless be suspected in younger age groups. Spontaneous remissions are usually only temporary, and medical or surgical treatment is required for its amelioration.

TICKS. An order of *arachnids closely related to, but larger than, mites; they are blood-sucking and can act as vectors of a number of diseases of both animals and man. Those of the latter include forms of *typhus, *relapsing fever and virus *encephalitis. Tick paralysis is a type of ascending motor paralysis reported from certain parts of the world and thought to be due to a toxin secreted by the tick (*Dermacentor andersoni*) itself.

TIMOTHY GRASS is a group of six grasses with sausage-shaped flower-spikes similar to the fox-tails, the two commonest being *Phleum pratense* and *Phleum bertolinii.* Their pollen is a cause of *hay fever.

TINCTURE. An alcoholic solution.

TINEA is any fungal infection of the skin. The site (or other characteristic) is usually designated, as for example in tinea barbae (beard), tinea capitis (scalp), tinea pedis ('athlete's foot'), tinea cruris (crotch), tinea circinata ('ringworm'), etc.

TINNITUS is a sensation of ringing, buzzing, or hissing in the ears. It can occur in a variety of conditions, particularly those involving the *cochlea and the *auditory nerve and as a side-effect of certain drugs (e.g. *quinine, *salicylates). As an isolated symptom it can be intractable and distressing.

TISSOT, SIMON ANDRE (1728–97). Swiss physician, MD Montpellier (1746). Tissot practised as a professor in Lausanne with a break from 1780 to 1783, when he occupied the chair of medicine in Pavia. He advocated 'variolation' in the prevention of *smallpox and claimed an effective treatment for this disease. He wrote on *epilepsy and nervous disease but was chiefly renowned for his popular works on personal hygiene, *balneotherapy, and *masturbation.

TISSUE. A collection of cells of similar type fulfilling a similar function, together with organizing and supportive elements such as connective tissue cells, blood vessels, etc.

TISSUE BANK. A stored supply of human tissues for future use, for example for grafting, tissue culture, etc.

TISSUE CULTURE is the maintenance of living tissue under artificial conditions separately from the organism from which it was derived.

TOBACCO is prepared in various ways, from the leaves and stalks of the tobacco plant, a solanaceous shrub *Nicotiana tabacum.* Tobacco is consumed chiefly by *smoking, in which form it is a potent cause of disease because of tar and carbon monoxide formation. These products are lacking when tobacco is used in ways that do not involve combustion (e.g. *snuff, *tobacco chewing) but which nevertheless allow absorption of the addictive alkaloid *nicotine; undesirable effects may then be only those related to local irritation, since it has not been established that nicotine itself plays a major part in the pathogenesis of the important smoking diseases.

TOBACCO AMBLYOPIA is a particular type of visual defect associated with heavy use of certain tobaccos. The mechanism is uncertain, but cyanide in smoke is probably a factor and alcohol may also play a part (tobacco-alcohol amblyopia).

TOBACCO CHEWING is one of the forms of tobacco use, less common now than formerly, in which the material is chewed and retained in the mouth for a period before being expectorated; *nicotine absorption occurs from the oral mucosa. The chewing of tobacco mixtures in certain parts of the world is associated with the occurrence of oral *cancers, though it is not established that tobacco itself is the cause. At best, however, the habit is aesthetically displeasing.

TOCOPHEROL is a fat-soluble *vitamin (vitamin E), essential for the correct synthesis of *porphyrins and *haemoglobin. Deficiency in human diets is unusual.

TODD, ROBERT BENTLEY (1809–60). Anglo-Irish physician, LRCSI (1831), DM Oxford (1836), FRCP (1837), FRS (1838), FRCS (1844). Todd trained in Dublin and became the first professor of physiology in King's College, London (1836–53). He was one of the founders and first physicians of *King's College Hospital (1838) and established a school of nursing at St John's House. He edited the *Cyclopaedia of Anatomy and Physiology* (1833–59).

***TODD REPORT*.** The report of a UK Royal Commission on medical education set up in 1956 under the chairmanship of Lord Todd, published in 1968. It contained a number of major recommendations concerning undergraduate and postgraduate medical education generally, and the reorganization of the London medical school system in particular. See MEDICAL EDUCATION IN THE UK AND EUROPE.

TOGAVIRUSES form a subgroup of the *arboviruses; they are ribonucleic acid (RNA) viruses named because of their host-derived envelope.

TOLERANCE, in pharmacology, is the ability to withstand without marked effect relatively large doses of a drug, which may be acquired as a result of previous administration of that drug (see TACHYPHYLAXIS) or of a substance related to it (illustrated by the resistance of chronic alcoholics to certain anaesthetic agents). Immunological tolerance refers to lack of reactivity on the part of the lymphoid *immune system to a specific *antigen (as distinct from general *immuno-suppression).

TOMB. A chamber, vault, excavation, or grave for the reception of a dead body or bodies; or a mound or tumulus raised over a dead body.

TOMOGRAPHY is a *radiographic technique which, by altering the geometrical relationship between the X-ray tube and the film during exposure, allows the visualization of structures in a single plane (or 'cut') and blurs images in other planes.

TONE usually refers to muscular tone (or tonus), the slight degree of tension which is normally present in healthy muscles when stretched and which can readily be assessed by passively moving the limbs.

TONICS. A term used to describe various medicinal preparations formerly prescribed with the intention of restoring tone and vigour to the system of those supposedly suffering from a deficiency of these qualities. Such *nostra might contain substances of therapeutic value when used under appropriate circumstances and in correct dosage, such as *vitamins and *iron salts, together with colouring, flavouring, *ethanol, and a variety of other ingredients (for example, harmless quantities of *strychnine or *arsenic salts). It is debatable whether the use of such *placebos can ever be justified.

TONOMETRY. The measurement of tension, particularly the indirect measurement of intra-ocular tension.

TONSILLECTOMY is the surgical removal of the *tonsils.

TONSILLITIS is inflammation of the *tonsils; a common accompaniment of viral and bacterial infections of the upper respiratory tract.

TONSILS. Two small almond-shaped masses of lymphoid tissue situated on either side of the throat, between the pillars of the *fauces.

TONUS. See TONE.

TOOTH. See TEETH.

TOPHUS. Tophi are localized deposits of aggregated crystals of monosodium urate monohydrate, characteristic of *gout; they occur in relation to cartilages, bones, tendons, and joints, and may be visible in the subcutaneous tissues, particularly over the external ear.

TORSION. Twisting about a long axis.

TORTI, FRANCESCO (1658–1741). Italian physician, MD Bologna (1678). Becoming professor of medicine at Modena in 1709, Torti established the value of *cinchona bark (quinine) in his widely read book on intermittent fevers (1712). He was responsible for introducing the term '*malaria'.

TORTICOLLIS is abnormal persistent contraction of neck muscles causing the head to be held in an unnatural and twisted position. Torticollis is also known as wryneck.

TORULA is an earlier name for *Cryptococcus neoformans*. See CRYPTOCOCCOSIS.

TOTAL ALLERGY SYNDROME is a condition in which there is supposed allergy to a wide variety of substances normally present in the environment, from which sufferers must therefore be protected by controlled, filtered ventilation, specially prepared food, etc. In fact, the condition is 'neither allergic nor total' (see ALLERGY); and other explanations should be sought for the patient's symptoms.

TOTAL PARENTERAL NUTRITION (TPN) is the administration through a catheter placed in a central vein of a patient's whole nutritional requirements, in situations in which alimentation via the alimentary canal is not possible.

TOURNIQUET. A constricting band encircling a limb, usually with the object of temporarily interrupting the arterial blood supply and preventing *haemorrhage from a site distal to the point of compression.

TOXAEMIA is the liberation of toxic bacterial products into the blood stream. The word assumes a rather different meaning in the term 'toxaemia of pregnancy' (now called pre-eclampsia), since it is unlikely that bacteria are involved in the causation of this syndrome (*oedema, *proteinuria, and *hypertension sometimes progressing to *encephalopathy and occurring during pregnancy or the puerperium: see OBSTETRICS).

TOXICOLOGY is the study of poisons and their effects. See POISONING.

TOXIN is any poison, but particularly a protein poison of animal or bacterial origin.

TOXOCARA CANIS is a common intestinal *nematode parasite of dogs, which can occasionally infect man with serious consequences. See DOGS AS CARRIERS OF DISEASE.

TOXOID. A bacterial *toxin which has been modified for purposes of *immunization.

TOXOPLASMOSIS is infection with the *protozoan parasite *Toxoplasma gondii*, common in birds and mammals; the domestic cat is particularly important in transmission. Human infection is also widespread in most communities in dry and temperate zones, though often producing only mild and transient disturbances. In two groups, however, infection is serious: fetuses, transplacentally infected; and patients with generalized depression of the *immune system. The eye (retinochoroiditis) and the brain are among the many organs and tissues which may be damaged by congenital toxoplasmosis.

TOYNBEE, JOSEPH (1815–66). See OTOLARYNGOLOGY.

TRACE ELEMENTS. Elements (metals and non-metals), found in only minute amounts in the tissues of the healthy body, which are nevertheless essential components of the human diet (for example, copper, manganese, fluorine, chromium, selenium, molybdenum) or which may be harmful if taken in excess.

TRACHEA. The windpipe, the tube connecting the *larynx to the right and left main *bronchi and forming part of the *airway by which atmospheric air reaches the lungs. Its wall is membranous and elastic, and lined with mucous membrane; it is kept patent by a series of incomplete rings of *cartilage.

TRACHEITIS is inflammation of the *trachea, a common accompaniment of upper respiratory infections.

TRACHEOSTOMY is the surgical creation of an opening into the *trachea from the front of the neck, an operation described by *Galen in the 2nd c. AD and said to have been performed by Alexander the Great with the point of his sword. Present-day indications include: upper respiratory obstruction and failure of laryngeal function; provision of an airway for *artificial respiration; and provision of access to the bronchial tree for manipulative purposes.

TRACHOMA is a chronic infectious eye disease due to a *chlamydia (*Chlamydia trachomatis*), a common cause of blindness in hot arid regions of the world. The organism is carried in the genital tract, and infection may occur at birth, in childhood, or in adult life.

TRACT. A collection of nerve *fibres travelling in the same direction and serving a similar function.

TRACTION is the exertion of a pulling force on a part, for example to maintain bone position during the healing of a fracture.

TRACTOTOMY is the surgical division of a nerve *tract, an operation sometimes undertaken in order to interrupt the pathways responsible for severe and intractable pain.

TRAINEE ASSISTANTS. See GENERAL MEDICAL PRACTICE.

TRAIT is a term used to denote the relatively asymptomatic *heterozygous state in *sickle cell disease.

TRANQUILLIZERS. A term used to describe a group of drugs used to calm the emotions but with lesser sedative and hypnotic actions than the *bromides and *barbiturates traditionally employed for this purpose. The tranquillizers are sometimes subdivided into major and minor, but the so-called 'major tranquillizers' (exemplified by the *phenothiazine derivatives, the butyrophenones, the thioxanthenes, and pimozide) are better termed 'antipsychotic drugs' (or 'neuroleptics'); they are used primarily for the treatment of *psychoses.

The alternative and perhaps better term for minor tranquillizers is 'anxiolytics', since their primary use is in the treatment of *anxiety states. They are almost all derivatives of *benzodiazepene (e.g. chlordiazepoxide or Librium®, diazepam or Valium®; oxazepam or Serenid-D®; lorazepam or Ativan®; clorazepate or Tranxene®; and a number of others, all with essentially the same action and differing only in speed and duration of action). It should be remembered that tolerance, dependence, and addiction all occur with these drugs. Other anxiolytics include benzoctamine, meprobamate, and beta-blocking agents such as *propranolol.

TRANSAMINASE is the name for any of the *enzymes which catalyse the transfer of an amino group between an *amino acid and a keto acid (transamination).

TRANSDUCTION is a technique of *genetic engineering whereby *deoxyribonucleic acid (DNA) is exchanged between bacteria.

TRANSFER FACTOR. An extract of *leucocytes which was originally thought to transfer specific immunocompetence to T *lymphocytes; the specificity, however, is now doubted.

TRANSFORMATION is a term used to denote the change undergone by a *cell when it becomes *malignant.

TRANSFUSION is the *infusion of whole blood or blood components. See BLOOD TRANSFUSION.

TRANSILLUMINATION is the examination of a part by placing a light source behind it and observing it from the front.

TRANSLOCATION is the exchange of genetic material between different *chromosomes. See GENETICS.

TRANSMISSION has various biomedical senses, but refers particularly to the passage of nervous impulses from one nerve cell to another or to a receptor organ (see NEUROTRANSMITTERS), or to the transfer of communicable diseases between individuals, or to the transfer of genetically determined characteristics to and through offspring.

TRANSPLANT. An organ or piece of tissue removed from its native site and re-established elsewhere, either in the same individual or in another individual of the same or another species: synonymous with *graft. For terminology, see ALLOGRAFT; see also TRANSPLANTATION OF HUMAN ORGANS.

TRANSPLANTATION OF HUMAN ORGANS.

The idea of replacing diseased tissues with grafts is ancient, but the realization of this dream had to await technical developments in surgery so that the biological barriers could be studied. According to legend, *Sts Cosmas and Damien, the twin patrons of medicine, removed a man's cancerous leg and with divine help, replaced it successfully with a leg removed from a corpse exhumed especially for the operation (Fig. 1). The depiction of this miraculous surgery in early European churches testifies to the general ethical approval of the procedure at a time when such operations were restricted to one specialist team!

History. In 1800 the Italian surgeon, Baronio, reported the first clearly defined scientific experiments on tissue grafting. He showed that free '*autografts' of skin taken from the animal to be grafted, took permanently if the surgery was skilful but skin '*allografts' taken from another individual were destroyed after a few days (Fig. 2).

More than a century later, this process was shown to be an immune reaction by the classic experiments of Gibson and Medawar (1943). They showed that after skin grafts taken from a donor rabbit were rejected by the recipient, 'second-set' grafts from the same donor were destroyed more

Fig. 2. Baronio's skin grafting experiment. Autografts below took satisfactorily; allografts above were rejected. (Reproduced by permission from Calne, R. Y. (1963), *Renal Transplantation*, London)

rapidly. As a result of exposure to the donor's skin, the recipient had become specifically sensitized in a manner analogous to the *immunity to *measles that follows infection with the measles virus. The animals would react normally to skin taken from a different donor. Corneal transplants (see OPHTHALMOLOGY) come into a special category because they survive without vascularization and therefore do not elicit (nor are they subject to) an immune response unless blood vessels inadvertently grow into the cornea.

Transplantation immunity. There has been intensive study of transplantation immunity, a central feature of which concerned the definition of inheritance of the 'transplantation antigens' that differ between individuals of the same species and are recognized as foreign in a graft by the recipient's immune system, which then reacts against the transplanted tissue and destroys it. Billingham *et al.* (1956) showed that the destructive immune response could be prevented if the donor's antigens were presented to the recipient *in utero* or during the neonatal period, before the *reticuloendothelial cells (the lymphocyte and macrophage system) of the immune system had developed. The recipient animals became unable to recognize these grafts as foreign and accepted subsequent grafts from the same donor origin. They had developed specific 'immunological tolerance'. Although this procedure has no direct clinical application, the work of Medawar and his colleagues in the 1950s was a potent stimulus to surgeons to attempt the grafting of organs to treat patients. For details concerning the graft-versus-host reaction see IMMUNOLOGY.

In this article, I shall summarize some of the important steps in the grafting of vascularized living organs which have been of therapeutic value. For information on blood transfusion and bone marrow transplantation see BLOOD TRANSFUSION; BONE MARROW GRAFTING.

Technical developments. No progress was possible until a reliable means of joining blood vessels together was devised; this was achieved by Alexis *Carrel at the turn of the century (Fig. 3) and

Fig. 1. Saints Cosmas and Damien miraculously replacing a leg from a dead donor to a patient afflicted with a tumour of his leg. (Reproduction of a painting attributed to Girolamo da Cremona (1463–5), appearing in *Brook Antiphonal*, Society of Antiquaries, London)

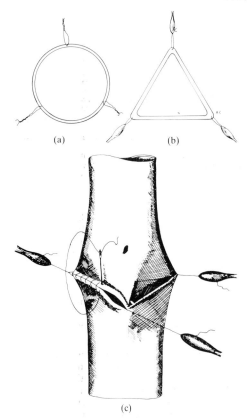

Fig. 3. Carrel's method of anastomosis. (a) Three silk-stay sutures are inserted from each other between the vessels to be anastomosed. (b) Slight tension results in triangulation which facilitates an over-and-over suture of fine silk (c). (Reproduced by permission from Calne, R. Y. (1975), *Organ Grafts*, London)

permitted surgeons to investigate grafts of organs. Carrel (1914) exploited his technique with a series of experimental kidney grafts, concluding that if the surgery were correctly performed, renal autografts were accepted permanently, whereas allografts after a period of function of a few days were destroyed. Thus, he had duplicated Baronio's experiments, but with a vascularized kidney instead of skin. Further studies of kidney grafting in the dog led to the first clinical renal transplantation at the Peter Bent Brigham Hospital in Boston. Hume *et al.* (1955) grafted renal allografts from unrelated donors, into nine patients with terminal renal failure. Despite the lack of effective *immunosuppression, some of these kidneys functioned for surprisingly long periods; one produced urine for $5\frac{1}{2}$ months. This was probably because patients with chronic *uraemia and any serious debilitating disease have impaired immune defences.

Confidence in the surgical technique of kidney

grafting had been established and the first successful therapeutic kidney grafts between identical *twins were performed by Murray *et al.* (1958), also at the Brigham. Some of their early patients still have functioning transplants 20–25 years later, demonstrating that when rejection is avoided a kidney graft can remain in excellent condition for at least a quarter of a century!

Further tentative trials of allografts from both unrelated and familial donors using large doses of total body X-irradiation to damage the immune system were failures, with two important exceptions. Both of these grafts were between non-identical twins; one was performed in Paris, the other at the Brigham. The advantage of familial donors has been established subsequently and the main transplantation tissue groups (the *major histocompatibility complex (MHC)) have been partly unravelled by work started by Dausset (1954), Payne and Rolfs (1958), Terasaki and McClelland (1964), and van Rood *et al.* (1958). The MHC products reside on the sixth human chromosome and there is a 1:4 chance that siblings will share these products (double haplotype match). Parents will usually be half matched for their children (single haplotype match) (see GENETICS).

Graft rejection. It became clear that without immunosuppressive treatment, rejection was to be expected of all grafts except those between identical twins, and that total body X-irradiation could not prevent rejection except in recipients of particularly well-matched familial donors. Rejection in the kidney is manifested by two destructive processes. *Lymphocytes from the blood penetrate the *capillary walls of the graft and divide rapidly in the substance of the kidney, causing swelling of the organ and impaired function. This cellular infiltration can often be dispersed with high doses of *corticosteroid drugs leaving little damage behind. The second immune response is due to circulating antibodies secreted by *plasma cells (secretory B lymphocytes) in the *lymph nodes and *spleen. The antibodies are specifically active against the graft blood vessels, causing destruction of their lining and eventually blocking their lumina. This humoral response is not easily controlled and much of the damage is irreversible.

Schwartz and Dameshek (1959) reported experiments on rabbits challenged with bovine gamma *globulin (BGG) and given the antileukaemia drug 6-mercaptopurine for the first 2 weeks after the protein injection. Antibody production was inhibited and subsequent injections of BGG after the 6-mercaptopurine treatment had been stopped, still failed to produce an immune response. However, a different protein, human serum *albumin, given in this phase elicited normal antibody production. A 'drug-induced immunological tolerance' had been produced. The rejection of renal allografts in dogs was also impaired by 6-mercaptopurine (Calne, 1960; Zukoski *et al.*, 1960) but did not produce a tolerant state. Elion (1951) at Burroughs Wellcome Laboratories, New York, had synthesized a number of antimetabolite analogues of purine bases. One of them, *azathioprine, a derivative of 6-mercaptopurine, was more effective than 6-mercaptopurine (Calne, 1961) and this, combined with corticosteroids, became the sheet anchor of clinical immunosuppressive treatment for recipients of organ grafts. Although corticosteroids had been investigated previously with unpredictable results, Goodwin et al. (1963) first showed a favourable response to rejection in a patient with a renal allograft and Zukoski et al. (1960) reported prolongation of renal allograft survival in dogs.

Transplantable organs. The kidney was the first organ requiring primary revascularization to be transplanted successfully because the surgery is straightforward: in addition, patients dying of kidney failure can be restored from a moribund state to reasonable health by recurrent *renal dialysis, which can also be used to maintain the patient if the graft is slow to function or suffers from a reversible rejection crisis. The pooled results of kidney grafting are shown in Table 1 from the *Thirteenth* (and final) *Report of the Human Renal Transplant Registry* (1977). The advantage of familial donors is clear. The patient survival is, of course, better in each category because most patients with failed grafts are rescued by dialysis and some receive further grafts. A number of adjuncts to azathioprine and corticosteroids have been tried but, with the exception of certain batches of *antilymphocyte globulin preparations extracted from the sera of animals injected with human lymphoid cells, none has been shown to improve the therapeutic index of the combination of azathioprine and corticosteroids. The side-effects of both these drugs can be unpleasant and dangerous. Azathioprine may damage the *bone marrow and cause leucopenia and thrombocytopenia (destruction of white blood cells and platelets). Corticosteroids cause disfiguring *Cushing's syndrome, stunt the growth of children, and can produce hip joint destruction from aseptic necrosis of the femoral head. Despite these disadvantages, many patients have survived for long periods after renal allografting. We have patients with unmatched cadaver grafts with good function still after more than 18 years.

Table 1. Kidney transplants—functioning grafts

	1 year (per cent)	5 years (per cent)
Sibling	75	60
Parent	70	50
Cadaver	50	30

The experimental studies of Starzl et al. (1959) and Lower et al. (1961) paved the way for clinical orthotopic transplantation of the liver and heart respectively. With both these procedures the organ had to become and remain life-sustaining immediately after grafting, there being no adequate substitute for function corresponding to dialysis for renal failure.

With the liver, rejection is less severe than with other organs, an intriguing observation that in some species can be remarkable (Figs. 4 and 5). In man, immunosuppressive drugs are needed but the main danger is the operation itself, which is a major trauma in an already sick patient.

The heart is more susceptible to rejection than the kidney, and additional immunosuppression with antilymphocyte globulin together with azathioprine and corticosteroids has usually been necessary. With both the liver and heart some encouraging successes have been reported. A number of patients are now surviving and well rehabilitated after more than 12 years (Gaudiani et al., 1981; Starzl et al., 1982b).

Organ preservation. Preservation of organs is an important requirement if the benefits of tissue typing are to be applied. Throughout the world there is a shortage of donor organs and in many countries superstitious *taboos preclude cadaveric transplantation. The ideal donor is a person, otherwise healthy, who has died as a result of head injury, intracranial haemorrhage, or primary *cerebral tumour, who does not harbour *sepsis or an extracranial *neoplasm. Such cases, managed

Fig. 4. Pig with orthotopic liver allograft treated with no immunosuppression, survived for 11 years, eventually dying of heart failure with a good functioning liver

Fig. 5. PVG rat with a DA orthotopic liver allograft. No immunosuppression. A DA skin graft has also taken satisfactorily. (PVG and DA simply identify specific strains of rats.) (Reproduced by courtesy of Dr Naoshi Kamada

on a *ventilator, can be maintained so that the organs to be grafted are in perfect condition until they are removed and cooled. They may be then stored in ice for several hours (48 for the kidney, 10 for the liver, and 4 for the heart) and transported to the hospital where the graft is to be performed. The world-wide shortage of donor organs means that many potential recipients do not get the chance of a graft. For example, of those cases accepted for liver grafting in the UK and USA, more than half die before a suitable liver becomes available.

Immunosuppression: new developments. With the availability of more powerful immunosuppression, namely *cyclosporin A (CyA) (see below), combined grafting of both lungs and the heart has been successfully accomplished by Reitz et al. (1982). There are a number of patients in whom both the heart and lungs are irreversibly diseased and grafting of one without the other will be of no help to the patient. The lung is especially liable to rejection and also damage from *ischaemia if there is a delay in transplantation. To avoid a long period of ischaemia the donor and recipient must be in the same hospital.

The chief obstacles to organ grafting are the shortage of donors and the limitations of current immunosuppression. Public education and conscientious help from within the medical profession are obvious ways to improve organ donation. Legislation permitting organ removal from dead people, provided that there has been no prior objection, has improved the supply of organs for grafting in France and allows organ removal without the necessity of what can be a traumatic interview with the relatives when they have just been bereaved. With presumed consent, the question of organ donation should be faced and a decision made before the death of the potential donor.

The goal of immunosuppression is to obtain graft acceptance in a specific manner so that the immune defences are not generally impaired. It seems likely that natural inhibitory control of aggressive immune reactions does occur spontaneously with time. Both cellular (suppressor T-cells derived from the *thymus) and humoral (enhancing antibodies) factors can play a part in the maintenance of a graft. Although experimentally there are examples of the production of specific tolerance in adult animals without the use of noxious agents, in man this has not yet been achieved. Better pharmacological immunosuppression is probably the more realistic next step but there have been many agents investigated that seemed promising in the laboratory but proved to be disappointing when applied clinically.

An interesting new agent is cyclosporin A (CyA), a fungal cyclic *peptide of 11 amino acids, a product investigated as an *antibiotic but found to be ineffective in that role. Borel (1976), working in the Sandoz company, showed that CyA had immunosuppressive properties and extended the

survival time of murine skin allografts. CyA was subsequently shown to be more effective than any other drug or combination of agents in controlling the rejection of experimental vascularized organ grafts (Kostakis et al., 1977a, 1977b). A cautious pilot study of CyA in clinical cadaveric renal allografts confirmed its immunosuppressive action, but also revealed nephrotoxic properties not observed in animals. The nephrotoxicity is loosely correlated with blood levels which are unpredictable following a given oral or intravenous dose, making the drug difficult to use. Renal function can be severely impaired but usually recovers on cessation of CyA treatment and changing to azathioprine and corticosteroids (Calne and White, 1982). In a multicentre randomized controlled *clinical trial (European Multicentre Trial, 1982) of CyA as the sole initial immunosuppressive agent in cadaveric renal transplantation, compared with azathioprine and corticosteroids, a clear advantage with CyA therapy was demonstrated (Fig. 6). CyA is also preferable to conventional treatment of recipients of liver grafts (Starzl et al., 1982b) and heart grafts (Oyer et al., 1982). The compound has been completely synthesized by chemists of the Sandoz company (Wenger, 1982).

Synthetic derivatives can be produced and natural analogues have been found. It is to be hoped that one of these will have equivalent or superior immunosuppressive action to CyA, but lack nephrotoxicity.

North American workers have combined CyA with corticosteroids but it remains to be seen if this combination has an improved therapeutic index.

Excessive immunosuppression leading to '*opportunistic' virus infections and the develop-

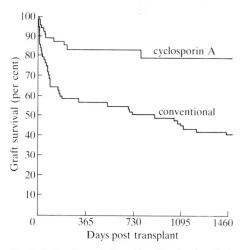

Fig. 6. Cadaveric renal allografting. Functional survival. A comparison of the actuarial survival of 75 patients treated with cyclosporin A compared with the actual survival of 16 patients treated conventionally with azathioprine and corticosteroids

ment of *lymphoma may result (Calne *et al.*, 1979). Late side-effects of CyA are not known; the longest period of treatment is only four years but the possibility of a drug-induced interstitial *nephritis has not been excluded. *Parenchymal *fibrosis in renal allografts is difficult to interpret, being a feature of rejection, infection, and hypertension. Renal function studies and ultimate morphological examination of grafted organs in recipients of hepatic and cardiac grafts should give more appropriate information. For the present, CyA represents an improvement over azathioprine and steroids, but more effective and less toxic agents are still required.

The future. Every organ in the body has now been transplanted experimentally, although in the case of the brain it is a philosophical point to decide if a grafted brain is really the transplantation of a body to the recipient of the brain. The fact that central nervous reconnections cannot take place means that this rather ghastly prospect can remain a source for theoretical dialogue. If immunosuppression were certain, safe, and cheap there would be a rapid change in the practice of surgery. The *pancreas would be grafted for *diabetes and other *endocrine glands could be transplanted. *Gonadal grafting would produce much debate: a child born of a donor's *sperm cells would have the biological identity of the graft and not the apparent parent. Limbs could be grafted because peripheral nerve regeneration will occur. Patients with malfunctioning or deficient *bowel, could have intestinal grafts. It is likely that tissue transplantation will develop along these lines.

Already pancreas grafting has been used in attempts to ameliorate the devastating microangiopathy (pathological changes in small blood vessels) that can complicate diabetes with blindness and kidney failure. Only a few patients have benefited, but the feasibility of this treatment has been demonstrated. Mechanical substitutes for diseased organs are a possible alternative in the case of organs whose function is understood, such as the pumping action of the heart and the mechanical requirements of joints—*hip replacement is already a successful treatment for many sufferers of hip arthritis (see ORTHOPAEDICS). However, for many tissues a biological graft would be preferable. From where will the extra organs come? Even with the utilization of all suitable cadaver organs there could well be a shortfall. Greater biological knowledge might allow grafting between species; the use of healthy organs of appropriate size taken from specially bred pigs would be attractive to most, anathema to some on religious grounds, and a matter of debate by a minority of *Homo sapiens* who might feel that the claim of swine for human organs would be a preferable moral choice. Perhaps it is our good fortune that this argument is not yet relevant because of our ignorance of the biological mechanisms that at present prevent *xenografting!   R. Y. CALNE

References

Billingham, M. E., Brent, L. and Medawar, P. B. (1956). The antigenic stimulus in transplantation immunity. *Nature (London)*, **178**, 514.

Borel, J. F. (1976). Comparative study of *in vitro* and *in vivo* drug effects on cell-mediated cytotoxicity. *Immunology*, **31**, 631.

Calne, R. Y. (1960). The rejection of renal homografts. Inhibition in dogs by 6-mercaptopurine. *Lancet*, **i**, 417.

Calne, R. Y. (1961). Inhibition of the rejection of renal homografts in dogs with purine analogues. *Transplantation Bulletin*, **28**, 445.

Calne, R. Y., Rolles, K., White, D. J. G., Thiru, S., Evans, D. B., McMaster, P., Dunn, D. C.,, Craddock, G. N., Henderson, R. G., Aziz, S. and Lewis, P. (1979). Cyclosporin A initially as the only immunosuppressant in 34 recipients of cadaveric organs: 32 kidneys, 2 pancreases and 2 livers. *Lancet*, **ii**, 1033.

Calne, R. Y. and White, D. J. G. (1982). The use of Cyclosporin A in clinical organ grafting. *Annals of Surgery*, **196**, 330.

Carrel, A. (1914). Transplantation of organs by Alexis Carrel. *New York Medical Journal*, **99**, 839.

Dausset, J. (1954). Leuco-agglutinins IV. Leuco-agglutinins and blood transfusion. *Vox Sanguinis*, **4**, 190.

Elion, G. B., Hitchings, G. H. and van der Werff, H. (1951). Antagonists of nucleic acid derivatives. IV. Purines. *Journal of Biological Chemistry*, **192**, 505.

European Multicentre Trial (1982). Cyclosporin A as sole immunosuppressive agent in recipients of kidney allografts from cadaver donors. Preliminary results. *Lancet*, **ii**, 57.

Gaudiani, V. A., Stinson, E. B., Alderman, E., Hunt, S. A., Schroeder, J. S., Perlroth, M. G., Bieber, C. P., Oyer, P. E., Reitz, B. A., Jamieson, S. W., Christopherson, L. and Shumway, N. E. (1981). Long-term survival and function after cardiac transplantation. *Annals of Surgery*, **194**, 381.

Gibson, T. and Medawar, P. B. (1943). The state of skin homografts in man. *Journal of Anatomy*, **77**, 299.

Goodwin, W. E., Kaufmann, J. J., Mims, M. M., Turner, R. D., Glassock, R., Goldman, R. and Maxwell, M. M. (1963). Human renal transplantation. I. Clinical experiences with six cases of renal homotransplantation. *Journal of Urology*, **89**, 13.

Hume, D. M., Merrill, J. P., Miller, B. R. and Thorn, G. W. (1955). Experience with renal homotransplantation in the human: Report of nine cases. *Journal of Clinical Investigation*, **34**, 327.

Kostakis, A. J. and Calne, R. Y. (1977). The immunosuppressive action of Metronidazole. *IRCS Journal of Medical Science*, **5**, 142.

Kostakis, A. J., White, D. J. G. and Calne, R. Y. (1977). Prolongation of the rat heart allograft survival by Cyclosporin A. *IRCS Journal of Medical Science*, **5**, 280.

Lower, R. R., Stofer, R. C. and Shumway, N. E. (1961). Homovital transplantation of the heart. *Journal of Thoracic Surgery*, **41**, 196.

Murray, J. E., Merrill, J. P. and Harrison, J. H. (1958). Kidney transplantation between seven pairs of identical twins. *Annals of Surgery*, **148**, 343.

Oyer, P. E., Stinson, E. B., Reitz, B. A., Jamieson, S. W., Hunt, S. A., Schroeder, J. S., Billingham, M. E., Wallwork, J., Bieber, C. P., Baumgartner, W. A., Gamberg, P. L., Miller, J. L. and Shumway, N. E. (1982). Preliminary results with Cyclosporin A in clinical cardiac transplantation. In White, D. J. G. (ed.) *Cyclosporin A*, Ch. 41, p. 461. Amsterdam.

Payne, R. and Rolfs, M. R. (1958). Fetomaternal leukocyte incompatibility. *Journal of Clinical Investigation*, **37**, 1756.

Reitz, B. A., Wallwork, J. L., Hunt, S. A., Pennock, J. L., Oyer, P. E., Stinson, E. B. and Shumway, N. E. (1982). Cyclosporin A for combined heart–lung transplantation. In White, D. J. G. (ed.), *Cyclosporin A*, Ch. 42, p. 473. Amsterdam.

Schwartz, R. and Dameshek, W. (1959). Drug induced immunologic tolerance. *Nature, London*, **183**, 1682.

Starzl, T. E., Bernhard, V. M., Benvenuto, R. and Cortes, N. (1959). A new method for one stage hepatectomy. *Surgery*, **46**, 880.

Starzl, T. E., Iwatsuki, S., Bahnson, H. B., van Thiel, D. H., Hardesty, R., Griffith, B., Shaw Jr, B. W., Klintmalm, G. B. G. and Porter, K. A. (1982a). Cyclosporin A and steroids for liver and heart transplantation. In White, D. J. G. (ed.), *Cyclosporin A*, Ch. 38, p. 431. Amsterdam.

Starzl, T. E., Iwatsuki, S., van Thiel, D. H., Gartner, J. C., Zitelli, B. J., Malatak, J. J., Schade, R. R., Shaw, B. W., Hakala, T. R., Rosenthal, J. T. and Porter, K. A. (1982b). Evolution of liver transplantation. *Hepatology*, **2**, 614.

Terasaki, P. I. and McClelland, J. D. (1964). Microdroplet assay of human serum cytotoxins. *Nature, London*, **204**, 998.

Thirteenth Report of the Human Renal Transplant Registry (1977). *Transplantation Proceedings*, **9**, 9.

van Rood, J., Errnisse, J. G., van Leeuwen, C. T. (1958). Leucocyte antibodies in sera from pregnant women. *Nature, London*, **181**, 1735.

Wenger, R. (1982). Chemistry of cyclosporin. In White, D. J. G. (ed.), *Cyclosporin A*, p. 19. Amsterdam.

Zukoski, C. F., Lee, H. M. and Hume, D. H. (1960). The prolongation of functional survival of canine renal homograft by 6-mercaptopurine. *Surgical Forum*, **11**, 470.

TRANSPOSITION usually refers to transposition of the great vessels, a developmental anomaly of the heart in which the *aorta arises from the right (instead of the left) ventricle and conversely the *pulmonary artery is on the left (instead of the right) side. The result is severe functional impairment of the circulation. Surgical amelioration is possible.

TRANSSEXUAL. An individual suffering from persistent paradoxical gender identification, or such a person who has undergone *sex change procedures.

TRANSUDATE is the fluid extruded from a tissue or through a membrane.

TRANSVESTISM is a morbid compulsion, also known as 'cross-dressing', to wear the clothing of the opposite sex. Transvestites are usually males who wear female underclothing in order to induce sexual excitement. There is a strong, though not exclusive, association with repressed *homosexuality. Transvestites may come to notice because of their tendency to steal articles of ladies' underwear. The condition may be regarded as a form of *fetishism.

TRANYLCYPROMINE is an *antidepressant drug

of the *monoamine oxidase inhibitor (MAOI) group. Like other MAOIs, tranylcypromine has a number of side-effects and can have potentially dangerous interactions with other drugs and with certain foodstuffs (see TYRAMINE).

TRAUBE, LUDWIG (1818–76). German physician, MD Berlin (1840). After study in Vienna and Paris, Traube was appointed professor of medicine in Berlin at the *Charité in 1857. He was the founder of experimental pathology in Germany, publishing his *Gesammelte Beiträge zur experimentelle Pathologie* (1871–8). He studied the pulmonary effects of vagal section (1846), suffocation (1847), and the rhythmic variations in vasomotor tone (Traube–Hering waves, 1865). He popularized the new methods of physical examination, introduced the *thermometer into clinical medicine (1850), described *pulsus alternans (1872), and the area of resonance to *percussion over the gastric air bubble (Traube's space).

TRAUMA. Injury. See SURGERY OF TRAUMA.

TREATMENT. The application of remedies to disease; the general management of illness. This is the central purpose and the *raison d'être* of the profession of medicine, the objectives of which were set down by the anonymous author of the 15th c. folk-saying: *guérir quelquefois, soulager souvent, consoler toujours* (to cure sometimes, to relieve often, to comfort always).

TREMATODE. See FLUKES.

TREMOR is a form of involuntary movement in which there is a constant high-frequency rhythmic oscillation of a body part or parts. The commonest type is postural tremor, which can most easily be observed (and palpated) in the fingers with the arms outstretched and the fingers separated. A very slight tremor can usually be detected in normal subjects; this is part of the physiological mechanism for maintaining posture. More obvious tremor can have a number of causes: it occurs in *anxiety states, *thyrotoxicosis, chronic *alcoholism (an important sign), as a result of certain *sympathomimetic and *antidepressive drugs, and in heavy metal poisoning; it may also result from structural brain disease (e.g. *neurosyphilis, *cerebellar disease, *Wilson's disease); one form, termed 'benign essential', is inherited and a similar tremor is characteristic of senility. Other types are rest or static tremor, which occurs in *Parkinson's disease and other extrapyramidal disorders, and intention tremor, which becomes greatly intensified when the patient makes a purposive movement; the latter indicates cerebellar or brainstem disease, due for example to *multiple sclerosis.

TRENCH FEVER is an infectious disease due to a *rickettsia-like organism (*Rochalimaea quintana*) transmitted by the human *body louse (*Pediculus* *humanus humanus*). As the name implies, trench fever flourished in Europe during the First World War; it remains endemic in parts of Europe, Africa, Asia, and America. It has features resembling *typhus but is rarely fatal; the course is characteristically recurrent, with eventual complete recovery. Like other diseases in the typhus group, it has many synonyms, for example five-day fever, quintan fever, Meuse fever, shin bone fever, Volhynia fever, and His–Werner disease.

TRENCH FOOT. See IMMERSION FOOT.

TRENDELENBURG, FRIEDRICH (1844–1924). German surgeon, MD Berlin (1866). A pupil of von *Langenbeck, Trendelenburg worked for a while with *Lister before being made professor of surgery at Rostock (1875) whence he moved to Bonn (1882) and later to Leipzig. He was the first to administer endotracheal *anaesthesia through a *tracheostomy (1869), to undertake gastrostomy (1877), and to operate for pulmonary *embolism (1908). His position of the supine patient with the pelvis elevated, his test for competence of the long saphenous vein, and his sign for dislocation of the hip are all familiar.

TRENDELENBURG'S POSITION. Lying on the back on a table which is angulated at the knees so that the thighs, trunk, neck, and head are sloping backwards and downwards at an angle of about 40° and the lower legs forwards and downwards by about the same amount.

TREPAN. An obsolete cylindrical saw for removing a circle of bone from the skull.

TREPHINE is the modern version of the *trepan: a crown saw with a central guiding pin, designed to remove a circular disc of bone, usually from the skull.

TREPONEMA **IMMOBILIZATION TEST.** A specific serological test for *syphilis, in which a positive result is the immobilization of a live motile culture of *Treponema pallidum* in the presence of *complement by *antibody in the patient's serum. Though highly accurate when properly performed, the test is expensive and laborious, and one of the many other tests available for detecting treponemal antibody is usually preferred.

TREPONEMA PALLIDUM is the spiral bacterium (spirochaete) which is the causative agent of *syphilis.

TREVES, SIR FREDERICK BT (1853–1923). British surgeon, FRCS (1878). Treves trained at the *London Hospital to which he became assistant surgeon in 1879 and surgeon in 1884. He was a renowned teacher of anatomy until 1893. He served as consulting surgeon to the Army in the South African War (1899), surgeon-extraordinary to Queen Victoria in 1900, serjeant-surgeon to Edward VII in 1902 and George V until 1910. He was created Companion of the Order of the Bath in 1900, and a baronet in 1902. Treves operated on King Edward VII for acute *appendicitis on 24 June 1902 which led to the coronation being postponed. He was the author of several textbooks as well as books of travel and *belles-lettres*. He was also the holder of a 'master mariner's ticket'.

TRIAGE is the assortment of casualties according to severity, urgency, nature of treatment required, and proposed disposal. See SURGERY OF TRAUMA.

TRIAMCINOLONE is a potent synthetic *glucocorticoid available in preparations for oral, intramuscular, intra-articular, and topical use.

TRIBADISM is mutual genital friction, or more elaborate simulation of heterosexual intercourse employing a prosthetic penile device, between female homosexuals.

TRICHINELLA SPIRALIS. See TRICHINIASIS.

TRICHINIASIS, also known as trichinosis and trichinellosis, is due to infestation with the small parasitic *nematode worm *Trichinella spiralis.* Infection, which is common and in many cases passes unnoticed, is acquired by eating inadequately cooked infected meat, almost always pork. Ingested larvae develop in the intestine into adult forms (sometimes causing gastrointestinal symptoms) and produce a second generation of larvae; these are then disseminated widely throughout the body via the blood and lymphatic circulation causing systemic symptoms, usually between 7 and 14 days after the initial infection. Among the various manifestations, fever, malaise, periorbital oedema, petechial haemorrhages, and muscle pain and tenderness are prominent. Complications are rare but can be serious; they include *pneumonia, *myocarditis, and *meningo-encephalitis. In their absence, the condition resolves in a few weeks. Larvae persist mostly in skeletal muscle, where they become encysted and eventually calcified. The prevalence of trichiniasis in pigs can be greatly reduced by not feeding them raw garbage.

TRICHOLOGY is the study of hair.

TRICHOMONIASIS is infection with one of the mobile flagellated protozoal organisms belonging to the genus *Trichomonas.* The species of importance in man is *T. vaginalis,* which causes irritation and discharge in the urogenital tract, mainly the vagina and the male urethra. Trichomoniasis is frequently transmitted by sexual intercourse. As it may be asymptomatic, it is important to investigate and if necessary to treat both members of a sexual partnership, in order to prevent 'ping-pong' infection.

Other trichomonad species are found in man (*T. hominis, T. tinax*) but are not pathogenic. Some cause disease of animals and are of importance in veterinary medicine, for example those causing mortality among young turkeys (*T. gallinarum*) and abortion in cattle (*T. fetus*).

TRICHOPHYTON is a genus of fungi, some species of which cause superficial infections of the skin, nails, and hair, including some cases of *ringworm.

TRICHROMAT. An individual with normal *colour vision.

TRICUSPID VALVE. The right atrioventricular valve. See VALVES, CARDIAC.

TRIGEMINAL NERVE. The Vth cranial nerve, which through its three divisions (ophthalmic, maxillary, and mandibular) carries nerve fibres responsible for sensation over the face, within the mouth and nasal cavity, and from the teeth; the mandibular division also carries motor fibres to the muscles of the jaw. See also TIC DOULOUREUX.

TRIGEMINAL NEURALGIA. See TIC DOULOUREUX.

TRI-IODOTHYRONINE is one of the two main *thyroid hormones, the other being *thyroxine. Tri-iodothyronine, often abbreviated to T3, is four times more active than thyroxine and is responsible for most of the metabolic effects of thyroid secretion.

TRI-ORTHO-CRESYL PHOSPHATE is a toxic organophosphorus compound which has caused outbreaks of polyneuropathy by contamination of bootleg liquor or illicit cooking oil. See POISONING.

TRISMUS is spasm of the jaw muscles, which may be due to a local inflammatory lesion or to the muscular rigidity of *tetanus; it may cause inability to open the mouth (lockjaw).

TRISOMY is a chromosomal abnormality in which an extra (third) *chromosome is present in addition to one of the normal 23 pairs, so that the total chromosome complement is 47 instead of 46. Trisomy 21 results in *Down's syndrome or mongolism; other developmental anomalies are produced by trisomy at other locations. See also GENETICS.

TROCAR. A stout surgical needle employed in conjunction with a *cannula to puncture body cavities, the trocar being subsequently withdrawn to allow the drainage of fluid.

TROCHANTERS. Two large protuberances below the neck of the femur (known as the greater and lesser trochanters) which serve as bases for the attachment of muscles.

TROILISM is the involvement of three individuals simultaneously in sexual activity.

TROPHOBLAST. The outer epithelial layer which encloses all embryonic structures in the placental mammal, from which the *chorion and the *amnion, and the embryonic side of the *placenta, are derived.

TROPHOBLAST BIOPSY is the removal of a fragment of *trophoblastic tissue at a very early stage of pregnancy (before *amniocentesis is possible) in order that cells of embryonic origin can be subjected to genetic analysis.

TROPICAL MEDICINE

Introduction. Tropical medicine is remarkable among the specialties of medicine in being defined neither by the organ of the body affected, nor the age of the patient, nor the agent of disease, but by the part of the world where the illness was acquired. It has been affected far more than most specialties, in its history and definition, by political realities and social values, and can best be understood in a historical perspective. At the present time, the subject has reached a critical point, with several different concepts of tropical medicine jostling for priority amid a good deal of confusion. A clear perception of the origins of the concepts may prevent some ill-judged decisions in relation to the future. The ties of tropical medicine to tropical hygiene and to the natural history of the agents and vectors of disease are sufficiently close that they have to be considered together, though the concepts involved in *parasitology are addressed elsewhere in this book.

History. The origins of medical practice in the tropics were the traditional medical systems of the indigenous peoples. With the notable exception of the use of *quinine among the Incas and its transfer to Europe and elsewhere as an antimalarial (first as Peruvian or Jesuits' bark of the cinchona tree), indigenous medical systems had little impact on 'tropical medicine', as usually defined, until the last decade. Rather, the subject arose from the problems encountered by explorers and the military, and developed as a necessary aspect of the colonial system.

Mortality amongst Europeans visiting the tropics, from the time of the earliest Portuguese and Spanish explorers, was very high. In addition to the nutritional problems of long sea voyages, visits to tropical ports were accompanied or shortly followed by fevers with or without jaundice, diarrhoeal diseases, and many other illnesses. In both West Africa and the Caribbean the most lethal were what we would now call *malaria and *yellow fever, with men of the garrisons in Jamaica dying at the rate of 13 per cent per year in the early 19th c. In South and South-East Asia, yellow fever was absent, but malaria and *dysentery were such that 45 per cent of members of the military expedition to Burma in 1824 died of disease. With so high a mortality, due to causes unexplained at the time, there was a clear need for understanding and control of the diseases of these tropical areas, and the military medical services had a large role in this.

The initial discovery that linked medicine in the tropics to specific biological issues was, however, made by a civilian British physician working in Amoy (Xiamen) in China on the spread of *elephantiasis (swelling of the limbs) which had been shown by Lewis and by *Bancroft to be caused by a filarial worm. Patrick *Manson (1878) demonstrated that the embryos, or microfilariae, of the worm were found in the peripheral blood only at night and that they underwent development in a night-biting mosquito which was responsible for transmission of the infection. This was the first demonstration of an insect vector of human disease, adding two further connotations to the idea of tropical diseases: first, that many are transmitted by insect vectors and, secondly, that the life cycle of many agents of tropical disease involves development outside the human body, and that this stage is temperature-dependent. Where the extrinsic part of the cycle (outside the human body) is in an insect or other organism living at environmental temperature, the association of the disease with a warm climate is explained.

In the decades which followed, corresponding to the golden age of bacteriology, *mosquitoes were shown to be responsible for the transmission of malaria and yellow fever, and many other diseases peculiar to the tropics were shown to be *insect-borne, while the role of *ticks and *snails in the transmission of infections was discovered, together with the role of mammalian reservoirs of viral, bacterial, and parasitic diseases. The strong zoological and natural history component of tropical medicine was thus established.

Epidemic disease control. These scientific advances in understanding parasitic disease transmission were accompanied by, and sometimes due to, concern for practical problems of epidemic disease control in the tropics. Interest in the Third World had moved from exploration to colonization, and the period 1890–1910 was marked by disease outbreaks on a scale that could not be ignored by governments. In particular, *sleeping sickness was responsible for the deaths of perhaps one-third of the population of southern Uganda, India was affected by epidemics of *plague and of *kala-azar, while the great Punjab malaria epidemic of 1908 led to an intensified interest in malariology. In the New World the building of the Panama canal depended on adequate measures for disease control. Both yellow fever and malaria were of crucial importance. These two decades of great activity saw the complex life cycles of the major parasitic and other vector-borne diseases elucidated, usually by the military or by expeditions from industrial countries, although the life cycle of *schistosomiasis was first determined by the Japanese in their own country.

The epidemics needed to be controlled, and in the absence of adequate *chemotherapy, emphasis had to be placed on the environmental control of vectors. This developed rapidly in the case of malaria and yellow fever, followed by that of sleeping sickness. It had been found early on that malaria was transmitted only by anopheline mosquitoes and that in a given area only a few species were important vectors. The breeding habitats of these were rather specific: some species lived in swamps, others in small sunlit pools, and yet others in shaded streams. Environmental modifications could be directed at the specific habitats of the major vectors and often achieved good results at moderate cost, an approach known as species sanitation. Sleeping sickness was similarly controlled by selective removal of vegetation to make the area unattractive to *tsetse flies, although in the Uganda epidemic the more drastic approach of removing the entire human population from the epidemic area was attempted. Subsequently, chemotherapy with arsenicals became available, but the treatment of sleeping sickness remained hazardous.

Tropical health care systems. Over the next few decades, as colonial governments became more involved with the welfare of indigenous populations as well as of the colonists, there was a gradual expansion of health care systems to the major towns, while the concept of a medical officer with responsibility for the defined population of a district developed. The doctors were expatriates. They might be of military or civilian origin, depending on the country. Thus in the French African territories a military system operated and has continued; in India the *Indian Medical Service was primarily military, but doctors could be seconded to the civil service; and in British parts of Africa a civil Colonial Service provided medical care. To train European doctors in the diseases peculiar to the tropics, schools of tropical medicine were set up at the beginning of the 20th c., gradually taking over the lead in this area from the military schools of medicine. A more stable basis for research than expeditions was needed, and there developed research institutes in South America, Malaysia, India, and later in Africa, devoted to tropical disease research and backed up by the European schools of tropical medicine.

The schools of tropical medicine in Europe reflected the shift from military and trading ventures to colonization. Thus they were usually sited at major ports such as London, Liverpool, Antwerp, Amsterdam, Hamburg, and Marseilles. This relationship was emphasized by the origins of the London school from the Dreadnought hospital at Greenwich, originally sited in the floating hulk of a warship, and by the title of the Hamburg Institute as 'für Schiffs-und Tropenkrankheiten'. The needs of traders in the tropics and of ship-owners, of comparable significance to those of governments and the military, were a very strong driving force in establishing both the subject of tropical medicine and the tropical schools. Then as colonization progressed, they became more associated with imperial power (e.g. the Royal Tropical Institute in Amsterdam), and although each had some global interests the focus tended to be on the corresponding national colonial territories. The Dutch Institute specialized in Indonesia and Guiana, the Belgian in Zaïre (then the Belgian Congo), Rwanda, and Burundi, and the German focus was on what were then Tanganyika and Togo. France and the UK, with a more widespread distribution of their colonies around the globe, tended to have a world-wide interest; thus there was a military medical basis in France together with the network of overseas *Pasteur Institutes.

Research laboratories were established in the tropics, often in response to a particular problem, but some had a broader function. A striking example, founded at the beginning of the century, is the Institute for Medical Research in Kuala Lumpur, which made decisive contributions to understanding the aetiology of *beriberi, the identification of scrub *typhus, and to our knowledge of *leptospirosis and the environmental control of malaria. By contrast, the *Rockefeller Foundation founded laboratories to study yellow fever specifically in Belem, in Trinidad, in Poona, and in several places in Africa. They uncovered a wealth of *arboviruses and more recently have evolved into laboratories with a wider remit. Other research institutes were of indigenous origin such as the Oswaldo Cruz Institute in Brazil.

In the UK, the early part of the 20th c. saw the gradual eclipse of the military schools of medicine, such as that at Netley, as centres of research, due to the emergence of the London and Liverpool schools (see LONDON SCHOOL OF HYGIENE AND TROPICAL MEDICINE) with a focus on East and West Africa respectively, as the intellectual centres. In the Indian subcontinent, the growth of research institutes initially staffed by the Indian Medical Services kept the focus of activity in the tropics, and the founding of the Calcutta School of Tropical Medicine and the growth of other research and university institutions in India provided bases for research on malaria under such workers as Christophers, Sinton, and Shortt who extended the pioneer work of *Ross, on *cholera by *Rogers, on kala-azar by Shortt, and on dysentery by *Boyd. They were gradually replaced in the field by a distinguished group of Indian national research workers.

The American tradition in tropical medicine has several strands. A strong military component was exemplified by the outstanding research work of Walter *Reed on the transmission of yellow fever, and its control, together with malaria in Cuba and Panama by *Gorgas. This has continued up to the present day with the Walter Reed Army Institute of Research in Washington playing a major part in parasitological research as have a series of naval research units in the tropics. In parallel with these military efforts, many American civilian parasitologists, usually biologists rather than physicians in background discipline, have done outstanding work in helminthology. Their activities developed during the *hookworm campaigns of the Rockefeller Foundation during the 1920s in the southern states of the USA. As malaria and various *helminths were endemic, the American civil tradition has been more national in its origins, though with a strong involvement in China during the pre-war period of the Peking Union Medical College and in the Philippines with schistosomiasis after the Second World War. That war was a notable stimulus to increased American involvement in tropical disease research in the field because for the first time disease was a great cause of morbidity rather than mortality affecting armies; the war speeded up the introduction of residual insecticides, synthetic antimalarials, and *antibacterial chemotherapy. Malaria and scrub typhus were major problems in the tropical campaigns.

Whereas before the Second World War the British role in tropical medicine could have been considered to be greatest in India, the post-war focus was on Africa, for the obvious reason of Indian political independence. The focus also shifted from sleeping sickness, epidemics of which had wrought such havoc in Uganda and the West African Sahel but were now under control, to the other parasitic infections. Malaria and filariasis were studied and especially the extreme degrees of malarial endemicity seen only in sub-Saharan Africa and New Guinea.

The recent past. *Malaria* dominated much of the world scene in tropical medicine until the 1960s and is returning to this position at present. Indeed, the largest international meetings in this subject area were known as the 'International congresses of tropical medicine and malaria' and the picture of malaria as constituting half the subject was realistic. During the post-war decade, *DDT became widely available and its use in the Mediterranean islands controlled malaria to a dramatic extent. This was because its persistent insecticidal properties for up to six months when sprayed on surfaces not only reduced mosquito numbers but in particular reduced the long-term mosquito survival which is needed for malaria transmission. Moreover, it was found that when spraying was discontinued after several years, in some instances malaria did not recur as the reservoir of infection in man had died out. This was developed into specific national campaigns aimed at the eradication of malaria, rather than its control, within specific time limits. These were capital projects (not annually recurrent budget items), of immense cost in relation to national health resources, and organized separately from the general health services of developing countries. They required international financing and specialized expertise. The latter was provided through the *World Health Organization (WHO) particularly, and during the 1950s and 1960s that organization achieved international importance through malaria eradication which dominated its activities. The programme was highly successful in the malarious areas of Europe and North America where malaria transmission had been of limited intensity and showed an epidemic pattern ('unstable malaria') and where general health services were relatively well developed for detecting residual human cases after the insecticidal attack phase. Notable successes were recorded in Venezuela and Guyana due to the effects of Gabaldon and Giglioli respectively. An initially successful campaign was also implemented in Asia, although it was followed by a resurgence of infection in the 1970s as residual cases persisted. In the highly endemic areas of stable malaria in sub-Saharan Africa little impact was made on the disease. The experiences of this period had a marked effect on subsequent health policies, especially because the all-or-nothing nature of eradication attempts, with their concomitant capital budget and need to oversell the programme, tend to be followed by dramatic collapse and strong reaction if they fail. In addition to socioeconomic factors, the problems of malaria control increased with the emergence of insecticide resistance among vectors and drug resistance among the parasites, twin problems of so many control campaigns.

Medicine in the tropics. At the same time as this intensive public health endeavour developed, medicine in Africa and the Caribbean was moving in other directions. Universities had been founded in the post-war period and they developed medical schools, often initially in partnership with UK schools of medicine. The teachers were largely expatriates at first and often came from the UK medical academic scene. Far fewer were recruited from the field research workers of the Colonial Medical Service. There was a strong emphasis on comparability of graduates with those from UK medical schools, and the research interests of the teaching staff initially derived from UK medicine. Heart disease and cancer in Africa were investigated and many important and fascinating new diseases and syndromes were studied: *endomyocardial fibrosis, *Burkitt's lymphoma, malarial *nephrotic syndrome, *Kaposi's sarcoma, *pyomyositis (tropical myositis), *Buruli ulcer, and in the Caribbean *veno-occlusive disease of the liver, for example. Thus grew up an interest in what has been called 'medicine in the tropics' to distinguish it from those parasitic infections which were the traditional content of 'tropical medicine'. The two approaches remained relatively separate in Africa, with parasitic diseases being the subject of research in specialized institutes, while the other diseases predominated in university research where time and resources were more limited except for facilities for clinical and histopathologi-

cal work. A consequence of this separation was that medical students were educated in the second tradition, and for too long, both there and elsewhere, the focus of the first generation of indigenous physicians educated in modern medicine was not primarily upon the tropical parasitic diseases. Nutritional research, after the early description of tropical vitamin deficiency syndromes, was given new impetus by the description of *kwashiorkor by Cicely Williams in Ghana, and research units flourished in Jamaica and Uganda. However, both these traditions were orthodox in medical terms, viewing tropical medicine as dealing with a particular group of diseases and as comprising a specialty of medicine. Both also owed much to the influence of such bodies as the British *Medical Research Council which not only financed research units in the tropics and supported individual research workers, but also provided a pattern, facilitating the formation of regional (as in the Caribbean) and national (in India) Medical Research Councils along the British pattern.

A more radical approach viewing tropical medicine as an integral part of socioeconomic development has subsequently grown up. The reason is not hard to seek. There is a substantial overlap between the underdeveloped, or poverty-stricken, state and a tropical location. A high *infant mortality is perhaps the best indicator of underdevelopment, even more so than the gross national product per head, and the link between health and development has been re-emphasized in the last decade and a half. There is a real sense in which it is a re-emphasis, since the original impetus for the founding of the British schools of tropical medicine was the perception by traders that health and trade went together and the Ross Institute focused similarly on improving the health of labour in tropical mines and plantations on the grounds that it made good economic sense for management as well as being a humanitarian gesture.

The late stages of WHO's efforts at malaria eradication prepared the way for changes in the perception of tropical medicine. It had become clear before 1970 that a prerequisite for the consolidation phase of eradication, when the insecticidal attack on mosquitoes was lifted and residual infections in man were detected and treated, was effective health service coverage. This in turn required better management and organization. The focus of attention moved away from building up excellent medical schools, with their accompanying teaching hospitals, in each tropical country in order to ensure that nationals of that country were qualified to international standards, and towards the periphery, with emphasis on health centres, rather than large hospitals, with attention concentrating on the surrounding community. Medical schools acquired teaching health centres and their adjacent small communities as pilot or demonstration areas, and during the 1960s can be thought of as discovering the 'population denominator' with all its implications, although these took time to be realized. There are three main ones: the relevance of 'coverage' by health services (better thought of in terms of effective access by the people to the service); recognition that disease control and health promotion may be the only feasible routes to follow, with attention moving toward the lower age groups where mortality is greatest; and an implied use of lower cost approaches if coverage was to be achieved.

The medicine of poverty. These issues were first crystallized in such books as *Medical Care in Developing Countries* by King (1966) and *Health in the Developing World* by Bryant (1969). They laid emphasis on coverage, and on achieving it by health care largely delivered by paramedical workers. They wrote at a time when malaria was under better control, globally, than at any other time before or since, and their reflection of the pilot surveys and 'community diagnosis' concepts recently introduced meant that the key causes of death and disability emerged as cosmopolitan infections such as tuberculosis and acute gastrointestinal and respiratory infections; the ages most at risk were the very young and mothers during delivery, and the importance of malnutrition was apparent. These were not intrinsically tropical problems—similar diseases predominated in the poverty-stricken parts of temperate countries, most dramatically during the industrial revolution—but they were the principal health problems of the tropics. Thus a third view of tropical medicine emerged, as the 'diseases of poverty', and this became the most influential view during the 1970s. It clearly united health with development, though in the converse of the earlier way. Instead of health being viewed as a prerequisite for economic productivity, disease in the tropics was thought of as primarily being a consequence of poverty, with socioeconomic development representing the road to health. Thus malnutrition might be reduced more effectively by land reform than by specifically nutritional supplementation. This change of viewpoint had three major implications for tropical health. If disease was due to poverty, the reduction of disease was, at least in the longer run, not primarily a matter of medical professional intervention. Either the doctor accepted that his role was peripheral or else he became involved in a complex web of developmental issues that required other than traditional medical skills. Secondly, whichever of the preceding options the doctor followed, to achieve the necessary population coverage he could no longer practice on a traditional doctor–patient basis; his role became that of a teacher and manager of paramedical workers. Thirdly, if tropical medicine comprises the diseases of poverty, it follows that the resources available per head, with which to provide medical care, will be extremely limited so that a rigorous assessment of priorities and acceptance of only low-cost interventions will be necessary (see HEALTH CARE

ECONOMICS). This requires particular skills of a non-traditional type and the possession of such skills can be thought of as making the key aspect of tropical medicine the 'medicine of poverty' rather than studying the diseases of poverty. These problems attract a very different sort of person from the clinically orientated physician. There is a strong component of humanitarian administration and a tendency to minimize professional skills of diagnosis and one-to-one patient care, while the elements of social engineering are often uncongenial to the independently minded physician.

The 'medicine of poverty' was most effectively practised by charismatic individuals, sometimes nationals of the tropical countries concerned and sometimes not, outside the government health services and in remote places. Religious groups often led the way (see MISSIONARIES, MEDICAL). Meanwhile, the WHO had progressed from the faltering attempts at malaria eradication—by the mid 1970s malaria had been eradicated from many countries and the duration of a sustainable campaign in the others had been largely exceeded—to an emphasis on building up basic health services which had proceeded but slowly. Therefore, with the inspiration derived from the non-governmental programmes based at village level, the WHO placed emphasis on self-help and 'community participation' in programmes directed still more towards total coverage. Locally recruited and trained paramedical staff provided preventative as well as curative 'primary health care'. This global programme, launched at a meeting at Alma Ata in 1978, marked the extreme of de-professionalizing tropical medicine in an effort to improve access to health care for the entire populations of tropical and other developing countries. Such a programme creates an immense need for cheap, simple, and effective interventions to treat, and preferably prevent (though here the need is often greater than the demand), the major diseases of the tropics. Safe, effective, cheap, and robust chemotherapy and vaccines against the infections which form the bulk of Third World diseases are needed.

Treatment and control interventions. In many ways one intervention has become the prototype of what is involved in a 'medicine of poverty'. This is the use of oral rehydration therapy for the acute watery *diarrhoeas. From the original empirical observations and studies of physiological mechanisms whereby a mixture of saline and glucose allowed fluid absorption, a series of investigations have determined how far other sugars or starches could be substituted for glucose; the possible replacement of bicarbonate by citrate for easier storage; whether packets of salts will be made up correctly in villages and how far domestic ingredients can substitute; as well as how best to make the therapy both available and widely used in villages of the tropics. Such studies have something in common with the research needed for successful environmental control of mosquito vectors of malaria: a detailed understanding of the ecological and cultural milieu, precise definition of a relatively simple and low cost intervention, and thorough field study of its operational deployment. Other agents for the treatment and prevention of tropical infections have involved more complex laboratory work.

The animal parasitic infections, both with *protozoa and with helminths, have posed particularly difficult chemotherapeutic and *immunological problems. They are *eukaryotic organisms and hence resemble their hosts in their metabolic pathways more closely than do most *bacteria and *rickettsiae, so that safe chemotherapy of tropical parasites has been an elusive goal. The size and complexity of parasites are associated with multiple *antigens, so that although the infected host produces multiple *antibodies, to determine which are protective and then to purify the corresponding antigens for use as *vaccines has been very difficult until recently, when there has been in the last decade a resurgence of interest by basic scientists in the problems of parasitic disease. The recent advances in molecular genetics have come in time to contribute substantially to progress in this field, with the use of *monoclonal antibodies in the identification of pathogens, and the production of biosynthetic antigens for diagnosis as well as the promise of vaccines (see GENETIC ENGINEERING). The USA, with its relative lack of post-colonial responsibilities and field experience of the tropics, has been particularly active in these new areas.

Tropical disease chemotherapy goes back, apart from the natural product quinine, to the first decade of the 20th c. when antitrypanosomal arsenic compounds were studied by *Ehrlich and others. Synthetic antimalarials date from the 1930s when *mepacrine and *chloroquine began to become available, but in general the chemotherapy of parasitic infections has moved slowly; thus, there are still no good drugs available for killing the adult *Onchocerca* worms that cause river blindness *onchocerciasis) nor for the South American trypanosomes causing *Chagas' disease. During the 1970s anthelminthic agents against intestinal worms and schistosomes have greatly improved while the malaria scene has rather tended to regress so that in parts of South-East Asia only combined chemotherapy with quinine and tetracycline provides an adequate cure of falciparum malaria.

There is as yet no operationally available vaccine against a human parasitic disease, but recent intensive efforts, most successfully in the case of anti-sporozoite immunization against malaria, and the possibility of bioengineering methods for synthesizing large quantities of protective antigens, make this an area of rapid progress. Vaccines against other tropically important infections such as neonatal *tetanus (prevented by maternal immunization) and *poliomyelitis are an important component of primary health care strategy, and the development of a relatively heat-stable *measles vaccine has made this an important way to reduce tropical child mortality.

The deployment of child immunizations has been encouraged by the WHO, and grew out of its dramatically successful *smallpox eradication campaign. WHO's other recent programme in tropical parasitic disease research has developed the interest of biomedical research workers in the scientific fascination of the problems of drug and vaccine development against malaria, trypanosomiasis, *leishmaniasis, schistosomiasis, the filariases, and *leprosy, while the diarrhoeal diseases programme has focused attention on oral rehydration and other aspects of the control of these major killing diseases and a respiratory disease programme is beginning, directed at the largest single cause of tropical mortality. There has also been a revived interest in environmental health, with renewed concern for the improvement of water supplies and sanitation and for habitat control of disease vectors, all of which were neglected in the post-war enthusiasm for insecticides and chemotherapy. The regulation of human population growth has repeatedly been raised, too, in discussion of the health of tropical populations.

The present day. The field once known as tropical medicine is therefore now one of great activity, and a good deal of conceptual confusion. The different aspects and perceptions of the subject, as parasitic disease, as diseases of poverty, as tropical variants of disease, and as the medicine of poverty, are all jostling for position in a rapidly evolving scene. The traditional subject may well be breaking up. Tropical medicine until the last few years has been the last 'vertical' specialty of medicine, where it was possible for one person to have expert knowledge and do research, to remain academically 'respectable', while working at the cellular level, the level of the sick patient, and at the level of the population or community. The rate of progress in all these fields is now such that this breadth of effective interest may be almost impossible to achieve at the research level, although it remains necessary for the doctor in a tropical country. The countries with a colonial tradition have maintained the unity of the subject up to the present. In the UK and the major European nations there are still those who combine long experience of field work with laboratory expertise and clinical experience, but that generation is ageing. That tradition was missing in the USA in large part, with the absence of colonies permitting a tropical career, and the predominance of biologists. However, a younger generation of medically qualified Americans is now working more in the tropics, partly stimulated by the increasing role overseas of the Centers for Disease Control (CDC) whose staff played a major part in the smallpox eradication programme.

In the UK a series of changes in the organization of tropical medicine has been taking place, often unperceived by government. The imperial structure provided an overseas career in the Colonial Service and Indian Medical Service. Those of academic ability could, late in their careers, return from the tropics and teach in the two schools of tropical medicine for a decade or so, thus passing on their experience and continuing their laboratory work. In addition they could often visit the tropics and assist, in the post-war era, the WHO and the British Ministry of Overseas Development (later the Overseas Development Agency, or ODA), who, perceiving their value, created extra posts at the schools. As colonial territories became independent and passed through an understandably xenophobic phase, the overseas career structure disappeared: many experienced staff joined WHO and others the two schools. The Medical Research Council created some research posts, after a time, and consolidated its tropical work in laboratories in the Gambia and Jamaica. The Wellcome Trust also maintains several tropical units. But the career structure has shrunk drastically and for a decade governments let the former colonial institutions decay without facing up to the future, while the side-effects of fiscal policy on overseas aid and foreign student fees have placed an almost intolerable burden on the system. The change towards a political and commercial aid policy has had similar consequences. Charitable organizations such as *Oxfam and the *Save the Children Fund had meanwhile become larger and more professional in their approach. They support innovative work on health care in the tropics and younger doctors thereby gain experience in developing countries, as do some employed on short contracts in overseas universities or by the ODA. This humanitarian impulse became combined with the tropical field experience of older workers and the British tradition of epidemiological work, and sustained the subject through the difficult late 1970s. Meanwhile, originating largely in the USA but filling a wider need, there was a resurgence of scientific interest in communicable diseases of temperate countries. This was fostered by service with CDC (during the Vietnam era) or at the cholera laboratory in Dacca, then in East Pakistan (now Dhaka, Bangladesh), so that many now senior American physicians were concerned with communicable disease and encouraged in that interest by the Rockefeller Foundation. The global incidence of such diseases, and their greater prevalence and importance in the tropics, directed attention back to the Third World. A similar process is taking place in the UK, more slowly, and the streams of tropical parasitic disease and communicable disease generally, at the clinical level, are tending to converge.   D. J. BRADLEY

Further reading
The original reports of many tropical medicine discoveries are in journals difficult of access. However, the majority of them have been reprinted in:
Kean, B. H., Mott, K. E. and Russell, A. J. (1978).

Tropical Medicine and Parasitology: Classic Investigations, 2 vols. Ithaca, New York.

There is no wholly satisfactory history of tropical medicine; the fullest now available in English is:
Scott, H. H. (1939). *A History of Tropical Medicine*. London.

There are several large textbooks of tropical medicine for those wishing to go into greater detail on the subject matter. The three listed here are the longest-standing British and American texts respectively, and the most recently written one:
Manson-Bahr, P. E. C. and Apted, F. I. C. (1982). *Manson's Tropical Diseases*. 18th edn., London.
Strickland, G. T. (ed.) (1984). *Hunters' Tropical Medicine*. 6th edn., Philadelphia.
Warren, K. S. and Mahmoud, A. A. F. (eds) (1984). *Tropical and Geographical Medicine*. New York.

On the community aspects of tropical health:
Bryant, J. (1969). *Health and the Developing World*. Ithaca, New York.
King, M. H. (1966). *Medical Care In Developing Countries*. Nairobi.
Lucas, A. O. and Gilles, H. M. (1984). *A Short Textbook of Preventive Medicine for the Tropics*. 2nd edn, London.
Macdonald, G. (1965). On the scientific basis of tropical hygiene. *Transactions of the Royal Society of Tropical Medicine and Hygiene*. **59**, 611–20.

TROPISM is a growth response to a stimulus, the direction of growth being either towards the stimulus (positive tropism) or away from it (negative tropism).

TROTTER, WILFRED BATTEN LEWIS (1872–1939). British surgeon and philosopher, MD London (1897), MS London (1900), FRCS (1899), FRS (1931). Trotter was trained at *University College Hospital, London and worked there throughout his professional life, becoming assistant surgeon in 1914 and surgeon in 1915. He was made surgeon-in-ordinary to George V in 1928 and promoted serjeant-surgeon in 1932. In addition to his superlative technical skill as a surgeon, his diagnostic acumen and his ability as a teacher, Trotter possessed intellectual qualities of a high order. His essays *The Instincts of the Herd in Peace and War* (1916) had a great influence on sociological thought.

TROTULA (11th c.). Italian physician. The existence of Trotula is uncertain. Some authorities held that she was a teacher at *Salerno and wife of Johannes Platerius, others that 'Trotula' was a nickname for all Saliternan midwives. Extensive writings, especially on *gynaecology and *midwifery, are attributed to her.

TROUSSEAU, ARMAND (1801–67). French physician, MD Paris (1825). Trousseau was the leading French clinician of his day, and became professor of therapy at the Faculté in 1839 and of medicine in 1850, moving from the Hôpital S.

Antoine to the *Hôtel-Dieu. In 1828 he visited Gibraltar with a commission to report on *yellow fever. He was the first to undertake *tracheostomy in Paris (1831), published an important monograph on laryngeal *tuberculosis (1837), and popularized pleural *paracentesis (1843) and *intubation (1851). He suggested the eponymic titles of *Graves' disease (1860) and *Addison's disease (1856), and described the spasm produced by compression of the nerves in latent *tetany (Trousseau's sign, 1864). His publication *Clinique médicale de l'Hôtel-Dieu de Paris* (1861) enjoyed immense success.

TRUDEAU, EDWARD LIVINGSTON (1848–1915). American physician, MD Columbia University (1871). Trudeau began practice in New York City, but soon developed symptoms of pulmonary *tuberculosis. He went to the Adirondack Mountains to rest, expecting to die of the disease, but his health gradually improved and he attributed that to rest and mountain air. He remained in the Adirondacks, founding and directing the Saranac Lake Sanatorium. Trudeau carried out some laboratory and animal experiments with tuberculosis, following discovery of the organism by *Koch. He became a leading US authority on pulmonary tuberculosis, and played a prominent part in national medical societies. He is sometimes credited with the well-known maxim, thought now to be a 15th c. folk-saying, of a physician's goal: 'to cure sometimes, to help often, to comfort always'.

TRUNK. The main undivided part of an anatomical structure, for example the trunk of the body, to which the neck, the four limbs, and the genital appendages are attached.

TRUSS. A device for maintaining pressure over a weak area of the abdominal wall in order to prevent a *hernia from protruding.

TRYPANOSOME. Any protozoal organism belonging to the genus *Trypanosoma* (see TRYPANOSOMIASIS). Those of importance to man include *T. gambiense* and *T. rhodesiense* (agents of African sleeping sickness); *T. cruzi* (Chagas' disease); and *T. vivax, T. congolense,* and *T. brucei* (trypanosomiasis of cattle and other domestic animals).

TRYPANOSOMIASIS is the name for a group of parasitic diseases of man and animals caused by various species of protozoa belonging to the genus *Trypanosoma*. Transmission occurs by means of certain tropical insects in which the trypanosomes spend part of their life-cycle and which inoculate the vertebrate hosts by biting or faecal contamination.

In man, the principal types of trypanosomiasis are: African sleeping sickness, which has two distinct clinical forms due to *T. gambiense* and *T. rhodesiense* respectively, and which is transmitted by *tsetse flies; and American trypanosomiasis or *Chagas' disease, due to *T. cruzi* and transmitted in the faeces of insects belonging to the family Reduviidae (variously known as cone-nose, kissing, or assassin bugs). Animal trypanosomiasis is also of importance to man, since in certain regions it constitutes a severe handicap to the farming of cattle and other domestic animals; the organisms chiefly concerned are *T. vivax, T. congolense,* and *T. brucei.*

TRYPTAMINE. See SEROTONIN.

TRYPTOPHAN is one of the eight 'essential' *amino acids, that is one which cannot be synthesized by the body and which is therefore a necessary component of the human diet. It is a metabolic precursor of nicotinic acid (and therefore tryptophan deficiency is of equal importance to that of *niacin in the causation of *pellagra), and of *serotonin; and it is required for normal growth and nitrogen metabolism.

TSETSE FLY. A genus (*Glossina*) of biting flies native to tropical Africa, some species of which (most notably *G. palpalis* and *G. morsitans*) are responsible for transmitting *trypanosomiasis to man and animals.

TSH. See THYROID-STIMULATING HORMONE.

TUBAL TIE. Tubal ligation: sterilization of the female by *ligation of the *Fallopian tubes.

TUBE. Any hollow cylindrical structure, particularly the Fallopian (or uterine) tube, the long slender tube which extends from the upper lateral angle of the *uterus to the region of the *ovary on each side and which provides a passage for shed ova into the uterine cavity.

TUBERCULIN is an extract prepared from tubercle bacilli used in diagnostic tests for *tuberculosis. See TUBERCULIN TEST.

TUBERCULIN TEST. A test to determine whether *tuberculous infection has occurred in a subject, involving the intracutaneous or subcutaneous injection of an extract of tubercle bacilli (tuberculin) and studying local and systemic reaction. The standard form of the test, also known as the Mantoux test, requires the intracutaneous injection of 0.1 ml of the purified protein derivative (PPD) of tuberculin containing 5 tuberculin units, the reaction being read 48–72 hours later; induration of more than 10 mm in diameter is interpreted as a positive reaction indicating infection with *Mycobacterium tuberculosis*. A negative test may be repeated with a larger dose. False negatives are not uncommon, probably as a result of non-specific immune depression. False positives when they occur are usually the result of infection with other *mycobacterial species.

TUBERCULOMA. A tuberculous *granuloma.

TUBERCULOSIS is infection with one of the two variants of the tubercle bacillus which commonly parasitize man (*Mycobacterium tuberculosis hominis* and *bovis*). Tuberculosis, which can involve almost any organ or tissue of the body, remains a common and serious disease, but both its terrors and its prevalence have been vastly reduced by the discovery and application of tuberculostatic chemotherapy. For a review of modern developments, see CHEST MEDICINE.

TUBERCULOSIS OFFICER. An appointment created by the UK Public Health Act 1913. The Act, which was aimed chiefly at tuberculosis, required county councils to prepare schemes for prevention and treatment that included, as well as the provision of dispensaries and sanatoria, nurses for home visiting, and other facilities, the appointment of a tuberculosis officer.

TUBEROSITY. A bony protuberance.

TUBEROUS SCLEROSIS is one of the *phacomatoses, also known as epiloia and Bourneville's disease. It is genetically transmitted as a *dominant characteristic, though with incomplete penetrance. The main features are fibrotic and depigmented skin lesions (adenoma sebaceum), mental deficiency, and *epilepsy, often with associated defects of brain, kidney, heart, lungs, and other organs.

TUBOCURARINE is a neuromuscular blocking agent, the active alkaloid of *curare.

TUBULE. Any small *tube.

TUERCK, LUDWIG (1810–68). Austrian physician, MD Vienna (1836). Tuerck became first physician to the neurological department of the *Allgemeines Krankenhaus in 1857 and carried out valuable work on the cutaneous distribution of the *spinal nerves (1863). In 1857 he became dextrous in the use of the *laryngoscope devised in 1855 by Manuel Garcia (1805–1906), a Spanish teacher of singing in London, and wrote a book on laryngeal diseases.

TUFFIER, MARIN THÉODORE (1857–1929). French surgeon, MD Paris (1885). Surgeon to the Paris hospitals in 1887 and *agrégé* in 1889, Tuffier became well-known as an experimentalist, working at the Sorbonne. He was noted for his work in urology and the operative treatment of fractures and was a pioneer of thoracic surgery. He popularized *spinal anaesthesia in France. During the First World War he became one of France's leading military surgeons both in operative and administrative fields.

TUKE, DANIEL HACK (1827–95). British psychiatrist, MD Heidelberg (1853), FRCP (1875).

Although destined for the law, Tuke began to study mental disease at The Retreat, York, which has been founded by his great-grandfather. He decided to train in medicine and qualified from *St Bartholomew's Hospital, London, in 1852. After travel in Europe he returned to practise in York, but was taken ill in 1860 and spent 15 years in Falmouth. He started consulting work in London in 1875 and became the leading opinion in his branch of medicine. He was lecturer in mental diseases at Charing Cross Hospital from 1892. He published *A Manual of Psychological Medicine* (1852; jointly with Bucknell) and the authoritative *Dictionary of Psychological Medicine* (1892).

TUKE, WILLIAM (1732–1822). British philanthropist. Tuke was inspired to found The Retreat for the insane at York after a friend had died in the County Asylum, possibly from maltreatment. He 'struck the chains from lunatics'. See PSYCHIATRY.

TULARAEMIA is a rare infectious disease known to occur in the USA, Japan, and Russia and having some resemblance to *plague, except that the animal reservoir is mainly in rabbits. When infection is due to the bite of an infected tick or deerfly, there is a local lesion at the site of inoculation associated with regional *lymphadenopathy. A pneumonic form also occurs. In many cases, the disease is mild and self-limiting; and the response to antibiotics is good. The causative organism is a small pleomorphic gram-negative bacillus named *Francisella tularensis.*

TULP, NICOLAAS (1593–1674). Dutch physician and anatomist, MD Leiden (1614). Born Pieterz, he assumed the name of Tulp (=tulip) from sculptures on his house. He practised in Amsterdam, where he also held civic office and acquired immortality in Rembrandt's painting, *The Anatomy Lesson of Dr Tulp* (1632) (see ART AND MEDICINE). He gave an early account of *beriberi (1652) and instituted the first Dutch *pharmacopoeia.

TUMOUR. Strictly, any swelling; but it normally signifies a new growth (neoplasm), either benign or malignant. See ONCOLOGY.

TUPPER, SIR CHARLES (1821–1915). Canadian physician and politician, MD Edinburgh (1843). Tupper was one of Canada's Fathers of Confederation and was born in Nova Scotia. He graduated MD from Edinburgh and took his licentiate of the Royal College of Surgeons there and became an excellent practitioner. Tupper served in the Nova Scotia legislature and in the House of Commons at Ottawa from 1855 to 1900. In Confederation year (1867) he was elected president of the Canadian Medical Association, an office which he held for three years. From 1884 to 1886 he was High Commissioner for Canada in London, returning to

Canada as Minister of Finance to be responsible for floating the large loan through which the Canadian Pacific Railway was completed to the west coast of Canada. He returned to London to represent Canada, but was subsequently brought back to Ottawa as Prime Minister of Canada. It had been Tupper's courage and determination which brought his native province into the Canadian confederation. *Osler wrote in his obituary notice of the survivor of 93 tempestuous years: 'His life is an illustration of the brilliant success of the doctor in politics.'

TÜRK, WILHELM (1871–1916). Austrian physician, MD Vienna (1903). Türk became associate professor in 1915. He published a large number of observations in clinical *haematology and described a circulating *plasma cell (Türk cell).

TURNER'S SYNDROME results from failure of the *gonads (ovaries) to develop as a result of deletion (or other anomaly) of the second X chromosome; in classical Turner's syndrome, the chromosome complement is therefore 45,XO and the patient is chromatin-negative on *nuclear sexing although phenotypically female. The cardinal features become obvious at *puberty: they include primary *amenorrhoea; *dwarfism; sexual *infantilism; musculoskeletal abnormalities such as webbing of the neck, low-set ears, and wide carrying angle at the elbow; and associated anomalies, of which an important one may be *coarctation of the aorta. See also GENETICS.

TWILIGHT SLEEP is a popular term for a state of semi-narcosis induced by the administration of *morphine and *scopolamine during labour; this drug combination produces both *analgesia and *amnesia, and was formerly widely employed in obstetric practice.

TWINS are two offspring produced in the same pregnancy. Dizygotic (fraternal or non-identical) twins result from the fertilization of two ova at the same time. A tendency to produce more than one ovum at *ovulation can be inherited, so that fraternal twins can run in families; multiple ovulation can also be stimulated by drugs and hormones administered to counteract infertility and may thus result in multiple pregnancy (see FERTILITY DRUG). Monozygotic or identical twins, on the other hand, develop from the two halves of a single fertilized ovum formed after its first division. It follows that monozygotic twins have identical *karyotypes and are genetically identical, whereas the genetic relationship of dizygotic twins is no closer than that of ordinary siblings and they are as likely to be of opposite sex.

TYMPANIC MEMBRANE. The eardrum, the membrane separating the external from the *middle ear; it transmits sound vibrations from the air to the chain of auditory *ossicles in the middle ear.

TYPHOID FEVER is a serious febrile infectious disease caused by one of the *Salmonella organisms, S. typhi. Infection is from person to person, being transmitted by the urine and faeces of patients or symptomless carriers. The typhoid bacilli first multiply in the lymphoid tissue of the small intestine (typhoid is also known as enteric fever), whence they invade the bloodstream, causing high fever and severe general illness often marked by delirium or stupor. Abdominal pain, enlargement of the spleen, and a rose-coloured macular rash are common manifestations, but almost any organ can be involved and serious complications may ensue; the commonest of these are intestinal haemorrhage and perforation of the small intestine. In favourable cases, improvement begins at about the fourth week. The untreated mortality rate is up to 25 per cent; modern antibiotic therapy reduces this to less than 5 per cent. A proportion of recovered patients become chronic typhoid *carriers, and unless the persistent infection is eliminated (by intensive *antibiotic therapy and sometimes removal of the *gall bladder) constitute a public health problem.

TYPHUS, or typhus fever, also known as epidemic, louse-borne or classic typhus and as gaol fever, is caused by a species of Rickettsia (R. prowazekii), a group of small intracellular organisms intermediate between bacteria and viruses. The only known reservoir of R. prowazekii is man, transmission being by means of the human *bodylouse (Pediculus humanus humanus). Epidemics of typhus occur in dirty overcrowded conditions favouring lice and their transfer between people. The disease is characterized by sudden onset, headache, prostration, high fever, a generalized macular rash, and signs of central nervous sytem involvement. In patients who recover, the condition resolves in about 16 days; the mortality, however, can be high, particularly in patients over 40 years, when *antibiotic treatment is not available.

There are a number of allied infections due to other species of Rickettsia with other arthropod vectors, such as scrub or mite-borne typhus (R. tsutsugamushi), murine or flea-borne typhus (R. typhi), Rocky Mountain spotted fever or tickborne typhus (R. rickettsii), and a number of others. Unlike epidemic typhus, these are all zoonoses having animal reservoirs of infection.

Interepidemic survival of R. prowazekii is due to persistence in the tissues of recovered patients, in whom subsequent recrudescence (known as Brill–Zinsser disease) sometimes occurs.

TYRAMINE is a substance derived from the *amino acid *tyrosine, closely related to *adrenaline and *noradrenaline; it occurs in certain articles of diet, notably ripe cheese, yoghurt, bananas, wine, and decaying meat. Its importance lies in its interaction with *antidepressant drugs of the *monoamide oxidase inhibitor (MOAI) group to produce abrupt *sympathomimetic effects and paroxysmal *hypertension. Patients taking MAOIs should be given clear instructions as to which foods they must avoid.

TYROSINE is a white crystalline *amino acid present in most proteins and important in body metabolism as a precursor of various physiological substances (e.g. *thyroxine, *catecholamines, etc.).

U

ULCER. A breach or discontinuity in skin or mucous membrane, usually one that is persistent.

ULCERATION is the formation of an *ulcer, or the ulcer itself.

ULCERATIVE COLITIS is a chronic relapsing inflammatory condition of the large bowel, usually including the rectum, involving the mucosal and submucosal layers and characterized by ulceration. The cardinal symptoms are rectal bleeding, diarrhoea, abdominal pain, weight loss, and fever. Patients are usually young or in early middle age, with a slight preponderance of females; remission and relapses are common. The disease is a serious one, with a significant mortality rate; and in many cases palliation can only be achieved by total removal of the colon, with permanent exteriorization of the terminal ileum to the abdominal surface (ileostomy). The causation is unknown, and has been the subject of much speculation. It is now generally thought that some disturbance of immunological mechanisms is involved.

ULTRACENTRIFUGE. A precision *centrifuge capable of very high speeds (up to 75 000 r.p.m.) at controlled temperatures. Preparative ultracentrifuges are used for the separation of large molecules or small particles from liquids, as in the isolation of viruses, the preparation of cell fractions, or the separation of protein mixtures. Analytical ultracentrifuges allow the determination of relative molecular masses (molecular weights), sedimentation coefficients, and diffusion coefficients.

ULTRAMICROSCOPY. An ultramicroscope demonstrates the presence of particles too small to be seen with the conventional microscope. A powerful beam of light is brought to a focus in the liquid being examined in such a way that suspended particles scatter the light and appear as bright specks (the Tyndall effect). See also MICROSCOPE.

ULTRASONICS IN MEDICINE

History of ultrasound. Modern medical ultrasound has its origins in the work on marine SONAR (SOund NAvigation and Ranging) during the First World War. At this time, a number of techniques for generating high-frequency sound waves were developed and the resulting radiations were shown to be capable of inflicting pain on human beings and of killing small animals such as fish. During the third decade of the 20th c., experiments were conducted into the possibility of using these high-frequency sound waves for medical diagnostic purposes. The initial experiments attempted to use sound in much the same way that *X-rays had been used to pass through a subject and form a shadowgraph image (Dussik *et al.,* 1947). They met with very little success. During the 1940s and 1950s several groups in the USA and Europe started experimenting with pulse echo systems (Howry and Bliss, 1952). These were more directly analogous to the marine SONAR as brief pulses of sound were transmitted into the patient and the returning echoes were collected. During the 1950s, the technique of scanning was devised whereby the sound transmission and receiving system (the transducer) was moved across the surface of the patient and an electro-mechanical system caused the time base on the cathode ray display to move in synchrony (Brown, 1960). Echoes from internal structures were collected and displayed as bright dots on the cathode ray screen, the location of each dot in the display being representative of the location of the structure within the patient which gave rise to the relevant echo. By this means, crude black and white images of the echo-producing structures within a 'slice' (a section of the body) were obtained. By the early 1960s, the image quality was sufficiently good for the technique to begin to gain clinical acceptance. The early apparatuses were applied predominantly to diagnosis in obstetrics and gynaecology, notably by Professor Ian Donald, at the University of Glasgow (Donald and Brown, 1961). In the late 1960s and early 1970s, a form of display was developed in which the brightness varied with the strength of the returning echoes (Kossoff and Garrett, 1972). This was termed 'grey scale display' and permitted useful information to be obtained from the solid organs such as the *liver, *kidney, and *placenta. Simultaneously, several workers were experimenting with automatic scanning systems and a wide range of both mechanical and electronic devices have now been developed which scan the sound beam rapidly and automatically through the area of interest. Most such systems produce images at a rate in excess of 20 frames per second, thereby giving the impression of continuous live movement. These scanners have been termed 'real-time scanners' and are now rapidly replacing the previous manually operated 'static scanners'.

The nature of ultrasound. All sound waves consist merely of mechanical vibrations conducted through a medium. Audible sound waves fall in the range of 20–20 000 cycles per second (now termed hertz or Hz); frequencies above this level are called ultrasound. The frequencies employed in medical diagnostic and therapeutic devices normally lie in the range of 1–10 million Hz (1–10 MHz). At this frequency, the sound can be focused in much the same way as light. Despite its high frequency, the sound is still conducted merely as mechanical vibrations within the tissues and is therefore devoid of the potentially damaging ionizations associated with *X-rays. As the sound travels through the tissues it is partly reflected at any point where there is change in tissue density, the strength of the echo being proportional to the density change at the interface. As the sound travels at a constant speed in soft tissues, echoes occurring from deeper structures take longer to return to the surface and thus the depth and direction of the tissue giving rise to an echo can be determined by appropriate electronic apparatus.

Therapeutic ultrasound. The early workers with ultrasound were quick to note that when the hand was placed in a water tank in which high-powered ultrasound was being generated intense physical pain resulted. If small fish were placed within the tank they were rapidly killed, and it was therefore appreciated that this new ultrasound had potential biological effects. Experiments were conducted to determine the mechanisms for these effects and to apply these in clinical medicine. It was found possible to destroy malignant tumours using ultrasound (Lynn and Putnam, 1944), but regrettably a high proportion of the normal tissue through which the sound passed was also destroyed. The power levels necessary to cause this sort of tissue damage were in the range of 10–100 watts (W) per cm². In the late 1960s, beneficial therapeutic effects were identified from power levels of the order of 1 W and it is now well accepted that the healing of skin ulcers and soft tissue injuries can be considerably accelerated by exposure to ultrasound at these power levels (Dyson et al., 1968). It must, however, be admitted that the exact mechanism of this beneficial effect remains uncertain, although some of the effect at least is due to tissue heating during absorption of the sound within the patient.

Ultrasound has been used in industry for the testing of metal structures for many years and recently ultrasound drills have also been developed. These consist of very small transducers delivering high-powered ultrasound which fragments the structure to which the transducer is applied. This technique has now been developed for the destruction of *stones within the biliary and urinary systems and also as an operative aid for emulsifying unwanted soft tissue structures such as tumours.

Diagnostic ultrasound. The diagnostic uses of ultrasound can be divided into those relying on the Doppler effect to detect movement and pulse echo systems to produce images. The Doppler devices normally employ continuous ultrasound transmission and are used for the detection of the beating fetal heart or for confirming the presence of blood flow within blood vessels. The power levels employed in these devices is generally of the order of 10–50 milliwatts (mW).

Pulse echo systems use either manual or automatic systems to scan the sound beam through the area of interest (see above). The resulting image is a representation of the echoes produced within the 'slice' of the patient interrogated by the ultrasound beam. An alternative form of display is available, where the distance and amplitude of movement of the structure, commonly a cardiac valve, has to be monitored. In this situation, the transducer is aimed at the structure of interest and the apparatus is used to draw out a graph of the movements plotted against a time axis. This form of display is termed 'motion mode' (M-mode) or 'time–position' scan (T–P scan). The power level used in pulse echo diagnostic systems is now normally in the range of 0.01–10 mW.

The specialty of obstetrics is currently the greatest user of diagnostic ultrasound. Modern obstetric practice generally requires that every patient should have an ultrasound examination approximately four months after the first missed period in order to confirm the duration of the pregnancy and to exclude twins and fetal or other abnormalities. A high proportion of patients will receive an additional examination at some stage during their pregnancy to confirm the position of the placenta within the uterus and to monitor the growth rate of the fetus.

A wide range of anatomical abnormalities of the fetus are now detectable by ultrasound imaging; the technique has been shown to be capable of diagnosing or excluding all significant spinal abnormalities early in pregnancy as well as diagnosing abnormalities of the intestinal, urinary, and cardiovascular systems (Hansmann, 1982).

As mentioned above, specialized apparatus is now available for investigating the heart. These devices generally consist of an automated real-time scanner which can be used to study both the anatomy and function of the heart valves and chambers. More recently, Doppler facilities have been added to some machines in order to permit the measurement of blood velocities within the chambers of the heart and the great vessels.

Within the abdomen many structures can be visualized, including the liver, kidneys, *gall bladder, *urinary bladder, and major blood vessels. The technique is normally used for assessing the size and shape of the structures and for looking for localized abnormalities such as tumours, *cysts, and stones (Meire and Farrant, 1982a) (Figs. 1 and 2). The *stomach and *intestines are poorly seen by this technique and are better investigated using barium X-ray examinations (see RADIOLOGY).

Useful diagnostic information can also be obtained from a wide range of other structures and organs including the eye, thyroid gland, breast,

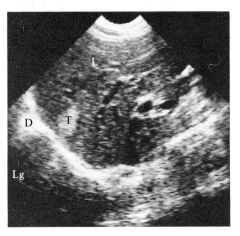

Fig. 1. Ultrasound scan of a liver (L) in which a highly reflective tumour (T) can be seen. The diaphragm (D) is also highly reflective and no useful information is obtained from the air-filled lung (Lg) above the diaphragm

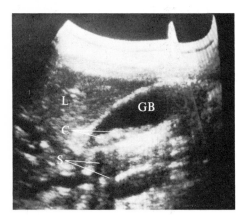

Fig. 2. Ultrasound scan of a gall bladder (GB) beneath the liver (L). No echoes are produced by the fluid bile, which therefore appears black. Two large and several small stones (C) are present in the gall bladder and are highly reflective. The large stones completely reflect the sound and give rise to areas of acoustic shadowing (S) beyond them

limbs, and the newborn baby's brain. Many of these applications require purpose-built apparatus.

The biological effects and hazards of medical ultrasound. It will be noted from the comments above that it is possible to produce quite catastrophic biological effects with ultrasound at high power levels. The beneficial effects are normally produced with powers in the region of 0.1–1 W, and a great deal of research has been conducted to attempt to identify any biological effects which may occur at the low power levels used in diagnostic apparatus. Apart from occasional

spurious results, which have proved to be unrepeatable, no adverse biological effects have yet been demonstrated at diagnostic power levels (Meire and Farrant, 1982b). It is important when considering potential biological effects to bear in mind the fact that ultrasound is rapidly attenuated as it passes through biological tissues. In most diagnostic apparatuses the power delivered to the unborn fetus, for instance, is likely to be less than one-thousandth of the output power of the apparatus. It therefore seems fairly clear that there is a very large margin of safety in current diagnostic ultrasound techniques.

The advantages of diagnostic ultrasound. The apparent complete freedom from hazard and biological effects confers a major advantage on diagnostic ultrasound examinations. The technique is also normally quick in application and does not require injections into the patient. Although the capital cost of the equipment is substantial, the potential for rapid patient throughput ensures that the cost for each examination is considerably less than that for conventional radiological investigations.

The limitations of diagnostic ultrasound. Ultrasound is totally reflected by air and almost totally reflected at the surface of bone. The air within the lungs renders them invisible to ultrasound examination and excessive gas within the bowel may impair the success of abdominal ultrasound examinations. The brain of newborn babies and infants can be readily examined through their thin skull vault but the much thicker adult *cranium severely limits the applications of ultrasound at this site. Hence detailed imaging of the brain is seldom possible in the adult but the echo from the highly reflective midline structure can be received and permits detection of displacement of the midline by disorders such as cerebral haemorrhage or tumour. This technique is called *echoencephalography or neurosonography. The other major limitation of the technique is its reliance upon a high degree of knowledge and skill in the equipment operator. Although an intelligently used ultrasound scanner is of enormous potential benefit to patients, even the most sophisticated apparatus becomes more of a liability than an asset when used by an untrained operator.

H. B. MEIRE

References

Brown, T. G. (1960). Direct contact ultrasonic scanning techniques for the visualisation of abdominal masses. In *Proceedings of the 2nd International Conference on Medical Electronics*, p. 358.

Donald, I. and Brown, T. G. (1961). Demonstration of tissue interfaces within the body by ultrasonic echo sounding. *British Journal of Radiology*, **34**, 539.

Dussik, K. T., Dussik, F. and Wyt, L. (1947). Auf dem Wege zur Hyper-phonographie des Gehirnes. *Wiener Medizinische Wochenschrift*, **97**, 425.

Dyson, M., Pond, J. B., Joseph, J. and Warwick, R. (1968). The stimulation of tissue regeneration by means of ultrasound. *Clinical Science*, **35**, 273.

Hansmann, M. (1982). Prenatal diagnosis of malformation. In Borruto, F. (ed.), *Fetal Ultrasonography, the Secret Prenatal Life*, p. 123. Chichester, Sussex.

Howry, D. H. and Bliss, W. R. (1952). Ultrasonic visualisation of soft tissue structures of the body. *Journal of Laboratory Clinical Medicine*, **40**, 579.

Kossoff, G. and Garrett, W. J. (1972). Ultrasonic film echoscopy for placental localisation. *Australia and New Zealand Journal of Obstetrics and Gynaecology*, **12**, 117.

Lynn, J. G. and Putnam, T. J. (1944). Histology of cerebral lesions produced by focused ultrasound. *American Journal of Pathology*, **20**, 637.

Meire, H. B. and Farrant, P. (1982a). Clinical application of ultrasound. In Meire, H. B. and Farrant, P., *Basic Clinical Ultrasound*, ch. 6, p. 53. London.

Meire, H. B. and Farrant, P. (1982b). Safety and biological effects of ultrasound. In Meire, H. B. and Farrant, P., *Basic Clinical Ultrasound*, ch. 3, p. 27. London.

ULTRASOUND. See ULTRASONICS.

ULTRAVIOLET LIGHT is electromagnetic *radiation of shorter wavelength than the shortest perceptible by the human eye (violet) but longer than that of *X-rays, the range being 5–400 nanometres. Sunlight is rich in ultraviolet radiation, but most of it is absorbed by the *ozone layer of the upper atmosphere. Acting on the skin, UV rays produce *sunburn and stimulate the formation of *vitamin D$_2$ from ergosterol (see RICKETS). UV radiation is generated artificially by the mercury vapour lamp.

UMBILICAL CORD. The structure, containing the two umbilical arteries and the umbilical vein together with supporting and vestigial tissues, which connects the fetal circulation with the maternal *placenta.

UMBILICUS. The scarred pit in the centre of the abdomen, also known as the navel, which marks the point of former attachment of the *umbilical cord.

UNCINATE ATTACKS are an uncommon variety of epileptic attacks associated with neuronal discharge arising in the region of the uncal gyrus of the temporal lobe. The characteristic feature is the occurrence of unpleasant olfactory hallucinations, thought to be related to the physiological function of the *uncus.

UNCONSCIOUSNESS is a state of insensibility and unawareness. See COMA.

UNCUS. An anatomical region of the *cerebral cortex, part of one of the convolutions on the inferior surface of the temporal lobe of the *cerebral hemisphere.

UNITED STATES NAVY MEDICAL CORPS. See ARMED FORCES IN THE USA.

UNITS. A unit may be defined as the quantity by reference to which other quantities are measured, the unit being taken as one. See, for example, SI UNITS.

UNIVERSITY COLLEGE HOSPITAL (UCH), London, arose partly out of reform of university education in general. Until 1826 this had been open in England only to members of the Anglican Church. The Council of the University of London was formed in that year and admission of students to the university was not based on religious discrimination. University College was opened in 1828 with a medical school to which Charles *Bell, of the *Middlesex Hospital, had been invited as professor of physiology and surgery. There were then no clinical facilities for medical students; it was expected that they would be found at the nearby Middlesex Hospital, but because of a blunder in negotiations this failed. A house in Gower Street, near the College, was bought to function as a hospital, but it was realized that a new hospital had to be built. The foundation stone was laid in 1833 and patients were admitted to the new hospital in 1834, opposite the College. It was the first hospital in London to be built for teaching as well as service. All the others were hospitals before becoming teaching centres. Over the years there have been many changes in governance of the hospital, but it is now part of the *National Health Service. The associated medical school remains with the University of London, and by an irony of fate it now works in combination with the medical school of the Middlesex Hospital.

At the start the staff included David Daniel Davis in midwifery, Robert *Liston (who had been invited from Edinburgh) in clinical surgery, and Richard *Quain in anatomy. Joseph *Lister was a student when Liston performed the first surgical operation in England under anaesthesia. Later Lister applied for the chair of surgery at UCH but was not appointed. The strong investigative and scientific tradition has continued at UCH. Of recent years famous physicians have included Sir Thomas *Lewis and Lord Rosenheim. The school and hospital still flourish in education and service.

UNIVERSITY GRANTS COMMITTEE (UGC). This UK body is responsible for allocating government funds to universities. The Committee receives a block grant from the government and formerly allocated it between individual universities on a quinquennial basis, after discussing their financial requirements with them during five-yearly 'grand visitations'. In the 1980s, owing to a change in government policy and cuts in spending, allocations have been made annually. The size of the overall government grant is determined after consideration of a submission by the UGC to the Secretary of State for Education and Science.

The relative independence of the UGC ensures that state support for scholarship is provided without state control. Although the secretariat is drawn from the Civil Service and the members are appointed by the Secretary of State, a majority of the latter are themselves active academics, with a leavening of representatives from industry and other branches of education. There is a full-time salaried chairman and two part-time salaried deputies. A subcommittee deals with matters related to medical education.

The UGC does not earmark its recurrent grants to universities but accompanies them with 'the fullest possible guidance'. Capital expenditure, apart from minor works, is provided independently and is earmarked.

It may be noted that something like 70 per cent of recurrent and 90 per cent of capital expenditure in UK universities is provided from public funds.

UNIVERSITY HEALTH MEDICAL CENTRES provide *primary health care for university students, sometimes with specialized services as well (e.g. psychiatry, family planning, etc.).

UNNA, PAUL GERSON (1850–1929). German dermatologist, MD Strasbourg (1875). After training in Vienna under *Hebra and *Kaposi, Unna returned to Hamburg and set up a private dermatological clinic (1881) and later a hospital for skin diseases (1884). He was granted the title of professor in 1907. After early pathological research he turned to the biochemistry of skin disease. He described *seborrhoeic eczema (1887–93) and introduced icthyol, resorcin, and zinc oxide paste (Unna's paste) into treatment (1886). See DERMATOLOGY.

URAEMIA is synonymous with *azotaemia.

URANIUM is a hard white naturally occurring radioactive metallic element (relative atomic mass 238.03, atomic number 92, symbol U). The natural element consists of a mixture of 99.3 per cent of the isotope uranium-238 (half-life 4.5 thousand million years) with 0.7 per cent of the isotope uranium-235 (half-life 710 million years); the latter is of greater importance in nuclear reactors and nuclear weapons. The principal ore is pitchblende.

UREA (NH_2CONH_2), also known as carbamide, is the end-product of protein *metabolism and the principal form in which nitrogen is excreted by the body. On an average daily dietary intake of about 100 g of protein (about 16 g of nitrogen), about 30 g of urea (14 g of nitrogen) are excreted in the urine, urea being formed in the liver from the breakdown of *amino acids. Urea, which was the first organic compound to be created artificially in the laboratory (by Wöhler in 1828), is sometimes employed in therapeutics as an osmotic *diuretic.

URETER. The tube, the wall of which has muscle as well as fibrous tissue, leading from each kidney to the *urinary bladder. In the adult, it is 40–45 cm long.

URETHRA. The membranous tube connecting the *urinary bladder to the exterior, through which the urine is voided. The female urethra is short (3.7 cm), passing below the pubis to open in front of the *vagina. In males it is much longer (about 20 cm), running downwards through the *prostate gland before turning forwards to traverse the length of the *penis. The male urinary tract is accordingly better protected from retrograde infection.

URETHRECTOMY is surgical excision of all or part of the urethra.

URETHRITIS is inflammation of the urethra. In many cases, though by no means all, urethritis is a manifestation of a sexually transmitted disease: see GONORRHOEA; NON-SPECIFIC URETHRITIS; VENEREOLOGY.

URETHROSCOPE. An *endoscope for inspecting the interior of the *urethra.

URIC ACID is the end-product of *nucleic acid metabolism, up to 1 g being normally excreted in the urine each day. Uric acid, which has a very low solubility, is often implicated in the formation of urinary *calculi; it also plays a central role in the pathogenesis of *gout.

URINARY BLADDER. The distensible and contractile muscular bag situated in the anterior part of the pelvic cavity which acts as a storage receptacle for the *urine prior to its intermittent discharge; it receives a continuous inflow from the kidneys via the two *ureters, the openings of which are guarded by valves, and is emptied through a *sphincter surrounding the exit of the *urethra at its lowest point.

URINATION is the act of voiding *urine.

URINE is the excretory product of the *kidneys, of which about 96 per cent is water (daily volume under normal conditions varying between about 1 and 2 litres). Volume and solute content reflect the critical role of the kidney in regulating the water, *electrolyte, and *acid–base composition of the body and body fluids (see NEPHROLOGY). The urine also contains many waste products, most notably those resulting from protein, muscle, and nucleic acid metabolism and the products of hormonal degradation. Examination of the urine is an essential part of routine physical examination, since abnormal constituents may give important diagnostic leads. Among those which are detected by simple inspection and routine testing by the examiner are: blood; haemoglobin; pus; bile; protein; sugar; ketone bodies; crystals of certain recognizable types; tubular *casts; epithelial cells; and certain parasites.

UROGRAPHY is *radiography of part of the urinary tract using a contrast medium, for example *nephrography, *pyelography, etc.

UROLITHIASIS is the occurrence of *calculi in the urinary tract.

UROLOGICAL SURGERY. Urology or urological surgery encompasses the care of the urinary tract and the male genital system. It overlaps: *nephrology, in the care of parenchymal renal diseases; *endocrinology, in the care of male infertility, adrenal diseases, and metabolic stone problems; *gynaecology, in the care of the female bladder and urethra (especially incontinence), and *radiology, in direct needle access to the kidney.

The symptoms of urological disease are most commonly disturbances in the voiding pattern. Frequent voidings (frequency), pain, or burning with voiding (dysuria) and the urgent need to void (urgency) are the most common, usually indicating inflammation or irritation of the lower urinary tract.

A slow stream or the need to strain to urinate are indicative of lower tract obstruction, while back or flank pain, nausea, and vomiting may accompany upper tract obstruction.

Cloudy urine and especially blood in the urine (haematuria) are indicative of urinary tract problems and should be investigated. Symptoms of renal failure (uraemia) may be seen in later stages of disease, and systemic symptoms of chills, fever, and malaise may accompany infection.

The development of urology was inseparable from the technological explosion of the late 19th and 20th c. Its practitioners were the intellectual descendants of the lithotomists (stone-cutters), the venereologists, and the surgeons. They became expert in the diagnosis of urinary tract disease through their mastery of urethral instrumentation, which included the use of the *cystoscope. This gave them the opportunity to compete with general surgeons for the care of certain patients, and eventually urology became a subspecialty of surgery. The Association Française d'Urologie was founded in 1896, the American Urological Association in 1902.

Stone disease. Some of the most colourful history concerns the treatment of urinary calculus or stone disease. Cutting for stone (which until less than 100 years ago included only bladder calculi) was separated from the main body of medicine and surgery long ago by *Hippocrates, who stated in his oath 'I will not cut persons labouring under the stone but will leave this to be done by practitioners in this work'. Hippocrates regarded wounds of the bladder as fatal ('Death commonly follows wounds of the brain, spinal cord, liver, diaphragm, bladder, and the great vessels'), and apparently preferred that his disciples should not be involved.

The earliest descriptions of the operations for stone were those in the Sushruta Samhita from India and of *Celsus, both written before AD 600, describing essentially the same operation, with a perineal exposure, going up through the bladder floor. The operation had changed little by the time

of Frère Jacques (1651–1714). He was an itinerant French lithotomist, setting up operating clinics in villages. Here he would line up his patients and prepare them for several days with *clysters, *bloodletting, and *purges. On the day of surgery, he and four assistants operated on all his patients and then moved on before the results of the surgery became known. After a long struggle with the medical establishment he was finally granted hospital privileges, where his errors soon caught up with him. Operating before crowds of up to 200 people, he 'cut' 60 patients in a four-month period. Twenty-five died soon after surgery and 13 were cured. The remaining 22 were 'beyond cure'. On one day seven patients died. He then went back to his itinerant practice, learned some more anatomy, modified his operation, and is said to have operated on 5000 people by the end of his career.

For a while the leadership in lithotomy went to England where *Cheselden, a trained anatomist who was also a lithotomist, tried the suprapubic approach, only to abandon it because of problems with patients straining. Straining was a help in the perineal approach since it helped to push the stone out of the incision, but with a suprapubic approach straining tended to push bowel into the incision and made it difficult to avoid opening the *peritoneum. With adequate relaxation the suprapubic approach is by far the safest and easiest, but it did not come into popular use until *anaesthesia was available.

Over the years numerous instruments were devised to break up calculi in the bladder so that they could be removed via the perineum. With the advent of anaesthesia, many of the constraints imposed by having the patient awake and straining were removed. About 1860 Sir Henry Thompson of London devised a workable lithotrite to crush bladder stones through the urethra and Henry Bigelow of Massachusetts in 1878 described a stronger instrument connected to an evacuator with a powerful rubber bulb, enabling the operator to crush and remove the entire calculus at one sitting.

The discovery of *X-rays in 1895 made early diagnosis possible. A kidney stone was visualized by McIntyre of Glasgow in 1896 and by 1918 sodium iodide was injected in a retrograde fashion via a *catheter into the urinary tract in order to visualize the kidney and *ureter, and surgery was no longer a last resort in the demonstration of stones. In 1929, Swik and Lichtenberg popularized the use of intravenously injected contrast media which visualized the kidneys.

Percutaneous nephrostomy, first devised by Goodwin and colleagues in 1965 and extended with the use of Seldinger *angiographic techniques, later allowed direct access to the kidney pelvis. With this technique a needle is introduced into the pelvis under radiographic *fluoroscopic guidance and is followed by a guide wire. Dilators are passed over the wire until operative instruments can be inserted. Renal stones can then be broken up and removed. Larger stones are usually fragmented with an ultrasonic probe acting as a miniature jackhammer and the fragments are irrigated out as they are produced.

For some of the larger or harder stones an electrohydraulic lithotriptor may be used. With this technique a spark gap is used to produce a shock wave in the irrigating fluid adjacent to the stone; this shock wave can either crack the stone or chip off small fragments. These *endoscopic techniques are much less traumatic than open surgery. Patients can be allowed out of bed almost immediately and usually go home within a few days, to resume normal activities.

A completely non-invasive method of treatment for renal calculi, which may supersede other techniques, in the majority of cases, has been developed in the past few years in Germany by Christian Chaussy. The patient is placed in a tub of water and an underwater spark-gap is used to produce a shock wave. This shock wave is then focused by an ellipsoidal reflector on the stone. The stone is strong to compressive forces, but as the shock wave passes through, a negative pressure is produced on the far side of the stone and pulls off small sandy fragments or dust which are then carried out by the urine.

While the surgical treatment of stone disease has been making these advances, our understanding of the metabolic causes of stone disease has been greatly augmented. Thirty years ago, apart from the stones which developed as a result of infection, we understood the mechanism of their formation in only a small proportion of cases. Now in only about 5 per cent of cases is the mechanism of formation obscure.

The commonest cause is an excess of *calcium in the urine (hypercalciuria), which may be classified into absorptive (too much calcium from the gut), resorptive (excess mobilization of calcium from the bone), or renal (tubular wasting and loss of calcium from the kidney). Increased oxalate (hyperoxaluria) or uric acid (hyperuricosuria) occur less frequently but can easily be determined by testing a 24-hour urine specimen.

Thus, as we have improved the surgical treatment of stone disease, we have also improved our capacity to prevent kidney and bladder stones, making surgical treatment less often necessary.

Instruments and strictures. The problem of an obstructed over-filled bladder must have been faced by man very early in history. The relief of urinary retention by reeds, straws, palm leaves, or leaves of the onion family is mentioned in the records of almost every civilization. Copper, bronze, and tin catheters were developed, but the most popular seems to have been the silver catheter, since it could be formed or bent and had some antiseptic properties. Woven catheters were used extensively and have only recently been replaced, first by rubber and then by silastic and now by a number of synthetic materials which can be designed for specific purposes. The double-lumened retention catheter with a balloon on the end to keep it in the bladder was invented as long ago as the 1820s by Reybard in France although credit usually goes to Foley, who designed the modern version in 1933.

Although the first *cystoscope was invented by Bozzini in 1804 and Nitze developed the first adequate lens system in 1879, the first really useful cystoscope had to await invention of the Edison electric light bulb in 1880. In 1887 Hartwig of Berlin and Leiter of Vienna both placed Edison's light in Nitze's scope and the interior of the bladder could be routinely and safely visualized. Modification of these instruments by Brown of Baltimore allowed insertion of catheters into the ureters and when X-rays were available contrast could be injected into the ureter to obtain an image of it for the first time. In the 1960s the Hopkins solid rod lens system increased the clarity considerably. *Fibre-optic light bundles increased the amount of light available and were much more reliable. The use of coherent fibre-optics allowed the image-carrying portion of the 'scope' to be flexible and led to the development of nephroscopes and ureter-scopes, permitting direct visualization of the entire urinary tract.

Although *venereal disease is discussed elsewhere, it is pertinent to note that the development of all the urological and urethral instruments tempted physicians to treat these afflictions aggressively, probably resulting in more harm than good. The reflection by Otis in 1883 noting that 'Gonorrhea runs its course in four weeks. Intensive therapy with irritating chemicals only prolongs the course of the disease', was neglected in favour of active interference, and many kinds of urethral irrigations and instrumentations were done. One of the more bizarre of these was an umbrella-like curette which was inserted into the urethra, then opened and withdrawn with the production of large amount of *pus which probably consisted mostly of urethral *mucosa. It was no wonder that so many *strictures resulted. These were almost invariably in the long male urethra, rarely if ever in the short urethra of the female. Indeed, urethral strictures following *gonorrhoea were so common in the 1920s and 1930s that their treatment made up a significant portion of the urological practice of the time. They were usually treated by frequent urethral dilatations achieved by passage into the male urethra of metal instruments called *bougies, used to keep the urethra open, but this never seemed to result in a cure.

Modern treatment for urethral strictures started with the open urethroplasties advocated by Johanson in 1953, later modified by Turner-Warwick and Blandy, and the grafting procedures of Horton and Devine. The use of an internal longitudinal incision (urethrotomy) through the area of stricture, a technique devised by Philip Syng *Physick of Philadelphia in 1795, but then discarded, was given new life by the advent of *antibiotics. Today it is usually done under direct urethroscopic vision as described by Sachse in 1972, with better control of the depth of the incision.

Tumours. The era of modern open urological surgery, as with all surgery, began with the development of anaesthesia and *asepsis. Simon carried out the first planned nephrectomy in 1869 for a postoperative ureteral *fistula. With the development of X-ray techniques a preoperative diagnosis could be made of most lesions. The removal of kidney stones, operable renal tumours, and obstructions all became routine procedures. This was not all good, because the easy access to the kidney led to the widespread use of the now discredited nephropexy (surgical fixation of the 'floating' kidney) on the assumption that renal ptosis (displacement) or hypermobility was the cause of ureteropelvic obstruction. The first of the modern operations for ureteropelvic obstruction was done by Thompson-Walker in 1906, and was followed by modifications introduced by von Lichtenberg in 1921, Foley in 1937, and the dismembered pyeloplasty by Anderson-Hynes in 1949. Kidney tumours are being demonstrated much earlier with the use of *computerized axial tomography (CAT) scans and ultrasonography than in the past, and inasmuch as the incidence of *metastatic spread is proportional to the size of the primary renal tumour, this should carry with it a better *prognosis.

In childhood renal tumours (Wilms tumour, nephroblastoma), even though the diagnosis is still usually made relatively late by the discovery of a large abdominal mass, the prognosis has changed from less than 40 per cent survival to better than 90 per cent survival, largely due to the advent of *antineoplastic chemotherapy and the exchange of information organized by the National Wilms Tumour Study Group.

The first recognized cause of bladder tumour was the so-called aniline dye workers' tumour described by Rehn in a German chemical plant in 1895. Actually, this tumour was probably produced by exposure to beta-naphthylamine, a by-product in the manufacture of alpha-naphthylamine, but that was not shown until the 1930s when Heuper was able to produce similar tumours in dogs by feeding beta-naphthylamine. Rats and mice metabolize naphthylamines in a different manner to that of humans and dogs and the same carcinogenic effects cannot be demonstrated in rodent experiments. Since then numerous chemicals, and even bracken fern have been reported as being carcinogenic to the bladder. The most important factor is, however, cigarette *smoking, which increases the incidence of bladder cancers fourfold.

Such tumours can now be reliably produced in animal models. In all tests of carcinogenicity the carcinogen is thought to be conjugated and detoxified in the liver, and excreted in inactive form in the urine, where the conjugate is broken up by urinary *enzymes to release the active carcinogen.

This hypothesis fits with clinical experience in two important respects: first, bladder tumours are 10 times as common as tumours of the renal pelvis where the urine rests for only a short time, and the carcinogen has not been released from its conjugated form; second, the clinical behaviour of the tumour with multiple recurrences over time in different parts of the bladder and even in the kidney and ureter can best be explained by the whole of the lining of the urinary tract being exposed to the same carcinogenic stimulus.

Over 90 per cent of these tumours are of the transitional-cell type. The relatively rare *adenocarcinomas and squamous carcinomas probably have different aetiologies and certainly a much poorer prognosis. Because of their tendency to recur, transitional-cell tumours require close follow-up with cystoscopy. This follow-up is helped by the use of urinary cytology and cytoflowmetry, which can detect malignant cells in the urine and provide evidence of tumour recurrence.

The prognosis of transitional cell tumours is related to the stage or depth of invasion and to the histological grade of the cells. The non-invasive (Stage 0) low grade tumours were formerly called *papillomas, a name now in disfavour because, although benign in appearance and prognosis, these tumours share the tendency to recur. These and the Stage A tumours, which extend through the basement membrane of the mucosa but not into muscle, are usually treated with transurethral resection and *cautery. More recently, locally applied chemotherapy (drugs instilled directly into the bladder) and *bacille Calmette–Guérin (BCG) (an attenuated tubercle bacillus used as an immune stimulator) have been used with some success. For widespread, frequently recurring disease, *radiotherapy can be used. One variation of this is the use of an intracavitary source of radiation to spare bladder muscle and avoid a post-treatment contracted bladder.

For Stage B tumours, which invade muscle, local resection and cautery often fail and the treatment seems to depend to some extent on what country the patient is in. In the UK, Bloom and co-workers use radiation as the primary modality, saving radical surgery for salvage in the case of radiation failure. In Holland, Van der Werf-Messing treats primarily with radiation with outstanding success, while in the USA preoperative radiation followed by cystectomy as described by Whitmore, is the standard procedure. Radiation therapy given before the cystectomy seems to improve the survival over that seen after surgery alone and may be the only treatment used if the tumour is through the muscle so that the prognosis is poor and not helped by surgery.

The removal of the bladder brings up the more general problem of urine flow diversion. Bringing the ureters out to the skin had been done as early as 1889 by LeDentu, but over a long term frequently resulted in stenosis (narrowing of the aperture). Nephrostomy with a catheter inserted directly into the renal pelvis was used until it was realized that the presence of the catheter caused infection and stone formation. Ureters were implanted into the bowel as a ureterosigmoidostomy but experience with this procedure over time was poor. Although a few patients did well, a majority had repeated ascending infections, reabsorption of urine from the bowel and gradual renal failure. Attempts to make a nipple or valve which would prevent reflux of the bowel flora into the kidney helped but were never reliable.

Bricker in 1950 developed what has been the most widely used diversion. Using a piece of *ileum in which the two ureters were implanted, the distal end of the ileum is then brought to the abdominal wall (an ileal bladder) where an appliance is worn to collect the urine. Moog latter recommended the use of large bowel in spite of the theoretical objections to the potentially higher pressures generated. The use of bowel as a substitute for various portions of the renal pelvis, ureter, and bladder was pioneered by Goodwin and has helped solve some difficult problems. Recently Koch has advocated a pouch which is a continent *ileostomy that must be catheterized every 4–6 hours but obviates the need for an external appliance.

Prostate gland. The prostate gland, forming a part of the sexual apparatus and responsible for the *ejaculatory contractions would be sorely missed by most males if totally absent. On the other hand, the prostate might be considered as the weak link of the male urinary tract as it suffers from three significant diseases: benign *hypertrophy, which affects at least one-third of men over 60 years of age and in somewhat over one-third of these ultimately necessitates a surgical procedure to remove obstructive tissue; *carcinoma of the prostate, which is one of the commonest male cancers and is present at least in some form in 80 per cent of men over 80 years of age; and prostatitis, which is one of the commoner male complaints between the ages of 25 and 50 years.

Bladder neck obstruction due to prostatic *hyperplasia has long been known and for many years the only treatment was regular catheterization. A patient would often carry his catheter around in his hat or even inside a shoe and lubricate it with saliva before use. More elegant was the walking cane or umbrella hollowed out to contain a catheter, occasionally even immersed in an antiseptic solution.

The first reported *prostatectomy as such was done by Amussat who in 1827 incidentally removed an obstructing intravesical prostate while removing a bladder calculus. The patient recovered completely. Eugene Fuller of New York is credited in 1894 with being the first to describe a technique for the complete suprapubic removal of a prostatic *adenoma. By this technique a suprapubic incision is made, the bladder is opened, and the prostate is enucleated through the bladder neck. There was a controversy about priority with Fryer, who with his large series, popularized the operation in the UK. In 1904 Young described his perineal approach to prostatectomy and then Terrence Millan in 1947 described the retropubic approach, coming down in front of the bladder directly on to the anterior prostatic capsule. The most common type of prostatectomy in the USA at present is, however, the transurethral resection. The first resectoscope was developed by Maximilian Stern in 1926, and was later improved by Davis and by McCarthy in order to have a square wave (spark gap) current for cutting and a sine wave current for coagulation. Some operators were able to remove several hundred grams of prostatic tissue at a single procedure, but now usually the larger glands are dealt with by open surgery. The advantage of the transurethral approach is that there is little discomfort and the patient may be out of the hospital two or three days after surgery.

Cancer of the prostate may be manifested late in the disease by pain from bone metastases. Until the 20th c. very little could be done for patients with prostatic cancer, except for the fortunate few (usually less than 5 per cent of the patients) in whom the disease was diagnosed while still localized. These could be subjected to the radical prostatectomy developed by Hugh Young in 1906, and later improved by Millan's retropubic approach. A radical prostatectomy differs from a simple prostatectomy in that the entire prostate adenoma (and 'surgical capsule' of prostate tissue) is removed, and the bladder is then sutured to the urethra. In a simple prostatectomy, as done for benign disease, only the adenoma is removed, leaving the 'capsule' intact. This difference is significant in two ways. In the radical procedure the chance of incontinence following the procedure is greater and with simple prostatectomy cancer can still develop in the remaining prostatic tissue.

The greatest real advance was the demonstration that prostate cancer is sometimes endocrine responsive. In 1941 *Huggins (an American urologist) published his work describing the hormonal control of the prostate in dogs and the use of *stilboestrol or *orchidectomy as a clinical treatment for carcinoma of the prostate. The results of orchidectomy were immediate, with dramatic relief of severe bone pain within a few hours. Huggins later received a Nobel prize for his work, the first surgeon to do so since Alexis *Carrel.

The results of hormonal therapy were so clearcut that most patients with non-operable disease were given hormonal therapy at the time the disease was discovered on the assumption that if it worked in advanced stages of disease, it should work in the early stages to retard the progress of the disease. About 20 years later, large-scale cooperative studies in the US *Veterans Administration hospitals produced findings that are now general guidelines. They showed that the immediate use of hormonal therapy did not prolong life when compared with the delayed use begun at the time of symptoms. They showed that the use of larger doses of *oestrogens (5 mg of stilboestrol compared with 2 mg) increased the death rate during the first six months of treatment, the excess deaths resulting from cardiovascular diseases. Endocrine therapy with *adrenal and *pituitary ablation has been tried but these approaches have been reserved for failures of standard therapy.

Radiation therapy for carcinoma of the prostate was not successful until Bagshaw reported on the use of megavoltage treatment in localized disease. It seems as good as radical surgery for up to 10 years, but is followed by an increased number of recurrences after this period. Another approach has been implantation of *radioactive material into the prostate. Originally a colloidal suspension of gold was used, but in recent years iodine-125 seeds have been used.

Significant side-effects occur after all forms of treatment of carcinoma of the prostate. *Impotence is expected after hormonal therapy or surgery and occurs in up to 60 per cent of patients after external beam therapy. Recent anatomical studies and investigations by Walsh in Baltimore suggest that perhaps careful attention to the neurovascular bundle on either side of the prostate may make it possible to maintain potency after a radical prostatectomy. Incontinence can follow radical surgery in 1–5 per cent of cases although the rate seems to be diminishing. Rectal and bladder irritability may occur following radiation therapy.

Paediatric urology. Studies have shown that about 40 per cent of the more serious congenital malformations occur in the genitourinary tract and most of the urological surgery in the young is concerned with their correction. In the past the management of these problems was in the hands of general surgeons and until Meredith Campbell published his textbook on paediatric urology in 1937 there was little concerted effort to pay special attention to paediatric urology. David Innes Williams held a similar position in the UK, as did Gregoire in France. The Pediatric Urology Society of America was formed in 1951 and the informal European Congress of Paediatric Urology first met in 1961.

Relief of obstruction and repair of badly dilated urinary tracts above the obstruction is the commonest problem. These obstructions are being recognized earlier, partly because of the availability of ultrasound scans, which are non-invasive. It is now commonplace to diagnose intrauterine obstruction and efforts are being made at times to drain some of these obstructions in utero so that upper tract damage is less severe at the time of birth.

Another area that has seen remarkable advances is the repair of hypospadias, a condition in which the urethra does not reach the end of the penis and may empty into the *perineum. The original techniques usually took several stages and were unreli-

able with many *fistulae and strictures resulting. There are now some 60–80 repair techniques available but in recent years the combined efforts of a plastic surgeon and a urologist, Horton and Devine, have brought major advances. Recently, attempts to bring the urethra all the way to the end of the penis rather than just to the corona of the glans have become more commonplace.

Urodynamics. It is important that urine is delivered to the outside at a low pressure and without infection. The recognition that urine flow is not simply a matter of static pressure but of dynamic flow has led to the development of a field of urology called urodynamics. The first scientific investigations were reported by Mosso and Pellacani in 1881. They developed a recording *manometer that could measure pressures in the bladder. They first described accommodation (the ability of the bladder to accept increasing quantities of fluid without a corresponding increase in pressure) and showed that the bladder muscle (detrusor) is integrated with the central nervous system. They were able to distinguish between abdominal pressure transmitted to the bladder and bladder pressure generated by the detrusor itself. The first clinical cystometer for measuring bladder (intravesical) pressure was devised by Rose in 1927 and a commercial aneroid model designed by Lewis in the 1940s was used for almost 20 years without significant modification. The present state of the art combining the use of fluoroscopic monitoring of bladder size and contractions with the measurement of bladder and rectal pressures was first described by Hinman and Miller in 1954. This has given a new insight into the co-ordination of the voiding and continence mechanisms.

Uncertainty as to the roles of the bladder neck and the urethral *sphincter in urinary continence led to the studies of Einhorning. He found that the highest pressures in the urethra occurred near the mid-urethra and that this differential was lost with stress incontinence. Later, Brown and Wickham devised techniques for the measurement of pressures while pulling out a catheter to produce a 'urethral pressure profile'. Other workers related flow rate to the total volume voided, that is, the larger the volume voided, the higher the flow rate.

A different approach was taken by Lapides using en bloc bladders and urethras removed from dogs. He demonstrated that these bladder preparations in vitro were continent (i.e. retained fluid). He then sliced lengths from the distal end of the urethra and urine was retained until the length of the urethra was less than 2–3 cm. Urine loss could then be stopped by stretching the remaining urethra to 4 cm. He then used intact animals and fashioned a bladder tube 4 cm in length, well away from the sphincter area, and showed that during voiding the contraction of the bladder funnelled and shortened the urethra and allowed voiding in the total absence of relaxation reflexes. The debate is not settled and much work continues to be done.

In spite of the incompleteness of our theoretical knowledge, much has been done in the practical treatment of incontinence. Female stress incontinence due to perineal relaxation has been a long-standing problem, often related to after-effects of childbearing. For years it was treated with *pessaries inserted into the vagina to hold the bladder in place. Then anterior vaginal repairs advocated by Kelly were done and gave considerable relief. In the 1950s the Marshall–Marchetti–Krantz procedure was devised. This involved suturing the periurethral and bladder neck tissue to the underside of the pubis to give a solid support to the bladder neck. Later Perrera with the modifications introduced by Stamey and Mason, developed a simpler technique, inserting a long needle down either side of the bladder neck and placing a stitch to lift the bladder neck up towards the abdominal wall. This procedure has gained wide popularity because of reliability and lack of morbidity.

Even more definitive is the development by Brantley Scott of the artificial sphincter. This consists of an inflatable silastic cuff which is placed around the urethra, a reservoir, and a pump or control valve which controls the flow between the reservoir and the cuff. The fluid (saline with a water-soluble contract medium) is pumped into the inflatable cuff to keep the patient continent and is released into the reservoir when the patient needs to empty the bladder.

In the upper collecting system, Hinman in the early 1900s studied the effects of obstruction, describing the sequence of dilatation and later *atrophy that occurs with acute obstruction. Kiil studied the active *peristalsis in the renal calyces and pelvis, and in the ureter, and Whitacre used the first dynamic flow of fluid to test for functional obstruction in the upper tracts.

The importance of these problems and the results of increased understanding are most obvious in the improved prognosis, both early and late, in patients with spinal cord injury. If the patient survived the acute injury or the first few years of life, the major cause of death in the past was renal failure, usually from a combination of obstruction, infection, and stone. Expectant treatment is now begun immediately and the disastrously damaged urinary tracts that were so common in paraplegics 15–20 years ago are now infrequently seen.

In patients with acute spinal cord injury, a programme of intermittent catheterization is begun almost immediately. Without the initial insult of an overdistended, often infected bladder, they are managed with either an intermittent catheterization programme, a sphincterotomy (cutting the sphincter to allow continual flow of urine), or a timed voiding programme. The situation is much the same in patients with *spina bifida and *meningomyelocoele. Previously, almost 100 per cent of the latter patients had some urinary tract abnormality appearing by the age of four years. Now many patients can be kept free of difficulty, either with medication or with intermittent catheterization.

W. H. CHAPMAN

Further reading

Herman, J. R. (1973). *Urology, A View Through the Retrospectroscope.* Hagerstown, Maryland.

Landes, R. R., Bush, R. B. and Zorgniotti, A. W. (1976–8). *Perspectives in Urology, The Official American Urological Association History of Urology.* Nutley, New Jersey.

Murphy, L. J. T. (1972). *The History of Urology.* Springfield, Illinois.

URTICARIA is the skin rash due to *allergy, also known as nettle rash or hives. Itchy blotches appear on the skin, with raised *erythematous patches of cutaneous *oedema (weals).

US PHARMACOPOEIA. Like its British equivalent, the *US Pharmacopoeia* (abbreviated to *USP*) is an official compilation of approved names and standards for substances and preparations used in medicine and pharmacy. It is published by the United States Pharmacopoeial Convention.

UTERINE SOUND. A slender surgical *probe or *bougie designed for introduction into the *cervix uteri for purposes of exploration and dilatation.

UTERUS. The womb. In the non-pregnant female adult the uterus is an elongated muscular organ about 8 cm long lying more or less vertically in the *pelvis behind the *urinary bladder. Above, its cavity communicates with the right and left *Fallopian tubes; below, the narrow lower section (the *cervix) protrudes into and communicates with the *vagina. The physiological changes which occur during pregnancy are associated with an increase of 30-fold or more in the weight of the uterine muscle (myometrium). See also MENSTRUATION; ENDOMETRIUM

UVEA. The vascular middle coat of the eye, comprising the *iris, the ciliary body, and the *choroid. See OPHTHALMOLOGY.

UVEITIS is inflammation of one or more of the structures comprising the *uvea, of which there may be many causes. See OPHTHALMOLOGY.

UVEOPAROTITIS is one of the clinical presentations of *sarcoidosis, in which the inflammatory process involves the *parotid gland and the structures of the *uvea; this variant is also known as uveoparotid fever.

UVULA. The small downwards midline projection of the soft *palate.

V

VACCINATION is immunization against any infectious disease by exposure to an appropriate *vaccine. The term was originally applied to immunization against *smallpox with *vaccinia virus, but *Pasteur extended the meaning to include all forms of active immunization with micro-organisms or their products.

VACCINE is any preparation of micro-organisms, killed or living but modified so as to reduce pathogenicity, administered in order to stimulate the production of *antibodies and hence to prevent or ameliorate the effects of infection with the natural or 'wild' organisms. Some vaccines, for example the Sabin vaccine against *poliomyelitis, are effective by mouth, but most have to be administered parenterally.

VACCINIA is the localized papulovesicular eruption which occurs at the site of inoculation with vaccinia virus (see COWPOX); it was formerly widely employed in immunization against *smallpox but now that the disease has been eradicated it is now indicated only in a few special groups, for example laboratory workers with *poxviruses. Rarely the eruption became generalized due to blood-borne spread of the virus ('generalized vaccinia') but without serious effects. 'Progressive vaccinia' or 'vaccinia gangrenosa' was a very much rarer and often fatal complication which followed vaccination of individuals whose *immune system had been depressed by disease or drugs.

VACUOLE. A small space within the cytoplasm of a *cell, initially formed by invagination of the cell membrane; material on the cell surface is thus engulfed into the vacuole—the process of *phagocytosis.

VAGINA. The sheath-like passage between the *vulva and the *cervix uteri which receives the *penis during sexual intercourse. The mucous lining of the vagina is under hormonal (*oestrogen) control.

VAGINISMUS is painful spasm of the muscles around the *vagina, making sexual intercourse difficult or impossible.

VAGINITIS is inflammation of the *vagina. *Candidiasis and *trichomoniasis are frequent causes. A type of atrophic (or senile) vaginitis occurs in postmenopausal women as a result of *oestrogen deficiency.

VAGOTOMY is the surgical division of one or both *vagus nerves.

VAGUS. The Xth cranial nerve, a major component of the *parasympathetic nervous system. The vagus is also a mixed nerve, so that as well as supplying parasympathetic fibres to and visceral afferents from the thoracic and abdominal organs, it carries sensory fibres from the ear, tongue, *pharynx, and *larynx and motor fibres to the pharynx, larynx, and *oesophagus.

VALERIAN is the dried rhizome and roots of the plant *Valeriana officinalis,* which has been used in the form of an extract, infusion, or tincture (often together with *bromides, *chloral hydrate, *phenobarbitone, or other sedatives) in the treatment of nervous conditions.

VALSALVA, ANTON MARIA (1666–1723). Italian physician and anatomist, MD Bologna (1687). Valsalva was a pupil of *Malpighi and became lecturer in anatomy in *Bologna, where he taught *Morgagni. His *De aura humana tractatus* (1704) contains an excellent account of the anatomy of the ear in which he names the *Eustachian tubes. He first described the aortic sinuses (sinuses of Valsalva). *Valsalva's manoeuvre provides a simple test of circulatory function.

VALSALVA MANOEUVRE. Forced expiration against a closed *glottis, a simple bedside test of circulatory function. In the normal subject, the increase in intrathoracic pressure hinders venous return to the heart, so that there is a fall in *cardiac output and hence in arterial *blood pressure; the resultant reflex *tachycardia can be detected in the arterial pulse at the wrist. When the manoeuvre is terminated (after about 10 seconds), the accumulated venous blood is pumped by the heart into a constricted vascular bed, causing an 'overshoot' of arterial pressure above the normal level and a consequent reflex *bradycardia. An alternative method of inducing a forced expiratory effort is to ask the subject to blow into the tube of a *sphygmomanometer against the mercury column, maintaining it at a level of about 40 mmHg for the same period of 10 seconds.

VALVE. In general, any fold or flap, or a system of these, in the lumen of a vessel, channel, or orifice which permits flow in only one direction. Many such valvular structures exist in the body: of particular note are those scattered throughout the veins (see VARICOSE VEINS) and those controlling the flow of blood between the chambers of the heart (see VALVES, CARDIAC).

VALVES, CARDIAC. A pair of *valves on each side control blood flow into and out of the right and left *ventricle of the *heart. They are the right and left atrioventricular valves (known also as tricuspid and mitral valves respectively), which open during *diastole to allow blood to flow into the ventricles from the atria and close during *systole to prevent retrograde flow; and the valves guarding the out-flow tracts of each ventricle (aortic and pulmonary valves) which open during systole to allow blood to flow into the pulmonary artery and the aorta and close during diastole to prevent backwards leakage. Each valve consists of three segments (cusps or leaflets) except the mitral, which usually only has two.

VALVULAR HEART DISEASE. Disease affecting the heart *valves, sometimes abbreviated to VHD. Defective valve function is of two types: stenosis, in which narrowing of the valve orifice restricts flow in the normal (forward) direction; and incompetence (or regurgitation), in which the defective valve fails to prevent retrograde flow. The major causes of VHD are *congenital heart disease, *rheumatic fever, and *infective endocarditis.

VAPOUR BATHS. Steam baths.

VARICELLA. See CHICKENPOX.

VARICOCELE. Varicosity (see VARICOSE VEINS) of the veins draining the *testis, usually the left. When symptomatic, the condition is easily dealt with surgically.

VARICOSE ULCER. A skin ulcer on the lower leg above the ankle associated with *varicose veins, due to impaired blood flow and hence impaired nutrition of the skin and subcutaneous tissues.

VARICOSE VEINS are the abnormally dilated and tortuous veins associated with conditions or circumstances resulting in persistently high venous pressure and with defective venous *valves allow-ing retrograde flow. Varicose veins are commonly manifest in the subcutaneous tissue of the legs, but may occur in other situations as a consequence of prolonged venous obstruction. There is usually held to be a genetic component in the aetiology, and predisposing conditions include obesity, pregnancy, ascites, and occupations which involve prolonged standing. Apart from cosmetic dis-figurement, varicose veins can cause aching of the legs and swelling of the ankles. Venous *throm-bosis and *ulceration of the skin over the lower parts of the legs (varicose ulcer) are troublesome complications.

VARIOLA. See SMALLPOX.

VARIX (pl. varices). A varicose vein.

VAROLIO, CONSTANZO (1543–75). Italian anatomist, MD Bologna (1567). Varolio was appointed professor of surgery in *Bologna (1567), and he moved to Rome as physician to Pope Gregory XIII in 1573. He described the ileocaecal valve (between the *ileum and *caecum) and, in *De nervis opticis* (1573), the pons Varolii.

VASCULAR SURGERY AND DISEASES OF ARTERIES AND VEINS

Introduction. If the central and peripheral nervous systems can be considered as the electrical messengers of the body, then the arteries and veins represent the plumbing. Like a house, the human body is full of pipes and without them it cannot function properly. These pipes fulfil four purposes:

1. They carry the requirements of the tissues from the *heart to the periphery. These include *oxygen, nutrient materials, and *hormones.
2. They clear away waste products of *metab-olism, in particular *carbon dioxide and acids, into the *lungs and *kidneys.
3. They operate as a 'reservoir' of fluid, which can be directed to various parts of the body accord-ing to need. A number of complicated switching mechanisms exist to accomplish this function.
4. They are concerned with the regulation of body *temperature. Human beings can operate only within a small temperature range, but are none the less capable of living anywhere from the North Pole to the Sahara. For this to be possible, it is necessary to control and alter blood-flow through the skin (see HOMEOSTASIS).

There are two systems of conducting pipes in the human body, the *arteries and the *veins, which have different functions, and will be discussed independently. (The third system, the *lym-phatics, lies outside the scope of this article.)

The arteries (Fig. 1) are thick-walled muscular tubes which convey blood from the left side of the heart to every part of the body, from the brain to the toes. The total amount of arterial tissue is less than 0.5 per cent of the whole, so that the average man weighing 70 kg, has about 350 g of artery in him. None the less, damage to this system of tubes represents the commonest cause of death in Western society, and it is conceivable that if *nutri-tion was adequate and *infection and *cancer eliminated throughout the world, arterial disease would turn out to be what stood between us and immortality. The arteries are tubes which work at high pressure, with high resistance, and fast flow. They make up a 'uni-cameral system' in that between the left *ventricle and the small vessels of the tissues, there is very little difference in *blood pressure. The main disease which affects arteries has various names such as *arteriosclerosis,

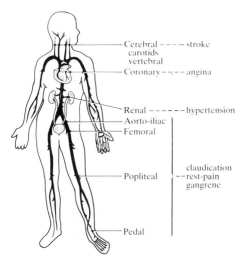

Fig. 1. The main arterial pathways

*atherosclerosis, and 'hardening of the arteries', and has been investigated with the greatest care over many years but without much progress. It is an observed fact that as a man (and to a lesser extent a woman) grows older, the arteries become rougher, harder, and prone to block, but why this should be so is uncertain. Two basic approaches to the problem have emerged. One school of thought relates this change to dietary handling of *cholesterol and related substances. Certainly, families who have a grossly abnormal cholesterol metabolism show a dangerous incidence of arterial disease, but whether this is actually relevant to the general population is still debatable. Others concentrate on the risk factor of high blood pressure (*hypertension), which is known to damage the lining of the arteries and can lead to *clotting of the blood, and eventual blockage. Here again, it is difficult to separate cause and effect. There is, however, one risk factor which is not only proved beyond all doubt, but is controllable: tobacco *smoking in any form worsens and accelerates arterial disease.

Because the arteries are the sole route of blood supply to the tissues, when they become blocked, harm results. A tissue which is able to function, though with less than its ideal requirement of blood and oxygen, starts to complain and become painful. Examples of this are pain in the heart felt during exercise by someone with narrowed coronary arteries, or pain in the legs on walking, due to impairment of flow through the femoral artery or its branches. This situation is termed ischaemia. Total blockage of an artery, particularly if it is an end artery (to take a geographical analogy, the only road into a village) results in death of local tissue, or *gangrene, unless there is a way around the block (the '*collateral circulation'). Death of tissue due to loss of blood supply is called *infarction. The pattern and position of the blocked vessel

are all-important. Thus if it supplies an arm or a leg, the result will be loss of that limb, which is bad enough. But if the artery supplies the muscle of the heart or the brain, then the result may be loss of life. This equally applies to the arteries to the abdominal organs. If the main artery to the *intestine becomes blocked, then the intestine becomes gangrenous, which precipitates a very unpleasant and painful death.

The great mass of the human body is concerned with locomotion, and is composed of the skeleton and muscles. It is nevertheless possible to live without limbs, and even without an intestine or a *bladder. What is not possible is to exist without the vital arteries, which accordingly have been extensively researched over the last century. It is logical when looking at individual arteries to start from the top.

The arteries to the brain. The heart gives off four arteries to the brain, two in front and two behind, the *carotid and vertebral arteries. These unite in a circle at the base of the brain, termed the *circle of Willis, after Queen Elizabeth I's physician, Thomas *Willis (Fig. 2). This is an efficient arrangement, in that if one or more of the four main routes into Willis's circle is closed, then the others can compensate and maintain flow. From the circle, smaller vessels run up into the brain itself. Interruption of one of these end-arteries produces a serious problem, because part of the brain then ceases to function, and a leg or an arm or even *breathing or *consciousness can fail. This is one mechanism of a '*stroke', *haemorrhage or bleeding into the brain tissue being another.

Years ago it was thought that the small arteries in the brain were the important factor in cerebral

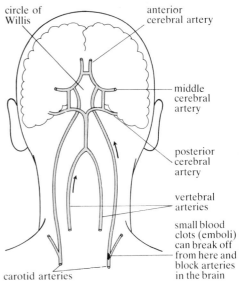

Fig. 2. The circle of Willis

function, and that these were frequently diseased. Recent research has shown that this is sometimes the case, but we also know now that it is often disease in the arteries in the neck, which are accessible to the surgeon, which determine events above them. Small clots known as *emboli become detached and block healthy arteries further on. Operations on the carotid arteries can stop this happening. Research continues on whether or not reconstruction of the vessels in the neck can actually improve cerebral function. More recently, surgeons have started to join up arteries between the scalp and the brain, in an effort to repair damage occasioned by a stroke, and even perhaps to improve mental function. The results of these operations appear encouraging, but have yet to be determined.

Chest arteries. Moving down into the chest, perhaps the most important arteries in the human body, in terms of sustaining life, are the first branches of the *aorta, the two coronary arteries which supply the heart muscle itself. Obstruction by a clot (coronary thrombosis) or narrowing of these vessels results in two types of illness. First is the person who experiences chest pain on exercise, the condition known as *angina pectoris. Angina may continue for years, and be consistent with a relatively normal life, but it always betokens trouble, and some of those who experience such symptoms progress to the next stage of ischaemic heart disease, a *myocardial infarction. This means that the ischaemia has become critical, in that the blood flow is so low that a part of the heart muscle actually dies. If a large area is affected then the heart will fail immediately and the person will die. More often, only a small part of the heart is involved, in which case the muscle will become replaced by a fibrous scar.

The treatment of heart disease and of *heart failure is outside the scope of this article, but the whole question has been revolutionized by the development of surgical techniques, designed to open up or bypass the coronary arteries, and to prevent further attacks. A small vein is taken from the leg, and attached to the aorta and to the coronary artery beyond the block, thus bypassing the occlusion (see CARDIOTHORACIC SURGERY). The operation of coronary artery bypass grafting (CABG) has developed into a large industry, and is in fact the second most frequently performed operation in the USA (the first being removal of the *gall bladder). Its effect on angina is well established and without doubt beneficial, and many middle-aged men who would otherwise be incapacitated are returned to useful life.

The effect of the operation on actual survival was initially thought to be doubtful, but it has now been established that it does in fact prolong life. Whether the operation will stand the test of time is another question. Obviously it is a simple mechanical solution to what is a complicated biochemical problem, and the effective answer must in the end be to develop a 'medical' treatment of ischaemic heart disease, which will prevent the accumulation of fatty deposits in the arterial wall. Already, many doctors believe that alterations in life-style in the USA have brought about a significant reduction in the frequency of these problems, and the same change appears to be under way in the UK. The important risk factors are again smoking, obesity, immobility, and high blood pressure.

Operations and treatment come and go with the advent of new knowledge, and one has only to contemplate the vast empire of *tuberculosis sanatoria of the 1920s and 1930s, described in Thomas Mann's *Magic Mountain,* which has been completely swept away by the advent of effective *antibiotics, to realize how soon a major advance becomes an anachronism. Perhaps CABG will be one such.

The kidneys. The kidney is not only an organ of excretion, it also has a function in the regulation of arterial blood pressure, and in the manufacture of red blood cells. Evolution has given the kidney a protective mechanism, whereby if the pressure in its artery falls below a certain level, then its cells produce 'pressor' substances (e.g. *angiotensin) which constrict blood vessels elsewhere in the body, thus raising the pressure and restoring its supply of oxygen. However, as often happens, an essentially benign biological mechanism can go awry, so that if a kidney is rendered ischaemic because of a narrowing or blockage in its artery, then it will respond by raising the blood pressure overall, which may be quite inappropriate, and lead to widespread arterial damage. Raised blood pressure (hypertension) is a potentially killing condition, and is discussed elsewhere in this book. One of its treatable (but uncommon) causes is a narrowed renal artery, which can be corrected surgically. The difficulty is to identify the people who really need this kind of surgical help. Most people with hypertension do not have abnormal renal arteries, but many were in the past none the less subjected to uncomfortable tests in case such a narrowing was present. It turned out that some of the patients in most need, that is to say young people with gross hypertension resistant to drugs, had narrowed vessels extending into the middle of their kidneys, which could not be operated upon. Short constrictions, which the surgeon could deal with, were usually found in older people, with widespread arterial disease. Even more disappointing, it was discovered that very often pressor substances were emerging from the 'better' kidney, which the surgeon was reluctant to approach, while the blocked renal artery on the 'bad' side protected its small vessels. In the early 1970s there appeared a new generation of drugs to reduce blood pressure, which were extremely effective, so that the operation more or less disappeared. It is not that it did not work. A successful reopening of the renal artery in selected cases succeeded not only in reducing blood pressure but in improving kidney function. However, the effort and expense of the selection process became unacceptable when measured against the ease with which blood pressure could be lowered by the new drugs. Recently, there has been a renewal of interest in the surgical approach, with the introduction of 'angioplasty'. This involves passing a long tube ending in a small tough balloon through the constricted artery; the balloon is then forcibly blown up. Because the new method is relatively safe and cheap, it has become again worth-while to consider opening a renal artery in a young person with raised blood pressure. It is too early to tell whether the initially promising results will last, or whether we will again witness the arrival of even more efficient drugs to lower arterial pressure.

There are, of course, many other causes of hypertension, not involving kidney disease; thus the activity of nervous centres in the *brainstem may be one factor. From this has arisen the interesting new approach of '*biofeedback' whereby through the exercise of deliberate introspection, a person can directly influence the behaviour of such centres of the brain and produce alterations in physical state, including lowering blood pressure.

The arteries to the gut. It might be thought that the arterial supply to the intestinal tract would be a major problem in human illness. Curiously, this is not the case. The design of the circulation to the bowel is so good that it practically never goes wrong. Accidents including infarction and ischaemia do happen in this territory, and have been the subject of much study by academic medical scientists, particularly surgeons, but they are comparatively unusual.

The limbs. The arms are hardly ever ischaemic unless they are injured, but the legs are quite different, and provide the vascular surgeon with his main activity. Why this should be so is not immediately apparent, but it is obvious that the legs are required to do much more work than the arms, in the way of simply carrying weight around; in addition their collateral circulation is better developed. When the arteries to the lower part of the body become narrowed or blocked, a very characteristic series of events take place. In the first place, the person complains of a symptom known as *intermittent claudication. This consists in the development of pain in one or both legs on walking for a set distance, which is relieved by rest. The description of the symptom is absolutely invariable and runs as follows: 'I have no problems when I am sitting or walking around the house, but as soon as I start to walk more than a few hundred yards up the street the muscles in my calf start to get crampy and painful, and I have to stop. After a few minutes' rest I am able to carry on, and can walk the same distance. This an embarrassment to me, particularly if I go for a walk, or do some shopping with friends, because I have to stop every few minutes. What is it due to and can anything be done about it?'

Many people with this problem get better, with or without 'treatment'. Careful evaluation is necessary before complicated tests and operations are undertaken. However, an unlucky minority progress to a further degree of vascular insufficiency, leading to pain at rest. The complaint then becomes different and runs 'Doctor, when I saw you a few months ago I was able to walk a certain distance, but now I can hardly walk at all, and I get pain in my foot at night, which keeps me awake, and the only relief I can obtain is by sitting out of bed and hanging my leg over the side. I cannot go on like this, please help me.'

This symptom means that the blood flow to the limb during resting conditions has become less than normal, so that cells of the tissues are unable to metabolize effectually, and they produce substances which irritate the nerves. In other words, claudication means that the legs cannot develop the increase in bloodflow which is required by activity, whereas rest pain means that the limb is at risk, because even when immobile, its oxygen needs are not being met.

Finally, the circulation may fail completely, in that the foot or leg is so badly deprived of blood that it is either on the point of death, or actually dead. Given this situation, the only possible remedy is *amputation which, not only to the victim, but also to an optimistic surgeon whose skill resides in restoring flow to arteries, seems a counsel of despair. Nevertheless, amputation of a dead limb can be a most helpful and life-enhancing operation. Absorption of poisonous substances from dead tissue profoundly affects the physical and mental well-being, quite apart from the intense pain which the presence of such tissue inflicts. Amputation is in many instances a passport to a new life. The provision of a modern light-weight artificial limb helps enormously (see REHABILITATION). However, it must be admitted that the life expectancy of somebody who loses a limb from vascular gangrene tends to be short, because of arterial disease elsewhere, and the enthusiasm and skill of the limb-fitter may be sadly frustrated.

Aneurysms. Curiously, the same disease process (atheroma) which leads to narrowed and blocked arteries, can also produce vessels which are weakened and thus become expanded by the pressure within them. A dilated artery is called an *aneurysm (in contrast to a varix, which is a dilated vein). Aneurysms have been recorded in mediaeval medicine, and were the subject of much professional argument in the 18th c., when John *Hunter introduced science into the practice of surgery. The commonest cause used to be *syphilis, but nowadays most aneurysms are the result of atheroma. Aneurysms are dangerous because as the arterial wall expands it becomes weaker, and eventually ruptures. The abdominal aorta is the vessel most frequently affected, and replacement of aneurysms of this vessel (first carried out by Dubost in Paris in 1948) is nowadays a standard operation. Interestingly, the life expectancy of someone who undergoes this operation is the same as that of a person who never had an aneurysm at all—this is in contrast to the patient with blocked arteries, who in actuarial terms is 10 years older than his recorded birth-date.

The techniques of arterial reconstruction. There are two ways of restoring flow to a blocked arterial circulation (Fig. 3). The first of these is termed 'disobliteration', 'thromboendarterectomy', or just 'rebore'. This consists in developing a plane (split) in the middle of the layers of the diseased artery, and removing the central piece which causes the obstruction. This simple surgical manoeuvre, which was developed in Portugal in the 1920s, has been the subject of much scientific enquiry.

The operation depends on two important surgical facts, which have yet to be explained. The first of these is that as arteries become older they become easier to operate upon because a split or plane develops at a particular level within the wall; this can be used by the surgeon. The obstructing material is removed, leaving a relatively smooth lining behind. However, for the operation to be successful, the thinned artery must be able to withstand high pressure: the second, and perhaps most surprising fact is that when the thick inner layers are taken away the remaining tube does not bulge and develop into an aneurysm. As originally devised, the operation of endarterectomy was applied to arteries all over the body, but most vascular surgeons nowadays would restrict it to short blocks of large vessels, such as the aortic bifurcation, or the main carotid arteries at the root of the neck.

The other way to deal with a closed artery is to introduce a bypass, which means stitching something in above and below the blocked segment so as to conduct the blood around it. This sounds simple, but unfortunately the problem is still not solved, because the human body tends to reject implanted materials, whether of biological or synthetic origin. The best bypass for a blocked artery is the person's own vein. We have more than enough veins in our body, and there is a particular one in the leg, known as the long saphenous vein (the word saphena is derived from the Arabic, and means easily seen), which is not only dispensable, but is strong enough to take arterial pressure. The saphenous vein is particularly useful in the coronary circulation, but is also the best bypass for a femoral artery, when that vessel is so severely blocked that the leg is threatened. Unfortunately, this vein is often removed early in life, for cosmetic reasons. Varicose veins, which will be discussed later, are unsightly, but do not in themselves amount to a disease, and most vascular specialists would agree that of the three competitors for the saphenous vein the cardiac surgeon should come first, the peripheral vascular surgeon second, and the varicose vein doctor nowhere at all!

The technique of bypassing an artery is finicky and difficult, but can be learned, and in most British hospitals, young surgeons are trained to carry out this type of operation. A proportion of patients who need a bypass do not have a usable vein, either because it has already been removed, or because it is anatomically unsuitable. It then becomes necessary to introduce some kind of synthetic conduit. For many years scientists have tried to devise an artificial artery, which would perform better than a natural vein, but no one has yet succeeded in this. However, grafts of synthetic materials are still widely used.

Arteries are living, pulsating, vibrating structures, which conduct blood from the left heart to the tissues in a rhythmical manner, and the rhythm is important. Additionally, they have a beautifully designed smooth lining, which discourages the accumulation of blockage or thrombosis. Hence the engineer who is attempting to produce an artificial artery has two problems. He has to provide a tube which not only remains pulsatile and vibrative, but whose lining remains attached and does not cause the blood to clot. Most researchers concentrate on the first problem, namely the compliance of the introduced tube, but recently more attention has been given to the physical attributes

For short blocks of large vessels
aorto-iliac
carotid   endarterectomy

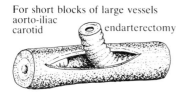

For long blocks of large vessels
aorto-femoral

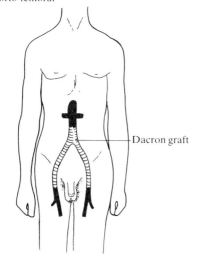

Dacron graft

Fig. 3. Some techniques of arterial reconstruction

of the lining. If it were possible to line a prosthetic tube with some kind of living human cell which would inhibit blood clotting, then this might perform better than the currently available prostheses. Work along these lines is concentrating on the properties of certain cells to produce substances known as 'prostacyclins' which have the capacity to diminish clotting and encourage flow. This type of research is exciting, but is still at an early stage. At present, we have to accept that a patient with a blocked artery, who has no immediately available vein, and who is not suitable for an endarterectomy, needs to have some kind of synthetic bypass, and all of the available devices are imperfect.

The veins. In contrast to the high-speed, high-pressure delivery system constituted by the arteries, the veins are thin-walled low-pressure tubes, which contain valves to direct their flow. Their main function is to return blood from the tissues, via the heart, into the lungs, for discharge of CO_2 and replenishment of oxygen. Additionally, they act as a reservoir in the pumping system, capable of expansion and contraction in response to the body's needs.

Evolution has largely been concerned with quadrupeds, and man as an upright biped is a fairly late development; this produces gravitational problems in the lower limbs. For this reason, most disorders affecting the venous system occur in the legs. If a person stands immobile for more than a few minutes the circulation to his brain will fail and he will faint and fall over. The reason for this is that the force generated by his heart cannot overcome the forces of gravity in order to drive the blood up from his toes to his brain. There is a compensatory mechanism in the veins of the legs, which ensures

that as their muscles contract, blood is propelled upwards against gravity, protected by the valves, to re-enter the circulation (Fig. 4). But this system has its defects. The return valves in the veins are subject to great pressure, and if they are not perfectly co-ordinated, may fail.

There are two systems of veins in the legs (see Figs. 5 and 6), the deep veins, which lie within the muscles and are subject to 'squeeze' effects, and thus operate at high pressure, and the superficial veins which run under the skin, in the fatty tissue which surrounds the muscle. These are not squeezed, and hence are at a much lower pressure. The superficial veins connect with the deep veins at certain anatomical points, and these connections are guarded by one-way valves, which prevent high-pressure deep venous blood from being ejec-

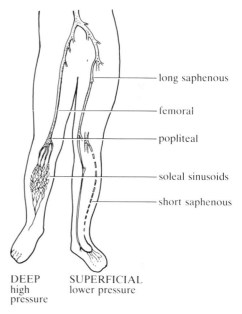

DEEP
high
pressure

SUPERFICIAL
lower pressure

— long saphenous

— femoral

— popliteal

— soleal sinusoids

— short saphenous

Fig. 5. The leg veins, seen from the front

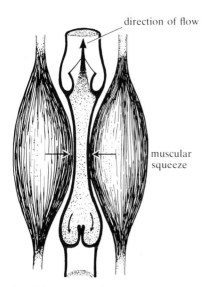

direction of flow

muscular
squeeze

Fig. 4. The venous valves

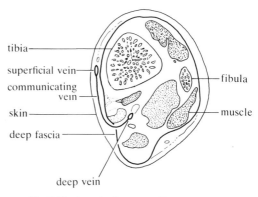

tibia —

superficial vein —

communicating
vein —

skin —

deep fascia —

— fibula

— muscle

deep vein

Fig. 6. The leg veins in cross-section

ted into the superficial veins. Should these valves fail, as quite often happens, then visible veins under the skin become congested and dilate, resulting in the appearance of varicosities. Varicose veins are an extremely common blemish, the incidence of which increases with age, so that almost everybody over the age of 40 has some enlarged veins on their legs. Whether such a common anatomical fault can properly be called a 'disease' is a matter of definition. Certainly, it is difficult to correlate appearance with symptoms, in that some individuals experience severe discomfort from quite small veins, whereas more stoical people tolerate enormous bunches of veins apparently without complaint. The cosmetic aspect of the problem is certainly most important.

Treatment of varicose veins consists either in injecting an irritant into the compressed vein, so as to cause its walls to adhere and eliminate the unsightly bulge, or in more advanced cases to remove the vein surgically. This usually involves removal of (or at least interference with) the long saphenous vein which, as already explained, is the best available substitute for a blocked artery, and hence should not be discarded lightly. Unless their appearance is very distressing, or they seem to be causing some discomfort, varicose veins are probably best left alone. Certainly, if they were no longer treated surgically, the effect on hospital waiting-lists would be quite dramatic.

In contrast to the common, but relatively innocent, problem of dilated superficial veins, disease in the deep system is a threat to health and even sometimes to life.

The deep veins in the legs are arranged in a sort of honeycomb network, which is very easily blocked by a blood clot (deep vein thrombosis, or DVT). This has two effects. In the first place, damage to the valves can impair the circulation to the skin, and result in swelling, discomfort, and eventually *varicose ulcers, which are a common health problem and very difficult to treat.

A great deal of research here has resulted in very little progress. The other problem is the venous occlusion which occurs in the patient immobilized in hospital, perhaps because of an operation. This is the silent accumulation of a large DVT extending up into the thigh. This can be very serious, as it may result in the dislodgment of a clot from the legs into the lungs, causing anything from a slight transient pain in the chest to sudden death. This is known as a pulmonary embolus. In 1898 the great German pathologist, Rudolf *Virchow, described a triad of preconditions, that is stasis (the immobilized patient), trauma to the vein wall (as may occur in unconsciousness or under anaesthesia), and finally hypercoagulability. As a natural defence mechanism, developed through evolution, injury or illness activates the clotting activity of the blood, thus preventing haemorrhage but at the price of inducing DVT. Prevention of this disaster therefore concentrates on mobility, protection of the veins, and some form of *antico-

agulant therapy designed to keep the blood fluid without at the same time causing surgical haemorrhage. There are signs that these efforts are being rewarded and that the incidence of DVT and pulmonary embolus is falling.

Small vessel disease. As mentioned at the outset, one of the functions of the circulation is to regulate body temperature by altering flow through the small vessels in the skin. This is done by nervous impulses stimulating the muscular walls of the vessels to contract, and by various chemical substances in the blood which operate directly on the muscle. There is a striking sex difference in the way the skin vessels behave, in that men on the whole maintain their vessels open, and hence lose some 10 per cent more of their body heat through the skin than do women, whose arterioles are more tightly controlled. The various *reflexes which influence the opening and shutting of the skin circulation were investigated by Sir Thomas *Lewis of University College, London, in the 1920s, using no more sophisticated equipment than pins, rubber bands, and warm water. Considering how commonly these reflexes are disturbed, leading to such afflictions as *chilblains, *sores, and excessive sweating (particularly in women) it is extraordinary how little our knowledge has advanced since his day. Research in this important area is badly needed.

Most clinical problems in the microcirculation arise from excessive activity of the muscle in the vessel wall, causing coldness, blueness, and numbness, and eventually even to ulceration and loss of tissue, particularly on the extremities. They are given a variety of names such as *Raynaud's disease (after the 19th c. French physician, Maurice *Raynaud, who described a peculiar series of colour and temperature changes in the fingers), *erythromelalgia, erythrocyanosis frigida, *acrocyanosis, and so forth (Fig. 7). In fact these complicated terms serve only to translate the patient's symptoms into Greek or Latin and add nothing to our understanding of the underlying mechanisms or how to treat them.

There are two ways of treating these disorders,

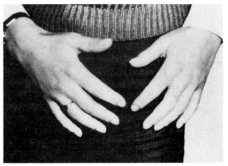

Fig. 7. Raynaud's phenomenon; note the pallor of the fingers

neither of which is particularly effective. '*Vaso-dilator' drugs are designed to counteract spasm in the peripheral vessels and to improve flow. These are very widely administered (in fact one particular product of French origin is the second most frequently prescribed in that country, after anti-biotics) but there is very little evidence, either from the laboratory or field trials that they actually work. One problem is that to be effective in over-coming arterial *spasm the drug has to be given in such high doses as to cause unacceptable side-effects. None the less, there is considerable com-mercial pressure, and vasodilators continue to be prescribed. It is unfortunately true that when doc-tors do not have an effective remedy for a disease they tend to use an ineffective one (provided that it is not positively harmful) rather than nothing at all.

The other line of treatment is surgical (sympathectomy), which consists in cutting the sympathetic nerves which constrict blood vessel walls. This is sometimes dramatically successful, but only too often the improvement is short-lived and after a few months the vessels regain their *tone and the symptoms come back. For this reason the operation has now been largely abandoned.

Summary. Although the arteries and the veins comprise a small proportion of the body mass, they are critical to health, and this applies particularly to the arteries, whose role is to sustain and nourish the tissues and organs. Obstruction to flow can result in a whole spectrum of disorders from the comparatively trivial (chilblains, varicose veins) to the catastrophic (myocardial infarction, stroke). Vascular disease is best prevented by avoidance of known risk factors such as smoking, obesity, inac-tivity, and certain forms of diet, but once damage has occurred, modern surgical techniques can often overcome or compensate for some of its worst effects.   A. MARSTON

Further reading
Birnstingl, M. (ed.) (1978). *Peripheral Vascular Surgery.* London.
Bunker, J. B., Barnes, B. A. and Mosteller, F. (1977). *Costs, Risks, and Benefits of Surgery.* Oxford.
Treasure, T. (1983). Coronary artery bypass surgery. *British Journal of Hospital Medicine,* **30,** 259.

VASCULITIS is inflammation of blood vessels; it is equivalent to *angiitis.

VASCULOTOXIC. Having a damaging effect on blood or lymph vessels.

VAS DEFERENS. The duct that carries *spermatozoa from the testis; after uniting with the duct from the *seminal vesicle, it joins the *urethra.

VASECTOMY is interruption of the *vasa deferentia by ligation or removal of a portion, frequently performed as a method of male steriliza-

tion; the operation is a simple one, because for part of its course the duct lies subcutaneously.

VASOCONSTRICTION is contraction of blood vessels with narrowing of their calibre, particularly of the *arterioles, which are the main determinant of total peripheral vascular resistance and the means by which adjustments in regional *perfusion occur.

VASODILATATION is relaxation of blood vessels with widening of their calibre, particularly of the *arterioles (cf. VASOCONSTRICTION).

VASOMOTOR. Affecting the calibre of blood ves-sels, particularly of *arterioles.

VASOPRESSIN is an alternative name for *anti-diuretic hormone (ADH). See PITUITARY GLAND.

VAUGHAN, VICTOR CLARENCE (1851–1929). American physician, MD University of Michigan (1978). Vaughan served in the University of Michi-gan as professor of therapeutics and of hygiene, and also as dean of the medical school. His research focused on the formation of poisonous substances by bacteria in foodstuffs (then called *ptomaines). He was influential in US academic medicine during the first quarter of the 20th c.

VAULT. Any structure with an arched roof, for example the vault of the *skull.

VECTOR is used in two medical senses: the usual scientific meaning of any quantity that requires a direction to be stated in order to define it com-pletely; and alternatively to denote an animal car-rier of the agent of a communicable disease (e.g. the anopheline *mosquito in the case of *malaria).

VECTORCARDIOGRAPHY is the recording and analysis of the *electrocardiogram in terms of a series of instantaneous mean *vectors, that is in terms of the moment-to-moment average magnitude and direction of the electrical forces generated during cardiac contraction. See also CAR-DIOLOGY I.

VEGAN. A strict *vegetarian, that is one who not only abstains from eating flesh but also from all other foods of animal origin, including milk, milk products, eggs, and honey.

VEGETARIANISM, strictly speaking, is absten-tion from all foods of animal origin, including dairy products, eggs, milk, and honey as well as meat and fish. In practice, most vegetarians abstain only from meat and fish, a diet which, providing it is adequately varied, is perfectly compatible with normal health. The term 'vegan' is often used to denote one who is strictly vegetarian; instances of *vitamin B$_{12}$ deficiency have been reported in such individuals.

The modern history of organized vegetarianism began in 1809 with the founding of the Bible Christian Church at Salford, near Manchester, by the Reverend William Cowherd and Joseph Brotherton, MP. In 1817 a group of 41 members emigrated to America and founded a similar church in Philadelphia, which also flourished. In 1847 some members of the Salford congregation, feeling that vegetarianism should not be a religious movement and acting in conjunction with a number of like-minded persons in the south of England, broke away to form the secular Vegetarian Society.

VEGETATION. One of the warty aggregations of *platelets, *fibrin, *erythrocytes, and sometimes *bacteria which form on the *endocardium of the heart *valves in rheumatic, bacterial, and other forms of *endocarditis.

VEHICLE. A base of non-active substance in which a drug or other medicinal agent is incorporated to facilitate administration; an *excipient.

VEIN. Any of the blood vessels in which blood returns from the tissues (and lungs) to the heart. Veins are distinguished from *arteries in having walls which are both much thinner (the intravascular pressure being correspondingly lower) and are collapsible, in carrying (except in the case of the pulmonary veins) deoxygenated blood and in having numerous *valves along their course.

VELPEAU, ALFRED ARMAND LOUIS MARIE (1795–1867). French surgeon, MD Paris (1823). After becoming *chef de clinique* at the Hôpital de la Faculté, Velpeau was surgeon successively to the Hôpital S.Antoine (1828), la Pitié (1830), and the Charité (1834). He wrote much and was a man of unflagging energy. His best known book was on diseases of the breast (1854). He also wrote on obstetrics (1835) in which he had a practice almost as extensive as that in surgery.

VENAE CAVAE. The two main venous channels which return blood to the right *atrium of the heart, known respectively as the superior vena cava and the inferior vena cava. The former drains venous blood from the head, neck, arms, and chest; the latter from the legs, pelvis, and abdomen. The two vessels enter the right atrium separately.

VENEPUNCTURE. See VENESECTION.

VENEREAL. Transmitted by sexual intercourse. See VENEREOLOGY.

VENEREAL DISEASE. See VENEREOLOGY.

VENEREAL DISEASE ACT 1917. This UK Act was passed to prevent the treatment of venereal disease (defined as *syphilis, *gonorrhoea, and soft chancre or *chancroid) otherwise than by duly qualified medical practitioners, to prohibit advertisements for the treatment of venereal disease, and to control the supply of venereal disease remedies. See also VENEREOLOGY.

VENEREOLOGY

Introduction. Venereology is the specialty of medicine which aims to study and to treat the venereal, or sexually transmitted, diseases. In recent years the field has enlarged, because of the realization that there are many conditions which are sexually transmissible, but which are not classified as venereal by existing laws or regulations, and which vary from country to country. In the UK, since 1970, the term *genitourinary medicine has come into use to describe the specialty. There is nothing new in that expression. It was mooted by Sir William *Osler when giving evidence to the Royal Commission on Venereal Diseases (1914).

In the UK since that Commission reported its findings in 1916, enacted in 1917, there have been specialists practising in venereology. Although a few doctors devoted much of their work to this field in the period between the two World Wars, it was not until the advent of the *National Health Service that many more devoted all their time to the subject. The situation, however, is very different in other countries. In continental Europe, venereology is a sub-specialty of *dermatology, dermatovenereology. In some other countries its practice is even more fragmented. Urologists treat men who have a *urethral discharge. Gynaecologists treat the female patient. Dermatologists treat many of the skin manifestations of sexually transmitted diseases. Elsewhere, notably in parts of the USA, venereology is considered to fall within the scope of the practice of *infectious disease.

Origins and development. There are records of venereal disease, most notably *gonorrhoea, from earliest times. Only with the development of the city and the concept of travel, be it in the context of war, commerce, or expedition, can it be said that there has been some practice of venereology. Gonorrhoea is mentioned by the ancient Egyptians, being described in the papyrus discovered by *Ebers. It is mentioned in the Old Testament in Leviticus 15:2–33: 'the man who has a running of the reins is unclean. And he must still be considered unclean, even though his defilement, at certain times, dries up and causes a stoppage' (Knox translation). The Greek and Roman writers, notably Herodotus, *Celsus, and *Galen, described gonorrhoea and its sequelae. In the Middle Ages *Avicenna of Baghdad wrote at length on urethral discharge recommending *irrigations. Moses *Maimonides of Cordoba aptly described gonorrhoea, being fluid escaping without erection or feeling of pleasure, doughy, and the result of disease including amorousness and excesses. By that time complications of gonorrhoea such as epididymo-orchitis were recognized. The infectiousness of gonorrhoea was realized and records note measures taken by civic authorities to control it both in cities abroad such as in Avignon (1347), and in London from the 12th c. onwards. In London the Winchester Stews (brothels) under the jurisdiction of the Bishop of Winchester at Southwark were to be notorious for 500 years.

*Scabies and *louse infestation was also recognized very early, although the concept of different causes for skin disease has developed only in the last 300 years. Genital warts, *condylomata acuminata, venereally acquired, have been recognized for 2000 years. Anal warts as a result of *sodomy were exemplified by Juvenal in his satires. Much later they were described by the Restoration surgeon Richard *Wiseman (1676) and the French physician John Astruc (1736).

*Syphilis is among the most interesting of diseases from a historical standpoint, not only because of arguments about its origin, but because of its influence on morality and measures towards public health and hygiene. There are conflicting views as to its origin in Europe. The pre-Columbian (Europeanist) theory is that syphilis was somehow endemic in Europe throughout the Middle Ages, becoming pandemic at the end of the 15th c. and venereally acquired. The Columbian (Americanist) theory is that in 1493 after the return of Christopher Columbus from the New World to Spain, his sailors brought back with them this new disease. Another idea is the Unitarian theory of Hudson (1946). *Yaws, a treponemal infection, is widespread in Equatorial regions. It has many similarities in its manifestations to syphilis. Hudson emphasized the evolutionary relationship of yaws, *pinta, endemic syphilis, and sporadic syphilis, regarding them all as varieties of one disease, caused by one parasite, *Treponema pallidum*. This concept considers sub-Saharan Africa to be the area where treponematosis originated. Whatever the origin of syphilis, its passage was well described after the siege of Naples (1495) and the disbandment of mercenaries throughout Europe. Public health edicts against the disease stemmed from that time. One such was at Nuremberg (1496), which inspired the celebrated drawing by Dürer of a syphilitic man (Fig. 1). Physicians, most notably the Italians such as Torella, very soon described the signs and symptoms of early syphilis as well as realizing the concept of congenital syphilis. From its first epidemic ravages, treatment for syphilis had been by inunction with mercury ointment (unguentum Saracenicum). Preparations of *mercury had long been in favour for the treatment of skin diseases. They had been used for this purpose by the Arabian physicians *Rhazes and *Avicenna in the 10th c. Mercury was also given in pill form, by inhalation and fumigation, and much later in the 19th c. by hypodermic injection. Among the many references to syphilis in Shakespeare is one to fumigation which was car-

Fig. 1. The earliest known portrayal of the eruption of secondary syphilis in a European cavalier, by Dürer. Prepared as an illustration for Theodoricus Ulsenius' Broadsheet of 1 August 1496. (Reproduced from *Graphishe und Typographische, Erstlinge der Syphilisliteratur aus den Jahren 1495 und 1496*, Munich, 1912)

ried out in the sweating tub, the patients often being confined for this purpose to the 'spital', the equivalent of the later lock-hospital, and the successor to the old lazar house. In *Henry V* (II, i), Pistol tells us that Doll Tearsheet is in 'the powd'ring tub of infamy', and that ' . . . my Nell is dead, the spital of malady of France' (V, i). In 1537 Barbarossa hearing that Francis I of France had acquired syphilis, sent him as a chivalrous gesture from one enemy in trouble to another, a present of mercury pills.

Guaiacum, an organic substance derived from a South American tree, was introduced as an alternative treatment. It was imported into Europe by the mercantile house of Fugger of Augsburg. Its most celebrated advocates were *Falloppius (1564) and *Fernel (1579), the latter maintaining that nearly all the late symptoms of syphilis were really due to mercury poisoning. The dread of mercury was such that guaiacum was kept in the *pharmacopoeia for 400 years, together with two other drugs used in treatment, sarsaparilla and sassafras.

It must of course be realized that early descriptions call syphilis the Great Pox or Morbus Gallicus, the French disease, or in that country the Neapolitan disease or Spanish disease. Jacques de Bethencourt of Rouen was the first to use the term venereal disease (lues venerea) in 1527. In 1530 Girolamo *Fracastoro of Verona wrote the celebrated poem 'Syphilus sive morbus gallicus'. Syphilus, a swineherd, was smitten when he refused to make sacrifices to Apollo. Syphilis must be the only disease to be named after an imaginary person in a poem. The term was not used in English literature until 1686 when the poet laureate Nahum Tate translated the work of Fracastoro. The first mention in English medical writing was the work of the surgeon-dermatologist Daniel Turner on *Syphilis* (1717).

Although in modern times gonorrhoea and syphilis have been regarded as different diseases this has not always been so. The confusion between syphilis and gonorrhoea seems to have been compounded during the first part of the 16th c. by *Paracelsus (von Hohenheim), who called Morbus Gallicus French gonorrhoea, dividing the disease into simple gonorrhoea and virulent gonorrhoea which developed constitutional symptoms. For the next 300 years until the final proof of their difference by the French physician Philippe *Ricord (1838), the medical world was split into two on the pathology of venereal diseases. There were monists, such as the celebrated 17th c. English physician Thomas *Sydenham, who believed syphilis and gonorrhoea were one and the same disease, and dualists who stuck out for there being two distinct conditions. The frequent association of gonorrhoea with syphilis as well as the discharge due to a urethral *chancre doubtless explains the tendency of the old writers to regard 'clap' as the early stage and syphilis the late stage of 'the pox', a view idealized by Pope, 'Time that at last matures a clap to pox'.

To understand the development of venereology an appreciation of important discoveries and progress in the field in the last 400 years is required. It must also be understood how progress is part of the heritage of the general body of European medicine.

In his posthumous work Falloppius (1564) described the indurated primary penile sore of syphilis as being typical of that disease. He also differentiated between condylomata lata (syphilitic) and condylomata acuminata (genital warts). He was a protagonist of the *condom as a form of *prophylaxis against venereal disease. He advised those in need to carry one at all times. Fernel (1579) added to the corpus of knowledge by stating that the 'virus' of the disease could not pass through intact skin. After Fallopius and Fernel there was a long period in the history of syphilis in the 17th c. during which nothing of special merit occurred. *Lancisi posthumously (1728) correlated dilatation of the heart with syphilis 'aneurysma gallicum'. In the same year the great innovative physician *Boerhaave of Leiden implicated syphilis as a cause of cardiovascular disease. In 1736 Jean Astruc, physician to Louis XV, summarized the whole corpus of knowledge on venereal disease to that time, in the most comprehensive and scholarly work on the subject yet written. He argued strongly for the American origin of the disease but at the same time shared the current belief that gonorrhoea and syphilis were two stages of the same venereal disease. Among his descriptions of minor conditions is an accurate one of *genital herpes. Van *Swieten, a pupil of Boerhaave, reinvigorated the teaching and practice of medicine in Vienna after 1749 and popularized more liberal treatment of syphilitics as well as the introduction of graduated dosage with mercury in its treatment, thus preventing troublesome sideeffects such as over-salivation (ptyalism), the 'shakes' (tremor), and renal disease.

In London, with the growth of the voluntary hospitals and their policy of exclusion of patients with venereal disease, there was obviously a need for facilities for treatment of the malady. In 1746 William Bromfield, a surgeon of *St George's Hospital, launched a philanthropic campaign which led to the foundation of the London Lock Hospital near Hyde Park Corner. This was the principal institution in the Metropolis for the treatment of venereal disease and was not to be closed, by which time it had been resited, until the advent of the *National Health Service in 1948. Later smaller so-called 'lock' hospitals (specifically for venereal disease) were founded in principal provincial cities. Almost every major continental city had special hospitals for the treatment of syphilis by the middle of the 18th c.

John *Hunter's book of 1786 *A Treatise on the Venereal Disease*, although notable for scientific objectivity, is not one of his greatest works, but such was his eminence that perhaps more importance has been attached to it than would have been the case with a lesser man. He described the venereal *sore characterized by indolent *induration, though that was nothing new. It is still to this day named after him, but he failed to appreciate soft sore (*chancroid). He also failed to appreciate the contagiousness of secondary syphilis. This view was also later held by Ricord. Hunter's most important error was, however, adhesion to the monist doctrine. It has until recently been thought that in the celebrated experiment in 1767, Hunter, to prove the view of the single identity of gonorrhoea and syphilis, inoculated himself with matter of gonorrhoea on to his prepuce and glans. Unfortunately he chose the inoculum from a patient suffering from syphilis *and* gonorrhoea, after which he further strengthened his single identity view. Two modern commentators, Qvist and Dempster, state that the experiment is described in the third person and they argue that there are reasons for believing the experiment was done on a patient. Hunter thought that the only difference between the two diseases depended on the nature of the surface to which the poison was applied, that it caused *ulceration when it acted on a cutaneous surface but only a purulent discharge without breach of surface, when applied to a mucous membrane.

In Edinburgh, Benjamin Bell (1793) in *A Treatise on Gonorrhoea Virulenta and Lues Venerea*, following work of *Morgagni and Francis Balfour, opposed the unity theory and presented strong arguments for the duality theory. A major point was that syphilis required mercury for a cure, whereas gonorrhoea did not. He observed that the symptoms and consequences of the two diseases were different, that gonorrhoea was a local disease while syphilis was not. He noted that the inoculation of gonorrhoea and syphilis between persons rarely produced the other disease and that even in severe cases of gonorrhoea no lues ensued and that no stage of pox had ever produced gonorrhoea. Bell carried out experiments on medical students to prove his arguments. The ethics of endangering the lives of his students may be questioned and it was left to Philippe Ricord in Paris in 1838 to show conclusively, by experiments on 667 mental hospital patients, that gonorrhoea and syphilis were different diseases. Ricord also classified syphilis into three stages, primary, secondary, and tertiary. He was the founder of a remarkable school of venereology in France in the 19th c.

That many doctors in the UK in the period between Bell and Ricord still accepted the old doctrine is shown by the warning which Sir Astley *Cooper gave in his lectures on venereal disease at *St Thomas's Hospital, which were published in the *Lancet* in 1824. He declared that 'a man who gives mercury in gonorrhoea deserves to be flogged out of the profession because he must be quite ignorant of the principle in which the disease is cured'.

Emphasis on the dangers of mercury, which meant that some surgeons forbade its use, led to a search for other drugs. Robert Williams of St Thomas's had used potassium iodide in secondary syphilis from 1831, but it was left to William Wallace of Dublin in 1835 to popularize its use in tertiary syphilis. The ethical standards of that time are again illustrated by the fact that Wallace deliberately inoculated his healthy out-patients from the secondary eruptions of syphilitic cases in order to prove that Ricord was wrong in teaching that secondary lesions were not infectious. Ricord refused to be convinced. Just at that time Wallace engaged in a dispute over priority with his Dublin colleague Abraham *Colles, who stated in his book *Practical Observations on the Venereal Disease* (1837) the principle later known as Colles's Law, that is 'that a syphilitic child cannot infect the mother'.

In the early 19th c., the recognition of the importance of other sexually transmitted diseases was also emerging. Thomas *Bateman (1814) in the fourth edition of *A Practical Synopsis of Cutaneous Disease* described herpes praeputalis (genitalis): 'It occurs in a situation where it is liable to occasion a practical mistake of serious consequence to the patient. The progress of the herpetic clusters when seated on the prepuce so closely resembles that of chancre, that it may be doubted whether it has not been frequently confounded with the latter.' He described the prodromal itching, formation, and breakdown of vesicles, 'so to the inaccurate or inexperienced observer, it may be readily mistaken for a chancre'. A later commentator, Jonathan *Hutchinson (1887), noted 'that once they had occurred once, they are very prone to occur again'.

Benjamin *Brodie of St George's Hospital in 1818 in his textbook on diseases of the joints, described what is now considered to be *Reiter's syndrome. His case was a man aged 45 with urethral discharge, fever, recurrent joint swellings, and *conjunctivitis. He mentioned similar cases he had seen in practice at that time, as did later Astley Cooper in 1824. Donné in Paris (1836), an ardent advocate of the use of the *microscope in medicine, using that instrument was able to describe in 1836 *Trichomonas vaginalis* (see TRICHOMONIASIS), mistakenly thinking at first that it was the causal agent of gonorrhoea.

Venereological progress can be made only within the framework of medicine as a whole and the 19th c. in its own way brought some enormous advances in the subject. After the reforms of Napoleon, the Paris medical school was to bring forward some of the most important changes in the first 40 years of the 19th c., out of which flowed the important contributions to dermatovenereology by such men as *Alibert, Ricord, and later *Fournier. Then from about 1840 under the leadership of *Skoda and *Rokitansky the Vienna medical school became the foremost in central Europe. The dermatological reforms under *Hebra, as a classifier of skin disease on the basis of underlying pathology, were to have an impact that influenced dermatovenereology in all the German-speaking countries for the next hundred years. Later, from about 1860 onwards the era of scientific medicine using laboratory techniques such as microscopy and the disciplines of *microbiology, *serology, *immunology, and inorganic chemistry, was to lead on to the advances which brought about the recognition of causal agents for syphilis, gonorrhoea, and serological tests and a cure for the former.

The first appointment of Hebra was to the lowly post in charge of *Krätzestation* (scabies station). By repeated findings of the *mite using the microscope and by auto-inoculation ('I was plagued by a strong itch that spread over my entire body'), he was able to show conclusively in 1844 that the mite was the cause of scabies. Under the guidance of Hebra a syphilis clinic was started in Vienna under the care of Sigmund von Ilanor, a refuter of the unitarian views on venereal disease, among other conceptions recognizing the dangers of gonococcal infection in both sexes, a new idea at that time.

In 1852 Bassereau, one of Ricord's pupils, exemplified soft sore (chancroid). It was definitely differentiated from syphilis in 1854 by Clerc, who showed the difference between the two diseases by a series of inoculation experiments. It was not until 1888 that Augusto *Ducrey was able to demonstrate the causal organism for chancroid (*Haemophilus ducreyi*).

The development of the recognition of chancroid led to a curious line of treatment called syphilization. Auzias Turenne about 1850 believed that repeated inoculations of matter from soft sore rendered patients less susceptible to syphilis. In 1865 it was tried out in the London Lock Hospital, but British surgeons decided very quickly that the remedy was worse than the disease it was intended to cure.

As could be expected, with growing industrialization, and poverty, slums, and overcrowding in cities, syphilis formed a substantial proportion of 19th c. medical practice. At St Bartholomew's Hospital, Sir James *Paget (1879) reckoned that his out-patients included about 48 per cent of venereal cases. There were no national *morbidity figures, but those that were available for the army and navy support this figure. In 1864 the government passed the euphemistically named Contagious Diseases Act, amended in 1867 and 1869, requiring the compulsory medical examination of all prostitutes in towns and seaports where army or navy personnel were housed. Syphilis had always been prevalent in the navy. Thomas Trotter, at the end of the 18th c., had obtained the abolition of the rule whereby a seaman who was found to be infected was fined two weeks' pay. Naturally this had led to concealment and to the spread of disease. By 1886, when the Contagious Diseases Act was repealed through the campaign against it led by Josephine Butler, the rate of infection in the services had been reduced to 27.5 per cent and by 1900 it was down to about 10 per cent.

Congenital syphilis had been recognized since the first epidemic manifestations of the new disease at the end of the 15th c. In 1854 Diday codified the whole of knowledge of congenital syphilis up to that time with descriptions of clinical features and discussions on prognosis and therapy. He advocated treatment of the apparently healthy child born to syphilitic parents. Between 1857 and 1863 Jonathan Hutchinson of the *London Hospital described in detail in several journals all the entities now known as *Hutchinson's triad (interstitial keratitis in the cornea, eighth cranial nerve deafness, and Hutchinson's teeth (notching of the incisors both in the juvenile and adult dentitions)), important signs of established congenital syphilis.

From the time of Boerhaave it had been realized that syphilis had an effect on the constitution, especially the *central nervous system. Moritz *Romberg (1846) had accurately described *tabes dorsalis but its aetiology was still unknown. As late as 1869 the eminent French neurologist *Charcot, although describing tabetic *arthropathy in

*locomotor ataxia, stated that syphilis had nothing to do with the disease. It was left to Alfred Fournier, the successor of Ricord, in 1875 to propose that syphilis was a cause of the symptoms of paralysis, motor incoordination and progressive locomotor ataxia. Fournier formed the concept of parasyphilis, 'those diseases of which syphilis is essentially the cause, but which are not directly the result of the syphilitic virus, namely general paralysis, tabes dorsalis, taboparesis, and primary optic atrophy'. Fournier was the chief exponent of the school of venereology of Paris of the late 19th c. He realized the dangers of syphilis, which often at first had few clinical signs in women, and the subsequent danger to the child of congenital syphilis. He was an excellent teacher, encouraging training not only of postgraduates but of undergraduates in venereal diseases. He was an advocate of the view that the intelligent lay public should also be informed about these diseases. He was the instigator of a new idea, for those days, of international co-operation as a policy for the prophylaxis of venereal disease. International conferences on the subject were held at Brussels in 1899 and 1902.

The treatment of venereal diseases in the UK for most of the 19th c. was in the hands of surgeons. Such was Hunter's influence that even after Ricord had differentiated gonorrhoea from syphilis in 1838 his views took a long time to be accepted by some surgeons. As late as 1876 one surgeon at the London Lock Hospital stated there was no such thing as a specific gonorrhoeal poison. It was not until 1879 that one microbe for the disease was generally accepted. Then Albert *Neisser, working as an assistant in the dermatology section at Breslau, using *Koch's staining methods, conclusively described the causal agent of gonorrhoea. Progress in the field of diagnosis and treatment of gonorrhoea succeeded quickly after Neisser's discovery. In 1881 *Credé of Leipzig introduced instillation of silver nitrate drops into the eyes of the newborn to prevent gonococcal ophthalmia neonatorum, in those days a common cause of blindness in infants. The gonococcus was grown in culture by Leistikow (1882) and Bumm (1885) and *Gram's stain (1884) brought a reliable staining technique into the microscopical diagnosis of gonorrhoea. In 1888 Ernest Finger of Vienna summarized the total knowledge on gonorrhoea till that time, especially focusing upon the importance of the disease in women. For about 100 years several commentators had noticed *urethritis which did not seem like gonorrhoea in its true sense. In 1907 Halberstaedter and *Prowazek found inclusions in the eye in infants with neonatal conjunctivitis and then from genital discharge in their mothers. Lindner (1909) in Vienna advanced knowledge into the aetiology of non-gonococcal urethritis when he demonstrated initial bodies and elementary bodies morphologically indistinguishable from those seen in inclusion conjunctivitis in urethral discharge.

Thus by the beginning of the 20th c. the realization of the aetiology of gonorrhoea and non-gonococcal urethritis was well under way. In the case of the latter it was to take 50 years before the entity of non-gonococcal urethritis was appreciated.

In the last 50 years of the 19th c. enormous progress was made in clinical observations on syphilis, not only by doctors who spent most of their time in venereology, such as Hutchinson in London, Fournier in Paris, von Baerensprung in Berlin, and Sigmund and Isidor Neumann in Vienna, but by physicians who were taking over from surgeons an interest in the systemic aspects of syphilis, such as Hughlings *Jackson, *Wilks, and *Gowers in London. New scientific methods were to come to the aid of knowledge of syphilis and to bring it out of an era merely of clinical observation to one of exact diagnosis and rational treatment.

Between 1875 and 1877 Edwin *Klebs of Prague had observed *spirochaetes in human syphilitic material, probably also transmitting the disease to monkeys. Experimental syphilis was reborn, when in 1903 *Metchnikoff and *Roux showed that syphilis could be consistently transmitted to chimpanzees. Fritz *Schaudinn, a protozoologist, collaborated with Erich Hoffmann, a dermatologist, in examining specimens of preparations of primary and secondary syphilis stained with aniline dye. On 3 March 1905 in the women's section of the dermatological clinic of the *Charité in Berlin, Schaudinn was able to demonstrate spirochaetes in one of Hoffmann's slides. The specimen was taken from a papule of the right *labia in a 25-year-old with secondary syphilis. The recognition of the spiral organism responsible for syphilis, Treponema pallidum, one of the group of spirochaetes, was more easily demonstrated in 1906 when *Landsteiner and Mucha were able to recognize it by dark field methods. The method is still in use today (see MICROSCOPE). In 1913 *Noguchi and Moore using a silver staining method were able to demonstrate Treponema pallidum in the brains from 12 patients with *general paralysis of the insane, thus proving definitely its causation.

Immunology had come into its own in the latter years of the 19th c. *Bordet and *Gengou (1901) had described the *complement fixation test, by means of which an infection could be diagnosed by finding its *antibody in the *serum. *Wassermann (1906) in Berlin, using a crude extract of the liver of an infant who had died from congenital syphilis, was able to show the value of the complement fixation test in the diagnosis of syphilis. It was not, however, till 1907 that Landsteiner and Müller in Vienna were able to explain the principles underlying the *Wassermann reaction. Over the next 40 years many different serological tests for syphilis were devised. It was not until the early 1940s that it was fully realized that many diseases could be responsible for a positive Wassermann reaction. The introduction of the first test for specific antibody, the *treponemal immobilization test by Nelson and Mayer in 1949, inaugurated an era of more accurate serological diagnosis.

From the first epidemic manifestations of syphilis at the end of the 15th c., the armamentarium of treatment had mainly depended on mercury, which at the most has a very weak treponemicidal activity in vivo. Iodides had been used especially in gummatous syphilis from 1836 onwards. In 1891 Paul *Ehrlich reported the successful treatment of malaria with methylene blue. From 1904 until his death in 1915, he worked continuously to produce synthetic agents which would cure infections. His work showed arsenicals to be promising, especially in trypanosomal infections. In 1907 Ehrlich patented the 606th compound synthesized, which was named *salvarsan, later arsphenamine. By 1909 it was found to be largely effective in syphilis in animals and in the spring of 1910 Ehrlich announced that arsphenamine could cure syphilis in humans. As could be imagined, Ehrlich was besieged by requests from all over the world for his magic bullet, therapeutica magnans. To his credit Ehrlich refused to supply the drug unless the recipient was a trained syphilologist and had adequate laboratory and clinical facilities.

In 1887 *Wagner-Jauregg had suggested that therapeutically induced fever might be useful in the treatment of psychotic patients. *Malaria and *erysipelas were suggested, but the latter proved unsatisfactory. In 1912 satisfactory results for treating paresis with mercury iodide combined with Koch's old *tuberculin were published. It was not until 1917, while looking after soldiers invalided from the Balkans, that the idea of malaria therapy was revived. A soldier with malaria had been accidentally admitted to one of Wagner-Jauregg's beds. Instead of being given quinine straight away, drops of his malarial blood were scarified into the skin of three paretic patients; the successful results were published in 1921. Malaria therapy became the main method of treating general paralysis of the insane until it was superseded by *penicillin 25 years later.

Although not as active as arsenicals, *bismuth, first suggested for its use in syphilis in the 19th c., was tried out and found to be effective by Sazerac and Levaditi in 1922. Until the advent of penicillin the alternative use of arsenicals and bismuth became a popular mode of treatment of syphilis. Bismuth is hardly ever used nowadays.

After the discovery in 1932 by *Domagk that the azo-dye, *prontosil, could protect mice from death due to *streptococcal septicaemia, the *sulphonamides were rapidly developed. They were soon successfully used in the treatment of gonorrhoea which, however, became resistant to sulphonamides in the latter part of the Second World War, luckily at just about the time penicillin was being developed. The use of penicillin in the effective treatment of syphilis was first reported by Mahoney and his co-workers from the USA in 1943. Forty years on, penicillin remains the main drug in the treatment of syphilis. Unfortunately certain strains of gonococci have shown growing resistance to penicillin. To the present the *pharmaceutical industry's endeavours in producing new preparations of other *antibiotics effective for more resistant strains of gonorrhoea have, however, been successful: to name some, an *aminoglycoside, spectinomycin, and the more recent *cephalosporins such as cefuroxime, cefotaxime, and ceftriaxone. The use of penicillin and the advent of other antimicrobials in recent years has altered the concept of control of venereal diseases, not the least in the attitudes of the public to those once taboo infections. It must, however, be realized that there are still no effective cures for some of the virally transmitted sexually transmitted diseases, such as herpes genitalis or ubiquitous genital warts. An effective vaccine for *hepatitis B, often sexually transmitted, especially in homosexuals, has brought new hope for the control of that viral sexually transmitted disease. A cure for genital herpes may be found in steady progress towards developing an effective vaccine for it.

The more common sexually transmitted diseases, after a list compiled by the *World Health Organization (report of a WHO Consultative Group, Geneva, 16–19 November 1982).

World-wide
1. *Gonorrhoea.*
Cause: *Neisseria gonorrhoeae.* This may cause uncomplicated urogenital infection in both sexes. In addition, especially after homosexual activity or oropharyngeal contact, there may be rectal and pharyngeal infections, respectively. If left untreated in the male, epididymo-orchitis and prostatitis may result, and in the female, pelvic inflammatory disease may occur, with resultant sterility. Disseminated infection may occur infrequently with variable skin, joint, and blood spread manifestations. Adult conjunctivitis is rare in developed countries, but commoner in under-developed countries where spread may be via *fomites. An untreated mother may give rise to a baby born with neonatal conjunctivitis. Prepubertal girls may occasionally contract a vulvovaginitis due to gonorrhoea. In the last 10 years, various strains of *N. gonorrhoeae* have developed which are completely resistant to penicillin and to some other antibiotics; many of them produce penicillinase, an *enzyme which destroys penicillin. These originated in West Africa, and South-East Asia, but are now found throughout the world.
Treatment: uncomplicated infections:
(i) penicillin-sensitive strains: penicillin and its analogues and *probenecid in high doses by mouth or intramuscular injection; alternatively, *tetracycline may be used.
(ii) penicillin-resistant strains: spectinomycin, cefotaxime, cefuroxime, or ceftriaxone by injection. Rectal, pharyngeal and systemic infections usually require more prolonged courses of treatment with the appropriate antibiotics.
2. *Non-specific genital infection.* (The name often used synonymously with non-gonococcal urethritis, non-specific urethritis.)
Cause: in 30–60 per cent of cases, *Chlamydia trachomatis,* other organisms implicated being *Ureaplasma urealyticum* and *Mycoplasma hominis.* May cause non-gonococcal urethritis, post-gonococcal urethritis, epididymitis, proctitis, cervicitis, infection of Bartholin's ducts, salpingitis, perihepatitis.
Infrequently in males, mostly after a urethritis, Reiter's syndrome may occur with associated arthritis, and conjunctivitis and other variable manifestations.
Treatment: tetracycline, or doxycycline by mouth for at least 7 days. If tetracyclines are contraindicated erythromycin and sulphonamides are needed for at least 7 days.
3. *Syphilis*
Cause: *Treponema pallidum*
(i) Early infections: the primary stage gives rise to sore, chancre with regional lymphadenopathy at site of inoculation, genitals, ano-rectum, mouth, pharynx; the secondary stage gives rise to systemic manifestations, especially skin rashes.
(ii) Early latent: latent of not more than 2 years' duration.
(iii) Latent: no manifestations but specific serological tests for syphilis positive.
(iv) Late syphilis (tertiary or late syphilis): may lead on to cardiovascular, neurological, and systemic complications.
(v) Congenital syphilis: acquired infection of the newborn from an untreated mother.
Treatment: according to stage, but generally with benzathine penicillin or procaine penicillin by injection in varying dosages. If the patient is allergic to penicillin, tetracycline, doxycycline, or erythromycin by mouth in prolonged courses of treatment. Follow-up after treatment necessary. Contact tracing of sexual contacts in early syphilis essential.
4. *Genital herpes simplex virus infections*
Cause: herpes simplex virus (Types II and I). Genital herpes infection is a viral disease that may be chronic and recurring. Symptoms are variable, starting with a small *blister (vesicle) and leading on to recurrent small genital sores. There may be systemic complications. There is a potential, more than a real, danger to the child born to a pregnant women who has had herpes genitalis. Her clinical attendants should be informed of her history. It is thought that there may be an increased risk of *carcinoma of the *cervix in certain circumstances following herpetic infection of the cervix.
Treatment: as yet no totally effective therapy. *Acyclovir—a new antiviral agent—may help in a particular event, but does not cure for ever.
5. *Venereal warts (condylomata acuminata)*
Cause: genital wart virus. Soft infectious warts may occur in the anogenital region after sexual contact with persons also infected with genital warts. Recently anogenital warts very occasionally have been linked to the development of cancer.

Atypical warts should be biopsied. Cervical cytology should be performed in women with genital warts.

Treatment: tincture of podophyllin, an organic substance, applied to the warts. Other alternatives are cryotherapy, using liquid nitrogen or solid carbon dioxide, electrosurgery, or surgical removal.

6. Molluscum contagiosum

Cause: a pox virus. This is not infrequently found in the genital region. Small horny papules, which may be mistaken for warts, are found in groups.

Treatment: by simple removal using varying techniques.

7. Trichomoniasis

Cause: Trichomonas vaginalis, a protozoon. This causes an unpleasant vaginal discharge. Men are symptomless carriers.

Treatment: with *metronidazole for the patient and her sexual partners.

8. Non-specific vaginitis (Gardnerella vaginalis)

Cause: Gardnerella, Haemophilus vaginalis, and various anerobic organisms. This may cause variable vaginal discharge. Its role is, however, still uncertain.

Treatment: with metronidazole for the patient and her sexual partners.

9. Genital candidiasis (thrush)

Cause: Candida albicans. This is a common disorder caused by a yeast C. albicans, which is often found on the skin and in the intestines and symptomless carriage is reported in the vagina. It may be associated with other systemic disease, especially in recurrent cases. It may occur after antibiotic treatment for other conditions. It is not a venereal disease, but as it may present with genital symptoms is included in this list for completeness. It commonly occurs: (i) in women, when it may present with a vaginitis; (ii) in men, when it may present with a balanoposthitis, inflammation of the glans and prepuce.

Treatment: with intravaginal pessaries or creams. Effective therapy can be with an antibiotic—*nystatin or newer synthetic imidazole derivatives such as clotrimazole or miconazole. Genital candidiasis usually does not require systemic treatment.

10. Skin parasite infections, sexually transmissible

(i) Scabies

Cause: a mite Sarcoptes scabiei. This causes an itchy rash. It is passed on by close body contact, which may include coitus.

Treatment: with benzyl benzoate or 1 per cent gamma benzene hexachloride lotions to the body. Close contacts should be treated.

(ii) Pediculosis pubis (vulgarly 'crabs')

Cause: a louse, Pediculosis pubis. This makes the patient itch. It may be found in the anogenital area and also in pubic, abdominal, and axillary hair.

Treatment: similar to that for scabies.

Tropical sexually transmitted diseases. These diseases are more commonly found in the tropics (see TROPICAL MEDICINE). Travellers may occasionally bring them back to more temperate latitudes. Recently chancroid has recurred in some industrial nations of Europe and in the USA and Canada.

1. *Lymphogranuloma venereum

Cause: Lymphogranuloma venereum (LGV), serotype of Chlamydia trachomatis. After an initial transient genital lesion, inguinal adenitis occurs followed by various constitutional symptoms. There may be late complications resulting from fibrotic changes occurring to the lymph drainage from the genitals.

Treatment: by prolonged courses of tetracycline or sulphonamides. In addition, surgical intervention may be needed for late cases.

2. Chancroid

Cause: Ducrey's bacillus (Haemophilus ducreyi). This may cause painful genital sores which lead on to inguinal *buboes (swellings with *abscess formation in the groins). It must be differentiated from syphilis, genital herpes, and granuloma inguinale.

Treatment: by co-trimoxazole, tetracyclines, or erythromycin by mouth. Trials suggest kanamycin by injection may be useful.

3. Donovanosis (Granuloma inguinale)

Cause: Calymmatabacterium granulomatis (Donovan body)—a bacterium. This disease was first described by tropical medicine specialists at the turn of the 20th c. in the Indian Medical Service. Ulcerating enlarging granulating sores leading to inguinal pseudo-buboes occur.

Treatment: by tetracycline or *chloramphenicol by mouth or streptomycin by injection.

Other diseases in which a sexually transmissible organism (and route) has been implicated

1. Bacteria

Listeria monocytogenes: disease in the fetus and neonate.

Campylobacter fetus: known as a cause of abortion in cattle; disease recently reported in women and neonates.

Group B Streptococcus: commonly found on genitals of promiscuous heterosexual adults. Only some types may be pathogenic. May lead on to neonatal sepsis.

*Haemophilus influenzae: cause of increasingly frequently recognized neonatal sepsis.

*Escherichia coli
Peptostreptococcus
Bacteroides spp.

All may be responsible, as well as N. gonorrhoeae, C. trachomatis, and M. hominis, for cases of pelvic inflammatory disease.

2. Viruses

*Epstein–Barr virus: cause of glandular fever-like illness in young adults. May be passed on by oral transmission at time of coitus.

*Cytomegalovirus: causes mild glandular fever-like symptoms in young adults. Serious cause of

neonatal congenital infection. Commonly found in USA in groups of homosexual men.

*Hepatitis A: cause of faecally transmitted jaundice, especially in homosexuals.

Hepatitis B: cause of jaundice and chronic ill health, especially in homosexuals. Some may be asymptomatic carriers. Can be prevented by effective vaccine.

*Marburg virus: this has been reported sexually transmitted in the case of a laboratory worker who became contaminated.

Infectious agents commoner in homosexual men, other than hepatitis (infectious causes of the 'gay bowel' syndrome)

Oro-anal contact, and to a lesser extent anogenital contact, as well as digital and manual penetration of the infected anus, may lead on to several diseases which can be caused by pathogens found in the infected intestine. In general the symptoms are those of diarrhoea, loose stools, abdominal cramps, and loss of weight. Appropriate examination of the stools is required. Organisms implicated are

1. *Bacteria*: Shigellosis (*Shigella sonnei* and *Shigella flexneri*); *Salmonella* spp. including *S. typhi; Campylobacter fetus,* subspecies *jejuni.*

2. *Viral*: Viral gastroenteritis is seen to be common in homosexual men. Among the causes are *rotavirus and Norwalk virus. (See below for acquired immune deficiency syndrome (AIDS).)

3. *Protozoal infections*:

(i) *Amoebiasis—*Entamoeba histolytica.* There have been outbreaks in New York, San Francisco, Seattle, and Berlin in recent years.

(ii) Giardiasis—*Giardia lamblia.* Though endemic throughout the world and waterborne, may be found not infrequently in homosexuals after oro-anal exposure.

(iii) Cryptosporidiosis. Established cause of human gastroenteritis, described in homosexual men recently especially in AIDS.

4. *Metazoal infections*:

(i) *Enterobius vermicularis* (pin-worms or *threadworms) commonly sexually transmitted in homosexual men.

(ii) *Strongyloides stercoralis.* Reports would suggest this can also be transmitted after homosexual practices.

Present situation. The first ten years of the 20th c. in the field of venereology were marked by amazing discoveries, all from Germany; the recognition of the spirochaete in 1905, the Wassermann reaction in 1906 and the introduction of salvarsan by Ehrlich in 1909. Because of these events, the very varying treatment facilities for the public within the UK, and the decline in syphilis and gonorrhoea in the services since 1885, with at the same time continued high levels of venereal disease amongst the civilian population, a Royal Commission on Venereal Diseases was set up in 1913. It took into consideration Parliamentary acts concerned with venereal disease since 1864 and

reviewed the prevalence and effects of venereal disease, together with means of alleviation and prevention, with recommendations of action to be taken. A large number of eminent witnesses in the field of venereal diseases, not only from the UK but also Europe, gave evidence and in 1916 its report was published, as the *Final Report of the Commissioners, Royal Commission on Venereal Disease, 1916.* Some startling facts emerged, such as the high mortality from late syphilis. To quote an example of mortality statistics for syphilis, 10 per cent of London working class males were found to be infected. Twenty-five per cent of infantile blindness was found to be due to gonococcal ophthalmia. The cost of chronic morbidity caused by venereal disease was found to be considerable.

Despite the stringencies of the First World War the recommendations of the Commission were embodied in the *Public Health (Venereal Diseases) Regulations* of 1916, in which the councils of counties and county boroughs were instructed to organize the free and confidential treatment of persons suspected to be suffering from venereal disease, at hours convenient to patients. These duties were taken over by the National Health Service in 1948. In 1917, the *Venereal Diseases Act was passed which prohibited under penalty unqualified persons from treating these diseases, and forbade advertisements by persons other than local authorities concerning their treatment or prevention. The same Act defined venereal disease as syphilis, gonorrhoea, and soft sore (chancroid). It is of interest that 25 years later in 1942, when the House of Lords was debating the compulsory treatment of venereal diseases under Defence Regulation 33B (a wartime measure), Lord Snell for the government stated explicitly that government policy at that time was based on the principles laid down by the Royal Commission of 1913–16. These principles were: (i) voluntary attendance for treatment without any system of notification or compulsory powers to secure attendance; (ii) treatment (both out-patient and institutional) should be available to everyone free of charge; (iii) laboratory facilities for diagnosis should be available to all practitioners free of charge; (iv) treatment by unqualified persons should be prohibited; and (v) education of the public should be an essential part of any arrangement for dealing with venereal diseases. (*Official Report,* House of Lords, 8 December 1942.) Forty-four years later these principles cannot be bettered.

From 1942 to 1947 an emergency measure was taken, Defence Regulation 33B, where a *Medical Officer of Health could require a person to be compulsorily examined, and if found to be infected, treated, if reported as being the source of infection by two others. This regulation had some value in wartime with the problem of control of venereal disease among military personnel.

A little-known statutory instrument is the *National Health Service (Venereal Diseases) Regulations 1974.* These reinforce the confidentiality of information with respect to persons examined or treated for any sexually transmitted disease and they also extend the scope of the service so as to include all sexually transmitted diseases, and not only those commonly known as venereal diseases.

From 1917 the clinic system under the control of specialists in venereal diseases was set up; it exists to this day. From 1925, national statistics for syphilis and gonorrhoea, obtained from returns collected throughout the country from clinics, came into being, although many local authorities have figures dating from 1916. From 1951, with increasing recognition of non-gonococcal urethritis, now called non-specific genital infection, figures have also been obtained for that disease. From 1971, figures have also been received for a variety of minor sexually transmissible infections, trichomoniasis, candidiasis, scabies, pediculosis pubis, herpes genitalis, genital warts, and genital molluscum contagiosum. Figures are also obtained for patients with non-venereal treponematosis, other conditions (often minor genital problems) requiring treatment at centres, and patients seen and examined but not found to have any disease, as well as patients referred to other hospital departments.

The Medical Society for the Study of Venereal Diseases was founded in 1922. It holds six meetings a year, five in London and one alternately in the provinces or abroad. It acts as a forum for discussion and liaison between venereologists and dissemination of recent advances in the subject. It has about 550 members, one-third living overseas. In recent years the Society has convened annually a seminar for postgraduate study for young doctors working in the specialty. The *British Journal of Venereal Diseases* (renamed *Genitourinary Medicine* in 1985), founded by the Medical Society for the Study of Venereal Diseases, is published six times a year and is the foremost journal of its kind in the world for the advancement of new knowledge and the results of research specifically in the field of venereal diseases and allied disorders.

Other countries such as the USA, Scandinavia, Holland, India, Australia, and New Zealand also have societies for the study of sexually transmitted diseases. In some European countries the professional organizations for the study of venereal diseases are combined with national societies for the study of dermatovenereology. The American Venereal Disease Association publishes *Sexually Transmitted Diseases,* a journal printed quarterly and gaining in importance. Many recent advances in the field are disseminated in journals devoted to general aspects of medicine, and much research applied to genitourinary medicine, as would be expected, has come from outside the specialty, especially in recent years from microbiology, virology, immunology, epidemiology, public health, and applied pharmacology.

It is implicit from the recommendations of 1916, that a prospective patient in venereology can seek medical attention from a specialist venereologist without being referred from his general practitioner, unlike the principle within the UK governing all other consultations in medicine. Nevertheless a certain number of patients are referred from general practitioners and close liaison between the hospital-based venereologist and his general practitioner colleagues is to be welcomed and encouraged. Clinics for the treatment of sexually transmitted disease are available throughout the UK in most of the larger centres of population. Even so, authorities far too frequently have been tardy in funding. Seventy years after the Royal Commission, some of the facilities and staffing arrangements are unfortunately not designed to encourage patients to attend. All the teaching hospitals in the UK have departments of genitourinary medicine (venereology). Instruction in the subject is given to undergraduates and postgraduates by consultants and junior doctors (registrars) specializing in the subject. In all the larger centres there are two or more consultants in genitourinary medicine. It is not felt by the specialty in the UK that there is a place for consultants who combine venereology with some other branch of medicine, be it dermatology or infectious diseases or general medicine.

In 1978 a professorial chair of genitourinary medicine was established at the *Middlesex Hospital Medical School, the first incumbent being M. W. Adler. This post, it is hoped, will be of importance in raising the academic standards in the subject and is already stimulating research and epidemiological studies in the field. The specialty has realized the need for entrants in the subject to have adequate postgraduate training in internal medicine. Membership of the Royal College of Physicians is the preferred mode of entry for training in the specialty, but other higher qualifications such as membership of the Royal College of Obstetricians and Gynaecologists, provided that there is enough internal medical experience, are acceptable.

Two postgraduate courses in venereology have been instituted in the UK, at Liverpool in 1967 and London in 1974. They are mainly to train future specialists from overseas but young British postgraduates in the subject may attend in a part-time capacity. Examinations take place at the end of the course, the successful candidates being granted a diploma.

No clinic for the treatment of venereal diseases can be run successfully unless there is locally adequate funding for equipment, nursing, and clerical staff. Neither can the service be claimed to be competent unless laboratory facilities are adequate both in the clinic and through those provided by microbiologists, for the very necessary serological and culture tests from specimens taken.

Contact tracing needs to be encouraged. Should a patient be found to have a sexually transmitted disease, adequate steps are taken within the clinic to encourage the patient to contact his or her sexual partners and encourage them to attend for investigation to exclude sexually transmitted disease. At the same time the patient will often need support and simple advice intelligible to the layman of the need for treatment and follow-up to make sure that the disease has been adequately cured. This work is done by a contact tracer. In the UK the contact tracer is called a health adviser in sexually transmitted diseases. Up to the present, entry has been from varying sources, for example health visitors and social workers, but it is hoped that in the future standardization of entry and an adequate training programme will be instituted. Since 1981 the Department of Health and Social Security has organized training courses at two centres in the UK for the adequate instruction of contact tracers and nurses working in the field of contact tracing.

Education of the public on sexually transmitted diseases in the UK, although adequate in some parts of the country, is perhaps not as good as in some other countries, especially Scandinavia and Holland, and needs to be improved.

As already stated, international co-operation between the medical profession in the field of venereology has a long history going back to the last years of the 19th c. The International Union against the Venereal Diseases and Treponematoses was founded in 1923 and meets regularly throughout the world, not only to discuss new advances in this field but to formulate policies and advise governments and international organizations, such as the World Health Organization, about the control of sexually transmitted diseases. In recent years there has been a plethora of international conferences on the subject. One such society holding conferences is the International Society for Sexually Transmitted Disease Research, founded by the co-operation of research workers in Europe and North America in the field of sexually transmitted diseases in the early 1970s. This body has now held five international meetings, its most recent being in Seattle, USA, in 1983. Its emphasis is on research in the field of microbiology and immunology as applied to sexually transmitted diseases. Some of the wealthier developed nations have also seconded researchers in the field of venereal disease to poorer countries, especially in South America, Asia, and Africa.

In the last 30 years there have been enormous changes in human behaviour which affect sexually transmitted disease; the breakdown of family life; migration to urban areas; much greater freedom to travel both in work and for pleasure; the subculture for so-called sexual freedom in the young adult of both sexes, together with improved means of contraception; generally greater prosperity, and with that rising health standards; changing legislation on prostitution throughout the world; freeing of morals and controls on homosexuality. Together with these behavioural changes, there has been increasing knowledge of diseases which can be sexually transmitted and which had not been previously realized, for example *anaerobic infec-

tions of the genital tract in women, and some infections not uncommonly found to be transmitted in homosexuals, such as hepatitis and a variety of enteric diseases. This constellation of various sexually transmitted diseases occurring in homosexual men has been given the phrase 'gay bowel syndrome', a group of anorectal and colon conditions found with unusual frequency in male homosexuals as a result of orogenital, ororectal, and proctogenital sexual contact.

The *acquired immune deficiency syndrome (AIDS) includes highly lethal opportunistic infections and rare malignancies in people with no apparent reason to be immunosuppressed. Cases have been probably appearing in the USA since 1978, but it was first described there in 1981. Up to September 1983 there had been 2000 cases in the USA and by 30 June 1983 the World Health Organization was aware of 153 European cases. These figures had trebled by 1985. There is a high mortality rate. The largest group of sufferers in both the USA and Europe has been homosexual in at least 70 per cent of cases. The final definitive cause of the syndrome is now known; many suggestions were postulated but it seems to be a retrovirus, human T-cell lymphotropic (leukaemia) virus type III (HTLV-III), which in appropriate circumstances initiates the start of the disease process.

The specialty of venereology is certainly not a static one. Very few Royal Commissions have had such widespread effects as that of 1916. It is to be hoped that those working in the specialty of genitourinary medicine will demand an outstanding service in the future for their patients and that the subject will continue to develop in years to come.

M. A. WAUGH

Further reading

Ackerknecht, E. H. (1967). *Medicine at the Paris Hospital, 1794–1848.* Baltimore.

Bloomfield, A. L. (1956). A bibliography of internal medicine, syphilis. *Stanford Medical Bulletin (San Francisco)*, **14**, 1–19; 77–91.

Catterall, R. D. (1981). Biological effects of sexual freedom. *Lancet*, 315–19.

Flegel, K. M. (1974). Changing concepts of the nosology of gonorrhea and syphilis. *Bulletin of the History of Medicine*, **48**, 571–88.

Lesky, E. (1976). *The Vienna Medical School of the 19th Century.* Baltimore and London.

Morton, R. S. (1977). *Gonorrhoea*, pp. 1–24. London, Philadelphia, and Toronto.

Panofsky, E. (1961). Homage to Fracastoro in a Germano-Flemish composition of about 1590 (in English). *Nederlands Kunsthistorisch Jaarboek*, pp. 1–33. Amsterdam.

Parish, L. C. *et al.* (1973, 1975). Bibliography of secondary sources on the history of dermatology. *Archives of Dermatology. Chicago.* **108**, 351–66; **111**, 1036–48; 1188–99.

Thomas, C. G. A. (1961). The light of many minds. *British Journal of Venereal Diseases*, **37**, 33–58.

Waugh, M. A. (1971). Attitudes of hospitals in London to venereal disease in the eighteenth and nineteenth centuries. *British Journal of Venereal Diseases*, **47**, 146–50.

Waugh, M. A. (1973). Venereal diseases in sixteenth-century England. *Medical History*, **17**, 192–9.

Weidmann, P. (1965). *Die Venereologie in Paris von 1800–1850* (in German). Zurich.

Willcox, R. R. (1967). Fifty years since the conception of an organized venereal diseases service in Great Britain. *British Journal of Venereal Diseases*, **43**, 1–9.

Wyke, T. J. (1973). Hospital facilities for, and diagnosis and treatment of, venereal disease in England 1800–1870. *British Journal of Venereal Diseases*, **49**, 78–85.

VENESECTION is the cutting of a vein to draw off blood or to insert, for example, a *cannula. The term is synonymous with 'phlebotomy'. It is sometimes used interchangeably with the more precise 'venepuncture', the puncturing of a vein with a needle in order to obtain a specimen of venous blood or to deliver an injection.

VENOGRAM. A *radiograph obtained by *phlebography.

VENOM is the poisonous material secreted and injected by certain stinging or biting *arthropods, reptiles, and fish.

VENO-OCCLUSIVE DISEASE OF THE LIVER is a syndrome produced by certain toxic substances; it has been reported from Jamaica following ingestion of plant alkaloids in so-called 'bush teas', and following *antineoplastic chemotherapy, for example with *cytarabine. The smaller branches of the hepatic veins become occluded by thrombosis, causing centrilobular necrosis of the liver, fibrosis, and *portal hypertension.

VENTILATION is the movement of air in and out of the lungs during breathing.

VENTILATOR. Any device for artificially ventilating the lungs. See also RESPIRATOR.

VENTOUSE. A cupping glass. See CUPPING.

VENTRICLE. A small cavity. The term ventricle usually means one of the several cavities of the *brain; or one of the two lower chambers of the *heart from which blood is expelled at each heart beat by the forcible muscular contraction of the ventricular walls.

VENTRICULAR FIBRILLATION is the most serious of all the cardiac *arrhythmias, in which normal co-ordinated contraction of the ventricular *myocardium ceases and is replaced by chaotic uncoordinated electromechanical activity at many independent foci. There is no effective *cardiac output, and the state is therefore incompatible with life for more than a minute or two unless the circulation is artificially restored and maintained. Ventricular fibrillation is the usual mode of sudden death following *coronary thrombosis. It can be reversed by *defibrillation, provided the circulation can be adequately supported until the defibrillating apparatus is available.

VENTRICULAR SEPTAL DEFECT is a developmental anomaly in which there is an abnormal opening in the interventricular septum of the heart, allowing blood to shunt from the chamber of higher pressure (normally the left ventricle) across to the other side. Ventricular septal defect (VSD), either alone or in combination with other cardiac malformations, is one of the commoner forms of *congenital heart disease and is what is usually meant by the term 'hole in the heart'.

VENTRICULOGRAM. A radiogram of the cerebral *ventricles after replacement of the *cerebrospinal fluid with air or other contrast medium.

VENTRICULOGRAPHY is the *radiographic visualization of the *cerebral ventricles by means of replacing the *cerebrospinal fluid with a contrast medium such as air. This technique, unlike *pneumoencephalography (air encephalography) in which the air is injected into the lumbar canal after lumbar puncture, involves direct injection into a lateral ventricle via a needle inserted through a burr-hole in the skull. Since the advent of *computerized axial tomography (CAT) scanning, it has rarely been needed.

VENULES are the smallest vessels of the venous system, connecting the *capillary bed to the *veins proper.

VERATRINE is a derivative of the hellebore plants (*Veratrum viride* and *V. album*), formerly used in the treatment of arterial *hypertension.

VERMIS. The central portion of the *cerebellum.

VERNEUIL, ARISTÉDE AUGUSTE STANISLAS (1823–95). French surgeon, MD Paris (1852). Verneuil became professor of experimental pathology in 1868, before moving to be chief of the surgical clinic at la Pitié in 1872. A distinguished anatomist, his contribution to surgery was in the treatment of *cold abscesses by instilling *iodoform. He was the founder in 1881 of the influential *Revue de chirurgerie*.

VERRUCA. A wart, a small benign epidermal tumour caused by a *virus of the *papovavirus group.

VERSION is the conversion, usually by manipulation, of an abnormal fetal position into a normal one.

VERTEBRA. See SPINE.

VERTIGO is a sensation of dizziness in which it seems to the sufferer that his immediate environment is rotating around him; the cause usually lies in the structures of the inner ear or their central nervous connections.

VERVET MONKEY DISEASE. A synonym for *Marburg disease.

VESALIUS, ANDREAS (1514–64). Flemish anatomist, MD Padua (1537). Vesalius studied in Louvain and Paris, before enrolling at *Padua where on graduation he was appointed demonstrator of anatomy. He established a great reputation as a teacher with unorthodox views. In 1542 he published his *De humani corporis fabrica,* probably the most influential of all medical works. He supervised its production himself, selecting the paper, the draughtsman, the block-cutters, and the printer (see ANATOMY). The anatomical descriptions, founded on his own observations and frequently differing from those of *Galen, aroused bitter antagonism, not least from his old teacher Johannes *Sylvius. Possibly on this account he left Padua in 1543 to serve the Emperor Charles V and after his abdication in 1555, his son Philip II. He achieved great renown in practice. He introduced surgical drainage of pleural *empyema (1547). In 1564 he was taken ill and shipwrecked on a voyage home from Palestine and died on the island of Zante. He had accepted an invitation to return to the chair of anatomy in Padua, left vacant by the death of *Falloppio.

VESICLE. A small blister, a localized epidermal swelling containing clear fluid. Cf. BULLA.

VESICOVAGINAL FISTULA. A *fistula connecting the *urinary bladder with the *vagina.

VESSEL. An *artery, *vein, or *lymphatic channel.

VESTIBULE. An anatomical space at the entrance to a canal.

VETERANS' ADMINISTRATION, US, AND ITS MEDICAL PROGRAMME. The Veterans' Administration (VA) makes a significant contribution to medical care in the USA. It presently operates about 170 hospitals, and more than 230 clinics throughout the country. Some 16 million clinic visits are made each year, and 1.3 million patients are treated in VA hospitals each year, amounting to about 7 per cent of all hospital admissions.

US programmes for the care and pensioning of veterans of military service (i.e. all former members of the Armed Forces) began after the American Revolutionary War. By the early part of the 19th c. there were 'homes' for elderly and disabled veterans in many parts of the nation, in which medical care often had to be provided. Following the American Civil War several veterans' hospitals were created, and maintained by the government, and by the early part of the 20th c. these had increased to some 50 in number. More hospitals were created after the two World Wars.

At present, more than 30 per cent of US males over the age of 17 years may be eligible for VA medical care. A system of priorities for such eligibility has been established. The highest priority is for illness or disability incurred in military service. The second category is the veteran who has been disabled to some extent in military service, but who needs care for some other form of disability. In the third category is the veteran with non-service-connected disability who claims to be unable to pay for medical care in other institutions. The question of inability to pay is answered largely by a statement made by the veteran.

At the close of the Second World War, arrangements began to be made for affiliation between VA hospitals and various medical schools. At present about three-quarters of all VA hospital staff members have medical school faculty appointments. This has been advantageous to both parties, and has undoubtedly been responsible for a general upgrading of the quality of medical care provided in veterans' hospitals.

The VA Department of Medicine and Surgery also sponsors biomedical research, both basic and developmental; this source of research funding is of importance in the overall research activity in the country today. Two VA scientists, R. S. Yallow and A. V. Schally, have received Nobel prizes in recognition of their work. The system of VA hospitals has provided an excellent base for multi-centre programmes to evaluate forms of therapy, for example, the *chemotherapy of *tuberculosis, and *coronary bypass surgery.

Several agencies of government were responsible for the funding of veterans' benefits, pensions, and care in the early part of the history of the USA, but these were all combined in 1930 with the formation of the Veterans' Administration. It was made an independent agency responsible directly to the President of the USA; it is exceeeded only by the Defense Department and the Postal Service in its number of federal employees. The motto of the Veterans' Administration is a phrase from the second inaugural address of Abraham Lincoln: 'To care for him who shall have borne the battle and for his widow, and his orphan'.

VETERINARY MEDICINE IN RELATION TO HUMAN MEDICINE

Early days of the British veterinary profession. British Army farriers were named veterinary surgeons in 1796 by the Board of General Officers, to differentiate them from human surgeons. They became a profession by Royal Charter in 1844. Their progress has been documented since 1828 by four journals of outstanding merit: the *Veterinarian* of 1828 to 1902, published monthly; the *Veterinary Journal* of 1875, also monthly, still published as *The British Veterinary Journal*; the *Veterinary Record* of 1888, still published weekly; the *Journal of Comparative Pathology and Therapeutics,* quarterly, also of 1888, still published as the *Journal of Comparative*

Pathology. Thus, the story of British veterinary art and science is readily available in domestic, political, and scientific detail.

On the title page of the first number of the *Veterinarian,* there is the 5th c. comment of Publius Vegetius Renatus, traveller and gentleman: 'Ars veterinaria post medicinam secunda est.' Perhaps so, if man truly be nobler than the beast. However, if beef, pork, mutton, milk, and eggs are deemed essential to human living, the ranking might be reversed.

Closest similarities between veterinary and human medicine are at the level of extrapolation of animal experiments to man. For example, in physiology, pharmacology, bacteriology, virology, immunology, and surgery, human medicine is significantly influenced by animal responses. Differences between the two professions are in their outlook and objectives. Human medicine is concerned with comfort for body and mind, and preservation of life: veterinary medicine operates in economic and social circumstances that frequently call for *euthanasia. Great areas of human medicine have little veterinary relevance, for example chronic disabling diseases, mental deterioration, cancer, and diseases of old age. Psychosomatic disease is of no veterinary concern, for animals do not imagine they are ill. By the same token, important veterinary matters such as genetics and nutrition for food production, or control by law of epidemic animal diseases, are minor medical matters. Differences in approach to the same problem, notably in public health, have sometimes caused friction, in which human medicine has usually been dominant because the drawing-room overlooks the stable. Over the years, however, attitudes have mellowed to the worthy compromise of mutual respect.

Formal veterinary education dates from 1762, when Claude Bourgelat founded a school in Lyons. A graduate from that school, Charles Vial de St Bel, was first principal of the first veterinary school in the UK, established in London in 1791 as a consequence of pressure from the Agricultural Society of Odiham in Hampshire.

Among rules for his school, St Bel insisted that medical students must not attend his lectures, 'because it might give a disgust to the residing pupils from their application to the veterinary medicine and many of them would change their mind and apply themselves to the anatomy of the human body, thinking that it would be more honorable for them to cure the human species than animals'.

This comment reflects accurately a difference in social status between veterinary and human medicine that persisted well into the 20th c. As recently as 1927 a doctor of medicine was called to examine an injured horse owned by the Prince of Wales, with a veterinary surgeon 'in consultation'. The point is made because time and again, this difference in social status has affected relationships between the professions and the public. It is odd,

really, because for 100 years medical doctors and veterinary surgeons in the UK had essentially similar backgrounds; often, indeed, they came from the same family. Yet the first veterinary surgeon to be knighted for purely veterinary achievement was George Brown, head of the Government Veterinary Department, in 1898.

A second veterinary school was established in Edinburgh by William Dick, son of a farrier. In 1818 Dick acquired a veterinary certificate after a few months' residence at the London school. On his return to his father's shoeing forge, he was encouraged by the anatomist Dr Barclay to give occasional veterinary lectures. By 1823 the Highland and Agricultural Society was prepared to recognize a course of veterinary instruction, and Dick's school dates from November of that year. The school was a personal venture, supported by funds from Dick's veterinary practice, and his name has been retained in the title of the Edinburgh school—the Royal (Dick) School of Veterinary Studies.

There were medical examiners in the early years of both schools. In London all the examiners were distinguished medical men, led by Sir Astley *Cooper. In Edinburgh both professions were represented, at very senior level. Each school gave a certificate of competence, regarded as being of equal merit by, for example, the army and the East India Company.

The close relationship with human medicine in the London school was the result of the early death of the first principal St Bel, and his replacement in 1794 by Edward Coleman. Coleman, 28 years old, was a friend of Astley Cooper, with whom he had shared rooms while they studied medicine in London. Coleman's urbanity pleased the school's governors, but his 45 years as principal did little for veterinary science. He opined that the horse only was worth consideration, and his documented ignorance of that animal is terrifying. He refused to be advised by veterinary surgeons, and he obstructed every attempt to have them as examiners, or even as subscribers to the school. Professional progress was impossible until he died in 1839.

It had been recognized before Coleman's death that a veterinary profession could be created only by charter, supported by Act of Parliament. Coleman's opposition to such ambition was absolute. Very soon after his death, however, a move was made by Thomas Mayer and his son Thomas Walton Mayer, practitioners in Newcastle under Lyme, to unite the London and Edinburgh schools into a profession. They created a committee of veterinary surgeons, who, after superhuman efforts, presented the required petition and were awarded a charter in 1844. Success was received with rejoicing. A veterinary profession had been created, centred on a Royal College of Veterinary Surgeons, that must organize examinations and set professional standards.

General anaesthesia. At about this time, surgery

stepped into the wonderful world of general *anaesthesia. *Nitrous oxide, then *ether, then *chloroform had been found to create temporary oblivion. In the 1840s they were under scrutiny, no less by veterinary than by medical men. Tales of surgery before that time are of sickening horror.

In 1847 Edward Mayhew (of the *Punch* Mayhew family) described in the *Veterinarian* the effect of ether on dogs and cats. He was satisfied that insensibility was eventually produced, but he was distressed by cries as the animals were losing or regaining consciousness. A passion for animal welfare had attracted Mayhew in middle age to the London veterinary school, from which he graduated in 1845, hence his concern about the apparent pain of anaesthesia. It had to be tested personally. Mayhew asked 'F. Normansell, Esq., the well known surgeon-dentist', to administer ether and extract one of his teeth. The dentist said that all the teeth were sound, but he was overruled and persuaded to set about the operation. To his dismay, he failed to draw the tooth (fang, Mayhew called it) before consciousness returned. However, the point had been made and Mayhew was satisfied that animal cries under anaesthesia were not of pain. Indeed, the most painful consequence of the episode was that the unextracted tooth had 'by the force employed been rendered sensitive'.

The cattle plague catastrophe of 1865. The most traumatic episode in British veterinary history was the epidemic of cattle plague (rinderpest) of 1865–6. The disease spread across the land, and in some 18 months killed an estimated half-million cattle and many sheep. Everyone was involved: farmers, cattle-dealers and butchers at the livelihood level; veterinary surgeons in attempting to halt the massacre; the medical profession in giving advice; the Press and general public in reviling authority for impotence and the veterinary profession for ignorance; and the clergy, by authority of the Primate, in praying 'Lord God Almighty . . . in compassion . . . stay . . . this plague . . . and shield our homes from its ravages . . . so shall we ever offer . . . praise and thanksgiving . . . Amen'. Eventual control of the disease resulted in a government veterinary department, from which is descended the Animal Health Division of the Ministry of Agriculture, Fisheries and Food.

Cattle plague caused havoc in the UK in the mid 18th c., but had disappeared by 1757. It was endemic in eastern Europe, however, and movement of armies during the Crimean war brought it to the notice of British veterinary surgeons. The Army experiences of cattle plague in 1855 of Thomas Walton Mayer (the same who had been involved with the professional charter) were described in the *Veterinarian* early in 1857: 'A dreadful murrain was destroying immense numbers of cattle in Asiatic Turkey . . . a disease of no ordinary character'. The editors of the *Veterinarian* (J. B. Simonds and W. J. T. Morton, professors at the London veterinary school in cattle pathology and chemistry, respectively) commented that 'a most destructive cattle epizootic, new to the present generation of Englishmen, will probably ere long be introduced into this country from the Continent'.

Heed was taken of this warning, and Simonds and a veterinary colleague William Ernes, who spoke several European languages, were commissioned later in 1857 to investigate cattle plague on the European continent. Their expenses were paid by the Royal Agricultural Society of England, the Highland and Agricultural Society of Scotland, and the Royal Agricultural Improvement Society of Ireland.

It was a remarkable enterprise, described in an equally remarkable report published in ten instalments in the *Veterinarian*—a definitive description of the disease, although, of course, the causative *virus was not then known. It was recognized to spread from animal to animal, and Simonds did not accept the common belief that it arose spontaneously. He reported emphatically that it could be controlled only by rigorous *quarantine and slaughter of affected animals. Measures against it were so stringent in countries to the west of Russia that he believed it was unlikely to reach the UK.

However, with increasingly efficient transport, trade was expanding rapidly, and eight years after Simonds's report a cargo of plague-affected cattle reached the UK from the Baltic, and mingled with a highly susceptible population. Simonds diagnosed the disease early in July 1865 in a London dairy, and reproduced it experimentally at the London veterinary school by contact between a healthy and an affected animal. As there was no veterinary organization, he warned the *Privy Council of devastation if no action were taken. He had previously made the prescient comment in the *Veterinarian* that if the disease appeared it would be new to most Englishmen. Certainly the disease was virtually unknown, but everyone, and his brother, and his cousin, knew a 'certain' cure. The result was chaos for some weeks, with cattle dying in thousands.

Simonds's advice, based on his experience in continental Europe, that the disease could be controlled only by stopping movement of livestock and slaughtering and burying affected animals, had support from the widely travelled John Gamgee, proprietor of the New veterinary school he had established in Edinburgh in 1857. Gamgee's warnings over several years, that cattle plague would eventually enter the UK if importation of live cattle were not controlled, had been unheeded. There was strong support for Simonds, also, from William *Budd, of Clifton, Bristol, a considerable epidemiologist.

Budd was fascinated by cattle plague and believed it to be similar to human *typhoid fever. He and Simonds were friends, and he had been impressed by Simonds's 'masterly report' following his visit to seek cattle plague in eastern Europe. It had been arranged some time before the appearance of cattle plague in the UK, that Budd would contribute to the *Veterinarian* (of which Simonds was a senior editor) an article on: 'The Siberian Cattle Plague; Or The Typhoid Fever Of The Ox'. Events overtook this publication, but resulted in an interesting footnote to the first instalment in October 1865:

The circumstances under which this little essay on Cattle Plague makes its appearance were . . . remarkable . . . every one reading the title will . . . suppose . . . that the essay was suggested by the recent outbreak of this formidable disease . . . this is not the case . . . at the Annual meeting of the British Medical Association . . . in August 1862, a resolution was passed . . . to take up at once the study of epidemic and epizootic diseases . . . I had the honour to receive . . . a request that I should draw up a scheme . . . I mentioned rinderpest, or cattle plague, as a disease . . . important to study . . . on account of the striking analogy . . . to the typhoid fever of our own species.

Clearly, Simonds and Budd had had many discussions, and the resulting essay, published in four instalments in the *Veterinarian* of 1865 and 1866, is an admirable contribution to the literature. Spontaneous generation was discarded absolutely, and in the final instalment the infective agent was surmised to be 'so low in the scale of being that the toadstool may be said to rank high in comparison'. Could the demon virus identified in 1902 have been more picturesquely humiliated?

As treatment after treatment proved useless, cattle plague in the UK became more terrifying. Eventually, pressed by the Royal Agricultural Society, through Simonds its veterinary adviser, the government hurriedly passed the Cattle Diseases Prevention Act of February 1866, to restrict movement of livestock and to enforce slaughter of affected animals. The result was dramatic: by the end of the year the epidemic was virtually over.

The consequences of the episode were profound: veterinary surgeons were promoted from ignorant slaughterers to responsible advisers; the medical profession accepted that certain diseases of animals were outside its competence; the government translated a temporary cattle plague office into a veterinary department. Later, when Simonds was appointed principal of the London veterinary school in 1872, the department was put in charge of his chief cattle plague inspector, G. T. Brown, whose professional and administrative competence established a permanent unit of government.

Louis Pasteur and immunity to anthrax. Cattle plague in the UK was conquered long before its cause was known. For some time evidence had been accumulating that animalcules might be associated with disease, but their origin was unknown: spontaneous generation was still a respectable explanation, in spite of *Pasteur's meticulous observations on their ubiquity and ability to multiply. Medical and veterinary journals of the day reflect the excitement of experiment and dis-

covery. *Koch's superlative paper of 1877 on the *anthrax bacillus established the concept of one organism, one disease. In 1880 Pasteur observed what he termed 'attenuation' of the chicken cholera organism, originally identified by Toussaint at the Lyons veterinary school.

Combining these observations, Pasteur tested the protective effect of attenuated anthrax *culture against virulent challenge. The proposed experiment caused world-wide interest, for it was to be observed by the Press, including M. de Blowitz, Paris correspondent of the London *Times*. Medical and veterinary men were interested, of course, especially the latter, because although rather rare in man, anthrax was—and still is—a fairly common, usually lethal disease of farm animals.

The experiment had been suggested to the Melun Agricultural Society by veterinary surgeon Rossignol. The chairman of the Society, Baron de la Rochette, passed the request to Pasteur. The chosen location was the farm of Pouilly-le-Fort near Melun; the Society provided the animals.

On 5 May 1881, in front of a large crowd, 24 sheep, 5 cows, 1 ox, and 1 goat received a first injection of attenuated anthrax culture. The same animals received a second injection of less attenuated culture on 17 May. Injection of virulent culture would be on the last day of the month.

Excitement was intense when the time came for challenge of equal numbers of treated and untreated animals. Veterinary surgeon Biot, a vocal sceptic, was permitted to shake the anthrax culture before injection, and his request was granted that a larger dose than planned should be given. The test was completed by mid-afternoon. Two of Pasteur's assistants, Chamberland and *Roux, visited the farm next day, and noted with satisfaction dullness in several sheep untreated before challenge. A telegram from Rossignol reached Pasteur on the morning of 2 June, announcing the death of 18 unprotected sheep and the others dying. All the pre-treated animals were clinically normal. The telegram ended with the words 'stunning success'.

Pasteur was at the farm by early afternoon, to be cheered by a huge crowd that included representatives from the Melun Agricultural Society, from medical and veterinary societies, and from the Central Council of Hygiene of Seine and Marne. *The Times* sent the story round the world. It was decided to alter the name of the farm from Pouilly-le-Fort to Clos Pasteur.

Small wonder that a few weeks later at the International Medical Congress of 1881 in London, Pasteur's paper: 'Vaccination in relation to chicken cholera and splenic fever' was rapturously received. He proposed that the terms *vaccine and *vaccination should be extended from *smallpox to all prophylactic inoculations 'au mérite et aux immenses services rendus par un des plus grands hommes de l'Angleterre, votre Jenner'.

Robert Koch and tuberculosis. In the meantime

Koch had been struggling with the problem of how to obtain micro-organisms in pure culture. This was eventually solved with brilliant simplicity by using solid, as distinct from liquid, nutrient media. Koch demonstrated the technique to a small group that included Pasteur, at the Physiological Laboratory of King's College, London, on the occasion of the International Medical Congress of 1881, at which Pasteur's paper on anthrax vaccination had been so enthusiastically received. Pasteur commented, 'C'est un grand progrès, Monsieur!'

Great progress indeed. So important that on 24 March of the following year Koch could announce to the Physiological Society in Berlin the greatest of all bacteriological discoveries—isolation of the *tubercle bacillus.

In retrospect, it is astonishing that a disease-producing organism of supreme importance in man and animals and fastidious in artificial culture, should have been the first specifically identified by Koch's pure culture technique. Almost as astonishing is that on the day after Koch's announcement of his discovery, *Ehrlich stained the tubercle bacillus differentially by the use of aniline dye, so that it was clearly visible under the *microscope. The cause of *tuberculosis could now be seen, but how to defeat this sly and terrible disease? Even those who had suspected widespread distribution were horrified by its apparent omnipresence. Medical men and veterinary surgeons faced an enormous task in attempting control: elimination seemed impossible. Koch's announcement of tuberculinum in 1890, therefore, was of unequalled moment.

The Tenth International Medical Congress was to be in Berlin in the summer of 1890. For some months there had been rumours that Koch had made another important discovery. Some said that he had found a cure for tuberculosis. Koch himself had made no comment, but to say nothing invites speculation by others. It was indicated to Koch, from the highest level, that an announcement at the forthcoming congress would be good for Germany. Reluctantly, Koch agreed to describe incomplete experiments with a fluid he had been studying.

Rumour brought multitudes to Berlin's Renzi circus amphitheatre to hear Koch's paper. He said that he had found a substance that prevented growth of the tubercle bacillus in both test tube and animal body. There was pandemonium that obliterated Koch's plea for caution in interpretation of unfinished experiments. The demand for further information was strident and continuous, to the extent that Koch retreated mute to his laboratory.

When, after a few weeks, the panic had subsided, Koch reported his discovery that subcutaneous injection of a small amount of an extract of a liquid culture of the tubercle bacillus into a healthy person caused no response, but in a case of tuberculosis there was a severe local and general reaction. He commented: 'I think I am justified in saying that the remedy will . . . form an indispensable aid to diagnosis.' He emphasized, also, that speculation of a cure for tuberculosis had been made by others interpreting his comments 'in an exaggerated and distorted form'. Koch's tuberculinum was soon abbreviated to *tuberculin.

The relative significance of tuberculin in human and in animal medicine exemplifies the difference in objectives of the two professions. In the former, life must always be preserved. In the latter, life can be sacrificed to prevent suffering, to prevent spread of disease, or to save money for the farmer if the flesh be sound. It follows that in veterinary medicine accurate *diagnosis is frequently more important than treatment. Tuberculin was of slight interest to medical men, but enormously important in the veterinary world.

Very soon after discovery, tuberculin was tested in cattle at the Tartu Veterinary Institute at Dorpat in Russia. Clinical response was measured by rectal temperature over a period of several hours after subcutaneous injection. From tests in many countries, it was soon clear that a majority of tuberculous cattle could be thus identified, even those showing no clinical sign of disease. This latter point was supremely important, because herds free from tuberculosis could now be created. However, tuberculosis-free herds on a significant scale were an academic dream for decades. The practical difficulties were great. A simpler test had to be devised, with rigorously standardized tuberculin, and considerable finance was necessary to compensate farmers for slaughter of animals that failed the test. Eradication of bovine tuberculosis was not achieved in the UK until after the Second World War.

Glanders. *Bacillus mallei*, the causal organism of glanders of horses, was described by *Loeffler and Schütz of the Berlin veterinary school within a few months of Koch's announcement of the tubercle bacillus. Because the first clinical trial in cattle of tuberculin was carried out at the Tartu veterinary laboratories in 1890, it is not surprising that a similar extract, mallein, of the glanders organism was prepared and tested in similar manner at the same institute. By early 1892, mallein was everywhere recognized to be an even more specific diagnostic agent than tuberculin. It, too, identified clinical and subclinical cases.

Characteristically, glanders is a chronic debilitating, eventually fatal, disease affecting lungs, lymphatic glands, and sometimes skin, with suppurative discharge from any focus of the organism, but typically from deep in the nasal pathways. Cattle are naturally immune, but the organism is highly dangerous for man. Indeed, one of the most excruciating papers in British veterinary literature is that of veterinary surgeon Gaiger in the September 1913 number of the *Journal of Comparative Pathology and Therapeutics*, describing months of torture after he contracted glanders. Shortly after graduation from the Liverpool veterinary school, in 1905, Gaiger was appointed lecturer in pathology and bacteriology at the Lahore veterinary school in India. In 1911 he contracted glanders from a pony, and was invalided back to the UK for treatment. Numerous *pus-discharging *sinuses had daily to be dressed by plugging with cotton-wool soaked in *iodine or *lysol. The exquisite pain of this procedure was deadened by injections of *morphia or *heroin. At the height of the disease an arm was amputated. *Immunity developed gradually, and in July 1913, some 27 months after contracting the disease, and after 27 operations under general anaesthesia, Gaiger declared: 'I have never been in better general health'. Indeed, he had many useful years ahead, especially in research on sheep diseases. In the early 1920s he was closely associated with development of the Animal Diseases Research Association, out of which grew the Moredun Institute of Edinburgh.

Why, it may be asked, if mallein was known in 1892 to be a specific diagnostic agent for glanders, was that disgusting and dangerous disease not eliminated from the UK for 26 more years? The answer is, because of ignorance, avarice, indecision, and indifference. Ignorance of infectious disease was widespread among ordinary folk long after scientists had discounted lightning, flood, and full moon as likely causes. In the grime of great cities, glanders was rife until the turn of the century. Avarice was of those who worked sick horses in fog or by night, holding them hidden from critical eyes by day. Indecision was in county councils that dithered about the Contagious Diseases (Animals) Act of 1878, and several later Orders, and would not pay compensation for slaughter of glandered horses reported to the police. What cabby or carter would thus discard his livelihood? Indifference was in government: glanders was a city problem, it disliked country air, fields, and open stables, so why pay compensation for slight national return? The annual handful of human cases was regretted, but inevitable.

In 1907, at last, the mallein test was made compulsory. The Mines Act of 1911 decreed that pit ponies had to pass the test. By 1920 compensation bore some relationship to market value. Glanders disappeared in 1928.

Griffith Evans and a trypanosome. Indifference to glanders was in the tradition of official British reaction to veterinary medicine until the second decade of the 20th c. It was to be expected, therefore, that when British Army Inspecting Veterinary Surgeon G. Evans, attached to the Punjab Frontier Force, suggested in a report dated 13 November 1880 that a disease of horses and camels called *surra* was caused by a *parasite in the blood, the official comment was of regret 'that no cure for *surra* had been observed'. Evans and his talents were transferred to other fields: for posterity, however, his splendid report established beyond peradventure that trypanosomes could cause disease (see TRYPANOSOMIASIS).

Griffith Evans, born in 1835, served a short medical pupillage before entering the London veterinary school. His imagination was caught by a lecture on what might be seen with a microscope. As no microscope was available for students, he bought one for £5 from Baker's in High Holborn. From that moment he was a microscopist, and in 1855 he became in addition a veterinary surgeon.

He was commissioned with the Royal Artillery, and when stationed in Montreal in 1861 with few routine duties, he registered as a medical student at McGill University, and graduated MD, CM in 1864. Always inquisitive and resourceful, he obtained an interview with American President Lincoln, and from him received permission to visit battlefields of the Civil War.

In 1877, still an Army veterinary surgeon, with microscopy a compulsive hobby, he was posted to India, to the Punjab, to investigate a fatal disease of horses. Being familiar with the work of Koch and Pasteur, he soon identified the disease as anthrax. He was then sent to Dera Ismael Khan to examine horses and camels on the Punjab frontier dying of a disease locally named *surra*. He wished to attempt experimental transmission of the disease, but was instructed to cure affected animals, not to kill others in addition to those already doomed. Happily, intervention by the governor of the Punjab made experimental observations possible.

Griffith Evans concluded that a blood parasite was the cause of *surra*. He transported the parasite *in vivo* in a dog to Simla, where it was seen by Timothy Lewis and recognized as similar to an apparently harmless organism known in rats (now named *Trypanosoma lewisi*). Why, asked authority, should a parasite be harmful to horse or camel and harmless to the rat? It was a strong criticism of Evans's conclusions, that were discounted. As has been said, he was transferred to other duties.

Fortunately for all, Evans had sent copies of his report to Koch and to Pasteur, both of whom accepted his conclusions. Recognition by these great experimental biologists resulted, eventually in acknowledgement that this was the first record of a pathogenic trypanosome. Evans's meticulous observations, published in a series of papers in the *Veterinary Journal* of 1881, were a foundation on which others, notably David *Bruce (*Trypanosoma brucei*) could build. The name of Evans's trypanosome had an interesting career: first, *Spirochaeta evansi*, then *Haematomonas evansi*, then *Trichomonas evansi*, and finally, in 1896, *Trypanosoma evansi*. Evans enjoyed the dual triumph of being proved right, and of living 100 years.

Transmission of disease by animals to man. Something has been said of three diseases—anthrax, tuberculosis, and glanders—of which the agents can harm both animals and man. Trypanosomes have been cited as a group of organisms morphologically similar to each other, some pathogenic for animals and others for man. A similar pattern embraces many other diseases. There is only one *rabies virus, the cause of terrible death in man and animals, but in the *Pasteurella* group of *bacteria, found widely in animals and man, only *Pasteurella pestis* (now *Yersinia pestis*) causes human *plague.

The interaction of disease between man and animals has been studied for over 100 years. The subject is now a specialty in the field of comparative medicine. The classic summary of these researches is that of Hubbert, McCulloch, and Schnurrenberger, first published in 1930 and in its sixth edition by 1975. This comprehensive work, by some 90 authors, covers bacterial, mycotic, parasitic, viral, and non-infectious diseases, of which the tabular summary extends to 22 closely printed pages.

United States Bureau of Animal Industry. The pre-eminence of Pasteur and Koch is inclined to overshadow achievements of other investigators of infectious diseases, especially outside Europe. A case in point is the discovery, by the US Bureau of Animal Industry, of the cause of Texas fever.

The Bureau was established in 1883 as a Veterinary Division of the Department of Agriculture. The objectives were to examine imported animals for evidence of disease, and to investigate diseases already in the country. Of the latter, Texas fever was a lethal disease of cattle, widespread in certain areas.

In 1888 Theobald *Smith of the Bureau found a parasite in the red blood cells of affected animals. In the following year F. L. Kilborne discovered that the parasite was passed from animal to animal by a *tick. Cooper Curtice unravelled the life history of the tick. These investigations were superbly developed and definitively described in 1893.

This was the first recognition that an aetiological agent (a piroplasm in this case) could be transmitted by an intermediate invertebrate host. This led to discovery of the mode of transmission of diseases of man such as *malaria, *yellow fever, and *typhus, and of diseases of animals such as piroplasmosis, theileriasis, and *louping-ill.

The US Bureau of Animal Industry has an outstanding record in veterinary research. The first director, D. E. *Salmon, is perpetually recalled by the disease salmonellosis, because, in 1885 with Theobald Smith, he isolated from pigs the first organism of that group, now named *Salmonella choleraesuis*.

Experiments involving animals. Welfare of wild and domesticated animals is an emotive subject in the UK. For some people it ranks above self-preservation; it simply *is,* and cannot be altered by persuasion or discussion. To these individuals, animal experimentation is unacceptable. Their point of view is recognized and respected, but, in many anxious discussions, it has been overruled by

the conclusion that controlled use of experimental animals is justified if there is clear prospect of new knowledge that will prolong life or lessen suffering. (See EXPERIMENTAL METHOD.)

Ghastly *vivisection was practised in French veterinary schools well beyond the middle of the 19th c. It was excused in the belief that students must achieve surgical dexterity by operating on living animals. One sickening report will suffice. It is from a horrified *Veterinarian* of October 1858. A Monsieur Sanson of the Toulouse veterinary school casually described the animal he used for 'an experiment . . . upon the blood' as: 'A small cow, very thin, which had undergone numerous operations, that is to say, which had suffered during the whole of the day the most extreme torture, was placed upon a table and killed by injection of air into the jugular vein'. The animal had been cut to pieces, literally, by students practising surgery, and then passed to M. Sanson for his 'experiment'.

The British Society for the Prevention of Cruelty to Animals was founded in 1824. It had veterinary members from its earliest days, notably Charles Spooner who was on the staff of the London veterinary school for 33 years, and was principal from 1853 to 1871. There was no question, therefore, of vivisection at the London school, and, indeed, there is no record of the practice in any British veterinary school. Certainly, surgical operation to acquire dexterity has never been permitted. However, there has always been in the UK use of animals for biological experiments. It can justly be said, however, that humanity has long been a prime consideration, expressed in the *Cruelty to Animals Act of 1876 that is implemented less by threats than by good faith and good behaviour.

The Act was—and still is—a remarkable achievement. It is a compromise, quietly and persistently successful through uncommon sense: there must not be unlimited use of animals for experiments, and each must appear in an annual return to the Home Office. For many people, dogs, cats, and horses are cherished companions; very well, let dogs, cats, and horses be treated differently from sheep, cattle, mice, rats, and the rest. They are so treated, and special permission is required for their inclusion in an experiment. Some experiments are more likely than others to cause pain: again, very well, let the two categories be distinguished, and let it be obligatory that an anaesthetic be used and special permission be obtained for painful experiments. In addition, if an animal has been seriously harmed, and if the objective of the experiment has been achieved, that animal must be killed before regaining consciousness. Every person who carries out animal experiments must hold a licence, signed by specifically nominated, responsible people, for example the president of the Royal College of Surgeons. The place where experiments are conducted must be registered and approved by the Home Office. All animals under experiment must be identifiable, and they must be individually entered in detailed permanent records kept by the person responsible for their welfare. The Home Office has inspectors to oversee these regulations, and they have the right of entry unannounced to any place concerned with animal experiments. This right is an extremely valuable safeguard against wilful, or unthinking, breach of regulations, because a Home Office inspector may appear at any moment.

There is no better example of the (now happily bygone) difference in status between medical and veterinary people, than the story of Home Office inspectors under the Cruelty to Animals Act 1876. In 1876 all appointments were of medical men, and the status quo was maintained for 87 years. In 1963 a dent appeared in the wall of the citadel when Robert Mitchell, with both medical and veterinary qualifications, was appointed an inspector. In 1965 came the first inspector with a veterinary qualification only, but his inspection was limited to places unconnected with human medicine, and he received a much lower salary than his medical colleagues. In the same year, however, the Little-wood Departmental Committee on Experimental Animals snubbed this silliness and said: 'The inspectorate should be recruited equally from persons with medical or veterinary qualifications'. This recommendation was implemented in 1969, when three veterinary surgeons became inspectors on the same terms as medically qualified inspectors. The ultimate was achieved in 1976 when a veterinary surgeon became Chief Inspector. He was succeeded in 1983 by another of the same.

This short veterinary story must end with eyes on the future, for there is no progress without search for a wider better world. A hundred years ago the veterinary profession was an uneasy mix of agricultural necessity and medical science, and when a veterinary practitioner was called to a house for consultation he was expected to go to the 'Tradesmen's entrance'. However, following the advice of its great leader John McFadyean, founder of veterinary research in the UK, the profession strove to demonstrate special skills before complaining of neglect. McFadyean felt as keenly as any veterinarian of the late Victorian era the low public opinion of his profession. He set about raising morale by insisting that hard work and integrity bring worthwhile rewards, a philosophy implicit in the verb 'to vet'.

McFadyean, son of a tenant farmer in Galloway, graduated from the Edinburgh veterinary school in 1876. Immediately afterwards he was appointed lecturer in anatomy at that school. During the following years he became increasingly aware of the researches of Pasteur and Koch. Thus stimulated, he enrolled for courses in medicine and science at Edinburgh university to acquire knowledge of the new worlds of *pathology, *bacteriology, and *immunology. He graduated in medicine in 1882, and in science a year later. These qualifications were but a means to an end, for McFadyean was first and always a veterinary surgeon. From Edinburgh he moved to London, to become principal of the London veterinary school in 1894. He led his profession in every field— science, education, administration—and in 1908 acquired as son-in-law Stewart Stockman, one of the UK's outstanding Chief Veterinary Officers.

McFadyean introduced to the UK, and tested, tuberculin and mallein. In 1888 he founded, and for 52 years edited, the *Journal of Comparative Pathology and Therapeutics* through which his colleagues were kept in immediate touch with veterinary advances throughout the world. He had special interest in bovine tuberculosis after publicly challenging Koch's pronouncement at the International Congress on Tuberculosis in London in 1901, that bovine tuberculosis was of no importance in human medicine. This assertion led directly to establishment shortly after the Congress of a Royal Commission on tuberculosis (with McFadyean a member) that, over a decade, proved that bovine tuberculosis is a hazard to man. He was knighted for this outstanding contribution to veterinary and human medicine.

McFadyean kept pressure on his veterinary colleagues to investigate farm animal diseases. In particular, he urged research and administrative action to control contagious abortion (*brucellosis), the scourge of dairy cows and cause of a persistent malaise in man. As a result, the Ministry of Agriculture accepted responsibility for veterinary research on diseases of national importance, and in 1917 opened the Central Veterinary Laboratory in Weybridge, Surrey. The brucellosis saga ended in 1981 with the official announcement that the disease had been eradicated from the UK.

Veterinary progress since the First World War has been astonishing. The Advisory Committee on Research into Diseases in Animals was unequivocal in reporting in 1922 that lack of government support for veterinary research was 'a national disgrace'. That conclusion was based on an estimated value for farm livestock in the UK of £400 million, annual losses from disease £5 million, and government money spent on veterinary research in 1921–2 (at the veterinary schools of London, Liverpool, Edinburgh, Glasgow, and Dublin) £3696. The first two figures were probably rounded to the nearest few millions, but the disgraceful third was probably accurate.

Institutes of animal pathology were established in London and Cambridge in the 1920s. The Agricultural Research Council dates from 1931, and since that time has been a guiding and funding agency for research in veterinary schools and at an ever-increasing number of veterinary units, departments, and institutes. Also in the 1930s, the principle was accepted of a national veterinary investigation service organized by the Ministry of Agriculture. In spite of war, the 1940s achieved a revolution in veterinary education, when the previously independent schools were absorbed into the university system. Since the Second World War veterinary research has been in crescendo, moving into new areas such as poultry, fish, and wildlife, besides continuing to care for the animals of farm and home.

In most veterinary schemes there is now a medical interest or dimension, for many animal diseases are recognized to have a counterpart in man.

Each to his own, not in rivalry but for each other.

I. PATTISON

Further reading
Bulloch, W. (1938). *The History of Bacteriology*. Oxford.
Development Commission. Advisory Committee on Research into Diseases of Animals (1922). *Report of the Advisory Committee on Research into Diseases of Animals*. London.
Ministry of Agriculture and Fisheries and Department of Agriculture for Scotland (1944). *Report of the Committee on Veterinary Education in Great Britain*. London.
Ministry of Agriculture, Fisheries and Food (1965). *Animal Health a Centenary: 1865–1965*. London.
Hubbert, W. T., McCulloch, W. F. and Schnurrenberger, P. R. (1975). *Diseases Transmitted from Animals to Man*. 6th edn, New York.
Pattison, I. (1981). *John McFadyean: A Great British Veterinarian*. London and New York.
Pattison, I. (1984). *The British Veterinary Profession: 1791–1948*. London and New York.
Pugh, L. P. (1962). *From Farriery To Veterinary Medicine: 1785–1795*. Cambridge.

VIBRIO is a genus of motile curved and rod-shaped Gram-negative *bacteria which includes the causative agent of *cholera, *Vibrio cholerae*.

VIBROMASSAGE is a method of *massage employing an electrically powered vibrating pad.

VICARY, THOMAS (d. 1561). British surgeon. Vicary was Master of the Barbers' Company in 1530 and in 1548 was made a governor of *St Bartholomew's Hospital in charge of the surgeons. Appointed surgeon to Henry VIII in 1528, he became serjeant-surgeon in 1536 and later to Edward VI, Mary, Philip, and Elizabeth I. He features in Holbein's painting, receiving from Henry VIII in 1541 the Act of Incorporation of the Company of *Barber-Surgeons, in the formation of which he was instrumental.

VICQ D'AZYR, FELIX (1748–94). French physician and anatomist, MD Paris (1774). Vicq d'Azyr was appointed physician to Marie Antoinette and continued in her service although obsessed by the fear that he would be arraigned before the Revolutionary Council. During this period he was permanent secretary of the Académie de Médicine of Paris, and the moving spirit in the reorganization of French medicine. A distinguished anatomist, his name is attached to the mammillothalamic fasciculus which joins the *mammillary bodies to the *thalamus (Bundle of Vicq d'Azyr).

VIDIUS, VIDUS (1508–69). See GUIDI, GUIDO.

VIERORDT, KARL VON (1818–84). German physiologist, MD Heidelberg (1841). Vierordt occupied the chair of theoretical medicine in Tübingen in 1849, moving to that of physiology in 1855. He was the first to devise a method of enumerating the red blood cells (1851) and worked on cardiovascular and respiratory physiology. He made the first *sphygmograph (1855).

VIEUSSENS, RAYMOND (c. 1635–1715). French physician and anatomist, MD Montpellier (1670). Although physician to the court and the Hôtel-Dieu S. Eloi, Vieussens never held a professorial post. In 1685 he published *Neurographia universalis* and there are several structures in the brain as well as the heart bearing his name. He first described *aortic incompetence and its characteristic pulse wave (1695) and *mitral stenosis (1705).

VILLEMIN, JEAN ANTOINE (1827–92). French physician, MD Paris (1853). Villemin joined the army medical service and eventually became professor at Val-de-Grâce. In 1868 he firmly established the infectivity of *tuberculosis by transferring it from man to rabbit. This was before *Koch had isolated the mycobacterium and Villemin's work was discounted.

VILLUS. A projection from a *membrane, usually with a rich blood supply.

VINBLASTINE is one of several *alkaloids extracted from the plant *Vinca rosea*, collectively known as the vinca alkaloids. They are cytotoxic, causing *metaphase arrest by interfering with *microtubule assembly, and are used as *antineoplastic agents. Vinblastine is employed particularly against *lymphomas and malignant *teratomas. It may cause toxic depression of the *bone marrow.

VINCI, LEONARDO DA. See LEONARDO DA VINCI.

VINCRISTINE is one of the vinca alkaloids (see VINBLASTINE), used in the management of *leukaemias and *lymphomas and in the treatment of some solid tumours. It may cause neurotoxic side-effects.

VINYL CHLORIDE (C_2H_3Cl), or chloroethylene, is also known as VCM (vinyl chloride monomer). The toxic effects of vinyl chloride, which is extensively used in the manufacture of PVC (polyvinyl chloride, to which it polymerizes) and other vinyl polymers and was also employed as a propellant in aerosol sprays and cosmetics, were only recognized in man after it had been shown to induce *tumours in animals. It is now known that exposure to it causes angiosarcoma of the liver, an otherwise unusual malignant tumour, as well as an unrelated condition called acro-osteolysis, a form of finger *clubbing associated with *scleroderma and *Raynaud's phenomenon. Occupational exposure in industry to vinyl chloride is now limited to a concentration of 10 parts per million, and its use as an aerosol propellant and in cosmetics is prohibited (1976 Directive of the Council of the European Communities). See also OCCUPATIONAL MEDICINE.

VIRCHOW, RUDOLF KARL (1821–1902). German pathologist, MD Berlin (1843). Virchow enrolled at the Friedrich-Wilhelms Institut in 1839 undertaking to serve in the army after graduation. In 1847 he became prosector at the *Charité. When he was sent to report on an epidemic of *typhus in Upper Silesia his experiences turned him into a politically active radical and his consequent part in the uprising of 1848 led to his expulsion from the Charité. He was made professor of pathological anatomy in Würzburg in 1849 and in the following seven years built such a reputation that in 1856 he was invited to the chair in Berlin and to be the director of the pathological institute. Elected to the City Council three years later, he initiated great improvements in Berlin's hygiene and public health. Later as a member of the Prussian Lower House his radical views and his taste for polemics led him to oppose Bismarck on more than one occasion. During the Franco-Prussian war he organized the ambulance corps for the Prussian army.

Virchow, an outstanding figure in 19th c. medicine, has been accounted the greatest pathologist of all time. Although not of great originality he avoided metaphysical speculation and his opinions were founded on his own observations and experience. His most famous work *Die Cellularpathologie* (1858) applied the *cell theory to *pathology and allowed him to proclaim his doctrine of '*omnis cellula e cellula*'. He regarded all disease as disease of cells. He described *leukaemia (1845), invented the term '*amyloid', studied *thrombosis and introduced the idea of *embolism (1846–56), and observed and defined *leucocytosis. He first described the *neuroglia (1846) and the cerebral perivascular spaces (Virchow–Robin spaces, 1851). In his later years he became interested in anthropology and wrote widely on the subject. In 1847 he founded the still extant *Archiv für pathologische Anatomie (Virchows Archiv)*. Virchow was a man of powerful personality, unbounded energy, and strongly held opinions. At the end of his life he not only enjoyed unparalleled renown in the international world of medicine, but was one of the great folk heroes of Germany. See also PATHOLOGY.

VIRILISM is synonymous with *masculinization.

VIROLOGY is the branch of *microbiology concerned with *viruses. See MICROBIOLOGY.

VIRULENCE is the ability of a particular micro-organism (bacterium, virus, protozoan, etc.) to cause infection or death. Epidemiologically, virulence is judged by severity of clinical disease or by case fatality rate. In the laboratory, virulence is quantified by measuring the dose of micro-organisms required to kill one half of a population of experimental animals (the median lethal dose or LD_{50}) or to produce some observable effect other than death (the median effective dose or ED_{50}).

VIRUS. An infectious micro-organism smaller than a *bacterium, usually beyond the resolution of the light *microscope, and consisting simply of a nucleic acid (*deoxyribonucleic acid (DNA) or *ribonucleic acid (RNA) but never both) genome in a protein envelope. Unlike bacteria, viruses can only reproduce inside host cells. See MICROBIOLOGY.

VISCOSITY is the property of a fluid whereby it tends to resist relative motion within itself. A viscous liquid (i.e. one of high viscosity) drags in a treacle-like manner. Viscosity is measured in newton seconds per square metre (SI units).

VISCUS. Any of the large organs of the body (plural:viscera).

VISION is the faculty of sight, or the act of seeing. Visual acuity, or sharpness of sight, depends on the ability of the eye to adjust its total refractive power so that both near and distant objects can be brought into focus on the retina (see LENS; OPHTHALMOLOGY). Too strong a refractive power relative to the anteroposterior length of the eye causes short-sight (myopia), too weak long-sight (hypermetropia).

VISNA is a slow virus infection of the central nervous system in sheep, characterized by progressive paralysis and the pathological changes of inflammation and demyelination; it is due to an enveloped ribonucleic acid (RNA) *retrovirus (cf. SCRAPIE).

VISUAL ACUITY is sharpness (i.e. power of *resolution) of vision, usually measured by means of standard *test types.

VISUAL FIELD. The area, assessed for each eye separately with the visual axis held in the straight forward direction, within which visual stimuli can be perceived; it can be roughly but usefully assessed at the bedside by 'confrontation' testing, that is by comparison with the examiner's (contralateral) visual field.

VISUAL PURPLE. See RHODOPSIN.

VITAL CAPACITY is the maximum volume of gas which can be expelled from the lungs after maximal inspiration. See RESPIRATORY PHYSIOLOGY.

VITALISM is the doctrine that the origin and manifestations of life are produced by a vital force or principle as distinct from chemical and physical forces.

VITAL STATISTICS is that branch of statistics, sometimes known as biostatistics, which deals with demographic data (birth rate, death rate, morbidity, etc.). See EPIDEMIOLOGY.

VITAMIN A, also known as retinol, is a fat-soluble vitamin which together with its precursor substance (or pro-vitamin) carotene is widely distributed in foodstuffs, particularly dairy products, fish liver oils, and vegetables. It is essential for the normal functioning of skin and mucous membranes and for adequate night vision (see CAROTENE; RHODOPSIN; NIGHT BLINDNESS; XEROPHTHALMIA). Very large doses of vitamin A are toxic.

VITAMIN B covers a number of essential water-soluble dietary components, collectively known as the vitamin B complex. They include thiamine, also known as aneurin or vitamin B_1 (see THIAMINE; BERIBERI); riboflavin or vitamin B_2, which functions as a *coenzyme in the processes of oxidative metabolism and which is plentiful in the normal Western diet; niacin or vitamin B_3, sometimes also called vitamin PP for 'pellagra-preventing', which is a mixture of nicotinic acid and nicotinamide (see NIACIN; PELLAGRA); pantothenic acid or vitamin B_5, essential as part of the coenzyme A molecule for normal metabolism but so available in the human diet that spontaneous deficiency does not occur; pyridoxine and related substances, collectively known as vitamin B_6, which are concerned particularly with amino acid metabolism and lack of which may be a cause of anaemia; and cyanocobalamin or vitamin B_{12} (see CYANOCOBALAMIN; PERNICIOUS ANAEMIA). Other substances usually classified with the vitamin B complex are *biotin (or vitamin H), *choline, and *folic acid, although spontaneous deficiency of the first two probably does not occur in man and choline is not strictly a vitamin (see MEGALOBLASTIC ANAEMIA).

VITAMIN C. See ASCORBIC ACID; SCURVY.

VITAMIN D. See CALCIFEROL; RICKETS; OSTEOMALACIA.

VITAMIN E. See TOCOPHEROL.

VITAMIN K. A group of fat-soluble vitamins which promotes the synthesis in the liver of *prothrombin and several other blood coagulation factors (see HAEMATOLOGY). Though the dietary content of vitamin K is normally adequate (and is supplemented by bacterial synthesis in the gastrointestinal tract), a deficiency may develop in conditions associated with *malabsorption of fat. Newborn infants may also suffer from a haemorrhagic state due to deficiency of vitamin K, while oral anticoagulant drugs such as the *coumarin group achieve their effect by inhibiting the K-dependent hepatic synthesis of clotting factors.

VITAMINS, or accessory food factors, comprise a group of unrelated organic compounds which have in common the twin attributes of being necessary in trace amounts to the normal metabolic functioning of an organism and yet not being capable of synthesis by it; the organism to remain healthy must therefore obtain them from the environment, in man normally from the diet. Vitamins are peculiar to species; what is a vitamin for one organism may be capable of synthesis by another and therefore not a vitamin for it. For example, vitamin C (*ascorbic acid) is an essential part of man's diet but of few other animals.

The defining qualifications 'organic' and 'in trace amounts' should be noted. Essential *amino acids and essential *trace elements are not classified as vitamins.

Adequate amounts of the various vitamins are necessary to the human diet to prevent corresponding deficiency disorders. For recommended daily dietary allowances, see NUTRITION, Tables 2 and 3. There is no good evidence that excessive amounts are ever beneficial, and, as in the case of vitamins A and D, they may be harmful.

Sir Frederick Gowland *Hopkins first proposed the existence of accessory food factors in 1906, though deficiency diseases like *scurvy, *beriberi, and *rickets had been empirically treated with appropriate foodstuffs for many years before that. See also NUTRITION.

VITILIGO is a skin disorder in which there is progressive destruction of epidermal melanocytes (*melanin-producing cells), probably as a result of an *autoimmune process, causing patches of depigmentation. The white areas are usually symmetrical, sharply defined, and with a scalloped and hyperpigmented border. Other autoimmune disorders may be associated.

VITREOUS. The transparent gel-like substance that occupies the posterior cavity of the eye, between the *lens and the *retina. See OPHTHALMOLOGY.

VIVISECTION is the performance of experiments on living animals involving surgical procedures. See LICENCES FOR ANIMAL EXPERIMENTATION; VETERINARY MEDICINE.

VOCAL CORDS. The two mucous membrane-covered ridges which form the V-shaped opening within the *larynx known as the *glottis, through which the breath passes; their length and tension determine the pitch of the voice, and they are drawn together as the glottis is closed during swallowing.

VOIT, KARL VON (1831–1908). German physiologist, MD Munich (1854). Voit studied chemistry with *Liebig (1852) and Wöhler (1855) and was elected to the chair of physiology in Munich in 1863. Much of his working life was devoted to metabolic research and especially to the chemistry of *nutrition. He worked with *Pettenkofer in devising a method of studying simultaneously the utilization of food, heat production, and respiratory exchange in large animals. Together they proved the conservation of energy in living animals.

VOLHARD, FRANZ (1872–1950). German physician, MD Halle (1897). Volhard's early interest was in metabolic diseases. He was made professor at Halle in 1918 and at Frankfurt in 1927, became a leading authority on kidney disease, and published with Karl Theodor Fahr (1877–1945) an important and influential book on the subject.

VOLKMANN, RICHARD VON (1830–89). German surgeon, MD Berlin (1854). Volkmann was appointed professor of surgery in Halle in 1867, but served in the army medical services in the wars of 1866 and 1870. A supporter of *Lister's views, he was the first to excise the rectum for cancer (1878). He described the fibrosis of muscle resulting from *ischaemia (Volkmann's ischaemic contracture, 1881), and recommended cod liver oil in surgical tuberculosis. Volkmann was also a poet of some distinction (under the name Richard Leander).

VOLVULUS. Twisting of a loop of *intestine and its mesenteric attachment, causing intestinal *ischaemia and obstruction.

VOMITING is the forcible regurgitation and ejection through the mouth of the contents of the stomach. Vomiting, which is a reflex action of obvious protective value when due, for example, to ingestion of an irritant substance, is preceded or accompanied by retching, nausea, sweating, and pallor. It involves reverse peristaltic contractions of the stomach and spasmodic contractions of the respiratory and abdominal muscles. Vomiting is controlled by vomiting centres in the *medulla oblongata of the brain, and can be precipitated by a variety of stimuli.

VORONOFF, SERGE (1866–1951). French physiologist and surgeon, MD Paris (1890). Born in Russia, Voronoff became a naturalized French citizen in 1897. He worked on the grafting of organs, with special reference to rejuvenation and the prevention of ageing through grafting testicular tissue.

VOYEURISM is a sexual deviation (or variation as some have it) in which vicarious pleasure is obtained from observation of the sexual activity of others, even sometimes of animals. It includes *troilism and the peeping-tom syndrome.

VULVA. The region of the female external genitalia, bounded by the mons veneris (mons pubis) and the two folds of skin and subcutaneous fat known as the *labia majora or greater pudendal lips and enclosing the labia minora or lesser pudendal lips, the *vaginal and *urethral orifices, and the *clitoris.

W

WAGNER-JAUREGG, JULIUS (1857–1941). Austrian psychiatrist, MD Vienna (1880). A friend of *Freud, Wagner-Jauregg became a psychiatrist by default, failing to obtain a medical post at a teaching hospital. In 1889 he succeeded *Krafft-Ebing in the chair of psychiatry at Graz. He was interested in the beneficial effect of *fever in psychotics, especially in those with dementia paralytica (*general paralysis of the insane). In 1917 he inoculated such a patient with benign tertian *malaria and noted striking improvement. He continued to develop the method for the next 20 years. In 1927 he was awarded the Nobel prize for his work.

WAKLEY, THOMAS (1795–1862). British physician, reformer, and editor, MRCS (1817). Wakley was a friend of William Cobbett and well aware of the jobbery and nepotism in the medical profession. He founded the *Lancet* in 1823, publishing reports of hospital lectures and operations and attacking hospital administration and the Royal College of Surgeons. He was involved in many law suits. He was coroner for West Middlesex from 1839 until his death and sat as Member of Parliament for Finsbury from 1835 until 1852. He obtained a pardon for the Tolpuddle Martyrs. Clauses from his Private Member's Bill were adopted in the *Medical Act 1858. He reduced adulteration by publishing analyses of foods in the *Lancet* (1851). Wakley led an unremitting battle against injustice, favouritism, and charlatanism. See also MEDICAL JOURNALS.

WAKSMAN, SELMAN ABRAHAM (1888–1973). American microbiologist, born in Russia, MS Rutgers University 1916. Waksman remained at Rutgers University throughout his career, becoming professor of microbiology. His field of study was the microbiology of soil. From various soil organisms he isolated *antibiotics, including *streptomycin, *neomycin, and *actinomycin. For his work on streptomycin, the first effective treatment for *tuberculosis, he received many honours, including the Nobel prize in 1952.

WALD, LILLIAN (1867–1940). See PUBLIC HEALTH IN THE USA.

WALDEYER-HARTZ, HEINRICH WILHELM GOTTFRIED VON (1836–1921). German anatomist, MD Berlin (1862). Professor of pathological anatomy at Breslau (1868), Strasbourg (1872), and Berlin (1883), Waldeyer-Hartz was a successful teacher and administrator. He studied the spread of *tumours and the mechanism of *metastasis (1867–72), discovered the germinal epithelium (1870), and described the pharyngeal lymphoid tissue (Waldeyer's ring). He suggested the terms '*chromosome' and '*neurone', showing that the second was the basic unit of the nervous system.

WALE, JOHANNES DE (Walaeus) (1604–49). Dutch physician, MD Leiden (1631). Wale was professor of medicine at Leiden and a strong supporter of *Harvey's views on the circulation. He confirmed these by showing that blood spurted from a ligated artery if an incision were made proximal to the ligature, but only oozed through one which was distal (1640).

WALLER, AUGUSTUS DESIRE (1856–1922). English physiologist, MB Aberdeen (1878), FRS (1892). Augustus Waller was the only child of the no less distinguished neurophysiologist Augustus Volny *Waller. He was born in Paris and received his early education in Geneva. When he was 14 his father died and his mother moved to Aberdeen, where Augustus attended the medical school, graduating MB ChB in 1878. He decided to devote himself to physiology and went to work with Burdon Sanderson in London and with Carl *Ludwig in Leipzig. He then settled in London, obtaining lectureships in physiology successively at the London School of Medicine for Women and St Mary's Hospital Medical School. Laboratory facilities at these institutions were not well developed and Waller carrried out much experimental work at home, at first in his mother's house and later, after his marriage to Alice Palmer, in his own, with her, in St John's Wood. In 1901, largely at Waller's initiative, a research physiology laboratory was established in the newly reconstructed University of London buildings in South Kensington, of which he was appointed director.

He investigated many topics, but always one at a time and with one method, with scrupulous accuracy. Most concerned the electrical response of tissues to stimulation. He used the capillary electrometer and the string galvanometer but his favourite instrument was the reflecting galvanometer. He made important advances in cardiac electrophysiology; he was the first to suggest the electric dipole model of the heart (1898), showing how the varying cardiac potentials could be measured at the body surface and how the human *electrocardiogram could be obtained. He also studied nerve excitation and the effect of narcotic and other drugs; and was led on from this to a consideration of the problems of general anaesthesia. During the war he turned his attention to the assessment of the physiological cost of different kinds of occupational work by measuring carbon dioxide production. During the latter part of his life he became interested in applying his galvanometers to the measurement of the emotional response of human subjects (the so-called 'psychogalvanic reflex'), anticipating the modern use of the *polygraph.

He published much, including an *Introduction to Physiology* in 1891 which was highly praised, and another book on *Animal Electricity*.

WALLER, AUGUSTUS VOLNEY (1816–70). British physiologist, MD Paris (1840), LSA (1841), FRS (1851). Waller gave up general practice in London for research first in Bonn (1851–6) and later in Paris (1856–8). He became professor of physiology in Birmingham in 1858 but left after two years to work in Bruges and subsequently in Geneva. He demonstrated the vasoconstrictor action of *sympathetic nerves and the function of the *posterior root ganglia. He described the *diapedesis of *leucocytes (1846) and the degeneration of the *myelin sheath of a *nerve after its section ('Wallerian degeneration', 1851).

WALSHE, SIR FRANCIS MARTIN ROUSE (1885–1973). British neurologist, MD London (1913), D.Sc. (1924), FRCP (1920), FRS (1946). In his early years Walshe undertook much neurophysiological research, working at one time under *Sherrington. In 1921 he was elected to the staff of the *National Hospital for Nervous Diseases, Queen Square, London, and in 1924 was given charge of a neurological department founded for him at *University College Hospital. His interest lay in the correlation of clinical and experimental findings, but in later years, he gained an international reputation as an acutely critical writer on *neurology.

WARBURG, OTTO HEINRICH (1883–1970). German biochemist, Ph.D. Berlin (1906). Warburg was professor of biochemistry in Freiburg and director (1931–53) to the Kaiser Wilhelm (now Max Planck) Institute for cell physiology in Berlin. His researches covered a wide field: he made many contributions to biochemical methodology; he identified cytochrome oxidase (1934) and *nicotinamide (1938); and he studied *photosynthesis, tissue *respiration, and the metabolism of *cancer cells. He was awarded the Nobel prize in 1931.

WARD, JOSHUA (1685–1761). British quack doctor. Although Ward was returned as Member of Parliament for Marlborough in 1716, he never took his seat and had to flee to France because of electoral irregularities. While abroad he devised his celebrated 'drop and pill' and returned to England with a pardon from the King whose dislocated thumb he had reduced. He received the Royal permission to drive his carriage through St James's Park. Ward, known as 'Spot' because of a facial birthmark, converted three houses in Pimlico into a hospital for the poor. He was exempted by name from the Apothecaries Act (1748), which disallowed unregistered prescription. His pill which contained *antimony is said to have killed as many as it cured.

WARDROP, JAMES (1782–1869). British surgeon, MD St Andrews (1834), FRCS Edinburgh (1804), FRCS England (1843). Wardrop practised in Edinburgh as an ophthalmic surgeon from 1804 until 1808 when he moved to London. He was appointed surgeon-extraordinary to the Prince Regent in 1818 and to George IV in 1823, becoming surgeon-in-ordinary in 1828. Wardrop was renowned for the operation of resection of the lower jaw and for distal ligature for *aneurysm. During the final illness of George IV he was offended by what he considered the unjust behaviour of his colleagues and withdrew from public life.

WARFARIN is one of the *coumarin group of oral *anticoagulant agents, used in the prophylaxis and treatment of venous thrombosis and its complications and in other situations where it is desired to inhibit blood coagulation. Warfarin is also used as rat poison.

WARREN, JOHN (1753–1815). American surgeon, AB Harvard (1863), MD Harvard (1866). Warren was born in Roxbury, Massachusetts, USA, and took an active part in the Boston Tea Party of 1773. At various times he was prominent in helping control of *smallpox and *yellow fever epidemics. He gave anatomical lectures at the military hospital in Boston, helped found the Boston Medical Society, and established the first school of medicine associated with *Harvard in 1782, becoming the first professor of anatomy and surgery there. Warren was a pioneer in many surgical procedures.

WARREN, JOHN COLLINS (1778–1856). American surgeon, MD Harvard (1819). John Collins Warren was born in Boston, USA, one of John *Warren's 17 children. He studied medicine with his father at *Harvard, and followed his father in the chair of anatomy and surgery. He was Dean of the medical school at Harvard from 1816 to 1819, and surgeon at *Massachusetts General Hospital. Warren performed the first operation for *strangulated hernia in the USA, and in 1846 invited the dentist *Morton to administer ether *anaesthesia to a patient from whom he removed a tumour of the neck. The Warren Museum of Harvard Medical School was founded on the geological, palaeontological, and other specimens he left. He was also a founder of the *New England Journal of Medicine and Surgery*.

WARREN, JOHN COLLINS (1842–1927). American surgeon, MD Harvard (1866). This John Collins Warren was grandson of John *Warren, the founder of the *Harvard medical school; several members of the Warren family held faculty appointments there, as well as staff appointments at the *Massachusetts General Hospital. He visited *Lister's clinic in Glasgow in 1869, and brought back to Boston the concept of *antisepsis in surgery. He was appointed to the surgical staff of the Massachusetts General Hospital, and became Moseley professor of surgery in 1899. With Henry P. *Bowditch he conceived and carried to fruition the plan to relocate the Harvard Medical School on its present site. Warren personally secured much of the needed funding for the project, which included construction of a dormitory for the medical students.

WARREN, SAMUEL (1807–77). British physician, barrister, and author, FRS (1835). Warren studied medicine at Edinburgh in 1826–7 but did not graduate, and was later called to the bar. He was elected FRS in 1835 and became a Queen's Counsel in 1851. From 1856 to 1859 he was Member of Parliament for Midhurst and from 1852 to 1874 Recorder of Hull. He was appointed a Master of Lunacy in 1845. He wrote many novels, tracts, and legal textbooks. Of his novels *Ten Thousand a Year* (1839) was the best known.

WART. See VERRUCA.

WASSERMANN, AUGUST-PAUL VON (1860–1925). German bacteriologist, MD Strasbourg (1888). One of *Koch's assistants (1891), Wassermann became director of the Institute of Experimental Therapy in Berlin and of Hygiene at the War Ministry (1913). He studied *complement fixation and described his test for syphilis in 1906 (Wassermann reaction). In later years he turned his attention to the *chemotherapy of cancer.

WASSERMANN REACTION. One of a number of serological tests for *syphilis which depend upon the fact that syphilitic patients (and occasionally those with other diseases) develop *antibodies to a normal component of many tissues called cardiolipin. See KAHN TEST.

WATER (H_2O) is the normal oxide of *hydrogen. Pure water (natural water is never quite pure) is a colourless odourless liquid of melting point 0 °C and boiling point 100 °C, with a maximum density of 1.000 gram per cubic centimetre at 4 °C. Liquid water consists of associated polar molecules with hydrogen bonds between the molecules. The human body (70 kg) contains about 40 litres of water.

WATER BED. A water-filled rubber mattress, the object of which is to ensure that the patient's weight is distributed evenly.

WATER BRASH is *regurgitation into the throat and mouth of acid sour-tasting fluid from the stomach, often accompanied by *heartburn.

WATER CLOSET. A device for flushing excreta into a drain by discharging the contents of a water cistern. Water closets first came into limited use in the latter half of the 18th c., when they constituted a potent source of infection because of the dry brick-built drains into which they emptied.

WATER-HAMMER PULSE is the term (named after a Victorian toy) given to a type of peripheral arterial *pulse wave in which there is an unusually sharp upstroke followed by a similarly abrupt diastolic collapse, so that the percussion wave gives a palpable shock to the examining fingers. The sign, also known as a collapsing pulse or Corrigan's pulse, is seen at its most marked in *aortic incompetence.

WATERHOUSE, BENJAMIN (1754–1846). American physician, MD Leiden (1780). Waterhouse studied medicine at Edinburgh, Leiden, and *Harvard. He practised in Boston, and became professor of the theory and practice of physic at Harvard. From about 1800 he began using *Jenner's method of cowpox *vaccination, to protect against *smallpox. This caused much controversy. He was supported in the matter by President Thomas Jefferson, and lived to see himself vindicated.

WATER SUPPLY. The object is to supply the community with an adequate quantity of clean, pure, odourless, and palatable water. In the UK local authorities are required under the Public Health Act of 1936 periodically to ascertain the adequacy and wholesomeness of supplies in their district. The Water Act of 1973 created 10 regional water authorities in England and Wales under the Department of Environment; in 1974, these became responsible for water conservation and supply, sewerage and sewage disposal, and for the obligations of the former river authorities. A National Water Council has an advisory role.

The two most important medical aspects of water supply are chemical and microbiological. *Dental caries is markedly influenced by the *fluorine content of water; areas in which the supply contains one part per million or more have a very low prevalence compared with those in which the content is much less. Hardness or softness, governed by the content of calcium and magnesium salts, is also important; there is a positive correlation between soft water and the incidence of sudden death from *coronary heart disease. A similar but weaker relationship exists with congenital malformations of the central nervous system. Iodine deficiency in water is a possible cause of *goitre.

Numerous virus, bacterial, and parasitic diseases may be transmitted by contaminated water. They include virus hepatitis, poliomyelitis, gastroenteritis, enteric fever, bacillary dysentery, leptospirosis, cholera, amoebiasis, hookworm, bilharzia, filariasis, and many others.

WATSON, DR is the companion, friend, foil, and chronicler to Sherlock Holmes in the much-loved stories of Sir Arthur Conan *Doyle. Dr Watson's medical practice was variously 'quiet', 'never very absorbing,' or 'could get along very well for a day or two'.

WAVE. A periodic disturbance in a medium or in space that involves the elastic displacement of material particles or a periodic change in some physical quantity (e.g. temperature, pressure, electric potential, etc.).

WAX BATHS. A technique of *physiotherapy for applying heat to a part of the body by immersing it in heated liquid wax.

WEAKNESS. Lack of strength, feebleness, ill health.

WEAL (alternative spelling, wheal). A raised streak or patch of cutaneous *oedema accompanied by *erythema, due to *trauma or *urticaria.

WEATHER AND DISEASE. See ENVIRONMENT AND DISEASE; TROPICAL MEDICINE; ECOLOGY; HEAT AS CAUSE OF DISEASE; FROSTBITE; CLIMATOTHERAPY; FAMINE.

WEBER, ERNST HEINRICH (1795–1878). German anatomist and physiologist, MD Wittenberg (1815). Weber was appointed professor of anatomy at Leipzig (1821) and was one of three brothers holding chairs there. With one of them, Eduard Friedrich Weber (1806–71), he applied the study of hydrodynamics to the circulation and measured the velocity of the *pulse wave (1825). They were the first to demonstrate the inhibitory effect of *vagal stimulation (1845). His later researches were into sensory functions, especially those of touch and temperature.

WEBER, FRIEDRICH EUGEN (1832–91). German otologist. In Weber's test for *deafness a vibrating tuning fork is applied to the vertex of the skull. If the air passages are blocked on one side the sound is best heard there. If the internal ear is affected by disease the sound is best heard on the unaffected side.

WEBER, FREDERICK PARKES (1863–1962). English physician, MB Cambridge (1889), MD (1892), FRCP (1898). Educated at Cambridge and *St Bartholomew's Hospital, Weber became physician to the German Hospital in 1894, a position which he held for 50 years. He was a supreme collector and describer of medical rarities, and his name is linked with familial *telangiectasia,

cerebral *angioma, and relapsing *panniculitis (*Weber–Christian disease). In his life of close on 100 years, he saw much and forgot little; his millenary of papers seem little more than the gleanings of his vast store of knowledge. He attended medical meetings well into his 80s, and published papers and annotations into his 90s.

WEBER, SIR HERMAN (1823–1918). London physician, MD Bonn (1846), FRCP (1859). Weber described the syndrome of *hemiplegia together with *paralysis of the *oculomotor nerve of the opposite side due to a lesion of the cerebral peduncle.

WEBER–CHRISTIAN DISEASE is a rare condition characterized by recurrent patches of inflammation in the subcutaneous layer of fat (panniculus adiposus), resolution of which leaves puckered dimples on the skin. The chief features are summarized in the alternative name; relapsing febrile nodular non-suppurative panniculitis. The aetiology is unknown but the prognosis is generally good.

WEEPING describes a wound or surface which is discharging clear serous fluid.

WEIGERT, KARL (1845–1904). German pathologist, MD Berlin (1866). A cousin of *Ehrlich, after being professor-extraordinary at Leipzig (1879) he became director of the pathological institute of the Senckenberg Foundation in Frankfurt. Weigert devised special stains for *myelin sheaths (1884), *fibrin (1887), and *elastic fibres (1898), and made valuable contributions on miliary tuberculosis, smallpox, and nephritis.

WEIGHT is defined as the force of attraction of the Earth on a given mass. It is therefore properly expressed in units of force, such as the newton (N). Strictly speaking, weight should not be expressed in units of mass, since the acceleration of free fall (g) varies with geographical position and the weight of a mass (m) is equal to mg.

WEIL'S DISEASE. See LEPTOSPIROSIS.

WELCH, WILLIAM HENRY (1850–1934). American pathologist and microbiologist, MD Columbia University (1875). Welch spent several years studying in various European clinics, then returned to the USA to teach pathology at *Bellevue Hospital, New York City. He moved on to *Johns Hopkins Hospital and Medical School when that institution opened in 1889, as the first professor of pathology. He exerted a powerful influence upon the incorporation of the scientific method and thought into the teaching and practice of medicine in the USA. His special interest was in infectious diseases. He demonstrated that *Staphylococcus epidermidis could cause wound infections, and first described an anaerobic organism—*Clostridium welchii*—isolated from patients with *gas gangrene. He served on many committees and boards, and played a prominent role in the formation of the *Rockefeller Institute in New York, where for many years he was chairman of the Board of Scientific Advisors.

WELLCOME, SIR HENRY SOLOMON (1853–1936). Anglo-American patron of science and medicine. With his compatriot, E. M. Burroughs he founded the pharmaceutical firm of Burroughs Wellcome in 1880. In 1924 he endowed the Wellcome Trust. He was naturalized a British citizen in 1910, knighted in 1932, and elected fellow of the Royal Society the same year.

WELLCOME FOUNDATION. This foundation ultimately arose from the partnership of two American pharmacists, Silas M. Burroughs and Henry S. *Wellcome in the firm of Burroughs Wellcome & Co. in London in 1880. This inaugurated a new era in pharmacy as American methods were introduced into the UK. Both partners became British subjects, and Wellcome was later knighted. Burroughs died in 1895, and in 1924 Wellcome brought together all his now extensive business interests into the Wellcome Foundation Ltd. On his death in 1936 the profits of the company were transferred under his will to the Wellcome Trust which is the largest endowed charitable trust supporting research in medicine in the UK. It has over the years made benefactions of about £92 million. The business interests are of large scale and world-wide. They conform with the ideas of the founders in 'the discovery, development, manufacture, and sale of products to promote the health and hygiene of man and animals'. The headquarters remains in Euston Road in London, with research and production facilities round the UK and abroad in many countries, including the USA in North Carolina. In the London building is housed the *Wellcome Institute for the History of Medicine.

WELLCOME INSTITUTE FOR THE HISTORY OF MEDICINE has arisen from the Wellcome Historical Medical Museum and Library set up by Sir Henry *Wellcome in the 40 years before he died in 1936. His will founded the Wellcome Trust, a charity devoted to supporting medical, scientific, and medical historical research. Its funds come from the trading profits of the international pharmaceutical company, the *Wellcome Foundation, whose sole shareholders are the Trustees. This is a most remarkable arrangement, having many beneficial results.

Wellcome had made a collection of books and artefacts with a major theme of medical history, and this forms the basis of the present library and museum, both of which have been added to in subsequent years. There is also a Wellcome Research Institution, and the present Institute includes this and the Library. Because of several factors, especially shortage of space at the building in Euston Road, London, the Museum has been loaned permanently to the Science Museum in South Kensington, where parts of it are on display. The Library remains at Euston Road and is probably the best library in Europe on medical history, with many rare documents and volumes among its 400 000 printed works. Research in medical history has been enhanced by links with the Unit of the History of Medicine of University College, London.

WELLCOME TRUST. See WELLCOME FOUNDATION.

WELLS, HORACE (1815–48). American dentist. Wells practised in Hartford, Connecticut, USA. Gardner Colton, a chemist, visited the town in 1844, and demonstrated laughing gas—now known as *nitrous oxide. Wells saw a person in the audience who hurt his leg while under its influence and yet felt no pain. The next day he induced Colton to administer the gas to him while Riggs, a fellow dentist, extracted a molar tooth. Wells felt no pain and used the gas in his practice. He gave a public demonstration of it, which unfortunately failed lamentably. This discredited the gas and also Wells himself. He left the practice of dentistry as a result and later commited suicide in despair about the episode. This is sad since nitrous oxide is still widely used in anaesthetic practice, yet its pioneer never had a chance to know this. See ANAESTHESIA.

WELLS, SIR THOMAS SPENCER, BT (1818–97). British surgeon, FRCS (1844). After studying at Leeds, Trinity College, Dublin, and *St Thomas's Hospital (1839–41) and after service in Malta as a naval surgeon from 1841 to 1848 Wells returned to London and was appointed to the staff of the Samaritan Hospital in 1854. He served during the Crimean war. In 1863 he became surgeon to the Royal Household and in 1883 became president of the Royal College of Surgeons, receiving a baronetcy the same year. Wells was one of the earliest of the great abdominal surgeons, particularly skilled in *ovariotomy, which he had carried out over 1000 times by 1880. He devised the well-known Spencer Wells artery *forceps.

WEN. A *sebaceous cyst of the skin.

WENCKEBACH, KAREL FREDERIK (1864–1940). Dutch physician, MD Utrecht (1888). After working in pathological anatomy at Utrecht, Wenckebach became professor of internal medicine at Groningen (1901), Strasbourg (1911–14), and Vienna (1929). He described a collection of fibres running from the superior *vena cava to the right atrium (Wenckebach's bundle), but his reputation was founded on his studies of the cardiac *arrhythmias (1903, 1914). He described a form of atrioventriculular block with progressive lengthening of the PR interval until conduction fails (Wenckebach periods, 1899). See also CARDIOLOGY I and II.

WERLHOF, PAUL GOTTLIEB (1699–1767). German physician, FRS (1735). Werlhof described *purpura haemorrhagica or Werlhof's disease in which there are spontaneous *haemorrhages into the skin and mucous membranes and many other tissues and organs. This is now known to be caused by a diminution of *platelets (thrombocytes) in the blood, but of unknown origin. The modern name for the malady is idiopathic thrombocytopenic purpura.

WERNICKE, KARL (1848–1905). German neuropsychiatrist, MD Breslau (1870). Wernicke was professor of neurology and psychiatry at Breslau (1885) and Halle (1904). He described sensory *aphasia (Wernicke's aphasia), the encephalopathy known by his name (*Wernicke's encephalopathy), and the hemianopic pupil reaction.

WERNICKE'S ENCEPHALOPATHY, sometimes known as cerebral *beriberi, is a syndrome caused by brain damage due to deficiency of *thiamine (vitamin B$_1$) and commonly though not invariably associated with severe chronic *alcoholism. The main features are *ophthalmoplegia, *nystagmus, and cerebellar *ataxia together with the *amnesia and *confabulation characteristic of *Korsakoff's syndrome. Pathological examination of the brain shows widespread symmetrical areas of *necrosis, *demyelination, *capillary proliferation, and *haemorrhage, especially in the *brainstem and *mammillary bodies. The condition is a dangerous one, and requires urgent administration of thiamine.

WERTHEIM, ERNST (1864–1920). Austrian gynaecologist, MD Graz (1888). After serving as director of the gynaecological department of the Elizabeth Hospital in Vienna, Wertheim took charge of the first University Women's Clinic in 1910. He devised his radical pan-*hysterectomy for *cervical carcinoma (Wertheim's operation) in 1898.

WESBROOK, FRANK FAIRCHILD (1868–1918). Canadian physician and educator, MD Manitoba (1891). Born in Ontario, Wesbrook grew up in Winnipeg, where his father was mayor. After his MD at Manitoba, he became John Lucas Walker fellow of Gonville and Caius College, Cambridge (1892–5), where he was closely associated with Michael *Foster, Charles *Sherrington, William Bateson, Almroth *Wright, George *Adami, Humphrey Davy *Rolleston, Horace Darwin, W. B. Hardy, and John Scott *Haldane. At the age of 27 Wesbrook was made professor of pathology at the University of Minnesota. By 1906 he was named their first full-time dean of medicine.

In 1913 he was made founding president of the University of British Columbia in Vancouver. He died in the influenza epidemic of 1918 aged 50 years. In his five hectic years he changed life on the west coast of Canada as much as any other Canadian in history.

WEST, CHARLES (1816–98). British physician, MD Berlin (1840), FRCP (1848). Born in London, West studied in Bonn, Paris, and Berlin, where he qualified in medicine. He failed in general practice in the City of London, so went to Dublin to study *midwifery. He returned to London as physician to the Infirmary for Women and Children, Waterloo Road, and lectured on midwifery at the *Middlesex Hospital and *St Bartholomew's. In 1852 he founded the Hospital for Sick Children in Richard *Mead's house in *Great Ormond Street and was physician there for 23 years. Those who helped the foundation included Lord Shaftesbury and Charles Dickens. The Hospital became and remains a great international institution.

WESTMINSTER HOSPITAL was founded in London in 1716 by public subscription, in response to the needs of the sick poor of the time. At first it was opposite Westminster Abbey, but moved to its present site about half a mile away in 1939. When the *National Health Service started it incorporated the Westminster Children's Hospital (1948) and is now the major part of a complex of hospitals. There is a Westminster Medical School and a Nursing School associated with it, the Medical School being part of the University of London.

WET NURSE. A woman who suckles another's child.

WHIPPLE, GEORGE HOYT (1878–1976). American pathologist, MD Johns Hopkins (1905). Whipple was a member of the department of pathology at *Johns Hopkins until 1914, when he became professor of pathology and director of the Hooper Foundation at the University of California. When a new medical school was being created at the University of Rochester he accepted an invitation to move there as head of the department of pathology and dean of the medical school in 1921. In his early work at Johns Hopkins he described a chronic inflammatory disease of the bowel, still called Whipple's disease. His later research concerned liver injury, protein regeneration, and iron metabolism. His finding that dogs with *anaemia due to exsanguination recovered rapidly when fed liver led to the use of liver in treatment of patients with *pernicious anaemia by *Minot and Murphy. The Nobel prize in 1934 was given to these three, for discovering the first successful treatment of pernicious anaemia.

WHITE, CHARLES (1728–1813). British surgeon. White became a member of the Corporation of Surgeons in 1762 and was elected fellow of the Royal Society in the same year. White was one of the founders of the Manchester Royal Infirmary and the Lying-in Hospital (later St Mary's Hospital). He has been described as the father of conservative surgery.

WHITE, PAUL DUDLEY (1886–1973). American physician, MD Harvard (1911). White spent his entire professional career in Boston, as a member of the staff of the *Massachusetts General Hospital. He limited his practice to the field of diseases of the heart, and over his long career he trained scores of young physicians in that specialty. His textbook *Heart Disease* was a standard reference work for many years. He was called to Denver, Colorado, in 1955, when President Eisenhower suffered a *myocardial infarct, and his care of the President, as well as his adroit handling of the news releases, was widely appreciated.

WHITE BLOOD CELLS. See LEUCOCYTES.

WHITLOW. A purulent infection of the terminal phalanx of a finger, around or underneath the nail; *paronychia.

WHOOPING COUGH. See PERTUSSIS.

WHYTT, ROBERT (1714–66). British physician, MD Reims (1736), MD St Andrews (1737), FRCP Edinburgh (1738), FRS (1752). Whytt became professor of the theory of medicine in Edinburgh in 1747. In 1761 he was appointed first physician to the King in Scotland and elected president of the Royal College of Physicians of Edinburgh in 1763. He attracted attention by attempting to dissolve stones in the bladder with lime water. He was strongly opposed to the doctrines of *Stahl, who attributed vital activities to an all-pervading 'anima' or soul. Whytt held that involuntary movements in animals were due to a 'stimulus acting on an unconscious sentient principle'.

WIDAL, GEORGES FERNAND ISIDORE (1862–1929). French microbiologist and serologist, MD Paris (1889). Widal was made professor of internal pathology in 1911 and placed in charge of a medical clinic in 1918. He made many studies of infections and described acquired *haemolytic anaemia (Hayem–Widal haemolytic jaundice, 1907). He is best known however for his work on *typhoid fever. With Chantemesse he pointed out the significance of coliform bacilli which did not ferment lactose (1887), devised the diagnostic *agglutination test (Widal's reaction, 1896), and initiated preventive *vaccination (1888).

WILDE, SIR WILLIAM ROBERT WILLS (1815–76). Irish surgeon and antiquary, MD Dublin (1837). He qualified as a surgeon in Dublin in 1837 and practised in Dublin as an ophthalmologist and otolaryngologist. In 1853 he was appointed surgeon-oculist to Queen Victoria in Ireland and in 1864 he was knighted. He wrote much on topographical subjects. He was the father of Oscar Wilde.

WILKS, SIR SAMUEL, BT (1824–1911). British physician, MD London (1850), FRCP (1856), FRS (1870). Wilks was appointed assistant physician to *Guy's Hospital, London, in 1856 and physician in 1866. He was president of the Royal College of Physicians from 1896 to 1899, and was made physician-extraordinary to Queen Victoria in 1897 and received a baronetcy the same year. Although a renowned teacher, editor, morbid anatomist, and a most erudite physician, Wilks was lacking in originality.

WILLAN, ROBERT (1757–1812). British dermatologist, MD Edinburgh (1780), LRCP (1785), FRS (1809). Willan became physician to the Public Dispensary in 1783 and was the first to devise a systematic description of skin diseases. It was set out in his classic work *The Description and Treatment of Cutaneous Diseases* (1798–1814). See DERMATOLOGY.

WILLIS, THOMAS (1621–75). British physician, DM Oxford (1660), FRCP (1664). Willis was appointed Sedleian professor of natural philosophy at Oxford in 1660, but in 1664 moved to London where he practised in St Martin's Lane. Willis was one of the founders and an original fellow of the Royal Society. He was the first to note the sweet taste of the urine in *diabetes mellitus. Richard *Lower assisted him in the preparation of *Cerebri anatome nervorumque descriptio et usus* (1664), in which he described the arterial system at the base of the brain (the *circle of Willis).

WILSON, CHARLES McMORAN (1st Baron Moran of Manton, created 1943) (1882–1977). English physician, MD London (1913), FRCP (1921). Wilson's medical education was in *St Mary's Hospital Medical School, of which institution he became dean for a quarter of a century (1920–45). He served with distinction in the First World War, and in 1945 he published *The Anatomy of Courage*. He became president of the Royal College of Physicians in 1941, and retained this office until 1950, covering the period of medico-political struggle which attended the formation of the *National Health Service, and he played an important positive role at that time. He also had the distinction of being physician to Winston Churchill during and after the Second World War; and this part of his experience he narrated, not without raising some ethical misgivings, in *Winston Churchill, The Struggle for Survival* (1966).

WILSON, EDWARD ADRIAN (1872–1912). British physician, explorer, and ornithologist, MB Cambridge (1900). Wilson accompanied Captain R. F. Scott on Antarctic expeditions, firstly in 1901–2, when he became an expert on Antarctic bird life, and secondly in 1911 when he died with him on about 29 March 1912.

WILSON, SAMUEL ALEXANDER KINNIER (1874–1937). British neurologist, MB Edinburgh (1902), FRCP (1914). Although born in the USA of Irish parents, and educated in Edinburgh, Wilson's work was in London, mainly at *King's College Hospital. He concentrated on neurology immediately after his house appointments. In 1912, he described the syndrome of familial hepatolenticular degeneration which bears his name (*Wilson's disease). He founded the *Journal of Neurology and Psychopathology* in 1920. His writings are marked by unusual clarity, and he was a gifted lecturer.

WILSON, SIR WILLIAM JAMES ERASMUS (1809–84). British surgeon and dermatologist, LSA (1830), MRCS (1831), FRCS (1843), FRS (1845). Wilson became lecturer in anatomy and physiology at the *Middlesex Hospital and later surgeon to the St Pancras Infirmary. After 1840 he limited his practice to dermatology. He was elected president of the Royal College of Surgeons of England in 1881 and received a knighthood the same year. He was a generous benefactor to the Royal College of Surgeons and a protagonist of bathing and Turkish baths. He paid for the transport of Cleopatra's needle (a carved granite obelisk, *c.* 1475 BC) from Egypt to London.

WILSON'S DISEASE is a rare genetic abnormality of copper metabolism. The disease, also known as hepatolenticular degeneration, is inherited as an autosomal *recessive characteristic and is marked by copper deposits in various tissues and organs, notably the liver, brain (especially the basal ganglia), kidney, and cornea. The major clinical manifestations are those of hepatic *cirrhosis, widespread neurological disturbances (in which slurred speech, tremor, muscular rigidity, and mental deterioration usually predominate), and pigmented rings at the corneal rims (Kayser–Fleischer rings). Treatment with a *chelating agent is of benefit if commenced early; *penicillamine is the drug of choice.

WIND is air or gas in the gastrointestinal tract. Wind, or flatus, may cause discomfort due to distention and is normally relieved by expulsion through the anus or oropharynx.

WINDPIPE. See TRACHEA.

WINE is the fermented juice of the grape used as a beverage. The therapeutic value of wine, though often extolled ('Drink no longer water, but use a little wine for thy stomach's sake and thine often infirmities,' I Timothy 5:23) is in most applications less certain than is the damaging effect of the abuse of *ethanol in any form. Where the pharmacological properties of alcohol are desired, wine may be substituted by suitably flavoured and diluted rectified spirit.

WINNICOTT, DONALD (1896–1971). London paediatrician, MB London (1920), FRCP (1944). Winnicott worked mainly at Paddington Green Hospital. He was a man of ideas in regard to the understanding of children, which derived something from *psychoanalysis and child *psychiatry, and he helped to alter attitudes to sick children. He was an outstanding teacher of this philosophy, which was of immense importance yet not capable of purely scientific analysis and measurement.

WISDOM TEETH. The third molar teeth, the last of the permanent dentition to erupt; they often do not appear until early adult life, and may not do so at all. See TEETH.

WISEMAN, RICHARD (?1622–76). British surgeon. Wiseman was apprenticed to the Barber-Surgeons' Company in 1637, made free in 1651, and became Master in 1665. He served in the Dutch navy in 1643, but in the following year he joined the Royalist Army of the West, becoming surgeon in attendance upon Prince Charles's troops and later to Prince Charles. He was taken prisoner at Worcester in 1651 and on release started practice in London. In 1654 he was imprisoned for giving aid to a royalist. At the Restoration he became 'surgein-in-ordinary to the person' in 1660 and serjeant-surgeon in 1671. Wiseman was the first of the great surgeons and did much to raise the craft of surgery to the status of a profession.

WISH FULFILMENT. In Freudian psychology, the attainment of an objective, the desire for which is not acknowledged at the level of the conscious mind.

WISTAR INSTITUTE, THE, in Philadelphia was founded in 1892 as a result of a benefaction of the Wistar family and the initiative of the University of Pennsylvania. At first it was dependent on the income from the endowment but now receives a major contribution from the US *National Institutes of Health. It has no clinical facilities though it co-operates with many hospitals. Its work is essentially devoted to the study of biological phenomena at cellular and subcellular levels. In these it has a world-wide reputation, and it has produced *vaccines against *rubella and *rabies which are now used universally, through sales by pharmaceutical companies. Current concerns are with ageing, nutrition, the cause of tumours, and the actions of viruses on cells. Research workers are drawn from many countries, for the Wistar Institute is international rather than national. Though it is not a degree-granting body students attend for long-term postdoctoral education. In this way the Wistar has influenced medical developments far afield, and this it also does by its associations with the *World Health Organization, and the Pan-American Health Organization.

WITCHCRAFT. Magic or sorcery; the supposed exercise of supernatural powers by witches and *witch-doctors.

WITCH DOCTOR. One who professes to cure disease by *magic arts. Alternatively, among African tribes, especially Kaffirs, one who professes to detect witches and to counteract the effects of their magic.

WITHDRAWAL SYMPTOMS are the symptoms experienced by drug and alcohol addicts during the early stages of abstinence from the addicting substance. See ADDICTION.

WITHERING, WILLIAM (1741–99). British physician and botanist, MD Edinburgh (1766), FRS (1785). Withering was appointed physician to the County Infirmary, Stafford, in 1767 and to the Birmingham General Hospital in 1775. A distinguished botanist, he was the first to use *digitalis, learning that foxglove was 'good for the dropsy' from an old country woman. He published *An Account of the Fox-Glove* (1776) and *The Botanical Arrangement of all the Vegetables Naturally Growing in Great Britain* (1776).

WOLCOT, JOHN (1738–1819). British physician, poet, and, satirist, MD Aberdeen (1767). Wolcot served as physician to the Governor of Jamaica in 1767 and two years later he was ordained. However he failed to obtain the anticipated living and renounced the clerical life. For a while he practised in Truro, but moved to London, where, as Peter Pindar, he wrote satirical verse and pamphlets.

WOLFF–PARKINSON–WHITE SYNDROME is the combination of paroxysmal *tachycardia with characteristic *electrocardiographic (ECG) abnormalities consisting of a short PR interval and a wide QRS complex. The syndrome is due to the presence of an accessory bundle of conducting tissue which short-circuits the normal atrioventricular conducting system and causes premature excitation of the right ventricle; thus the ventricles contract asynchronously and the ventricular complex is splayed out. A re-entry mechanism utilizing the accessory bundle accounts for the paroxysmal tachycardia.

WOLFSON FOUNDATION, THE, was started in 1955 out of the munificence of the businessman, Sir Isaac Wolfson. It has a distinguished board of trustees and makes grants to education, technology, health, and social welfare, the arts, and historic buildings. In 25 years from its founding, over £10 million was granted to health and social welfare projects, about half being for education and research; £17 million went to universities and £10 million to technology.

WOLLASTON, WILLIAM HYDE (1766–1828). British physician and chemist, MD Cambridge (1793), FRS (1794). Wollaston was the nephew of William *Heberden the Elder. He was elected a fellow of Gonville and Caius College, Cambridge, and practised in Huntingdon and Bury St Edmunds before moving to London in 1797. He retired from practice in 1800 and established a chemical laboratory. His many discoveries included the metals palladium (1803) and rhodium (1804); how to render platinum malleable; that *gouty joints contained urates; and that some *calculi were composed of cystine. From his own visual disorders he suggested the semi-decussation of the *optic nerves (1824). He was secretary of the Royal Society (1804) and president from June to November 1820, retiring to allow the election of *Davy.

WOMB. See UTERUS.

WOMEN IN MEDICINE I. Throughout history women have been healers, nurses, midwives, herbalists, and some have assisted with, or made important scientific discoveries. Others have been benefactors and founded hospitals. In existing primitive societies, as in ancient sophisticated ones, medicine, magic, and religion are interwoven.

Ancient history to the fall of Rome. Wall paintings, inscriptions, clay tablets, burial artefacts, and early writings provide evidence of medical practice by women with or without priestly functions. Little is known of their training in Egypt, Sumeria, the Indus Valley, or Greece.

Clay tablets (*c.* 3500 BC) give prescriptions collected by an unknown physician for her students. Queen Shubad of Ur (*c.* 3500 BC) was buried with flint and bronze surgical instruments and prescriptions. The inscription on an Egyptian High Priest's tomb (*c.* 2730 BC) describes his mother as 'chief physician'. Specialization was practised at this period. Circumstantial evidence of treatment of women and children by women is confirmed by the Kahun papyrus (*c.* 2500 BC), an obstetrical and gynaecological treatise.

Atossa, consort of Darius I (522–486 BC) was treated by women for a breast abscess, confinements, and threatened miscarriages.

Herodotus (485–422 BC) wrote of women skilfully removing breasts and performing *Caesarean sections with stone knives and setting and splinting broken bones.

There appear to be no direct references to Indian women practitioners in early records (Thorwald, 1962). During the 1st millennium BC there were midwives, surgeons, and herbalists in China and in Siam, where the poor made no payment. In the 3rd c. BC both men and women worked in Buddhist hospitals in India and Ceylon.

The early history of Greek medicine contains many myths, but Homeric writings (8th–7th c. BC) refer to women treating injuries, nursing the sicᵏ, and administering pain-killing drugs. Painted pottery depicts them letting blood, and tombstones of women physicians and obstetricians have been found. Hippocratic writings (5th–4th c. BC) instruct midwives to pay particular attention to cleanliness of nails, and to restrict themselves to non-interfering techniques, except for retained placentae and necessary versions.

Women physicians were neither writers nor innovators; their work was expected to be so inconspicuous that 'after they were dead, no one would know they had lived'. Some escaped oblivion, amongst them Agnodice (reputedly a pupil of *Herophilus (c. 290 BC) in Alexandria), who returned to a successful Athenian practice. When arraigned by the Tribunal for false pretences, as she wore masculine dress, her patients secured her release.

Pythagoras (c. 530 BC) was assisted in his medical interests by his wife and daughters. *Aristotle acknowledged his wife Pythias for aiding his work on embryos and generation.

Soranus of Ephesus (AD 98–138) wrote a textbook of obstetrics and gynaecology for women students. Possibly Cleopatra (not the queen) was his contemporary; her treatise on these subjects was long lived.

When Corinth fell (146 BC), women prisoners with medical knowledge commanded the highest prices in Roman slave markets.

Roman and Etruscan medicine. Horace (55–8 BC) was impressed by the quality of work of women. Although Plautus (c. 254–184 BC), Terence (c. 195–159 BC), and Ovid (43 BC–AD 18) had pilloried disreputable midwives, highly respected *medicae-obstetricae* flourished during the reigns of Augustus (63 BC–AD 14) and Tiberius (AD 14–37). The writer Cornelius *Celsus described pleasant remedies, and the slaves and instruments of women practitioners. Their private hospitals provided better care than the public ones. References were made by *Pliny the Elder and Scribonius Largus, the companion of Claudius (10 BC–AD 54), to women doctors and those interested in drugs. *Galen valued the remedies of Margareta, an army surgeon and of Antiochus, a colleague at the Esquiline Hill medical school, who studied *arthritis, *sciatica, and *splenic disorders.

Apasia (2nd c. AD) removed uterine tumours, performed cystostomies for urinary retention and herniorrhaphies.

On the Mediterranean littoral, tombstones erected by families and grateful patients provide evidence for women physicians (Hurd-Mead, 1938).

Herbal remedies and drugs. In ancient Egypt rusty wheat was used for uterine bleeding (see ERGOT). 'Rotten bread' *poultices were applied to *boils and septic wounds thereby using the *antibiotic properties of moulds, but the discoverers of these remedies are unknown. Helen of Troy was reputed to have studied in Egypt and to have returned with 'nepenthe' with which to cure pain in friends and to dispose of enemies. Household remedies were prized by Greek and Roman women, the Empress Messalina using them to no good end (i.e. as poisons).

Benefactresses. Queen Semiramis of Persia (c.800 BC) encouraged men and women to study medicine, some going to Egypt.

Pagan and Christian women founded and worked in hospitals for slaves, travellers, and the poor. St Jerome (c. AD 347–420) wrote of women who served patients without fees.

Aurelian's granddaughter is credited with introducing Greek medicine to Persia when she became queen. The school at Edessa was under her protection.

The sack of Rome to the fifteenth century. The sack of Rome (AD 410), destruction of libraries, distintegration of the orderly Roman Empire, constant wars, famines, and plagues, and uncritical adherence to works of Aristotle, *Dioscorides, and Galen stultified intellectual progress. Four major factors contributed to the revival of medicine and learning. Convents and monasteries had continued to care for the sick and preserved and copied ancient manuscripts; *Nestorian heretics took Greek medicine to the Arabs in Syria, Baghdad, and Jundishapur and had learnt from Arabian medicine; Muslim conquests brought men and a few women physicians and surgeons to North Africa and Spain, together with translations of Greek and Roman texts, and later, works of *Rhazes and the Persian *Avicenna. Lastly the European discovery of printing in 1440 expedited the spread of knowledge and reduced the prohibitive cost of books, for example the medical faculty of the University of Paris had only 15 books in the early 14th c.

Influential and intelligent nuns and lay women, some royal, were responsible for the care of the sick in Britain and Europe from the 5th to 15th c. In Italy they replaced men in many hospitals since they were neat and clean and reduced diseases due to faulty diet and dirt. However in 1312 the Council of Vienna decreed that laity should supervise hospitals so that 'the sick be cared for more decently'. The best of the religious were practical, guided by observation and experience rather than the garbled traditions and astrology later dispensed by most universities. They taught girls who were expected to cater for the needs of families, guests, dependents, and, at times, battle casualties. Evidence of their work exists in contemporary pictures, literature (Boccaccio, Chaucer, Piers Plowman), the Paston Letters (family correspondence and state papers, regarded as invaluable sources of social information in England 1422–1509), and their own writings. One of the most famous hospitals was *St Bartholomew's in London, founded in 1100, where the prioress and nuns evidently had considerable knowledge.

The first formal European school of medicine

developed in *Salerno around the 9th c., and continued to 1811 when it was closed by Napoleon. Monks of Monte Cassino, Arabs, Jews, Greeks, Romans, men and women, contributed to the institution. The most famous teacher and practitioner was *Trotula (d. ?1085 or 1097). She was observant, practical, consulted by men and women, an effective teacher, and a skilful surgeon. She devised a classic *perineal repair and stressed the need for cleanliness. She classified diseases as inherited, contagious and 'other'. Her pharmacopoiea and hypotheses were no better or worse than those of her time; unfortunately later plagiarized editions of her writings refer to fetishes and charms.

*Montpellier (1141) was also a school in which women studied and taught; some were private students of Arab, Jewish, or Spanish physicians, the languages of instruction being Arabic, Hebrew, and Latin.

Decrees governing entrance to many European universities founded in the 12th and 13th c. debarred women. Most physicians were clergy and forbidden to shed blood or to be surgeons by the Councils of Tours (1125) and the Lateran (1139), and therefore such tasks were left to laymen or to women. *Bologna was exceptional: not only was *dissection of the human body allowed, but also Mondino de Luzzi (*Mundinus), author of the first modern anatomical textbook, was indebted to Alessandra Giliani for her superb prosections which 'brought him great fame and credit' [sic].

Three 14th c. women alumni of Salerno were Abella, a surgeon, Mercuriade, and Rebecca of Guernica who wrote on fevers, urine, and the embryo (Lipinska, 1900). Other named Italians include Constantia Mammona (d. 1308), a midwife, and two Venetians, Ghilietta Medica and Beatrice di Candida.

In 1345 distinctions were drawn between physicians, surgeons, and women who examined urine, and classes of medical men and women were later defined. Pictures of *apothecaries' shops showed women preparing and directing the work. In 1349 15 women were licensed to practise in Frankfurt-am-Main. Three were eye specialists and one, Margaret of Naples, was appointed physician to King Laslaux. The city had a list of 15 Jewish women practising various specialties and paying high taxes.

Elsewhere, formal education of men and, in particular, of medical women became increasingly difficult during the 14th c. In 1311 the University of Paris decreed 'no surgeon or apothecary, man or woman shall undertake work for which he or she has not been licensed or approved'. Such approval was obtained by successful examinations before the Master Surgeons' Corporation until Charles VIII (1470–98) forbade licensing of women surgeons, even if working under male supervision.

In England the Surgeons' Guild (1368) restricted the practice of barbers and in 1390 the Mayor of London appointed four surgeons to scrutinize men and women surgeons. Possibly some of the latter had gone abroad to the more liberal Italian schools for the physicians prayed that 'no man or woman should be allowed to practice but have a long time, y used the Scoles of Fisyk withynne some universitee and be graduated in the same' (cited by Hurd-Mead, 1938). In 1414 an edict was issued that 'other than university physicians might be licensed by a bishop on recommendation of the Faculty'. In 1421 the Church forbade women, on pain of imprisonment, to practise medicine or surgery. Finally Pope Sixtus IV (who reigned 1471–84) forbade practice by Jews or Gentiles (men or women) who were not university graduates.

Nevertheless there is ample evidence of women physicians and surgeons as well as nuns in Britain, France, Germany, and Italy. Protection was probably due to overriding popular need, poor communications, and powerful patrons and benefactors who endowed religious houses and hospitals. Licensing was not always administered judiciously, and some unlicensed women (and men) must have had lucrative practices as fines were paid repeatedly in London and Paris.

Other patrons included Queen Matilda (d. 1118) and Margaret Beaufort (1448–1509), mother of Henry VII. In France the Countess of Artois sought advice in Paris about suitable designs for infirmaries in convents. Eleanor of Aquitaine (c. 1122–1204), Blanche of Castile, her sisters Berengaria and Urraca of Portugal all endowed hospitals. Elizabeth of Aragon, Queen of Portugal, founded Coimbra Hospital, and Queen Isabella (1451–1504) provided tented hospitals for her army and later, after expulsion of the Moors, presided over building permanent ones and appointed some women to the staff.

Sixteenth to eighteenth centuries. This eventful period began with the Reformation and ended with the American (1775–83) and French Revolutions (1789–95). The many scientific discoveries included those of *Harvey, *Boyle, *Malpighi, *Willis, van *Leeuwenhoek, *Lavoisier and *Cuvier. The Industrial Revolution brought many advances at the cost of poverty, ill health, and exploitation of the workers. After puritanical subordination and neglect of women's education, their emancipation began, partly through the work and literacy and medical writings of women, but also through the support of Defoe, Dr Johnson, and Mary Wollstonecraft Godwin (a passionate advocate of women's rights to social equality with men, who was a 'disgusting and unwomanly creature' according to Horace Walpole) and by the opposing philosophies of revolution and of devout Nonconformists such as John Wesley (1703–91).

The 16th and 17th c. were marred by obsessional witch-hunting and by the Thirty Years War (1618–48) which was preceded and succeeded by constant wars and which involved France and the Hapsburgs of Spain and Austria, while Germany and other continental countries joined either party. Britain was involved in constitutional crises culminating in the Civil War and the rise of Puritanism. All these factors and repressive edicts adversely affected the education of women other than the wealthy, but a few exceptions were made possible in Italy and Germany.

In Britain the situation was confused. In 1511 an edict permitted the Bishop of London or the Dean of St Paul's to grant licences to men and women apprenticed to physicians and examined successfully by four expert physicians. Women were expected to treat only the poor, and without a fee. An Act of 1511, ratified in 1518 and 1523 (and never repealed) empowered the College of Physicians and the Archbishop of Canterbury to license physicians and surgeons. At least 66 women were known to have obtained these licences. The dissolution of the monasteries deprived the poor of nursing care and women of obtaining medical training. No substitute was provided, although St Bartholomew's hospital escaped. In 1614 licences to practise surgery were withdrawn from women (the 1511 Act was forgotten), but women of all classes continued to practise. In 1617 they were forbidden to be apothecaries. Between 1642 and 1652, 52 licences were granted to obstetricians and midwives after exacting examinations. Unfortunately thereafter payment of fees were the only requirements. Many men and women practitioners were unlicensed in Britain and on the European Continent, some clearly being affluent since again fines were paid on several occasions.

In 1560 French midwives who learnt from books, families, and licensed teachers were obliged to join the Fraternity of *Sts Cosmas and Damien, to attend dissections of female bodies and to forswear abortifacients. In 1755 Parliament decreed that no woman should associate with any Institute or practise any form of surgery, except midwifery. In 1768 a dispensation was granted to *accoucheuses so that they might attend lectures and dissections in the University of Paris. An exception was made also for Sister Martha of Besançon, an army surgeon.

During the 16th c. the governments of Spain appointed women to examine prostitutes. In 1516 the Elector of Brandenberg set up a panel of physicians and midwives to investigate *abortions and suspected *infanticides and in 1555 and 1595 ordinaries were promulgated in Regensburg, Frankfurt-am-Main, and Passau governing the practice of midwifery.

Women were still responsible for the care of dependents and guests, and wealthy ones had access to increasing numbers of books, and might be taught by medical fathers, husbands, and by tutors to their brothers, and some were pupils of distinguished practitioners.

Among these were aristocratic British women such as Anne, mother of Francis Bacon and Lady Burleigh, her sister, Lady Anne Clifford and her daughter-in-law, Lady Hoby, Lady Halkett, and two medical authoresses, the Countess of Kent and Lady Arundell. Mrs Colfe (d. 1644) 'was above 40 years, willing nurse, midwife, surgeon and in part, physician to all, both rich and poore'. The study of 'Physic and Surgery' consoled the Countess of Newcastle for her husband's infidelities. Louise of Savoy, mother of François I was well educated in literature, politics, and medicine, and Catherine de Medici (1519–89) (see MEDICI FAMILY) was said to be a skilful physician. Diane de Poitiers, mistress of Henry II (who reigned 1547–59) had a medical library, but whether she practised is debatable.

In spite of (perhaps because of) the devastations of war, medical studies were fashionable in Germany. Hurd-Mead (1938) cites one empress, four princesses, three duchesses, and three countesses, each of whom published books on medical subjects. Marguerite Fuss (d. 1626) of Heidelberg, taught by her mother (an aristocratic accoucheuse) also studied in Strasbourg and Cologne after being deserted by a worthless husband. A highly skilled midwife, and delightfully eccentric, she was in demand all over Germany, Holland, and Denmark.

Claudia Felicitas (1640–1705), wife of Emperor Leopold I of Austria, had received some formal medical and surgical training and 'worked as laboriously as a man' during the siege of Vienna. Another queen, Elena, third wife of Ferdinand III of Spain, studied in the lying-in hospital in Vienna and subsequently became a teacher and skilled accoucheuse.

Baroness von Calisch and her daughter had a flourishing surgical and obstetric practice in Buda in the 18th c. Salomée Ann Roussietski (1718–?) was an adventurous and highly skilled Polish doctor, who finally became physician to the harem of the Mustapha of Constantinople in 1759, after desertion by two husbands, each of whom decamped with all her money.

The widow of Bromfel, the Swiss botanist, was a good student at Montpellier and an excellent physician in Basle around the end of the 16th c. and at the beginning of the 17th c. Marie Clinet, taught by her husband Fabricius of Hilden, was known to work in Berne between 1585 and 1587 as an operative obstetrician and bone-setter.

In the liberal University of Bologna, Anne Morandi Manzolini (1716–74) wife of the professor, an expert model-maker, became an excellent assistant, after he succumbed to *tuberculosis, and she discovered the insertions of the oblique muscles of the eye. During his illness she was appointed lecturer and after his death the rector confirmed the appointment, although she lacked a degree. In 1750 she became professor and *modellatrice*, for her work was internationally famous. Laura Maria Caterina Bassi-Veralti (1711–78) became doctor of philosophy (*fu laureate*) in 1731 or 1732, and later a popular professor of anatomy. Maria della Donne (1776–1842), the first woman to seek and obtain the MD (*fu laureate*) in 1799, was appointed professor of obstetrics by Napoleon in 1802; she then became director of the School for Midwives in 1804 and a member of the French Academy in 1807.

Padua appointed Angelina to the chair of obstetrics and Elena Lucretia Cormero as lecturer in medicine and mathematics in the mid 17th c. Maria Pettracini obtained a medical degree from Florence in 1780, and her daughter, claimed by Florence and Bologna, graduated in 1800. Both were anatomists and medical practitioners in Ferrara.

By special intervention of Frederick the Great, Dorothea Christina Leporir-Erzhelen (1715–62) was admitted to the University of Halle in 1741, and after illness and domestic interruption to her studies graduated MD in 1754 and practised until her death from carcinoma of the breast. In 1773 Jernne Wuttenbach (d. 1830) graduated in medicine from Marburg. Regina Joseph Henning von Siebold was doctor of obstetrics of Giessen (*honoris causa*) having obtained her diploma as *Sage Femme* in Würzburg.

Three Frenchwomen were talented anatomists: Mme de Staël Delaunay (1693–1750) was one; another was Mme Geneviève Charlotte d'Arconville (1720–1805) who among other works, translated Alexander *Monro's Osteology,* and wrote on a number of topics including movements of the heart. Mlle Biheron (b. 1730) was impoverished 'but earnest in her studies', an expert anatomical model-maker, who unfortunately never developed her technique.

Rachael, daughter of Fredrick *Ruysch (1638–1731), the anatomist, followed her father and also became a pathologist and the first woman director of an anatomical museum. She and her father mounted specimens in fantastic postures and settings. Unfortunately when their collection was bought by Peter the Great, many specimens were vandalized aboard ship in transit to Russia and thrown away by the sailors.

At least two women practised surgery in London during the 18th c.: Catherine Bowles operated on *hernias, *hydrocoeles, and bladder *stones; in 1718, Lady Read offered skilled *ophthalmological treatment 'gratis to His Majesty's soldiers and sailors'. During this period some of the greatest medical women were obstetricians and midwives, but were rivalled by the male obstetricians, amongst them *Chamberlen, *Smellie, and William *Hunter, who gradually began to take over this specialty of medicine.

Pride of place goes to the French. Louyse (Louise) Bourgeois (1553–1638), friend and pupil of *Paré, published the first of three books in 1609. It was based on the personal observation of 2000 cases; 12 presentations and rules for the delivery of each type were described. She deplored meddlesome midwives, superstitions, and delivery rooms filled with spectators, and gave instructions on cleanliness and on avoiding infection and cross-infection. Unfortunately the Faculty of Medicine of Paris refused to let her give instruction to less skilled midwives. Her private pupil Marguerite de

Tertre de la Marche, superior midwife of the *Hôtel-Dieu, reorganized training and also wrote a book (1677). This was enlarged in 1759 by her own pupil Louise Leboursier du Caudray who managed to ameliorate some of the awful conditions in hospitals.

Jean Louis Baudelocque (1746–1810), chief obstetrician to the Hôtel-Dieu, professor at La Maternité in 1797, learnt his craft from the midwives. Marie Louise Dugés (1769–1821), granddaughter of Mme Bourgeois, educated by her mother and in Heidelberg, organized the hospital at Port Royale and published three volumes based on her experience of 40 000 cases. Baudelocque's classification of 94 fetal positions was reduced to 22. She seldom used *forceps, described *versions and treatment of *placenta praevia and early perineal repairs. The length of *pregnancy, duration of *labour, and incidence of dystocia were all calculated from her statistics.

Justina Siegmundie (b. 1545), an orphan, was virtually self-educated, after disillusionment by personal experience of midwives. She obtained de *Graaf's book *On Generation.* Initially treating the poor, she became state midwife in Liegnitz and midwife to the Prussian royal family and to the Kürfürst of Brandenburg. Her book was based on case records.

In England, midwives were less famous but Jane Sharp published the popular *Compleat Midwives Companion* in 1671, based on 30 years' experience. A Mrs Cellier urged midwives to unite and improve the profession. Her own practice was a successful one, and her view, based on her own experience, was that at least two-thirds of maternal and infant deaths were preventable. Her plans for a Royal Hospital, training school, and orphanage gained no support and the King failed to fulfil the promise of a Royal Charter.

Scandinavian records give little evidence of medical women working during this period, but thanks to the teaching of Saxotorph (1740–1800), professor in Copenhagen, to midwives and to doctors, the mortality and morbidity rates and infant mortality were commendably low.

Vrou Gertrude Kramer (1653–1744), trained by van *Deventer and Cyprianus practised obstetrics for over 50 years in Holland and kept a record of over 4000 patients: unfortunately, this was not published until 1920; her results were excellent for the time.

The cruelties of witch-hunting in the 16th and 17th c. inhibited study of medicinal plants and brought about the persecution and death of innocent women. However, Lady Willoughby, daughter of a medical man, gathered herbs and made medicaments as well as being an obstetrician and diagnostician. Anna Sophia, Princess of Denmark (married to August I of Saxony in 1643) planted a famous botanical garden with medicinal herbs and founded an apothecary's shop that lasted for over 300 years. The two most outstanding *herbalists were, first, Elizabeth Blackwell (1712–

70), author of *The Curious Herbal* (1737) in which the 500 engravings were coloured by herself. She studied medicine with her husband, a physician graduate of Aberdeen, and was later a student of Smellie. The second was Mrs Hutton, a botanist and herbalist of Shropshire who sold her remedy of *digitalis to William *Withering in 1785. In France Mme Marion Jeanne Roland, a philanthropist and herbalist, was executed in 1793 for outspoken opposition to the French Revolution.

Three lay women brought great medical benefit to Europe and the world. The Countess of Chinchon, vicereine of Peru was cured of *malaria by *Peruvian or Jesuit bark in 1636 and brought it to Europe in 1639, where the disease was endemic; for 300 years quinine, derived from Peruvian bark, was the only specific treatment. Lady Mary Wortley Montague (1689–1762), wife of the British ambassador to Turkey, noted the benefits of *inoculation against *smallpox, had her own children inoculated and introduced the practice to her friends and to the Royal family. Empress Maria Theresa of Austria (1717–80) came to the throne in 1740 and commanded van *Swieten, a pupil of *Boerhaave, to reorganize the medical school and hospital, and to establish a maternity hospital and training school; the *Allgemeines Krankenhaus was the result.

In France Mme Suzanne Necker (1740–1817) studied medicine and architecture, aiming to reform the appalling conditions of Parisian hospitals. A convent was converted to a clean, comfortable, 120-bedded hospital in 1778, and her book (1790) was to prove that good medical and nursing practice cost little more than the existing squalor.

Nineteenth and twentieth centuries. Despite world and localized endemic wars, attempted genocide, political persecution, revolutions, and natural and man-made disasters, this has been a period of unprecedented development ranging from opening up continents to the explosion of information combined with improvements in communication and transport. The repercussions on medical services and education have been incalculable. Since the First World War, *preventive medicine has become of world-wide concern.

Women have been affected by, and have effected, changes in education and suffrage, and have been involved in many humanitarian enterprises, including medicine in its widest connotation. Medical education, dependent upon secondary education, has become available to women in all countries, although to varying extents. They pioneered and are still preponderant in nursing (which was transformed by Florence *Nightingale), in hospital dietetics, and in physiotherapy, speech, and occupational therapy. Many radiographers and laboratory scientists and technicians who contribute to basic research and diagnosis are women. In 1894 Mary Stewart, appointed to the *Royal Free Hospital as the first lady almoner in the UK,

was the forerunner of hospital social services. Lady *almoners, now hospital social workers, allay patients' anxieties over family welfare while they are in hospital, and arrange convalescence and aftercare. When they are given an opportunity to meet the therapeutic team, they help to inculcate a more holistic approach to the effects of physical and social environment upon illness and responses to treatment and rehabilitation. They and the psychiatric social workers bridge the gap between the artificialities of hospitalization and the realities of the community.

Europe. At the beginning of the 19th c., the future of medical women seemed doomed to failure, since, at their best, medical education and practice were based increasingly upon science; and few women had access to general education. The outstanding female practitioners included Anne Victoria Boivin (1773–1847), an author, translator, and accomplished accoucheuse trained at La Maternité by Madame Lachapelle. She received no university recognition in France, but was awarded an honorary MD of Marburgh. Regina J. H. von Siebold received the honorary title of doctor of obstetrics of Giessen; her daughter, Charlotte, acquired the same degree by examination in 1817 and in 1819 delivered the future Queen Victoria.

By the middle of the 19th c. a few American women had acquired recognized medical qualifications (see WOMEN IN MEDICINE II). Their example, support, and skill were significant in establishing formal medical education for women in Europe and in the UK with her increasing influence as a world power. In the UK and parts of Europe this battle was bitter during the greater part of the 19th c.

In the UK reaction to Georgian licence was prudery and artificial ladylike delicacy. Bevies of unemployed daughters with trivial pastimes interspersed with home nursing and distributions to the deserving poor were status symbols for the middle class. Squalid conditions in medical schools and hospitals were deterrents to parental consent; nursing and midwifery were slovenly. Furthermore Queen Victoria deplored 'the mad wicked folly of women's rights'.

Investigations of the Select Committee appointed in 1834 to examine haphazard medical training culminated in the *Medical Act of 1858. The imposition of standards of training and compulsory registration with the newly formed *General Medical Council placed no embargo on the eligibility of women, but that lay in the hands of faculties of medicine and examining bodies where opposition to the admission of women was strong and increasing. One Englishwoman, Elizabeth *Blackwell, trained in the USA, could not be excluded from the Medical Register.

Elizabeth Blackwell and Emily Davies, founder and first Mistress of Girton College, Cambridge inspired Elizabeth Garrett (later *Anderson) to embark on an arduous and piecemeal training. The

Worshipful Company of Apothecaries of London had to accept her as a candidate for the licentiateship under threat of litigation by her father. They changed the regulations immediately after she qualified in 1865.

Also in 1865 the Faculty of Medicine of Zurich accepted women, and those with foreign medical qualifications or certificates of study were eligible to take examinations for doctorates. Basle, Berne, Geneva, and Lausanne followed suit, although few Swiss women could offer the appropriate requirements. In 1869 German universities accepted women with foreign diplomas or certificates for 'practical therapy' although women medical undergraduates were not accepted until 1908. In 1868 the University of Paris received four applications from women; reassured by the Swiss precedent, the dean and faculty accepted these women: Elizabeth Garrett and Putnam Jacobi of the USA became doctors of medicine of the Sorbonne in 1870 and 1871 respectively. None of these degrees were registrable in the UK.

Meanwhile in the UK a group of well-educated women fired by the example of the Americans, and by that of Drs Blackwell and Garrett, determined to acquire registrable British qualifications. Their leader was Sophia *Jex-Blake. The injustices experienced in Edinburgh (e.g. denial of the Hope Scholarship to Edith Pechey, solely on the grounds of sex, and a ruling, on technical grounds, that matriculated and fee-paying women could not take the final examination) evoked powerful support for the *London School of Medicine for Women (LSMW) which she founded in 1874. However, no examining body or general hospital would accept the students at first. The Enabling Bill was passed in 1876 and removed any statutory ban to the acceptance of women medical students. The school faced closure in 1877, but the King's and Queen's College of Physicians of Dublin accepted foreign doctorates and recognized the course of the LSMW. Also in 1877 clinical teaching was arranged in the *Royal Free Hospital in exchange for fees and an indemnity against loss of support from disapproving subscribers. A potentially disastrous rift between Sophia Jex-Blake and Elizabeth Garrett Anderson was staved off by the altruism of a most able woman, Isobel Thorne, one of 'the seven against Edinburgh'. By accepting the honorary secretaryship of the school, she had to abandon qualification, and became an important benefactor of British medical women and foreign students of the School. The final breach between Sophia Jex-Blake and Elizabeth Garrett Anderson came when the former went to Edinburgh and founded her second medical school.

Britain's world-wide political power gave the School a disproportionately influential role in India and Burma, and provided some of the earliest medical women to practise in South Africa and Australia.

The Queen's University of Belfast was the first British university to accept women medical students. The University of London, which had rejected applications from Jessie Meriton White in 1856 and Elizabeth Garrett in 1862, opened all faculties to women in 1878. This concession had the active support of men such as Sir James *Paget and the distinguished Council of LSMW owed much to the professional excellence, common sense, and moderation of Elizabeth Garrett Anderson. The first two to qualify were Mary Scharlieb and Miss Shove. In 1894 Edinburgh University opened medical degrees to women. By 1947 all medical schools in the UK had women students.

The General Medical Council's proposal to open a separate *Medical Register based on separate examinations for women was circumvented by Elizabeth Garrett Anderson. In a letter to *The Times* (5 May 1878) she proposed the formation of a Conjoint Board of Examining Bodies with uniform standards in medicine, surgery, and obstetrics for all candidates. The Royal Colleges of Edinburgh and Glasgow and the Irish Boards admitted women well before 1900; the London Board yielded in 1909 after receiving a memorial signed by hundreds of distinguished medical men, including Charles *Sherrington. The first women fellows of the Royal College of Surgeons of Ireland, England, and Edinburgh were Cecilia Williamson in 1910, Eleanor Davies-Colley in 1911, and Gertrude Hertzfeld in 1920 respectively. The Royal College of Physicians of London amended its regulations in 1926, and elected Helen Marion Macpherson MacKay to the fellowship in 1934.

After the Crimean War (1854–6) sporadic training was given to women in the Military Academy of Medicine, St Petersburg, an important factor being the need to cater for the families of Muslim Cossacks. Other women received permission to practise on return from France, Germany, or Switzerland. In 1872 a special Institute for Women was opened in St Petersburg with strong support from the Muslim provinces and tuition was provided by courageous professors, led by the composer *Borodin (1833–87), then professor of organic and physiological chemistry. By 1877 there were 700 graduates but despite protest, the school was closed, reopening in 1897. Other schools were established in Moscow and Kharkov and by 1926 there were 18 Russian medical schools.

The first native Swiss woman to graduate entered the faculty of Zurich in 1868. The numbers were small, partly owing to the state of secondary, and in particular scientific, education for girls. The humanitarian services to refugees gained great respect.

In Sweden permission to practise was granted in 1870, but was taken up slowly. The first woman to enter the Karolinska Institute, Karolina Widerström, was kindly received in 1878. She graduated in 1888 and after a distinguished obstetrical and gynaecological career was awarded an honorary degree.

The faculty of medicine in the University of Copenhagen accepted women in 1877, and the first two graduated in 1885 and 1886. Norwegian faculties were opened for women by Act of Parliament in 1884; the first graduate (1893), Marie Spangberg-Holth, was later health officer in the department of venereal disease in Oslo University.

In the Netherlands Aletta Jacobs entered the Medical School of Groningen in 1871 and graduated from Utrecht in 1878.

In 1889 Manuella Solis qualified in Valencia and was later the first woman elected to the Spanish Society of Gynaecologists. Also in 1889 Eliza Correia graduated from Coimbra, Portugal.

There was much opposition to women doctors from the profession (and probably the public) in the Austro-Hungarian Empire. Nevertheless, the scandal of two avoidable suicides in a fashionable girls' school (because of the lack of women doctors to whom these young ladies could go) led to the intervention of Franz Joseph I in the mid-1890s. Women with recognized foreign qualifications could register for practice, and girls with the entry requirements were to be admitted to medical faculties throughout the Empire (Vienna, Prague, Brno, Bratislava, and the Austrian part of Poland). The enrolment in national schools was slow, the first to graduate from Vienna did so in 1904, and in Sofia it was 1921. The débâcle of the Empire led to restrictive practices after the First World War. Women, who had to be nationals, practised without payment and mostly in subservient positions. Their status deteriorated still further with the Nazi occupation.

New Zealand and Australia. New Zealand had advanced views on women's suffrage and education. The University of Otago (founded 1876) had six out of 34 medical students in 1896 but numbers fluctuated until the outbreak of the First World War, when they increased abruptly as in the rest of the English-speaking world. After demobilization of men, hospital appointments seldom went to women on pleas of lack of funds and accommodation; they were absorbed into long-standing state and school services, or private practice.

In Australia women were first admitted to the faculties of Melbourne, Sydney, and Adelaide, in 1877, 1885, and the early 1890s respectively and *ab initio* to those of newer universities on the mainland, Tasmania, and Port Moresby. The first woman doctor, Constance Stone graduated in 1886 from the Women's Medical College of Pennsylvania, USA; her sisters, Grace and Mary graduated from Melbourne in 1892 and 1893 respectively, and three women entered Sydney Medical School at about the same period. Lilian Balcam, a Melbourne graduate (1891) became the first woman general surgeon in the city.

Women have played a notable part in health education by all the media, including the valuable radio services to out-stations, as well as contributing to the *flying doctor services.

They have been most active in the Medical Women's International Association, the first inter-national medical association. This provides a useful forum for discussion of medical problems of women in developed and developing countries.

India and Burma. Much is owed to women missionaries whose work revealed the needs of segregated women. The first were Americans whose generous work still continues. Once the LSMW was established, British women medical missionaries and civilian doctors were more numerous and had more influence with administrators. Three most significant events were the graduation of Mary Scharlieb, the introduction of nursing and medical training for Indian women, and the establishment of the Indian Women's Medical Service.

Mary Scharlieb, wife of an English barrister practising in Madras, qualified as a medical licentiate from Madras University in 1875. She later graduated MB BS (London) with great distinction in 1882 and was presented to the Queen with her colleague Miss Edith Shove by Elizabeth Garrett Anderson. The Queen requested a full and frank account of the medical problems of her 'beloved Indian subjects'. Her concern was translated into action, and the vicereine set up the Dufferin and Ava Fund which established many small hospitals and clinics in India and Burma. The staff were women who now gained royal approval and respectability.

The North India School of Medicine for Christian Women at Ludhiana was founded in 1894 by Edith Brown (1864–1956), three years after qualification, with a borrowed hospital, £50, six old school rooms, and three members of staff. The first session was for dispensers and midwives, the second began a four-year course for medical assistants. By 1953 the school became coeducational. It had trained hundreds of nurses, dispensers, midwives, and doctors, and 50 out of 600 applicants were selected for the MB BS degrees of the University of the Punjab. The outstanding contribution of this school was probably the early establishment of domiciliary visits and of one of the most comprehensive services in *community health.

In the late 19th and early 20th c. Indian girls of suitable education went abroad to train for degrees and diplomas. The first two who trained in the USA died of tuberculosis. Dr Rukmabai, the first of many, entered the LSMW in 1894 and returned to serve in civil hospitals and later the Indian Women's Medical Service.

On the instigation of two delegations led by Mrs Scharlieb the British government inaugurated the Indian Women's Medical Service, staffed by women doctors. This provided an organized service throughout India and Burma, conducted research, collected epidemiological evidence, and trained Indian women; and as a result the Lady Harding Medical School and Hospital were established.

Ida Scudder (1870–1960), a notable medical missionary, trained in the Pennsylvania School and founded Vellore Christian Medical College in 1918. From its small beginnings of training subassistants and licentiates it became a part of the University of Madras and a coeducational school in 1947 under the direction of Hilda Lazarus, a distinguished Indian graduate of the university. The Hospital still has an international reputation, particularly for treatment and rehabilitation of patients with *leprosy.

Women are now admitted to all medical faculties in the Indian subcontinent, and, where custom demands, as in Pakistan, separate schools are provided.

In Burma all students are admitted on merit and without sex discrimination, for girls and boys have equal opportunities at primary and secondary schools. The Universities of Rangoon and Mandalay and the Military Institute have women members of staff, including professors.

Africa. Much of this vast continent was opened up only during the last 150 years. Its cultures and customs vary from the ancient and sophisticated to simple hunters and gatherers. Climate and terrain go from one extreme to the other. It has been invaded by many over thousands of years, and more recent colonial powers have varied in enlightenment and concern for education and medical services. Although there were Arab women physicians in Spain and North Africa in the 1st millennium, conditions became deplorable in many areas. Attempts by Potin, Director of the Medical School of Algiers, resulted in the establishment of a commission and in 1871 a plan to educate women, including doctors, was abandoned for political reasons. In 1895 Mme Chellier-Fumat was admitted to the school and subsequently practised amongst native women. Every encouragement was given to Frenchwomen, many of whom accepted the challenge.

In Egypt expatriate women were responsible for the medical care of women by women; students were sent overseas until conditions became suitable for local training. With emancipation, schools in Egypt accepted women students and academic staff, some at professorial level but not as heads of departments. But throughout the continent women still do not usually serve in remote rural areas. In the early to mid 1900s, East and West African women tended to go to LSMW for training as coeducation was not acceptable. Subsequently this changed and with the establishment of many new universities and medical faculties, some once in a special relationship with London, women are now accepted on merit.

South Africa. The first woman to practise was Miss Waterston, one of the first students of LSMW. White women are now accepted, but in a minority. In 1940 the University of Witwatersrand admitted the first African student. Mary Susan Mapahlele qualified in 1947.

Sudan. In the Sudan the Kitchener School of

Medicine founded for men in 1923 became the University College of Khartoum in 1950, also in a special relationship with London. Women were admitted once suitable accommodation with a resident warden was obtained. There is now no discrimination and women doctors are highly respected.

Far East. In the Far East, in Singapore, Malaysia and Thailand women are accepted in all medical faculties. Earlier many attended the LSMW, while many from the Philippines and parts of China went to the Pennsylvania School until their own faculties were established.

Japan. A brief reference to women trained in obstetrics and gynaecology in the 8th c. was followed by silence until the first quarter of the 19th c. when a few women were in practice. In 1870 they were legally banned. A coeducational school was founded by Dr Takahashi in 1876 but closed in 1901. Dr Ogina of Tokyo graduated from a male school in 1882 but could not practise until 1884. Excellent training was later obtained with difficulty but in 1945 women received suffrage and were accepted in the universities.

War service. From Homeric times women have attended battle casualties, but were rarely mentioned by name. Muhammad's army was accompanied by them and mediaeval romances and French and English records of the 11th to 13th c. refer to women *fisiciennes* at the Crusades. The Hospitaller Order of Knights of *St John of Jerusalem included a few sisters, one of whom, Edina Rittle, a nun from St Bartholomew's, London, was in charge of the Pantacrator Hospital, Constantinople.

A Lady Hoby treated soldiers of James I's army and during the English Civil War, Royalist Lady Anne Halkett rendered outstanding surgical services, while Lucy Hutchinson accompanied her Parliamentarian husband to Nottingham prison and treated the wounded of both armies.

Sister Martha Besançon (d. 1824), a nun, and surgeon to the French Army, treated French and enemy casualties with skill and kindness that earned decorations from France, Austria, Russia, and Prussia (Hurd-Mead, 1938).

James (Miranda Stewart) Barrie (Barry), masquerading as a man, graduated MD of Edinburgh in 1812. She joined the army in 1813, was promoted from Hospital Mate to Assistant Surgeon during the battle of Waterloo (1815), reaching the supreme rank of Inspector-General of Hospitals in 1858, and was noted for her concern for soldiers and their families. She served in the West Indies, Cape of Good Hope, Canada, and in the Crimea. Bitterly critical of the disgraceful conditions, she brooked no criticisms from civilian Florence Nightingale. The secret of her sex was preserved, until after her death (1865), through her peppery temper and her remarkable skill as a pistol duellist.

The Union Army employed one woman, Mary

Walker, as contract surgeon during the American Civil War.

Senior students of the first Russian School of Medicine in St Petersburg were assigned to military posts in the Russo-Turkish war (1877–8) and when they graduated, Tsar Alexander II gave each a medal struck in their honour.

During the South African War (1899–1902) two British women doctors served with the army, receiving equal pay and campaign medals.

Treatment was less generous during the First World War. Twenty per cent of women doctors volunteered and served in the medical services. One Canadian woman served in England and France and 14 Australians and New Zealanders paid their own way to join the war effort, while those remaining at home worked beyond the call of duty, taking the places of men.

Conditions of service were deplorable, sometimes humiliating in the three categories of employment: Civilian Medical Practitioners were part-time assistants in hospitals, clinics, and recruiting boards; Civil Officers were recruited in 1916 for service in Egypt, Malta, UK, and in some instances, in Belgium and France treating military and civilian casualties and refugees. The third category were appointed Medical Officers to the Women's Auxiliary Army Corps, which was organized by Mona Chalmers Watson, in 1917 with Jane Turnbull as CMO for 50 000 women stationed in the UK, and Laura Sandeman for 8000 behind the lines in France. Later in 1917, Dorothy Hare was appointed Medical Advisor to the Women's Royal Naval Service which never numbered more than 9000. Laetitia Fairfield was appointed Chief Medical Officer to the Women's Royal Air Force founded in 1918.

Many of the personnel suffered from the effects of rickets, malnutrition, and rheumatic heart disease. Venereal disease was rife and pregnancies were frequent. Valuable knowledge of the health needs of large female communities was built up on past experience as factory and school doctors. General health standards of hygiene and education improved, to the lasting benefit of the whole population.

Barrie Lambert formed a Corps of Physiotherapists and was appointed Inspector of Military Massage and Electric Services.

Many voluntary units employed women for relief work overseas. Three founded by women were outstanding. Louisa Garrett Anderson completely equipped a hospital, staffed by women. This was rejected by the establishment and accepted by the French *Red Cross. Their work so impressed Sir Alfred Keogh that they were later transferred to London where over 26 000 serious military surgical and medical cases were treated. Elsie Maud Inglis (1864–1917) founded the Scottish Women's Hospitals which served with heroism and great efficiency in France and Serbia, Corsica, Salonika, Romania, Russia, and briefly in Malta. Dr Inglis and her colleagues received some of the highest decorations from France and Serbia. The only ones accorded to Dr Inglis in the UK were a magnificent funeral in Edinburgh and a permanent exhibit in the Imperial War Museum. The latter was also the only British honour given to Mrs St Clair Stobart for the magnificent and equally heroic work of her Ambulance Brigade in the Balkans. Miss Garrett Anderson and several colleagues were amongst the first women appointed Companions of the Order of the British Empire in the civilian division, although also awarded the 1914–1918 and Victory medals.

The women's medical services disappeared in the interwar years, but were revived in 1939 with improved conditions, although no commissions were granted. In the Royal Army Medical Corps women were allowed uniforms, equivalent rank, equal pay, and unequal allowances. At first the Royal Air Force disallowed titles of rank. A civilian Advisor Surgeon and Agent was appointed in 1939 to examine WRNS recruits, and in 1940 was appointed to the staff of the Medical Director General as Surgeon Lieutenant RNVR.

In December 1940 the Army appointed women specialists with the field rank of Major. Lieutenant-Colonel Laetitia Fairfield was appointed Woman Medical Advisor to the Director General of Army Medical Services (DGAMS) and the Director of the Auxiliary Territorial Service (ATS) with a seat on the Army Council. The War Office Woman Medical Advisor became an Assistant Director General. Wing Commander Butler-Jones was appointed Woman Medical Liaison Officer to the Air Ministry. The Army and Air Force created posts at command level to deal with medical problems of the women's services.

In 1941 women medical officers were granted commissions into the women's forces but not into the appropriate medical arm of their respective service. That privilege was granted after the war.

Co-operation between the three services, at the highest levels and between men and women, was harmonious. The health of the women's units was enhanced. Although working mainly with women's forces, the medical officers encountered little or no objection from men when they were assigned to mixed units.

In all theatres of war, occupied territories, and prison camps, UK civilian women doctors had heavy medical duties and problems with evacuees and refugees. In occupied territories many served with the Resistance. In both World Wars and in subsequent conflicts they have demonstrated capacities of endurance, courage, efficiency, and organizational talent.

Tribute is due to the lay women who volunteered as nursing aides and others who turned their houses into hospitals and convalescent homes and to ambulance drivers and stretcher bearers who rescued victims of air raids. The conduct of medical women in the First World War was one of the most telling contributions to the granting of suffrage in the UK.

Achievements of women. The early pioneers in all countries during the last two centuries have campaigned for social reform and improved services, particularly for women, children, and civil liberties. A few have been Ministers of Health. They have contributed to all branches of medicine and surgery, but have tended towards paediatrics, obstetrics, gynaecology, ophthalmology, anaesthetics, pathology, radiology, community medicine, and rehabilitation. They founded training schools, hospitals, and the most recent development of hospices for terminally ill patients is mainly due to Dame Cicely Saunders (see DEATH, DYING, AND THE HOSPICE MOVEMENT). The first hospital for early treatment of non-certifiable mental and nervous disorders was established by Helen Boyle and Mabel Jones, in the Lady Chichester Hospital (1898), and the School in Vienna produced some distinguished women psychiatrists. Maria *Montessori, the first woman doctor to graduate from Rome (1894) revolutionized the education of subnormal and normal children.

Notable studies of infantile malnutrition were made by Helen MacKay and Cicely Williams, the discoverer of the cause of *kwashiorkor; Dr Gerta *Cori shared the Nobel prize (1947) with her husband and Professor Houssay for studies of carbohydrate metabolism.

Many medically qualified women serve in or direct laboratories of the *Medical Research Council and/or universities. Others serve on Medical Councils and Academic Councils.

Of the non-medically qualified who have influenced medicine profoundly are Marie *Curie and her daughter Irène Joliot-Curie with their work on *radium and *isotopes; Marjorie Stephenson (1885–1948), one of the first women to become a fellow of the Royal Society, a chemical *microbiologist who made fundamental discoveries on *bacterial metabolism. Other women fellows still living have made important contributions to pharmacology, endocrinology, biochemistry, immunology, immunochemistry, immunogenetics, blood grouping, and nutrition.

The present position of women in medicine (see also MEDICAL PRACTICE). Women constitute a minority of the medical workforce in the USA and Canada (10 per cent), Norway (14 per cent), Austria (20 per cent), Australia, Denmark, France, and Sweden (20–30 per cent). Twenty per cent of British registered medical practitioners are women, although not all are fully employed (Day, 1982). In developing countries and some Eastern cultures, slowly changing tradition and a paucity of secondary schools for girls (excepting in Burma where girls have had equal rights to schooling for years) restrict numbers of eligible students. However, all of the universities once in a special relationship with the University of London in Jamaica, West and East Africa, and Singapore had no restrictions to entry on the same terms as men. Women's colleges cater for the needs of Saudi Arabia and Pakistan where purdah persists. During the 1960s 77 per cent of the profession were women in the USSR but recent policy has lowered entry requirements for men in order to achieve equal proportions by the year 2000. There, as in other countries, women have a disproportionately low representation in prestigious posts in hospital specialties and administration. Although found in all specialties, they gravitate towards psychiatry, paediatrics, anaesthetics, radiology, and community medicine and general practice (see Council for Postgraduate Medical Education, 1981, for UK figures). This is not entirely due to willingness to compromise, rather than be unemployed, for women have made notable contributions in community and social medicine.

There is a steady general rise in women entrants and medical graduates throughout the European Economic Community (1983). In 1981 the percentages of entrants and graduates ranged from 20 to 50 and 10 to 44.8 respectively.

In 1947 British medical schools had to admit at least 5 per cent of women, but the national average in 1980 was 38 per cent. The Royal Free Hospital School of Medicine (formerly for women) reached its goal of equal numbers by 1957 and at least three others have done so recently, giving a good working atmosphere and engendering mutual understanding of problems of combining family and professional life.

Undergraduate wastage in the UK is lower for women than men, and their examination results are better. Since the 1950s reports of disappointingly low postgraduate achievement and a measure of unemployment led some to demand reintroduction of quotas, despite legal obligations to provide equality of opportunity on grounds of merit. In 1976 88.2 per cent of men and 82.7 per cent of women were in practice. These figures included all ages and no account was taken of women likely to return when children reached school age.

Hutt *et al.* (1979) reported that 62 per cent of men and 45 per cent of women were practising their specialty of first choice. In an analysis of careers and marital status of two cohorts of women qualifying in 1949–51 and 1965 Ward (1981) gave strikingly different figures but showed improvement from 24 per cent to 34 per cent for the later group. Eighty-three per cent of the first and 88 per cent of the younger group were married; their average numbers of children were 2.61 and 2.21. Ninety-one per cent of both groups were in full- or part-time practice with participation indices of 0.73 and 0.65 respectively. A bimodal pattern of work was apparent in both groups. In the nine years since graduation the younger women had achieved more than the older at a corresponding stage and promised longer periods of service. Seventy-four per cent of the first group and 77 per cent of the younger considered that marriage had affected the posts for which they could apply. Particular difficulty was encountered when they were married to doctors in training. The increasing tendency for women in the UK to work, and to return to interesting and prestigious posts is emphasized in *Women and Employment: a Lifetime Perspective* (Martin and Roberts, 1984).

Department of Health and Social Security publications (1982, 1984) reveal little improvement in prospects of hospital consultancies for women in the near future. Merit awards are disproportionately low for women. Poor representation on decision-making committees is possibly due to reluctance to accept appointments in addition to heavy domestic commitments.

In many of the developing countries, all but the richest women work, often in arduous conditions. Education is highly prized and confers status and responsibility to serve. Despite diminishing help from extended families few women fail to practise. Some hold important administrative posts such as Chief Medical Officer in a busy West African port or clinical professorial appointments in university teaching hospitals.

Part-time training posts for women with domestic commitments were pioneered in the Oxford region in 1966. They ranked as senior house officers, registrars, and since 1972, senior registrars. In 1977, Scheme A, a bridging operation, provided training for general practitioners or specialists, and Scheme B provided *ad hoc* training if offering only one or two sessions a week. Circumstances permitting, transfer from B to A is encouraged. By 1981 48 per cent had become hospital consultants and the rest associate specialists or clinical assistants. The Doctors' Retainer Schemes, details of which are available from the DHSS and Scottish Home and Health Department (SHHD) allow women to offer a minimum requirement of one monthly session, but membership of a Defence Society (see PROFESSIONAL PROTECTION SOCIETIES) and regular subscription to a journal are obligatory. The end in view is greater participation in the future. Useful as these schemes are, there are administrative problems and varying interpretations imposed by autonomous Health Authorities. They do not tackle the fundamental problems of the *National Health Service, the unsatisfactory conditions of service, and legitimate career prospects of both men and women, all highlighted by the Fourth Report of the Social Services Committee (Short, 1981).

Virtually full medical employment has been achieved in the USSR and Sweden (Day, 1982). In Russia, content and hours of work for all healthy adults are rigidly controlled. Women tend to work fewer and more regular hours than men. Nurseries, schools, and places of recreation are provided for children; loyalty to the state overrides all personal wishes.

As Swedish women entrants to medicine increased, radical reforms of practice and postgraduate training were introduced in 1970. Doctors in state employment became whole-time civil servants working 40 hours a week with options for longer or shorter periods; 64.8 per cent of women

and 56.4 per cent of men worked 40–44 hours. Despite falls in productivity and income, a massive survey by the Swedish Medical Association showed that few wished to return to old-style practice. By 1979, 14 000 out of 17 500 doctors had entered the Service, of which 23 per cent were women. Out of 96.8 per cent of registered practitioners responding to the questionnaire, 0.002 per cent of men and 2.4 per cent of women were not practising. All postgraduate hospital training was available in a relatively small geographical area, as all services were levelled up and co-ordinated with benefit to patients and doctors. Generous maternal and paternal leave was introduced in 1970, and from 1978 both parents could accept reduced hours and a 25 per cent cut in income until a child was eight, the appointments remaining open and secure.

Although neither scheme could be transplanted unchanged to other societies, features of both merit serious consideration. Women's role in childbearing is immutable; organizations and regulations are not. Preservation of all the good features in the welfare state, the reforms needed to utilize fully talents, skill, and fruits of education, and to fulfil legitimate and reasonable aspirations of men and women are a worthy challenge. (See also WOMEN IN MEDICINE II.)   RUTH E. M. BOWDEN

References
Council for Postgraduate Medical Education (1981). *Part-time in Medicine*, London.
Day, P. (1982). *Women Doctors, Choices and Constraints, in Policies for Medical Manpower*. London.
Hurd-Mead, K. C. (1938). *A History of Women in Medicine from the Earlier Times to the Beginning of the Nineteenth Century*. Haddam, Connecticut.
Hutt, R., Parsons, D., and Pearson, R. (1979). *The Determinants of Doctors' Career Decisions*. Report by the Institute of Manpower Studies to the DHSS and SHHD. London.
Lipinska, M. (1900). *Histoire des Femmes Médicins, depuis l'antiquité jusqu'á nos jours*. Paris.
Martin, J. and Roberts, C. (1984). *Women and Employment: a lifetime perspective*. London.
Short, R. (1981). Chairman. (4th Report for the Social Services Committee Session 1980–81). *Medical Education with Special Reference to the Number of Doctors and the Career Structures in Hospitals*. Vol. 1, London.
Thorwald, J. (1962). *Science and the Secrets of Early Medicine, Egypt, Babylonia, India, China, Mexico, Peru*. London.
Ward, A. (1981). *Careers for Medical Women*. Medical Care Research Unit, Sheffield.

Further information and reading
Archives of the Elizabeth Garrett Anderson Hospital.
Archives of the Fawcett Society.
Archives of the Medical Women's Federation.
Archives of the Royal Free Hospital School of Medicine and the Royal Free Hospital.
Balfour, M. I. and Young, R. (1929). *The Work of Medical Women in India*. Oxford.
Bell, B. H. C. Moberly (1953). *Storming the Citadel: The Rise of the Woman Doctor*. London.
Dictionary of National Biography.

Dictionary of National Biography of Women, ed. Elizabeth Vallance. In press.

Fox-Hume, R. (1964). *Great Women of Medicine*. New York.

Frey, H. (1978). *The Woman Physician in Sweden*. Part III. Uppsala.

Hellstedt, L. M. (1978). *Women Physicians of the World*. New York, London.

HMSO (1981). *Government Response to the Short Report*. Cmnd. 8970. London.

Jex-Blake, S. (1867). *A visit to some American Schools and Colleges*. London.

Lawrence, M. (1971). *Shadow of Swords: A Biography of Elsie Inglis*. London.

Lipinska, M. (1930). *Les Femmes et le Progrés des Sciences Médicales*. Paris.

Lives of Fellows of the Royal Society, London.

Lovejoy, D. P. (1957). *Women Doctors of the World*. London.

Manton, J. (1965). *Elizabeth Garrett Anderson*. London.

Medical Education, Journal of the Association for the Study of Medical Education. Numerous articles on careers of women doctors.

Murray, F. (1920). *Women as Army Surgeons: Being the History of the Women's Hospital Corps in Paris, Wimereux and Endell Street*. September 1914–October 1919. London.

Newman, C. (1957). *The Evolution of Medical Education in the Nineteenth Century*. Oxford.

Obituaries in: *British Medical Journal* and *Lancet*.

Putnam, R. (ed.) (1925). *Life and Letters of Mary Putnam Jacobi*. New York.

Todd, M. (1918). *Life of Sophia Jex-Blake*. London.

Tovell, A. (1966). *Women on the Warpath: the Story of the Women of the First World War*. London.

Winner, Albertine, Dame. (1975). Women in medicine. Caroline Hazlett Lecture. *Journal of the Royal Society of Arts*, 337–48.

WOMEN IN MEDICINE II

Introduction. The history of the medical profession on the North American continent and the entry of women into that profession was influenced greatly by the fact that the colonists and, later, immigrants, were those who for one reason or another—personal, familial, social, political, economic—had broken with tradition. These effects continue to the present day.

Early Jamestown (1607) and Plymouth (1620) colonists had no established medical profession, nor had they any of the accoutrements of a profession: schools, hospitals, medical societies, licensing standards, or journals. Medical care was a makeshift unsystematic affair. Faith healing and folk remedies, many of them borrowed from the native Indians, were popular. Anyone who wished could call himself or herself a 'doctor' and could collect fees for services. On the other hand, *midwifery was the exclusive domain of the women and remained so for approximately 150 years (until about 1750). Given the long distances midwives travelled to confinements, the frequency of confinements, the large number of children per family, the high disease rate, and the scarcity of trained practitioners of any sort, it would seem only natural that midwives would care for other family members and thereby build a reputation as 'doctresses' as well. But even in that primitive society, the number of doctresses was small.

The early practitioners. Probably the first woman to practise medicine in America was Elizabeth Pott, wife of Dr John Pott, who cared for the Jamestown residents beginning in the 1620s. It is likely that she learned her skills from her husband and that her work was an extension of his.

In the Massachusetts Bay Colony, Bridgit Fuller (d. 1633) was held 'in great esteem as a midwife'. Anne Hutchinson (d. 1643), who practised midwifery and preaching, was banished, on the other hand, to Rhode Island. Doctress Margaret Jones (d. 1648), like other women who fell foul of the authorities, was hanged for witchcraft.

In Connecticut Colony and in Maryland women were also recorded as doctresses and midwives.

From about 1700, women were gradually driven out of general medical practice and were more and more confined exclusively to midwifery. In addition, beginning in about 1730, a few of the more affluent young men began to go to Europe for formal training, as the colonies did not yet have a medical school. Returning home with an enhanced status, a knowledge of the new 'English *obstetrics', and skill in using the improved *forceps, these men were able to bring to a successful conclusion cases which failed the midwife. Female midwives would continue practising for decades, but in this increasingly affluent and sophisticated American society, the death knell for female midwifery had been sounded.

In the late 1760s the colonies acquired two native medical schools, one in Philadelphia and one in New York City, and by 1800 the USA had five—as well as native hospitals, medical societies, and licensing procedures, even a medical journal. But women, lacking the necessary preparatory education, were not admitted to the medical schools. Women disappeared from medical practice and, except for some rural areas, from midwifery as well.

The nineteenth century. By the beginning of the 19th c., a generation after the Revolutionary War, the mood of the young country was one of optimism. The swelling population had passed the 5 000 000 mark, the birth rate continued high, life expectancy was believed to be on the rise, and material wealth was increasing. At the same time, profound shifts were taking place in the role of women and in society's attitude toward them. The public and private spheres were becoming more sharply differentiated, with men moving outside the home to work and women remaining within the home. Since the women no longer contributed to the economy, but had their material needs supplied by men, they became prized objects, much praised for delicacy, deportment, and spirituality. While also praised for their intellectual capacities, it was unthinkable that any refined woman would enter the coarse, vulgar public sphere.

Nor could women study medicine, for to take one into the dissecting room would destroy her 'refined sensibility' and 'those moral qualities of character, which are essential to the office'. Thus, opposition to the study of medicine by women in America was based not on intellectual inferiority, but on decorum, or seemliness. Ironically, this same argument of feminine modesty was to be used only a generation later in reverse fashion in favour of permitting women to enter medical school so that female patients would not suffer the indignity of examination by a male physician or, worse, die as the result of no examination at all.

The rapid growth of the country also brought its problems. At the beginning of the 19th c. a man could become a licensed practitioner in either of two ways: by apprenticeship to an established physician followed by examination, or by graduation from one of the five medical schools existing at that time and registration of his diploma. Only the latter were MDs, but it was largely theoretical since neither the law nor the public made any practical distinction between the two types of practitioners. Both were considered 'regular' physicians.

Gradually, however, changes and abuses crept in. Apprenticeships were shortened, preceptors grew lax, even dishonest, and so-called proprietary schools, founded for profit and chartered to award the MD degree, began proliferating at an astonishing rate. Fewer than half had hospitals where students could receive clinical training. In some cases a man could receive his MD in less than a year; virtually any man who could read and write could become an MD. As a result, by mid-century the MD degree had lost prestige and the profession the esteem it had enjoyed at the beginning of the 19th c.

Into this void, created on the one hand by laxity of the profession and on the other by a society clamouring for change and egalitarianism, rushed the medical sects and cults, the so-called 'irregular' physicians, who eschewed both the scientific method and traditional medicine in favour of doctrines idiosyncratic to their own beliefs. The 'regulars' fought vigorously against the 'irregulars', who were claiming a large share of the medical dollar, perhaps the largest, but it was a losing battle. With the 'irregulars' added to the already large number of 'regular' practitioners, the physician–population ratio in 1840 was the highest in the world. Especially unwanted in this overcrowded profession were large, new, easily identifiable groups such as blacks and women.

The 1840s were chaotic, but they were also the incubator for three singular events that occurred near their close. These three events, each in its own way, profoundly affected the history of women physicians.

In May 1846, a group of 'regular' physicians, alarmed at the increasing numbers of 'irregulars', met in New York City and proposed, among other matters, that a 'uniform and elevated standard' be set for the MD degree and that a code of ethics that would apply to the entire profession be set up. These proposals were passed at a second meeting in 1847 in Philadelphia and thus was born the *American Medical Association. The Code of Ethics and its wording adopted at the Philadelphia session were to become important to women physicians some 20 years later when its language was studied to determine whether women could ethically be admitted to the Association and whether, indeed, a 'regular' physician could even ethically consult with a woman physician, or with a 'regular' physician if he taught at a woman's medical school.

The second decisive event occurred in November 1847, just six months later. After two and a half years of apprentice training with physicians in the Carolinas, Elizabeth *Blackwell entered Geneva College, a 'regular' proprietary country medical school. Fifteen months later, in January 1849, she became the first woman to receive the MD degree in North America. The school was severely censured, but Blackwell had broken the gender barrier at last.

The third decisive event occurred in July 1848, in Seneca Falls, New York, a small town not far from where Blackwell was studying medicine. A group of women led by Elizabeth Cady Stanton (1815–1902) and Lucretia Mott (1793–1880) passed resolutions that called for equality for men and women and for female suffrage. It was the official beginning of the Women's Rights Movement in the USA.

These three events, coming within months of each other and seemingly unrelated, arose in the chaos of the 1840s, but their effects would interact over the next nearly 150 years, down to the present. The 1840s were the nidus from which women entered the practice of medicine as professionals and by which, in mutual influence, much of their subsequent course would be determined.

If the admission of Elizabeth Blackwell to Geneva Medical College promised a dawn for women professionals, it was a false dawn, for Geneva refused to admit any more women for 16 years; the second, and last, woman to receive an MD degree from Geneva Medical College was Martha Rogers, who graduated in 1865. Nor would any of the other 'regular' medical schools admit women. Although 20 other women received the MD degree from four other medical colleges between 1849 and 1852, none could be considered 'regular' practitioners. Only with the awarding of the degree to Nancy Clark (1825–1901) by Cleveland Medical College, the Medical Department of Western Reserve College, in March 1852, did North America have its second female 'regular' physician. Although the distinction between 'regular' and 'irregular' physicians made no practical difference in the practice of medicine, it was to have grave consequences for women when they sought to join organized medicine and to be recognized as professionals with the same rights and privileges as male physicians.

Even so, when Nancy Clark, MD, applied for admission to the Massachusetts Medical Society in January 1853, the Board of Censors found her qualified for membership in so far as her medical credentials were concerned, but because the application was 'of a character never contemplated by the founders of the Society', that is, the application was from a 'female', 'it was voted unanimously not to license Mrs. Nancy E. Clark'. Nearly 20 years were to pass before the first state medical societies—those of Rhode Island, Kansas, and Iowa—were to admit women and it was 1876 before the first woman was admitted to the American Medical Association.

The women of this third quarter of the 19th c. were not only the first to break the sexual barriers in the medical schools, but they themselves were also the early founders of medical schools for women and of clinics, infirmaries, and hospitals where women could obtain clinical training not open to them elsewhere and where women patients might obtain treatment from someone of their own sex.

Although Blackwell was the first to receive the MD degree, she was still not the first woman to practise medicine in this turbulent century. Trained solely by apprenticeship, Harriot Kezia Hunt (1805–75), with her sister, Sarah, were in practice in Boston in 1835, nearly 15 years before Blackwell graduated. Harriot continued well into the 1870s, amassing a sizeable fortune. In 1847, wishing to legitimize her practice, she applied to *Harvard Medical School for permission to attend the public medical lectures. Oliver Wendell *Holmes, MD, as dean, was favourably inclined, but he was overruled. Harriot tried again, in 1850, and this time was accepted for attendance at the lectures only. Meanwhile, Harvard had also accepted three black men to the MD programme, and the medical students protested publicly against all four. Hunt and the three men withdrew. Nearly a hundred years passed before Harvard admitted women, though many eminently qualified students applied. Although Hunt's practice was 'irregular' and she had no degree (save for an honorary MD she was awarded by the Female Medical College of Pennsylvania in 1853), she is accredited as the first woman 'to practise medicine successfully' in the USA. Her lifelong efforts to secure equal educational opportunities for women, as well as her visible example in the practice of medicine, make her a true forerunner of women physicians.

Meanwhile, Elizabeth Blackwell did not rest on her laurels. With her characteristic energy, decisiveness, and high ideals, she went to Paris, hoping to train as a surgeon. Again she encountered obstacles, but was accepted as a student midwife at the Maternité. An eye infection forced her to abandon hope of being a surgeon and in 1850 she went to London where she studied with James *Paget at *St Bartholomew's Hospital. In 1851, after more than two years of postgraduate study in Paris and London, she returned to New York City to set up practice, but once again there were obstacles to be overcome. No *dispensary or hospital would allow her to see patients. She wrote of this period:

The first seven years of New York life were years of very difficult, though steady, uphill work . . . patients came very slowly to consult me. I had no medical companionship, the profession stood aloof, and society was distrustful of the innovation. Insolent letters occasionally came by post, and my pecuniary position was a source of constant anxiety.

In 1853, with the support of some members of the Society of Friends, she opened her own small, one-room dispensary where she saw destitute patients three times a week. By 1857, through her persistent efforts at writing, lecturing, and patient care, and the support of her Quaker friends, the dispensary had grown into the New York Infirmary for Women and Children. She was also joined by two other women physicians, her sister, Emily, who had received her MD from Cleveland Medical College, the Medical Department of Western Reserve College in 1854, and Marie Zakrzewska, who received her MD from the same institution in 1856. In 1858 Elizabeth returned to England to assist in opening the medical profession there to women, greatly inspiring Elizabeth Garrett (later *Anderson). On 1 January 1859, Blackwell became the first woman ever to be enrolled in the *Medical Register of the UK.

During this trip plans were also formulated for a medical college for women in New York City, but the Civil War forced a delay until 1868. The Women's Medical College of the New York Infirmary, as it was called, set standards higher than many of the men's medical colleges, and it continued to function until 1899, when medical coeducation became possible at Cornell University Medical School in New York. Elizabeth, however, returned once again to her native England, where she supported Garrett and Sophia *Jex-Blake in their pioneer efforts in the medical profession there. In 1875 she accepted the chair of gynaecology at Garrett's New Hospital and London School of Medicine for Women, but was forced to retire after a year because of ill health.

Emily Blackwell (1826–1910) was actually the sustaining American member of the Blackwell team in her devotion to the New York Infirmary and its Women's Medical College. Like her sister, she studied medicine by apprenticeship and then applied, unsuccessfully, to 11 medical schools. She was finally accepted at Rush Medical College in Chicago in 1852, but had to leave after only one year when the Illinois State Medical Society censured the school for admitting a woman. The following year she was admitted to Cleveland Medical College, which had closed its doors to women after the graduation of Nancy Clark in 1852, but which now reversed its policy. She received her degree from the Cleveland school in 1854 and, again like Elizabeth, went abroad for postgraduate study. In Edinburgh she studied with Sir James Young

*Simpson, in London with William *Jenner, and in Dresden with Franz von Winckel; she also studied in Paris and Berlin. Returning to New York in 1856, she joined her sister at the Infirmary, which grew steadily under her expert management into a recognized hospital for women and children and a clinical training ground for women physicians who could not study abroad. After the Women's Medical College of the New York Infirmary was established in 1868 by Elizabeth, Emily also took over its management, serving as dean and professor of obstetrics and diseases of women for the next 30 years. In 1899, because the newly established Cornell University Medical College in New York was accepting both women and men, she closed the Infirmary school in keeping with her belief that women should be educated with men. In its 31 years of existence, the Women's Medical College of the New York Infirmary awarded 346 MD degrees to women. The New York Infirmary for Women and Children, which had begun as a one-room dispensary and then as a modest hospital of 16 beds between 1853 and 1858, still exists.

The third member of this extraordinary triumvirate who did so much for early women physicians was Marie Zakrzewska (pronounced Zak-*Shef*-ska) (1829–1902). Born in Berlin and trained as a midwife, as was her mother, she emigrated to the USA in 1853 in order to study medicine. A year later she met Elizabeth Blackwell and through her efforts was admitted to Cleveland Medical College, one of four women in a class of some 200 men. She was awarded the MD degree in 1856 and returned to New York, where she assisted the Blackwell sisters during the first two years of their New York Infirmary for Women and Children. In 1859, lured by the prospect of starting a new hospital in Boston where women patients might be treated by physicians of their own sex and where female medical students might obtain clinical training, she became professor of obstetrics and diseases of women and children at the New England Female Medical College of Boston. Zakrzewska soon resigned, however, and in 1862 founded the 10-bed New England Hospital for Women and Children in Boston, where it still stands. For more than 35 years she devoted herself to the hospital, to the education of women physicians, and to the care of patients.

One of those assisting Marie Zakrzewska at the New England Hospital for Women and Children was Lucy Sewall (1838–1890). Born into a prominent Boston family, she received her MD from the New England Female Medical College in 1862 and, after a year's postgraduate study in Paris and London, where she inspired Sophia Jex-Blake to enter medicine, returned to Boston to join Marie Zakrzewska at her newly founded New England Hospital for Women and Children. She remained at the hospital for her entire career, treating the poor, and, in 1869, becoming its director. In 1881, Lucy Sewall, Marie Zakrzewska, Emily Blackwell, and Mary Putnam-Jacobi offered Harvard University £50 000 if it would open its doors to women for medical study. Their efforts were unavailing.

Other pioneer women physicians of note were:

Lydia Folger Fowler (1822–79) received her MD in 1850 from Central Medical College, Rochester, New York (Eclectic). She is usually credited with being the second woman in the USA to receive an MD degree even though the school was 'irregular'. She also became the first woman physician to hold a professorship in a medical school when, in 1851, she accepted the position of professor of midwifery and diseases of women and children at Central Medical College.

Sarah Read Adamson Dolley (1829–1909) received her MD in 1851 from Central Medical College, New York (Eclectic). She became the first female intern in the USA, serving at the famed Blockley Almshouse Hospital in Philadelphia in 1851–2.

Ann Preston (1813–72), having been refused admission to several of the all-male medical colleges in Philadelphia, was 37 years old when she, together with seven other women, was admitted to the first class (1850) of the Female Medical College of Pennsylvania, founded exclusively for women by a group of Quakers. When the class graduated on 31 December 1851, they brought the total number of women physicians in the USA to 14. After a year's postgraduate work at the College, Preston was appointed its professor of physiology and hygiene in 1853, a position she held until her death. Because of its 'irregular' status, students and graduates of the College were barred from clinical training in Philadelphia and from membership in the local medical society. In response, Ann Preston founded the Woman's Hospital in 1861. In 1866, the College made her its first woman dean. As dean, she fought successfully to have her students take their clinical training at 'the Blockley' and at the Pennsylvania Hospital. The College, which was renamed Woman's Medical College of Pennsylvania in 1868, remains in existence today as the Medical College of Pennsylvania (coeducational).

Hannah E. Myers Longshore (1819–1901) was also a member of the first graduating class of the Female Medical College of Pennsylvania in 1851. She is often credited with being the first woman in the USA to be a faculty member of a medical college, serving as demonstrator in anatomy at her Alma Mater in 1851.

Clemence Herned Lozier (1813–88) entered Central Medical College of Rochester, New York, an 'irregular' school, but the only coeducational school available. She finished her training at Syracuse (New York) Medical College, also an 'irregular' institution, in 1853. In New York City Clemence Lozier specialized in obstetrics and surgery for women, including the removal of tumours. In the mid 1860s her income reached £25 000 per year. Divorced in 1861, she turned her efforts to founding a medical college for women. On 14 April 1863 the New York State legislature chartered the New York Medical College and

Hospital for Women, a homoeopathic institution. Clemence Lozier served as its dean and professor of gynaecology and obstetrics until her death. The institution itself continued until 1918, when it became part of the New York Medical College of the Flower and Fifth Avenue Hospitals.

Emeline Horton Cleveland (1829–78) graduated from the Female Medical College of Pennsylvania in 1855 and joined its faculty as professor of anatomy and histology. As a protegé of Ann Preston, she was sent for a year's postgraduate work at the School of Obstetrics of the Maternité in Paris so that, on her return, she might take over as chief resident in the new Woman's Hospital being planned by Ann Preston and others. She accepted the post when the hospital opened in 1861 and the following year also became professor of obstetrics and diseases of women at the College. As a surgeon, she is credited with being the first woman to perform major abdominal surgery in the USA (1875) and also as the first woman to perform an *ovariotomy in the USA. In 1872 she succeeded Ann Preston as dean of Woman's Medical College, but was compelled to resign two years later because of ill health.

Mary Edwards Walker (1832–1919), who received her MD in 1855 from Syracuse (New York) Medical College (Eclectic), is as controversial today as she was during her lifetime. During the Civil War she served as a contract surgeon for the Union Army and in 1864/5 became the first woman named Acting Assistant Surgeon to the United States Army. She caused an outrage when she began her lifelong practice of wearing men's trousers. She received the Congressional Medal of Honor, a military decoration, but it was rescinded in 1917, when Walker was 84 years old. President Carter restored it in 1977. In 1982, a commemorative first-class postage stamp was issued by the United States Postal Service. She and Elizabeth Blackwell are the only American women physicians to be so honoured, although in 1984 the American Medical Association passed a resolution requesting that Alice Hamilton, MD, also be so honoured.

Four other women physicians deserve mention among the pioneers, for, in addition to being among the early physicians of their sex in the USA, they were also pioneers of their race.

Rebecca Lee (*c*. 1840–?) received her MD degree in 1864 from the New England Female Medical College. She is generally acknowledged to be the first black woman to receive the degree.

Rebecca Cole (1846–1922), also black, graduated from the Female Medical College of Pennsylvania in 1867. She practised in Washington, DC, and was superintendent of the government home for children and elderly women.

Susan Smith McKinney (1847–1918), the third black woman in the USA to hold the MD degree, graduated from the New York Homeopathic Medical College and Hospital for Women in 1870. She practised in Brooklyn for nearly a quarter of a century and then in Montana, Nebraska, and Ohio.

Susan La Flesche (1865–1915), a member of the Omaha Indian Tribe, received her MD degree from Woman's Medical College of Pennsylvania in 1889. She carried on her practice among the 1300 widely scattered members of her tribe, acquiring an influence that made her *de facto* leader of the tribe.

Women in medicine in Canada. Canadian women did not enter the medical profession until nearly 30 years after Elizabeth Blackwell received her degree. Emily Howard Jennings Stowe (1831–1903), unable to obtain admission to the all-male Toronto University, graduated from the New York Homeopathic Medical College for Women, and returned to Toronto to practise medicine in 1867, becoming the first Canadian woman to do so. Jennie Kidd Trout (1841–1921), on the other hand, although she did not receive her degree until 1875, from the Woman's Medical College of Pennsylvania, was the first Canadian woman licensed in Canada to practise medicine. Emily Stowe's daughter, Augusta Stowe-Gullen (1857–1935), was the first Canadian woman to receive an MD from a Canadian school. She graduated from Victoria College (via the Toronto School of Medicine) in 1883. Probably the strangest story in Canadian medicine, however, is that of James Miranda Stewart Barry (1795–1865) (MD University of Edinburgh (1812)), who masqueraded as a man for her entire adult life. A British Army medical officer, she was appointed Inspector-General of Hospitals for both Upper and Lower Canada in 1857. Barry thus receives the distinction of being the first woman to practise medicine in Canada—although believed at the time to be a man.

Career opportunities for women. Difficult as it was to obtain a medical education, early generations of women physicians faced the additional obstacle of competing in an already overcrowded market place. This they did successfully by serving the underserved, such as women and children, the poor, and the recent immigrants. They also practised in under-represented areas of medicine such as *preventive medicine, including hygiene, sanitation, and health and sex education for women. In this way countless women made a lasting contribution to American medicine.

A third and very popular choice was to serve in the foreign missions (see also MISSIONARIES, MEDICAL). A steady stream of women, most of them graduates of Woman's Medical College of Pennsylvania, made their way to the Far East and India to teach, to found hospitals and schools, and to care for the sick, especially women who were under the law of purdah. The first of these was Clara A. Swain (1834–1910) (MD Woman's Medical College of Pennsylvania (1869)), who went to India in 1870. In 1874 she opened the first hospital for women in India in Bareilly, which still stands as the Clara Swain Hospital. Twenty-five years later, Ida

Scudder (1870–1960) (MD Cornell Medical College (1899)) established a network of roadside clinics in rural India and also founded the Christian Medical College and Hospital in Vellore, South India. This huge institution is also still in operation.

As educational opportunities for women increased, some of the early women were able to join the mainstream of clinical medicine, publishing their clinical observations and commanding the academic respect of their male peers. Two of the most important were Mary Harris Thompson (1829–95) and Mary Putnam-Jacobi (1842–1906). Mary Thompson, trained by the Blackwells and Zakrzewska, graduated from the New England Female Medical College in 1863 and went immediately to Chicago. There she founded the Chicago Hospital for Women and Children in 1865 and the Woman's Hospital Medical College in 1870. When both were destroyed by the Great Fire of 1871, both were rebuilt. The school was absorbed into Northwestern University in 1891 as a separate department for women students and was closed in 1902 after all medical colleges in Chicago became coeducational. The hospital is still in operation as the Mary Thompson Hospital. Thompson became one of the most influential women in the nation. The surgeon Atton *Ochsner said she 'convinced many of us that it was possible for a woman to be a real physician and surgeon'.

Jacobi was equally notable and also trained by Zakrzewska, but received her degree from the Female Medical College of Pennsylvania (1863). In 1868, she entered the École de Médecine in Paris, which had never before admitted a woman, and graduated with honours in 1871. Insisting on high professional standards, she published more than 100 papers and rapidly became the leading woman physician in the USA. In an anonymous essay contest she won Harvard's coveted Boylston prize in 1876 for her essay 'The Question of Rest for Women during Menstruation'.

A third woman, who promised an equally brilliant career, was Susan Dimock (1847–75). After early training by Zakrzewska, she applied to Harvard Medical School along with Sophia Jex-Blake, but both were refused admission. She received her MD from the University of Zurich in 1871, but before her career could mature she was lost in a shipwreck. Samuel Cabot said publicly that she would have become a 'great surgeon'.

Regarded as one of the 'most highly esteemed women in American medicine' at the close of the 19th c., Marie Josepha Mergler (1851–1901) graduated from Thompson's Woman's Medical College in Chicago in 1879 and rose to become dean of its faculty. Frank Billings called her 'the best informed, the most rational and the broadest-minded medical and surgical practitioner among all the women [physicians] I have ever known'.

Women and organized medicine. Organized medicine was still an obstacle to achieving full professional status, however. The question of 'female practitioners' was first raised at the 1867 convention of the American Medical Association and referred to its Committee on Medical Ethics. The following year the Committee concluded that AMA members could ethically consult with any physician who had a 'regular' medical education, regardless of sex. When the matter came before the delegates, however, a vote on the Committee's recommendation was postponed indefinitely. Similar questions arose in succeeding conventions and again action was postponed. Finally, in 1876, Sarah Hackett Stevenson (1841–1909), a graduate of Thompson's Woman's Hospital Medical College of Chicago in 1874, became the first woman member of the American Medical Association when she was elected by the Illinois State Medical Society to be a delegate to the national convention. Because of the Federation structure of the Association, however, membership in the national body remained difficult since it depended on prior membership in local and state bodies, whose policies varied widely. Thus, in 1915, Bertha Van Hoosen (1863–1952) (MD University of Michigan Medical Department (1888)), a prominent Chicago surgeon and pioneer in the use of *scopolamine–morphine obstetric *anaesthesia, founded and was first president of the American Medical Women's Association (AMWA).

Although the official barriers have long since been removed, American women have been slow to join organized medicine. Of the some 64 200 women physicians in the USA in 1982, 23 000, or 36 per cent were members of the AMA. By way of contrast 52 per cent of the nearly 438 000 men physicians were members. Likewise, membership in AMWA numbered about 4000, or only 6 per cent of the total number of women physicians. Nevertheless, since 1876 countless women have held the top office in their state and local societies and three women have served as vice-presidents of the American Medical Association: Lillian H. South (1875–1967) (MD 1913/14); Alice Hamilton (1869–1970) (MD 1914/15); and M. Louise Gloeckner (1904–78) (MD 1969/70). In 1984/5, five women were delegates in the 343-member House of Delegates, the official policy-making body of the AMA, and 15 were alternate delegates. One member of the board of trustees is a medical student.

The Canadian Medical Association (CMA) admitted its first woman physician, Helen Reynolds Ryan (1860–1947) at its seventh annual meeting in 1887. In 1974, Bette Stephenson became the first woman to head the CMA.

Only after the early generations had opened the medical profession to women, established schools and hospitals for them, and achieved a secure professional status could later generations go on to make the substantial contributions to basic and clinical research that culminated in the awarding of the Nobel prize for physiology or medicine to an American woman, Gerty Cori (in conjunction with Carl Cori and Bernardo Houssay), in 1947. Only a few of these women, with their major achievements, can be listed here. More information can be found in *Notable American Women* (Vols I–III; The Modern Period).

Major contributions of medical women. Anna Wessels Williams (1863–1954) (MD Women's Medical College of the New York Infirmary (1891)) in collaboration with William Park isolated a strain of the *diphtheria bacillus in 1894 which has become known world-wide as the Park–Williams No. 8 strain and which is still used for commercial toxin production. In 1905, she developed a rapid staining method for the detection of *Negri bodies, which remained in use until 1939.

Alice Hamilton (1869–1970) (MD University of Michigan (1893)) was the founder of *occupational medicine in the USA and one of the world's authorities on *lead poisoning and industrial *toxins. Author of two widely used textbooks (1925, 1949), she was also the first woman professor ever at Harvard Medical School (1919).

Elizabeth Hurdon (1868–1941) (MD Trinity College of the University of Toronto (1895)) co-authored *The Vermiform Appendix and Its Diseases* with Howard A. Kelly, at Johns Hopkins Medical School, where she was also the first woman faculty member (1898). In England, she pioneered the use of *radium for gynaecological *cancer and was made a Commander of the Order of the British Empire (1938).

Florence Rena Sabin, (1871–1953) (MD Johns Hopkins Medical School (1900)), a superb researcher and teacher, demonstrated that the *lymphatics arise directly from the embryo's veins. In middle life she demonstrated the role of monocytes in the cellular aspects of *immunity. In 'retirement' she reformed the *public health system of Colorado. She was the first woman to be elected to the *National Academy of Sciences (1925).

Dorothy Reed Mendenhall (1874–1964) (MD Johns Hopkins Medical School (1900)) proved conclusively that *tuberculosis and *Hodgkin's disease are separate diseases by demonstrating the presence of a distinctive cell in the latter (1902). The cell is still known as the Reed cell or the Reed–Sternberg cell. She also made important international contributions in maternal and child welfare, especially in mortality studies and nutritional needs.

Gladys Dick (1881–1963) (MD John Hopkins University School of Medicine (1907)), with her husband George Dick demonstrated that *scarlet fever is caused by haemolytic *streptococci (1923) and developed a skin test ('Dick test') for susceptibility to the disease. For this they were nominated for the Nobel prize in 1925, but no prize in physiology or medicine was awarded that year.

Karen Horney (1885–1952) (MD University of Berlin (1911)), disciple of *Freud, soon departed from orthodox *psychoanalysis and founded her own school of psychoanalysis in New York City in which she emphasized the sociocultural factors operative in *neurosis and especially their importance in the psychology of women. She founded and edited the *American Journal of Psychoanalysis* (1941).

Louise Pearce (1885–1959) (MD Johns Hopkins University School of Medicine (1912)) is best remembered for the Brown–Pearce tumour, a transplantable *carcinoma of the rabbit that had world-wide importance in cancer research. She was also one of the developers of tryparsamide for African *sleeping sickness. For this she was awarded the Order of the Crown of Belgium, the King Leopold II prize, and the Royal Order of the Lion.

Helene Deutsch (1884–1982) (MD University of Vienna School of Medicine (1912)) was trained in psychoanalysis by Freud and did important work in the concept of the borderline personality. Her two-volume work, *The Psychology of Women: A Psychoanalytic Interpretation* (1944), though Freudian in orientation, remains the only systematic study of feminine psychology.

Gerty Cori (1896–1957) (MD Medical School of the German University of Prague (1920)) was the first American woman to win the Nobel prize for physiology or medicine (1947), which she shared with her husband Carl and Bernardo *Houssay of Argentina. Working on the intermediary *metabolism of *carbohydrates, the Coris isolated phosphorylase and synthesized *glycogen. They were also among the first to demonstrate that *enzyme defects can cause *heritable diseases.

Virginia Frantz (1896–1967) (MD College of Physicians and Surgeons of Columbia University (1922)), a pathologist, was the first to describe *insulin-secreting tumours of the *pancreas, in collaboration with the surgeon Allen O. Whipple.

Elizabeth Hazen (1885–1975) (Ph.D. Columbia University (1927)) in collaboration with Rachel Brown, discovered *nystatin (1948), an *antibiotic which is used in the treatment of fungal infections. Royalties from commercial production of the antifungal agent were used to fund research and to assist women in scientific careers.

H. Flanders Dunbar (1902–59) (MD Yale University School of Medicine (1930)) was a recognized Dante scholar, a theologian, a physician, and a psychoanalyst who pioneered in *psychosomatic medicine. She developed *personality profiles for various somatic diseases and was the first to describe the accident-prone personality. She founded and edited *Psychosomatic Medicine* (1938).

Grace Goldsmith (1904–75) (MD Tulane University School of Medicine (1932)) pioneered in the field of nutritional *deficiency diseases, especially those involving *vitamin C and the B-complex vitamins. She was the first to report on the use of *folic acid in the treatment of macrocytic *anaemia.

Virginia Apgar (1909–74) (MD College of Physicians and Surgeons, Columbia University (1933)) developed the well-known '*Apgar Score' (1952), a rapid clinical method of assessing a newborn's condition at birth and predicting which infants needed immediate special care.

Judith Pool (1919–75) (Ph.D. University of Chicago (1946)) developed cryoprecipitate, which facilitated the successful treatment of persons with *haemophilia (1964).

Among Canadian women, **Maude Abbott** (1869–1940) (MD, Bishop's College, 1894) was pre-eminent. Noted for her work in *congenital heart disease, she was also curator of the McGill Medical Museum and author of the well-known *Atlas of Congenital Cardiac Diseases*, the section on congenital heart disease in Sir William *Osler's textbook of medicine, and *History of Medicine in the Province of Quebec*.

In the 135 years since Elizabeth Blackwell received her degree women have made great strides in as well as great contributions to medicine. On the other hand, much of the progress in numbers in the USA has just come since 1970, when the Women's Equity Action League (WEAL) filed a class action suit against every medical school in the country for their failure to admit more women. Between 1930 and 1960 the number of women in the entering (freshman) class held steady at 4.5–6 per cent of the total number of students in the class. In 1970 it was 9 per cent, but by 1980 it had reached 28 per cent and by 1983 almost 32 per cent. In 1982–3, nearly 12 000 women applied for admission to medical school and 5500 were accepted; nearly half the women who wished to study medicine were able to do so.

In terms of the total number of physicians, however, the women are still catching up. In 1981, of the 485 000 physicians in the USA, women accounted for slightly more than 59 000, or about 12 per cent of the total. By far the largest number, 19 per cent, were under the age of 35, reflecting their fairly recent admission to medical school in larger numbers.

In terms of practice, more than half the women chose one of five specialties: internal medicine (16 per cent), paediatrics (15 per cent), general practice (9 per cent), psychiatry (8 per cent), and obstetrics and gynaecology (6 per cent). The remainder are represented in virtually all the other specialties.

Although women are catching up in terms of numbers, they are still deficient in terms of self-determination. They are under-represented, for example, in positions of leadership in academia and in organized medicine, where they can share institutional power and help to set policy. Recent consciousness of this problem, however, promises that gains can soon be expected in this area as well.

In the 1980s there also remain other unresolved problems of a more immediate nature that both men and women physicians must face. They have their roots partly in biology, partly in cultural tradition, and partly in the fact that American society is once again in a state of rapid transition.

Although officially sanctioned, maternity leave for women in training is often a problem at the local level. Tax credits for child care and household help are sought for all working women, but there remains the problem of finding suitable help in a country where few people are trained to provide these services. While helpful for some working women, day-care centres present scheduling problems for the woman professional. Dual-physician marriages or other dual-career marriages have the unique problem of the site of the primary home. It is not rare for one or other spouse to be a weekly intercity commuter, even a transcontinental commuter, for extended periods. And not the least is the problem many women have, one perhaps peculiar to women, of dividing their emotional commitment between family and profession. In cases such as this, it is not uncommon for a woman to absent herself from the profession temporarily and then to return after a period of retraining. This particular problem faces all working women, of course, but it seems to be especially acute for women physicians working in a profession where rapid progress in research quickly makes current information obsolete. Moreover, retraining programmes and split-time residencies are only a partial solution for the woman physician with a family; they do not greatly help the woman who is in a 'fast-track' competitive career environment.

Although all of these problems are urgent concerns at the present time, there is no reason why they will not also be overcome, just as were the barriers and obstacles that have faced women in the medical profession over the past 150 years, when Harriot Hunt began her practice in Boston without a degree.

(See also WOMEN IN MEDICINE I.)

M. THERESE SOUTHGATE

Further reading

Abbott, M. E. (1931). *History of Medicine in the Province of Quebec*. Montreal.

Alsop, G. F. (1950). *History of the Women's Medical College, Philadelphia, Pennsylvania, 1850–1950*. Philadelphia.

American Medical Association (1984). *House of Delegates 1984–1985*. Chicago.

Blackwell, E. (1895). *Pioneer Work in Opening the Medical Profession to Women*. London.

Chaff, S. L., Hainsbach, R., Fenichel, C. H. and Woodside, N. B. (eds) (1977). *Women in Medicine: A Bibliography of the Literature on Women Physicians*. Metuchen, New Jersey.

Deutsch, H. (1973). *Confrontations with Myself: An Epilogue*. New York.

Donegan, J. B. (1978). *Women and Men Midwives: Medicine, Morality, and Misogyny in Early America*. Westport, Connecticut.

Eiler, M. A. (1984). *Physician Characteristics and Distribution in the US* (1983 edition). American Medical Association. Chicago.

Fleming, A. (1964). *Doctors in Petticoats*. Philadelphia.

Hacker, C. (1974). *The Indomitable Lady Doctors*. Toronto.

Hughes, M. J. (1943). *Women in Medieval Life and Literature*. Reprint (1968), Freeport, New York.

Hurd-Mead, K. C. (1933). *Medical Women of America: A Short History of the Pioneer Medical Women of America and a Few of their Colleagues in England*. New York.

James, E. T. (ed.) (1971). *Notable American Women 1607–1950. A Biographical Dictionary*. Cambridge, Massachusetts.

Jex-Blake, S. (1886). *Medical Women: A Thesis and a History*. Edinburgh. Reprint (1970), New York.

King, L. S. (1984). *American Medicine Comes of Age 1890–1920*. American Medical Association, Chicago.

Lopate, C. (1968). *Women in Medicine*. Baltimore, Maryland.

Lovejoy, E. P. (1957). *Women Doctors of the World*. New York.

Marks, G. and Beatty, W. K. (1972). *Women in White*. New York.

Morantz, R. M. (1982). From art to science: women physicians in American medicine, 1600–1980. In Morantz, R. M. *et al.*, *In Her Own Words*. Westport, Connecticut.

Morantz, R. M., Pomerleau, C. S. and Fenichel, C. H. (eds) (1982). *In Her Own Words: Oral Histories of Women Physicians*. Westport, Connecticut.

Packard, F. R. (1901). *The History of Medicine in the United States*. Philadelphia.

Putnam-Jacobi, M. (1877). *The Question of Rest for Women During Menstruation* (the Boylston Prize Essay of Harvard University for 1876). New York.

Putnam-Jacobi, M. (1891). Women in medicine. In Meyer, A. N. M. (ed.), *Woman's Work in America*. New York.

Shryock, R. M. (1966). *Medicine in America: Historical Essays*. Baltimore, Maryland.

Sicherman, B., and Green, C. H. (eds) (1980). *Notable American Women: The Modern Period. A Biographical Dictionary*. Cambridge, Massachusetts.

Walsh, M. R. (1977). *Doctors Wanted: No Women Need Apply. Sexual Barriers in the Medical Profession, 1835–1975*. New Haven, Connecticut.

WOOD, PAUL HAMILTON (1907–62). Anglo-Australian physician, MD Melbourne (1940) FRCP (1940). Wood was made physician to the National Heart Hospital, London, in 1937, cardiologist to the *Royal Postgraduate Medical School in 1940, and to the Brompton Hospital in 1949. Paul Wood rapidly established a world-wide reputation as a cardiologist with an original and acute mind. He published a classic textbook *Diseases of the Heart and Circulation* (1950).

WOODALL, JOHN (?1556–1643). British surgeon. Woodall served as surgeon to Lord Willoughby's regiment in Europe in 1591 and remained on the Continent for eight years. In 1599 he was admitted to the *Barber-Surgeons' Company, becoming Master in 1633. He was appointed surgeon to *St Bartholomew's Hospital in 1616 and was made the first surgeon-general to the East India Company in 1612. He was involved with the Virginia Company in 1620 and later. He published *The Surgeon's Mate* (1617), in which he recommended lemon juice for the treatment of *scurvy, and *Viaticum, being the Pathway to the Surgeon's Chest* (1628).

WORKMEN'S COMPENSATION ACTS. A series of Workmen's Compensation Acts dating from 1897 which sought to deal with the increasing problems arising against the background of a rapidly changing and increasingly mechanized industrial system in the UK. They were replaced by the *National Insurance (Industrial Injuries) Act of 1946.

WORLD HEALTH ORGANIZATION (WHO) was established in 1948 by the United Nations. It took over the functions of the Health Organization of the League of Nations and the International Office of Public Health in Paris. These had been concerned with control of epidemics, quarantine measures, and drug standardization. Now the WHO has a remit which covers all aspects of health of all peoples, and in a variety of ways it assists countries to improve the health of their own populations. The head office is in Geneva, Switzerland, and there are regional offices in Egypt, the Congo, Denmark, India, the Philippines, and the USA. There is a staff of over 3500 in these offices and in the field, supported by contributions made by member states of the World Health Assembly, which determines broad policy annually. Its tools for assistance to countries include information and education on all aspects of health; sponsoring measures for the control of epidemics and other disorders by mass programmes, particularly of vaccination, immunization, antibiotics and chemotherapy, and the setting up of laboratory and clinical facilities for early diagnosis and prevention of disease, improving water supplies and health education; and helping to strengthen public health adminstration locally in countries where this is needed. The work of WHO was largely responsible for the eradication of *smallpox from the world a few years ago. It also sponsors doctors and health care professionals of all kinds to go to countries to help with their problems and to teach. It is miniscule by comparison with the tasks which lie ahead of it in the drive for international good health, but its help is often visible in areas where it is most needed. Its work must surely grow in future for far too much of the world is poor, malnourished, and prey to preventable diseases and overpopulation in all of which problems the weak need the stronger to assist them. Given more resources the WHO can do this. In 1981 the World Health Assembly adopted a policy of health for all by the year 2000. This tall order requires the recognition of health as a fundamental right; the elimination of inequalities in health care; community involvement in health care and attention to the socioeconomic factors on which it depends; political commitment by states to health care; national self-reliance in health care; integration of health care with all other factors such as agriculture, animal husbandry, food, education, housing, public works, and communications; and better use of the world's resources. In every way open to it the WHO intends to help with all these aims.

WORLD MEDICAL ASSOCIATION, THE, with

headquarters in Ferney-Voltaire, France, was founded in 1947. It represents the coming together of representatives from National Medical Associations, which have to be free associations for doctors and bona fide medical students only, and not subject to or controlled by any organ of government. Such associations may not exist in countries with totalitarian regimes, so these have no representation in the WMA. Nevertheless 41 countries have membership. 'The purpose of the Association shall be to serve humanity by endeavouring to achieve the highest international standards in medical education, medical science, medical art, and medical ethics, and health care for all people of the world.' It has few direct powers, and is unable to enforce its decisions on its member associations without their agreement. It might therefore be considered to be simply a talking-shop for the relatively few doctors with an interest in medical politics, and hence suspect among the generality of the profession. Nevertheless, and perhaps surprisingly, this is not the case and the WMA has attained considerable prestige and influence by many of its pronouncements. These have been issued from time to time from various places where the WMA Assembly has met, for there are regional organizations covering Europe, Asia, the Pacific region, Latin America, Africa, and North America. With so many different cultural and political backgrounds to the practice of medicine it is most remarkable that it has been possible to promulgate common standards of ethics to which by far the majority of doctors can assent. Moreover they can be and have been used to change attitudes and lighten repression on doctors and their patients from whatever quarters those malign influences have come.

Among the successful publications have been:

Regulations in Time of Armed Conflict (Havana, 1956; Istanbul, 1957)

Computers and Confidentiality (Munich, 1973)

Twelve Principles of Social Security and Medical Care (1963)

Family Planning (Madrid, 1967; Paris, 1969)

Declaration of Tokyo (1975). 'Guidelines for Medical Doctors concerning Torture and Other Cruel, Inhuman or Degrading Treatment or Punishment in relation to Detention and Imprisonment.'

Declaration of Helsinki (1964): revised Tokyo (1975). 'Recommendations guiding medical doctors in biomedical research involving human subjects.'

The Use and Misuse of Psychotropic Drugs (1975)

Declaration of Sydney (1968). Statement on death especially with regard to the use of organs for transplantation

Statement on Pollution (São Paulo, 1976)

Statement on Therapeutic Abortion (Oslo, 1970)

International Code of Medical Ethics (London, 1949; Sydney, 1968) which includes (*a*) *Duties of Doctors in General*, (*b*) *Duties of Doctors to the Sick*, (*c*) *Duties of Doctors to Each Other*.

Declaration of Geneva (1948; Sydney 1968). This is a form of updating of the ancient *Hippocratic Oath to meet modern conditions.

Recommendations concerning Medical Care in Rural Areas (1977)

Principles of Health Care for Sports Medicine (Lisbon, 1981). Defines the use of drugs in sports.

The Rights of the Patient (Lisbon, 1981).

This abbreviated list shows that the medical profession is capable of transcending local and apparently insistent considerations of the moment and of being ever reminded of its higher nobler duties, established for centuries, yet needing constant restatement in practical applicable terms.

The Assembly now meets every two years. The *World Medical Journal* is published in English every two months.

WORMS parasitic in man (helminths) fall into one of three broad groups: roundworms or nematodes; flukes or trematodes; and tapeworms or cestodes. (The latter two groups both come under the phylum of flatworms or platyhelminths.) For their further classification, see NEMATODES; FLUKES; and TAPEWORMS; and under the names of individual worms and their diseases.

WOUND INFECTION. Postoperative wound infections vary in incidence and type with the nature of the surgical procedure, the degree of surgical skill, and the adequacy of aseptic technique before, during, and after the operation. Staphylococci and coliform bacilli are the commonest organisms responsible but others, including haemolytic streptococci, may be identified: all are potentially dangerous.

WOUNDS. Lesions produced by external mechanical force involving damage to the normal continuity of tissues, such as bruises (contusions), cuts (incisions), tears (lacerations), stabs (punctures), breaks (fractures), etc.

WREN, SIR CHRISTOPHER (1632–1723). Wren was born in East Knoyle, Wiltshire, England, and educated at Westminster School and Wadham College, Oxford. He became a fellow of All Souls College in 1653 and took some interest in medicine but later researched in astronomy. In 1657 he became professor of astronomy at Gresham College, London. Some problems arose during the Cromwellian era and the Restoration of the monarchy and he moved between Oxford and London. In 1661 he was made Savilian professor of astronomy at Oxford. He was inspired by *Descartes, worked with *Boyle, knew *Newton, and was a major figure in a remarkable century. Why he changed to architecture is not fully known. He had been involved in some building projects prior to the Great Fire of London of 1666, and he became King's Surveyor in 1669. He was a founder of the Royal Society and president 1681–3. Wren rebuilt over 50 City of London churches, the most famous being St Paul's Cathedral. There he is buried and on his memorial is inscribed 'Si monumentum requiris, circumspice' (If you seek a monument, look around you).

WRIGHT, SIR ALMROTH EDWARD (1861–1947). British bacteriologist, MD Trinity College, Dublin (1889), FRCP (1938), FRS (1906). After service from 1892 to 1902 as professor of pathology at the Army Medical School, Netley, Wright was appointed pathologist to *St Mary's Hospital, London, in 1902. He served as Colonel AMS in the First World War as adviser in bacteriology. He was knighted in 1906, made Companion of the Order of the Bath in 1915. Wright introduced the routine antityphoid vaccination into the Army. He developed and exploited therapeutic immunization by vaccines at his Institute at St Mary's Hospital and his work inspired Bernard Shaw's *The Doctor's Dilemma*.

WRITER'S CRAMP. See OCCUPATIONAL CRAMP.

WRY-NECK. See TORTICOLLIS.

WUNDERLICH, KARL REINHOLD AUGUST (1815–77). German physician, MD Tübingen (1839). Wunderlich was professor of medicine first in Tübingen (1843) and later in Leipzig (1850). He made the thermometer an indispensable clinical tool, describing his findings in *Das Verhaltern der Eigenwärme in Krankheiten* (1868). He was an authority also on climatology and *balneotherapy and an erudite medical historian.

WYNDHAM, SIR CHARLES (1841–1919). British physician and actor, MRCS (1857), MD Giessen (1859). Wyndham was born Charles Culverwell, changing his name when he went on to the stage in 1862. He served as a surgeon in the Federal Army during the American Civil War. He was manager of the Criterion Theatre in London from 1876 until 1899 when he opened Wyndham's Theatre. He was knighted in 1902.

X

XANTHINE is a nitrogenous base from which a number of pharmacologically active compounds are derived; they include *caffeine, *theophylline, theobromine, and aminophylline. Xanthine derivatives have *bronchodilator, myocardial stimulant, respiratory stimulant and *diuretic properties.

XANTHOCHROMIA is a yellowish discoloration, particularly with reference to the normally colourless *cerebrospinal fluid.

XANTHOMA. A yellow plaque or nodule in the skin, due to the deposition of *lipids.

XENOGRAFT. A transplant of organ or tissue between individuals of different species. Cf. ALLOGRAFT; AUTOGRAFT; SYNGRAFT.

XENOPHOBIA is a pathological fear of strangers, or a dislike of foreigners.

XENOPSYLLA is a genus of rat *fleas, many species of which are vectors of human disease, particularly *plague (notably the Asiatic rat flea, *Xenopsylla cheopis*).

XENOPUS PREGNANCY TEST. A *urinary test for *pregnancy, based on the rate of egg deposition by the female African toad (*Xenopus laevis*) following the injection of 2 ml of the specimen into the dorsal lymph sac.

XERODERMA is any condition in which the skin is abnormally dry, for example *ichthyosis.

XERODERMA PIGMENTOSUM is a recessively transmitted defect of the *enzyme system for *deoxyribonucleic acid (DNA) repair, resulting in a syndrome of sun-sensitivity with freckling, dryness and atrophy of the skin, *telangiectasia, and the development of cutaneous malignant tumours. The condition becomes apparent in early childhood and death from *metastases or intercurrent infection is usual by the third decade.

XEROGRAPHY is a dry process for producing *radiographs.

XEROPHTHALMIA is dryness of the conjunctiva and cornea due to *vitamin A deficiency. See also NIGHT BLINDNESS.

X-LINKED DISEASE. *Sex linkage in which the abnormal gene responsible for the disease is carried on the X chromosome. In the case of a dominant gene, an affected father will transmit the condition to all his daughters but none of his sons, an affected heterozygous mother to half her children of whatever sex.
Recessive X-linked conditions are much commoner; they occur only in males, who are hemizygous, and are transmitted only through heterozygous females (the classic example being *haemophilia); females are only affected in the improbable case of a homozygote resulting from the union of a male sufferer with a female carrier. See also GENETICS.

X-RAY MICROANALYSIS is the analysis of minute quantities of material by means of *X-ray spectra.

X-RAYS are electromagnetic *radiation (i.e. radiation of the same non-particulate type as light, *gamma rays, and radio waves) whose wavelength is shorter than that of *ultraviolet light but longer than that of gamma rays, ranging from 5 nanometres to 6 picometres. See also RADIOLOGY; RADIOTHERAPY; RADIATION, IONIZING.

XXX SYNDROME. Females with the triple X syndrome, that is with 47 chromosomes due to the addition of an extra X or female chromosome, are not uncommon in the general population, since the XXX *genotype is found in about 1 in 2000 of all live births. Many are clinically normal, and may be fertile, but it is known that this genotype is significantly associated with low intelligence.

XYY SYNDROME is a common genetic abnormality (one in 700 live male births) in which the patient's cells have 47 chromosomes, the extra one being an additional male or Y chromosome. Many normal individuals in the population possess this *genotype, but there is an established association with tallness; and studies of populations of men with aggressive, psychopathic, and criminal tendencies have shown an increased incidence of XYY constitution.

Y

YANG AND YIN are the two opposing principles or essences of Chinese philosophy and medicine, influencing destiny and health. Yin is negative, feminine, and dark, dominating earth, moon, winter, and water; Yang is positive, masculine, and light, dominating heaven, sun, summer, and fire. For good health, the two must be perfectly balanced; imbalance leads to disease. An elaborate system of interrelationships between tissues and organs is constructed from this simplistic concept, and deductions about them are made by studying the character of the arterial pulse.

YAWN. A semi-voluntary wide opening of the mouth, which may be associated with deep inspiration and sometimes with stretching of the limbs; a manifestation of fatigue, boredom, or anxiety.

YAWS is a chronic non-venereal spirochaetal infection of the tropics, usually acquired in childhood, which has many features resembling *syphilis. The causative organism is *Treponema pertenue*, very similar to *Treponema pallidum*.

YEAST is a general term for single-celled fungi belonging to the class Ascomycetes. Yeasts typically multiply by a budding process.

YEAST EXTRACT is a preparation derived from a culture of *yeast, a byproduct of the brewing and baking industries. It is a source of *protein and *vitamins of the B complex.

YELLOW FEVER is an acute viral infection of tropical Africa and America transmitted by biting mosquitoes of the *Aedes* and *Haemagogus* genera; the causative agent is an enveloped ribonucleic acid (RNA) *virus of the flavivirus group. Yellow fever varies in severity from a mild influenza-like episode to a dangerous and sometimes fatal illness marked by jaundice due to liver necrosis, haemorrhagic manifestations, and renal failure. Immunization with live attenuated vaccine provides safe, effective, and long-lived (at least 10 years) protection, and is essential for travellers to endemic areas. Yellow fever is one of the six diseases internationally notifiable to the *World Health Organization.

YERSIN, ALEXANDRE (1863–1943). Swiss bacteriologist, MD Paris (1888). After working with *Roux at the Institut Pasteur in Paris on *diphtheria toxin and the bactericidal properties of the blood (1888), Yersin went to Indo-China and became a medical officer in the French Colonial Service (1894). He found the cause of *plague (*Pasteurella pestis*, now known as *Yersinia pestis*) independently of *Kitasato (1894) and made an effective serum (1896). He did much to control epidemics in Indo-China and became director of the Pasteur Institute in Annam.

YOGA is a system of mental concentration, abstract meditation, asceticism, and physical discipline derived from Hindu philosophy and practised with the object of emancipating the soul and achieving union with a supreme spirit.

YOUNG, FRANCIS BRETT (1884–1954). British physician and novelist, MB Birmingham (1907). Young practised little, but served in the Royal Army Medical Corps in East Africa during the First World War. He wrote many novels, the best known of which were *Portrait of Clare* (1927), *My Brother Jonathan* (1928), and *They Seek a Country* (1937).

YOUNG, HENRY ESSON (1867–1939). Public health pioneer and educator, BA Queens University, Kingston, Ontario (1883), MD, CM McGill (1888). Young was one of *Osler's favourite pupils, following him to Pennsylvania in vacations. He became general practitioner in Atlin, BC, on the Alaskan border. He was elected to the Provincial Legislature 1903, and was Minister of Education and Provincial Secretary from 1907 until 1916 when the government was defeated. Thereafter he served as Provincial Health Officer. He was 'the father of the University of British Columbia', and a pioneer in mental health, the provincial library, archives, and museum, and a civil service based on merit. With advice from Osler and *Sherrington he selected Frank Fairchild *Wesbrook, then dean of medicine at the University of Minnesota, to be first (outstandingly successful) president of the University of British Columbia.

YOUNG, HUGH HAMPTON (1870–1945). American urological surgeon, MD University of Virginia (1894). Young became a resident surgeon at the *Johns Hopkins Hospital, and later was named to head a division of urological surgery. This became a major training site in that field of surgery. Young wrote scores of articles on urological diseases, and on surgical treatment, and edited the *Journal of Urology* for many years. He was elected to honorary membership in the urological societies of many other countries.

YOUNG, THOMAS (1773–1829). British physician and polymath, MD Göttingen (1796), MD Cambridge (1808), FRCP (1809), FRS (1794). Young started practice in London in 1799 and became professor of natural philosophy at the Royal Institution in 1801. He was elected physician to *St George's Hospital in 1811 and remained in office until his death. He was known at Cambridge, 'with a mixture of respect and derision', as 'Phenomenon Young'. By the age of 19 he had mastered Latin, Greek, Hebrew, Chaldee, Arabic, Syriac, Persian, Samaritan, French, Italian, Spanish, and German. He was the founder of physiological optics (Young's theory of *colour vision); he supervised the *Nautical Almanac*; he propounded the first theory of capillary action; and he deciphered the demotic text of the Rosetta stone. As a mathematician he devised Young's modulus. He did not however 'shine at the bedside, nor in the practical work of his profession'. He retired from practice in 1814.

YULE, GEORGE UDNY (1871–1951). British statistician. At University College, London, Yule met Karl *Pearson who started Yule's interest in *statistics, then just seriously beginning. He was lecturer at University College and at Cambridge University. He wrote the standard textbook, *Introduction to the Theory of Statistics* (1911), and made many contributions of lasting value to the subject, and to Mendelian *inheritance and *epidemiology. Yule was elected a fellow of the Royal Society in 1921. Nearing retirement he studied Latin with a view to reading Thomas à Kempis and others in the original. Because of authorship controversies he proposed the statistical study of works of doubtful authorship and published *The Statistical Study of Literary Vocabulary* (1944).

Z

ZEISS, CARL (1816–88). German optician, Dr Phil. (hon.) Jena (1881). Zeiss was born in Weimar, East Germany. In 1846 he opened his optical glass works in Jena, in the east of Germany, and produced the finest of optical instruments, including *microscopes. Abbe, a physicist joined him, and so did Schott, a glass chemist who developed over 100 types of optical and heat-resistant glass. After the death of Zeiss, Abbe gave the firm, in which he was then a partner, to start the Carl Zeiss Foundation. Schott added his share later to the same cause. At the end of the war in 1945 the Foundation was moved to West Germany at Heidenheim. Zeiss instruments are still among the best in the world for scientific purposes, and are widely used in medicine.

ZEN DIET is generally *vegetarian, but the distinguished Zen Buddhist Christmas Humphreys wrote:

With regard to the killing of animals for food, it is obvious that the purer the food we eat the more fit will our bodies become for the functioning of our inner faculties, but once more common sense must be employed. A Buddhist's first requirement is a healthy body in which to work. He must therefore eat such food as long experience has shown to be, not the most pleasing to his palate, but most suited to his health. To make oneself ill by insufficient nutriment is a form of vanity. Diet is not a matter of religion, but of climate, occupation and individual temperament. Indeed, Narasu quotes the Buddha as saying: 'My disciples have permission to eat whatever food it is customary to eat in any place or country provided it is done without indulgence of the appetite, or evil desire'. (*Buddhism* (1962) 3rd edn, London).

ZENKER, FRIEDRICH ALBERT (1825–98). German pathologist, MD Leipzig (1851). Zenker was professor of pathological anatomy in Leipzig (1855) and later in Erlangen (1862). He is best known for his description of waxy degeneration in muscle (Zenker's degeneration). He gave an excellent description of *trichiniasis in 1860.

ZHIVAGO, DR is the eponymous young doctor and poet of the novel by Boris Pasternak (1890–1960), himself an important poet of the early Soviet period. *Dr Zhivago*, which in the Russian original is partly in verse, recounts the experiences of Yuri Zhivago during the Russian Revolution; it contains some explicit anti-Marxist passages, particularly in the conversations between Yuri and his uncle Kolya. Publication was initially suppressed in the Soviet Union, and the first version to appear was an Italian translation in 1957. An English translation was published in 1958, the same year that Pasternak was awarded, but felt obliged to reject, the Nobel prize for literature.

ZIEGLER, ERNST (1849–1905). Swiss pathologist, MD Würzburg (1872). Ziegler served as professor of pathological anatomy in Zurich (1881), Tübingen (1882), and Freiburg-im-Bresgau (1889). One of the leading morbid anatomists of his time, his textbook of pathological anatomy (1881) circulated widely. He founded the influential journal *Beiträge zur pathologischen Anatomie* (1886).

ZINC is a hard bluish-white metallic element (relative atomic mass 65.37, atomic number 30, symbol Zn). Zinc is a constituent of a number of important body *enzymes and is an essential dietary *trace element; deficiency is associated with dwarfism, hypogonadism, anaemia, and impaired wound healing. Zinc salts are mildly astringent and antiseptic and in medicine are used in various lotions, ointments, and dusting powders (calamine is zinc oxide).

ZINSSER, HANS (1878–1940). American bacteriologist and immunologist, MD Columbia University (1901). After a short period of medical practice in New York Zinsser joined the department of bacteriology at Columbia; then he became head of the department of bacteriology and immunology at Harvard in 1923. He was co-editor (first with His, then with Bayne-Jones) of a widely used textbook of bacteriology and immunology. Much of his research was directed toward elucidation of the role of immunological mechanisms in the manifestations and courses of *infectious diseases. During the First World War he served in Europe on the Typhus Commission; thereafter he maintained an intense interest in *rickettsial diseases. By using epidemiological information he produced persuasive evidence that *Brill's disease is a recrudescence, in older adults, of *typhus fever contracted in early life. His popular book, *Rats, Lice and History* was enjoyed by both medical and lay readers.

ZOLLINGER–ELLISON SYNDROME is a condition due to a *gastrin-secreting tumour, situated usually in the *pancreas, which causes marked gastric hypersecretion and in the majority of cases a *peptic ulcer in the *duodenum or stomach. Other endocrine abnormalities are often also present.

ZONDEK, BERNHARD (1891–1966). German gynaecologist, MD Berlin (1912). Zondek worked with *Aschheim on the first reliable *pregnancy test. He attended the medical school of the University of Berlin, and became associate professor of obstetrics and gynaecology at the *Charité, and in 1929 director of obstetrics and gynaecology in the Berlin-Spandau Hospital. He left Germany as a result of Nazi persecution and in 1934 was made professor of obstetrics and gynaecology at the Hebrew University-Hadassah Medical School in Jerusalem. He was Aschheim's junior by 13 years and worked with him in Berlin.

ZOOLOGY IN RELATION TO MEDICINE. Ever since *Galen dissected apes and pigs, the advance of medicine has depended crucially on the scientific study of animals. This debt is not confined to human anatomy, embryology, and physiology, though zoology remains an important premedical subject in the education of most doctors. Pharmacology, nutrition, microbiology, genetics, experimental pathology, operative surgery, psychology, parasitology, and the human zoonoses are but a few of the branches of medicine where animal studies have always been of paramount importance. See also VETERINARY MEDICINE.

ZOONOSIS. Any disease of animals which may be transmitted to man, for example, *rabies, *plague, *brucellosis, *ornithosis, and numerous others.

ZOSTER. See HERPES ZOSTER.

ZUCKERKANDL, EMIL (1849–1901). Viennese anatomist. Zuckerkandl studied at the University of Vienna, and later was a demonstrator in Vienna and Amsterdam, and was appointed professor with *Rokitansky in Vienna in 1879. He described paraganglia (now known as *chromaffin tissue) in the vicinity of the abdominal *aorta, the subcallosal sulcus of the brain, and a vein running between the nasal cavities and the brain. All were named after him for some time, though eponymous structures are disappearing now from anatomical vocabulary.

ZYGOTE. The cell produced by fusion of male and female *gametes (spermatozoon and ovum respectively), that is the fertilized ovum.

APPENDIX I

MAJOR MEDICAL AND RELATED QUALIFICATIONS

AAPSW	Associate of the Association of Psychiatric Social Workers
AB	Bachelor of Arts
A.B.Ps.S.	Associate of the British Psychological Society
AFOM	Associate of the Faculty of Occupational Medicine
AIMBI	Associate of the Institute of Medical and Biological Illustration
AIMLS	Associate of the Institute of Medical Laboratory Science
AIMSW	Associate of the Institute of Medical Social Workers
AM	Master of Arts
ARPS	Associate of the Royal Photographic Society
BA	Bachelor of Arts
BAO	Bachelor of the Art of Obstetrics
BC	Bachelor of Surgery
B.Ch.	Bachelor of Surgery
B.Ch.D.	Bachelor of Dental Surgery
B.Chir.	Bachelor of Surgery
BDS	Bachelor of Dental Surgery
B.D.Sc.	Bachelor of Dental Science
B.Hyg.	Bachelor of Hygiene
BM	Bachelor of Medicine
B.Med.Sc.	Bachelor of Medical Science
B.Pharm.	Bachelor of Pharmacy
B. Phil.	Bachelor of Philosophy
BS	Bachelor of Surgery; Bachelor of Science
B.Sc.	Bachelor of Science
BVMS	Bachelor of Veterinary Medicine and Surgery
C.Chem.	Chartered Chemist
Ch.B.	Bachelor of Surgery
Ch.M.	Master of Surgery
CM	Master of Surgery
CPH	Certificate in Public Health
CRCP(C)	Certificant, Royal College of Physicians of Canada
DA	Diploma in Anaesthesia
DABR	Diplomate of the American Board of Radiology
DASS	Diploma in Applied Social Studies
DBA	Doctor of Business Administration
DCCH	Diploma in Child and Community Health
DCD	Diploma in Chest Diseases
DCH	Diploma in Child Health
D.Ch.	Doctor of Surgery
DCMHE	Diploma of Contents and Methods of Health Education
DCMT	Diploma in Clinical Medicine of the Tropics
DCP	Diploma in Clinical Pathology

DCR(R)	Diploma of the College of Radiographers (Diagnostic Radiology)
DCR(T)	Diploma of the College of Radiographers (Radiotherapy)
DD	Doctor of Divinity
DDM	Diploma in Dermatological Medicine
DDO	Diploma in Dental Orthopaedics
DDPH	Diploma in Dental Public Health
DDR	Diploma in Diagnostic Radiology
DDS	Doctor of Dental Surgery
D.D.Sc.	Doctor of Dental Science
D en M	Docteur en Médecine
DGO	Diploma in Obstetrics and Gynaecology
DHMSA	Diploma in the History of Medicine (Society of Apothecaries)
D.Hyg.	Doctor of Hygiene
DIH	Diploma in Industrial Health
Dip.B.M.S.	Diploma in Basic Medical Science
Dip.Ven.	Diploma in Venereology
DLO	Diploma in Laryngology and Otology
DM	Doctor of Medicine
DMD	Diploma in Medical Dentistry
DMHS	Diploma in Medical and Health Services
DMJ	Diploma in Medical Jurisprudence
DMJ(Path.)	Diploma in Medical Jurisprudence (Pathology)
DMR	Diploma in Radiology
DMRD	Diploma in Medical Radiological Diagnosis
DMRE	Diploma in Medical Radiology and Electronics
DMRT	Diploma in Medical Radiotherapy
DMSA	Diploma in Medical Service Administration
DMV	Doctor of Veterinary Medicine
DNS	Doctor of Nursing Science
D.N.Sc.	Doctor of Nursing Science
DO	Diploma in Ophthalmology
D.Obst.R.C.O.G.	Diploma in Obstetrics, Royal College of Obstetricians and Gynae-cologists
DOMS	Diploma in Ophthalmic Medicine and Surgery
D.Orth.	Diploma in Orthodontics
DPD	Diploma in Public Dentistry
DPH	Diploma in Public Health
D.Phil.	Doctor of Philosophy
DPM	Diploma in Psychological Medicine
DR	Diploma in Radiology
DRD	Diploma in Restorative Dentistry
Dr.P.H.	Doctor of Public Health
Dr.Phil.	Doctor of Philosophy
DS	Doctor of Science
D.Sc.	Doctor of Science
DSM	Diploma in Social Medicine
DSN	Doctor of the Science of Nursing
DTCD	Diploma in Tubercular and Chest Diseases
DTCH	Diploma in Tropical Child Health
DTD	Diploma in Tubercular Diseases
DTH	Diploma in Tropical Hygiene
DTM	Diploma in Tropical Medicine
DTM&H	Diploma in Tropical Medicine and Hygiene
DTPH	Diploma in Tropical Public Health
DV&D	Diploma in Venereology and Dermatology
DVM	Doctor of Veterinary Medicine
DVMS	Doctor of Veterinary Medicine and Surgery

DVS	Doctor of Veterinary Surgery
D.V.Sc.	Doctor of Veterinary Science
Ed.D	Doctor of Education
EOPH	Examined Officer in Public Health
FAAFP	Fellow of the American Academy of Family Physicians
FAAN	Fellow of the American Academy of Nursing
FACC	Fellow of the American College of Cardiology
FACCP	Fellow of the American College of Chest Physicians
FACD	Fellow of the American College of Dentistry
FACDS	Fellow of the Australian College of Dental Surgeons
FACFP	Fellow of the American College of Family Practice
FACG	Fellow of the American College of Gastroenterology
FACN	Fellow of the American College of Nutrition
FACO	Fellow of the American College of Otolaryngology
FACOG	Fellow of the American College of Obstetricians and Gynecologists
FACP	Fellow of the American College of Physicians
FACPM	Fellow of the American College of Preventive Medicine
FACR	Fellow of the American College of Radiologists
FACS	Fellow of the American College of Surgeons
FACTM	Fellow of the American College of Tropical Medicine
FAGO	Fellowship in Australia in Obstetrics and Gynaecology
FAMA	Fellow of the American Medical Association
FAPA	Fellow of the American Psychiatric Association
FAPHA	Fellow of the American Public Health Association
F.B.Ps.S.	Fellow of the British Psychological Society
FCAP	Fellow of the College of American Pathologists
F.Ch.S.	Fellow of the Society of Chiropodists
FCMS	Fellow of the College of Medicine and Surgery
FCOG(SA)	Fellow of the South African College of Obstetricians and Gynaecologists
FCP(SoAf)	Fellow of the College of Physicians, South Africa
FCSP	Fellow of the Chartered Society of Physiotherapists
FCSSA	Fellow of the College of Surgeons, South Africa
FCST	Fellow of the College of Speech Therapists
FDS	Fellow in Dental Surgery
FDSRCPS(Glasg.)	Fellow in Dental Surgery, Royal College of Physicians and Surgeons of Glasgow
FDSRCS	Fellow in Dental Surgery, Royal College of Surgeons of England
FDSRCS(Ed.)	Fellow in Dental Surgery, Royal College of Surgeons of Edinburgh
FFARACS	Fellow of the Faculty of Anaesthetists, Royal Australasian College of Surgeons
FFARCS	Fellow of the Faculty of Anaesthetists, Royal College of Surgeons of England
FFARCS(Irel.)	Fellow of the Faculty of Anaesthetists, Royal College of Surgeons in Ireland
FFDRSC(Irel.)	Fellow of the Faculty of Dentistry, Royal College of Surgeons in Ireland
FFCM	Fellow of the Faculty of Community Medicine
F.F.Hom.	Fellow of the Faculty of Homoeopathy
FFOM	Fellow of the Faculty of Occupational Medicine
FHA	Fellow of the Institute of Health Service Administrators
F.I.Biol.	Fellow of the Institute of Biology
FICS	Fellow of the International College of Surgeons

FIHE	Fellow of the Institute of Health Education
F.I.Hosp.E.	Fellow of the Institute of Hospital Engineers
FIMLS	Fellow of the Institute of Medical Laboratory Sciences
F.Inst.P.	Fellow of the Institute of Physics
FIPHE	Fellow of the Institute of Public Health Engineers
FLA	Fellow of the Library Association
FLS	Fellow of the Linnean Society
FPS	Fellow of the Pharmaceutical Society
FRACDS	Fellow of the Royal Australian College of Dental Surgeons
FRACGP	Fellow of the Royal Australian College of General Practitioners
FRACMA	Fellow of the Royal Australian College of Medical Administrators
FRACO	Fellow of the Royal Australian College of Ophthalmologists
FRACOG	Fellow of the Royal Australasian College of Obstetricians and Gynaecologists
FRACP	Fellow of the Royal Australasian College of Physicians
FRACR	Fellow of the Royal Australasian College of Radiologists
FRACS	Fellow of the Royal Australasian College of Surgeons
FRANZCP	Fellow of the Royal Australian and New Zealand College of Psychiatrists
FRCGP	Fellow of the Royal College of General Practitioners
FRCN	Fellow of the Royal College of Nursing
FRCOG	Fellow of the Royal College of Obstetricians and Gynaecologists
FRCP	Fellow of the Royal College of Physicians of London
FRCPA	Fellow of the Royal College of Pathologists of Australia
F.R.C.Path.	Fellow of the Royal College of Pathologists
FRCP(C)	Fellow of the Royal College of Physicians of Canada
FRCP(Ed. or Edin.)	Fellow of the Royal College of Physicians, Edinburgh
FRCP(Glasg.)	Fellow of the Royal College of Physicians and Surgeons of Glasgow
FRCPI	Fellow of the Royal College of Physicians of Ireland
FRCP&S(Canada)	Fellow of the Royal College of Physicians and Surgeons of Canada
F.R.C.Psych.	Fellow of the Royal College of Psychiatrists
FRCR	Fellow of the Royal College of Radiologists
FRCS	Fellow of the Royal College of Surgeons of England
FRCS(C)	Fellow of the Royal College of Surgeons of Canada
FRCS(Ed. or Edin.)	Fellow of the Royal College of Surgeons of Edinburgh
FRCS(Glasg.)	Fellow of the Royal College of Physicians and Surgeons of Glasgow
FRCS(Irel.)	Fellow of the Royal College of Surgeons in Ireland
FRCVS	Fellow of the Royal College of Veterinary Science
FRIPHH	Fellow of the Royal Institute of Public Health and Hygiene
FRPS	Fellow of the Royal Photographic Society
FRS	Fellow of the Royal Society
FRSC	Fellow of the Royal Society of Canada
FRSE	Fellow of the Royal Society of Edinburgh
FRSH	Fellow of the Royal Society for the Promotion of Health
FRSTM&H	Fellow of the Royal Society of Tropical Medicine and Hygiene
HDD	Higher Dental Diploma
KLJ	Knight of St Lazarus of Jerusalem
LAH	Licentiate of the Apothecaries' Hall, Dublin
L.Ch.	Licentiate in Surgery
LCST	Licentiate of the College of Speech Therapists
LDS	Licentiate in Dental Surgery
LHD	*Literarum Humaniorum Doctor*, Doctor of Literature

Lic.Med.	Licentiate in Medicine
LLB	Bachelor of Law
LM	Licentiate in Midwifery
LMCC	Licentiate of the Medical Council of Canada
L.Med.	Licentiate in Medicine
LMSSA	Licentiate in Medicine and Surgery of the Society of Apothecaries
LRCP	Licentiate of the Royal College of Physicians of London
LRCP(Ed. *or* Edin.)	Licentiate of the Royal College of Physicians, Edinburgh
LRCPI	Licentiate of the Royal College of Physicians of Ireland
LRCPS(Glasg.)	Licentiate of the Royal College of Physicians and Surgeons of Glasgow
LRCS	Licentiate of the Royal College of Surgeons of England
LRCS(Ed. *or* Edin.)	Licentiate of the Royal College of Surgeons of Edinburgh
LRCS(Irel.)	Licentiate of the Royal College of Surgeons in Ireland
LSA	Licentiate of the Society of Apothecaries
MA	Master of Arts
MACP	Master of the American College of Physicians
MAO	Master of the Art of Obstetrics
MB	Bachelor of Medicine
MB BS	Bachelor of Medicine and Bachelor of Surgery
MC	Master of Surgery
M.Ch.	Master of Surgery
M.Ch.D.	Master of Dental Surgery
M.Chir.	Master of Surgery
M.Ch.Orth.	Master of Orthopaedic Surgery
M.Ch.Otol.	Master of Otology
M.Ch.S.	Member of the Society of Chiropodists
M.Cl.Sc.	Master of Clinical Science
M.Comm.H.	Master of Community Health
MCR(R)	Member of the College of Radiographers (Diagnostic Radiography)
MCR(T)	Member of the College of Radiographers (Radiotherapy)
MCSP	Member of the Chartered Society of Physiotherapists
MD	Doctor of Medicine
M.Dent.Sc.	Master of Dental Science
MDS	Master of Dental Surgery
MFCM	Member of the Faculty of Community Medicine
M.F.Hom.	Member of the Faculty of Homoeopathy
MFOM	Member of the Faculty of Occupational Medicine
M.Hyg.	Master of Hygiene
MIH	Master of Industrial Health
MIPR	Member of the Institute of Public Relations
ML	Licentiate in Medicine
M.Med.	Master of Medicine
M.Med.Sc.	Master of Medical Science
MMSA	Master of Midwifery (Society of Apothecaries)
MNAS	Member of the National Academy of Sciences
MO&G	Master of Obstetrics and Gynaecology
MPH	Master of Public Health
M.Phil.	Master of Philosophy
MPS	Member of the Pharmaceutical Society
MPSI	Member of the Pharmaceutical Society of Ireland
MPSNI	Member of the Pharmaceutical Society of Northern Ireland
M.Psy.Med.	Master of Psychological Medicine
MRACP	Member of the Royal Australasian College of Physicians
MRACS	Member of the Royal Australasian College of Surgeons

M.Rad.	Master of Radiology
MRCGP	Member of the Royal College of General Practitioners
MRCOG	Member of the Royal College of Obstetricians and Gynaecologists
MRCP	Member of the Royal College of Physicians of London
MRCPA	Member of the Royal College of Pathologists of Australia
M.R.C.Path.	Member of the Royal College of Pathologists
MRCP(Ed. *or* Edin.)	Member of the Royal College of Physicians, Edinburgh
MRCP(Glasg.)	Member of the Royal College of Physicians and Surgeons of Glasgow
MRCPI	Member of the Royal College of Physicians of Ireland
M.R.C.Psych.	Member of the Royal College of Psychiatrists
MRCR	Member of the Royal College of Radiologists
MRCS	Member of the Royal College of Surgeons of England
MRCS(Ed. *or* Edin.)	Member of the Royal College of Surgeons of Edinburgh
MRCS(Irel.)	Member of the Royal College of Surgeons in Ireland
MRCVS	Member of the Royal College of Veterinary Science
MRSH	Member of the Royal Society for the Promotion of Health
MS	Master of Surgery; Master of Science
MSA	Member of the Society of Apothecaries
M.Sc.	Master of Science
M.Sc.D.	Master of Dental Science
MTD	Midwife Teacher's Diploma
ND	Doctor of Nursing
NP	Nurse-practitioner
OHNC	Occupational Health Nursing Certificate
PD	Doctor of Pharmacy
Ph.B.	Bachelor of Philosophy
Ph.D.	Doctor of Philosophy
Ph.M.	Master of Philosophy
PRCOG	President of the Royal College of Obstetricians and Gynaecologists
PRCP	President of the Royal College of Physicians of London
PRCP(Ed. *or* Edin.)	President of the Royal College of Physicians, Edinburgh
PRCS	President of the Royal College of Surgeons of England
PRCS(Ed. *or* Edin.)	President of the Royal College of Surgeons of Edinburgh
PRS	President of the Royal Society
PRSE	President of the Royal Society of Edinburgh
RCNT	Registered Clinical Nurse Teacher
RFN	Registered Fever Nurse
RGN	Registered General Nurse
RHV	Registered Health Visitor
RM	Registered Midwife
RMN	Registered Mental Nurse
RN	Registered Nurse
RNMD	Registered Nurse for Mental Defectives
RNMH	Registered Nurse for the Mentally Handicapped
RNMS	Registered Nurse for the Mentally Subnormal
RNT	Registered Nurse Tutor
RSCN	Registered Sick Children's Nurse
SB	Bachelor of Science
Sc.D.	Doctor of Science
SCM	State Certified Midwife

SEN	State Enrolled Nurse
SM	Master of Science
SRN	State Registered Nurse
SRP	State Registered Physiotherapist

Selected honours in the UK and Commonwealth conferred by the Crown (including awards for gallantry in military service).

AFC	Air Force Cross
Bart	Baronet
BEM	British Empire Medal
Bt	Baronet
CB	Companion of the Order of the Bath
CBE	Commander of the Order of the British Empire
CH	Companion of Honour
CMG	Companion of the Order of St Michael and St George
CVO	Companion of the Royal Victorian Order
DBE	Dame Commander of the Order of the British Empire
DCB	Dame Commander of the Order of the Bath
DCM	Distinguished Conduct Medal
DCMG	Dame Commander of the Order of St Michael and St George
DCVO	Dame Commander of the Royal Victorian Order
DFC	Distinguished Flying Cross
DSO	Companion of the Distinguished Service Order
ERD	Emergency Reserve Decoration (Army)
GBE	Knight or Dame Grand Cross of the Order of the British Empire
GC	George Cross
GCB	Knight Grand Cross of the Order of the Bath
GCMG	Knight or Dame Grand Cross of the Order of St Michael and St George
GCVO	Knight or Dame Grand Cross of the Royal Victorian Order
GM	George Medal
KBE	Knight Commander of the Order of the British Empire
KCB	Knight Commander of the Order of the Bath
KCMG	Knight Commander of the Order of St Michael and St George
KCVO	Knight Commander of the Royal Victorian Order
KG	Knight of the Order of the Garter
KT	Knight of the Order of the Thistle
Kt	Knight
MBE	Member of the Order of the British Empire
MC	Military Cross
MVO	Member of the Royal Victorian Order
OBE	Officer of the Order of the British Empire
OM	Order of Merit
TD	Territorial Efficiency Decoration
VC	Victoria Cross
VD	Royal Naval Volunteer Reserve Officers' Decoration (now VRD)

APPENDIX II

MEDICAL ABBREVIATIONS

A	argon
A_2	aortic second sound
AA	(i) Alcoholics Anonymous
	(ii) achievement age
AAA	aneurysm of the abdominal aorta
AADR	American Association for Dental Research
AAMC	Association of American Medical Colleges
AAP	Association of American Physicians
AAV	adenovirus-associated virus
Ab	antibody
ABG	arterial blood gases
ABN	Association of British Neurologists
ABP	arterial blood pressure
ABPI	Association of the British Pharmaceutical Industry
ABRC	Advisory Board for the Research Councils
Ac	actinium
a.c.	*ante cibum* (before meals)
ACCME	Accreditation Council for Continuing Medical Education
ACD	acid–citrate–dextrose
ACE	angiotensin converting enzyme
ACG	apex cardiogram
ACGIH	American Conference of Governmental Industrial Hygienists
ACGME	Accreditation Council for Graduate Medical Education
ACh	acetylcholine
ACP	American College of Physicians
ACS	(i) American Cancer Society
	(ii) American College of Surgeons
ACTH	adrenocorticotrophic hormone
ACTH-RH	ACTH releasing hormone
ADA	American Dental Association
ADH	antidiuretic hormone
ADI	acceptable daily intake
ADMS	Assistant Director of Medical Services
ADP	(i) adenosine diphosphate
	(ii) automatic data processing
ADTA	American Dental Trade Association
A & E	accident and emergency
AEA	Atomic Energy Authority
AEG	air encephalogram
AERE	Atomic Energy Research Establishment
aet.	*aetas* (age)
AF	atrial fibrillation
AFB	(i) American Foundation for the Blind
	(ii) acid-fast bacillus
AFIP	Armed Forces Institute of Pathology
AFP	alpha-fetoprotein

Ag	(i) silver
	(ii) antigen
A/G ratio	albumin/globulin ratio
AGL	acute granulocytic leukaemia
AGN	acute glomerulonephritis
AHA	(i) Area Health Authority
	(ii) American Heart Association
AHG	antihaemophilic globulin
AI	(i) aortic incompetence
	(ii) artificial insemination
AID	artificial insemination from donor
AIDS	acquired immune deficiency syndrome
AIH	artificial insemination from husband
AIIMS	All India Institute of Medical Sciences
AJ	ankle jerk
AK	above knee
ALT	alanine transaminase
Al	aluminium
Ala	alanine
ALAC	Artificial Limb and Appliance Centre
ALG	antilymphocytic globulin
ALL	acute lymphoblastic leukaemia
ALS	(i) antilymphocytic serum
	(ii) amyotrophic lateral sclerosis
ALT	alanine aminotransferase
alt. dieb.	*alternis diebus* (every other day)
AM	actomyosin
AMA	American Medical Association
AMI	acute myocardial infarction
AML	acute myelogenous leukaemia
AMP	adenosine monophosphate
AMS	Army Medical Service
a.m.u.	atomic mass unit
ANF	(i) antinuclear factor
	(ii) American Nurses' Foundation
ANP	atrial natriuretic peptide
AP	(i) anteroposterior
	(ii) artificial pneumothorax
APA	American Psychiatric Association
APC	aspirin, phenacetin, and caffeine
APE	anterior pituitary extract
APGAR	(see text entry)
APH	ante-partum haemorrhage
APKD	adult polycystic kidney disease
APT	alum-precipitated toxoid
APTT	activated partial thromboplastin time
APUD	(see text entry)
AQ	achievement quotient
AR	(i) Analytical Reagent
	(ii) artificial respiration
	(iii) aortic regurgitation
ara-A	adenine arabinoside
ara-C	cytosine arabinoside
ARC	Arthritis and Rheumatism Council
ARD	acute respiratory disease
ARDS	adult respiratory distress syndrome
Arg	arginine

ARI	acute respiratory infection
ARIA	automated radioimmunoassay
ARM	artificial rupture of the membranes
ARV	AIDS-associated retrovirus
AS	(i) aortic stenosis
	(ii) ankylosing spondylitis
As	arsenic
ASA	(i) American Surgical Association
	(ii) acetylsalicylic acid
ASB	anencephaly and spina bifida
ASD	atrial septal defect
ASH	Action on Smoking and Health
ASME	Association for the Study of Medical Education
Asn	asparagine
ASO	antistreptolysin-O
Asp	aspartic acid
ASS	anterior superior spine
AST	aspartate transaminase
ATA	antithyroglobulin antibody
ATP	adenosine triphosphate
ATPase	adenosine triphosphatase
Au	gold
AV	(i) atrioventricular
	(ii) arteriovenous
AVB	atrioventricular block
AVP	arginine vasopressin
AW	above the waist
A&W	alive and well
AZT	Aschheim–Zondek test
B	boron
Ba	barium
BAAS	British Association for the Advancement of Science
BaE	barium enema
BAL	(i) British Anti-Lewisite
	(ii) blood alcohol level
BaM	barium meal
BBA	born before arrival
BBB	(i) bundle branch block
	(ii) blood–brain barrier
BC/BS	Blue Cross/Blue Shield
BCG	(i) bacille Calmette–Guérin
	(ii) ballistocardiogram
BCS	British Cardiac Society
b.d.	*bis die* (twice a day)
BDA	British Dental Association
BDL	below detectable limits
Be	beryllium
BERBOH	British Examining and Registration Board in Occupational Hygiene
BGG	bovine gamma globulin
BHL	biological half-life
Bi	bismuth
BIBRA	British Industrial Biological Research Association
BID	brought in dead
b.i.d.	*bis in die* (twice daily)
BIPP	bismuth, iodoform, and paraffin paste (Morison's paste)

BK	below knee
BLAR	British League Against Rheumatism
BMA	British Medical Association
BMI	body mass index
BMR	basal metabolic rate
BMSA	British Medical Students' Association
BNA	*Basel Nomina Anatomica*
BNF	*British National Formulary*
BNO	bowels not opened
BO	(i) bowels opened
	(ii) body odour
BOD	biological oxygen demand
BP	(i) *British Pharmacopoeia*
	(ii) blood pressure
b.p.	boiling point
BPA	British Paediatric Association
BPC	*British Pharmaceutical Codex*
BPH	benign prostatic hypertrophy
BPMF	British Postgraduate Medical Federation
BR	*Birmingham Revision*
Br	bromine
BS	(i) breath sounds
	(ii) blood sugar
BSA	body surface area
BSI	British Standards Institution
BSP	bromsulphthalein
BSR	(i) blood sedimentation rate
	(ii) British Society of Rheumatology
BSS	buffered saline solution
BT	bleeding time
BUN	blood urea nitrogen
BUPA	British United Provident Association
BV	(i) blood vessel
	(ii) blood volume
BW	(i) below the waist
	(ii) body water
	(iii) body weight
C	carbon
C1, C2, etc.	cervical vertebrae
C_5	pentamethonium
C_6	hexamethonium
C_{10}	decamethonium
CA	(i) chronological age
	(ii) cardiac arrest
Ca	(i) calcium
	(ii) carcinoma
CABG	coronary artery bypass graft
CACMS	Committee on Accreditation of Canadian Medical Schools
CAH	(i) chronic active hepatitis
	(ii) congenital adrenal hyperplasia
CALLA	common acute lymphoblastic leukaemia antigen
CAM	chorio-allantoic membrane
cAMP	cyclic adenosine monophosphate
CAMR	Centre for Applied Microbiology and Research
CAPD	continous ambulatory peritoneal dialysis
CASPE	Clinical Accountability, Service Planning, and Evaluation

CAT	computerized (computed) axial tomography
CBA	cost–benefit analysis
CBD	common bile duct
CBF	cerebral blood flow
CBG	corticosteroid-binding globulin
CBR	complete bed rest
CBW	chemical and biological warfare
CCCM	Central Committee for Community Medicine (BMA)
CCCR	closed chest cardiac resuscitation
CCF	congestive cardiac failure
CCHMS	Central Committee for Hospital Medical Services
CCK	cholecystokinin
CCL	carcinoma cell line
C_{cr}	creatinine clearance
CCS	casualty clearing station
CCU	coronary care unit
CD	controlled drug
Cd	cadmium
CDC	Center for Disease Control
CDH	congenital disease of the heart
CDSC	Communicable Disease Surveillance Centre
CEA	(i) cost–effectiveness analysis
	(ii) carcinoembryonic antigen
CEC	Central Ethical Committee (BMA)
CERD	chronic end-stage renal disease
CF	(i) cystic fibrosis
	(ii) complement fixation
CFA	(i) complement-fixing antibody
	(ii) complete Freund's adjuvant
CFT	complement fixation test
CFU	colony-forming unit
CGH	chorionic gonadotrophin hormone
CGL	chronic granulocytic leukaemia
CGN	chronic glomerulonephritis
c.g.s.	centimetre–gram–second system
CHA	chronic haemolytic anaemia
CHAMPUS	Civilian Health and Medical Program of the Uniformed Services
CHB	complete heart block
CHC	Community Health Council
CHD	coronary heart disease
ChE	cholinesterase
CHF	congestive heart failure
CHO	carbohydrate
CI	(i) cardiac index
	(ii) colour index
CID	cytomegalic inclusion disease
C_{in}	inulin clearance
CIOMS	Council for International Organizations of Medical Sciences
CJD	Creutzfeldt–Jacob disease
CK	creatine kinase
Cl	chlorine
CLL	chronic lymphocytic leukaemia
CLT	clot lysis time
CMA	Canadian Medical Association
CMB	Central Midwives' Board
CMC	carpometacarpal
CMI	cell-mediated immunity

CML	chronic myeloid (myelogenous) leukaemia
CMN	cystic medial necrosis
CMO	Chief Medical Officer
CMR	cerebral metabolic rate
$CMRO_2$	cerebral metabolic rate for oxygen
CMV	*Cytomegalovirus*
CNA	Canadian Nurses' Association
CNAA	Council for National Academic Awards
CNS	central nervous system
CO	(i) cardiac output
	(ii) carbon monoxide
CO_2	carbon dioxide
Co	(i) cobalt
	(ii) coenzyme
	(iii) *compositus* (compound)
C/O	complains of
CoA	coenzyme A
COAD	chronic obstructive airways disease
COBT	chronic obstruction of the biliary tract
COD	(i) cause of death
	(ii) chemical oxygen demand
COHb	carboxyhaemoglobin
COLD	chronic obstructive lung disease
COMA	Committee on Medical Aspects of Food Policy
COMT	catechol-O-methyltransferase
CON	cyclopropane, oxygen, and nitrogen
COOH	carboxyl group
COP	colloid osmotic pressure
COPD	chronic obstructive pulmonary disease
CoR	Congo red
CP	(i) chemically pure
	(ii) cor pulmonale
C/P	cholesterol/phospholipid ratio
C&P	cystoscopy and pyelography
C_{pah}	para-aminohippurate clearance
CPAP	continuous positive airway pressure
CPB	cardiopulmonary bypass
CPC	clinicopathological conference
CPD	(i) cephalopelvic disproportion
	(ii) citrate–phosphate–dextrose
CPE	chronic pulmonary emphysema
CPK	creatine phosphokinase
CPKD	childhood polycystic kidney disease
CPM	counts per minute
CPME	Council for Postgraduate Medical Education
CPP	cerebral perfusion pressure
CPPB	constant positive pressure breathing
CPPV	continuous positive pressure ventilation
CPR	cardiopulmonary resuscitation
c.p.s.	cycles per second
CPU	central processing unit
CR	(i) conditioned reflex
	(ii) crown-rump
Cr	chromium
C&R	convalescence and rehabilitation
CRAO	central retinal artery occlusion
CRC	(i) Cancer Research Campaign

CRC	(ii) Clinical Research Centre
CRE	cumulative radiation effect
CRF	corticotrophin-releasing factor
CRH	corticotrophin-releasing hormone
CRL	crown-rump length
CRM	cross-reacting material
CRP	C-reactive protein
CrP	creatine phosphate
CRS	congenital rubella syndrome
CRT	cathode ray tube
CS	caesarean section
CSF	cerebrospinal fluid
Cs	caesium
CSM	(i) Committee on Safety of Medicines
	(ii) cerebrospinal meningitis
CSOM	chronic suppurative otitis media
CSP	Chartered Society of Physiotherapy
CSSD	Central Sterile Supply Department
CST	(i) cavernous sinus thrombosis
	(ii) convulsive shock therapy
CSU	catheter specimen of urine
CT	(i) computerized (computed) tomography
	(ii) coronary thrombosis
	(iii) cerebral thrombosis
	(iv) cerebral tumour
CTC	Clinical Trial Certificate
CTR	cardiothoracic ratio
CTS	carpal tunnel syndrome
Cu	copper
CV	(i) cardiovascular
	(ii) cerebrovascular
CVA	cerebrovascular accident
CVP	central venous pressure
CVR	cerebrovascular resistance
CVS	cardiovascular system
CWI	cardiac work index
CX	cervix
CXR	chest X-ray
CyA	cyclosporin A
Cys	cysteine
Cys–Cys	cystine
D	deuterium
DA	developmental age
D&C	dilatation and curettage
DADMS	Deputy Assistant Director of Medical Services
DAH	disordered action of the heart
DAO	Duly Authorized Officer
DBP	diastolic blood pressure
DBW	desirable body weight
DCS	dorsal column stimulation
DD	(i) dangerous drug
	(ii) differential diagnosis
DDMS	Deputy Director of Medical Services
DDRB	Doctors' and Dentists' Review Body
DDS	dapsone (diamino-diphenyl-sulphone)
DDSO	diamino-diphenyl-sulphoxide

DDST	Denver Developmental Screening Test
DDT	dichloro-diphenyl-trichloroethane
DEA	dehydroepiandrosterone
DEC	diethylcarbamazine
decd.	deceased
decub.	*decubitus* (lying down)
DES	(i) diethylstilboestrol
	(ii) Department of Education and Science
DF	degrees of freedom
DFO	District Finance Officer
DFR	(dihydro) folate reductase
DGAMS	Director General, Army Medical Services
DGMS	Director General, Medical Services
1,25-DHCC	1,25-dihydroxycholecalciferol
DHA	District Health Authority
DHE	dihydroergotamine
DHEW	Department of Health, Education and Welfare
DHHS	Department of Health and Human Services
DHR	delayed hypersensitivity reaction
DHSS	Department of Health and Social Security
DI	diabetes insipidus
DIC	disseminated intravascular coagulopathy
DIP	distal interphalangeal joint
DLE	(i) discoid lupus erythematosus
	(ii) disseminated lupus erythematosus
DLF	Disabled Living Foundation
DM	(i) diabetes mellitus
	(ii) diastolic murmur
DMF	decayed, missing, and filled (teeth)
DMO	District Medical Officer
DMP	dimethylphthalate
DMS	Director of Medical Services
DMSO	dimethyl sulphoxide
DNA	(i) deoxyribonucleic acid
	(ii) did not attend
DNMS	Director of Naval Medical Services
DNO	District Nursing Officer
DNOC	dinitro-ortho-cresol
DNR	do not resuscitate
D_2O	deuterium oxide (heavy water)
DOA	dead on arrival
DOB	date of birth
DOC	11-deoxycorticosterone
DOCA	deoxycorticosterone acetate
DOE	(i) dyspnoea on effort
	(ii) Department of the Environment
dopa	dihydroxyphenylalanine
DP	data processing
DPAG	Dangerous Pathogens Advisory Group
DRG	diagnostic-related group
DS	(i) disseminated (multiple) sclerosis
	(ii) Down's syndrome
	(iii) dead space
D/S	dextrose saline
DSA	digital subtraction angiography
DSS	dioctyl sodium sulphosuccinate
DST	dexamethasone suppression test

DT	delirium tremens
DTP	(i) distal tingling on percussion
	(ii) diphtheria, tetanus, pertussis
DTR	deep tendon reflex
DU	duodenal ulcer
D&V	diarrhoea and vomiting
DVT	deep vein thrombosis
D/W	dextrose in water
Dx	diagnosis
DXR	deep X-ray
DXRT	deep X-ray therapy
DZ	dizygotic
EACA	epsilon-aminocaproic acid
EAE	experimental allergic encephalomyelitis
EAHF	eczema, asthma, hay fever
EAM	external auditory meatus
EB	epidermolysis bullosa
EBF	erythroblastosis fetalis
EBI	emetine bismuth iodide
EBS	Emergency Bed Service
EBV	Epstein–Barr virus
EC	electron capture
ECAT	emission computerized (computed) axial tomography
ECBO	(i) enteric cytopathic bovine orphan (virus)
	(ii) European Cell Biology Organization
ECF	extracellular fluid
ECFMG	Educational Commission for Foreign Medical Graduates
ECG	electrocardiogram
ECHO	(i) Equipment to Charity Hospitals Overseas
	(ii) enteric cytopathic human orphan (virus)
ECT	electroconvulsive therapy
ECV	extracellular volume
ED	erythema dose
ED_{50}	median effective dose
EDD	expected date of delivery
EDM	early diastolic murmur
EDP	(i) end-diastolic pressure
	(ii) electron dense particles
EDS	Ehlers–Danlos syndrome
EDTA	(i) ethylenediamine tetraacetic acid (edetic acid)
	(ii) European Dialysis and Transplant Association
EDV	end-diastolic volume
EEC	European Economic Community
EEE	eastern equine encephalitis
EEG	electroencephalogram
EFA	essential fatty acids
EFE	endocardial fibroelastosis
EGDF	embryonic growth and development factor
EGF	epidermal growth factor
EHC	enterohepatic circulation
EHL	effective half-life
EHV	equine herpes virus
EIA	enzyme immunoassay
EIS	Epidemic Intelligence Service
EJ	elbow jerk
EKG	see ECG

ELISA	enzyme-linked immunosorbent assay
ELSS	Emergency Life Support System
EM	electron microscopy
E–M	Embden–Meyerhof pathway
EMAS	Employment Medical Advisory Service
EMBL	European Molecular Biology Laboratory
EMBO	European Molecular Biology Organization
EMF	(i) electromotive force
	(ii) endomyocardial fibrosis
EMG	electromyogram
EMRC	European Medical Research Councils
EMS	Emergency Medical Service
EN	erythema nodosum
ENL	erythema nodosum leprosum
ENT	ear, nose, and throat
EOA	examination, opinion, and advice
EOG	electro-oculogram
EOL	end of life
EORTC	European Organization for Research into the Treatment of Cancer
EP	*Extra Pharmacopoeia*
EPA	Environmental Protection Agency
EPP	end-plate potential
ERA	estrogen (oestrogen) receptor assay
ERBF	effective renal blood flow
ERCP	endoscopic retrograde cholangiopancreatography
ERPC	evacuation of retained products of conception
ERPF	effective renal plasma flow
ERT	estrogen (oestrogen) replacement therapy
ERV	expiratory reserve volume
ESF	European Science Foundation
ESN	educationally subnormal
ESP	(i) extrasensory perception
	(ii) end-systolic pressure
ESR	(i) electron spin resonance
	(ii) erythrocyte sedimentation rate
ESRC	(i) Economic and Social Research Council
	(ii) European Science Research Councils
ESRD	end-stage renal disease
ESV	end-systolic volume
ETC	estimated time of conception
ETEC	enterotoxigenic *Escherichia coli*
ETO	estimated time of ovulation
ETR	effective thyroxine ratio
ETT	exercise tolerance test
EUA	examination under anaesthesia
EULAR	European League Against Rheumatism
EWL	evaporative water loss
F	fluorine
FA	fluorescent antibody
Fab	fragment, antigen-binding (of IgG molecule)
FAD	familial autonomic dysfunction
FAH	Federation of American Hospitals
FANY	First Aid Nursing Yeomanry
FAO	Food and Agricultural Organization (United Nations)
FAS	fetal alcohol syndrome

FB	foreign body
FBC	full blood count
Fc	fragment, crystallizable (of IgG molecule)
FCA	Freund's complete adjuvant
FCM	Faculty of Community Medicine
FCO	Foreign and Commonwealth Office
FDA	Food and Drug Administration
FDIU	fetal death *in utero*
FDP	fibrin degradation products
Fe	iron
FEUO	for external use only
FEV	forced expiratory volume
FEV_1	forced expiratory volume in one second
FF	filtration fraction
FFA	free fatty acids
FFD	focus–film distance
FFI	fit and free from infection
FFP	fresh frozen plasma
FFT	flicker fusion threshold
FH	(i) family history
	(ii) familial hypercholesterolaemia
	(iii) fetal heart
FHH	fetal heart heard
FHNH	fetal heart not heard
FHR	fetal heart rate
FIF	fibroblast interferon
FIGLU	formiminoglutamic acid
FIP	Fédération Internationale Pharmaceutique
FIUO	for internal use only
FMDV	foot-and-mouth disease virus
FMS	fat-mobilizing substance
F–N	finger–nose
FOB	faecal occult blood
FOM	Faculty of Occupational Medicine
f.p.	freezing point
f.p.s.	foot–pound–second system
FPA	Family Planning Association
FPB	femoropopliteal bypass
FPC	(i) Family Practitioner Committee
	(ii) family planning clinic
FRC	functional residual capacity
FRF	see FSH-RF
FRJM	full range of joint movement
FSD	focus–skin distance
f.s.d.	full-scale deflection
FSH	follicle-stimulating hormone
FSH-RF	FSH releasing factor
FSH-RH	FSH releasing hormone
FT	(i) full term
	(ii) formol toxoid
FT_4	free thyroxine
FTA	fluorescent treponemal antibody test
FTBD	full term, born dead
FT_4I	free thyroxine index
FTE	full-time equivalent
FTM	fractional test meal
FTND	full term, normal delivery

FTT	failure to thrive
FU	follow up
FUO	fever of uncertain origin
FVC	forced vital capacity
Fx	fracture
GA	(i) general anaesthesia
	(ii) gestational age
Ga	gallium
GABA	gamma-aminobutyric acid
GADS	gonococcal arthritis/dermatitis syndrome
Gal	galactose
GALT	gut-associated lymphoid tissue
GB	gall-bladder
GBM	glomerular basement membrane
GBS	Guillain–Barré syndrome
GC	(i) gas chromatography
	(ii) gonococcal
GCE	General Certificate of Education
GCFT	gonococcal complement fixation test
GCMS	gas chromatography with mass spectrometry
GCS	Glasgow Coma Score
GD	gonadal dysgenesis
GDB	Guide Dogs for the Blind
GDC	General Dental Council
GDH	glutamate dehydrogenase
GDMO	General Duties Medical Officer
GE	gastroenterology
GET	gastric emptying time
GF	(i) growth factor
	(ii) glomerular filtrate
GFR	glomerular filtration rate
GGT	gamma-glutamyl transpeptidase
GH	growth hormone
GHRF	GH releasing factor
GI	gastrointestinal
GIK	glucose, insulin, and potassium
GIP	gastric inhibitory peptide
GIS	gastrointestinal series
GITT	glucose insulin tolerance test
GLC	gas–liquid chromatography
Gln	glutamine
Glu	glutamic acid
Gly	glycine
GM	Geiger–Müller
GMAG	Genetic Manipulation Advisory Group
GMC	General Medical Council
GMSC	General Medical Services Committee
GN	glomerulonephritis
GNC	General Nursing Council
GNP	gross national product
GOS	Great Ormond Street
GOT	glutamic-oxaloacetic transaminase
GP	general practitioner
G-6-P	glucose-6-phosphate
GPB	glossopharyngeal breathing
G-6-PD	glucose-6-phosphate dehydrogenase

GPI	general paralysis (paresis) of the insane
GPT	glutamic-pyruvic transaminase
GRAS	generally recognized as safe (food additives)
GRID	gay-related immunodeficiency
GSD	glycogen storage disease
GSE	gluten-sensitive enteropathy
GSW	gunshot wound
GTH	gonadotrophic hormone
GTP	glutamyl transpeptidase
GTT	glucose tolerance test
GU	(i) gastric ulcer
	(ii) genitourinary
GVH	graft-versus-host (reaction, disease)
H	hydrogen
HA	haemagglutination
HAA	(i) Hospital Activity Analysis
	(ii) hepatitis-associated antigen
HAI	haemagglutination inhibition
HAV	hepatitis A virus
Hb	haemoglobin
HbA	adult haemoglobin
HBAb	hepatitis B antibody
HBAg	hepatitis B antigen
HB_cAg	hepatitis B core antigen
HBD	has been drinking
HBF	hepatic blood flow
HbF	fetal haemoglobin
HbH	haemoglobin H
HbO_2	oxyhaemoglobin
HbS	sickle-cell haemoglobin
HB_sAg	hepatitis B surface antigen
HBV	hepatitis B virus
HC	hereditary coproporphyria
HCC	hepatocellular carcinoma
HCD	heavy chain disease
HCG	human chorionic gonadotrophin
HCL	hairy cell leukaemia
HCVD	hypertensive cardiovascular disease
HD	Hodgkin's disease
HDA	Hospital Doctors' Association
HDL	high density lipoprotein
HDLC	high density lipoprotein cholesterol
HDN	haemolytic disease of the newborn
HDU	haemodialysis unit
He	helium
H & E	(i) haematoxylin and eosin
	(ii) haemorrhages and exudates
HEC	Health Education Council
HeLa	Helen Lake (tumour cell line)
HFIF	human fibroblast interferon
HFPPV	high frequency positive pressure ventilation
Hg	mercury
HGG	human gamma globulin
HGH	human growth hormone
HHT	hereditary haemorrhagic telangiectasia
5-HIAA	5-hydroxyindole acetic acid

His	histidine
HJR	hepatojugular reflex
HJSC	Hospital Junior Staff Council (BMA)
HLA	(see text entry)
HLH	human luteinizing hormone
HMD	hyaline membrane disease
HMMA	4-hydroxy-3-methoxymandelic acid
HMO	Health Maintenance Organization
HMP	hexose monophosphate
HNA	higher nervous activity
HNP	herniated nucleus pulposus
HOCM	hypertrophic obstructive cardiomyopathy
HP	house physician
Hp	haptoglobin
HPA	hypothalamus–pituitary–adrenal
HPG	human pituitary gonadotrophin
HPI	history of present illness
HPL	human placental lactogen
HPLC	high pressure liquid chromatography
HPNS	high pressure nervous syndrome
HPOA	hypertrophic pulmonary osteoarthropathy
hPRL	prolactin
HR	heart rate
HRH	hypothalamic releasing hormone
HRT	hormone replacement therapy
HS	house surgeon
HSA	human serum albumin
HSC	Health and Safety Commission
HSE	(i) Health and Safety Executive
	(ii) herpes simplex encephalitis
HSR	health services research
HSRB	Health Services Research Board
HSV	herpes simplex virus
5-HT	5-hydroxytryptamine
HTLV	human T-cell lymphoma (leukaemia) virus
HUS	haemolytic-uraemic syndrome
HV	*Herpesvirus*
HVA	homovanillic acid
HVG	host-versus-graft
HVH	*Herpesvirus hominis*
I	iodine
IA	intra-arterial
IADR	International Association for Dental Research
IAEA	International Atomic Energy Agency
IAM	Institute of Aviation Medicine
IAPB	International Agency for the Prevention of Blindness
IARC	International Agency for Research on Cancer
IASP	International Association for the Study of Pain
IBRO	International Brain Research Organization
IBS	irritable bowel syndrome
IBW	ideal body weight
IC	internal conversion
ICD	(i) International Classification of Disease
	(ii) immune complex disease
ICF	intracellular fluid
ICLA	International Committee on Laboratory Animals

ICP	intracranial pressure
ICRF	Imperial Cancer Research Fund
ICRP	International Commission on Radiological Protection
ICSH	interstitial cell-stimulating hormone
ICSU	International Council of Scientific Unions
ICU	intensive care unit
I&D	incision and drainage
IDD	insulin-dependent diabetes
IDK	internal derangement of knee
IDL	intermediate density lipoprotein
IDU	idoxuridine
IDV	intermittent demand ventilation
IEM	inborn error of metabolism
IEP	immunoelectrophoresis
IF	intrinsic factor
IFA	immunofluorescence assay
Ig	immunoglobulin
IgA	immunoglobulin A
IgD	immunoglobulin D
IgE	immunoglobulin E
IgG	immunoglobulin G
IgM	immunoglobulin M
IHD	ischaemic heart disease
ILAE	International League Against Epilepsy
Ile	isoleucine
ILO	International Labour Organization
IM	(i) intramuscular
	(ii) infectious mononucleosis
IME	Institute of Medical Ethics
IMLS	Institute of Medical Laboratory Science
IMS	Indian Medical Service
In	indium
INH	isoniazid (isonicotinic acid hydrazide)
INI	intranuclear inclusion
INM	Institute of Naval Medicine
I&O	intake and output
IOD	injured on duty
IOFB	intra-ocular foreign body
IOM	Institute of Medicine
IOP	intra-ocular pressure
IP	(i) *International Pharmacopoeia*
	(ii) interphalangeal
IPD	intermittent peritoneal dialysis
IPPA	inspection, palpation, percussion, auscultation
IPPF	International Planned Parenthood Federation
IPPNW	International Physicians for the Prevention of Nuclear War
IPPR	intermittent positive pressure respiration
IPPV	intermittent positive pressure ventilation
IQ	intelligence quotient
IR	infra-red
Ir	iridium
IRDS	idiopathic respiratory distress syndrome
IRMA	International Rehabilitation Medicine Association
IRV	inspiratory reserve volume
ISE	ion-sensitive electrode
ISF	interstitial fluid
ISO	International Standards Organization

ISQ	*in statu quo* (unchanged)
IST	insulin shock therapy
IT	isomeric transition
ITP	idiopathic thrombocytopenic purpura
ITT	insulin tolerance test
IU	international unit
IUD	(i) intrauterine device
	(ii) intrauterine death
IUGR	intrauterine growth retardation
IUP	intrauterine pressure
IUT	intrauterine transfusion
IV	intravenous
i.v.	iodine value
IVC	inferior vena cava
IVCD	intraventricular conduction defect
IVD	intervertebral disc
IVF	*in vitro* fertilization
IVGTT	intravenous glucose tolerance test
IVH	intraventricular haemorrhage
IVP	intravenous pyelogram
IVS	interventricular septum
IVSD	interventricular septal defect
IVT	intravenous transfusion
IZS	insulin zinc suspension
JACNE	Joint Advisory Committee on Nutrition Education
JCC	Joint Consultants Committee
JCHMT	Joint Committee on Higher Medical Training
JCHST	Joint Committee on Higher Surgical Training
JDM	juvenile diabetes mellitus
JEE	Japanese equine encephalitis
JG	juxtaglomerular
JGA	juxtaglomerular apparatus
JHDA	Junior Hospital Doctors' Association
JHMO	Junior Hospital Medical Officer
JHU	Johns Hopkins University
JJ	jaw jerk
JNA	*Jena Nomina Anatomica*
JND	just noticeable difference
JOD	juvenile onset diabetes
JV	jugular vein
JVP	jugular venous pressure (or pulse)
K	potassium
17-K	17-ketosteroids
KA	King–Armstrong (units of alkaline phosphate)
KB	ketone bodies
kb	kilobase
kcal	kilocalorie (1000 calories or 1 Calorie)
K_e	exchangeable body potassium
K–F rings	Kayser–Fleischer rings
17-KGS	17-ketogenic steroids
KJ	knee jerk
KLS	kidney, liver, spleen
KO	knock-out
KP	keratin precipitates (in keratitis punctata)
Kr	krypton

KS	Kaposi's sarcoma
17-KS	17-ketosteroids
KUB	kidney, ureter, bladder
K–WS	Kimmelstiel–Wilson syndrome
L1, L2, etc.	lumbar vertebrae
LA	(i) left atrial
	(ii) latex agglutination
L&A	light and accommodation
LAA	leucocyte ascorbic acid
LAD	(i) left axis deviation
	(ii) lactic acid dehydrogenase
LAF	laminar air flow
LAH	(i) left anterior hemiblock
	(ii) left atrial hypertrophy
LAIT	latex agglutination inhibition test
LAP	(i) leucine aminopeptidase
	(ii) leucocyte alkaline phosphatase
L-ASP	L-asparaginase
LAT	latex agglutination test
LATS	long-acting thyroid stimulator
LATS-P	LATS-protector substance
LBB	left bundle branch
LBBB	left bundle branch block
LBF	liver blood flow
LBH	length, breadth, height
LBL	lymphoblastic lymphoma
LBM	lean body mass
LBP	low back pain
LBW	low birth weight
LCD	liquid crystal display
LCFA	long-chain fatty acid
LCM	lymphocytic choriomeningitis
LCME	Liaison Committee on Medical Education
LCMV	LCM virus
LD	Legionnaires' disease
LD_{50}	median lethal dose
LDH	lactate dehydrogenase
LDL	low-density lipoprotein
LDLC	low-density lipoprotein cholesterol
LE	lupus erythematosus
LED	light-emitting diode
LES	lower oesophageal (esophageal) sphincter
LET	linear energy transfer
Leu	leucine
LFD	least fatal dose
LFT	(i) liver function tests
	(ii) latex fixation test
LFV	Lassa fever virus
LGH	lactogenic hormone
LGV	lymphogranuloma venereum
LH	luteinizing hormone
LHC	Local Health Council
LHRF	luteinizing hormone releasing factor
LHRH	luteinizing hormone releasing hormone
LHS	left heart strain
Li	lithium

LIF	left iliac fossa
LIH	left inguinal hernia
LKS	liver, kidney, spleen
LLO	*Legionella*-like organisms
LLQ	left lower quadrant
LMC	Local Medical Committee
LMN	lower motor neurone
LMP	last menstrual period
LOM	limitation of movement
LOPS	length of patient stay
LP	lumbar puncture
LPF	low-power field
LPH	left posterior hemiblock
LPL	lipoprotein lipase
LRF	see LHRF
LRH	see LHRH
LRT	lower respiratory tract
LRTI	LRT infection
LSCS	lower segment caesarean section
LSD	lysergic acid diethylamide (lysergide)
LSF	lymphocyte-stimulating factor
LSK	liver, spleen, kidney
LSMW	London School of Medicine for Women
LTC	long-term care
LTF	lymphocyte-transforming factor
LUQ	left upper quadrant
LV	left ventricle
LVEDP	left ventricular end-diastolic pressure
LVEDV	left ventricular end-diastolic volume
LVF	left ventricular failure
LVH	left ventricular hypertrophy
LVN	low viscosity nitrocellulose
LVS	left ventricular strain
L&W	living and well
Lys	lysine
LZM	lysozyme
M_1	first heart sound, mitral area
M_2	second heart sound, mitral area
MA	mental age
MABP	mean arterial blood pressure
MAC	maximum allowable concentration
MAF	macrophage activating factor
MAHA	microangiopathic haemolytic anaemia
MAKA	major karyotypic abnormality
MAL	mid-axillary line
mal	malate
MAO	monoamine oxidase
MAOI	monoamine oxidase inhibitor
MAP	(i) mean arterial pressure
	(ii) muscle action potential
MAS	Medical Advisory Service
MASC	Medical Academic Staff Council (BMA)
MASH	Mobile Army Surgical Hospital
MBC	maximum breathing capacity
MBD	minimal brain dysfunction
MBL	(i) Marine Biological Laboratory

MBL	(ii) menstrual blood loss
MBP	mean blood pressure
MCAT	Medical College Admission Test
McB	McBurney's point
MCCU	mobile coronary care unit
MCD	mean corpuscular diameter
MCH	mean corpuscular haemoglobin
MCHC	mean corpuscular haemoglobin concentration
MCKD	multicystic kidney disease
MCL	midclavicular line
MCP	metacarpophalangeal
MCQ	multiple-choice question
MCT	mean circulation time
MCTD	mixed connective tissue disease
MCV	mean corpuscular volume
MD	(i) mentally deficient
	(ii) muscular dystrophy
MDM	mid-diastolic murmur
MDH	malic dehydrogenase
M-dopa	methyl-dopa
MDQ	minimum detectable quantity
MDR	minimum daily requirement
MDU	Medical Defence Union
MEA	multiple endocrine adenomatosis
MEC	minimum effective concentration
MED	(i) minimum effective dose
	(ii) minimum erythema dose
MEDLARS	Medical Literature Analysis and Retrieval System
MEDLINE	MEDLARS on-line
MEF	mean expiratory flow rate
MELAS	mitochondrial encephalomyopathy, lactic acidosis, and stroke
MEN	multiple endocrine neoplasia
MEP	motor end-plate
MEPP	miniature end-plate potential
Met	methionine
metHb	methaemoglobin
MF	myelofibrosis
M/F	male/female
MFD	minimum fatal dose
MG	macroglobulinaemia
Mg	magnesium
MGH	Massachusetts General Hospital
MHC	major histocompatibility complex
MHD	minimum haemolytic dose
MHI	malignant histiocytosis of the intestine
MI	(i) myocardial infarction
	(ii) mitral incompetence
	(iii) medical inspection
MIC	minimum inhibitory concentration
MICU	mobile intensive care unit
MID	minimum infective dose
MIF	migration-inhibition factor
MIFR	maximum inspiratory flow rate
MIKA	minor karyotypic abnormalities
MIMS	Monthly Index of Medical Specialities
MIO	minimum identifiable odour
MIT	mono-iodotyrosine

MK	monkey kidney
m.k.s.	metre–kilogram–second system
MLC	mixed lymphocyte culture
MLD	minimum lethal dose
MLSO	medical laboratory scientific officer
MLV	murine leukaemia virus
MM	(i) multiple myeloma
	(ii) mucous membrane
mmHg	millimetres of mercury
MMPI	Minnesota Multiphasic Personality Inventory
MMR	mass miniature radiography
Mn	manganese
MND	motor neurone disease
MO	medical officer
Mo	molybdenum
MOC	maximum oxygen consumption
MOD	(i) maturity onset diabetes
	(ii) Ministry of Defence
MOH	Medical Officer of Health
MOUS	multiple occurrence of unexplained symptoms
m.p.	melting point
6-MP	6-mercaptopurine
MPB	male pattern baldness
MPC	maximum permissible concentration
MPD	maximum permissible dose
MPE	maximum possible error
MPGN	membranoproliferative glomerulonephritis
MPI	maximum permissible intake
MPL	maximum permissible level
MPU	Medical Practitioners Union
MPV	mean platelet volume
MR	mitral regurgitation
MRC	Medical Research Council
MRD	minimal residual disease
mRNA	messenger RNA
MRV	minute respiratory volume
MS	(i) multiple sclerosis
	(ii) mitral stenosis
MSG	monosodium glutamate
MSH	melanocyte-stimulating hormone
MST	mean survival time
MSU	mid-stream specimen of urine
MSUD	maple syrup urine disease
MSV	murine sarcoma virus
MTC	medullary thyroid carcinoma
MTP	metatarsophalangeal
MTT	mean transit time
MTU	methylthiouracil
MTX	methotrexate
MV	mitral valve
MVP	mitral valve prolapse
MVR	mitral valve replacement
MW	molecular weight
MWF	Medical Women's Federation
MZ	monozygotic
N	nitrogen

NA	(i) *Nomina Anatomica*
	(ii) numerical aperture
Na	sodium
NAA	no apparent abnormalities
NAD	(i) nicotinamide adenine dinucleotide
	(ii) nil abnormal discovered
NADP	nicotinamide adenine dinucleotide phosphate
Na_e	exchangeable body sodium
NAI	non-accidental injury
NALP	neuroadenolysis of the pituitary
NANBH	non-A, non-B hepatitis
NAR	nasal airway resistance
NAS	National Academy of Sciences
NAS–NRC	NAS–National Research Council
NAWCH	National Association for the Welfare of Children in Hospital
NBI	no bone injury
NBM	nil by mouth
NBME	National Board of Medical Examiners
NBTS	National Blood Transfusion Service
NCD	normal childhood disorders
NCI	National Cancer Institute
NCIB	National Collection of Industrial Bacteria
NCTC	National Collection of Type Cultures
NDA	no detectable activity
NDE	near death experience
NDI	nephrogenic diabetes insipidus
NDV	Newcastle disease virus
NE	niacin equivalent
Ne	neon
NEC	necrotizing enterocolitis
NED	no evidence of disease
NEFA	non-esterified fatty acids
NET	nasoendotracheal tube
NF	*National Formulary*
NFTD	normal full-term delivery
NGF	nerve growth factor
NGU	non-gonococcal urethritis
NHI	National Health Insurance
NHL	non-Hodgkin lymphoma
NHLBI	National Heart, Lung and Blood Institute
NHS	National Health Service
Ni	nickel
NIADDK	National Institute of Arthritis, Diabetes, and Digestive and Kidney Diseases
NIAID	National Institute of Allergy and Infectious Diseases
NIAMD	National Institute of Arthritis and Metabolic Diseases
NIB	National Institute for the Blind
NIBSC	National Institute for Biological Standards and Control
NICHHD	National Institute of Child Health and Human Development
NICM	Nuffield Institute of Comparative Medicine
NICU	neonatal intensive care unit
NIDD	non-insulin-dependent diabetes
NIDR	National Institute for Dental Research
NIH	National Institutes of Health
NIHL	noise-induced hearing loss
NIMH	National Institute of Mental Health
NIMR	National Institute for Medical Research

NINDB	National Institute of Neurological Diseases and Blindness
NINDS	National Institute of Neurological Diseases and Stroke
NIOSH	National Institute for Occupational Safety and Health
NLM	National Library of Medicine
NLN	no longer needed
NMR	nuclear magnetic resonance
NND	neonatal death
NNR	New and Non-official Remedies
NOPWC	National Old People's Welfare Council
NP	nurse practitioner
n.p.	*nomen proprium* (label with its own name)
NPHT	Nuffield Provincial Hospitals Trust
NPL	National Physical Laboratory
NPN	non-protein nitrogen
NRPB	National Radiological Protection Board
NRS	normal rabbit serum
NS	normal saline
NSAID	non-steroidal anti-inflammatory drug
NSD	(i) normal spontaneous delivery
	(ii) nominal standard dose
NSR	normal sinus rhythm
NSU	non-specific urethritis
NTD	neural tube defect
NTG	nitroglycerine
NTP	normal temperature and pressure
N&V	nausea and vomiting
NVM	non-volatile matter
NWB	non-weight-bearing
NYD	not yet diagnosed
NZB	New Zealand Black (mice)
O	oxygen
OA	osteoarthropathy (osteoarthritis, osteoarthrosis)
OAD	obstructive airways disease
OB	(i) obstetrics
	(ii) occult blood
OBD	organic brain disease
OC	oral contraceptive
O&C	onset and course
OCP	oral contraceptive pill
OD	overdose
ODA	(i) Overseas Development Administration (FCO)
	(ii) Overseas Doctors' Association
OECD	Organization for Economic Cooperation and Development
OER	oxygen enhancement ratio
O&G	obstetrics and gynaecology
OGTT	oral glucose tolerance test
25-OHCC	25-hydroxycholecalciferol
17-OHCS	17-hydroxycorticosteroids
17-OHP	17-hydroxyprogesterone
OHS	obesity hypoventilation syndrome
OI	opsonic index
OIHP	Office International d'Hygiene Publique
OND	other neurological disorders
ONTR	orders not to resuscitate
OP	(i) outpatient
	(ii) over proof

OPCA	olivopontocerebellar atrophy
OPCS	Office of Population, Censuses and Surveys
OPD	out-patient department
OPV	oral poliomyelitis vaccine
OR	operating room
O–R	oxidation–reduction
ORIF	open reduction with internal fixation
Orn	ornithine
ORT	oral rehydration therapy
OS	opening snap
OSHA	Occupational Safety and Health Administration
OSRD	Office of Scientific Research and Development
OT	(i) occupational therapist
	(ii) old tuberculin
OVX	ovariectomized
o/w	oil in water
P	phosphorus
p	probability
P_1	pulmonary first sound
P_2	pulmonary second sound
PA	(i) pernicious anaemia
	(ii) pulmonary artery
PABA	para-aminobenzoic acid
p_aCO_2	arterial partial pressure of carbon dioxide
PAF	platelet activating factor
PAG	(i) polyacrylamide gel electrophoresis
	(ii) periaqueductal grey matter
PAH	para-aminohippuric acid
PAHO	Pan-American Health Organization
PAL	posterior axillary line
PAM	penicillin aluminium monostearate
PAMA	post-amputation mobility aid
PANLAR	Pan-American League Against Rheumatism
p_aO_2	arterial partial pressure of oxygen
PAP	peak airway pressure
Pap.	Papanicolaou (smear, etc.)
PAPP	pregnancy-associated plasma protein
PARU	post-anaesthetic recovery unit
PAS	(i) para-aminosalicylic acid
	(ii) periodic-acid Schiff
PASB	Pan-American Sanitary Bureau
PAT	paroxysmal atrial tachycardia
PAWP	pulmonary artery wedge pressure
Pb	lead
PBC	primary biliary cirrhosis
PBG	porphobilinogen
PBI	protein-bound iodine
PBP	progressive bulbar palsy
PBV	pulmonary blood volume
PBZ	phenylbutazone
p.c.	*post cibum* (after food)
PCA	passive cutaneous anaphylaxis
PCB	(i) post-coital bleeding
	(ii) polychlorinated biphenyls
PCC	(i) phaeochromocytoma
	(ii) Professional Conduct Committee (GMC)

PCD	polycystic disease
PCE	pseudocholinesterase
PCG	phonocardiogram
PCH	paroxysmal cold haemoglobinuria
PCKD	polycystic kidney disease
PCL	persistent corpus luteum
PCM	protein-calorie malnutrition
pCO_2	partial pressure of carbon dioxide
PCP	phencyclidine
PCS	post-cardiotomy syndrome
PCT	(i) prothrombin consumption test
	(ii) porphyria cutanea tarda
PCV	packed cell volume
PD	(i) potential difference
	(ii) pupillary difference
PDA	patent ductus arteriosus
PECT	positron emission computerized (computed) tomography
PEEP	positive end-expiratory pressure
PEF	peak expiratory flow rate
PEG	pneumoencephalogram
PEM	protein-energy malnutrition
PERLA	pupils equal, react to light and accommodation
PES	pre-excitation syndrome
PET	(i) positron emission tomography
	(ii) pre-eclamptic toxaemia
PETN	pentaerythritol tetranitrate
PEV	peak expiratory volume
PFK	phosphofructokinase
PFO	patent foramen ovale
PFP	platelet-free plasma
PFR	peak flow rate
PFT	pulmonary function tests
PG	prostaglandin (also PGA, PGB, etc.)
PGC	primordial germ cell
PGH	pituitary growth hormone
PGM	phosphoglucomutase
PGN	proliferative glomerulonephritis
PH	previous history
pH	(see text entry)
PHA	phytohaemagglutinin
Phe	phenylalanine
PHI	permanent health insurance
PHK	post-mortem human kidney
PHLS	Public Health Laboratory Service
PHR	peak heart rate
PHS	Public Health Service
PI	pulmonary incompetence
PICU	paediatric intensive care unit
PID	(i) prolapsed intervertebral disc
	(ii) pelvic inflammatory disease
PIE	pulmonary infiltration with eosinophilia
PIF	prolactin-inhibiting factor
PIFR	peak inspiratory flow rate
PIP	proximal interphalangeal (joint)
PISCES	percutaneously implanted spinal cord epidural stimulation
PIV	parainfluenza virus
PK	(i) pyruvate kinase

PK	(ii) Prausnitz–Kustner (reaction)
pK	dissociation constant
PKD	polycystic kidney disease
PKU	phenylketonuria
PLAB	Professional and Linguistic Assessment Board
PLG	plasminogen
PLM	polarized light microscopy
PM	(i) photomultiplier
	(ii) post-mortem
PMA	progressive muscular atrophy
PMB	post-menopausal bleeding
PMC	pseudomembraneous colitis
PMF	progressive massive fibrosis
PMI	point of maximum impulse
PML	progressive multifocal leucoencephalopathy
PMO	Principal Medical Officer
PMR	polymyalgia rheumatica
PMRAFNS	Princess Mary's Royal Air Force Nursing Service
PMT	premenstrual tension
PN	percussion note
Pn	plutonium
PNA	*Paris Nomina Anatomica*
PND	paroxysmal nocturnal dyspnoea
PNH	paroxysmal nocturnal haemoglobinuria
PNO	Principal Nursing Officer
pO_2	partial pressure of oxygen
POA	primary optic atrophy
PoE	portal of entry
PoM	prescription-only medicine
POMR	problem-orientated medical record
POP	plaster of Paris
POSM	patient-operated selector mechanism
POSSUM	patient-operated selector mechanism
PP	(i) placenta praevia
	(ii) private patient
PPB	positive pressure breathing
PPC	(i) progressive patient care
	(ii) Preliminary Proceedings Committee (GMC)
PPD	purified protein derivative (tuberculin)
PPF	pellagra-preventing factor
PPH	post-partum haemorrhage
PPLO	pleuropneumonia-like organisms
p.p.m.	parts per million
PR	(i) *per rectum*
	(ii) pulse rate
	(iii) pre-registration (year)
PRA	(i) progesterone receptor assay
	(ii) plasma renin activity
PRF	prolactin-releasing factor
p.r.n.	*pro re nata* (as and when required)
Pro	proline
PROM	premature rupture of membranes
PRP	platelet-rich plasma
PRU	peripheral resistance unit
PRV	polycythaemia rubra vera
PS	pulmonary stenosis
P/S	polyunsaturated/saturated ratio

PSGN	post-streptococcal glomerulonephritis
PSS	progressive systemic sclerosis
PSVT	paroxysmal supraventricular tachycardia
PSW	psychiatric social worker
Pt	platinum
PTA	prior to admission
PTC	(i) phenylthiocarbamide
	(ii) plasma thromboplastin component (Factor IX)
PTD	permament total disability
PTF	plasma thromboplastin factor (Factor X)
PTH	parathyroid hormone
PTT	partial thromboplastin time
PTU	propylthiouracil
PTx	parathyroidectomy
PU	(i) passed urine
	(ii) peptic ulcer
PUFA	polyunsaturated fatty acids
PUO	pyrexia of uncertain (or unknown) origin
PUVA	psoralens and ultraviolet A
PV	(i) *per vaginam*
	(ii) polyoma virus
PVB	premature ventricular beat
PVC	polyvinyl chloride
PVD	peripheral vascular disease
PVG	periventricular grey matter
PVP	polyvinylpyrrolidone (povidone)
PVR	(i) peripheral vascular resistance
	(ii) pulmonary vascular resistance
PVT	paroxysmal ventricular tachycardia
PWM	pokeweed mitogen
PWP	pulmonary wedge pressure
PZ	pancreozymin
PZI	protamine zinc insulin
QALY	quality-adjusted life years
QARANC	Queen Alexandra's Royal Army Nursing Corps
QARNNS	Queen Alexandra's Royal Naval Nursing Service
q.i.d.	*quater in die* (four times a day)
QNS	quantity not sufficient
q.s.	sufficient quantity
QT	Quick's test
RA	(i) right atrium
	(ii) rheumatoid arthritis
Ra	radium
RACGP	Royal Australian College of General Practitioners
RACP	Royal Australasian College of Physicians
RACS	Royal Australasian College of Surgeons
RAD	right axis deviation
rad	(see text entry)
R&D	research and development
RADAR	Royal Association for Disability and Rehabilitation
RAIU	radioactive iodine uptake
RAM	relative atomic mass
RAMC	Royal Army Medical Corps
R.A.N.Z. Psych.	Royal Australian and New Zealand College of Psychiatrists
RAP	right atrial pressure

Rb	rubidium
RBB	right bundle branch
RBBB	right bundle branch block
RBC	red blood cell(s)
RBE	relative biological effectiveness
RBF	renal blood flow
RBN	retrobulbar neuritis
RBP	retinol binding protein
RCF	relative centrifugal force
RCGP	Royal College of General Practitioners
RCM	red cell mass
RCN	Royal College of Nursing
RCOG	Royal College of Obstetricians and Gynaecologists
RCP	Royal College of Physicians of London
R.C.Path.	Royal College of Pathologists
RCP(Ed. *or* Edin.)	Royal College of Physicians, Edinburgh
RCPI	Royal College of Physicians of Ireland
RCPS(C)	Royal College of Physicians and Surgeons of Canada
RCPS(Glasg.)	Royal College of Physicians and Surgeons of Glasgow
R.C.Psych.	Royal College of Psychiatrists
RCR	Royal College of Radiologists
RCS	Royal College of Surgeons of England
RCS(Ed. *or* Edin.)	Royal College of Surgeons of Edinburgh
RCS(Irel.)	Royal College of Surgeons in Ireland
RCT	randomized clinical trial
RD	(i) relative density
	(ii) reaction of degeneration
RDA	recommended daily allowance
RDE	receptor-destroying enzyme
rDNA	recombinant DNA
RDS	respiratory distress syndrome
redox	reduction–oxidation
REF	renal erythropoietic factor
REM	rapid eye movements
rem	roentgen equivalent man
RER	respiratory exchange ratio
RES	reticuloendothelial system
R factor	resistance factor
RH	relative humidity
Rh	rhesus
RHA	Regional Health Authority
RHB	Regional Hospital Board
RHD	(i) rheumatic heart disease
	(ii) rhesus haemolytic disease
RHF	right heart failure
RI	refractive index
RIA	radioimmunoassay
RIF	right iliac fossa
RIH	right inguinal hernia
RLC	residual lung capacity
RLF	retrolental fibroplasia
RMM	relative molecular mass
RMO	(i) resident medical officer
	(ii) Regional Medical Officer
RMS	root mean square
RMV	respiratory minute volume
Rn	radon

RNA	ribonucleic acid
RNase	ribonuclease
RNIB	Royal National Institute for the Blind
ROM	rupture of membranes
RPF	renal plasma flow
RPGN	rapidly progressive glomerulonephritis
RPMS	Royal Postgraduate Medical School
RPP	retropubic prostatectomy
RPS	renal pressor substance
RQ	respiratory quotient
RRA	radioreceptor assay
rRNA	ribosomal RNA
RRP	relative refractory period
RS	Royal Society
RSF	rheumatoid serum factor
RSM	Royal Society of Medicine
RSO	resident surgical officer
RSR	regular sinus rhythm
RSV	respiratory syncytial virus
RT	reaction time
RTA	renal tubular acidosis
RTF	resistance transfer factor
RTI	respiratory tract infection
RV	(i) right ventricle
	(ii) residual volume
RVH	right ventricular hypertrophy
RW	Rideal–Walker (coefficient)
S	sulphur
SACE	serum angiotensin converting enzyme
SAH	subarachnoid haemorrhage
SAMI	socially acceptable monitoring instrument
SAN	sinoatrial node
SAS	sterile aqueous suspension
SB	stillbirth
Sb	antimony
SBA	sick bay attendant
SBE	subacute bacterial endocarditis
SBP	systolic blood pressure
SBR	strict bed rest
SC	subcutaneous
SCA	sickle cell anaemia
SCAN	suspected child abuse and neglect
SCAT	sheep cell agglutination test
SCBU	special care baby unit
SCD	subacute combined degeneration
SCE	sister chromatid exchange
SCI	spinal cord injury
SCG	sodium cromoglycate
SCM	State Certified Midwife
SCU	Special Care Unit
SCUBA	self-contained underwater breathing apparatus
SD	standard deviation
SDA	specific dynamic action
SDHD	sudden death heart disease
SE	standard error
Se	selenium

SED	skin erythema dose
SEM	scanning electron microscope
SEN	State Enrolled Nurse
SEP	systolic ejection period
Ser	serine
SES	socioeconomic status
SFD	small for dates
SG	specific gravity
SGOT	serum glutamic-oxaloacetic transaminase
SGPT	serum glutamic-pyruvic transaminase
SH	(i) serum hepatitis
	(ii) social history
SHHD	Scottish Home and Health Department
SHMO	Senior Hospital Medical Officer
SHO	Senior House Officer
SI units	(see text entry)
Si	silicon
SIADH	syndrome of inappropriate ADH secretion
SIDS	sudden infant death syndrome
sig.	*signetur* (let it be labelled)
SIW	self-inflicted wound
SK	streptokinase
SLE	systemic lupus erythematosus
SLR	straight leg raising
SM	systolic murmur
SMAC	Standing Medical Advisory Committee
SMD	senile macular degeneration
SMO	Senior Medical Officer
SMON	subacute myelo-optic neuropathy
SMR	standardized mortality rate
SMX	sulphamethoxazole
Sn	tin
S/N	signal to noise ratio
SOB	shortness of breath
SOL	space-occupying lesion
SOP	standard operating procedure
sp.	species (singular)
SPA	stimulus-produced analgesia
SPECT	single photon emission computerized (computed) tomography
SPF	specific pathogen-free
SPP	suprapubic prostatectomy
spp.	species (plural)
SPV	Shope papilloma virus
SR	(i) Senior Registrar
	(ii) sinus rhythm
Sr	strontium
SRN	State Registered Nurse
SRNS	steroid-responsive nephrotic syndrome
SRR	Society for Research in Rehabilitation
SRS-A	slow reacting substance of anaphylaxis
SSPE	subacute sclerosing panencephalitis
SSS	sick sinus syndrome
stat.	*statim* (at once)
STD	(i) sexually transmitted diseases
	(ii) skin test dose
STEM	scanning transmission electron microscopy
STH	somatotrophic hormone

STI	serum trypsin inhibitor
STOP	suction termination of pregnancy
s.t.p.	standard temperature and pressure
SV	stroke volume
SVC	superior vena cava
SVR	systemic vascular resistance
SVT	supraventricular tachycardia
SWD	short-wave diathermy
T1, T2, etc.	thoracic vertebrae
T$_{\frac{1}{2}}$	half-life
T$_3$	triiodothyronine
T$_4$	thyroxine
T&A	tonsils and adenoids
TAB	typhoid, paratyphoid A and B
TAF	toxin–antitoxin floccules
TAH	total abdominal hysterectomy
TAPV	totally anomalous pulmonary veins
TAT	Thematic Apperception Test
TB	tuberculosis
TBE	tick-borne encephalitis
TBG	thyroxine-binding globulin
TBI	total body irradiation
TBM	tuberculous meningitis
TBP	thyroxine-binding protein
TBPA	thyroxine-binding pre-albumin
TBW	total body water
Tc	technetium
TCA	(i) tricyclic antidepressant
	(ii) trichloroacetic acid
TCB	tumour cell burden
TCI	to come in
T-CLL	T-cell chronic lymphatic leukaemia
TCO	carbon monoxide transfer factor
TCT	thyrocalcitonin
TDD	thoracic duct drainage
TDE	total digestible energy
t.d.s.	*ter die sumendum* (to be taken three times a day)
TE	alpha-tocopherol equivalent
Te	tellurium
TEAB	tetraethylammonium bromide
TEAC	tetraethylammonium chloride
TED	threshold erythema dose
TEE	total energy expenditure
TEM	transmission electron microscopy
TES	transcutaneous electrical stimulation
TEV	talipes equinovarus
TF	transfer factor
TFA	total fatty acids
TFS	testicular feminization syndrome
TG	(i) triglycerides
	(ii) thyroglobulin
TGA	transposition of the great arteries
TGE	transmissible gastroenteritis
TGT	thromboplastin generation time
TGV	transposition of the great vessels
THC	tetrahydrocannabinol

Thr	threonine
THRF	thyrotrophic hormone releasing factor
TI	tricuspid incompetence
Ti	titanium
TIA	transient ischaemic attack
TIBC	total iron-binding capacity
t.i.d.	*ter in die* (thrice a day)
TJ	triceps jerk
TK	thymidine kinase
Tl	thallium
TLC	(i) thin-layer chromatography
	(ii) total lung capacity
TLD	thoracic lymph duct
TLE	thin-layer electrophoresis
TLV	(i) total lung volume
	(ii) threshold limit value
T_m	maximum tubular reabsorption
TMA	thyroid microsomal antibody
TME	total metabolizable energy
TMJ	temporomandibular joint
TMP/SMX	trimethoprin/sulphamethoxazole
TMV	tobacco mosaic virus
TNF	tumour necrosis factor
TNS	transcutaneous nerve stimulation
TNT	trinitrotoluene
TNTC	too numerous to count
TOF	tetralogy of Fallot
TOP	termination of pregnancy
TOPS	take off pounds sensibly
TPI	*Treponema pallidum* immobilization test
TPN	total parenteral nutrition
TPR	total peripheral resistance
TR	tricuspid regurgitation
TRCH	tanned red cell haemagglutination test
TRH	thyrotrophin-releasing hormone
TRIAC	triiodothyroacetic acid
TRIC	trachoma-inclusion conjunctivitis
tRNA	transfer RNA
TRP	(i) tubular reabsorption of phosphate
	(ii) total refractory period
Trp	tryptophane
T_3RU	triiodothyronine resin uptake test
TS	tricuspid stenosis
TSA	tumour specific antigen
TSH	thyroid-stimulating hormone
TSH-RF	thyroid-stimulating hormone-releasing factor
TSI	thyroid-stimulating immunoglobulin
TSP	total serum protein
TSS	toxic shock syndrome
TT	(i) tetanus toxoid
	(ii) tuberculin tested
TURP	transurethral resection of prostate
TVF	tactile vocal fremitus
TVP	tricuspid valve prolapse
TVU	total volume of urine (24 hours)
TX	thromboxane
Tyr	tyrosine

U	uranium
UCD	usual childhood diseases
UCG	urinary chorionic gonadotrophin
UCH	University College Hospital
UCR	usual, customary, and reasonable
UFAW	University Federation for Animal Welfare
UGC	University Grants Committee
UICC	Union Internationale Contre le Cancer (International Union Against Cancer)
UKCC	United Kingdom Central Council (for Nursing, Midwifery, and Health Visiting)
UMN	upper motor neurone
UMT	unit of medical time
UNEP	United Nations Environment Programme
UNESCO	United Nations Educational, Scientific and Cultural Organization
UNICEF	United Nations Children's Fund (originally United Nations International Children's Emergency Fund)
UNRRA	United Nations Relief and Rehabilitation Administration
UO	urinary output
UP	under proof
URF	uterine relaxing factor
URI	upper respiratory infection
URT	upper respiratory tract
USAN	United States Adopted Name
USNF	*United States National Formulary*
USP	*United States Pharmacopoeia*
USRDA	United States Recommended Dietary Allowance
USS	ultrasound scanning
UTI	urinary tract infection
u.v.	ultraviolet
UVA	ultraviolet light, long wave
V	vanadium
VA	Veterans' Administration
V_a	alveolar ventilation (l/min)
VAD	Voluntary Aid Detachment
Val	valine
VAT	ventricular activation time
VBL	vinblastine
VC	vital capacity
VCC	vasoconstrictor centre
VCG	vectorcardiogram
VCO_2	carbon dioxide production (l/min)
VCR	vincristine (Oncovin®)
VD	venereal disease
VDC	vasodilator centre
VDH	valvular disease of the heart
VDRL	Venereal Disease Research Laboratory test
VE	vaginal examination
VEB	ventricular ectopic beats
VEE	Venezuelan equine encephalitis
VER	visual evoked response
VF	ventricular fibrillation
VGH	very good health
VI	virgo intacta
VIC	vasoinhibitory centre
VIP	vasoactive intestinal peptide

VLDL	very low density lipoprotein
VLP	virus-like particle
VMA	vannillylmandelic acid
VMC	vasomotor centre
VNA	Visiting Nurse Association
VO_2	oxygen consumption (l/min)
VOD	veno-occlusive disease
VON	Victorian Order of Nurses
VOR	vestibulo-ocular reflex
VP	variegate porphyria
VPB	ventricular premature beat
VR	vocal resonance
VRI	viral respiratory infection
VS	vesicular sounds
VSS	vital signs stable
VSD	ventricular septal defect
VT	ventricular tachycardia
Vt	tidal volume
VU	varicose ulcer
VUR	vesicoureteric reflex
VWD	von Willebrand's disease
VWF	von Willebrand factor
Vx	vertex
V-Z	varicella-zoster
V-ZV	varicella-zoster virus

WAIS	Wechsler Adult Intelligence Scale
WBA	whole body activity
WBC	white blood cell(s)
WBR	whole body radiation
WBS	whole body scan
WBT	wet bulb temperature
WD	Wallerian degeneration
WDLL	well-differentiated lymphatic lymphoma
WEE	Western equine encephalitis
WFN	World Federation of Neurology
WHML	Wellcome Historical Medical Library
WHO	World Health Organization
WL	waiting list
WMA	World Medical Association
WNL	within normal limits
WO	wash out
w/o	(i) water in oil
	(ii) without
WPW	Wolff–Parkinson–White (syndrome)
WR	Wassermann reaction
WS	water soluble
wt.	weight

Xan	xanthine
XDH	xanthine dehydrogenase
XDP	xeroderma pigmentosum
Xe	Xenon
XLP	X-linked lymphoproliferative syndrome
XO	xanthine oxidase
XR	X-ray
XRT	X-ray therapy

XS	cross-section
XX	sex chromosomes (normal female)
XY	sex chromosomes (normal male)
Xyl	xylose
Y	yttrium
yr.	year
YS	yellow spot (macula retinae)
ZES	Zollinger–Ellison syndrome
ZF	zona fasciculata
ZG	zona glomerulosa
ZN	Ziehl–Neelson
Zn	zinc
ZR	zona reticularis
Zr	zirconium